Protest, Power, and Change

GARLAND REFERENCE LIBRARY OF THE HUMANITIES (VOL. 1625)

Advisory Board

Protest, Power, and Change

An Encyclopedia of Nonviolent Action
from ACT-UP to Women's Suffrage

Editors
Roger S. Powers
William B. Vogele

Associate Editors
Christopher Kruegler
Ronald M. McCarthy

GARLAND PUBLISHING, INC.
New York & London
1997

Library of Congress Cataloging-in-Publication Data

Protest, power, and change : an encyclopedia of nonviolent action from ACT-UP
    to women's suffrage / editors, Roger S. Powers, William B. Vogele; associate
    editors, Christopher Kruegler, Ronald M. McCarthy.
            p.   cm. — (Garland reference library of the humanities ;
    vol. 1625)
        Includes bibliographical references and index.
        ISBN 0-8153-0913-9 (alk. paper)
        1. Nonviolence—Encyclopedias.   I. Powers, Roger S.   II. Vogele,
    William B.   III. Series.
        HM278.P76   1997
        303.61'03—dc20   96-26869
                                                                  CIP

Cover photograph: The Rev. Dr. Martin Luther King, Jr., waves to supporters
    during the March on Washington, August 28, 1963. AP/Wide World Photos.

Cover design: Lawrence Wolfson Design, N.Y.

Printed on acid-free, 250-year-life paper
Manufactured in the United States of America

To my partner, Susan Quass, for her love and encouragement
RSP

To the memory of Gabriel Alderman Farren (1985–1994)
WBV

To my parents, Rose Mary and James Kruegler
CK

Contents

ix   Acknowledgments

xi   Introduction

xiii   Categorical Listing
of Entries

xvii   Editors

xviii   Contributors

3   The Encyclopedia

587   Index

Acknowledgments

To acknowledge all of the people who have helped make this book possible is a daunting task. First and foremost, the work would not have been possible at all without the generous participation of all of the contributors. Their essays in this book offer a wealth of profound and provocative insights about the nature, history, and dynamics of nonviolent action. We are deeply grateful to have worked with them.

We are also indebted to the Albert Einstein Institution and to the intellectual contributions of Gene Sharp to the topic of nonviolent action which made this book possible. The Institution provided the material support necessary to produce the book—providing the space and resources that are often unavailable for projects of this scope. More profoundly, however, it has been the continuous intellectual effort of Gene Sharp to define and promote the importance of this topic that enabled this book to be born. Without Gene's years of struggle, analysis, and leadership in this area of study it would have been impossible to even conceive of an encyclopedia of nonviolent action. We hope this book stands as a modest acknowledgment of our deep personal and professional thanks.

Several contributors deserve special thanks and recognition. Doug Bond, Chaiwat Satha Anand, Linda Forcey, Robin Alison Remington, Adam Roberts, Peggy Scranton, Gene Sharp, and Carolyn Stephenson all served as advisors to the project as well as contributors. They offered guidance and encouragement throughout the project, suggesting topics, challenging our assumptions, and offering good-natured moral support. In particular, we were fortunate to have the ready good counsel of Doug Bond on matters of substance and conception.

Several other individuals provided invaluable assistance. Brad Bennett authored dozens of entries ranging from biographies, to summaries of important events, to explanations of nonviolent methods. He combined an uncanny sense of what was important with energy and effort that were unmatched. His contributions throughout this book were crucial to the whole project. We'd also like to thank Patricia Chilton, Maria Figueroa, Kimberley Pyles, Paul Ropp, and Ed Steinfeld for their help and advice over the course of the project.

We are indebted to Jeff Conrad at Garland, who first approached us with the idea of editing an encyclopedia on the subject of nonviolent action, and to Kennie Lyman, Marianne Lown, and Adrienne Makowski, also at Garland, who shepherded us through the process. They kept us on course and along the way were unerringly supportive and helpful. Research for, and work on the book took place, in part, at the Center for International Affairs at Harvard University. David Maybury-Lewis, director of the Program on Nonviolent Sanctions and Cultural Survival at the Center, generously provided the institutional space necessary for completing the project. We owe thanks, also, to the many individuals and archives that provided photographs for this volume, especially AP/Wide World Photos, the Fellowship of Reconciliation, the Sophia Smith

Collection at Smith College, the Swarthmore College Peace Collection, and the War Resisters League. Their generosity has added an important visual dimension to the book.

With any publishing project, the behind-the-scenes support of family is irreplaceable—with a project of this scope and duration the forebearance demanded of them has been exceptional. Our love and thanks to Susan Quass, Connie Parrish, Katie Vogele, Sarah Vogele, Gillian Price, Marianne McCarthy, and Brendan McCarthy.

Finally, in this book, as in any edited work, a variety of views are expressed. This is by design. However, it also means that no one of the contributors or editors necessarily agrees with everything that is in the book. We therefore offer this standard disclaimer: The views expressed are those of the individual contributors only and do not necessarily reflect the views of any other participant.

Roger S. Powers
William B. Vogele
Christopher Kruegler
Ronald M. McCarthy

x

Introduction

Every day one can find evidence of nonviolent struggle in world events. Labor strikes, protest marches, and the defiance of governmental authority by groups of people in all parts of the world are common stories in the news. No form of government appears to be free from nonviolent challenges, neither the most repressive nor the most democratic. Nor are examples limited to the current period: Historical research reveals examples of nonviolent action going back as far as the Roman Empire. And nonviolent action has been used throughout the ages by people as varied as members of medieval guilds, African-American slaves, and upper-class English women.

But like the prose that Molière's Monsieur Jourdain discovered he had been speaking all his life, nonviolent action has not had a distinctive identity as such. Most people associate nonviolent action with the movements led by Mahatma Gandhi and Martin Luther King, Jr., but they are unaware of the larger history of its use. A much smaller group of people practice nonviolent action, but they usually call it "protest," in keeping with the purposes of their activities. Some scholars study nonviolent action, but they often call it "collective action." And reporters frequently write about nonviolent action, but they tend to call it by the particular method being used, a "demonstration," a "march," a "rally," or a "boycott."

Thus, nonviolent action remains poorly understood as a distinctive phenomenon. Because it overlaps with other areas of human behavior that receive much more study on their own (such as social conflicts, state violence and repression, war, and collective action and protest), nonviolent action has been subsumed into these fields, to the extent that it is studied at all. As a result, behavior that clearly qualifies as nonviolent action has not been studied as such; rather, it has been treated as a marginal part of other areas of interest, or worse, misinterpreted completely. Further, the field of research on nonviolent action itself generally lacks clear definition as the study of a genuinely empirical category of human actions in conflicts.

The central purpose of this *Encyclopedia* is to provide a standard reference work for an important domain of human behavior that has been well studied but incompletely identified. In this sense we wish to name the phenomenon to give it identity and coherence. Nonviolent action is defined here as a range of methods for actively waging conflict without directly threatening or inflicting physical harm to human beings. This deceptively simple definition locates nonviolent action within the realm of social conflict and identifies it as a distinctive form of conflict behavior—one that eschews violence and physical force.

Our goal has been to develop a reference work that is at once focused and eclectic. It is focused empirically on the human experience—and therefore the great diversity—of applying nonviolent methods of action in social and political conflicts. Our conviction that nonviolent action is a universal phenomenon, transcending cultures, political systems, and even historical periods, demanded that we strive to represent much of that experience. Our selections of the many cases of nonviolent struggle provide a rich set of examples.

At the same time, our volume is eclectic in reaching out to scholars and activists whose work in other areas directly informs the study, and even the definition, of nonviolent action. The *Encyclopedia*, therefore, is also an exercise in interdisciplinary discourse.

What will the reader find in this book? The *Encyclopedia* includes case studies of nonviolent struggle, selected methods of nonviolent action, and profiles of people and organizations that have contributed through their arguments or actions (or both) to advancing the knowledge or practice of nonviolent struggle. In selecting these entries, we have sought to be representative rather than exhaustive. Our aim was to compile a body of work that would present the diversity of applications of nonviolent action, as well as cases that hold particular lessons. That said, we must also acknowledge that the *Encyclopedia* has two biases. It contains much more on the twentieth century than on other periods in history. And it focuses on the United States more than on other parts of the world.

The *Encyclopedia* also contains essays on topics directly related to the study of nonviolent action, as well as on themes not commonly associated with that enterprise. These entries offer integrative insights that can inform our reading of the empirical case study entries. In some cases they may also provide a certain creative tension. For example, the entry on strategy suggests that the exercise of strategic analysis, commonly undertaken by military professionals can, and should, be applied to nonviolent struggle. Indeed, when one then reads the essays on abolition, the Indian independence movement, or women's suffrage, the moments of strategic dilemma and choice appear sharply, and we can think about whether the choices made were wise or foolish. Similarly, the entry on methods of nonviolent action elaborates on the technique approach to studying nonviolent action, arguing that ethical motivations should not be part of the definition of nonviolent action. Nevertheless, ethics as well as politics and strategy have often influenced the course of nonviolent struggle, as the essays on pacifism, Gandhi, and King, among others, clearly show. (A categorical listing of the *Encyclopedia*'s contents follows this introduction as an aid to finding one's way through the volume's contents.)

We hope our efforts here contribute to defining a field of study and facilitate productive thought and action by many persons. We see this volume as a place where one might begin an inquiry on this important topic, be engaged by mature debates, and be struck by new insights.

Roger S. Powers
William B. Vogele
Christopher Kruegler
Ronald M. McCarthy

Categorical Listing of Entries

Campaigns, Events, Locations

Abolitionist Movement (United States)
Ahmedabad Labor Satyagraha (India), 1918
Albany, Georgia, 1961–1962
Algeria, French Generals' Revolt of 1961
Australia, a History of Nonviolent Action
Baliapal Movement (India), 1985–1992
Baltic Independence Movements, 1987–1991
Bardoli Campaign (India), 1928
Beit Sahour (Occupied West Bank), 1988–1989
Berlin Wall Destruction, 1989–1990
Birmingham, Alabama, 1963
Bosnia-Herzegovina, Resistance to Civil War, 1991–1992
Burma, Democracy Movement, 1988–1989
Catonsville Nine, 1968
Chile, Civic Strike, 1931
Chile, Transition to Democracy
China
Chipko Movement (India)
Civil Rights Movement (United States)
Colombia, Civic Strike, 1957
Czechoslovakia, 1968 Resistance Movement
Democracy Wall Movement (China)
Denmark, Evacuation of Danish Jews, 1943
Denmark, Resistance to Nazi Occupation
Desaparecidos Movement in Latin America
Dharasana Salt Works Raid (India), 1930
Dominican Republic, Civic Strike, 1961
East Timor, Resistance to Indonesian Occupation
Egyptian Demonstrations against British Rule, 1919–1922
El Salvador, Civic Strike, 1944
France, Politics and Protest
Freedom Rides, 1961
Freedom Summer Project, Mississippi, 1964
Gay Rights Movement
Ghana, Anticolonial Movement, 1947–1951

Golan Heights Druze Resistance, 1981–1982
Greenham Common Peace Camp, 1981–1993
Guatemala, Overthrow of Jorge Ubico, 1944
Haiti, Fall of Duvalier, 1985–1986
Hungarian National Movement, 1848–1867
Independence Club Movement (Korea), 1896–1898
Indian National Movement
Intifada (Palestinian Uprising), 1987–1990
IRA Hunger Strikes, 1980–1981
Iranian Revolution, 1963–1979
Iraq Uprising, 1948
Italy, Social Movements and the Evolution of Strategy
Japan, Security Treaty Protests, 1959–1960
Jewish Resistance to the Holocaust
Kapp Putsch (Germany), 1920
Korea, Democratic Struggle in the South
Kosova, Albanian National Movement
Kwangju Uprising (Korea), 1980
Larzac (France), 1971–1981
Le Chambon Sur Lignon, France
Maori Movement, 1870–1900
March First Independence Movement (Korea), 1919
March on Washington, 1963
Mau Noncooperation (Western Samoa), 1924–1936
May Fourth Movement (China), 1919
Mexico, Nonviolent Action and Political Processes
Montgomery Bus Boycott, 1955–1956
Namibia, Campaign for Freedom
Native American Treaty Rights Movements, 1950s–1990s
Nazism, Civilian Resistance, 1939–1945
Nepal, Movement for Restoration of Democracy, 1990
Nicaragua, Civic Strike, 1944

Nicaragua, Nonviolence and Revolution
Norway, Resistance to German Occupation, 1940–1945
Nuclear Energy Opposition
Nuclear Weapons Opposition
Palestine, Arab Revolt, 1936–1939
Palestine, Illegal Jewish Immigration, 1939–1948
Panama, Civic Crusade, 1987–1989
Pathan Defiance, 1929–1938
Persia, Reform Movement, 1880–1909
Philippines People Power Revolution, 1986
Poor People's Campaign, 1968
Rainbow Warrior
Revolutions of 1989
Rosenstraße Protest (Germany), 1943
Rowlatt Bills, Opposition (India), 1919
Ruhrkampf (Germany), 1923
Russian Revolution of 1905
Salt March (India), 1930
San Francisco General Strike, 1934
Sanctuary Movement
Seattle General Strike, 1919
Selma-to-Montgomery March, 1965
Serbia, Antiwar Activity, 1991–1994
Solidarity (Poland)
South Africa, Antiapartheid Sanctions
South Africa, Opposition to Racial Oppression
Soviet Union, Coup Attempt, 1991
Soweto Uprising (South Africa), 1976
Sudan Rebellion, 1985
Thailand, Democracy Movement, 1992
Tiananmen Square, Democracy Movement, Beijing, 1989
Tibetan Resistance, 1950–present
United States, Independence Movement, 1765–1775
Vietnam War Opposition
Vykom Campaign (India), 1924–1925
Women's Suffrage
Zambia, Anticolonial Movement, 1953–1964

Methods of Nonviolent Action

Air Raids, Nonviolent
Blacklisting
Blockades
Boycotts
Civic Strike
Civil Disobedience
Conscientious Objection
Diplomatic Sanctions
Disappearance, Collective
Disrobing, Protest
Emigration, Protest *(Hijrat)*
Fasting
Funerals, Demonstrative
Graffiti
Guerrilla Theater
Harassment, Nonviolent
Hartal
Hijrat. See Emigration, Protest
International Economic Sanctions
Land Seizure
Lightning Strike
Monkeywrenching
Mutiny
Nullification and Interposition
Outing
Picketing
Property, Destruction of One's Own
Publishing, Underground
Reverse Strike
Reverse Trial
Sit-ins, Sit-downs, and Building Occupations
Skywriting and Earthwriting
Social Boycott
Sports Boycott
Strikes
Suicide, Protest
Teach-in
Vigil
Voyages, Protest
War Tax Resistance
Withdrawal, Symbolic

Organizations

ACT-UP (AIDS Coalition to Unleash Power)
ADAPT (American Disabled for Attendant Programs Today)
African National Congress of South Africa
American Friends Service Committee
Brookwood Labor College
Campaign for Nuclear Disarmament
Catholic Worker Movement
Charter 77 (Czechoslovakia)
Clamshell Alliance
Committee for Nonviolent Action
Committee of 100 (Great Britain)
Community for Creative Non-Violence
Congress of Racial Equality
Direct Action Committee against Nuclear War (Great Britain)
Doukhobors (Canada)
Fellowship of Reconciliation, International
Freedom Council (Denmark)
Greenpeace
Highlander Folk School
Indian National Congress

Industrial Workers of the World
Madres de Plaza de Mayo
Movement for a New Society
National Woman Suffrage Association
Nonviolent Alternatives
Northern Ireland Civil Rights Association
Pax Christi International
Peace Brigades International
Peace People, Community of the (Northern
    Ireland)
Peace Pledge Union (Great Britain)
Plowshares Movement
Quakers (Religious Society of Friends)
Queer Nation
SANE (National Committee for a Sane
    Nuclear Policy)
Southern Christian Leadership Conference
Student Nonviolent Coordinating Committee
United Farm Workers Organizing Committee
War Resisters' International
White Rose (Germany)
Witness for Peace
Women Strike for Peace (United States)
Women's International League for Peace and
    Freedom, U.S. Section

People
Addams, Jane (1860–1935)
Allen, Devere (1891–1955)
Anthony, Susan Brownell (1820–1906)
Aquino, Corazon (b. 1933)
Aung San Suu Kyi (b. 1945)
Ballou, Adin (1803–1890)
Berrigan, Daniel (b. 1921)
Berrigan, Philip (b. 1923)
Bhave, Vinoba (1895–1982)
Bigelow, Albert Smith (1906–1993)
Bose, Subhas Chandra (1897–1945)
Bstan-dzin-rgya-mtsho, Dalai Lama XIV
    (b. 1935)
Burritt, Elihu (1810–1879)
Camara, Dom Helder (b. 1909)
Case, Clarence Marsh (1874–1946)
Chavez, Cesar Estrada (1927–1993)
Clausewitz, Carl von (1780–1831)
Corrigan, Mairead (b. 1944); Williams, Betty
    (b. 1943)
Dalai Lama XIV. See Bstan-dzin-rgya-mtsho
Day, Dorothy (1897–1980)
de Ligt, Barthélemy (Bart) (1883–1938)
Deming, Barbara (1917–1984)
Dolci, Danilo (b. 1928)
Douglass, Frederick (1818?–1895)
Dubček, Alexander (1921–1992)

Fox, George (1624–1691)
Gandhi, Mohandas Karamchand (1869–1948)
Garrison, William Lloyd (1805–1879)
Goldman, Emma (1869–1940)
Goss-Mayr, Hildegard (b. 1930) and Jean
    (1912–1991)
Gregg, Richard (1885–1974)
Griffith, Arthur (1871–1922)
Grimké, Sarah Moore (1792–1873) and
    Angelina Emily (1805–1879)
Havel, Václav (b. 1936)
Jagerstatter, Franz (1907–1943)
Jefferson, Thomas (1743–1826)
Jones, "Mother" Mary Harris (1830–1930)
Khan Abdul Ghaffar Khan (1890–1988)
King, Coretta Scott (b. 1929)
King, Martin Luther, Jr. (1929–1968)
King-Hall, Baron Stephen (1893–1966)
La Boétie, Etienne de (1530–1563)
Lanza del Vasto, Joseph Jean (1901–1981)
Liddell Hart, Captain Sir Basil Henry (1895–
    1970)
Lutuli, Albert John (1898–1967)
Mandela, Nelson Rolihlahia (b. 1918)
Menchú Tum, Rigoberta (b. 1959)
Merton, Thomas (1915–1968)
Mott, Lucretia Coffin (1793–1880)
Muste, Abraham John (1885–1967)
Nehru, Jawaharlal (1889–1964)
Nhat Hanh, Thich (b. 1926)
Nixon, E.D. (1899–1987)
Parks, Rosa (b. 1913)
Paul, Alice (1885–1977)
Peck, James (1914–1993)
Pérez Esquivel, Adolfo (b. 1931)
Sayre, John Nevin (1884–1977)
Sharp, Gene (b. 1928)
Shridharani, Krishnalal (1911–1960)
Sivaraksa, Sulak (b. 1933)
Stanton, Elizabeth Cady (1815–1902)
Thoreau, Henry David (1817–1862)
Tolstoy, Leo Nikolaevich (1828–1910)
Truth, Sojourner (1797?–1883)
Tubman, Harriet (1820?–1913)
Tutu, Archbishop Desmond Mpilo (b. 1931)
Walesa, Lech (b. 1943)
Williams, Betty. See Corrigan, Mairead

Related Topics
Ahimsa
Civil Society
Civilian-Based Defense
Conflict Resolution
Conflict Theories

Constructive Program
Coups d'état
Democratization
Environmental Movements
Ethnic Conflict
Everyday Forms of Resistance
Feminism
Geography and Nonviolent Action
Human Rights
Identity Theory
Jihad
Leadership
Mechanisms of Direct Action
Methods of Nonviolent Action
Nobel Peace Prize
Nonviolence, Principled
Nonviolent Struggle: The Contemporary Practice of Nonviolent Action

Organization in Social Movements
Pacifism
Peace Studies
Religion and Nonviolent Action
Revolution
Sanctions
Satyagraha
Social Movements
Social Power
Solidarity
Strategy
Training for Nonviolent Action
Transarmament
Transformational Politics
Voluntary Servitude, Discourse on *(Discours de la Servitude Volontaire)*
Women and Nonviolent Action in the United States since 1950

Editors

Roger S. Powers is a researcher, writer, and lecturer on aspects of nonviolent struggle, peacemaking, and conflict resolution. He holds an M.A. in international politics from the University of Denver. He is a member of the Fellowship of Reconciliation and serves on the National Committee of the Presbyterian Peace Fellowship.

William B. Vogele is a professor of political science at Pine Manor College and a research associate with the Program on Nonviolent Sanctions and Cultural Survival at the Center for International Affairs at Harvard University. Vogele is the author of numerous publications on nonviolent struggle and international affairs, including *Stepping Back: Nuclear Arms Control and the End of the Cold War*.

Christopher Kruegler is a co-author of *Strategic Nonviolent Conflict*, a former director of the Program on Nonviolent Sanctions at Harvard University, and a past president of the Albert Einstein Institution in Cambridge, Massachusetts. He has taught aspects of nonviolent action at Syracuse University, the University of Missouri-Colombia, and the College of the Holy Cross.

Ronald M. McCarthy is a professor of sociology at Merrimack College and director of Research and the Fellows Program at the Albert Einstein Institution. McCarthy is the co-editor, with Gene Sharp, of *Nonviolent Action: A Research Guide*.

Contributors

Irwin Abrams is Distinguished University Professor Emeritus at Antioch University and author of *The Nobel Prize and the Laureates*.

Peter Ackerman is the managing director of Rockport Capital, Ltd., and co-author of *Strategic Nonviolent Conflict*.

John A. Agnew is a professor of geography at the University of California in Los Angeles and co-author of *Mastering Space: Hegemony, Territory, and International Political Economy*.

Harriet Hyman Alonso is a professor of history at Fitchburg State College in Massachusetts and author of *Peace as a Women's Issue*.

Margaret Hope Bacon is the author of *Mothers of Feminism* and other works of Quaker and women's history.

Steven E. Barkan is a professor of sociology at the University of Maine in Orono and author of *Protesters on Trial*.

Bernice McNair Barnett is a professor of Educational Policy Studies at the University of Illinois at Urbana-Champagne.

Yehuda Bauer is a professor of Holocaust studies at the Hebrew University in Jerusalem and author of *Jews For Sale?*.

Hugo Adam Bedau is a professor of philosophy at Tufts University in Medford, Massachusetts, and editor of *Civil Disobedience in Focus*.

Brad Bennett teaches primary education at the Thoreau School in Concord, Massachusetts.

Michael Berenbaum is the director of the United States Holocaust Research Institute in Washington, D.C., professor of theology at Georgetown University, and author of *The World Must Know*.

Lennart Bergfeldt is a senior lecturer in political science in the School of Social Sciences at Växjö University in Sweden.

Elez Biberaj is the chief of the Albanian Service for Voice of America in Washington, D.C., and author of *Kosova: The Balkan Powderkeg*.

Molly Blank is a member of the Atlantis Community in Denver, Colorado, and an activist with ADAPT.

Roland Bleiker is a scholar at the Australian National University in Canberra studying critical theory and civil resistance.

Doug Bond is an associate director of the Program on Nonviolent Sanctions and Cultural Survival at Harvard University.

Judith M. Brown is the Beit Professor of the History of the British Commonwealth at Oxford University and author of *Gandhi: Prisoner of Hope.*

Janusz Bugajski is the director of East European Studies at the Center for Strategic and International Studies in Washington, D.C., and author of *Czechoslovakia: Charter 77's Decade of Dissent* and *Nations in Turmoil: Conflict and Cooperation in Eastern Europe.*

Paul Buhle is a professor of American civilization at Brown University in Providence, Rhode Island, and co-editor of the *Encyclopedia of the American Left.*

Clayborne Carson is a professor of history and director of the Martin Luther King, Jr. Papers Project at Stanford University and senior editor of *The Papers of Martin Luther King, Jr.*

Vipan Chandra is a professor of history at Wheaton College in Norton, Massachusetts, and author of *Imperialism, Resistance, and Reform in Late Nineteenth-Century Korea.*

Charles Chatfield is a professor of history at Wittenberg University in Ohio and author of *The American Peace Movement: Ideals and Activism.*

Paul A. Chilton teaches at Warwick University in Coventry, England, and is author of *Orwellian Language and the Media.*

Patricia M. Chuchryk is a professor of sociology at the University of Lethbridge in Alberta, Canada, and a scholar of women's political movements in Latin America.

Christina A. Clamp teaches in the Community Economic Development Program at New Hampshire College.

Donald N. Clark is a professor of history at Trinity University in San Antonio, Texas, and editor of *The Kwangju Uprising.*

Howard Clark is an activist and director of War Resisters' International in London and author of *Making Nonviolent Revolution.*

Walter C. Clemens, Jr. is a professor of political science at Boston University and author of many books on the former Soviet Union, including *Baltic Independence and Russian Empire.*

Walter H. Conser, Jr. is a professor of religion and history at the University of North Carolina at Wilmington and co-editor of *Resistance, Politics and the American Struggle for Independence 1765–1775.*

Patrick G. Coy is active with Peace Brigades International and editor of *A Revolution of the Heart: Essays on the Catholic Worker.*

Souad Dajani is a sociologist and author of *Eyes Without Country: Searching for a Palestinian Strategy of Liberation.*

Stephen M. Davis is the president of Davis Global Advisors in Newton, Massachusetts, and formerly served as the senior South Africa analyst at the Investor Responsibility Research Center, Inc., based in Washington, D.C.

Richard L. Deats is the editor of *Fellowship* magazine at the Fellowship of Reconciliation, in Nyack, New York.

Donatella della Porta is a professor of local government in the Faculty of Political Science at the University of Florence, Italy.

Wonmo Dong is a professor of political science at Southern Methodist University.

Eknath Easwaran is the founder-director of the Blue Mountain Center of Meditation in Tomales, California, and author of, among many works, *A Man to Match His Mountains, Gandhi: The Man,* and *The Bhagavad-Gita for Daily Living.*

Kimberly Ann Elliott is a senior researcher at the Institute for International Economics in Washington, D.C., and co-author of *Economic Sanctions Reconsidered.*

Douglas J. Elwood is a cofounder and codirector of Little Children of the World, Inc., in Etowah, Tennessee, and author of *Toward a Theology of People Power: Reflections on the Philippine February Phenomenon.*

Glenn T. Eskew is a professor of history at Georgia State University in Atlanta.

Joseph J. Fahey is a professor of religious studies and director of the Peace Studies Program at Manhattan College in New York.

Maria Figueroa is a research assistant in the Office of Development Studies at the United Nations Development Program.

Valerie Flessati is on the staff of the Department of Peace Studies at Bradford University, England, and is vice-president of the British Section of Pax Christi International.

Linda Rennie Forcey is a professor of Women's Studies and Human Development at Binghamton University in New York, author of *Mothers and Sons: Toward an Understanding of Responsibility* and editor of, among many works, *Peace: Meanings, Politics, Strategies.*

Nathalie J. Frensley is a professor of government at the University of Texas at Austin.

Duane K. Friesen is a professor of Bible and religion at Bethel College in Kansas, and author of *Christian Peacemaking and International Conflict.*

J. William Frost is a professor of religion and director of the Friends Historical Library at Swarthmore College.

Arun Gandhi is the director of the M. K. Gandhi Institute in Memphis, Tennessee.

Deborah J. Gerner is a professor of political science at the University of Kansas in Lawrence and author of *One Land, Two Peoples: The Conflict Over Palestine.*

Kristian Skrede Gleditsch is a past member of the editorial staff of *Ikkevold* and a graduate student in political science at the University of Maryland.

Ed Griffin-Nolan is the author of *Witness for Peace: A Story of Resistance.*

Abdusalam Gusseinov is a professor of moral philosophy and director of the Institute of Philosophy in Moscow, Russia.

Walter Harding is the founding secretary of the Thoreau Society in Geneseo, New York.

Barbara Harmel is the former director of the South Africa Program of the Albert Einstein Institution at the University of the Witwatersrand in Johannesburg, South Africa.

Ed Hedemann is an activist and author of *War Tax Resistance*.

James Hinton is a professor of history at Warwick University in Coventry, England, and author of *Protests and Visions: Peace Politics in Twentieth-Century Britain*.

Eric L. Hirsch is a professor of sociology at Providence College in Rhode Island and author of *Urban Revolt: Ethnic Politics in the Nineteenth-Century Chicago Labor Movement*.

Marjorie Hope is a scholar, activist, and co-author of *The Struggle for Humanity: Agents of Nonviolent Change in a Violent World*.

Charles F. Howlett is a teacher, and author of *Brookwood Labor College and the Struggle for Peace and Social Justice in America*.

Hu Ping is the chief commentator for *Beijing Spring Monthly*.

Douglas R. Imig is a professor of public administration at the University of Nevada in Las Vegas and author of *Poverty and Power: The Political Representation of Poor Americans*.

H. Larry Ingle is a professor of history at the University of Tennessee at Chattanooga, and author of *First Among Friends: George Fox and the Creation of Quakerism*.

Cynthia L. Irvin is a professor of political science at the University of Kentucky.

Robert A. Irwin is a sociologist, activist, and author of *Building a Peace System*.

Christian Joppke is a professor of sociology at the University of Southern California and author of *Mobilizing Against Nuclear Energy*.

Milton S. Katz is a professor and chair of the Liberal Arts Department at the Kansas Art Institute and author of *Ban the Bomb: A History of SANE*.

Neil H. Katz is a professor of public affairs at Syracuse University and co-author of *Conflict Resolution: Building Bridges* and several other books and essays on conflict resolution and nonviolent action.

Louis Kriesberg is a professor of sociology and Maxwell Professor of Conflict Studies at Syracuse University and author of numerous books and articles on conflict and conflict resolution, including *International Conflict Resolution*.

Roman Laba is a professor at the Naval Postgraduate School in Monterey, California, and author of *The Roots of Solidarity: A Political Sociology of Working Class Democratization*.

Gary L. Lehring is a professor of government at Smith College in Northampton, Massachusetts, and author of *Officially Gay*.

Li Fang is a professor of political science at the Chinese Academy of Social Sciences in Beijing.

Bertil Lintner is the special correspondent on Burma and Laos for the *Far Eastern Economic Review.*

David C. List teaches at Metropolitan State University in Minnesota.

Tom Lodge is a professor of political studies at the University of the Witwatersrand in Johannesburg, South Africa, and co-author of *All Here and Now: Black Politics in South Africa in the 1980s.*

Brian S. Mandell is a professor of international relations and policy studies at the John F. Kennedy School of Government in Cambridge, Massachusetts, and co-author of *International Conflict Resolution for the Twenty-first Century.*

Kenneth Martin teaches at the Community College of Philadelphia, served as the associate executive director of the American Friends Service Committee, and served as a consultant and writer for the Namibia Program of the AFSC.

Sam Marullo is a professor of sociology at Georgetown University in Washington, D.C., and author of *Ending the Cold War at Home.*

James Masselos is a reader in history at the University of Sydney in Australia and author of several works on Indian politics and history, including *Indian Nationalism: An History* and *Struggling and Ruling: The Indian National Congress, 1885–1985.*

Dragan Matic is a doctoral candidate in political science at the University of Missouri in Columbia.

Doug McAdam is a professor of sociology at the University of Arizona in Tucson, and author of *Freedom Summer.*

Pam McAllister is an activist, musician, poet, and author of books on women and nonviolence, including *You Can't Kill the Spirit, This River of Courage,* and *Reweaving the Web of Life: Feminism and Nonviolence.*

John D. McCarthy is a professor of sociology at the Catholic University of America in Washington, D.C., and co-editor of *The Dynamics of Social Movements.*

David S. Meyer is a professor of political science at the City University of New York and author of *A Winter of Discontent: The Nuclear Freeze and American Politics.*

Jane Meyerding is the editor of *We Are All Part of One Another: A Barbara Deming Reader.*

Joseph V. Montville is the director of the program on preventive diplomacy at the Center for Strategic and International Studies in Washington, D.C., and editor of *Conflict and Peacemaking in Multi-ethnic Societies.*

Aldon D. Morris is a professor of sociology at Northwestern University in Evanston, Illinois, and author of *The Origins of the Civil Rights Movement.*

Marysa Navarro is Charles Collin Professor of History at Dartmouth College in Hanover, New Hampshire.

Sharon Erickson Nepstad is a sociologist and scholar of nonviolent movements for change in Latin America.

Terrell A. Northrup is a professor of political science and international relations at Syracuse University and co-editor of *Intractable Conflicts and Their Transformation.*

Padraig O'Malley is a senior fellow at the John McCormack Institute of Politics at the University of Massachusetts in Boston and author of *Biting at the Grave: The Irish Hunger Strikes and the Politics of Despair.*

Patricia Parkman is the author of *Nonviolent Insurrection in El Salvador.*

Kimberley A. Pyles is a public relations associate with Professional Media Services, Inc., in Newton, Massachusetts.

Robin Alison Remington is a professor of political science at the University of Missouri in Columbia.

Adam Roberts is Montague Burton Professor of International Relations at Balliol College, Oxford University, and author of numerous books on international relations and international organization.

Jo Ann Ooiman Robinson is a professor of history at Morgan State College in Baltimore, Maryland, and author of *Abraham Went Out: A Biography of A.J. Muste.*

Thomas D. Rojas is a political scientist and scholar of Mexican politics.

Elihu Rose is an adjunct associate professor of history at New York University, and chairman of American Historical Publications.

Paul Routledge is a lecturer in geography at the University of Glasgow in Scotland and author of *Terrains of Resistance.*

R.J. Rummel is a professor emeritus of political science at the University of Hawaii-Manoa in Honolulu and author of *Death by Government.*

Michael Salla is a professor in the Peace and Conflict Resolution Program of the School of International Service at American University and author of *Islamic Radicalism, Muslim Nations and the West.*

Chaiwat Satha-Anand is a professor of political science and dean at Thammasat University in Bangkok.

Margaret E. Scranton is a professor of political science at the University of Arkansas at Little Rock and author of *The Noriega Years.*

Jacques Semelin is a senior research associate at the Laboratoire Communication et Politique in Paris and author of *Unarmed Against Hitler.*

Gene Sharp is the founder and president of the Albert Einstein Institution and author of several books on nonviolent action and civilian-based defense, including *The Politics of Nonviolent Action.*

Lynne Shivers teaches English at the Community College of Philadelphia, has led nonviolence training workshops in various countries since 1968, and is the author of over fifty articles and books.

Carolyn M. Stephenson is a professor of political science at the University of Hawaii-Manoa in Honolulu.

Brett C. Stockdill is an activist and doctoral candidate in sociology at Northwestern University in Evanston, Illinois.

Nathan Stoltzfus is a professor of history at Florida State University in Tallahassee and author of *Resistance of the Heart: Jewish-German Intermarriage in Nazi Germany*.

Ralph Summy is a senior lecturer in political science and coordinator of the Peace and Conflict Studies Program at the University of Queensland, Australia; co-editor of the journal *Social Alternatives*; and author of, among other works, *The Australian Peace Movement* and *Why the Cold War Ended*.

Amy Swerdlow is a professor emerita at Sarah Lawrence College, author of *Women Strike for Peace: Traditional Motherhood and Radical Politics in the 1960s*, and numerous articles and essays on the U.S. women's peace movement.

Susan Neiburg Terkel is an independent writer and author of books on social and medical issues.

Ralph A. Thaxton Jr., is a professor of politics at Brandeis University in Waltham, Massachusetts, and author of *China Turned Rightside Up*.

Dorothy Thompson is a founder and member of END and the Helsinki Citizen's Assembly, Fellow of the Royal Historical Society, and editor of *Over Our Dead Bodies: Women Against the Bomb*.

Bassam Tibi is head of the Center of International Relations at Göttingen University in Germany and author of numerous books on Islamic politics, culture, and international relations in German and English, including *The Crisis of Modern Islam*, *Islam and the Cultural Accommodation of Social Change*, and *Conflict and War in the Middle East*.

Michael True is a professor of English at Assumption College in Worcester, Massachusetts, and author of *To Construct Peace* and *An Energy Field More Intense than War: The Nonviolent Tradition in American Literature*.

Peter van den Dungen is a lecturer in the Department of Peace Studies at the University of Bradford in England, and co-editor of *Twentieth Century Peace Movements*.

Fred A. Wilcox teaches creative and expository writing at Ithaca College in New York and is the author of *Uncommon Martyrs: How the Berrigans and Others are Turning Swords into Plowshares*.

George Willoughby is a Quaker activist and an original member of the Movement for a New Society.

Frank L. Wilson is a professor of political science at Purdue University in Indiana and author of *European Politics Today: The Democratic Experience*.

Lynne M. Woehrle is an activist, sociologist, and author of several works on feminism and nonviolence.

Robert Woito is an activist and director of the World Without War Council office in Chicago.

Peter Woodrow is a mediator, activist, and nonviolence trainer in Boulder, Colorado.

L. William Yolton is a former executive director of the National Interreligious Service Board for Conscientious Objectors in Washington, D.C.

James Herbert Young is a scholar, activist, and co-author of *The Struggle for Humanity: Agents of Nonviolent Change in a Violent World.*

Gordon C. Zahn is the author of *In Solitary Witness: The Life and Death of Franz Jagerstatter.*

Valarie H. Ziegler is a professor of religious studies at DePauw University and author of *The Advocates of Peace in Antebellum America.*

Betty H. Zisk is a professor of political science at Boston University and author of *The Politics of Transformation.*

Protest, Power, and Change

A

Abolitionist Movement (United States)

Nineteenth-century reform movement dedicated to abolishing African-American slavery, initially through the use of nonviolent means. The movement attracted a wide variety of adherents, from those who advocated the emigration of freed slaves to Africa to those who saw in abolitionism the opportunity to create a society in which blacks and whites, as well as women and men, lived in equality. In the early 1830s, abolitionists of all temperaments agreed that nonviolent means were essential to their cause. They urged their compatriots to conform to Jesus' admonition in the Sermon on the Mount to "resist not evil." As political tensions over the antislavery movement increased, however, many abolitionists were increasingly drawn to the use of violence to secure freedom for the slaves. The coming of the Civil War in 1861 presented nonviolent abolitionists with their sternest test—reconciling their desire to free the slaves with their commitment to nonviolent means.

Abolitionism appeared as an organized movement in 1816, with the formation of the American Colonization Society (ACS). Coinciding with the rise of abolitionism was the emergence of a northern peace movement. The New York Peace Society and the Massachusetts Peace Society, formed in 1815, represented the first organized efforts in American history—outside those of the historic peace churches such as the Quakers—to work systematically for world peace. In 1828, the various local and state peace societies united to form the American Peace Society (APS).

Though the APS never officially designated abolitionism among its goals, many APS members active in the antislavery movement understood abolitionism as concomitant to the work of peace reform. The violence inherent in slavery was inimical, they believed, to the ethic of love advocated in the New Testament. APS members interpreted the Sermon on the Mount as a divine command to love all persons, regardless of the consequences. When enough Christians embraced that ethic of love, the APS argued, the kingdom of God would dawn and all political evils would pass away. Until then, peace advocates ought to work both to create a Congress of Nations to adjudicate disputes among nations and to educate common people about the evils of war.

Prior to 1831, the principal dissension to wrack the APS centered on the question of the state's use of violence. Some members argued that the New Testament's admonition to love one's enemies and eschew violence admitted no exceptions. The state ought never resort to violence, even if foreign powers should invade it. More conservative members disagreed, noting that the apostle Paul had stated in Romans 13 that God ordained government to punish wrongdoers. In its police function, therefore, the state had no choice but to obey an ethic of coercion. When dealing with criminals (or with foreign invaders who threatened its sovereignty), the state could not in good conscience follow the ethic of love; it must rely upon coercion.

The relative tranquility of the APS was shattered by the rise of a new breed of peace reformers—abolitionists who identified themselves as "nonresistants" and who advocated an antislavery strategy called "immediatism." In the 1820s and early 1830s, a number of younger antislavery reformers concluded that the goals of the Colonization Society were immoral. The ACS had proposed compensating slave owners and then returning freed slaves to Africa. To this new generation of abolitionists, everything about that policy was wrong.

Compensating owners meant conceding that slaveholders legitimately regarded African-American slaves as property—a position the immediatists found abhorrent. Moreover, according to the immediatists, the ACS desire to resettle freed slaves in Africa was a racist attempt to deny African Americans their right to live in the nation for which they had labored without recompense. The proper aim of emancipation, the immediatists concluded, was to create a biracial society in which blacks and whites lived together as equals.

Led by William Lloyd Garrison, who in 1831 began publishing a weekly antislavery journal called the *Liberator,* a contingent of immediatists declared themselves to be "nonresistants," or radical pacifists. They admitted no exceptions to the ethic of love delineated in the Sermon on the Mount. Arguing that the perfection of God's kingdom was attainable to all who would forswear sin, the Garrisonian nonresistants called upon every American to refuse to cooperate with institutions that supported violence. Since the Garrisonians defined slavery as a form of violence, they urged individuals to denounce slavery. The Garrisonians conceded that such renunciations would not in themselves end slavery, but argued that the first step toward its abolition consisted of the individual's "immediate" decision to refuse to collaborate with institutions tainted by slavery.

Disavowing violence also entailed a withdrawal from politics. Because the state was inherently violent, employing a standing army and using coercion to enforce its laws, nonresistants not only declined to serve in the military or with the police; they also refused to vote or hold political office. The Garrisonians rejected the APS argument that the state was at times obliged to use violent means in order to obey God's mandate to govern. Violence, they concluded, always violated the ethic of love. The Garrisonians conceded that it was better for sinful people and governments to use violence in behalf of freedom and justice than in the service of oppression. But it was better still to renounce violence altogether. Obedience to the ethic of love, without regard for the consequences, was the way of perfection.

The Garrisonian nonresistants developed an interest in the APS in the early 1830s. Dismayed that the APS refused to condemn defensive wars and the police function of the state, the Garrisonians urged APS members to advance to the "higher ground" of absolute nonresistance. Fiery debates erupted as peace advocates disputed what tactics were best suited to convince Americans to renounce violence.

The Garrisonians argued that the peace reformer was like a gadfly—the goal was to irritate and disturb people until they took action against social evils. Above all, the peace reformer was to renounce the sin of "gradualism." Rather than proposing halfway measures that fell short of perfection, peace reformers should act as prophets. They should identify sin wherever they saw it and challenge the guilty to disavow their evil ways. Immediatism worked in peace advocacy as it did in abolitionism—the goal of both reforms was to convince individuals to abjure corrupt practices and institutions.

Members of the APS were unsure how to respond to the Garrisonian nonresistants. It had always been an APS strategy to appeal to influential Americans. Rather than risk alienating persons inclined to be friendly to the cause of peace by proclaiming a radical program of reform, the APS had chosen to define its goals more modestly. The APS, for example, had been careful in its constitution not to mention defensive wars at all, thereby opening membership to anyone of any opinion on the question. Though some members were eager for the APS to denounce all wars as sinful, embracing nonresistance would be a controversial move. Undoubtedly the APS would, by such an action, estrange its conservative members, as well as sacrifice its public image as a mainstream reform society. In addition, APS members opposed to the Garrisonians insisted that attaching "extraneous" reforms (such as abolitionism) to the cause of peace destroyed the integrity of peace advocacy.

While, from 1833 to 1838, the APS was debating the changes proposed by the Garrisonians, a similar discussion was occurring in the American Anti-Slavery Society (AASS). The AASS was formed in 1833 by several groups of immediatists who pledged themselves, in the AASS Declaration of Sentiments, to "reject, and to entreat the oppressed to reject, the use of all carnal weapons for deliverance from bondage." From 1835 to 1838, nonviolent abolitionism prospered, growing from about 500 societies to 1,350 societies, with approximately 250,000 members.

The various societies proved resourceful in devising "immediate" ways to resist slavery. Members launched massive postal campaigns, hoping to saturate the nation with abolitionist literature. Petition drives were also popular. In 1838 alone, 415,000 petitions for the abolition of slavery were sent to the federal government in Washington. Abolitionists organized boycotts of goods produced by slave labor. Defying Northern segregation laws, black and white abolitionists publicly traveled and dined together in an effort to resist the racism endemic to American society. In time, an antislavery subculture arose in which virtually every daily act was connected to abolitionism. Abolitionists furnished their tables with bowls and plates embossed with antislavery slogans; they wrote letters upon antislavery stationery, sealed with wafers denoting the evils of slavery; they gave antislavery handkerchiefs to their children while denying them toy soldiers; they withdrew from churches perceived to be friendly to slavery and founded churches dedicated to freedom; they observed the Fourth of July as a day of mourning, but celebrated August 1 (the date of the abolition of slavery in the British West Indies).

United in their opposition to slavery, abolitionists nevertheless continued to debate their commitment to nonviolence. The Garrisonians played a major role in the AASS, but an even more powerful faction was led by Arthur and Lewis Tappan. The Tappans were New York businessmen who also belonged to the APS. While joining the Garrisonians in denouncing colonization as a strategy for emancipation, the Tappans were more moderate in assessing the sins of the state. Ultimately, they would decide not to renounce political means as an abolitionist tool.

In 1837, an event occurred that grabbed the attention of abolitionists and peace advocates throughout the nation. In Alton, Illinois, a proslavery mob demanded that an abolitionist publisher named Elijah Lovejoy surrender his printing press. The mayor of Alton informed Lovejoy that the town was unable to protect him. As proslavery men were setting fire to the roof of the warehouse occupied by Lovejoy and his press, Lovejoy came out of the building to shoot at them. Before he could get back inside, men from the proslavery crowd had shot him dead.

Lovejoy's death forced peace and antislavery reformers to ask themselves just how committed they were to nonviolence. Conservatives in the APS exclaimed that Lovejoy's death was the logical result of Garrisonian radicalism. They condemned the Garrisonians for inciting people to violence. Moderate immediatists who belonged to the AASS and the APS, such as the Tappans, took a different approach. They could not condemn Lovejoy for protecting his property and his life. Instead, they published an address by Beriah Green, who compared Lovejoy to Stephen, the first Christian martyr. Garrisonian attempts in 1838 to persuade the AASS to declare Lovejoy's actions inconsistent with the principles of the AASS failed. Both conservative and moderate reformers feared that the Garrisonian insistence that it is sinful to use force to uphold government laws would lead to social anarchy.

The Garrisonian nonresistants feared anarchy less than most people. Since they thought that American society was mired in sin, the prospect of sweeping reform appealed to them. By 1838, they were vigorously advocating the issue of women's rights in both the AASS and the APS. Dismissing nineteenth-century notions that woman's place was in the home, the Garrisonians contended that both the APS and the AASS should permit women to function as full members, with speaking and voting privileges. Among the regenerate who followed the New Testament ethic of love, claimed the Garrisonians, gender inequalities were as unacceptable as racial prejudice.

Such sentiments were shocking, even to progressive social reformers, in an age when women were not permitted to speak in "promiscuous" assemblies of males and females. Sensing that they would never convince the APS to abjure sexism, the Garrisonians abandoned the APS and formed the New England Non-Resistance Society (NENRS) and immediately elected women officers. Adopting the phrase "Resist not evil— Jesus Christ" for the masthead of the society's journal, the *Non-Resistant,* the NENRS gave notice that the Sermon on the Mount was the core of its movement. The NENRS repudiated all forms of violence and coercion, denouncing lawsuits, criminal codes, voting, and the holding of political office as well as self-defense, murder, war, and slavery. The nonresistants, as "come-outers," urged Americans to abandon all institutions—whether they were churches, reform societies, or government itself—that fell short of the ethic of love delineated in the Sermon on the Mount.

The moderate immediatists in the AASS could not reconcile themselves to the prospect of accepting women as full members. Moreover, the moderates were not convinced, as were the

Garrisonians, of the futility or sinfulness of political reform. Increasingly, they were intrigued by the notion of creating an antislavery political party. Rather than debate women's rights or the morality of the state, the moderates decided to leave the AASS to the Garrisonians. In 1840, with the financial support of the Tappans, the moderate immediatists founded the American and Foreign Anti-Slavery Society (AFASS).

That split left unresolved another potentially divisive issue: the role of African Americans in the antislavery movement. Characteristically, the Garrisonians were initially more assertive in making personal contacts with free Northern blacks. In return, New England African Americans provided crucial financial support for Garrison's *Liberator*. But the establishment of genuine mutuality between white and black abolitionists was difficult. Although by the end of the 1830s most abolitionist societies admitted blacks as members, few black abolitionists emerged as officers of abolitionist societies or as editors of antislavery journals. Instead, abolitionist societies preferred to hire black abolitionists to lecture, raise funds, or compose antislavery pamphlets.

The most celebrated black male abolitionist was Frederick Douglass. An escaped slave living in Massachusetts, Douglass was recruited by Garrison in 1841 as a lecturer for the Massachusetts Anti-Slavery Society. Douglass gained international fame for his eloquence, but he never felt truly accepted as part of the Garrisonians' inner circle. In the face of vigorous opposition from his co-workers, he decided to leave the Garrisonians in 1847 to edit his own abolitionist paper, the *North Star*. By the 1850s, he, like many other black reformers, had embraced political means as well as moral means as appropriate to the antislavery campaign. Conscious that the overwhelming majority of free Northern black workers could find employment only at menial labor, black abolitionists were more inclined than their white counterparts to stress economic and civil rights for free blacks.

Ironically, it was the movement for women's rights that offered white and black abolitionists the most harmonious working relationships. White women feminists, peace advocates, and abolitionists like Angelina and Sarah Grimké and Lucretia Mott worked hard at overcoming prejudice and paternalism in seeking to establish genuinely mutual relationships with black reformers. Black abolitionists like

Douglass and Sojourner Truth were important figures in the women's movement. Indeed, Sojourner Truth emerged as one of the most striking figures of antebellum reform. Raised in slavery and unalterably committed to racial and gender uplift, as well as to nonviolence, she had adopted the name Sojourner Truth as a symbol of her determination to work for freedom, equality, and peace.

All of which is not to say that the women's movement provided a haven for black and white reformers. The question of using violence to further the antislavery cause would cut across the women's movement as well as across abolitionism. Black abolitionist Harriet Tubman would support John Brown, and Frederick Douglass would lobby the federal government to raise regiments of black troops, while Sojourner Truth would remain committed to nonviolence. Postwar legislation that gave black men the right to vote, but denied suffrage to women of all races, would strain relationships between black and white reformers who had labored for women's rights as well as for abolitionism.

Nevertheless, regardless of how many issues threatened to divide abolitionists, one fact had become clear by 1840: antislavery efforts were making an impact in the South. Indeed, as the various antislavery groups agitated for reform, Southern slaveholders increasingly resented and feared their efforts. They successfully lobbied for legislation designed to foil abolitionist efforts, from regulations that made the mailing or possession of abolitionist literature illegal in the South, to the Fugitive Slave Law of 1850. As a result, many abolitionists came to wonder if nonviolent means were sufficiently forceful to battle the slaveholding interests. The Fugitive Slave Law, which required Northerners to assist in the capture of escaped slaves living in the North, was particularly galling. Moderate and conservative abolitionists, who had placed their hopes on the possibilities of government-sponsored emancipation, were forced instead to watch the government defend slavery. And nonresistants, who had counseled one another to "resist not evil," found it almost impossible to stand by while escaped slaves were returned to their owners.

An equally disturbing issue was the question of extending slavery to western territories. Both the APS and the NENRS were convinced that the government had declared war on Mexico in 1846 to add Texas to the Union as a slave state. Civil unrest in Kansas in the 1850s

Executive Committee of the Philadelphia Anti-Slavery Society, 1851. Back row, l. to r.: Mary Grew, E.M. Davis, Haworth Wetherald, Abby Kimber, J. Miller McKim, Sarah Pugh. Front row, l. to r.: Oliver Johnson, Margaret James Burleigh, Benjamin C. Bacon, Robert Purvis, Lucretia Mott, James Mott. Sophia Smith Collection/Smith College (Photo by F. Gutekunst).

degenerated into open warfare between slavery and antislavery factions. A new generation of abolitionists, disinclined toward the pacifist sentiments typical of the movement's founders, advocated the use of violence to prevent the spread of slavery.

The presidential election of 1856 offered special temptations for nonresistants. The newly formed Republican Party nominated John C. Frémont, and the prospect of voting for an antislavery candidate was enticing, even if it did entail participating in a proslavery constitutional system. Also in 1856, the Supreme Court's Dred Scott decision opened up both the western territories and the free states for the expansion of slavery. Given the signs of the times, it was no surprise that many nonresistants took secret pleasure from John Brown's raid on the arsenal in Harpers Ferry, Virginia, in 1859. While the APS condemned Brown as a criminal who set himself above the law, the nonresistants respected him for facing his execution bravely and without complaint. If one had to resort to violence, many nonresistants thought, John Brown was a prophetic model.

The 1860 election of Lincoln as president prompted the secession of a number of Southern states and eventually led to war between the Union and the newly formed Confederacy. Even though emancipating the slaves was not one of the original Union war goals, most abolitionists believed that a Union victory would bring an end to slavery. By 1861 few abolitionists were committed to nonviolence, and most of them wholeheartedly supported the Union war effort.

For abolitionists associated with the APS or Garrisonian nonresistance, however, the situation was not so clear cut. The APS, since the departure of the Garrisonians in 1838, had been careful to label abolitionism as an extraneous cause unrelated to peace reform. Led by the conservative George Beckwith, the APS had defined the goals of peace reform ever more narrowly. Beckwith insisted that issues like capital punishment, self-defense, and even defensive wars were irrelevant to the cause of peace. The sole purpose of the APS, he argued, was to outlaw wars of aggression.

The antigovernment sentiments of the nonresistants especially horrified Beckwith. Under his leadership, the APS increasingly had come to defend government as a divinely mandated institution. Pointing to Romans 13 as the ground of governmental authority, the APS had noted throughout the 1850s that the state was obliged to use coercion to repress those who disobeyed the law. When the Southern states seceded, the APS applauded the possibility of a bloodless breakup of the Union. But when the South initiated hostilities by firing on Fort Sumter, the APS called for swift and decisive retribution against the secessionist "criminals" who had dared to use violence against a duly established government.

For the next four years, the APS argued that the war was in fact not a war, but a criminal action that the federal government was obliged to punish. Almost all APS members supported the Union's efforts to "punish" the South for the "gigantic crime" of attempting to overthrow a divinely mandated government. Prominent abolitionists associated with the APS—such as Charles Sumner, Gerrit Smith, and Amasa Walker—were known throughout the nation for their zealous support of the Union war effort.

The war put the nonresistants in a painful position. Unlike the APS, the nonresistants did not acknowledge that Romans 13 could ever supersede the Sermon on the Mount. For the nonresistants, violence was always immoral, even when wielded judiciously by the state on behalf of public interests. Since the command to love one's enemies and return no evil for evil admitted no exceptions, the nonresistants could not appeal to Romans 13 to legitimate the Union's violent response to Southern secession.

Nevertheless, the nonresistants saw the war as the best hope for the abolition of slavery, and they did not wish to hinder the Union war effort. Ultimately, Garrison argued that the time had come for the prophetic voices of nonresistant abolitionism to be silent. He had argued for decades that slavery violated not only the New Testament ethic of love, but also the ideals of the Declaration of Independence. Garrison conceded that the Declaration was the product of a violent effort to expel British rule from American soil. Even so, the Declaration held up ideals of justice that were inimical to the institution of slavery.

Most Americans, Garrison said, had never gained the moral purity to follow the path of nonresistant love. Most never would. But at least they could follow the highest values available to the ethic of coercion; they could fight for freedom rather than for slavery. The war, Garrison concluded, was God's judgment on a land that was inherently violent. Americans had resisted moral suasion. They had not expelled the sin of slavery from their land. It was God's decree that they answer for their failures with their own blood; but expel slavery they must.

Garrison counseled the nonresistants not to take part in the war, but not to criticize the Union war effort either. In time, Lincoln designated emancipation as a Union war aim. There could be no further doubt that the war meant an end to slavery. The abolitionists associated with nonresistance had never advocated violence, and they did not resort to it now. They remained nonviolent to the end. But they had labored for decades to abolish slavery, and they chose to do nothing to hinder Unionists who, in the hour of extremity, took up arms on behalf of the slaves.

For abolitionists committed to nonviolent means, the Civil War presented an almost unbearable dilemma. For the most part, neither nonresistants nor members of the APS had the heart to campaign for peace during the war. As nonresistant Henry C. Wright wrote to the North in the November 2, 1862, edition of the *Liberator:* "'I BLESS YOU FOR PREFERRING WAR TO SUCH A PEACE!' Be this your slogan: 'DEATH TO SLAVERY! the sum of all villainy, the concocted essence of theft, rape, robbery, prostitution, incest, piracy and murder!'"

Valarie H. Ziegler

References

Brock, Peter. *Radical Pacifists in Antebellum America.* Princeton: Princeton University Press, 1968.

Curti, Merle. *The American Peace Crusade, 1815–1860.* New York: Octagon, 1965.

Demos, John. "The Antislavery Movement and the Problem of Violent 'Means.'" *New England Quarterly* 37 (December 1964): 501–526.

Friedman, Lawrence J. *Gregarious Saints: Self and Community in American Abolitionism.* Cambridge: Cambridge University Press, 1982.

Kraditor, Aileen. *Means and Ends in American Abolitionism.* New York: Pantheon, 1969.

Pease, William H., and Jane H. Pease. "Freedom and Peace: A Nineteenth-Century Dilemma." *Midwest Quarterly Review*

20 (Winter 1968): 768–782.

Perry, Lewis. *Radical Abolitionism: Anarchy and the Government of God in Antislavery Thought*. Ithaca, N.Y.: Cornell University Press, 1973.

Stewart, James Brewer. *Holy Warriors: The Abolitionists and American Slavery*. American Century Series. New York: Hill and Wang, 1976.

Walters, Ronald G. *The Antislavery Appeal: American Abolitionism after 1830*. Baltimore: Johns Hopkins Press, 1976.

Ziegler, Valarie H. *The Advocates of Peace in Antebellum America*. Bloomington: Indiana University Press, 1992.

See also BALLOU, ADIN; BURRITT, ELIHU; DOUGLASS, FREDERICK; GARRISON, WILLIAM LLOYD; GRIMKÉ, SARAH MOORE AND ANGELINA EMILY ; MOTT, LUCRETIA COFFIN; NONVIOLENCE, PRINCIPLED; PACIFISM; THOREAU, HENRY DAVID; TRUTH, SOJOURNER; TUBMAN, HARRIET

ACT-UP (AIDS Coalition to Unleash Power)

An organization formed in 1987 by a group of New York AIDS activists—most of them gay and lesbian, and many of them living with HIV/AIDS—frustrated with the lack of concerted action to fight the AIDS crisis. The nonhierarchical direct-action group, now with chapters in numerous cities across the country, has developed confrontational nonviolent campaigns targeting multiple aspects of the AIDS crisis, including exorbitant drug prices, inadequate government funding for research and prevention, sluggish medical research, inaccessible clinical drug trials, negligent AIDS service organizations, and biased media coverage.

After engaging in extensive research and discussion, ACT-UP has employed nonviolent tactics such as phone and fax zaps, marches, rallies, die-ins, office take-overs, art, video, and agit-prop (agitational propaganda). In one action illustrating ACT-UP's creativity and determination, ACT-UP/Chicago led a protest against the failure of the Cook County Board of Commissioners to establish an AIDS ward for women at Cook County Hospital. ACT-UP's Women's Caucus, supported by the PISD (People with Immune System Disorders) Caucus and the People of Color Caucus, created a symbolic AIDS ward by placing sixteen mattresses, wrapped in sheets covered with slogans about women and AIDS, in the center of a busy intersection, blocking traffic. The women lay down on the beds and refused to move. Over one hundred people were arrested in the demonstration. The AIDS ward was opened the next day.

Along with such direct-action tactics, ACT-UP has challenged the homophobia and heterosexism that have fueled the fire of the AIDS crisis. Sociologist Josh Gamson observes that "ACT-UP mixes strategic action and material targets with expressive action and cultural targets; their cultural activity takes the form of boundary-crossing and the contesting of images." This cultural defiance includes speaking explicitly and positively about lesbian and gay male sex, publicly displaying homosexual affection, distributing thousands of condoms, as well as unfurling banners promoting safer sex at major league baseball games, the Republican national convention, and other public events. As ACT-UP works to expose how homophobia and other forms of oppression are intertwined with AIDS, the organization has sought to humanize people with AIDS and has urged people to vocally defy the status quo as symbolized in the ACT-UP slogan "Silence = Death."

As in other movements, there has been considerable in-fighting around issues relating to race, class, and gender in several ACT-UP chapters, including Chicago, Los Angeles, New York, and San Francisco. A significant number of ACT-UP members, typically, but not exclusively, white gay men, have been reluctant to focus on how racism and sexism are connected to AIDS. Simultaneously, they frequently have been reluctant to accept leadership by women and people of color—many of whom have had prior activist experience. In some chapters, this faction of white men has maintained that race and gender are not integrally linked to AIDS and that time spent on these issues would be better spent focusing on AIDS treatment issues and finding a cure.

In contrast, other members of ACT-UP have argued strongly that systemic racial and gender oppression are part and parcel of the AIDS crisis. People-of-color caucuses were formed in many ACT-UP chapters to do educational outreach in communities of color. These caucuses have put together educational workshops to challenge racism within the organization, sponsored conferences on AIDS in communities of color, and worked with community-based organizations to improve AIDS services. Virtually all of these caucuses are now defunct, with many of the members having left the organization to do work elsewhere.

Women, particularly lesbians, have provided key leadership in ACT-UP. In response to the pervasive gender inequality that exacerbates the threat of AIDS among women, women's caucuses have pushed for more research on, and services for, women with HIV/AIDS. In order to confront a situation in which women died of AIDS without ever being diagnosed (due to perceptions of AIDS as a gay male disease, the Center for Disease Control's narrow definition of AIDS, and other factors), women created the slogan "Women don't get AIDS. They just die from it." Women's caucuses have also utilized direct action to challenge the societal neglect of women with AIDS. For example, women in ACT-UP led several nonviolent protests—disrupting conferences and sitting in at the CDC offices—with the goal of forcing the CDC to change its definition of AIDS to include the primary manifestations of AIDS in women. Significantly, lesbians in many ACT-UP chapters have stimulated internal dialogues on race, class, and gender and have played a central role in pushing for collective action around these and related issues, such as AIDS among prisoners and injection drug users.

While not as severe as the political repression targeting movements of the 1960s and early 1970s, the repression ACT-UP has faced has included police violence, FBI surveillance and harassment, and the use of the judicial system to intimidate ACT-UP members. George M. Carter writes: "Incidents of police brutality include physical assault and verbal abuse sustained by AIDS activists in Chicago, Philadelphia, New York and elsewhere. This affects AIDS activism directly. The point of AIDS demonstrations is lost in the story of violence while activists continue to face the threat of police brutality."

FBI files released under the Freedom of Information Act show that ACT-UP has been the subject of "Domestic Terrorism" and "Civil Unrest" investigations since its birth in 1987. A campaign of harassing phone calls and death threats targeted ACT-UP women nationally, and multiple felony charges were filed against the Houston Three (members of ACT-UP/New York) at the 1992 Republican Party Convention. Echoing government attempts to divide earlier movements, a grand jury was used to divide queer/AIDS activists in Colorado and to indict three members of ACT-UP/Denver on felony charges in 1993 for their participation in an action protesting the AIDSphobia and homophobia of the Catholic Church.

ACT-UP's combination of provocative education and social protest has been integral in raising awareness about HIV and AIDS in the gay and lesbian community and broader society, increasing government AIDS budgets, opening up experimental trials, and making treatment more accessible for people with AIDS. ACT-UP chapters in several cities have been key players in the formation of clean needle exchanges and improved AIDS programs and services for women and for prisoners.

Beginning in 1991, various factors have contributed to a reduction in the ranks of ACT-UP. Many members have died, and others are simply burned out after years of physically and emotionally draining work. Some ACT-UPers have moved into paid positions in the ever-expanding AIDS service industry. A lack of interest on the part of society in general and the news media in particular as well as an increasingly conservative political climate have also made AIDS activism increasingly difficult. However, in 1995, the organization persists in many cities and continues to ACT-UP against AIDS.

Brett C. Stockdill

References

ACT-UP/New York—Women and AIDS Book Group. *Women, AIDS and Activism.* Boston: South End, 1992.

Arno, Peter S., and Karyn L. Feiden. *Against the Odds: The Story of AIDS Drug Development, Politics and Profits.* New York: HarperCollins, 1992.

Carter, George M. *ACT-UP, the AIDS War and Activism.* Westfield, N.J.: Open Magazine Pamphlet Series, 1992.

Corea, Gena. *The Invisible Epidemic: The Story of Women and AIDS.* New York: HarperCollins, 1992.

Crimp, Douglas. *AIDS demo graphics.* Seattle: Bay, 1990.

Gamson, Josh. "Silence, Death, and the Invisible Enemy: AIDS Activism and Social Movement Newness." *Social Problems* 36, no. 4 (1989): 351–367.

Kramer, Larry. *Reports from the Holocaust: The Making of an AIDS Activist.* New York: St. Martin's, 1989.

McKenzie, Nancy F., ed. *The AIDS Reader: Social, Political, Ethical Issues.* New York: Penguin, 1991.

Patton, C. *Inventing AIDS.* New York: Routledge, 1990.

See also GAY RIGHTS MOVEMENT; QUEER NATION

ADAPT (American Disabled for Attendant Programs Today)

A project of the Atlantis Community (an independent living center in Denver, Colorado), for the purpose of empowering people who have severe disabilities and training them to use nonviolent action to gain the civil rights denied them. Founded in 1983 by Wade Blank and Mike Auberger, ADAPT currently has chapters throughout the United States and in England and Sweden. The group's original name, American Disabled for Accessible Public Transportation, reflects its first struggle—to win a federal mandate for wheelchair access on all public transit systems. As ADAPT activist Mark Johnson explained, "Black people fought for the right to ride on the front of the bus. We're fighting for the right to get on the bus."

After nearly seven years of nonviolent struggle, ADAPT achieved its initial goal: a national mandate that all buses bought with public funds be equipped with wheelchair lifts. News media coverage of disabled activists in wheelchairs being dragged to jail proved so dramatic that ADAPT also succeeded in creating a national awareness of the disability rights movement. The struggle, in fact, helped create the Americans with Disabilities Act, a 1990 law that guarantees equality to citizens with disabilities.

The seeds for ADAPT began in 1975, when Reverend Wade Blank, a veteran of both the civil rights and Vietnam antiwar movements, founded the Atlantis Community to provide attendant care to people with severe disabilities who choose to live independently. In order to integrate Atlantis members into the community, Blank recognized the dire need for accessible public transportation.

At the time, Denver, like most communities in the United States, could legally discriminate against people on the basis of their disabilities. Wheelchair users were routinely asked to leave restaurants, theaters, and other places where they were regarded as "fire hazards," and they were subject to arrest if they failed to comply.

ADAPT Logo.

People with disabilities also lacked wheelchair access to most housing, retail stores, classrooms, places of worship, and places of employment. People with severe disabilities, who need to rely on others for their physical needs, were frequently treated in a paternalistic and sheltered manner. They failed to appreciate the extent to which their civil rights were being denied by such policies, conditions, and barriers. In short, people with disabilities needed to be awakened to the idea that they share the same basic civil rights as everyone else and deserve to fight for those rights—and to inform the general public of their needs and rights.

In the group's first major nonviolent action, on July 5, 1978, forty-five people in wheelchairs surrounded two city buses, bringing traffic at a busy intersection to a halt. Nineteen people held the buses hostage through the night. Today, a plaque marks the site of the Denver protest—the first public monument in the United States to the struggle for civil rights for people with disabilities.

After five years of similar actions, during which numerous people with disabilities were arrested, the group from the Atlantis Community gained a commitment from Denver's Regional Transit District (RTD) to provide wheelchair lifts on all its buses. With this victory, the now-seasoned activists elevated their struggle to a national level in order to extend the same right to the estimated 3 million Americans in wheelchairs. They decided to take on the American

Public Transit Authority (APTA) because it is the professional and lobbying group for all public transit systems in the nation. To carry out this national struggle, Atlantis established ADAPT as a training and organizing tool.

The group's ironclad commitment was still to 100 percent access, and it relied on the same nonviolent strategy and tactics: sidestep federal bureaucracy by targeting an opponent whom activists can see face-to-face; confront that opponent primarily at national conventions; and finally, mobilize those people who have the most at stake in the issue, no matter how poor or disabled, to undertake nonviolent direct action.

ADAPT also embraced a unique perspective on training, given that most of its members are so severely disabled. Atlantis provides financial assistance for predominantly low-income, severely disabled people from around the country to be brought to an action site. There, Atlantis staff members serve as volunteer trainers and attendants. After brief classroom instruction on organizing skills, civil rights, and strategy development, staffers lead trainees in conducting a direct action, such as a "crawl-in." Outside a restaurant, for example, trainees will throw themselves from their wheelchairs and crawl to the front door in order to dramatize the restaurant's failure to remove barriers to wheelchair accessibility. With this kind of training, disabled activists return to their home cities equipped to challenge barriers there and to win.

Each year, ADAPT members conducted a series of protests at the national transit convention. As hundreds of transit executives would arrive at the convention center, disabled activists would wedge their wheelchairs into the doors of the convention hall, blocking the entrance. Others threw themselves out of their wheelchairs, sprawling out on the sidewalk to further block access to the building. Still others would hand out leaflets explaining their grievances and demands.

When they could enter the main hall, ADAPT members unfurled protest banners and disrupted the speakers by shouting "Access, access, we want access" and other slogans. On still other occasions, dozens of disabled activists did sit-ins (refusing to leave until arrested) at the office suites of government officials and transit administrators, demanding to be heard and heeded.

As publicity about the direct actions spread, ADAPT membership burgeoned. In time, ADAPT began winning concessions of meetings, legislation, and more widespread attention to their issues and concerns. Nevertheless, by March 1990, after years of fighting, their major goal still eluded them. A comprehensive bill that would guarantee access to all public transportation and buildings, protection against employment, housing, and other discrimination, as well as other issues, lay stalled in congressional committee.

To move the bill out of committee and urge its passage, ADAPT members staged a major nonviolent direct-action campaign. On the first day of the campaign, over a thousand people walked or rode in wheelchairs, in a protest march along Pennsylvania Avenue, from the White House to the Capitol building. Then, in a symbolic protest, about sixty disabled activists abandoned their wheelchairs to ascend the eighty-three steep marble steps of the federal building.

The next day, others occupied the Capitol building Rotunda, chaining their wheelchairs together and refusing to leave, an illegal action that forced police to work for four hours, prying apart the protesters with large cutting tools and blow torches, before they could arrest 104 of them.

Finally, on July 26, 1990, after hundreds of disabled people had engaged in heroic protest actions and been arrested, after some of them had been tipped or thrown from their wheelchairs, carried by their necks, or forced into solitary confinement, after much determination, planning, hard work, and many setbacks, the U.S. Senate passed the Americans with Disabilities Act.

After this victory, the group changed its name to American Disabled for Attendant Programs Today. As the new name suggests, ADAPT turned its attention to the problem of people confined to nursing homes and other institutions because community-based options are not available that would allow them to stay in their own homes. Using the same confrontational approach, and again targeting a single opponent (the American Health Care Association, the nursing home industry's Washington lobby group), ADAPT activists seek to divert one-fourth of Medicare and Medicaid budgets away from nursing homes and into community-based programs and independent living assistance.

ADAPT is only one of many groups that have shared the fight for disability rights, especially for passage of the Americans with Disabilities Act. With its call to incitement and nonviolent direct action, however, ADAPT has stayed on the cutting edge of the disabilities rights movement, and in the opinion of its critics, on its militant fringes as well. ADAPT has not received the extensive press coverage or notoriety of other nonviolent direct-action groups, such as the Freedom Riders, Greenpeace, or ACT-UP. But, to its credit, ADAPT has transformed some of the most severely disabled people alive into powerful nonviolent warriors.

Molly Blank
Susan Neiburg Terkel

References

Shapiro, Joseph. *No Pity*. New York: Random House, 1993.

Addams, Jane (1860–1935)

Social reformer instrumental in launching the settlement movement in the United States, leader of women's peace activism, and co-winner of the 1931 Nobel Peace Prize. She was born in Cedarville, Illinois, on September 6, 1860, and died in Chicago on May 21, 1935.

Addams graduated from Rockford (Ill.) Female Seminary in 1881. On a trip to London's East End in 1888, she was inspired by a visit to the Toynbee Hall settlement house. The following year, she founded Hull House in Chicago's immigrant ward with long-time friend and labor activist Ellen Gates Starr. Under the direction of Addams and Starr, Hull House grew to include thirteen buildings and a summer campground and provided a range of social services and cultural activities for poor European immigrants. Hull House attracted many women activists, most notably Alice Hamilton, Julia Lathrop, Florence Kelley, and Grace Abbott, who worked to promote organized labor, expose sweatshop working conditions, abolish child labor, and advocate workers' compensation legislation.

Addams lectured and wrote numerous articles, pamphlets, and books, including *Democracy and Social Ethics* (1902), *Newer Ideals of Peace* (1907), *Twenty Years at Hull House* (1910), *Peace and Bread in Time of War* (1922), *The Second Twenty Years at Hull House* (1930), *The Excellent becomes the Permanent* (1932), and *My Friend, Julia Lathrop* (1935).

In addition to working for labor reform, Addams joined the campaign for women's suf-

Jane Addams and Mary McDowell at the Democratic National Convention, 1932. Swarthmore College Peace Collection.

frage in 1907 and served as vice president of the National American Woman Suffrage Association from 1911 to 1914.

Addams was greatly influenced by the writings of Tolstoy and visited his estate outside Moscow in 1896. That, with her horror at the outbreak of the Spanish-American War in 1898, pushed Addams toward pacifism. In 1915, as World War I engulfed Europe, Addams helped found the Woman's Peace Party and was elected president of the International Congress of Women at The Hague. With other delegates, she visited leaders of the warring countries to urge peace negotiations and mediation.

After her return to the United States, she caused an uproar when she claimed that young men on Europe's battlefields were finding it necessary to use stimulants before they could engage in bayonet charges. After this statement was reported in the press, Addams, once venerated as a popular heroine, was ridiculed and vilified as an anti-American traitor. For several years she suffered a decline in popularity as well as health.

In 1919 she attended the Women's Conference in Zurich where she was elected president of the newly formed Women's International

League for Peace and Freedom, a post that she held until 1929. Addams regained some of her self-confidence during this time and spent the next few years traveling abroad, where she was greeted by enthusiastic crowds in Europe and Asia.

Although most of her efforts supported women's peace activism, Addams also participated in launching such organizations as the National Association for the Advancement of Colored People and the American Civil Liberties Union. In the 1930s, controversy surrounding Addams subsided and she was awarded many tributes, most notably the Nobel Peace Prize in 1931.

Pam McAllister

References

Cooney, Robert, and Helen Michalowski, eds. *The Power of the People: Active Nonviolence in the United States.* From an original text by Marty Jezer. Culver City, Calif.: Peace Press, 1977. 2nd ed. Philadelphia, Pa.: New Society, 1987.

Davis, Allen F. *American Heroine: The Life and Legend of Jane Addams.* London: Oxford University Press, 1973.

See also NOBEL PEACE PRIZE; WOMEN AND NONVIOLENT ACTION IN THE UNITED STATES SINCE 1950; WOMEN'S INTERNATIONAL LEAGUE FOR PEACE AND FREEDOM, U.S. SECTION; WOMEN'S SUFFRAGE

African National Congress of South Africa

Founded in 1912, the oldest national liberation movement of the African continent. In April 1994, the African National Congress of South Africa (ANC) was voted into office as the majority political party in South Africa's Government of National Unity. The organization's electoral victory signaled the end of over eighty years of struggle against minority domination and racist exclusion. By far the largest and most significant participant of that struggle, the ANC had initially dedicated itself to exclusively nonviolent methods of direct action. In 1961, it adopted a significant policy shift and embarked on armed warfare. By the 1980s, the ANC was engaged in battle on a variety of fronts, international and domestic, violent and nonviolent.

Originally established as the South African Native National Congress (SANNC) in Bloem-

fontein on January 8, 1912, its several hundred members came from a small strata of black professionals, chiefs, and businessmen. Under the presidency of John Dube, the Congress's early concerns lay primarily in protecting the interests of this elite. Deputations, delegations, and consultations formed the organization's main protest activities. These efforts brought no relief from the increasing number of segregation laws. For the most part the Congress disassociated itself from the broad mass of the majority population. By the 1930s the ANC (the change of name occurred in 1923) was practically moribund, its national significance overshadowed by the Industrial and Commercial Workers Union.

The years of World War II witnessed a surge of political activity in South Africa. Blacks flocked into the country's cities in response to a substantial expansion in industry. The development of a rapidly growing black urban population was accompanied by a rise in militancy, typified by labor strikes, bus boycotts, rent strikes, and land occupations by squatters. From most of these the ANC leadership stood aloof although its then president, Josiah Gumede, was able to sway his executive committee into supporting antipass campaigns organized by the Communist Party of South Africa. But generally the ANC largely immersed its energies in an advisory body established by the government, the Natives' Representative Council. Although increasing disillusionment with the efficacy of negotiations through government channels crept into the ANC, the leadership remained reluctant to turn to more radical tactics.

The transformation of the organization was spawned by a new generation within the ANC. Establishing themselves as the Congress Youth League, these young men were fired by ideals of African nationalism and were impatient with the passivity of their leaders, which contrasted so starkly with the militancy of labor and other popular movements of the war years. By 1949 several Youth Leaguers had won places on the ANC's National Executive Committee (NEC) and had succeeded in having their Program of Action adopted by the NEC. Included among the new leadership were Nelson Mandela, Walter Sisulu, and Oliver Tambo. The Program of Action was dedicated to "immediate and active boycott, strikes, civil disobedience, noncooperation and such other means as may bring about the accomplishment and realization of our aspirations."

The 1950s were to become the classical period of nonviolent direct action in South Africa. An alliance was formed by the ANC in partnership with the Indian, colored, white, and trade union congresses, and together they launched a series of campaigns throughout the decade. The Communist Party, by then illegal, was also a close collaborator in the Congress Alliance. But, despite the energy and enthusiasm of the leadership, the campaigns brought no immediate gains. From the first and most successful of the ANC's mass actions, the Defiance Campaign of 1952, police brutality and legislated repression characterized the state's response. Attracting thousands of "volunteers" to participate in acts of defiance against six—"unjust"—discriminatory laws, many of whom went to prison rather than paying fines, the campaign ended in police shootings, riots, bannings of leaders, and proscriptions on public meetings.

In 1960, police opened fire and killed sixty-seven unarmed demonstrators who were protesting the pass laws outside the police station in Sharpeville. Although the demonstration was organized by the ANC's rival organization, the Pan Africanist Congress, the government outlawed both organizations in the wake of uprisings following the Sharpeville massacre. In December 1961, the ANC announced the formation of its military wing, *Umkhonto we Sizwe* (MK), and its shift from exclusively nonviolent forms of action.

The lack of immediate gains wrought by the ANC's nonviolent campaigns and its subsequent adoption of armed struggle lay in a complex web of causes. Throughout the 1950s, the ANC was continually hampered by severe financial constraints, which exacerbated already limited communication and organizational capacities. The black population was struggling under the duress of both a postwar recession and a stream of newly enacted apartheid laws. The most acute repercussions of those processes—economic hardship and alarming rises in the rate of pass offenses—were not the focus of the ANC campaigns of the 1950s. Instead these concerns were left to a weakened trade union movement and to the women's branch of the ANC in campaigns for a minimum wage and against the proposed introduction of passes for women. While some of the ANC campaigns won a solid measure of popular support—including the campaign against Bantu education, a potato boycott against farm prison conditions for pass offenders, the Congress of the People

to adopt a program for a nonracist democracy, and the Freedom Charter—the organization's membership never reached more than one hundred thousand.

Pressures for greater militancy mounted through the decade, in particular from black urban youth and the black peasantry. The enormity of embarking on guerrilla warfare, its potential consequences of a racial conflagration, and the implications of abandoning the ANC's image as a nonviolent movement weighed heavily on important sections of the leadership. Ultimately, the fear of being overtaken by more militant organizations and a belief in the impotence of mass action held sway. A decision was taken to form a military wing, in partnership with, but independent of, the ANC. In 1960 Oliver Tambo was sent abroad to arrange for military training of MK cadres as well as to establish an international boycott. Nelson Mandela joined him briefly in meetings with various African and other leaders in 1961–1962. A high command of MK was formed to orchestrate operations inside the country.

Although various acts of sabotage inside the country were conducted and several hundred supporters left for training camps outside South Africa, MK's first few years were marked by disaster. The entire high command were discovered in their underground headquarters and sentenced to life imprisonment. The introduction of a ninety-day detention act, solitary confinement, and torture quickly devastated the movement. By 1964 almost all of MK's internal structures were destroyed. It was not until the aftermath of the students' uprising in 1976, begun in Soweto, that new life was breathed into the organization as thousands of young people fled the country and made their way to MK training camps.

The prestige of the ANC rose dramatically in the following years. Guerrilla activities inside South Africa were resumed in 1977. An international antiapartheid movement, led by the ANC's external mission, expanded dramatically, bringing increasing isolation to the country from an arms embargo, boycotts of sports teams, cultural groups, and South African products, and the passage of the 1986 U.S. sanctions bill. When the United Democratic Front (UDF) was created in South Africa in 1983, several ANC stalwarts, together with new recruits recently released from imprisonment on Robbin Island, were highly influential in winning the front's support for and liaison with the ANC in exile in Lusaka, Zambia.

A

By the late 1980s, despite continuing government repression inside the country, sanctions busting, and an energetic diplomatic and violent counterattack on the anti-apartheid movement, the government was forced to change its strategy. Ongoing actions in the black townships (nonviolent and violent), economic decline, and hardening international hostility finally prompted a move toward negotiated change. Secret discussions began with Nelson Mandela while he was still in prison and later with other ANC leaders in exile, with the objective of creating some form of power sharing. By 1990, the ANC was legalized, its top leadership released from prison and returned from exile, and formal negotiations were begun with the ruling National Party.

Heading an alliance among the ANC, the newly legalized South African Communist Party, and the Congress of South African Trade Unions, Nelson Mandela became the country's first black president in April 1994. Mandela's election represents not only the end of minority rule in South Africa but also the triumph of the ideals of nonracism that were forged in the bleak years of the 1950s. In office, the ANC renounced its dedication to nationalization of major industries and committed itself to a program of Reconstruction and Development and affirmative action. It vigorously wooed international investment. During its first few months in office, it was vociferously confronted, as the major party in the Government of National Unity, with manifestations of the profound problems facing the country. Ongoing labor strikes and land occupations signaled the dire inequalities wrought by the apartheid system.

In 1994 the ANC successfully brought about closure to its first prolonged battle as a liberation movement. Thirty years earlier, Mandela had declared that it would be "no easy walk to freedom." The ANC now faces a new struggle that may also be no easy walk: the establishment of a democratic society in place of the authoritarianism, racism, and intolerances of the old South Africa.

Barbara Harmel

References

Lutlui, Albert John. *Let My People Go*. New York: McGraw-Hill, 1962.

Mandela, Nelson. *Long Walk to Freedom: The Autobiography of Nelson Mandela*. London: Little Brown, 1994.

———. *The Struggle Is My Life*. 3d ed. London: IDAF Publications, 1990.

See also LUTULI, ALBERT JOHN; MANDELA, NELSON ROLIHLAHIA; NAMIBIA, CAMPAIGN FOR FREEDOM; SOUTH AFRICA, ANTIAPARTHEID SANCTIONS; SOUTH AFRICA, OPPOSITION TO RACIAL OPPRESSION; SOWETO UPRISING, 1976; TUTU, ARCHBISHOP DESMOND MPILO

Ahimsa

A Sanskrit word brought to global prominence by Mohandas K. Gandhi through his political philosophy and nonviolent campaigns. *Ahimsa* is usually translated in English to mean "nonviolence," and its root, *himsa,* is usually translated as "violence." Neither translation quite reveals the essence of the Sanskrit word, however. Ahimsa actually conveys a comprehensive meaning of nonviolence in word, deed, thought—in all aspects of human life.

Ahimsa is an ethical precept found in the Jain, Buddhist, and Hindu religions. In Jainism, ahimsa is the first and most important of five vows, the central tenet of its ethical system. For followers of Jainism, ahimsa means absolute nonharm, particularly, nonkilling of any form of life. It includes not only renunciation of the physical act of killing but also renunciation of the will to kill or do harm. Jains embrace nonviolence in their quest for purity, self-perfection, and self-realization. For Buddhists, ahimsa is only slightly less important than it is for Jains. It is part of "right conduct," the fourth principle of the Noble Eightfold Path. In Buddhism, ahimsa means nonharm but also involves an attitude of compassion toward the suffering of all beings. Ahimsa is also an important concept in Hinduism. Indeed, Gandhi considered it the "core of Hinduism."

For Gandhi, ahimsa was more than a negative concept of doing no harm. It was a positive, dynamic, active concept that he identified with love. Love, he said, was the "active state of ahimsa." He sometimes called ahimsa the "law of love." In this sense, for Gandhi, ahimsa was similar to the concept of Christian charity and the Greek word for love, *agape*. From this perspective, Gandhi argued that killing, in certain circumstances, such as putting a dying animal out of its misery, could be considered ahimsa, because ending the animal's suffering was the most loving thing to do.

For example, at one time at the ashram in Ahmedabad there was an incurably ill calf. Although the calf's agony was severe, there was nothing that could be done to save the animal or ease its pain. A sharp debate arose among members of the ashram, in which one argued against killing the calf on the grounds that the right to take life is vested only in the one who gives life. Gandhi argued that in this case taking the calf's life was not motivated by self-interest, and that the agony of the creature could not be ignored. Ultimately he decided to end the calf's misery and asked the doctor to do it as quickly and painlessly as possible.

When asked whether he would use the same argument for human beings, for someone he loves, or for himself, Gandhi argued categorically that he would apply it to himself and to those whom he loved without exception. If a person is in a position to decide for himself whether to live or die, he must make that decision. If not, Gandhi believed, those who are closest to the person must make the decision for him. Gandhi recognized the difficulty of making such choices but nevertheless argued against a narrow and absolutist interpretation of ahimsa as simply avoiding direct physical harm.

Gandhi insisted that nonviolence can be understood only through understanding the depth, scope, and expanse of violence committed by human beings. The gruesome realities of physical violence tend to overshadow the subtleties of what Gandhi called "passive violence" (that is, harsh words, harsh judgments, ill will, anger, spite, lust, cruelty). It was, in his view, more urgent to deal with passive violence because it fuels physical violence. If the absence of war does not mean peace, by the same token, the absence of street violence does not mean the community lives in harmony. In ahimsa Gandhi sought to enlarge the understanding of passive violence and suggest ways in which individuals and societies could overcome all forms of violence. Similarly, ahimsa could not be separated from the idea of satyagraha as the process of struggle to transform individuals and society.

Arun Gandhi

References
Gandhi, Mohandas K. "The Fiery Ordeal." *Young India,* 1928.

See also GANDHI, MOHANDAS KARAMCHAND; NONVIOLENCE, PRINCIPLED; PACIFISM; SATYAGRAHA

Ahmedabad Labor Satyagraha (India), 1918

A labor strike of textile mill workers in Ahmedabad, the principal city of the state of Gujarat, arising out of a dispute over wage bonuses. The bonuses, originally given during a plague in 1917 as an enticement for workers to remain at their jobs, constituted up to 80 percent of workers' wages. When mill owners decided to withdraw the bonuses in 1918, workers asked for a 50 percent cost of living increase. Owners offered only a 20 percent increase and threatened to fire workers who did not accept these terms.

Mohandas K. Gandhi entered the dispute in an attempt to find a compromise at 35 percent. When his arbitration failed, thousands of workers struck the mills, beginning February 26, 1918. Strikers pledged to observe the principles of nonviolence consistent with Gandhi's concept of satyagraha. They swore to avoid assaults on mill owners, looting and destruction of mill owners' property, and to refrain from indecent language. Gandhi also began programs of self-help in health and sanitary education, the provision of medical aid, the distribution of educational bulletins, and the organization of daily meetings. He discouraged the acceptance of external financial assistance and urged workers to find alternative sources of support.

Forty days into the strike Gandhi pledged to refuse food and the use of a car until a satisfactory solution was reached. The fast was a symbolic act designed to publicly reaffirm the goals of the satyagraha, to rekindle morale among the striking workers, and to draw attention to the conflict. Although the fast brought indirect pressure upon the mill owners, Gandhi's primary objective with the fast was to strengthen unity among the workers participating in the satyagraha campaign. In July, mill owners agreed to implement a cost of living increase of 35 percent as partial replacement for the lost wage bonuses. The strike also inspired workers to create the Ahmedabad Textile Labor Association, which became a model for future Indian trade unions.

Maria Figueroa

References
Dikwakar, Ranganath R. *Saga of Satyagraha.* Delhi, India: Kapur, 1969.

See also GANDHI, MOHANDAS KARAMCHAND; STRIKES

Air Raids, Nonviolent

Use of airplanes, helicopters, balloons, or other air transport to enter an opponent's air space to communicate with, or bring gifts for, the population. One common form of air raid is dropping leaflets designed to persuade the population to resist the ruling military or civilian government. This method is intended to have a psychological effect. Sometimes the method is used in conjunction with other nonviolent tactics. It may also be used within overwhelmingly violent struggles, however, and is commonly considered a tactic of "psychological warfare."

One example of a nonviolent air raid occurred during the 1920 Kapp Putsch in Germany. On Tuesday, March 16, an airplane from the exiled German government in Stuttgart dropped leaflets entitled "The Collapse of the Military Dictatorship" on Berlin. Many Berliners reading these leaflets cheered so loudly that the Allied Commission of Control rushed to their windows to see what the uproar was about. Other examples took place in 1965, in the midst of the Vietnam War. United States planes dropped toys and clothes over villages near Hanoi in an attempt to convince North Vietnamese civilians of American good will. American planes also hovered over National Liberation Front positions in South Vietnam and played tape recordings of family sounds with a plea to desert and go home to North Vietnam.

References
Sharp, Gene. *The Politics of Nonviolent Action.* Boston: Porter Sargent, 1973.

See also KAPP PUTSCH

Albany, Georgia, 1961–1962

Significant campaign of the U.S. civil rights movement, widely regarded both within and outside of the movement as a failure. The Albany protests emerged in response to the student sit-ins of 1960 and the Freedom Rides of 1961. Local organizers worked with the Student Nonviolent Coordinating Committee (SNCC) and the Southern Christian Leadership Conference (SCLC) to mount a series of nonviolent protests to end the segregation of all public facilities in the city, including bus and train stations, lunch counters, schools, parks, swimming pools, hospitals, and libraries. The campaign involved protest marches, sit-ins, and consumer boycotts. But after months of demon-strations and more than one thousand arrests, the campaign had produced few tangible gains. The bus boycott bankrupted the bus company, and the city finally desegregated its bus terminals to comply with an Interstate Commerce Commission ruling, but all other public facilities either remained segregated or closed rather than be integrated.

There were several reasons for the campaign's failure. First, the campaign lacked a specific, achievable goal. It was too ambitious. Instead of attempting to desegregate all public facilities in Albany at one time, it should have focused on one or two well-defined targets. Second, the campaign lacked unity. There was constant infighting between SNCC and SCLC, and the campaign was unable to enlist the support of many older African Americans in Albany. Third, Police Chief Laurie Pritchett "met nonviolence with nonviolence," effectively undermining the impact of the nonviolent protests. He had studied the nonviolent tactics of the civil rights movement and was prepared to respond with shrewd tactics of his own. He treated protesters with restraint, and even politeness, when arresting them; imprisoned them in the jails of neighboring towns to keep the Albany jail from filling up; and arranged for Martin Luther King, Jr., to be released from jail quickly. Pritchett's tactics were calculated to diffuse rather than concentrate the protests' energy, and the tactics worked. Finally, King's strategic choices emphasized conciliation rather than coercion. The first time he was arrested in Albany, he agreed to be released on bail after local organizers had negotiated a verbal "truce" with city officials, saying that he did "not want to stand in the way of peaceful negotiation." Later, when a federal court injunction banned civil rights demonstrations in Albany, King agreed to obey the injunction. Both of these decisions caused the campaign to lose momentum. The lessons learned in Albany, Georgia, however, proved especially useful in 1963 when the SCLC mounted its next campaign, in Birmingham, Alabama.

Roger S. Powers

References
Colaiaco, James A. *Martin Luther King, Jr.: Apostle of Militant Nonviolence.* New York: St. Martin's, 1988.

See also BIRMINGHAM, ALABAMA, 1963; CIVIL RIGHTS MOVEMENT; FREEDOM RIDES,

1961; KING, MARTIN LUTHER, JR.; MONT-GOMERY BUS BOYCOTT, 1955–1956; SOUTH-ERN CHRISTIAN LEADERSHIP CONFERENCE; STUDENT NONVIOLENT COORDINATING COM-MITTEE

Algeria, French Generals' Revolt of 1961

A brief attempt by units of the French Army in Algeria to seize power in late April 1961; at that time, Algeria was administered as part of France. This coup d'état, or seizure of power, was an attempt by senior French officers to prevent the French government from negotiating independence with the Algerian nationalist forces. It was also seen as a possible prelude to a seizure of power in France itself. The coup d'état was strongly opposed in both Algeria and France, and collapsed after four days. Civil resistance was one important factor leading to this outcome.

The background to these events was the Algerian nationalist revolt, which had begun in 1954. The rebels of the *Front de Libération Nationale* (National Liberation Front, commonly known as FLN) used methods of guerrilla warfare and urban terrorism. The French forces engaged in tough counterinsurgency methods and are known to have resorted to torture. As the French Fourth Republic collapsed in 1958, General Charles de Gaulle was brought to power by a coalition of pro-colonial political groups and the military. De Gaulle led the creation of a new constitution and formed the Fifth Republic, of which he became president. Yet by April 1961 de Gaulle had indicated publicly that he was prepared to enter into negotiations with the FLN. Many senior officers sought to exercise pressure to prevent any French capitulation to the FLN.

The "Generals' Revolt" began on the night of April 21–22, 1961. French military units captured control of the city of Algiers and other key points in Algeria. Led by four recently retired generals (Maurice Challe, Edmond Jouhaud, André Zeller, and Raoul Salan), the putsch secured support from many senior serving officers, as well as from the European population in Algeria. The leaders issued a proclamation declaring that all power in Algeria had passed to the military authority and that action would be taken against "individuals who have taken a direct part in the attempt to abandon Algeria and the Sahara." Several generals who remained loyal to President de Gaulle were arrested.

There were widespread fears that the putsch would be followed by a parallel action in metropolitan France itself. Of the French armed forces, some 500,000 men, constituting the majority of operational units, were in Algeria. President de Gaulle had to reckon with the twin possibilities of an airborne invasion from Algeria and a military insurrection within France.

Both in France and in Algeria, opposition to the putsch built up on Saturday and Sunday, April 22 and 23. In a broadcast on the evening of Sunday, April 23, President de Gaulle, who assumed sweeping emergency powers during this crisis, declared: "I order that all means—I repeat all means—be employed to bar the way everywhere to these men until they are brought down. I forbid every Frenchman, and in the first place every soldier, to carry out any of their orders." Later the same evening, the prime minister, Michel Debré, expressed concern about the possibility of an airborne invasion from Algeria, and called on the people "to convince the mistaken soldiers of their huge error." French political parties and trade unions called for a one-hour general strike at 5 P.M. on Monday, April 24. Some 10 million workers throughout France participated in this remarkable demonstration of civilian solidarity with the Paris government.

In Algeria, although the coup leaders controlled all the newspapers and main radio transmitters, they could not stop people, including soldiers, from listening to broadcasts from France. The message of resistance spread quickly throughout Algeria, especially after de Gaulle's Sunday broadcast. Air force pilots flew empty transport planes (which might otherwise have been used for an invasion) to France; French army conscripts refused to cooperate with the putsch; communications and transport got delayed.

By Tuesday, April 25, it became clear to leaders of the putsch that they were incapable of ruling even Algeria effectively. Eventually they decided to liquidate the affair. On the night of April 25–26 the First Foreign Legion Parachute Regiment withdrew from Algiers, and government buildings were abandoned by the rebels.

This outcome was achieved by essentially nonviolent means. Although de Gaulle relied for protection on armed police units and had called for the use of "all means" against the rebels, at no time was a single shot fired against any of the rebel forces. After the collapse of the coup, some of the rebels went on to take part in an unsuccessful campaign of violence and terror in the name of *Algérie française*. Algeria became an independent state in 1962.

Adam Roberts

References

Fauvet, Jacques, and Jean Planchais. *La Fronde des Généraux*. Paris: Arthaud, 1961.

Kelly, George Armstrong. *Lost Soldiers: The French Army and Empire in Crisis 1947–1962*. Cambridge: MIT Press, 1965.

Roberts, Adam. "Civil Resistance to Military Coups." *Journal of Peace Research* (Oslo), 1 (1975): 19–36.

See also COUPS D'ÉTAT

Devere Allen. Photo by Bachrach.

Allen, Devere (1891–1955)

Socialist pacifist journalist prominent in the American antiwar movement in the twentieth century. Allen was born in Providence, Rhode Island, on June 24, 1891, and died on August 27, 1955. He was an important analyst of pacifism, who advocated nonviolent action as the only way to prevent aggression and war.

Devere Allen began his antiwar activities as a college student and then as executive secretary of Young Democracy, a political youth organization founded in 1918. From 1921 to 1933, Allen edited *World Tomorrow,* the journal of the Fellowship of Reconciliation, a religious pacifist organization. In 1929, Allen edited a collection of essays applying the concept of pacifism to social problems; it was called *Pacifism in the Modern World*. In 1930, he published *The Fight for Peace,* which documented the American peace movement and analyzed alternative peace-making strategies. Allen urged pacifists to develop a realistic way to combat oppression in the world. He advocated the use of three types of nonviolent action: nonviolent noncooperation with aggressors, nonviolent "attack" to effect positive social change, and mass nonviolent direct action to prevent war. Although he was one of the leaders of the Fellowship of Reconciliation, Allen focused on ethical rather than religious pacifism.

In addition to his writing and editing, Allen was an advocate of internationalist pacifism. While covering the Spanish civil war, Allen was inspired by the war to urge international pacifists to embrace socialist revolutionary aims as well. In 1933, Allen and his wife, Marie, founded an international news clearinghouse called the No-Frontier News Service (later renamed Worldover Press), in which they reported and analyzed events overlooked by traditional press services, in an effort to cater to peace constituencies. By 1955, the service boasted over seven hundred subscribers across the globe.

Allen was also involved in socialist politics and activities. As a board member of the League for Industrial Democracy, he opposed the use of violence by workers and instead urged mass nonviolent direct action. As a long-time member of the Socialist Party, he was a prominent proponent of nonviolent war resistance. During the 1934 Socialist Party national meeting, Allen authored the Declaration of Principles, which advocated the general strike as the best strategy to defeat fascism. For forty years, Devere Allen championed the cause of socialist internationalism and revolutionary nonviolent resistance.

Brad Bennett

References

Allen, Devere. *Devere Allen: Life and Writings*. Edited by Charles Chatfield. New York: Garland, 1976.

Cooney, Robert, and Helen Michalowski,

eds. *The Power of the People: Active Nonviolence in the United States.* From an original text by Marty Jezer. Culver City, Calif.: Peace Press, 1977. 2nd ed. Philadelphia: New Society, 1987.

See also FELLOWSHIP OF RECONCILIATION, INTERNATIONAL; PACIFISM

American Friends Service Committee

Relief organization seeking to implement the Quaker peace testimony. Quakers from many American Yearly Meetings with differing theological and social perspectives created the American Friends Service Committee (AFSC) in the spring of 1917, immediately after the U.S. entrance into World War I. The AFSC's purpose was to provide a "service of love in wartime"; that is, the AFSC would give conscientious objectors, who for religious reasons opposed all wars, an opportunity to show their patriotism and love of God by engaging in relief and reconstruction work in France. Operating under the auspices of the American Red Cross, the AFSC sent to Europe 550 young men and 50 women to join in the ongoing relief efforts of English Quakers. During the war, AFSC workers built prefabricated houses or repaired homes damaged in the war, provided medical care for civilians, taught modern agricultural methods to peasants, and helped care for refugees. Because of wartime restrictions, they were not allowed to talk openly about their pacifist religious beliefs.

What began as a temporary agency became a permanent relief organization after the war. The French entrusted the AFSC with reconstruction work in the area around Verdun. Because of their accomplishments in France, their fair treatment of German prisoners of war after the Armistice, and their reputation as pacifists, they were entrusted by the German and American governments with the responsibility for feeding German children. With funding provided largely from the American Relief Association, the AFSC in 1920 began supervising the feeding of over one million German children and undertook relief projects in Russia, Serbia, Poland, and Austria. The AFSC viewed its relief work in Europe as an effort at reconciliation and a means of creating the conditions for future peace.

The Service Committee operates today under a pattern first developed before 1920.

The organization is not a missionary body and does not proselytize. Its personnel profess adherence to the Quaker peace testimony by renouncing a reliance upon war and seeking to promote harmony through working nonviolently for social justice. Those who receive aid are not subjected to religious or political tests, and the AFSC attempts to enlist local personnel in designing and implementing projects. The AFSC is not committed to any one philosophy of nonviolent activity, believing that "our deeds carry the message." Originally the AFSC depended upon a few paid supervisors, unpaid part-time volunteers, and conscientious objectors who received a subsistence allowance. Now the overseas and headquarters workers are likely to have professional expertise.

The Service Committee attempts to combine Quaker "sense of the meeting" procedures (where there is no voting) with modern bureaucratic techniques. Policy is set by a board whose members are Quakers, but the staff has always included some non-Quakers. In the 1960s, the AFSC attempted to recruit as staff people of similar ethnic background to those it was trying to help. One result is that Quakers now constitute less than 15 percent of the total staff. Most funding has always come from non-Quaker sources. International and national programs are implemented from the headquarters in Philadelphia, but regional offices have autonomy for local activities. The AFSC cooperates closely with its British Quaker counterpart, the Friends Service Council.

From its beginning, the AFSC has been criticized within and outside the Society of Friends. Its personnel have been generally more liberal than other Quakers or the general public. It has been denounced by political conservatives as pro-German, pro-Communist, pro-Israeli, pro-Palestinian, pro-black, and pro-homosexual. Those Quakers who are fundamentalist or right-wing evangelicals oppose its emphasis upon material improvements and neglect of proselytization.

The AFSC is best known for its relief work for the victims of war. In the 1930s, it worked with refugees from the Spanish civil war and attempted to help Jews emigrate from Germany and Austria. During World War II, Congress barred American conscientious objectors from working abroad, but a few Americans not subject to the draft worked in China. In the postwar period the AFSC was active in Europe, Palestine, India, and China. While relief work remains the most well-known AFSC program, the organization has from its beginnings attempted to foster grassroots social change with various projects. For example, programs have run kindergartens for Palestinian refugees in Israeli-occupied Gaza, introduced new agricultural methods in sub-Saharan Africa, and trained women in pre- and postnatal care in Brazil. In general, the AFSC relief programs concentrate upon human-made rather than natural disasters. Since the 1920s, limited financial resources required AFSC programs to be smaller and to have more community involvement than those undertaken by the Red Cross, the United Nations, or the U.S. government.

The AFSC has been a persistent critic of American military interventions and supporter of disarmament and arms control. In World War II, it raised money for and ran Civilian Public Service camps for conscientious objectors. The AFSC opposed the war in Vietnam, disobeyed a U.S. government embargo by sending medical supplies to North Vietnam, and worked with wounded civilians and refugees in South Vietnam. In the 1980s, it provided medical care, worked for economic development, and sent observers to monitor the conduct of the U.S.-backed government in El Salvador. In all of America's recent wars it has provided draft counseling and legal advice to young men dealing with the Selective Service System, visited imprisoned conscientious objectors, and advised men in the army who sought a discharge for reasons of conscience. The AFSC is not a registered lobbying organization and does not participate directly in political affairs.

Since the 1920s, beginning with aid to the children of striking coal miners, the AFSC has engaged in programs of relief and peace education in the United States. During the 1930s, the AFSC promoted a homestead program for unemployed coal miners and has continued to the present with programs for migrant workers. One section within the AFSC attempts to overcome economic and social discrimination and to promote integration and good relations among the races. Peace education, a second type of domestic program, has taken many forms: peace caravans that visited college campuses, work camps for young people, essay contests, news releases, movies, conferences, tracts, and demonstrations. After World War II, the AFSC commissioned groups of experts to produce a series of books with policy recommendations on major issues of foreign and domestic policy,

including the cold war, the Arab-Israeli conflict, Vietnam, the arms race, abortion, and AIDS. The AFSC led and cooperated with other peace groups demonstrating in Washington and elsewhere for civil rights for African Americans and for nuclear disarmament. Its publications and speakers keep a wide public informed on issues affecting peace.

In some international conflicts, the AFSC has played a mediating role. AFSC representatives acted as confidential messengers between Nasser and Ben Gurion in 1955 and between the Ibo generals and the Nigerian government during their civil war in the 1970s. In the late 1940s and 1950s, the AFSC sponsored cultural contacts with Soviet peace groups, and it has hosted off-the-record conferences among hostile groups, such as the Israelis and Palestinians. The AFSC is often caught between its wishes to help oppressed peoples (whose struggles for freedom may be violent) and its desires to promote peace and to serve as a neutral facilitator of meaningful dialogue between enemies.

During its early years, the AFSC worked closely with the U.S. government. Its programs in France and in Germany had official support. During the Depression, the AFSC's programs complemented those of the New Deal. After experiencing official restrictions during World War II as well as the government's tactics used to oppose communism during the cold war, the AFSC drew back from official cooperation with Washington on relief activities. It now independently sponsors wide-ranging domestic and foreign programs. The AFSC, as a part of the general American peace movement, has since 1917 supported a wide variety of means to foster peace: international organizations including the League of Nations and the United Nations, disarmament and arms control, racial justice, Gandhian protest tactics, and conflict resolution. The AFSC seeks incremental changes, not violent revolution, by improving the lives of the poor and oppressed through nonviolent social change.

J. William Frost

References

Forbes, John. *The Quaker Star under Seven Flags, 1917–1927.* Philadelphia: University of Pennsylvania, 1962.

Frost, J. William. "'Our Deeds Carry Our Message': The Early History of the American Friends Service Committee." *Quaker History* 81 (Spring 1992): 1–51.

Jones, Rufus. *A Service of Love in Wartime: American Friends Relief Work in Europe, 1917–1919.* New York: Macmillan, 1920.

Weisbord, Marvin. *Some Form of Peace: True Stories of the American Friends Service Committee at Home and Abroad.* New York: Viking, 1967.

See also NOBEL PEACE PRIZE; PACIFISM; QUAKERS

Anthony, Susan Brownell (1820–1906)

Social reformer and leader of the U.S. women's rights movement. She was born in Adams, Massachusetts, on February 15, 1820, and died in Rochester, New York, on March 13, 1906.

Anthony was educated first at home and then in a Quaker boarding school outside of Philadelphia. She worked for a number of years as a teacher and, in 1846, became headmistress of the female department of an academy west of Albany, New York. There, claiming to be tired of theory, she joined the Daughters of Temperance.

In 1849, she rejoined her parents on a farm outside of Rochester, New York, and became involved in the antislavery cause inspired by abolitionist leaders William Lloyd Garrison, Wendell Phillips, Frederick Douglass, and Stephen and Abby Foster. Near the Canadian border, Rochester was a strategically located stop on the Underground Railroad and, in the early 1850s, Anthony provided sanctuary for a number of escaped slaves. Her primary commitment, however, was to the temperance cause, through which she met Amelia Bloomer, Lucy Stone, and the woman who became the catalyst for Anthony's feminism—Elizabeth Cady Stanton.

In 1852, when women were refused permission to speak at an Albany temperance rally, Anthony formed the Woman's State Temperance Society. For the next decade, Anthony made links between the temperance, abolitionist, and women's rights causes, lecturing, petitioning, and raising funds throughout the state. She campaigned for a liberalization of laws regarding married women's property rights and served as an agent of Garrison's American Anti-Slavery Society.

After the Civil War, Anthony increasingly focused her organizing skills on the cause of women's suffrage and, in 1866, became corre-

Susan B. Anthony at 48. Sophia Smith Collection/ Smith College.

sponding secretary of the American Equal Rights Association. With Elizabeth Cady Stanton, she began publishing a periodical, *Revolution,* in 1868, and the following year the two women formed the National Woman Suffrage Association (NWSA). Anthony traveled throughout the country to support women's suffrage efforts in various states. In addition to writing and lecturing, Anthony sometimes engaged in nonviolent actions to disrupt and challenge business as usual. In 1872, she was arrested, convicted, and fined for attempting to vote in a presidential election. (She refused to pay the fine.) On the Fourth of July in 1876, Anthony and several other activists disrupted the nation's centennial celebration in Philadelphia by distributing and reading aloud the Woman's Declaration of Rights.

With Elizabeth Cady Stanton and Matilda Joslyn Gage, Anthony wrote *The History of Woman Suffrage,* which was published in four volumes in 1881, 1882, 1886, and 1902. In 1888, Anthony helped found the International Council of Women and was warmly received on trips to London and Berlin as head of the U.S. delegation to the council. By the 1890s, Anthony was a national heroine, though women's suffrage was still unrealized. In 1890, the more conservative American Woman Suffrage Association merged with NWSA. Anthony served as president of the new National American Woman Suffrage Association from 1892 to 1900.

Pam McAllister

A

References

Bacon, Margaret Hope. *Mothers of Feminism: The Story of Quaker Women in America*. San Francisco: Harper and Row, 1986.

Barry, Kathleen. *Susan B. Anthony: A Biography of a Singular Feminist*. New York: Ballantine, 1988.

See also ABOLITIONIST MOVEMENT; DOUGLASS, FREDERICK; GARRISON, WILLIAM LLOYD; NATIONAL WOMAN SUFFRAGE ASSOCIATION; STANTON, ELIZABETH CADY; WOMEN AND NONVIOLENT ACTION IN THE UNITED STATES SINCE 1950; WOMEN'S SUFFRAGE

Aquino, Corazon (b. 1933)

President of the Philippines who came to office following a predominantly nonviolent "people power" revolution overthrowing dictator Ferdinand Marcos in February 1986. As an opposition leader before assuming the presidency, Aquino advocated nonviolent direct action to overthrow the repressive and corrupt Marcos regime.

Corazon Aquino was born in Manila on January 25, 1933. Her husband, Benigno Aquino, served as a senator in the Filipino parliament from 1967 to 1972, was imprisoned for his opposition activities from September 1972 to May 1980, and then spent three years in exile in the United States. He was assassinated upon his return to the Philippines on August 21, 1983. Throughout those years, Corazon Aquino had supported her husband's career and raised their children. Following his assassination, however, she gradually assumed a leadership role in the anti-Marcos opposition movement. During the next two years, she advocated fighting nonviolently for liberation. After months of urging by supporters to run against Marcos for the presidency, Aquino announced her candidacy in early December 1985.

When the official results of the election gave victory to Marcos, Aquino addressed over 2 million people at a "Triumph of the People" prayer rally on February 16, 1986. She called for a widespread campaign of nonviolent struggle, including a general strike, a boycott of the Marcos-controlled press, an economic boycott of companies owned by Marcos and his cronies, delaying payment of utility bills, and overloading government agencies with loan applications.

Before this campaign could be carried out, the crisis came to a head on February 22, when military leaders of a suspected coup plot were being rounded up. Over 1 million Filipinos gathered in the capital of Manila to protect these renegade officers and to form human barricades in front of military forces. In the face of this nonviolent resistance and with declining U.S. government support, Marcos fled the country, and Aquino was inaugurated on February 25, 1986. The Aquino government neglected promised land reforms and maintained a counterinsurgency war against communist and Muslim rebels. Aquino was voted out of office and replaced by Fidel Ramos in May 1992.

Brad Bennett

References

Komisar, Lucy. *Corazon Aquino: The Story of a Revolution*. New York: George Braziller, 1987.

White, Mel. *Aquino*. Dallas: Word, 1989.

See also PHILIPPINES PEOPLE POWER REVOLUTION, 1986

Aung San Suu Kyi (b. 1945)

Recipient of the 1991 Nobel Prize in Peace, Suu Kyi became the leader and symbol of Burma's democracy movement beginning in 1988. In 1989, Suu Kyi began a long-term detention under house arrest on orders of the military government officially known as the State Law and Order Restoration Council (SLORC). Although not free in her personal circumstances, she nevertheless continued to set a standard for freedom and human rights in Burma and elsewhere. When the Nobel Committee announced that Suu Kyi had won the Peace Prize for her "nonviolent struggle for democracy and human rights," it called the struggle "one of the most extraordinary examples of civil courage in Asia in recent decades."

Suu Kyi is the daughter of Burma's most revered national hero, General Aung San, who had brought the country to the brink of independence before he was assassinated in 1947, but she did not make a life of politics. As a teenager, she lived in New Delhi, India, where her mother was Burma's ambassador. Later she studied philosophy and politics at Oxford University, taking her degree in 1967, and then worked for three years for the United Nations

Secretariat in New York. In January 1972 she married Michael Aris, a British scholar of Tibetan literature. They lived in England for sixteen years.

Suu Kyi returned to Burma in March 1988 to care for her mother, who had suffered a severe stroke. A prodemocracy movement emerged, organized mostly by students, with the aim of ending the twenty-six-year rule of General Ne Win. In August, Suu Kyi joined, and electrified, the movement. On a hot day, thousands of Burmese crowded the grounds of the great Schwedagon pagoda in Rangoon to hear her, although she was little known personally and many knew only that she was Aung San's daughter. But her own articulate and passionate speech established her identity and leadership.

The opposition movement caused the resignation of Ne Win, but the new SLORC government was rapidly created as the new generals brutally suppressed the movement. To maintain an air of legitimacy, however, the SLORC generals said they would turn over power to a civilian government after elections. Suu Kyi became the leader of the National League for Democracy Party, traveling the countryside by bullock cart and speaking to a thousand meetings in defiance of a SLORC ban on political gatherings of more than four people. In her speeches Suu Kyi emphasized human rights as the democratic goal and nonviolence as the means to attain it, basing her arguments on Buddhist tenets. On one occasion, as she was walking down the street with her associates, soldiers lined up in front of her with their rifles at the ready, threatening to shoot if she advanced any further. She calmly walked on and at the last moment a higher officer countermanded the order to fire.

Shortly after the government placed her under "restrictive residence" in 1989, Suu Kyi began a twelve-day hunger strike protesting the treatment of her jailed political associates—she demanded that she be jailed just as her supporters had. The strike ended after promises that her supporters would not be maltreated. Despite her house arrest, and the fact that she was not allowed to run, the election of May 1990 was a resounding victory for the National League for Democracy Party. The SLORC government, nevertheless ignored the election, jailed the elected NLD representatives, and remained in power.

On July 11, 1995, Suu Kyi was released. This followed various international appeals, international pressure, and continuous attention—including a 1993 attempt by other Nobel Laureates to enter Burma from Thailand to demand her freedom.

Irwin Abrams

References

Abrams, Irwin. "The Nobel Prize in Peace." In *The Nobel Prize Annual 1991*. Edited by International Merchandising Group. New York: IMG, 1992.

Aung San Suu Kyi. *Freedom from Fear*. Edited by Michael Aris. London: Viking, 1991.

See also BURMA, DEMOCRACY MOVEMENT, 1988–1989; NOBEL PEACE PRIZE

Australia, a History of Nonviolent Action

Australia's more than two-hundred-year history of white settlement records many examples of nonviolent action. Until very recently, however, they were never classified as such; they were simply called protests, rallies, strikes, squattings, resistances, and so on, and then subdivided into those actions that "turned violent" and those that "remained peaceful." Disinterested observers, as well as the protagonists themselves, may have often disagreed about the nature of an action, but they all accepted the conventional terminology. If nonviolence had any meaning, it was equated with pacifism, passivity, or nonresistance, and associated with the Christianity of a tiny group of "peace churches."

Notwithstanding the principled nonviolence conducted by this handful of Christians, most of the participating population resorted to nonviolent action because of its tactical or strategic advantage. It was seen as an effective political tool for implementing the *vox populi,* and thus it can be identified with the strong egalitarian strain present among the less powerful Australian classes. Since the focal point of opposition to elite domination has occurred in the arena of extraparliamentary politics, nonviolent action, at the tactical and strategic levels, arguably defines a major, though unacknowledged, part of Australian history.

The traces of nonviolent action go back to the early years of Australia's settlement as a penal colony. The convicts often defied their jailers with protests of tactically inspired nonviolent insolence and idleness, "bolting," or brawling. Typically met with extremely harsh measures, these primarily nonviolent actions were quickly quelled or else they degenerated, on both sides, into violent clashes (such as the Castle Hill Rebellion in 1804), leaving the convicts shot, hanged, or mercilessly flogged and thrown into solitary confinement. Only rarely did their suffering and perseverance bring instrumental success, or did they manage to escape into the bush. Some of these escapees, along with fellow ex-convicts ("emancipists"), who had stolen stock from free settlers, drove their flocks and herds into the wilderness and nonviolently occupied lands to which they had no claim. More respectable colonists soon imitated this process, which became known as "squatting." During the second quarter of the nineteenth century the squatters gained so much land and power that the governor of New South Wales was forced to accede to them legal title over properties constituting tens and even hundreds of thousands of acres. From humble beginnings of nonviolent defiance a new elite of pastoralists called the "squattocracy" came to dominate the politics of eastern Australia.

They were challenged by the democratic spirit emanating from the gold fields discovered in the 1850s. Some of the richest diggings were located in the newly created colony of Victoria. As the diggers found the license fees an unbearable tax burden, those working the Ballarat fields rebelled, burning their licenses in a huge bonfire and demanding extensive democratic reforms to the Victorian electoral and parliamentary systems. When the more fanatical armed themselves and erected a stockade at Eureka in Ballarat, it was assaulted by troops, and twenty-five of the diggers and four of the troopers lost their lives. With the exception of the killing of the indigenous peoples, this was the most violent incident in Australia's entire history. Despite the military defeat, other diggers continued to struggle nonviolently, refusing to pay their fees and petitioning the governor for relief. Within a few months most of their demands were met. Popular opinion had developed so strongly in favor of the diggers that only thirteen of the Eureka Stockade rebels were ever brought to trial, and they were subsequently acquitted.

Struggles for Aboriginal Rights
The physical and cultural genocide that Australia's indigenous people faced with the arrival of the Europeans has evoked many forms of resistance. During the late eighteenth and nineteenth centuries the Aborigines often responded violently (if they were not wiped out by smallpox and venereal disease), but they also tried to negotiate agreements with the white occupiers of their land. When frustrated they would reoccupy the land. When forced into Aboriginal settlements for their "own protection," they would often practice silent noncooperation to preserve their culture and identity. In more recent times—beginning in 1963 when the Yirrkala tribe submitted to the federal government a bark petition in their tribal language protesting the operations of the mining company Nabalco on their Northern Territory reserve—the Aborigines have intensified their nonviolent resistance, focusing on the issues of civil rights and sacred sites but mainly on their special relationship to the land.

Although the Yirrkala eventually lost their land rights claim in the High Court, other struggles have had greater, though often only symbolic, success. In 1966–1967, the decision of the Gurindji people in the Northern Territory to walk off a foreign-owned cattle station and begin a nine-year strike for wages and land rights, captured the nation's imagination. A song, "The Gurindji Blues," even briefly topped the Australian pop charts. The Gurindji sought the return of some of their traditional land, amounting to less than 10 percent of the six thousand square miles of the Wave Hill pastoral lease held by the British company Vesteys. As a first step they established their own township settlement at Wattie Creek. Despite gaining broad support for their struggle from whites, the Gurindji waited until 1975 for the federal government to respond, and then they received only twenty-five of the five hundred square miles they claimed.

However, a number of campaigns generated a momentum for change. In 1965, the young black leader Charles Perkins, inspired by the nonviolent civil rights campaigns in America, organized "freedom rides" to combat racist attitudes and practices in northwestern New South Wales. The rides featured mixed groups of Aborigines and white university students arriving in towns where blacks were unofficially segregated from certain residential sections and from local facilities such as swimming pools, veterans clubs, hotels, and pubs, and then occupying the offending areas. The challenge of the riders to local customs evoked scenes of hatred and violence from the townspeople that set in motion a classical case of "political jiu-jitsu." Moderate whites throughout Australia were horrified to discover the depth of racism in their country and, where possible, pressured the communities of "the deep north" to alter their policies and practices. The strong revulsion to blatant forms of racism subsequently was reflected in the 1967 Commonwealth referendum, in which nearly 92 percent of non-Aboriginal Australians voted to confer citizenship on Aborigines and have them counted in the official census.

Nevertheless, lacking the requisite electoral and financial influence, the Aborigines continued to eschew parliamentary and lobbying politics. To gain empowerment—and self-preservation—they set up, in 1971, autonomous black-controlled bodies to service their legal and health needs. The issue of land rights was brought to the attention of whites with the establishment, on Australia Day 1972, of an Aboriginal Tent Embassy on the lawn outside Parliament House in Canberra. Repeatedly razed on orders of the government and then resurrected by the Aborigines, it stood for years as a bleak reminder that the nation faced an inescapable problem. Harvard-educated black activist Bobby Sykes credits this campaign with eventually having a greater impact on the lives of Aborigines than the 1967 referendum. It was during this period that the Aboriginal flag of black, gold, and red, symbolizing the integration of the people, sun, and earth, was first unfurled. During the 1980s, demands mounted for an Aboriginal Treaty in order to erase, among other things, the legal fiction of *terra nullius* which had denied recognition of Aboriginal land occupancy and hence entitlement to its control. This campaign continued into the 1990s with most Aborigines calling for a sovereign treaty recognizable by international rather than Australian law.

The most dramatic nonviolent action staged by Aborigines occurred on January 26, 1988, when they denounced the whites' bicentennial birthday celebrations of European settlement with the slogan "Bugger the Bicentenary," and some fifty thousand blacks (nearly a fifth of their population) came to Sydney in "freedom buses" and on foot to mourn the invasion of their country and the end of their freedom. The action upstaged the expensive formal festivities and generally drew the strong condemnation of officials, news media, and the general public, who called it "disruptive" and "insensitive."

As the memory of the bicentennial faded, arguably the most lasting impression became the demands of a long-suffering people for some long-overdue justice. That message also was transmitted to the outside world. Indeed, on the same day that the First Fleet's arrival was being re-enacted in Sydney, the black artist and actor Burnam Burnam raised the Aboriginal flag at Dover, England, from where the fleet had set sail, claiming the "Mother Country" in the name of all Aborigines.

This case of nonviolent theater was followed by many other black actions to demonstrate their invincibility. Campaigns have been waged to return Aboriginal remains and relics that have been pilfered over the years and are now held in museums at home and abroad. Tasmanian black leader Michael Mansell was successful in securing from Britain a commitment for the shipment of ancestral bones back to Australia.

Numerous protests have been conducted to preserve burial sites threatened by tourist and mining development. One of the most prolonged of these struggles occurred at the site of the old Swan brewery in Perth, where business interests wanted to build a tourist center. Blacks claimed that this would disturb Wagyl, the rainbow serpent, who rested there on his journey to create all the waterways. In December 1988, Aborigines, together with many white supporters, set up a tent protest to thwart the government's $28 million redevelopment plan. Despite periodic arrests for trespassing, the protesters persisted over the next two years, took their case to the High Court on the grounds that it contravened the Aboriginal Heritage Act of Western Australia, and received a favorable verdict that, at least temporarily, respected the peace of the Wagyl Spirit.

A new mood of growing confidence among Aborigines is reflected in their establishment of an Aboriginal Provisional Government to provide an independent voice in determining their structures of decision making and behavior, rather than becoming dependent on Australian government-controlled bodies. Persistence with these and many other nonviolent initiatives has contributed to a more sympathetic treatment from the mass media and nascent signs from the public that there might exist a "white problem." Yet one of the most pressing Aboriginal concerns—that of black deaths in police custody—continues to defy solution despite the highly visible black demonstrations each time a death occurs.

Great changes in white attitudes to blacks are reflected in some of the enduring elite institutions such as the churches, schools, and

A

courts. Of arguably greatest impact has been the High Court's decision in *Mabo* v. *State of Queensland* (1992) that common law can confer land title to blacks if they are able to establish continuous occupation. Traditional Aboriginal landowners are thus protected from government acquisition of their lands without just compensation. In drafting legislation to incorporate the principles of this ruling, the federal government attempted to reconcile the interests of miners, developers, and pastoralists with those of black leaders, whose political pressure came largely from a constituency engaging in a wide range of nonviolent actions. Beyond their effect on the legislative process, these actions served to heighten the consciousness and solidarity of the indigenous people themselves, as well as form part of the white community's ongoing education.

The Peace Movement

The protests of environmental, feminist, labor, and peace activists represent more self-consciously tactical and strategic applications of nonviolent methods. Nonviolent action has been the principal form of political activity of the Australian peace movement, dating back to the 1885 opposition to participation in the British intervention in the Sudan. Some of these campaigns helped to create the salient issues of their day.

The first to engage the nation's attention stemmed from opposition to the provisions of the Labor government's Defense Act of 1910, which introduced compulsory military training for young men. To repeal these compulsory clauses, some Quakers formed a group called the Australian Freedom League (AFL), which, according to Tanner, quickly "showed signs of becoming a mass movement." In less than three years, the AFL claimed a broadly based membership of fifty-five thousand—at a time when Australia's total population was less than 5 million. The organization's success can be measured by the extensive resistance to the act. By mid-1914, the Labor government had been forced to institute 27,749 prosecutions. While most of these led to fines, 5,732 youths were imprisoned for varying periods in military fortresses or civilian jails.

The widespread defiance brought the government under increasing pressure, so that arguably it would have had to rescind the offensive provisions had it not been for the tremendous patriotic fervor that attended the outbreak of the First World War. Initially, volunteers flocked to enlist, but after two years of inconclusive fighting, as casualties mounted and the pool of replacements dried up, a revitalized peace movement pressed its case to dissuade the government from conscripting men for overseas service.

Although the movement had been protesting a wide range of issues, it was conscription for the battlefields of Europe that evoked the public's hue and cry. A split emerged within the Labor Party, forcing the pro-conscription majority in the Labor government to try to consolidate its position with the support of a popular mandate. The announcement of a referendum for October 28, 1916, signaled the beginning of a massive grassroots campaign on the part of the "No Conscription" forces. Radical socialists, trade unionists, disaffected Labor Party members, Christian pacifists, Irish Catholics, feminists, and liberal internationalists forged an alliance that conducted nonviolent actions across the country, achieving an upset victory at the polls that ranks among Australia's most outstanding examples of "people power." A hopelessly divided Labor Party, no longer able to govern, gave way to a new government comprising the parliamentary opposition and a rump of pro-conscription Labor parliamentarians. Prime Minister William Hughes retained his position by heading the newly created Nationalist Party. Believing it was the disunity of his former Labor Party that had brought about the initial defeat, Hughes called for a second referendum to be held on December 20, 1917. Again, the "No" forces rallied with nonviolent actions across the country to defeat the proposal. On this occasion, however, voting divided along party lines and the government did not fall.

The peace movement's influence waned in the years immediately following World War I, but its reduced forces campaigned vigorously for disarmament and the principles of the League of Nations. With the rise of the Axis powers, it sponsored rallies, conferences, and the visits of overseas figures to alert the public to the dangers of fascism and to canvass ways to overcome the prevailing moods of appeasement and isolationism. One of the most dynamic actions (partly within an isolationist framework) occurred in November 1938, when dock workers refused to load a large shipment of pig iron onto the steamer *Dalfram* bound for Japan. Though the strikers were forced to capitulate two months later—due to the company's retaliatory dismissal of four thousand steelworkers—their action, at great personal loss in wages and abuse by government officials, is now considered a high-water mark in the folklore of Australian trade unionism.

Another success of workers' actions in the peace movement occurred at the end of the Second World War, when the Dutch attempted to forcibly re-impose control over their former colony of Indonesia. The maritime unions refused to allow Dutch access to Australian ports. The unionists placed bans on all goods that might assist the Dutch, including clothing and food. Ships and aircraft were denied refueling and repairs. These actions, in turn, were supported by student-led demonstrations. Although a Labor government was initially reluctant to take a firm stand in support of this defiance, it eventually chose to side with the unionists and their allies.

During the 1950s and early 1960s, the peace movement conducted many campaigns against nuclear testing, the arms build-up, Australia's involvement in SEATO (the Southeast Asian Treaty Organization), the establishment of a U.S. radio base in western Australia, and the government's support for counterrevolutionary forces in the Third World.

For seven years after the government announced its intention to send combat troops, including conscripts, to South Vietnam in April 1965, the twin issues of Vietnam and conscription dominated the political agenda. Citizen groups, Christian clergy and laity, trade unions, professional associations, and wide sections of a self-conscious youth class engaged in numerous nonviolent campaigns. Activities reached a peak in a series of nationwide moratoriums in 1970 and 1971. In August 1971, the government announced that the last Australian battalion would be withdrawn before the end of the year. The national mood, as reflected in the news media's greater tolerance for dissident views, had noticeably changed, which helped the Labor Party to triumph at the polls in December 1972 after twenty-three years on the opposition benches.

Broadening Nonviolent Struggle

Despite an immediate decline in peace activity after Labor's victory, a generation of middle-class youth had been radicalized, and techniques of nonviolent action were now applied to issues of the environment, patriarchy, Aboriginal advancement, civil liberties, sexual preference, and the general devolution of power structures. Peace issues merged with some of these other issues and were reflected, around 1977, in a revival of protest that centered on Australia's participation in the nuclear-power cycle. Campaigns were mobilized to "keep Australian uranium in the ground" and to prevent its sale abroad.

In response to well-publicized nonviolent actions conducted by students, unionists, feminists, and alarmed citizens generally, the Gallup polls consistently disclosed the public's resistance to the overseas sale of Australian uranium.

During the 1980s, the peace movement turned its attention to opposing the reinvigorated nuclear confrontation of the superpowers and, in particular, the deepening involvement of Australia in the U.S. nuclear strategic network. Demonstrations were staged against the U.S. surveillance and communication bases (officially called "joint facilities") at Pine Gap, North-West Cape, and Nurrungar. Located in remote parts of the country, these bases became the targets of highly publicized pilgrimages over long weekend holidays. On a couple of occasions the campaigns, modeled after those at Greenham Common (England) and Comiso (Italy), were declared to be exclusively for women and children. Women also set up an exclusive "Peace Camp" in western Australia against the berthing of American submarines at Stirling Naval Base in order to, in their words, "express their opposition to nuclear madness through creative, nonviolent action." In addition, women regularly intervened in the annual war memorial marches, drawing attention to the link between militarism and sexism. By focusing their remembrances on the victims of rape and pillage at a ceremony honoring male valor, they provoked the ire of war veteran leaders and other traditionally minded Australians, but proved highly successful in initiating the debate they desired.

Women figured prominently in all the campaigns of the revived peace movement. They represented a disproportionate number of the antinuclear protesters at the massive Palm Sunday rallies, which reached a national peak of about 350,000 in 1985 (or 2 percent of the population). Increasingly, women assumed leadership positions—Dr. Helen Caldicott and Senator Jo Vallentine becoming especially well

A

known. Among the many other nonviolent campaigns in which women featured prominently were direct actions waged against the home porting of nuclear-armed and nuclear-powered ships in Sydney, Melbourne, Brisbane, and Fremantle, as well as grants of staging rights to American B-52 bombers in Darwin.

The end of the cold war brought about a sharp decline in peace activities, but the organizational infrastructure and experience, for the most part, remained intact. Thus, protest quickly mobilized in opposition to the government's decision to provide naval assistance in the 1991 Persian Gulf War. Many movement members also rallied behind, and helped to energetically publicize, the Australian contingent who traveled to the Middle East to engage in nonviolent actions with the international Gulf Peace Team. However, mass protests receded once Desert Storm commenced. Nonviolent actions following the war were mainly confined to protesting government-sponsored arms bazaars, the sale of weapons abroad, the failure to reduce the defense budget significantly, and the government's equivocal positions on Bougainville and East Timor.

On other issues, however, the use of nonviolent struggle has not been declining. Indeed, on many of these issues nonviolent actions virtually have become an acceptable, and indeed expected, feature of contemporary politics.

The environmental movement became the forerunner in nonviolent struggle activities from the early 1970s on. The most important examples were the green ban campaign in Sydney between 1971 and 1974 and the Franklin Dam action in the wilderness of Tasmania in 1982 and 1983. Both campaigns attracted worldwide attention.

The first green ban occurred in the fashionable suburb of Hunters Hill in Sidney. A group of women residents, after exhausting all conventional political avenues, appealed to the idealistic trade union the NSW Builders Labourers Federation (BLF) to help them save Kelly's Bush, the last remnant of open space in the area. The BLF took a position that "all work performed should be of a socially useful and of an ecologically benign nature."

Kelly's Bush was under threat from a giant developer, which proposed to build luxury houses on the site. The union told the "Battlers for Kelly's Bush" (as the women became known) that they had to demonstrate substantial community support for their request before

labor would participate in the resistance. When over six hundred people from the small suburb attended a meeting and formally sought the union's assistance, the workers agreed to issue a green ban.

The developer, Jennings Industries, responded by bringing in nonunion labor. BLF members working on a Jennings office project in another part of the city threatened, "If you attempt to build on Kelly's Bush, even if there is the loss of one tree, this half-completed building will remain so forever, as a monument to Kelly's Bush." In the face of this threat of nonviolent coercion, the company capitulated and Kelly's Bush survived as an open public reserve.

In the course of four years, forty-two green bans were declared, preventing or transforming well over $3 billion worth of planned development. More than one hundred buildings considered by the National Trust to be worthy of preservation were rescued from demolition.

As the green ban movement captured the imagination of Australia it posed a challenge to the established social order, with the result that the radical New South Wales branch of the BLF was brought under more conservative control by the national office. In addition, the New South Wales branch in general failed to attract significant support from mainstream labor organizations.

The Franklin Dam Blockade campaign began when the Tasmanian Hydro-Electric Commission (HEC), with state government approval, announced plans to build a dam that would generate cheap power in order to attract much-needed industry to the state. The process involved the flooding of vast areas of primal forest. Led by the Tasmanian Wilderness Society (TWS), a massive nonviolent blockade began in the remote region where the HEC works were located. Almost three thousand people came to the debarkation town of Strahan, and were given "crash courses" in nonviolent training before being sent up river to the contested dam site. Small and close-knit affinity groups were the basis of much of the action, but the overall strategy was planned and implemented by the TWS, which also conducted a highly effective media campaign and coordinated diverse external support, raising a budget of over $150,000, and through its charismatic leader Dr. Robert Brown, projecting an image of middle-class respectability.

As a federal election approached, the Labor Party endorsed the blockade action. The position of the non-Labor Coalition government was more circumspect. Labor won the election, in no small measure due to the seats it picked up in the state of Victoria, where concern about the Franklin issue ran especially high. The new government supported a legal action leading to a High Court ruling that the international obligation of a World Heritage declaration was binding upon state governments. The last blockaders pulled out in July 1983, ending a campaign about which eminent sociologist Bob Connell stated, "Nonviolent direct mass action has rarely had a more spectacular success."

The environmental movement has engaged in many other successful campaigns—such as actions to protect rain forests in northern Queensland, and to preserve marine life at the Great Barrier Reef. In the cities, actions have been taken to curb air pollution, to protest the building of a third runway at Sydney's airport, to eliminate various health hazards, and to save parklands and open fields from becoming toxic waste dumps. When the opposition has denied basic civil liberties, as occurred in Queensland from the 1960s to the mid-1980s, movement participants have had to resort to nonviolent struggle to gain the right to exercise nonviolence in other campaigns.

While in all these campaigns nonviolence was used almost exclusively as a tactical or strategic technique, a few leading activists were committed to nonviolence as a way of life. Influenced by Gandhian ideas, they have gathered in groups like Melbourne's Rainforest Action Group (RAG), which is dedicated to preventing the destruction of the world's rain forests. Its immediate objective is to halt the import of timber into Australia, and they employ a strategy of research, education, negotiations, as well as nonviolent action. The latter takes the form of blockading incoming ships that carry timber from the rain forests of Sarawak, Malaysia, negotiating with unions to impose bans, calling for consumer boycotts, and picketing at the timber-processing sites.

RAG campaigns, however, are conducted according to a principled conception of nonviolence, in which secrecy and sabotage are renounced; a genuine endeavor is made to build positive relationships with unionists, police, and representatives of the timber industry; the focus is on generating grassroots action rather than appealing directly to elite decision makers; and the long-term aim of creating a nonviolent society guides each and every action.

Similarly influenced, some activists make personal statements of conscience, like that of political scientist Robert J. Burrowes, who, since 1983, has been redirecting that proportion of his taxes devoted to the military budget into what he considers socially useful purposes. Burrowes has used both the courtroom and mini-dramas staged outside the offices of the Australian Taxation Department to publicize his position. When the government has declined to accept his offers to pay delinquent taxes with shovels, trees, or the return of a trailer-load of land to the Aborigines, Burrowes has written out checks for the amounts to Aboriginal groups and to the privately funded Peace and Development Foundation. The shovels and trees have gone to an overseas aid organization and to local schools, respectively. Though declared bankrupt by the court for his resistance, he has yet to be imprisoned.

Despite the limited acceptance of nonviolence at the level of principle, it is these practitioners who are beginning to exert its greatest impact at the strategic/tactical level. They are the ones, for example, that provided most of the nonviolent training for the Franklin Dam actionists. Moreover, as the so-called new social movements wax and wane, the philosophically committed among the nonviolent actionists tend to represent the more permanent element, keeping the movements intact during their lean periods. Though still few in number, the proponents of principled nonviolence are an expanding body, and therefore may have a greater influence on Australia's future than they have had in the past.

Ralph Summy

References

Ansara, Martha. *Always Was, Always Will Be.* Balmain, NSW: Privately printed, 1989.

Burgmann, Verity. *Power and Protest: Movements for Change in Australian Society.* Sydney: Allen and Unwin, 1993.

Burrowes, Robert J. "Defence Statement of Robert J. Burrowes, Tax Resister." *Social Alternatives* 11, no. 2 (1992): 43–48.

———. "Kooris Stride toward Freedom." *Nonviolence Today* 17 (1990): 7–9.

Cairns, Brendan. "Stop the Drop." In *Staining the Wattle: A People's History of Australia since 1788,* edited by Verity Burgmann and Jenny Lee. Fitzroy, Victoria: McPhee Gribble/Penguin, 1988.

Connell, Bob. "Socialism: Moving On." In *Moving Left: The Future of Socialism in Australia,* edited by David McKnight. Sydney: Pluto, 1986.

Greenhill, Lisa. "Nonviolence Yesterday." *Nonviolence Today* 13 (1990): 7.

Lockwood, Rupert. *Black Armada: Australia and the Struggle for Indonesian Independence.* Sydney: Hale and Iremonger, 1982.

Love, Peter. "From Convicts to Communist." In *Staining the Wattle: A People's History of Australia since 1788,* edited by Verity Burgmann and Jenny Lee. Fitzroy, Victoria: McPhee Gribble/Penguin, 1988.

McQueen, James. *The Franklin: Not Just a River.* Ringwood, Victoria: Penguin, 1983.

Mundey, Jack. "From Red to Green: Citizen-Worker Alliance." In *Green Politics in Australia,* edited by Drew Hutton. North Ryde, NSW: Angus and Robertson, 1987.

Plunkett, Mark, and Ralph Summy. "Civil Liberties in Queensland." *Social Alternatives* 1, no. 6/7 (1980): 73–90.

Reynolds, Henry. *The Other Side of the Frontier: Aboriginal Resistance to the European Invasion of Australia.* Ringwood, Victoria: Penguin, 1982.

Richardson, Len. *The Bitter Years: Wollongong during the Great Depression.* Sydney: Hale and Iremonger, 1984.

Saunders, Malcolm, and Ralph Summy. *The Australian Peace Movement: A Short History.* Canberra: Australian National University Peace Research Centre, 1986.

Smith, Carolyn. "Sound Women's Peace Camp." *Peace Studies* 7 (1984): 4.

Sykes, Roberta B. *Black Majority.* Hawthorn, Victoria: Hudson, 1989.

Tanner, Thomas W. *Compulsory Citizen Soldiers.* Sydney: Alternative Publishing Cooperative, 1980.

Weber, Thomas, and Robert J. Burrowes. "Nonviolence: An Introduction." *Peace Dossier* 27 (1991): 1–10.

See also EAST TIMOR, RESISTANCE TO INDONESIAN OCCUPATION; ENVIRONMENTAL MOVEMENTS; NONVIOLENCE, PRINCIPLED; NUCLEAR ENERGY OPPOSITION; NUCLEAR WEAPONS OPPOSITION; WOMEN AND NONVIOLENT ACTION IN THE UNITED STATES SINCE 1950

B

Baliapal Movement (India), 1985–1992
Nonviolent peasant movement that opposed the establishment of a new missile testing site that would have necessitated the forced eviction of over 100,000 farmers and fisherfolk (according to local estimates) from their homes and lands. The Baliapal movement emerged in 1985 in response to the Indian central government's decision to locate the National Testing Range (NTR)—a base for the research, production, and launching of missiles and satellites—in the area of Baliapal in the north of the Orissa state on India's Bay of Bengal coast. By 1992, Baliapal villagers had returned to their agricultural activities, having for the time being prevented establishment of the testing range.

Resistance by the local population was motivated by both economic and cultural factors. Baliapal's lucrative cash crop economy, whose principal product, *paan* (betel), is cultivated by most of the residents of the area, has provided a degree of prosperity to all residents. Indeed all castes and classes have an (albeit unequal) stake in the land, sea, and resources of the area. Combined with this was a powerful connection of the Baliapalis to the land, since the earth is revered as a manifestation of the Great Goddess, or mother, Durga (Kali). The movement was characterized by an almost unique (for India) solidarity across caste, class, and gender lines, reflecting the perceived threat to all inhabitants' livelihood that the NTR represented and the important role of women, who conduct most of the cultivation in the homestead economy in addition to their household work and child-rearing.

The cultural expressions of resistance reflected both a moral commitment to nonviolence and a strategic use of place-specific sanc-

tions, spanning methods of intervention, noncooperation, and protest and persuasion. In order to prevent government officials from entering the Baliapal area (of approximately 130 villages), barricades across the entrance roads to the area were erected and staffed around the clock. Whenever the state attempted to enter the area, conch shells were blown and *thalis* (metal plates) were beaten to summon thousands of peasants to the barricades, where they formed human roadblocks to prevent the government's entry. The movement also established a *Maran Sena* (suicide squad) consisting of five thousand people (a third of whom were women). These people pledged before the Hindu warrior goddess Durga to give their lives by throwing themselves in front of approaching government vehicles if the barricades were breached. When the government suggested that the Baliapalis were to be relocated in new villages outside the area, the movement dispatched Demolition Squads to destroy the model village under construction.

Villagers engaged in noncooperation as well, by refusing to pay loans and taxes, organizing strikes of local shops, and by reviving the *Vichar* institution, through which village problems (such as land disputes) are discussed and solved in a consensus process without recourse to the law enforcement and judicial establishment. The movement also used many methods of protest and persuasion, including conducting *Dharnas* (sitting in protest) outside of the district collector's office and outside of local police stations.

The movement's ideology was articulated as *Beeta Maati* ("our soil, our earth, our land") and drew upon the cultural and economic dimensions of the peasant's everyday reality. Using religious and mythical tools, it converted the cultural sentiment for the land—the peasant's sense of place—into a political demand for the absolute right to its continued use. Movement ideology was articulated in songs and dramas that emerged as potent expressions of the Baliapal resistance.

The government's response to the movement spanned the spectrum of seduction, coercion, and mediation. Seduction came in the form of the rehabilitation and compensation scheme designed to persuade the peasants to leave their homes and lands. The government's coercive tactics included an economic blockade of the area, which prevented importation of kerosene and other goods and imposed fines on bullock carts and vehicles leaving the area with produce bound for market. Activists were arrested and detained without trial, and preventive arrests were made at many of the large demonstrations. In May 1988, eight thousand armed police were deployed around the Baliapal area when the Orissa government decided to launch a military assault to evict the peasants. Mediation talks between the movement and the state government ultimately defused the situation and prevented the attack.

Paul Routledge

References

Routledge, Paul. *Terrains of Resistance: Nonviolent Social Movements and the Contestation of Place in India.* Westport, Conn.: Praeger, 1993.

Ballou, Adin (1803–1890)

American clergyman, pamphleteer, and nonviolent theorist. Before Tolstoy and Gandhi, who studied Ballou's carefully reasoned and generous-spirited writings, Adin Ballou contributed more to people's understanding of the concept of nonviolence, perhaps, than anyone. A popular preacher, Ballou exercised considerable influence through his writings in pacifist and abolitionist journals, including *The Non-resistant and Practical Christian* (1845–1849), and he co-founded and served as president of one of the nineteenth century's principal utopian communities. Although he regarded himself as "no antagonist to human government," Ballou denied a preeminent role to the state. As with Thoreau in "Civil Disobedience," Ballou regarded government as "a mere cypher" with "no rightful claim to the allegiance of man."

Born April 23, 1803, in Cumberland, Rhode Island, Adin Ballou was descended from the founders of that New England colony. At eighteen, he responded to what he regarded as a supernatural call to the ministry, and eventually led Universalist societies in New York City and Milford, Massachusetts. A vigorous debater, with a remarkable sense of the practical implications of nonviolence, Ballou skillfully challenged the so-called just war theory.

If self-preservation is the best method of protecting and preserving human life, Ballou said, why have "fourteen thousand millions of human beings been slain by human means, in war and otherwise?" If everyone since the conflict of Cain and Abel had responded to robbery, murder, and killing with nonresistance, he asked, "would as many lives have been sacrificed, or as much real misery have been experienced by the human race" as have been sacrificed to meet injury with injury?

In 1839, at a meeting of Boston's Non-Resistance Society, Ballou stressed the obligation to "disobey parents, patriarchs, priests, kings, nobles, presidents, governors, generals, legislatures, constitutions, armies, mobs, all rather than disobey God . . . and then patiently endure the penal consequences." Two years later, he co-founded the Hopedale Community on 250 acres of land near Milford, Massachusetts. Based upon radical Christian principles, Hopedale was an effort "to establish a state of society governed by divine moral principles, with as little as possible of mere human restraint."

For Ballou, as for Tolstoy, the informing "sub-principle of Christian nonresistance" is that "evil can be overcome only with good." Among the "commandments" that conscientious followers of Jesus must obey were never to "kill, maim, or otherwise *absolutely injure* any human being, in personal self-defense, or for the sake of his family, or any thing he holds dear." Nor can they belong to "any voluntary association, however orderly, respectable or allowable by law and general consent" that "approves as commendable in practice, *war, capital* punishment, or any other absolute personal injury."

During the Civil War, as his old friends and fellow nonresistants—William Lloyd Garrison and Stephen Symonds Foster—forgot their commitment to nonviolence, Ballou remained steadfast, and in his autobiography, he set their earlier statements beside their later justifications of war. In his final years, Ballou devoted himself to family and community history, while continuing to live the values and principles of nonviolence formulated in his writings a half-century earlier.

Michael True

References

Ballou, Adin *Autobiography of Adin Ballou, 1803–1890, Containing an Elaborate Record and Narrative of His Life from Infancy to Old Age, with Appendixes* [1896]. Edited by William S. Heywood. Philadelphia: Porcupine, 1975.

———. *Christian Non-Resistance, in All Its Important Bearings, Illustrated and Defended.* Philadelphia: J. Miller M'Kim, 1846.

———. *Practical Christian Socialism: A Conversational Exposition of the True System of Human Society.* New York: Fowlers and Wells, 1854.

See also ABOLITIONIST MOVEMENT; GARRISON, WILLIAM LLOYD; NONVIOLENCE, PRINCIPLED; PACIFISM; THOREAU, HENRY DAVID; TOLSTOY, LEO NIKOLAEVICH

Baltic Independence Movements, 1987–1991

The people in the Baltic republics of Estonia, Lithuania, and Latvia were the first within the USSR to demand statehood, ultimately succeeding in mid-1991, shortly before the Soviet Union dissolved. They used only nonviolent methods to pursue this goal, even when provoked and attacked by Soviet military and paramilitary forces. Some Balts called their drive for independence in the 1980s a "singing revolution." Literally, the term denoted the song festivals held in each Baltic republic since the late nineteenth century, which were conducted with renewed nationalist fervor in the 1980s. Figuratively, the term referred to the whole panoply of nonviolent actions used by Balts to break from Soviet dominion.

Background: Subservience and Defiance

Estonians, Latvians, and Lithuanians have lived on the shores of the Baltic Sea for four millennia. At various times in their histories each group has struggled against foreign rule or absorption. Estonians and Latvians fought the Teutonic Knights but were conquered in the thirteenth century. Lithuanians drove off the Germans and conquered much of today's Belarus and Ukraine in the fourteenth century. As Russia grew stronger, however, Lithuania, allied with Poland, was gradually absorbed by Poland. In the early eighteenth century, Russia took what is now Estonia and Latvia from Sweden; later in the century Russia annexed Lithuania as well, along with much of Poland.

In the nineteenth century a network of roads and railroads began to link Baltic rural communities that had previously been isolated. Inspired by Johann Gottfried von Herder and a growing interest in folklore throughout Europe, each Baltic people sought to recover and articulate its own national spirit. Rural teachers and village priests cultivated the indigenous tongues. Parish choirs sang the old songs. When they met with other parishes in folksong festivals, a new pride and confidence took root.

The development of national consciousness was also a response to oppression. Estonians and Latvians chafed under Germanic "Baltic barons" who dominated Baltic towns and rural estates, even when Sweden and then Russia formally ruled the region. Seeking relief from Germanization, some Balts joined the Orthodox Church, only to be greeted by Russification. In 1905, Balts joined the waves of revolution that shook the foundations of the Russian empire.

When imperial Russia collapsed in early 1917, Baltic leaders hoped for a Finnish-style autonomy within a democratic Russia. After the Bolsheviks seized power in November 1917 and civil war spread throughout the former Russian empire, nationalist leaders in Estonia, Latvia, and Lithuania declared independence. Soviet Russia signed a treaty in March 1918 consigning the Baltic region and Ukraine to imperial German rule. But when the German kaiser fell, the Red Army, working with Baltic Communists, sought to regain the Baltic littoral for Soviet Russia. Using their own small armies, buttressed by economic, moral, and military support from Britain, France, and Finland, the three Baltic governments repulsed the Red Army and compelled the Soviet regime to recognize their independence in 1920.

Independent statehood ended in June 1940 as Soviet military and police agents occupied each Baltic country; arrested and exiled local political, economic, literary, and religious leaders; and rigged parliamentary elections. These compliant legislatures then requested admission for each Baltic nation into the USSR

B

as a Soviet Socialist Republic. Nazi forces evicted local Communists a year later, but Stalinism returned with a vengeance in 1944 and 1945. Mass deportations, executions, and arrests were carried out. After 1945, the three Baltic republics were both "Sovietized" and Russified. Soviet politicians sought to supplant Baltic languages with Russian. The Kremlin dispatched huge waves of Russian settlers to replace dead and exiled Balts and to work in new industries mandated by central planners in Moscow. For the Kremlin, the Baltic littoral was at once a buffer defending northern Russia and a staging area from which to threaten Poland, western Europe, and the Nordic countries. The region became one of the most militarized in the world.

Intense repression led many observers to believe that the three remaining Baltic cultures would follow the path of Old Prussian—dead since the seventeenth century. But beneath the iceberg of Soviet rule, demands for self-determination survived. In the 1970s and 1980s, such demands were sustained by many forces. Living standards in the Baltics were higher than in any other part of the USSR, and yet much poorer than in Sweden and Finland, leading Balts to believe that they could do much better if liberated from Soviet oppression and central planning. Cultural contacts provided information about other struggles, especially in Poland. Balts watched as Solidarity defied Soviet and local Communist rule. Many Estonians followed world events on television from Helsinki in Finnish. Within the Conference on Security and Cooperation in Europe (CSCE), the human rights section of the 1975 Helsinki Final Act authorized periodic reviews of human rights performance in each signatory country. Balts wrote to the CSCE complaining of Soviet violation of their rights. They demanded national self-determination and demilitarization. Soviet authorities in the late 1970s and early 1980s tried to repress such campaigns but failed. One batch of dissidents could be put away, but others took its place.

The churches in each country provided important institutional and cultural support for independence activities. The Vatican and local bishops supported independence for Lithuania. Local Lutheran clerics in Estonia and Latvia began to associate themselves with national self-determination.

Finally, Baltic nationalists appealed to the fact that since the mid-nineteenth century, the

United States had rejected the right of conquest. After 1940, the United States refused to recognize Soviet annexation of the Baltics even when Washington sought to buttress Stalin in the war against fascism. Official U.S. maps, congressional resolutions, and the Voice of America reiterated U.S. nonrecognition policy. Furthermore, no other Western governments except Sweden, and, for a time, New Zealand, recognized Soviet annexation. International denial of Soviet legitimacy nourished Baltic hopes that independence could be regained.

The Gorbachev Revolution
Taking power in Moscow in 1985, Mikhail S. Gorbachev promoted perestroika (economic restructuring), glasnost (openness), *demokratizatsiya,* and devotion to a "law-governed state." Balts seized upon these slogans to work for their own liberation. Previous Soviet leaders had permitted economic experiments in the Baltic republics, and Gorbachev hoped that the Balts would show the way to successful perestroika. He realized that economic reform would require more openness and democracy, but he did not appreciate the depths of national consciousness that his slogans would unleash.

Each Baltic republic had been damaged not just by industrialization but also by militarization, including military maneuvers and the dumping of hazardous wastes. Encouraged by the recent success of Russians who managed to stop projects to reverse the flow of Siberian rivers, Baltic scientists, poets, and common people began to demonstrate against vast new projects that threatened already weakened ecosystems. Estonians, for example, demanded that Moscow halt its plans to increase phosphate mining. Notably, these and similar demands in Latvia and Lithuania were basically within the bounds authorized by the new openness.

Local dissidents were emboldened by the quiescent response of Soviet authorities to these first signs of Baltic independence. Local historical societies demanded that the "blank pages" in Baltic–Soviet relations be filled in. Beginning in 1987, Balts held large demonstrations on August 23 to demand publication in the USSR of the secret protocols to the August 23, 1939, Molotov–Ribbentrop pact between Germany and the Soviet Union that ceded the Baltic republics and eastern Poland to Stalin. In 1989, on the pact's fiftieth anniversary, some 2 million Balts joined in a "hands-across-the-Baltic" human chain from Tallinn to Vilnius. Spurred by such pressures, the USSR Supreme Soviet in December 1989 condemned the protocols as "legally untenable and invalid from the moment they were signed," an admission that delegitimized the 1940 annexation. Balts also began to honor other "calendar days," such as their first declarations of "independence," the first deportations in 1940, and the bombing of Tallinn by Soviet planes in 1944.

"Popular fronts" took shape in Estonia, Latvia, and Lithuania *(Sajudis)* in 1988. Ostensibly formed to support perestroika, these bodies quickly demanded for each republic "autonomy," then "sovereignty," and—still later—"independence." The fronts were meant to unite Communists and non-Communists, and initially had Moscow's blessing. But Communists quickly lost ground to nationalist anti-Communists.

The old flags of the interwar years reappeared, supplementing and then supplanting the Soviet Republic flags. Baltic Communists tried to join the nationalist bandwagon. In 1988, the Supreme Soviet of Estonia proclaimed the superiority of republican laws to those of the central government in Moscow. Lithuania's Supreme Soviet in 1989 asserted that the only laws in force in Lithuania were those passed by the national parliament or by referendum. All three Baltic parliaments claimed republic control of land, sea, and other natural resources. When authorities in Moscow sought to reassert control, the republican parliaments remained defiant.

Balts Begin to Act As Though They Are Free

In the late 1980s, Baltic governments began to claim the rights and privileges that had long existed on paper under the USSR constitution but had never been used—including the right to secede. They rationalized each bold step toward freedom in terms of Gorbachev's goal of a "law-governed state."

Native Balts had to deal not just with Moscow but also with Soviet troops garrisoned on their territory and with large numbers of Russian and other settlers from other parts of the USSR. Leaving the troops aside, settlers made up nearly half of Latvia's population in the late 1980s, 40 percent of Estonia's, and 20 percent of Lithuania's. Some settlers welcomed movement toward Baltic independence, but most feared any steps that might undermine their existing privileges. Signs appeared in Russian: "The Army and People Are One." The implication: The Soviet Armed Forces, domi-

nated by Russians, would side with the Russian-speaking settlers.

Settlers organized "international movements" fronts to defend their Soviet-era privileges against Baltic nationalists. The fronts, often backed by Russian factory managers supported by Moscow, appealed to the Kremlin and to the Red Army garrisons. They sought to influence local elections and organized strikes to show how settler power could sabotage the republic economies.

Baltic nationalists saw Russian settlers and troops as exploitative imperialists who had no right to usurp Baltic living space. Still, most Balts sought to avoid confrontations with the outsiders. Most tried to present their movements toward independence in a nonthreatening way to Russian troops and workers, but they gained few allies.

Estonians and Latvians welcomed Russians who would endorse their demands for independence and gave settlers token representation on popular councils that sought to bypass the supreme soviets of each republic. But they failed to make clear under what circumstances settlers could become citizens in independent Baltic states. Although few Russians attempted to learn the local tongue, Balts made little effort to interest Russians in their language and culture.

Some Lithuanian nationalists sought to ally with and encourage the growing nationalism of Russians against Soviet imperialism. Several hundred pre-1917 Russian flags were manufactured in Kaunas and taken by two hundred Lithuanians to Moscow, where they distributed them to Russian demonstrators. In addition, underground publications for the Ukraine, Belarus, and Kazakhstan were published in the Baltic republics.

Estonians often took the first steps toward national self-determination in the late 1980s, presenting them in a nonprovocative manner. On March 11, 1990, however, Lithuania—spurred by *Sajudis* leader Vytautis Landsbergis—asserted its independence outright. Lithuania, like Estonia and Latvia, declared that the Kremlin had usurped power for fifty years. Lithuania took the lead in proclaiming an end to compulsory duty in the Soviet armed forces. For all this, Lithuania paid a price. Soviet military and paramilitary forces sought to displace Landsbergis in 1990 and again in 1991.

Resistance to the Soviets came from many sources. Audrius Butkevičius, a young psychia-

B

trist, mobilized representatives from each of forty-five districts in Lithuania for a trip to Siberia to collect the remains of Lithuanians who had perished in Soviet camps. This action reminded Lithuanians in every corner of the republic how their people had suffered under Soviet rule. Learning that Soviet forces would attack Landsbergis early in 1991, Butkevičius (then director-general of the Department of National Defense) asked for volunteers from each county to join a human shield, a "living ring," surrounding the parliament building. They came immediately and formed a barrier that the Soviets hesitated to pierce by force, especially since foreign television crews were present.

The nonviolent defiance of Landsbergis and his defenders worked, although the clash killed more than a dozen and wounded seven hundred Lithuanians. The (pro-Soviet) Committee for National Salvation collapsed and the "Black Berets" (Soviet special forces) withdrew. Seeking to undermine any future Soviet takeover, the Lithuanian parliament in February 1991 declared as invalid in Lithuania any structures, laws, or court decisions the USSR might try to impose. It obliged government officials, and requested all citizens, to refuse cooperation with any Soviet occupation. During 1990 and 1991, Estonian and Latvian leaders also asked their countrymen to disobey any rules set down by occupying forces. Civilian resistance in Estonia in May 1990 and in Latvia in January 1991 helped their countries to repulse putsch efforts smaller in scale than those against Lithuania, although four Latvians were killed by Soviet forces on January 20.

In September 1991, Gorbachev's Kremlin acknowledged the independence of the three Baltic republics. Within months each of the remaining twelve Union Republics proclaimed its independence. The USSR collapsed in December 1991. Most of the new states entered the loose Commonwealth of Independent States, but the Baltic states and Georgia (until 1993) refused to take part in any device that might perpetuate Russian hegemony.

After Independence

Ethnic feuding began in many of the new states of the former Soviet Union even before independence. After independence it got worse, especially in the Caucasus, where state fought state and ethnic majority repressed ethnic minority. Violence begot violence. The bloodletting in much of the former USSR underscored the utility, for all parties, of the Baltic commitment to nonviolent action. The Balts had no capacity to force the Russian troops to leave, but pressured them in negotiations and by soliciting Western support. Balts offered to build housing for the troops in Russia, provided others paid for the materials. In the confused transition to Russian independence, Moscow seemed reluctant to deal with the troops issue. But the Kremlin removed almost all of its forces from the Baltics by 1994.

Butkevičius, who became Lithuania's first defense minister since the 1930s, stated in September 1991 that Lithuania would "never have an army big enough to defeat an invader. Our goal has to be to win not physically, but morally, economically, and politically." He counted on the Lithuanian army to resist militarily any attack on the country. In addition, he sought to incorporate civilian-based resistance into Lithuanian defense policy so that, if Lithuania were attacked, the entire population could mount strikes and other actions to paralyze the country. Already the government possessed radio systems that could broadcast directly into Soviet tanks, transmitting information and disinformation. Butkevičius hoped to have five hundred paratroopers for rapid response to crises, a unit to deal with environmental disasters, and units trained in psychological warfare. He expected total armed forces to number no more than twenty thousand under arms (compared with thirty-two thousand troops in the 1930s).

Literature on nonviolent action and civilian-based defense was translated and published in Estonian, Latvian, and Lithuanian, with backing from each republic's defense ministry. As Baltic defense planners perceived the situation, the principal threat to their independence was not so much from a massive Russian onslaught as from smaller-scale attacks that might destabilize Baltic governments but which Moscow could plausibly deny, random moves by renegade Russian units, and collaboration between the Russian military and Russian settlers. Such concerns pushed all three Baltic republics to consider a blend of military and civilian-based defense forces.

An atmosphere of lawlessness in the Baltics, violent crime, smuggling through porous borders, black markets, and sporadic violence by the remaining Russian forces raised pressures in each new republic to form strong border units as well as conventional defense forces. In 1993, Butkevičius rejected neutrality and urged that Lithuania develop defense structures that could easily fuse with west European security mechanisms. But he reiterated that Lithuania should depend on what he called the "intelligence and sabotage" alternative. Conventional forces were bolstered in February 1993 as Lithuania acquired from Kyrgyzstan four almost new training jets made in Czechoslovakia for the giveaway price of $21,000 each. In April 1993, Poland's defense minister predicted that his country would provide military equipment and training to Latvia, Estonia, and probably Lithuania.

Balts gave the world an example of how nonviolent resistance, even when not carefully planned or financed, could help small nations to break from imperial control. But the Balts' success depended on the failure of Russia's imperial will, analogous to India's peaceful split from the British Empire. The coup de grace for the Soviet system came, not from the Baltics or elsewhere on the periphery or beyond, but from Kremlin hardliners who sought to stem decay at the core.

Once independence had been achieved, Balts lost much of the *élan vital* that had made their singing revolution so powerful. There was little coordination among the three republics and precious little dialogue between the indigenous leaders and the Russian settlers who remained. Balts seemed to give less thought to how to rule than how to seize power.

Walter C. Clemens, Jr.

References

Clemens, Walter C., Jr. *Baltic Independence and Russian Empire.* New York: St. Martin's, 1991.

Eglitis, Olgerts. *Nonviolent Action in the Liberation of Latvia.* Cambridge, Mass.: Albert Einstein Institution, 1993.

Lieven, Anatol. *The Baltic Revolution: Estonia, Latvia, Lithuania and the Path to Independence.* New Haven: Yale University Press, 1993.

Misiunas, Romuald J., and Rein Taagepera. *The Baltic States: Years of Dependence, 1940–1990.* Berkeley: University of California Press, 1993.

Raun, Toivo U. *Estonia and the Estonians.* 2nd ed. Stanford: Stanford University Press, 1991.

Taagepera, Rein. *Estonia: Return to Independence.* Boulder, Colo.: Westview, 1993.

See also CIVILIAN-BASED DEFENSE; REVOLUTIONS OF 1989

Bardoli Campaign (India), 1928

Nonviolent protest waged by residents of the Bardoli *taluka,* in the Surat district of India, against officials of the Bombay government. This campaign was exemplary for its adherence to the Gandhian principles of satyagraha, which include the clear identification of a "truth" objective and an adherence to nonviolent tactics of protest. The dispute centered around a land revenue assessment, or land tax, of 30 percent established by the Revenue Department. Protests from the peasant populations in the area succeeded in gaining a reduction of the tax from 30 to 22 percent. This was still an unacceptably high figure, but continued complaints from the peasantry did not result in further concessions. Under the leadership of Sardar Vallabhbhai Patel, a movement was organized to protest the arbitrary means by which the assessment was evaluated. On February 12, 1928, a resolution was adopted by the protesters that pledged to refuse payment of the increased assessment until an impartial inquiry was begun into the matter. Two hundred and fifty satyagrahis and over eighty-five thousand local sympathizers organized themselves into sixteen organizational camps. Through daily news bulletins, songs, and petition drives, villagers were educated about the goals of the protest and the necessity of adhering to a pledge of nonviolence. Police and government officials reacted by seizing lands and property, arresting protesters, intimidating people with violence, and mounting propaganda campaigns. Such actions were countered by tactics of noncooperation, submission to arrest, technical trespass (continued use of land and property although it had legally changed ownership), resignation of government positions by local authorities, and rejection of violent tactics. On August 4, 1928, after six months of protest, the demands of the protesters were met. Forfeited lands were restored, local officials who had resigned their posts were reinstated, all satyagrahi who had been arrested were released, and an inquiry group, called the Broomfield Committee, was appointed. The final recommendation of this committee was a land assessment increase of only 6.25 percent, and after taking into consideration factors that the committee had previously disregarded, the assessment subsequently was reduced to an even lower amount. In his writings in *Young India,* Gandhi cited the Bardoli campaign as a testament to the strength of a united peasantry and as a model for future resistance against the imposition of arbitrary and unjust taxes.

Maria Figueroa

References

Bondurant, Joan V. *Conquest of Violence: The Gandhian Philosophy of Conflict.* Princeton: Princeton University Press, 1958, 1988.

See also GANDHI, MOHANDAS KARAMCHAND; INDIAN NATIONAL MOVEMENT; SATYAGRAHA

Beit Sahour (Occupied West Bank), 1988–1989

Collective tax refusal and noncooperation with Israeli occupation policies by a predominantly Christian village near Bethlehem. By refusing to pay taxes funding the occupation and by creating parallel institutions in the face of a curfew and blockade by Israeli authorities, villagers contributed to intifada efforts to hurt the Israeli economy and further Palestinian moves toward economic and political self-sufficiency.

By the spring of 1988, many Palestinians were refusing to pay income taxes to the Israeli government. In July, after soldiers and tax collectors raided Beit Sahour, impounding cars and other property to pay outstanding taxes and entering homes to seize identification papers, several hundred villagers returned their identification cards to protest the crackdown. Israeli forces countered by imposing a two-week curfew on the town and by blocking food and other supplies from entering the village.

The residents of Beit Sahour and the surrounding area responded by organizing parallel institutions. They planted "victory gardens" and began to harvest their own food. "Popular Committees" were formed to clean streets, collect garbage, educate children, resolve disputes, and distribute assistance to the needy. A medical clinic started during this period grew to receiving fifteen hundred patients a day in the Bethlehem area. Beit Sahour villagers even pretended they were enjoying the curfew to defy Israeli authorities. These activities continued during 1989, despite decreased morale caused by unilateral but unreciprocated concessions to the mediating United States made by Palestine Liberation Organization leader Yassar Arafat. The

town was again subjected to a six-week Israeli curfew starting in September 1989. Storekeepers conducted a three-month commercial boycott in protest against millions of dollars of confiscated property taken during this siege.

Although they continued to suffer under Israeli repression, the villagers of Beit Sahour made a major contribution to the resistance of the intifada and succeeded in making significant strides toward self-sufficiency.

Brad Bennett

References

Hunter, F. Robert. *The Palestinian Uprising: A War by Other Means.* Revised and expanded. Berkeley: University of California Press, 1993.

Rigby, Andrew. *Living the Intifada.* London: Zed, 1991.

Vogele, William B. "Learning and Nonviolent Struggle in the Intifadah." *Peace and Change* 17 (July 1992): 312–340.

See also INTIFADA

Berlin Wall Destruction, 1989–1990

Demonstrations calling for the destruction of the Berlin Wall separating East and West Berlin and subsequent physical tearing down of the wall.

The Berlin Wall had served as a physical and political barrier between East and West Germany and a symbol of the cold war since 1961. During 1989, many Soviet-bloc members began to renounce communism, embrace reform, and open their borders. Demonstrations erupted throughout East Germany. Thousands protested for perestroika (economic restructuring), glasnost (openness), democracy, and freedom to travel. Violent police repression helped to fuel the movement to open the border, and a pro-democracy group called "New Forum" was organized. On October 18, 1989, the hardline East German leader Erich Honecker resigned, but the protests continued. On November 4, over 500,000 people demonstrated in East Berlin, the largest protest since an uprising in 1953. On November 7, the entire East German cabinet resigned. The next day, both the Communist Party Politburo and Central Committee resigned.

Finally, on November 9, 1989, the Berlin Wall was opened up. Both East and West Berliners participated in spontaneous celebrations all along the wall. Citizens and souvenir hunters

*Philip Berrigan (center) and Daniel Berrigan (right) burning draft records taken from the draft board of-
fice in Catonsville, Maryland, May 17, 1968. AP/Wide World Photos.*

chipped away at the structure with chisels and hammers, and large sections of the wall were destroyed in the next few months. The two Germanys eventually united on October 3, 1990.

Brad Bennett

References
Bornstein, Jerry. *The Wall Came Tumbling Down: The Berlin Wall and the Fall of Communism.* New York: Arch Cape, 1990.
McClelland, Charles E. "The Berlin Wall: From Cold War Symbol to Cultural Artifact." In *Up against It: Photographs of the Berlin Wall,* edited by Leland Rice. Albuquerque: University of New Mexico Press, 1991.

See also REVOLUTIONS OF 1989

Berrigan, Daniel (b. 1921)

American poet, clergyman, teacher, and nonviolent activist. Daniel Berrigan first came to prominence as a nonviolent activist in 1968, when he and eight other people burned draft records at Catonsville, Maryland, in an effort to end conscription during the Vietnam War. Already well known as a poet and religious writer, he was subsequently sentenced to two years in a Danbury, Connecticut, federal prison for war resistance. Since 1980, as a participant in Plowshares actions, he has served numerous briefer periods in jail for attempting to disarm nuclear weapons at military bases and arms manufacturers throughout the United States The author of over fifty books of poetry, drama, and prose, Father Berrigan has taught religion and literature at colleges and universities throughout the United States, including Cornell, Yale, and DePaul universities, and he has conducted religious retreats in various countries throughout Europe and the Americas. Through his writings, he is a major influence on Catholic social thought.

The fifth of six sons of an Irish railroad man and a devout, willful German woman, Daniel Berrigan was born in Virginia, Minnesota, on May 9, 1921, but grew up near Syracuse, New York. Entering the Society of Jesus in 1939 and later ordained a priest, he studied and taught in various Jesuit schools and colleges, including Le Moyne College in Syracuse, 1957–1964. He admired the worker priest movement in France, where he spent a sabbatical year in 1964, and traveled to eastern Europe, where he found the Catholic Church persecuted, but clear in its resistance to the war-making state. On returning to the United States, Berrigan became involved in the movement against the war in Southeast Asia, co-founded Clergy and Laymen Concerned about Vietnam, and was exiled to Latin America by the cardinal archbishop of New York—an experience that only deepened Berrigan's resistance to U.S. imperialism in various parts of the world.

Shortly after accompanying Howard Zinn, the American historian and activist, on a peace mission to Hanoi, Daniel Berrigan joined his brother Philip Berrigan and seven other men and women in burning registration forms at a draft board in Catonsville, Maryland, on May 17, 1968. In the subsequent trial, the basis of his popular award-winning play, *The Trial of the Catonsville Nine* (1970), Daniel Berrigan and his fellow religionists helped to sustain the first major peace movement among Roman Catholics in the United States. Later, through actions and trials associated with the Plowshares movement, including the film *In the King of Prussia* (1982), Berrigan remained at the cen-

ter of nonviolent opposition to the escalating nuclear arms race during the Reagan and Bush administrations of the 1980s.

Father Berrigan once wrote that he is "concerned with so simple a thing as language." In the name of the Gospel, he condemns "the speech of power politics, the speech of military murder, the language of religious mystification, all language that indicates the death of the mind, the studied obscenity, the speech that portends to human dignity and the truth while in fact it brings down the world." Winner of the Lamont Poetry Prize of the Academy of American Poets for *Time without Number* (1957), Berrigan's work has also received the Obie Drama Award, Los Angeles Drama Critics Award, Melcher Book Award, and Thomas More Association Medal. He is the subject of a film, *Holy Outlaw* (1970), and served as a consultant for the feature film *The Mission* (1990), in which he also made a cameo appearance.

Michael True

References

Berrigan, Daniel. *Daniel Berrigan: Poetry, Drama, Prose.* Edited by Michael True. Maryknoll, N.Y.: Orbis, 1988.
———.*To Dwell in Peace: An Autobiography.* New York: Harper and Row, 1987.
du Plessix Gray, Francine. *Divine Disobedience.* New York: Random House, 1969.
Klejment, Anne. *The Berrigans: A Bibliography of Published Works by Daniel, Philip, and Elizabeth McAlister Berrigan.* New York: Garland, 1979.

See also BERRIGAN, PHILIP; CATONSVILLE NINE, 1968; NUCLEAR WEAPONS OPPOSITION; PLOWSHARES MOVEMENT; VIETNAM WAR OPPOSITION

Berrigan, Philip (b. 1923)

American nonviolent activist and writer. Since 1967, Philip Berrigan has been arrested over one hundred times for nonviolent resistance to conscription during the Vietnam War and to the making and deployment of nuclear weapons. In articles, books, and documentary films, he has recounted his religious resistance to injustice and war, beginning with the civil rights movement in the South in the 1950s. A major figure in the so-called Catholic conspiracy against the Vietnam War, he co-founded the resistance community Jonah House in Baltimore in 1973, the Plowshares movement, and the Atlantic Life Community.

Born in Two Harbors, Minnesota, on October 5, 1923, the sixth son of Thomas and Freda Fromhart Berrigan, Philip Berrigan attended Catholic parochial schools in Syracuse, New York, and the University of Toronto, before enlisting in the U.S. Army during World War II. As a paratrooper he witnessed the destruction of Dresden by Allied bombers, an event that left a deep impression on him. After graduating from the College of the Holy Cross in 1950, Berrigan entered the Society of St. Joseph, a men's religious order with a special ministry among African Americans, and was ordained a priest. Teaching at a high school in New Orleans, he became involved, through the Congress of Racial Equality, in the civil rights movement, and co-founded the Catholic Peace Fellowship, a pacifist organization associated with the Fellowship of Reconciliation, in 1964.

After a brief appointment at the Josephite seminary in Newburgh, New York, in 1965, Berrigan was assigned to an African-American parish in Baltimore. There, in 1967, he, Tom Lewis, and two other men poured blood on draft records in an effort to halt conscription and to halt the American war in Southeast Asia. Six months later, Berrigan and eight others, including his brother Daniel Berrigan, burned draft files in nearby Catonsville, Maryland. During court testimony in the trial that followed, Philip Berrigan exhibited an extensive knowledge of Southeast Asia, as well as of the American tradition of nonviolence. Shipped from jail to jail, Berrigan was spied on by fellow prisoners whom he befriended, and the Federal Bureau of Investigation tried to discredit him by releasing letters about his romantic involvement with Elizabeth McAlister. Their marriage, on April 7, 1969—formally announced four years later—meant the end of his formal ministry as a Catholic priest.

Philip Berrigan's involvement with the Plowshares 8, which hammered the nose cone of an MX missile at the General Electric Plant in King of Prussia, Pennsylvania, in 1980, led to over forty similar symbolic actions against nuclear weapons by activists throughout the United States, in Germany, Australia, England, and the Netherlands.

Jailed periodically for civil disobedience and war resistance, sometimes for extended periods, Berrigan lives at Jonah House, Baltimore, with his wife and their three children, and other resisters. He regards family life, prayer, and contemplation as central to his vocation as a nonviolent activist. The author of six books, he writes regularly for the newsletter *Year One,* and speaks on campuses and in communities throughout this country and abroad.

Michael True

References

Berrigan, Philip. *A Punishment for Peace.* New York: Macmillan, 1969.

Berrigan, Philip, and Elizabeth McAlister. *The Time's Discipline: The Beatitudes and Nuclear Resistance.* Baltimore: Fortkamp, 1989.

Klejment, Anne. *The Berrigans: A Bibliography of Published Works by Daniel, Philip, and Elizabeth McAlister Berrigan.* New York: Garland, 1979.

See also BERRIGAN, DANIEL; CATONSVILLE NINE, 1968; PLOWSHARES MOVEMENT; NUCLEAR WEAPONS OPPOSITION; VIETNAM WAR OPPOSITION

Bhave, Vinoba (1895–1982)

Indian philosopher, social worker, and follower of Mohandas Gandhi. Vinoba Bhave advocated the renunciation of worldy goods, especially land, as a way to continue the nonviolent revolution in India following independence. Active until the end of his life, he died on November 15, 1982, in Paunar, India.

Bhave was born Vinayak Narahari Bhave on September 11, 1895, in Gogoda in the Maharashtra state of British India. In 1916, he joined Gandhi's ashram at Sabarmati, near Ahmadabad. Bhave participated in many of the nonviolent campaigns of the Indian national movement and strongly supported the concepts of self-sufficiency and self-rule. He was imprisoned by British colonial authorities for a total of two years.

Bhave is most noted for founding the Bhoodan Yajna (land-gift sacrifice) movement in 1951. He walked from village to village, holding prayer meetings, listening to local problems, and urging individual land owners to donate acreage to be redistributed among landless peasants in each community. Land was donated voluntarily and redistributed on the basis of need. By the end of 1956, more than 4 million acres had been collected. While this was far short of his goal of 50 million acres (one-sixth of the country's arable land), it was enough for people to consider the movement one of the most significant in India's history. Bhave's program later expanded to include Gramdan (village-gift), in which entire villages pledged to donate their land for redistribution.

By 1970, the Bhoodan movement had redistributed over a million acres of land, and about one-third of the villages in India (160,000) had been declared Gramdan villages.

Maria Figueroa

References
Shepard, Mark. *Gandhi Today: A Report on Mahatma Gandhi's Successors*. Arcata, Calif.: Simple, 1987.

See also CONSTRUCTIVE PROGRAM; GANDHI, MOHANDAS KARAMCHAND; INDIAN NATIONAL MOVEMENT

Bigelow, Albert Smith (1906–1993)

Pacifist and one of the founders of the Committee for Nonviolent Action who led an attempt to sail into the United States atomic-test area in the Marshall Islands in 1958. The attempted voyage of the *Golden Rule* was an application of the principles of Gandhian "nonviolence." The action and subsequent trial and imprisonment received widespread international attention. He died October 1, 1993, in Walpole, Massachusetts.

Albert Bigelow was born on May 1, 1906, in Brookline, Massachusetts. A lieutenant commander in the U.S. Navy during World War II, he resigned his commission in the Naval Reserve several years later. He was active in religious service committees during the 1950s and helped found the original ad hoc committee called Non-Violent Action against Nuclear Weapons in June 1957, which became the Committee for Nonviolent Action (CNVA). With CNVA, Bigelow helped to organize a vigil and civil disobedience action in August 1957 to protest atomic energy testing in Nevada. He also participated in a month-long "Prayer and Conscience Vigil" at the White House in November 1957.

In September 1957, the United States announced that it would be conducting atomic tests in the Marshall Islands in April 1958. CNVA sponsored Bigelow and three others as they bought and outfitted a ketch named the *Golden Rule* and prepared to sail openly into the Marshall Islands test site to protest the atomic bomb tests. Bigelow considered the action a case of "considerate disobedience," following principles outlined by Gandhi and Thoreau. Sailing from Honolulu on May 1, 1958, in spite of a court injunction against them, Bigelow and his crew were arrested and towed back to port. During their appeal of their guilty finding, they attempted another thwarted voyage in early June. A second ketch, the *Phoenix,* inspired by the *Golden Rule,* successfully sailed into the testing area, and its crew were arrested in early July.

During the court case and the subsequent nine-week jail term, the *Golden Rule* gained international publicity and support. There were sympathy picket lines in several U.S. cities as well as in London and Montreal. In San Francisco, over four hundred people petitioned the U.S. district attorney to take action against them because they supported the crew of the *Golden Rule*. Bigelow wrote a personal account of the action, which was published in 1959. The voyage of the *Golden Rule* was one of the most important examples of nonviolent action against atomic testing up to that time.

Brad Bennett

References
Bigelow, Albert. *The Voyage of the* Golden Rule: *An Experiment with Truth*. Garden City, N.Y.: Doubleday, 1959.
Cooney, Robert, and Helen Michalowski, eds. *The Power of the People: Active Nonviolence in the United States*. From an original text by Marty Jezer. Culver City, Calif.: Peace, 1977. 2nd ed. Philadelphia: New Society, 1987.

See also COMMITTEE FOR NONVIOLENT ACTION; VOYAGES, PROTEST

Birmingham, Alabama, 1963

At the time, one of the most segregated cities in the South, which became the center of a dramatic nonviolent direct action campaign for civil rights led by the Southern Christian Leadership Conference (SCLC). The campaign led to an agreement with city officials that downtown Birmingham lunch counters, restrooms, and water fountains would be desegregated, that businesses would adopt nondiscriminatory hiring practices, and that a biracial committee would be formed to implement further desegregation. Moreover, the Birmingham struggle inspired hundreds of civil rights demonstrations across the country and pushed President John F. Kennedy to introduce comprehensive civil rights legislation into Congress.

The SCLC began planning the Birmingham campaign in January 1963. They wanted to create a crisis in the city that would force whites to negotiate in good faith with black leaders and agree to end racial segregation in Birmingham. They decided to focus on downtown merchants, using the only leverage blacks had—their buying power in downtown stores. By withholding their dollars from white-owned stores, they would be able to impose a cost on part of the white business community. At the same time they would disrupt business as usual by holding sit-ins at the "whites only" lunch counters of downtown stores.

The boycott and lunch counter sit-ins began on April 3, 1963. In the first three days there were thirty-five arrests. However, that was not enough to command major news media attention. On April 6, Fred Shuttlesworth led a small procession toward City Hall, but the marchers were stopped after only a few blocks and forty-two were arrested. The next day, Palm Sunday, the brother of Martin Luther King, Jr., A.D. King, led another small protest march toward downtown. However, this time, as the two dozen marchers were being arrested, a large crowd of black spectators gathered. One of the spectators was attacked by a police dog, and then police officers wielding clubs and two more police dogs rushed the crowd. This incident of police brutality received widespread press coverage, giving the Birmingham campaign a much needed boost. Small protest marches continued until April 10, when the city administration obtained a court injunction banning further demonstrations.

After much deliberation, Martin Luther King, Jr., decided to defy the court injunction. On April 12, Good Friday, King led a group of fifty marchers and was arrested. While in jail he wrote his "Letter from Birmingham Jail," in which he responded to criticism (from white Birmingham clergy) of the nonviolent direct-action campaign.

On April 20, after eight days in jail, King was released on bond. By that time, the Birmingham campaign was losing momentum. SCLC organizers were finding it hard to recruit more volunteers from the black community for nonviolent direct action. It was at this point that SCLC staffer James Bevel suggested that school children be recruited to join the protests. This became the next phase of the Birmingham campaign. SCLC staffers visited high schools and colleges, inviting hundreds of black students to attend mass meetings and nonviolence training sessions. By May they had succeeded in recruiting and training some six thousand schoolchildren for a Children's Crusade for freedom.

On Thursday, May 2, more than a thousand black schoolchildren marched from the Sixteenth Street Baptist Church toward the downtown area singing freedom songs. More than nine hundred of them were arrested.

The next day, another thousand black schoolchildren filled the Sixteenth Street Baptist Church. This time, however, Public Safety Commissioner Eugene "Bull" Connor was determined to prevent them from marching. He ordered police to barricade the church doors. But about half of the children managed to escape from the church and joined the crowd that had assembled across the street in Kelly Ingram Park. When they refused to return to the church, Bull Connor ordered police and firefighters to "let 'em have it." Police charged into the crowd with billy clubs and police dogs. Firefighters turned fire hoses on the crowd. Most of the people in the park did not retaliate, but some, who had not received nonviolence training, threw bottles and rocks at the police and firefighters. More than two hundred were arrested. Film footage of the brutal attack on black schoolchildren and adults was shown on national television that evening and the story appeared on the front page of the nation's newspapers the next morning.

On Saturday, May 4, President Kennedy responded by putting pressure on Birmingham's business leaders and by sending Assistant Attorney General Burke Marshall to mediate. On Sunday, May 5, white businessmen met together for most of the day to discuss their alternatives. That same afternoon, Bull Connor attempted to stop another march of several hundred people, ordering firefighters to turn their hoses on the demonstrators. This time, however, the firefighters refused to obey Connor's order. The marchers, who had stopped and knelt in prayer, got up and continued their march as police stepped aside. Connor was losing his ability to repress the movement.

On May 6, another thousand black schoolchildren were arrested, filling the jails. The next day, almost three thousand blacks gathered in downtown Birmingham, stopping traffic and disrupting commerce. Governor George Wallace sent in more than eight hundred state troopers at Connor's request.

This demonstration finally made it clear to Birmingham's white elite that they would have to compromise on race reform if the protests were to end. The Senior Citizen's Committee, a group of prominent Birmingham businessmen, held all-night negotiating sessions with black protest leaders. On May 8, to show good faith in the negotiations, King called a twenty-four-hour truce. President Kennedy publicly urged the two to reach an agreement. Finally, on May 10, an agreement was reached. Most of the protesters' demands would be met. In exchange, the boycott and demonstrations would end.

White racists tried to undermine the agreement, bombing SCLC headquarters and the home of A.D. King. Angry young blacks responded by rioting in downtown Birmingham. Again, President Kennedy intervened, declaring that the Birmingham agreement had the full support of the federal government and sending three thousand federal troops to Birmingham to maintain order.

On May 20, the U.S. Supreme Court declared Alabama's segregation laws unconstitutional, and in June, President Kennedy sent the Civil Rights Bill to Congress.

Roger S. Powers

References
Colaiaco, James A. *Martin Luther King, Jr.: Apostle of Militant Nonviolence.* New York: St. Martin's, 1993.
Garrow, David J. *Bearing the Cross: Martin Luther King, Jr. and the Southern Christian Leadership Conference.* New York: Vintage, 1988.
————, ed. *Birmingham, Alabama, 1956–1963: The Black Struggle for Civil Rights.* New York: Carlson, 1989.

See also CIVIL RIGHTS MOVEMENT; KING, MARTIN LUTHER, JR.

Blacklisting
Listing of names of persons, businesses, firms, institutions, or nations with which commercial or social relationships are prohibited. If such a list remains unpublished, it is considered a "graylist," and may cause the listee to lose time and money waiting for a transaction without knowing that it is being boycotted.

Examples of blacklisting range from international to subnational levels. On the international level, one government may seek to block trade with another government or company by prohibiting transactions with a published blacklist of traders. The U.S. government used the method of graylisting as a standard practice during World War II. Blacklisting can also be used by a federal government against a segment of its own population. An investigation by the U.S. House on Un-American Activities Committee in 1947–1951 led to the blacklisting of many Hollywood producers, directors, screenwriters, actors, and technical workers suspected of holding Communist political beliefs. Many of these people lost jobs and were banned from filmmaking.

References
Buhle, Mary Jo, Paul Buhle, and Dan Georgakas, eds. *Encyclopedia of the American Left.* New York and London: Garland, 1990.
Sharp, Gene. *The Politics of Nonviolent Action.* Boston: Porter Sargent, 1973.

See also SOCIAL BOYCOTT

Blockades
Physical prevention of some activity by an opponent or third party. Blockades can occur on land or at sea, and usually require large numbers of people or vehicles.

One type of blockade, preventing supplies from reaching an intended destination, may take place within a variety of conflict situations. Such action can occur during an international war or as part of an international embargo. If a blockade is a military tactic, it is no longer nonviolent, however. One recent example of an international blockade of supplies was the embargo on Haiti in 1994.

Another type of blockade is the denial of access to a given location by interposing in some way. The actionists may use their bodies to block an entrance to a building by sitting, standing, or lying down, en masse. This type of blockade is usually called a "sit-in." They may attempt to block a moving land vehicle, like a train, truck, or tank, by placing their bodies in front of it. Examples of people physically blockading access include two famous incidents, Fili-

During a visit of the nuclear-powered, nuclear-armed submarine U.S.S. Pintado *to Auckland, New Zealand, a massive fleet of antinuclear protest vessels blocked the harbor entrance, bringing the submarine to a halt and compelling it to go astern. Fellowship of Reconciliation Archives.*

pinos blocking tanks in Manila in 1986 and Chinese students blocking tanks in Tiananmen Square in 1989.

Similarly, actionists may try to block marine vessels by maneuvering rowboats, canoes, kayaks, or "Zodiacs" in front of them. Examples of marine blockades are numerous. In July 1971, a group of people in canoes attempted to paddle in front of a Pakistani ship in Baltimore Harbor to protest U.S. military aid to the Pakistani government in their war against Bangladesh. The international environmental organization Greenpeace has used the tactic of interposing themselves between the harpoon guns of whaling ships and the whales being hunted. French and Scottish fishermen conducted a blockade of numerous ports to publicize their economic woes in 1975. New

Zealand's "peace squadrons" regularly attempted to blockade ports against entry by nuclear weapons–carrying vessels of other nations.

Blockades can be used with two major objectives in mind. If the actionists intend total obstruction, a formidable physical barrier must be created, and change is induced by manipulating the physical environment ("nonviolent obstruction"). If the actionists desire to place themselves between their opponents and the opponents' intended destination, but do so in such a way that the barrier can be overcome, then they are trying to induce the opponents to change their behavior or risk inflicting injury or death on the actionists themselves (by walking, climbing, driving, or sailing over the actionist). Thus, the mechanisms of change inherent in this objective ("nonviolent interjection") include appeal and psychological coercion.

References

Cargill, Gavin. *Blockade '75: The Story of the Fishermen's Blockade of the Ports.* Glasgow: Molendinar, 1976.

Newnham, Tom. *Peace Squadron: The Sharp End of Nuclear Protest in New Zealand.* Auckland: Graphic, 1986.

Sharp, Gene. *The Politics of Nonviolent Action.* Boston: Porter Sargent, 1973.

Taylor, Richard K. Blockade. Maryknoll, N.Y.: Orbis, 1977.

See also GREENPEACE; MECHANISMS OF DI-RECT ACTION; NEPAL, MOVEMENT FOR RESTO-RATION OF DEMOCRACY, 1990; PHILIPPINES PEOPLE POWER REVOLUTION, 1986; TIANAN-MEN SQUARE DEMOCRACY MOVEMENT, BEIJING, 1989

Bose, Subhas Chandra (1897–1945)

Charismatic socialist member of the Indian National Congress from 1921 to 1939 and a radical anti-imperialist. Bose was born on January 23, 1897, in Cuttack, Bengal, India, and was killed in a plane crash on August 18, 1945. He is perhaps best known for his gradual move away from adherence to nonviolent Gandhian strategies of struggle to the advocacy of armed resistance as a necessary last resort for the Indian national movement.

Bose joined the Indian nationalist struggle in 1921. An initial supporter of Gandhian satyagraha, he organized *hartals* (general strikes), boycotts, and flood relief in Bengal in the early 1920s. Bose was jailed seven times for his participation in Indian nationalist campaigns, and during one prison term in February 1926, he led a successful hunger strike for more humane treatment.

Bose became increasingly disillusioned with Gandhi and his strategy during the 1920s and 1930s. He disagreed with Gandhi for strategic reasons. First, while Gandhi rejected violence absolutely, Bose believed in the necessity of armed rebellion as a last resort. Secondly, he criticized Gandhi's strategy of compromise with the British. Bose advocated a complete boycott of the British in all societal spheres. Thirdly, Bose considered Gandhi a reformist—Bose wanted total revolution for India, including a complete economic overhaul. This personal conflict reached its peak in 1939, when Bose opposed Gandhi's wishes and won re-election as president of the Indian National Congress. Gandhi and his allies opposed Bose's leadership, eventually purging Bose from the Congress that same year.

Following his expulsion from Congress in 1939, Bose embarked upon a campaign to organize armed resistance to the British Raj. He left India and solicited German and Italian collaboration to create an external liberation army. Bose was heavily criticized by many Indians for collaborating with these fascist governments. He set up a provisional government, recruited troops for an Indian National Army mainly from the Indian population living in Southeast Asia, and launched an unsuccessful armed revolt to liberate India.

Brad Bennett

References

Chattopadhyay, Subhash Chandra. *Subhas Chandra Bose: Man, Mission and Means.* Calcutta: Minerva, 1989.

Kar, Jasobanta. *Subhas Chandra Bose: The Man and His Mind.* Calcutta: Minerva, 1988.

See also GANDHI, MOHANDAS KARAMCHAND; HARTAL; INDIAN NATIONAL CONGRESS; INDIAN NATIONAL MOVEMENT; SATYAGRAHA

Bosnia-Herzegovina, Resistance to Civil War, 1991–1992

One-year period from May 1991 to May 1992 representing the life span of the collective nonviolent action to forestall war in Bosnia-Herzegovina as the former Yugoslav republic collapsed. The movement represented each of the three main national groups—Bosnian Muslims (44 percent), Serbs (32 percent), and Croats (17 percent). Nonviolent action to keep Bosnia-Herzegovina out of war developed largely as a response to political polarization, which endangered the existence of Yugoslavia, and to threats from local paramilitaries operating in Bosnia-Herzegovina after civil war began in Croatia in June 1991.

In December 1990, three nationalist parties won the election in Bosnia-Herzegovina. The predominantly Muslim Party for Democratic Action (SDA), led by Alija Izetbegovic, who became leader of the Coalition Presidency of the Republic, received 38 percent of the popular votes. The SDA ruled in coalition with the Serbian Democratic Party (SDS), led by

Radovan Karadzic, current president of the self-proclaimed Bosnian *Republica Srpska* (Republic of Serbia), and the Croatian Democratic Union (HDZ) led by Stjepan Kljujic. Initially this coalition government avoided responding to the October 8 Slovene and Croatian platform for a decentralized Yugoslav confederation. However, when the presidency of Yugoslavia countered in January 1991 by proposing an integrated federation in line with Serbian preferences, pressure intensified for Bosnia-Herzegovina to declare its stand on the future of Yugoslavia. Within days President Izetbegovic warned that the emerging constitutional conflict could result in a "chain reaction" that risked igniting civil war throughout all of Yugoslavia.

By spring 1991, the predicted crisis had escalated. The federal presidency clashed over the state of emergency attempted in response to the opposition's March 9 demonstration in Belgrade and the May 15 scheduled rotation of Croatian representative Stjepan Mesic as a president of the federal presidency. The Serbian and Montenegrin governments, which objected to Mesic on the basis that he would foster the secession of Croatia and Slovenia, maneuvered to block him from taking the position and thereby created a self-fulfilled prophecy. The country was on the verge of breakup. On June 6, Izetbegovic and Macedonian President Kiro Gligorov presented a compromise plan to save Yugoslavia based on the formation of a union of Yugoslav republics less decentralized than the Slovene and Croatian plan and far less centralized than the proposed federal alternative. On the same day, the Bosnian president gave an interview stressing the necessity for the country to stay together as a precondition for peace.

All these efforts to forestall the collapse of the country failed. Slovenia and Croatia declared independence on June 25. Fighting broke out in late June in Slovenia and soon moved to Croatia. The Bosnia-Herzegovina leadership and citizens of all national groups feared that their historically peaceful, multiethnic republic was next in line.

Throughout May and June the political tension in Bosnia-Herzegovina increased in response to the Mesic crisis in the federal presidency. When the federal government's show of force backfired into a shooting confrontation, the European Community (EC) temporarily monitored a compromise. On July 7, EC representatives and all parties to the Yugoslav crisis signed the Brioni Declaration, in which they agreed to enforce a cease-fire and continue negotiations on the future of Yugoslavia for a three-month period. Slovenia and the federal government soon reached a peaceful agreement, but the fighting in Croatia escalated.

Presented with the possibility of large-scale war and legitimized by President Izetbegovic's call for peace and attempts to broker compromise, the first collective nonviolent action came in the form of demands by the "Assembly for peace, life together and successful democratic compromise" on July 20. This appeared to be a loose coalition of various social groups including women, children's advocacy groups, and soldiers' rights associations. The coalition issued a declaration calling for an end to rearmament, to militarization of the economy, and to military mobilization. The declaration accused the local paramilitaries and the federal army of being involved in the clashes in Croatia and appealed to citizens of all national ethnic groups to join in the search for peaceful solutions. Vice president of Bosnia-Herzegovina, Ejup Ganic, further encouraged nonviolent action on August 2 by insisting that the destiny of Bosnia was to remain neutral and within Yugoslavia.

The news media contributed significantly to mobilizing support for nonviolent action. Television was the most important news outlet, as 88 percent of the population owned television sets. Although the official news media were under the control of the three national parties, the independent television station Yugoslav Television (YUTEL), increasingly unwelcome in both Belgrade (the capital of Serbia and the failing Yugoslav federal state) and Zagreb (capital of Croatia), now operated out of Sarajevo and maintained its pro-Yugoslav orientation. YUTEL set the tone for nonviolent action devoted not only to stopping the war from coming to Bosnia-Herzegovina but also to keeping Yugoslavia together. YUTEL both mobilized and publicized the nonviolent resistance to war. Popularity of the independent television station reached a peak in August 1991, when it organized the largest peace rally in Yugoslavia since 1945. More than 100,000 people of all nationalities and from all over the disintegrating Yugoslavia gathered in Sarajevo calling for democracy and peace.

The shared goals of the Bosnia-Herzegovina political leaders and the participants in the nonviolent action to forestall civil war undergirded an International Peace Convoy organized by the Helsinki Parliament of Citizens that traveled across Yugoslavia to Sarajevo in September

1991. The convoy, which included four hundred people from fourteen European countries as well as local peace groups, musicians, and actors, promoted a peaceful settlement of the emerging conflict through negotiations.

On October 14, the Bosnia-Herzegovina Parliament adopted a Memorandum on Sovereignty. The memorandum stated that Bosnia-Herzegovina would not stay in a Yugoslavia that did not include both Serbia and Croatia. Bosnian Serbs immediately declared the memorandum illegitimate because it meant that since Croatia was breaking away from Yugoslavia, Bosnia-Herzegovina would as well. Juridically, the memorandum violated the constitutional rules that decreed such decisions must be taken by consensus among all three nations. However, still more important, it evoked memories for Bosnian Serbs of atrocities they suffered during World War II when Bosnia-Herzegovina was within the fascist Independent State of Croatia, allied with Nazi Germany.

After October 1991, the situation drastically changed due to internal and external pressure. During his visit to Germany in November, Izetbegovic warned Germany and the EC of the danger from premature recognition of Croatia and Slovenia. He repeated his warning in December, joined by former Secretary-General of the UN Javier Perez de Quellar and UN troubleshooter for the cease-fire in Croatia, former U.S. Secretary of State Cyrus Vance. Nonetheless, the EC established December 23 as the due date for all the breakaway republics to request recognition, making recognition of Bosnia-Herzegovina contingent on a referendum rather than a negotiated settlement among the three constituent nations of the republic. Well before the EC recognition of Slovenia and Croatia on January 15, 1992, the Bosnian Serb referendum of November 1991 had made clear that if Bosnia-Herzegovina opted for independence, the Serbian population intended to stay with what was left of Yugoslavia. Meanwhile, the Bosnian Serb leadership called upon its constituency to boycott the proposed referendum on independence.

By recognizing Slovenia and Croatia, the EC placed Bosnia-Herzegovina in an increasingly dangerous position. President Izetbegovic had warned that if the republic responded to the EC offer of recognition, civil war would come to Bosnia-Herzegovina. In these circumstances it became more and more difficult to organize nonviolent action in support of peace. More-over, an estimated one-seventh of the population already had arms in the beginning of 1992. Once the political leadership went forward with the referendum on independence on February 29 and March 1, an unbridgeable gap grew between the government and the antiwar groups. As predicted, Bosnian Serbs boycotted the referendum while Bosnian Croats and Muslims voted for independence. Two days later, on March 2 and 3, all three national parties openly supported their members who set up barricades dividing Sarajevo. However, in response, citizens of all three nations gathered in a mass peaceful protest that succeeded in forcing the political leaders to postpone the inevitable clash.

Undoubtedly this nonviolent action was a factor in the March 18 Lisbon Agreement, in which President Izetbegovic joined the Bosnian Serbs and Croats in a plan for peaceful partition of the republic. The agreement was the best deal for Bosnian Muslims by far because they were to receive 44 percent of the land and to have only 18 percent of the Muslim population outside of Muslim-administered provinces. Nonetheless, encouraged by the Bush administration, Izetbegovic withdrew from the Lisbon Agreement on March 26.

On the eve of EC April 6 recognition of Bosnia-Herzegovina, ten thousand residents of Sarajevo again braved snipers and paramilitaries and went into the streets. They occupied the republic's parliament, demanding the resignations of the leaders of all three parties. The failure of the "All People's Parliament" ended what was probably the last chance for peace. On April 7, U.S. recognition of Bosnia-Herzegovina followed. According to a former National Security Council official, David Gompert, Washington pushed the EC to recognize Bosnia-Herzegovina in return for U.S. recognition of Croatia and Slovenia.

Ultimately, nonviolent action in search of peace could not succeed once the alliance between its supporters and the political leaders of Bosnia-Herzegovina had collapsed under pressure generated by EC and U.S. policy recognizing Slovenia, Croatia, and finally Bosnia-Herzegovina itself. Participants in collective nonviolent action had limited success in delaying the civil war. However they subsequently became a crucial element in Sarajevo's survival of the state of siege imposed by war, and they provide an important resource for future attempts to reestablish the spirit of Sarajevo as a peaceful multiethnic community when peace returns.

Dragan Matic

References

Glenny, Misha. *The Fall of Yugoslavia: The Third Balkan War.* Rev. ed. London: Penguin, 1994.

Goati, Vladimir. "Political Life in Bosnia and Herzegovina 1989–1992." *In Bosnia and Herzegovina in between War and Peace,* edited by Dusan Janic and Poul Shoup. Belgrade-Sarajevo: Forum for Ethnic Relations, 1992.

Gompert, David. "How to Defeat Serbia." *Foreign Affairs* 73 (July–August 1994): 30–48.

Hayden, M. Robert. "The Partition of Bosnia and Herzegovnia, 1990–1993." *RFE/RL Research Report* 2 (May 28, 1993): 1–14.

Remington, A. Robin. "Bosnia: The Tangled Web." *Current History* 92 (November 1993): 364–370.

See also KOSOVA, ALBANIAN NATIONAL MOVEMENT; REVOLUTIONS OF 1989; SERBIA, ANTIWAR ACTIVITY, 1991–1994

Boycotts

Methods of nonviolent noncooperation in which parties refuse to continue or to enter into economic, social, or political relationships with another party in order to influence the behavior of that party. In a consumers' boycott, consumers refuse to purchase or use the goods of targeted producers. In a producers' boycott, producers refuse to sell to a given party. Similarly, the notion has been extended to various aspects of social and political relationships, such as the ostracism of individuals through a social boycott, or the refusal to participate in voting procedures in an election boycott. The term *boycott* was first used in Ireland in 1880, when tenant farmers retaliated against a particularly punitive landholder, one Captain Charles Cunningham Boycott, by refusing to maintain any social or economic relations with him or his family.

Economic boycotts and trade embargoes are staples of international economic sanctions. One of the best known examples is the boycott of Israeli products, as well as the products of firms doing business with Israel, initiated by the Arab League in 1948. Countries often will impose a prohibition on the sale within their territory of another country's products, which amounts to a national consumer boycott (although not one in which all the nation's consumers voluntarily elect to do without the goods).

By far the most common form of economic boycott is that initiated within a country by nongovernmental groups. The target and scope of boycotts have varied. In Colonial America, pro-independence activists initiated a boycott of British tea. Under Gandhi's direction, Indians began a boycott of British textiles in the 1930s and began producing and using locally made cloth instead. Throughout the American South in the 1950s and early 1960s, black consumers in towns and cities refused to support local businesses and services in protest against segregationist laws or practices.

Two of the most well-known consumer boycotts in the United States were the boycott of domestic table grapes in the late 1960s, initiated by Cesar Chavez and the United Farm Workers Organizing Committee (UFWOC), and the boycott of Nestlé products in the 1980s to protest sales of infant formula in developing countries. The UFW campaign engaged American consumers in the farmworkers' efforts to organize and gain better working conditions and pay. Produce retailers were the direct focus of economic pressure as consumers refused to purchase non-UFW-approved grapes. These merchants, in turn, ceased to purchase grapes from producers, thus shifting the pressure to the target of the UFW campaigns. The grape boycott lasted from 1965 to 1970 and produced significant gains for agricultural labor in the United States. A renewed grape boycott by the union in the 1980s, however, failed to have similar effect.

The boycott organized against Nestlé grew from public health activists' concerns about the consequences of marketing infant formula in developing countries. In the view of activists and many experts in the World Health Organization of the United Nations, promoting the use of infant formula in developing economies had avoidable negative public health effects: purchasing the formula depleted the meager resources of families; insufficient nutrition was provided because mothers excessively diluted the mixtures (responding to the cost of the product); formula was mixed with unpotable water; and babies were unnecessarily deprived of the nutritional and immunological benefits of natural breast milk. The Infant Formula Action Coalition (INFACT) began a consumer education and boycott campaign in 1977, targeting Nestlé because it was a major producer of both infant formula marketed worldwide and numerous common food products that consumers could identify. Consumers were encouraged to boycott products like Nescafé instant coffee and Nestlé Quik milk flavorings until the company altered its infant formula marketing practices to be more socially responsible. By 1984 INFACT and Nestlé reached an agreement that sufficient progress had been made, and the boycott ended.

Successful consumer boycotts seem to have three ingredients. First, the target company or country must be vulnerable to a disruption in demand. If the sales of a product in a particular market do not contribute significantly to revenues, the coercive potential of a boycott is diminished. Second, participation of a substantial portion of the relevant consumers is essential. How large this group must be depends, of course, on the vulnerability of the target company or country to decreased demand. Applying economic pressure to a single-product company serving a localized market (such as the retailers in southern towns and cities) will require fewer boycotters than is the case for a diversified corporation serving extensive markets. Finally, the boycott must be sustainable long enough to have an effect. In practical terms, either the economic costs to boycott participants must be minimized or the social value of participation must be enhanced. The costs of a boycott are reduced when substitutable products are available at a reasonable cost, or the boycotted product is highly discretionary—for example, consumers of gold coins could purchase the Canadian Maple Leaf coin in place of the South African Krugerrand, and consumers of U.S. table grapes could switch to another fruit. During the Montgomery bus boycott, the organizers had to find alternative transportation for black commuters. When costs to participants are not easily reduced, as was the case in Montgomery, increasing the social benefits of the boycott can help sustain the action. The broad goals of independence and civil rights were powerful sources of cohesion and consensus in the Indian independence campaigns and the U.S. civil rights movement, respectively, and they helped make the costs of boycott activities more bearable.

William B. Vogele

References

Sharp, Gene. *The Politics of Nonviolent Action.* Boston: Porter Sargent, 1973.
Smith, N. Craig. *Morality and the Market: Consumer Pressure for Corporate Accountability.* London: Routledge, 1990.

See also Chavez, Cesar Estrada; Gandhi, Mohandas Karamchand; Indian National Movement; International Economic Sanctions; Montgomery Bus Boycott, 1955–1956; Sanctions; Social Boycott; South Africa, Antiapartheid Sanctions; South Africa, Opposition to Racial Oppression; United Farm Workers Organizing Committee; United States, Independence Movement, 1765–1775

Brookwood Labor College

Noted residential school for workers established between the world wars and located in Katonah, New York. Brookwood was created without the support of mainstream American labor. It was supported by and worked closely with the peace organization, Fellowship of Reconciliation (FOR), in applying nonviolent methods to labor conflicts. Both organizations worked individually and in collaboration on some of the period's most important labor disputes. Brookwood was thus the focal point for intensive efforts to promote nonviolent action in labor struggles in the first half of the twentieth century.

The college had a full-time staff that included some of the country's most influential labor and peace activists—A.J. Muste, the nation's most famous pacifist clergyman of the twentieth century; Tucker P. Smith, vice-presidential candidate on the Socialist Party ticket in 1948; David J. Saposs, labor historian; John C. Kennedy, organizer of the Chicago Peace Society; Arthur W. Calhoun, former professor of sociology and author of the acclaimed three-volume *Social History of the American Family;* Tom Tippett, labor organizer in the Midwest and author of *When Southern Labor Stirs;* and Mark Starr, labor educator from Great Britain and later director of the education department of the International Ladies Garment Workers Union.

Brookwood offered a two-year workers' education program, reduced to one year in 1928, rooted in the social sciences and humanities, as well as practical courses in union organizing.

Fostering an alliance of progressive trade unionists and sympathetic intellectuals, Brookwood criticized the conservatism of the American Federation of Labor's craft unionist policies. In 1928, the executive council of the AFL advised its affiliates to sever ties with the college. The debate over Brookwood and progressive workers' education continued into the 1930s. During the Great Depression, Brookwood promoted the organization of unskilled industrial workers. Some graduates such as Len DeCaux and Rose Pesotta became influential leaders in the Congress of Industrial Organizations.

The college also maintained that war was a fundamental cause of industrial oppression. It established a theatrical program to dramatize its support for peace and nonviolence, in addition to labor rights. Performing at labor colleges and union halls throughout the nation, students performed antiwar plays such as "Coal Digger Mule Goes to War," "Guncotton," and "Uncle Sam Wants You." In 1936, Brookwood operated a Workers' Anti-War Summer School providing intensive training for peace activity in the labor movement. A news service on peace and world problems was provided for some four hundred labor groups as part of the effort of Brookwood and the Emergency Peace Campaign to keep America out of the next world war. In 1937, the college closed as the lasting effects of the economic depression and continuing competition between the AFL and CIO finally depleted its treasury.

Brookwood and labor's interest in nonviolence originated with American involvement in the Great War. Members of the religious-pacifist organization Fellowship of Reconciliation, such as John Nevin Sayre, William and Helen Fincke, Norman Thomas, and Robert William Dunn, were responsible for creating Brookwood and then linking it to the labor movement. At Brookwood and within the FOR, pacifists were troubled by the postwar state of industrial conditions. The suppression of strikes by local and state authorities, encouraged by industrialists, negated labor's effort to establish a just society. The suspension of civil rights and use of partial military law often led to violence. Anti-union campaigns often were characterized by red-baiting, the open shop, the use of "yellow-dog" contracts, and frequent employment of strike breakers. Leaders at Brookwood and FOR entered the industrial-labor relations field to establish labor peace and economic justice through unionization.

In addition, the tactics of nonviolence were used effectively in a number of labor conflicts between the wars, most commonly peaceful picketing outside the factory or the sit-down strike. When attacked by militia or arrested by local authorities, strikers did not retaliate with force. Their objective was to win sympathy for their cause from the public at large. Many of the individuals central to Brookwood also played key roles in these developments.

In 1919, prior to his arrival at Brookwood, Muste was involved in the Lawrence (Massachusetts) textile strike. During sixteen long and bitter weeks, Muste emerged as chairman of the strike executive committee. Despite the threats of police and state militia to break the strike by provoking picketers, Muste applied his pacifism to labor organizing and contract disputes. The strikers held firm to nonviolence when clubbed by mounted police. It proved to be one of the first examples of collective, pacifist pro-labor action in American history.

In the 1920s and 1930s, nonviolence was regularly employed in labor disputes that were connected to the FOR and Brookwood. One important test for labor pacifists occurred during the long textile strike in Passaic, New Jersey. A.J. Muste and Brookwood student Anna Kula created an Emergency Committee for Strikers' Relief. They helped raise money and distributed leaflets calling for economic and social justice. Muste's efforts were also supported by fellow pacifists Norman Thomas, George Collins, William Spofford, Willard Simpson, and noted anti–World War I clergyman John Haynes Holmes. When mass picketing led to clashes with the police, who used tear gas and firemen's hoses to disperse the strikers, Muste kept the striking workers in line by warning them "that our real power was in our solidarity in our capacity to endure suffering rather than give up the fight for the right to organize; that no one could 'weave wool with machine guns.'" For seventeen months, September 1925 to February 1927, workers walked the picket line in protest against a 10 percent wage cut. Throughout the ordeal, nonresistance succeeded despite the wrath of mounted patrolmen and the local Ku Klux Klan, American Legion, and National Security League.

In 1930, in Nazareth, Pennsylvania, FOR industrial organizer Charles C. Webber personally assisted in mediating the Kraemer Hosiery Mill strike. The following summer at Allentown, Pennsylvania, Webber's peaceful actions won praise from local law enforcement officials. When five thousand silk workers went out on strike against repeated wage reductions, Webber took the lead in the struggle for a uniform living wage and union recognition. The sheriff of Allentown and the United States commissioner of labor noted Webber's actions for personally preventing bloodshed between strikers and employers. As he approached strike headquarters he saw a large crowd of strikers gathered around an automobile, the windows shattered by gunfire. One striker had been wounded by gunmen hired by the mill owners. The strikers were calling for revenge. Webber addressed the crowd and marched them to the mill where they gave verbal, not physical, vent to their feelings. Webber's leadership and the strikers' peaceful protest led to a resolution of the conflict.

The ideological underpinning of Brookwood's and the FOR's nonviolent labor strategies were stated succinctly by George "Shorty" Collins, the FOR's first field secretary of racial and industrial affairs: "As labor gains in strength violence can be expected to diminish. Violence has been especially the weapon of the weak—those who were hard pressed. If the workers are strong enough to win, in a labor struggle violence is unnecessary, while if they are weak enough to need violence the chances are against their winning anyway."

One of the greatest ideological challenges to nonviolence in labor disputes, a threat to Brookwood and the FOR's views and actions, took place in 1933, when pacifists were asked to choose between force and pacifism. Under the impact of the misery and despair of the Great Depression, many labor activists began qualifying their pacifist beliefs. Joseph B. Matthews, the FOR's executive secretary, was one who favored more violent militancy in the workers' cause. Matthews argued that capitalism used the educational system to prevent the spread of radical ideas. Pacifists, while refusing all participation in international wars, may be allowed to employ coercion in the class struggle against capitalism. The FOR polled its membership on the question, "Should the F.O.R. hold on to nonviolence in the class war as well as the international war?" On both counts the answer was overwhelmingly in favor of the nonresisters. Matthews was forced to resign. Brookwood and the FOR continued pursuing nonviolent tactics.

The FOR promoted its position of nonviolence in labor conflicts in a series of articles that were published in its journal, *Fellowship,* during the 1930s. Pacifist Claud Nelson presented the most compelling reason when reflecting upon militia repression in the southern textile strikes of 1929–1931: "On practical grounds the case against the use of violence by the workers is strengthened as the conflict covers wider areas of territory and of population. Without violence, workers have some likelihood of winning public support, preventing the use of National Guards, and obtaining justice or an increasing measure of justice through codes and courts." The magazine carried a special piece on the FOR's role in assisting the California fruit pickers in 1935. Jerome Davis wrote the story under the title "Nonviolent Techniques in Industrial Justice." Another writer, Howard Alexander, extolled the virtues of why "Labor Chooses Nonviolence." Ralph Galt wrote of the merits of nonviolence and its successful application in the August 1939 milk strike in New York State.

The most noted application of nonviolence took place during the industrial organizing drives in the auto industry of the mid-1930s. Gandhian nonviolence was successfully employed, resulting in the recognition of the United Auto Workers and their affiliation with the Congress of Industrial Organization. Two former Brookwood students, Roy Reuther and Merlin D. Bishop, played instrumental roles during the General Motors strike in Flint, Michigan. As union organizers, Reuther and Bishop utilized the passive nonresistance tactic, the sit-down, which they had learned about while studying at Brookwood. Bishop helped organize the sit-down strike by leading workers in singing concerts while barricaded inside the factory walls. The sit-down at Flint marked a turning point in union strategy. One Brookwood educator, Joel Seidman, observed: "The sit-down is a challenge to constituted authority, but so is every picket line. . . . It is of no value to the employer to eject the strikers if by so doing he loses public sympathy. . . . A bitter struggle within the plant, moreover, may result in damage to valuable machinery."

Another example of successful labor nonresistance was the effort of union pacifists Elwood Keppley, Donald Rhoads, Eugene Geisinger, and Herbert G. Bohn. In the fall of 1936 and winter of 1937, these unionists counseled their fellow strikers against using violence during the bitter walkout at the Berkshire Knitting Mills in Reading, Pennsylvania. Despite the usual confrontational tactics of employer-instigated riots, tear gas bombs, and clubbing attacks by state police, the picketers turned the other cheek. Over a series of weeks, inspired by their faith in the possibilities of nonviolence, coupled with the plant owner's unsuccessful resort to violence, the demonstrators put up no resistance when arrested and put in jail. Nearly thirty strikers were jailed each day without incident. This legion of peaceful proletariats went "through with this new technique (nonviolence) even unto death because the cause for which they were doing it was a just cause, not only for themselves but for others among them and those who would follow."

Thus, labor pacifists during the interwar years successfully helped to alter traditional attitudes of Americans toward the working class and toward the use of force in labor disputes. They were able to "define an ethic of conflict, dealing with force as an instrument for social control and rejecting violent means." The perpetuation of democracy and the destiny of the American labor movement had been shaped by the nonviolent worker struggles of the 1920s and 1930s.

Charles F. Howlett

References

Chatfield, Charles. *For Peace and Justice: Pacifism in America, 1914–1941*. Knoxville: University of Tennessee Press, 1971.

Howlett, Charles F. *Brookwood Labor College and the Struggle for Peace and Social Justice in America*. Lewiston, N.Y.: Edwin Mellen Press, 1993.

———. "Fellowship with Workers: F.O.R. Pacifists and the Interwar Labor Movement." *Peace Research* 23 (1991): 63–74.

Morris, James O. *Conflict within the AFL: A Study of Craft versus Industrial Unionism*. Ithaca, N.Y.: Cornell University Press, 1958.

Nelson, John K. *The Peace Prophets: American Pacifist Thought, 1919–1941*. Chapel Hill: University of North Carolina Press, 1967.

Robinson, Jo Ann O. *Abraham Went Out: A Biography of A.J. Muste*. Philadelphia: Temple University Press, 1981.

Seidman, Joel. *Sit-Down*. Detroit: League for Industrial Democracy, 1937.

See also FELLOWSHIP OF RECONCILIATION, INTERNATIONAL; MUSTE, ABRAHAM JOHN; STRIKES

Bstan-dzin-rgya-mtsho, Dalai Lama XIV (b. 1935)

B

Fourteenth Dalai Lama, the spiritual and political leader of Tibetan Buddhists, and recipient of the 1989 Nobel Prize for Peace. Born to a farmer in northeastern Tibet, he was identified through spiritual signs and portents as the reincarnation of the thirteenth Dalai Lama. He was renamed Tenzin Gyatso and sent to the Tibetan capital, Lhasa, for a rigorous secular and religious education. During his youth a regent ruled the country. At fifteen, however, he took the reins of government when Chinese troops invaded, occupied, and ultimately incorporated Tibet into the Chinese state in 1950.

The Dalai Lama tried to cooperate with the Chinese while preserving the cultural and religious heritage of his country. But Chinese policies of cultural and religious eradication fueled growing resistance. Despite his efforts to keep peace, rioting broke out in 1959 and spread to Lhasa. In the face of military repression by the Chinese, the Dalai Lama fled to asylum in India. From his exile in the Himalayan city of Dharmsala, the Dalai Lama administers the refugee community, primarily in India, and provides a beacon for nonviolent resistance both within Tibet and in the larger international community. Despite the fact that perhaps more than a million Tibetans have died as the direct result of the Chinese occupation, and many thousands have been imprisoned, demonstrations within Tibet continue.

While denouncing China's oppression of his people, the Dalai Lama has continued to seek a peaceful resolution of the conflict. He has ceaselessly urged Tibetans to avoid violence in their struggle, not only because of Buddhist teachings, but also for practical reasons. After Chinese troops fired on demonstrators in Lhasa in 1988, he declared, "Nonviolence is for us the only way. Quite patently, in our case violence would be tantamount to suicide."

In his speech accepting the Nobel Prize, the Dalai Lama connected his struggle with the activities of Chinese students who were repressed in June 1989, as well as with other expressions of people power elsewhere. "With the cold war era apparently drawing to a close," he declared, "people everywhere live with renewed hope. Sadly, the courageous efforts of the Chinese people to bring similar change to their country were brutally crushed last June. But their efforts too are a source of hope. I particularly admire the fact that these young people who have been taught that 'power grows from the barrel of the gun' chose instead to use nonviolence as their weapon. These positive changes indicate that reason, courage, determination, and the inextinguishable desire for freedom can ultimately win. In the struggle between forces of war, violence, and oppression on the one hand, and peace, reason, and freedom on the other, the latter are gaining the upper hand."

Irwin Abrams

References

Bstan-dzin-rgya-mtsho, Dalai Lama XIV. *Freedom in Exile: The Autobiography of the Dalai Lama.* New York: Harper Collins, 1990.
———. *My Land, My People: Memoirs of the Dalai Lama of Tibet.* New York: McGraw-Hill, 1962.

See also NOBEL PEACE PRIZE; RELIGION AND NONVIOLENT ACTION; TIBETAN RESISTANCE, 1950–PRESENT

Burma, Democracy Movement, 1988–1989

Nonviolent mass movement that mounted the most serious challenge to the iron-fisted rule of General Ne Win since he had overthrown Burma's last democratically elected government and seized power in a coup d'état in 1962. The pro-democracy movement had two periods. The first period, from March to September 1988, was characterized by mass demonstrations led by students and Buddhist monks, the development of an alternative civil administration, and brutal repression by the military. The second period began after a military crackdown on September 18 put an end to mass street protests. It consisted of electoral campaigning by newly established opposition parties, but under the strict limitations of martial law. Aung San Suu Kyi, who emerged as leader of the pro-democracy movement, crisscrossed the country giving speeches until she was placed under house arrest in July 1989, which effectively suppressed the movement.

In 1962, General Ne Win and the military introduced a "Burmese Way to Socialism"—which brought near complete isolation to the country and a steady economic decline of what once was one of Asia's most prosperous economies. These reactionary policies made Ne Win rich, but the country became desperately poor.

The per capita income of Burma's 40 million well-educated and talented people was just U.S. $170 annually—one of the lowest in the world.

By March 1988, twenty-six years of pent-up frustration with the repressive dictatorship of Ne Win exploded with an unprecedented fury, taking everyone, probably the Burmese themselves included, by complete surprise. Burma's students, always at the forefront of any political movement in the country's history, took to the streets by the thousands. Their protests were met with unbelievable brutality. Police and army units opened fire, killing hundreds of teenagers and youths in their early twenties. Thousands were arrested and there were credible reports of female students having been raped in police custody.

But this only outraged even more people and on August 8 a general strike was launched. Millions of people marched against the government in nearly every city, town, and major village across the country. An estimated one to three thousand people were killed in Rangoon alone as heavily armed troops sprayed automatic rifle fire into crowds of unarmed demonstrators. Armored cars equipped with machine guns fired indiscriminately into neighborhoods, killing people even inside their own homes.

The streets reeked of blood and cordite and the government operated Rangoon's crematoria around the clock to burn the corpses of the people who had been massacred. The capital's general hospital was full of wounded. Poorly equipped in the best of times, it was now rapidly running out of blood plasma, anesthetics, and even bandages. On August 10, a group of nurses emerged from the hospital carrying the national flag and a banner with the message: "Doctors, nurses, and hospital workers who are treating the wounded urge the soldiers to stop shooting!" The response was a salvo of automatic rifle fire—on the hospital workers. Three nurses were severely wounded, two others were slightly hurt. Several civilians—blood donors and relatives looking for their kin—were killed. By the time Aung San Suu Kyi made her first public appearance on August 26, the movement had caught fire throughout the country.

The organized mass movement of 1988 had its origin in the collapse of the old order that followed in the wake of the August massacre. The first steps toward forming an alternative civil administration had actually been taken during the killings; in several neighborhoods in central Rangoon, people had decided to donate one blanket and one pillow per household to the Rangoon General Hospital, which was running desperately short of all kinds of supplies for the wounded. Even the black marketeers had handed over, free of charge, the contraband medicines they had in stock.

From this spontaneous effort emerged local citizens' committees, usually consisting of Buddhist monks, community elders, and students. After they took over the functions of civil administration, including the distribution of foodstuffs and gasoline, a major problem was the maintenance of law and order. Bamboo fences with guarded gates and even watchtowers were erected around the various localities to keep a close watch on movements in and out of them, especially at night. Crime was increasing and monks often functioned as interrogators and judges whenever a culprit was caught. In the northern city of Mandalay, monks organized day-to-day affairs like rubbish collection; they made sure the water supply was working, and even acted as traffic policemen. The maintenance of law and order was also in the hands of the Buddhist clergy in Mandalay—and the criminals who were caught were often given rather unorthodox sentences. One visitor to Mandalay in August saw a man chained to a lamppost outside the railway station who shouted all day: "I'm a thief! I'm a thief!"

Daily mass demonstrations occurred in virtually every city, town, and major village across the country. In Rangoon, professional groups joined and formed their own sections in the marches. There were lawyers in their court robes, doctors and nurses in hospital white, bankers, businessmen, laborers, writers, artists, film actors, civil servants from various ministries, housewives banging pots and pans to voice their demands, long processions of rickshaw drivers, Buddhist monks in saffron robes, Muslims brandishing green banners, Christian clergymen chanting "Jesus loves democracy," and even fringe groups such as columns of blind people and transvestites demanding equal rights. To demonstrate their unity, most demonstrators wore red headbands with a white dove, symbolizing peace. It was a true "parliament of the streets" in the striking phrase of Cardinal Sin of the Philippines.

The traditional creativeness of the Burmese psyche flourished again after twenty-six years of silence. By the end of August, Rangoon alone had almost forty independent newspapers and magazines, full of political commentaries, biting satires, and cartoons ridiculing the ruling elite.

The mass protests in the streets came to an abrupt end on September 18 when the military decided to stage a coup, not to overthrow a failing government but to shore up a regime overwhelmed by popular protests. Ne Win had already officially resigned in July, but few Burmese had any doubts whatsoever that he remained the real power behind the two men who succeeded him in rapid sequence: his close protégé Sein Lwin, from July 25 until August 12, and Dr. Maung Maung, another of his old associates, from August 12 until September 18. This third time, he chose the army chief, General Saw Maung, who set up the so-called State Law and Order Restoration Council (SLORC). By using brute force once again—thousands more people were killed in a second round of mass killings when he assumed power—the population was cowed into submission. Or, at least, that was what Ne Win thought, as they were no longer demonstrating in the streets.

To placate the restive crowds and to appease the international community, which had condemned the carnage in Rangoon, Saw Maung allowed the opposition to set up their own parties—and, to the surprise of many, he also promised general elections. There was no real freedom, of course. The country was placed under martial law, and the notorious SLORC decree 2/88 banned public gatherings of five or more people. The news media were also firmly controlled by the military; there was only one newspaper, the SLORC-controlled propaganda sheet *Working People's Daily* (since renamed the *New Light of Myanmar*).

But within the strict limitations of the new martial law regime, the opposition continued the struggle for democracy that had begun several months before. On September 24, the National League for Democracy (NLD) was formed with Aung San Suu Kyi as its general secretary. She boldly declared that her NLD was indeed going to participate in the election that the SLORC, after all, had promised.

In 1989, she embarked on a strenuous program, traveling to virtually every part of Burma. Her insistence on Gandhian principles of nonviolent confrontation came to play a crucial role in transforming the Burmese uprising into a sustained and remarkably coordinated movement. Even when the Ne Win regime threatened her, she continued to speak out. A new move-

B

ment was taking shape, and it was clear that it was of a completely different nature than the joyful, spontaneous uprising of August–September 1988. The large crowds around Aung San Suu Kyi did not shout slogans and wave banners in 1989; they listened attentively to her speeches and afterwards asked intelligent, relevant questions. Perhaps even more important, the troops that had been sent out to disperse the crowds began to get down from their trucks—to listen to her message.

From the SLORC's point of view, a new, dangerous situation was emerging. More than twenty thousand fresh troops moved into Rangoon and, on July 20, the ruling military placed Aung San Suu Kyi under house arrest in her own home on University Avenue in Rangoon. Thousands of NLD workers were arrested all over the country.

But regardless of these measures, it soon became evident that Aung San Suu Kyi's basic message had begun to take root firmly among the population at large. Between her first appearance in August 1988 and the time when she was placed under house arrest in July 1989, she had delivered more than a thousand speeches across the country. These had echoed themes of her father's that had emerged during her research abroad: the dependence of freedom on discipline, strictly fair treatment of political opponents, and a deep distaste for power-mongering and behind-the-scenes maneuvering. More informal talks had focused on the importance of reading books or of the people's taking responsibility for their own neighborhoods—where grassroot democracy should begin.

With Aung San Suu Kyi muzzled, the pro-democracy movement suppressed, and the Burmese people fearful, the SLORC had probably hoped that the elections it had promised to hold would mean little. That was a gross miscalculation. When the Burmese eventually went to the polls on May 27, 1990, they began to form lines at 5 A.M., immediately after the night curfew and an hour before voting booths opened. By the end of the day, the NLD had captured 392 out of 485 seats in the national assembly. Everywhere, the name that won the votes was Aung San Suu Kyi. Said one diplomat: "Burmese throughout the country were often unaware of the local NLD candidate they were actually voting for. But they all had heard of Aung San Suu Kyi. It was yes to her and no to Ne Win."

But still, as of 1995, the SLORC had refused to convene the elected assembly, and had even declined to open a dialogue with the NLD. Aung San Suu Kyi remained under house arrest until July 11, 1995, when she was released.

Bertil Lintner

References

Aung San Suu Kyi. *Freedom from Fear.* London: Penguin, 1991.

Kanbawza Win. *Aung San Suu Kyi, the Nobel Laureate: A Burmese Perspective.* Bangkok: CPDSK, 1992.

Lintner, Bertil. *Aung San Suu Kyi and Burma's Unfinished Renaissance.* Bangkok: White Lotus, 1991.

———. *Outrage: Burma's Struggle for Democracy.* London: White Lotus UK, 1990.

Mya Maung. *Totalitarianism in Burma.* New York: Paragon House, 1992.

O'Brien, Harriet. *Forgotten Land: A Rediscovery of Burma.* London: Michael Joseph, 1991.

Steinberg, David. *The Future of Burma: Crisis and Choice in Myanmar.* New York: Asia Society, 1990.

See also AUNG SAN SUU KYI; NOBEL PEACE PRIZE

Burritt, Elihu (1810–1879)

Born in New Britain, Connecticut, this dedicated American pacifist and social reformer also is known as "the learned blacksmith." During his youth, as an iron worker, he devoted much time to the study of languages and became self-educated and proficient in more than fifty languages. A strong advocate of temperance, abolition, and world peace, he advanced these causes by editing numerous publications, organizing conferences, giving lectures, and proposing innovative plans that would further those ideas. Through easily understandable arguments published in *The Christian Citizen,* a weekly paper that Burritt ran from 1844 to 1851, he sought to persuade the common man of the importance of striving to achieve world peace. As tensions increased in 1846 between America and England over the possession of the Oregon Territory, Burritt organized the distribution of fifteen hundred *Olive Leaves,* leaflets of information and statistics containing arguments against the war. These publications also advocated "people's di-

Elihu Burritt (ca. 1846). Papers of Elihu Burritt/ Swarthmore College Peace Collection.

plomacy," the active participation of citizens in the movement to bring peace. In 1847, Burritt founded the League of Universal Brotherhood, a secular pacifist organization with branches in the United States and Britain. Efforts to prevent a war between England and France led him to continue his efforts abroad. From 1847 to 1851 he organized the annual Popular International Peace Congress, a body of members that passed resolutions advocating the reduction of arma-

ments, the arbitration of future disputes, and the increase of antiwar propaganda. These conferences also encouraged the establishment of a Court of Nations, in which all members of the international community would be represented in order to prevent the outbreak of war by means of ongoing arbitration. Although these congresses were supported by intellectuals and liberals, they failed to gain much support from the revolutionary and working-class parties. While abroad, Burritt also proposed the Ocean Penny Postage program, aimed at reducing the cost of transatlantic postage in order to increase the level of international communication. In this way he believed misunderstanding among groups of people could be reduced and conflict could be avoided.

As an abolitionist, he advocated the idea of "compensated emancipation." This program, based on the model used in the British West Indies, would provide monetary compensation to planters who released their slaves. Revenue for the program would come from the sale of the unoccupied western territories and would include a strong national commitment to the assistance and education of freed blacks. This idea was proposed at an 1856 conference in Cleveland, Ohio, and gained the support of many prominent pacifists, intellectuals, and politicians, including Abraham Lincoln. However, the conference was unable to secure the full support of any major political party.

Maria Figueroa

References
Curti, Merle. *The Learned Blacksmith*. New York: Wilson-Erickson, 1937.

See also ABOLITIONIST MOVEMENT

C

Camara, Dom Helder (b. 1909)

Brazilian clergyman, liberation theologian, and activist. Long before the Second Vatican Council encouraged Latin American bishops at Medellin (1968) and Puebla (1979) to commit themselves to "a preferential option for the poor," Helder Camara had already done so. In organizing base communities and initiating the National Conference of Brazilian Bishops (CNBB) in 1952, he helped to develop church-sponsored schools that brought poor city dwellers and landless peasants together to examine critically the poverty, malnutrition, and illiteracy of their region. "Opting for nonviolence," he said, "means believing more strongly in the power of truth, justice, and love than in the power of wars, weapons, and hatred."

Basic tools for Camara's movement for nonviolent social change were the Bible and the educational philosophy of Paulo Freire, enhanced by his familiarity with Gandhi and Martin Luther King, Jr. Camara's campaigns included picketing factories whose poisonous wastes endangered the livelihood of thousands of poor fishermen in 1964 and initiating Operation Hope to help people rebuild their homes after floods devastated the area in 1966. Two years later, he organized a "living chain" of 130 priests who placed themselves between police and students protesting the policies of the military government, and he mobilized three thousand workers, housewives, clergy, and peasants in support of workers striking for better conditions and wages. Camara's continued resistance to the policies of the military government after 1964 led to several death threats. The national media slandered his name and blacklisted him for nine years.

Born February 7, 1909, in Fortaleza, on the northeastern coast of Brazil, Helder Pesoa Camara was one of thirteen children of a devout Catholic mother and a father who taught that "it is possible to be good without being religious." At fourteen, Camara entered the seminary and spent the first five years after ordination in his native city. Attracted to the "Green Shirts," a Brazilian fascist party, because of its militant anticommunism, he acknowledges that his naiveté at that time made it easier for him later to understand others similarly misled.

Transferred to Rio de Janeiro in 1936, Camara gradually came to realize "the fallaciousness of the communism–anticommunism dichotomy." Underfed people living in shacks and without hope dramatized for him that "the most threatening clash of our time is not between East and West but rather between the developed and underdeveloped countries." Injustice results, he insisted, not from "occasional events," but from structures and corporations that "ally themselves to military power and to governments."

As a participant in the Second Vatican Council in the 1960s, Camara urged the church to go boldly "in search of her lost poverty." Censored by the Roman curia for suggesting that they address social issues more directly, he encouraged his brothers at the council to forgo privileges and decorative attire that distance working-class Catholics from the clergy.

Named archbishop of Olinda and Recife by Pope Paul VI in 1964, the same year that the military overthrew a reformist president, Camara initiated the Action, Justice, and Peace Association, to support a just wage among underpaid workers. As the political repression worsened in Brazil, Camara's close associate, a

Dom Helder Camara. Photo by Stefan Merken.

chaplain at the University of Recife, was murdered; the military machine-gunned Camara's residence and terrorized other progressives in the city. Throughout efforts to discredit him, Camara insisted that his inspiration came not from the writings of Karl Marx, but from papal encyclicals and Catholic social teaching. A well-known poster quotes him as saying, "When I give food to the poor, they call me a saint. When I ask why the poor have no food, they call me a communist." Although retired—and replaced by a prelate less concerned about justice issues—Helder Camara remains "a presence" in Brazil and wherever the Catholic church lives out its preferential option for the poor.

Michael True

References
Camara, Helder. *The Church and Colonialism: The Betrayal of the Third World.* Translated by William McSweeney. Densville, N.Y.: Dimension, 1969.

———. *The Desert Is Fertile.* Translated by Dinah Livingstone. Maryknoll, N.Y.: Orbis, 1974.

De Broucker, Jose. *Dom Helder Camara: The Violence of a Peacemaker.* Translated by Herma Briffault. Maryknoll, N.Y.: Orbis, 1970.

Lernoux, Penny. *Cry of the People: United States Involvement in the Rise of Fascism, Torture, and Murder and the Persecution of the Catholic Church in Latin America.* New York: Doubleday, 1980.

See also NONVIOLENT ALTERNATIVES; PAX CHRISTI INTERNATIONAL

Campaign for Nuclear Disarmament

Main organization of the nuclear disarmament movement in Britain, campaigning for the unilateral abandonment of British nuclear weapons and the removal of all U.S. nuclear weapons from British territory. Since its founding in 1958, the campaign went through two major waves of activity: from 1958 to 1962 and from 1979 to 1984.

The first wave was triggered by British testing of its first H-bomb in the aftermath of the Suez crisis of 1956, which had done much to break up the postwar foreign policy consensus in Britain. The high point of this wave of activity came in 1960, when the annual conference of the main opposition party, the Labour Party, adopted the position of unilateral nuclear disarmament in defiance of the party leadership. After this decision was reversed a year later, the movement went into decline, especially when superpower relations improved sufficiently following the Cuban missile crisis to permit a Partial Test Ban Treaty in 1963.

CND's second wave was triggered by the revival of the cold war in the late 1970s, in particular the British decision to replace its aging Polaris ballistic missile submarines with Trident submarines, and the NATO decision to deploy cruise missiles in Europe. This time the Labour Party—again out of office—was supportive from the outset. The re-election of Margaret Thatcher in 1983 and the defeat of left-wing parties on the Continent, however, made the deployment of cruise missiles inevitable, and the movement again began to loose steam.

At its peak in the early 1980s, CND claimed 90,000 national members and a further 250,000 in local branches. This made it one of the largest political organizations in Britain and probably the largest single peace movement in the world (outside the state-sponsored movements of the Communist bloc). Its demonstration in London on the eve of cruise missile deployment in October 1983 was among the largest in British history. While membership came from all parts of the political and social spectrum, the ethos of CND was essentially that of middle-class radicalism. The first wave had many of the characteristics of a youth movement, as young people adopted the black and white CND symbol as the badge of a more generalized revolt against the suffocating conformism of postwar Britain. This was less true of the second wave, which appealed as much to the generation that had launched CND in the 1950s as it did to their children.

CND was formed by a self-appointed group of radical notables in February 1958. They inherited a network of local branches from a campaign against nuclear testing and an Easter march from London to Aldermaston (the main nuclear bomb factory in Britain), which had already been planned by the Direct Action Campaign. In later years the direction of the march was reversed, in order to emphasize that CND addressed itself primarily to politicians in London rather than to defense workers at Aldermaston. The annual Aldermaston marches became the main campaigning tool of CND's first wave.

From the outset there was tension between those who sought to work through conventional political channels and those of a more anarchist disposition. The mainstream of the campaign combined mass, but legal, protest in the streets with pressure-group activity in conventional politics, particularly in the Labour Party and in trade unions, where it put down strong roots among activists. Most of those in the direct-action wing of the movement had little faith in the strategy of winning over the Labour Party and then getting it elected. They organized sit-down blockades at nuclear bases, which were acceptable to the CND leadership, and mass civil disobedience in central London, which was not. CND leaders argued that a campaign of civil disobedience designed to force what was still, regrettably, a minority view in the government was neither democratic nor truly nonviolent. During the first wave of action in 1960, this issue led to a formal split, when the Committee of 100 went ahead with plans for a central London sit-down.

In the second wave a formal split was avoided. CND actively participated in direct action, notably in organizing the "cruise-watch"

network that tracked missile convoys when they were deployed to secret firing sites in the countryside. Most local CND branches held a dual loyalty to national CND and to the independent initiative of the peace camps outside nuclear bases, particularly the women's camp at Greenham Common, the first base designated for cruise missiles. The Greenham women were responsible for the most imaginative and effective direct action in these years, but their opposition to mixed-sex activities at the base led to major conflicts within CND, particularly when cruise missiles were deployed at the end of 1983.

Neither wave of CND was notably successful in its main objective of converting the British public to unilateralism. Indeed, the main response of the Labour Party to the second wave of the campaign was eventually to abandon unilateralism, which it had quietly adopted during the 1970s, on the grounds that by embracing CND's position it had contributed to its own unelectability in 1983. Even after the end of the cold war and the collapse of the Soviet Union, British nuclear weapons continued to enjoy majority support. CND was more in tune with majority opinion in its opposition to U.S. nuclear bases in Britain, probably because on that issue it was cutting with the grain of nationalism rather than against it.

CND still exists and has active local branches throughout Britain. Its national membership of around fifty-five thousand (1993) provides a substantially larger core of support than it maintained between the first two waves. While the end of the cold war removed much of the original rationale for the campaign, it is unlikely to disappear so long as Britain continues to cling to nuclear weapons.

James Hinton

References

Byrne, Paul. *The Campaign for Nuclear Disarmament.* London: Croom Helm, 1988.
———. "CND: The Second Phase." *International Social Movement Research* 3 (1991): 67–90.
Driver, Christopher. *The Disarmers: A Study in Protest.* London: Hodder and Stoughton, 1964.
Hinton, James. *Protests and Visions: Peace Politics in Twentieth-Century Britain.* London: Radius, 1989.
Parkin, Frank. *Middle-Class Radicalism: The Social Bases of CND.* Manchester, UK: Manchester University Press, 1968.

Taylor, Richard. *Against the Bomb: The British Peace Movement, 1958–1965.* Oxford: Clarendon, 1988.

See also COMMITTEE OF 100; DIRECT ACTION COMMITTEE AGAINST NUCLEAR WAR; GREENHAM COMMON PEACE CAMP, 1981–1993; NUCLEAR WEAPONS OPPOSITION; PEACE PLEDGE UNION

Case, Clarence Marsh (1874–1946)

Sociologist, professor, Quaker minister, and author of *Non-Violent Coercion: A Study in Methods of Social Pressure,* an important contribution to the conception of pragmatic nonviolent action. He was born on January 18, 1874, in Indianapolis, Indiana, and died on July 20, 1946.

Non-Violent Coercion, published in 1923, is considered the first systematic attempt to portray coercive acts like boycotts and strikes as examples of nonviolent action. Case argued that past studies of conflict had overlooked the importance of "antagonistic cooperation." In *Non-Violent Coercion,* Case first presented a history of the use of nonviolent action by various pacifists and war resisters up to World War I. He then discussed the efficacy of nonviolent action and attempted to dispel the myth that practitioners of this technique are cowards. He ended with documentation of modern examples of several methods of nonviolent action. Throughout the book, Case also examined nonviolent action and methodology in terms of psychosocial theory. *Non-Violent Coercion* made a valuable contribution to the field of conflict analysis and to the conceptualization of nonviolent action.

Brad Bennett

References

Case, Clarence Marsh. *Non-Violent Coercion. A Study in Methods of Social Pressure.* New York and London: Garland, 1972.

Catholic Worker Movement

Lay movement founded in New York City in 1933 in response to the love ethic of Jesus, the social teachings of the Catholic Church, and the Great Depression. Peter Maurin, an itinerant street philosopher, and Dorothy Day, a radical journalist, created a lay movement within the Catholic Church that has provided a spiritual home for generations of Catholics committed to Gospel nonviolence.

The movement emphasizes voluntary poverty, pacifism, community living, and a philosophy of personalism in the pages of its popular periodical, *The Catholic Worker.* The Catholic Worker (CW) movement is known for it ubiquitous urban houses of hospitality, where the poor are fed, clothed, and given shelter, and from whence nonviolent direct actions on behalf of peace, disarmament, and racial and economic justice are launched. The movement's peace witness exerted a profound effect on the U.S. Catholic Church, resulting in pacifism being officially recognized for the first time by the U.S. bishops in 1983 as a fully viable Catholic position in times of war.

The CW movement was the primary advocate for Catholic conscientious objectors during World War II, both within the church and in society. By applying the church's just war theory to the conditions of modern war, and by highlighting Christ's Gospel teachings on love and nonviolence, the movement argues that pacifism and nonviolence are the only genuine options for Christians in the nuclear age. The movement counsels Catholics to consider refusing to do war-related work and to perform works of mercy instead.

Catholic Worker personalism or anarchism challenges the power of the state over the individual and society. The CW has refused to accept tax-exempt status from the state, arguing that works of charity and justice should be acts of conscience that come at a personal sacrifice, without government approval or reward. Movement members advocate and engage in federal income tax refusal as a Christian duty of resistance to the violent state.

From 1955 to 1961, during the height of the cold war, New York City held annual civil defense drills that simulated nuclear war conditions. All citizens were required to take shelter during the drills. Ammon Hennacy and Dorothy Day of the CW organized annual civil disobedience protests to these drills, publicly refusing to "play this silly war game." They were regularly arrested and imprisoned for thirty days. Although only twenty-eight others joined them the first year, by 1961 there were over two thousand who publicly refused to take shelter and courted arrest. The drills were stopped the following year.

During the Vietnam War era, Catholic Workers were some of the first to publicly burn their draft cards in protest of the war and the conscription system. The CW movement also provided many of the participants in the draft board raid movement, in which conscription records were seized and destroyed in nonviolent acts of civil disobedience against U.S. policies in Vietnam. Similarly, a significant proportion of the participants in the Plowshares movement of the 1980s and 1990s, in which nuclear installations are penetrated and weaponry is symbolically destroyed, have come from Catholic Worker communities.

Catholic Workers live in supportive community with the poor and homeless, sharing finances, work, and daily prayer. It is a lifestyle designed to make service to the poor and a radical peace activism that often leads to long prison terms more tenable. Historically, the various Catholic Worker houses of hospitality (there are over one hundred in the United States alone) engage in a broad range of nonviolent actions.

Prayer vigils are held for those facing the death penalty, arms bazaars are picketed, economic boycotts are publicized and promoted in the movement's paper, and public fasting in behalf of peace and the rights of the poor is common. Many CW houses organize alternative public observances on Christian holidays, including neighborhood religious processions that stop to pray at sites that are symbolic of racial and economic injustice, and at military installations where nonviolent civil disobedience is conducted.

Patrick G. Coy

References

Coy, Patrick G., ed. *A Revolution of the Heart: Essays on the Catholic Worker.* Philadelphia: Temple University Press, 1988. 2nd ed. Philadelphia: New Society, 1992.

———. "Leaving It to the Laity: Conscription and the Catholic Conscience in World War II." In *American Catholic Pacifism,* edited by Anne Klejment and Nancy Roberts. New York: Praeger, 1994.

Forest, Jim. *Love Is the Measure: A Biography of Dorothy Day.* New York: Paulist, 1986.

Klejment, Anne, and Alice Klejment, eds. *Dorothy Day and "The Catholic Worker": A Bibliography and Index.* New York: Garland, 1986.

McNeal, Patricia. *Harder than War: Catholic Peacemaking in the Twentieth Century.*
New Brunswick: Rutgers University Press, 1992.

Miller, William D. *A Harsh and Dreadful Love: Dorothy Day and the Catholic Worker Movement.* New York: Liveright, 1973.

Piehl, Mel. *Breaking Bread: The Catholic Worker and the Origins of Catholic Radicalism in America.* Philadelphia: Temple University Press, 1982.

See also DAY, DOROTHY; NONVIOLENCE, PRINCIPLED; PACIFISM; PLOWSHARES MOVEMENT; VIETNAM WAR OPPOSITION

Catonsville Nine, 1968

A group of radical Catholic pacifists who destroyed draft files with homemade napalm to protest the Vietnam War. Considered one of the precursors to the Plowshares actions of the 1980s, the Catonsville Nine action was controversial within the antiwar movement, primarily because of the destruction of property it entailed. The significance of the action also grew during the ensuing trial, which garnered national publicity.

The Catonsville Nine action was preceded by a similar event during the previous year. On October 27, 1967, four Catholic pacifists entered the Selective Service office in Baltimore and poured blood on draft files to protest the Vietnam War. Two of the four, Philip Berrigan and Thomas Lewis, fasted for one week in jail to continue their protest. They were convicted of a federal crime in April 1968 and sentenced after the Catonsville action. The Baltimore Four, as they were known, had escalated the intensity of war-protest tactics in the United States to the level of nonviolent destruction of government property.

The Catonsville Nine action continued this new strategy of property destruction. On May 17, 1968, Daniel and Philip Berrigan and seven other Catholics (David Darst, John Hogan, Thomas Lewis, Marjorie and Thomas Melville, George Mische, and Mary Moylan) entered the draft board office in Catonsville, Maryland. Three of the nine were clothed in Roman Catholic clerical attire. They seized 378 file folders containing the names of men soon to be called to serve in the armed forces, dumped the files into metal waste baskets they had brought with them, and carried the baskets outside to the parking lot. They then poured homemade napalm (made from a formula in a Green Beret handbook) on the files and lit them on fire. The activists had alerted the news media ahead of time to ensure widespread publicity for their action. The group then prayed and waited for the FBI to arrest them.

The major significance of the Catonsville Nine action occurred during the trial proceedings of October 5–9, 1968. During the trial, conducted by federal judge Thomsen, the defendants were allowed to present testimony concerning their motivations for their action. The nine were allowed to express their religious, moral, and political justifications for their behavior. However, Judge Thomsen later refused to allow their testimony to be considered by the jury. Nevertheless, the trial of the Catonsville Nine presented an unprecedented opportunity for antiwar activists to use the courtroom as a venue for expression of their political beliefs.

The defendants used the trial to publicize their protest and to put the government "on trial" for waging what, in their view, was a criminal war. In effect, they conducted a "reverse trial" in the courtroom. In addition, over two thousand supporters assembled in Baltimore for the week, conducting rallies, marches, and street theater, and imploring draft board employees to resign. On October 9, the jury gave a guilty verdict and all nine were sentenced to up to three years in prison, though none served the entire term. They were imprisoned in March 1970 after the Supreme Court rejected their appeal. Two of the nine, Philip Berrigan and Tom Lewis, conducted a hunger strike in a federal prison in Lewisburg, Pennsylvania. The Berrigans also organized an inmate strike to protest prison working conditions.

Reaction to the Catonsville Nine protest varied from total support to outright condemnation. Some of the controversy focused on the method of direct action employed by the Catonsville Nine. Some anti–Vietnam War activists criticized the destruction of property as violent and therefore unjustifiable. Others were inspired by the action to stage similar protests. On September 24, 1968, two weeks prior to the Catonsville trial, the "Milwaukee Fourteen" broke into a Selective Service office, seized thousands of draft records, and burned them with homemade napalm. These three incidents of property destruction initiated a new form of religious pacifist resistance in the United States that was to re-emerge in the 1980s in the Plowshares movement against nuclear weapons. In addition, the trial of the Catonsville Nine became a historically important venue for anti–Vietnam War protest.

Brad Bennett

References

Berrigan, Daniel. *The Trial of the Catonsville Nine.* Boston: Beacon Press, 1970.

Gray, Francine du Plessix. *Divine Disobedience: Profiles in Catholic Radicalism.* New York: Alfred A. Knopf, 1970.

Wilcox, Fred A. *Uncommon Martyrs: The Berrigans, the Catholic Left, and the Plowshares Movement.* Reading, Mass.: Addison-Wesley, 1991.

See also BERRIGAN, DANIEL; BERRIGAN, PHILIP; PLOWSHARES MOVEMENT; VIETNAM WAR OPPOSITION

Charter 77 (Czechoslovakia)

Human rights and dissident movement organized by intellectuals in Communist Czechoslovakia that helped spawn the peaceful "Velvet Revolution" in the fall of 1989. Charter 77 was the product of debate among disenfranchised intellectuals and reformers purged from the Communist Party after the 1968 Soviet invasion. The charter's initial signatories represented a broad spectrum of Czechoslovak society, including writers, academics, journalists, former politicians, party functionaries, technicians, students, and a smattering of blue-collar workers. The instigators of the charter sought the widest possible movement of citizens in defense of fundamental civil liberties.

According to its founding declaration, dated January 1, 1977, "Charter 77 is a free, informal, and open community of people of different convictions, different faiths, and different professions, united by the will to strive, individually and collectively, for the respect of civic and human rights." The Chartists stressed that they were not establishing a political organization, because Charter 77 had no rules, statutes, permanent bodies, or formal membership. Furthermore, the charter did not avowedly propose a program of political reform, but wished to conduct a constructive dialogue with the state authorities.

Charter 77 urged the involvement of citizens in guarding a spectrum of civil rights. The Chartists demanded that Prague obey its own laws and respect the international obligations it had freely undertaken, including the Helsinki Final Act signed in 1975. The appearance of Charter 77 was psychologically important, because it breached the barrier of fear that the regime had cultivated since 1968. The avoidance of political overtones and its commitment to act openly and strictly within the law broadened the charter's appeal. Though the founders harbored few illusions that the authorities would respond positively to their propositions, they reasoned that Charter 77 could at least create a climate in which far-ranging political changes could eventually materialize.

The question of whether the Chartists should function openly or clandestinely was resolved early on. It was decided that secretive and anonymous activities would be counterproductive, because they would provide the government with a clear-cut excuse for strangling the movement at birth and dismissing it as an "anti-state conspiracy." Instead, by operating openly and disclosing the names of its signatories from the outset, Charter 77 depicted itself as a fully legal human rights campaign without subversive intentions. Moreover, by declaring itself in favor of "constructive dialogue" with the government, the Chartists could further deflect the inevitable official offensive.

Anyone was at liberty to sign the charter, but because the movement lacked any formal structure there was little need to recruit masses of activists. Moreover, the Chartists evidently did not rate their success according to the number of signatories, but rather by their effectiveness in influencing the regime and stimulating autonomous citizens' initiatives. The majority of Chartists reasoned that the best compromise between restricted and mass membership was to encourage various cultural and educational pursuits parallel to those controlled by the state.

Charter 77 combined several political and nonpolitical groups and individuals. The charter did not constitute a formal union or federation of these groups, did not publicly represent any of them, nor did it evolve into a mouthpiece for their views. It simply provided a platform and an opportunity for action by people who could subordinate their personal opinions and ideological orientations to the larger human rights cause. When the charter was launched, one of the largest groups to sign was made up of "ex-Communists" or reform Communists, including former Minister of Foreign Affairs Jiri Hajek. Initially, they formed about half the signatories, but over the years their percentage of

the total declined to a small minority. The influence of reform Communists within Charter 77 was most noticeable in the signatories' repeated calls for dialogue with the regime and in the underlying belief that the party was still capable of instigating reform.

A second sizable group within Charter 77 consisted of a mixture of "democratic socialists" and "independent liberals," including such notable figures as the sociologist Rudolf Battek. A number of them periodically criticized the ex-Communists for unnecessary moderation and urged more direct political activism. Although many of the "independents" envisaged little prospect for systematic reform, they conceded that given the political impasse only the application of consistent pressure on the authorities could bring dividends. A campaign for human rights seemed to offer the most realistic chance of success and could ultimately evolve into a more substantive opposition force if circumstances became more favorable. The independent liberals appeared to have been the most ardent supporters of independent initiatives in culture and education, and fully supported the pursuit of international contacts with Eastern dissidents and Western sympathizers.

The third significant element within Charter 77 consisted of religious activists, including the much persecuted Catholic priest Father Václav Maly. The movement provided a forum that helped Protestants, Catholics, and other denominations unite around the campaign for freedom of belief, worship, and assembly. The religious groups did not adopt any specific political orientation, but instead espoused a practical humanism that enabled them to act in concert with nonreligious Chartists. A growing number of practicing Christians joined the campaign or provided support; some were also involved in the unofficial "underground church."

In addition to the better-defined groups and tendencies, Charter 77 attracted an assortment of unaffiliated intellectuals such as the acclaimed playwright Václav Havel, young people from the "cultural underground," and ordinary citizens without strong political views. The wide spectrum of orientations within the charter did not include any explicitly nationalist elements. Splinter groups or factions did not materialize and a general unity of purpose was maintained.

The number of Charter 77 signatories stood at under two thousand in 1988, but there were certainly many more active supporters or passive sympathizers. How many is difficult to know. Charter 77 proved unable to kindle widespread and active support among the majority of the population. The crushing of the Prague Spring reforms and two decades of paralyzing "normalization" left most Czechoslovaks in a resigned mood. Although a majority was latently hostile to the regime, there was little immediate prospect for citizens to exert real influence on government policies. Like subjects in most other communist states, Czechoslovaks remained skeptical about the advisability of independent action and preferred to devote their attention to private or consumer concerns. Irrespective of how many thousands were actually involved in human rights activities, underlying, if inchoate, popular support proved sufficient to enable the movement's active minority to persevere despite constant government harassment.

The backbone of Charter 77 activities consisted of compiling, producing, and disseminating various unofficial texts. These included communiqués and statements signed by the three annually selected spokespersons, letters, petitions, political or literary essays *(feuilletons),* and situation reports. These documents explained charter initiatives and outlined concrete proposals for economic and political reform. They were intended for domestic and international audiences by highlighting conditions in Czechoslovakia and canvassing support for the human rights campaign. Besides defending civil liberties and sponsoring independent publishing, educational, and cultural pursuits, Charter 77 sought to restore "humanism" in social relations. It stressed ethics, morality, honesty, and individual responsibility. Chartists maintained that people did not need to become members of any specific organization or even sign the charter; they should simply aim to recreate "elementary human values" in a hostile political setting that favored bribery, dishonesty, corruption, greed, and selfishness.

In the late 1980s, on the eve of the Communist collapse, Charter 77 increasingly spoke out in favor of political pluralism and announced that it was ready to support and defend almost any independent political endeavor. However, the movement also cautioned that it would continue to avoid formulating any political program or establishing an oppositionist grouping under its auspices. Charter 77 also attempted to become more visible and gain wider influence by organizing outdoor rallies, symposia, and demonstrations on pertinent occasions. For example, Chartists tried to arrange rallies in Prague on Human Rights Day each December. The Chartists also appealed for greater grassroots activism in all manner of independent pursuits. Their objective was to expand public activities beyond the narrow confines of the traditional dissident circles. The cautious reforms enacted by the Prague regime in 1989 were clearly insufficient to satisfy dissident demands and growing popular aspirations for liberty. After a series of mass demonstrations and strikes in November and December 1989, the Communist government fell in what became known as the "Velvet Revolution."

Janusz Bugajski

References

Bugajski, Janusz. *Czechoslovakia: Charter 77's Decade of Dissent.* Westport, Conn.: Praeger, 1987.

Bugajski, Janusz, and Maxine Pollack. *East European Fault Lines: Dissent, Opposition, and Social Activism.* Boulder, Colo.: Westview, 1989.

See also HAVEL, VÁCLAV; HUMAN RIGHTS; REVOLUTIONS OF 1989

Chavez, Cesar Estrada (1927–1993)

Born near Yuma, Arizona, on March 31, 1927, the son of migrant laborers, Chavez helped to organize farm workers in California into unions and to lead protests against growers of table grapes in the region for increased benefits and rights for migrant Filipino and Mexican laborers. From 1952 to 1962 he was a member, and then director, of the Community Service Organization (CSO) in San Jose, California, which helped with immigration problems of recently arrived Chicanos and organized voter registration drives. When the organization did not support Chavez's efforts to organize a farm workers' union, he established the National Farm Workers Association (NFWA), an organization dedicated to the provision of social services for farm workers. In three years' time (1962–1965), the union registered over seventeen thousand families. In September 1965, when Filipino workers began to strike in protest of the lower wages paid to the recently arrived Mexican laborers, the NFWA and Chavez joined the cause against the grape growers of Delano, California.

Nonviolent tactics of protest were fundamental to the ideology of NFWA members.

C

Cesar Estrada Chavez. Fellowship of Reconciliation Archives.

Only in this way, they believed, would they maintain respect for their cause. Protests took the forms of pickets, sit-ins, and processions, but were also accompanied by a strong religious component. Catholic masses often were held to encourage morale among the strikers. In addition, many clergy members participated in the movement. In February 1968, in order to prevent protesters from turning to violent means of action, to draw national attention to the strike, and to present publicly his personal militant devotion to the strike, Chavez began a twenty-five-day fast. Between 1968 and 1969 protest efforts expanded to include a national boycott of California grapes. On July 26, 1970, a contract was signed by the twenty-six Delano growers recognizing the United Farm Workers Organizing Committee (the successor organization to the NFWA) and giving control of 50 percent of the grape harvest to the UFWOC.

Chavez remained the leading figure in the UFW until his death on April 23, 1993. Through the union and his personal connections with California's governor, Edmund G. Brown, Jr., he helped secure the 1974 Agricultural Labor Relations Act in that state. Throughout the 1970s and 1980s Chavez used his personal commitment to nonviolence and to *la causa* to publicize and promote union activities. In 1988 he maintained a thirty-six-day water-only fast to support a new boycott of California table grapes, which had begun in 1982 and ended in 1992. Chavez's personality could not overcome the changes in agricultural economics that worked against the UFW by the early 1990s. At the time of his death the union had suffered dramatic membership declines and faced political and legal pressures.

Maria Figueroa

References
Day, Mark. *Forty Acres: Cesar Chavez and the Farm Workers*. New York: Praeger, 1971.
Taylor, Ronald B. *Chavez and the Farm Workers*. Boston: Beacon, 1975.

See also BOYCOTTS; UNITED FARM WORKERS ORGANIZING COMMITTEE

Chile, Civic Strike, 1931

A phase of the movement to end rule of military dictator Carlos Ibáñez del Campo that began in 1931 on July 21 and ended with the resignation of Ibáñez on July 26. University students went on strike, followed by physicians, lawyers, architects, dentists, public school teachers, pharmacists, accountants, bank employees, and other commercial employees. Shops closed in Santiago, the capital city, on July 25.

Facing an acute financial crisis, Ibáñez had appointed a reform cabinet on July 13 whose key officials demanded a return to constitutional government as the price of their participation. The resignation of this cabinet precipitated spontaneous street demonstrations and some property destruction. Troops and police became involved in fights with people in the streets, which also erupted on July 23 and 24. Reports of casualties varied, but at least one police officer and three civilians were killed.

Meanwhile, on July 22, students at the national (state-supported) and the Catholic universities jointly called upon all citizens to strike. On the same day, the Unión Civilista (Antimilitary Union), a group of opposition professional men, decided to organize a strike. Work stoppages by professionals and white-collar workers developed over the next three days. Engineers voted to suspend work, which would have cut off electricity and water in Santiago, as of Monday, July 27. Blue-collar workers generally were not involved, though there were reports that some were prepared to strike on July 27. At some point all the municipal authorities in the city of Concepción resigned.

A second cabinet resigned on July 23, and in the congress on July 25, deputies of three political parties introduced a resolution asking the president to retire. One researcher reported divisions and demoralization within the armed forces by July 25 (Nunn, 165). Standing almost alone and dismayed by the bloodshed in the streets, Ibáñez gave up.

Patricia Parkman

References

Marín Balmaceda, Raúl. *La caída de un régimen: Julio de 1931*. Santiago, Chile: Imprenta Universitaria, 1933.
Nunn, Frederick. *Chilean Politics, 1920–1931: The Honorable Mission of the Armed Forces*. Albuquerque: New Mexico Press, 1970.
Ochoa Mena, H. *La revolución de julio: La caída de la tiranía militar en Chile*. Santiago, Chile: Imprenta "Cisneros," 1931.
Parkman, Patricia. *Insurrectionary Civic Strikes in Latin America 1931–1961*. Cambridge, Mass.: The Albert Einstein Institution, 1990.

See also CIVIC STRIKE

Chile, Transition to Democracy

Period from 1983 to 1988 during which political parties, social movements, and the civilian population in general used predominantly nonviolent methods to challenge, resist, and oppose the military regime and bring about a return to democracy in Chile.

On September 11, 1973, the Chilean military, with assistance from the United States, violently overthrew the democratically elected government of Salvador Allende Gossens, ushering in fifteen years of military rule established and maintained by violence, repression, and a culture of fear. During the first ten years the regime faced no significant organized public opposition with the exception of the Catholic Church, the only institution through which dissent could be expressed or channeled. Massive public social dissent began in May 1983. With a few exceptions, these were nonviolent expressions of resistance and opposition, to which the state responded with violence. From 1983 to 1986 opposition political parties, social movements, and labor unions attempted to develop coherent unified strategies to hasten the return to democratic rule. By the end of 1986, these actions had pushed the regime in two directions: the government offered a half-hearted invitation to the opposition to open a dialogue (called *apertura* in Spanish), and at the same time it increased political repression. By 1988, the opposition shifted its mainstream strategy from protest to working within the regime's own legal and political system, using mechanisms from General Pinochet's own constitution of 1980 to defeat him at the polls on October 5, 1988. This plebiscite required that Chileans accept or reject Pinochet for a continuing nine-year term as president of the republic. In December 1989, a center-left coalition, the *Concertación de Partidos por la Democracia* (Coalition of Parties for Democracy—CPD) won the presidential election and a majority in parliament. Patricio Aylwin, leader of the Christian Democratic Party, became the new president of Chile on March 11, 1990.

During the first years of military rule, the state dismantled all the traditional mechanisms for political participation and expression. Political parties were outlawed, labor unions were severely restricted, congress was dissolved, elected officials and university administrators were replaced by military officers, the news media were restricted and censored, and many people associated (or suspected of having been associated) with the previous government were exiled, executed, imprisoned, or disappeared. Repression was so effective and severe that public opposition was clearly foolhardy and dangerous. During this time, the Church was the only national institution sufficiently powerful and protected to express political dissent. The Vicariate of Solidarity was created to assist victims of the repression, often providing food, shelter, and clothing in addition to legal assistance. In 1975, the Church established the Academy of Christian Humanism, an umbrella organization offering sponsorship and protection to a variety of alternative research centers staffed primarily by academics and intellectuals dismissed from their university posts by the military.

This was a time when the average citizen scrambled for survival. Many social and political organizations also struggled, often clandestinely, to survive. There were no mass mobilizations, and Garretón describes the spontaneous expressions of dissent and resistance that did exist as "isolated incidences, erratic, and generally brief in duration." Nevertheless, people resisted in a variety of ways. Popular economic organizations *(organizaciones económicas populares)* such as community kitchens, shopping cooperatives, and income-generating workshops were developed nominally to meet subsistence needs, proliferating as a response to the harsh economic policies of the regime. Human rights organizations formed; the Association of Relatives of the Detained and Disappeared, a group of women organized to pressure the government to disclose the whereabouts of their disappeared loved ones, was the first such organization to oppose the regime publicly. Artists, actors, and musicians also found ways to express their opposition, most notably in the *canto nuevo* (new song) movement. Though often threatened, censored, and repressed, news media workers continued efforts to publicize the actions of the state, while social scientists revealed the negative consequences of state political and economic policies. The only pre-1983 attempt to generate a self-sustaining public political opposition was the response, coordinated by Christian Democrats

(PDC), to Pinochet's 1980 constitution; this was rendered ineffectual by the lack of a coordinated strategy with other opposition constituencies.

The economic crisis of 1981–1982 left even the middle class in severe economic distress. So when Rodolfo Seguel, leader of the Confederation of Copper Workers, called for a National Day of Protest in May 1983, middle- and working-class people cooperated for the first time in years. This marked the beginning of the National Days of Protest, a cycle of grassroots social mobilizations that continued through 1986. Protest activities included strikes, work slowdowns, workplace absenteeism, campus assemblies, and demonstrations. Young children stayed out of school; people refrained from shopping and declined to use public transportation; drivers honked their horns in the main thoroughfares of Santiago; and citizens turned off their lights at a designated hour and banged pots and pans (a symbolic act, reminiscent of protests against Allende in 1972–1973). While the labor movement and political parties experienced tensions over the leadership of these protests, the protests themselves increasingly exacerbated tensions between political party elites and the grassroots.

The social mobilizations of 1983 to 1986 marked the collective loss of inhibiting fear and the beginning of the repoliticization of Chilean society. One of the most significant aspects of these grassroots mobilizations is the extent to which "civil society" (not of the state, the military, or political parties) began to organize independently of political parties and to occupy "political space" *(espacio político)*. New social actors emerged, among them the women's, human rights, *poblador,* and students' movements, as well as a reconstituted labor movement. Perhaps the most significant of these was the women's movement, noted for its pluralist and nonsectarian organizing strategies. A gathering in December 1983, for example, convoked by the nonpartisan *Mujeres Por la Vida* (Women for Life) drew ten thousand women to the Caupolicán theater to model unity and solidarity to the opposition.

In an atmosphere made heady by the loss of fear on the part of average citizens and the regime's apparent willingness to open up a dialogue, attempts were made to create a united opposition front. *The Alianza Democrática* (Democratic Alliance—AD), formed in August 1983 as a coalition comprising the Christian Democrats (PDC), a branch of the Socialist Party known as "renovated" socialists, several

C

other center and center-left political parties, and some right-wing groups. Thinking it might be possible to negotiate with the newly appointed minister of the interior, Sergio Onofre Jarpa, the AD developed a program for the replacement of the military dictatorship and advocated a number of reforms to the 1980 constitution.

The mainstream opposition abhorred violence and tended to isolate and marginalize those groups advocating and engaging in violent resistance. For this reason, the AD excluded advocates of armed insurrection like the Movement of the Revolutionary Left (MIR) and the Communist Party (PC)—the latter being traditionally an important party in the Chilean political landscape. In reaction, the PC, together with the MIR, the Almeyda Socialists, and some smaller left-wing parties, formed the *Movimiento Democrático Popular* (Democratic Popular Movement). This coalition believed that protests would destabilize the regime and force its leadership to step down.

Another attempt at alliance was initiated by the Church when, along with a number of political parties, it signed the *Acuerdo Nacional* (National Accord) in August 1985—a document that proposed mechanisms by which a peaceful transition to democracy might occur. In early 1986, in yet another attempt to build a coherent and unified opposition, members of a variety of opposition groups formed the *Asamblea de la Civilidad* (Civic Assembly—AC). Composed of representatives of labor unions, women's groups, *poblador* organizations, student federations, professional associations, human rights organizations, and other groups from civil society, the AC called an effective two-day national strike in July 1986 and drafted the *Demanda de Chile* (Demand of Chile), a published list of demands for the return to democratic rule.

None of these efforts met with success, either as coalitions or alternatives acceptable to the military rulers. And while Pinochet appointed Jarpa as minister of the interior ostensibly to open dialogue with the opposition, the most that was accomplished was that some exiles were permitted to return to Chile, and some opposition journals were permitted to publish. Furthermore, *apertura* was accompanied by increased repression, culminating in 1986 with the burning death of Rodrigo Rojas and the disfigurement and severe injury of Carmen Gloria Quintana, in an incident that refocused international attention on the Chilean

military junta. Moreover by 1986, middle-income sectors became increasingly reluctant to participate in the protests, leaving students and *pobladores* (shantytown residents) to dominate the monthly mobilizations. These protests became more and more violent owing to the increased use of repressive tactics by the state and increasing levels of frustration on the part of students and *pobladores*. Political parties began to withdraw support from the protests and search for an alternative strategy. They found one in the 1980 constitution.

By the end of 1987 and the beginning of 1988, the opposition (excepting the PC, the MIR, and some other marginal groups) decided that the best strategy was to defeat Pinochet at the polls in the October 1988 plebiscite. The 1980 constitution allowed for Pinochet to remain president of Chile for sixteen years, provided he first be acclaimed by a majority of the electorate in a plebiscite in 1988. If acclaimed, he would be entitled to rule until 1996, at which time he could choose to remain as head of the armed forces for another eight years. A coalition of opposition groups formed the *Comando Por el No* (Command for the No) in February 1988 and established an intensive campaign to encourage eligible voters to register, and registered voters to vote "no." During this time, the opposition was also able to negotiate access to television and permission for the exiled to return to Chile, which, among other things, allowed for a more level political playing field. It was as much in the interests of the state for the plebiscite to appear legitimate (unlike the 1980 constitutional plebiscite) as it was for the opposition to ensure that it would be so. Additionally, the United States provided financial assistance for poll watchers and sophisticated computer technology for a parallel vote count. The opposition was risking a great deal playing by Pinochet's rules, but they proved successful, securing the first major step in the Chilean transition to democracy. On October 5, 1988, 55 percent of registered voters (and an unprecedented 90 percent of those eligible to register did so) voted "no," effectively ending fifteen years of military rule.

The strategic emphasis on electoral issues placed political parties back in the forefront of the opposition movement, even though the organizational capacities of the social movements played a decisive role in the victory of the "no" vote. The *Commando Por el No* was transformed into the *Concertación de Partidos Por* la *Democracia* (Coalition of Parties for Democracy—CPD), a sixteen-party alliance poised to contest the presidential and parliamentary elections in 1989. In addition, the opposition was able to negotiate a number of changes to the 1980 constitution—changes that assisted in the transition process.

In December 1989, the CPD won the elections, and on March 11, 1990, Patricio Aylwin, leader of the Christian Democrats, was installed as Chile's first civilian president since 1973. Democracy in Chile remains constrained by the 1980 constitution and the powers still resident in Pinochet, the National Security Council, and the nine Pinochet-appointed senators. Nevertheless, it is a continuing and stable transition. The CPD holds firm, and on March 11, 1994, Eduardo Frei, new leader of the Christian Democrats and coalition candidate, was sworn in as president of Chile.

Over the course of fifteen years of rule by a brutal and repressive military dictatorship, dissent, resistance, and protest took a variety of forms. In general, however, Chileans rejected the use of violence to oppose state-sanctioned violence. Mainline opposition groups were quick to distance themselves from groups advocating and engaging in the use of violence, such as the *Frente Patriótico Manuel Rodríguez* (Manuel Rodríguez Patriotic Front), the *Milícias Rodriguistas* (both connected to the PC), and the MIR.

There were enduring consequences of the process of democratic transition in Chile, including the emergence of new social actors independent of political parties, principally human rights groups, cultural organizations, and women's movements. These grassroots organizations challenged the traditional hegemony of political parties and successfully contested the terrain of political "space." They remain significant even though orthodox parties have resumed their dominance of political life and social participation.

Patricia M. Chuchryk

References

Bowers, Stephen R. "Pinochet's Plebiscite and the Catholics: The Dual Role of the Chilean Church." *World Affairs* 150 (1988): 51–58.

Chuchryk, Patricia M. "From Dictatorship to Democracy: The Women's Movement in Chile." In *The Women's Movement in Latin America: Feminism and the Transition to Democracy,* 2nd ed., edited by Jane S. Jaquette. Boulder, Colo.: Westview, 1994.

Constable, Pamela, and Arturo Valenzuela. *A Nation of Enemies: Chile under Pinochet.* New York: Norton, 1991.

Drake, Paul W., and Iván Jaksic, eds. *The Struggle for Democracy in Chile 1982–1990.* Lincoln: University of Nebraska Press, 1991.

Falcoff, Mark. *Modern Chile 1970–1989: A Critical History.* New Brunswick, N.J.: Transaction, 1989.

Garretón, Manuel Antonio. "Popular Mobilization and the Military Regime in Chile: The Complexities of the Invisible Transition." In *Power and Popular Protest: Latin American Social Movements,* edited by Susan Eckstein. Berkeley: University of California Press, 1989.

———. "The Political Opposition and the Party System under the Military Regime." In *The Struggle for Democracy in Chile 1982–1990,* edited by Paul W. Drake and Iván Jaksic. Lincoln: University of Nebraska Press, 1991.

Livermore, J.D. "The Search of an Elusive Consensus: Democracy, Dictatorship and 'Apertura' in Chile, 1983–1986." *Canadian Journal of Latin American and Caribbean Studies/Revue canadienne des études latino-américaines et caraíbes* 13 (1989): 29–43.

Morris, Nancy J. "Canto porque es necesario cantar: The New Song Movement in Chile: 1973–1983." *Latin American Research Review* 21 (1986): 117–136.

Oppenheim, Lois Hecht. *Politics in Chile: Democracy, Authoritarianism, and the Search for Development.* Boulder, Colo.: Westview, 1993.

China

The most populous country in the world with a rich, but little-known, history of nonviolent action. While examples of nonviolent action in China can be found dating back to ancient times, by far the largest number of examples come from the twentieth century. The Chinese engaged in nonviolent action in the 1920s and early 1930s against the influence of foreign powers, especially the Japanese. From 1945 to 1949, nonviolent action against the Guomindang (GMD or Nationalist Party) government was one of the factors that led to the collapse of that regime under Chiang Kai-shek and contributed to the establishment of the communist government. Since the Communists took power in 1949, nonviolent action has become an increasingly visible aspect of opposition to the Chinese Communist Party (CCP), although its appearance has risen and fallen with the severity of repression imposed by the Beijing leadership. Notably throughout the twentieth century, intellectuals and students acted as the most common carriers of resistance.

Several philosophical perspectives form a long cultural thread that frames a Chinese basis for understanding nonviolence and nonviolent action. The central spirit of Confucianism is Etiquette, or Rite *(Li)*, and Benevolence *(Ren)*. One ancient motto was "The spirit of Li is peace." Another important philosophical perspective, Taoism, made similar points: "You can use softness to conquer hardness," a view similar to modern notions of nonviolent action. Similarly, the doctrine of the school of Mohism was: "To love each other equally (without discrimination)," and "To fight only in self-defense." While these philosophical teachings provided some basis for legitimizing nonviolent action, the structure of Chinese society tended to be hierarchical and was often repressive, which generally impeded popular resort to nonviolent struggle. By the end of the nineteenth century, as the final empire collapsed and China became increasingly influenced by the ideas and politics of the rest of the world, the scope and frequency of nonviolent action increased.

Nonviolent Action against Foreign Influence
The modern development of nonviolent action in China was strongly influenced by Western civilization. The Opium War of 1839–1842 pried China open to Western influence. In a critical period of social change, hundreds of students studied in the West and were influenced by the Western ideas of the imperial powers (in addition to those of Christian missionaries teaching in China). These students emerged as a new intellectual elite, much more independent of the state than their predecessors. As late as 1900, traditional education and scholarship, emphasizing Chinese classical study and bound to the dying imperial social structure, prevailed. However, the generation of new scholars born in the 1890s, John King Fairbank observes, struggled to reconcile their initial traditional training with their exposure to Western ideas, technologies, and social

forms. It was this group that emerged as a new independent stratum of intellectuals, informed by the West as well as China's history. When they engaged in political struggles, they frequently adopted the ideas, organization, and forms of nonviolent action of the West, demanding free expression and national self-determination, forming associations, conducting strikes, organizing demonstrations, and the like.

In addition, at the turn of the century the internal empire of the Qing dynasty collapsed under the pressures of internal fragmentation and external predation. Following the Opium War, the European powers and Japan established treaty ports and "concession areas" within these and other cities. Concession areas ceded Chinese sovereignty to foreign powers under perpetual leases; within these areas the foreign powers governed themselves independently of Chinese authority, both legally and culturally. Over the course of the next decades, networks of trade and resource extraction developed that linked the interior and the coast by rail and waterway. Fairbank notes: "In 1898 France, Germany, Great Britain, Japan and Russia all occupied or claimed spheres of influence in China. These usually consisted of a major port as a naval base, a railway through its hinterland, and mines to develop along it." Antiforeign and nationalist sentiments grew as the Qing empire's power over the country eroded. The empire's support for the "Boxer" movement in North China during the rebellion of 1898–1901 thus produced two results. First, the emperor and the empress dowager fled Beijing, and the city was subsequently looted and thousands of Chinese killed in retribution attacks by German soldiers. Second, provincial governors in central and south China dismissed the rebellion. Imperial rule, and three hundred years of bureaucratic control by a central authority, collapsed.

The years from 1912 to 1949 are known as China's "republican" period, to distinguish it from the preceding empire and the subsequent regime of the Communist Party. The moment of republican revolution in 1912 rapidly turned to autocratic rule, and for nearly thirty years no central government was sufficiently powerful to resist continuing foreign pressures. Between the Boxer Rebellion and the consolidation of control by Chiang Kai-shek and the Guomindang or Nationalist Party (GMD; known as the Kuomintang, KMT, under the Wade-Giles romanization system) in 1927, a period of fragmented and often despotic government prevailed under the rule of regional warlords. The Nationalist government provided something close to a unified national authority, but faced substantial threats from within, in the form of regional challengers and the Communist Party (CCP), as well as externally from Japanese invasion and occupation after 1931.

Several forms of nonviolent action became pervasive elements of the revolutionary period leading to GMD consolidation in 1927, the anti-Japanese resistance, and the GMD-CCP struggles. Strikes by industrial workers, general strikes by students and other Chinese in various regions and cities, mass demonstrations, and boycotts of foreign products emerged as central tactics. The organization and direction of many of these efforts were controlled by the CCP. Other events arose more or less spontaneously, often in reaction to specific acts of repression or violence by ruling elites. These crucial tactics in the Chinese revolutionary struggle took place within an intensely violent and militarized social and political context.

The first large-scale nonviolent action in modern China was the May Fourth Movement of 1919. During World War I, China declared neutrality, which it maintained with some difficulty in the face of Japanese interests and influence. Japan, allied with Great Britain and already controlling important areas of northeast China as the result of its victory over Russia in 1905, expanded its control against German interests. At the Paris Peace Conference following the war, European delegates stripped Germany of the privileges it had enjoyed in Shandong province, southeast of Beijing, and gave them to Japan, instead of returning full control of the territory to China. In protest, thousands of students in Beijing and in cities across China mounted demonstrations and went on strike. Many students were arrested and some were injured and killed in clashes with police. Merchants joined the protests, closing their shops; labor unions staged strikes in the most widespread outpouring of national sentiment ever seen in China. Although the Chinese government of the northern warlords generally complied with Japanese interests, it retreated in the face of such popular pressure, releasing the arrested students, dismissing the three officials who were responsible for negotiating the treaty with Japan, and refusing to sign the Paris Peace Treaty. The May Fourth Movement opened a new era of nonviolent action in China. It became a rallying point for student activism, and new student mobilizations often occurred on its anniversary.

Over the next twenty years, China endured both continuing predation by increasingly ambitious Japanese governments and internal strife. Throughout this period several moments of nonviolent struggle occurred. In 1923, Chinese railway workers, directed by the CCP, established a federation of trade unions at Zhengzhou, an act prohibited by the regional warlord Wu Peifu. The workers moved the federation to Hankou (Hankow) and protested with a general strike. Starting on February 4, all railway transportation in China running north and south stopped. Wu, supported by the British, brutally suppressed workers at Zhengzhou, Hankou, and other places. More than forty were killed, hundreds wounded, dozens arrested, and more than one thousand fired from their jobs. The leaders, nevertheless, remained undaunted. Owing to strong pressure, the strike stopped on February 9.

A strike by Chinese workers at Japanese textile mills in Shanghai in mid-May 1925 led to an intensified anti-imperialist movement across the country. On May 15, Japanese guards at the factories fired on the workers who had closed and occupied a mill; one worker, a Communist leader, died from his wounds. Students and labor, the latter organized by the CCP, demonstrated at the International Settlement in Shanghai, leading to many arrests. New demonstrations promoted demands for the release of the students and more broadly for the end of the "unequal treaties" that gave foreign powers special privileges. Chinese workers at other mills struck.

On May 30 more than 2,000 students from eight colleges in the Shanghai area converged in the International Settlement to protest both the unequal treaty system and the rule of China by military warlords. British Settlement police arrested more than 100 students and more than 10,000 people gathered before the police in the Settlement, demanding release of the students and shouting "Down with the imperialists!" Constables fired on the crowd, killing 4 immediately and wounding many, several of whom later died. On June 1, more than 300,000 workers, students, and merchants went on strike. They established organizations and put forward their demands, which included punishing the murderers, canceling consular jurisdiction, and withdrawing all foreign armies.

C

Although these events began as a political-labor action against Japanese mill owners, they had a generalized impact, which C. Martin Wilbur describes: "[The May Thirtieth incident] gave a tremendous spur to the nationalist movement. Local leaders and political activists in Shanghai immediately organized a city-wide protest, which developed to a general strike on Monday June 1. Further rioting, countered by police repression, lasted several days. Ten more Chinese died. The International Settlement became an armed camp; 1300 marines from the five powers patrolled. . . . Demonstrations occurred in at least twenty-eight cities." On June 23, Chinese parading in Guangzhou (Canton) were fired upon with machine guns from the Shamian concession, killing fifty-two and wounding over one hundred. This violence set off a sixteen-month general strike and boycotts of British goods and merchants in Guangzhou and Hong Kong. Wilbur notes that the "May Thirtieth Movement" was a nationwide protest that aroused and focused both Chinese public opinion and international public opinion against the "archaic treaty system." The protracted strikes and boycotts imposed considerable economic pressure on the merchant and financial communities in the treaty ports and concession cities, which began to influence the policies of the foreign powers.

In Hunan Province Chinese protested the Japanese imposition of a series of political and economic demands. They organized protest associations and boycotted Japanese products. On June 6, 1925, when people went to the river port of Changsha to inspect goods, Japanese soldiers shot at them from a warship, killing two and wounding dozens. Tens of thousands of people demonstrated, carrying the coffins of the dead.

The nominal national government in Beijing was weak and inclined to conciliation with foreign powers. In fact, one of the goals of British foreign policy during this period of political fragmentation and regional violence by rival warlords was to support Beijing as the best hope for serving British interests. But none of the foreign powers were above exploiting the chaotic situation of Chinese politics. For example, in mid-March 1926, the eight foreign signatories to the 1901 Boxer Protocol demanded that the government of warlord Duan Qirui in Beijing provide unimpeded access to the sea, as the protocol stipulated. On March 18, 1926, more than five thousand people,

many of them students, gathered in Tiananmen Square in Beijing to protest and demonstrate, calling on the government to refuse the demands of the eight countries and to end all unequal treaties. The Beijing government's guards fired on the demonstrators. Forty-seven people died and more than one hundred were wounded, which substantially weakened the Duan government and further aroused nationalist and revolutionary sentiment.

Throughout 1926 and 1927, as the nationalist revolution under Chiang Kai-shek's direction gained momentum and scored military victories moving northward from the Guangdong province in the southeast toward Beijing, demonstrations, strikes, and boycotts became recurrent tactics. General strikes in the cities tended to be organized by the CCP. More or less spontaneous rural revolts erupted in conjunction with the nationalist revolution, often directed against landlords to address the economic despair produced by years of warlord rule and accompanied by much violence. Mao Zedong recognized the revolutionary potential of these revolts, but, largely because of the ideological and political guidance the CCP received from Moscow, rural areas were not yet a primary focus of communist organizing.

Similarly, boycotts were part of the general nationalist movement that mobilized the emergent merchant and bourgeois classes. Marie-Claire Bergère observes: "The economic boycott represented the bourgeois method par excellence for nationalist mobilization. . . . After 1919, and in the nationalist excitement created by the May Fourth Movement, the boycott became semi-permanent. The movement of 1919–21 was followed by that of 1923, which carried over into 1924, became general in 1925–26, and thereafter was incorporated into the strategy of revolutionary struggle."

At the beginning of 1927, as Chiang's faction of the Guomindang (GMD) consolidated its control of the revolution by turning violently against the GMD-left and the CCP within the GMD, concession areas in Hankou, Nanjing (Nanking), and Shanghai were overrun and seized by crowds. When Chiang established the Nationalist government in Nanjing in April 1927, he had created a more unified national authority than had existed in China for several decades. Nevertheless, political violence shifted to a civil struggle between the military and political forces of the GMD right wing under Chiang, and the Communist Party. Some foreign powers reluctantly adapted to this new situation. Britain recognized that its interests were probably best served by developing new relations with Chiang. Japan, however, sought to consolidate and extend its influence in the Northeast region of Manchuria.

At the end of 1931, Japanese control in China became more intense and more direct. On November 18, 1931, Japanese military forces occupied Northeast China and then penetrated North China. They established a puppet government and asked the Nationalist government to allow North China to become relatively autonomous. The Chiang government had been engaged in the civil war against the CCP, and may well have intended to submit to Japanese demands. Popular pressure, especially among students, quickly arose demanding an end to intraparty fights and a common front against the Japanese. Chiang resigned his leadership positions in the government on December 15 and left Nanjing. On December 29, 1931, more than six thousand students from Beijing University, Qinghua University, and others demonstrated, promoting such slogans as "Stop the civil war," "National front against Japanese aggressors," "Down with the Japanese imperialists," "Down with traitors," and "Freedom of speech, the press and association." The interim government arrested many, and the next day more than ten thousand students and citizens demonstrated once again. This time, three hundred were wounded. Thirty-five cities expressed support for the students and many anti-Japanese organizations were established. The weak regime under Sun Ke (Sun Yatsen's son) collapsed within a month and Chiang returned to power at the end of January 1932. This anti-Japanese movement increased the patriotism of the people and promoted the establishment of the United Front of GMD and CCP forces to resist the Japanese invasion. Chiang's continuing war against the Chinese Communists, however, was so unpopular that he was kidnaped by one of his own generals in Xian in December 1936. He was forced to call off the civil war and to join the Communists in a United Front against Japan. This was followed, in 1937, by Japan's invasion of China, and the beginning of World War II in East Asia.

Nonviolent Action against the Guomindang

As suggested above, the condition of the central government within China was perilous and fragile, even after the Nationalist government was established in 1927. Throughout World War II the Guomindang and the Chinese Communist Party cooperated in a common resistance struggle against Japanese occupation. At the end of the war, however, the civil struggle reemerged immediately as the GMD government intended to unify the country and crush the CCP within three months, while the CCP revolted and attacked the GMD. Japanese occupation had isolated China and deeply damaged its economy. Between 1945 and 1949, as the civil war renewed, the economy plunged further, suffering both depression and hyper-inflation. Thus the national power of Chiang and the GMD was substantially reduced, to the point that military and political envoys from both Britain and the United States saw Chiang as little more than the leader of a small militarist faction. Owing to its loss of popular sympathy, the GMD could not resist popular movements, and anti-GMD nonviolent action became a second front of the civil war that led to the collapse of the GMD government.

A powerful movement of intellectuals and students emerged between the end of 1945 and 1948 focused on economic hardships and opposing the renewed civil war and the political stigmatizing of all teachers and students who had taught in or graduated from schools under Japanese collaboration. On November 25, 1945, six thousand students gathered on the campus of the Southwest Associated University in Kunming (capital of the southern province of Yunnan) for an anti–civil war rally. Soldiers and police encircled the campus, fired to frighten the students, and cordoned off the area. The next day, the students went on a general strike. On December 1, soldiers and police broke into the schools, attacked the students, and even threw grenades. Four students were killed and at least ten were wounded.

In January 1946, the Chinese people grew extremely anxious about the future peace of the country as the civil war intensified. Prompted by public opinion and American pressure and encouragement, a Political Consultative Conference between GMD and CCP representatives convened in January to establish terms for a ceasefire and power-sharing. In the midst of the conference, on January 25, almost ten thousand students, many marching long distances to the wartime provisional capital of Chongqing, gathered before the gates of the conference. They petitioned and demonstrated, condemning the civil war and insisting that the conference must bring it to an end.

C

The Anti–Hunger Anti–Civil War movement of students and intellectuals expanded through 1947 and became increasingly opposed to the GMD government, including its support by the United States, in part because of some crimes committed by American soldiers in China and because of strong U.S. support for the postwar Japanese government. Anti-American demonstrations erupted in December 1946 and January 1947, prompted by the rape of a female student of Beijing University on December 24, 1946. More generally, however, students challenged the presence of American troops in the first place, as a continuing violation of Chinese sovereignty.

In May 1947, students of all the universities and colleges in Nanjing demonstrated and petitioned the Ministry of Education and the Council of Ministers for increases in their stipends and food allowances, which had eroded enormously in the face of hyperinflation, but they received no positive response. Their demonstration was actively supported by students throughout the country, even by the most conservative and strictly controlled schools of the GMD, which sent representatives to Nanjing to join the movement.

Student slogans were carefully worked out to represent the demands of the whole country at the time and became known as the "three counters"—counter-starvation, counter-civil war, and counter-persecution. The students determined to demonstrate again on May 20. The government hastily published "The Provisionary Regulations for Social Security" (similar to martial law) and Chiang Kai-shek himself gave a threatening speech. Student demonstrators broke through a blockade and demonstrated in front of military police on horseback. More than one hundred students were wounded in this action and dozens arrested.

The same day, similar demonstrations were held in Shanghai, Tianjin, and other cities. Many students were wounded in Tianjin. The wide and violent repression of the May 20 demonstrations prompted similar demonstrations and disturbances in other places. It also was symptomatic of the Chiang government's loss of legitimacy. The government interpreted these challenges as evidence of Communist agitators, rather than popular sentiment. Thus the government's reactions were often brutal, including abduction, torture, and summary execution of students. As a result, the legitimacy

of the government eroded at an accelerating rate leading to its final collapse in 1949.

Nonviolent Action in China since 1949

Under the CCP regime, no political action is permitted except that organized by and for the government; participants in unauthorized movements, including those who publicly challenge the regime's policies or doctrines, are severely persecuted. Although this suppression of dissent has been clear, and to some degree effective, in the years since the party came to power, suppression of dissent and independent action also took place within the Communist struggle against the Nationalists and the Japanese.

In one example, students at the anti-Japanese military college run by the party in the 1940s, many of whom came from the arduous conditions of the front and would return there after graduation, rose in a rebellion against the relatively luxurious lives of the party leadership. They went on strike, protested in wall posters, and killed all the pigs that they had fed so as to deprive the leadership. The party considered this strike a reactionary incident, and arrested and executed most of the student strikers.

In a similar incident in 1942, two well-known young intellectuals, Wang Shiwei and Ding Ling, arrived at the CCP headquarters in Yan'an, which the party had established after the Long March of 1934–35. Like the military academy students, Wang and Ding criticized the disparities in privileges and rankings that prevailed. Wang charged that while the poor and sick lacked food and medicine, high party officials lived luxuriously. Ding accused the party of neglecting the needs of common women and mothers, while wives of party leaders obtained extra care. For their dissent both authors were denounced and expelled from the party; Wang was executed.

After 1949, the CCP's reluctance to accept criticism and the corruption bred by its own hierarchy continued. Cases of nonviolent action against the regime became more numerous, although most of these actions were concealed from the outside world. In May 1956 the party opened the Hundred Flowers Campaign, aimed at promoting a relatively candid discussion of the regime's politics and governance. At the time Mao felt that only a very small portion of the country's intellectuals and students actually opposed the party; he thought that even if they were not party members, the vast majority of intellectuals supported and approved of the regime. Thus, he assumed that criticism would not be severe and would generally be constructive. For a year intellectuals held their tongues. When they began to speak, in May 1957, the rush of criticism, covering all topics from theory to administrative practice, shocked the leadership. The movement gained momentum through big-character posters, newspaper articles, forums, and even meetings and demonstrations. The campaign was terminated after five weeks.

The party believed that this was a prelude to disturbances and insurrections like those of Poland and Hungary in the previous year. In response, Mao initiated an "Anti-Rightist" campaign that targeted intellectuals. More than 600,000 intellectuals, especially the most best-known among them, were publicly denounced and condemned as "enemies of the people." They were punished by demotion in rank, and often by forced hard labor. Some were executed. The Anti-Rightist campaign drastically alienated intellectuals from both public service and loyalty to the party. This replacement of intellectuals by more ideologically fervent bureaucrats and local leaders began a process that accelerated with the Cultural Revolution of the next decade.

Large-scale nonviolent action disappeared for almost two decades as Mao mobilized the country in the Great Leap Forward and then the Cultural Revolution. Each of these, especially the latter, increased rewards for ideological purity and intensified suppression of dissent, either real or imagined. The broad economic impoverishment and social violence that these policies engendered gradually eroded unquestioning support for Mao's personal leadership.

The death of Zhou Enlai in January 1976 prompted the next major nonviolent demonstration. Zhou had been Mao's close compatriot since the 1920s and as premier was his chosen principal assistant. Although Zhou implemented many of Mao's policies, he was also known as something of a reformer. In the previous two years he had rehabilitated Deng Xiaoping, and had him elevated to the post of first vice premier, largely because of Deng's support for economic reform. Just before his death Zhou promoted the "Four Modernizations," calling for economic restructuring and greater efficiency. These positions set Zhou and Deng against the so-called Gang of Four, led by Mao's wife, Jiang Qing, who had been central to the Cultural Revolution.

When Zhou died, the Gang of Four prohibited mourning. In early April, however, when Chinese traditionally mark an annual day of mourning for the dead, hundreds of thousands of people went into the streets to express their grief. They placed wreaths, mourning couplets antithetical to Mao, posters, and mourning articles along Chang'an Jie (Avenue of Eternal Peace), Tiananmen Square, and especially at the Monument to the Martyrs of the People in the Square. Some of them gave public speeches, and small bottles were hung on trees to express support for Deng Xiaoping (the pronunciation of "small bottle" is *xiao ping*). Some writings apparently criticized the Gang of Four and Mao himself. This large-scale nonviolent movement held special Chinese features similar to those at the commencement of the democracy movement that would occur in 1989 and harkening back to the May Fourth Movement of 1919.

The traditional Qing Ming Jie (mourning festival) came soon after the cremation of Zhou. The same spectacle occurred again, but with more people, more flowers, and posters. Some of the mourning wreaths were three to four meters high, made of hard materials, and weighing tons in order that they not be moved away by the police. Many posters jeered at the Gang of Four, and some were even directed at Mao himself. The situation threatened the government. Mao saw this as a reactionary insurrection and ordered the violent clearing of Tiananmen Square. No one knows how many people died and how many thousands were arrested. It took the government more than one week to clean the blood from the square. Deng was once again removed from his positions and denounced as an "evil backstage manipulator" of the movement. The crackdown deprived the government of all its remaining support and led to the collapse of the Gang of Four shortly after Mao's death in September 1976.

After Mao's death and the removal of the Gang of Four, a power struggle ensued in which Deng Xiaoping and other party reformers emerged victorious. Deng began a series of economic reforms, following Zhou's orientation toward the need for modernization, and the CCP permitted some expressions of new political views.

During 1978, a new expression of protest, which became known as the Democracy Wall movement, appeared. Large character posters and periodicals produced independently of the party were placed on the Xidan Qiang, a streetside wall in Xidan, a central area of Beijing. The Xidan wall came to be known in the West as Democracy Wall. For a period of time, this center was as open as Hyde Park in London. People asked in their wall posters for freedom, democracy, justice, and human rights. Some even denounced Deng's ambition for a new dictatorship. Deng did not tolerate this degree of political liberalization and he turned against the campaign. He suddenly closed the Xidan Wall, imprisoned many of the protesters, and amended the constitution to forbid demonstrations.

During this period, hundred of thousands of people came to Beijing or to the provincial capitals to petition or demonstrate for the redress of their grievances. They included recent graduates compelled to work in the countryside, dismissed workers, unjustly treated cadres, veterans, and peasants. Among them were representatives of fifty thousand recent high school graduates who led a general strike in Yunnan Province on December 9, 1978. Other students conducted a strike in Shanghai in February 1979. Both of these became well known and had a wide influence, although both were severely suppressed by the regime.

Economic reforms without corresponding political reforms gave officials, their children, and relatives plentiful opportunity to gain wealth through corrupt means. Rapid inflation steadily worsened the daily life of the people. As a result, students in the large cities demonstrated during 1985 and 1986, despite restrictions by the government. These demonstrations advocated political reform, democracy, freedom, and human rights. Deng was prepared to suppress the movement, and the students retreated before the threats. Like that of his predecessor, Mao, Deng's response was to remove the party's general secretary, Hu Yaobang, and carry out a campaign against "bourgeois liberalization."

Student demands for political and economic reform emerged again powerfully in 1989. The movement began, as had the April 5 events of 1976, with public expression of mourning for a leading party reformer, Hu Yaobang, who had died in April 1989. This time students took the lead, and their criticism of the government was more blunt. The regime's criticism and dismissal of the students' petitions, coupled with mixed signals from a divided Politburo, prompted a massive demonstration of up to 1 million students in Tiananmen Square, opposite the government buildings.

As the confrontation intensified under the attentive eye of the international news media (in Beijing to cover Soviet leader Mikhail Gorbachev's visit), several students began a hunger strike on May 13. By early June, with the hunger strikers weakening and the regime apparently unmoved, demonstration leaders debated new tactics. In the early morning hours of June 4, units of the army moved against the students with force, including the use of machine guns and tanks. An indeterminate number were killed and scores were arrested.

The events of May and June 1989 had two consequences. First, they drew widespread international condemnation and heightened scrutiny of the CCP regime's human rights violations. Some countries imposed economic sanctions; many countries gave support to Chinese dissidents who fled. Second, while the Beijing government's action suppressed the student demonstration, it did not eliminate internal dissent and agitation for democratic reforms. If anything, among intellectuals and students, alienation intensified and dissent remained high.

Conclusions

Nonviolent struggle in China in the twentieth century is significant in many respects. Mass nonviolent action was mobilized as a central part of both the nationalist and republican revolutions, and in connection with the success of the Communist Party's rise to power. Chinese groups engaged in tactics ranging from demonstrations and strikes to economic boycotts. All of this took place in a social context in which the population suffered a great many threats from violence, economic hardship, and political persecution. Although many demands for change arose in reaction to repression or at moments of political transition in the leadership, many others were consciously part of a pattern of dissent and resistance.

In the era of Communist Party rule, dissent was more effectively suppressed, but it did not disappear. Crucially, the Communist regime intensified the isolation and alienation of the intellectual classes that had become important carriers of demands for social reform, including democracy, since the time of the Imperial collapse. Liberalizing economic policies, while meeting the threats of dissent expressed through nonviolent action, will continue to be the challenge the regime has created for itself.

Li Fang

References

Bergère, Marie-Claire. "The Chinese Bourgeoisie, 1911–37." In *Cambridge History of China*, Volume 12, *Republican China, 1912–1949*, Part 1, edited by John King Fairbank. New York: Cambridge University Press, 1983.

Ding Shu. *The Open Plot—Before and after the Anti-Rightist Struggle*. Hong Kong: Press of Nineteen Nineties, 1991.

Fairbank, John King. *China: A New History*. Cambridge: Harvard University Press, 1992.

Hua Binqing. *History of the May Twentieth Demonstration*. P.R. China: Press of Nanjing University, 1989.

Pepper, Suzanne. "The KMT-CCP Conflict, 1945–1949." In *Cambridge History of China*, Volume 13, *Republican China, 1912–1949*, Part 2, edited by John King Fairbank and Albert Feuerwerker. New York: Cambridge University Press, 1986.

Wilbur, C. Martin. "The Nationalist Revolution: From Canton to Nanking, 1923–28." In *Cambridge History of China*, Volume 12, *Republican China, 1912–1949*, Part 1, edited by John King Fairbank. New York: Cambridge University Press, 1983.

Xing Guoqiang. *Records of the Anti-Human Rights Deeds of the CCP*. Taiwan: Press of National University of Politics, 1981.

Zhang Yu-fa. *Contemporary History of China*. Taiwan: East China Press, 1983.

See also DEMOCRACY WALL MOVEMENT; EVERYDAY FORMS OF RESISTANCE; MAY FOURTH MOVEMENT; TIANANMEN SQUARE DEMOCRACY MOVEMENT, BEIJING, 1989

Chipko Movement (India)

Nonviolent ecological movement organized by Gandhian *Sarvodaya* activists in the Uttarkhand hill districts of the state of Uttar Pradesh in 1972. The Chipko movement emerged in response to an ongoing process of resource exploitation in the area, which had resulted in deforestation and destruction of much of the viable agricultural and pasture land. The movement, which is still active today, takes its name from the Hindi word meaning to hug, since one of the principal nonviolent tactics used by its members is to hug trees to prevent them from being cut down. It is notable for the significant participation of women.

At the local level, Chipko's actions have resulted in ecological and economic improvements in some villages. Women have become more empowered in village life through their continued involvement in the movement, and some of the arduousness of their work has been alleviated. The movement has brought together different castes, age groups, and ethnic groups. It also has raised environmental consciousness across the Uttar Pradesh Himalayas and has inspired many other ecological movements throughout India. However, the rate at which trees are cut down in the region has slowed only slightly.

The cultural expressions of resistance are motivated by economic, ecological, and religious concerns. For example, to signify their close relationship to the trees, women tie yellow *rakhis* (sacred threads) around the trees to provide symbolic protection, and readings of the *Bhagavad Gita* (a sacred Hindu text) often accompany movement actions. Religious stories, or *Bhagwat Kathas*, are told to increase environmental consciousness, referring to stories about the Hindu deity Krishna detailing the usefulness and sanctity of the trees. The resistance also finds expression in songs and poems that carry potent ecological and religious messages. By deliberately associating sacred Hindu texts with the forests, the movement has provided a religious and moral justification for protecting the trees. A series of symbolic Chipko marches called *padyatras* (evoking the image of religious pilgrimages) were undertaken throughout the Himalayas to spread the Chipko word and gain support. The movement also initiated reforestation programs and held eco-development camps to educate villagers and plan strategies concerning ecological issues.

Other methods of nonviolent intervention have included the disruption of auctions where tree plots were to be sold to timber contractors, mass protective sit-in blockades of forests slated for cutting, and the uprooting of eucalyptus saplings in government-run tree nurseries to protest the planting of ecologically unsuitable tree species. In the Doon Valley during 1986–1988, activists buried themselves up to their waists in the middle of an access road to a quarrying site that had been responsible for depleting water resources in the area. The movement organized many demonstrations, and some of the movement's leaders conducted fasts in protest of state government policy.

Paul Routledge

References

Routledge, Paul. *Terrains of Resistance: Non-violent Social Movements and the Contestation of Place in India*. Westport, Conn.: Praeger, 1993.

See also ENVIRONMENTAL MOVEMENTS

Civic Strike

Collective suspension of normal activity—economic and noneconomic—by diverse groups to achieve common political ends.

Numerous civic strikes have occurred in Latin America, where such a suspension of activity is occasionally denoted by the Spanish words *paro cívico* (civic strike) or *paro civil* (civil, or civilian, strike). The more common term in Latin American countries is "general strike." However, this phrase, borrowed from the labor movement, is misleading because the phenomenon is not primarily a labor action. (Conversely, the name *paro cívico* was given to two national strikes called by Colombian labor unions in 1977 and 1981 that involved supporting often violent demonstrations, but that included minimal suspension of normal activity by groups outside the unions. These last have been excluded from the present discussion.)

Scholarly examination of this phenomenon to date consists of Patricia Parkman's study of the use of insurrectionary civic strikes to remove heads of state in Latin America between 1931 and 1961, and the work of Colombian scholars on civic strikes over local issues in Colombian cities from 1958 to 1980.

Parkman's study compared fifteen cases in which strikes, or attempts to organize strikes, figured in successful or unsuccessful civilian movements to overthrow governments. Labor unions initiated two of these movements, but the others were led by university students, middle-class professionals, and even members of the upper classes. While the activities involved varied from one civic strike to another, typically shops closed and university students walked out. Physicians, lawyers, commercial employees, and government employees also struck in a number of cases. Working-class participation in some of these movements was weak, and organized labor actually opposed one of them.

These strikes usually climaxed movements that developed over months or years. In most cases, other actions, such as street demonstrations, occupations, and efforts to stop traffic, accompanied the shutdown itself. Not infrequently, these complementary actions led to violent clashes with police or soldiers, but nine of the fifteen civic strikes were completely or almost completely nonviolent.

The comparative analysis of these cases points to a number of factors that appear to have contributed to successful outcomes. Defiance by citizens reached a level that seriously threatened the government's ability to function. Key collaborators, such as cabinet officials, deserted the president. The head of state, or of the armed forces, or both, found killing civilians unacceptable. Military leaders did not feel their own position to be threatened by the movement. They either stood aside or turned against the president and forced his resignation. In two cases, U.S. intervention contributed to the ouster of the government.

Variants on the model of insurrectionary civic strikes defined by this study have been identified. Some civic strikes have provided civilian support for military movements against established governments, as in Venezuela in 1958 and Cuba in 1959. The first successful use of strikes to end rule by the armed forces occurred in Bolivia in September 1982. The labor federation there shut down one city after another (with the cooperation of business organizations in at least two cities) over a ten-day period, ending with the departure of the military regime.

The Colombian studies identified 144 local *paros cívicos*. The majority of these strikes put pressure on government authorities to provide better public services (such as water, electricity, transportation, or schools), to improve roads, or to rescind increases in the cost of essential services. Others protested government repression, demanded the dismissal of mayors or heads of schools, and supported the demands of particular groups. Most took place in the smaller cities of Colombia between 1971 and 1980.

Typically, the movement began with the organization of a broad coalition, including business organizations, civic improvement groups, neighborhood organizations, unions, and student groups, around a problem that affected the community as a whole. Petitions to public officials, public meetings, and demonstrations followed. In some cases local legislative bodies and, less frequently, mayors, unable to meet the demands, threw their support to a movement directed at the national government. In the majority of cases, a formal "civic committee" was elected in a public assembly to conduct negotiations and issue calls for action. Pressure for more vigorous direct action generally came from the less privileged (and less powerful) groups in the coalition—for example, residents of poor neighborhoods, manual laborers, and small shopkeepers—and the coalition often split over the strike. Auxiliary actions such as street demonstrations, occupations, and blockading roads normally accompanied the strikes.

The authorities usually temporized, postponing action, trying to divide the coalitions, wearing down the communities, and threatening them with repression. Santana's study of the 128 civic strikes recorded between 1971 and 1980 found that repression occurred in over a third of the cases: military occupation of neighborhoods, curfews, mass arrests, shutting down business establishments and popular organizations, or violent confrontations with citizens in the streets. Nevertheless, 35 of these strikes resulted in agreements that were very favorable to the demands of the participants, and another 17 achieved some of their objectives. Santana did not attempt to account for the outcomes beyond noting that the government consistently refused to take actions that would require immediate large investments of money, and suggesting that wider, more "radical," mobilization would have been required to force a different response.

Still other civic strikes on record illustrate the variety of purposes for which this form of political action has been used. In the state of Pernambuco, Brazil, for example, a business-labor coalition had wrested control of the city of Recife away from the landed oligarchy in 1955. Both groups then became the targets of repression by state authorities. Joined by the peasant unions and small proprietors of the interior, the opposition responded in 1956 by shutting down, as Moraes recounts, "all economic and financial activities in Pernambuco: banks, commerce, industry and agriculture." In 1978, the city of Managua, Nicaragua, shut down to protest the assassination of antigovernment newspaper publisher Joaquín Chamorro. A civic strike in June 1984 figured in the con-

flict over the terms of the election that ended military rule in Uruguay several months later. Further research may well reveal an even wider variety of civic strikes, not only in Latin America, but in other parts of the world as well.

Patricia Parkman

References

"Bolivia." *Latin America Weekly Report,* September 10, 17, 24, 1982.

Carrillo Bedoya, Jaime. *Los paros cívicos en Colombia.* Bogotá, Colombia: Editorial La Oveja Negra, 1981.

Moraes, Clodomir. "Peasant Leagues in Brazil." In *Agrarian Problems and Peasant Movements in Latin America,* edited by Rodolfo Stavenhagen. Garden City, N.Y.: Anchor, 1970.

Parkman, Patricia. *Insurrectionary Civic Strikes in Latin America 1931–1961.* Cambridge, Mass.: The Albert Einstein Institution, 1990.

———. *Nonviolent Insurrection in El Salvador: The Fall of Maximiliano Hernández Martínez.* Tucson: University of Arizona Press, 1988.

Santana R., Pedro. *Desarrollo regional y paros cívicos en Colombia.* Bogotá, Colombia: Centro de Investigación y Educación Popular, 1983.

Santana R., Pedro, Hernán Suarez J., and Efraán Aldana. *El Paro Cívico 1981.* [Bogotá, Colombia]: Editorial CINEP [Centro de Investigación y Educación Popular] *Serie Controversia* No. 101, n.d.

"Uruguay." *Latin America Regional Report/ Southern Cone,* August 3, 1984. London: Latin American Newsletters.

See also CHILE, CIVIC STRIKE, 1931; CHILE, TRANSITION TO DEMOCRACY; COLOMBIA, CIVIC STRIKE, 1957; DOMINICAN REPUBLIC, CIVIC STRIKE, 1961; EL SALVADOR, CIVIC STRIKE, 1944; GUATEMALA, OVERTHROW OF JORGE UBICO, 1944; NICARAGUA CIVIC STRIKE, 1944; NICARAGUA, NONVIOLENCE AND REVOLUTION; PANAMA, CIVIC CRUSADE, 1987–1989

Civil Disobedience

Deliberate violation of the law in order to protest injustice. Civil disobedience attracted worldwide attention earlier in the twentieth century through the efforts of Mohandas K. Gandhi in the campaigns he organized, first against racial laws in South Africa and then against British rule in India. In the United States, mass civil disobedience became a central tactic during the civil rights movement, classically explained in the 1963 "Letter from Birmingham Jail" by Martin Luther King, Jr. It was also a tactic a few years later in protest against the Vietnam War; one such episode was the destruction of draft board files in 1968 by the so-called Catonsville Nine, led by Daniel Berrigan and his brother Philip Berrigan both Catholic priests. But the history of such disobedience is far older than events in this century.

Henry David Thoreau is usually credited with coining and popularizing the term *civil disobedience*. He does not actually use the phrase, however, and the title "Civil Disobedience" was given to his essay "Resistance to Civil Government" only posthumously. Thoreau's protest of the Mexican War, the Fugitive Slave Act, and chattel slavery in the South took the form of refusing to pay the state poll tax, an act for which he was arrested and briefly jailed. That act was not, however, part of an organized nonviolent campaign to reform law and policy (as was true of Gandhi and King), nor did Thoreau go to jail (as many later civil disobedients would) in order to attest to his underlying fidelity to the legal order. It is also unclear whether he saw as centrally important the nonviolent character of his protest and whether he hoped his act of disobedience would arouse the conscience of the majority to the injustices he protested. In some ways, Thoreau's conduct was more akin to the conscientious refusal practiced by religious minorities stretching back to the post-Biblical Jews and Christians who were unwilling to acknowledge the Roman gods. In other words, disobedient conduct such as Thoreau's is more nearly a personal act of conscientious refusal, bearing witness in protest to public wrongs without concern for the political consequences of the act, rather than an act of civil disobedience of the sort practiced by Gandhi, King, or the Berrigans in the hope of actually bringing about change in the law.

Definition

Civil disobedience may take many different forms, but it always involves breaking the law. Legal protest (such as boycotts, strikes, and poster parades in democratic societies) may be linked with illegal protest, but the former involves no disobedience of the law in the strict sense of the term.

Civil disobedience may also be either direct or indirect. One who refuses to be drafted into military service because he believes the system of conscription itself is unjust is engaged in direct disobedience. Refusal to be drafted because one objects to participation in an unjust war is indirect disobedience. Tax refusal is thus usually, although not invariably, a form of indirect disobedience. Civil disobedience often must be indirect because the protesters have no direct access to the injustice they seek to protest. It is not possible to use direct civil disobedience, for example, to protest the failure of the government to enact or enforce antipollution laws. Yet indirect civil disobedience invariably communicates a mixed message, the more so as the causal connection between the law being broken and the injustice being protested becomes remote and attenuated.

From Thoreau to King, civil disobedience is usually assumed to be nonviolent, but many would disagree on the grounds that the term *civil* refers not to the civility of the tactics used, but to the role the protest plays in the civic life of the community. Thus, the Boston Tea Party (1773) is often cited as an example of civil disobedience even though it involved illegal destruction of private property—as the damage to draft board records by the Catonsville Nine involved destruction of government property. Any narrow definition of civil disobedience that incorporates nonviolence as an essential element would, of course, have to exclude such acts.

Unlike ordinary criminal law-breaking and even some conscientious refusal, civil disobedience aims at bringing public attention to social injustice and so must be conducted in the full light of publicity.

Civil disobedience and conscientious refusal share, however, a conscious and sincere reliance on moral principle. But because the civil disobedient hopes to change the law, the principle being relied upon must be one that is (or at least is believed to be) shared with the majority. It is this belief in an underlying shared moral principle that provides the leverage exerted by the illegal protest in the direction of social change. Whereas conscientious disobedients want respect for their acts, civil disobedients want to persuade others to agree with them.

Finally, civil disobedience usually proceeds from within a tacit acceptance of the current constitutional order. Thus, typical civil disobedients accept without protest whatever punishment is meted out for their illegal conduct. It is possible, however, to imagine revolutionary aims carried out by means of nonviolent civil disobedience.

As these considerations show, civil disobedience can be distinguished from a variety of other kinds of protest, legal and illegal, selfish and public-spirited; it must be defined in a manner neutral to several basic distinctions (such as direct versus indirect, violent versus nonviolent, and individual versus organized).

Justification

Historically, the justification of civil disobedience has taken various forms, including appeals to natural law, divine law, conscience, and secular moral principles. Antigone of Thebes, in Sophocles' drama, is portrayed as appealing to natural law to vindicate her defiance of the tyrant Creon's edict. Not only Judaism and Christianity but virtually all religions have insisted that their devotees must refuse to obey human laws when they clash with divine law. Far more popular and widespread, however, is a simple appeal to conscience and its priority. But the appeal to conscience is both ambiguous and inconclusive: Is it the sincerity and earnestness of one's convictions that carry the justificatory weight? Or is it the content of those convictions, the principles themselves, that really matters? Since one can be earnestly devoted to dubious or even immoral principles, it must be the justice of one's cause, not the earnestness or sincerity with which one acts, that justifies one's disobedience (if anything does).

In a constitutional democracy, where minority rights of public protest are respected by law and where participation in the political process is guaranteed to all, civil disobedience is not easily justified—for two reasons. First, the state arguably already recognizes and embodies the basic principles of social and political justice. Second, the disruption of community life that results from deliberate and organized law-breaking may do more harm than whatever good comes from protesting undesirable laws that are not basic injustices. To the extent this is true, illegal protest often remains at the margins of political activity and is unlikely to arouse the conscience of the majority.

Nevertheless, these reflections do suggest general criteria of justification for civil disobedience conducted in a constitutional democracy (criteria proposed and popularized by the philosopher John Rawls). First, the target of protest must be a basic injustice, such as failure to extend the franchise to all adult citizens (thus excluding such targets as the current tax on tobacco). Second, legitimate methods of public protest must have been tried and seen to be ineffective (thus excluding using illegal protest without any prior attempt to influence the legislature by petition and assembly). Third, the protesters must agree that others in their society similarly situated, with their sense of justice deeply offended by some other law or policy, also have the right to engage in civil disobedience (thus ruling out any claim to exclusivity or special privilege). Finally, there must be some reasonable prospect of success resulting from the protest (though, of course, success need not be measured solely by reference to immediately ending the injustice under protest).

Observations

Organizers of civil disobedience in the U.S. civil rights movement appealed to the fundamental political rights of equality and justice as articulated in the federal Constitution. They focused on the basic injustice of laws and constitutional interpretations that failed to accommodate full participation of all persons in the political, social, and economic life of the nation, regardless of race. This led many constitutional lawyers at the time to argue that the civil rights movement really involved little or no civil disobedience; instead, the protests involved breaking local and state laws that were unlawful—they were inconsistent with the federal constitution—and so the first requirement of genuine civil disobedience, illegal conduct, was not satisfied. Thus, although the civil rights movement touched divisive social issues, the basis of its appeals kept its tactics of illegal protest from becoming marginalized.

By contrast, civil disobedience against U.S. involvement in the Vietnam War was marginalized to a far greater extent, not only because the tactics often involved property destruction and the protesters refused to acquiesce in their own punishment, but mainly because the nation itself was deeply divided over the wisdom of the war, and there seemed to be no basis for appeal to any shared but tacit fundamental moral principle. Similar controversy attends the justification of the most publicized acts of civil disobedience in the United States in the 1990s—illegal trespass (whether or not accompanied by violent tactics) organized by anti-abortion organizations trying to close down abortion clinics.

Mass civil disobedience by itself, even if strictly nonviolent, is unlikely to bring about fundamental social change. In societies that flout human rights, civil disobedience always verges on futility and martyrdom. In societies that respect human rights, time-consuming methods of legal protest may nevertheless suffice. Public education in the justice of the protester's cause must be carried out by the most effective tools, including earnest dialogue to win over the undecided and patience in the face of hostility and resistance. Illegal nonviolent protest by itself, however just the cause, will rarely prove sufficient to effect political change.

Hugo Adam Bedau

References

Bedau, H.A., ed. *Civil Disobedience: Theory and Practice.* New York: Pegasus, 1969.
———, ed. *Civil Disobedience in Focus.* London: Routledge, 1991.
Greenawalt, Kent. *Conflicts of Law and Morality.* New York: Oxford University Press, 1987.
Haksar, Vinit. *Civil Disobedience, Threats and Offers: Gandhi and Rawls.* Delhi: Oxford University Press, 1986.
Singer, Peter. *Democracy and Disobedience.* Oxford: Clarendon, 1973.
Zweibach, Burton. *Civility and Disobedience.* New York: Cambridge University Press, 1975.

See also CATONSVILLE NINE, 1968; CIVIL RIGHTS MOVEMENT; GANDHI, MOHANDAS KARAMCHAND; INDIAN NATIONAL MOVEMENT; KING, MARTIN LUTHER, JR.; THOREAU, HENRY DAVID; VIETNAM WAR OPPOSITION

Civil Rights Movement (United States)

The movement that championed the use of nonviolent direct action as a viable form of social protest in the United States. The Reverend Dr. Martin Luther King, Jr., the premier leader of the racial awakening during the 1950s and 1960s, combined Gandhian resistance with Christian repentance in a new philosophy of nonviolence unique to the African-American community. The movement achieved its immediate goals but floundered over demands for structural changes to the system.

A deep tradition of nonviolent resistance to racial oppression within the black community nourished the modern civil rights struggle. Forced to accommodate to the master's paternalism, slaves resisted the harsher, dehumanizing aspects of slavery. Emancipation following the Civil War of 1861–1865 briefly opened up new opportunities for African Americans. Under Reconstruction, states ratified the Fourteenth and Fifteenth amendments to the Constitution in an effort to guarantee citizenship and voting rights for freedmen. In southern cities, black protests prevented the imposition of segregation laws. Indeed, former slaves eagerly participated in the political system until violently forced from the polls by the Ku Klux Klan. After the federal government refused to protect the freedmen, the social revolution of Reconstruction came to an end, leaving a legacy of constitutional—but unprotected—civil rights.

At the turn of the century when the white South adopted Jim Crow laws that institutionalized racial proscription, African Americans again organized boycotts in protest. Homer A. Plessy filed suit against the Louisiana railroad officials who ejected him from the "whites-only" car of a train. The infamous United States Supreme Court decision of *Plessy* v. *Ferguson* (1896) upheld the doctrine of separate but equal that enabled southern states to circumvent the Fourteenth Amendment's requirement for equal protection under the law. Encouraged by the court's ruling, southern whites legally segregated the races. In cities across the South such as Savannah, Charleston, New Orleans, and Richmond, African Americans conducted boycotts against streetcar companies that enforced the new ordinances. In some border-state cities such as Louisville, Kentucky, black protest prevented the enactment of Jim Crow laws. In most of the South however, strict segregation triumphed by the first decade of the twentieth century. African Americans resisted the new social order in various ways. Some people confronted authorities outright and suffered violent consequences such as lynching. Others followed the leadership of Booker T. Washington and accommodated to segregation.

Violence and the threat of violence maintained the South's segregated social structure, which in turn reinforced the region's colonial-style economy. Since the days of King Cotton, the South had grown increasingly dependent on

The Rev. Dr. Martin Luther King, Jr., the charismatic leader of the U.S. civil rights movement, waves to supporters during the March on Washington, August, 28, 1963. AP/Wide World Photos.

staple crop agriculture. Despite the ballyhoo of the New South boosters, the region's stunted industrial development presented no threat to the prevailing low-wage agricultural system. Like planters, absentee-owned corporations profited from a racial division of labor that relegated African Americans to unskilled jobs as laborers, sharecroppers, and domestics. Night riders kept down black people who attempted to rise above these inferior positions. Although whites earned slightly more, the combined wages of black and white workers fell far below the national average as the South remained a distinct region that processed raw materials and produced unfinished manufactured goods.

During the 1920s and 1930s the old plantation system collapsed. The boll weevil infestation and the bottoming out of market prices made cotton production unprofitable. As a result, thousands of black and white sharecroppers were forced from the fields. Old-fashioned paternalistic labor relations gave way to modern commodity labor relations. At the same time, New Deal federal policies encouraged economic development and social change in the region. With World War II, military contracts provided a stimulus for growth that was sustained into the postwar period. A highly competitive and dynamic consumer market arose. Structural shifts in the region's political economy made traditional forms of race relations appear increasingly archaic as demands for changes in the South's social structure increased.

Although southern efforts at race reform during the period failed, forces outside the region succeeded in slowly altering federal policy toward the South. Organized in the 1930s, some indigenous southern reform groups were race-baited and red-baited out of existence by the 1950s. In contrast, the National Association for the Advancement of Colored People (NAACP), with its headquarters and main sources of support located outside the region, proved more effective. The oldest of the mainstream civil rights groups, the NAACP directed a legal battle for equality that dismantled the South's segregated social structure. In *Smith* v. *Allwright* (1944), the NAACP convinced the Supreme Court to outlaw the white primary that prevented black participation in the democratic process. The case represented the first significant reinterpretation by the courts of the Fourteenth and Fifteenth amendments. Other rulings soon followed that challenged segregated seating in interstate travel and dual university systems that provided unequal educational opportunities for graduate students and professionals. Through its Legal Defense and Educational Fund, the NAACP steadily chipped away at the separate but equal principle behind legalized segregation in the South. The effort culminated in the 1954 Supreme Court decision of *Brown* v. *Board of Education,* which overturned *Plessy* v. *Ferguson* by declaring the South's racially separate and unequal school systems unconstitutional. Yet, implementing the hard-won legal precedents proved even more difficult than winning the rulings.

A less than activist federal government slowed the external drive for race reform in the South. During the 1930s, President Franklin D. Roosevelt had promoted racial equality through his support for the biracial Congress of Industrial Organizations and the Fair Employment Practices Committee, the latter resulting from pressure by A. Philip Randolph, the president of the Brotherhood of Sleeping Car Porters. Yet a shift rightward during World War II curtailed the federal government's halting intervention in behalf of racial equality in the region. President Harry S. Truman oversaw the desegregation of the armed services but did little else despite his much-acclaimed civil rights plank of 1948. While overseeing the desegregation of Washington, D.C., President Dwight D. Eisenhower not only regretted the *Brown* decision but also hesitated to defend the Constitution when forced to do so at Little Rock. These administrations fashioned federal policy around the conservative goal of citizenship rights for African Americans achieved through the registration of qualified Negro voters. Indeed, the federal government moved more slowly on race reform than the federal courts.

In response to the landmark legal decisions and the subtle changes in federal policy, southern conservatives coordinated the rise of massive resistance to school desegregation in the 1950s. Citizens' councils mobilized the white community against the implementation of the *Brown* decision. While some leaders, such as the businessmen in Atlanta who promoted a civic image of racial moderation, acquiesced to demands for desegregation, other leaders, such as the politicians in Birmingham who violently maintained racial separation, ignored the court rulings. Thus, on the eve of the modern civil rights movement, much of the white South defended a segregated social structure that had grown increasingly obsolete in the face of a modernizing economy and external pressure for race reform. The moment was ripe for indigenous protest.

Emergence of a Movement, 1953–1960

Although most people date the beginning of the modern civil rights movement with the Montgomery bus boycott of 1955–1956, a similar boycott had occurred just two years before in Baton Rouge, Louisiana. That successful protest shared similar characteristics with the streetcar boycotts of fifty years before and with later campaigns that developed elsewhere in the region. In Baton Rouge, the Reverend T. J. Jemison, a charismatic minister and newcomer to the city, headed an indigenous protest movement centered in the black church. He combined activist congregations with middle-class civic groups to form an umbrella organization that coordinated a boycott of city buses. During June 1953, Baton Rouge's black community stayed off the buses until the city agreed to provide black patrons with better seating arrangements. Mass meetings mobilized the black community behind the boycott. Modeled on church services, the meetings kept African Americans abreast of the boycott, reinforced the community's resolve, and raised revenues for the protest. Indeed, Baton Rouge—with its charismatic leadership style, organizational structure, and moral tenor—reflected an evolving movement culture in the South centered in the black church.

Events in Montgomery, Alabama, brought the emerging protest to the nation's attention. For months, black civic groups headed by Jo Ann Robinson and E.D. Nixon had planned a boycott of city buses in order to achieve more equitable seating and courteous treatment on public transportation. When Rosa Parks refused to move from a seat in the white section of the bus on December 1, 1955, and was arrested for violating the city's segregation ordinance, Robinson and Nixon asked her to serve as a focal point for the protest. Parks was a highly respected member of the black community and a leader in the local NAACP who had recently attended a workshop on racial equality at the radical Highlander Folk School. She readily agreed to endorse the campaign. As Robinson printed leaflets announcing a one-day boycott of the buses, Nixon contacted the Reverend Ralph Abernathy and other black ministers to enlist the church in the December 5

event. After most African Americans stayed off the buses that morning, the civic leaders and ministers organized an umbrella group, the Montgomery Improvement Association (MIA), and named King as president. King had recently accepted the pastorate of Dexter Avenue Baptist Church but had yet to participate in local activities. The selection of this untried minister from a prominent family in Atlanta proved most propitious. Aware of the previous boycott, King contacted Jemison for advice and later borrowed strategy from that successful movement. His oratory also expressed to the nation the nonviolent movement's goals and aspirations. Following a rousing speech by King, black Montgomery opted to stay off the buses until the movement's demands were met.

The boycott lasted just over a year. During that time, the MIA broadened its protest to include a legal challenge to bus segregation. The civil case *Browder* v. *Gayle* followed the appeals process into federal court where, in light of *Brown* and other recent decisions, the judges ruled segregated seating on public transportation unconstitutional. On December 21, 1956, official notification of the Supreme Court's decision upholding the lower court's ruling finally reached Montgomery. King called off the boycott, boarded the bus for the first time in a year, and sat up front in the formerly white section. A national news media increasingly interested in southern race relations identified King as a new leader in black America.

Over the course of the Montgomery bus boycott, King developed a philosophy of nonviolence. He combined the tradition of resistance within the black community and the religious imperatives of the black church with an understanding of Gandhian ideology to propose something new. A third-generation preacher, King had grown up in the black Baptist church. As a student at Morehouse College and at Crozer Theological Seminary, he had heard of Mohandas K. Gandhi's nonviolent campaign against British imperialism in India. He had read the works of Henry David Thoreau on civil disobedience, Walter Rauschenbusch on the social gospel, and Reinhold Niebuhr on moral man's struggle in an immoral society. He had discovered the dialectic of G.W.F. Hegel while in the doctoral program at Boston University. Yet it was not until he found himself at the head of a mass movement in Montgomery that King conceptualized a philosophy of nonviolence.

C

National civil rights organizations helped King. In February 1956, the Fellowship of Reconciliation (FOR) sent the white Reverend Glenn E. Smiley, and the War Resisters League sent African American Bayard Rustin to Montgomery to report on the bus boycott and to offer assistance to its leaders. Both organizations advocated Christian pacifism. In 1947, the biracial FOR, with its 1942 offshoot the Congress of Racial Equality (CORE), had undertaken a Journey of Reconciliation through the Upper South to test compliance with a recent Supreme Court ruling desegregating interstate bus travel. The challenge resulted in several arrests but little violence, and it was considered a success. As opposed to passive boycotts, FOR and CORE promoted nonviolent direct action best symbolized in the sit-in technique that CORE pioneered by combining Gandhian nonviolence with the sit-down strike of the United Auto Workers. Several years passed before a similar protest led by students independently erupted across the South.

In Montgomery, Smiley found an interested King who nonetheless had little knowledge of Gandhi or satyagraha. Smiley explained that retaliation against evil actually multiplied the evil and that Gandhian nonviolence required one to refuse to retaliate. He shared tracts on the subject with King and other leaders in the MIA and later spoke at a mass meeting where he was warmly received. A former member of FOR, Rustin had participated in the Journey of Reconciliation. With the encouragement of A. Philip Randolph, he traveled to Montgomery to discuss nonviolence with King and the MIA staff. Both Rustin and Smiley hoped King would emerge as a black Gandhi to lead a nonviolent movement for race reform in the South. Already the national news media had compared the Montgomery bus boycott to the independence movement in India.

Applying his academic knowledge to the social reality of the movement, King used the concepts of thesis, antithesis, and synthesis to work out his own satyagraha. On the one hand, African Americans could accommodate to segregation in a process King described as acquiescence. On the other hand, they could violently resist racial discrimination. Neither outcome was acceptable to King, who argued instead for a synthesis of the two. His conception of nonviolent resistance enabled one to refuse to participate in an evil system while rejecting physical aggression against one's opponent. He

contrasted this passive resistance to the segregationist massive resistance. In place of hatred for the oppressor, King substituted the Gandhian hatred for oppression and unconditional love for those who oppress. At the same time he emphasized Christian moral persuasion to convince the oppressor of the injustice of oppression. King posited that through nonviolence, African Americans could end racial oppression, free themselves and their white oppressors from the sin of racial discrimination, and then build a beloved community based on equality and Christian love.

While King increasingly articulated a philosophy that made nonviolence a way of life, many members of the indigenous movement interpreted Gandhian techniques through the lens of black theology. Nonviolence offered a practical strategy with which to counter violent white resistance. During the course of the struggle, civil rights activists systematically trained volunteers in the practice of nonviolence. Experts such as Rustin and Smiley traveled across the South to meet with movement leaders and to hold workshops where staged sociodramas approximated racist attacks in an effort to demonstrate nonviolent responses to provocation. Volunteers signed pledges not to retaliate but to turn the other cheek. Over time, the movement trained hundreds of activists disciplined in nonviolence.

Indigenous civil rights movements emerged in other southern cities during the Montgomery bus boycott. The lengthy struggle against bus segregation in New Orleans was typical. The first protest occurred in January 1956 and periodically resumed until complete desegregation resulted in 1958. The Reverend A.L. Davis headed the New Orleans movement, which derived strength from students. In May 1956, students provoked a bus boycott in Tallahassee, Florida, that evolved into a mass movement led by the Reverend C.K. Steele. The next month, the Reverend Fred L. Shuttlesworth organized the Alabama Christian Movement for Human Rights (ACMHR) in Birmingham in response to a state injunction prohibiting the NAACP. Davis, Steele, and Shuttlesworth were aware of Jemison's earlier protest in Baton Rouge, and they had observed the organizational meetings of the MIA. While they borrowed strategy from these earlier boycotts, the protests in New Orleans, Tallahassee, and Birmingham remained locally inspired and controlled. During the late 1950s, various movement centers were the locus of civil rights protest.

Following the successful resolution of the Montgomery bus boycott, black ministers and activists organized the Southern Christian Leadership Conference (SCLC) in 1957. The effort received direction from In Friendship, a New York civil rights group that included Rustin, Randolph, white lawyer Stanley Levison, and black activist Ella Baker. Previously Rustin had urged King to join with Steele, Shuttlesworth, Davis, and Jemison in formalizing the regional protest. Rustin remained an adviser to King throughout the struggle, and Levison became King's personal attorney. In many ways, SCLC functioned as an extension of King's will, for as president he alone made the final decisions. The organization itself cultivated King's public image and capitalized upon his prestige. Although Baker would later clash with SCLC's autocratic leadership, she at first contributed her enormous organizational skills to get the fledgling conference off the ground. As there were no bus boycotts to support, SCLC emphasized voting rights with a Crusade for Citizenship coordinated by Baker. The lack of nonviolent protest and the conservative shift to voter registration drives reflected SCLC's unclear purpose. Baker and Shuttlesworth unsuccessfully appealed to King for a more activist approach to race reform. Not until black students initiated the sit-in movement in 1960 did SCLC, scrambling to catch up, find its mission.

The Lunch Counter Sit-ins, 1960

The spontaneous decision by four young black men to sit down at the whites-only lunch counter and request service from the F.W. Woolworth store in Greensboro, North Carolina, on February 1, 1960, triggered a regional protest by black students that in many ways marked the real beginning of the modern civil rights movement. Of course, well-publicized previous events such as the Montgomery bus boycott and the 1955 lynching of Emmitt Till had influenced the students. Whereas the bus boycotts had used passive forms of resistance, the sit-in movement signified the widespread adoption of nonviolent direct action by a new protest movement within the black community. Unlike the ministers who operated out of movement centers and willingly negotiated with white leaders, the students refused to compromise their demands for immediate access to the system. The inexperienced youth initially accepted the assistance of older civil rights orga-

nizations, but in time they broke with the mainstream movement.

The pattern in Greensboro reoccurred across the South. The Woolworth stores denied the black activists service although the students remained at the counter until closing time. The next day they returned with several friends and repeated the sit-in. At the behest of white municipal leaders, the black students suspended the sit-ins to work out an agreement, but when the negotiations fell through they resumed the protest. With the addition of a boycott of white businesses, the students succeeded in pressuring Greensboro merchants to desegregate by July 1960. Press reports the first week of the protest carried the idea to two other cities in North Carolina. Coverage increased the second week as the indigenous movement spread outside the state. Dozens of cities across the South experienced sit-ins during February and March 1960.

Caught completely off guard, SCLC and CORE dispatched advisers to the sit-ins to train the activists in nonviolence and to offer organizational support. The formerly personal and unplanned protests took on more formal structure with selected leaders who notified white officials of demands for desegregation. The students recognized the advantage of forming an association to tie the various protest groups into a network that could share legal and financial resources. The SCLC and CORE sponsored the formation of the Student Nonviolent Coordinating Committee (SNCC) in April 1960. Two adults in particular helped the students: Ella Baker and the Reverend James M. Lawson, Jr. As acting executive director, Baker increasingly resented King's benevolent dictatorship at SCLC, and she warned the students to keep SNCC autonomous. Lawson, a field secretary of FOR and a black divinity student at Vanderbilt University, had advised the participants in the Nashville sit-ins. Actually, the student movement there predated the Greensboro protest by a few months, reflecting the overall rise in expectations experienced by black youth. In November 1959, Lawson had conducted a series of workshops on nonviolence that had concluded with an attempted sit-in at a downtown department store. The outbreak of sit-ins in February sparked renewed protest in Nashville. Some whites responded violently, and police arrested the demonstrators. Efforts to negotiate a truce failed, resulting in a black boycott of white businesses. After night riders bombed the house of the movement's lawyer, Nashville's black community staged a silent protest march on city hall. Sit-in leader Diane Nash asked the mayor if he found racial discrimination at lunch counters immoral. His affirmative response broke the stalemate in civil rights as white merchants negotiated desegregation with movement leaders. To silence him, Vanderbilt University expelled Lawson for his civil rights activities, but the young pacifist had already influenced the sit-in movement through his teachings of Gandhian resistance. Nashville students such as Nash, Marion Barry, James Bevel, John Lewis, Bernard Lafayette, and C.T. Vivian took Lawson's legacy of disciplined nonviolent direct action with them into SNCC.

The Freedom Rides, 1961

The Freedom Rides of 1961 reinvigorated the waning sit-in movement and reinforced the decided shift toward nonviolent direct action. Similar to CORE's Journey of Reconciliation, the Freedom Ride tested the Supreme Court's decision of *Boynton* v. *Virginia,* which desegregated lunch counters and rest rooms in interstate travel. This time, CORE staged the protest in the Deep South. Seven black and six white integrationists left Washington, D.C., on May 4, 1961, headed for New Orleans. In the Upper South, the activists met little resistance as they desegregated bus terminal facilities. In Anniston, Alabama, however, the Klan firebombed one bus and boarded the other. When the Trailways bus pulled into Birmingham, a mob attacked the already brutalized integrationists, savagely beating James Peck, a veteran of the 1947 ride.

The outbreak of violence during the Freedom Ride shocked the nation. Newly inaugurated President John F. Kennedy attempted to limit the negative international reaction. The protest again caught the SCLC off guard, although affiliates and movement centers such as the ACMHR in Birmingham had been notified of the challenge by CORE. In response, Shuttlesworth sent movement cars to collect the integrationists nearly killed by smoke inhalation, and he rescued the activists beaten by the Klan. The ACMHR provided much needed resources. Shaken by the extensive damage and violence, CORE halted the Freedom Ride; yet SNCC members in Nashville and Atlanta determined the protest must go on. Student volunteers arrived in Birmingham to continue the journey. The Kennedy administration worked with local and state law enforcement to arrange another bus ride. On May 20, 1961, state troopers escorted a Greyhound bus carrying eighteen integrationists out of Birmingham. When the bus reached Montgomery, the highway patrol disappeared, leaving the black and white activists at the mercy of the mob that awaited them. Again the vigilante violence provoked a presidential response. Working behind the scenes, Attorney General Robert Kennedy struck an agreement with Alabama and Mississippi officials that ended the Klan brutality but did not protect the constitutional rights of the integrationists. The Kennedy administration implemented a policy of "federalism" that left the enforcement of civil rights up to local officials. Authorities in Jackson, Mississippi, quietly arrested the activists, quickly arraigned and convicted them and, once the local jails filled up, sent them off to the state penitentiary at Parchman. SNCC activists had refused to post bond, thus extending to the Freedom Rides the jail-in strategy developed during a January 1961 sit-in at Rock Hill, South Carolina. By serving their prison sentences, SNCC members demonstrated their commitment to nonviolence. The experience galvanized those involved, including James Farmer of CORE and Stokely Carmichael. The Freedom Rides also underscored President Kennedy's reluctance to support civil rights reform and the national news media's preoccupation with sensationalism. The protest proved less successful in achieving desegregation.

The Albany Campaign, 1961–1962

The black community in Albany, Georgia, responded to the arrival of Freedom Riders and SNCC workers by forming the Albany Movement in November 1961 as an umbrella group to coordinate the protest activities of the local NAACP, SCLC, and SNCC affiliates. Street demonstrations followed the arrest of more Freedom Riders on December 10. For the first time since the Montgomery bus boycott, an entire black community mobilized behind the indigenous movement. On December 15, 1961, King addressed the mass meeting. The next day he led a protest march on city hall that resulted in his arrest. King joined more than seven hundred demonstrators already behind bars. The national media reported on events in Albany as city officials and movement leaders hastily arranged a verbal agreement that suspended the marches, released most of the prisoners, desegregated the bus and train station, and guaranteed biracial negotiations. Although he had promised to stay in jail until Christmas, King returned to Atlanta, leaving behind no tangible victory and a deflated Albany Movement.

The truce collapsed by the New Year. The arrest of a black teenager for refusing to leave the white section of a municipal bus sparked a boycott that ultimately bankrupted the bus company. SNCC initiated new protests against segregation in all of its manifestations. Sit-ins occurred at the bus station and downtown drugstores. Activists picketed white merchants who refused to desegregate and hire black clerks. Demonstrators marched on city hall. Yet with no clearly defined target, the widespread protests proved ineffectual. King's return to Albany in July 1962 for sentencing in connection with his December arrest reinvigorated the movement. This time he planned to serve his jail term. Protest marches resumed. Students staged kneel-ins at area churches, read-ins at the library, and swim-ins at the pool.

To ease racial tensions, Police Chief Laurie Pritchett arranged for a black man to pay King's fine, thus releasing the civil rights leader from jail. Pritchett had read King's account of the Montgomery bus boycott, and he responded to the nonviolence and Gandhian tactic of filling the jail by politely arresting the protesters and locking them up in nearby jails so that his facility remained nearly empty. As a result, the national news media and the Kennedy administration praised Pritchett for his restraint. At the height of the summer protests, the city received a court injunction against movement leaders. King obeyed the ruling since he viewed the federal judiciary as an ally, but the demonstrations stalled as SCLC filed an appeal. After the injunction was lifted later in July, King was arrested for holding a protest outside city hall. He spent a week in jail awaiting trial. The judge convicted King of disturbing the peace but released him with a suspended sentence. This time a frustrated King willingly left for Atlanta. White resistance had worn down the resolve of the SCLC. It had also suggested just how difficult it would be to use moral persuasion to convince the oppressor of the evils of oppression. By August 1962, the Albany Movement had little to show for months of demonstrations and hundreds of arrests. The national press declared King a failure and Albany a defeat.

A badly bruised SCLC withdrew to Atlanta and regrouped, analyzing the experience to draw lessons from Albany. As executive director, the Reverend Wyatt Tee Walker had been partially responsible for SCLC's activities in Albany. He had coordinated sit-ins and other protests, but his autocratic nature had alienated many followers, especially students. Infighting among SNCC, SCLC, and NAACP leaders within the Albany Movement had hindered the protest. The spontaneous approach of SNCC workers made a coordinated strategy difficult. SNCC had followed its philosophy of organizing a grassroots movement by branching out into the surrounding southwest Georgia countryside. Having cultivated the black community in Albany from the outset, SNCC activists had resented SCLC coming in from out of town, taking over the movement, and benefiting from their hard work. Walker's attitude had made matters worse.

In assessing the failure of the Albany campaign, Walker and King reached several conclusions. The SCLC had entered Albany unprepared, suggesting King had naively expected another Montgomery miracle. The lack of a clear strategy had wasted movement resources. Competition with other civil rights groups, especially SNCC, had contributed to the problem. Therefore King and Walker decided that the next protest they undertook would be totally controlled by SCLC and would follow a prearranged strategy that limited targets for effectiveness. Nonetheless, the movement remained committed to moral persuasion through nonviolent direct action.

The Birmingham Campaign, 1963

Birmingham, Alabama, fit the SCLC's new criteria perfectly. For years Shuttlesworth and the ACMHR had struggled against entrenched white resistance led by City Commissioner T. Eugene "Bull" Connor. By 1962 Shuttlesworth had grown tired of winning piecemeal reforms, so he invited King and SCLC to join him in an all-out assault against segregation. The ACMHR was the only civil rights organization in town, and it was one of SCLC's strongest affiliates. The tough reputation of Birmingham guaranteed coverage by the national news media and encouraged the belief within SCLC that a victory in the "Johannesburg of the South" would toll the death knell for segregation. King also hoped to restore his damaged reputation as a civil rights leader. Yet the movement had no reason to expect federal intervention by the Kennedy administration on behalf of civil rights.

A police dog attacks a civil rights protester in Birmingham, Alabama, May 3, 1963. AP/Wide World Photos.

During the winter of 1963, Walker made elaborate plans for a spring offensive. He selected primary, secondary, and tertiary targets for movement sit-ins, noting the number of seats at lunch counters and the best methods of access and egress. He met with ACMHR members willing to protest and risk jail, and he consulted black attorneys about potential fines. Walker intended the sit-ins to draw attention to a black boycott of white businesses that the SCLC hoped would, through moral persuasion, convince the city to desegregate. The focus on merchants contrasted sharply with the Albany movement's lack of focus, which was interpreted as a confrontation with white politicians who feared few reprisals from the disenfranchised black electorate. In Birmingham, SCLC planned no marches and no mass arrests, for the opponent was not city hall and the objective was not to fill the jail. Indeed, in the weeks before the campaign, King and Shuttlesworth appealed to northern liberals for bail money. Having learned from Albany, Walker and King proposed a tightly organized protest. The campaign unfolded accordingly, but the dynamics of the protest quickly exceeded Walker's narrow plan as SCLC—reflecting the fluidity of social movements—altered its strategy to suit its immediate needs.

Birmingham provided SCLC with its greatest success, yet the campaign's inauspicious beginning threatened another Albany. The sit-ins and selective buying campaign began on April 3, 1963, amid little fanfare within the black community. White resistance proved particularly troublesome. Connor, who had also learned from Albany, refrained from violence. Instead of desegregating, many lunch counters closed, forcing the movement to run through its list of targets within the first two weeks of the campaign. With no mass arrests, the national news media found little to report. When the city commission refused to grant a permit to picket downtown department stores, Shuttlesworth responded by leading a march on city hall that resulted in forty-two arrests. Movement strategy had unintentionally broadened. It would change forever the next day. During the arrest of demonstrators on April 7, 1963, Bull Connor set police dogs upon unruly black bystanders, prompting an excited Walker to call King with the news of the police brutality. Walker recognized the importance of appearances, for instead of the actual handful of movement members, the news media saw hundreds of participants being savagely attacked by dogs. To generate more sensational coverage that exposed the often hidden brutality behind racial oppression, Walker staged events to provoke a violent response in a new strategy described by some scholars as nonviolent coercion. King remained wedded to his belief in moral persuasion, but he acquiesced to the new direction the movement had taken. Others, such as James Forman of SNCC, criticized the development.

The movement stumbled along for much of April as Connor kept the dogs at bay. To generate interest in the campaign, King announced plans to lead a march on April 12. White leaders attempted to derail the effort by issuing a court order enjoining King and the movement from protesting. In Albany, King had obeyed a similar injunction and the movement had lost momentum. In Birmingham, King violated the court order and was arrested. While behind bars, King responded to a local letter in the newspaper by eight prominent clergymen criticizing the demonstrations as unwise. The result, his "Letter from Birmingham Jail," stands as the clearest expression of nonviolence and moral persuasion to come out of the movement. Dismissing the epithet of outside agitator, King compared himself to the missionary Saint Paul. He confessed his impatience with those white liberals unpersuaded by the nonviolent movement, and he justified the use of direct action by explaining that the movement created tension in order to force the white community to confront racial oppression. King then called on all moral people to violate unjust laws. While King's eloquent "Letter" would join the ranks of universal literature, it went largely unnoticed at the time of its release. For the rest of the month, SCLC concerned itself with court cases as fewer people volunteered to sit in. Even King's release from jail failed to revive the movement.

Just as it appeared the campaign would collapse, movement strategy shifted again. SCLC staffers had taught high school students freedom songs and nonviolent resistance. Bevel approached Walker about letting the youngsters demonstrate. On May 2, 1963, they sent hundreds of school children out the door of Sixteenth Street Baptist Church and into the arms of waiting policemen. King had not approved the use of school children, but he defended the action after seeing its effect. Officers arrested hundreds of black boys and girls, using school buses to haul them off to jail. The children's crusade saved the campaign, for it created the tension King needed to force a resolution to the local and national stalemate on civil rights. The decision marked the turning point in Birmingham. It also reinforced the cynicism behind nonviolent coercion. To contain the demonstrations, Connor stationed firemen around Kelly Ingram Park the next day. He turned on the hoses when the students marched out of the church. With the first blast, the nonviolent protesters dropped to their knees and held on to each other. As the water pressure increased, clothes ripped away and bodies tumbled down the street. At times the water was hard enough to tear bark from trees and shatter car windows. The country sat horrified as television stations broadcast footage of the brutality. Kennedy ordered emissaries to Birmingham to arrange a settlement. Biracial negotiations resumed in earnest. Soon Connor had arrested so many school children that they filled the jail. At noon on May 7, 1963, civil order collapsed in Birmingham as thousands of African Americans converged on the downtown business district in a general strike that shut offices and paralyzed traffic. A crazed Connor re-exerted control through brute force, letting the dogs loose and the hoses roar. Ready to end the negative publicity, Birmingham's white power structure ne-

C

gotiated a truce with movement leaders. They promised limited desegregation if the demonstrations ended. Sensing a personal victory, King accepted the terms.

The Kennedy administration had brokered the Birmingham accord, and it believed it had ended the protests without altering its policy of federalism. Yet coverage of the movement had spawned hundreds of demonstrations across the country as a national Negro Revolution took up the cry of "Freedom Now." In Washington, Kennedy realized that the demonstrations had wider effect than solely in Birmingham, for suddenly everyone was talking about the need for race reform. In a televised address on June 11, 1963, the president announced plans for sweeping legislation designed to remove race as an issue in American society. His proposed bill would be adopted as the landmark Civil Rights Act of 1964. The legislation outlawed racial discrimination in the marketplace by ensuring African Americans equal job opportunities and equal access as consumers. The Supreme Court cited the interstate commerce clause and Fourteenth Amendment to the Constitution in upholding the law. Thus, leading to this watershed in American race relations, the climax of the civil rights struggle occurred in Birmingham.

The march on Washington in the summer of 1963 was, in many ways, a celebration of the victory in Birmingham. Nearly a quarter of a million people gathered at the steps of the Lincoln Memorial on August 28 to hear orations by civil rights leaders. King's stirring "I Have a Dream" speech captured the mood of the movement with its emotional call for African-American assimilation into the system. Since the march also acted as a political rally supporting the civil rights bill, organizers forced John Lewis of SNCC to edit criticism of Kennedy out of his address. A. Philip Randolph gloried in the culmination of a protest that he had envisioned in 1941 as the March on Washington Movement. His colleague, Bayard Rustin, coordinated the day's event, which came to symbolize the highwater mark of the united movement. Birmingham had vindicated nonviolence and underscored the moral offensive of the civil rights struggle.

After Birmingham, white resistance turned deadly. In Jackson, Mississippi, on the night of Kennedy's televised speech, a vigilante murdered Medgar Evers, the head of Mississippi's NAACP. Klansmen bombed the Sixteenth Street Baptist Church in Birmingham on September 15, killing four black girls. Indeed, Kennedy's assassination on November 22, 1963, reflected a national shift toward violence later seen in urban riots and the war in Vietnam. As a tribute to the slain leader, President Lyndon B. Johnson convinced Congress to adopt Kennedy's proposed civil rights legislation. Southern senators filibustered the bill while the SCLC staged demonstrations in St. Augustine, Florida, to emphasize discrimination in public accommodations. The use of night marches to prompt Klan violence, a tactic developed by the Reverend Hosea Williams, reinforced SCLC's shift to nonviolent coercion. This time however, the strategy backfired. St. Augustine lacked a well-developed indigenous protest group. Swim-ins forced the issue of desegregation, but they disrupted tourism and alienated the white community, making moral persuasion difficult. Vigilante violence generated negative publicity about St. Augustine but little sympathy for civil rights. To extricate SCLC from another failed campaign, King accepted an empty truce. Only with the new civil rights act did St. Augustine concede race reform.

The Drive for Voting Rights, 1964–1965

Having defeated segregation, the movement turned to voting rights. SNCC workers functioned as the vanguard of the new struggle. They moved into rural communities across the South where African Americans were a majority of the population but were denied the vote. SNCC sponsored voter registration drives, established freedom schools, and created co-ops in an effort to change the way black people thought and lived. Robert Moses orchestrated SNCC's campaign in Mississippi, where a grassroots movement had existed since the Freedom Rides. Moses and other activists sponsored the Mississippi Freedom Democratic Party (MFDP) as a challenge to the state's racist political system. White students from northern campuses were invited to participate in the Mississippi Freedom Summer. In preparation they trained in nonviolence. No sooner had the voting rights campaign gotten underway in June 1964 than three SNCC volunteers disappeared in Philadelphia, Mississippi. For the rest of the summer an intense manhunt searched the piney woods of the state, finally locating the bodies of James Chaney, Andrew Goodman, and Michael Schwerner in an earthen dam. Their murder by the Klan, and the refusal of the Johnson administration to protect civil rights activists, fueled the campaign. After the state Democratic Party adopted a platform condemning civil rights, the MFDP attempted to unseat the "unloyal" democratic regulars by sending its own delegates to the Democratic National Convention in 1964. During the credentials committee hearings on the matter, Fannie Lou Hamer of the Mississippi Delta mesmerized the news media and the country with her testimony of brutality endured for the ballot. An embarrassed President Johnson marshaled party officials against the MFDP. Compromised by their northeastern allies in a lesson of hardball politics, a dejected MFDP returned to Mississippi. The experience radicalized many SNCC activists who had lost faith in the political system. It embittered Moses, who withdrew from SNCC and contemplated black nationalism.

In Alabama's black belt, SNCC activists worked hard to register voters but met with limited success. SCLC decided to capitalize on the grassroots movement. King led a voting rights march in Selma on February 1, 1965, that resulted in hundreds of arrests but no brutality. Organizers hoped that with enough creative tension, Dallas County Sheriff Jim Clark would brutalize nonviolent activists. Following the police shooting of black youth Jimmie Lee Jackson in nearby Marion, SCLC's James Bevel proposed a march to Montgomery to emphasize the denial of voting rights. On "Bloody Sunday," March 7, 1965, some five hundred activists led by John Lewis of SNCC and Hosea Williams of SCLC crossed the Alabama River headed to the state capital. Just beyond the Edmund Pettus Bridge stood state troopers and a mounted posse of local white vigilantes. When the marchers reached the foot of the bridge they were told to disperse. As they knelt in prayer, the cavalry charged and the troopers followed firing tear gas, swinging billy clubs, and poking cattle prods. The officials routed the nonviolent demonstrators. Televised accounts of the police repression provoked public outrage.

Two days later, King, who had missed the first march, followed a court-ordered compromise that required the second march to return to Selma after crossing the bridge. He avoided an opportunity for nonviolent coercion and was excoriated for "Turnaround Tuesday." Since Albany, many SNCC workers had grown hostile to SCLC because of its willingness to compromise, its religiosity, and its faith in nonviolence. That night vigilantes killed a white minister. President Johnson responded to the violence in Selma by announcing on television plans to reform voter registration in the South, an area inadequately addressed in the Civil Rights Act of 1964. Johnson federalized the Alabama National Guard and sent troops to secure the Selma to Montgomery highway for SCLC. The courts opened the way for the protest, which began on March 21. Four days later nearly twenty-five thousand people gathered around the base of the state capitol and listened to King speak. That night vigilantes killed Viola Liuzzo, a white volunteer from Detroit.

Over the summer, Congress debated Johnson's proposed legislation. On August 6, 1965, the president signed into law the Voting Rights Act, which enforced the Fifteenth Amendment to the Constitution by outlawing educational requirements for the ballot and by sending federal registrars into the South to register voters. With the Civil Rights Act of 1964 and the Voting Rights Act of 1965, the movement achieved its original goals through the enforcement of constitutional rights.

The Decline of the Civil Rights Movement, 1966–1968

After the Selma campaign, the civil rights movement disintegrated. In early 1966 King took SCLC to Chicago in an effort to organize the movement in the North. He put his family in the ghetto to emphasize the need for fair housing. Instead of an economic target such as a real estate board, however, SCLC focused on a political one, Mayor Richard Daley who successfully outmaneuvered King, causing the protest to fall flat. In negotiations with the mayor, King compromised on a threatened march through the white neighborhood of Cicero and won nothing in return. Unlike the South, there was no indigenous movement in Chicago, although SCLC did establish Operation Breadbasket. King left Chicago blaming capitalism for the extent of racial discrimination in the world. His criticism of the war in Vietnam also alienated him from mainstream America, other civil rights leaders, and the Johnson administration. As he grew increasingly radical, King nonetheless remained true to his philosophy of nonviolence. The same cannot be said of SNCC. In June 1966 James Meredith, who had integrated the University of Mississippi in 1962, proposed a March against Fear from Memphis to Jackson. He was shot after crossing the state line. Members from SCLC, SNCC, and CORE agreed to continue the march. Yet one month earlier, a militant minority in SNCC had ousted John Lewis as chairman and elected Stokely Carmichael, in a move that reflected a general shift toward black nationalism. These SNCC workers had been influenced by Malcolm X. They repudiated nonviolence as a way of life although they retained it as a tactic. At CORE, the replacement of James Farmer by Floyd McKissick marked a similar development. When the Meredith march reached Greenwood, Carmichael signaled SNCC's open rebellion against nonviolence by replacing the slogan "Freedom Now" with the ominous sounding "Black Power." No longer did the young activists see integration and the vote as the answer. With Black Power came the call for separatism. On June 26, 1966, the Meredith March concluded in Jackson with the permanent division of the movement.

An increasingly depressed King turned SCLC's attention to fighting poverty. He planned a Poor People's Campaign as a massive nonviolent protest in Washington, D.C., that would emphasize the need for fundamental structural changes in the distribution of wealth in America. Poor people of all races were to march into the capital, build a shantytown on government property, and wage sit-ins in federal office buildings until Congress adopted legislation that guaranteed a decent standard of living and adequate shelter for all Americans. As SCLC planned the new protest in the winter of 1968, King answered a call to support a strike of sanitation workers in Memphis, Tennessee. The protest had the appearance of the earlier indigenous movements, with charismatic ministers such as James Lawson leading mass meetings and conducting nonviolent demonstrations. Yet when King led a protest on March 28, militant black street thugs disrupted the proceedings with violence that turned into looting. The national news media pointed to the inability of SCLC to control the riot and suggested a similar upheaval would occur in Washington during the Poor People's Campaign. SCLC had not organized the march, and a chagrined King denounced the violence. Yet he worried about maintaining nonviolence in an age of urban uprisings. After much discussion, SCLC decided to continue the Poor People's Campaign and to return to Memphis to lead another march and thus demonstrate the effectiveness of nonviolence.

On April 4, 1968, a white assassin, James Earl Ray, shot King as he stood on the balcony of the Lorraine Motel. King's murder begat violence as urban rioting erupted in dozens of cities across America. His death helped end the Memphis strike in favor of the garbage collectors, and it contributed to the passage of the Civil Rights Act of 1968, which included fair housing measures. Yet the spirit was gone. A devastated SCLC carried on with the Poor People's Campaign, but dissension among the ranks and inadequate planning doomed the enterprise. The modern civil rights movement had ended. In the South, old activists staged occasional protests but received limited support from the black community. The SNCC workers advocating separatism joined the Black Panthers and were violently suppressed by white authorities. By King's death, most African Americans accepted the political system as the proper arena for race reform.

Glenn T. Eskew

References

Bartley, Numan V. *The Rise of Massive Resistance: Race and Politics in the South during the 1950s.* Baton Rouge: Louisiana State University Press, 1969.

Bloom, Jack M. *Class, Race, and the Civil Rights Movement.* Bloomington: Indiana University Press, 1987.

Carson, Clayborne. *In Struggle: SNCC and the Black Awakening of the 1960s.* Cambridge: Harvard University Press, 1981.

Dittmer, John. *Local People: The Struggle for Civil Rights in Mississippi.* Urbana: University of Illinois Press, 1994.

Fairclough, Adam. *To Redeem the Soul of America: The Southern Christian Leadership Conference and Martin Luther King, Jr.* Athens: University of Georgia Press, 1987.

Garrow, David J., ed. *Martin Luther King, Jr. and the Civil Rights Movement.* 18 Volumes. Brooklyn, N.Y.: Carlson, 1989.

King, Martin Luther, Jr. *Stride toward Freedom: The Montgomery Story.* New York: Harper and Row, 1958.

Meier, August, and Elliott Rudwick. *CORE: A Study in the Civil Rights Movement, 1942–1968.* Urbana: University of Illinois Press, 1975.

Morris, Aldon D. *The Origins of the Civil Rights Movement: Black Communities Organizing for Change.* New York: Free Press, 1984.

Rustin, Bayard. *Strategies for Freedom: The Changing Patterns of Black Protest.* New York: Columbia University Press, 1976.

Walton, Hanes Jr. *The Political Philosophy of Martin Luther King, Jr.* Westport, Conn.: Greenwood, 1971.

Zinn, Howard. *SNCC: The New Abolitionists.* Westport, Conn.: Greenwood, 1985, ©1964.

See also ALBANY, GEORGIA, 1961–1962; BIRMINGHAM, ALABAMA, 1963; CONGRESS OF RACIAL EQUALITY; FELLOWSHIP OF RECONCILIATION, INTERNATIONAL; FREEDOM RIDES, 1961; FREEDOM SUMMER PROJECT, MISSISSIPPI, 1964; GANDHI, MOHANDAS KARAMCHAND; HIGHLANDER FOLK SCHOOL; KING, MARTIN LUTHER, JR.; MARCH ON WASHINGTON, 1963; MONTGOMERY BUS BOYCOTT, 1955–1956; NIXON, E.D.; PARKS, ROSA; POOR PEOPLE'S CAMPAIGN, 1968; SELMA-TO-MONTGOMERY MARCH, 1965; SOUTHERN CHRISTIAN LEADERSHIP CONFERENCE; STUDENT NONVIOLENT COORDINATING COMMITTEE

Civil Society

Sphere of society in which pluralistic interests and ideas compete for hegemonic status (the widespread support and acceptance as legitimate and moral by a majority of the population) without being directly controlled by the state. The concept of civil society is relevant to the study of nonviolent direct action in two ways. First, before a resistance movement against an authoritarian regime can emerge and organize its activities, at least some aspects of civil society have to be isolated from encroachment by the state. Second, if a nonviolent direct action is to have a realistic chance of emerging victorious in a struggle with a state apparatus of coercion, activists must first assume leadership within civil society.

Although the dichotomy between civil society and the state goes back to at least eighteenth-century political theory and is imbued with multiple and contradictory meanings, the concept is mostly associated with Antonio Gramsci. The majority of Gramsci's ideas are contained in the notebooks and letters that he wrote during his confinement in the prisons of fascist Italy between 1928 and his death in 1937.

Gramsci's separation of the state and civil society corresponds to two realms, one of coercion and one of consent. The economic sphere represents the third analytical component, but will not receive further attention here. The state, being the sphere of coercion, contains such elements as the police, the army, the secret service, and the bureaucracy. These are the means of domination and repression at the disposal of the ruling group. Civil society is the sphere of consent, where contrasting opinions compete against each other for hegemonic status. In short, this refers to the noneconomic aspects of a society that exist independently of direct state control.

Hegemony is the crux of Antonio Gramsci's ideas. This term refers to the existence of a dominant world view that extends throughout all aspects of a society and encompasses ideology, morality, culture, language, and power. This world view is disseminated through subtle and hidden mechanisms, which conceal and support the dominance of one social group over others. Hegemony thus constitutes what Michel Foucault called a system of exclusion: an explicitly and subconsciously diffused set of fundamental assumptions that determine, at a particular time and place, what is right and wrong, moral and immoral, good and evil, true and untrue.

The state, with its means of coercion and indoctrination, plays an important role in the creation of hegemony. Gramsci employed the concept to facilitate understanding of the way ruling groups can engineer popular support by disseminating a particular *Weltanschauung* ("worldview" or "ideology" in a very broad sense) that favors their interests. Despite the key role played by the state, it is within civil society that hegemony ultimately emerges out of conflicting and competing ideas. By looking at this sphere of consent from the vantage point of the suppressed part of the populace, Gramsci attempted to comprehend the conditions under which segments of a society opposing the regime can promote social change.

The boundaries of the state and civil society are always in flux. Depending upon the level of direct state control, such institutions as trade unions, the news media, religious organizations, schools, or universities may either belong to the state's apparatus of propaganda and repression or be part of the pluralistic struggle for hegemony within civil society. In a liberal society, the state may assume a relatively minor role, leaving social dynamics open to market forces and the evolution of competing and conflicting interests. In a totalitarian society, the state's role

C

may be dominant to the point that it virtually annihilates civil society (such as in Albania under the rule of Enver Hoxha or North Korea under Kim Il Sung).

No element in the dynamics of nonviolent direct action is necessarily contingent upon the prior existence of a strong and independent civil society. Power structures ultimately depend upon popular consent and if certain external and domestic preconditions are favorable, this consent can be withdrawn. Yet, a certain breathing space from the encroachment of the state is necessary for the emergence of opinions critical of the regime and their organized expression in the form of mass scale popular dissent. If a regime controls virtually all social aspects and is able to seal off the population from so-called subversive external influences, it may be able to create popular support for its selfish, class-related interests. Consequently, the regime can minimize the forces that would otherwise lead toward a fundamental societal change.

Such an attempt can be undermined by defending or establishing a sphere of consent even in an authoritarian society. German social scientists aptly call this an *Ersatzöffentlichkeit,* a substitute for the suppressed public sphere. Such a quasi-substitute for an independent civil society can be created through various means. In Gramsci's sense, an ideal (and thus rare) precondition for a revolutionary change through nonviolent action exists if regime-hostile discourse has already infiltrated and taken over the classically autonomous institutions of civil society, such as the news media, schools, churches, political parties, sports organizations, and the like. A more common, and in normal circumstances more realistic, way of defending civil society is the creation of social movements and grassroots organizations that challenge the official politico-ideological discourse. The regime's attempt to annihilate civil society through indoctrination also can be countered by the infiltration of critical information sources from outside the system. Such a case occurred, for example, when Western television and radio broadcasts undermined the attempt by authoritarian regimes in central and eastern Europe to impose legitimacy through indoctrination and the control of information. Thus, even if institutions of civil society are suppressed by a repressive state, a sphere of ideological competition can be created in the minds of the people.

If such an arduously carved out sphere of consent exists, official ideological discourse must compete with contrasting opinions for popular support. The result of this process decisively influences the potential and limits of popular movements that employ nonviolent resistance against a totalitarian regime.

A nonviolent resistance movement can establish a new and stable order only if the classes or social groups that conduct the struggle enjoy widespread popular support and dominate the institutions of civil society before attempting to seize state power. Gramsci recognized this in his emphasis on the need for a coalition between the Italian proletariat and the intellectual elite, an unusual position at the time. Without first winning this so-called "war of position" and achieving hegemonic leadership throughout civil society, the staying power of the repressive state apparatus most likely will remain strong enough to silence dissident voices from below.

This aspect of Gramsci's thought is of utmost importance for judging a nonviolent struggle's likelihood of success. It suggests that social change through nonviolent struggle becomes a realistic possibility only from the moment when regime-hostile social segments have achieved a substantial degree of hegemonic consent within civil society. That is, when their proposed ideological alternative to the established order has infiltrated most social levels and is considered moral and legitimate by a substantial part of the population.

Roland Bleiker

References

Bleiker, Roland. *Nonviolent Struggle and the Revolution in East Germany.* Cambridge, Mass.: Albert Einstein Institution, 1993.

Bocock, Robert. *Hegemony.* Sussex: Ellis Horwood, 1986.

Cohen, Jean L., and Andrew Arato. *Civil Society and Political Theory.* Cambridge: MIT Press, 1992.

Gramsci, Antonio. *Selections from the Prison Notebooks, 1928–1937.* Edited and translated by Q. Hoare and G.N. Smith. New York: International, 1971.

Habermas, Jürgen. *The Structural Transformation of the Public Sphere.* Translated by Thomas Burger with the assistance of Frederick Lawrence. Cambridge: MIT Press, 1989.

Keane, John, ed. *Civil Society and the State:*

New European Perspectives. London: Verso, 1988.

Civilian-Based Defense

A developing defense policy designed to deter and defeat both foreign military occupations and internal take-overs by prepared noncooperation and political defiance by trained populations. It employs social, economic, political, and psychological "weapons" (or specific methods of action). This policy would operate by preventing the attackers from ruling the attacked society, denying them their other objectives, subverting their troops and functionaries, and mobilizing international opposition to the attack. All this is to be done in ways that are most difficult for the attackers to counter.

The term *civilian-based defense* indicates defense by civilians (as distinguished from military personnel) using civilian means of struggle (as distinct from military or paramilitary means). Weapons of violence are not required and would in fact be counterproductive. This policy has also variously been called "social defense," "nonmilitary defense," and "nonviolent defense." (However, the term *social defense* has also become closely associated with various ideological approaches to wider social change.)

One of the ways in which civilian-based defense differs from conventional military defense is that it focuses on the defense of the society by the members and institutions of the society itself. This policy defends social and political space, not points of geography, terrain, or physical space. When successful, civilian-based defense of the society would lead to the geographical withdrawal of the invaders or collapse of the internal usurpers.

Instead of attempting to provide defense by fighting over geographical points, people applying civilian-based defense actively defend their way of life, institutions, and freedoms directly. The priorities of action are regarded as crucial. The maintenance of a free press, for example, or keeping the attackers' propaganda out of the schools, are seen to be of more direct importance to democracy and independence than, say, possession of a given mountain or building, or the killing of young conscripts in the invaders' army.

Civilian-based defense is based on the insight that attacks occur for some purpose. Possible purposes include replacing the government and establishing political control of the country, economic exploitation, ideological indoctrination, expansion of an empire, as well as others. An effective societal defense is considered possible because neither a coup nor an invasion immediately gives the attackers their specific objectives and control of the population, social institutions, and governmental structure. Even in the absence of resistance, those objectives and control take time and effort to achieve. In the face of well-prepared noncooperation and defiance, the achievement of those ends may not only be slowed, but may be blocked by a skilled and determined civilian population.

Theorists of civilian-based defense argue that it is important to understand clearly the meaning of defense as protection, preservation, and the warding off of dangers arising from attacks. Defense is not simply retaliation for an attack, nor should it be equated with military conflict in general. Deterrence as used in the literature of this field refers to the capacity to prevent an attack by the perceived strength to repel it. Deterrence, then, comes from the capacity to defend, not from the ability to retaliate, which may occur without any effective defense.

Civilian-based defense is meant to be waged on the foundation of advance preparations, planning, and training. These would be based upon the findings of basic research into this type of resistance and the systems of the attacker, and also upon intensive problem-solving research. The latter needs to focus on ways to improve the effectiveness of such resistance, to meet impediments, and to solve problems in its application, especially against ruthless regimes. Understanding the basic requirements for effectiveness of these forms of struggle and also of ways to aggravate weaknesses of the attackers' regime is the foundation for developing successful strategies of civilian-based defense.

Civilian-based defense offers both widespread and selective noncooperation and political defiance. This would involve the training of the population and leaders of institutions. This advance work would be comparable to, but more extensive than, preparations for military warfare. The defensive measures involved are designed to be applied by the general population, particular population groups most affected by the attackers' objectives and actions, and by the various institutions of the society. Which of these are most involved differs with the attackers' aims—whether they are economic, ideological, political, or something else.

In the event of an attack, civilian defenders would aim to make the attacked society unrulable by foreign or internal aggressors; maintain control of their own society despite the attack; effectively resist the imposition of an unwanted government over the population (whether this is a foreign administration, a puppet regime, or a government of usurpers); convert the society's institutions into pervasive resistance organizations; deny the attackers their objectives; and make the costs of the attack and attempted domination unacceptable to the attackers. In this struggle, noncooperation by personnel and institutions, and by departments and ministries, should prevent the attackers from taking over the governmental structure. Meanwhile, the earlier policies and laws of the attacked regime would be respected and obeyed by the population. The people would work together through their independent associations and institutions to meet their needs as far as possible without cooperation with the attackers.

In some circumstances, the defenders would attempt to destroy the attackers' military and administrative forces by subverting the loyalty and reliability of the attackers' troops and functionaries, especially in carrying out orders for repression, and even to induce them to mutiny. They would also report the attack, resistance, and repression to the population of the attackers' homeland or their usual supporters; encourage dissension and opposition among the attackers' home population and usual supporters; stimulate international opposition to the attack by diplomatic, economic, and public opinion pressures against the attackers; and seek international support for the defenders in communications, finances, food, diplomacy, and other resources. The defense would thereby operate primarily in the attacked country, secondarily in the attackers' country or among their usual supporters, and to some degree internationally.

The development of this defense policy, which relies on massive nonviolent noncooperation and political defiance, has been greatly influenced by the following: (1) improvised defense struggles against foreign invasions (the Ruhr in 1923 and Czechoslovakia in 1968–1969, for example) and against coups d'état (Germany in 1920, France in 1961, and the Soviet Union in 1991); (2) the thinking of various social radicals and pacifists in Europe and the United States and Mohandas K. Gandhi in India in the 1920s,

1930s, and 1940s about how fascist aggression could be resisted without war; (3) the thinking of two military historians and strategists—Carl von Clausewitz's concept of "defense in depth" and Sir Basil Liddell Hart's "indirect approach" to strategy and his exploratory comments on the potential and later practice of nonviolent resistance, especially against Nazi aggression; and (4) the exploratory analyses by several scholars in Europe and the United States from the 1950s to the present of the potential for a defense policy based on nonviolent noncooperation and political defiance and how this could be developed, prepared, and strategically applied.

The prototype cases of improvised nonviolent resistance to dictatorships, foreign aggression and occupation, and internal coups d'état, include several struggles in Europe, among them those waged in Communist-ruled nations during the decades of totalitarian domination. Since the Second World War, powerful nonviolent struggles have occurred in East Germany (1953 and 1989), in Hungary (1956–1957 and 1988–1989), in Poland (1956, 1970–1971, and 1980–1989), in Czechoslovakia (1968–1969 and 1989), and in the Baltic states (1987–1991). The results of these struggles range from short-term defeats, to partial successes, to full successes. Due to their improvised nature, these prototypes are imperfect, but they do provide a basis for development and refinement.

In recent years, especially in late 1989, the peoples of these regions exhibited stunning power in dissolving well-entrenched dictatorships through largely nonviolent means. The democratic revolutions of 1989 and 1990 self-reliantly liberated several nations and millions of people. This was done with far fewer casualties and much less destruction than would have accompanied massive violent uprisings or invasions by foreign liberating armies.

Moreover, in Lithuania, Latvia, and Estonia, high government officials have confirmed that their defense recommendations during the crises of 1991 were based primarily on writings about civilian-based defense, supplemented by other ideas.

These cases of civilian resistance for national defense are not examples of civilian-based defense, for they were all improvised and lacked the advantages of planning, preparations, and training—elements that are regarded as essential by strategists of this policy. They do, however, offer evidence of the potential viability of a prepared civilian-based defense policy that should operate in refined and significantly strengthened forms.

The weapons used in the past improvised cases have included, among many others, the following: paralysis of transportation, general strikes, economic shutdown, political noncooperation, adoption of false identities, economic boycotts, publication of banned newspapers, deliberate inefficiency in carrying out orders, defiance by the legislature, judicial resistance, noncooperation by civil servants, defiant continuation of the previous policies and laws, refusal of collaboration, maintaining the autonomy of independent organizations and institutions and creation of new ones, and subversion of the attackers' troops.

Such weapons or methods employed in civilian-based defense will be most effective if they are applied as component parts of a comprehensive plan of defense—that is, a carefully chosen strategy of defense. Then, particular tactics (plans for limited actions) and specific methods are used to implement the strategy.

Strategies of civilian-based defense might be grouped initially into two broad categories, "general resistance"—following advance guidelines on when and how to resist—and "organized resistance"—resisting according to new specific instructions.

No matter how well prepared it is, the initial defense campaign should be regarded as simply the opening phase of a struggle that, like a military campaign, may require a longer period of intense effort to achieve victory. In the event that the attack does not collapse in the initial phase of resistance, a shift in defense strategy may be required to make it possible to carry on a sustained defense.

Civilian-based defense may be intended either as a supplement to military means or as a full alternative to them to deter and defend a society against attacks. While civilian-based defense can be developed as a full defense policy, its advocates recognize that it will be fully adopted only when and if there is confidence in its strength to provide both defense and deterrence. In some countries, such as Sweden, Lithuania, Latvia, Estonia, and Thailand, there is interest in the use of these means as components for special purposes and in particular circumstances only. Such components might, for example, be used only if military defense against a military giant is obviously futile, or if military means have been used and have failed. They might also be applied against a coup d'état, whether by a military clique, a political party, or in cooperation with a foreign intelligence agency.

There can be no single blueprint for the use of this weapons system. The application of civilian-based defense offers a variety of possible strategies and weapons of resistance. It needs to be adjusted to defeat both the attackers' efforts to gain political control and any other specific objective.

Steps in the consideration and implementation of civilian-based defense that have been advocated in literature on the subject include the following: (1) strategic analyses and research on related phenomena; (2) public education; (3) developing a core of civilian-based defense strategists; (4) constitutional and legal changes to support civilian-based defense; (5) establishing appropriate institutions to assist with the preparations for and conduct of civilian-based defense; (6) determination of the feasible modes of transarmament and implementation in stages; (7) preparations and training; and (8) international support and civilian-based defense mutual assistance treaties.

As with military security policies, civilian-based defense works best when it helps to prevent an attack. A key aim of this policy is to help dissuade and deter possible attackers. The deterrence capacity of civilian-based defense has two key elements: the actual ability of the society to defend itself, and the potential attackers' perception of that ability. Whether the aim of the attack is political domination, economic exploitation, ideological indoctrination, or some other, achievement of the aim will most likely require the cooperation of at least some of the inhabitants of the attacked country. If it is clear that such cooperation will be firmly denied as a consequence of the civilian-based defense preparations, the attackers may reconsider whether their objectives can actually be obtained. Therefore, understanding the deterrence capacity of civilian-based defense depends on understanding the actual defense strategies and capacities of this policy.

Any deterrence policy, whether military-based or civilian-based, can fail, for any number of reasons. In contrast to nuclear deterrence, however, if civilian-based deterrence fails, the policy of civilian-based defense still provides a viable defense option to combat the attack without the risk of massive destruction and immense casualties.

Civilian-based defense is not free of risks, however. Aggressors facing concerted noncooperation and defiance may be seriously threatened and are likely to respond with repression. The killings by Soviet troops in Vilnius and Riga in January 1991 are among the tragic examples of this. Nonviolent defiance often risks casualties, sometimes serious ones, but according to preliminary research it almost always produces far fewer casualties than when both sides use violence.

Success in civilian-based defense depends on several key factors. These include, among others, the spirit of resistance, the solidarity of the defending population, the ability of resisters to control and utilize the sources of political power, the strength of the defending social institutions, the ability of the people to persist in resistance with nonviolent discipline and to withstand repression, the vulnerabilities of the attackers, and, very importantly, the wisdom of the defense strategies.

Exponents of civilian-based defense have suggested that in addition to its contribution to deterrence and defense and maintenance of national independence, it also has implications for the vitality of a functioning democracy. By placing a major part of the responsibility for defense on the people themselves, this policy would encourage citizens to recognize qualities of the society worthy of defense and to explore how any less meritorious aspects could be improved. In addition, while civilian-based defense policies would have financial costs, they would not require the massive sums of money and industrial production that modern military weaponry requires.

Civilian-based defense rests on the theory that political power, whether of domestic or foreign origin, is derived from sources within each society. By denying or severing these sources of power, populations can control rulers and defeat foreign aggressors.

Gene Sharp

References

Eglitis, Olgerts. *Nonviolent Action in the Liberation of Latvia.* Cambridge, Mass.: Albert Einstein Institution, 1993.
Holst, Johan Jørgen. *Civilian-Based Defense in a New Era.* Cambridge, Mass.: Albert Einstein Institution, 1990.
Roberts, Adam, ed. *Civilian Resistance As a National Defense* Harrisburg, Pa.: Stackpole, 1967. British ed.: *The Strategy of Civilian Defence.* London: Faber and Faber, 1967.
Sharp, Gene, with Bruce Jenkins. *Civilian-Based Defense: A Post-Military Weapons System.* Princeton: Princeton University Press, 1990.

See also ALGERIA, FRENCH GENERALS' REVOLT OF 1961; BALTIC INDEPENDENCE MOVEMENTS, 1987–1991; CLAUSEWITZ, CARL VON; COUPS D'ÉTAT; CZECHOSLOVAKIA, 1968 RESISTANCE MOVEMENT; LIDDELL HART, CAPTAIN SIR BASIL HENRY; REVOLUTIONS OF 1989; RUHRKAMPF; TRANSARMAMENT

Clamshell Alliance

A protest group organized against the Seabrook nuclear power plant in Seabrook, New Hampshire. Formed in July 1976, the Clamshell Alliance was the first organized antinuclear group to engage in direct protests, and its early successes and publicity led to the formation of similar groups across the country. By the late 1970s, protests at nuclear power plants occurred throughout the United States. They adopted as a common protest tactic the Clamshell Alliance's use of nonviolent civil disobedience, in the form of occupations of nuclear plant sites, and its consensus style of decision making involving the use of affinity groups.

Seabrook residents had opposed the nuclear power plant in hearings before regulatory agencies and in a town meeting vote. Because plans for constructing the plant were still proceeding, people at a July 1976 meeting decided that direct action was necessary. They were inspired by a 1975 protest at a nuclear power plant construction site in Whyl, West Germany, where almost thirty thousand citizens occupied the site for nearly a year and forced the cancellation of the construction.

The Clamshell Alliance's first protest at the Seabrook site took place on August 1, 1976, with a rally of 600 people. Eighteen protesters were arrested for trespassing onto the site. At another rally three weeks later, 180 people were arrested.

The alliance's largest and most celebrated protest took place on April 30, 1977, when 1,414 participants were arrested for trespassing. The protesters were kept for two weeks in National Guard armories before being released on personal recognizance. Their act of nonviolent civil disobedience and subsequent incarceration

A Clamshell Alliance affinity group meeting at the Seabrook Nuclear Power Plant site, in Seabrook, New Hampshire, April 30, 1977. Photo © Ellen Shub 1995.

in the armories captured news media attention across the nation.

The alliance was later beset by internal divisions over the use of civil disobedience, consensus decision making, and other matters that ultimately led to its demise. These divisions first manifested themselves at the armories after the April 30 protest, as alliance members disagreed over the extent to which they should cooperate with the National Guard. A year later the alliance was planning another illegal occupation of the Seabrook site in June 1978. The state of New Hampshire offered part of the site to the alliance for a legal rally. Clamshell members from the Seabrook area felt they should accept the state's offer, while members from other parts of New England felt they should continue with the planned illegal occupation. The alliance's coordinating group of affinity group representatives decided to hold the legal rally without sending the issue back, as required, to the affinity groups themselves. Although the legal rally attracted twenty thousand people, the decision to hold it left many Clamshell members disenchanted.

A year later Clamshell members favoring continued illegal occupations split off from the alliance and formed the Coalition for Direct Action at Seabrook. After two attempted occupations of the Seabrook site in October 1979

and May 1980 were prevented by police, the coalition eventually disbanded by early 1982. The remaining members of the Clamshell Alliance continued to meet until early 1981, when it, too, ceased to exist.

Steven E. Barkan

References

Barkan, Steven E. "Strategic, Tactical, and Organizational Dilemmas of the Protest Movement against Nuclear Power." *Social Problems* 27 (1979): 19–37.

Downey, Gary L. "Ideology and the Clamshell Identity: Organizational Dilemmas in the Anti-Nuclear Power Movement." *Social Problems* 33 (1986): 357–373.

Joppke, Christian. *Mobilizing against Nuclear Energy: A Comparison of Germany and the United States.* Berkeley: University of California Press, 1993.

Price, Jerome. *The Antinuclear Movement.* Boston, Mass.: Twayne, 1990.

See also NUCLEAR ENERGY OPPOSITION

Clausewitz, Carl von (1780–1831)

Considered one of the most influential modern writers on the subjects of strategy and war. Born in Burg, Germany, of a Prussian military family, his military career began at the age of twelve with a campaign to drive Napoleonic forces out of Prussian territory, and throughout he remained a staunch opponent of Napoleon. At the age of twenty-one, Clausewitz was accepted into the highly prestigious War Academy in Berlin and after graduating first in his class, he was appointed to the position of military tutor for the Prussian Crown Prince. From 1818 to 1830 he was the director of the War Academy. He died in 1831 of cholera.

Among his numerous writings, his most famous is a series of works entitled *On War*, published posthumously in 1833. This collection of eight books is an inquiry into the definition and analysis of war as it interacts with the political and social realms. His careful study of various military campaigns sought to identify the changes taking place in the methods and strategies of warfare during his time. For Clausewitz, the ideal form of military strategy was a concept he called "total/absolute war," in which "absolute violence [ends] in the total destruction of one side by the other." However, he recognized that war does not occur as an isolated incident; rather, it functions with external influences from the political, social, economic, and technological realms. That is why he believed that political leadership, rather than military authority, should determine the goals and course of a war, for the political authorities would ultimately be responsible for leadership in the aftermath of conflict. Furthermore, he acknowledged that the psychological and moral components of a strategy are equally as important as the material and military strength components.

Clausewitz's views on issues of strategy and warfare, as well as his integration of both theoretical and practical argumentation on the nature of war, provide a basis for understanding the dynamics of other conflicts, including nonviolent struggle. The effective application of nonviolent action in a conflict benefits from attention to the whole range of possibilities for action. Strategic choices, following Clausewitz's guidance, must relate politics, economics, and social forces to the objectives and tactics of a campaign.

Maria Figueroa

References

Aron, Raymon. *Clausewitz: Philosopher of War*. New York: Simon and Schuster, 1983.

Clausewitz, Carl von. *On War*. Edited and translated by Michael Howard and Peter Paret. Princeton: Princeton University Press, 1984.

Paret, Peter. *Understanding War: Essays on Clausewitz and the History of Military Power*. Princeton: Princeton University Press, 1992

See also CIVILIAN-BASED DEFENSE; KING-HALL, BARON STEPHEN; LIDDELL HART, CAPTAIN SIR BASIL HENRY; STRATEGY

Colombia, Civic Strike, 1957

The movement during the first nine days of May 1957 that led to the removal of dictator Gustavo Rojas Pinilla. It included university student strikes in at least five cities, as well as strikes by professors and physicians and general shutdowns by the owners of stores, factories, and banks in Bogotá (the capital), Cali, Medellín, and other cities. The Catholic labor federation supported the movement, as did Cali union leaders. The rectors of private universities in Bogotá closed them, independent newspapers throughout the country suspended publication, and a few transportation companies suspended service. Catholic clergy gave significant moral support.

General Rojas Pinilla came to power through a military coup in 1953. The National Assembly subsequently elected him to serve as president from 1954 to 1958. In March 1957 he convened a hand-picked constituent assembly, which in April began considering constitutional amendments that would give the assembly power to re-elect Rojas Pinilla.

Meanwhile, in 1956, leaders of the traditional Liberal and Conservative parties had united in a Civic Front, demanding free election of the next president. The Civic Front named its candidate, Conservative Guillermo León Valencia, on April 8, 1957.

The action began in Cali, where the social clubs planned a tribute to Valencia on May 1. The governor suddenly ordered them to get prior approval for all gatherings, precipitating the decision of Cali social clubs to suspend activities on May 1. Social clubs in five other cities followed suit the next day. Meanwhile, troops surrounded the house where Valencia was staying. Students in Cali, Bogotá, Popoyán, and Medellín declared strikes on May 2. The organization of the civic strike began on May 3, and the shutdown spread from May 4 to 7.

Constant street demonstrations in Bogotá and Cali led to fights with police and soldiers, resulting in numerous casualties. In Cali, a clandestine radio station kept citizens informed about the progress of the movement and carried repeated appeals for calm and nonviolence.

Opposition to Rojas Pinilla had existed within the Colombian armed forces for months, but there is no evidence of any military plot against the government before the civic strike. As the civilian uprising developed, the attempt to control constant demonstrations exhausted the troops, and officers feared the growth of antimilitary public sentiment. Military disaffection spread when the government nationalized the banks on May 8 in order to reopen them. With no palatable alternative available, armed forces leaders agreed on May 9 to demand the immediate resignation of the president and also reached agreement with representatives of the Civic Front about what would replace his rule.

Rojas Pinilla turned the government over to a military junta on May 10. Shortly thereafter, the junta announced the formation of a cabinet consisting of three generals and ten civilians, suspended the constituent assembly, and scheduled the election of a new president for May 1958. The election was held, and Colombia returned to civilian, constitutional government.

Patricia Parkman

References

Berardo García, José. *La explosión de mayo.* Cali, Colombia: Imprenta Departmental, 1957.

Londoño Marín, Abelardo, and Flavio Correa Restrepo. *"Soldados sin coraza" Historia de una revolución.* Medellín, Colombia: Editorial Bedout, 1957.

Parkman, Patricia. *Insurrectionary Civic Strikes in Latin America, 1931–1961.* Cambridge, Mass.: The Albert Einstein Institution, 1990.

See also CIVIC STRIKE

Committee for Nonviolent Action

Radical pacifist group dedicated to the uses of nonviolent direct action. After a series of meetings in spring 1957, peace leaders launched two organizations to rejuvenate the American peace movement and lead a spirited attack against increased nuclear testing and acceptance of militarism. One organization, later to become the National Committee for a SANE Nuclear Policy (SANE), became the home of nuclear pacifists who used traditional peace education approaches such as rallies, speeches, newspaper articles, and advertisements. The other organization, later to become the Committee for Nonviolent Action (CNVA), would be more daring and provocative. The radical pacifists linked to CNVA adopted a more comprehensive and revolutionary antimilitaristic stance. More important, CNVA's strategy and tactics emphasized confrontational nonviolent action methods including civil disobedience, the intentional breaking of "unjust" laws. For the next ten years, CNVA served as the organizational base for radical pacifists to organize and implement dramatic nonviolent efforts toward peace and justice.

During its existence, CNVA primarily served two distinct and important functions. First, it served as a rallying point and identity base for radical pacifists who believed that nonviolent direct action and civil disobedience were the most effective tactics to use, both for personal witness and for awakening a public too long silenced by the effects of McCarthyism, the Korean War, and the cold war. The second purpose CNVA served was to be the recognized vanguard, or "cutting edge," of the pacifist movement in thought as well as action. CNVA's experiments in direct action were complemented by daring proposals for demilitarizing and democratizing both American society and the world at large. Thus, both in form and content, CNVA presented a constant challenge to the rest of the peace movement.

CNVA was organized as a collection of individuals who coalesced around certain projects or campaigns that captured their imagination and interests. Leaders were a combination of well-established peace figures such as Larry Scott of the American Friends Service Committee and A.J. Muste of the Fellowship of Reconciliation and less well known visionaries like Brad Lyttle, a young writer and advocate of Gandhian nonviolent action.

Scott, Muste, Lyttle and others took the lead in launching several highly dramatic efforts to promote their cause. The first of these occurred in August 1957 when, on the twelfth anniversary of the Hiroshima bombing, eleven pacifists led by Larry Scott were arrested at an Atomic Energy Commission bomb test site in Nevada for deliberately trespassing onto military territory. The

CNVA *San Francisco-to-Moscow peace walkers in Pennsylvania, May 21, 1961. Theodore B. Hetzel Photograph Collection/Swarthmore College Peace Collection.*

following year, four CNVA members sailed a small ketch, the *Golden Rule,* into the Pacific Ocean in a symbolic protest against hydrogen bomb tests. Refusing to comply with a government issued injunction, the pacifists twice attempted to sail into the forbidden area and were arrested both times. In this project CNVA was publicly supported by SANE and other pacifist groups who led popular protests to "stop the bomb tests, not the *Golden Rule.*"

The news media coverage and public outcry in support of the CNVA team noticeably increased when Earle Reynolds, an anthropology professor and former National Academy of Sciences employee, and his family successfully sailed their small boat, the *Phoenix,* into the nuclear test zone. The favorable publicity resulting from the conversion of these nonpacifists to strident opponents of nuclear testing was the first indication of the radical pacifists' potential influence.

In 1958, CNVA shifted its focus from the atomic testing issue to a more inclusive antimilitarism. At the first American base being con-

structed for the placement of intercontinental ballistic missiles (ICBMs) in Cheyenne, Wyoming, Brad Lyttle led a cadre of CNVA militants in a series of obstructionist sit-ins at the entrance and temporarily prevented vehicles from entering the base. In Omaha, Nebraska, CNVA militants, led by seventy-five-year-old A.J. Muste, defiantly climbed over the base's entrance fence and were summarily arrested.

In 1960, CNVA, under Lyttle's leadership, began one of its most ambitious and well-known efforts—the San Francisco-to-Moscow peace walk. The nine-month, six-thousand-mile journey across the United States and across Europe to Moscow gave CNVA activists an opportunity to spread their message in rallies, speeches, interviews, and newspaper articles in the United States, Poland, and Russia. Mass media accounts, though quick to blame "the other side" for the arms race, praised the radical pacifists for their "spirit and endurance, as well as their consistency in raising the same plea in both the U.S. and the U.S.S.R."

During 1963–1964, CNVA forged ahead in its "cutting edge" role, linking both peace and justice concerns in its daring and ambitious Quebec-Washington-Guantanamo walk for peace. By sending an integrated walk team on the Canada-to-Cuba walk, CNVA linked protest against the U.S. diplomatic oppression in Cuba with protest against domestic segregation at home. Though unsuccessful in traveling to Cuba, the CNVA team was successful in demonstrating at several military installations along the march route and in forging a link between the peace and civil rights movements. The link became particularly visible when the CNVA walk team was jailed for two months in Albany, Georgia, for protesting laws prohibiting integrated demonstrations in the downtown area. After a successful "jail-in" and public fast, CNVA was able to negotiate a compromise agreement with Albany officials to walk a small integrated team quickly through the "white only" section of downtown. This small "victory" was important in invigorating the civil rights movement in this heretofore strictly segregated town.

During the escalation of the Vietnam War in the mid to late 1960s, CNVA played a limited yet significant role in the effort against America's increasingly larger involvement in the war. In 1966, CNVA sent its own six-member team to Saigon to show the Vietnamese that some Americans opposed the war. In the United States, CNVA organized anti–Vietnam War actions such as a tax resistance campaign, protests at munitions plants, teach-ins on college campuses, speak-outs at the Pentagon, draft card burnings, and picket lines at induction centers. In addition, CNVA joined in coalitions with New Left groups in large anti–Vietnam War coalition demonstrations.

Though CNVA's participation in the mass anti–Vietnam War protests ensured it some influence with large numbers of peace workers, the radical pacifists became overshadowed by the more flamboyant, provocative media figures of the New Left. Besides, CNVA's once daring stress on nonviolent action, including civil disobedience, was no longer unique. "The nonviolent action it had pioneered had long since been adapted by the movement as a whole" (Merger) as the peace movement began to adopt "unrespected massive dislocation efforts" to "jam the war machine" (McReynolds). When CNVA decided to merge into the War Resisters League in 1967, it could claim considerable credit for shaping and directing the American peace movement's use of nonviolent action and infusing it with a recognition that a direct action component could supplement standard forms of political discourse, broaden the power base, and bring pressure to bear on important public policy issues.

Neil H. Katz

References
CNVA Manuscript Collection. Swarthmore College Peace Collection, Swarthmore, Pa.
Katz, Milton S., and Neil H. Katz. "Pragmatists and Visionaries in the Post–World War II American Peace Movement: SANE and CNVA." In *Doves and Diplomats,* edited by Solomon Wank. Westport, Conn.: Greenwood, 1978.
Katz, Neil H. "Radical Pacifism and the Contemporary American Peace Movement: The Committee for Nonviolent Action, 1957–1967." Unpublished Ph.D. dissertation, University of Maryland, 1974.
Lyttle, Bradford. *You Come with Naked Hands—The Story of the San Francisco to Moscow Walk for Peace.* Raymond, N.H.: Greenleaf, 1966.
McReynolds, David. "Teaching Pacifists a Lesson." *WRL News* (July–August 1963).
"Merger." *WRL News* (March–April 1968).

See also MUSTE, ABRAHAM JOHN; NUCLEAR WEAPONS OPPOSITION; SANE; VIETNAM WAR OPPOSITION; VOYAGES, PROTEST

Committee of 100 (Great Britain)

Organization committed to mass civil disobedience against nuclear weapons. Acting under a motto of "Act or Perish," the Committee of 100 attempted to mobilize large groups of people in order to create civil disorder and thereby compel the British government to implement disarmament and change its foreign and military policies.

The first meeting of the Committee of 100 was held on October 22, 1960. Many of the leaders of the group were members of the soon-to-be dissolved Direct Action Committee Against Nuclear War. Others were prominent people recruited by Bertrand Russell and his colleagues through letters inviting participation in a new organization opposing nuclear missile production. The committee's first demonstration occurred on February 18, 1961, outside the Ministry of Defense, where over two thousand people conducted a march and sit-in. Throughout the spring, committee members staged several other obstructive demonstrations.

British authorities gradually increased their punitive response to the Committee of 100. In order to forestall planned mass demonstrations on September 17, the government arrested and sentenced thirty-two members of the group (including Russell) for inciting a breach of the peace. Imprisoning the eighty-nine-year-old Russell fueled press coverage and public sentiment against the authorities. The September 17 Trafalgar Square demonstrations were widely attended (12,000 people conducted a sit-in and over 1,300 were arrested) and widely covered (nationally and internationally). This event marked the high point in the lifespan of the Committee of 100 and the culmination of a move away from small, controlled Gandhian actions to mass direct action as a form of resistance.

Primarily due to a strategic decision to decentralize, their next step was to undertake an ambitious series of dispersed demonstrations at seven locations on December 9, 1961. The government acted to hinder the demonstrations, erecting barbed wire around the Wethersfield base, raiding the committee's headquarters on December 6, and arresting several committee workers on December 8. Because of this repression and other factors, the demonstrations, given their own expectations, were not well attended and they failed to immobilize one or more of the military bases (one of their stated objectives). In February 1962, the committee members arrested in December were tried under the Official Secrets Act. Each was found guilty and sentenced to eighteen months in prison.

The committee organized numerous demonstrations during 1962, including a June march to Greenham Common and the subsequent twenty-three-hour-long immobilization of the base. A "Troops against the Bomb" campaign was conducted during October and November 1962 with the aim of converting British servicemen to support the antinuclear weapons movement.

From 1962 to 1968, the Committee of 100 continued to engage in direct action but gradually became less effective and popular. They became increasingly anarchistic in ideology and organization. In 1963 and 1964, a subgroup of the committee, the "Spies for Peace," engaged in covert illegal direct action to discover and publish information regarding regional seats of government, from which authorities would administer the country in the event of a nuclear attack. This activity sparked a controversy regarding whether nonviolent direct actionists should keep their activities secret. The committee's focus also shifted to more disparate issues. For example, in July 1963, they organized a series of demonstrations against visiting Queen Frederika of Greece to protest Greek authoritarian oppression. The group finally disbanded in September 1968.

Brad Bennett

References

Randle, Michael. "Non-Violent Direct Action in the 1950s and 1960s." In *Campaigns for Peace: British Peace Movements in the Twentieth Century,* edited by Richard Taylor and Nigel Young. Manchester: Manchester University Press, 1987.

Taylor, Richard. *Against the Bomb: The British Peace Movement, 1958–1965.* Oxford: Clarendon, 1988.

See also CAMPAIGN FOR NUCLEAR DISARMAMENT; DIRECT ACTION COMMITTEE AGAINST NUCLEAR WAR; NUCLEAR WEAPONS OPPOSITION

Community for Creative Non-Violence

Founded in 1970 by a small group of activists with deep religious convictions and a commitment to social justice, the Community for Creative Non-Violence (CCNV) emerged in the 1980s at the forefront of the American homelessness movement. Under the brilliant strategic direction of Mitch Snyder, CCNV undertook nonviolent direct action in order to equalize the dialogue between the poor and more powerful voices in national politics. Acknowledging the weakness of poor people as a traditional political force, CCNV reasoned that the poor have their lives, freedom, and health to bring to the bargaining table.

Through the 1980s, national newspapers regularly carried articles chronicling the battle between CCNV activists and the administration of President Ronald Reagan. Collectively, CCNV members launched a series of acts of civil disobedience that offered scathing condemnations of both White House policy and national insensitivity to hunger and homelessness.

Early in 1981, CCNV raised a tent city in Lafayette Park (across from the White House). Nicknamed "Reaganville" after the Hooverville encampments of the Great Depression, the CCNV tent city was the site of ongoing protest, regular press conferences, occasional large-scale rallies and demonstrations, and several well-publicized fasts. The tent city was periodically dismantled by park police as "permanent shelter." These regular roustings and arrests raised the level of news media attention directed toward the camp and brought the support of the American Civil Liberties Union, which argued that the camp represented symbolic speech by the homeless, who have no other means of political expression.

In addition to tent cities, demonstrations, and sit-ins, CCNV added fasting to the repertoire of homeless protest in the 1980s. In July 1983, CCNV members fasted for thirty days in Kansas City to protest the federal stockpiling of surplus agricultural products in the face of widespread hunger. In response to this protest, the administration agreed to give more government-owned food to the poor.

CCNV launched the most significant fast of the movement in September 1984. Twelve members of the group, including Mitch Snyder and Carol Fennelly, began an open-ended fast in conjunction with a sit-in in the Lafayette Park tent city. The fast, according to Snyder, would continue "until the Reagan administration changes its policy on street people." Meanwhile, in the weeks leading up to the November election, CCNV also orchestrated a "Call to Civil Disobedience" in which small groups of demonstrators took turns taking direct action, being arrested, and commanding a steady share of news media coverage. Demonstrators raised a scarecrow effigy of the president, laid sleeping mats across the White House driveway and declared the area a homeless shelter, chained themselves to the White House fence, and released paper bags of cockroaches on the White House tour. All the while, Snyder's fast continued.

By mid-November, after having lost over sixty pounds, Snyder lay near death in the Reaganville shantytown. The White House, keenly aware of the potential they faced to make a martyr for the homeless movement, began to negotiate with Snyder for an end to his fast. After fifty-one days without solid food, Snyder agreed to break the fast in return for the administration's pledge to fund needed renovations of CCNV's shelter.

These promised funds became the focus of much CCNV activity over the next two years. Whereas earlier protests by the group had condemned "meanspiritedness," or "Reaganomics," later actions increasingly called for full funding of the promised renovations. In June of 1985, for example, two hundred people marched with CCNV members to the White House to protest President Reagan's apparent reneging on his promise to fund the D.C. shelter. A year later, Snyder declared that there was no point in believing the White House intended to ever live up to its pledge to fund renovations of the shelter and, therefore, that he would resume the fast truncated in November of 1984. Four days into this fast Congress released $1.5 million in renovation funds.

This victory irrevocably refashioned the group into a direct service provider. After years of battling from outside institutional channels for a better level of care for the homeless, the group became part of the institutional infrastructure providing care for that same population and found themselves having to provide the better care they claimed was possible. Reviews of their ability to do this have been mixed.

Through the early 1990s, CCNV functioned both as a direct service provider and as a political action organization. In its role as service provider, CCNV maintained the administration of the fifteen-hundred-bed Federal City Shelter in Washington, D.C. In conjunction with this massive shelter operation, CCNV provided educational and drug-treatment programs, oversaw several Alcoholics Anonymous chapters, and ran an in-house health clinic and day care center. In effect, the existence of the shelter represented both the proof and the shackling of CCNV's power as a political action group.

CCNV continued to lead direct action events through the 1980s and early 1990s, including a second massive call to civil disobedience before the 1988 elections. Hollywood celebrities and national politicians began to join Mitch Snyder and CCNV on subsequent political actions, including the "Grate American Sleep-Out," in which they huddled over heating grates on a cold D.C. night, demanding passage of the Stuart McKinney Homeless Assistance Act.

The combination of funding for CCNV's Federal City Shelter in 1986, passage of the McKinney Act in 1987, and Mitch Snyder's suicide in 1991 (apparently resulting from personal problems) led the organization to redirect much of its energy inward and to greatly reduce its subsequent level of nonviolent direct action.

Douglas R. Imig

References

Imig, Douglas R. *Poverty and Power: The Political Representation of Poor Americans*. Lincoln: University of Nebraska Press, 1995.

Rader, Victoria. *Signal through the Flames: Mitch Snyder and America's Homeless*. Kansas City, Mo.: Sheed and Ward, 1986.

Conflict Resolution

Part of the growing repertoire of methods and approaches for addressing social conflict. Conflict resolution refers to the processes and outcomes necessary for conflict to be truly resolved—that is, transformed to a state within a relational context that, as Ronald J. Fisher notes, "is self-supporting, self-correcting, and sustainable for the foreseeable future." While assuming some forms of conflict to be constructive, the challenge for conflict resolutionists is to resolve escalated, protracted, mutually destructive conflicts in ways that will both prevent and deal effectively with future conflicts between individuals and groups. Conflict resolution, then, involves nothing less than the transformation of the conflict relationship in ways that remove the problems that caused the conflict in the first place.

Conflict resolution techniques should not be confused with nonviolent direct action, which is a technique for waging conflict. However, despite the differences between these approaches, there are also potential areas of complementarity. Conflict resolution and nonviolent direct action techniques can be employed together in a conflict (either consecutively or simultaneously) to realize goals of democracy, human rights, and individual/group security.

Methods of Conflict Resolution

Parties in social conflict have several choices they can make among procedures for addressing their conflict. In the realm of conflict resolution, disputants may choose to resolve their conflict by way of relationship- and interest-oriented, joint decision-making processes such as negotiation and mediation. In these voluntary procedures, parties maintain maximum control over the resolution process and outcomes. Alternatively, parties may choose to resolve their conflict by way of such rights-oriented, third-party decision-making procedures as arbitration and adjudication. These procedures mix voluntary and involuntary elements, leaving parties with minimal control over the outcome of the resolution process.

Joint decision making, through negotiation or mediation, is most likely to occur, according to Pruitt and Carnevale, when "all parties are willing to participate; negotiation and mediation are understood to be viable mechanisms for reconciling separate interests; and some degree of trust and communication prevails, motivating the parties to produce satisfying and lasting solutions that contribute to a positive future relationship."

In negotiation the conflicting parties have high control over both the process and the outcome. Negotiation, as Jeff Rubin puts it, is a voluntary process in which two or more parties to a conflict resolve incompatible goals and use the exchange of offers and ideas to create a mutually acceptable agreement. The agreements achieved in negotiation may involve new divisions of resources, new rules of behavior, or the creation of new institutions. Negotiation takes place only under conditions of interdependence and where parties need to communicate for persuasion. If a disputant can achieve its goals without assistance, however, then negotiation will be neither feasible nor desirable.

Negotiation is at the root of many norms and societal structures that govern society. Social norms have, in turn, a strong impact on negotiation and the boundaries of social conflict. For example, negotiation depends upon reciprocity and fairness—both of which encourage efforts to achieve equitable concessions and outcomes. As Pruitt and Carnevale argue, "Social norms may prevent conflict altogether, regulate the way conflict is conducted and provide a solution when conflict arises." From the perspective of nonviolent direct action, however, prevailing social norms can also exacerbate conflict, compelling people to fight an "unjust" norm, for example, or defend their rights.

In mediation, the conflicting parties have a moderate degree of control over the process, but a high level of control over the outcome. As another type of voluntary, nonbinding process focused on joint decision making, problem solving, and the maintenance of relationships, mediation is best characterized as third-party-assisted negotiations. Mediation can be distinguished from arbitration, in which the third party makes a binding decision regarding the issues in question. As Pruitt and Carnevale suggest, "Mediation preserves the voluntary joint features of negotiation, with the disputants retaining the right to accept or reject any suggestion made by the mediator." Seen from this perspective, then, mediation is best understood as part of the broader context of negotiations and the parties' own efforts to manage their conflict. Mediation changes the structure of interaction in a conflict, with mediators bringing their own agendas and assumptions into the resolution process.

In arbitration, parties have extensive control over the process but low control over the outcome. More adversarial and rights-oriented than negotiation or mediation, arbitration (along with adjudication) is a form of binding third-party decision making. According to Goldberg, Sanders, and Rogers: "Arbitration is a private dispute resolution procedure designed by the parties to serve their particular needs, and contains the essential elements of court adjudication: proofs and arguments are submitted to a neutral third party who has the power to issue a binding decision." Arbitration possesses a number of potential advantages over court-based adjudication: it takes into account the decision maker's specialized expertise rather than simply imposing a random officer of the court; its decisions are final and there are no appeals; its proceedings are private and informal; its costs are low; and it offers speedy resolution.

In contrast to mediation, the neutral third party, not the disputing parties themselves, retains control over the outcome in an arbitrated settlement. Thus, as Frank Sander argues, the benefits flowing from a mutually agreed upon resolution or compromise by the parties cannot be realistically anticipated through arbitration. Nor is arbitration likely to lead to the high degree of voluntary compliance associated with negotiated or mediated settlements. Typically, there are no formal sanctions for failing to comply with an arbitrator's decision.

In adjudication, the conflicting parties have low control over both the process and the outcome. Whereas arbitration is a private, voluntary process, adjudication is a public, involuntary process in which public resources and public officials are involved in a process driven by active public participation. These "third party" officials possess a power defined and conferred by public law rather than private agreement. The job of judges, as Sander notes, "is not to maximize the ends of private parties, nor simply to secure the peace, but to explicate and give force to the values embodied in authoritative texts such as the Constitution and statutes. . . . This duty is not discharged when the parties settle." Therefore, the larger goal of adjudication is justice and not merely a settlement arrived at through plea bargaining and capitulation to the norms and conditions of mass society.

Conflict Resolution versus Nonviolent Direct Action

The methods of conflict resolution are all directed toward the nonviolent resolution of conflict. While none of the methods discussed above would claim to produce ideal outcomes and justice for all, they do aim to resolve differences without resort to war and violence. In contrast, nonviolent direct action does not seek to resolve conflict, but to wage it. It is a means of prosecuting a conflict, using all direct methods of punishment and persuasion to strategically undermine an opponent's objectives or to protect one's own interests short of physical harm, force, or violence. In short, conflict is a campaign to be won. Integrative, win-win solutions are not the central goals of parties that engage in strikes, boycotts, defiance campaigns, the creation of parallel institutions, and acts of civil disobedience. These actions all create costs for some parties to a conflict and, in so doing, contribute to a shift in the relative power of the conflicting parties. When parties adopt such a contending approach to conflict, the focus is not on problem solving or generating reciprocal concessions; the bulk of effort is directed toward exploiting those conflict conditions that permit a shifting of loyalties and power balances.

Conflict resolution assumes that conflict deescalation and creative compromise represent a high-priority social value that can be achieved through negotiation and mediation. Proponents of nonviolent direct action make no such presumptions about the purposes and methods of addressing social conflict; instead, they understand conflict to be an inherently adversarial process among contenders for power and loyalties. Nonviolent direct actionists insist there are circumstances in which escalating and waging conflict by nonviolent methods may be a more effective strategy than either compromise or violent conflict. This is especially the case where certain social objectives must be advanced or defended by active means. Using such nonviolent sanctions as protest, persuasion, noncooperation, and intervention, direct actionists seek to inflict costs on opponents and, as a result, to shift the relative power among contenders in conflict.

Choices at the Moment of Impasse

Having reviewed the predominant procedures for addressing social conflict, we can now ask which strategic choices from among them parties should consider at the moment of impasse. Let us assume here that conflict resolution (as opposed to "winning") is the higher order value and a condition to be achieved. Nonviolent direct action (a contending and struggle-oriented approach) can serve as a precursor or catalyst to the more collaborative decision-making mode of conflict resolution. From this perspective, it is feasible to imagine nonviolent direct action accomplishing several tasks necessary for effective conflict resolution. For example, direct action, as an expression of one party's power, may create a new equilibrium so that bargaining becomes possible. Nonviolent direct action may also raise the salience of a claim to rights, as in the U.S. civil rights campaigns of the 1960s. It is possible that the powerful expression of interests without violence may shift attitudes and perceptions of "the other" (as in the Palestinian intifada) thereby turning a perceived enemy into a potential negotiating partner. Innovative use of information technology may improve communications. Finally, nonviolent direct action may create space for parties to avoid capitulation and the costs of violent struggle, thereby making it easier for them to find areas of common agreement. The pursuit of violent struggle, by contrast, only ensures a further polarization of disputants.

Techniques of conflict resolution and nonviolent direct action are also employed simultaneously in certain conflict situations. The most common example of this is the use of strikes by labor unions concurrent with contract negotiations. Waging conflict could generate the "opening" necessary for a more collaborative mode of interaction wherein negotiation and mediation become possible. And should such potential collaboration prove impossible or short-lived, a new or extended impasse could serve as the catalyst for the continued use of nonviolent direct action.

Conclusions

This brief review of the means and methods by which conflict resolution addresses social conflict suggests we need to think more comparatively about conflict theory. In doing so, we will be better situated to evaluate the relative effectiveness of conflict resolution and nonviolent direct-action techniques across the spectrum of social conflict. The separate discourses on responses to social conflict—all purporting to have the best strategies and means for creating the conditions necessary for sustaining global peace—need to be synthesized and integrated. Thinking and acting comparatively, then, necessarily means breaking down the privileged differences that tend to separate and define proponents of the conflict resolution and nonviolent direct action communities. Each community, for example, has tended to assume that at the moment of impasse, disputants have only a narrow and restricted range of strategic options from which they can choose to approach their conflict. As this essay clearly shows, however, this is simply not so: they have a rich repertoire of credible "moves" to draw from. Thus conflict prosecution and conflict resolution can, and must, coexist on the continuum of approaches for addressing social conflict.

Brian S. Mandell

References

Ackerman, Peter, and Christopher Kruegler. *Strategic Nonviolent Conflict: The Dynamics of People Power in the Twentieth Century.* Westport, Conn.: Praeger, 1994.

Fisher, Ronald J. "Generic Principles for Resolving Intergroup Conflict." *Journal of Social Issues* 50, no. 1 (1994): 47–66.

Goldberg, Stephen B., Frank E.A. Sander, and Nancy H. Rogers. *Dispute Resolution: Negotiation, Mediation and Other Processes.* 2nd ed. Boston: Little Brown, 1992.

Pruitt, Dean G., and Peter J. Carnevale. *Negotiation in Social Conflict.* Pacific Grove, Calif.: Brooks/Cole, 1993.

Rubin, Jeffrey Z. "Models of Conflict Management." *Journal of Social Issues* 50, no. 1 (1994): 33–46.

See also CONFLICT THEORIES; MECHANISMS OF DIRECT ACTION; METHODS OF NONVIOLENT ACTION; NONVIOLENCE, PRINCIPLED

Conflict Theories

Review of various contending explanations to account for the emergence, escalation, and termination of a wide variety of social conflicts. This contribution does not discuss conflict-based theories of society, which seek to explain social change, social stratification, or social system maintenance. It draws from theories and research about social conflicts in general and also theories about revolutions, ethnic struggles, class conflicts, marital fights, labor-management conflicts, community disputes, and other specific conflicts insofar as they pertain to conflicts generally.

The Phenomenon of Social Conflicts

Social conflicts vary greatly in regard to the issues in contention (for example, borders, ideology, power, religion, social recognition, and environmental policy). They also vary in the arena in which they are conducted (such as cities, factories, universities, families, countries, regions of the world, or urban neighborhoods). They vary in the size and degree of organization of the adversaries (such as trade union and management organizations, individual persons, national governments, social classes, ethnic communities, and neighborhood gangs). They vary in innumerable other ways, but the emphasis here is on commonalities among conflicts.

Social conflicts that are the focus of attention in the theoretical literature, and will be in this review, are ones that are relatively non-regulated and that are waged with violence and other kinds of coercion, or their threatened use. Nonviolent actions are often coercive and whether coercive or not, they are challenging to official ways of managing conflicts. When conflicts are conducted according to highly institutionalized rules, they may be viewed as a game, as in electoral politics or judicial trials in some countries at some times.

Furthermore, the theories pertain to conflicts among relatively clearly defined human antagonists, not among general social or physical forces nor among supernatural actors. The human actors can range in number from one person to the population of a country that is represented by a government or person who can commit that population to action in a particular conflict. There is a fundamental distinction between a person acting for herself alone and a person acting as if she represents a constituency. A person with a constituency needs to keep the support or at least acquiescence of that constituency to remain a leader of her side in the struggle. The constituency is often a source of pressure to intensify the struggle, but sometimes it is a pressure to limit the fight or to settle it.

Finally, social conflicts are discussed here as if they have an observable beginning, middle, and end. This presumption that a conflict may be isolated from the general social-historical context in which it is embedded does not assume that this is objectively true, independent of the beliefs of the partisans. The presumption is that the partisans or analysts create this sense of a distinct conflict, specific war, or particular revolution. People interact and collectively characterize a set of events as constituting a conflict; it is socially constructed.

The great variety of social conflicts stimulate different kinds of questions, as discussed next. Different questions generate different answers, as subsequently discussed. Finally, I suggest some specifications of theories of conflicts.

Questions Theories Seek to Answer

Theories offer explanations of selected aspects of a complex, loosely bounded variety of phenomena. The explanations may be derived from general assumptions or propositions about human nature or about the nature of social life. Explanations may be less formal, providing understandings by offering insights from the perspectives of the parties to the conflict. Explanations may be historically grounded, the present being a result of what has been. In any case, theories help make sense of what otherwise seems unintelligible.

Theories differ not only in the kind of explanation they provide, but in what they seek to explain. In this review, I will examine theories in terms of the kinds of questions they attempt to answer.

Most theoretical work about conflicts focuses on explaining why conflicts erupt. Officials, the public, and academic analysts alike are fascinated with the outbreak of violent conflicts. The most natural questions seem to be, why did World War I happen? what caused the French Revolution of 1789? or what caused the 1992 riots in Los Angeles?

Other questions that are frequently asked include, Why did the conflict escalate as much as it did? Why did the partisans resort to violence, particularly to extensive violence, destroying many lives? For example, there has been much theorizing about the causes of wars, a particularly violent way of conducting intergovernmental conflicts.

Questions about other aspects or phases of conflicts have been relatively infrequently asked in the past, but are increasingly being raised. The resort to violence is more often now viewed as problematic, so the questions asked pertain to the use of alternative ways to wage a conflict, including nonviolent coercion, positive sanctions, and persuasion. Nonviolent action variously combines coercion, rewards, and persuasive efforts. For example, nonviolent action in the form of symbolic acts opposing official policy may be a form of witnessing, seeking to persuade others, or it may be massive resistance that disrupts official functions and thus is largely coercive.

Questions about limiting or interrupting conflict escalation and about transitions away from protracted conflicts toward de-escalation and settlement are increasingly being asked. These kinds of inquiries have been stimulated by the growth of the conflict resolution field. This leads to studies of conflicts that did not take a destructive course and to the consideration of ways destructive conflicts can be avoided.

Questions about the consequences of conflicts have been asked in the past, often about the unintended consequences, for example for the growth of the state. More often now, questions are asked about the success of the protagonists in achieving their goals and the effectiveness of different means of struggle. In addition, Coser posed the question about the function conflicts serve not only for the adversaries, but for the larger social system of which they are a part.

Theoretical Approaches to Answers

A wide variety of folk and academic theories have provided answers to many of the questions posed. They include beliefs about the will of God; but the theories discussed here are socialscientific ones, grounded on some empirical evidence. Three classes of theories will be distinguished, those emphasizing the factors internal to one or all of the adversary parties, those emphasizing the relationship between the parties, and those stressing the social context within which the adversaries exist.

Internal Factors

Among the theoretical approaches that stress internal factors are ones focusing on psycho-logical processes and characteristics. Some theorists have proposed that humans have innate aggressive or other drives that generate human conflicts. The variability in forms of conflict are so great, however, that innate drives cannot be a full or major explanation of their origin. Other theorists note the prevalence of psychological processes such as projection (by which undesirable attributes of one's own are projected onto an external party) and displacement (whereby resentments arising from dissatisfaction from one source are displaced on another group as the scapegoat). Extrapolating from such individual processes to group processes, however, must be done warily, not assuming that collectivities exhibit such processes as a unit. Members of collectivities may exhibit a variety of them. For example, psychological and social psychological processes affect decision makers representing their constituencies. Leaders and would-be leaders also can try to mobilize a constituency's support for various policies, using appeals based on such processes. Additional internal factors pertain to the structure and culture of the adversaries, whether societies, communities, or organizations. One or more of the adversary parties may have developed an internal group whose task it is to wage conflicts and to prepare to do so; in societies this may be a military-industrial complex that has a vested interest in developing the readiness to wage war. In general, leaders of communities and of organizations as well as of countries often represent their constituencies in relations with nonmembers. Depending on the culture of the party and the character of the leaders, such representation is varyingly confrontational.

Cultural factors may be seen in the varying sensibility different groups have to upholding one's honor and sensing challenges to it. Feminist scholars, such as Harris and King, have noted that the prevalent socialization practices are gender-related, with men learning to be fighters and warriors as part of their self-identity as men.

Adversary Relations

Many theories about conflicts emphasize the relations between possible adversaries. The history of relations between adversaries is often seen as a source of future conflict and an explanation of its course. Parties with a history of past fights inculcate their members with the memories of past losses and humiliations and tend to glorify their own selves and denigrate their enemies. When the opportunity appears, retribution is sought and a fight erupts, perhaps conducted more viciously than the issues at stake seem to warrant.

Many theories emphasize that parties with low material conditions, low status, or little power will seek to improve their position and challenge others who are better off. Some theorists, such as Gurr, stress that it is not the actual position, but the relative standing that brings on feelings of deprivation. Very often, however, conflicts are begun by the relatively stronger party; wars are not usually started by the weaker side. This suggests that it is the capacity to wage a conflict and not only the feeling of dissatisfaction that fuels a fight. Thus revolutions break out not necessarily when many people are deprived, but when the ruling group appears vulnerable. These differing views have been disputed, particularly among theorists of revolutions and of social movements.

One aspect of the relationship between possible adversaries has received a great deal of theoretical attention: relative power. Since many approaches to conflict stress the importance of coercion in the waging of conflict, the relative ability to harm or threaten harm is given most attention. Associated with that idea is an emphasis on the rational calculation of the likely benefits of coercive struggle versus the likely costs. In the study of international relations, those considerations occupy a central role in the "realist" approach.

Adversaries are in various kinds of relationships affected by power differences. Often the relatively powerful adversary claims legitimate authority over the challenging party. When this authority is acknowledged by the subordinate group, a conflict may remain submerged and emerge into overt struggle when other circumstances change.

Coercive power is too often assumed to refer only to violence and the threat of violence. Of course, coercion can include many forms of nonviolent action. This may include imposing negative sanctions such as withholding labor, as in strikes, or in refusing to cooperate, as in civil disobedience. Many of these coercive sanctions depend upon a pre-existing mutual dependency between the adversaries. This is important to recognize. A conflict between two parties never involves only a relationship in which what one side gains the other loses (a zero-sum conflict or relationship). There are always some possibilities of mutual gain and mutual loss. The parties always have some shared and complementary interests, even if these are lost sight of when a conflict intensifies.

Conflicts, moreover, are not waged only by the use or threatened use of coercive power. In addition, one side may offer positive sanctions to an adversary in order to win its cooperation or compliance. Cash payments, deference, grants of autonomy, or other benefits may be promised or awarded. Again, this depends on the existence of a relationship with some mutual dependency. Many feminist and conflict resolution theorists stress the importance of the ongoing relations among protagonists, noting that in such a context, conflicts are not zero-sum and may be conducted in noncoercive ways.

Conflicts are even waged by resort to persuasive efforts and normative claims. Each side in a conflict typically offers reasons why the adversary ought to agree to its requests or demands. Such persuasive efforts are likely to be effective insofar as the parties share values and norms. For example, the claims of African Americans in the civil rights struggles of the 1960s were made within the shared discourse of Americans about equal rights and the primacy of the U.S. Constitution; the claims made in those terms convinced many people, won allies, and divided adversaries. As Kriesberg argued in 1992, even the cold war was waged and ended through extensive persuasive efforts, through people-to-people exchanges, and by the Soviet and U.S. governments seeking to influence each other's peoples.

Another way of considering the relationship between possible adversaries as a factor in social conflicts is to consider the kind of issues about which adversaries contend. On many issues, the possible opponents agree about the desirability of some matter. For example, they want the same land or access to the same resources, and they strive for prestige and power. These are disputes over consensual issues. On other matters, however, the parties do not agree about what is desirable; for example, they differ about political ideology or religion and seek to convert another party or to impose their preferences. These are dissensual conflicts. While every actual social conflict involves some mixture of consensual and dissensual components, one or the other usually predominates.

Conflicts always involve many issues. What appears to be a single issue can be fractionated into subissues, and additional issues are readily linked. As conflicts escalate, more and more issues are likely to be engaged, as past grievances are brought up, as new hurts need to be redressed, and as new interests are created by the struggle. This complexity hinders conflict de-escalation, but it can also provide a basis for negotiated settlements. The multiplicity of issues allows for tradeoffs so that packages may be designed by which each side may yield on matters of low priority and gain on matters of high priority to it. These possibilities have been elaborated in the extensive research and theory-building about negotiations, for example, in the work of Howard Raiffa.

Context

Parties to a conflict never struggle in isolation. They are part of a larger system of relationships and structures. Some theoretical perspectives, such as that of Ross, stress the system context to explain the eruption and course of social conflicts. One major part of the system context are the institutions within which the parties are embedded. Every social system has some procedures for managing disputes among its members. In contemporary, large societies, this is institutionalized in the form of electoral and judicial systems. Conflict theorists give particular attention to those disputes that are not handled through such institutions.

One mechanism for managing conflicts, which is varyingly institutionalized, is mediation. A body of literature, discussed by Pruitt and Rubin, has developed about the roles that an organization, group, or person who is not an active partisan in a conflict can play to limit a conflict's escalation, hasten its settlement, and reach a fair and enduring resolution. A variety of mediating functions may be served by a formally designated mediator or even by those who are not so designated. These include constructing new options, facilitating communication among enemies, giving legitimacy and credibility to possible terms of settlement, and modifying one or more side's expectations of what will happen if the conflict continues and escalates.

Another way of considering the context of a conflict relates to the location of the adversaries within a larger stratified social system. A social system may be regarded as consisting of actors with varying degrees of power, with each one seeking to maximize its gains and forming coalitions as a way to do so. Previous relations, shared cultures, and other kinds of special

bonds may impede easy, calculated shifts among coalition partners.

Every social system is differentiated in many different ways. Persons and groups differ in their rankings of status, power, and material resources; they differ in institutional affiliations; they differ in place of residence and of work, and in various other ways. These differences can become lines of cleavage and if they coincide, they may reinforce each other making a conflict along those lines more intense. If the lines of cleavage crosscut each other, on the other hand, a conflict is likely to be inhibited and its destructiveness muted.

Finally, adversaries are usually members of the same or similar cultures. That shared culture provides shared understandings about the nature of conflict and how it should be waged and settled. This is especially the case for members of the same society, but even in international conflicts, often the adversaries are part of the same civilization. Cultural differences, nevertheless, are present to some degree, and they complicate negotiating settlements as well as contribute to the emergence of conflicts.

Specifying Theoretical Answers

The variety of theories about social conflicts is bewildering, and integrating or choosing among them seems impossible, given the variety of questions posed and the wide range of social conflicts. The existing social science evidence is still limited to tiny bits of the vast field of conflict studies and is inadequate to disconfirm major components of the theories in the field. Yet combining various theoretical ideas and examining a wide range of conflicts enriches our understanding of each.

To assess the validity or plausibility of various theories, it is necessary to specify under what circumstances various theoretical propositions are likely to be applicable. In this article, I consider two sets of specifying conditions: the kind of conflict being studied and the stage of the conflict about which questions are posed.

Kinds of Conflicts

One of the many ways conflicts vary is the arena in which they occur: for example, a family, a country, an organization, a city, or a global region. A critical aspect of the variation in arenas is the degree to which institutionalized conflict settlement procedures exist. Insofar as conflicts are regulated, the internal features of possible adversaries are not likely to be the primary sources of conflicts or determinants of how they are waged and resolved. Contextual factors correspondingly are likely to be major explanatory factors.

Another important variation among conflicts are the adversaries' relations with each other. For example, often adversaries are in a hierarchical relationship, with great differences in power and authority. This is the case in many bureaucratic organizations and in societal political systems dominated by a small elite. In such cases, conflicts are often covert or suppressed, but when they do erupt they may be fiercely coercive, as in class-based revolutions, ethnic-based secessionist fights, prison riots, and army mutinies. Variations in the relative power of the possible adversaries, then, are especially significant.

Theories stressing the relations between adversaries are particularly likely to be relevant for such kinds of conflicts; this may include attention to calculations of the likelihood of benefits outweighing costs; attention to group and perceptual processes affecting judgments of expected costs and the likelihood of various outcomes; and attention to the ways social and political discourse by the ruling group are inculcated and accepted.

Another way conflicts vary is the nature of the adversaries themselves. They may be more or less differentiated, large, clearly bounded, and with different repertoires for conducting conflicts. Many or few may be engaged in conflict.

Finally, conflicts differ regarding the matters in contention. One kind of variation is the degree to which each party believes its vital interests are at stake in the fight. This variation certainly affects the way a conflict is waged and the kinds of outcomes that may be reached.

Conflict Stages

Theories differ in the kind of questions they seek to answer, and one dimension along which the questions differ is the stage of a conflict for which they are pertinent. Four stages will be noted here: emergence, escalation, de-escalation, and settlement.

Many theories are especially relevant for explaining the emergence or eruption of conflicts, and are varyingly significant for different kinds of conflicts. One set of theories stresses the characteristics of the adversaries, typically the one challenging the dominant party. This approach is most relevant for conflicts in which the adversaries are interdependent, forming a single social system—for example, workers and managers in a factory or a subordinated ethnic group in a country dominated by another ethnic group.

These theories generally emphasize the sense of grievance felt by the challenging group and its belief that the grievance can be redressed by getting the dominant group to change its conduct. The challenging group may act from desperation, but more typically, it acts from the belief that the dominant group is vulnerable because it is weakening or because the challengers are growing in strength.

Clearly, however, the nature of the relationship between the possible adversaries is not sufficient to account for the eruption of a coercively conducted, overt conflict. The system context also contributes to the eruption. That system context varyingly allows for alternative ways of conducting the struggle. Those ways include open electoral and judicial processes; they also include the acceptable repertoire of demonstrations, boycotts, and so on.

Theories about conflicts generally give attention to the escalation of conflicts, and they often focus on the interaction between the adversaries, as they mutually threaten and harm each other. Such interactions lead to polarization, misunderstandings, and even dehumanization of the opponents. A value of nonviolent escalation is that such means are less likely to foster dehumanization.

Destructive conflict escalation is exacerbated by psychological mechanisms, by which members of each adversary group justify themselves and castigate the enemy. Organizational processes also promote escalation, including the development of vested interests in continuing the fight, the avoidance of admitting having made sacrifices in vain, and the exclusion of doubters from the leadership engaged in the struggle.

The external context sets parameters for conflict escalation. The idea that there is a repertoire of methods that particular sets of people think of using at given historical periods is an important insight offered by Tilly. The role of other parties, external to the immediate conflict is also important, either in intervening to escalate the struggle or to inhibit the conflict's escalation.

Only recently has work in the theory of conflicts given systematic attention to conflict de-escalation. Conventional and traditional

C

thinking has stressed that conflicts de-escalate with the victory of one side and the surrender by the other. In actuality, conflicts often begin to move toward de-escalation and settlement without a clear, unilaterally imposed defeat. As Touval and Zartman suggest, this movement frequently arises when there is a mutually hurting stalemate and a formula for a mutually acceptable settlement is created.

Although ideas about internal factors that promote conflict escalation are much more developed, there are some theoretical propositions linking internal factors to conflict de-escalation. For example, waging a struggle both imposes costs and provides benefits to members of an adversary party. But those costs and benefits are not evenly distributed. Insofar as they are differentially borne, there is a greater likelihood of dissension and a weakening of resolve to persevere in the struggle.

Where parties to a conflict are embedded in institutions and associations that transcend them, parties who are not directly engaged in the struggle are likely to set limits to the conflict's escalation. Some of them may intervene and facilitate or impose constraints or even settlements. The social context of a conflict provides models and examples of the way in which conflicts are waged and ended.

Finally, theories provide explanations about the ending and consequences of conflicts. Traditional approaches have stressed endings in which one side defeats the other and gains what the other loses. Clearly, outcomes are nearly always much more mixed, with all parties losing something if the conflict was waged destructively. Often the major contenders may lose or gain together, relative to other parties in the social system to which they belong. As the newer ideas of conflict resolution stress, outcomes also may be mutually harmful or mutually beneficial.

The newly developing theories about conflict resolution provide much insight about factors that bring about mutually satisfactory settlements and resolutions of conflicts. They tend to stress the way the adversaries relate to each other, particularly when negotiations are undertaken. They also give attention to the ways in which mediating parties help to bring about settlements, and particularly ones that are mutually beneficial.

In considering the consequences of conflicts, the indirect and unintended effects deserve attention as well as the intended ones. Functionalist theoretical approaches, such as that of Coser, provide ideas about the unintended consequences of social conflicts, particularly for the social system within which they are waged. Recently, attention is being given to the effectiveness of different means of conducting conflicts in attaining the objectives sought by the antagonists.

Theoretical Issues

Many controversies continue as theorists of conflicts offer their explanations. I will note four issues that generate controversy. First, theoretical approaches differ in the degree to which they regard conflicts as based on an objective reality or as socially constructed by the adversaries. Rather than viewing these as dichotomous alternatives, some theorists try to take an integrative approach. For example, they may stress that criteria which analysts may use to characterize a class or ethnic group are varyingly used by partisans to form a collective identity and thus become a party to a conflict.

Another set of theoretical issues are related to assumptions about human nature. These include assumptions about the flexibility of human nature, the primacy of various needs, the power-seeking nature of humans, and their reliance on aggression and coercion.

Related to the preceding issues is the controversy about the realistic or unrealistic character of social conflicts. Some theorists tend to emphasize that conflicts are unrealistic in the sense that they are based on misunderstandings between adversaries or driven by internal forces, unrelated to the presumed adversary. Others emphasize the reality of the differences between adversaries and the rationality of using coercion and even violence to maximize benefits in a situation where one party will gain at the expense of the other. Some analysts offer syntheses, noting that there are many real bases for conflicts, but only some are actualized, and once a conflict begins to escalate, processes enter that exacerbate the conflict and engender misunderstandings.

Finally, there are controversies about the application of theory to the practice of conducting and settling conflicts. These controversies are complicated by the involvement that theorists have with ongoing conflicts. Yet engagement provides insights and the possibility of testing ideas that enrich understanding.

Conclusions

The theoretical analysis of social conflicts is a particularly exciting intellectual field at present.

Many competing theoretical approaches in the social sciences are relevant to the analysis of social conflicts and are being brought to bear. What adds to the excitement is the pervasiveness of social conflicts and their growing destructiveness with advances in the technology of violence.

How adversaries think about the analysis of conflicts affects how the adversaries wage conflicts and resolve them. The recognition of that phenomenon by analysts helps fuel their debates in the field, since the outcomes of the debates are likely to affect how fights are waged.

Theory and practice will be advanced as analysts more explicitly provide explanations for particular kinds of conflicts and for specific phases and aspects of the conflicts' course. One single general theory of social conflicts, answering all questions we may pose about them, does not and never will exist. General approaches are useful, as are specific explanations for specific matters about conflicts.

Louis Kriesberg

References

Coser, Lewis A. *The Functions of Social Conflict*. New York: Free Press, 1956.

Goldstone, Jack A., ed. *Revolutions: Theoretical, Comparative, and Historical Studies*. San Diego: Harcourt Brace Jovanovich, 1986.

Gurr, Ted R. *Why Men Rebel*. Princeton: Princeton University Press, 1970.

Harris, Adrienne, and Ynestra King, eds. *Rocking the Ship of State: Toward a Feminist Peace Politics*. Boulder, Colo.: Westview, 1990.

Kriesberg, Louis. *International Conflict Resolution*. New Haven and London: Yale University Press, 1992.

———. *Social Conflicts*. 2nd ed. Englewood Cliffs, N.J.: Prentice-Hall, 1982.

Pruitt, Dean G., and Jeffrey Z. Rubin. *Social Conflict: Escalation, Stalemate, and Settlement*. New York: Random House, 1986.

Raiffa, Howard. *The Art and Science of Negotiation*. Cambridge, Mass., and London: Harvard University Press, 1982.

Ross, Marc Howard. *The Culture of Conflict*. New Haven and London: Yale University Press, 1993.

Tilly, Charles. *From Mobilization to Revolution*. Reading, Mass.: Addison-Wesley, 1978.

Touval, Saadia, and I. William Zartman, eds. *International Mediation in Theory and Practice*. Boulder, Colo.: Westview, 1985.

C

Congress of Racial Equality

An important organization of the American civil rights movement, formed in 1942 by a small interracial group in Chicago. The Congress of Racial Equality (CORE) emerged more than a decade before the modern civil rights movement developed in the mid-1950s. Because of its prior experience with nonviolent direct action, CORE was able to facilitate the development of the modern civil rights movement. It found itself in a position to assist the movement tactically, and it provided the movement with one of its major charismatic leaders, as well as other experienced activists.

CORE was founded by an interracial group of six pacifists, all members of the Fellowship of Reconciliation (FOR). James Farmer and George Houser were FOR staff members. Bernice Fisher, Joe Guinn, Homer Jack, and James R. Robinson were students at the University of Chicago and were members of an FOR group on campus. Four of the founders were white and two were black. They were educated and came from middle-class backgrounds.

These individuals were opposed to racial inequality and racial discrimination, and they believed that the kind of nonviolent direct action developed by Gandhi in India could be utilized to eradicate America's racial problem. In fact, they idolized Gandhi as a charismatic saint, and they studied his method of nonviolent direct action in a systematic fashion. Krishnalal Shridharani's *War without Violence: A Study of Gandhi's Method and Its Accomplishments* (1939) became the group's bible. They were especially attracted to the spiritual dimension of Gandhi's movement. Like Gandhi, they believed that the proper use of nonviolent direct action would transform the heart of the oppressor, enabling him to desist discriminatory behavior and become a loving human being in the process.

Gandhi laid out precise steps for activists to follow in undertaking nonviolent direct action. The original CORE group adopted them in total. The first step called for a full investigation of an unjust situation. The investigation was to be followed by negotiations with the perpetrators of the unjust actions. If negotiations failed, the demands for change were made public so they could be understood by the larger community. If the oppressor refused to yield to public scrutiny, the activists were to engage in a self-purification process readying themselves to engage in peaceful protest. Finally, direct action was to be initiated if the prior steps proved unsuccessful.

CORE's founders were convinced that America should be a color-blind society where race was irrelevant in human affairs. Their ideals stood in sharp contrast to the racial realities of the 1940s. The American South was characterized by institutionalized legal segregation backed by lynch mobs and white supremacist organizations. De facto segregation and racial discrimination were pervasive in the North. For example, in Chicago in 1942 many public facilities were racially segregated, as were residential neighborhoods. In reality, then, this small interracial CORE group could not dine together in many restaurants, live in the same neighborhood, or skate together in the local roller rink. The original CORE group believed that nonviolent resistance could change these practices and the nation.

Thus, in Chicago in 1942, the CORE group attacked housing segregation when some of its black and white members moved into a house in a white residential area. After legal maneuvers, the CORE group prevailed. This was followed by demonstrations at a roller skating rink that discriminated against blacks. Because of the effectiveness of CORE's picket line, the owners of the rink began admitting blacks. The next demonstration occurred at Jack Sprat, a Chicago restaurant that refused to serve blacks. Approximately two dozen CORE demonstrators initiated a sit-in in Jack Sprat, forcing its owners to change its racist policies. All of these Chicago demonstrations followed the Gandhian methods of nonviolent resistance and served as a model for other CORE groups that emerged in northern cities. These small CORE groups began attacking racial discrimination in public accommodation and other arenas. Often they disappeared following a demonstration. They operated with meager funds and were never able to develop a mass base. Moreover, the majority of CORE members were white and relatively privileged in contrast to the poor masses of African Americans.

In April 1947, in an attempt to gain more national attention, CORE, together with the FOR, organized the first freedom ride, from Washington, D.C., to Louisville, Kentucky, and back again. This Journey of Reconciliation, as it was called, tested the 1946 U.S. Supreme Court decision banning segregated seating on interstate buses. However, with few arrests and relatively little violence during the course of the journey, it did not receive the national publicity that organizers had hoped for. Still, it provided a model for the later Freedom Rides of 1961.

By the mid-1950s, CORE still did not have national visibility. It was not active in the deep South, where racial segregation was most rampant. Nevertheless, by this time CORE activists had developed a repertoire of direct-action tactics and an understanding of the philosophy of nonviolent resistance. Within the organization were talented and skilled leaders of nonviolent resistance, including James Farmer and Bayard Rustin. With these experiences and resources, CORE was poised to play a major role in the American civil rights movement. CORE had envisioned the possibility of a nonviolent mass movement against racial inequality from its inception.

The Montgomery bus boycott of 1955–1956 was the watershed of the modern civil rights movement, for it proved that a successful nonviolent mass movement against racial inequality was possible. The boycott mobilized the entire black population of Montgomery, Alabama, against segregation on the local buses and achieved victory after sustaining a year-long mass movement. The boycott catapulted the charismatic Martin Luther King, Jr., into the national limelight and sent an unmistakable message to the nation that the black masses were ready to move against racial segregation.

This message was not lost on CORE. Like the Southern Christian Leadership Conference (SCLC), CORE began establishing chapters in the South during the late 1950s with the intent of generating mass action against racial segregation. The breakthrough occurred in 1960. On February 1, four college students at North Carolina A&T College conducted a sit-in at the lunch counter of the local Woolworth store, where blacks were prohibited. College students from across the South followed this model and conducted similar sit-ins in their local areas. CORE made major contributions to this sit-in movement. It assisted in the nonviolent training of many of these students and provided important resources that helped the sit-in movement to become a major force. As a result, CORE began to gain national visibility and attract resources that enabled it to become a major civil rights organization.

It was the Freedom Rides of 1961 that brought fame to CORE and established it as one of the leading organizations of the civil rights movement. In December 1960, the U.S. Supreme Court extended the ban on segregation in interstate transportation to include terminal facilities. CORE decided to test the court's decision with integrated teams of riders on a Greyhound and a Trailways bus in May of 1961. The trip was to begin in Washington, D.C., and end in the deep South. The outcome was predictable. When the buses reached the South, they were fire bombed and the CORE activists were severely beaten. A stunned nation watched the violence on television. The federal government and other civil rights organizations—especially the Student Nonviolent Coordinating Committee (SNCC) and SCLC—had to intervene on behalf of CORE before the rides could be completed. James Farmer, one of CORE's founding members, participated in the Freedom Rides and, as a result, became one of the key leaders of the civil rights movement. The Freedom Rides became a small mass movement in and of themselves, as activists throughout the movement initiated Freedom Rides in 1961. These protests led to the desegregation of interstate travel.

The Freedom Rides elevated CORE to the enviable position of sharing the spotlight with SCLC and SNCC as the major direct-action organizations of the civil rights movement. CORE became a household name and garnered the financial resources and prestige required to increase the size of its staff and to play an active role in the unfolding movement. The organization was able to become involved in many of the communitywide movements in the South during the early 1960s that attempted to break the backbone of segregation. Farmer was probably second only to King in terms of the charismatic influence he wielded in the movement during this period. Additionally, CORE worked with other groups to achieve the franchise for Southern blacks. CORE played an important role in creating the conditions that led to the passage of the 1964 Civil Rights Act and the 1965 Voting Rights Act. These measures brought an end to the formal system of racial segregation in the United States.

By the mid to late 1960s it was becoming clear that the formal system of racial segregation was only one of the factors responsible for racial inequality. The unequal distribution of economic and social power between blacks and whites proved to be a major problem as well. Indeed, large numbers of black people during this period began questioning the efficacy of racial integration. The goal of racial integration had been the umbrella that united the major civil rights organizations. This fragile consensus began to crumble when black leaders began to ask how racial integration would enable African Americans to exercise power within their own communities. They asked how racial integration could generate economic solutions to the vast poverty that gripped much of the black community. On a cultural level, many wondered whether racial integration could embrace black culture and black pride. Large numbers of grassroots black people began to openly reject the goal of racial integration. They reasoned that whites, including white liberals, were not willing to share power and economic resources with black people. As a result, they began to demand "Black Power" and black self-determination. The urban rebellions of the late 1960s exemplified this thrust.

This development signaled the decline of CORE. From the beginning, CORE was vulnerable to the charge that it was dominated by whites and responded to the black community in a paternalistic fashion. Moreover, most whites in CORE could not resonate with the goals of Black Power, community control, and black self-determinism. To white CORE members, such goals led to racial chauvinism, not a color-blind society. The claim by some that blacks had a right to defend themselves was also bothersome to traditional CORE members, because for them such a posture was likely to lead to violence, which they detested.

Nevertheless, by the late 1960s whites in CORE along with some blacks were losing the battle to keep the organization interracial and firmly committed to racial integration and peaceful protest. As early as 1966, the newly ascendant black CORE leaders, including Floyd McKissick and Roy Innis, began to embrace the concept of Black Power. Social movements and external social forces are always engaged in an intricate dance where each wishes to lead the other. By the late 1960s, CORE was forced to yield to the winds of change that sought black empowerment often through radical and unconventional means. But CORE was not alone in this predicament. SNCC was a victim of such a quest, and Martin Luther King, Jr., was wrestling with this dilemma when an assassin's bullet cut short his brilliant leadership.

When CORE's leadership embraced Black Power, its white members fell away, as did the bulk of the organization's financial resources. As CORE approaches the twenty-first century, it is only a shell of the organization that flourished in the early 1960s. Its future is uncertain. But what is certain is that CORE made major contributions to the modern civil rights movement. The tactical and philosophical knowledge that CORE brought to that struggle, along with skilled activists and leaders, served to quicken the pace of the civil rights movement and enhanced its ability to become one of the distinctive forces of the twentieth century.

Aldon D. Morris

References

Farmer, James. *Freedom—When?* New York: Random House, 1965.

Meier, August, and Elliott Rudwick. *CORE: A Study in the Civil Rights Movement, 1942–1968.* New York: Oxford University Press, 1973.

Morris, Aldon D. *The Origins of the Civil Rights Movement.* New York: Free Press, 1984.

Shridharani, Krishnalal. *War without Violence: A Study of Gandhi's Method and Its Accomplishments.* New York: Harcourt, Brace, 1939.

See also CIVIL RIGHTS MOVEMENT; FELLOWSHIP OF RECONCILIATION, INTERNATIONAL; FREEDOM RIDES, 1961; GANDHI, MOHANDAS KARAMCHAND; KING, MARTIN LUTHER, JR.; MONTGOMERY BUS BOYCOTT, 1955–1956; PACIFISM; SATYAGRAHA; SHRIDHARANI, KRISHNALAL; SOUTHERN CHRISTIAN LEADERSHIP CONFERENCE; STUDENT NONVIOLENT COORDINATING COMMITTEE

Conscientious Objection

A sincere belief that participation in war is wrong. This objection may apply to all forms or to particular aspects of war. Such a conviction is said to be known in the conscience, the center of moral awareness; thus, to compel conscientious objectors (COs) to serve in the military would violate their human rights.

Generally, conscientious objection has pertained to principled objection to all wars. Some understandings of conscientious objection have focused on the use or threat of lethal force, others stress the collective organization of violence. Conscientious objection to particular wars and forms of warfare has received very limited recognition.

From the seventeenth century until World War II, the grounds for conscientious objection were communally held religious beliefs. In the late twentieth century, however, the narrow scope of permitted grounds has been greatly broadened. The reasons for conscientious objection now range beyond religious and moral-ethical beliefs to philosophical, sociological, and political grounds. In some countries, the mere fact of a personal objection to participation in war is treated as an instance of conscientious objection.

Conscientious objection is becoming a worldwide phenomenon. As of 1994 the right to conscientious objection has become recognized in twenty-three countries, including states in the former Soviet Union and in the Southern Hemisphere. Other states may make informal provision by reassigning COs to other duties, such as work battalions. Government provision for conscientious objection is correlated with democratic regimes. The United Nations Commission on Human Rights has asserted it as a human right, and international law has begun to incorporate it, as, for example, in the International Covenant on Civil and Political Rights.

Generally, there are five variations of conscientious objection, each with different implications for action.

1. Conscientious objectors who will accept no service in the military: These persons, if drafted, are assigned to alternative service under civilian direction. If serving in the military when their beliefs "crystallize," they may be discharged.

2. Conscientious objectors who will accept service in the military: These persons, if conscripted, are assigned to noncombatant service, usually in the medical corps. If serving in the military when their beliefs "crystallize," they will be assigned to noncombatant duties.

3. Absolutist conscientious objectors. These are persons who will not cooperate in any way with the military, the war system, and preparations for war or organized violence. They will not register for conscription, and in some cases, when brought to trial will not participate in their own defense.

4. Objectors to a particular war or form of armed conflict. Often called "selective conscientious objectors," these are persons who are sincerely opposed to participation in what they believe to be an "unjust" war, but would participate in a "just war." For example, some people were opposed to the Vietnam War, but would have participated in World War II. These objectors, who make discriminate judgments about the justifiableness of conflicts and weapons, may seek exemption from military service during a period of conscription, and may request discharge or reassignment if in the armed forces.

   Nuclear pacifists are a subset of just-war objectors. Their consciences would not allow them to participate in a nuclear war, or what they believe would become a nuclear war. Some nuclear pacifists are opposed to participation in all war because of their belief that *any* war fought today could lead to the use of nuclear weapons.

5. Conscientious objectors to paying taxes for war. These are persons whose consciences forbid them to pay the military portion of their taxes because of religious and moral beliefs about participation in war. A few such objectors refuse to pay any federal tax since their taxes are commingled in the general treasury and will be used to pay for war and preparations for war.

The Early History of Conscientious Objection

The early Christians are now understood to have refused to participate in war and in the military, not only on the basis of teachings against killing, but also on the grounds of abhorrence of idolatrous worship in the Roman legions. Theologians from Tertullian to Origen supported conscientious objection. St. Martin of Tours is celebrated today for his decision to leave the military after his conversion and for his refusal to oppose the barbarian siege of the city. There is a direct line from this tradition through the medieval prohibitions on the clergy and members of religious orders, who comprised the church, from direct participation in violence and the shedding of blood, to the redefinition of the church in the radical Reformation to include the entire community of believers who share the same duty to refrain from warfare.

The Anabaptist sects in the Reformation of the sixteenth century took upon themselves the duty to be the church, shared belief in obeying the teaching of Jesus, and accepted suffering with him on behalf of others. Central to their belief is a rejection of participation in war. Persecuted in Europe they fled to America, where provisions in colonial charters gave them freedom of religion, or those rights developed subsequently. Among these groups were the closely related Mennonites and Amish. Smaller groups such as the Moravians and Schwenkfelders followed in the eighteenth century. The German Baptists, Dunkers, who combined pietist and Anabaptist distinctives, prospered in America, coming as a small band following their organization in 1708 at Swarztenau in the Rhineland. The followers of George Fox, the Society of Friends (Quakers), who grew out of the religious ferment in seventeenth-century England, came in numbers to the proprietary colony of William Penn, but they immigrated to the other colonies, also, so that they were one of the five most numerous denominations in America at the end of the eighteenth century. Other millenarian sects from England, such as the Christadelphians, Shakers, and Plymouth Brethren, also migrated to America during the Colonial period.

The current provisions for conscientious objection stem from the American Colonial-era exemptions given members of religious bodies, primarily the "historic peace churches," Mennonites, Brethren, and Quakers, who held beliefs that opposed participation in war. The exemptions were therefore intended to apply only to those persons opposed to all wars because of their religion. They were exempted in statutes that date from 1657 (Massachusetts) and 1662 (Rhode Island). Because the Quaker establishment in Pennsylvania was not willing to prosecute the wars against the Indians nor implement a militia, their principles led to their loss of political control in the Commonwealth at the time of the French and Indian Wars.

During the American Revolution when his troops attempted to force Quakers to bear arms at Valley Forge, George Washington directed that they be set free to return home. At the time of the Civil War, there was no federal policy about conscientious objection in the United States. When conscription was initiated in 1862 in the Confederacy, there were exemptions for Quakers, Mennonites, Dunkards, and Moravians. When conscription was instituted in 1863 by the Union, conscientious objection was not allowed at first, but was soon provided for somewhat sporadically. With the availability of the open frontier, many Brethren moved to the West to escape conscription and thus to protect the conscientious objector men among them from military service. The provisions for COs echoed those of the Colonial era: a CO had to find a substitute or pay a commutation fee, often nearly a year's wages.

Conscientious Objection during World War I

In Britain at World War I, when conscription was instituted in 1916, sixteen thousand registered as conscientious objectors. Petitioners for CO status were regularly rejected by the hostile local tribunals and sent to jail. Thirty were sentenced to death, though secretly the sentences were countermanded. Fifty were sent to France in an effort to put them into combat and make them subject to a firing squad for disobeying orders. Harsh measures, such as isolation in prison, bread and water, "crucifixion"—being tied up, arms spread, tilted forward for hours at a time—failed to stop the movement of COs. Fourteen New Zealand COs were shipped to England and then to France, in an unsuccessful effort to force them into submission. One of them, Mark Briggs, was tied with a cable and dragged a mile until his clothes were torn off and his body was bleeding. Every founding member of the No-Conscription Fellowship was imprisoned, as was every editor of their newsletter, *The Tribunal*. The campaign of abuse was mitigated and over four thousand served in "work of national importance." "Conchies," some of whom had been imprisoned and released several times in a "cat and mouse" pattern, worked at various tasks, including moving granite stones for no clear purpose.

In the United States during World War I, the Selective Draft Act of 1917 mimicked some elements of the just-enacted law in Britain. The lobbying of the National Service Association, which in 1913 had established training camps for prospective officers, sought a tough law without consideration for COs.

Efforts to stem the recognition of conscientious objectors were widespread. The Molokans, a pacifist sect that fled Russia to the western United States, were particularly subject to persecution, for they were not willing to participate in conscription, holding worship services outside the places of registration. They were among the five hundred men imprisoned for their beliefs in opposition to participation in war. The Hutterites, like the Mennonites, an Anabaptist sect dating from 1524, were also subject to persecution. Prejudice against their German speech and their communal lifestyle were contributing factors and led many colonies to flee from the Dakotas and Montana to safety in Canada. Two Hofer brothers and Jacob Wipf were imprisoned at Alcatraz. They refused to wear a military uniform and were denied other clothing. Hosed down in freezing weather, they contracted pneumonia, and they were shipped to Ft. Leavenworth. The two Hofers died. Their bodies were returned to their families, and when the coffin of one was opened he was dressed in the uniform that he had refused to wear in life.

Among the absolutists, 142 were sentenced to life imprisonment, and 17 to death, though their sentences were commuted. Seventeen died in prison from other causes. The last CO from World War I was released in 1934. When COs refused to cooperate in compulsory work programs in prison, during the times that other prisoners were at work they were hung by their thumbs until their toes barely touched the floor.

Mennonite leaders trustingly discussed with the secretary of war, Newton B. Baker, plans to conscript Mennonite men into the military and then grant them CO status, while his deputy, Judge Advocate General Crowder, was planning ways to force them to abandon their beliefs to get them to serve in the regular military.

Crowder had been the principal author of the Selective Service Act, with encouragement from the National Service Association. The act provided that members "of any well-recognized religious sects or organization whose existing creed or religious principles forbid its members to participate in war in any form" shall not be compelled to serve in any of the forces herein, except none shall be "exempted from service in any capacity the President shall declare to be noncombatant." Several denominations made special efforts to assert conscientious objector beliefs in order to protect the COs in their midst.

Of the 56,830 conscientious objector claims approved by local boards, only 3,989 persisted in their beliefs so that their CO status was sustained by the military after induction. About half were found unfit for service, but 16,000 were pressured into abandoning their position after induction. The FBI framed the leaders of the Church of God in Christ, a black denomination then mostly confined to the deep South and southern California. The church taught a form of pacifism on biblical grounds that would have allowed adherents to claim conscientious objector status under the Selective Service Act. The government, claiming they were agents of the kaiser, prosecuted and jailed the leaders. In the South, the draft board authority gave local leaders new and federal powers to control blacks in their community through manipulating their deferment.

After much delay, provisions for assignment of COs in "work of national importance" were determined by President Wilson. Some thirteen hundred were furloughed to farm work. Only in the last four months of the war were one hundred men allowed to work in Quaker war relief work in France. When the American Friends Service Committee was founded to provide service opportunities for COs, Quakers had hoped it would provide a principal vehicle for civilian service for COs. At World War II the pattern of alternative service "under civilian direction" "in lieu of military service" was put in place at last, and it has become the recognized international standard.

Conscientious Objection during World War II

In Great Britain, the government became much more tolerant of COs during World War II. Over 60,000 men and women claimed CO status. Only 1,050 were court martialed. Some were court martialed several times, however. Isolated instances of brutality still occurred. But, in the midst of a war for survival, even selective objectors were allowed by some tribunals. COs did relief work, and even a few absolutists did not do anything officially to aid in the war.

In 1940, the U.S. government enacted conscription under the Burke-Wadsworth Act, which provided for civilian-controlled alternative service in Civilian Public Service camps and, eventually, in detached service in mental hospitals and schools for the mentally retarded. After three years of lobbying, the statute was considerably modified from the World War I version. The qualification for conscientious objection was changed to a general definition of religious objection to participation in all wars. Against the testimony of religious leaders who favored a broad conscience-based test as existed in Britain, the Senate committee added the com-

promise requirement worked out by leading Friends that conscientious objection must be based on "religious training and belief." Thus the Congress believed it had continued the World War I restrictions on conscientious objectors without the constitutional infirmities of an establishment of particular religions.

The number of COs in the United States during World War II is not accurately determinable. Perhaps 25,000 to 50,000 were noncombatants in the military. Over 12,000 served in the civilian public service camps. The number of claims made is not determinable, since Selective Service did not keep centralized records. (The same records problem persisted through the Vietnam era.) Perhaps as many as 100,000 claimed CO status. Six thousand went to prison as COs, 5,000 of whom were Jehovah's Witnesses. Nine seminarians out of twenty-one who had declared their opposition to registration on October 16, 1940, publicly refused and within a month were in Danbury prison for a year.

The treatment of COs during the war was much better than it had been during World War I. Ostracism and vilification were the extent of public reactions. The churches worked together to develop a program for COs that they partially financed. Mennonites contributed over $5 million of the $8 million to finance it. The relative success of the new program of civilian service became a pattern for international standards.

Conscientious Objection since World War II

In 1948, conscription was revived as the Universal Military Training and Service Act, with the addition of a requirement that conscientious objectors had to believe in a Supreme Being. At first there was no service requirement for COs. The act was amended in 1950 to provide that COs classified as 1–Ws would serve in individualized settings in alternative service.

Conscription was delayed during the Korean War, for the Department of Defense relied at first on reservists. When conscription of COs began again, as many COs (12,000) were placed in alternative service as there had been during World War II, out of a much smaller number of registrants. Conscription and CO classification and placement continued at very low levels and with general acceptance until the war in Vietnam.

During the Vietnam era, at least 171,000 claims for conscientious objector classification were made, and more than half were granted.

The number of claims may be estimated to have been considerably greater since local board records were kept independently, and the Selective Service did not have a central record-keeping system except as classifications were actually made. From extreme hostility to COs in the early stages of the twelve-year conflict, the public support for COs shifted until in 1972 more CO claims were granted than there were inductees.

Supporters of COs led the way in organizing draft counseling programs, at first through campus ministry centers and then in community-based programs often under church sponsorship. National organizations such as the National Interreligious Service Board for Conscientious Objectors (previously known as the National Service Board for Religious Objectors), the Central Committee for Conscientious Objectors, which was spun off from NSBRO in 1948, and AFSC carried out programs of training and support for local attorneys and counselors. New programs for alternative service were initiated to accommodate the large number of COs that Selective Service was unable to place. A national Interfaith Committee on Draft and Military Counseling coordinated work among the agencies.

A separate organization of National Black Draft Counselors was founded to deal with the special problems of discriminatory treatment, including the allocation of resources. Although individual black COs, such as Bayard Rustin during World War II, are notable in other periods, for the first time African-American COs emerged as a significant group with their own understanding, which included recognition of the racist pattern of war. The leadership of Martin Luther King, Jr., in opposing the war in Vietnam was matched among younger COs by the appeal of the Student Nonviolent Coordinating Committee.

After draft registration was restored in 1980, virtually all of the public resisters were conscientious objectors. Against the backdrop of nuclear war protest in the early 1980s, conscientious objection was a thoughtful position of many participants in that movement. The decade proved to be a time of conscientization for young people all over the world.

When the war in the Persian Gulf developed in late 1990, the CO counseling agencies were overwhelmed with requests for assistance. Despite assurances that a draft was not likely, attorneys and peace activists, many of whom had been active at the end of the Vietnam era, began training programs again. The requests for assistance from emerging COs in the armed forces were similarly unprecedented. In the short period of three months, as many counseling cases were begun as would previously have been initiated over the course of several years, or in a full year during the Vietnam era. The significant number of cases of racial minority Marines, whose consciences were stimulated by the elements of Third World oppression, showed a shift from the usual pattern of CO claims in the military. Though commanders sought to limit the number of CO claims and sought to block their fair processing, many of the unfair convictions have been reversed. Pentagon officials now recognize a need to develop skilled counseling and a fairer procedure to protect the rights of COs.

L. William Yolton

References

Boyle, Beth, ed. *Words of Conscience: Religious Statements on Conscientious Objection.* 10th ed. Washington, D.C.: National Interreligious Service Board for Conscientious Objection, 1982.

Keim, Albert N., and Grant M. Stoltzfus. *The Politics of Conscience: The Historic Peace Churches and America at War, 1917–1955.* Scottsdale, Pa.: Herald, 1988.

Moorhead, Caroline. *Troublesome People: The Warriors of Pacifism.* Bethesda, Md.: Adler and Adler, 1987.

Moskos, Charles C., and John Whiteclay Chambers II, eds. *The New Conscientious Objection: From Sacred to Secular Resistance.* New York: Oxford University Press, 1993.

Sibley, Mulford Q., and Philip E. Jacob. *Conscription of Conscience: The American State and Conscientious Objector, 1940–1947.* Ithaca, N.Y.: Cornell University Press, 1952.

See also JAGERSTATTER, FRANZ; NONVIOLENCE, PRINCIPLED; PACIFISM; VIETNAM WAR OPPOSITION; WAR TAX RESISTANCE

Constructive Program

Effort by Mohandas K. Gandhi to apply the principles of satyagraha to the process of concrete social change. Satyagraha, which for Gandhi meant "the pursuit of truth," grew out of Gandhi's belief that a nonviolent movement

The spinning wheel symbolized Gandhi's "constructive program." (Photo taken in 1946 by Life *photographer Margaret Bourke-White.) AP/Wide World Photos.*

should do more than simply protest an injustice. Satyagraha was conceived as a people's movement that would empower and inspire people to work for social change and for the nonviolent resolution of social conflicts.

Gandhi believed that if people in a free society wished to enjoy rights they must also shoulder responsibilities. Building a cohesive society, Gandhi felt, required the active involvement of the people through their daily lives. Simply electing governments and expecting them to take care of all problems was unrealistic, in his view. Thus, satyagraha, which was a means to liberate both the individual and the nation, also required a "constructive program" by which change was implemented by individuals and local communities in ways designed to change individual attitudes as well as social structures.

Gandhi argued that people practice two forms of violence—passive and physical. Pas-

sive violence results in dissatisfaction and anger and ultimately explodes into physical violence. In the broadest sense, he would say that the absence of war does not mean there is peace. It was Gandhi's concern about the consequences of individual and collective "passive" violence that encouraged his search for a "people's solution" to this "people's problem." The constructive program, therefore, reflected the essence of satyagraha; getting people involved in their own search for solutions helped make them more committed, caring, and concerned for the larger society and helped them overcome the effects of passive violence.

The breadth of Gandhi's concept of satyagraha offered many opportunities for people to be involved in different aspects of their own liberation struggle. Consequently, the overall satyagraha campaign in India was greatly diversified into programs dealing with village-level education, health, and hygiene, overcoming divisions among religious communities, improving the condition of women, and promoting economic self-reliance.

Most other leaders in the Indian independence campaign felt Gandhi was dissipating his own energy and that of the people by developing programs which, they argued, could wait until after independence from British rule had been achieved. Gandhi, however, was convinced that an Indian government could be as ineffective in solving these social problems as was the British administration. This reflected his view, embodied in satyagraha, that *swaraj,* or self-rule, meant liberation in every sense of the word, not simply political emancipation.

Aspects of the constructive program, which Gandhi articulated most clearly in a pamphlet by the same name published in 1941, included *swadeshi,* or the home production movement, the production of *khadi* (home-spun cloth), and the broader *khaddar* movement of hand spinning and hand weaving, the creation of other village-level industries that would provide self-sufficiency, abolition of untouchability in Hindu society, and improved education for adults as well as for children.

Each of these activities served Indian independence in ways that were, for Gandhi, both highly personal and broadly collective, and that were aimed at spiritual as well as social transformation. For example, the *khaddar* movement provided work and livelihood for numerous individuals as handspun thread was exchanged for handwoven cloth and garments. The spinning wheel and the adoption of Indian dress (in place of Western attire) provided powerful collective symbols that forged a common identity. Finally, the replacement of British textiles with Indian materials exerted economic pressure on the British administration. In a similar vein, Gandhi recognized that the invidious prejudices of caste could be overcome only by working directly with those in need, especially those deemed "untouchables," rather than by lecturing them on how they should change their behavior. In this way the erosion of divisive attitudes among individuals would contribute to improvement in the material conditions for many.

Arun Gandhi

References

Gandhi, Mohandas K. "The Constructive Programme: Its Meaning and Place." In *The Collected Works of Mahatma Gandhi,* vol. 75. New Delhi: Publication Division, Ministry of Information and Broadcasting, 1979.

See also GANDHI, MOHANDAS KARAMCHAND; INDIAN NATIONAL MOVEMENT; SATYAGRAHA

Corrigan, Mairead (b. 1944); Williams, Betty (b. 1943)

Founders of the Community of the Peace People in Northern Ireland, in 1976, an interdenominational group seeking an end to the violence used by both sides in the conflict. The women were awarded the 1976 Nobel Prize for Peace in 1977, the prize committee having delayed presenting the honor to any individual or group in 1976. Corrigan and Williams were thrust together by an automobile accident in August 1976 that gravely injured Corrigan's sister, Anne Maguire, and three of Maguire's children. Following a shoot-out, British soldiers that had been pursuing Irish Republican Army gunmen shot dead the driver of their car, which then went out of control and smashed the Maguire family against an iron railing.

Mairead Corrigan grew up in a Catholic home, fearing both the British soldiers and the Irish Republican Army. She never considered herself a revolutionary, and she watched the increasing violence in her community with dismay. She sympathized with the British-held political prisoners of both sides, whom she visited in her work with the Legion of Mary, a Catholic welfare organization. However, she felt that the acts of violence of which they were accused were not consistent with the way of Christ, and she told them so. Interviewed the evening after her family's tragedy, she declared, "It's not violence that people want. Only 1 percent of the people in this province want this slaughter." With courage, she condemned those who encouraged young people to join the paramilitary groups.

Betty Williams had witnessed the accident, and she immediately set about walking the streets of her neighborhood, collecting signatures to a petition demanding peace and a stop to the violence. In two days she announced over television that she had six thousand signatures. She asked all women, both Protestant and Catholic, to help "rid our community of this riffraff." Williams was the daughter of a Catholic mother and a Protestant father; her maternal grandmother was a Polish Jew. She attended Catholic schools and married a non-Catholic.

She had originally sympathized with the Northern Irish revolutionaries, but came to believe that violence only breeds violence and makes victims of the innocent. In 1972, she joined a movement started by a Protestant clergyman to try to end the violence.

Corrigan joined Williams in leading a peace march of ten thousand women to the new graves of the Maguire children. Protestants marched with Catholics and persisted in the face of physical assaults by IRA supporters. The next week, thirty-five thousand marched from a Catholic to a Protestant area of Belfast. With encouragement from Ciaran McKeown, a newspaper reporter, Corrigan and Williams formed the Community of the Peace People.

The movement captured the imagination of the world and was given wide publicity. A campaign by newspapers and civic organizations in Norway, where it was too late for a nomination for the Peace Prize, raised $340,000. The Peace People used the contributions to arrange nonsectarian activities, to repair damaged factories and schools, and to make loans for small businesses. In accepting the 1976 prize in 1977, Williams spoke of the role of women in the pursuit of peace: "The voice of women has a special role and a special soul-force in the struggle for a nonviolent world. We do not wish to replace religious sectarianism, or ideological division with sexism or any kind of militant feminism. But we do believe . . . that women have a leading role to play in this great struggle." She called on women everywhere to encourage men to have the courage to say no to war.

Irwin Abrams

References

Deutsch, Richard. *Mairead Corrigan, Betty Williams*. New York: Woodberry, 1977.
McKeown, Ciaran. *The Passion of Peace.* Belfast: Blackstaff, 1984.

See also IRA HUNGER STRIKES, 1980–1981; NOBEL PEACE PRIZE; NORTHERN IRELAND CIVIL RIGHTS ASSOCIATION; PEACE PEOPLE, COMMUNITY OF THE; WOMEN AND NONVIOLENT ACTION IN THE UNITED STATES SINCE 1950

Coups d'état

A coup d'état is a rapid seizure of physical and political control of the state apparatus by the illegal action of a conspiratorial group backed by the threat or use of violence. The previous government is deposed and the coup group or its appointees rapidly occupy the centers of command, decision making, and administration. Coups are one of the principal means by which governments are changed. Coups have overthrown constitutional democratic governments, halted movements toward greater democracy, and imposed new dictatorships. Coups may precipitate civil wars and other internal or international crises.

Coups are most often conducted by a critical part of the military forces, acting alone or in alliance with political cliques, intelligence organizations (domestic or foreign), or police forces. Sometimes coups have been usurpations by an established president or prime minister. Coups also have been conducted by a dictatorial political party, with or without its own paramilitary forces. Coups may also be initiated by a section of the ruling elite backed by other groups.

If a coup is to succeed it is important that nonparticipants in the coup be supportive, remain passive, or be made ineffective. One prerequisite of a successful coup is that the putschists' organizational and repressive forces be believed to be more powerful than the other institutions and forces of the society. These other sectors of the society, then, will often readily capitulate in the face of the seemingly overwhelming forces supporting the coup. They may have active sympathy for the putschists, or simply not know what to do in opposition.

In some countries a coup of internal origin appears unthinkable, as in Norway and Switzerland, for example, because democratic constitutional procedures to change governments exist and are respected, and the groups capable of conducting a coup—such as the army—respect the limits on their authority. Also, where the independent civil, nongovernmental institutions of the society are strong, and military institutions and antidemocratic political parties are comparatively weaker, a coup is not likely to occur.

In many constitutional democracies it has been assumed that if the constitution and laws prohibit coups d'état, then the democracy is safe. That is demonstrably not true, as the examples of Greece in 1967, Chile in 1973, and Argentina in 1976 illustrate. A lack of preparations for anticoup defense has left the prospects for a lasting democratic system very doubtful in many countries, especially in those with a history of coups.

However, despite often disadvantageous conditions, popular resistance has at times been able to block these illegal attempts to seize state power. The defeat of the attempted hardline takeover in the former Soviet Union in August 1991 is one recent case of mass noncooperation against a coup. The methods used included large demonstrations at the Soviet parliament building, blocking streets with vehicles, publication of banned newspapers, defiant radio and television broadcasts, appeals to troops to disobey the putschists, several cases of entire military units deserting to the defenders, and defiance by city and republic governments. Prominent earlier cases of successful anticoup defense occurred in Germany in 1920 against the Kapp Putsch (which threatened the new Weimar Republic) and in France in 1961 against the Algiers generals' revolt (which aimed to keep Algeria French by ousting the de Gaulle–Debré government).

In the German case, the legal government called for obedience to it only and for the provinces to refuse all cooperation with the putschists. A workers' general strike was matched with large-scale noncooperation by civil servants and conservative government bureaucrats. Prominent persons refused to accept ministerial posts. The police joined in demanding that the putschists step down.

In the French case, political parties and trade unions held massive demonstrations and short general strikes. President Charles de Gaulle (by radio) urged people to defy and disobey the rebels. High army officers in Algeria found that their troops were disobeying them in support of the legal government, and four days later the parachute regiment that had seized the city of Algiers withdrew, signaling the collapse of the coup.

Only occasionally, as during the 1991 coup in the Soviet Union, has serious supportive international diplomatic and economic action been threatened or taken.

Historical examples therefore exist which suggest that an effective defense against coups d'état is possible. The essence of such a policy appears to be twofold. First, those who are conducting a coup must be denied all legitimacy. Second, they must be denied all cooperation—no one in the government or in the population should assist or obey them in any way. If both legitimacy and cooperation are denied, the coup may die of political starvation.

The use of nonviolent struggle in anticoup defense avoids fighting the putschists with military weapons, with which the usurpers usually have the advantage. The nonviolent technique also, as in the past examples, maximizes the power of the defenders, vastly increases the possible number of resisters compared with those able and willing to use violence, and, very importantly, may help to undermine the morale and reliability of the putschists' soldiers.

The methods of nonviolent struggle—such as strikes, boycotts, types of political noncooperation, and mutiny—may be the most effective means to defeat attempted coups if they are applied as components of a comprehensive, carefully chosen strategy. Adherents of this approach also stress that it is important to give primary responsibility to those methods that directly counter the putschists' initial objectives. In particular, action should (1) show repudiation of the putschists' claims to legitimacy; (2) block their taking control of the political machinery of the state (as by noncooperation of civil servants, police, military forces, and lower levels of government); (3) demonstrate the population's rejection of the coup and its noncooperation and disobedience against it; (4) block the putschists' efforts to control the means of communication and instead maintain this through various means including print media and telecommunications; and (5) defy the putschists' efforts to neutralize or control the independent institutions of the society. It follows that if the means of defense cited here can be applied massively and effectively to achieve these aims, the coup can only collapse.

The intended cumulative impact of such institutional noncooperation is to break the link between the coup leaders' physical control of the government facilities and the political control of the state, thus preventing them from controlling both the government and the society as a whole. The putschists are expected to apply brutal repression when confronted with such resistance (though it has often been and is most likely to be much less severe than in the case of violent resistance). The putschists may also deliberately seek to provoke the resisters to use violence in order to create the appearance that violent repression is justified to crush the resistance.

Success in using nonviolent struggle in anticoup defense has depended on several key factors. These include, among others, the spirit of resistance, the solidarity of the defending population, the strength of the defending society, the ability of the people to maintain resistance and nonviolent discipline, the strengths and weaknesses of the putschists, the choice of the putschists' strategy of attack, and the wisdom of the defense strategies.

Well-prepared defense capacities utilizing nonviolent struggle against coups d'état are currently being studied and may be implemented with the expectation that they can constitute a formidable deterrent against would-be putschists. When a society is known to have a well-prepared anticoup defense, would-be usurpers anticipating at best a very hard struggle and at worst an ignominious defeat may well never even attempt a coup.

The objective of such a defense policy against coups d'état is to preserve constitutional government by blocking the imposition of viable government by the putschists, making the attacked society unrulable by the attackers, and enabling the population to maintain control and self-direction of their society even when under attack. The responsibility for this preservation of constitutional government thus rests with the whole population.

Gene Sharp

References

Finer, Samuel E. *Man on Horseback: The Role of the Military in Politics.* London: Pall Mall, 1967; New York: Praeger, 1967.

Goodspeed, Donald J. *The Conspirators: A Study in the Coup d'Etat.* Toronto and London: Macmillan, 1962; New York: St. Martin's, 1962.

Sharp, Gene, Bruce Jenkins, and Charles Norchi. *Human Rights and Coups d'Etat* (pamphlet). Occasional Paper no. 2. New York: International League for Human Rights, 1994.

See also ALGERIA, FRENCH GENERALS' REVOLT OF 1961; CIVILIAN-BASED DEFENSE; KAPP PUTSCH

Czechoslovakia, 1968 Resistance Movement

Massive popular nonviolent resistance to occupation by "allied socialist forces" of the Soviet Union, Bulgaria, Poland, East Germany, and Hungary to put an end to the Czechoslovak reform communist movement known as the Prague Spring.

The Prague Spring of 1968 provided a prototype for perestroika and glasnost policies undertaken by former Soviet President Mikhail Gorbachev, leading to the fall of the Berlin Wall, the Czechoslovak "velvet revolution" in November 1989, and the collapse of the Soviet Union itself in December 1991. The earlier Czech and Slovak party reformers, however, were two decades ahead of their time in attempting to overhaul Soviet-style socialism. Their efforts to transform Czechoslovak communism so as to adjust to the scientific, technical, and information revolution of the twentieth century backfired. The Prague Spring's search for "socialism with a human face" became a long, hot summer. On August 21 the "allied socialist troops" marched into Czechoslovakia to prevent what their orthodox communist leaders viewed as "counterrevolution."

With regard to nonviolent struggle, the issue is not the substance of the Prague Spring so much as the reaction of the Czechoslovak party and society when confronted with socialist soldiers sent by Moscow and allied socialist governments. Over the course of roughly eight months from the military intervention in August 1968 to April 1969, when Gustav Husák replaced Alexander Dubček as head of the Czechoslovak Communist Party (KSC), the resistance moved through two distinct phases. The first phase, which lasted only a week, demonstrated the potential power of nonviolent struggle. The longer second phase suggests the difficulty of maintaining popular struggle when strategies and goals become incompatible.

Initial Reactions (August 21–28, 1968)

This period is one of the most dramatic success stories of collective nonviolent resistance in the twentieth century. At 2 A.M., August 21, the KSC party presidium issued a proclamation declaring the occupation of Czechoslovakia illegal, contrary to socialist principles, and a violation of international law. It ordered the army, state security, and militia not to use force to defend the country. It called upon citizens to remain calm. Although instructed not to resist the invading armies, citizens were directed to refuse to obey orders other than those of the legitimate Czechoslovak authorities and institutions. The party presidium emphasized that party and government leaders had no advance knowledge of the invasion and that all leading officials would remain on the job. Thus it simultaneously signaled other levels of government and bureaucracy to follow the top leadership's example while reassuring people that the government was not collaborating with the occupation forces.

Czechoslovak state radio, which was controlled by supporters of reform, broadcast the presidium message to the people. These broadcasts continually warned the population to avoid provocations and clashes and to resist all exercise of illegal authority. Statements of support for the proclamation poured in from all around the country. Radio workers refused to spread propaganda of the occupying forces and told their listeners to obey only "legal" Radio Czechoslovakia.

This triggered a demonstration effect with all intermediate levels of authority joining the resistance to occupation. The resulting organizational and individual bandwagon made would-be collaborators' actions illegitimate in the eyes of friends and colleagues. Thus, before the invading troops reached Prague, the population had become committed to noncooperation. Those who resisted felt neither isolated nor helpless.

Street signs went down. Commanders of the invading forces could not find easily identifiable "counterrevolutionaries," the "healthy forces" that they had been told had invited them, or much of anything else. An old woman in front of Radio Czechoslovakia told them it was a sewing machine factory. Whether or not the story is apocryphal, these troops were sufficiently disoriented to allow Czechoslovak radio to go underground and stay on the air, reportedly aided by ministries of interior and defense. This media link between the party and the people was essential to building morale, solidarity, and national cohesiveness. Soon underground presses appeared, further disseminating news from Czechoslovak radio. In the tradition of World War II, these presses provided for local participation. Meanwhile, the walls and sidewalks of Prague became a protest gallery of political art.

Although the invading troops kidnaped the Czechoslovak party and government leadership and moved them to Moscow, their chosen leader of a transitional government, seventy-three-year-old hero of the Soviet Union, Ludvik Svoboda, refused to cooperate. On August 22, the Fourteenth Extraordinary Party Congress took place in a Prague factory whereupon some twelve hundred delegates condemned the occupation. This established the KSC's "leading role" and legitimate authority despite the fact that Dubček and other top party leaders were

prisoners in Moscow. A massive one-hour protest strike on August 23 demonstrated the potential power of the resistance to bring the country to an economic standstill.

By August 28 the Czechoslovak resistance won the return of the reform leadership to Prague. There was a promise of troop removal and a promise to continue the reforms begun in January 1968. Return of the leadership was a genuine victory. But the promises proved to be illusions.

Erosion of Resistance at the Top (August 28, 1968–April 17, 1969)

Before being returned from Moscow, the Czechoslovak leadership signed an agreement declaring the Fourteenth Extraordinary Congress invalid. The document linked removal of Soviet troops to an ambiguously defined "normalization," thereby allowing a return to Soviet meddling in Czechoslovak domestic political choices.

Nonetheless, the leaders who signed the Moscow document genuinely believed that it left room to continue reforms, even as it satisfied the Soviet need to legitimate any scaling back of what the Kremlin saw as the most dangerous aspects of the Prague Spring. The agreement pledged to stand against "anti-socialist forces" and to get Czechoslovak news media under control. With regard to the second point, the name of the game was implementation, and, aside from pleas for self-censorship, the press remained remarkably free throughout 1968.

Popular resistance continued with a massive student strike opposing the October 16, 1968, treaty legalizing Soviet troops on Czechoslovak territory and continued censorship. Some sixty thousand students struck for almost a week in support of the reform action program. They were supported by workers in surrounding factories and fed by local contributions. The Metal Workers Union signed a formal agreement with the Union of Students to oppose the policy of continual concessions to outside pressure.

Although the November party plenum did criticize "antisocialist forces," Dubček continued to defend the main themes of reform. He refused to concede that the situation in Czechoslovakia was "counterrevolutionary" or to support the legitimacy of Soviet occupation. When twenty-one-year-old Jan Palach burned himself to death in front of the National Museum demanding the abolition of censorship and the end of the Soviet-published occupation newspaper, *Zpravy*, at least two government ministers and many prominent reform leaders joined the hundreds of thousands who paid their respects at his funeral parade on January 25, 1969. Soon there were three more fiery suicides, in Pilsen, Bruno, and Prague, that were less well known because the government deliberately attempted to prevent the news from spreading.

By spring of 1969 Czechoslovak–Soviet relations were in a tense holding pattern. Without paying a cost that Soviet leaders were unwilling to pay, Moscow could not impose its own version of normalization. At the same time the Dubček regime could not gain popular support for a policy of compromise acceptable to the Kremlin that would lead to the removal of Soviet troops.

In the jubilant celebration that followed the Czechoslovak ice hockey victory against the Soviets in Stockholm, March 21 and 28, 1969, anti-Soviet vandalism became the excuse for breaking the stalemate. An estimated 150,000 people went into the streets after the second four-to-three victory. Police agents under the direction of the Czechoslovak minister of interior had conveniently piled paving stones in front of the Soviet Aeroflot office on Wenceslas Square. Whether or not demonstrators joined the security agents throwing rocks through Aeroflot windows, the result was the same.

This was the precipitating incident for Soviet demands that the Dubček government call out the Czechoslovak army followed by a visit from the Soviet defense minister, Marshal Andrei A. Grechko, and V. S. Semyonov, Soviet deputy foreign minister in charge of military affairs. Another eight thousand Soviet troops moved into Czechoslovakia. There was a threat that in case of further demonstrations, Soviet troops would use their own weapons around their garrisons. In short, Moscow turned up the political and military heat in order to get rid of Dubček and fatally wound reform forces.

Yet in reality it was far more important that party reformers themselves were deeply split. As Dubček acknowledged in his autobiography, the pro-reform group was disintegrating, and his own support had dwindled to the point where it "hinged on one or two votes." After the ice hockey incident, Dubček saw his resignation as a means to avoid mass repression. He maneuvered unsuccessfully to prevent Gustav Husák from taking over as head of the party. That failure meant that Moscow defined normalization and began to rewrite the history of the Prague Spring.

As Karel Kosik had predicted, Soviet dictate prescribed the formulas for capitulation. It was only a matter of time before Slovaks and Czechs who wanted to remain in the room at the top began to play the Soviet game and search for "counterrevolutionary" scapegoats to secure their own positions. Small wonder that twenty years later Husák was deeply threatened by the "profound connection" that Dubček and some of Gorbachev's advisers saw between Soviet perestroika and the Prague Spring.

The Balance Sheet

The two stages of nonviolent struggle of the Czechoslovak resistance to Soviet occupation and abortion of the Prague Spring reform agendas contain important differences. First, in terms of mobilization of the resistance movement, Eidlin emphasizes the importance of the fact that people were asked to do what they normally did, to go about their business and to resist outside authority. This worked because it was grounded in habit and normal social interaction. During this heady week, there was a limited goal of bringing back the kidnaped reform leadership. There was solidarity between the party leaders in Prague and the population.

During the second stage, the task became more complex and the goals of keeping the reform on track and getting rid of Soviet troops became mutually incompatible. If the party had retained its cohesion, then perhaps a significant amount of reform could have continued in the shadow of Moscow's military presence, as it eventually did in Hungary after 1956. However, the reformers who were willing to dump Dubček for Husák in 1969 lost on both counts—Czechoslovakia would get neither political reform nor the removal of the Soviet troops that Husák saw as his insurance.

Much of the popular resistance movement went underground into a form of "inner emigration" in which the resisters of 1968 turned to surviving the long winter of discontent, helping families of those who were in prison or unemployed, and creating a counterculture. Other opposition figures focused on opportunities provided by the 1975 Helsinki Agreements on Human Rights. These signers of the Charter of 1977—including the 1994 president of the Czech Republic, Václav Havel—in turn became a nucleus for the "velvet revolution"

C

that set Czechoslovakia on the road to political democracy and a market economy in 1989.

Yet in the post–cold war Europe there was no place for reform communism with or without a human face. Instead defenders of the nation took advantage of the multiparty political environment to open the Pandora's box of Czech and Slovak ethnonational political grievances and economic conflict that led to dissolution of seven decades of Czechoslovak federation in January 1993.

Robin Alison Remington

References

Dubček, Alexander. *Hope Dies Last: The Autobiography of Alexander Dubček*. Edited and translated by Jiri Hochman. New York: Kodansha, 1993.

———. Interview in *L'Unita* (Rome), January 10, 1988.

Eidlin, Fred H. *The Logic of Normalization: The Soviet Intervention in Czechoslovakia of 21 August 1968 and the Czechoslovak Response*. New York: Columbia University Press, 1980.

Golan, Galia. *Reform Rule in Czechoslovakia: The Dubček Era 1968–1969*. Cambridge: Cambridge University Press, 1973.

Littell, Robert, ed. *The Czech Black Book: An Eyewitness, Documented Account of the Invasion of Czechoslovakia*. New York: Frederick A. Praeger, 1969.

Remington, Robin Alison. *Winter in Prague: Documents on Czechoslovak Communism in Crisis*. Cambridge: MIT Press, 1969.

See also CHARTER 77; CIVILIAN-BASED DEFENSE; DUBČEK, ALEXANDER; HAVEL, VÁCLAV; KOSOVA, ALBANIAN NATIONAL MOVEMENT; REVOLUTIONS OF 1989; RUHRKAMPF; SOLIDARITY (POLAND); SUICIDE, PROTEST

D

Dalai Lama XIV
See Bstan-dzin-rgya-mtsho, Dalai Lama XIV

Day, Dorothy (1897–1980)
Pacifist activist, journalist, and co-founder of the Catholic Worker movement, born in Brooklyn, New York, on November 8, 1897, and died in New York City on November 29, 1980.

Born into a lower-middle-class family, Day grew up in New York, Oakland, and Chicago. In 1914, she entered the University of Illinois, where she joined the Socialist Party. She left the university after two years and returned to New York City to pursue a career in journalism. Taking up residence in the immigrant quarter of the Lower East Side, Day worked for several years as a reporter for socialist newspapers and journals. Day became involved in the women's suffrage movement and in 1917 joined in picketing the White House. When she was arrested and imprisoned, she joined other women activists in a hunger strike.

For a time, Day was a part of New York City's sophisticated "Village set" and a close companion of playwright Eugene O'Neill. She eventually became disaffected with this milieu and left to work at a succession of jobs in New York and Chicago. In 1924 she wrote and published a novel, *The Eleventh Virgin,* and bought a house on Staten Island. There, Day entered into a common-law marriage with an atheistic anarchist and, in 1926, gave birth to a daughter, Tamar. Having the baby baptized a Catholic marked both the end of her marriage and the beginning of her commitment to Catholicism.

In December 1932, Day met Peter Maurin, a French peasant who advocated Catholic populism, voluntary poverty, and the transition of society to a functional anarchy of small units. Day, inspired by Maurin's vision, responded by starting a newspaper that would address social issues from a progressive Catholic perspective. The first issue of the *Catholic Worker* was distributed on May 1, 1933, at a Communist rally in New York City. Within two years, the circulation had grown to 150,000.

The Catholic Worker became a movement of lay people, with farming communes and Houses of Hospitality opening around the country. During this time, Day traveled, lectured, and wrote, reporting frequently on labor union activities.

Day articulated the Worker's adherence to pacifism, a position she found inherent in the commandments of Jesus. In 1936, with the outbreak of the civil war in Spain, and later, with the beginnings of World War II, Day's pacifist writings resulted in thousands of canceled subscriptions and nearly split the movement in two. In 1939, in response to Hitler's regime, she helped found the Committee of Catholics to Fight Anti-Semitism. In the 1950s, Day and other members of the Catholic Worker movement protested against preparations for nuclear war by fasting, advocating tax resistance, occupying missile bases, and refusing to cooperate with compulsory civil defense drills. Day was repeatedly imprisoned for her part in civil disobedience actions. In 1952, she published an autobiography, *The Long Loneliness.* Late in her life, Day traveled extensively, spreading the news of the Catholic Worker movement in Cuba, Mexico, England, Italy, the Soviet Union, and India. Her last arrest, in 1973 when she was seventy-five, was on a United Farm Workers'

Dorothy Day, 1960. Photo © Diana Davies.

picket line in California in the nonviolent struggle led by Cesar Chavez.

Pam McAllister

References
Ellsberg, Robert, ed. *By Little and By Little: The Selected Writings of Dorothy Day.* New York: Alfred A. Knopf, 1983.

See also CATHOLIC WORKER MOVEMENT; NONVIOLENCE, PRINCIPLED; PACIFISM

de Ligt, Barthélemy (Bart) (1883–1938)

Dutch theorist of nonviolent action and radical antimilitarist. Born on July 17, 1883, in Schalkwijk, the Netherlands, Bart de Ligt studied theology (1903–1909) and became a pastor. In 1909, he joined the Union of Christian Socialists and became its leading member over the next decade, speaking out against capitalism, militarism, and colonialism, and sharply criticizing the state, the church, and the monarchy. He was imprisoned in 1915 and 1921 for his antimilitarist activities, which contributed greatly to passage of the first Dutch law on conscientious objection to military service in 1923. From Geneva, where he had moved in 1925, he played a central role in coordinating and strengthening the antimilitarist movement, both in the Netherlands and internationally. He was in constant communication with the leading figures of the radical peace movement and addressed a series of open letters to Mohandas Gandhi (1928–1929), expressing criticism of Gandhi's abandonment of principled pacifism on several occasions.

De Ligt rejected the use of violence in the struggle against capitalism and militarism on both ethical and pragmatic grounds, arguing instead for the possibility and greater effectiveness of nonviolent struggle. His whole life and work was characterized by efforts to demonstrate (in theory, and in history) that true revolution necessitated revolutionary (that is, nonviolent) methods of struggle; "the more violence, the less revolution" is one of his most often quoted phrases. Furthermore, it also required the transformation not merely of social structures and institutions but also of individual beliefs and attitudes. Influenced by Asian philosophies, he developed a "cosmic consciousness" that expressed a deeply felt sympathy with all of creation.

De Ligt was the first to document the universality, in time and space, of nonviolent action (especially to combat war). He contends that nonviolent struggle extends into every branch of human civilization and demands a systematic, intellectual, and moral readiness that we have not, by any means, reached. De Ligt was the first to develop a systematic "Plan of Campaign against All War and All Preparation for War" as a means to develop that "readiness." Presented at the International conference of the War Resisters International at Welwyn (Herts, England), in July 1934, de Ligt's plan laid out strategic and tactical considerations for the voluntary mobilization of all antiwar forces and specified direct individual as well as collective action. Sympathetic critics of de Ligt such as George Lakey and Gene Sharp have noted his failure to convincingly relate nonviolent struggle to the conflicts of his time, such as the Spanish civil war and the rise of Hitler in Germany.

In order to promote the theory and practice of nonviolent action, de Ligt, with his wife, founded a Peace Academy that held its first meeting near Paris in August 1938. Creation of the academy, along with his inaugural lecture, "The Science of Peace," foreshadowed the emergence of peace research in the second half of the twentieth century. Sadly, de Ligt was too ill to deliver his own lecture; he died on September 3, 1938, in Nantes, France.

Modern students of his work regard him as the most creative theoretician of the European antimilitarist movement of the interwar period, who played an important role in helping to reveal the effectiveness of nonviolent struggle and power potential rooted in people.

Peter van den Dungen

References
de Ligt, Bart. *The Conquest of Violence: An Essay on War and Revolution.* London: Routledge, 1937. New ed., London: Pluto, 1989 and Winchester, Mass.: Unwin Hyman, 1989.

———. *La Paix Créatrice: Histoire des Principes et des Tactiques de l'Action Directe Contre la Guerre.* Paris: Marcel Rivière, 1934.

Jochheim, Gernot. *Antimilitaristische Aktionstheorie, Soziale Revolution und Soziale Verteidigung.* Assen/Amsterdam: Van Gorcum, 1977; Frankfurt/Main: Haag and Herchen, 1977.

van den Dungen, Peter, Herman Noordegraaf, and Wim Robben. *Bart de Ligt (1883–1938): Peace Activist and Peace Researcher.* Boxtel, Netherlands: Bart de Ligt Fund; Zwolle, Netherlands: Foundation for Information on Active Nonviolence, 1990.

Deming, Barbara (1917–1984)

Peace and civil rights activist, pacifist-feminist, lesbian, writer, born in New York City on July 23, 1917, and died in Sugarloaf Key, Florida, on August 2, 1984.

Deming was educated in Quaker schools through high school and studied literature and theater at Bennington College in Vermont. After holding a variety of jobs, she was hired in 1942 as a film analyst for a Library of Congress project. Her first book, *Running Away from Myself—A Dream Portrait of America Drawn from the Films of the '40s,* written during this period, was not published until 1969.

In the mid-1940s she began to devote herself to writing essays, theater reviews, poems, and short stories. *A Humming under My Feet: A Book of Travail,* an autobiographical book based on a year of travel in Europe, was begun in 1952, completed years later, and published posthumously in 1985.

After traveling to India in the late 1950s, Deming read Gandhi's work and began to identify as a pacifist, but it was her trip to Cuba in 1960 and a personal encounter with Fidel Castro that pushed her toward both nonviolent activism and the role of journalist. That same year, Deming was inspired by members of two radical pacifist groups, the Committee for Nonviolent Action and the Peacemakers. Her subsequent activism in the 1960s ranged from fasting for the abolition of the CIA in 1961 to numerous arrests and imprisonments for antiwar and civil rights protests.

In 1964, Deming joined the Quebec-Washington-Guantanamo Walk for Peace. The protesters were arrested in Albany, Georgia, for attempting to walk through the town as an interracial group. *Prison Notes,* written during her month in Albany jail, was published in 1966 and is widely regarded as a classic prison narrative. During the war in Indochina, Deming spent eleven days in North Vietnam with three other women and returned home to speak and write about her experiences of U.S. bombing raids. Deming's best-known essay, "On Revolution and Equilibrium," published in *Liberation* in 1968, articulated her argument for nonviolence, using as counterpoint Frantz Fanon's *The Wretched of the Earth.* In the summer of 1968 she lived in Resurrection City, a community established by poor people on the mall in Washington, D.C.

Deming was seriously injured in a car accident in September 1971, and struggled with

Barbara Deming, 1973. Photo ©Diana Davies.

physical frailty and ill health for the rest of her life. She turned to letter writing as a form of activism and became a respected voice in the emerging feminist movement of the 1970s. Self-identified as a lesbian since the age of sixteen, Deming publicly came out in 1973 and added her pacifist perspective to the new movement for lesbian/gay rights. In 1975, with money from a settlement she received after the car accident, Deming established the Money for Women Fund to provide grants to feminists in the arts.

Books by Deming published in the 1970s and 1980s include: *Revolution and Equilibrium* (essays, 1971); *Wash Us and Comb Us* (short stories, 1972); *We Cannot Live without Our Lives* (essays, letters, poems, 1974); *Remembering Who We Are* (essays, letters, poems, 1981); and a collection of writings, *We Are All Part of One Another: A Barbara Deming Reader* (1984).

In the summer of 1983, Deming was one of fifty-four women arrested at the Seneca Women's Peace Encampment in upstate New York. Her essay about that experience, "A New Spirit Moves among Us," was published posthumously in 1985 in the book *Prisons that Could Not Hold: Prison Notes 1964–Seneca 1984.*

Grace Paley called Deming "a great reconciler with a wonderful stubborn streak," and Judith McDaniel, executor of the Barbara Deming Archives, wrote that Deming's work "was to highlight for us the connection between issues of oppression."

Pam McAllister

References

Meigs, Mary. "Remembering Barbara Deming." *Women's Review of Books* 2 (October 1984).

Meyerding, Jane. "Introduction." In *We Are All Part of One Another: A Barbara Deming Reader,* edited by Jane Meyerding with a foreword by Barbara Smith. Philadelphia: New Society, 1984.

Segrest, Mab. "Feminism and Disobedience: Conversations with Barbara Deming." In *Reweaving the Web of Life: Feminism and Nonviolence,* edited by Pam McAllister. Philadelphia: New Society, 1982.

See also COMMITTEE FOR NONVIOLENT ACTION; FEMINISM; WOMEN AND NONVIOLENT ACTION IN THE UNITED STATES SINCE 1950

Democracy Wall Movement (China)

A movement that called for increased freedom and democracy in the People's Republic of China, lasting from the fall of 1978 to the spring of 1981. The movement emerged in the form of political posters, which authorities tacitly permitted, and expanded to include publication of unofficial journals. These activities were declared illegal only in late 1979, and even then, some publications were maintained until early 1981.

In November 1978, numerous posters, written with very large characters to make them easily readable, appeared on a wall approximately two hundred meters long and two and a half meters high on west Chang'an Avenue in Beijing. These posters, which criticized Mao Zedong and the Great Cultural Revolution, demanded freedom and democracy. They received wide attention and were the subject of heated discussions. The wall became known as the Democracy Wall. In December 1978, some who were active at the wall began to publish mimeographed journals and have them posted on, and circulated and sold around, the wall. They also organized discussions, speeches, and demonstrations in the name of the journals' editorial offices and the Joint Conference of unofficial journals. During the same time, similar political discussions and

Democracy Wall, Beijing, China, 1979. Photo by Hu Ping.

unofficial mimeographed journals appeared in Shanghai, Guangzhou, and about two dozen other cities in China. It is estimated that there were over forty such journals in Beijing alone. About two thousand people are thought to have been directly involved in these publications, most of them workers and students in their twenties and thirties.

China's Communist government initially tolerated the activities of the Democracy Wall movement but soon became repressive. It arrested a number of activists in March, April, and November of 1979. The authorities put the wall off limits in December 1979 and banned big-character posters and unofficial journals soon afterward. Unofficial journals in all parts of China were forced to cease publication at the end of 1979. A small number of activists continued to publish their journals as "study references" and did not distribute them publicly. At the end of 1980, they prepared for the establishment of a national association of unofficial publications. In April 1981, the group was arrested and convicted by the authorities. This

wave of repression signified the end of the Democracy Wall movement.

The Democracy Wall movement was the first large-scale effort to advance democracy in the People's Republic after Mao's death. The fall of the "Gang of Four" at that time allowed what had been the orthodox ideology to be widely questioned. Within the Communist Party, reformers were trying to make use of people's discontent to prevail over the conservatives in a power struggle. This situation gave rise to certain opportunities for the appearance and dissemination of dissenting political opinions. Because of their deeply felt fear and loathing of the widespread and cruel political persecution experienced during the Cultural Revolution of the 1960s, ordinary Chinese showed considerable interest and sympathy toward calls for freedom and democracy. The young activists of the movement acquired their faith in, and began their pursuit of, freedom and democracy mainly through their own bitter experience, and not because of foreign influence, as alleged by the government. The vast majority of these activists adhered to the principle of nonviolence because they believed nonviolent actions to be right, and because they considered nonviolent means effective and feasible.

The basic course of action of the Democracy Wall movement was the independent publication of journals and the free expression of political opinions. Freedom of speech and freedom of the press were common goals of the activists. A number of important viewpoints were developed during the movement. These included critical evaluation of Mao Zedong and the "Gang of Four," a critique of the existing socialist system, elaboration of the principles of freedom of thought and freedom of artistic expression, the call for democracy and economic reforms, and enunciation of the concepts of human rights and humanitarianism.

The Democracy Wall movement, however, was not a homogeneous movement. Participants' ideological positions ranged from near neo-Marxism to liberalism. Politically, some emphasized the need to support the reformers inside the Communist Party. Others were more thoroughly critical of the political system, and still others tried to find a way to gradually do away with totalitarianism and establish guarantees for individual rights.

The movement made an important contribution to de-Maofication and the emancipation of thought in China. It also provided a rich source of ideas and examples of personal integrity, supporting the spread of concepts like freedom and the growth of the democracy movement. Because of suppression by the authorities and the unrealistic hopes that many people had had about reforms within the system, the movement's impact at the time was rather limited. As time passes, though, its significance becomes more widely recognized. The prevailing views and ideals expressed during the movement continued to gain recognition and acceptance, and many of the Democracy Wall activists continued their efforts and played vital roles in the democracy movements that followed.

Hu Ping

References

Hu Ping. *Reflection on Chinese Democracy.* Hong Kong: Oxford University Press, 1992.

Institute for the Study of Chinese Communist Problems. *A Collection of Underground Publications Circulated on Chinese Mainland,* vols. 1–20. Taipei, Taiwan: 1981.

Nathan, Andrew. *Chinese Democracy.* New York: Alfred A. Knopf, 1985.

See also CHINA; MAY FOURTH MOVEMENT, 1919; TIANANMEN SQUARE, DEMOCRACY MOVEMENT, BEIJING, 1989

Democratization

The process through which a political system becomes democratic. This raises three questions: What is the meaning of democracy, the result of this process? What is the process that achieves this end? How is this end to be evaluated?

Democracy may be defined by its inherent nature and by its empirical conditions. As to its nature, Aristotle defined democracy as rule by the people (Greek *demokratia: demos,* "the people" + *kratein,* "to rule"), and this idea that in some way the people govern themselves is still the core meaning of democracy. But around this idea several related themes have developed that are now thought integral to what democracy means. One is that the people govern themselves by regular elections through which their highest leaders are periodically determined (representative democracy) or policies governing them are chosen (direct democracy).

A second is that the right to vote includes virtually all adults. This is an entirely modern addition. Not so long ago governments were called democratic that excluded from the franchise all slaves, women, and free men who did not meet certain property or literacy requirements. Now it is considered perverse to call democratic any country so restricting the franchise—as, for example, the South Africa apartheid regime that limited voting to minority whites.

A third is the acceptance of certain so-called democratic rights, particularly the right to vote, the right to have one's vote count equally, the right to run for the highest office, and the right to organize political groups or parties.

And finally, there is above the state a law to which all authorities adhere, that provides the framework for democratic rule, and that protects democratic rights. Democracy, therefore, now generally means that a people rule themselves through periodic elections of their highest leaders in which nearly all adults can participate, for which offices they are eligible, and under the rule of law.

In addition to this basic meaning, there is wide agreement on the empirical conditions that either give substance to what democracy means or that must be present for democracy to exist. One is that the newspapers and other communication media are free to criticize government policies and leaders. A second is that there is open competition allowed for political office, which usually is translated to mean that there is more than one political party competing for power. A third is that there be a popularly and regularly elected legislature and head of government. Moreover, it is now deemed necessary that election ballots be cast secretly, but that debate and voting by democratically elected representatives be public. Then there is also the widely accepted belief that democracies cannot coexist with lack of religious freedom or the right to hold and express unpopular ideas. Finally, for there to be a rule of law there must be fundamental documents that structure the government, elaborate the reciprocal rights and duties of government and the people, and which all governing officials and their policies must obey. This is a constitution, either in the form of a single document, as for the United States, or a set of documents, statutes, and signed agreements, as for Great Britain.

These are the generally accepted conditions of democracy. Among some democratic theorists and activists, however, it is also believed that democracy is inconsistent with a command economy, or that there must be guarantees of minority rights, or that government must be limited. Some also insist that democracy can exist only when the people also have economic power. But these and other such elaborations are really defining types of democracies (such as democratic socialist or democratic individualist) rather than the basic ideal or its conditions.

How is the ideal to be achieved? There appears to be no one process of democratization. What agreement there is on how best to achieve a stable democracy favors slow incremental development. Great Britain is, of course, the example of the gradual change over centuries from absolute monarchy to one of the world's most enduring democracies. However, such an incremental process seems neither necessary nor sufficient for democracy, nor for its stability. Great Britain is an example of a bottom-up process, where the nongoverning elite or lower classes made incessant demands for an extension of rights and voting power that, by government concession after concession, chipped away at ruling authority. Not all such democratization is so gradual, and indeed many instances appear revolutionary. The American Revolution, the French Revolution, the Chinese Revolution of 1912, and the Russian Revolution of 1917 that preceded the Bolshevik coup are examples, only the first of which established a long-lasting democracy.

The process of democratization may also be carried out by the governing elite themselves, as has often happened in South America, and indeed, one will find authoritarian leaders who claim that their rule is required to create the conditions for democracy. However, this top-down process has more often ended in an unstable democracy, unless it has been responsive to revolutionary pressure and pro-democratic violence from those below.

Democracy may also be created and midwifed by foreign powers. This is how the democracies of Japan and West Germany were created. After the Second World War, the United States occupied Japan and with the help of democratic-minded Japanese intellectuals and politicians reconstructed the Japanese government, wrote the so-called MacArthur Constitution, and carried out social reforms, such as land reform, that would strengthen democracy. This top-down, foreign-imposed democratization produced a democracy stable enough to see in 1993 one of the longest lasting and most powerful governing parties among democracies thrown out of power by the Japanese people. Similarly, the new postwar democratic West German government, erected with the help and under the watchful eyes of Great Britain, France, and the United States, has been stable and effective. Notably, it managed to accommodate both dramatic enlargement and economic strain as it absorbed the former East Germany into a single German state in 1990.

Colonization, especially by Great Britain, has provided an incubation period for democracy in a number of countries, which with independence became full-fledged and stable democracies. Canada, New Zealand, and Australia are good examples. India is also an example, although its democracy has come under severe strain, and its survival is all the more remarkable given regional religious, linguistic, and ethnic centrifugal forces.

Rather than define a process of democratization, many have tried to define the empirical conditions necessary for the creation and success of democracy. In some of this work there tends to be confusion between the conditions of democracy itself, such as a free press and political parties, and that of successful democratization. If we understand the latter to mean those conditions that facilitate the creation of democracy and its stability, confusion can be avoided. In these terms most stress the importance of economic development to democratization, with the concomitant high levels of literacy and education, and modern communications. It is believed that democracy requires an aware and relatively educated electorate, and that moreover, where poverty and inequality is as severe as it is in the least economically developed nations, democracy cannot take root.

But also there is the role of culture. Many democratic theorists now accept that democracy requires a political culture of negotiation, compromise, accommodation, and a willingness to lose. Where this culture is absent, democracy, even if created through revolution by the people themselves, cannot succeed. However, as one considers such democracies as Japan, France, Germany, or India, their predemocratic cultures were most conducive to authoritarian rule of some kind. It is only with the development of democracy that their political cultures gradually became democratic. Whether political democracy or democratic culture came first is clearly a chicken-and-egg question, but whether it comes before or after democracy is created, it is widely recognized as essential to democratic stability. Other conditions have been proposed, such as the importance of a vigorous, bourgeois middle class, or the necessity for a depoliticized military.

Finally there is the question of why one should want democratization. One argument is that people are all in nature equal, that it is a natural right that people govern themselves, that they be free in a democratic sense. Since each person is an individual with free will and is equal in this sense to any other individual, the only system of natural governance is one in which all individuals collectively rule themselves. Another argument is that democracy is the social contract to which people in a state of nature would agree collectively had they no foreknowledge as to how they would personally benefit (as in gaining or losing property).

Of all arguments for democracy, however, the most popular are the utilitarian ones. De-

mocracy creates the greatest happiness of the greatest number; it promotes economic and personal development; public policy is most effective because of its incremental nature and the feedback of democratic elections; people are freer and minorities better protected; equality is promoted and enhanced; it enables gradual and incremental revolutionary change.

But especially important here is the argument that democracy institutionalizes a means of nonviolent conflict resolution—the willingness to negotiate, compromise, and debate, rather than fight. Moreover, the ballot rather than the bullet is the very democratic ideal of voting to resolve differences and choose leaders. It is what we mean by democracy.

Empirical research supports this argument. Especially well established is the finding that democracies do not make war on each other. Moreover, the more democracy the less likely violent rebellion, revolution, civil war, bloody riots, antigovernment terrorism, and such. Finally, democratic leaders generally do not kill their own people through genocide, massacres, extrajudicial executions, and other forms of mass murder.

R.J. Rummel

References

Dahl, Robert A. *A Preface to Democratic Theory.* Chicago: University of Chicago Press, 1956.

Diamond, Larry, Juan J. Linz, and Seymour Martin Lipset, eds. *Democracy in Developing Countries.* Vols. 1–4. Boulder: Lynne Rienner, 1988–1989.

Held, David. *Models of Democracy.* Cambridge: Polity, 1987.

Holden, Barry. *The Nature of Democracy.* New York: Harper and Row, 1974.

Huntington, Samuel. *The Third Wave.* Norman: University of Oklahoma Press, 1991.

Linz, Juan J., and Alfred Stepan, eds. *The Breakdown of Democratic Regimes: Crisis, Breakdown and Reequilibrium.* Baltimore: Johns Hopkins University Press, 1978.

O'Donnell, Guillermo, and Philippe C. Schmitter. *Transitions from Authoritarian Rule: Tentative Conclusions about Uncertain Democracies.* Baltimore: Johns Hopkins University Press, 1986.

O'Donnell, Guillermo, Philippe C. Schmitter, and Laurence Whitehead, eds. *Transi-*

tions from *Authoritarian Rule: Comparative Perspectives*. Baltimore: Johns Hopkins University Press, 1988.

Rummel, R.J. *Death by Government: Genocide and Mass Murder since 1900*. New Brunswick: Transaction, 1994.

Russett, Bruce. *Grasping the Democratic Peace: Principles for a Post–Cold War World*. Princeton: Princeton University Press, 1993.

Sørensen, Georg. *Democracy and Democratization: Processes and Prospects in a Changing World*. Boulder: Westview Press, 1993.

Denmark, Evacuation of Danish Jews, 1943

Coordinated action of many sectors of Danish society to warn, protect, and finally to save some seventy-two hundred members of the eight-thousand-person Jewish community from deportation. The German seizure of Denmark in April 1940 was marked in its early stages by efforts to gain a measure of Danish acquiescence in the occupation. In this context, German officials in Denmark hesitated to introduce rigorous occupation policies. Additionally, the early date of the occupation meant that the policies and mechanisms of the Holocaust were not yet fully in operation. Danish government policy was defensive, granting certain concessions to Germany while protecting Danish institutions and citizens. On April 15, 1940, for example, Danish officials informed the German official in charge, Cecil von Renthe-Finck, that unspecified disturbances might follow German interference with Jews and leftists, or the creation of a secret police force. This was an indirect warning that interference in important internal matters might threaten the Danish accommodation with the occupation regime. In turn, Denmark complied to some extent with German expectations, such as signing the November 1941 Anti-Comintern Pact. In some respects, for the Danish people the safety of Jews and the preservation of a level of civil freedoms was a test of German intentions to live up to promises of a limited occupation system.

Following the June 1941 occupation of the Soviet Union, and particularly after the January 1942 Wannsee Conference on plans to carry out the destruction of the European Jews, pressure on Denmark to address its "Jewish problem" increased. Both Renthe-Finck and his successor as Germany's representative in Denmark, Werner Best, were strongly interested in maintaining the relative political peace in the country. To that end, both officials found various ways of avoiding the day when harsh measures would be taken in Denmark, enlisting Foreign Ministry colleagues in delaying tactics. Time ran out on this policy in August 1943, with the declaration of a state of emergency in Denmark that led to a September decision to deport Danish Jews.

Werner Best's own conduct and motives at this time were ambiguous, because he drafted and carried out the state of emergency plan, while at the same time making it known clandestinely that the seizure of Jews was about to begin. Shortly before the date of the attack on Danish Jews (the night of October 1–2, during Rosh Hashannah), Best revealed his plan to Georg Duckwitz, a German used occasionally as a go-between. Duckwitz in turn informed his contacts among the Danish Social Democrats, who spread their knowledge widely. On the morning of September 30, Rabbi Marcus Melchior delivered a warning at services that Denmark's Jews must act to save themselves.

Beginning on October 1 and lasting approximately three weeks, the rescue unfolded in three stages: warning, secreting of Jews in temporary locations, and transferring them by sea to Sweden. The Jewish community had followed the broader political line of relying on the king and legal political institutions in a nonconfrontational policy of maintaining freedoms and national identity under occupation. No preparations had been made for flight. Christians had been primed by a letter from their bishops, read in churches on September 29, condemning the persecution of Jews and calling on parishioners to obey their consciences and fight for their fellow citizens. According to Glenthoj, spontaneous mass efforts emerged to locate and warn Jews of the danger. The Freedom Council issued a statement of solidarity that included all citizens and instructed civil servants, police, and workers to "reject all cooperation" with the occupation. Yahil writes that a majority of Jews left their homes in the first hours, finding shelter in the apartments and houses of people who were often complete strangers, as well as in schools and hospitals, both in the countryside and in Copenhagen.

Although the idea of helping Jews to escape to Sweden predated October 1, it was several days until the necessity of evacuating all Jews was realized. The small country of Denmark offered little security for lengthy hiding of hunted people.

A variety of methods were created to effect the third stage, moving people out of the country. In greater or lesser numbers, groups were moved clandestinely through the cities and villages, staying briefly in various places until being transferred to the ports. There, under cover of darkness, groups were taken across the strait in fishing vessels to neutral Sweden and safety. Ad hoc organizations arose for each of these functions, as well as for collecting funds to pay the fishing boat owners for passage, fuel, and food for the evacuees.

The very limited success of the German operation to deport Danish Jews is not entirely explained by the failure of the Germans to mount a full-fledged effort, although Yahil stresses that many Germans outside the special forces directly engaged in this campaign offered little assistance. Some Jews were captured in the initial sweep, followed by others caught in transit, totaling over 400 persons. Of the entire community of nearly 8,000, 7,200 were evacuated safely; those captured were sent to Theresienstadt concentration camp in Czechoslovakia. Nearly all survived, in part because of the continued concern of the Danish government for their safety.

As Yahil writes, "Double dealing was one of the ingredients of Nazi rule." Werner Best's policies, and his studied revelations to Duckwitz, can be understood as balancing his wish to preserve civil peace under Nazi rule, to his own benefit, with his duty to his hardline superiors. (Indeed, self-serving postwar accounts by both men cloud the full extent of their complicity.) In this sense, Germany's (and German functionaries') multiple and contradictory objectives in Denmark set the stage for the successful clandestine evacuation of Danish Jews. Nevertheless, writers on the subject stress that the attack upon Danish Jewry, which occurred at the same time as the internment of forty thousand Danish military personnel in Germany, triggered action rather than acquiescence on the part of the populace. Rejecting the Nazi view that Jews could not be full citizens of the state, Danes of all religious backgrounds insisted that Jews possessed the same rights as every other citizen, and that an attack upon Jews was an attack upon all.

Ronald M. McCarthy

References

Brustein-Berenstein, Tatiana. "The Historiographic Treatment of the Abortive Attempt to Deport the Danish Jews." In *The Nazi Holocaust: Historical Articles on the Destruction of European Jewry,* edited by Michael Marrus. Westport, Conn. and London: Meckler, 1989.

Glenthoj, Jorgen. "The Little Dunkerque: The Danish Rescue of Jews in October 1943." In *Human Responses to the Holocaust: Perpetrators and Victims, Bystanders and Resisters,* edited by Michael D. Ryan. New York and Toronto: Edwin Mellen, 1981.

Yahil, Leni. *The Holocaust: The Fate of European Jewry, 1932–1945.* New York and Oxford: Oxford University Press, 1990.

———. *The Rescue of Danish Jewry: Test of a Democracy.* Philadelphia: Jewish Publication Society of America, 1969, 1983.

See also DENMARK, RESISTANCE TO NAZI OCCUPATION; FREEDOM COUNCIL; JEWISH RESISTANCE TO THE HOLOCAUST; LE CHAMBON SUR LIGNON, FRANCE; NAZISM, CIVILIAN RESISTANCE, 1939–1945; ROSENSTRAßE PROTEST, 1943; WHITE ROSE

Denmark, Resistance to Nazi Occupation

Under the direction of the Danish government (which remained in place until August 1943) and an underground resistance movement, the Danish population engaged in various forms of nonviolent resistance to the Nazi occupation between April 1940 and May 1945, including political noncooperation, social boycotts, strikes, and sabotage.

On April 9, 1940, the German army swept over the two small Scandinavian countries of Denmark and Norway. Its chief objective was control of the transport lines of Swedish iron ore via the Norwegian port of Narvik, as well as the militarily important harbors further south on the west coast. The official justification was to preclude a suspected French and British military strike in the same direction. In addition, German leaders nurtured the hope of converting the Nordic peoples to the Nazi ideology.

When German troops crossed the Danish border, the German ambassador to Denmark presented a note to the Danish minister of foreign affairs, stating the reasons behind the attack and making a number of promises and demands. The Danish government found the German military superiority overwhelming and decided to yield under protest.

Superficially, the case may be seen as a confrontation between two states, Germany and Denmark. It happened, however, within the framework of the larger struggle of World War II. The Danish resistance that evolved through the coming months and years must therefore be seen as one example of a series of largely improvised collective actions that took place, in most European countries, in reaction to the German occupation. Although their struggle was not totally nonviolent, the Danish people showed an impressive capacity to resist nonviolently German demands and influence in Danish affairs.

Unlike the case in several other occupied countries, the Danish government decided to stay and offer an unequal fight instead of fleeing the country. A national unity government was formed, representing the four major democratic parties. Its weapons of choice were nonviolent methods for social survival and civilian resistance, including persuasion and appeals to the promises and good faith of the antagonist, as well as efforts at cementing the relative internal unity of the people against the foreign influence.

However, the full picture of the conflict was not simple. There were important internal splits and contradictions within each of the two adversaries. On the side of the aggressor, the Nazi-governed Third Reich, there was some divergence between party and state authorities, as well as contradictions between political and military authorities in occupied Denmark. For example, party representatives wanted to push forward with Nazification, but state representatives wanted to keep the situation calm in order to profit from Danish production.

On the Danish side, the internal differences crystallized around two opposite poles, the traditional political and social establishment and the resistance movement. The establishment centered around the government and the leading democratic politicians. Its policy was characterized by a careful defensive attitude that left room primarily for "passive resistance." The resistance movement had its original base in an unusual alliance between the politically extreme left and the extreme, but anti-Nazi, right. Its attitude was more explicitly hostile toward the

occupier, its policy was more offensive, and it did not refrain from taking violent actions.

Thus, the differences on the Danish side were grounded in both strategy and ideology. In addition, the character and role of the resistance movement changed over time and, in many ways, functioned as an Allied proxy in Denmark—especially during the year and a half after August 1943.

In the beginning of the occupation, the Danish strategy as formulated by the government contained a defensive and protective "wait-and-see" element, but hardly the notion of "struggle." The government acted and adjusted its policies according to the prospects of various situations as they evolved. Through negotiations, a chief tactic was to resist firmly in areas of main importance to Danish society—for example, to stay neutral and preserve the political system, culture, and welfare—while yielding the fewest possible concessions on relatively less important points. A complicating factor was that the official stance also held the door open for some types of questionable collaboration, above all economic collaboration.

Although the official policy was generally supported by the Danes, the challenging alternative strategy of the resistance movement gradually gained acceptance among broader circles. From the autumn of 1943 until the summer of 1945, the situation may be characterized in terms of "dual support," popular loyalty to the "old order" temporarily superseded by support to the resistance movement.

Throughout the occupation, the Danish general population played the role of the grievance group. At times, important sections were involved in direct action, but its chief function was supportive. A national unity movement provided support for the negotiation policy of the government. It had a stronghold in the popular organizations, which also, due to the very special circumstances, developed new organizational forms and activities, such as the Danish Youth League, which was an umbrella organization for many different youth groups and movements. It cooperated with the Council of Elders, which originated in the Folk High School movement and worked to inspire popular action against Nazism. The council served as an advisory board and helped finance the work of the Youth League.

Finally, foreign third parties played important roles. England was the most important Allied contact for Denmark, along with the

D

geographically adjacent and ethnically similar Sweden. Although in quite different ways, both supported the Danish case and struggle. Both relationships rested on longtime close and friendly ties. The British Special Operations Executive (SOE) helped to establish underground resistance groups in the occupied countries of mainland Europe, including Denmark. These groups were to engage in sabotage and subversion and to prepare for small-scale war behind German lines in the event of an Allied offensive. The British provided materials and training. The British Foreign Office even supported "passive resistance" in Danish broadcasts of the BBC. The Swedish role was determined by its close geographic location and national and cultural similarities. In the beginning of the occupation, Danes could cross the narrow sound relatively easily by ferry. Later illegal—and much more dangerous—boats continued to bring resisters and Jewish refugees to safety in Sweden. In addition, Swedish news was easily available in Denmark. Toward the end, Sweden hosted the paramilitary Danish Brigade and furnished the underground forces with weapons.

Nonviolent means were more frequently used than is usually realized or acknowledged. The nonviolent approach was wider in scope than violent resistance, and it was used by all groups and on practically all levels of society. The large number of methods used indicates the complexity of the struggle and the inventiveness of the resisters in finding both expressive and instrumental nonviolent means of civilian resistance.

For example, the Danish political establishment used various forms of protests and appeals, protracted negotiations, bureaucratic procrastination, and delaying tactics, as well as fraternization. It also provided economic and political contacts to the resistance movement during the last years of the occupation. The general population used such methods as community singing, wearing national symbols, social boycotts of individuals, strikes, and mutual support. Even the resistance movement used nonviolent means to a greater extent than is commonly recognized. For example, the movement developed an underground press and other alternative communication systems, instigated and led certain general strikes, and facilitated the hiding, escape, and creation of false identities for individuals sought by the occupiers. The nonviolent methods of the resistance

movement gained in importance especially in the summer of 1944, when a series of People's Strikes peaked with the famous Copenhagen People's Strike. They were also consciously applied by the Freedom Council, the coordinating body of the Danish resistance.

The borders between the nonviolent and violent means were never clear cut, and sometimes the two complemented one another. Although the Danish resistance movement is best known for its sabotage, some of this involved the limited destruction of their own property. Indeed, the sabotage may be viewed as nonviolent action, mainly because the resisters consciously tried to avoid casualties. Another form of resistance on the border between nonviolent and violent action was the activity of the secret intelligence service, which was nonviolent in itself but contributed to the Allied war effort.

Overall, most nonviolent methods of resistance worked effectively to achieve their goals, and there were few negative effects; however, some methods stand out as relatively more effective. Protest and persuasion generally strengthened the internal unity. Two related methods of political noncooperation, protracted negotiations and passive bureaucratic resistance, were applied effectively by the Danish political establishment. The social boycott was taken up at an early stage and applied through the rest of the occupation. With great symbolic effects, it defined and contained the conflict groups. The strike weapon was applied during sharply limited periods but its symbolic functions were clear. Finally, the underground press and its forerunners, occasional chain letters and pamphlets, as well as touring speakers, seem to have functioned rather efficiently, both as channels for uncensored news and as a means of propaganda against the occupation.

With respect to the German military goals, the results of the Danish resistance were quite modest. In relation to the secondary, economic goals of the occupation, the resistance was more successful. Notable results were achieved by various forms of both sabotage and strikes. The greatest strength of the Danish resistance rested in the political, ideological, and cultural struggle by the national revival movement and the popular defensive resistance. This part of the full resistance emphasized the ideological content of the conflict, and this was the sector within which Danish society had its largest resources. The great differences between the two main parties to the conflict facilitated the political mobilization and polarization necessary to ignite the spark of resistance, and to keep it burning.

Lennart Bergfeldt

References

Bergfeldt, Lennart. *The Intelligent Resistance: How the Danes Withstood German Occupation.* Westport, Conn.: Praeger, 1997.

See also NAZISM, CIVILIAN RESISTANCE, 1939–1945

Desaparecidos Movement in Latin America

A movement throughout Latin America, predominantly of women, which arose in response to a form of state repression consisting of "disappearing" people. It is also known as the mothers' movement. Beginning in the late 1960s, women in several Latin American and Caribbean countries formed organizations to search for their sons, daughters, husbands, and other relatives who had been "disappeared" by brutal and repressive authoritarian regimes. These countries include El Salvador, Honduras, Haiti, Nicaragua, Guatemala, Mexico, Colombia, Bolivia, Brazil, Chile, Argentina, Uruguay, Paraguay, Ecuador, and Peru. In many cases, these groups were the first to publicly protest against these regimes. Hence they became symbols of resistance and national conscience. Despite a later move toward more democratic rule in many of these countries, and the diminishing use of disappearance as a tool of repression, these groups continued to try to bring those responsible to justice. This movement is perhaps best known for "politicizing motherhood" in Latin America.

The disappeared (*desaparecido* in Spanish) specifically refers to people forcibly abducted from their homes or places of work, or sometimes off the street or out of classrooms, by heavily armed death squads, police, or soldiers usually in civilian dress. Prisoners typically are taken to concentration camps or clandestine torture centers, where they are interrogated and physically and psychologically assaulted. Many are later killed and their mutilated and unrecognizable bodies thrown away on body dumps (El Salvador), thrown from helicopters into the ocean (Argentina), or buried in mass graves (Chile, Guatemala, Argentina). There is little or no paperwork on these prisoners and when questioned, the complicitous authorities generally deny all knowledge of them, often claiming

that they are guerrillas or subversives who have gone underground or that they have voluntarily left the country. The term *detenido-desaparecido* (detained-disappeared) often is used to indicate the involvement of government security agencies. It is estimated by del Olmo that approximately ninety thousand Latin Americans have disappeared since 1966.

Across Latin America, the response to this form of state-sanctioned terrorism was remarkably consistent. Beginning in 1967 with the Committee of Families of the Disappeared in Guatemala, female relatives of the disappeared formed groups to pressure the authorities to disclose the whereabouts of their loved ones. Perhaps the best-known of these organizations are the Association of Relatives of the Detained and Disappeared (formed in 1974 in Chile); the Committee of Mothers and Relatives of Prisoners, the Disappeared, and the Politically Assassinated Monsignor Oscar Arnulfo Romero (formed in 1975 in El Salvador); the Mothers and Grandmothers of the Plaza de Mayo (formed in Argentina in 1977); and the Mutual Support Group for the Appearance, Alive, of our Children, Spouses, Parents, and Brothers and Sisters in Guatemala (formed in 1984). In 1980, the Latin American Federation of Relatives of the Detained-Disappeared (FEDEFAM) was created with member organizations from twenty-one countries.

The evolution of these groups was similar across national boundaries. Women would encounter each other outside of prisons, police stations, military barracks, hospitals, morgues, and in government offices, and eventually they would become aware of the potential benefits of acting collectively. In many cases, the Church provided space, guidance, and legal expertise in addition to a minimally effective protective shield.

The women came from all social sectors. In Chile and Argentina, for example, they were mostly middle- and working-class housewives. In El Salvador and Guatemala, they were mostly poor, rural, and indigenous women. Most of these women lacked previous political experience of any kind. In many countries, the women organized around their identities as wives and mothers searching for their disappeared husbands or children. With only a couple of exceptions, such as the Madres of Argentina, whose membership was limited to mothers of disappeared children, these groups grew to include some men and extended to a variety of familial relationships.

These groups employed a variety of legal and extralegal strategies. Generally they would begin with recourse to the criminal justice system, specifically habeus corpus, which requires that a person be brought before a court or a judge to determine whether there is sufficient evidence to justify a legal detention. In some instances, collective writs of habeus corpus were presented on behalf of many individuals at the same time. In Argentina in 1977, for example, a collective writ was filed on behalf of 159 disappeared persons. The groups also applied pressure through the use of the international and national press. The *denuncia* (denunciation) was a common strategy in which affected individuals would reveal all they knew about a situation, usually at press conferences. As these strategies were not particularly effective, women's organizations evolved less conventional (and increasingly extralegal) nonviolent strategies including hunger strikes, marches, demonstrations, the distribution of flyers and pamphlets in churches, marketplaces, and neighborhoods, the seizure of offices and churches, sit-ins, and, in Chile, chaining themselves to the gates of government and international buildings.

Because these groups typically were nonpartisan, nonsectarian, and unburdened by prevailing societal ideological divisions, they were able to develop novel strategies and political symbols. In El Salvador, for example, women wore black dresses, white kerchiefs, and carried red and white carnations—black dresses for grieving, white kerchiefs for peace and justice, red carnations for spilled blood, white carnations for the detained-disappeared, and the green leaves for hope. In Argentina, the Mothers wore white head scarves, embroidered with the name, age, and date of disappearance of their loved ones, as they marched silently around the pyramidal monument in the central square Plaza de Mayo, every Thursday afternoon from 3:30 to 4:00 P.M. In other countries women wore photographs of the disappeared sewn on their clothing. A very dramatic strategy, used in both Chile and Argentina, was to march carrying cardboard silhouettes of disappeared people bearing only their names, or to paste silhouettes of disappeared people on sidewalks and walls, also bearing their names. At one point, there were thirty thousand of these silhouettes in Buenos Aires.

The activities of *desaparecido* groups were not limited to resistance and political pressure, but included a wide variety of supportive functions, such as visits with political prisoners and the provision of assistance to their families, the creation of health care clinics, day care centers, homes for orphaned children, and the organization of educational, self-help, and income-generating workshops. Fourteen women from the Chilean Association of Relatives of the Detained-Disappeared, for example, formed a folkloric troupe that served both therapeutic and educational functions.

The *desaparecido* movement "politicized motherhood" as an authentic symbol of resistance. Although the dominant social and political norms in Latin America valued a particular, repressive notion of motherhood, the political and economic reality of the region made it difficult for women to fulfill even these idealized roles. Nor did the traditional notion of motherhood protect women from state terrorism, as the case of Argentina, whose "dirty war" is well known for the persecution of pregnant women, so dramatically illustrates. Yet motherhood is not a wholly accurate metaphor for this movement, since in the far reaches of Latin America, participation included men and women of all ages, social classes, and relationships to the disappeared.

In addition to the formation of their own international federation, FEDEFAM, these associations were also linked to the larger human rights movement in Latin America and to similar organizations such as the Associations of Relatives of the Exiled, Political Prisoners, and Politically Executed (Chile), the National Coordinator of Widows (Guatemala), and the Mothers and Relatives of Those Tried by Military Justice (Uruguay). Some individuals participated actively in national movements opposing military and authoritarian regimes. Some also were linked to the women's movements in their countries and developed a politicized gender consciousness.

It is difficult to assess the effectiveness of this movement. Some disappeared persons were located, but the numbers are insignificant relative to the enormity of the atrocities. Movement-generated international media attention led to some people being freed shortly after they disappeared. It is possible that these groups were more effective in preventing further disappearances on a mass scale, especially by the beginning of the 1980s.

The comment of one Guatemalan general, that "[t]o take steps toward the reappearance alive of the disappeared is a subversive act," reflects the way in which various Latin American military regimes generally regarded these organizations. Many participants suffered death threats, and some were detained, tortured, raped, assassinated, or themselves disappeared. Among the many documented cases of the abduction and disappearance of movement activists are that of Azucena Villaflor de Vicenti (1977), a founding member of the Madres de Plaza de Mayo; the assassination of Marianella García Villas (1983), a prominent human rights lawyer in El Salvador; and the abduction and murder of the vice president of the Mutual Support Group (along with her brother and two-year-old son) in Guatemala (1985).

In most countries these groups continued into the 1990s and through transition to democratic rule in various countries. They generally opposed amnesty for those responsible for the atrocities and worked very hard to bring about justice. In Argentina, and other countries, they continued to press for *aparición con vida* (reappearance with life). They represented not only a national but also an international collective conscience to ensure that justice is done, that these crimes do not occur again, and that societies do not forget.

Patricia M. Chuchryk

References

Chuchryk, Patricia. "Subversive Mothers: The Women's Opposition to the Military Regime in Chile." In *Women, the State, and Development,* edited by Sue Ellen Charlton, Jana Everett, and Kathleen Staudt. Albany: State University of New York Press, 1989.

del Olmo, Rosa. "Women and the Search for the Detained/Disappeared Persons of Latin America." *Resources for Feminist Research* 15, no. 1 (1986): 42–44.

Fisher, Jo. *Out of the Shadows: Women, Resistance and Politics in South America.* London: Latin American Bureau, 1993.

Miller, Francesca. *Latin American Women and the Search for Social Justice.* Hanover, N.H.: University Press of New England, 1991.

Navarro, Marysa. "The Personal is Political: Las Madres de Plaza de Mayo." In *Power and Popular Protest: Latin American Social Movements,* edited by Susan Eckstein. Berkeley: University of California Press, 1989.

Nunca Mas. *A Report by Argentina's Commission on Disappeared People.* London: Faber and Faber, 1986.

Schirmer, Jennifer. "The Seeking of Truth and the Gendering of Consciousness: The CoMadres of El Salvador and the CONAVIGUA Widows of Guatemala." In *"Viva": Women and Popular Protest in Latin America.* London: Routledge, 1993.
———. "'Those Who Die for Life Cannot Be Called Dead': Women and Human Rights Protest in Latin America." *Feminist Review* 32 (1989): 3–29.

See also MADRES DE PLAZA DE MAYO

Dharasana Salt Works Raid (India), 1930

Effort by several thousand satyagrahis to occupy the salt storage facilities controlled by the colonial British government. The attempted raids, following Mohandas Gandhi's march to Dandi in defiance of the British Salt Acts and lasting from May 12 to June 6, were part of the larger civil disobedience movement of 1930–1931. The raids at Dharasana failed in their tangible goal of seizing possession of the works. But, through the nonviolent endurance of brutal police repression by thousands of volunteers, the raids established a moral high ground for the independence movement.

The actions at Dharasana began on May 12 with a march of about sixty satyagrahis to the works led by the elderly Abbas Tyabji, in which all were arrested before their arrival. Between May 13 and May 20, several new attempts to reach the works, each involving larger numbers of volunteers, were frustrated by police cordons. On these occasions, the protest resulted in a stand-off, often in a mutual sit-down confrontation between the marchers and the police. More vigorous efforts to actually reach and occupy the facilities began on May 21 and lasted until June 6. On May 21, between fifteen hundred and twenty-five hundred volunteers approached the works and tried to enter. Their leaders carried ropes with which to pull down the fences and wire cutters for opening the barbed wire.

Volunteers were met with consistent, and, over time, escalating, police violence. Police beat approaching protesters with *lathi* (steel-tipped clubs), often until they were senseless, and despite the volunteers total restraint from retaliation. Aid workers among the satyagrahis continuously carried off their bloodied comrades as new groups of protesters stepped forward into the police lines. Although some eyewitnesses reported that a few police appeared reluctant or upset by the violence of their actions, as the protests continued police action became less restrained. By the final days of the campaign, protesters regularly received dozens of blows, many were kicked as they fell, and others dragged to shallow ditches. In all, thousands of protesters were beaten and thousands were arrested.

The campaign on the Dharasana works galvanized a national moral outrage among Indians, as well as bringing international opprobrium on the British rule. J.C. Kumarappa wrote, in evaluating the events, that the goal of the effort, in deliberately inviting violence without retaliation in turn, was to "show the world at large the fangs and claws of the Government in all its ugliness and ferocity. In this we have succeeded beyond all measure."

Maria Figueroa
William B. Vogele

References

Ackerman, Peter, and Christopher Kruegler. *Strategic Nonviolent Conflict: The Dynamics of People Power in the Twentieth Century.* Westport, Conn.: Praeger, 1994.

Bondurant, Joan V. *Conquest of Violence: The Gandhian Philosophy of Conflict.* Princeton: Princeton University Press, 1958. Rev. ed., 1988.

Sharp, Gene. *Gandhi Wields the Weapon of Moral Power.* Ahmedabad, India: Navajivan, 1960.

See also GANDHI, MOHANDAS KARAMCHAND; INDIAN NATIONAL MOVEMENT; SALT MARCH, 1930; SATYAGRAHA

Diplomatic Sanctions

A series of methods of international noncooperation between governments. The methods range from relatively benign symbolic actions to more extreme actions that disrupt normal diplomatic, commercial, or social interactions. These sanctions can be classified as those occurring between nations directly, and those that take place in the context of an international organization.

One example of a state-to-state action is to change the status of diplomatic relations without making a total break; these sanctions include recalling diplomats and closing consulates. Governments may also deliberately delay or cancel diplomatic events to show displeasure with the events or policies of the other party. If one government objects to the legitimacy of a newly formed government, they may withhold diplomatic recognition. And a nation may unilaterally sever all diplomatic relations with another, or two nations can mutually break off all relations. This can happen as a prelude to declarations of war or as a distinct sanction in a context that never erupts into war.

Governments may also attempt to engage in protest noncooperation in the context of international organizations or bodies. They may withdraw their membership or participation, or withhold financial support, to express dissatisfaction. Conversely, an international organization may take action against a single government by refusing membership or by expelling members who violate policy.

References

Sharp, Gene. *The Politics of Nonviolent Action.* Boston: Porter Sargent, 1973.

See also SANCTIONS; SPORTS BOYCOTT

Direct Action Committee against Nuclear War (Great Britain)

Gandhian radical pacifist organization in the British nuclear disarmament movement. While the Direct Action Committee against Nuclear War (DAC) had as its ultimate goal the creation of a nonviolent society, it focused its energies on promoting unilateral nuclear disarmament.

The Emergency Committee for Direct Action against Nuclear War (soon shortened to Direct Action Committee against Nuclear War) was founded in April 1957. Its precursors in the direct action movement were Operation Gandhi and Non-Violent Resistance, two groups that organized demonstrations against the atomic bomb in the early 1950s. The initial impetus behind the formation of DAC was the organization and financing of an unsuccessful attempt to sail into the British nuclear testing area at Christmas Island to prevent testing. DAC launched its first big direct-action campaign in the spring of 1958, a march from London to the Atomic Weapons Research Establishment (AWRE) in Aldermaston. Over five thousand people participated, and press coverage was extensive. The march ended with a week-long vigil and picket at AWRE. DAC later organized a nine-week vigil and picket at AWRE from July 20 to September 22, 1958, ending in a sit-down demonstration on the last day.

DAC's strategy continued to focus on direct action at key military installations. In contrast to the strategy of the newly formed Campaign for Nuclear Disarmament, which advocated working within the liberal Labour Party using constitutional means, DAC concentrated on building a grassroots movement of workers and others using extraparliamentary means. DAC activists organized demonstrations and the nonviolent obstruction of construction at a missile base in North Pickenham in the winter of 1958–1959. DAC also launched the Voters' Veto campaign of 1959, during which it encouraged voters to vote only for candidates committed to unilateral nuclear disarmament. During 1959 and 1960, DAC continued to organize a large number of nuclear missile base demonstrations, marches, and vigils, sometimes involving civil disobedience.

A major aspect of DAC strategy was its "industrial campaign," an attempt to arouse workers directly involved in nuclear armaments production by educating them about their individual responsibility in the arms race. Organizers sought to stimulate these workers to strike, so as to cripple the military-industrial complex. The effects of this campaign were marginal, however. Another major aspect of DAC's activities was the organization and cosponsorship of international actions. DAC cosponsored the Sahara Protest Expedition in the winter of 1959–1960, in which an international team attempted to walk onto the French atomic test site in Algeria. DAC also cosponsored the San Francisco to Moscow March of 1961 to protest nuclear weapons and the cold war, which marched through England.

The last DAC campaign was the Holy Loch action of 1961, a six-week march during spring and summer from London to the Holy Loch naval base where nuclear submarines were moored. Along the route, rallies, meetings, and demonstrations were held, some intended to organize trade union support. The march ended with a package of direct actions, including two marches, a nonviolent occupation of two piers used by naval crews, and an attempt to nonviolently board the nuclear submarines.

After this campaign, many DAC members joined the newly formed Committee of 100, and DAC itself disbanded in late 1961. DAC had demonstrated a strong commitment to using and developing the techniques of nonviolent direct action. In fact, the Committee of 100 continued the strategy of DAC, but on a larger scale.

Brad Bennett

References

Randle, Michael. "Non-Violent Direct Action in the 1950s and 1960s." In *Campaigns for Peace: British Peace Movements in the Twentieth Century,* edited by Richard Taylor and Nigel Young. Manchester: Manchester University Press, 1987.

Taylor, Richard. *Against the Bomb: The British Peace Movement, 1958–1965.* Oxford: Clarendon, 1988.

See also CAMPAIGN FOR NUCLEAR DISARMAMENT; COMMITTEE OF 100; NUCLEAR WEAPONS OPPOSITION

Disappearance, Collective

Act of noncooperation in which a small population (for example, a town or village) severs all social contact with an opponent by "disappearing" or abandoning their homes, thereby impeding the opponent's ability to rule effectively or to control an occupied area without resistance. The villagers usually remain in hiding somewhere nearby and do not flee from the nation or political unit as a whole, thus distinguishing this method from "protest emigration."

Peasants in Kanara in South India opposed British attempts to rule them by collectively disappearing in 1799 and 1800. When a British officer approached a village, the local people left and traveled to another village. Another example occurred during the Japanese occupation of China in 1939. Whenever a Japanese military unit approached a northern Chinese village, the inhabitants would completely evacuate, taking with them all food, animals, and tools. They would relocate to the hills surrounding the village. This tactic of collective disappearance forced the Japanese to bring with them everything they would need for their own support, making it more difficult to occupy the territory.

References

Sharp, Gene. *The Politics of Nonviolent Action.* Boston: Porter Sargent, 1973.

See also EMIGRATION, PROTEST

Disrobing, Protest

Method of protest in which one publicly removes one's clothes to express religious or political disapproval. By doing so, one is calling attention to a specific issue and attempting to embarrass an opponent. The actionist appeals to the opponent to change his or her position on the issue.

Probably the most famous practitioners of this method are the Doukhobors, a religious sect in British Columbia, Canada. In the first half of the twentieth century, they conducted numerous "nude parades" to protest government interference and oppression. On May 28, 1962, when Canadian Prime Minister John Diefenbaker was attending a political rally in Trail, British Columbia, a group of Doukhobor women whose husbands were charged with terrorist acts interrupted the meeting and took off their clothes to protest the government's treatment of Doukhobors. Another example occurred in Grinnell, Iowa, on February 5, 1969, when students staged a "nude-in" during a speech by a *Playboy* magazine representative to protest the magazine's portrayal of sex

References

Sharp, Gene. *The Politics of Nonviolent Action.* Boston: Porter Sargent, 1973.

See also DOUKHOBORS

Dolci, Danilo (b. 1928)

Italian writer, poet, and social reformer who used nonviolent techniques to promote social reform in western Sicily, Italy. A proponent of revolutionary nonviolent transformation of society, he publicized and worked to improve the social conditions of poor Sicilians and campaigned against the Mafia. Dolci was dubbed the "Gandhi of Sicily" and is considered one of the most effective activists to apply Gandhian techniques to the European context. The two techniques he is most known for are the hunger strike and the "reverse strike."

Dolci was born on June 28, 1928, in Sesana, Italy (Trieste, now part of Slovenia), and was trained as an architect. In solidarity with the poor, he renounced his middle-class heritage, however, and started living in Sicily in 1952. He soon began a campaign to alleviate poverty in western Sicily that was to continue for twenty years. His first publicized use of

Danilo Dolci. Fellowship of Reconciliation Archives.

nonviolent action occurred when he conducted a nine-day hunger strike in 1952 to dramatize the hunger of the children in the town of Trappeto. In response to this fast, authorities spent 100 million lire in relief for Trappeto over the subsequent two years. Dolci continued to use the hunger strike as one of his primary tactics. For Dolci, fasting was undertaken, not with a sense of martyrdom, but as a strategic initiative.

Dolci's activism was based on a conviction that social change campaigns must start with research into problems and their causes. Over the years, Dolci and his associates published pamphlets and books documenting the squalor of western Sicily. In 1955, Dolci founded a *Centro di studi e iniziative* ("The Center") to promote the study of long-range social change. Research, in his view, was the first step in a larger five-stage process. It was followed by community discussions, the formation of "action groups," the study of strategic alternatives, and the use of a variety of nonviolent techniques. This process was employed toward a long-term goal of revolutionary transformation of the economy and power relations of the Italian society. He distinguished the revolutionary nonviolent action he proposed from both passive nonresistance and nonviolent tactics used merely to fight individual evils.

While researching the social conditions of Sicily, Dolci discovered that dams were necessary for economic development and that the Mafia controlled the allocation of water resources on the parched island. This realization ignited a campaign to pressure the government to build dams and an anti-Mafia campaign to wrestle power away from the powerful secret society.

On February 2, 1956, Dolci led a group of unemployed workers in a "reverse strike" to repair a road necessary for dam construction and to publicize and test the citizens' right to work as guaranteed by the Italian constitution. When authorities arrested Dolci and six others, Dolci went limp and had to be carried to the police car. For this act, Dolci was sentenced to fifty days in jail. The subsequent trial, however, garnered international support for Dolci and for the Sicilian cause. Friends of Danilo Dolci committees were formed in several European cities. In November 1957, Dolci hosted an international Congress for Full Employment.

Another famous incident occurred in September 1965, when Dolci and his colleague, Franco Alasia, accused members of the Christian Democrat Party of association with the Mafia. Dolci and Alasia were sued for libel, and during the ensuing trial they were able to present documents and witnesses to demonstrate the corruption of the Mafia and related politicians. In December 1966, when the judge prevented any more testimony toward this cause, Dolci boycotted his own trial. He led a six-day march in February 1967 to protest the Mafia and the trial. Later that year, he was sentenced to two years in jail, but he appealed and successfully avoided the sentence.

In the two decades of campaigning against poverty and the Mafia, Dolci and western Sicilians achieved some significant success. Several dams were built during the late 1950s and early 1960s. The standard of living in western Sicily rose 50 percent, Mafia influence significantly decreased, and more people were moving to Sicily than were leaving the island. During the 1970s, Dolci moved away from nonviolent action toward the cause of educational development. He helped establish an educational center in 1975. By the mid-1970s, "The Center" had transformed into a cultural center. For two decades, however, Dolci and his associates had maintained a successful non-violent campaign against poverty and Mafia corruption.

Brad Bennett

References

Amato, Joseph. "Danilo Dolci: A Nonviolent Reformer." In *Nonviolent Action and Social Change,* edited by Severyn T. Bruyn and Paula M. Rayman. New York: Irvington, 1981.

Hope, Marjorie, and James Young. *The Struggle for Humanity: Agents of Nonviolent Change in a Violent World.* Maryknoll, N.Y.: Orbis, 1977.

See also FASTING; REVERSE STRIKE; REVOLUTION

Dominican Republic, Civic Strike, 1961

Movement to force the resignation of President Joaquín Balaguer of the Dominican Republic, which lasted from November 28 to December 9, 1961. Organized by the predominantly middle- and upper-class opposition coalition, the Unión Cívica Nacional (National Civic Union, UCN), the strike ended when Balaguer agreed with the UCN on the formation of a Council of State to govern the country, from which he would resign within six weeks.

Balaguer had succeeded to the presidency after the assassination of dictator Rafael Trujillo on May 31, 1961. The UCN, composed primarily of business and professional people, emerged in July, campaigning for the removal of all vestiges of the Trujillo regime before the election of a new president, scheduled for May 1962. In November, the Balaguer regime attempted to reach agreement with the UCN on a new interim government. When Balaguer refused to step down, the UCN called the civic strike.

The associations of lawyers and students and some infant labor unions joined the strike. Stores, banks, offices, and gas stations in the capital city closed. Buses and taxis did not run, and almost no stevedores were at work on the docks. Sugar mills closed, while the coffee and cocoa crops went unharvested.

Troops maintained essential services, led mobs in breaking open and looting closed stores, and on one occasion attacked striking bus drivers at their union headquarters. Police and soldiers also attempted to break up crowds and at least two organized demonstrations in Santo Domingo with teargas, tanks, or gunfire,

D

but no fatalities and few injuries were reported. The UCN leadership, which repeatedly called for calm and nonviolence, discouraged street demonstrations.

Some proprietors who closed their businesses paid their employees in advance of the strike, or at least gave them food money. The UCN collected funds to sustain strikers in certain key sectors. Nevertheless, by December 3 opposition leaders were expressing concern about the effect of the strike on poor and working-class people, and the *New York Times* correspondent in Santo Domingo reported that the strike was beginning to weaken. On December 7, in anticipation of the December 9 agreement between the UCN and Balaguer, more taxis and buses appeared in the streets and public offices returned to normal.

The armed forces leadership as a whole supported Balaguer and opposed the agreement of December 9. On December 10, Balaguer reneged on the agreement, announcing his intention to remain in office until August 1962. The UCN did not call for renewal of the strike, which at that point had failed.

Meanwhile, the position of the United States shifted. For some months after the death of Trujillo, U.S. government officials favored Balaguer's continuation in office as the best guarantee of stability until a new president could be elected. On November 20, 1961, U.S. representatives became involved in the negotiations between Balaguer and the UCN to create a new interim government, though it is not clear when the State Department decided that Balaguer would have to go. The breakdown of the December 9 agreement confronted the U.S. government with a crisis in which it felt compelled to intervene. All the leverage it possessed—support for ending the sanctions the Organization of American States had imposed on the Trujillo regime, recognition of the interim government, resumption of U.S.–Dominican trade, and the implicit threat of warships lying off the coast of the island—were brought to bear on Balaguer and the Dominican military. On December 17 they accepted a new plan under which Balaguer would leave office by February 27, 1962.

Patricia Parkman

References

Parkman, Patricia. *Insurrectionary Civic Strikes in Latin America, 1931–1961.* Cambridge, Mass.: The Albert Einstein Institution, 1990.

Frederick Douglass. Sophia Smith Collection/Smith College.

See also CIVIC STRIKE

Douglass, Frederick (1818?–1895)

Fugitive slave and one of the most famous African-American abolitionists. Douglass was born in 1817 or 1818 in Talbot County, Maryland, and died on February 20, 1895, in Washington, D.C. As a writer, editor, and orator, he championed the cause of emancipation and equal rights for former slaves. As a runaway slave, he constantly risked being identified and returned to captivity during his many public acts of protest against slavery and inequality.

In 1838, at the age of twenty, Frederick Bailey escaped from his Baltimore slavery to New York. He subsequently married a free African-American woman, settled in New Bedford, Massachusetts, and changed his name to Douglass to protect his identity. Douglass heard the famous abolitionist William Lloyd Garrison speak at an antislavery meeting in 1839, gave the first major public speech of his own in August 1841, and soon became one of the period's most compelling and popular orators on abolitionism. He became an agent of antislavery societies, and over the next fifty years, Douglass made countless public appearances to advocate abolition, emancipation, and equal rights (for women as well as blacks).

In addition to oration, Douglass was well known for his writing. He published three autobiographical works. The first, *Narrative of the Life of Frederick Douglass, an American Slave,* was published in 1845 and soon became the most noted slave narrative. Because of this document, Douglass feared for his safety and toured Britain for over a year. He also edited four journals or newspapers between 1847 and 1874. His first paper, called *North Star,* was first published in 1847. He continued to write throughout his life.

During the early 1840s, Douglass joined Garrison in advocating "nonresistance," or nonviolent agitation, to advance the abolitionist cause. Upon publishing *North Star,* however, he broke with Garrison, and gradually began to support armed insurrection. As a friend of John Brown, who led an unsuccessful raid in 1859 on a federal arsenal to procure arms for a slave revolt, Douglass evaded arrest for conspiracy by again leaving the country until Southern outrage died down. Douglass embraced a variety of means for achieving emancipation, including nonviolent protest, the Underground Railroad (an illegal network that aided runaway slaves), constitutionalism, armed rebellion, and ultimately war on the slave-holding South. In contrast to Garrison, Douglass did not believe the abolitionist movement was successful, because he felt it had not changed the hearts of the American people.

Brad Bennett

References

McFeely, William S. *Frederick Douglass.* New York: W.W. Norton, 1991.

Stewart, James Brewer. *William Lloyd Garrison and the Challenge of Emancipation.* Arlington Heights, Ill.: Harlan Davidson, 1992.

See also ABOLITIONIST MOVEMENT; GARRISON, WILLIAM LLOYD

Doukhobors (Canada)

Pacifist sect of Russian Christians, many of whom immigrated to the Canadian Northwest Territories in 1898–1899. They have maintained a consistent attempt to resist assimilation into the religious, economic, educational, and political systems of the Canadian government. In challenging external authority and modern materialism, they have utilized tactics of nonviolent direct action and property destruction. Their tactical style has often been one of sudden inspiration and unpremeditated actions.

Perhaps the first famous incident of noncooperation of Doukhobors occurred in the Caucasus in 1895, when villagers burned their firearms and refused to accept military service demanded by czarist authorities. Upon immigration to Canada, Doukhobors resisted assimilation and external authority regarding six major issues: militarization, materialism, land allocation, registration, taxation, and mandatory education. They claimed, and were granted, exemption from military service due to religious conscientious objection. They also engaged in noncooperation, deliberate withholding of information, deception, and tax refusal. A radical minority Doukhobor faction called the "Sons of Freedom" began protesting against assimilation and materialism as early as 1902.

Much of the radical direct action from 1902 to 1962 is attributed to the Sons of Freedom. Their primary tactics included nude demonstrations and parades, burning their own property, and destroying public property. Initially, the exhibitions of nakedness and the burning of their own property were merely expressions of innocence and a renunciation of wealth and material possessions. They slowly transformed into demonstrations of antimaterial protest and began to include the burning of other Doukhobors' houses in an attempt, they reasoned, to divest others of corrupting material possessions. Many of these activities were conducted so as to court arrest and martyrdom.

Beginning in 1923, the Sons of Freedom began to express resistance to both the Canadian government and the traditional Doukhobor leadership. Some members of the Sons of Freedom engaged in arson and dynamiting of public property to protest government authority of different forms. The most frequent targets were schools built by the Canadian government or the majority Doukhobors. The Sons of Freedom burned down or blew up most of these schools to prevent mandatory education. In contrast to direct action prior to 1923, many of these acts of destruction were secret, and Sons of Freedom called them "black work."

Some of the largest Doukhobor direct action campaigns included a pilgrimage in 1902;

mass nude demonstrations and parades in 1932 (in which almost one thousand people were arrested and imprisoned for three years under a newly enacted law against public nudity); a 1943–1944 campaign of noncooperation with conscription that included demonstrations, strikes, nude parades, and the burning of personal property and public property (schools); and a "Great March" in 1962.

Brad Bennett

References

Tarasoff, Koozma J. *Plakun Trava: The Doukhobors*. Grand Forks, B.C.: MIR, 1982.

Woodcock, George, and Ivan Avakumovic. *The Doukhobors*. Ottawa: McClelland and Stewart, 1977.

See also DISROBING, PROTEST; PROPERTY, DESTRUCTION OF ONE'S OWN

Dubček, Alexander (1921–1992)

Political reformer and first secretary of the Czechoslovak Communist Party during the period of liberalization in 1968 known as the "Prague Spring" and during the ensuing invasion and occupation of Czechoslovakia by Soviet-led forces. Born in Slovakia on November 21, 1921, Alexander Dubček spent eight years of his childhood in Pishpek, a village of Kirghizia located in Soviet Central Asia. Then, in 1933, he and his family moved to Gorkiy, an industrial town 250 miles east of Moscow. Growing up in the Soviet Union, Dubček saw the extent of terror, starvation, oppression, and poverty under which people lived. Eventually, the Dubčeks returned home to Slovakia in 1938.

After World War II, Dubček worked his way through the ranks of the Communist Party and was eventually elected to the Czechoslovak Party Presidium in 1962. At a 1967 meeting of the Central Committee in Prague, Dubček rallied party reformers and Slovak nationalists against the conservative Stalinist leadership of Antonin Novotny. On January 5, 1968, Novotny was forced to resign, and Dubček succeeded him to become first secretary of the Czechoslovak Communist Party.

Dubček became a rallying symbol for groups seeking the liberalization of Czechoslovak society. Under his leadership, a movement for political and economic reform in Czechoslovakia blossomed and became known as the "Prague Spring." Press censorship was virtually eliminated. Soviet influence in the Czechoslovak Communist Party and in trade unions was reduced. The arbitrary powers of the secret police were taken away. Freedom was in the air.

Threatened by this turn of events, the Soviet Union intervened, leading several Warsaw Pact allies in an invasion of Czechoslovakia on the night of August 20–21, 1968. The Soviet leadership feared that the future of socialism in Czechoslovakia was at risk, that the Communist Party had lost control of that nation, and that Dubček himself had no control of the party. Dubček was accused of allowing policy decisions to be made in the streets and in the editorial offices of Prague rather than in the Central Committee building.

Dubček and five other presidium members were arrested and taken to Moscow. Within a week, however, nonviolent resistance to the Soviet occupation of Czechoslovakia won the return of the Czechoslovak leadership to Prague. Nevertheless, before returning from Moscow the Czech leaders signed a document that would ultimately be used to legitimize "normalization" and the reversal of reforms.

Dubček continued to support democratic reform and refused to give any legitimacy to the Soviet occupation. He remained head of the Czechoslovak Communist Party until April 17, 1969, when he was replaced by Gustav Husák, who brought an end to the democratization process, reinstating government censorship of the press and dissolving reform groups that had emerged during the Prague Spring. Dubček was expelled from the party and soon dropped out of public life.

It was not until December of 1989 that Dubček returned to prominence in Czechoslovak politics, when the Communist Party yielded its dominant power to participate in a coalition government. In a compromise between the Communists and the Czechs and Slovaks, Dubček was elected chairman of the Federal Assembly on December 28, 1989. Dubček died November 7, 1992.

Kimberley A. Pyles

References

Dubček, Alexander. *Czechoslovakia's Blueprint for "Freedom: Unity, Socialism and Humanity."* Introduction and analysis by Paul Ello. Washington: Acropolis, 1968.

D

———. *Hope Dies Last: The Autobiography of Alexander Dubček*. Edited and translated by Jiri Hochman. New York: Kodansha International, 1993.

Kusin, Vladimir V. *From Dubček to Charter 77: A Study of "Normalisation" in Czechoslovakia, 1968–1978*. New York: St. Martin's, 1978.

See also CHARTER 77; CZECHOSLOVAKIA, 1968 RESISTANCE MOVEMENT; HAVEL, VÁCLAV; REVOLUTIONS OF 1989

E

East Timor, Resistance to Indonesian Occupation

Former Portuguese territory within the Indonesian archipelago, invaded and occupied by Indonesian forces in December 1975 and formally annexed by Indonesia on July 15, 1976. East Timor has been the site of nonviolent resistance and guerrilla warfare since the Indonesian invasion. Nonviolent resistance is based on two distinct but complementary political forces opposed in whole or in part to Indonesia's forcible integration of the region. One is linked with Falantil (the East Timorese guerrilla army fighting Indonesian military forces and the military arm of the East Timorese political party Fretilin), while the second is associated with the Catholic Church. Despite determined efforts by Indonesian authorities to eliminate or nullify all forms of resistance, nonviolent struggle is attracting increasing domestic support and international attention.

The "Clandestine Front" *(Frente Clandestine)* is a term used by East Timorese to describe political resistance to *integrasi* (the Indonesian term describing East Timor's integration as the twenty-seventh province of Indonesia) and support for an independent East Timor. It is nonviolent insofar as a deliberate effort is made to avoid armed force in the protests, demonstrations, and other activities organized by the Clandestine Front. This strategy is deemed to be most effective in gaining domestic and international support for the goals of the resistance. Much of the Clandestine Front is centrally run and organized by Falantil, but an appreciable part of the front comprises a collection of individuals or groups with no formal association with Falantil.

East Timor's Clandestine Front has three distinct branches. The first relays information between Falantil and externally based Timorese groups concerning reports of clashes, casualties, Indonesian troop movements, and military repression of the civilian population. It also coordinates the activities of politically active East Timorese individuals and organizations.

The second branch comprises politically active students and youth that organize or participate in demonstrations and protests (such as raising the banned Fretilin flag or shouting pro-independence slogans) when foreign dignitaries and international news media representatives visit East Timor. They also contact foreign tourists to relate stories of human rights abuses by the military and to appeal for international support for their struggle for self-determination.

The third branch of the Clandestine Front is found in Indonesian universities, where hundreds of East Timorese are enrolled. One of the goals of this branch is to have political issues associated with East Timor included on the agenda of the Indonesian pro-democracy movement. Another goal is to maintain contact with supportive Indonesian human rights organizations and pass on information about abuses, detentions, or protests in East Timor.

The Catholic Church is a focal point for nonviolent resistance to the religious, cultural, and economic aspects of *integrasi*. In contrast to the Clandestine Front, the nonviolent resistance of the Church is motivated by a principled rejection of violence as outlined by biblical precepts and practices. The main goals of the resistance are exposing human rights abuses by the Indonesian military, countering the effects of Indonesian immigration to East Timor and monopolistic economic practices, maintaining East Timor's Catholic heritage in the face of the widespread promotion of Islam, and protecting East Timorese culture. The nonviolent methods used include public statements criticizing Indonesian policies made by Catholic clergy and encouraging traditional East Timorese cultural practices. In addition, the Church maintains an East Timorese curriculum in schools and seminaries, a chief feature of which is the use of Tetun, the region's main indigenous language, thereby elevating it to an unofficial second language after Bahasa Indonesian. Though there is a clear emphasis on "dialogue" as opposed to more confrontational activity such as protests, the Church continues to provide support for those participating in or organizing protests and demonstrations.

Under the leadership of Bishop Carlos Ximenes Belo, the Catholic Church pursues a nonpolitical agenda insofar as the bishop avoids statements that would make the Church a partisan actor in the conflict. He tries to steer a middle course between the uncompromising demands for independence by the guerrilla resistance and Clandestine Front and the hardline Indonesian generals who wish to eliminate all political opposition.

A feature of this nonpartisan political stance is an emphasis on the cultural and economic aspects of *integrasi* and the importance of resisting many of these. According to Bishop Belo, East Timorese must "fight for a kind of autonomy, at least at the social and cultural level." He uses the term *Indonization* to encapsulate the unsavory aspects of *integrasi,* which would permanently transform East Timorese culture, and political and economic conditions, thereby more closely integrating the region with the rest of Indonesia and curtailing support for political dissent.

The most visible element of Indonization is the demographic effect of the population influx from other provinces, including business migrants, military and police personnel, public servants, and those arriving as part of Indonesia's transmigration policy. Another aspect of Indonization is the influx of Muslims and the perceived promotion of Islam in East Timor. Not surprisingly, this is viewed by the Catholic Church as a threat to East Timor's Catholic heritage and national identity.

Nonviolent action to preserve East Timor's religious heritage was exemplified in July 1994 by the reaction to the abuse of church sacraments by two Muslim soldiers who had pretended to be Catholics. This act of sacrilege sparked one of the largest protests ever in Dili, East Timor's capital. Nearly three hundred protesters carried large crosses and pictures of the Virgin Mary in a two-kilometer walk from the site of the incident to the governor's office. This was soon followed by another incident in which four Indonesian men harassed two nuns. In response, hundreds of students attempted to march from the University of East Timor to the governor's office until the march was stopped by security forces.

The Indonesian government and security forces pursue a number of strategies to nullify the nonviolent activities of the Clandestine Front and the Catholic Church. These include direct repression and intimidation of activists and Church officials, hampering Church efforts to prevent harassment or detention of parishioners, and withdrawing scholarships for East Timorese students in Dili or in Indonesian universities. The military has used informants and agent provocateurs to draw out members of the Clandestine Front and has undertaken mass round ups of suspected activists prior to visits by dignitaries or before important anniversaries. In addition, the Indonesian government has strategically used development funds earmarked for East Timor to coopt or silence significant elements of the East Timorese community. The most dramatic and violent act of repression occurred on November 12, 1991, when Indonesian police opened fire on a nonviolent demonstration at the Santa Cruz Cemetary in Dili, killing up to 270 protesters.

While the nonviolent resistance of the Catholic Church is analytically distinct from that of the Clandestine Front, the two cannot be easily disassociated due to their overlapping goals and bases of support. Those participating in Clandestine Front activities, for example, are also Catholics who will work for cultural, religious, and economic rights pursued by the Church. Also, the political consequences of many Church proposals, such as Bishop Belo's referendum proposal, are aligned with political sentiments in the Clandestine Front. Consequently, the nonviolent resistance of the Catholic Church and the Clandestine Front are intertwined in a movement that continues to grow in popular support despite Indonesian efforts to counter it.

Michael Salla

References

Gunn, Geoffrey. *A Critical View of Western Journalism and Scholarship on East Timor.* Manila: Journal of Contemporary Asian Publishers, 1994.

Taylor, John G. *Indonesia's Forgotten War: The Hidden History of East Timor.* Atlantic Highlands, N.J.: Zed, 1991.

Egyptian Demonstrations against British Rule, 1919–1922

A nationalist movement against British rule that included demonstrations, widespread strikes, and political boycotts. Opposition became widespread after World War I and led to limited Egyptian independence in 1922.

At the outbreak of World War I, Britain proclaimed Egypt a British Protectorate and declared martial law. Despite a prior pledge, citizens were conscripted into the Labour Corps, resources were expropriated, and censorship was enforced to aid the British war effort. Several small expressions of protest against this unwanted militarization of Egyptian society occurred prior to mass resistance, including a 1915 boycott by law students of a visit from a British-backed Turkish Sultan and a 1916 Cairo demonstration.

After the Armistice was signed in 1918, nationalist leaders petitioned the Crown demanding formation of an Egyptian delegation to facilitate independence. Political leader Saad Zaghlul organized a permanent body, called *Al-Wafd al-Misri,* to agitate for independence. On March 8, 1919, the British arrested Zaghlul and other prominent nationalists and exiled them to Malta. This action provoked demonstrations in major Egyptian cities and strikes by students, transport workers, judges, and lawyers. Some of the demonstrations included violent destruction of public property and Anglo newspaper offices. Demonstrators were brutally attacked by the British military, and there were deaths on both sides. Peaceful demonstrations and violent riots continued throughout Egypt.

Although the Wafd leaders were released and a new Egyptian government was formed in April, the Paris Peace Conference endorsed the British Protectorate over Egypt, and strikes and demonstrations continued through April. The Wafd published and distributed leaflets and illegal newspapers. Many sectors of the populations of Cairo and Alexandra went on strike, including government officials. This civil strike collapsed, however, under threat of dismissal by British authorities. Other workers soon followed suit and went back to work.

When Lord Milner led an inquiry to study the Egyptian conflict from December 1919 to April 1920, the Wafd led a political boycott against the Milner mission. The Milner report, published in February 1921, recommended that Britain abandon the Protectorate arrangement, and General Allenby granted Egypt limited independence in February 1922. Nationalist demonstrations continued through this transition period. Zaghlul organized a large demonstration in Cairo in December 1921. All political meetings were banned, Wafd leaders defied this prohibition, and Zaghlul and others were deported to Suez.

Although there was some violence, primarily directed at public property, the Wafd-led nationalist movement was predominantly nonviolent. The most effective weapon, in terms of influencing the Milner mission, was the political boycott. The nationalist movement led to limited change in the British policy toward Egypt. Total independence from British influence and control was not accomplished until 1952.

Brad Bennett

References

Bennett, Brad. "Arab-Muslim Cases of Nonviolent Struggle." In *Arab Nonviolent Political Struggle in the Middle East,* edited by Ralph E. Crow, Philip Grant, and Saad E. Ibrahim. Boulder and London: Lynne Rienner, 1990.

Carter, B.L. *The Copts in Egyptian Politics.* London: Croom Helm, 1986.

Young, George. *Egypt.* New York: Charles Scribner's Sons, 1927.

See also SOCIAL BOYCOTT

El Salvador, Civic Strike, 1944

A movement that ended the rule of dictator Maximiliano Hernández Martínez. It began with the declaration of a university student strike on April 24. Martínez resigned on May 9, but the strike continued until he left the country on May 11.

At its height on May 8, the strike involved most of the population of San Salvador, the capital, and was beginning to spread to other cities. Participants included physicians, dentists, pharmacists, lawyers, justices of the peace, and employees of all national and municipal government departments, as well as market vendors, commercial employees, railroad workers, taxi drivers, and some artisans and factory workers. Banks and schools in San Salvador closed.

Opposition to Martínez grew after he engineered an amendment of the constitution to allow his reelection to a third presidential term in February 1944. An unsuccessful military uprising on April 2 led to the execution of a number of participants. Intense public indignation and fear that others implicated in the revolt would be executed fueled the strike, which was organized primarily by university students. The organizers avoided demonstrations to minimize the possibility of repression until May 7, when police shot and killed the son of a North American father who had married into a prominent Salvadoran family. Massive, though peaceful, crowds then appeared in the streets, and unfounded rumors of U.S. intervention circulated.

Martínez's cabinet resigned on May 8. With essential sectors of the economy paralyzed, the president was left with no collaborators and no power base except the commanders of the armed forces. The latter remained loyal, but the April 2 uprising had demonstrated the unreliability of their subordinates. Martínez chose not to try to hold on by resorting to violent repression. After all-day negotiations with opposition leaders, he agreed to step down immediately.

Patricia Parkman

References

Parkman, Patricia. *Nonviolent Insurrection in El Salvador: The Fall of Maximiliano Hernández Martínez.* Tucson: University of Arizona Press, 1988.

See also CIVIC STRIKE

Emigration, Protest (Hijrat)

Method of extreme noncooperation in which a person or group deliberately migrates from a country to protest specific injustices or general oppression attributed to that state's government. It represents a withdrawal of all consent with or severence of all forms of social cooperation from the social system. Nonviolent action theorist Joan Bondurant calls this method "voluntary exile." The protest emigration is often intended to be permanent. Sometimes, however, the emigration is intended to be temporary and is designed to appeal to or coerce the opponent by withdrawing consent, especially if that opponent desires the emigrants' cooperation. The larger the population that emigrates, the more it becomes a method of large-scale noncooperation.

Called *hijrat* in India, this method was used extensively in various campaigns against British rule. It developed as an offshoot of "no-tax" campaigns. Gandhi advocated *hijrat* as a last resort in satyagraha campaigns if the repression was too severe to bear. The physical withdrawal or self-imposed exile from territory controlled by the state, while a sacrifical burden to the emigrants, provided a nonviolent alternative to taking up arms in situations of severe repression or oppression. Peasants in the state of Gujarat migrated to Baroda (an area outside of British jurisdiction) to avoid repression during their 1930–1931 tax-refusal campaign.

This method was also used by Japanese peasants during the Tokugawa period (1603–1867) and was called *chosan,* or desertion. In reaction to oppressive feudal lords or corrupt officials, entire villages of peasants would move into a neighboring fief. They would then petition that lord to be allowed to remain under his rule, or they would ask him to intervene on their behalf in the conflict with their former lord. One study estimates that *chosan* made up 9 percent of all peasant uprisings during the Tukugawa period.

During the May Fourth Movement in China in the early twentieth century, Chinese students studying in Japan returned home en masse to protest Japanese and European policies regarding the World War I peace settlements.

Sometimes protest emigration is undertaken to escape religious persecution. Large numbers of Prussian Mennonites immigrated to Pennsylvania and Russia in the late 1700s and early 1800s to avoid compulsory military service, which was against their religious beliefs.

References

Borton, Hugh. *Peasant Uprisings in Japan of the Tokugawa Period.* New York: Paragon, 1968.

Sharp, Gene. *The Politics of Nonviolent Action.* Boston: Porter Sargent, 1973.

See also INDIAN NATIONAL MOVEMENT; MAY FOURTH MOVEMENT, 1919; REVOLUTIONS OF 1989

Environmental Movements

Movements that have used scientific expertise, legal expertise, political advocacy, and nonviolent direct action in attempts to protect the earth from ecological destruction and its inhabitants from extinction.

Environmental groups have pressed for the conservation of wilderness areas and the preservation of endangered species. They have fought for pollution controls, for the cleanup of toxic wastes, and for an end to the production and use of hazardous nuclear materials. They have worked against environmentally damaging development, deforestation, and the wanton exploitation of the earth's natural resources. They have championed the cause of animal rights. Over time, some environmental groups have emerged that take a more interventionist approach to these issues, with direct action playing an increasingly important role in their strategy for change. These include Greenpeace, Earth First! and Chipko.

Emergence of Environmental Consciousness

Contemporary environmental movements trace the emergence of environmental protection to the conservation movement. Among the first environmental organizations were the Audubon Society and the Sierra Club, founded in the late nineteenth century. These groups began by focusing on the protection of endangered species and the preservation of wilderness areas. In the United States, some of the first national parks were established as a result of their work. This tradition remains strong in the United States and in other parts of the world. In other countries, conservation efforts have established national parks and wildlife refuges, and provided legal protection for endangered species, such as elephants, rhinoceroses, whales, and birds. International agreements such as the Convention on International Trade in Endangered Species of Wild Flora and Fauna (CITES), adopted in 1973, grew out of this approach. Increasingly, it became clear that preservation of a species demanded more than regulating or prohibiting international trade. Preservation of species required the preservation, or at least conservation, of the territory and ecosystem in which the species lived.

After decades of conservation activity, popular environmental consciousness made a significant shift in the 1960s, owing among other things to the publication of two books. Rachel Carson's 1962 book *Silent Spring* raised the issue of pesticides in the food chain, sparking serious public concern about these chemicals and focusing attention on the interrelated issues of air, water, and other pollution. Health problems associated with overexposure to pesticides were felt particularly acutely among farmworkers, who experienced daily chemical contact in their work and living conditions. Pesticide-related deaths were recorded as early as 1952, but it was only in 1968, after the stir caused by Carson's book, that organizations such as the United Farm Workers of California began to take up the issue for action. In March 1969, the United Farm Workers' Organizing Committee sued to open pesticide application records and to end the use of DDT, and it made pesticide use the primary issue in negotiations with table-grape growers that summer. Strikes by the United Farm Workers and especially the UFW-led consumer boycott of grapes have become legendary in the history of nonviolent action.

The publication in 1968 of Paul Ehrlich's *The Population Bomb* focused attention on the environmental impact of human population growth. While Thomas Malthus had linked food supply to population in the previous century, Ehrlich's book took hold of the public imagination in ways that were significant for action. Similarly, Garrett Hardin's 1968 essay "The Tragedy of the Commons" focused on the pressure population growth puts on limited resources and the tragic consequences that can result. Subsequent work by the Club of Rome highlighted the links between population, food supply, industrial capacity, resources, and pollution. Education and changing people's ways of thinking about the environment were central among forms of action.

After hearing Ehrlich speak in September 1969, Senator Gaylord Nelson decided, borrowing a method from antiwar activists, to hold an environmental teach-in. He hired Denis Hayes and proceeded to develop Earth Day for April 22, 1970, a nationwide environmental teach-in that has been held annually ever since. Friends of the Earth, a spin-off from the Sierra Club, published *The Environmental Handbook* as a guide for Earth Day on philosophy, issues, and what it called eco-tactics, both for individual change and political action.

Nevertheless, the world has been slow to acknowledge the need for population control. The UN World Population Conferences of 1974, 1984, and 1994 were plagued with debates over birth control, with clearer consensus about the need to control world population coming only in the 1994 conference.

E

Environmental Actions and Strategies

In most instances, nonviolent direct actions are not isolated incidents in environmental campaigns, but are carefully choreographed as part of a larger strategy that often includes scientific, legal, and political research, lobbying, negotiation, lawsuits, monitoring, photography, and media work, as well as participation in governmental and international policymaking. Groups such as the Sierra Club, Greenpeace, Friends of the Earth, the Audubon Society, the National Wildlife Federation, the World Wildlife Federation, the Wilderness Society, Zero Population Growth, and countless local groups all over the world have worked separately and together, using a variety of such strategies, to stop specific instances of pollution or harmful development as well as to influence the policies of governments and international organizations.

A debate over working within or outside the system is echoed in the debate over tactics. At one end of the spectrum are those who work actively with governments and international organizations to frame, write, and administer policy. Most movements and organizations also do public education, and many create demonstration projects and offer alternative models for policies they oppose. Monitoring is also an important part of environmental-group activities. On the other end of the spectrum are those groups who focus on nonviolent direct action such as strikes, boycotts, and blockades of development projects. The direct blockage of toxic waste discharge and other forms of pollution from factories and the monitoring and labeling of environmentally damaging practices are also common. Symbolic actions often are directly related to the problem addressed. For example, environmental vigilantes poured oil in the reflecting pool in front of the Standard Oil building in San Francisco to bring attention to the oil slicks that were discoloring offshore waters. And on Fifth Avenue in New York City, demonstrators held up fish killed by pollution to say, "You're next, people!"

The debate over tactics in environmental movements extends to one's definition of nonviolence—whether or not the destruction of property is acceptable. The Sea Shepherd Conservation Society, for example, considers sabotage legitimate. Formed in 1977 by Paul Watson after he was expelled from Greenpeace for his radical tactics, the society is dedicated to the protection of marine mammals through means that have included ramming a pirate whaling

ship. The Sea Shepherds are part of a small radical wing of the environmental movement. Animal rights groups such as the Animal Liberation Front are also in this category, utilizing sabotage to save animals from medical experiments and from being killed for furs.

Earth First! is probably the best known of the radical environmental groups. Its philosophy is based loosely on the "deep ecology" thought formulated largely by Norwegian Arne Naess, who also has written on civilian-based defense and other aspects of nonviolent action. Earth First! believes that human life and other life on earth have equal and independent value and that world population must be drastically reduced because it interferes with the ability of both nature and human beings to flourish. Earth First! activists have used such tactics as throwing themselves in front of logging trucks, pulling up stakes for an oil exploration project, chaining themselves to ancient trees marked for logging, and driving iron spikes into trees to make it dangerous for loggers to cut them.

From the late 1950s through the 1980s, antinuclear activity proved to be an important link between antiwar and environmental movements, as did protest against the use of agent orange, a defoliant used during the Vietnam War. For example, Greenpeace formed in 1971 and began with a protest voyage into the U.S. nuclear test zone at Amchitka Island, Alaska. The repeated sit-ins and sympathy demonstrations against the Seabrook, New Hampshire, nuclear power plant, among others, linked antiwar activists with community concerns about accidents, nuclear waste safety, and other adverse environmental impacts of nuclear power. Similarly, both antiwar and environmental concerns motivated the repeated flotillas of small boats in New Zealand, San Francisco, and elsewhere that attempted to blockade ships carrying nuclear weapons.

Other issues that have been central to environmental movements include whaling and the killing of dolphins, driftnet fishing, tropical deforestation and clear-cutting, water and air quality, various types of pollution, global warming, the creation of dams, and toxic waste sites. While some actions on these issues were motivated by an attitude of "not in my backyard" (or "NIMBY"), many more involved integrated campaigns that opposed not only a particular location for some environmentally damaging activity, but also opposed the activity worldwide. Various types of nonviolent ac-

Greenpeace activists attempt to prevent whaling by Japanese ship Kyo Maru No. 1, *December 20, 1991. Photo © Greenpeace/Culley.*

tion were pursued in all of these campaigns, which became increasingly international.

Internationalization and Environmental Action Networks

While environmental movements and actors appear to have had their origin largely in Western, developed countries, they spread rapidly to other areas of the world. Some of this was an echo effect, some the result of deliberate movement and network building. In 1972, the United Nations held its first Conference on the Human Environment in Stockholm. Environmental activists decided to attend the conference, both to lobby it and to talk among themselves. The Swedish government then created an alternative conference, the Forum, where environmental activists demonstrated alternative energy technologies such as solar cookers and developed environmental thinking that was widely recognized to be far more important than what came out of the official conference. But the official conference resulted in the creation of the UN Environment Program (UNEP) in 1975 with headquarters in Nairobi, Kenya. To have access to this new international environmental organization, several nongovernmental organizations (NGOs) formed the Environmental Liaison Centre, both to facilitate liaison with UNEP and to help catalyze and develop networks among movements in Africa and developing countries. They were tremendously successful, and linkages began to form rapidly between such groups as the already existent Chipko Movement founded in 1972 in India, Friends of the Earth Malaysia, the Brazilian rainforest group led by Chico Mendez, and rainforest groups in the United States and the Canadian Pacific Northwest, together forming the Rainforest Action Network to share research, strategies, and tactics. Other networks formed as well.

Resisting deforestation was coupled with promoting reforestation. In the Greenbelt Movement founded by Wangari Maathai, a Kenyan biologist, women planted trees to help stop desertification while raising their own political consciousness. The Treepeople in Southern California have used similar tree-planting actions since 1977 both to raise consciousness and to combat air pollution, with seedlings provided by the California Forestry Division. That inspired similar groups in Utah and San Diego, and led to the establishment of the Global ReLeaf Program. Other tactics have ranged from Chipko's

hugging of trees to direct blockage of bulldozers beginning ranch development in Brazil to demonstrating alternative and traditional uses of the rainforest, as Chico Mendez did with rubber tapping and the harvesting of Brazil nuts, before his murder by ranchers. Coupled with the direct resistance actions and alternative use demonstrations were the revival of traditional cultural patterns and the marketing of alternative rainforest products. Ben and Jerry's ice cream, for example, introduced Rainforest Crunch in 1989, buying the nuts from Community Products, which donates 40 percent of its profits to rainforest-related projects, and which buys from Cultural Survival, which in turn buys from Brazilian rubber tapper and indigenous people's organizations.

The Taiga forests of Eastern Siberia, which surround Lake Baikal, also have been the focus of international action. The case demonstrates how actions are linked together in integrated campaigns. In 1992, Friends of the Earth Japan and the Japanese Tropical Action Network (JATAN) contacted the Korean Citizens Coalition for Economic Justice for aid in stopping the Hyundai Company's logging operations in the old-growth boreal forests. A Korean activist was invited to an International Boreal Forest Conference in Sweden, where he heard from the chair of the Russian Socio-Ecological Union, Russia's largest environmental NGO, about their efforts to save the Taiga forest. While international NGOs threatened a boycott of Hyundai products and agreed to place ads to that effect in the *New York Times,* Greenpeace blockaded Svetlaya Harbor, and the Korean activist went to speak with the chair of Hyundai, who was by then a candidate for president. He reminded the Hyundai chairman that his party symbol was the Korean tiger, a relative of which his company was destroying in the Taiga forest. He suggested that this symbolism might not work to his advantage in the upcoming election. The company soon announced its intention to stop logging operations.

Similar campaigns have been mounted concerning the Three Gorges Dam in China, a World Bank dam project in India, the development of debt-for-nature swaps, and the creation of biosphere reserves. The World Wildlife Fund and the African Wildlife Fund worked together to develop first, in 1986, quotas, and then, in 1990, a ban on the ivory trade through CITES. Campaigns also have been mounted against toxic waste dumps in Love Canal, New York, along the Miramichi River in eastern Canada, and in South Africa.

The United Nations Conference on Environment and Development in Rio de Janeiro in the summer of 1992 was an occasion for tremendous growth in environmental actions and networking. As at the 1972 Stockholm environment conference, Forum '92 was the confluence of actions and discussions by hundreds of environmental and other NGOs. Activities included demonstrations of alternative technology, celebrations, discussions, and lobbying. A new technique, the signing of nongovernmental "treaties" on specific areas of environmental concern, also appeared. Participants together wrote and signed treaties on forests, sustainable agriculture, oceans, and other subjects, committing themselves to future action. While some environmentalists judged this to be a diversion from real attempts at influencing governmental policy, others felt that creating their own alternative systems was a more constructive step.

Carolyn M. Stephenson

References
Caldwell, Lynton. *In Defense of Earth*. Bloomington: Indiana University Press, 1972.
Carson, Rachel. *Silent Spring*. Greenwich, Conn.: Fawcett, 1962.
Davis, John, ed. *The Earth First! Reader: Ten Years of Radical Environmentalism*. Salt Lake City, Utah: Peregrine Smith, 1991.
De Bell, Garrett, ed. *The Environmental Handbook: Prepared for the First Environmental Teach-In*. New York: Ballantine, 1970.
Ehrlich, Paul. *The Population Bomb*. New York: Ballantine, 1968.
French, Hilary. *Green Revolutions: Environmental Reconstruction in Eastern Europe and the Soviet Union*. Worldwatch Paper 99. Washington, D.C.: Worldwatch Institute, November 1990.
Hardin, Garrett. "The Tragedy of the Commons." *Science* 162 (December 13, 1968): 1243–1248.
Jancar-Webster, Barbara. *Environmental Action in Eastern Europe*. Armonk, N.Y.: M.E. Sharpe, 1993.
Manes, Christopher. *Green Rage: Radical Environmentalism and the Unmaking of Civilization*. Boston: Little, Brown, 1990
Mitchell, John G., with Constance L. Stallings, eds. *Ecotactics: The Sierra Club Handbook for Environment Activists*. New York: Pocket Books, 1970.
Scarce, Rik. *Eco-Warriors: Understanding the Radical Environmental Movement*. Chicago: Noble, 1990.
Shabecoff, Philip. *A Fierce Green Fire*. New York: Hill and Wang, 1993.

See also CHIPKO MOVEMENT; CLAMSHELL ALLIANCE; GREENPEACE; MONKEYWRENCHING; NUCLEAR ENERGY OPPOSITION; NUCLEAR WEAPONS OPPOSITION; *RAINBOW WARRIOR;* UNITED FARM WORKERS ORGANIZING COMMITTEE

Ethnic Conflict
A domain of conflict among groups and nations, often rooted in political and economic disagreements, but profoundly colored by incompatible definitions of identity. Understanding the roots of ethnic conflicts requires analysis of immediate structural and historical circumstances in each case. The potential virulence of conflicts that threaten identity, however, makes these particularly difficult either to resolve, or for the participants to wage with nonviolent means. This is not to say that nonviolent methods have not been used in ethnically based conflicts to pursue a group's goals or to attempt to break a spiral of violence: some Azeris have attempted nonviolent action in the Azerbaijan-Armenia conflict; ethnic Albanians in Kosova have resisted being drawn into the larger civil war in former Yugoslavia; and diverse groups have used nonviolent methods in various of India's conflicts. The challenge is in determining how an ethnically based nonviolent campaign can substitute for the more easily expressed, and less organized, violence.

Rodolfo Stevenhagen defines ethnic conflict as a "confrontation (at any level: political, social, military) in which the contending actors or parties identify themselves or each other (or are so identified by outsiders) in ethnic terms, that is, using ethnic criteria." The criteria can be language, religion, culture, or nationality, either alone or in combination. However, the terms *identity group* or *survival group* may offer a broader analytic sweep and help account for the intercommunal violence in Somalia, for example, where clans sharing the same religion, language, culture, and ethnos or nationality have been fighting miniwars motivated by fear of subjugation, and possibly extinction, by other clans. The operative words are subjugation, extinction, and especially "other," as will soon be seen.

To many, the puzzling and shocking intercommunal violence and murder, often extending to genocide, that seems to dominate the news is quite novel, the unanticipated result of the collapse of communism in Europe and the end of the cold war. The bipolar tension in the U.S.–Soviet enmity contained lesser conflicts even in Asia, Africa, and Latin America, and when the enmity disappeared so too did the constraints. As H.D.S. Greenway wrote in a first-rate series for the *Boston Globe* in 1992, "The customs, laws and civility that allowed people of different cultures to live in peace together are going down all over Europe and beyond. From the brutality of Bosnia's civil war to the outrages against outsiders in Germany, and the communal violence that . . . swept India, the beast of ethnic hatred is loose."

In early 1994, Gurr and Harff counted twenty-three "hot" wars being fought around the world. All but five were ethnic conflicts. According to data through 1993, the authors report, there were over 18 million refugees and 24 million internally displaced persons fleeing ethnic violence and state repression. One informed estimate predicted the refugee number could rise to 100 million by the year 2000. In the current inventory of conflicts some 4 million people, almost entirely civilians, have died, 700,000 in 1992–1993 alone.

Social scientists who study ethnic conflict tend to pay close attention to structural or systemic factors in the genesis of political violence. This contrasts with the dynamically oriented psychologists, psychiatrists, and (by definition) psychoanalysts whose great strength is the explanation of group psychology and especially conscious and unconscious group motivation. The wisest of both communities of scholars recognize that knowledge of both systemic and group psychological factors and their interaction is critical to understanding ethnic conflict and prescribing approaches to managing and resolving it.

In the most comprehensive sense, structural factors, more literally the failure of the state, were critical in the outbreak of the ethnic wars in former Yugoslavia and the former Soviet Union. The civil and cross-border wars in Moldova, Armenia-Azerbaijan, Georgia-Abkhazia-Ossetia, and Tadjikistan resulted in good part from the loss of the security structure—the Red Army and KGB internal security forces—that accompanied the collapse of the Soviet Union.

A less apocalyptic view of structural factors contributing to the potential outbreak of domestic political violence is offered in Dipak Gupta's *The Economics of Political Violence.* The author explores a wide range of economic, social, political, and demographic structural imbalance theories. Under the economics heading, unemployment, inflation, and income inequality are prominent.

Interestingly, several studies Gupta cites show a greater correlation between unemployment and political violence in more developed countries, explained, perhaps, by greater prevalence of real social safety nets in more traditional societies. High inflation demonstrably contributes to political tensions in any society. It was an important factor in President Jimmy Carter's electoral defeat in 1980; it helped precipitate military coups in Latin America; and it stimulated the rise of radical regimes in Europe in the post–World War I period, most notably Hitler's in Germany. Hyperinflation helped destroy Chiang Kai-shek's regime in China and bring Mao Zedong to power after World War II. Gupta presents interesting survey findings on the relationship between poverty and political violence in that it is not existential poverty so much as the concentration of wealth in a small percentage of a population that is a potential precipitating factor.

Social structural strain factors come closer to explaining particularly ethnic conflict where imbalances in (non-Marxian) class status structure can contribute to political strife and violence. Here discrimination based on race, religion, color, or language is a major factor. Not only are those groups who feel kept down likely to fight back, but also those groups that have lost income and thus suffer from "status strain." Into this category fall lower-middle- and working-class Germans attacking Turks and other foreign "guest workers," Frenchmen competing with North African immigrants, or "Anglos" in America feeling crowded in some labor markets by blacks, Hispanics, or Asian immigrants.

In the category of political structural strain, emphasis is on the legitimacy of ruling elites and their ability to ensure political stability. The theory is that social injustice and relative deprivation of income or just access to income are only necessary preconditions for political tension. It is the perception of the regime's political illegitimacy that moves the situation toward violence. Another factor contributing to political stress is new knowledge provided by modern mass communications on how much better off other societies are both economically and in political freedoms.

Under demographic strain must be included high levels of migration, which intensify population pressure on the existing economic resource base, for example Bengalis into Assam state in India, Yugoslav refugees into Germany, or Salvadorans into Honduras, precipitating the "Soccer War" of 1969. Then there is the problem of rapid rural migration to cities, which can overwhelm a society's capacity to provide public goods and services. Shah Mohammed Reza Pahlavi's unrealistic drive to raise the Iranian economy to the level of Italy's by the year 2000 brought large numbers of migrants from villages to the cities. Predictable gridlock paralyzed the development campaign and helped persuade an uprooted, newly unemployed, and angry Iranian proletariat that the shah had to go.

A more recently recognized source of systemic or structural stress is that generated by environmental degradation. The public health costs of Soviet-style industrialization have been documented in Feshbach's and Friendly's extraordinary *Ecocide in the USSR*. The growing level of public anger at the costs over the years of environmental indifference of Communist planners in the (particularly Slavic) Soviet Union and in Eastern Europe paved the way for political insurgencies on "green" platforms as Gorbachev deconstructed the Warsaw Pact imperium.

In a broad sense, many of the systemic or structural weaknesses just reviewed, especially the economic, demographic, and environmental stresses are ethnically neutral. They can cause rulers extreme distress in homogeneous societies and are not automatic indicators of potential ethnic violence. For these one must look more closely at political-psychological factors.

The concept of the "self" in developmental psychology is essential to understanding the origins, predictability, and perpetuation of intergroup or interethnic conflict. The late Heinz Kohut, a psychoanalyst, is credited by his peers with having developed a persuasive definition of the self and preparing the way for the idea of the *extended self,* which might be used inter-changeably with the terms *group self, identity group,* or *survival group.* The self in Kohut's view related to the essence of the personality make-up of the child, which evolves from the interplay with its mother or immediate caregivers. The self combines basic ambitions, idealized goals, skills, and talents, and the ability to manage desires realistically. The self is the physical person, a learner and an actor.

A strong, stable sense of self is the most important psychological defense against the human existential fear of death. According to psychiatrist Gregory Rochlin, "Narcissism, this love of self, is the human psychological process through which preserving the self is assured. . . . And, when narcissism is threatened, we are humiliated, *our self-esteem is injured* and *aggression appears.*" In fact, "From our earliest years narcissism and aggression are found to be linked in an invisible bond."

The self, however, does not exist in a vacuum. Our selfhood is defined in relationships with others, our immediate families in infancy and childhood, and our peer groups, communities, and nations as we move through adolescence and young adulthood. Our sense of self and security in the self derives from the judgments of our family, peers, and associates in work and society. We work hard to win the esteem of others, and when we fail, or esteem is withdrawn, the defensive response is aggression externalized to return the hurt to others— to reject the rejecters—or aggression directed inwardly toward ourselves.

Here is where the extended or group-self as a psychological concept illuminates the phenomenon of ethnic conflict. As Rochlin explains, "As an infant and young child, man survives only through the care, help and protection others give him. From his earliest years, the debt owed to others for the security of his existence makes those relationships inseparable from the sense of self. The security of our existence, always precariously held, rests on an ineradicable commitment to others." Thus the use of the terms *identity group* and *survival group* takes on more meaning when one asks the question why individuals are willing to sacrifice their lives in defense of the ethnic group or nation.

Rochlin sees the willingness to die for the sake of the nation as reflecting a dread of the degradation of the self. "To give up one's life to satisfy one's narcissism on the surface may appear to be a contradiction. But, of the two, it seems that narcissism is the more important. The self is best served by maintaining self-regard. If in order to do so, life must be forfeited [then so be it], the risk to our existence comes from whatever menaces our narcissism." In light of this insight, the American cold war slogan "Better Dead than Red" is more easily understood.

Insult or aggression from outside groups or nations wounds the sense of group or national self and triggers various forms of group aggression in defense of the collective self. In the eighteenth and nineteenth centuries, Germany struggled to recover from the double burdens of consistent disdain in the eyes of the culturally superior French and the Napoleanic invasions. It was a painful time as German intellectuals in particular worked to construct a sense of collective self-worth for their nation. The narcissistic injury to Germany is indicated in the following declaration and oath by the nationalist poet Arndt quoted in Liah Greenfeld: "I hate all Frenchmen without distinction in the name of God and of my people, I teach this hatred to my son, I teach it to the sons of my people. . . . I shall work all my life that the contempt and hatred for this people strike the deepest roots in German hearts."

In light of the above, it is remarkable to consider the depth of Franco–German reconciliation created after World War II (after three German invasions). Together France and Germany laid the foundation stone of the contemporary European Union, but only after the expenditure of enormous spiritual as well as intellectual and material effort in both countries to rebuild mutual respect based on recognition of the wounded narcissism of both traumatized nations. They set an enduring model for genuine ethnic conflict resolution.

Yet, in the post–cold war era, the depressing resurgence of ethnic conflict in eastern Europe and the former Soviet republics attests to the durability of wounds to the collective self, be it in Serbia, Armenia, or Georgia. Of course ethnic conflicts in Africa flourished even during the cold war, and Asia and Latin America have had more than a fair share of this tragic human dilemma. In the United States, a small, vicious ethnic conflict between fundamentally unreconciled black and white America washes the nation in violent crime and erupts periodically in mass rioting.

Psychiatrist John Mack is quoted in Greenway's essays saying that the Los Angeles riots of 1992 showed examples of urban survival groups. In this case, "The gang was the primary identification for them because they found nothing in the city or the nation with which to identify." He continued, saying, "The psychological functions served by that identification are common to all conflicts: survival, a sense of self-worth. These are all fundamental psychological principles, a sense of having power versus powerlessness."

When a history of narcissistic wounding combines with unusual systemic economic or political stress or breakdown, the stage is set for ethnic conflict of increasing levels of virulence. One can only hint in this limited space at the forms and processes an ethnic conflict-resolution strategy might take. But there is reason to be hopeful that with new knowledge available to practitioners of ethnic conflict resolution as part of a newly vital preventive diplomacy and with the development of strategic nonviolent action as a means of waging conflict, humankind need not be perpetually subject to violence and destruction in the solving of political problems in the future.

Joseph V. Montville

References

Feshbach, Murray, and Alfred Friendly, Jr. *Ecocide in the USSR.* New York: Basic, 1992.

Greenfeld, Liah. *Nationalism: Five Roads to Modernity.* Cambridge: Harvard University Press, 1992.

Greenway, H.D.S. "Roots of Ethnic Hatred." *Boston Globe,* December 13–16, 1992.

Gupta, Dipak K. *The Economics of Political Violence.* New York: Praeger, 1990.

Gurr, Ted Robert. *Minorities at Risk.* Washington, D.C.: U.S. Institute of Peace, 1993.

Gurr, Ted Robert, and Barbara Harff. "Conceptual Research, and Policy Issues in Early Warning Research: An Overview." *Journal of Ethno-Development* 4 (1994): 3–14.

Horowitz, Donald L. *Ethnic Groups in Conflict.* Berkeley: University of California Press, 1985.

Kohut, Heinz. *The Analysis of the Self.* New York: International Universities Press, 1976.

Montville, Joseph V. *Conflict and Peacemaking in Multiethnic Societies.* Lexington, Mass.: Lexington, 1989.

———. "Facing Ethnic Conflict: A Problem-

Solving Diplomacy for the Clinton Administration." *Harvard Journal of World Affairs* 2 (1993): 1–14.

———. "The Healing Function in Political Conflict Resolution." In *Conflict Resolution Theory and Practice,* edited by Dennis Sandole and Hugo Van Der Merwe. Manchester: Manchester University Press, 1993.

———. "Complicated Mourning and Mobilization for Nationalism." In *Social Pathology in Comparative Perspective,* edited by Jerome Braun. Westport, Conn.: Praeger, 1995.

Rochlin, Gregory. *Man's Aggression.* Boston: Gambit, 1973.

Stevenhagen, Rodolfo. "Reflections on Some Theories of Ethnic Conflict." *Journal of Ethno-Development* 4 (1994): 15–19.

Volkan, Vamik. *The Need to Have Enemies and Allies.* Northvale, N.J.: Jason Aronson, 1994.

See also BOSNIA-HERZEGOVINA RESISTANCE TO CIVIL WAR, 1991–1992; EAST TIMOR, RESISTANCE TO INDONESIAN OCCUPATION; KOSOVA, ALBANIAN NATIONAL MOVEMENT

Everyday Forms of Resistance

Barely visible, low-profile actions against rulers by subordinate, powerless groups, commonly occurring in agrarian societies such as Colombia, Peru, the Philippines, and China. James C. Scott and a host of other astute scholars of political conflict in agrarian systems have called these actions "everyday forms of resistance."

Such "everyday resistance" might encompass underreporting or concealment of harvests, silent noncooperation with tax collectors, avoidance of military conscription, spreading false rumors about government intentions, character assassination aimed at corrupt officials, and acts of arson. These forms of resistance are often the weapon of choice for rural people living in political systems where, according to Scott, "open defiance is impossible or entails mortal danger." Such acts are taken against rulers precisely because their practitioners are fearful of detection, apprehension, and punishment by political authorities who have closed off civil discourse and who prefer to settle disputes by force. Seldom, if ever, do these acts constitute an open, direct,

and contentious political challenge to the regime in question, and indeed most are undertaken initially to avoid confrontations with government officials.

Such daily forms of resistance are seldom reported in the history of protest and rebellion sanctioned by traditional state powerholders, colonial administrations, or socialist governments. The targets of everyday resistance vary from country to country. This form of resistance has characterized struggles to regain the land seized by European colonizers. Consequently, it has emerged in response to capitalist land seizures accompanying the spread of colonial force, as in Zimbabwe and Algeria. This type of resistance also has formed in response to what Charles Tilly has termed "statemaking," that is, the attempt of national governments to regiment peasant communities in order to draw up their resources for state use. Peasant resistance to Bolshevik seizures of harvests in Russia under Stalin and to Communist Party procurement of harvests in Maoist China during the era of collectivization reflect everyday struggles against the intrusion of the fiscal apparatus of centralized statemaking. On the other hand, everyday resistance also has been waged against the rival claimants of central governments.

Tax struggles in contemporary China constitute a vivid example of everyday resistance. Ever since the failure of the Great Leap Forward in the late 1950s, the central government of China has been caught in a revenue crisis that, given its draconian schemes for extracting resources from the rural population, is in part of its own making. This crisis nonetheless also owes its origins substantially to the protracted formation of everyday forms of peasant resistance to the attempt of the central state and its local agents to take away resources from the small landholders who make up the vast majority of peasant producers in rural China. Since the mid-1980s, routine peasant resistance to the multiplication of demands by rival local government claimants has become more common than resistance to the claims of the central government. Such opposition can be seen in vivid detail.

Western social scientists and news correspondents have reported peasant discontent over taxation by Chinese government officials at all levels. Resulting popular indignation has ignited a wide range of tax resistance, running the gamut from petitions to reduce taxes, to voiced refusals to pay taxes, to open confrontations with officials demanding taxes for construction of township office buildings, highways, and educational facilities. In much of the deep countryside, popular antitax sentiments have been expressed in low-profile, relatively silent forms of peasant resistance that have culminated in a hidden but powerful rebellion against government tax injustice. Four forms of such resistance stand out and pose an obstacle to the fiscal goals of China's centrally placed statemakers and, more important, to rival local tax regimes.

One of the most common, and often the most effective, forms of everyday peasant resistance to government appropriation has been the voiced threat of work stoppages—that is, the declared intention to suspend agricultural production in order to persuade officials to lower taxes. In 1992, the peasants of Zigang village, in Hebei province, told local tax officials they were not going to farm the land anymore if they had to pay exorbitant grain taxes—they literally threatened to leave the land to go work on construction sites in the cities instead. This form of resistance apparently is widespread. In one Anhui county, for example, nearly one-third of the peasants stopped tilling the land because high taxes, among other things, made agricultural production seem irrational. This kind of resistance has frightened provincial and county officials, and in some cases resulted in a reduction of the government wheat tax, which by 1993 posed a threat to the gains peasants were able to secure from working their family lands.

A second form of daily antitax activity involves the popular manufacture of rumor. Between 1982 and 1992, in the first decade of China's household-based farming system, local government leaders often piled onto the central government tax claim more than twenty other kinds of tax fees. Since local tax-gouging officials attempted to pass on these surtaxes as part of the central government's claim, not all peasants knew about them. Many only knew they had to pay so much a year, and that the center's announced claim was minimal. In the absence of village leaders who were committed to accurately transmit central government tax policy, a growing number of peasants in one Henan village took it on themselves to spread rumors that the central government did not allow village leaders to collect any tax at all from villagers, portraying all of the taxes taken by local tax agents as illegal. The popular dissemination of

such false rumors has fueled arguments about the legitimacy of state taxation at the village level, and is a constant source of headache for party leaders charged with collecting taxes from household heads with different levels of knowledge of state tax policy.

Yet another form of everyday resistance in the 1990s is tax evasion. Several techniques of evasion are commonly practiced in the countryside. One is footdragging, which means intentionally delaying payment of taxes. Another is underreporting. Peasants know that the grain collected by government tax collectors is not to exceed 5 percent of their total previous year's income—a limit that was established by the central government. Thus, they habitually underreport household income to protect against gouging by local tax collectors, all the while reminding them of disciplinary action by superiors if they exceed the 5 percent limit. When evasion has not worked, some villagers have petitioned village tax agents for tax reductions. More and more, these village-based tax brokers find the people who make such remedialist appeals to be "difficult to deal with," and local tax supervisors are worried that if they do not accommodate such appeals there is a good chance that informal petitioning will give way to refusal to pay.

Prior to 1990, refusal to pay was not the most frequently practiced form of routine resistance, but this fourth form of tax resistance is on the rise in contemporary rural China. Increasingly, the peasant refusals to pay the grain tax to district level governments have led to stand-offs between villagers and district tax officials and to police interventions on behalf of the officials.

There are many other forms of everyday resistance besides tax resistance. For example, peasants have pursued various strategies of resistance to the central government's birth control policy of one child per family since 1990. The most common weapon in popular attempts to get around birth control regulations has been bribery. Time and time again peasants have resisted the family planning campaigns by bribery, which has taken the form of giving lavish gifts to corrupt party cadres, all in an attempt to persuade them to turn blind eyes to the birth of a second or third child. Another strategy of resistance is feigned sterilization. Once the central government tightened up on the single child policy in the countryside, township family planners insisted that village women who already had one child present themselves for tubal ligations in the township hospitals. Yet many of the women who have undergone such operations have still become pregnant. In reality, the "failure" of this surgical procedure has been discreetly prearranged between peasant families and rural folk doctors who, though working for the township, are still village residents, in sympathy with the strong desires of peasants to bear sons to continue family lines. They are easily persuaded to perform the operations without actually tying the tubes, thus allowing the female patients to give birth to a second, "accidental child" while feigning ignorance and innocence to the state family planning officials.

Much of everyday resistance takes place at the microlevel of village and neighborhood settings and seldom finds a voice, or impact, beyond this village today or that district tomorrow. It is ultralocal and without regional and national political consequence. Thus it cannot automatically be considered to be a widely based collective political movement. Nevertheless, under certain political conditions, everyday forms of resistance are repeated simultaneously and often enough from one locality to the next, giving rise to contagion and cooperation among the resisters, and ultimately producing collective actions that are ramified across districts, counties, provinces, and regions. When this pattern of resistance develops, a movement of subordinate rural subjects may evolve the potential for thwarting, if not defeating, the appropriation schemes of statemakers.

Thus the concept of everyday resistance helps us understand how such low-key, silent forms of seemingly isolated and harmless struggle can suddenly well up in loosely coordinated fashion to potently serve peasant efforts to keep state tax claims fair and tolerable. An example of how such everyday resistance has become ramified in contemporary rural China, and how it has produced collective popular opposition to government taxation illustrates the concept in action. In 1993, the district government's unreasonable grain tax incited a collective tax refusal by the peasant inhabitants of Jing Degu village in Jing Degu district in Nanle county (Henan province). When the police attempted to force the issue, a crowd of villagers waged nonviolent resistance against them and eventually drove the police out of the village. They subsequently joined with peasants in other villages to rush to Jing Degu township, where they physically abused the head of the township government. The rural people behind this collective action, which grew from the minute acts of smaller groups waging everyday resistance to taxation in the microuniverses of different villages, were not punished. In fact, they went to the nearby prefectural court to sue Communist Party township government leaders for overtaxing them and won their lawsuit. Consequently, the Jing Degu township government leaders were ordered to return part of the grain tax payment to the village, and the head of Jing Degu township was criticized and transferred to another place. Local knowledge of this victory spread, and by 1994 this pattern of resistance was catching on in many other districts of Nanle county, so that it constituted a democratic break from below on state appropriation.

Ralph A. Thaxton, Jr.

References

Duara, Pransenjit. *Culture, Power and the State.* Stanford, Calif.: Stanford University Press, 1988.

Herbst, Jeffry. "How the Weak Succeed." In *Everyday Forms of Peasant Resistance,* edited by Forrest D. Colburn. New York: M.E. Sharpe, 1989.

Scott, James C. "Everyday Forms of Resistance." In *Everyday Forms of Peasant Resistance,* edited by Forrest D. Colburn. New York: M.E. Sharpe, 1989.

Tilly, Charles. *The Contentious French.* Cambridge: Harvard University Press, 1986.

Wang Shaoguang. *Zhongguo Guojia Nengli Baogao.* Liaoning Renmin Chubanshe, 1993.

Wolf, Eric R. *Peasant Wars of the Twentieth Century.* New York: Harper and Row, 1968.

WuDunn, Sheryl. "China is Sowing Discontent with 'Taxes' on the Peasants." *New York Times,* May 19, 1993.

See also CHINA; METHODS OF NONVIOLENT ACTION

E

F

Fasting

Method of psychological intervention or moral protest whereby the nonviolent actionist abstains from certain or all foods. The fast can be conducted with the intent to persuade (using altruistic appeal) or to coerce (using moral pressure). Most major religions have historically incorporated fasting into rituals for spiritual purity or strength. Fasting is a method of nonviolent action only when it is undertaken for a political reason or to effect social change. In *The Politics of Nonviolent Action,* Sharp delineates three major types of political fasts: the fast of moral pressure, the hunger strike, and the satyagrahic fast.

Fasts of moral pressure are usually undertaken to appeal to a third party or an opponent in order to achieve an objective. Often, the actionist who engages in a fast is appealing to altruism or some other moral, religious, or legal ideal supposedly shared by both parties. A major goal of the fast of moral pressure is to call attention to a specific issue. Saint Patrick fasted to urge King Trian of Ulster to deal compassionately with his slaves. The Virginia House of Burgesses voted on May 24, 1774, to create a day of "Fasting, Humiliation, and Prayer" to invoke divine assistance in preventing the British from denying them their civil rights. Other Colonial governments endorsed fasts during the next year. Italian Danilo Dolci employed an individual fast to call attention to poverty in 1952 and organized a collective fast by fishermen to protest unemployment in 1956.

The hunger striker attempts to coerce an opponent to change certain policies or behaviors. The hunger strike may last a certain length of time or be undertaken until death. Hunger strikes have historically been a prominent aspect of Irish legal and political struggles. It was the legal duty of Irish plaintiffs in ancient times to "fast on" the defendant if they did not feel justice was obtained by other means. Irish political prisoners have conducted hunger strikes, sometimes to death, against the British in their nationalist struggle in the twentieth century. English and American women's suffragists used hunger strikes in prison to press for the vote, sometimes being subjected to force-feeding. This method has been used extensively for a variety of causes throughout the globe.

The satyagrahic fast is of Gandhian origin. Gandhi regarded hunger strikes as coercive and, by contrast, claimed that the satyagrahic fast was conducted in an attempt to convert the other person(s). Gandhi considered fasting the highest form of satyagraha and demanded that an activist be spiritually prepared before undertaking a fast and share some sort of mutual personal bond with the target of the fast. Gandhi's most famous fast was undertaken in Delhi in 1948 to press for Hindu–Muslim unity and peace.

As noted above, fasting can be undertaken by individuals or groups. In the United States in recent years, fasting has often been undertaken by famous individuals in order to coerce an opponent to act before receiving unwanted negative publicity. One of the more famous of these fasts is Cesar Chavez's 1968 twenty-five-day penitential fast to appeal for unity among migrant farm workers, which seemed to transform itself into a more coercive act as his supporters began to fear for his life. Comedian Dick Gregory fasted in protest against American involvement in Vietnam in 1966. Mitch Snyder of the Community for Creative Non-Violence used a fast in 1985 to call attention to the plight of the homeless. This type of fast can often blur the distinctions between the mechanisms of appeal and coercion.

Brad Bennett

References

Brooks, Svevo, John Burkhart, Dorothy Granada, and Charles Gray. *A Guide to Political Fasting*. Cottage Grove, Ore.: Larry Langdon, 1982.

Rogers, Eric N. *Fasting: The Phenomenon of Self-Denial*. Nashville: Thomas Nelson, 1976.

Sharp, Gene. *The Politics of Nonviolent Action*. Boston: Porter Sargent, 1973.

See also CHAVEZ, CESAR ESTRADA; COMMUNITY FOR CREATIVE NON-VIOLENCE; DOLCI, DANILO; GANDHI, MOHANDAS KARAMCHAND; IRA HUNGER STRIKES, 1980–1981; SATYAGRAHA

Fellowship of Reconciliation, International

An international and interfaith peace organization that began in Europe at the outset of World War I. With branches and affiliated movements in over forty countries, its international secretariat is in Alkmaar, Holland. IFOR has consultative status as a nongovernmental organization with the United Nations. It publishes *Reconciliation International* six times a year.

IFOR's beginning can be traced to an ecumenical conference held in Constance, Switzerland, in August 1914. The onset of World War I during the meeting caused the conference to break up early. Two persons who attended the conference, Henry Hodgkin, a British Quaker, and Frederich Siegmund-Schültze, a German Lutheran and chaplain to the kaiser, pledged that they would refuse to support the war and would carry out a ministry of reconciliation. Out of this pledge the first branch of the Fellowship of Reconciliation was founded at Cambridge University in December 1914 as a Christian fellowship whose loyalty to country, humanity, the universal church, and to Jesus Christ led them to work for "the enthronement of Love in personal, social, commercial and national life [the original Basis for FOR]." The FOR spread to other countries in Europe and to the United States, where its members supported conscientious objectors, exposed wartime propaganda, assisted refugees and war resisters, and worked for the conditions to build reconciliation. In October 1919, fifty women and men from ten countries met in Bilthoven, Holland, to found the International Fellowship of Reconciliation.

Between the two world wars, the International Fellowship of Reconciliation worked for universal understanding and peace among nations, amnesty for war resisters, and for the establishment of the right of conscientious objection. Through its Swiss secretary, Pierre Ceresole, IFOR fostered the work camp movement that brought together volunteers from former enemy nations to carry out reconstruction projects in war-ravaged areas in Europe. Its concern for economic justice led members such as American A.J. Muste (1885–1967) to help establish the rights of laborers to organize into unions and to develop nonviolent tactics for their protests. In 1932, in support of the Geneva World Disarmament Conference, the IFOR led a Youth Crusade across Europe calling for total disarmament.

IFOR opposed the emerging totalitarianism and the growing threat of war in the 1930s by establishing Embassies of Reconciliation in Europe, the United States, and Asia that initiated peace efforts with various world leaders. For example, IFOR sponsored the British Labor leader George Lansbury in meetings with U.S. President Franklin Delano Roosevelt, German Chancellor Adolph Hitler, and Italian Prime Minister Benito Mussolini. IFOR also contacted Gandhi and gave support to the nonviolent liberation struggle in India. When Gandhi came to London to attend the Round Table Conference in 1932, he stayed at Kingsley Hall in the East End, whose founder, Muriel Lester, was a longtime friend. Later, Lester, as an IFOR traveling secretary, did extensive work for peace throughout the world.

During World War II, many IFOR members were imprisoned for conscientious objection and other acts of war resistance. Some joined the nonviolent underground resistance to totalitarianism, including efforts to rescue Jews and other victims of the war. For example, in the French village of Le Chambon, Magda and André Trocmé led the extraordinary nonviolent effort by which thousands of Jews found sanctuary and escaped the Vichy and Nazi attempts to arrest them. In 1944 the publication of Vera Brittain's "Massacre by Bombing" by the U.S. branch of IFOR brought international attention to the devastating effects of the Allies' obliteration bombing of European cities and heightened widespread awareness of the savagery of modern warfare. The end of the war brought intensified

Founding conference of the International Fellowship of Reconciliation in Bilthoven, The Netherlands, October 4–11, 1919. International Fellowship of Reconciliation Archives.

F

efforts by the IFOR and its various branches to aid the victims of war and to promote reconciliation among former enemies. For the next four decades, the organization opposed the cold war and worked for East–West reconciliation.

IFOR condemned the atomic bombing of Hiroshima and Nagasaki and the subsequent development and testing of nuclear weapons as well as all other weapons of mass destruction. This opposition was expressed in such efforts as petitions, marches, rallies, and acts of civil disobedience such as refusing to take shelter during air raid drills and walking into forbidden zones where nuclear weapons were tested or stored.

IFOR's activities extended beyond war resistance to other issues of social justice. IFOR long opposed racism and apartheid. Its U.S. branch was a pioneer in civil rights. In 1947 the U.S. FOR sponsored an interracial team on the first "freedom ride" to test the court decision outlawing discrimination in interstate travel. It also sponsored training in nonviolent action in the South, and FOR Field Secretary Glenn Smiley worked with Martin Luther King, Jr., throughout the Montgomery bus boycott in 1956.

Through its contact with the Gandhian movement, Buddhists during the Vietnam War, and pacifists of other traditions, IFOR's work became increasingly interfaith, developing training in active nonviolence in many countries. Jean and Hildegard Goss-Mayr, several times nominated for the Nobel Peace Prize, trained thousands of persons throughout Latin America, Africa, and Asia. They helped lay the groundwork for the "people power" revolution in the Philippines and the founding of Servicio Paz y Justicia in Latin America.

Richard L. Deats

References

Brittain, Vera. *The Rebel Passion*. Nyack, N.Y.: Fellowship, 1964.

Chatfield, Charles. *For Peace & Justice: Pacifism in America, 1914–1941*. Knoxville: University of Tennessee Press, 1971.

Fellowship. Serial: United States Fellowship

of Reconciliation. Box 271, Nyack, NY 10960.

Reconciliation International. Serial: International Fellowship of Reconciliation. Spoorstraat 38, 1815 BK Alkmaar, Holland.

See also GOSS-MAYR, HILDEGARD AND JEAN; LE CHAMBON SUR LIGNON, FRANCE; MONTGOMERY BUS BOYCOTT, 1955–1956; MUSTE, ABRAHAM JOHN; NUCLEAR WEAPONS OPPOSITION; PHILIPPINES PEOPLE POWER REVOLUTION, 1986; SAYRE, JOHN NEVIN; VIETNAM WAR OPPOSITION

Feminism

Feminism argues that our gender identity is one of the factors that shapes our experiences and how we understand the construction of society. These social structures force most women to live their daily lives within the framework of male dominance, or patriarchy. Feminists argue that social systems of oppression are a context in which conceptions of violence and nonviolence are embedded. Thus the difference established by the reproduction of gender roles and relationships frames the way that men and women think about nonviolence theory and nonviolent action.

Some feminists choose nonviolent action as a challenge to the oppression of patriarchy. Yet despite the extensive contributions by women to nonviolent action, the particular experiences of women are seldom included in the development of theory about nonviolence. Not all feminists choose nonviolence, but those who do see it as integral to their commitment to feminism. Furthermore, women who choose nonviolent action, especially "Third World" women, often do not call themselves feminists.

Women choose nonviolence for many reasons: it is a means of breaking the cycle of violence; it is a moral method of social change; it requires human commitment but not military might; and it seeks to change but not to destroy relationships. Gender analysis suggests that we must consider the differing experiences of men and women when we theorize and when we take action. Thus feminism provides a new standpoint for analyzing and developing theories about both violence and nonviolent action.

Feminists expand traditional perceptions of violence to include patriarchal violence against women. This violence is intended to enforce the system of male dominance. Violence against women is both physical and psychological; both individual and systemic. Feminists argue that violence is present in the private as well as the public spheres of social relations. The model of nation-state violence and domination is paralleled by violence in the home and the workplace. Besides common forms of violence in society, women's specific experiences of violence include battering, rape, sexual harassment, incest, sexist language and educational systems, social inequality, and socially learned low self-esteem. Because violence against women is often predicated on their biological sex or gender category, nonviolent strategies for women must be diverse and connected to a movement to end sexist oppression. The violence of sexist oppression ranges from explicitly physical attacks to women's internalized belief that men's lives are more important than their own.

Feminism is instrumental in making women aware of the violence they live with, and providing a channel for response. In practice and theory, feminism provides a basis for a gender analysis of violence. For example, sociological analysis suggests that women are, more often than men, raised to be nonviolent, and men are, more often than women, raised to be violent. Feminism argues that women are actually socialized to be not-violent, and to be passive. Women are rewarded for responding to a situation by compromising their needs.

While both men and women must change socialized habits in order to effectively participate in nonviolent action, feminism can help us see that men and women have different challenges to face in developing principled and pragmatic commitments to nonviolence. Because women and men experience violence in different forms, they experience nonviolence differently. In developing the ability to be nonviolent, women need to learn to replace passivity with assertion, and men need to learn to use nonviolent assertions rather than aggression.

These different approaches to becoming nonviolent are related to the unequal distribution of power in our society. The primary structure shaping power in a patriarchal society is the relationship of dominant-submissive. Power is primarily defined as control over people, property, and the power to make decisions regarding the allocation of resources. Thus power is seen as the ability to do or to make others do something. It is viewed as a limited commodity and something that must be taken. It is significant that the predominant theories of nonviolent action are based on the idea of refusing to let those in power make you "do." Nonviolent campaigns are based on the idea of redistributing this power and continue to connect power with controlling resources, ideology, or people in some way. Often the very bases of this problematic power, the systemic structures of inequality, are not addressed.

Most feminists argue that we must do more than change the hands that hold power; instead we must transform power by redefining what constitutes it. Power based on control of others is "power-over," and should be reconstituted as "power-with." Transformed power comes from within through the process of individual and group empowerment. Power-with is used by feminists to end white and patriarchal domination. Power transformed is a creative force based on a sense of self-worth, a belief in our own competence, and it builds on our energy to be and to act. Its strength is the web of community. We draw on our own energy and combine it with that of others rather than controlling and using their energy for our own purposes. Power-with is found in unity, in taking responsibility for oneself, and in one's relationship to others.

An important step is to reject the traditional mechanisms of power and replace them with processes that empower all people. The idea of empowerment is that by practicing power-with instead of dominance we can raise self-esteem and create resourceful people to take action for social change. Empowerment comes from acting with people to find the resources to effect change. Feminists call for resistance to power-over in both the public and private spheres. Nonviolent resistance against dominance is important at all levels of social relations, including transforming power in personal relationships and even in movements for nonviolent social change.

In relating techniques for organizing, most of the writings by women about nonviolence refer to notions of "collective action," "affinity groups," and "networks" or "networking." These are the mechanisms that are used to send out messages, to make small group decisions, to form coalitions, to organize support for an action, and to extend support and the feeling of empowerment to our everyday lives.

Besides redefining what is considered violence, and calling for a transformation of the construction of power, feminism encourages women to take a critical view of nonviolence formulated on the bases of exclusively male experiences. Awareness of sexist oppression helps raise recognition of the violence in silencing women's voices in nonviolent action and especially in the development of theory about nonviolence. Besides demanding the inclusion of women's experiences and women's texts in the curriculum of nonviolence, feminists call for the integration of women's ideas into theory-building. Feminism challenges several assumptions that are central to much discussion of both principled and pragmatic nonviolence, such as self-suffering, universal love, withdrawing consent, controlling or denying emotions, and the complete rejection of all violent responses to violence.

The ideals of suffering, humility, and sacrifice are central to Gandhian nonviolence. The Feminism and Nonviolence Study Group in Britain argues, however, that women already experience extensive physical and emotional suffering in their daily lives, so why seek more? Feminists wonder what the goal is in seeking more suffering merely for the idea that suffering makes a more moral human being. As a diverse group, women are already on the margins, and there is little to be gained by reinforcing their willingness to suffer for others because men already expect women to suffer for them. Instead, feminists such as Barbara Deming call on women to demand their rights while simultaneously remembering to treat "the other" with respect.

Historically, women have suffered daily for others, especially for men. For example, in the United States at least a quarter of all women experience sexual assault and abuse by the time they are eighteen. Most women experience sex-related violence at some point in their lives. Feminism points out the depths of women's suffering and helps women to refuse to continue suffering. Knowing that women are in a socialized position of suffering, it seems counterproductive to bring more pain and responsibility into their lives.

Kate McGuinness argues that power is not always based on consent. She argues that the socialized coercion of women to accept man's dominance draws into question whether Gene Sharp's core argument that power is based on consent and can always be withdrawn is relevant to the experience of women. McGuinness argues that in patriarchal systems women are not constituted as full citizens and therefore are not given the choice to consent or to withdraw consent. Men's role as ruler is enforced with violence against women's bodies and self-esteem.

The vast range of women-centered self-defense programs that emerged in the 1970s and continue to prosper today is based on the idea that women need to learn to defend their bodies and develop a sense of personal empowerment. Often the first step is to be in touch with the emotions one feels when oppressed, especially anger or rage. Rage is about recognizing what patriarchy does to women's self-esteem, what ethnocentrism does to women's self-image, and what structures of violence do to children. Accepting and channeling emotions to a creative space is an important step for women in reaching resourceful space. In an empowered state women can then choose to act nonviolently or to live by principled nonviolence, or both.

Years of research, personal accounts, and case studies suggest that despite the potential problems involved, women consistently participate in nonviolent action. However, women choose nonviolence not because they wish to improve themselves through additional suffering, but because the strategy fits their values and their resources. Yet a question remains: how can we best prepare women to be nonviolent activists without increasing their vulnerability and suffering through sexist oppression? For feminists women must choose ways of acting that challenge rather than reinforce the patriarchal system of male dominance.

Programs and actions that empower women teach them that they should not suffer in silence. Women are encouraged to defend themselves verbally, and if necessary physically, in ways that cause minimal suffering to others. Many of the same feminists who encourage women to learn to "fight back" and defend themselves also advocate nonviolence as both a pragmatic strategy and as a philosophical basis for social organization. This is not seen as paradoxical because men's oppression of women, it is argued, means that women have less power to begin with and therefore must be empowered. As long as men attack women to control them, women may find at times it is necessary and conscionable to respond with violence in self-defense.

Another example of a situation where women may struggle with a seemingly contradictory situation emerges around the practice of abortion. In the masculinist paradigm of nonviolence, which excludes all violent acts, a feminist nonviolent activist's participation in the pro-choice movement may seem contradictory. Feminism moves the issue from the specifics of abortion to a struggle over who controls women's bodies and a critique of the structures of sexist oppression. In the transition it becomes clear that there are many levels of violence surrounding this issue. In that transition, nonviolence becomes not just an immediate strategy but part of a larger end that may for some women include the right to choose now, with the goal of a changed society in the future, a society in which men equally share the responsibility for birth control and child-rearing.

Feminism provides a framework for identifying the difference between "not-violent" and nonviolence or nonviolent action. From a feminist standpoint nonviolence must be understood within the structural violence of power as domination that characterizes patriarchal society. Seeing the social context within which nonviolence is practiced helps increase our understanding of the various ways we experience nonviolence. Naming the patriarchal organizing principles of our society helps frame what it might mean to practice nonviolence.

Socialization processes mean that women have a different task in developing nonviolent social action, which may include learning to be assertive and angry as part of the path to a commitment to nonviolence. It may also mean at times reacting violently to defend an individual self. Feminists do not see it as impossible to one's momentary action to be violent for practical reasons, while the goal of nonviolence underlies one's daily lifestyle.

Feminism helps raise the complexities for women of participation in nonviolence as principled and pragmatic. The core of literature on nonviolence developed without the inclusion of the many specific experiences women have that shape their relationship to nonviolence. Feminism gives the gift of multiplicity to nonviolent action and theories of nonviolence. It recognizes that women bring important gifts to the process of nonviolent action. Feminism is a catalyst that helps women and men see new perspectives on nonviolence that emerge from the standpoint of being a woman.

The ethic of care for self and others is the basis of most women's value systems. Combining it with the need for women to learn to express anger or rage, to assert their needs, and to maintain relationships, provides the basis for women's nonviolence. Feminism, a praxis that highlights social-structural bases for systemic violence, helps to open a space for women's voices and experiences in practicing and theorizing about nonviolence. Feminism makes it clear that men and women experience different sorts of violence and thus the development of a nonviolent praxis is linked to one's gender, race, class, sexual preference—one's social identity—and its place in the structures of society.

Lynne M. Woehrle

References

Bromley, Marion. "Feminism and Nonviolent Revolution." In *Reweaving the Web of Life: Feminism and Nonviolence,* edited by Pam McAllister. Philadelphia: New Society, 1982.

Deming, Barbara. *We Are All Part of One Another.* Philadelphia: New Society, 1984.

Feminism and Nonviolence Study Group. *Piecing It Together: Feminism and Nonviolence.* Devon, UK: Feminism and Nonviolence Study Group, 1983.

McAllister, Pam. *Reweaving the Web of Life: Feminism and Nonviolence.* Philadelphia: New Society, 1982.

———. *You Can't Kill the Spirit.* Philadelphia: New Society, 1988.

McGuinness, Kate. "Gene Sharp's Theory of Power: A Feminist Critique of Consent." *Journal of Peace Research* 30, no. 1 (1993): 101–115.

Shiva, Vandana. *Staying Alive: Women, Ecology, and Development.* UK: Zed, 1989.

Woehrle, Lynne. "Feminist Debates about Nonviolence." In *Nonviolence: Social and Psychological Issues,* edited by V.K. Kool. Landsdowne, Md.: University Press of America, 1993.

See also DEMING, BARBARA; WOMEN AND NONVIOLENT ACTION

Fox, George (1624–1691)

Principal founder and organizer of the Religious Society of Friends (or Quakers), one of the three historic peace churches. Fox was born in Drayton-in-the-Clay (now Fenny Drayton), England, and, except for four relatively brief trips abroad, spent most of his life traveling and preaching throughout that country. He was an exponent of the active pacifism that, following the Stuart Restoration in 1660, came to be identified with the Friends; his followers used the tactic of nonviolent resistance to challenge the authorities before and after the Restoration.

Taking advantage of the upheavals of the English Revolution and the opportunities it offered, Fox and his disciples represented a major threat to the Cromwellian Interregnum by 1659. However nonviolent, the sect had numerous adherents within the New Model Army and caused uneasy authorities to fear its influence. As a result, Fox was jailed on several occasions for "blaspheming," a rather loose and catchall charge. Although the Quakers did not formally adopt a pacifist position until 1661, Fox revealed his own personal decision not to engage in war a decade before, when, from his Derby jail cell during one of his incarcerations, he informed soldiers pressing him to become their captain that he "lived in the virtue of that life and power that took away the occasion of all wars."

Significantly, Fox did not repudiate the idea that a ruler might use the sword in a just cause. The basis of Fox's pacifism was his belief that the millennium was at hand because, as he preached, "Christ has come to teach his people himself." The Children of the Light, the name the first Friends gave themselves, would then replace the old regime and institute a kingdom of righteousness. Marked by these views as dangerous radicals, they represented a continuing threat to the existing order.

Fox's followers petitioned parliament to end compulsory church dues tithing—on one occasion in 1658, they did the unheard of and mobilized seven thousand women to sign. They took advantage of the end of official censorship to flood the country's bookstalls with pamphlets publicizing their ideas. They adopted a confrontational stance, refusing to pay tithes, swear oaths, and use the plural "you" or doff their hats to their betters.

These nonviolent tactics brought the Children into conflict with the law, and when hauled into court, their obstinacy on points that seemed minor irritated judges and resulted in their ready incarceration. Hundreds were imprisoned in England during the 1650s, and four suffered death by hanging in Massachusetts for violating legal restrictions against proclaiming the Quaker message. By 1659, as the Cromwellian Interregnum wound down, Fox and his followers realized that they could not replace it, and watched in dismay as angry public and of-

F

George Fox (etching on stone by A. Newsam).
Friends Historical Library/Swarthmore College.

arrest. Thousands, including even some children, were rounded up in massive acts of civil disobedience; in fact Fox suffered his two longest and most debilitating imprisonments in this period, once in the 1660s and again in the mid-1670s, both results of his refusal to take an oath.

Fox died in London on January 13, 1691, leader of a movement numbering more than sixty thousand. Over the last decade and a half of his life he was less active in carrying his message to non-Quakers, but he had stabilized the Society of Friends under the control of substantial leadership, which, though more conservative than in the exuberant 1650s, maintained a commitment to peace and what later generations referred to as "nonviolence."

H. Larry Ingle

References

Ingle, H. Larry. *First among Friends: George Fox and the Creation of Quakerism.* New York: Oxford University Press, 1994.

Journal of George Fox. Edited by John L. Nickalls. Cambridge: Cambridge University Press, 1952.

See also QUAKERS

France, Politics and Protest

Often called the "contentious" country, France stands out as a modern democracy particularly prone to the disruptive politics of protest and even civil violence. French politics do tend to be more colorful than those in other democracies, but not necessarily more volatile; notably, most political demonstrations are nonviolent and carefully controlled. The politics of protest and nonviolent action in France, however, illuminate important aspects of the relationship between state power and popular action, the rewards and effectiveness of protest, and the relationship between nonviolent action and a democratic polity.

Even casual visitors to Paris rarely miss the excitement of a French political demonstration. Gym teachers protest the reduction of physical education requirements and funding by jogging through the streets of Paris; motorcyclists cruise the boulevards protesting helmet and antinoise laws; farmers bring their tractors to block streets in opposition to European Community trade policies or reductions in farm subsidies;

ficial opinion linked them to an abortive plot by other millenarians in 1661.

In a withdrawal from political activity, Fox and eleven other men, speaking for the church, issued their famous "Peace Testimony" in January. This move affirmed that they would not violate the principles to which Christ had led them: "All bloody principles and practices we . . . do utterly deny, with all outward wars and strife, and fightings with outward weapons, for any end, or under any pretence whatsoever: and this is our testimony to the whole world." Although some dissented, and rumors circulated for the next three decades that Friends were involved in plots to overthrow the government, the Testimony was never repudiated and has remained the formal position of the Religious Society of Friends ever since.

The document had the desired effect on the Stuart kings, successors to the Interregnum government, but not Parliament, whose members still saw the Friends as a threat. Hence, until 1689 and passage of the Act of Toleration, which granted dissenters the right to worship freely and freed Quakers from the necessity of swearing most oaths, attempts to suppress the sect continued.

Unlike other dissenters, like the Baptists, Fox advised his followers not to secrete themselves away but to meet openly and thus court parents march through the city beating saucepans with ladles to protect state subsidies to private schools. Such events disrupt the city and often attract national and even international attention to whatever cause has motivated the demonstration. Similar events occur elsewhere in the country.

In spite of their frequency, French political demonstrations are generally nonviolent. This absence of violence comes in spite of a long tradition of barricades and in a setting where the rhetorical violence is often great. It is common to hear protesters talk of occupying buildings, confronting the riot police, or erecting barricades; it is far less common to see these verbal threats fulfilled. The language is fiery; the acts are much more prosaic. Occasionally, French protests produce property damage, but no more frequently than in other countries. Violence against persons is very rare and usually accidental rather than purposeful. Injuries or deaths are highly counterproductive to the protesters' hopes of achieving their goals. For example, the emerging antinuclear power movement came to a halt in the mid-1970s when a demonstrator was killed.

Most organizers of political demonstrations in France pride themselves on the skill of their own monitors in keeping the crowd under control. The monitors protect the fringes of the action in order to keep their own people in line and to protect the demonstrators from provocateurs. The state has well-trained and disciplined riot police able to prevent disorder without provocation in most cases of political protest. As a result, the vast majority of French protest demonstrations are free of property damage or personal injuries. The few exceptions are usually limited to relatively minor, often symbolic property damage; rarely are there injuries and almost never do modern French protests lead to deaths. The "events of May 1968" offer an illustration of the joint ability of demonstrators and police to limit violence. In this month-long revolt of students and workers, there were many minor injuries but only three fatalities. A few days of rioting in South-Central Los Angeles in 1992 produced many more casualties and fatalities.

While property damage, injuries, and deaths are unusual in routine acts of direct political action, France is troubled by violence associated with terrorism. Domestic terrorists based on ideology (such as Action Directe) or ethnic claims (such as Breton or Corsican nationalist groups) are less restricted than are the usual political demonstrators. In addition, France is a privileged asylum for political refugees, resulting in occasional episodes of international terrorism. International terrorists in France usually target non-French immigrants, but the violence spills over into the native population. As a consequence, terrorism accounts for a large percentage of political violence in France.

The French propensity to political protest is not new; even before the Revolution of 1789, protest was an established practice. Centuries of regular political upheaval and protest have earned the French the reputation for being "contentious." One French observer points to the frequency of political demonstrations and declares rioting to be "a national sport." De Gaulle referred to his country's "perpetual political effervescence." However, the French pattern of nonviolent protest differs little from what is now common in other European democracies, such as Britain, Germany, or Italy. It is more salient in France, and protest often takes the form of revolts that threaten the very existence of a regime. Several of the dozen or so regimes that have come and gone in France since 1789 succumbed to such revolts. Even the seemingly well-entrenched Fifth Republic tottered on the brink of collapse during the student-worker revolt of May 1968.

More frequently, however, protest in the form of marches, sit-ins, and demonstrations is "politics as usual" in France. It is turned to with little hesitation by all types of groups to pursue many kinds of political objectives. Political parties in and out of the "system" resort to protest; deputies disrupt parliamentary sessions by banging their desk tops and disorderly outbursts; organized and spontaneous groups representing all social classes and widely divergent causes turn to protest as part of their usual political activities. Protest demonstrations are not "unconventional" in France in any sense of the word. Protest is conventional in that it is common in occurrence, normal as a tactic in the usual range of repertoire of political action, expected by the government, and accepted as an integral and even essential part of the democratic process.

Incidence of Political Protest

While political protest is on the rise everywhere, there is widespread agreement that protest is now and has always been more common in France than elsewhere. In fact, several empirical studies provide only partial support for these beliefs. One survey of public opinion in eleven West European countries and the United States during the early 1980s showed that French approval of various types of protest politics was not strikingly different from that found in other Western democracies. French citizens were not the most inclined to protest; the Swiss were the unlikely European leader in such forms of protest politics as lawful demonstrations, boycotts, and the occupations of buildings. Except for the occupation of buildings, French opinion was only slightly above the average of all twelve surveyed countries. The French did show the highest acceptance of personal violence but the vast majority of these respondents expressed their possible intent rather than claiming to have already engaged in violence.

Another set of cross-national data on political protest based on "disruptive events" between 1948 and 1978 suggests that the incidence of political protest in France is the lowest of major Western democracies except for West Germany. Only between 1958 and 1967 did France lead the four large European countries in the total episodes of political protest: 1958–1967. In the thirty-year total, France ranks fourth out of the five large Western democracies in the number of protest events.

Finally, a study by Hanspeter Kriesi and his colleagues measured mobilization in protest activities in France, Germany, the Netherlands, and Switzerland, drawing on a sample of events between 1975 and 1989. When adjusted for differences in the size of populations, participation in unconventional political actions is remarkably similar among the four countries. While the French may be no more contentious than other Europeans—including such seemingly pacific peoples as the Swiss or Dutch—there is some evidence that protest in France is more likely to be disruptive. Kriesi's study found that French protests were more likely to be violent than demonstrations in the other countries. Overall, however, these studies suggest that the French do not engage in peaceful protests more often than do peoples in other democracies and that the French tendency toward more violent outbursts is also limited.

From Nonviolent Demonstrations to Violent Protest and Revolt

Even if French protest is no more common than direct action in other Western democracies, France still bears the image of a polity charac-terized by its vulnerability to violent protest. Civil uprisings have a prominent place in French history. If separate protest actions focused on specific issues are no more common in France than elsewhere, this is not the case of more sweeping protest movements. Such broad-based, collective movements have been relatively frequent events throughout the course of French history. Approximately every twenty years or so—usually once in each generation—there are vast collective movements that threaten to or actually topple the entire regime: May 1968, the Resistance, the 1936 general strike, the Dreyfus affair, Boulangism, the Paris Commune, the 1848 revolts, the 1830 revolt, and the Revolution in 1789. The link between protest politics and regime overthrow is well established and makes contemporary protest events more interesting to both domestic and foreign observers.

It is these vast, regime-threatening protest movements that are responsible for most violent incidents in France. The dynamics that change isolated and specific protests into regime-threatening, mass collective action remain mysterious. At times, widespread and well-grounded dissent portends threats to the existence of the regime and then nothing happens. Other times, seemingly small disputes escalate very rapidly into outright revolts that threaten or bring regime change. No one, not the participants, their leaders, or the government, can control the flow of events. This uncertainty means that knowledgeable observers of France must pay especially close attention to the otherwise common protest phenomenon.

The tactics of protest are more colorful. The French are highly adept at using eye-catching and newsworthy protest techniques. For example, in early 1993, French fishermen swept onto the docks to destroy fish imported from Russia by spilling the fresh fish on the ground and pouring kerosene on them. British fishermen were similarly aggrieved and mounted perhaps even better-organized protests. They set up blockades of fishing boats across the harbor openings to close the seaports to all vessels. But few took note of these less picturesque activities. It is much better television to see French fishermen pouring oil on fish carcasses than it is to have long distance shots of British fishing boats forming an amorphous barrier across a harbor. The difficulty with such political spectacles is that they can harm those who organize and participate in them. Events that stir emotions to the point that they are good television are often unpredictable and uncontrollable.

Effectiveness of Protest Politics

Assessments of the effects of protest politics are highly subjective and therefore difficult for a careful observer to make in general terms. Final policy decisions are usually taken well after the protest event and reflect many other considerations and interests. But protest can affect more than specific policy decisions on the issue that provoked dissent. Protest may also, and with greater significance, bring change in the policy process and even changes in social values. It is not necessary for a protest movement to succeed in its immediate policy objective in order to accomplish changes in the policy process or social values. The protesters may compel policymakers to include them in decision processes that previously excluded them. They may bring new issues onto the political agenda. They may also provoke major shifts in value structures or the political culture, such as new attitudes toward the role of women in society.

Another effect of protest should be calculated into assessments of the effectiveness of protest: the consequences for the protesting groups and individuals. These internal gains are not negligible; they alone may be valuable enough to justify even those protests that fail to change policy, the policy process, or social values. The organizing groups can benefit from the cohesion, élan, and sense of solidarity that nearly always emerges during a protest. There are personal rewards of camaraderie, a sense of being involved in something significant, and happy memories of daring adventures that are long remembered by demonstrators. Obviously, these internal rewards of protest are most common when the direct political action is accomplished without violence. But it is not uncommon for contemporary, nonviolent demonstrations to evoke the memories of martyrs from past revolts or protests.

French protests, both violent and nonviolent, rarely achieve the specific policy aims that brought the demonstration. Protest nonetheless is seen as important in the French political process. Crozier contends that mass protest is the only means to achieve change. He sees France caught in cycles of protest and order: long periods of routine and static politics followed by short periods of change induced by crisis and protest. Hoffmann sees crises of massive political protest bringing forward heroic leaders,

such as de Gaulle, to carry out social and political changes that were impossible in ordinary times. Tarrow sees cycles of protest as bringing fundamental political and social changes.

In the same spirit, many point to the presumed sweeping effects of the "Events of May" in 1968. However, the changes that finally are institutionalized in the wake of a civil uprising are not necessarily those sought by the initial leaders of the protest movement or their supporters. The demonstrators in May 1968 called for dramatic changes in the social pattern of citizen participation; they got modest salary increases, a forty-hour work week, and some token university reforms. Many other factors are at work in reshaping the polity even after very disruptive events. Few would deny that French political culture and relationships changed dramatically in the years following the Events of May but it is much more difficult to isolate the effect of that revolt from the other social and political factors that determined the actual changes. Indeed, there are many who see very few enduring effects of this most recent near insurrection. And the changes that do occur may not be those sought by the protesters. Thus, there is a generation of *soixante-huitards,* but they have seen the achievement of very few of their goals.

There are some important limitations on the achievements of even the best-organized and largest protests. First, protest is nearly always an attempt to veto policy decisions rather than to promote new policies. On those few occasions when protests are successful, they are negative in that they are most likely to succeed in blocking government-proposed changes that they see as detrimental to their interests. There are very few examples of protests succeeding in forcing government to initiate policy. Nor is it easy for groups to organize demonstrations to propose innovative policies. For example, in the 1970s, when state economic planning was still fashionable, the CFDT (Confederation Française et Democratique du Travail) never could mount a successful workers' demonstration to support their innovative economic counterplans; the Communist CGT (Confederation Generale du Travail) had no difficulty in mobilizing its supporters to protest (albeit unsuccessfully) the government's economic plan.

Second, groups seek to publicize their actions in order to draw public attention to their position and the issue that concerns them. French groups, as noted earlier, are highly successful in using colorful tactics that attract the news media and especially television. Most of them seem well aware of the importance of the visual and the entertaining elements of their actions. As Gamson and Wolsfeld characterize the distinction between a movement's motivations and its public presentation, "Fire in the belly is fine, but fire on the ground photographs better." The problem with such tactics is that they can lead to violence and injuries. Leaders and demonstrators may be jailed. Beyond these dangers to the organizations and individuals involved, spectacular protest may bring public revulsion against the excesses and property damage by the protesters that will further reduce the likelihood of achieving their policy goals.

Third, there are very real costs to any large protest. The preparation of a successful demonstration requires major investments in staff time and group funds. Volunteers must be recruited to provide security and marshal the marchers; flyers and posters must be printed and distributed; charter buses and trains need to be arranged and paid for to bring in supporters from the provinces; housing for these out-of-town participants must be arranged; and so on. There are also direct and indirect costs peculiar to many protest actions. Farmers who spoil their own crops suffer an additional loss; truck drivers who leave their rigs running must pay for the fuel; strikers may undermine the competitiveness of their firm. In addition, protesters make a personal investment of their time and this often means losing a day's pay. These are very real and often high costs to the protesters and need to be considered in assessing the cost effectiveness of protest politics. As a result, protest tactics are nearly always reserved for extreme cases where the group fears major damage to its members' interests and all other means have proved unsuccessful.

Finally, there is also the déjà vu factor: protest is sufficiently frequent in France that it has lost much of its power to catch the public's or the government's attention. This tradition immunizes the political system against isolated protests and even very large demonstrations. As a result, protest organizers must find a way to set their demonstration apart from the many others and this leads to increasingly colorful and spectacular forms of protest. They also find it difficult to use the tactic on a regular basis for fear that their action will not match the success or numbers of their own earlier protests. For example, through great exertion one group brought 100,000 people into the streets for a particular protest. In subsequent years it feared any new action that mobilized fewer protesters would be taken as a sign that the group had lost support or that its cause was not as deeply felt as had been the earlier issue.

The Strength of the State

Protest in France is engendered by the remoteness of the state from the people. It is a polity where the attention of the government is more easily attracted by a disruptive event than by a need. It is widely described as a "strong state" capable of making decisions, even unpopular ones, and implementing them with only general reference to the public's views. The power of the state over society leaves those unhappy with its decisions few options other than protest. But the same strength that allows the state to proceed without the people also is used to channel, control, coopt, or crush protesters.

From long experience with protest, the state has acquired the expertise and the means to regulate conflict and protest. Observers of French protest are usually surprised not only by the demonstrators' antics but also by the massive presence of forces of order at these events. There are always bus loads of specially trained riot police sitting around, ready to step in should there be any excesses. Usually such force is not needed. Suzanne Berger suggests the state uses a "feather quilt" strategy to handle disruptive events. It seeks to absorb and limit violence and property damage without responding to the issues while waiting for the demonstrators to tire or dissolve in internal conflicts. In most cases, these tactics work in limiting conflict and allowing the state to ignore the specific demands of the protesters.

In some cases, the government will offer headline-attracting concessions during the heat of a protest and then retract or deform them once the demonstrators are demobilized. An example can be found in a 1982 truckers' demonstration over increases in diesel fuel taxes. Trucks clogged the cities and blocked the autoroutes all over France for several days. Eventually, the prime minister agreed to meet with the truckers' leaders. When the meeting took place headlines reported the prime minister had pledged to cut the tax to benefit the truckers. But when the details were announced more quietly over a week later, the concessions were spread over five years and a new value-added tax affecting the truckers virtually wiped out even these token concessions. By then, of course, the truckers were demobilized and demoralized. The government got credit for ending the bothersome demonstration and for appearing conciliatory and responsive; the truckers got nothing. Instead, they had the enormous costs of time lost from work and of organizing a nationwide protest.

Organizational and Personal Benefits of Protest

Many demonstrations can justify their costs by the contributions they make to the organization and individuals involved. Groups and causes can establish their credibility and importance among their supporters as the result of a well-organized protest. It shows supporters that the group is "doing something" even if the leadership fails to achieve its policy goals. It is a way for the group to express its concerns when its members know that any expression of their views will be futile. This expressive role of protest is very useful to the group's leaders in justifying their inability to influence politics as their members see the futility even of a well-orchestrated demonstration. Throughout French history, there have been groups where the leaders justify their existence mainly by organizing demonstrations. The groups change over time but there are still "bureaucrats of protest" in today's France.

Groups may not even be very aggrieved to feel a need to "show the colors" by taking their supporters into the streets. The group may want not only to impress the government but also to demonstrate its strength to rival groups. It is not unusual for demonstration leaders to admit publicly that the group took to the streets simply to "affirm its presence" and to limit the ambitions of rival groups while planning to continue usual patterns of consultation with the government.

Protest demonstrations usually allow groups to achieve unity and cohesion. Personal rivalries and ideological differences are put aside in order to present a united front against the "enemy" state. The fragmented trade union movement, for example, organized "days of action" less for the causes they sought than for the temporary unity among otherwise divided unions. Protests and demonstrations encourage a sense of solidarity among participants who want to be "standing on the same side of the barricades" as those with whom they share an interest. Such unity often breaks down after the event, but protest can give even divided groups a temporary sense of cohesion and solidarity.

There are also personal rewards to the individuals who give of their time to make the protest. Most protests produce pleasant memories of excitement and adventure. They give individuals a sense of involvement and significance whatever the outcome of the event. Out of these events emerges a special sense of camaraderie and bonding with their companions that cannot be obtained in other ways. Strangers become fast friends; personal animosities are put aside at least temporarily. Protest allows people today to share in the historical traditions of revolutionary France with a minimum of danger to themselves or to others. Their mothers and fathers have told them about May 1968; their grandparents have reminisced about the Liberation; they have read about the Commune and the Revolution. This is a way for contemporaries to relive and participate in these grand events.

Protest Politics or Ritual Politics?

In France, contemporary political protests flow out of a rich history of contention that is full of drama and passion. Protest has become an important popular art in France. There are sites and methods of protest that establish guidelines for protest organizers. A leftist march nearly always goes between Place de la Nation and Place de la Bastille; conservatives gather at the Arc de Triomphe; the extreme Right assembles at the statue of Jeanne d'Arc just off Rivoli. When defenders of private schools marched through the streets in 1984 banging pots and pans with ladles they were conforming to tradition. The banner slogans, chants, and songs of the protesters are the same ones used for decades and even centuries. There is room for innovation but always within the traditions of the past that confer legitimacy upon the political action and evoke deep emotions among the participants. The conformity to tradition is deliberate and self-conscious.

By now, the dangerous elements of protest are minimal. Nearly all protests are nonviolent by intention and by the skills of the organizers and riot police. The prospect of regime change is also much less in the 1990s than it was in the 1950s or before. Protest politics can become street theater in which participants act out glorious events from the past in a safe but memorable manner. Because of the usual avoidance of violence, major protests are nearly always festive events. They are gay but not frivolous. While grievances are often serious and deeply felt by the protesters, that is not often revealed by the demeanor of participants. There are occasional demonstrations where the participants are mean-spirited and nasty. But protests are usually happy events, with participants remaining orderly and peaceful and waving to onlookers with no malice or threat. The protest events are often accompanied by street dances and small gatherings in bars before and after the march. These social events have as much significance to the participants as do the actual demonstrations.

None of this diminishes the political importance or the serious nature of protest politics in France. Ritual has an important role in the political process, and the ritual of protest serves both expressive and integrative purposes. Indeed, protest and demonstrations in France are perhaps less acts of political participation than political rites with much the same meaning as Americans pledging allegiance to the flag. It is the importance of this ritual of protest that makes political demonstrations in France, where the incidence and success rates of protest are little different from those of other Western democracies, so prominent a feature of politics.

Frank L. Wilson

References

Baumgartner, Frank R. *Conflict and Rhetoric in French Policymaking.* Pittsburgh: University of Pittsburgh Press, 1989.

Berger, Suzanne. *Peasants against Politics: Rural Organizations in Brittany, 1911–1967.* Cambridge: Harvard University Press, 1972.

Crozier, Michel. *The Stalled Society.* New York: Viking, 1973.

Gamson, William, and Gadi Wolsfeld. "Movements and Media as Interacting Systems." *Annals of the Academy of Political and Social Science* (July 1993): 114–126.

Hoffmann, Stanley. *Decline or Renewal? France since the 1930s.* New York: Viking, 1974.

Kriesi, Hanspeter, et al. "New Social Movements and Political Opportunities in Western Europe." *European Journal of Political Research* 22 (1982): 219–244.

Schonfeld, William R. *Obedience and Revolt: French Political Behavior toward Authority.* Beverly Hills, Calif.: Sage, 1976.

Tarrow, Sidney. *Democracy and Disorder: Protest and Politics in Italy 1965–1975.* Oxford: Oxford University Press, 1989.

———. "Modular Collective Action and the Rise of the Social Movement: Why the French Revolution Was Not Enough." *Politics & Society* 21 (1993): 69–90.

Tilly, Charles. *The Contentious French.* Cambridge: Harvard University Press, 1986.

Freedom Council (Denmark)

Body that provided national coordination of the various Danish resistance groups during the Nazi German occupation from 1940 to 1945. Established on September 16, 1943, the Freedom Council claimed leadership of the entire Danish resistance struggle. Seven resistance leaders formed the original council, six representing clandestine organizations plus one independent member.

For several months the council had to fight for recognition, as many groups within Danish society were reluctant to acknowledge its claim to authority. Therefore, when appealing for joint action toward national independence, freedom, and democracy, it refrained from identifying with any political party or group. In November, the council published a joint political platform for the resistance movement, *When Denmark Is Free Again,* stating the goals of an immediate postwar return to democracy and a judicial settlement in full accordance with Danish concepts of justice. The chief purpose of the pamphlet was to counter the critique that the council was dominated by "enemies of the system," in effect Communists, and to make the council politically acceptable to as wide circles as possible. In order to do this, it always had to emphasize a national identity and democratic attitude, balancing carefully all demands and recommendations issued.

The council's primary task according to its founding statement was "to organize the resistance against the Germans in all fields and by all popular methods available." Additionally, it intended to fight "the Danish Nazis, renegades and defeatists." Thus, the council promoted resistance without an explicit commitment to nonviolent resistance. During its twenty-month life, however, the council often encouraged nonviolent struggle and cautioned against the use of violence. For example, in October 1943, the council explicitly warned resisters against shooting Germans. Similarly, sabotage actions were to be directed only against material facilities of vital interest to the Germans. The council also intervened to encourage and guide the resistance during the final stages of the Copenhagen People's Strike—the most famous single example of Danish collective resistance during the German occupation. Here the strike was "rediscovered" as an effective weapon, and it was consciously applied in several later instances.

At its height, the council carried traits of an underground government. It had special bodies and committees, for example, for military matters, for sabotage, and for arresting and trying traitors. It issued central directives and appeals for both general resistance and specific actions. And it engaged in international negotiations. However, the hard times demanded a united posture by the Danish people. Therefore, in August 1944, the underground Contact Committee was established to connect representatives of the political parties and members of the council, which after the German capitulation resulted in a transitional "Liberation" government.

Lennart Bergfeldt

References

Bergfeldt, Lennart. *The Intelligent Resistance: How the Danes Withstood German Occupation.* Westport, Conn.: Praeger, 1997.

Freedom Rides, 1961

Effort to test the 1960 U.S. Supreme Court decision in *Boynton* v. *Commonwealth of Virginia,* which banned segregation in interstate transportation facilities, such as bus station restaurants, waiting rooms, and rest rooms. Interracial teams of civil rights activists rode buses through the South and attempted to integrate bus terminal facilities at stops along the way.

The Freedom Rides of 1961 were modeled after an earlier freedom ride in 1947, organized by the Congress of Racial Equality (CORE) and the Fellowship of Reconciliation. Known as the Journey of Reconciliation, it tested the 1946 U.S. Supreme Court ruling in *Morgan* v. *Virginia,* which declared segregated seating unconstitutional on interstate buses. Unlike the later Freedom Rides, it had nothing to do with terminal facilities, nor was it met with violence.

As desegregation made legal progress through the 1950s, CORE was determined to make desegregation on buses and in bus stations a reality and not just a legal doctrine, especially in the Deep South. The group initially

arranged for an interracial and interregional team of thirteen people to ride a Greyhound bus and a Trailways bus through several southern states and to use the related bus terminal facilities. The ride was scheduled to begin on May 4 in Washington, D.C, and end in New Orleans on May 17, the anniversary of the 1954 school desegregation ruling.

Anticipating the likely animosity their effort would provoke, CORE trained the riders in the philosophy and methods of nonviolent action. In the event of arrest, they each agreed to stay in jail and not accept the alternative fine or bail payments.

Although the first few days of travel were uneventful, the riders eventually did meet with major opposition, first in Rock Hill, South Carolina, where two riders were beaten, and then in Anniston, Alabama. In Anniston, thirty to forty whites attacked the Greyhound bus with chains and iron bars as it entered the station. When the bus stopped, the angry crowd pulled the Freedom Riders off the bus and severely beat them as policemen stood by and watched. Eventually, police broke up the mob and escorted the bus back onto the street, where it immediately departed for Birmingham. The white rioters jumped in their cars and chased the bus six miles down the road until one of its already damaged tires blew, and the bus was forced to stop. The crowd again attacked the bus and threw a homemade bomb inside, which temporarily trapped passengers in the resulting flames and smoke. They were able to escape, but many passengers suffered from smoke inhalation; and the beatings continued. Soon after the police arrived, several cars carrying Freedom Ride supporters arrived and drove the riders to Birmingham, where they were treated for their injuries. Back at the Anniston station, the Trailways bus arrived an hour after the Greyhound bus and was met with similar violence. When the Trailways bus finally arrived in Birmingham, the Freedom Riders again were attacked and beaten mercilessly by a large mob. Unable to find bus drivers to take them to Montgomery, the CORE Freedom Riders completed their journey to New Orleans by airplane.

A few days later, the Student Nonviolent Coordinating Committee (SNCC) assembled a team of twenty-one Freedom Riders to continue the journey. When they arrived in Montgomery on May 20, they, too, were beaten by a racist mob. At this point, the federal government prevailed upon the governor of Mississippi to call

F

in the Mississippi National Guard to protect the Freedom Riders on the next leg of their journey to Jackson, Mississippi. In Jackson, they were arrested for attempting to integrate the bus terminal facilities. Through the summer, Freedom Riders continued to stream into Jackson and were arrested. As the support grew, so did the violence and anger. By the end of the summer, 360 people had been arrested.

Eventually, on September 22, in response to a request by U.S. Attorney General Robert F. Kennedy, the Interstate Commerce Commission issued rules for desegregation of terminals and related terminal facilities effective November 1, 1961. Desegregation of both interstate transportation and facilities finally became a reality.

Kimberley A. Pyles

References

Cooney, Robert, and Helen Michalowski, eds. *The Power of the People: Active Nonviolence in the United States.* From an original text by Marty Jezer. Culver City, Calif.: Peace Press, 1977. 2nd ed. Philadelphia: New Society, 1987.

Laue, James H. *Direct Action and Desegregation, 1960–1962: Toward a Theory of the Rationalization of Protest.* Brooklyn: Carlson, 1989.

Viorst, Milton. *Fire in the Streets: America in the 1960s.* New York: Simon and Schuster, 1979.

See also CIVIL RIGHTS MOVEMENT; CONGRESS OF RACIAL EQUALITY; FELLOWSHIP OF RECONCILIATON, INTERNATIONAL; STUDENT NONVIOLENT COORDINATING COMMITTEE

Freedom Summer Project, Mississippi, 1964

The Summer Project was one of the most audacious and celebrated campaigns of the U.S. civil rights movement. Though nominally sponsored by a coalition of civil rights organizations, the project was principally the work of the Student Nonviolent Coordinating Committee (SNCC). Not only did the idea for the project originate within SNCC, but the organization also supplied staff for four-fifths of the local projects that composed the overall campaign. The project pursued three main programs over the course of the summer—creating alternative "freedom schools," registering black voters, and organizing the Mississippi Democratic Party to challenge the existing state Democratic Party. The project was born of SNCC's frustration at the stalemate it faced in Mississippi after three years of grueling and dangerous organizing there. Despite a string of celebrated atrocities by segregationists over that period of time, SNCC had been unable to persuade federal officials to intervene more forcefully in the state. Nor had the national news media shown the same level of interest in events there as they had in the actions of Martin Luther King, Jr. Lacking the glare of media coverage or any real federal presence in the state, SNCC came to realize that it had little chance of effecting change in what remained the most recalcitrant of southern states. Freedom Summer was a response to the dilemma in which the organization found itself. By recruiting outside volunteers—one thousand principally white, northern, college students—to work in the state, SNCC hoped to bring the news media as well and with it the kind of public attention and pressure that would compel federal action and break the strategic stalemate in the state.

With the "help" of Mississippi's segregationists, project organizers were able to accomplish these broad aims. Barely a day into the campaign, three project participants, James Chaney, Andrew Goodman, and Michael Schwerner, disappeared while investigating the bombing of a black church near Philadelphia, Mississippi. Their bodies would not be recovered until August, but the disappearance made headlines and assured SNCC the kind of news media attention and stepped-up federal presence they had been unable to compel during the previous three years. Nor did the disappearance of the three workers mark the end of the violence against the project. Over the course of the summer one other volunteer was killed, eighty others were badly beaten, and an additional one thousand arrested. In addition, some sixty-seven churches, homes, and businesses were burned or bombed. The ongoing violence kept the project on the front pages and the nightly news throughout the summer.

The campaign itself was composed of some forty-four local projects scattered throughout Mississippi's five congressional districts. SNCC was responsible for the projects in four of the five districts, while the Congress of Racial Equality (CORE) oversaw operations in the remaining district. Most of the local projects featured two principal components: a "freedom school" and a voter registration campaign. The freedom schools were an ambitious effort on the part of

SNCC to counteract the debilitating effects of Mississippi's public school system on its black students. To put the necessary curricular flesh on this basic idea, the National Council of Churches sponsored a March 1964 planning session in New York City. There, educators, clergy, and SNCC staff members hammered out a basic curriculum for the schools emphasizing four principal topic areas: remedial education, leadership development, contemporary issues, and nonacademic curriculum. Teachers were then recruited and trained at a special orientation held in June at Western College for Women in Oxford, Ohio. By any standard, the freedom schools were a success. Where project organizers had hoped to attract one thousand or so students, between three thousand and thirty-five hundred showed up. And those who overflowed the makeshift classrooms were exposed to the kind of impassioned, alternative education long denied them by the state.

On the face of it, the voter registration component of the summer project was far less successful than the freedom school program. Barely sixteen hundred residents were registered over the course of the summer. But these numbers tell only a part of the story. In all, seventeen thousand black residents attempted to register as a part of the project. And the countless instances of intimidation, harassment, and discrimination visited upon the prospective registrants by Mississippi's white registrars served as crucial supporting evidence in later legislative testimony leading to the passage of the Voting Rights Act of 1965.

Knowing full well the intransigence of the state's political establishment, project organizers also founded the Mississippi Freedom Democratic Party (MFDP) as an alternative to the state's lily-white Democratic Party, and established a parallel primary process to grant blacks a means of political expression during that year's presidential campaign. As a practical matter, this meant that project participants were simultaneously engaged in two tasks: trying to persuade blacks to attempt to register as official voters and "freedom-registering" voters on behalf of the MFDP. As the summer wore on, however, the MFDP effort came increasingly to dominate the project's political program. While project organizers initially conceived of the MFDP as a demonstration of and protest against Mississippi's closed political system, they soon came to view the MFDP effort more ambitiously. Emboldened by support

from around the nation and their own success in freedom-registering voters, the MFDP braintrust set for themselves the audacious task of unseating the state Democratic Party delegation to the Democratic National Convention to be held in Atlantic City in August. The road there wound through the same tiered primary process the party regulars were subject to, culminating in the election of sixty-eight delegates at the state MFDP convention held August 6 in Jackson, Mississippi.

From there the delegates traveled to Atlantic City for their showdown with the Democratic Party establishment. By now the outcome of that confrontation is the stuff of American political history. Despite an intensive lobbying campaign and a highly dramatic appearance before the convention's Credentials Committee, the MFDP delegation failed to unseat the Mississippi Party regulars. Fearing the erosion of southern Democratic support, Lyndon Johnson spared no effort in sabotaging the challenge. In the end, Johnson's hardball politics proved effective. Support for the challenge evaporated in the Credentials Committee, and the MFDP forces were left to consider a rather weak compromise proposal: two at-large convention seats and a promise to review the whole matter of racial exclusion prior to the 1968 convention. The MFDP delegation overwhelmingly rejected the compromise. That was not quite the end of it, though. Using credentials borrowed from sympathetic delegates from other states, a contingent of MFDP members gained access to the convention floor and staged a sit-in in the Mississippi section. The sight of black Mississippians being carried from the convention floor by uniformed, white security officers was but the ultimate ironic denouement to Freedom Summer.

While the MFDP challenge marked the end of the summer project, the effects of the campaign are still evident today. Three specific effects are worth noting. First, as touched on above, the project proved instrumental in the drafting and ultimate passage of the Voting Rights Act of 1965. In turn, the act redemocratized voting rights in the South and ushered in a new era in southern—and, indeed, national—politics.

Second, the project served as a kind of activist "basic training" for a disproportionate number of those who would go on to play important pioneering roles in the other major movements of the era. Specifically, project volunteers were conspicuous by their presence in the ranks of the early student, antiwar, and women's liberation movements. And through the influence of the volunteers, these movements, and the New Left in general, came to draw heavily on the ideologies, tactics, and organizational style of the summer project and its parent organization, SNCC.

Alas, for SNCC itself, the project exacerbated interpersonal tensions and philosophical differences that had been building in the organization for some time. The result was a prolonged period of intense organizational debate and reflection that marked the effective end of SNCC's long-standing commitments to nonviolence, the politics of moral witness, and, perhaps most important, interracialism as a guiding principle of the organization. SNCC's increasing hostility to whites, coupled with its own internal crisis, foreclosed the possibility of massive northern student involvement in the organization at precisely the moment when Freedom Summer had awakened students to the appeal and possibility of civil rights work. The ultimate shape of the New Left would owe much to this estrangement.

Doug McAdam

References

Carson, Clayborne. *In Struggle.* Cambridge: Harvard University Press, 1981.
McAdam, Doug. *Freedom Summer.* New York: Oxford University Press, 1988.

See also CIVIL RIGHTS MOVEMENT; STUDENT NONVIOLENT COORDINATING COMMITTEE

Funerals, Demonstrative

Memorial, funeral service, or procession for people who died during a protest or resistance movement, or who were killed by an opponent. The conduct of the event is meant to communicate condemnation of the perpetrator of that specific death, of a general government policy, or of the whole regime. The event often takes place during a time of political unrest and may help to solidify a campaign or movement. The protest is usually expressed by some kind of visual symbol, dramatic gesture, song, or speech. Demonstrative funerals often include large numbers of people, as when the crowd is marking the death of a prominent opposition leader.

Historical examples of demonstrative funerals are common. During American Colonial resistance to the Townshend Acts in 1770, an eleven-year-old boy, part of a crowd of children protesting an importer who was violating a boycott, was killed by a pro-British informer. The boy's funeral became a large demonstration, and the boy was declared a hero and a martyr for the cause. During the Russian Revolution of 1905, funeral processions and services for dead antigovernment activists were transformed into huge political demonstrations. Over half a million Czechoslovaks attended a funeral on January 25, 1969, for Jan Palach, a student who burned himself in a plea for political freedom. Thousands of mourners filed past his coffin in the center of Prague, the national anthem was played, and people hung national flags with black sashes. The funeral grew into a nationwide demonstration of protest against the Soviet-led invasion of the previous August.

References

Sharp, Gene. *The Politics of Nonviolent Action.* Boston: Porter Sargent, 1973.

See also CZECHOSLOVAKIA, 1968 RESISTANCE MOVEMENT

G

Gandhi, Mohandas Karamchand (1869–1948)

Known as "Mahatma" (Great Soul), a major Indian nationalist leader and exponent of non-violent action, first in South Africa on behalf of Indian migrants and then in India against the British Raj.

Gandhi was born in Gujarat, western India (October 2, 1869), into a family of middling social status. He was educated locally before traveling to England in 1888 to train as a lawyer in London, where he stayed for three years. Thereafter he failed in legal practice in India and went in 1893 on a year's contract as a legal adviser to an Indian firm in South Africa. He stayed until 1914 to help Indians combat increasing white settler discrimination. Gandhi returned to India finally in 1915, and spent five years in comparative obscurity, founding an *ashram* (religious community), and apparently not considering a political career.

In 1920, he assumed unexpected dominance in the Indian National Congress, the main organ of nationalist action and aspiration, advising those who attended, and the country at large, to take up noncooperation against the Raj. He led three major all-India campaigns of nonviolent resistance to the British, in 1920–1922, 1930–1934, and 1940–1942. None of these, in contrast to various local campaigns of nonviolence on single issues, as in 1917, 1918, and 1928, lived up to his ideal of nonviolence, nor did they dislodge the British. But they were a significant addition to the political repertoire of Indian nationalism and profoundly affected a developing sense of Indian national identity.

Independence in 1947 was accompanied by the partition of the subcontinent, when Muslim Pakistan was separated from predominantly Hindu India. Although Gandhi had argued for decades that Muslims and Hindus belonged to one nation, a Hindu assassinated him (January 30, 1948) in New Delhi, holding him responsible for partition because of his sensitivity to India's Muslim minority. Indians were deeply shocked and grieved, and he is still widely revered as the Father of the Nation. But few followed his nonviolent path in India after his death, and he is now more influential as an inspiration to people outside India who have drawn vision and strength from his life and teaching.

South Africa

His years in South Africa transformed Gandhi. The shy, unsuccessful lawyer without political connections became a public figure, journalist, and political activist, motivated by a newly found spiritual vision. Outwardly he appeared for a decade as a lawyer building up a successful practice, a settled married man with four sons, living a comfortable and Westernized lifestyle. Gradually he simplified his living, cutting down his needs and possessions, until he founded his two ashram communities, Phoenix near Durban (1904) and Tolstoy Farm (1910) near Johannesburg. There he worked out a spartan religious life for his family, a group of close friends that included Europeans, and those who were associated with him in nonviolent action. These experiments in a new manner of living were the outward signs of an inner spiritual growth, which culminated in 1906 in his vow of celibacy and dedication to a life following after ultimate Truth, expressed in service to the wider family of humanity. It must be admitted that Gandhi led this life often at the expense

Mohandas K. Gandhi, 1931. AP/Wide World Photos.

of his sons and his wife, Kasturbai, who married him when they were both in their teens, and stayed with him through his experiments in living and nonviolence, enduring and sometimes sharing his jail sentences, until her death in 1944.

The origins of Gandhi's spiritual vision, which undergirded his dedication to nonviolence, lay in the Hindu and Jain religious traditions with which he was familiar from his upbringing in western India. He remained a devout Hindu throughout his life, despite his condemnation of many practices associated with Hinduism, and despite his deep sense of divine disclosure in other religions. Indeed in Hinduism he experienced a sense of personal relationship with God that he described as an "inner voice." Both Hinduism and Jainism stress the religious importance of nonviolence, ahimsa, and the Jains speak of ultimate truth as "many-sided" like a diamond, an insight that strengthened Gandhi's growing belief that, as individuals could grasp only facets of truth and never the whole, any conflict must be resolved through nonviolent means that safeguarded the integrity of all parties to the conflict. What might have been theological abstraction was still a reality in Gujarat, where practical traditions of nonviolent confrontation and pressure persisted into the nineteenth century. Although the roots of Gandhian ahimsa lay deep within Indian tradition and example, his beliefs were

reinforced by his exposure to the Sermon on the Mount and his reading in South Africa of some of the works of Western exponents of nonviolence, particularly Thoreau and Tolstoy.

However, there was also an element of pragmatism in Gandhi's transformation of ahimsa into a practical mode of political action. He began to experiment with forms of nonviolent resistance as an answer to Indian dilemmas in South Africa—and well before he had refined the concept of what he was to call satyagraha or holding fast to truth. This Gujarati name for nonviolent resistance signified how different it was in Gandhi's mind from what English-speakers called passive resistance. For him, satyagraha was a weapon not of the weak but of the courageous and morally strong; it was for those who had clarified their vision of truth and strengthened themselves to follow truth and become satyagrahis by a life of simplicity and self-denial.

Gandhi increasingly believed that satyagraha was a morally transforming mode of action that purified any encounter and resolved the issue of means and ends. For him, ends could never justify the means; but in satyagraha there was an instrument that he felt generated a morally good outcome by its very action. By 1909, when he wrote the booklet *Hind Swaraj* (Indian Home Rule), his vision of satyagraha was fully formed, though he went on "experimenting with truth," to use the metaphor he constantly used himself and made the subtitle of his *Autobiography*.

In South Africa, Gandhi taught himself to be a publicist and a politician. He learned by trial and error a wide range of political skills, and developed many political strategies—using the press, calling public meetings, going on deputations to government officials, forming political organizations. But none of these proved adequate in dealing with mounting Indian grievances in South Africa, which ranged from physical segregation from white people to compulsory registration, problems relating to leases for trade, taxes on former indentured laborers who did not return to India, the invalidation of non-Christian marriages, entry restrictions, and non-enfranchisement.

After years of more "normal" political petitioning and campaigning it became clear to Gandhi that although Indians were nominally equal citizens with white people within the British Empire, the imperial government in London could do nothing to secure this equality and redress their grievances in South Africa. At last in 1907–1908 he exhorted Indians to peacefully resist the injustice of the Transvaal "Black Act" by refusing to register as the act demanded, and later by dramatically burning certificates of registration voluntarily when it seemed that the local government had gone back on a compromise reached on the issue. Resistance continued until 1911, when an agreement was reached with the government of the new Union of South Africa, but then it broke out again in 1913 on further issues, leading to a campaign of law-breaking and jail-going, including the symbolic "invasion" of Transvaal by a select group of Indians from Phoenix who had no permits to enter. Indian women were also brought into the campaign, which was a dramatic break with traditional norms of seclusion. In 1913, Gandhi himself led a group of two thousand satyagrahis across the Transvaal border in the sure knowledge that they would be deported to Natal, prosecuted, and jailed. It was in South Africa that Gandhi himself first went to jail, starting the process that culminated in India, whereby a mark of deep shame became a badge of honor in the fight against the imperial Raj.

Satyagraha in South Africa was an enormously important experience in terms of Gandhi's own spiritual and political maturation. He returned to India convinced of its political efficacy and its morally transforming qualities. It was also highly significant in creating a new Indian sense of community and of self-esteem among Indian migrants, although rifts between "African-born" and newer arrivals persisted, despite Gandhi's efforts to create a new unity. The "achievements" of nonviolent resistance in relation to Indian grievances were limited, however. Although Gandhi's personal relationship with Interior Minister Jan Christian Smuts and the compromises they achieved appeared to resolve some of the main issues between Indians and the white settler governments by 1911, others remained, even after a commission of enquiry's recommendations were enacted in 1914 to deal, for example, with the marital status of Indian women and the tax on ex-indentured laborers. Satyagraha had been most effective in moving governments when it coincided with industrial action and international pressure, as in 1913. But on a permanent basis it did not provide the sort of political pressure that could influence government policy, not least because the Indian community was a minority and governments had other sources of political support. Despite Gandhi's vision of moral transformation, it had not succeeded in changing the attitudes of white South Africans, as Indians and black Africans were to find to their detriment in subsequent decades.

Return to India: A Pilgrim in Search of Truth

The mature Gandhi who returned to India in 1915, renowned now in his homeland as well as in South Africa and honored by the British government in India for services to Indians in Africa, was in his own eyes still a pilgrim after truth. He was not a political philosopher, and he consistently refused to accept that there was a body of belief that constituted "Gandhi-ism," or to make a definitive exposition of his ideas. He often said that to be truly consistent with the pursuit of truth was to be prepared to go on learning and changing according to deepening vision and the challenge of new circumstances. In the absence of any treatise on nonviolence, those who would understand his thinking now as in his lifetime must rely on his few extended pieces of didactic writing *(Hind Swaraj, An Autobiography, Satyagraha in South Africa)* and a vast array of occasional pieces, speeches, letters, and articles, through which he strove to propagate his vision of nonviolence and of a new India. But more than anything he had written, he advised people to study his life, because this was his message. He saw his life partly in the nature of a scientific experiment with nonviolence, and his campaigns as "laboratories" of nonviolence, as he said in Rajkot in 1939.

From his actions and expositions it is possible to elaborate certain key themes in his understanding of nonviolence as both moral and practical politics. At the outset, the aim of any satyagraha campaign was not to force the opponent into submission, but to change the dynamics of the relationship of those engaged in conflict, by the deepening of the understanding of truth by both parties. To change the heart was always Gandhi's goal, in relation to his countrymen and to the British; for this was in his eyes the ground of truly radical change, change from the individual upward. It followed from this that satyagraha could properly be used only in relation to issues where the opponent could change the situation, following a change of attitude. Furthermore, the satyagrahi must always be prepared to engage in negotiation before or during a confrontation, in order to achieve such a change of attitude, and also to accept a compromise as a settlement of a conflict, provided that no fundamental moral principles were sacrificed. In his own life this openness to negotiation was clear, from his relations with Smuts in South Africa to the famous "pact" with Lord Irwin, the Viceroy of India, in 1931, that temporarily halted an all-India satyagraha and paved the way for Gandhi to attend a constitutional conference in London.

Nonviolent confrontation was always the last resort for Gandhi, not least because he realized that nonviolence in practice was highly problematic. In his own experience he struggled through rigorous self-discipline to prepare himself for selfless and fearless nonviolent resistance to wrong. But he realized that few people shared his vision of ahimsa and of truth or had fashioned the lifestyle that he considered essential training for a true satyagrahi. Even the ashrams he founded in India, to be spiritual nurseries of those dedicated to truth and nonviolence, were rent with squabbles and feuds, and his political associates often paid lip-service to the notion of nonviolence and saw satyagraha as a convenient tool in certain situations rather than as the only moral way of resolving wrongs.

Recognizing the risk of violence and discord in any large-scale campaign, Gandhi experimented with a whole range of symbolic and small-scale modes of satyagraha, such as refusing to wear foreign cloth, selling banned books and papers, making salt illegally, or observing *hartal*, a cessation of public business as a sign of grief. Only rarely did he sanction the nonpayment of taxes or similarly overt forms of outright noncooperation with or civil disobedience to the Raj. Often he restricted the numbers and types of people who were permitted to become satyagrahis, for example in his 1930 march to Dandi to make salt, or in the "individual" protest against participation in the war in 1940–1941. When he did sanction mass satyagraha he made great efforts to educate the participating public in nonviolence, both in relation to the British and their compatriots.

Numbers for Gandhi were not the essence of satyagraha—rather, the moral force of a campaign came from the spiritual strength and moral uprightness of the satyagrahis. It followed that even one satyagrahi might truly change a situation of conflict, as he himself attempted to demonstrate during the communal violence that engulfed Bengal in 1946, when he walked unarmed through the conflict-torn areas. Moreover, whenever it seemed that satyagraha had "failed," he claimed, as he did

after the violence that accompanied the Quit India campaign of 1942, that it had not been properly tried.

Similarly, faced with the profound dilemma of applying his principles to the approaching world war at the end of the 1930s, Gandhi stressed the importance of nonviolent resistance. Particularly as the naked violence confronting Europe's Jews became clear, he admitted, "If there ever could be a justifiable war in the name of and for humanity, a war against Germany, to prevent the wanton prosecution of a whole race, would be completely justified," although he added, "I do not believe in any war." To Jewish victims he offered only the suggestion of large-scale nonviolent resistance, which he thought might have some effect even upon those like Hitler and Mussolini, and would at least maintain the resisters' self-respect. Even if that took them all to death it would not signify a failure of nonviolence, but a triumph of the human spirit in pursuit of truth.

In the context of India's particular political situation, Gandhi was clear that satyagraha had an important but limited role. He believed that the presence of the colonial ruler was a sign and a result of India's own moral crisis. If India were to withstand the British, Indians must first transform themselves and their relations with each other. His goal on his return to India was a total moral reconstruction of Indian society, which would in turn be the basis for true political change. Political independence without moral and social transformation would just mean a "brown raj," in which Indian rulers would not differ from the British they displaced.

Key aspects of the essential social reconstruction that would bring in swaraj, self-rule, were the observation of *swadeshi* (using Indian-made goods as a sign of Indian social unity as well as a way of lessening imperial economic interest in India), of which the spinning wheel was the symbol; the creation of fraternity and tolerance between India's religious communities; and the abolition of inhumanity and gross inequality among Indians so abundantly plain in the observation of Untouchability. The better he knew the reality of India after his return from South Africa, the stronger became his condemnation of the "wrongs" he saw in Indian society. He extended his criticism to caste itself and to the treatment of women. He also began to engage with the problems of a proper educational system for all Indians, and of the health and economics of India's villages, urging a return to a simpler life for the nation, uncorrupted by the violence and greed he assumed to be the fruit of an economy built on industrialization.

In this total package of national reconstruction, where lay the role for satyagraha in the form of nonviolent resistance to the British Raj? Gandhi insisted that civil disobedience was the inherent right of every citizen, though there could properly be questions about the wisdom of applying it in any particular instance. Furthermore, its scope and area should always be limited "to the barest necessity of the case." But, Gandhi wrote in *Young India* in 1922, it became "a sacred duty when the State has become lawless, or . . . corrupt. And a citizen that barters with such a State shares its corruption or lawlessness." As early as 1920, he had become convinced that the British government in India was one with which he could not cooperate. The Amritsar shooting of 1919 and the treatment of the Sultan of Turkey, the Muslims' Khalifa, by the victorious allies after the First World War convinced him that the Raj was "satanic." Yet he still maintained that civil disobedience to it should be undertaken only with extreme care and caution, on appropriate issues.

Almost twenty years later in a pamphlet on the "constructive program" through which he still hoped to attain true independence nonviolently, Gandhi outlined the three functions of civil disobedience: to achieve redress of a local wrong; to rouse consciousness of a particular wrong (without trying to redress it); and as part of the struggle for political freedom, to concentrate on a particular issue such as freedom of speech. He warned, "Civil disobedience can never be directed for a general cause such as independence. The issue must be definite and capable of being clearly understood and within the power of the opponent to yield."

It is hardly surprising that Gandhi's social and economic priorities, seemingly at the expense of political freedom, his commitment to nonviolence, and his scrupulous concern over its use, mystified most Indian politicians whose main goal was to gain power from the British, culminating in independence. Some felt that violence was an inevitable if regrettable part of the anticolonial struggle. Others felt that Gandhi's political style was a denial of democratic and rational politics. Few shared his ideal of rural simplicity for free India. Even Jawaharlal Nehru, one of his closest friends and political colleagues, was irritated by his religiosity and unpredictability in terms of normal political calculations, and found distasteful Gandhi's references to his "inner voice," which seemed to get in the way of an all-out struggle for freedom. Some knowledge of Gandhi's role in Indian politics is therefore essential for an understanding of his influence in Indian political life and of the practice of satyagraha in India after his return from Africa.

Gandhi and Indian Politics: Satyagraha in Action

Gandhi was never a political careerist, even after his growing distrust of British rule had drawn him into national politics in 1919–1920. He remained a spiritual seeker, living in his ashram homes, attempting the reconstruction of Indian people and Indian society from the roots upward. And he was willing to engage in either local or national politics only when he sensed that there was a way in which satyagraha could change the situation, and when his compatriots would accept his advice and leadership. He regarded himself as an "expert" on the subject of civil disobedience: "I regard it as my own independent discovery, and I look upon it as my *dharma* [duty] to show from time to time its applicability and its limitations." His role in the Indian National Congress was therefore an ambiguous one. He was never a leader with a strong local following that he could use to influence the Congress; nor did he have within the Congress a group who were committed to his ideals. His fluctuating influence in the Congress rested very largely on the way his particular political style and tactics at times enabled congressmen to achieve unity among themselves, and to gain a measure of genuine popular support. So enabled, the Congress could pressure the British rulers with a nonviolent political program that undercut British legitimacy and threatened the cooperation of the millions of their Indian subjects on which their Raj rested. Thus, Gandhi and satyagraha were, at certain times, invaluable to many congressmen. His significance was enhanced by his powerfully attractive personality, and the way his strength of purpose, his courage even to the point of imprisonment, and his vision of a transformed India, helped many to throw off the psychological yoke of the colonial presence, and to believe in the possibility of a new and free India.

Yet satyagraha at times precipitated violence or led the Congress into a political impasse in relation to the British, when other political strategies such as cooperation in new constitutional arrangements promised more immediate political power. At such times, the Congress did not hesitate to abandon Gandhi's leadership and nonviolent programs, even though disentangling from Gandhi could be prolonged and painful, as in 1933–1934. Ultimately, when independence was in sight after the Second World War, Congress leadership fell to others. In these circumstances Gandhi was able to offer the Congress little, and he recognized that his words now carried little weight.

The attitude and priorities of congressmen were, therefore, a tight constraint on Gandhi's ability to practice satyagraha on a national scale or on a national issue. So too was the fact that the Congress was not a well-organized national party with clear lines of authority and sound finances. It was composed of loose alliances of local political groups, and satyagraha, like any all-India strategy, depended for its acceptance on their attitudes and the requirements of their often very different local situations. Moreover the identity of the Indian nation was itself often bitterly contested, despite the Congress's claims to speak for the nation. And social and religious divisions became a further impediment to the practice of satyagraha and the observance of nonviolence. Such cleavages generated violent hostility to Gandhi himself, among many Muslims and Untouchables, for example, who saw him as a Hindu symbol and spokesman, despite his evident concern for minorities, religious tolerance, and vision of an embracing cultural inheritance.

Gandhian satyagraha was at its most authentic, and perhaps its most successful, in dealing with a range of local "wrongs" or issues that Gandhi took up in India, where the diversities of Indian society and the ambiguities of all-India politics did not intrude on limited and clearly defined goals. Among the most famous of these local movements of nonviolent resistance were those in Champaran, Bihar (1917), against the methods by which indigo planters coerced their tenants; in 1918 in Ahmedabad, Gujarat, for mill workers against their Indian employers on the issue of pay, and in Kaira district of Gujarat against an enhanced land revenue assessment; and in 1928 in Bardoli district of Gujarat, again in protest of the land revenue assessment. In each instance the issue was small scale and local, comprehensible and directly relevant to local people. The people involved in the struggles were comparatively few in number (in Champaran, Gandhi was the only satyagrahi, by refusing to leave the district) and were often a homogeneous and close-knit group. Because of this and their unity in a limited purpose, discipline and nonviolence were comparatively easy to maintain.

These local movements did not all achieve similar outcomes, however. Where the issue was resolved "successfully" from the viewpoint of the activists, in practical political rather than in Gandhian moral terms, this tended to be because the opponent was vulnerable to the type of resistance offered, because of the structure of power or the force of external opinion. In Champaran and in Bardoli the local government was in each case forced to compromise by a government in Delhi with different, pan-Indian priorities. A "failed" local satyagraha in the princely state of Rajkot in 1939 indicated the importance of the opponent's vulnerability to such pressure and the ineffectiveness of satyagraha when used for political ends that were unclear and controversial because of the diversities of local society.

The potential problems inherent in satyagraha, visible even in these small-scale campaigns, were manifest the moment Gandhi launched any all-India program. His first attempt, against the "Rowlatt Acts" in 1919, was quickly aborted because of the outbreak of violence among activists and sympathizers. He had launched the campaign somewhat quixotically with no all-India support or following. His subsequent campaigns all had the Congress imprimatur and the backing of its organization: in 1920–1922 for a broad range of acts of noncooperation with government; in 1930–1934 for a loosely coordinated civil disobedience movement, with an intermission in 1931 while Gandhi represented the Congress at a Round Table Conference in London; in 1940–1941 when he led "individual" resistance to the war effort; and in 1942 when the Congress launched the so-called "Quit India" movement, which erupted into violence upon the arrest of all the major leaders and in the absence of any well-thought-out all-India strategy of resistance. In all these instances, the Congress followed Gandhi into satyagraha because other political strategies seemed incapable of shifting the colonial government. To take one example, the Congress followed Gandhi into satyagraha in 1930 after widespread political protests and demonstrations had failed to turn back the 1928 Simon Commission or prevail on the British to grant far-reaching political concessions in 1929.

But satyagraha was also adopted as a means of maintaining unity in Congress, without which the pressure it could exert on the British was very limited. This was the case when Congress followed Gandhi's plans in 1941, as in 1930 or 1920. On each occasion Gandhi had to launch campaigns on limited issues that were symptomatic or symbolic of the larger "wrong" of imperial rule, but would maintain as much unity as possible among Indian politicians and activists. The search for unity lay behind his agonizing over the issue for resistance in 1930, which culminated in disobedience against the government's salt monopoly by the illegal manufacture of salt. It also led him a decade later to the tactic of "individual" resistance to the war effort, when congressmen were bitterly divided on the issue of supporting or opposing the war effort of a colonial regime that was itself fighting a fascist alliance to which most congressmen were also hostile.

The perennial danger of violence erupting against the British or among Indians also influenced Gandhi's choice of issue and of tactics and styles of satyagraha. In 1919 he had learned the bitter lesson of how easily mass violence could break out if people were encouraged to break the law. He confessed then that he had made a "Himalayan miscalculation" in thinking that people were prepared for nonviolence. In 1922 he felt compelled to call off noncooperation because a mob in northern India killed twenty-two policemen. Thereafter he took extreme care over the types of action allowed and the people permitted to participate in satyagraha, for not only was violence sinful in his eyes, but it would also alienate many peripheral, moderate sympathizers of the nationalist movement, at home and abroad, and would inevitably draw out the repressive forces of the Raj, as it did in 1942.

Therefore, wherever possible Gandhi gave strict instructions about courteous and nonviolent behavior, to the country at large through his speeches and journalism, and by instructions to specific and potentially turbulent social groups such as the peasantry and students. He encouraged women to enter the public arena in his campaigns, believing them to be particularly suited to becoming exponents of nonviolence, for example as peaceful pickets outside cloth and liquor shops. At its most extreme, Gandhi's quality control of satyagrahis occurred in 1941–1942, when he personally selected those who were permitted to participate. Furthermore, he attempted to stage his campaigns so that the chances of potentially violent confrontations were minimized, often choosing symbolic actions before permitting the breaking of significant laws or the nonpayment of taxes.

Yet mass campaigns on all-India issues regularly proved uncontrollable, not least because at the local level popular participation rested on people's perceptions and interpretations of Gandhi's message and program, which were often markedly different from their originator's intentions. Where popular peasant participation occurred, for example in 1920–1921 in the United Provinces, it rested on miracle stories of Gandhi's powers and the hope that he and his satyagraha would solve the local problems caused by landlord pressure and rising prices. It was hardly surprising that violence erupted.

After Gandhi had felt forced to call off noncooperation in 1922 as a result of mob violence, he had to rethink his response to such violence, for he recognized that the political credibility of satyagraha and of his leadership would be undermined if people knew that in similar circumstances he would call off subsequent campaigns. Thereafter he argued that "peripheral" violence might well occur because of the inherent violence of the colonial relationship, but that what was essential was that committed satyagrahis remain nonviolent. He wrote in 1930 that although it was likely that violence would occur during the impending civil disobedience campaign, satyagraha would not cause it—rather, the reverse. "Violence is there already corroding the whole body politic. Civil disobedience will be but a purifying process and may bring to the surface what is burrowing under and into the whole body. . . . With the evidence I have of the constitution of the country and with the unquenchable faith I have in the method of civil resistance, I must not be deterred from the course the inward voice seems to be leading me to."

This also seems to have been his attitude in 1942, when the Congress embarked on "Quit India." For Gandhi, potential violence and even anarchy was a lesser evil than inaction in the face of war, possible Japanese invasion, and the imperial hold on India. He had an apocalyptic faith in the power of satyagraha in the face of the worst evil that seemed to be engulfing India. "This is the time to prove that there is no power stronger than ahimsa in this world," he argued in June 1942.

Impact and Legacy

As Gandhi sadly recognized in the final years of his life, his compatriots had never engaged in the true satyagraha of his vision; and the result was an independence marred by violent political and religious conflict, culminating in the partition of the country. Furthermore, Indians had been as little convinced by his constructive program as they were by nonviolence. And independence was not Gandhian *swaraj* but the "brown Raj" he had feared as early as 1909. But he never lost his indomitable hope in the perfectibility of human nature, nor his vision of truth as an active, divine presence at work in his own life and in the world, although he knew Indians paid little heed to his ideals and that leadership of the new India had passed into younger hands.

To the end, despite increasing frailty, he urged the Congress to engage in radical reconstruction rather than party politics, and he continued to preach the religious tolerance he saw as essential to a diverse society with so many minority groups—a tolerance that eventually cost him his life at the hands of a Hindu fanatic.

Although nonviolent protest is often thought of as Gandhi's peculiar contribution to the Indian nationalist movement, in retrospect it is evident that satyagraha never fundamentally weakened the power of the British Raj. By a mixture of political strategy and force the Raj was able to withstand each of the all-India movements against them. When they decided to quit India their decision was the result of the exigencies of war and long-term international and economic pressures as much as the domestic demand for independence. They were able to deal with each of the national satyagrahas not least because they could depend on the alliance of the many Indians who continued to work with them in their political structures, in their police, armed, and civilian services, and who continued to pay their taxes.

Yet Gandhi's preaching and campaigns were central to the development of a powerful new sense of Indian identity and to a significant erosion of imperial legitimacy, as satyagraha increasingly seized for the nationalists the high moral ground, in the estimation of many thousands in and outside India who watched the conflict even if they did not participate. Despite its limited role in achieving major and large-scale political change in India, Gandhi's experiments in the politics of nonviolence added to the political repertoire of his contemporaries and of those who came after him, not only in India.

As a political thinker Gandhi also had serious weaknesses. His wish to return to simpler political and socioeconomic arrangements in India rested on the belief that only small-scale communities could conduct their affairs morally and nonviolently. He thus never came to grips with the reality of the modern state and its potential, and therefore in a sense left the nationalist movement with a paucity of creative political thinking as India faced the challenges of independence in a fast-changing world.

His major significance perhaps was that he insisted that there could never be different standards in private and public life. He believed that the public and political domain, as much as the life of the individual, must be seen as a moral enterprise, as the arena in which men and women must seek after ultimate truth and live according to it.

Judith M. Brown

References

Brown, Judith M. *Gandhi: Prisoner of Hope.* New Haven and London: Yale University Press, 1989.

Chatterjee, M. *Gandhi's Religious Thought.* London: Macmillan, 1983.

Copley, A. *Gandhi: Against the Tide.* Oxford: Basil Blackwell, 1987.

Gandhi, Mohandas K. *An Autobiography: The Story of My Experiments with Truth* [1927 in serial form] London: J. Cape, 1966.

———. *The Collected Works of Mahatma Gandhi.* 90 volumes. New Delhi: Government of India, 1957–1984.

———. *Satyagraha in South Africa* [1928]. Ahmedabad: Navajivan, 1961.

Iyer, R., ed. *The Moral and Political Thought of Mahatma Gandhi.* New York: Oxford University Press, 1973.

———. *The Moral and Political Writings of Mahatma Gandhi.* Volume III, *Non-Violent Resistance and Social Transformation.* Oxford: Clarendon Press, 1987.

Nanda, B.R. *Gandhi and His Critics.* Delhi: Oxford University Press, 1985.

Parekh, B. *Colonialism, Tradition and Reform: An Analysis of Gandhi's Political Discourse.* Sage, New Delhi: Newbury Park and London, 1989.

———. *Gandhi's Political Philosophy: A Critical Examination.* Basingstoke and London: Macmillan, 1989.

Swan, M. *Gandhi. The South African Experi-*

ence. Johannesburg: Ravan, 1985.

See also Ahimsa; Ahmedabad Labor
Satyagraha, 1918; Bardoli Campaign,
1928; Civil Disobedience; Constructive
Program; Indian National Congress; Indian National Movement; Nehru,
Jawaharlal; Rowlatt Bills, Opposition,
1919; Salt March, 1930; Satyagraha;
Vykom Campaign, 1924–1925

Garrison, William Lloyd (1805–1879)

Newspaper editor and one of the most vocal
and famous American abolitionists, Garrison
campaigned for the immediate emancipation of
slaves, the dismantling of racial segregation and
discrimination, equality for women, and temperance. Garrison was born on December 10,
1805, in Newburyport, Massachusetts, and
died on May 24, 1879, in New York City. As
an avowed pacifist and editor of *The Liberator,*
an abolitionist newspaper, from 1831 to 1865,
he developed a theory and strategy of "nonresistance" to accomplish his goals.

William Lloyd Garrison. Friends Historical Library/Swarthmore College.

Garrison embarked on a long career as an
activist in 1826, when, as editor of the *National Philanthropist,* he first publicly championed the cause of temperance. He quickly embraced a different cause, and his career as an
abolitionist began as co-editor of the *Genius
of Universal Emancipation* in 1829. In opposing both gradual emancipation and the recolonization of American blacks to Africa,
Garrison espoused a goal of immediate emancipation. He began publishing *The Liberator*
in 1831, and it soon became one of the primary voices of the abolition movement and an
object of antipathy from pro-slavery forces. In
fact, the newspaper was banned by several
southern states, and the Georgia legislature
proposed a bill offering a reward for Garrison's capture.

Garrison helped organize the New England
Anti-Slavery Society in 1832 and the American
Anti-Slavery Society in 1833. As a leader of the
American Anti-Slavery Society, Garrison drew
up its manifesto, in which he advocated employing tactics borrowed from the evangelical
revivalist religious movement. He urged the use
of "moral suasion" of opponents through militant nonviolent action, including defiance of
"immoral" laws and civil disruption of the "illegitimate" institutions of organized religion
and the state. In 1834, he spearheaded a postal

campaign in which thousands of essays, newspapers, and texts of sermons were mailed to
individuals in both the North and the South.
The American Anti-Slavery Society also presented petitions demanding abolition to congressmen without seeking customary approval
from local political authorities. Because of some
of these radical tactics, Garrisonian abolitionists were targets of repeated anti-abolition attacks during the 1830s. Garrison was once
forced to take refuge in jail for a night to escape
an angry mob in Boston.

Garrison soon took this policy of moral
suasion one step further in his strategy of
"nonresistance," a radical pacifism in which
abolitionists refused to vote, refused to hold
political offices, and repudiated any honors to
avoid being complicit with "unjust laws" and
"illegitimate authority." This position led to a
split in the abolitionist movement in 1840 between Garrisonians and those who believed in
traditional electoral change. In early 1842,
Garrison called for the secession of northern
states from southern slave states in a campaign
of "No Union with Slaveholders." In 1854,
Garrison burned copies of the Fugitive Slave
Act and the U.S. Constitution in a public protest.

In addition to these national activities,
Garrison worked on the local level to eradicate

racial segregation. He often traveled to speaking engagements in "blacks only" railroad cars with his African-American friends and colleagues. He collaborated with African-American activists in an eleven-year campaign to desegregate Boston schools that finally ended successfully in 1855 when Massachusetts outlawed segregation in public schools. Garrison also was active in the struggle for women's equality. He boycotted the World Anti-Slavery Convention of 1840 after women were rejected as voting delegates.

During the 1850s, Garrison publicly began to modify his radical pacifist and abolitionist stance. While he maintained his personal pacifism, he started to support armed insurrection by others in support of emancipation, including the famous 1859 raid on Harpers Ferry, West Virginia, to procure arms to free slaves led by John Brown. He also began to align with Republican politicians who included emancipation in their platform, and eventually met with President Lincoln to urge him to use military force to emancipate the slaves. Garrison was overjoyed when the Thirteenth Amendment was submitted to individual states for ratification and when the Confederate forces surrendered in 1865. He left the American Anti-Slavery Society soon thereafter and retired *The Liberator* because he felt that his goal had been accomplished.

Throughout his abolitionist career, Garrison was a subject of controversy because of his tactics, strategy, and theory of radical nonresistance. He remains, however, one of the most famous abolitionists and a symbol of the antislavery movement.

Brad Bennett

References

Filler, Louis. *Crusade against Slavery: Friends, Foes, and Reforms, 1820–1860.* Algonac, Mich.: Reference Publications, 1986.

Kraditor, Aileen S. *Means and Ends in American Abolitionism: Garrison and His Critics on Strategy and Tactics, 1834–1850.* New York: Pantheon, 1967.

Stewart, James Brewer. *William Lloyd Garrison and the Challenge of Emancipation.* Arlington Heights, Ill.: Harlan Davidson, 1992.

See also ABOLITIONIST MOVEMENT

Gay Rights Movement

Social movement first established in Germany at the turn of the century, today consisting of many separate organizations in many countries, with the common goal of ending the persecution and oppression of, and legal discrimination against, gays and lesbians. The contemporary activist movement in the United States emerged through three distinct periods, each of which contributed a crucial element—from legitimizing efforts for legal reform and interest-group organization in the 1960s to a mobilization of radical activism in the 1970s, to a political activism that combined reform efforts with nonviolent direct action in the 1980s. In many ways, despite successful efforts to remove social and legal stigma from individuals' sexual orientation, mobilization and activism continue to reflect shifts of the political culture and the issues of the moment. In the face of a conservative backlash in the mid-1990s, efforts for gay liberation returned to defending legal rights and reforms and moved away from direct action.

The Early "Homosexual" Rights Movement

In 1871, the German Reichstag added paragraph 175 to the new German penal code, criminalizing homosexual acts between men. Paragraph 175 would become the impetus for the very first gay and lesbian political organization: The Scientific Humanitarian Committee (SHC). Established in 1897 by Dr. Magnus Hirschfeld, the motto for the SHC was *per scientiam ad justitiam* (justice through science), and most of its members were medical doctors and scientists who believed homosexuality should not be punished as a crime, but treated as an inborn medical condition over which the individual had no control. According to these early "sexologists," as they called themselves, a homosexual was not someone who chose to break the law, or commit a sin, but someone whose innate sexual desire led him to express himself sexually in a manner different from the majority of society.

The shift from an emphasis on sexual acts (sodomy) to one of a medicalized identity (homosexuality) was an important first step in the development of a group identity and consciousness, an essential part of any social movement. The stated goals of the SHC were threefold: repeal Paragraph 175; enlighten the public about homosexuality; and generate interest among "the homosexual himself in the struggle for his rights." To accomplish the first goal, the

SHC collected thousands of signatures on a petition calling for the repeal of Paragraph 175, forcing public debates both within and without the Reichstag. In January 1898, the petition and the repeal of Germany's sodomy law were the subject of debate in the Reichstag, and in 1907, more than two thousand people attended a public debate on Paragraph 175, sponsored by the SHC.

Hirschfeld became a world-renowned figure and was the driving force of the SHC for most of its thirty-five-year existence. He organized international conferences and delivered public lectures around the world in his effort to educate both the public and medical communities. Hirschfeld traveled extensively throughout Europe, and in 1930 he launched a world speaking tour that took him as far as the United States and China. Under his tutelage, the SHC grew to twenty-five branches in Germany and one in London, England, each dedicated to the advancement of the rights of gays and lesbians. In 1921, Hirschfeld established the World League of Sexual Reform, also in Germany, which grew to 130,000 members worldwide before the decade was over.

Although other countries had thriving gay subcultures and some academic or medical organizations dedicated to the study of homosexuality in fin-de-siècle Europe, only the Scientific Humanitarian Committee and the World League of Sexual Reform were dedicated to legal reform and establishing rights for homosexuals.

The rise of fascism in Europe in the 1930s, and especially of the Nazi Party in Germany, created a virulent backlash against the legal reform movement. Hirschfeld's Institute for Sexual Science in Berlin was one of the first targets of Nazi book burning in 1933. Hirschfeld fled to Nice, France, where he died in 1935. For thousands of homosexuals in Europe, the following decade meant violent persecution as they were swept into the Nazi Holocaust. The public emblem forced upon homosexual prisoners by the Nazis, the pink triangle, was re-appropriated decades later by gay and lesbian activists as a symbol of identification, community pride, and remembrance.

Gays and Lesbians after World War II

Despite the persecution of gays and lesbians by the Nazis, World War II served to lay the groundwork for the future gay and lesbian civil rights movement by providing many gay men and lesbians with their first exposure to a gay subculture. In large European and American cities, a gay subculture that included bars, restaurants, and public meeting places, had existed since the turn of the century. The massive mobilization of human resources required for the war effort brought thousands of young gay men and women from small towns and farms across the United States into big cities like New York, Boston, Providence, and San Francisco, fueling an expanding and more visible lesbian and gay night life and social scene. More important, the wartime mobilization ended the isolation for many gay men and lesbians who never had met another person like themselves.

Although there was a wide divergence in the way individual gays and lesbians were treated by the U.S. military during the war—some were accepted by their peers and commanding officers, while others were imprisoned, humiliated, and abused—immediately after the war military policy became increasingly hostile. The military labeled homosexuals a security threat and demanded their discharge. Gay and lesbian service persons who were discharged for homosexuality were given "undesirable discharges," a discharge reserved solely for gays and lesbians. A "dishonorable discharge" was given for all other infractions of military law. Requiring many employers to review military discharge papers of soldiers returning to civilian life before providing them with employment, the federal government ensured that the effect of an "undesirable discharge" was to reveal a former soldier's sexuality to future employers, making it difficult for many gays and lesbians to find employment in civilian fields.

Still, not all gays and lesbians who were discovered were discharged. Some were able to continue serving even after revealing their sexuality to their superior officers. For example, shortly after the Japanese bombing of Pearl Harbor, then General Dwight D. Eisenhower turned a blind eye to the emerging policy restrictions. Having asked a close assistant to ferret out the lesbians in her WAC battalion, the young woman replied that she would be happy to do the investigation, but her name would be the first one on the list. Not wanting to lose a trusted assistant, Eisenhower suspended the investigation.

The U.S. military often relaxed its exclusionary policy in time of great emergencies and need, only to pursue it again with renewed vigor when the emergency had passed. This was especially true during the Vietnam War and the 1992 Persian Gulf War, leading many in Congress to call for an end to the ban against gays and lesbians in the military.

Most gays and lesbians accepted their discharges from the U. S. military without a legal battle, but over time more and more gay and lesbian service personnel began to contest their discharges, bringing their mistreatment and the discriminatory military policy into the federal court system. Today, of all the North Atlantic Treaty Organization (NATO) members, only the United States and Great Britain still have policies that refuse to allow gays and lesbians to serve openly in their countries' armed forces. Federal appeals courts in the United States have disagreed as to the constitutionality of the military ban, making it likely that the Supreme Court will be forced to rule on this issue.

The 1950s proved to be a very difficult time for gays and lesbians. In a pattern that would continue for years, the military intensified its purge of gays and lesbians. More important, the attitude toward nonconformity of all kinds shifted in society as a whole. The cold war era began with a U.S. government witchhunt led by Senator Joseph McCarthy in one house of Congress and the House Un-American Activities Committee in the other. The stated goal of these congressional investigations was to discover and remove suspected Communist spies from the government, and from public life in general, but the real intent was to marshal the political, economic, and social lives of all Americans into a single-minded, monolithic, anti-Soviet force. Homosexuals and any other nonconformists, in addition to those suspected of having Communist sympathies, were subjected to congressional investigation and fired from their jobs. Hundreds of gay men were fired from positions in the State Department alone as alleged security risks. The claim was that their homosexuality made them more vulnerable to blackmail from Soviet spies seeking classified information. It was almost impossible for individuals to fight these government purges, and many loyal government employees lost their careers in the McCarthy witchhunts.

Difficult as the 1950s were for most gays and lesbians in the United States, it was in this period that the first U.S. gay rights organization was formed in Los Angeles. Founded in 1950 and disguised with a name borrowed from a secret Medieval Society of unmarried French men who conducted rituals and dances during festivals, the Mattachine Society organized its members into secret cells along the lines of the Communist Party, in which the founders had been active. In their mission statement, the Mattachine Society proposed to foster an "ethical homosexual culture" comparable to "the emerging culture of our fellow minorities—the Negro, Mexican and Jewish Peoples." Stressing the importance of education, unity, and consciousness raising, they also called for their members to engage in "political action to erase from our law books the discriminatory and oppressive legislation directed at the homosexual minority."

In practice, the Mattachine Society did help men in trouble with the law, winning court cases against the police for entrapment. The Mattachine Society grew quickly, and with this growth came divisions over the organization's political orientation. In 1953, when conservative members wrested control of the organization away from Mattachine Society founder Harry Hay, he and his friends resigned.

Over the decade, the Mattachine Society, and another early gay rights organization, One Inc., published America's first gay magazines, *The Mattachine Review* and *One*. These organizations primarily benefited men, but a third organization, The Daughters of Bilitis (DOB), was formed in San Francisco specifically for lesbians. Started in 1955, DOB's primary goal was to educate lesbians and the general public about lesbianism. Like One and the Mattachine Society, the Daughters of Bilitis also published a newsletter, entitled *The Ladder,* which served as an inspiration and lifeline to many lesbians across the country who had no other contact with a lesbian culture.

The First Wave of Gay Activism: Gay Liberation

In the 1960s many gay rights organizations on both coasts joined in regional and national federations, hoping to build a homosexual rights movement modeled after the black civil rights movement. Still seeking to end discrimination and gain some level of public acceptance, chapters of the Mattachine Society along the East Coast joined with the Janus Society of Philadelphia and Daughters of Bilitis–New York to form an organization called Eastern Regional Coalitions of Homophile Organizations (ERCHO). After attending an annual ERCHO conference, leaders of homosexual rights groups across the country created a National American Conference of Homophile Organizations (NACHO), whose purpose was to tie together legal reform efforts across the country. Small by today's standards, these organizations were plagued by disagreements over both strategy and political philosophy. Although size and disagreements limited their effectiveness, the existence of the organizations during the 1960s laid the groundwork for much of what would follow.

Although early political organizations were important first steps in raising the political and social consciousness of many men and women, the gay bar was still the primary meeting place for most gay men and lesbians in the United States. But gay bars were often dangerous places. With laws on the books in many cities that made same sex dancing or cross-dressing illegal, gay bars existed only with the sufferance of the local police. In large cities, many of these bars had connections to organized crime. Even when bar owners bribed local police officials, police raids were commonplace. Making matters worse, many city newspapers published the names of those arrested, and bar patrons risked having their sexual identity revealed to friends and family, bosses and co-workers, for nothing other than socializing with other gay men or lesbians.

On June 28, 1969, a raid on a Greenwich Village bar called the Stonewall Inn proved to be different from the many routine raids of gay bars conducted by the New York City Police Department. Part of a crackdown on unlicensed gay bars believed to have connections to organized crime, the raid on the Stonewall was different because this time, those arrested chose to fight back.

Led by drag queens, hustlers, street kids, and people of color, Stonewall patrons refused to disperse after police emptied the bar. Instead they gathered in the street outside taunting the police with chants of "Gay Power." When the police began to make arrests, forcing protesters into a nearby paddy wagon, the crowd began to throw beer cans, bottles, bricks, and other debris at officers who, surprised and unaccustomed to this reaction by gays, retreated into the bar. Tearing a parking meter from the ground, the crowd used it as a battering ram, attacking the door to the bar that had been barricaded by the policemen inside. Hurling a garbage can through the bar's plate glass window, the demonstrators set the building afire. Police reinforcements were summoned, but even with the assistance of New York's Tactical Patrol Force (a highly trained riot

control squad), it was hours before the crowd would disperse. The riot moved from in front of the bar to the streets, and whenever the Tactical Patrol Force, replete with tear gas, billy clubs, riot helmets, and shields charged down the street brandishing their clubs, the crowd would slowly retreat. At the end of the street the crowd would disperse only momentarily before running around the block and regrouping behind the police, where they again hurled bottles and bricks.

Newspaper accounts of the Stonewall riot brought thousands of gays and lesbians out to the streets, where confrontations between lesbians and gays and the New York City police continued for several nights. The riots served as a catalyst to greater action. In the days following the riots, rallies and meetings were planned, and many new gay liberation organizations were formed to combat police harassment and to free lesbians and gay men from societal discrimination. Both the Mattachine Society and the Daughters of Bilitis had branches in New York City before the Stonewall riots, but many new groups sprang up in the weeks that followed, many with a decidedly radical agenda. Organizations such as Women's International Terrorist Conspiracy from Hell (WITCH) and the Gay Liberation Front (GLF) represented the radical turn gay activism in New York was to take in the 1970s.

Antiwar and anticapitalist, these organizations shared the counterculture's disdain of marriage and family and believed both society and government in the United States were corrupt and must be radically altered if gay oppression, like race oppression and the oppression of women, were ever to be overturned. But the Gay Liberation Front quickly split, and those seeking cultural reform rather than cultural revolution left the GLF and formed the Gay Activists Alliance (GAA). The tensions and differences in approach to gay liberation that mark these two organizations are noteworthy because they echo the earlier split of the Mattachine Society in the 1950s. Radicals seeking comprehensive and sweeping economic and social change squared off against reformers who sought integration and equal rights for lesbians and gays. The former group's tactics included confrontation and violent protest, while the latter group believed societal change could be pursued through legal and legislative channels.

As the decade wore on, the GAA's civil liberties approach was the one most often emulated by other gay organizations around the country, but the tension between radicals and reformers would be replayed in many cities around the United States, where many new organizations joined the struggle for gay liberation.

Today, the Stonewall riots are seen as the beginning of the modern gay rights movement, and every June commemorative parades and protests are held in cities across the country. Bringing thousands of gays and lesbians into some form of political activism for the first time and providing a symbol of collective resistance, Stonewall was of great significance. But the gay liberation movement of the 1970s owes a larger debt. Many of the gay liberationists, and many involved directly in the Stonewall riots, drew on the rhetoric and tactics of the New Left, the civil rights movement, the women's movement, and the less confrontational gay rights organizations that had been in existence since the 1950s.

The 1970s witnessed an explosion of societal interest in gay and lesbian culture by mainstream America. Periodicals like *Time Magazine* explored the private lives and social and political activities of gays and lesbians for the first time. This brought increased awareness of the daily discrimination and mistreatment homosexuals experienced to society at large, while also making membership in gay and lesbian organizations less threatening.

Although there were major political and philosophical differences between the many organizations that constituted the 1970s gay and lesbian political movement, with growing memberships and increased activism came some important political successes. Many cities passed laws protecting homosexuals from housing and job discrimination. Police harassment of gay bars was curbed after the laws making their existence illegal were struck down by the courts. And in San Francisco, Harvey Milk was elected city supervisor in 1977, becoming the first openly gay city official in American history.

But greater success meant greater hostility from some segments of American society. Anita Bryant's "Save the Children" campaign led to a repeal of gay rights ordinances in Dade County, Florida, and in several other cities. In a 1978 California state ballot initiative, voters narrowly defeated a proposal that would have required schools to fire homosexual teachers or any teacher that mentioned homosexuality positively in the classroom. And in November of that year, San Francisco City Supervisor

Harvey Milk and gay-friendly Mayor George Moscone were assassinated in their offices by fellow City Supervisor Dan White. The night of the assassinations, forty thousand San Franciscans gathered for a candlelight vigil, marching the many blocks from Castro Street to City Hall in shocked but powerful silence, tens of thousands of candles burning in tribute to the murdered men. Although the police feared violence, the march was peaceful.

Five months later, White's attorneys used what later would be called "the Twinkie defense" and pleaded "diminished capacity" for their client, arguing that White had overdosed on sugar and was not responsible for his actions. A jury agreed with the defense and found White not guilty of murder, sentencing him to seven years in prison for manslaughter. White was paroled after serving five years of his sentence.

Following the White verdict, over five thousand gay people took to the streets of San Francisco. Outraged by the verdict, they marched to the city hall and smashed in the front doors. They overturned police cars, setting many on fire. Ordered not to fight the city hall protesters by the chief of police, swarms of angry police officers invaded the Castro (a gay neighborhood in San Francisco), and attacked men and women on the street. Entering a gay bar called the Elephant Walk, police beat more gay men and destroyed the bar. Over one hundred gay people and sixty-one police officers were hospitalized before the "White Night Riots" were over.

In the aftermath of the turbulent 1970s, gay men and women succeeded in establishing themselves as a powerful political force. With slogans of "Gay Is Good" and "We Are Everywhere," a new self-acceptance and sense of personal empowerment led many people to "come out of the closet" and admit their sexual identity publicly. But the conservative backlash that began in the late 1970s would intensify in the 1980s, at the same time that a mysterious disease began to kill many gay men. As the decade continued, so too did the death toll, and with no cure for AIDS (acquired immune deficiency syndrome) in sight, gays and lesbians turned their activist energies toward their own community, taking care of the sick and dying that American society had seemingly abandoned. Far-right conservatives used AIDS to again link homosexuality with disease, and anti-gay violence increased.

In the 1986 case *Bowers* v. *Hardwick,* the U.S. Supreme Court ruled that state sodomy laws were constitutional and that the right to privacy did not extend to the protection of gay relationships. Faced with substantial political and social obstacles and thousands of deaths from a disease with no cure, the gay movement persisted in part because of a new activism that arose from the rage of societal and governmental indifference to the AIDS epidemic.

The Second Wave: Queer Activism

During the 1980s, in attempts to drive homosexuality back into the closet, the far right blamed social tolerance for homosexuality for the decline in "family values." Although doing so made many of them visible targets of this new political backlash, gays and lesbians continued to support gay and lesbian organizations. In the 1980s, groups dedicated to other aspects of one's identity were testimony to the strides that had been made in societal acceptance of homosexuals. As homosexuality became simply one of many aspects of a person's life and not the single driving force, the concept of identity could be expanded to encompass things other than one's sexuality. Organizations for gay Asians, gay outdoorspersons, gay elderly, and gay youth were born, bringing thousands of new gays and lesbians into social activities. The explosion of gay and lesbian groups that addressed issues of identity made the movement stronger, even as it dispersed the focused political and reformist energies that gay liberation in the 1970s had created.

On the political front, organizations like the National Gay Rights Advocates, Lambda Legal Defense Fund, the Human Rights Campaign Fund, and the National Gay and Lesbian Task Forces pressed for reform in the nation's courts and in the U.S. Congress. The gay political movement had come of age, drawing 600,000 people for a march on Washington in 1987 and over 1 million people for a second national demonstration in 1992. Yet many people still felt excluded in the national gay organizations' vision of what it meant to be gay. Drag queens, lesbian separatists, gay minorities, working-class people, and people with AIDS often felt excluded by a national gay power structure they felt was overwhelmingly white, wealthy, and male.

The radical spirit of gay liberation present in the early Mattachine Society and later in the Gay Liberation Front again infused the gay political movement in the mid-1980s in response to the AIDS epidemic. An organization called AIDS Coalition to Unleash Power (ACT-UP) formed local organizations in over sixty American cities in just a few short years. With "Silence = Death" as a slogan, they set out to bring attention to the many gay men who were dying of AIDS, as a result of government indifference. ACT-UP blamed the Reagan administration for failing to respond either in time or with sufficient resources to an escalating public health crisis. ACT-UP members wrapped a government building in red tape to symbolize the bureaucratic delays that were costing lives. They burned effigies of President Reagan at a sit-in at the Food and Drug Administration, claiming that government delays and the laborious testing procedures for new drugs kept many medications off the market that might prolong the lives of those terminally ill from AIDS. Chaining themselves to a balcony in the New York Stock Exchange, they protested the exorbitant profits drug companies were making from the epidemic, and they spray-painted outlines of bodies on city streets to represent those who had already died from AIDS. ACT-UP disrupted meetings, passed out safe sex literature and condoms at high schools and shopping malls, and used civil disobedience and guerrilla theater to jolt the conscience of a nation they felt had abandoned them. ACT-UP was successful in bringing about greater awareness to the plight of those with AIDS, and in bringing changes to federal government procedures governing drug research and regulation.

In 1990, a second radical organization was born. Queer Nation (QN) was originally founded in response to the disenchantment many gays and lesbians felt for ACT-UP, because of the latter group's narrow focus on issues surrounding the AIDS epidemic. Like ACT-UP, Queer Nation had many chapters around the country and employed direct confrontation and guerrilla theater tactics to increase awareness and visibility of gay and lesbian people and to combat the homophobia they face. Updating civil rights–era techniques such as sit-ins, boycotts, and picket lines, Queer Nation members came to these demonstrations dressed and cross dressed as "go-go boys," "motorcycle dykes," and "drag queens," forcing heterosexuals to openly confront stereotypes of who and what gays and lesbians are. QN is most notable for its use of modern technology, such as the Internet computer network and facsimile machines, and its innovative appropriation of public space to further its political agenda. Originating the slogan "We're Here, We're Queer, Get Used To It" to symbolize the merger of their personal identities with the political struggle for social justice and legal equality, QN believed in confronting closeted gay public figures with calls to "Come Out."

While some ACT-UP and Queer Nation chapters are still active today, membership has waned. Their emphasis on radical tactics alienated many within the gay and lesbian community who might normally have been supportive of attempts to create social change.

Gay Liberation in the Future

The future of gay liberation is unclear. The far-right backlash continues, and equal rights ordinances that protect gays and lesbians from discrimination in housing and employment are again being repealed in many cities. Worse still, ballot questions that would prohibit local towns and cities from including gays and lesbians among protected groups in equal rights laws are appearing on many state ballots across the country. In 1994, eleven states included such a question on their annual ballot. In addition to fighting the far right over equal protection laws, gays and lesbians are working to end the ban against their participation in the military, and to alter federal guidelines that include homosexuality among the reasons an employee can be denied a government security clearance. The passage of a federal civil rights law protecting gays and lesbians has been introduced in Congress repeatedly but has not yet been brought to the floor of either the House of Representatives or the Senate for a vote.

On a more personal note, gays and lesbians are fighting to have their personal relationships validated by both religious organizations and by the state, seeking equal treatment by law in issues of gay marriage, partnership benefits, custody cases, gay adoption, and gay foster-parenting. All of this, while still seeking to end police harassment, sexuality-related hate-crimes, and AIDS discrimination. Formidable obstacles still face gays and lesbians as they continue their search for equality and justice in the United States. But in less than fifty years, gays and lesbians have moved from obscurity and isolation to the forefront of American politics, forcing all Americans to explore their understanding of, and commitment to, a tolerant and diverse political community.

Gary L. Lehring

References

Adam, Barry. *The Rise of a Gay and Lesbian Movement*. Boston: Twayne, 1987.

Altman, Dennis. *Homosexual Oppression and Liberation*. New York: New York University Press, 1971.

Cruikshank, Margaret. *The Gay and Lesbian Liberation Movement*. New York: Routledge, Chapman and Hall, 1992.

Duberman, Martin. *Stonewall*. New York: Dutton, 1993.

Lehring, Gary. "Difference and Identity, Difference As Identity: Theoretical Strategies in American Politics and Policy." Ph.D. dissertation, University of Massachusetts, Amherst, 1993.

Marotta, Toby. *The Politics of Homosexuality*. Boston: Houghton Mifflin, 1981.

New York Public Library. "Becoming Visible: The Legacy of Stonewall." 1994.

Shilts, Randy. *The Mayor of Castro Street: The Life and Times of Harvey Milk*. New York: St. Martin's, 1982.

Signorile, Michelangelo. *Queer in America: Sex, the Media, and the Closets of Power*. New York: Random House, 1993.

Weiss, Andrea, and Greta Schiller. *Before Stonewall: The Making of a Gay and Lesbian Community*. Florida: Naiad, 1988.

See also ACT-UP; QUEER NATION

Geography and Nonviolent Action

The impact of space-time settings on the possibility, origins, and course of nonviolent action. Geography can take on many meanings, but in a social science context two senses predominate. One is as the manifestation in particular settings of abstract social processes, such as state building, social stratification, and ideological hegemony. From this point of view spatial differences in social organization and political life are produced extra-geographically by abstract forces of class, ethnicity, or discursive hegemony (dominant ideas). The second main sense is as the real geographical ground where social processes are mediated through individual and collective action. From this perspective geography refers to the process whereby social worlds and human agency interact to create particular space-time contexts (or "places") for political action. The pairing of space and time indicates that contexts are not set spatially for all time but are in a state of flux as individuals and groups redefine the institutional scope and geographical horizons of their political activities.

It is only in the 1980s that thinking and research about nonviolent action began to take seriously the second understanding of geography. Three philosophical issues at the heart of much debate within the social sciences have probably done most to stimulate this interest. The first is the issue of a universal theoretical and political foundationalism. This refers to the controversy over whether overarching or universal theories can explain all instances of a named phenomenon, such as "development," "social movements," or "political parties," as resulting from causes or forces without attention to the distinctive spatial and historical contexts of each instance of political action. The second is the issue of the nature of power. In much conventional social science, power is seen as a force emanating from institutions rather than a human capability. However, the withdrawal of popular consent from established institutions and resistance to armed coercion suggest that power is not a global or nationwide "force-field" structuring individual agency but rather a potential intrinsic to agency itself as it is realized in particular contexts. The third issue is what Seidman has called "the malaise of theory in its disciplinary mode." Some social scientists have begun to reject theoretical claims that are missing explicit moral intent. In this construction moral and political conflicts about symbolic and material interests should not be reduced to technical and metatheoretical disputes about the meaning of terms or methods of inquiry. So, for example, stories of social development or political activity should be centered on the basic geographical units of social action (or places) in order to avoid the reified categories and systematic ignoring of differences entailed in the grand evolutionary narratives and universal behavioral models of orthodox social science.

There are four features of studies of geography and nonviolent action. The first concerns the link between nonviolent action, cultural identity, and state building. The second involves the critical analysis of the geopolitics of "foreign" relations. The third addresses the geography of intergroup conflict. The fourth surveys the geographical origins and spread of nonviolent political movements.

Cultural Identity and State Building

Ideas about what is right, proper, and just are communicated through space and time, especially through the linked processes of cultural identity formation and state building. Consequently, what becomes accepted as appropriate behavior or activity is structured geographically. Through the division of space into public and private and the designation of places (such as sites of battles, birthplaces of national heroes, monuments, war memorials, and palaces) as having particular importance in expressing national identity, political commitments and ideas of historical roots are defined and channeled. Notions of order and appropriate action are built into the landscape. Major public buildings containing political representatives and civil servants recruited in legitimate ways are one major manifestation. The conceptual existence of the state is embodied in the physical landscape, especially that of capital cities. Anything that undermines the order in this landscape can become a threat to the security of the state.

From the viewpoint of the individual citizen, the existence of the state is revealed not only through the services that its institutions provide, but also through the rituals (such as oaths of allegiance, voting, and serving in the military) that receive solid expression through the geographical presence of the state in the everyday routines of citizens. Demonstrations, civil disobedience, and other forms of nonviolent action transgress the received and accepted ordering of space associated with state building. Loyalty, maturity, even sanity—the everyday "geography of normality"—are called into question when the established spatial order is violated. The geography of normality is profoundly disturbed by nonviolent action directed toward state institutions.

The civil rights movement in the United States and the European movement for nuclear disarmament provide recent examples of nonviolent political movements that challenged the geography of normality. Each movement threatened the dominant "normality" in everyday life by demanding a substantial change—the extension of civil rights to African Americans, and European nuclear disarmament, respectively. Each movement also made sure it both used and violated the "sacred" places of statehood that were associated with the ideas and practices that it opposed or that represented sentiments to which it was appealing. Thus, the civil rights movement organized voter registration in the capitals of southern U.S. states and appealed to principles of justice and emancipation at the Lincoln Memorial in Washington, D.C. The European disarmament movement maintained vigils at nuclear weapons bases and appealed to popular rule in the British House of Commons.

Geopolitics and "Foreign" Relations

Foreign policy is constructed through practices of geographical differentiation and exclusion. A practical geopolitics informs how states relate to one another by sharply distinguishing the ordered and "safe" space of the state from the dangerous anarchic world beyond the state's boundaries. The pursuit of the political virtues, justice and liberty, is confined by the geographical borders of statehood. Outside these limits, diplomacy and force rather than common identity and collective reasoning are the major means of interaction. The boundary between "community" and anarchy becomes a Manichean divide between "good" and "evil." In the process the complex human geography of peoples and places becomes eviscerated. States lose their quality as socially constructed geographical places and become abstract entities in a geopolitical power game. The world "out there" is thus perceived as prone to violence and disorder.

This dehumanized geopolitics is illustrated in the speeches and policy statements of the Bush administration in the United States during the Persian Gulf War of 1991. Certain recurring themes indicate how the administration reasoned about the war. First, policymakers stated the motivations for the deployment of U.S. forces, such as securing oil supplies and establishing a "new world order" after the cold war. Second they provided frames of reference that justified the war in terms of previous conflicts, such as the failure of appeasement policies at the onset of World War II, and the allegedly ineffective policies of slow escalation during the Vietnam War. Third, they positioned the Persian Gulf in terms of specific global divisions—Islamic expansionism versus Western "just war" doctrines, and Iraqi primitivism versus Western technological sophistication. Coverage of the Gulf War by the American mass media merged these themes in an overarching vision of the war as a spectacle. Geopolitical speculation, usually the preserve of military and foreign policy elites, became a popular sport, with the actual killing taking on the appearance in American living rooms of a large-scale video game. The war essentially escaped from being about real people in real places into something like the fantasy realm of video games (Campbell; Dalby; Luke). Many critics of the war pointed out how its representation facilitated an acceptance of violence as a solution to international conflicts.

Intergroup Conflict

Although people like to claim that the cultural and political divisions that they create are natural, there is considerable evidence that they are historical and largely arbitrary. But cultural and political boundary making are universal, and we all take the resulting boundaries very seriously. As groups form historically they come to celebrate their uniqueness in terms of how they differ from others. Though objectified in the process of learning, the meaning of distinguishing symbols, be they religious, linguistic, or other, is ambiguous so that "traditions" are never static but constantly reinvented and reinterpreted. Given the possibility of group disintegration, geographical differentiation has been one of the most important strategies for establishing and reinforcing group distinctions. Intergroup conflicts, therefore, tend to take on a clear territorial character. ·

Some social groups, such as ethnic groups, are closely tied to exclusive spatial claims that serve to define group identity. Others are not. For example, social forms such as many churches are nonspatial. But most social groups have an important spatial fixity such that, as Spykman argued, "The proximity or distance, the uniqueness or the plurality which characterize the relations of social groups to their territory are therefore often the root and symbol of their structure." It is in this context that one can identify the key spatial and temporal sources of difficulty in resolving intergroup, such as ethnic, conflicts. For instance, groups can have rival claims to the same territory; conflict encourages enhanced identity between group and territory; and intergroup conflict increases the dehumanization of other groups through the use of a military-spatial vocabulary—"no-go areas," "target populations," "ethnic cleansing"—all of which mitigate against conflict mediation and resolution.

The Spread of Social Movements

The collective identity that often inspires participation in political movements that do not have fairly immediate material payoffs can have a variety of origins. In recent years, however, numerous commentators have argued that collective identity and consciousness are frequently constituted through place-specific social relations. A number of studies have paid special attention to the geographical development of nonviolent protest movements by drawing broadly from the social science literature on popular struggles and protest movements. A major theme of this general literature is the relation between time and place in the "repertoires" of popular collective action. Tilly argues that as "the interests and organization of ordinary people [shift] away from local affairs and powerful patrons to national affairs and major concentrations of power and capital," forms of protest such as seizures of grain and invasions of fields are replaced by public meetings, demonstrations, and social movements that search for recruits and make claims for their relevance beyond the bounds of their places of initial organization.

The spatial mediation of social processes in the growth of social movements committed to nonviolent action has been the focus of studies of the Chipko and Baliapal movements in India (Routledge) and U.S. peace movement organizations (Miller). Routledge uses the term *terrains of resistance* to signify the real geographical ground upon which the process of economic development sponsored by the Indian state meets with the resistance of groups devoted to other ends. The nature of the places in which the movements originate and put down roots is seen as key to understanding the movements. Similarly, Miller investigates several peace movements in an American metropolitan area in terms of the differences in levels of organization and activism between different communities. Differences in political mobilization are attributed to local variations in political efficacy (such as the relative openness of local political institutions to influence from peace groups) and collective identity (such as the degree to which a sense of place helps to create or retard a sense of common fate).

The application of the "geographical imagination" to the major problem areas of the field of nonviolent action is in its early days. Further progress will be limited unless the sense that geography is more than a mapping of the effects of natural or abstract social processes is replaced by an understanding of geography as intrinsic to nonviolent action itself. Certainly, spatial terms such as *core* and *periphery, territory,* and *location* have become increasingly common in the social sciences and humanities. By and large, however, the use of these terms has been descrip-

tive and metaphorical. Terms such as *territory* and *location* can evoke images of difference in power and wealth without any commitment to a geography of difference in itself. This "alienation of place" is not only theoretically deficient, as the emerging literature on geography and nonviolent action suggests, it also denies the political significance of seeing beyond and beneath the boundaries of the territorial states that have monopolized and terrorized thinking about political activities of all types.

John A. Agnew

References

Agnew, John. "Beyond Reason: Spatial and Temporal Sources of Ethnic Conflicts." In *Intractable Conflicts and Their Transformation,* edited by Louis Kriesberg, Terrell A. Northrup, and Stuart J. Thorson. Syracuse, N.Y.: Syracuse University Press, 1989.

————. "Timeless Space and State-Centrism: The Geographical Assumptions of International Relations Theory." In *The Global Economy As Political Space,* edited by Stephen Rosow, Naeem Inayatullah, and Mark Rupert. Boulder, Colo.: Lynne Rienner, 1994.

Agnew, John, and James S. Duncan, eds. *The Power of Place: Bringing Together Geographical and Sociological Imaginations.* Boston: Unwin Hyman, 1989.

Campbell, David. *Writing Security: United States Foreign Policy and the Politics of Identity.* Minneapolis: University of Minnesota Press, 1992.

Dalby, Simon. "American Security Discourse: The Persistence of Geopolitics." *Political Geography Quarterly* 9 (1990): 171–188.

Luke, Timothy W. "The Discipline of Security Studies and the Codes of Containment: Learning from Kuwait." *Alternatives* 16 (1991): 315–344.

Miller, Byron. "Collective Action and Rational Choice: Place, Community, and the Limits of Individual Self-Interest." *Economic Geography* 68 (1992): 22–42.

Northrup, Terrell A. "The Dynamic of Identity in Personal and Social Conflict." In *Intractable Conflicts and Their Transformation,* edited by Louis Kriesberg, Terrell A. Northrup, and Stuart J. Thorson. Syracuse, N.Y.: Syracuse University Press, 1989.

G

Routledge, Paul. *Terrains of Resistance: Non-violent Social Movements and the Contestation of Place in India.* Westport, Conn.: Praeger, 1993.

Seidman, Steven. "Postmodern Social Theory As Narrative with Moral Intent." In *Postmodernism and Social Theory,* edited by Steven Seidman and Donald Wagner. Cambridge, Mass.: Blackwell, 1992.

Spykman, Nicholas J. *The Social Theory of Georg Simmel.* New York: Russell and Russell, 1925.

Tilly, Charles. *The Contentious French: Four Centuries of Popular Struggle.* Cambridge, Mass.: Harvard University Press, 1986.

Ghana Anticolonial Movement, 1947–1951

Mass campaign for self-government in the Gold Coast, a former British colony that became independent Ghana in 1957. Led by Kwame Nkrumah, the people of the Gold Coast used widespread demonstrations, boycotts, and a general strike to agitate for "self-government now." Nkrumah developed a strategy of nonviolent "positive action" to coerce the British into granting independence.

The British governor of the Gold Coast, Sir Alan Burns, enacted a new constitution in 1946 that was intended to set the stage for a transition to self-government. Though hailed by some as one of the most advanced constitutions in Africa, it enabled the governor to retain a majority in the Executive Council and gave him absolute power to pass any law he desired. Many people of the Gold Coast were not satisfied with this arrangement. In August 1947, the United Gold Coast Convention (UGCC) was created by middle-class and professional people to press for self-government, using "legitimate and constitutional means." Kwame Nkrumah, who had recently returned from abroad, was asked to be general secretary of the UGCC beginning in December.

UGCC agitation began to intensify during late 1947 and early 1948. Nkrumah and other UGCC leaders traveled from village to village, building national unity for the movement. In addition, economic problems had arisen following World War II, and Gold Coast Africans were beginning to voice their complaints. On January 11, 1948, an Accran chief, Nii Kwabena Bonne III, called a boycott on the purchase of European-imported goods to force the lowering of prices in the Gold Coast. This widespread boycott lasted through most of February. Pressure to comply with the boycott was significant, in that native administrations imposed fines on those who failed to cooperate, and young men used force to maintain strict compliance. During the boycott, posters throughout the city called on African police to go on strike and defy English officers. In late February, the Accra Chamber of Commerce finally agreed to lower prices for a trial period. In a letter circulated to members of the UGCC Working Committee during this time, Nkrumah called for demonstrations, boycotts, and strikes to agitate for self-government.

On February 28, the Ex-Servicemen's Union, dissatisfied with unfulfilled promises made to them during their service in World War II, marched in Accra to present their grievances to the governor. Police fired on the march, killing two and provoking widespread looting and violent clashes around the country on February 28 and 29. Over twenty people were killed and over two hundred were injured. The UGCC was blamed for the riots, and Nkrumah was among movement leaders to be arrested and temporarily detained. In response to this violence, Nkrumah again publicized his call for nonviolent demonstrations, boycotts, and strikes as the "only weapons to support our pressure for self-government." During this period, the movement's ultimate goal—the end of colonial rule—was solidified.

A commission headed by A.K. Watson, sent by the British government to investigate the February riots, condemned the administration and recommended a new and more democratic constitution. By this time, Nkrumah and his followers had organized villagers and youths across the country into over five hundred branches of the UGCC. The *Accra Evening News,* an important daily newspaper supporting the national liberation movement, was founded in September 1948. However, disagreements had emerged between Nkrumah and UGCC leaders who were working with the government to create new governing proposals. On June 12, 1949, at the largest rally ever in Accra, Nkrumah helped to form the Convention People's Party (CPP), which split with the UGCC one month later. The CPP became the dominant political party in the national liberation movement.

In October 1949, Nkrumah published a pamphlet entitled *What I Mean by Positive*

Action and threatened to call for a widespread campaign of nonviolent action in the form of strikes, boycotts, and noncooperation. A gathering of ninety thousand attended a "Representative Assembly" on November 20, at which Nkrumah outlined his agenda for "positive action without violence for full self-government now." At a December 15 meeting of the CPP, Nkrumah made a passionate plea for complete nonviolence during the campaign of resistance. Nkrumah's "weapons of positive action" consisted of legitimate political advocacy, newspaper propaganda, educational campaigns, and nonviolent direct action as a last resort.

The British authorities quickly acted to smash the CPP, arresting and prosecuting members, banning conferences, and prohibiting protest cablegrams from being sent outside the country. On January 8, 1950, Nkrumah called for a countrywide general strike, excluding public utilities and police. The response was immediate and widespread, and the country came to a complete economic standstill. In response, the government declared a state of emergency, raided CPP headquarters, banned the *Accra Evening News,* and arrested and jailed Nkrumah and other leaders. The strike lasted until January 19, but the state of emergency continued through April 1. The Positive Action campaign was aborted on January 21.

During 1950, the CPP rebuilt its headquarters and continued to meet secretly. CPP representatives began to win municipal elections later that year. During the first general election under the new constitution in February 1951, Nkrumah was elected to the Executive Council while still in jail. He gained over 90 percent of the votes cast. Nkrumah was subsequently released from jail to dictate his own terms in the formation of a new government of self-rule. He was appointed leader of government business until he became prime minister in 1952, ruling in that capacity until a military overthrow in 1966. The Gold Coast became the nation of Ghana and officially gained its independence in 1957.

Because of Nkrumah's leadership in designing a "positive action" campaign of nonviolent direct action, and because the Burns administration had paved the way, the transition to self-government was relatively smooth and free of violence. The independence movement in Ghana was in the forefront of African anticolonial resistance movements.

Brad Bennett

References
Bourret, F.M. *Ghana: The Road to Independence, 1919–1957.* Stanford, Calif.: Stanford University Press, 1960.
James, C.L.R. *Nkrumah and the Ghana Revolution.* London: Allison and Busby, 1977.
Timothy, Bankole. *Kwame Nkrumah from Cradle to Grave.* Dorchester, Dorset, UK: Gavin, 1981.

Golan Heights Druze Resistance, 1981–1982

Nonviolent noncooperation campaign waged by Arab villagers against Israeli occupation. On December 14, 1981, the Israeli government formally annexed the Golan Heights region of Syrian territory, which it had occupied since the 1973 Yom Kippur War. The Druze, a sect synthesizing Shi'ite Islam and other religious traditions and centered in the Golan and the mountains of neighboring Lebanon and Syria, reacted to the annexation and forced assimilation by Israel with widespread resistance. Through sustained nonviolent noncooperation, the Druze were able to force Israel to halt a state of siege and back off from some of its more authoritarian and repressive occupation policies.

The Golani Druze immediately resisted the annexation and the accompanying mandatory identification cards and forced Israeli citizenship. Noncooperation took many forms, including defying curfews and orders not to fraternize, staging demonstrations, and conducting strikes. Druze who accepted Israeli identification cards were subjected to a complete social boycott by the entire community. At one demonstration, women surrounded Israeli soldiers, nonviolently took their weapons away, and returned them after they were finished demonstrating. One village organized a "reverse strike": when the Israeli government denied them funds to complete a major sewer project, the villagers installed the pipeline themselves. Striking Druze workers from four villages crippled northern Israeli industries for several weeks. Villagers organized cooperative economic structures and schools.

After four months of protracted negotiations, Israel escalated its military repression on April 1, 1982, and imposed a state of siege that lasted for forty-three days. The period was characterized by arrests, violent supression of demonstrations, destruction of houses, and a blockade of food and energy supplies.

G

The Druze continued their campaign of nonviolent noncooperation. Morale and discipline among Israeli soldiers started to break down in the face of Druze persistence. Israel finally lifted the siege as a result of this Druze resolve. The Golani Druze continued to resist Israeli efforts to control the region and force assimilation. Strikes continued until July 1982, when a compromise agreement was reached. However, Israel did not fulfill most of the conditions of the settlement. Noncooperation with identification card procedures continued. In September 1983, thirty-five thousand people participated in a memorial service for one of the leaders of the 1982 strike. Although Israel continues to occupy the region, Druze nonviolent tactics forced modification of some of its severe assimilation tactics.

Brad Bennett

References
Bennett, Brad. "Arab-Muslim Cases of Nonviolent Struggle." In *Arab Nonviolent Political Struggle in the Middle East,* edited by Ralph E. Crow, Philip Grant, and Saad E. Ibrahim. Boulder, Colo., and London: Lynne Rienner, 1990.
Kennedy, R. Scott. "The Druze of the Golan: A Case of Nonviolent Resistance." In *Nonviolence in Theory and Practice,* edited by Robert L. Holmes. Belmont, Calif.: Wadsworth, 1990.

See also BEIT SAHOUR, 1988–1989; INTIFADA, 1987–1990

Goldman, Emma (1869–1940)

Anarchist, labor agitator, activist, and lecturer, born in Kaunas (or Kovno), Lithuania, on June 27, 1869, and died in Toronto, Canada, on May 14, 1940.

Born into a Jewish ghetto family, Goldman immigrated to the United States in 1885 at the age of sixteen, after limited formal education and early association with radical students in St. Petersburg. First in Rochester, New York, and then in New Haven, Connecticut, Goldman worked in clothing factories, where she was influenced by socialist and anarchist groups among the workers. In 1887 she was married to Jacob Kersner.

In 1889, she moved to New York City. There she met Alexander Berkman, a young Russian émigré, and became involved in the anarchist cause. In 1892, Berkman was imprisoned for an attempt to assassinate Henry Clay Frick during a steel strike. The following year, after Goldman delivered a fiery speech to a group of unemployed workers in New York City, she was charged with inciting to riot and was sentenced to one year's imprisonment on Blackwell's Island in New York. After her release, Goldman traveled extensively on lecture tours in the United States and Europe, defending free speech and anarchism and advocating women's rights. She considered the right of suffrage largely irrelevant.

In 1906, Berkman was released from prison and was reunited with Goldman. That same year, Goldman founded a radical monthly periodical, *Mother Earth,* which was published until it was suppressed by the U.S. government in 1917. Though deprived of her U.S. citizenship in 1908, she continued to lecture and write. In 1910, she published *Anarchism and Other Essays.* Goldman also lectured and wrote about the new European drama, birth control, and "free love," the belief that intimate human relationships should be free of coercion by church or state. Goldman was jailed briefly in 1916 for her advocacy of birth control.

In 1917, she was sentenced to two years for agitating against military conscription. Shortly after she was released from prison in 1919, she and Berkman and 247 others were victims of the postwar "Red Scare" and were deported to the Soviet Union. There she came to believe that the new government was suppressing political dissent and emerging as a totalitarian state. In 1923, she published *My Disillusionment in Russia.*

For the rest of her life, Goldman continued to write and lecture in Europe and Canada. She married James Colton in 1925 to obtain British citizenship. Her autobiography, *Living My Life,* was published in 1931. In 1936, shortly after Berkman committed suicide, Goldman transcended her grief by responding to an appeal from friends in Spain to help fight Franco. She died in Toronto, Canada, while working energetically on behalf of the antifascist forces in the Spanish civil war.

Pam McAllister

References
Goldman, Emma. *Living My Life.* Edited by Richard Drinnon and Anna Maria Drinnon. New York: New American Library, 1977.

Jean and Hildegard Goss-Mayr. Photo by Jim Forest.

Goss-Mayr, Hildegard (b. 1930) and Jean (1912–1991)

Teachers and trainers of active nonviolence throughout the world for over three decades. They served the International Fellowship of Reconciliation (IFOR) as traveling secretaries, vice presidents, and honorary presidents. An Austrian/French Catholic couple, they were nominated several times for the Nobel Peace Prize and were recipients of the Award for Commitment to Human Rights Work of the Dr. Bruno Kreisky Foundation and the Pope Paul VI "Teacher for Peace" award of Pax Christi U.S.A. Their publications include *Revolution ohne Gewalt: Christen ost und West in Gespräch* (Revolution without Violence: Christians East and West in Conversation) and Gerard Houver's book interview, *Jean et Hildegard Goss: La nonviolence, c'est la vie* (A Nonviolent Lifestyle: Conversations with Jean and Hildegard Goss-Mayr).

Jean Goss was born in Lyons, France, and worked in a print shop, a book bindery, a biscuit factory, and later for the French railways. Active as a trade unionist, he led a general strike in 1953. He served in the French army in World War II and was decorated with the Croix de Guerre. He was taken as a prisoner of war by the Nazis. During imprisonment he was converted to nonviolence. Released after five years as a prisoner, Goss learned about Gandhi and the nonviolent movement through the French FOR. He subsequently became a conscientious objector and gave back to the French military his war decorations and citations for gallantry.

In 1958, Jean Goss married Hildegard Mayr, the daughter of Kaspar Mayr, Austrian co-founder of the International FOR. Residents of Vienna, she and her family were persecuted by the Nazis. In 1953, Hildegard received her Ph.D. from the University of Vienna *sub auspiciis praesidentis*, the first time this highest degree was received by a woman. In 1953, she became a traveling secretary of the International FOR, work that she and Jean continued after their marriage.

The Goss-Mayrs worked for postwar reconciliation and East–West dialogue during the height of the cold war. As lobbyists at Vatican Council II, they were largely responsible for inclusion in *Gaudium et Spes* of passages recognizing the rights of conscientious objectors and commending nonviolence. During the 1960s and 1970s, they worked in Latin America with labor unions, base communities, and churches for human rights, peace, and justice. In 1974, they helped organize the continental network

Graffiti Wall: THIS IS HUNGER'S WALL: TELL IT LIKE IT IS. *Theodore B. Hetzel Photograph Collection/ Swarthmore College Peace Collection.*

Servicio Paz y Justicia. They worked with leading bishops such as Dom Helder Camara, Dom Aloisio Lorscheider, and Mons. Leonidas Proano.

The Goss-Mayrs held seminars on active nonviolence throughout Africa, Asia, and Europe, showing the relationship of radical religious faith to the methodology and philosophy of Gandhian nonviolence. Their seminars in 1984 and 1985 in the Philippines helped lay the groundwork for the nonviolent overthrow of the Marcos dictatorship.

Hildegard Goss-Mayr continued her work as honorary president of IFOR after Jean's death. She received the prestigious Niwano Peace Prize for her contributions to world peace and the enhancement of culture, and she addressed the 1982 Second United Nations Special Session on Disarmament. Her writings include *Der Mensch vor dem Unrecht: Spiritualität und Praxis gewaltloser Befreiung* (Humankind Confronting Injustice: The Spirituality and Practice of Nonviolent Liberation) (published in four languages), *Geschenk der Armen an die Reichen: Zeugnisse aus dem gewaltfreien Kampf in Lateinamerika* (Gift of the Poor to the Rich: Experiences of Nonviolent Struggle in Latin America), and *Die Macht der Gewaltlosen* (The Power of Nonviolent People).

Richard L. Deats

See also FELLOWSHIP OF RECONCILIATION, INTERNATIONAL; TRAINING FOR NONVIOLENT ACTION

Graffiti

Painting slogans, caricatures, and symbols on surfaces to express protest. The surfaces can be publicly owned, such as the walls of government buildings or public transport vehicles, or privately owned, such as factories or billboards. Whether the target is public or private, the act of creating graffiti is generally done secretly, without permission, and is usually illegal. Often graffiti alter an existing image or message (for example, by changing words or by defacing portraits). While graffiti primarily present a symbolic appeal, the act itself also manipulates the physical environment and disregards laws against vandalism and trespassing. Because graffiti deface public or private property, the question of whether this method is nonviolent is controversial.

Graffiti have been prevalent throughout history and especially in the twentieth century. In 1941–1942, the "Baum Group," a resistance circle of Jewish young people in Berlin, conducted a night campaign of painting slogans on walls to protest the Nazi regime. In 1962, graffiti actionists in Eisenbach altered a huge picture of East German leader Walter Ulbricht by painting a rope around his neck to protest his regime. British feminist and antismoking groups in the 1970s and 1980s encouraged activists to spray paint on advertising billboards and posters with images that would symbolically deride or challenge their intended message.

References

Posener, Jill. *Spray It Loud.* London: Routledge and Kegan Paul, 1982.
Sharp, Gene. *The Politics of Nonviolent Action.* Boston: Porter Sargent, 1973.

See also MONKEYWRENCHING

Greenham Common, January 1, 1983, dawn. Women dance on silos being built to house cruise missiles. They were subsequently charged with breach of the peace and imprisoned for fourteen days. Photo by Raissa Page.

Greenham Common Peace Camp, 1981–1993

Women's peace camp at a proposed cruise missile site in Southern England. The Greenham Common peace camp was part of the campaign against nuclear weapons that revived in Britain and in other parts of the world in the early 1980s in response to the proposal to site cruise missiles in Europe. As part of the protests, camps were set up at some of the proposed sites, including Comiso in Southern Italy and Greenham Common in Berkshire, South-West England. The women's peace camp at Greenham Common provided a dramatic focus for the British and European resistance and attracted new forces to the British peace movement, particularly women and young people.

The proposal to site the missiles in Britain became public in December 1979. The Campaign for Nuclear Disarmament, which had been in existence since 1958 but which had been fairly quiescent during the 1960s and 1970s, was aroused by the new threat and launched a campaign of opposition. Other groups throughout Britain were alerted and looked for ways to protest. In the summer of 1981, a group of women in Wales, some of them members of CND, and others not hitherto involved in public peace ac-

tivity, decided to march to Greenham Common in protest against the proposed siting of the missiles.

They called themselves "Women for Life on Earth," and they arranged for public outdoor meetings to be held by local peace groups at points along the route. As they marched they discussed questions raised by the government's nuclear strategy, and by the time they arrived at Greenham they had clarified their ideas. A few of the women decided to use a tactic from the women's suffrage movement; they chained themselves to the fence at Greenham until a senior government spokesperson agreed to come and engage in a public debate with them. No such person was forthcoming, and eventually the women campaigners set up camps at the gates to the missile base and announced their intention of staying there to prevent the arrival of the missiles. After some debate within the peace movement and its supporters, all-female camps were established at all the access gates to the site.

There were three main reasons why the women opposed the siting of cruise missiles at Greenham Common. First, they were absolutely opposed to nuclear weapons in any form. Second, they objected to the fact that these weapons were under the control of a foreign power, the United States, whose recent history gave little encouragement to those who looked for the peaceful solution of international conflicts. Third, they opposed the use of common land, nominally the property of the community, for the establishment of a secret installation from which the public was barred.

From the beginning the camps were confined to women only, although an enormous amount of support in terms of financing, goods such as tents and blankets, and transportation came from peace groups and other organizations supported by both men and women.

Each year on December 12, the anniversary of the decision to site the missiles in Europe, campers organized demonstrations using images and actions that emphasized the nonviolent and feminine nature of the camps. The first such demonstration was called through network propaganda rather than through public announcements. It brought together around thirty thousand women to "embrace the base." The women joined arms, embracing the nine miles of perimeter fence that surrounded the base. They saw themselves in the role of a mother embracing an unruly child rather than beating it, quieting it by reason and affection rather than by aggression. The pictures on television taken by helicopters overhead were seen all over the country and were some of the most impressive images of nonviolent protest of the whole peace campaign. Other later demonstrations included "rough music" (blowing whistles, banging kettles, and making other loud and raucous noises every hour for a whole day), outbreaks of "keening" (a traditional form of public mourning), and different forms of singing, dancing, and proclaiming. In addition to large demonstrations, smaller groups of women broke into the fenced enclosures, decorated the fences with flowers and children's clothing, tracked missile-bearing vehicles when these left the base, and blocked the path of trucks entering or leaving the base by lying in the road. All their forms of activity were nonviolent, but some were illegal. When arrested the women usually refused to accept orders from the magistrates to keep the peace, declaring that this was what they were trying to do, and a number served terms of imprisonment for their activities.

The camps were conducted on ultrademocratic lines with no official leaders or officers. Delegates went to other parts of the world, and women from many countries, including Japanese survivors from Hiroshima and Buddhist nuns as well as women from most parts of Europe and America, visited the camps.

As the cold war collapsed and the missiles were withdrawn, the large-scale camps dispersed, but small groups remained to remind the public of the unfulfilled promise by the authorities to return the site to its use as common land.

Dorothy Thompson

See also CAMPAIGN FOR NUCLEAR DISARMAMENT; NUCLEAR WEAPONS OPPOSITION; WOMEN AND NONVIOLENT ACTION IN THE UNITED STATES SINCE 1950

Greenpeace

International environmental organization founded in 1969 during a nonviolent direct action campaign against U.S. nuclear weapons testing in Alaska. Greenpeace probably has been the most successful of the many environmental organizations that use nonviolent action. Certainly it was one of the first, and by combining a philosophical base, clear strategic design, scientific research, political and legal research and lobbying, courageous direct action, and brilliant use of media attention, it has made tremendous gains both for the organization itself and for the environment it has sought to protect.

Greenpeace's activities and membership have grown beyond its direct action origins so that it now employs a combination of nonviolent direct action, scientific inquiry, and political action to oppose such problems as toxic waste shipment and disposal, acid rain, the slaughter of seal pups and kangaroos, nuclear weapons at sea, whaling, driftnet fishing, and ocean pollution. By 1976 Greenpeace's active membership was eight thousand, with thirteen "very active" branches around the world and twenty-eight "heard from occasionally," according to the Vancouver *Sun*. By 1980 Boston alone counted twenty-five thousand contributors, and about fifty different actions took place in that year alone. By 1991 a Greenpeace publication listed offices in twenty-three countries. In the mid-1990s, however, declining membership and financial concerns forced the organization to close several local offices.

Greenpeace had its origins in nonviolent action. In October 1969, the newly formed Don't Make a Wave Committee discussed how to continue the momentum of what was both an antiwar and environmental movement protesting

U.S. underground nuclear testing at Amchitka Island, Alaska. American Marie Bohlen who, with her husband, Jim, had been one of the founders of the British Columbia chapter of the Sierra Club, suggested sailing a boat to Amchitka and mooring it near the bomb site. At a later meeting, as American Quaker Irving Stowe left the meeting with his usual peace sign, Canadian Bill Darnell added, "Make it a green peace." Jim Bohlen said they could name the boat *Greenpeace* if they ever found one.

Following in the Quaker tradition of "bearing witness" and the Quaker protest voyages of the *Phoenix* and the *Golden Rule* against U.S. nuclear tests in the 1950s and early 1960s Greenpeace sailed to the Amchitka test zone from Vancouver in September 1971. Although the first nuclear explosion to be protested was canceled and the second occurred before the ship arrived, the voyages grabbed mass media attention, in a pattern that would work well for Greenpeace on many new issues. Shortly after the second voyage, the U.S. military ended its use of the Alaskan area for nuclear testing.

Few of Greenpeace's antinuclear campaigns are better known than the last voyage of the *Rainbow Warrior,* the ship that was sunk on July 10, 1985, by French government agents in the harbor of Auckland, New Zealand, while on a trip to protest French nuclear testing at Moruroa Atoll. This trip demonstrated two of the techniques that had been central to Greenpeace's work. First, members of Greenpeace were to bear witness to nuclear testing by putting themselves in harm's way in the test area. Second, members took others out of harm's way. Prior to the Auckland stop, the *Rainbow Warrior* had taken four trips from Rongelap to Mejato to relocate three hundred islanders whose home had been contaminated by radioactive fallout from U.S. nuclear tests conducted between 1946 and 1958.

The sabotage of the *Rainbow Warrior,* which also killed Greenpeace photographer Fernando Pereira, led New Zealanders to display the slogan "You can't sink a rainbow" in the streets of Wellington as they began to raise money for Greenpeace. After the discovery that it was French agents who had carried out the bombing, the UN secretary general mediated the resulting dispute between New Zealand and France. Greenpeace, which suffered in the loss of life, loss of the ship, and cancellation of the immediate campaign, nevertheless gained publicity that tremendously increased its member-

ship. When its French office was reopened in 1989, for example, it gained 13,500 members in the first year alone.

In the mid-1970s the activities of the organization had expanded as it embraced more singularly environmental issues. Among the first of these was the antiwhaling campaign. Combining scientific research with the direct action of placing their bodies and ships between the Soviet and Japanese whaling fleets and the whales, Greenpeace brought the issue of whaling to public attention. Their skillful photography of their direct actions was used widely in the news media. This combination became a trademark of Greenpeace work. What was not so obvious to public view, and what is not so clearly played up in Greenpeace publicity, is that this publicly visible action was accompanied by the less visible but no less important action of Greenpeace lawyers and scientists who were lobbying the International Whaling Commission. In time this combination began to have an effect on the positions of countries represented on the commission, and more serious restrictions on whaling began to come out of the commission.

Among other Greenpeace efforts have been the campaign to save Newfoundland harp seal pups from being slaughtered for fur by commercial sealing fleets from Norway and Canada, the campaign to save Antarctica by turning it into an international park, and the campaign to stop several European nations from ocean dumping of radioactive nuclear waste. In this last campaign, again, Greenpeace combined the techniques of careful scientific, political, and legal research, with direct action (banners, painting emblems on ships, placing themselves in the way of barrels of nuclear waste being dumped), photography of the direct action which was then fed to the news media, and direct negotiation with the London Dumping Convention, which regulates the disposal of nuclear waste.

One of the key factors in Greenpeace's success in capturing the interest of the public was the consistency of the direct-action technique employed with the objective Greenpeace was attempting to accomplish. The David and Goliath image was particularly effective in pictures of Greenpeace members on an iceberg hugging seal pups as the iceberg was about to be hit by a government ship, and pictures of Zodiac rafts harassing the freighter *Pacific Fisher* as it carried nuclear fuel rods from Japan to France and Britain. Another common technique was the physical obstruction of something they wished to stop, such as when the Greenpeace ship *Sirius* attempted to block the arrival of the *Pacific Crane,* which was carrying spent nuclear fuel rods from Japan into France's Cherbourg harbor. A similar technique was also used to advantage in many of Greenpeace's acid rain and toxic waste campaigns when activists blocked factory smokestacks and outflow pipes. In 1987, for example, demonstrators scaled two smokestacks of a garbage incinerator in Tacoma, Washington, and plugged them with giant makeshift corks.

Greenpeace has always used the technique of exposing the aspects of a debate that might be hidden. For example, Greenpeace pictures of whaling, driftnet fishing, sealing, and toxic waste operations graphically brought issues to the attention of the international community that might not otherwise have seen the light of day. One unique example, less dramatic but no less effective, was the chance a Greenpeace member offered the public to see the Seattle mayor's own garbage after a raid on his trash can a few nights before. The mayor had been advocating the building of an incinerator in the south end of the city, but not in his back yard.

Greenpeace's international network has enabled it to make connections between different levels and locations of a problem and to help others to make connections as well. When Thor (a corporation from the United Kingdom) and American Cyanamid (a U.S. business) exported toxic waste to South Africa, Greenpeace took samples in the Valley of the 1000 Hills, worked with local organizations to educate people on the danger, and worked with Earthlife Africa to discredit an illegal waste dump and to expose water supply problems. Most of Africa is now off limits to toxic waste dumping as a result of such work.

Since its beginning there have been signs of unity and of disunity within Greenpeace. Greenpeace's philosophy has been rooted in nonviolence and internationalism. In its willingness to employ direct action the organization moved beyond the activities of traditional conservation groups. But Greenpeace's diversity was both its strength and its weakness. Composed of scientists, journalists, antinuclear activists, and people from various walks of life, Greenpeace experienced the usual difficulties of a family on their first voyage. As it grew and became more successful, there were two kinds of conflict. First, growth and bureaucratization led to accusations from more radical activists that Greenpeace was losing its direct-action impetus to more conventional political lobbying. Always in Greenpeace there has been that tension between those involved in direct action and those involved in influencing the legal and political system by a combination of scientific expertise and lobbying. But, as the examples above suggest, this combination has also been Greenpeace's strength.

The second kind of conflict that Greenpeace experienced was due to the tremendous growth in its membership during the 1970s. Offices had varying fund-raising capabilities, and many experienced difficulties juggling assets, expenses, debts, and campaigns. Factionalism grew, resulting at one point in a lawsuit between the Vancouver and San Francisco offices. When Robert Hunter resigned as president in April 1977, Patrick Moore tried unsuccessfully to set up an international board of directors. Resolution of the various crises came when David McTaggert stitched together an agreement in which Greenpeace Europe paid off Vancouver's debts, and the U.S., Canadian, and European groups formed the new umbrella organization, Greenpeace International, headquartered in the Netherlands.

In the 1990s, Greenpeace remains the premier environmental organization, combining traditional political activities and coalitions with nonviolent direct action. As such, and largely because of its innovative uses of nonviolent action, it has had a large influence on both the agenda of the global environmental movement and various national and international policies.

Carolyn M. Stephenson

References

Brown, Michael, and John May. *The Greenpeace Story.* New York: Dorling Kindersley, 1989.

Hunter, Robert. *Warriors of the Rainbow: A Chronicle of the Greenpeace Movement.* New York: Holt, Rinehart and Winston, 1979.

Hunter, Robert, and Rex Weyler. *To Save a Whale: The Voyages of Greenpeace.* San Francisco: Chronicle, 1978.

Robie, David. *Eyes of Fire: The Last Voyage of the Rainbow Warrior.* Philadelphia: New Society, 1986.

Sunday Times Insight Team. *Rainbow War-*

rior: The French Attempt to Sink Green-peace. London: Century Hutchison, 1986.

See also ENVIRONMENTAL MOVEMENTS; NUCLEAR ENERGY OPPOSITION; *RAINBOW WARRIOR;* VOYAGES, PROTEST

Gregg, Richard (1885–1974)

American labor lawyer and an important pioneer in the field of nonviolent action and civilian-based defense. Gregg was born in 1885 in Colorado Springs, Colorado, and died on January 27, 1974. His book *The Power of Nonviolence* remains an important historical contribution to the development of the technique of nonviolent struggle.

Gregg traveled to India in the 1920s to study Mohandas K. Gandhi's campaigns for independence from British rule. In his subsequent analysis of Gandhian strategy, Gregg published *The Power of Nonviolence* in 1935. In this discussion of the power of nonviolent action, he articulated the concept of "moral jiu-jitsu" to denote the emotional or psychological effects of the perseverance of nonviolent action on repressive opponents. Gregg suggested that this jiu-jitsu was accomplished through persuading and loving one's enemies. In the book, he also described how a campaign of mass nonviolent resistance would work, emphasizing the importance of training and discipline. He was one of the first analysts of conflict to consider nonviolent resistance as a functional equivalent for war.

Brad Bennett

References
Gregg, Richard B. *The Power of Nonviolence.* New York: Schocken, 1966.

Griffith, Arthur (1871–1922)

Leader of the Irish nationalist movement during the early part of the twentieth century. Griffith was born on March 31, 1871, in Ulster County, Ireland, and died on August 12, 1922. A noted journalist and editor, he wrote a pamphlet entitled *The Resurrection of Hungary, a Parallel for Ireland* in 1904, in which he claimed that Hungarians won their independence by ignoring Austrian "illegal" suspension of the 1848 Hungarian constitution and by refusing to participate in a solely Austrian government. He advocated a similar campaign of Irish noncooperation with "illegal" British policies and practices that eclipsed the 1783 British Renunciation Act, and he called for nonviolent resistance to British domination. As a founder and leader of nationalist organizations like *Cumann na nGaedheal* and *Sinn Fein* ("Ourselves Alone"), Griffith advocated unity among Irish nationalist groups, educating the public, and a peaceful transition toward Irish independence.

Brad Bennett

References
Davis, Richard P. *Arthur Griffith and Non-Violent Sinn Fein.* Dublin: Anvil, 1974.
Younger, Calton. *Arthur Griffith.* Dublin: Gill and Macmillan, 1981.

See also HUNGARIAN NATIONAL MOVEMENT, 1848–1867; NORTHERN IRELAND CIVIL RIGHTS ASSOCIATION

Grimké, Sarah Moore (1792–1873) and Angelina Emily (1805–1879)

Sisters, Quaker social reformers, abolitionists, and feminist activists. Sarah was born in Charleston, South Carolina, on November 26, 1792, the sixth child of John and Mary Grimké. Angelina, the fourteenth and final child, was born on February 20, 1805. Both sisters died in Boston, Massachusetts, Sarah on December 23, 1873, and Angelina on October 26, 1879.

Though born into a slave-holding family of the Charleston aristocracy, Sarah Grimké never accepted plantation life—neither the severe limitations imposed on her as a girl nor the indifference to the suffering of the enslaved African people. At age four, having witnessed the whipping of a slave woman, Sarah was found at the waterfront searching for a sea captain who could take her someplace where such things didn't happen. Several years later, she deliberately "defied the laws of South Carolina" by teaching her waiting-maid to read. As a young woman, she rebelled against educational restrictions imposed on her own life and studied her father's law books in secret.

In 1805, when Angelina was born, Sarah, almost thirteen, was eager to cultivate an ally and resolved to protect and educate her sister. For the next thirty years, Angelina called Sarah "Mother."

In 1818, Judge Grimké became seriously ill and was sent north to be treated by a doctor in Philadelphia. Sarah accompanied him and lodged, for a brief time, with a Quaker family. After her father's death, she encountered Quakers again on her trip home and was exposed to the antislavery writings of John Woolman. In 1821, Sarah defied society's expectations of an unmarried southern woman when she moved north and joined the Society of Friends.

Angelina, like Sarah, rebelled against the oppression of women and the persecution of the enslaved African men and women. She intended to remain in the South and challenge the cruelties she witnessed daily, but, expelled from the Presbyterian Church and subjected to rumors of mental instability, she fled to the North in 1829 to join her sister.

In 1835, when antislavery activists were targets of mob violence, Angelina wrote a letter in defense of free speech that was published in William Lloyd Garrison's abolitionist paper, *The Liberator.* She encouraged antislavery activists to face persecution bravely and wrote: "The ground upon which you stand is holy ground: never—never surrender it." Angelina's letter was widely reproduced. Encouraged, she penned an antislavery tract, *An Appeal to the Christian Women of the South,* urging mothers, sisters, and wives of men who make the laws to pray about and speak against the injustice of slavery and to free their own slaves.

Though initially uneasy about Angelina's activism, Sarah soon risked personal involvement and was the first to explicitly address the relationship of race and sex in society, stating: "The similarities of the woman's and the Negroes' problems are not accidental. They were . . . originally determined in a paternalistic order of society." In 1836, her essay *An Epistle of the Clergy of the Southern States* openly challenged Christian clergy's acceptance and advocacy of slavery.

The sisters became the first female abolitionist agents in the United States, organizing women's antislavery organizations in northern cities. They were denounced by the clergy in a public pastoral letter and criticized by some abolitionists who feared that the demand for women's rights would complicate and weaken the antislavery cause. Nevertheless, Sarah and Angelina continued to write tracts, circulate petitions, lead workshops, and lecture to gatherings of thousands in Boston and throughout New England. They personally challenged segregation by sitting on the "colored bench" at church services.

In 1838, when Angelina married the prominent abolitionist Theodore Weld, the Society of Friends "disowned" the sisters—Angelina for marrying outside the faith and Sarah for attending the wedding ceremony. Weld and the two sisters shared a household and, in 1839, published *American Slavery As It Is: Testimony of a Thousand Witnesses,* which sold over 100,000 copies in the first year.

After that joint venture the sisters were only minimally involved in social change. In the early 1850s they participated in a brief experiment with a utopian cooperative. In 1870, they joined forty other women and their male escorts in a procession through a blizzard to a polling place where they voted with mock ballots. Both sisters served as officers of the Massachusetts Woman Suffrage Association, founded in 1870. At the age of seventy-nine, Sarah walked miles, going door-to-door to sell copies of John Stuart Mill's work *The Subjection of Women.*

Pam McAllister

References

Caplair, Larry, ed. *The Public Years of Sarah and Angelina Grimké: Selected Writings, 1835–1839.* New York: Columbia University Press, 1989.

Lerner, Gerda. *The Grimké Sisters from South Carolina: Pioneers for Woman's Rights and Abolition.* New York: Shocken, 1967.

Nies, Judith. *Seven Women: Portraits from the American Radical Tradition.* New York: Viking, 1977.

See also ABOLITIONIST MOVEMENT; WOMEN'S SUFFRAGE

Guatemala, Overthrow of Jorge Ubico, 1944

A nonviolent popular movement of the urban elite—students, teachers, and business professionals—that successfully organized against the last great dictator of Guatemala, Jorge Ubico, in May and June 1944. The movement was inspired by the overthrow of Maximiliano Hernandez Martínez in El Salvador in May 1944 and Allied rhetoric best articulated in the Atlantic Charter and Franklin D. Roosevelt's speech "The Four Freedoms." The wartime disruption of an economy heavily dependent on Germany and the strong presence of U.S. military in the country resulted in inflation and further diminished the power of Ubico.

In October 1943, the University Students Association (AEU) was founded at the University of San Carlos with students from various schools. In May 1944, a small group of Ubico's political opponents formed an opposition party, the Social Democratic Party (SDP). Both groups agreed to work together, with the SDP responsible for negotiations with the diplomatic corps, Ubico, and his ministers. In June, school teachers joined the AEU.

In early June, a group of forty-five lawyers requested the removal of a judge, and Ubico allowed their charges to be published in the newspaper *Nuestro Diario*. Two hundred teachers petitioned for a salary increase and organized a boycott of the Teacher's Day parade, in which teachers were required to march. The government responded by dismissing all teachers, arresting some teachers and students, and trying for sedition the two teachers who had organized the petition.

On June 22, the AEU sent an ultimatum to Ubico demanding the release of arrested students and teachers, the reinstatement of suspended teachers, abolition of the paramilitary teachers' parade, and various university reforms. They threatened a general strike if their demands were not met. When the government responded favorably to some of their demands, the students and teachers escalated their demands to include complete autonomy for the university and the resignation of Ubico. The government then suspended constitutional guarantees. On June 23, students, teachers, and lawyers went on strike. A petition to Ubico by 311 distinguished citizens asked for the restoration of constitutional guarantees and consideration of the students' demands.

The popular movement took to the streets, gaining support from workers. It used various nonviolent methods, such as public marches, the use of public silence, the wearing of black to mourn the suspension of constitutional guarantees, and the singing of the national anthem and the Marseillaise. In the marches, people walked two by two, since Guatemalan law forbade assemblies of more than two people on the street. In a women's march on June 25, the women carried candles and rosaries and wore black as a symbol of political mourning. When a teacher in the women's march was killed by the military, public sentiment coalesced in support of a complete economic shutdown. All businesses and transportation systems closed on June 26. The conflict ended five days later when Ubico resigned, on July 1.

Christina A. Clamp

References

Clamp, Christina. *The Overthrow of Jorge Ubico: A Case of Nonviolent Action in Guatemala.* Unpublished bachelor's thesis, Friends World College, 1976.
———. "Towards an Analysis of Protest: The Case of Guatemala." Unpublished Master's paper, Boston College, 1977.

See also CIVIC STRIKE; EL SALVADOR, CIVIC STRIKE, 1944

Guerrilla Theater

Skit, dramatic presentation, or performance piece that is intended to disrupt a speech, lecture, meeting, or other proceedings of a group or institution. The term is also used to describe politically motivated spontaneous theater usually performed in a nontraditional venue (such as on the street). This second form of guerrilla theater is also called *agitprop*. In the first case, guerrilla theater takes the form of nonviolent social intervention. The second use is one of nonviolent protest and persuasion, as the actors deliberately intend to communicate a political message or educate audiences about specific issues. In both cases, the actors are symbolically appealing to an audience, whether it be an opponent or a third party. If the drama disrupts an opponent's activity, the dramatists are attempting to manipulate a change in behavior directly. Guerrilla theater often uses parody and satire to deliver a symbolic message.

Guerrilla theater was widely used in the United States in the 1960s. A group called the Yippies engaged in dramatic actions to call attention to specific issues and disrupt "business as usual." In 1967, they dropped dollar bills onto the New York Stock Exchange to symbolically denounce the American preoccupation with money. Also in the 1960s, groups adopted a tactic they called "zap actions" to denote short skits that delivered a political message. More recently, feminist groups in the United States such as Ladies Against Women and the Women's Action Coalition have performed small skits to protest patriarchal oppression of women.

References

Buhle, Mary Jo, Paul Buhle, and Dan Georgakas, eds. *Encyclopedia of the American Left.* New York and London: Garland, 1990.

Sharp, Gene. *The Politics of Nonviolent Action.* Boston: Porter Sargent, 1973.

H

Haiti, Fall of Duvalier, 1985–1986

Predominantly nonviolent struggle that brought an end to the Duvalier dictatorship. Haiti, the poorest country in the Western Hemisphere, was ruled by the Duvalier family for twenty-eight years, first by François "Papa Doc" Duvalier, and then by his son, Jean-Claude "Baby Doc" Duvalier. In the mid-1980s, four forces converged in Haiti that led to the fall of Jean-Claude Duvalier. The Church criticized the regime for its indifference to the extreme poverty in the country. Haitian peasants engaged in street protests against the Duvalier government. Members of the Haitian elite conspired to oust Duvalier. And the U.S. government, which had always propped up the regime, withdrew its support when it was clear the regime was going to fall.

The Roman Catholic Church began to oppose the Duvalier regime in the early 1980s. Parish priests influenced by liberation theology spoke out for social justice and against economic and political oppression. Jean-Bertrand Aristide, a young Salesian priest ordained in 1982, became the most prominent among them, known for his prophetic sermons critical of the Duvalier government. The visit of Pope John Paul II, on March 9, 1983, galvanized the Church's opposition to the regime, leading 860 priests and Church workers to sign a statement calling for the Church to take bold new action to help the poor. The bishops of Haiti soon made a similar statement. Protestant churches, especially the Anglicans and Methodists, also criticized the government. Church radio stations, such as Radio Soleil and Radio Lumière, became voices of dissent.

The first street protests came in May 1984, soon after Michèle Bennett Duvalier, Jean-Claude's wife, held a lavish May ball for the Haitian elite and had it televised across the country. This display of opulence raised the level of anger and frustration among the Haitian poor to a fever pitch. In the city of Gonaïves, food riots broke out when rumors circulated that food aid from the nongovernmental organization CARE was going to be sold on the black market. The crowds ransacked the CARE warehouse and went on to attack shops of Duvalier supporters, beating soldiers that tried to stand in their way. In the repression that followed, at least forty were killed by government soldiers. Similar events occurred in other provincial towns.

Economic conditions in Haiti deteriorated further in 1985. The Duvaliers had plundered the country's treasury, stashing millions away in foreign bank accounts. Their spending also was extravagant. In 1985, Michèle and two dozen of her friends went on a European shopping spree, spending $85,000 on first-class plane tickets alone and buying furs, clothes, and artwork at a cost of $1.7 million. The money came out of the government's foreign reserves. This, together with substantial cuts in U.S. aid, created a foreign currency shortage for the government. Fuel tankers stopped coming to Haiti because the government no longer had the foreign currency to pay for it. The resulting fuel shortages caused long lines at gas pumps, and worse, starvation, since food could not be transported to the countryside.

Meanwhile, a conspiracy to oust Duvalier was hatched by Gérard C. Noel, a lawyer; Lieutenant General Henri Namphy, the army chief of staff; and Colonel Williams Regala, inspector general of the armed forces. They wanted to get rid of Duvalier and the excesses of his regime in a bloodless coup, to form an interim coalition government, and then to hold elections as soon as possible.

Through the year, Duvalier made attempts to gain favor with the Haitian people. He promised reforms, legalized political parties, released thirty-six political prisoners, made changes in his cabinet, abolished the death penalty for political crimes, and fired Roger Lafontant, the hated minister of the interior who was in charge of the police and army. But to the Haitian people, these concessions only indicated that the regime was weakening. Protests became bolder.

On November 27, 1985, again in Gonaïves, children and young people marched through the streets protesting hunger and poverty. Protesters burned tires at intersections, displayed anti-Duvalierist signs, and sang anti-Duvalierist songs. By midday, schools were closed. When demonstrations continued the next day, government soldiers shot and killed three students. In response, protests erupted throughout Haiti.

On December 5, Duvalier shut down the Church radio stations, Radio Soleil and Radio Lumière. Later, the Catholic Bishops Conference issued its annual Christmas Eve message, calling for change and further legitimizing the opposition movement. Protests spread.

Duvalier reshuffled his cabinet again on December 31, 1985. In early January, he announced a 10 percent reduction in government-controlled prices for flour, cooking oil, and diesel fuel. But by that time, nothing short of a bloody crackdown could quell the opposition. On January 6 and 7, antigovernment demonstrations, timed with the scheduled reopening of the schools, spread to several cities, including Port-au-Prince. Father Jean-Bertrand Aristide, of the St.-Jean-Bosco parish in Port-au-Prince, was one of the principal organizers of the urban protests. Duvalier closed the schools on January 8, but the demonstrations continued. Protesters blocked roads with burning tires and threw rocks at police and government soldiers. Workers went on strike and shops closed, bringing the entire country to a standstill. Military troops and members of the Tonton Macoutes (the Duvalier regime's "security forces") beat and arrested demonstrators and fired automatic weapons into crowds to disperse them.

By mid-January, Duvalier was being criticized from every quarter. Protestant religious leaders issued a joint statement criticizing the violence, corruption, and lack of human rights in Haiti. Duvalier was also condemned by the Haitian Human Rights League, the Haitian Committee of Members of Religious Orders, the Haitian Medical Association, and the Haitian Industrialists Association. Even Duvalier's own voodoo priests condemned him, saying that the spirits were angry with him and wanted him to leave.

Student-led demonstrations erupted again in Cap Haitien on January 25, following the government's announcement that three soldiers had been charged with murder in the November 28 shooting deaths of the three students in Gonaïves. The demonstrations in Cap Haitien peaked on January 27, with forty thousand out of a total population of sixty-five thousand participating.

In late January, the U.S. government also began to pull away from the Duvalier regime. The Reagan administration announced that it would cut off aid to Haiti. And at the beginning of February, U.S. Secretary of State George Shultz called for democracy in Haiti. U.S. Ambassador Clayton E. McManaway, Jr., put pressure on Duvalier to step down, as did Haitian Foreign Minister Georges Salomon and other members of the Haitian elite.

On January 31, White House spokesman Larry Speakes announced that Duvalier had left Haiti. But this was an erroneous report and was later retracted. Duvalier and his family would not leave until February 7, 1986. The U.S. provided an Air Force military transport plane and negotiated temporary political asylum for him in France. He was replaced by an interim coalition government headed by Lieutenant General Henri Namphy.

Following the departure of Duvalier, there were celebrations in the streets. But jubilation quickly turned to vengeance, as Haitians attacked Duvalierists and Tonton Macoutes in a process of popular justice they called *dechoukaj* (the uprooting).

In the end, the National Council of Government (CNG) turned out to be more repressive than the Duvalier regime. According to Haitian anthropologist Michel-Rolph Trouillot: "By the end of its first year in office the CNG, generously helped by the U.S. taxpayers' money, had openly gunned down more civilians than Jean-Claude Duvalier's government had done in fifteen years." The CNG's policies simply amounted to "Duvalierism without Duvalier."

Jean-Bertrand Aristide, a central opposition figure during this period, became Haiti's first freely elected president on February 7, 1991, only to be ousted in a military coup d'état on September 30 and forced into exile. Three years and fifteen days later, on October 15, 1994, Aristide was returned to power through the combined influence of international economic sanctions, diplomatic pressure, and the threat of U.S. military intervention.

Roger S. Powers

References

Abbott, Elizabeth. *Haiti: An Insider's Story of the Rise and Fall of the Duvaliers.* New York: Simon and Schuster, 1988.

Farmer, Paul. *The Uses of Haiti.* Monroe, Maine: Common Courage, 1994.

Trouillot, Michel-Rolph. *Haiti: State against Nation.* New York: Monthly Review, 1990.

Weinstein, Brian, and Aaron Segal. *Haiti: The Failure of Politics.* New York: Praeger, 1992.

Harassment, Nonviolent

Methods used to pressure individuals to change their behavior, either through persuasion or psychological intervention. Examples of nonviolent harassment designed to persuade individuals include "haunting" public officials (by following them about and thereby constantly reminding them of their unacceptable behavior or the determination of the resistance), taunting individuals (by mocking, name-calling, and insulting), and fraternization (by subjecting them to intense influence and propaganda, often positive in nature).

Nonviolent harassment as a means of psychological intervention often consists of a stronger and more persistent use of "haunting" and taunting. Often harassment includes some form of accusation or condemnation as well. Sometimes a combination of pressures (such as taunting, heckling, and accusatory posters) is used in a campaign against a person or group. The object of this type of nonviolent harassment is to stop certain behavior rather than persuade the opponents to change their beliefs.

Indian volunteers "haunted" officials during the 1928 Bardoli campaign, following them everywhere and camping next to officials' residences. Fraternization by Czech citizens with invading Soviet soldiers in 1968 led to doubts and morale problems among the soldiers and necessitated the rotation and replacement of troops. More intense harassment was used by U.S. abolitionists against slave hunters who captured and returned escaped slaves to their Southern owners. Posters naming and describing these slave hunters were plastered in public places and abolitionists were encouraged to follow and surround the slave hunters wherever they went, so as to hinder their task. American anti-abortion activists have harassed women entering abortion clinics in the 1980s and 1990s.

References

Sharp, Gene. *The Politics of Nonviolent Action.* Boston: Porter Sargent, 1973.

See also ABOLITIONIST MOVEMENT; BARDOLI CAMPAIGN, 1928; CZECHOSLOVAKIA, 1968 RESISTANCE MOVEMENT; OUTING

Hartal

Indian method of temporarily suspending the economic life of an area on a voluntary basis to demonstrate dissatisfaction with or enmity toward a policy, situation, action, or regime. The *hartal* usually lasts one day, but it may be extended in extreme situations. It is composed of a combination of labor strikes and economic closures. Laborers often solicit permission from their employers to abstain from work, because one major emphasis of the *hartal* is that it must be voluntary. Shop owners and businesspeople also participate by closing their factories and businesses. The *hartal* is differentiated from the general strike in that it is used primarily to communicate opinions and feelings rather than wield economic pressure. Thus, while the *hartal* is a form of economic noncooperation, the primary mechanism of action is one of appeal through symbolic protest. The *hartal* is usually citywide or villagewide, although it may be expanded to a nationwide level.

The *hartal* has been used in India since ancient times, often to communicate disapproval of a specific government policy to a prince or king. Mohandas K. Gandhi often used this method at the beginning of a resistance campaign so as to purify and solidify the movement. For example, a *hartal* was used in the opening stages of both the 1919 satyagraha campaign against the Rowlatt Bills and the 1930–1931 independence campaign.

References

Sharp, Gene. *The Politics of Nonviolent Action*. Boston: Porter Sargent, 1973.

See also INDIAN NATIONAL MOVEMENT; ROWLATT BILLS, OPPOSITION, 1919; SATYAGRAHA

Havel, Václav (b. 1936)

Czech playwright and political dissident, born in Prague on October 6, 1936. Active in the effort to reinstate democratic government in Czechoslovakia, and a primary founder and leader of Charter 77 and the Civic Forum, Havel became president of the Czech and Slovak Republic in December 1989 following the "Velvet Revolution" that ended Communist rule.

As a young man, Havel was denied access to the university because he was from a wealthy, non–Communist Party family. He educated himself by studying independently and by actively participating in a group he formed called the Thirty-Sixers. Open only to his friends born in 1936, the Thirty-Sixers was a discussion group that focused on politics, economics, and literature.

Under the political repression of the Communist Party's rule, Havel found that the theater, where he worked initially as a stage hand, was the only place he could distinguish himself. He eventually became resident playwright of the Theatre of the Balustrade company in 1968, the same year that Alexander Dubček attempted to liberalize communism in Czechoslovakia.

As Dubček's reforms began to spread, Havel promoted the political engagement of intellectuals in the liberalization process. He established and chaired the Independent Writer's Circle in 1968, and he helped to create two other groups that formed a nascent opposition party to the Communists. KAN (which stood for the Club for Committed Non-Party Activists) and K231 (for those who had been previously imprisoned by the Communists for political reasons under Article 231 of the criminal code) each rapidly drew thousands of members from largely disaffected intellectuals and Communist Party renegades. In May 1968, Havel and many of his supporters demanded the reinstatement of the Social Democratic Party.

In August, the Soviets led an invasion of Czechoslovakia to crush the reforms. Czechs responded with nonviolent resistance that im-posed moral and psychological pressure on the Soviet occupation troops. Havel and his friends set up a clandestine radio station and broadcast scripts written by Havel to support the resistance. The Czechs eventually were forced into submission. Censorship was reimposed, and KAN and K231 were suppressed. Havel's plays were banned and his passport was confiscated.

As Soviet oppression of Czechoslovakia continued, Havel continued to fight. He was arrested several times and interrogated by police concerning his many activities denouncing "normalization." In 1975, Havel wrote a letter to Czech Communist Party leader Gustav Husák, who was attempting to normalize the country on Moscow's behalf. The letter brought about major international controversy because it directly addressed the idea that the Czechs were being driven by fear to obey and to conform to their oppressors.

Just before New Year's Day in 1977, Havel and several other dissidents established Charter 77, named for the pending year. Their document, which had 240 original signatories, declared Charter 77 "a free and open association." It maintained that human rights were being infringed in the normalization process and that the Czech government was violating several international agreements, including the Final Act of the Helsinki Accords on cooperation and security in Europe, signed in 1976. Members of Charter 77 provided information about the status of political and civil freedoms in Czechoslovakia to Western journalists who then publicized it through international news media. The London newspapers called the efforts of Charter 77 "the first signs of liberal dissent since 1968."

In the early part of 1977, Havel was interrogated and his home searched daily by police. One such search lasted thirteen hours. Others who were involved in Charter 77 had similar experiences. Every night, Havel and his friends met at his apartment to compare notes, which would then be passed on to foreign journalists. The leadership became aware of such meetings and took more drastic steps to control Havel and his dissident activities. Throughout the 1970s and 1980s, Havel was repeatedly arrested, and he served a total of four years in prison.

Living under such conditions, Havel was inspired to write an essay entitled "Power of the Powerless," in which he argued that under circumstances of oppression people must nevertheless "live within the truth." By the essential action of refusing to "live the lie" of obeisance to the forms of dictatorship, Havel argued that individuals, and then society "from below," could reclaim their freedom.

In 1989, anti-Communist revolutions erupted throughout eastern Europe, which among other things led to the fall of the Berlin Wall. Communist Party membership and power were in deep decline. This was a dream come true for Havel. During the revolution, Havel helped to establish and became the leader of the Civic Forum, a non-Communist opposition group that urged democratic reform. By December, the Communist Party surrendered its losing battle and formed a cooperative government with Civic Forum. As a result of this alliance, Havel was elected president of Czechoslovakia on December 29, 1989.

Over the next three years, political and economic divisions eroded the bond between the Czech and Slovak republics in the new democratic state. On January 1, 1993, Havel presided over the "velvet divorce" and became the first president of the new Czech Republic.

Kimberley A. Pyles

References

Havel, Václav, et al. *Power of the Powerless: Citizens against the State in Central-Eastern Europe.* Introduction by Steven Lukes. Edited by John Keane. Armonk, N.Y.: M.E. Sharpe, 1985.

Kriseová, Eda. *Václav Havel: The Authorized Biography.* New York: St. Martin's, 1993.

Simmons, Michael. *The Reluctant President: A Political Life of Vaclav Havel.* London: Methuen, 1991.

Wheaton, Bernard, and Zdenek Kavan. *The Velvet Revolution: Czechoslovakia, 1968–1991.* Boulder, Colo.: Westview, 1992.

See also CHARTER 77; CZECHOSLOVAKIA, 1968 RESISTANCE MOVEMENT; DUBČEK, ALEXANDER; REVOLUTIONS OF 1989

Highlander Folk School

Community adult education school and training center for developing leadership in labor, community, and civil rights movements. Committed to integrating education and action, the Highlander Folk School analyzed goals, strategy, and tactics (including nonviolent direct action) in social movements against oppression in the South. The school faculty advocated a strategic analysis of all aspects of struggles, in the hopes that education would facilitate successful action.

Founded by Myles Horton in 1932 near Monteagle, Tennessee, for the purpose of educating rural and labor leaders to create a "new social order," the Highlander Folk School (HFS) initially focused primarily on labor struggles. The faculty held workshops for potential labor leaders, organized unions, and assisted with strikes. While early strike actions were largely unsuccessful, HFS gained valuable knowledge regarding education for social change. Two of the more significant campaigns were the 1933 "Bugwood" strike and the 1939 "Stay-In." During the strike by Bugwood (a Tennessee wood used for fuel) cutters, HFS conducted crisis-oriented community education in support of the strike. In February 1939, striking Works Progress Adminstration (WPA) workers and their families refused to leave the Tracy City, Tennessee, Relief Office without promise of jobs. HFS organized workshops, rallies, and a jobless parade, again engaging in education in a protest situation. Despite limited gains in both of these campaigns, HFS received practical experience in combining education and action for social change. From 1937 to 1941, HFS became an integral part of the training of labor leaders for the Congress of Industrial Organizations union organizing drive.

The Highlander Folk School was also active in other campaigns to educate and empower oppressed peoples. It focused on local indigenous impoverished people and their problems. It also attempted to organize small farmers into a union, and in the late 1940s HFS attempted unsuccessfully to build a labor–farmer coalition in the South. From 1953 to 1961, organizers conducted the Highlander Community Leadership Training Program, designed to educate poor blacks so they could register to vote.

From the beginning, the Highlander Folk School was devoted to racial integration in education. In the 1950s and early 1960s, HFS began a campaign to bring about integration in public schools and later became an educational center for the black civil rights movement. Rosa Parks, whose refusal to yield her seat to a white passenger triggered the 1955 Montgomery bus boycott, had attended a desegregation work-

H

shop at HFS the previous summer. Many of the leaders of the student sit-ins for racial desegregation in the early 1960s were veterans of HFS workshops and continued to meet there to discuss goals and strategy. The popular song of the civil rights movement, "We Shall Overcome," first gained prominence at HFS.

From its genesis, the Highlander Folk School faced a barrage of criticism, threats, and hostile investigations by opponents. Perhaps the most damaging campaign was an anti-Communist offensive that resulted in the state's revoking the HFS charter and confiscating its land in 1962. Anticipating this consequence, HFS leaders founded a new organization, the Highlander Research and Education Center in Knoxville in 1961 (it moved to New Market, Tennessee, in 1971). From 1932 to 1962, the Highlander Folk School played an important role in education and organization for social change in southern labor and civil rights movements.

Brad Bennett

References

Glen, John M. *Highlander: No Ordinary School, 1932–1962.* Lexington: University Press of Kentucky, 1988.

Horton, Aimee Isgrig. *The Highlander Folk School: A History of Its Major Programs, 1932–1961.* Brooklyn, N.Y.: Carlson, 1989.

See also CIVIL RIGHTS MOVEMENT; PARKS, ROSA; TRAINING FOR NONVIOLENT ACTION

Hijrat

See EMIGRATION, PROTEST

Human Rights

That due a person, or a claim a person has by virtue of being a human being. The term *human rights* is relatively recent. It was first used by U.S. President Franklin Delano Roosevelt in a 1941 message to the U.S. Congress in which he propounded four freedoms: freedoms of speech and religion and freedoms from want and fear. The idea of human rights is an elaboration of what used to be called natural rights or the rights of man.

These are a particularly Western idea that grew out of the medieval concern for the rights of specific groups, such as lords, barons, churchmen, kings, guilds, or towns. With the Enlightenment, philosophers began to consider whether people in general had any rights. John Locke in particular argued in his influential *Second Treatise of Government* (1690) that all people have a natural right to freedom, equality, and property. He directly influenced the American Declaration of Independence, which almost a century later (1776) declared that "We hold these Truths to be self-evident, that all Men are created equal, that they are endowed by their Creator with certain unalienable Rights, that among these are Life, Liberty, and the pursuit of Happiness." During the French Revolution the French National Assembly approved the Declaration of the Rights of Man and the Citizen (1789), which proclaimed that the goal of political association is the preservation of the natural and inalienable rights of man, of liberty, private property, personal security, and resistance to oppression.

Such rights were further defined in the Bill of Rights, the first ten amendments to the Constitution of the United States, among them the freedom of speech, religion, and assembly. These and other rights have been included in many other constitutions and now are part of an International Bill of Rights. This comprises the 1945 United Nations Charter (Articles 1 and 55), the 1948 Universal Declaration of Human Rights (UDHR) adopted by the UN General Assembly, and the two international covenants passed by the General Assembly in 1966, one on Civil and Political Rights (CPR) and the other on Economic, Social, and Cultural Rights (ESCR). There is now a UN Human Rights Commission that can investigate alleged violations of human rights and also receive and consider individual complaints, a momentous advance for human rights in the state-centered international system. And there is the Helsinki process that began with the Helsinki Accord of 1975, with its Basket Three on human rights and periodic meetings to assess the progress of human rights among the signatories.

In addition, human rights have been pursued in several regions. To mention just some of this activity, the Council of Europe adopted the European Convention on Human Rights, and Europe now has the European Court of Human Rights and the European Commission on Human Rights. The Organization of American States also adopted the American Declaration on Human Rights, and further the American states have created the Inter-American Convention and Court on Human Rights. And due to the Organization for African Unity, there is now the African Charter of Human and People's Rights. Moreover, there have been numerous formal conferences among states and interested international government organizations on human rights such as the World Conference on Human Rights among 183 nations in Vienna during June 1993.

Human rights have also been the concern of numerous private organizations that have sought to further define and extend human rights (such as to a clean environment), observe their implementation among governments, publicize violations by governments (such as of the right against torture and summary execution), or pressure governments to cease their violations. Some of the many such organizations include the International Committee of the Red Cross, the Anti-Slavery Society, Amnesty International, the International League for Human Rights, and the International Commission of Jurists.

In sum, human rights now are very much a part of international relations and law. They define fundamental moral canons for criticizing international and national conditions and behavior. As such they are imbedded in the practice of nations and treaty prescriptions. Many states now even include human rights monitors or representatives within their foreign ministries. For example, the United States Department of State has a Bureau of Human Rights and Humanitarian Affairs run by an assistant secretary.

States have even generally agreed to moderate their warfare to preserve certain human rights, as precisely defined in the 1949 Geneva Conventions and their 1977 Additional Protocols. And under international law there is now a fundamental core of human rights, for which there is universal jurisdiction, that no state can violate without risking mandated sanctions by the UN Security Council. Such include piracy, slavery, and genocide, for example.

Along with all this activity on human rights, the number of such rights has multiplied in the last half-century. There are at least forty human rights listed in the basic UDHR, CPR, and ESCR international documents on human rights, and even these have been further extended, as for the right to development, which was declared "an inalienable human right" by the UN General Assembly in 1982.

All these rights may be divided into those that concern *individuals* and those regarding *collectivities*. The former, which comprise the vast majority of rights, may be further divided into those *rights of the individual against the state*, usually the traditional Western rights, and those *rights that make claims on the state*. We can list an internationally recognized core of rights against the state from those listed in the UDHR. These include the rights

- to life, liberty, security of the person, recognition as a person before the law, equal protection of the law, remedy for violation of rights, fair and public trial, the presumption of innocence until proven guilty if charged with a penal offense, leave any country and return, seek asylum from persecution, nationality, marriage, property, the secret ballot and periodic elections, freely chosen representatives, form and join trade unions, equal access to public service, and participation in cultural life;
- to freedom of movement and residence, thought, conscience and religion, opinion and expression, peaceful assembly and association, and of parents to choose their children's education;
- and to freedom from slavery or servitude, torture, degrading or inhuman treatment or punishment, arbitrary arrest or detention or exile, arbitrary interference with privacy or family or home or correspondence, deprivation of nationality, arbitrary deprivation of property, and being compelled to join an association.

Those that are claims on the state mainly comprise the rights to social security; work and free choice of employment; just and favorable conditions of work; protection against unemployment; equal pay for equal work; just and favorable remuneration (and that is supplemented if necessary); rest and leisure including periodic holidays with pay; adequate standard of living; special care and assistance for motherhood and childhood; education (including free education in elementary and fundamental stages); protection of the family; protection of one's scientific, literary, or artistic production; protection from attacks on one's honor or reputation; and the assurance to individuals and their families of an existence worthy of human dignity.

In addition there are collective rights not mentioned in the UDHR that include the right

H

to economic development and the right to self-determination of a people. Nor does it explicitly include those rights whose violation we call war crimes or crimes against humanity.

Obviously, the list of internationalized human rights has gone far beyond the American Bill of Rights, and one may well ask what defines and justifies a human right. Philosophers have argued much about this question, especially in terms of natural rights. In its original meaning, a natural right was one that commended itself to reason. It was one that reasonable people for good reasons could agree on as a right of all people. For example, the right to life and equal freedom were two of the original natural rights that presumably fit this definition. But reasonable people often disagree on fundamentals, and there consequently have been various attempts to find less apparently subjective grounds for natural or human rights. Such is the appeal to utility—people have certain rights as they ensure the happiness of the greatest number. This in fact may be the underlying justification for the acceptance of many of the rights listed above.

Another justification is that there is one core natural right that is self-evident, which is that of each individual to equal freedom, and that any other right must be a derivation or specialization of this right, as are the freedoms of religion, assembly, and speech. Otherwise what is alleged to be a natural or human right is only a human want or need, and other justification must be found to satisfy it.

Human rights may also be justified by a social contract. That is, these are the rights that in the state of nature all people, contracting to form a common government for their welfare, would impartially agree upon. A variant of this is to ask the question of all people as to what rights they would want to be guaranteed if they were completely free to re-create their society and state, while ignorant of their original position or status in it. Those rights theoretically agreed upon would then define our human rights.

Finally, there is the positivists' justification by the behavior and practices of states. These, it is said, are what rights the world community has agreed to in their international deliberative assemblies, organizations, and treaties. And therefore they describe the multicultural, multinational consensus as to what rights human beings as human beings are entitled to and may justly claim.

Besides justification there is the question whether these rights are absolute, so fundamental as rights that they should not be abridged ever. This used to be a question raised with regard to basic civil rights such as that of the freedom of religion, and the answer was that no right could be absolute. For one, in concrete situations rights may contradict each other (as when one person's religion dictates the limitation of another's freedom of speech). For another, even what are considered the most important rights have to be circumscribed to promote a just social order. For example, even in the United States with its Bill of Rights and Supreme Court jurists like Justice Hugo Black who have proclaimed that freedom of speech is absolute, a person is not legally free to publish a defamation of the character or reputation of a nonpublic person.

In any case, this question assumes that all human rights already have a legal status in international and municipal laws. Some do, such as certain political and civil rights in democratic constitutions, but internationally these and the other human rights collectively are not what may be presently demanded of a state such that their denial enables legal or international action to be taken against a government. Rather, together they are goals of state and international behavior. This is made clear in the preamble to the UDHR, for example, which proclaims the document "as a common standard of achievement for all peoples and all nations, to the end that every individual and every organ of society . . . shall strive by teaching and education to promote respect for these rights and freedoms and by progressive measures, national and international to secure their universal and effective recognition and observance."

Given this status of human rights and their very large number, are some rights more basic than others such that their satisfaction takes precedence over the others? Even though the UN General Assembly resolved in 1977 that all human rights and fundamental freedoms are "inalienable and indivisible" and that all should be given "equal attention," this question of precedence has caused much international debate on human rights. Usually the democracies and in particular Western countries have argued that civil and political rights must take precedence, that without such rights as to the ballot and freely elected representatives, and the freedoms of religion, speech, and assembly, no one can be secure in any social, economic, or cultural rights. On the other side, many of the leaders of nondemocratic and less economically developed states argue that this should be the other way around, that the drive to achieve economic development, a fair standard of living, social security, and other such internationally specified rights, initially precludes certain civil and political rights. Some of these leaders even go further and argue that Western nations have pursued a kind of cultural imperialism by interfering in their internal affairs—as by tying economic aid to human rights progress—and trying to impose on them alien, inappropriate, or untimely human rights. Their human rights progress, they argue, should be judged within their own cultural context by their own "particularities."

This debate is implicitly about the means for achieving certain social, economic, and cultural rights. Those subscribing to the Western tradition of liberal individualism seek civil and political rights, what are ordinarily called liberal democratic freedoms, as not only rights in themselves, but also as means for achieving other rights, such as rights to development, social security, employment, a reasonable standard of living, and the like. That is, they argue that when a people are free under a limited constitutional government, a free social and economic market naturally follows, and this will create the wealth and diversity to automatically secure social and economic human rights, such as development and employment. The opposing position is that government must be fully involved in the economy and society through government ownership and control and intervention to achieve social, economic, and cultural rights. The main international human rights debate then reduces to the empirical question as to the best route to social, economic, and cultural development and human happiness and satisfaction. This is then a debate along two traditional dimensions, that between democrats and authoritarians, and that between individualists and socialists.

This debate notwithstanding, the international community has established certain rights as so basic that there is virtually no nation today dissenting in public from them. In practice they are neither goals nor are they to be held in abeyance while achieving other rights. They now exist for all people. Such is the right to be free from piracy, racism, torture, summary executions, slavery, starvation, and genocide. Even the foremost proponents of cultural relativism do not argue that nations or people should be free to violate these rights. They thus form a universal core of existing international human rights.

Of major interest to students of nonviolence, many proponents of human rights have seen them as not only promoting the human dignity and worth of the person, but also as facilitating more peaceful relations among and within nations. Article 55 of the UN Charter reads: "With a view to the creation of conditions of stability and well-being which are necessary for peaceful and friendly relations among nations, . . . the UN shall promote . . . universal respect for, and observance of, human rights and fundamental freedoms for all without distinction as to race, sex, language, or religion."

This view of the close relationship between peace and human rights, particularly those civil and political rights that define democracy, has received considerable research support in recent decades. Indeed, a more general empirical statement of this relationship can be made. Among those nations that most observe human rights, the democracies, war does not occur, domestic collective violence is on average the least, and there is virtually no domestic genocide or mass murder by their governments. Among those nations that least observe human rights, aggressive war is most common, internal violence is greatest, and genocide and mass murder are most pervasive, often accounting for millions of victims. Accordingly, one might argue that respect for human rights in practice reduces to the respect for and nonviolent preservation of human life, the most fundamental human right of all.

R.J. Rummel

References

Donnelly, Jack. *International Human Rights*. Boulder, Colo.: Westview, 1993.

Donnelly, Jack, and Rhoda Howard, eds. *International Handbook on Human Rights*. Westport, Conn.: Greenwood, 1987.

Forsythe, David P. *The Internationalization of Human Rights*. Lexington, Mass.: Lexington, 1991.

Glaser, Kurt, and Stefan T. Possony. *Victims of Politics: The State of Human Rights*. New York: Columbia University Press, 1979.

Humana, Charles. *World Human Rights Guide*. London: Economist, 1986.

Lawson, Edward H. *Encyclopedia of Human*

Rights. New York: Taylor and Francis, 1990.

Rummel, R.J. *Death by Government: Genocide and Mass Murder since 1900.* New Brunswick, N.J.: Transaction, 1994.

Sieghart, Paul. *The International Law of Human Rights.* Oxford: Oxford University Press, 1985.

Strauss, Leo. *Natural Right and History.* Chicago: University of Chicago Press, 1953.

United Nations Yearbook on Human Rights. Geneva: United Nations, biennial.

See also DEMOCRATIZATION

Hungarian National Movement, 1848–1867

Hungarian movement for independence from the Austrian monarchy, characterized by nonviolent and military resistance in 1848 and 1849, and mostly nonviolent resistance thereafter. A spring 1848 drive for constitutional reform was led by Louis Kossuth and Arthur Gorgey, who also subsequently led a military defense against invading Croatian, Austrian, and Russian troops in 1848–1849. Nationalist resistance in the form of a complete political boycott was led primarily by Francis Deak from 1850 to 1867.

Under Austrian rule since 1526, Hungarians clashed periodically with their foreign rulers. Although Hungary was governed constitutionally in 1848, the hereditary right of the Austrian Hapsburgs to rule over Hungary remained. It was this fact that fueled the Hungarian resistance movement. This agitation first peaked in March 1848, when Hungarians, led by Kossuth, demonstrated in the streets of Buda-Pest and pressed for constitutional reform in the Hungarian Diet. On March 15, thousands marched to the Pest City Council to demand the adoption of the "Twelve Points," a list of legislative reforms. They formed the Committee of Public Safety and printed and distributed copies of the twelve points and the national song, an act that violated censorship laws. Upon gaining significant concessions at the Pest City Council, they then marched across the Danube River to the Buda City Council, again demanding and receiving several concessions. A huge celebration ensued that night in Buda-Pest to mark the reforms won by nonviolent demonstrations. Among these reforms were the final emancipation of peasants, royal consent for independence, the right to unite with Transylvania and other separated territories, and other economic and social changes.

The reforms were short lived, however. Following the adoption of a new constitution in April, civil war erupted with the Serbs in the summer of 1848. Hungarian forces then fought invasions by Croats in September, Austrians in December, and Austria's Russian allies in June 1849. In August, Hungarian troops surrendered, and the country remained under absolutist Austrian control.

The dispute over Hungarian self-determination continued. After defeat in the War of 1859 with Sardinia, Austria appointed Hungarian representatives to the Imperial Parliament in Vienna. Most of these politicians refused their appointments. In 1860, Emperor Franz Josef revived the defunct 1847 constitution. In response, Hungarian county councils refused to pass legislation enabling military recruitment and taxation. In 1861, prominent politician Francis Deak led a campaign by the Hungarian Diet to refuse to send representatives to the Imperial Paliament. On August 12, 1861, Emperor Franz Josef dissolved the Hungarian Diet. The Diet members refused to acknowledge the legality of this act, and marched to the Diet but were turned back by Austrian soldiers. The Pest County Council protested the illegal dissolution of the Hungarian Diet, and they too were dissolved by the emperor. When they were removed by force, these council members were praised by a crowd of people singing the Hungarian national anthem. County officials throughout Hungary refused to serve the Austrian government and anarchy resulted. A military governor was appointed who proclaimed martial law. Deak pleaded against violence and called for "passive resistance," which he felt was more powerful than armed rebellion. People refused to pay taxes or serve in the Austrian army. People defied decrees and filled the jails.

The Hapsburg regime continued to push for a unified monarchy. The Hungarians, on the other hand, pressed for a dualistic framework, whereby Austria and Hungary would have autonomy over domestic affairs, but the monarchy would control international and military matters. The Hungarians remained firm in their nonviolent noncooperation, maintaining their political boycott for several years. In 1865, Emperor Franz Josef visited Pest and was greeted with disdain and flags of independent Hungary hanging from the houses in Pest. Witnessing the Hungarian resolve firsthand, the emperor finally abolished the Imperial Parliament in September 1865 and the new Hungarian Parliament opened in December. Although Franz Josef was crowned King of Hungary, the June 8, 1867, Compromise Agreement with the Austrian House gave Hungary an equal political partnership with Austria. This power was won primarily by the persistent refusal of Hungarians to cooperate with Austrian measures. This Hungarian resistance was later to inspire Arthur Griffith, a leader of a similar nationalist movement in Ireland in the early twentieth century.

Brad Bennett

References

Deak, Istvan. *The Lawful Revolution: Louis Kossuth and the Hungarians, 1848–1849*. New York: Columbia University Press, 1979.

Griffith, Arthur. *The Resurrection of Hungary: A Parallel for Ireland*. Dublin: Whelan and Son, 1918.

May, Arthur J. *The Hapsburg Monarchy, 1867–1914*. Cambridge: Harvard University Press, 1951.

See also GRIFFITH, ARTHUR

H

I

Identity Theory

A set of theoretical approaches that attempts to explain the role of group membership–related self-conceptions in social and political conflicts. These theories, which may be grounded in sociology, psychology, or political science, posit that group identity plays a major role in the development, escalation, deescalation, and transformation of conflicts and that a full understanding of particular conflicts requires an examination of the involvement of identity. Identity theory appears to have particular applicability to ethnic, racial, religious, and other culturally based conflicts that in the post–cold war world are erupting into a variety of nationalist struggles. Similarly, the manner in which identity is constructed in a conflict may influence the types of action chosen by participants. Those strategies may contribute to escalation, but they may also lead to transformation of the conflict through nonviolent action, for example.

Identity is seen as a particular dynamic underlying the processes of escalation and rigidification in intractable conflicts. It is considered to be one significant contributor to the development and maintenance of intractability, but it is not the only factor. Economic, political, or social issues are also usually involved, and in the case of conflicts that are protracted it is likely that all of these elements interact with identity in complex ways to reproduce the conflict over time.

Identity has been defined in a variety of ways, but in a general sense it can be viewed as an interrelated set of beliefs that constitute a relatively stable sense of self and the relationship of the self to the world. Most theorists, either implicitly or explicitly, suggest that an abiding sense of identity is desirable, if not a requirement. John Burton, for example, considers identity a basic human "need." George Kelly argues that the system of beliefs that is the self makes life relatively predictable rather than disorganized and random. This notion of self does not, however, imply that identity is static. It may be to some extent fluid and changeable in order to deal with novel circumstances and new information. A system that is too fluid would not provide enough predictability to be able to function, while a system that is too rigid would not allow for adaptation and growth. Since identity is considered a need, and since it is postulated to contribute to a sense of safety and predictability, the possibility of major change in identity is likely to create a sense of threat.

The notion of identity becomes useful in the context of social theory when it is extended beyond its obvious psychological context to a social context. Henri Tajfel, a leading theorist of social identity, suggests that people have both personal (individual) and group (social) identities. Social identity was defined by Tajfel as a person's knowledge of belonging to a group "together with some emotional and value significance to him of the group membership." To the extent that group membership is central to a person's conception of self it will also be core to the personal sense of self. It is likely, then, that individuals or identity groups will be motivated to preserve their identity; the greater the threat to identity the greater the push to protect it. Further, it is not simply the group itself that group members will attempt to preserve, but the character of the group.

In the case of ethnic identity it is the particular components of group life, such as religious practices, language, customs, history, blood lines, and land, for example, that may represent the central meaning of the group. Anthony Smith has provided rich descriptions of the myths of origin, descent, and future rebirth often passed on from generation to generation within an ethnic group in order to protect these meanings. On the surface it may appear almost self-destructive when some groups refuse to take part in nonviolent solutions to ethnic or culture-related conflicts (such as peace talks, power sharing, or diplomatic moves toward integration). To the extent that such solutions seem to lead to assimilation, however, they may be seen as threatening to the preservation of a distinctive sense of identity. From this perspective, participation in cooperative solutions is seen as likely to result in self-destruction.

Identity, then, plays a central role in the creation, escalation, and protraction of social and political conflicts. When a conflict between parties involves threats to core aspects of identity, the conflict is more likely to become intractable. On the other hand, for conflict that originally had little involvement of identity concerns, the more protracted the fight becomes, the more likely it is that identity will become salient. Identity, in effect, is nonnegotiable. In the case where each party sees the mere existence of the other party as threatening to its own identity, one might expect to find the most protracted and virulent conflicts. A case in point is the Middle East, where both Israelis and Palestinians invest a significant part of their identity in the same areas of land. Loss of the land, or the threat of its loss, or the threat of not being able to obtain it, carries a meaning greater than loss of territory; it implies a loss of something that is experienced as inherent to group identity. Each group sees the successful accomplishment of the nationalistic goals of the other as equivalent to its own destruction.

Social psychological and psychoanalytic identity theorists (such as Ralph White, Jay Rothman, and Vamik Volkan) draw attention to a variety of psychological processes that are viewed as manifesting themselves within and between conflicting groups. They discuss the role of such processes as distorted perception, rigidification of constructions of the other party, deindividuation (viewing all people who are members of the opposing group as only opponents, not individuals), dehumanization (seeing all members of the other group as less than human or savage), group polarization, in-group conformity, and images of the other group as the enemy. All of these processes serve to separate conflicting parties from one another and to reproduce the terms of the conflict over time. In its most extreme form, it has been suggested, the dispute reaches a stage in which the parties appear to cooperate to keep the conflict alive. To the extent that the conflict has been integrated into the sense of identity, it becomes threatening to each party to move toward conciliation.

In such circumstances, several processes may occur:

1. Severe rigidification, including extreme separation that permeates many aspects of society, dehumanization of the out-group, and tolerance of extreme groups
2. Early socialization of children into conflict-preserving attitudes and behaviors
3. Frequent framing of the conflict as a core concern
4. Interaction of identity concerns with other factors to reproduce the conflict—for example, the creation of new material stakes
5. The presence of severe rewards and sanctions the purpose of which is to maintain separation and therefore the conflict
6. Sabotage of conciliatory efforts, including increased tolerance or popularity of extreme groups and of violence, and the use of identity by elites to mobilize group members to action
7. The movement of extreme groups toward the center during extreme circumstances
8. A tolerance of violence or description of violence as justified; the institutionalization of violence; the social regulation of violence at a level that maintains the conflict but is not so high that society disintegrates
9. The tendency for group identity to take on greater importance than individual identity, making personal sacrifice seem acceptable or desirable

The prospects for nonviolent, productive, and enduring solutions to conflicts involving identity vary depending on the depth and centrality of the involvement of identity concerns. When the conflict has reached a stage in which the conflict itself has become a part of the meaning of group life, change is far more difficult. Some theorists suggest that the impetus for change may have to come from outside in such cases. Others argue that particular types of interventions are required to foster change when such conflicts have become relatively intractable, as in the case of the Middle East, Northern Ireland, or the former Yugoslavia. Some social scientists have attempted to apply the principles of conflict resolution to problem-solving workshops aimed at second-level officials who informally represent disputing groups.

The prospects for nonviolent action in intractable conflicts seem mixed. Since identity theory argues that parties in relatively intractable conflicts are motivated to preserve the conflict, and since, in addition, there are very strong forces within each group for coherence and conformity, the possibilities for the emergence of a dissenting voice within either group seem grim and fraught with risk for participants. Nonetheless, there have been dissenting voices in such cases, such as the peace movement in Northern Ireland and the push for and participation in integrated education in that region.

In fact, the process of nonviolent action can in itself become a source of identity transformation that has the potential for leading to powerful political change. Participation in, being the target of, or merely observing nonviolent action may foster shifts in identity, leading to position change rather than escalation. For example, during the civil rights movement in the United States, news media images of the hosing and clubbing of peaceful marchers by police led to important changes in the sense of identity of many Americans. Many white U.S. citizens, for the first time, felt compelled to face the effects of racism in their country, and to acknowledge the impact of different treatment on people of different races. Current identity theory has not yet accounted for the contributions of such moves toward transformation, integration, and conciliation, and this seems a fruitful direction for theorists to take.

Terrell A. Northrup

References

Burton, John, ed. *Conflict: Human Needs Theory.* New York: St. Martin's, 1990.

Fisher, Ronald J. "Developing the Field of Interactive Conflict Resolution: Issues in Training, Funding and Institutionalization." *Political Psychology* 14 (1993): 123–138.

Kelly, George A. *A Theory of Personality: The Psychology of Personal Constructs.* New York: W.W. Norton, 1955.

Northrup, Terrell A. "The Dynamic of Identity in Personal and Social Conflict." In *Intractable Conflicts and Their Transformation,* edited by Louis Kriesberg, Terrell A. Northrup, and Stuart J. Thorson. Syracuse: Syracuse University Press, 1989.

Rothman, Jay. *From Confrontation to Cooperation: Resolving Ethnic and Regional Conflict.* Newbury Park, Calif.: Sage, 1992.

Smith, Anthony D. "Ethnic Identity and World Order." *Millennium* 12 (1983): 149–161.

Tajfel, Henri, ed. *Social Identity and Intergroup Relations.* Cambridge: Cambridge University Press, 1982.

Volkan, Vamik. *The Need to Have Enemies and Allies: From Clinical Practice to International Relationships.* Northvale, N.J.: Aronson, 1988.

White, Ralph. *Fearful Warriors: A Psychological Profile of U.S.-Soviet Relations.* New York: Free Press, 1984.

See also CONFLICT RESOLUTION; CONFLICT THEORIES; ETHNIC CONFLICT

Independence Club Movement (Korea), 1896–1898

Celebrated but short-lived public pressure group that stands out among the many Korean attempts at national transformation both for the comprehensiveness of its goals, for its nonviolent, civil-society-type actions, and for its broad-based leadership. The club's founders stressed the role of public education and used the press to promote new reform ideas and to serve as a unifying influence in the country. The *Tongnip Sinmun* (Independent Newspaper) was established in April 1896 and quickly gained a nationwide audience. The birth of the club itself centered around the construction of three commemorative monuments: Independence Gate, Independence Park, and Independence Hall. These monuments, though modest, carried much symbolic meaning in the context of Korea's newly won status as an independent state—won in 1895 as a consequence of the defeat of China, Korea's traditional overlord, at the hands of Japan.

Across east Asia in the late nineteenth century, public discussions often focused on the themes of tradition and change. In Korea, the most articulate responses to this debate and the most organized pressure for change came from the Independence Club. The club's imaginative focus on national independence and its enlistment of royal patronage made it easy for officials to accept it as a desirable organization. Royal endorsement in fact made it mandatory for most senior officials to join the club. By the end of 1896 the club reported a membership of some twenty-four hundred. Also, the *Tongnip Sinmun* was supported financially by the government. The *Tongnip Sinmun* and the Independence Club worked hand in hand, and for all practical purposes the newspaper became the mouthpiece of the group.

The club's internal structure and procedures conformed to certain democratic principles, such as absence of class, wealth, religious, and gender barriers. Provisions were made for regular general and special meetings, well-defined functions of officers, the maintenance of accounts under control of the general body, the adoption of all decisions by majority vote after due deliberation, and the incorporation of these and related stipulations into the club's charter. The charter, enacted in July 1896, was Korea's first formal statement governing the functioning of a voluntary association according to democratic principles. The club's debating society followed *Robert's Rules of Order*.

As the club grew, however, inherent incongruities and latent tensions soon surfaced. As the club openly confronted divisive questions on its larger aims, such as reform of the class structure and popular participation in government, a steadily increasing polarization between its progressive and conservative office-holders emerged. The club aired these issues in a series of weekly public debates. The debates proved a potent force. They lifted the mystique of government as a distant, nonresponsive, repressive entity, and audiences of the debates thereby acquired a new sense of self-esteem. Ultimately, however, the result was the alienation, and eventual exit, of the conservatives.

The club played an important role in forging a new national identity through the use of symbols, especially in its promotion of the native Korean script, *Han'gŭl*. Nationalist ideology was linked to the theme of national power and prosperity. Its leaders wrote at length about how best to promote the economic, political, and military strength of the nation. The leaders illuminated the connections among these ideas,

even as numerous concessions were being made by the government to the Japanese, Westerners, and Russians. The *Tongnip Sinmun* called upon the government to establish vocational schools as well as factories. The club also recommended measures for further development of modern banking in the country as an indispensable part of the new economic infrastructure.

These then were the major dimensions of the Independence Club's ideology of nationalism. Ideas, rather than carefully conceived long-term strategies, were at the heart of the club's nationalism. While the *how* did not escape the club's attention, the *what*—what should be done?—was the subject of its focus, not because ideas alone were seen as offering practical solutions but because they were building blocks of a new national consciousness. The club seems to have assumed that once its appeals had been heard by enough people across the country, many national plans for meeting Korea's needs would evolve by themselves along with viable strategies for their implementation.

As Russian and other foreign powers encroached upon Korea, the club mobilized popular support in mass demonstrations and rallies to promote its vision of an independent Korean state and citizenship. A significant victory was won in this campaign for national self-assertion when Russia withdrew some of its military instructors and financial advisers. Faced with the impressive show of popular support, Emperor Kojong also bowed to the pressure for liberalization, including granting the club's demand for a partly elected national assembly. Still, he viewed the club as a tool to be used by government, and not as a movement to redefine and limit the authority of the monarch. This divergence portended the club's demise as the emperor first moved to thwart the leadership through cooptation and, later, dissolved the club on charges that it was trying to create a "republic."

The Independence Club came to a quick end. It failed to establish any enduring institutional means for the Korean people to participate in their government. The most obvious failure was one of leadership. At critical junctures, the leadership chose the path of least resistance over continued dedication to the cause they had raised and fostered. Leaders' actions often failed to match the rhetoric of their own platform calling for extraordinary self-abnegation and risk-taking. Although many Koreans were unable to fully comprehend the more sophisticated elements of the club's rhetoric, they sensed in it a sincere concern for national well-being and human rights. More important, they saw the club as an instrument for translating inchoate personal desires into political action. But there was something very tenuous and fragile in this popular support. As long as the club had the monarch's patronage, or even grudging tolerance, the people stayed with it and were keen to go along with the calls for reform in the government. However, as soon as they concluded that the club was undermining the monarchy, they quickly abandoned it.

The club also failed to significantly improve Korea's security against foreign aggression. The club did achieve some success against Russia by crafting and staging an impressive display of solidarity between the government and the people. This solidarity was to be linked with political liberalism, and was projected by the club as the foremost bulwark against future foreign domination over Korea. With the demise of the club, Korea again became a hotbed of open and relentless foreign schemes, especially Japanese, against its territorial integrity.

Vipan Chandra

References

Chandra, Vipan. *Imperialism, Resistance, and Reform in Late-Nineteenth-Century Korea Enlightenment and the Independence Club*. Berkeley, Calif.: Institute of East Asian Studies, 1988.

See also KOREA, DEMOCRATIC STRUGGLE IN THE SOUTH; KWANGJU UPRISING, 1980; MARCH FIRST INDEPENDENCE MOVEMENT, 1919; MAY FOURTH MOVEMENT, 1919

Indian National Congress

The spectacularly successful organization that carried the main thrust of the Indian independence movement following its founding in 1885. The Indian National Congress managed to develop and evolve according to changing circumstances from its foundation through to independence, attracting along the way a galaxy of extraordinarily capable leaders and creating novel techniques of agitation and building up bases for support throughout the countryside.

The Indian National Congress was founded in 1885 but was preceded by public and political associations going back to the 1850s. Even earlier leading Indian public men and local politicians in Calcutta, Bombay, and Madras had come together in various kinds of voluntary associations. It was not until 1851, when it became clear that some concerted action was needed to put Indian views before the British Parliament about the renewal of the East India Company's charter in 1854, that clearly identifiable political bodies developed. In the three main British port cities of Calcutta, Madras, and Bombay, and the former capital of the Maratha confederation, Poona, associations formed to petition Parliament on the issue. The first established was the British Indian Association in Calcutta on October 29, 1851. Others followed: the Deccan Association in Poona, a branch of the British Indian Association in Madras, and in August 1852 a Bombay Association. Each represented some kind of alliance between a new Western-educated intelligentsia and local elites—wealthy merchants, landlords, and even local nobility—but there was no interaction with the wider population, nor any desire to establish it, since the role of the bodies was merely to present reasoned arguments to the government on the issue of charter renewal and later on other measures. Some tensions resulted from the social blend of the memberships, and conflicts occurred within the organizations, which stopped functioning during the Great Revolt of 1857 (or, as the British knew it, the Indian Mutiny).

Some of the associations were revived in the 1860s, and in the 1870s more energetic and radical ones were established, such as the Poona Sarvajanik Sabha in 1870 under Justice M.G. Ranade, and the Indian Association in 1876 led by Surendranath Banerjea. The first attempt to bring together the various regional associations into some kind of all-India structure occurred in Delhi at the end of 1876 during a *durbar* (ceremony) organized by the viceroy, Lytton, to proclaim Queen Victoria empress of India. While the official ceremonies were going on, representatives of the associations met and decided to form a national, in the sense of India-wide, body. Because of government suspicion and a period of increasingly repressive rule, the new national body had only a limited life and undertook little activity.

The political climate changed in the early 1880s with the arrival of a new Liberal Party viceroy, Lord Ripon, and the public associations became increasingly active both as organizers of petitions and as champions of Indian causes. They built up support bases in a few sections of the countryside. During 1883, Europeans in India actively campaigned against the viceroy's advocacy of the Ilbert Bill, which gave Indian judges in the countryside the right to try Europeans. Indian politicians noted the impact of the white campaign and organized themselves to support the viceroy and attack the racism of the bill's opponents.

By this time politicians around the country had established contact with one another and had learned to operate as effective lobbying groups in their own regions. One of the people who helped maintain the links was a former Indian civil servant, A.O. Hume. Hume had been affected by the way Hinduism was currently being reasserted as a major religion by people like Dayananda Saraswati and his Arya Samaj and particularly by Madame Blavatsky and Colonel Olcott, whose Theosophical Society dated to the late 1870s in the main cities of India. The Theosophists met annually in national session in the first years of the 1880s, and through them Hume established contacts with the political groups active in regional affairs. He built up further links during the Ilbert Bill agitation and in 1885 was the driving force behind a national gathering of delegates from around India.

The first session of the Indian National Congress was held in December 1885 in Bombay. Concurrently, Surendranath Banerjea and others in Bengal connected to the Indian Association were convening at a national conference in Calcutta. The following year, in 1886, they joined the Congress, which became the dominant expression of an India-wide gathering of delegates who were mainly middle class and urban. At its formation it was not clear whether the Congress was the product of an idea of Indian nationalism, but it was argued that it would produce such feelings if they did not already exist.

In its early years, the Indian National Congress functioned mainly as an annual gathering of delegates from around the country. They assembled shortly after Christmas; a president made a long address; and various resolutions relating to political and administrative matters were adopted. Hume, as secretary, maintained such ongoing Congress functions as were needed during the year, and the various local associations continued with their activities and sent delegates to the annual sessions. The Congress attempted to build up support in the countryside and educate people politically. It also tried to prevent divisive issues from reaching the annual meeting. Social reform matters were excluded, while matters affecting religious communities required the assent of the community involved. This did not prevent an opposition Muslim movement developing under the leadership of Sir Sayyid Ahmed Khan from his base in northern India at what became a Muslim university, Aligarh College.

Under Sir Sayyid's leadership most Muslims remained aloof if not antagonistic to the Congress until the second decade of the next century. The primary initial Congress activity was to lobby for further constitutional advances from the British Parliament, which eventually made some concessions to Indian representation in the Indian Councils Act of 1892—but it did not satisfy elite political opinion.

The Congress began to change, socially and politically, in the first decade of the twentieth century. Home Rule leagues, organized by a British radical feminist and Theosophist, Annie Besant, and Indian nationalist radical Bal Gangadhar Tilak, created a broader basis for a nationalist ideology throughout the country. Besant was elected president of the Congress in 1917, the first woman and the first European to be elected to the position. The Congress also adopted a demand for complete autonomy from Britain, not just greater rights for Indians within the empire. The new position divided the Congress. Moderate politicians in the Congress seceded in 1918, leaving new forces in control.

For the first time, the Congress had a clear national objective of home rule, although it was limited by a probable intention to remain within the British Empire. For the first time also the politics of the Congress were dominated by an India-wide leadership and membership base, even though it was still largely urban, elite, and middle class.

The activities of Mohandas Gandhi following his return to India from South Africa in 1915 created a new factor in nationalist politics. Gandhi's success in organizing and leading local nonviolent campaigns for economic and social rights pointed toward a new form of political activity and organization. By 1920, the Congress recognized the powerful political force of Gandhi, who had heretofore operated outside of the party. Gandhi was invited to draft a new constitution for the Congress. In fact, the Congress found itself following Gandhi, as he continued to act independently (as in his undertaking of the 1920 noncooperation movement prior to the Congress's approval). Institutionally, the Congress was not converted to Gandhi so much as it was forced to work with him to partake of the benefits of popular mobilization and creative challenge to the Raj that he represented.

At the end of 1920 a dramatically different Congress convened in Nagpur to debate the noncooperation program Gandhi was organizing and to approve the Gandhi-drafted constitution. Political power had shifted from the traditional, Westernized, and educated elite to encompass a wider mass base. The new constitution reflected these political demographics, as well as the need to mobilize effectively for independence. The Congress became more accurately representative of India's linguistic and regional differences. It also became a continuously operating organization, directed by a small permanent executive of fifteen ("The Working Committee"), in which the president gained power and importance. The Congress, under the challenge of Gandhi and the needs of the times, transformed itself from a debating society of elites into a potentially powerful organization for struggle.

Following the failure of the noncooperation campaign in 1922, Congress moderates reasserted control through an internal faction, the Congress Swaraj Party. The Congress became more focused on waging the independence struggle by exploiting and possibly manipulating existing institutional channels, such as local council elections, and by opposing British rule from within the councils. India's diversity, especially the particularistic demands of local leaders, circumstances, and communal groups, threatened the unity of the organization.

Gandhi's return to leadership of the Congress came at the end of 1928 when he responded to the growing disunity within the Congress. A key division was between moderates arguing for gradual self-rule within the British Empire and radicals seeking immediate and complete independence. A second rift was growing between Hindus and Muslims in India generally, and was reflected in the wariness of many Congress members to make concessions to the Muslim League.

By the mid-1930s, the Congress's position of secular nationalism was challenged by a number of other organizations externally, while within the Congress a group formed as the Congress Socialist Party to push socialist objectives. Concurrently, Gandhi withdrew from specific formal direction of the affairs of the Congress, its presidency being filled by younger men even though he continued to influence its affairs from outside. That Congress remained predominant and that its organizational tactics and platform were attractive became clear in 1937 after elections to the new legislative councils established under the Government of India Act of 1935. The Congress won majorities in seven provinces and after much soul searching and factional division decided to form ministries in them. Because the Muslim League was unable to form a government even in Muslim-majority provinces, it became more separatist in attitude. Finally, in 1940, the League adopted the Lahore Resolution, after the city in which it met, and opted for a separate Muslim homeland as its primary objective.

When war broke out in 1939, the Congress and the government again moved into a collision course. The Congress ministers resigned because Indians had not been consulted before the formal declaration of India's involvement in the war. The Congress rejected as inadequate Viceroy Lord Linlithgow's statement of war aims and future concessions, and in July resolved that its primary task was to fight for freedom rather than against fascism.

Separation between the Congress and the Muslim League grew during the war and could not be bridged. Negotiations involving Gandhi, Jawaharlal Nehru, Mohammed Ali Jinnah (the League's leader), and a British cabinet delegation failed in the face of Muslim demands for a separate nation. The Congress inaugurated Quit India, its final satyagraha campaign, in August 1942 to drive the British out of India. Though massive in its extent and unprecedented in its social depth, the movement did not succeed. On the release of Congress detainees late in the war, further negotiations between the three parties, the Congress, the League, and the British, did not achieve a settlement of conflicting demands. Eventually, the last viceroy, Lord Mountbatten, possessed of plenipotentiary powers, announced that India would be partitioned into two nations in June 1948. The spread of communal riots and the disasters of communal anarchy compelled him to move forward the date to August 15, 1947. Congress leaders, guided by Jawaharlal Nehru and driven by the threat of a descent into communal war and by the desire for a strong and centralized even if divided state, agreed reluctantly to accept the terms. British India was partitioned into two successor nations, and India assumed power and sovereignty on the midnight hour of August 15, 1947.

Jim Masselos

References

Masselos, Jim, ed. *Struggling and Ruling: The Indian National Congress, 1885–1985.* Delhi: Sterling, 1987.

See also GANDHI, MOHANDAS KARAMCHAND; INDIAN NATIONAL MOVEMENT; NEHRU, JAWAHARLAL

Indian National Movement

Begun as an organized movement in the late nineteenth century in reaction against British rule over the subcontinent. Indian nationalism appeared throughout the earlier part of the century in less organized forms in the resistance of various groups in the country. Each appearance was expressed differently and at different times during the nineteenth and twentieth centuries and had its own characteristic shape. Apart from the presence of a common political antagonist, the imperial overlord, and the existence of economic drives inherent in the contrasts of wealth and economic exploitation, a diffuse but pervasive social and cultural similarity provided a basis for bringing people together through awareness of emotional similarity.

The nationalist movement, or movements, attempted to establish structures to unite people within a single organization defined by accepted objectives as to how freedom should be won and what was to be the content of that freedom. In one sense, freedom was won with the achievement of Indian independence in August 1947. India's deep regional, ethnic, social, and religious diversity, however, prevented the consolidation of a truly unified "Indian" identity. As a result, independence reflected competing claims, unreconciled differences, and was achieved at the cost of social division and political separation.

The single most important organizational expression of Indian nationalism was the Indian National Congress. Established in 1885, the Congress brought together political elites and organizations from around the country. Reflecting, in part, the combination of dominance by urban social elites and diverse regional and communal interests, the Congress never was a tightly controlled and coherent political organization. Nevertheless, it provided both ideological focus for nationalist movements and, frequently, the organizational infrastructure to wage antiimperial campaigns.

In the 1890s, some congressmen were developing a critique of British imperialism based on the economic impact of British rule on India. Dadabhai Naoroji, a Bombay Parsi, had earlier developed an analysis of the drain of Indian wealth to Britain and expressed it so strongly that it became the dominant economic critique of imperialism later in the movement. Other ideas were also explored in the 1890s with the beginnings of a cultural nationalism emphasizing Indian and Hindu values. In Bengal, novelists like Bankim Chandra Chatterjee metaphorically expressed ideas of opposition by focusing on Hindu opposition to pre-British rulers. In a less systematic manner, some marginalized groups like the Mundas, a tribal community in eastern India, rose in their jungle fastness against British rule, as had armed gangs earlier in western India in the 1870s such as that led by a Brahman, Vasudeo Phadke.

In the 1890s, another Marathi Brahman, Bal Gangadhar Tilak, began to articulate a strident antagonism to British rule and evolve techniques of opposition that mobilized large numbers of people through the use of indigenous rallying points. From 1893, Tilak developed a popular regional festival devoted to the worship of the elephant-headed god, Ganapati or Ganesh, and used it to carry messages of cultural and religious patriotism directly and indirectly opposed to the British Raj. Tilak also used the memory of the great Marathi leader Shivaji, who had risen against the Mughal Empire in the seventeenth century, as another rallying point, establishing a festival celebrating his birth.

While Tilak was changing the political vocabulary of resistance, other groups began to turn to more violent physical means to attack the British. A group of terrorists emerged who were inspired by Tilak and possibly had close connections with him. Immediate reasons for opposition were provided by the British handling of a plague epidemic that began in 1896. In 1897, terrorists killed the plague commissioner, and Tilak was jailed for his seditious writings and his influence in promoting an "atmosphere conducive to a terrorist mentality."

Cultural nationalism and active opposition to British rule combined again in 1905 when the

Mohandas K. Gandhi, seen here addressing an audience in 1934, became a major leader of the Indian National Movement. AP/Wide World Photos.

viceroy, Lord Curzon, partitioned Bengal. Bengal's middle groups, the *bhadralok,* protested vigorously, as did many of its artisan classes. While most Hindus joined in the opposition, many Muslims supported the division because they were a majority in East Bengal and thought they would benefit from dominating the new administrative division. In western Bengal, widespread protests were not limited to the presentation of memorials and petitions. The movement became increasingly innovative and adopted a widespread boycott of British-manufactured goods in favor of those made within India—*swadeshi* (literally "of one's own country"). The boycott was not merely an assertion of the need to support Indian manufactures but was also an attempt to attack Britain's economic base in its cottonmills.

The escalating momentum of the Bengal agitation caused tensions within the Congress. Leaders in western India disliked the use of violence and were unwilling to see the boycott adopted outside Bengal, although they did advocate the use of *swadeshi* goods. Gopal Krishna Gokhale, from Poona, and Pherozeshah Mehta, in Bombay, preferred a more moderate approach through petitions and lobbying the British Parliament. Their political opponents, who called themselves the "New Party," wanted an activist approach to achieve self-rule for India. As Tilak stated, *"Swaraj* [self-rule] is my birthright and I will have it." He, along with B.C. Pal from Bengal and Lala Lajpat Rai from the Punjab, attempted to win control of the Congress from the faction known as "moderates." After Tilak was jailed by the British government on sedition charges in 1908, however, moderates like Gokhale retained control of the organization.

The British government adopted a two-pronged strategy to handle the agitation. While it used military and police force to control and repress violence and terrorism, it also sought to mollify moderate opinion by offering constitutional concessions. These latter measures included a package of reforms (the Morley-Minto reforms) implemented in 1909, when representatives were voted from limited electorates to the provincial and central councils. Muslims were given separate electorates in fulfillment of a promise given by the viceroy to a Muslim delegation of elite leaders in 1906. An increasing Muslim separation from the Congress was marked by the formation of the All India Muslim League late in 1906. The two organizations continued on separate paths until 1916, when the Congress and the League agreed to work together in what became known as the Lucknow Pact (named for the city in which the agreement was reached).

By 1916, India's political geography had changed. The older generation of moderates had died or disappeared from the scene. New faces were entering nationalist politics and reacting to the situation created by the First World War. Turkey's entry into the war on the side of Germany, the issue of Muslim holy places in West Asia, and the defense of the sultan of Turkey, who, as Khalifah was the spiritual leader of Islam, evoked strong pan-Islamic feeling in India and an anti-British movement among Muslims. During the war Muslims became more stridently anti-British as Muslim intellectuals and theologians reevaluated the position of Islam under British imperialism during previous decades.

The war also sparked other antagonisms toward British rule. Home Rule leagues were established throughout India, led by Annie Besant, a former British feminist radical and then director of the Theosophical Society in India; she creatively adapted the agitational and organizational model of the movements with which she had earlier been involved in England. Following his release from jail, Tilak also set up a Home Rule League organization in his region of influence, the Marathi-speaking areas of Bombay Presidency.

The impact was potent. Attempting to control her activity and limit her popularity, the Madras government interned Besant in 1917. However, this won her India-wide popularity, helped convert the Congress to a Home Rule platform, and dramatically broadened the organization's base of support beyond the urban intellectual class of its origins.

In 1915 Mohandas K. Gandhi returned to India from South Africa, where he had led successful campaigns against racial discrimination. In doing so he had evolved new methods of agitation, as represented in satyagraha, or "truth force"—the application of nonviolence to political objectives.

It was unclear whether Gandhi's techniques could be applied to Indian circumstances and whether his abilities would be recognized in a different and much larger environment.

Gokhale, one of the Congress stalwarts and a leader much admired by Gandhi, advised him to spend a year in travel around the country, to develop a sensitivity to current Indian concerns, rather than to speak out immediately.

By the end of 1916, Gandhi became involved in regional problems. He was approached by leaders from Champaran, a district in Bihar, to take up the local cause of indigo workers. After examining the situation, he began his first Indian satyagraha there in 1917. He quickly won the workers' support and faced equally strong opposition from the British administration, which tried to expel him from the region. Gandhi refused to leave and in a classic court case articulated for the first time in India his theory of nonviolence. His opposition won him India-wide coverage in the press and persuaded the government to set up a commission of inquiry that eventually improved the conditions of the indigo workers.

Through the Champaran campaign and subsequent satyagrahas in the Kheda (or Kaira) District in Gujarat and in behalf of mill workers in Ahmedabad, Gandhi showed that his style of political activism was applicable to India. These campaigns also gave him political bases in Bihar and Gujarat among the regional political leadership and rural society. Gandhi was now a key figure on the Indian political scene, independent from the Congress network.

Until his experiences in 1917 and 1918, however, Gandhi's attitude toward British rule was ambivalent. His first campaigns were not directed against imperialism but against fairly specific and local administrative measures. During the war he unsuccessfully recruited volunteers for the British army. His attitude changed in 1918. A number of different issues coalesced to bring him to the forefront of agitational nationalism. The viceroy, Lord Chelmsford, was concerned with the growth of radical opinion and introduced the Rowlatt Bills, which limited basic freedom of expression. Virtually all groups of Indian politicians opposed the bills, as did the broader, Westernized middle class, already influenced by the Home Rule League movements.

On April 6, 1919, Gandhi inaugurated the Rowlatt Satyagraha as a means of focusing opposition. He creatively adopted the *hartal*, traditionally a period in which work stopped as a form of mourning, to symbolize the loss of liberties and respect that would result from the bills' implementation. The satyagraha began, among Gandhi and other committed satyagrahis, as a day of purification and prayer. Throughout the main cities of India, as well as in some rural areas, large numbers of people stopped work and many attended prayer meetings. Selected acts of civil disobedience, including sale of prohibited literature, also occurred. Nothing like this had happened before, either India-wide or regionally.

Nonviolent discipline, however, could not be maintained among the masses of popular participants, who were suddenly mobilized from a previously quiescent state. Rioting broke out in Delhi, Lahore, and even Gandhi's home town of Ahmedabad in Gujarat. When Gandhi attempted to go to Delhi to help calm the situation, he was returned to Bombay. Rumors of his "arrest" spread and more riots broke out in Bombay and in Gujarat. In the Punjab at Amritsar on April 13, a peaceful meeting at Jallianwala Bagh was stopped by General Richard Dyer, who ordered his soldiers to fire on the gathering. Several hundred people were killed and repressive martial law was immediately applied to the province.

Gandhi called off the satyagraha and undertook a three-day fast. He stated that he had made a "Himalayan miscalculation," referring to his optimistic expectations that the difficult discipline of satyagraha could be observed if people were simply encouraged en masse to disobey the law. This mistake in judgment about the tenor of Indian frustration at British reforms had been reinforced by the difficult organizational task of maintaining control in such a countrywide undertaking.

During 1919, the British Parliament fulfilled wartime promises by implementing the Montagu–Chelmsford reforms, named after the secretary of state for India and the viceroy. Concessions included establishing a wider electorate and opening nonessential provincial ministerial positions to elected Indians. Congress considered the proposals at its session in Amritsar at the end of 1919, but other events soon overtook the debate. The critical issue during 1920 centered around the Allies' treatment of Turkey and the control of Muslim holy places. The British prime minister, Harold Lloyd George, assured an Indian Muslim deputation that Turkey would not be dismembered, even though this was precisely what was provided for in the subsequent Treaty of Sèvres. In February, a Central Khilafat Committee brought together various Khilafat organizations under Gandhi's leadership.

In May, the group decided to inaugurate satyagraha against the government. In May, also, the report of the Congress inquiry into British repression in the Punjab evoked strong reactions. Gandhi decided to inaugurate satyagraha in August to redress the Punjab, the Rowlatt Bills, and the Khilafat wrongs, though he still did not have Congress support. In September, at a special meeting, the Congress narrowly voted for satyagraha and reaffirmed this decision in December with the objective of achieving *swaraj* (self-rule).

The resulting noncooperation campaign began with a boycott of government activities starting with the elections to the new legislative councils. Gandhi also asked people to renounce British titles, to withdraw from the British educational system, to refuse to use the courts of law, and generally not to participate in any government activity. He banned the use of British cloth or other manufactures. People were to use *swadeshi* goods (those made in India), especially *khadi* (cloth spun and woven by hand). Concurrently, Gandhi reorganized the Congress to give it a clearer regional and mass base.

The noncooperation campaign won massive support from virtually all religious and social groups in the city and countryside. Between twenty and thirty thousand people were jailed for sedition. However, some violence erupted. A Muslim community in Kerala, the Moplahs, violently rebelled to establish a "Khilafat Raj." In Bombay, a complete economic stoppage protesting a visit by the prince of Wales ended in rioting. Gandhi tried to stop such outbreaks, and, in 1922, after demonstrators in Chauri Chaura in the United Provinces set fire to a police post killing the policemen, Gandhi called off the entire campaign.

In the aftermath of the campaign, congressmen argued as to what should be done. One section, led by Motilal Nehru from the United Provinces and C.R. Das from Bengal, wanted the Congress to contest the council elections and fight the British from within the councils. They formed themselves into a Swaraj Party within the Congress, contested elections, and did surprisingly well. Initially they opposed government measures but soon found themselves involved in legislative decisions. Over the next few years political control of the Congress shifted back to these more moderate leaders, and Gandhi concentrated on the goals of his "constructive program," promoting self-sufficient values and activities such as home spinning, khadi, anti-untouchability, and Hindu–Muslim unity. Factional divisions, between radicals and moderates, between the national party and local organizations, and between Hindus and Muslims, gradually dominated the Congress and Indian politics.

In 1928, the Simon Commission, which had been appointed by the British Parliament to suggest further constitutional modifications, arrived in India to discuss proposals. Indians reacted strongly to being excluded from its membership and boycotted the commission. In the streets, demonstrators met police beatings, which resulted in the death of Lala Lajpat Rai. An All Parties Conference, chaired by Motilal Nehru, drafted proposals for a self-governing India, including dominion status within the British Empire and a political structure in which the rights of Muslims within the Hindu-dominated polity would be protected. Motilal's son, Jawaharlal, and other radical leaders like Subhas Chandra Bose, meanwhile, argued for an India completely free and outside the empire.

The Congress adopted the report of the elder Nehru, and Gandhi issued an ultimatum to the government that if the report were not accepted by the end of 1929, the Congress would inaugurate a new campaign of noncooperation to achieve *purna swaraj* (complete independence). In January 1930, Congress workers solemnly took an Independence Vow.

Gandhi took time to consider how best to initiate this new campaign of civil disobedience. He limited the campaign to the issue of the salt tax. Strategically, the salt tax represented a potent symbol of independence denied—Indians paid the tax to the Raj for the use of an essential commodity that was produced locally under British monopoly. Challenging the salt tax, therefore, attacked an issue felt immediately by Indians and understood as injustice by observers around the world. At the same time, however, defying the tax actually posed a very limited economic challenge to the British and seemed to be an issue that would not encourage uncontrollably violent passions by Indians or forcible responses by the government.

On March 12, 1930, Gandhi began a march from Ahmedabad to the seaside town of Dandi where, on April 6, the anniversary of the Rowlatt Satyagraha, he picked up a handful of brackish mud and declared that he had manufactured salt and broken the salt laws. This gesture marked the beginning of the campaign throughout India, and people began manufac-

turing salt illegally. Civil resisters were arrested, but others followed in their footsteps. Gandhi was arrested in early May, although technically not for breaking the salt laws. The campaign broadened to include the boycott of foreign cloth throughout India, as well as local variations, such as defiance of forestry laws in the Central Provinces, of liquor laws in Bihar, and land tax refusal in rural areas. The tens of thousands who were arrested represented a small fraction of the Indian population affected by the campaign. In addition, the movement mobilized new sectors of society, including the middle classes and women.

Gandhi was released from jail in early 1931 and reached an understanding with the viceroy, Lord Irwin. Under the Gandhi–Irwin settlement, the Congress agreed to discontinue the noncooperation campaign, and the government agreed to release jailed disobedients, return forfeited land, and end special police powers. The Congress, at a meeting in Karachi in March, ratified the settlement, with support that included members of the radical faction.

In September, the Second Indian Round Table Conference convened in London, and Gandhi attended as the Congress's representative. Little was accomplished in terms of establishing the Indian right to full independence. Furthermore, political conflicts between the Congress and Muslim and other minority members at the conference over who represented India undermined Gandhi's influence and reflected India's divisions. Gandhi sought to be the voice of a united India, whereas Muslim leaders demanded continued separate electorates as protection against domination by the Hindu majority. The British government, in turn, exploited minority interests to weaken the Congress's power.

On Gandhi's return to India in December, the civil disobedience campaign was renewed. Government reaction was harsh, and Gandhi was soon arrested, as were the Congress leadership and large numbers of satyagrahis. From jail Gandhi resisted the political fragmentation of the movement and began a fast to protest a proposal giving untouchables separate electorates. In the face of the fast, the untouchable leader, Dr. B.R. Ambedkar, agreed to a compromise which kept untouchables within the mainstream of Indian politics, unlike the Muslims, who were increasingly following a separatist path.

The second civil disobedience campaign was called off in the mid-1930s, as it had run out of momentum. By then a number of other nationalist organizations had emerged, reflecting alternative philosophies. A Communist Party of India had been formed in 1925, and in 1934 socialists established the Congress Socialist Party within the Congress. Hindu-based nationalist bodies like the RSS and the Hindu Mahasabha formed in the 1920s and developed clearly defined antisecular Hindu nationalist positions centered around V.D. Savarkar's idea of *Hindutva* (Hinduness). On the Muslim side, the word *Pakistan* was first used in 1933, when Mohammed Iqbal, Muslim poet and 1930 president of the Muslim League, promoted the idea of a separate homeland for Muslims.

The Congress's goal of a secular nationalist movement was fraying. Muslim nationalism, in particular, increased rather than diminished. The Congress remained the primary organizational focus, however. When war broke out in 1939, the Congress and the government again moved into a collision course. The Congress ministers who had been elected to power in most provinces in 1937 under a new constitution resigned because Indians had not been consulted before the formal declaration of India's involvement. The Congress rejected as inadequate the statement of the viceroy, Lord Linlithgow, specifying British war aims and future concessions. In July, the Congress resolved that its primary task was to fight for freedom rather than against fascism.

By 1942, with the Allied position in Asia endangered after the fall of Rangoon, Sir Stafford Cripps came to India on a mission from Parliament to make yet further political concessions. Both the Congress and the Muslim League found these unsatisfactory. Consequently, on August 8, the Congress undertook the Quit India Movement to drive the British out. The movement's effectiveness was limited initially by the immediate arrest of Gandhi and the Congress High Command. There was, however, a spontaneous popular reaction to the arrests in the form of widespread strikes, *hartals,* and various forms of civil disobedience. Congress socialists who had escaped jail sabotaged railway and telegraph lines and virtually cut off eastern India from the rest of the country. Parallel governments were established in Bengal and in Maharashtra that survived until 1944.

While Gandhi unswervingly advocated nonviolence from jail, the movement outside veered more and more toward violence, which the government controlled only because of the large numbers of Allied soldiers stationed in India. There was a different approach outside India. A former Congress president, Subhas Chandra Bose, had escaped to Germany and had then gone to Japan and Southeast Asia, where he built up an Indian National Army (INA) from Indian soldiers captured in the fall of Singapore. He wanted the INA to liberate India with Japanese help; but he was unsuccessful.

A three-cornered situation arose in India when the Muslim League's position improved with its success in council elections in 1943. By then it had established a virtually unassailable position as the representative of India's Muslims. Its position was confirmed when leader Mohammed Ali Jinnah held unsuccessful talks with Gandhi on his release from jail.

By 1945, it was clear the British would have to make significant concessions to India, but how it was to do so was complicated by the negotiations between the Congress, the League, and the British, as well as by Congress distrust of British intentions and Muslim distrust of the Congress's promises. In June 1945, the viceroy, Lord Wavell, announced proposals for an independent India involving a weak center and strong provinces. He also released the Congress High Command from jail; they traveled to Simla to discuss the proposals. These talks collapsed and Wavell announced new elections under the 1935 act. The elections demonstrated that only Congress and the League had extensive popular support. In 1946, the new British Labour government, tied to a policy of giving India freedom, attempted to resolve the deadlock with a special cabinet mission. But this approach failed in the face of Jinnah's unwillingness to accept anything short of a separate Muslim nation. Later, in July 1946, a constituent assembly met to work out the structure of India's postindependence government but it, too, was hampered by the stalemate between the two parties.

On August 16, Jinnah declared a "Day of Direct Action." Intended to be a peaceful assertion of the Muslim demand, it provoked communal rioting in Calcutta. Rioting spread to other places, adding urgency to the negotiations between the viceroy and the nationalist leadership. The Congress formed an interim government at the center that was again stalemated by the entry of the League. Clement Attlee, the British prime minister, convened discussions in London between Jinnah and Jawaharlal Nehru but could not achieve a compromise between the conflicting objectives of a separate Muslim state and the secular nation wanted by the Congress. In February, Attlee appointed Lord Mountbatten to cut the Gordian knot and transfer India from British to Indian control by June 1948.

Intensification of communal rioting rapidly convinced Mountbatten that independence should come sooner and that there should be two successor nations. On June 3, he announced Britain would transfer power to two new nations, India and Pakistan, on August 15, 1947. The Congress had no choice but to accept a truncated territory on either side of India. There were hence two nations established on August 14 and 15, 1947, each representing different ideas of nationhood and drawing upon differing popular bases. The nationalist movements had achieved a mass unity between people at all levels of society but had also divided them.

Jim Masselos

References

Brown, Judith M. *Gandhi: Prisoner of Hope.* New Haven and London: Yale University Press, 1989.
———. *Gandhi's Rise to Power.* Cambridge: Cambridge University Press, 1972.
Guha, Ranajit, ed. *Subaltern Studies I: Writings on South Asian History and Society.* Delhi: Oxford University Press, 1982.
Low, D.A. *Congress and the Raj: Facets of the Indian Struggle, 1917–1947.* London: Arnold-Heinemann, 1977.
Masselos, Jim. *Indian Nationalism: An History.* Delhi: Sterling, 1993.
———, ed. *Struggling and Ruling: The Indian National Congress, 1885–1985.* Delhi: Sterling, 1987.
Seal, Anil. *The Emergence of Indian Nationalism: Competition and Collaboration in the Later Nineteenth Century.* Cambridge: Cambridge University Press, 1968.

See also GANDHI, MOHANDAS KARAMCHAND; INDIAN NATIONAL CONGRESS; NEHRU, JAWAHARLAL; SALT MARCH, 1930; SATYAGRAHA

Industrial Workers of the World

Revolutionary anticapitalist labor organization that popularized new and little-known organizing and strike tactics during the early twentieth century. Founded in Chicago in 1905 by western miners, socialists, and independent radicals, the IWW waged major strikes and campaigns prior to 1918, after which government prosecutions decimated the organization. The union's members called themselves "Wobblies," a term whose origin remains obscure. Despite its brief tenure as a major force, the IWW's innovative use of nonviolent tactics won critical struggles over wages and working conditions, as well as paving a path for activists in the labor, civil rights, and peace movements.

One of the first events to draw national attention to the IWW was its successful two-month textile strike in Lawrence, Massachusetts, during 1912. With the aid of IWW organizers, a mainly female work force of over twenty nationalities overturned wage cuts and won raises. During the strike, the union mobilized thousands of workers into mobile mass picket lines that defied police and militia. Strikers threaded in and out of city stores and staged spontaneous sit-ins on sidewalks when ordered to disperse. National IWW organizer Elizabeth Gurley Flynn (1890–1964) staged a public relations coup when she orchestrated a protest emigration of strikers' children and child workers from the city. In an act of self-defeating brutality, police used clubs to beat the children at the Lawrence train station. Subsequent press coverage and a congressional investigation of child labor helped pressure the employers into a settlement.

The IWW encouraged slowdown strikes, the practice of remaining at work while reducing output. Wobblies used slowdowns extensively during successful recruiting drives among midwestern migratory farm workers and Pacific Northwest lumberjacks between 1915 and 1917. IWW timber workers also used the related tactic of leaving work after eight hours in a successful campaign to abolish ten-hour work days. Wobblies borrowed the term *sabotage* from French labor radicals to describe slowdown strikes. The term was not yet in widespread usage in the United States and was cited by the union's adversaries to label the IWW as violent.

In fact, the union's leaders overwhelmingly opposed both violence against people and property destruction. William ("Big Bill") Haywood (1869–1928), the union's best-known leader and a veteran of armed mine union battles in the 1890s, asserted in 1915 that worker violence

IWW Silent Agitator sticker. From Memoirs of a Wobbly, *by Henry E. McGuckin (Chicago: C.H. Kerr Publishing, 1987).*

was "old fashioned." Confident in the power of the working class, both Haywood and Flynn called for "passive resistance." While the union's national leaders clearly saw themselves as revolutionaries, Haywood predicted it would be "a revolution without blood."

Most of the union's leaders were neither pacifists nor advocates of principled nonviolence in labor struggles. Instead, they chose nonviolent tactics mainly for pragmatic reasons. Organizers appreciated the public relations value of avoiding violence, especially in the face of physical attacks by police or company guards. Such a pragmatic view of nonviolence left Wobblies free to use violence in self-defense, and some carried guns. This approach, in combination with the union's revolutionary goals and fierce rhetoric, made the IWW an easy target for those who would label the group dangerously violent. Prosecutors conducted at least six murder trials of Wobblies between 1906 and 1917; three acquittals and three convictions resulted, but the convictions were all based on ambiguous evidence. The net result was that generally nonviolent Wobblies acquired an unearned reputation for brutality.

In one of their most dramatic tactical innovations, the "Free Speech Fights," IWW activists actually demonstrated a remarkable capacity to endure violence without retaliating. The Free Speech Fights were campaigns in which jail-filling was used to pressure town governments to permit street corner speeches. The union found street speaking a valuable tool for organizing farm workers, lumberjacks, and miners, all of whom were often hired through urban employment agencies. When a municipality passed a law banning street speaking, the union would recruit members from across the nation to come to town for the purpose of defying the law and going to jail. The tactic was used in over fifty towns and cities between about 1909 and 1916, sometimes with spectacular success. Members were sometimes beaten during or after arrest, but never responded in kind. In Spokane, Washington, Wobblies endured fire hoses in their jail cells, while after the San Diego, California, Free Speech Fight, members had to be hospitalized for beatings.

The Free Speech Fights were also notable for the participants' creative use of resistance tactics while in jail. Wobblies often kept jailers awake by singing labor songs and at times engaged in hunger strikes and strikes against prison work. An IWW trademark was "building a battleship," which involved making as much noise as possible by stamping on floors, pounding on bars, and sometimes breaking the doors off their cells. Determined to win their struggles, Wobblies did not attempt to escape jail even when they clearly could have done so.

The entry of the United States into World War I in 1917 led to massive government repression of the IWW. Although the union's press had previously proposed the idea of draft resistance and antiwar strikes against capitalist wars, once Congress had declared war, IWW leaders were circumspect on those issues. Nonetheless, the federal government obtained convictions against virtually every national or local IWW leader for seeking to obstruct the war and the draft, and a number of state and local governments brought prosecutions as well. A few hundred rank-and-file Wobblies also were jailed in Minnesota, Illinois, Montana, Michigan, and elsewhere when they chose not to cooperate with the draft.

The IWW never recovered from the wartime prosecutions. It maintained a presence among timber workers into the 1920s, and a few scattered locals exist today among small cooperative businesses. Essentially, the union has functioned since the 1930s as a vehicle to promote the concept of worker solidarity and nonviolent forms of "direct action," a term used throughout the union's history to describe strikes and slowdowns.

The IWW left a valuable legacy to nonviolent activists. Its Free Speech Fights provided a model for jail-ins used later in labor, black civil rights, and antiwar movements. Slowdown strikes have repeatedly been used by unions. The enormous success of the United Automobile Workers union (UAW) in the 1930s grew directly out of the use of the sit-down strike, a tactic that the IWW employed in an abortive electrical workers' strike in Schenectady, New York, during 1906. The IWW also helped train activists who were later key figures in labor and socialist organizations such as the Socialist Workers Party and the United Automobile Workers. Elizabeth Gurley Flynn was one of several Wobblies who became national leaders of the U.S. Communist Party. Others, such as IWW organizer and songwriter Ralph Chaplin (1887–1961), would play a part in combating the influence of Communists among unions such as the International Brotherhood of Teamsters. Perhaps the most widely known legacy of the IWW is the labor song "Solidarity Forever," penned by Chaplin after a West Virginia coal miners' strike.

David C. List

References

Baxandall, Rosalyn Fraad. *Words on Fire: The Life and Writing of Elizabeth Gurley Flynn.* New Brunswick, N.J.: Rutgers University Press, 1987.

Conlin, Joseph. *Bread and Roses Too: Studies of the Wobblies.* Westport, Conn.: Greenwood, 1969.

Dubofsky, Melvyn. *We Shall Be All: A History of the IWW.* New York: Quadrangle, 1969.

Foner, Philip. *History of the Labor Movement in the United States.* Vol. 4, *The Industrial Workers of the World, 1905–1917.* New York: International, 1965.

Kornbluh, Joyce, ed. *Rebel Voices: An IWW Anthology.* Rev. ed. Chicago: Charles H. Kerr, 1988.

Salerno, Sal. *Red November, Black November: Culture and Community in the Industrial Workers of the World.* Albany: State University of New York, 1989.

International Economic Sanctions

Deliberate interruption or termination of normal economic relations intended to deter, punish, or coerce another country to change its behavior. Economic sanctions may be unilateral—imposed by a single country—or multilateral—imposed by a group of countries. They may range from quite modest measures, such as reducing or suspending foreign aid, to comprehensive sanctions cutting off all trade and financial relations with a targeted country. Sanctions are intended to raise the cost to the sanctioned country of a particular course of action to the point where the costs of that action exceed the benefits. Even if they fail to change behavior, however, sanctions may serve a useful purpose by signaling displeasure, which may reinforce international norms, support dissident groups in the sanctioned country, or deter third countries that are observing the international community's reaction to events.

Economic sanctions may be used as an alternative to military action in deterring or contributing to the resolution of a conflict or other threat to international peace and security, as in Haiti (1993) and Yugoslavia (1991–1993). Sanctions also may be employed as a prelude to military action, as in Iraq (1990–1991), or as an accompaniment to military action, as in World Wars I and II. Prior to the twentieth century, embargoes (the refusal to sell goods to a particular country), boycotts (the refusal to buy goods from a particular country), and blockades (physical interdiction of a target country's trade) were used primarily in support of military action during time of war. Examples include the Union naval blockade of Southern ports during the American Civil War and the British blockade of France during the Napoleonic wars of the early nineteenth century.

Using economic sanctions as an alternative to military force was first attempted by the League of Nations, established after World War I. The mere threat of multilateral sanctions by League members prevented Yugoslavia from expanding its territory at the expense of Albania in 1921. A similar threat in 1925 induced Greece to withdraw from Bulgaria. But the League faded into irrelevance in the 1930s when it could not muster forceful responses to military expansion by Japan, Italy, and Germany. No economic sanctions were imposed against Japan for its predations in Asia and the Pacific, or against Germany when Adolph Hitler violated treaty obligations by rearming and by occupying the Rhineland. Some economic sanctions were imposed against Italy following its invasion of Abyssinia (now Ethiopia) in 1935, although these did not include an embargo of oil sales to Italy. As a result, the sanctions were largely ineffective and Mussolini's aggression was undeterred.

The trauma of World War II reinforced the desire to find alternatives to military conflict for resolving disputes and enforcing collective security. Thus, Article 39 of the United Nations charter provides for the Security Council to determine when there is "any threat to the peace, breach of the peace, or act of aggression," and Article 41 authorizes nonmilitary responses, including "complete or partial interruption of economic relations and of rail, sea, air, postal, telegraphic, radio, and other means of communications, and the severance of diplomatic relations." Prior to the collapse of the Berlin Wall in 1989, however, the UN Security Council had approved binding sanctions resolutions on only two occasions, both against minority white governments in Africa—comprehensive, though leaky, sanctions against Rhodesia from 1966 to 1979, and an arms embargo of South Africa begun in 1977.

Economic sanctions in the period from 1945 to 1990 were adopted primarily by the two superpowers and, in particular, by the United States. By the count in the study by Hufbauer, Schott, and Elliott of more than one hundred instances of economic sanctions used in this period, the United States was the primary or single sanctioning country in seventy cases. U.S. objectives in these episodes varied, ranging from settling expropriation claims to improving human rights to destabilizing Fidel Castro to confronting the Soviet Union over its invasion of Afghanistan. The Soviet Union has also used economic sanctions, primarily to prevent or punish countries attempting to escape its embrace, as, for example, against Yugoslavia in the 1940s and 1950s and against Albania and China in the 1960s.

After the end of the cold war, however, the United Nations more actively used economic sanctions. It imposed arms embargoes against Somalia, Liberia, and Sudan, oil and arms embargoes against Haiti and the UNITA rebels in Angola, and an air traffic embargo against Libya. Comprehensive sanctions were applied against Iraq in 1990, for its invasion of Kuwait, and against the rump state of Yugoslavia (Serbia and Montenegro) in 1991 and 1992 for its role

in fomenting and supporting the civil wars in Croatia and Bosnia-Herzegovina.

The analysis by Hufbauer, Schott, and Elliott of all known economic sanctions cases from World War I through 1989 concluded that sanctions had contributed, at least modestly, to successful policy outcomes, from the perspective of the sanctioning country, in about a third of the 115 episodes documented. Sanctions are most likely to achieve foreign policy goals when the following conditions are met.

When the objective sought by the sanctioning country or coalition is relatively modest, the importance of multilateral cooperation (which often is difficult to obtain) is reduced; the chances that a rival power will provide offsetting assistance to the target country may also be smaller. However, if significant international cooperation is achieved—as in the Iraq case— a sanctioning coalition may be able to pursue more difficult goals.

Sanctions are more effective when the targeted country is much smaller than the country or countries imposing sanctions, and is also economically weak and politically unstable. Similarly, the leverage of sanctions improves when the sanctioning and targeted countries are friendly toward one another and conduct substantial trade with each other. The study of sanctions showed that the sanctioning country or countries accounted for 28 percent of the average target's trade in successful cases but only 19 percent in episodes of failed sanctions.

When sanctions are imposed quickly and comprehensively, they have the maximum economic, and presumably political, impact. The average cost to the target as a percentage of GNP was 2.4 percent in successful cases and only 1 percent in failures. Successful imposition of sanctions lasted an average of less than three years, while the duration of failures was eight years. Sanctions decisively imposed inhibit the ability of the target country to adjust, and enhance the political credibility of the sanctioning country or coalition, signaling its commitment to the sanctioning effort. Finally, sanctions are most effective when the sanctioning country or coalition avoids high costs to itself.

Because collective security goals typically will be ambitious, international cooperation, agreement on objectives, and commitment to enforcement of the sanctions are crucial in making them effective. Comparison of the implementation of the comprehensive UN sanctions against Iraq and Serbia suggests that many obstacles to effective multilateral economic sanctions remain, despite the end of the cold war. These cases suggest broad agreement within the international community that cross-border invasions are a threat to collective security that must be vigorously countered. They also suggest there is much less consensus on the appropriate response to internal conflicts and civil wars, which are likely to be far more common in the post–cold war era.

Even though the formal UN sanctions against Serbia are quite similar to those imposed against Iraq, the embargo of Iraq remains unique among sanctions efforts in this century. The economic embargo was agreed to by the UN Security Council less than a week after the invasion of Kuwait. Within a month, the council had approved the use of naval forces to enforce the sanctions. Within two months, the UN added an air embargo and authorized secondary boycotts of countries violating the resolutions. History suggests that the sanctions had a high probability of achieving the UN's goals— withdrawal of Iraqi forces from Kuwait and the restoration of Kuwaiti sovereignty—if given time.

By contrast, it was two to three weeks after the outbreak of civil war in Croatia before the European Community (EC) and United States embargoed arms against the belligerents. It was three months before the UN called on its members to embargo arms shipments and almost a year after the fighting had begun before comprehensive sanctions were mandated by the Security Council. Also, because the former Yugoslavia serves as a land route for Turkey to eastern and central Europe, and the Danube River is a major transportation route for eastern and central Europe to open water, a major loophole in the sanctions allowed for continued transshipment of goods, including petroleum and products, through Serbia. Not until November 1992, more than a year after the crisis had erupted and five months after the sanctions had been mandated, did the Security Council approve naval interdiction on the Adriatic to enforce the sanctions, call on Serbia's neighbors to crack down on abuse of the transshipment allowance, and approve the placement of UN-provided customs officers on the ground in neighboring countries to monitor enforcement.

Even the tightest sanctions usually weaken over time, in part because the high costs to the sanctioning coalition may erode support for the coercive measures. To counter this tendency during the Middle East crisis in 1990–1991, the United States and its allies went to extraordinary lengths to reduce the costs, especially for the hardest hit. Saudi Arabia and other oil exporters boosted oil production to offset losses from Iraqi and Kuwaiti production, and the United States took the lead in organizing the recycling of short-term windfall profits gained by the Saudis and other oil producers, and encouraging Japan and Germany to provide grants and low-cost loans to developing countries hurt by higher oil prices and lost trade and workers' remittances. The International Monetary Fund and World Bank also provided concessional loans to developing countries suffering balance-of-payments stresses because of the sudden jump in oil prices. There was no provision in the Serbian case for secondary sanctions and no compensation scheme for countries severely injured by enforcing the sanctions.

It should also be noted, however, that national and multinational sanctions are not the only alternative for supporting nonviolent struggles. Private, grassroots actions by individuals and nongovernmental organizations (NGOs) can also be important in putting pressure on governments—both domestic and foreign. The battle against apartheid in South Africa is a good example of the influence that private actions can have on governments.

Despite a series of reports and General Assembly resolutions opposing apartheid beginning in the 1960s, the United Nations was unable to agree on any mandatory action other than an arms embargo, and that not until November 1977. As early as March 1977, several American multinational corporations announced they would abide by key principles relating to equal opportunity in the workplace articulated by Rev. Leon Sullivan, the first African-American member of the General Motors board of directors. This was followed by similar actions in Canada and the European Community.

Although the number of companies committed to the Sullivan principles expanded in the following years, by 1983 Sullivan called for sanctions imposed by the U.S. government to put additional pressure on the South African regime. Public pressure increased for both the U.S. government and private companies to demonstrate their opposition to apartheid. Activists began a long-running protest outside the South African embassy in Washington, D.C., to keep the issue in the public eye. In 1986, the U.S. Congress passed the Comprehensive Anti-Apartheid Act, imposing sanctions on South Africa over President Ronald Reagan's veto.

Many analysts, however, believe the greatest economic pressure on South Africa came from the financial squeeze created when major private international banks suspended credit and firms operating in South Africa began to divest. These private decisions were triggered in part by concerns about the political risks associated with investing in South Africa following that regime's declaration of a state of emergency in the summer of 1985. But these decisions also were driven in no small part by the pressure of grassroots organizations. By the end of 1991, opponents of apartheid had convinced twenty-eight states—including California, Connecticut, Maryland, Massachusetts, and Michigan—twenty-five counties and ninety-one cities—including Boston, New York, Philadelphia, and Washington—to restrict their investments and other economic relations with South Africa.

To the extent that external pressure played a role in the ending of apartheid, and it was probably modest relative to internal factors, private, grassroots pressure must be given a large share of the credit. Grassroots pressure around the world contributed to private decisions by firms, as well as public decisions by governments at various levels, to reduce or eliminate their presence in South Africa.

In sum, economic sanctions may be an important tool for supporting nonviolent struggles against repressive regimes, and they are often one of the few alternatives to military action. It must also be noted, however, that they are not completely nonviolent. The combined effects of the aerial bombardment of Iraq in early 1991 and the continuation of the economic embargo following the war reportedly contributed to a sharp increase in infant and child mortality in that country as a result of the destroyed infrastructure, degraded diet, and reduced availability of medical supplies. Although food and medical supplies are typically excluded from economic sanctions, when normal commercial relations are interrupted, supplies of those commodities inevitably are affected.

The effects of sanctions on populations in countries governed by dictators such as Saddam Hussein are of particular concern because those who suffer most are likely to have little or no influence on their government's actions. Sanctions against extremely poor countries, such as Haiti, also raise special problems because stiff economic sanctions could slow economic development for years to come, even after the sanctions have been lifted. In such cases, sanctions threaten not only the livelihood of current generations but of future generations as well. The expected benefits of sanctions, then, must be weighed carefully against the costs, as well as against the effects of alternative policy instruments.

Kimberly Ann Elliott

References
American Friends Service Committee. *Dollars or Bombs: The Search for Justice through International Economic Sanctions.* Philadelphia, 1992.

Davis, Jennifer. "Squeezing Apartheid." *Bulletin of the Atomic Scientists* (November 1993): 16–19.

Doxey, Margaret. *International Economic Sanctions in Contemporary Perspective.* New York: St. Martin's, 1987.

Hufbauer, Gary Clyde, Jeffrey J. Schott, and Kimberly Ann Elliott. *Economic Sanctions Reconsidered.* 2 vols., rev. Washington, D.C.: Institute for International Economics, 1990.

Martin, Lisa. *Coercive Cooperation: Explaining Multilateral Economic Sanctions.* Princeton: Princeton University Press, 1992.

See also Blockades; Sanctions; South Africa, Antiapartheid Sanctions

Intifada (Palestinian Uprising), 1987–1990

A Palestinian movement against Israeli political and military occupation of the West Bank and Gaza Strip (the remaining areas of Mandate Palestine, which Israel captured from Jordan and Egypt in the June 1967 War). The intifada broke out in the Gaza Strip on December 8, 1987, before spreading to encompass the whole of the Israeli-occupied West Bank and Gaza Strip. The intifada was distinguished from earlier forms of Palestinian resistance in these areas by its universality across the Occupied Palestinian Territories and by its general adherence to nonviolent means of struggle.

Palestinians effectively used nonviolent methods such as protests, strikes, and boycotts, as well as more sophisticated means such as noncooperation, including civil disobedience, and the creation of alternative institutions. Palestinians sought to demonstrate that they could no longer be governed by Israel. By using these tactics, Palestinians asserted their noncooperation with the Israeli regime and their determination to unlink the Occupied Palestinian Territories from their dependence on Israel. Palestinians anticipated that their sustained direct action would put pressure on Israel and the international community to address the issue of Israel's continued occupation of Palestinian lands. They hoped that this would lead to a just settlement of the conflict based on the national rights of both peoples to independence and statehood.

By the beginning of the Gulf crisis in August 1990—which was precipitated by Iraq's invasion of Kuwait—the momentum of the intifada already had slowed. Severe Israeli repression, growing Palestinian weariness, increased factional divisions and infighting within the Palestinian community, disagreements over the course of future struggle, as well as various regional developments all converged and took their toll. Palestinian resistance did not end at that time, but individual cases of armed attacks against Israeli forces increased and overshadowed the types of mass demonstrations and community-wide resistance efforts characteristic of the first two years of the uprising.

Meanwhile, Israel had devised new tactics in response to the intifada, especially an increased use of collective punishment. For example, Israel launched massive raids into communities engaged in tax resistance. It also created the undercover units—specially trained Israeli soldiers—armed and dressed as Arabs or women, who penetrated Arab communities, pursued and often killed "wanted" youth, and spread fear among the Palestinian inhabitants. In the face of these pressures, many Palestinians felt isolated and demoralized and simply began to await help from abroad.

The term *intifada* originates from a root word in Arabic that means "to shake up" or "to shake off." By the time of its inception, Palestinians already had endured twenty-five years of occupation and had reached the conclusion that they would need to take matters into their own hands to shake off Israeli rule. Palestinian resistance against Israeli occupation had never ceased during the entire occupation. Protests, strikes, sit-ins, demonstrations, and other forms of noncooperation, as well as sporadic acts of violence, were frequent responses to repressive Israeli measures such as the confiscation of Arab lands, the construction of Jewish settlements, restrictive military orders, and the arrest and expulsion of dozens of Palestinians. However, Palestinian resistance was never organized on a mass scale throughout the Occupied Territories and had usually taken place in reaction to specific Israeli measures. Throughout these years, Palestinians under occupation were assigned a largely passive role in the wider Palestinian National Movement. They were to remain as "a thorn at Israel's side," a reminder to Israel of their presence and of the unresolved conflict. *"Sumud"* became the rallying call of pre-intifada resistance—this meant steadfastness, remaining on the land, preserving the Palestinian identity, and resisting Israeli attempts to dislodge them. Inside the Occupied Territories, Palestinians concentrated on developing their society and strengthening their social institutions. In the meantime, the Palestine Liberation Organization (PLO) outside was responsible for charting and conducting the general struggle against Israel.

Beginning in the mid-1970s, programs for development and steadfastness got seriously underway in the Occupied Territories, preparing Palestinians for the broader civilian struggle of the intifada. Palestinians began to organize themselves in grassroots and popular committees, in areas such as medical care, women's concerns, agricultural priorities, and cooperative efforts. They were mobilized and encouraged to develop their own indigenous alternatives to the institutions of the Israeli regime. Although these specific efforts were directed more at strengthening the Palestinian community than at resisting Israel, they provided a vital training ground for the quick mobilization, organization, coordination, and expansion of what later became the local committees that evolved to administer the intifada.

Acts of violent resistance against the occupation from within the Occupied Palestinian Territories did occur during this period, but the locus of these activities rested largely with the PLO outside. The PLO reserved for itself the right to conduct "armed struggle" against Israel, even as it was exploring political and diplomatic avenues of change. The notion of civilian resistance—granting the people under occupation responsibility for conducting its own struggle through largely nonviolent means—was slow to enter the lexicon of legitimate forms of struggle until the outbreak of the intifada made this change possible.

During this uprising, and especially during its first two years (1987–1989), Palestinians decided deliberately and consciously to concentrate on nonviolent means of struggle. Palestinians regarded civilian resistance and nonviolent civil disobedience as perhaps the most effective techniques that were available to them at the time to establish their nongovernability by Israel and shake off the occupation. Nonviolent methods had the advantage of empowering Palestinians and impelling them to action while putting their opponent off balance and causing demoralization, confusion, and splits within Israeli ranks. At the same time, there would be no mistaking Palestinian intentions—ending the occupation without posing any threat to the existence of the state of Israel itself or harming its citizens. Palestinians anticipated that nonviolent action would serve at once to unify their own community in its struggle and to split their opponent from within. They expected that this would force Israel to finally address the political issue of occupation unencumbered by the usual warnings and forebodings concerning violence. Israel's initial response to the intifada was confused and revealed the effectiveness of Palestinian nonviolent action. Through their sustained direct action, Palestinians had succeeded in putting Israel on the defensive, forcing it to react to Palestinian initiatives and struggling to quickly contain the impact of this uprising.

Palestinians engaged in various kinds of demonstrations and strikes, such as the general strike that brought all economic activity to a halt in the Occupied Territories. They boycotted Israeli products and redirected their productive capacity to the creation of indigenous alternatives, such as foods and medicines. They withdrew their cooperation with the Israeli regime by resigning from their posts with the civil administration, as did many Palestinian police officers. Palestinians also organized alternative institutions for health care, education, and agriculture. The "home economies," for example, were small communal plots of land that the inhabitants converted into areas for growing vegetables to supply subsistence needs. They also devised innovative means of nonviolent protest, such as whistle-blowing, clanging pots and pans, marching with olive branches in their hands, and the chanting and ululations of women confronting Israeli soldiers.

Across the Occupied Territories, Palestinians responded to the call for a campaign of civil disobedience—as they referred to their uprising—and they succeeded in attracting international attention and sympathy to their plight. The image of stone-throwing children pitted against well-armed and often brutal Israeli soldiers quickly captured world attention, and contributed significantly to challenging prevailing assumptions about Palestinians and to sensitizing international public opinion to the legitimacy of their cause.

Not only was Israel confounded by this uprising. The shake-up permeated Israeli and Palestinian society alike with both positive and negative consequences. Within Palestinian society, the intifada shook up traditional social structures and forms of authority and domination. Youth activists (shebab) played a leading role in the uprising. Their groups dominated the streets and set the tone of resistance against the Israeli forces. Women played an important part in the intifada, and their increased activism challenged patriarchal structures and values at all levels. This led to a call for more mobilization, participation, and especially more democratization throughout Palestinian society. Factional differences that had simmered for many years were bridged. Likewise, religious differences, differences between city and village, refugee and nonrefugee, were all superseded by the interests of the immediate national cause. For the first two years, Palestinians exhibited a degree of solidarity, unity, fearlessness, determination, and sense of purpose that had rarely been seen in these areas. The Unified Nationalist Leadership of the Uprising (UNLU), a body that represented all major factions of the PLO in the Occupied Territories, was established early in the intifada to chart the course of the uprising and to decide its tactics and methods in coordination with the nationalist leadership outside.

As the intifada wore on, Palestinians became disillusioned and began to weary of their struggle. They perceived that they were making enormous sacrifices without any discernible political gains. Although they had been trying to force Israel to address the political issue of occupation, Israel was responding to the intifada with intensified repression and violence against Palestinians. Palestinian casualties mounted. By the end of 1990, close to one thousand had been killed—one-third of whom were children under sixteen years of age—and over 100,000 had been injured. Collective punishment became commonplace and was used extensively by Israel to try to quell the intifada. Repressive methods included imposition of curfews, demolition of houses, mass arrests, tax raids, banning of popular committees, and deportations. Outside the Occupied Territories, the United States broke off the dialogue with the PLO that it had established barely a year before. This dialogue had been initiated in response to the PLO's official recognition of Israel and the renunciation of terrorism that had followed the declaration of Palestinian statehood by the Palestine National Council (PNC) in November 1989. Meanwhile, a right-wing government had been elected in Israel that publicly proclaimed its commitment to suppress the intifada and clearly stated its refusal to negotiate any Palestinian national rights.

An inevitable backlash ensued as Palestinians were forced to turn their attention inward, away from their opponent, to address problems emerging in their own communities. Among the issues Palestinians had to contend with was the increased scope of infighting between different political factions and the rise in the number of killings of suspected collaborators. Of special concern was the emergence of a strong extremist fundamentalist trend—embodied in *Hamas,* the Islamic Resistance Movement—that began in the Gaza Strip and spread to parts of the West Bank. This movement was fueled by the growing despair and weariness of the population under occupation. *Hamas* posed a serious challenge to the secular Palestinian leadership in the face of that leadership's failure to achieve political gains and its inability to protect the Palestinian community. The backlash from this movement also permeated other areas of Palestinian society. For example, women were called upon to return to their homes and abandon their participation in active public life and in the resistance against the occupation. *Hamas* called upon Palestinians to return to tradition and Islam so as to successfully confront the alien opponent. Such developments set the stage for a prolonged Palestinian reevaluation of the intifada and of resistance in general, and brought into sharper focus the type of future society they envisioned for themselves. This process of reevaluation was to some extent preempted by the Gulf War in January and February 1991 and the beginning of the peace talks between Israelis and Arabs at the Madrid Conference in October 1991.

Souad Dajani

References

Al-Haq. *A Nation under Siege. Al-Haq Annual Report on Human Rights in the Occupied Palestinian Territories 1989.* Ramallah: Al-Haq, 1990.

———. *Punishing a Nation. Human Rights Violations during the Palestinian Uprising, December 1987–December 1988.* Ramallah: Al-Haq, 1989.

Dajani, Souad R. *Eyes without Country: Searching for a Palestinian Strategy of Liberation.* Philadelphia: Temple University Press, 1994.

Journal of Palestine Studies. Selected issues, 1988–1990.

Lockman, Zachary, and Joel Beinin, eds. *Intifada: The Palestinian Uprising against Occupation.* Boston, Mass.: South End, 1989.

Marshall, Phil. *Intifada: Zionism, Imperialism and Palestinian Resistance.* London: Zed, 1989.

Nassar, Jamal, and Roger Heacock, eds. *Intifada: Palestine at the Crossroads.* New York: Praeger, 1990.

Palestine Human Rights Information Center. *Human Rights Updates.* Washington, D.C.: PHRIC.

Peretz, Don. *Intifada: The Palestinian Uprising.* Boulder, Colo.: Westview, 1990.

Schiff, Ze'ev, and Ehud Ya'ari. *Intifada: The Palestinian Uprising—Israel's Third Front.* New York: Simon and Schuster, 1989.

Sharp, Gene. "The Intifadah and Nonviolent Struggle." *Journal of Palestine Studies* 73 (Autumn 1989): 3–14.

Strum, Philippa. *The Women Are Marching: The Second Sex and the Palestinian Revolution.* New York: Lawrence Hill, 1992.

See also PALESTINE, ARAB REVOLT, 1936–1939

IRA Hunger Strikes, 1980–1981

Campaign by Irish Republican Army (IRA) members in Belfast, Northern Ireland, who wanted political or "special category" status as prisoners. The campaign's climax came on May 5, 1981, when Bobby Sands, an IRA prisoner at the Maze/Long Kesh prison, died after a hunger strike that lasted sixty-six days. Nine other hunger strikers also died in the campaign, which revitalized the IRA and provided the catalyst for negotiations between the British and Irish governments and the signing four years later of the Anglo-Irish Agreement.

The campaign started in 1976 when IRA prisoners refused to wear prison clothing, the badge of an ordinary criminal, and covered themselves with the only clothing at hand—their blankets. The "blanket protest" became the "dirty protest" when the prisoners smeared their excrement on the walls, floors, and ceilings of their cells. And when that didn't work, seven prisoners embarked on a hunger strike in October 1980 for the right to wear their own clothes, to associate freely, and not to have to do prison work. That hunger strike lasted fifty-three days, ending when the prisoners announced that they were satisfied that the government had agreed to meet the substance of their demands.

But the government had not—hence Sands's hunger strike and the ones that followed. Over a three-month period, twenty-three prisoners went on hunger strike and ten died, their deaths coming staccatolike in clusters of twos and threes, and for each hunger striker who died, another prisoner stepped forward to take his place.

Sands's hunger strike was initially met with little enthusiasm in his community. But that changed when the member of Parliament for Fermanagh–South Tyrone died suddenly, and the Republican movement nominated Sands for the seat. The election attracted international attention. Sands's campaign message was simple: the Catholic community should not stand by and let prisoners die. By electing Sands, voters would save his life—for it seemed inconceivable to the Catholic community that the British prime minister, Margaret Thatcher, would allow an elected member of the British Parliament to starve himself to death.

Sands won—in voting along strictly sectarian lines—and the news media of the world gathered in Belfast to chronicle Sands's deterioration, eager to capture the violence they had confidently predicted, their presence ensuring it would follow, adding to the forebodings that accompanied the death watch.

Sands's picture was everywhere. The relative inseverity of the crime for which he had been convicted and the severity of the sentence he had received (fourteen years for the possession of firearms), the fact that he had spent every Christmas since he was eighteen behind barbed wire or locked up in a cell, that he was not associated with any acts of violence, and that he had a visible family—father, mother, and sisters—transformed his persona. He became a son, a brother, a victim of discrimination and the inequities of the criminal-justice system, a young writer whose powerful descriptions of the H-block prison conditions conveyed a sensitivity that was difficult to associate with the hard men of violence and brutal acts of murder.

"The Performance of Myth"

The death watch became a communal vigil; each change in Sands's condition was front-page news, every rumor of his death intensifying fears on both sides of the divide and provoking riots and violence. As Sands edged closer to what had become his inevitable death, his stature grew. His hunger strike now fulfilled the criteria of mythology. It was in the ancient tradition of the historic quest, embedded in the hidden recesses of the Celtic consciousness. He had become a hero, retaining control of his destiny even beyond his death. He was history, which historian John Thompson describes as "the performance of myth . . . the embodiment of transcendence." The almost incomprehensible finality of his protest, a gesture of profound impotence in the face of insurmountable opposition, could be understood only in the context of the imagination, imagination that caught "the music of infinity and [made] the individual bear witness to it in his own moment of time."

When he died, his name was known in the most obscure corners of the world. He was hero, martyr, Bobby Sands MP, lonely agitator. He had pitted his fragile psyche against the impersonal power of a government, and he had won. In death, he was accorded the political recognition he had sought. Attention and empathy were worldwide. "By willing his own death," a *New York Times* editorial read, "Bobby Sands has earned a place in Ireland's long roll of martyrs and bested an implacable British Prime Minister." Mrs. Thatcher won the battle of wills—the hunger strikers abandoned their fast on October 3, 1981, 217 days after the protest started—but little else. The British government lost the propaganda war, resuscitated an ailing IRA, and politicized militant Republicanism.

The hunger strikers allowed the IRA to reestablish itself in the heroic mold and to reaffirm its legitimacy in a historical context, thereby making it more difficult to dismiss the IRA as mere terrorists with no political constituency. To the roster of martyrs that includes Tone, FitzGerald, Connolly, and Pearse were added the names of Sands, Hughes, O'Hara, McCreesh, McDonnell, Hurson, Lynch, Doherty, McIlwee, and Devine. They too, like the men of 1916 eulogized by Yeats, would be seen as having died because of an "excess of love."

Symbols of the Prison Question

The extraordinary emotive impact of the hunger strikes also drew its intensity from another source: they were symbolic of the prison question. Although most nationalists in both parts of Ireland were unequivocal in their condemnation of IRA terrorism, many also qualified their condemnation. There was a pervasive belief that the prisoners were somehow "special," that they would not be in prison if the "troubles" did not exist. Their actions were seen as the result of the conflict, not the cause of it. The prisoners, too, were victims. And they had been tried under special circumstances and in special courts—the one-judge, nonjury Diplock Courts.

The hunger strikes taught the Republican movement valuable lessons. They recognized that mobilization of public opinion around a particular issue, especially an emotional issue where support for the principles involved could be exploited as support for the movement, was a powerful propaganda tool. They also saw that contesting elections provided a base upon which to build an enduring political organization. And finally, they acknowledged that a political organization was a necessary prerequisite for taking power.

The hunger strikes were the catalyst for change in the 1980s and even into the 1990s. Sinn Fein, the political wing of the IRA, secured a third of the nationalist vote in the October 1982 election for the Northern Ireland Assembly. In response, the major nationalist parties in Ireland—the Labour Party, Fine Gael, and Fianna Fail from the South, and the Social Democratic and Labour party (SDLP) from the North—came together in the New Ireland Forum to spell out ways in which they hoped to achieve the unity of Ireland. When Sinn Fein received 43 percent of the Catholic/nationalist vote in the British general elections in 1983 and Gerry Adams, president of Sinn Fein, was elected to the British Parliament, the need to find some way to shore up constitutional nationalism and to address Catholic alienation intensified.

As a result, the British and Irish governments began a dialogue that led to signing the Anglo-Irish Agreement in November 1985. The agreement gave the Irish government a consultative role in the affairs of Northern Ireland and put Anglo-Irish relations on a new footing. "The Anglo-Irish Agreement," said Garret FitzGerald, who was Irish prime minister during much of the hunger strikes, "is the result of the IRA's performance on the hunger strike. They may not like to accept that, just as they would claim at times there are things we did that helped them, unintentionally, I'm sure. What they did helped Anglo-Irish relations enormously." The talks, which intermittently took place in 1991 and 1992 among these parties and the constitutional parties in Northern Ireland and the British and Irish governments, were aimed at finding mutually acceptable governance structures for Northern Ireland and a North–South relationship that satisfied the aspirations of both communities, resulting in an agreement that would supersede the Anglo-Irish Agreement. In this sense, these talks, too, had their origins in the hunger strikes.

In an ironic way, Sinn Fein, originally the most conspicuous beneficiary of the hunger strikes, may also have been their most conspicuous casualty. After the hunger strikes, the party pursued a dual strategy: a campaign of violence in Northern Ireland coupled with participation in the electoral processes in both Northern Ireland and the Republic of Ireland. However, the greater its commitment to armed struggle in the North, the less the appeal of Sinn Fein to voters in the South—in the 1992 general election, the party received less than 2 percent of the vote—and the more it exposed the IRA's lack of legitimacy in Ireland as a whole.

Dignity—at Last—in Death

And what of the hunger strikers themselves? They were ordinary young men who came, for the most part, from large families, more often than not from either staunchly Republican families or staunchly Republican areas. The validity of each of their deaths depended on its being followed by another; the solidarity that counted was with those who had died rather than with the living. It was clear, following Joe McDonnell's death (the fifth), that the hunger strikes were a failure as a tool of coercion; thus the decisions of other prisoners either to participate or continue were made with the certainty that their deaths would achieve nothing. They were left with nothing to live for and nothing to die for, except their dignity. Their acts of self-abnegation were an assertion in death of what life had denied them: a moment of self-realization and freedom transcending the strictures of cause, a reaffirmation of their own sense of worth. In death they became whole. Ultimately, what was at stake was not so much their belief in the justice of their cause but their belief in their own dignity as human beings. When all means of asserting it were appropriated, they used what was left them—their own lives. The prisoners' worlds had somehow deconstructed during the years of being on the blanket and dirty protests, of having endured physical deprivation to the point where their reaction to it had become existential: The physical self was something that existed outside the real self, and thus was something that could be discarded.

Protest itself and the maintenance of protest, rather than the purpose of protest, became the focus around which daily life was organized. The limitations and deprivations of their physical circumstances opened to them a new world in which the organization of their own deaths became the object of their survival. Endurance became more important than the end for which it was employed, bearing witness more exigent than success; to refuse help that was always at hand was a more pivotal concern than the other-world of ordinary commerce and discourse. Familiar things receded; with death came the final act of solidarity that brought rebirth, fulfillment, and fusion.

Hence the absolute finality of their protest. What began as a protest for five demands became a struggle for self-worth. The years on the blanket and dirty protests fostered among the prisoners a sense of camaraderie, of shared values that changed their sense of deprivation. They did not choose to die in the face of indeterminate sentences or the grim prospects of life behind bars. Rather, a metamorphosis occurred. They stumbled, unwittingly, or perhaps out of necessity, into a belief that the freedom to which they would return was no freedom at all. They came to an understanding, however tentative, that their collective acts, like a leap of faith or a creative impulse, were what artist Patrick Graham calls "a leap from the mortal chains of delusion—a kind of impermanent presence."

Padraig O'Malley

References

O'Malley, Padraig. *Biting at the Grave. The Irish Hunger Strikes and the Politics of Despair.* Boston: Beacon, 1990.

See also CORRIGAN, MAIREAD, AND BETTY WILLIAMS; FASTING; NORTHERN IRELAND CIVIL RIGHTS ASSOCIATION; PEACE PEOPLE, COMMUNITY OF THE

Iranian Revolution, 1963–1979

Revolution that removed the shah of Iran from power in 1979. The revolution had a visible final thrust in 1978, but the anti-shah sentiment that spawned it had been present since 1963. In spite of Western perceptions, the revolution was essentially nonviolent, involving marches, strikes, boycotts, noncooperation, petitions, symbolic clothing, self-sacrifice, walkouts, and general strikes.

The Iranian revolution is notable, in part, because the regime that was brought to power through nonviolent struggle did not remain obviously committed to nonviolence. Americans recoiled at the long ordeal of their diplomats held hostage (although unharmed) in the Teheran embassy for over one year. More significantly, perhaps, was the eight-year war with Iraq, persecution of dissidents, and political and material support for terrorist groups in the Middle East and elsewhere. These subsequent events make the nonviolent character of the anti-shah revolution all the more compelling.

The shah of Iran, Mohammed Reza Pahlavi, returned to power in 1953 through intervention by the Central Intelligence Agency of the United States. The secret police (the SAVAK) was created in 1957 supposedly to fight communism. However, its main goal became to bolster the shah's government by creating a climate of fear that would eliminate all resistance. Eventually there were five thousand officials and sixty thousand people hired to collect information. It seemed that SAVAK agents were everywhere in Iran, but that is not quite accurate. What was everywhere was the fear of the SAVAK. As resistance grew, more people disappeared or were tortured. A state of terror developed nationwide.

In 1963, the shah started a massive "Westernization" plan whose liberal-sounding goals served mainly to increase the power of the already privileged. It also deeply alienated a large majority of the population whose traditions, culture, and religious values were being attacked. The "White Revolution"—the set of agricultural reform policies—for example, ended up concentrating land in larger holdings where it could be used for the production of export crops. This forced hundreds of thousands of peasants off the land into marginal urban existence.

Khomeini was only one of the many prominent people who criticized the shah. But his condemnation was pivotal because, since 1923, he had consistently criticized the government when an earlier shah had attempted to reduce the clergy's authority. In 1941, Khomeini published a book called *Discovery of Secrets,* an attack on the Pahlavi dynasty, in which he called for an end to foreign domination in Iran.

After Imam Ruhallah Al-Musavi Al-Khomeini spoke against the White Revolution in 1963, the first anti-shah demonstration took place in Qom, followed shortly thereafter by demonstrations in other cities. The army's response was brutal; thousands were killed. Many prominent religious leaders were imprisoned or tortured, and Khomeini was forced into exile, first to Turkey, then to Iraq. From that point until January 1978, the resistance was entirely underground.

Those armed guerrilla groups that formed were usually heavily infiltrated by SAVAK agents, so they remained small and unimportant until the very end of the revolution, when they, too, joined the mass movement. For the next twenty-five years, it was mainly students who carried on the resistance.

It was virtually impossible to work in large groups because the SAVAK was so powerful. Therefore, people in the resistance did not know each other; most work was done singly. Some mosques were used as meeting places; after 2 A.M., the door was locked and a few students would meet with an ayatollah to discuss problems and issues. Resistance participants often woke in the morning to find explicit instructions on a paper slipped under the door.

The most important preparation for resistance came through people learning more about their Islamic culture and values as well as cutting dependence with the West and Western values. It was customary for a central committee of ayatollahs to recommend religious readings that would reach all students in the national public school system. Between 1975 and 1977, these recommended readings had significance to the developing resistance that students would understand.

Students' initial political analysis of the Iranian situation was Marxist. But many found it difficult to apply Marxism to their situation. Since the 1917 Russian Revolution, the USSR had had designs on Iran. In addition, Marxist analysis denied the existence or importance of spiritual values. Thus, students more frequently turned to the work of Ali Shariati, an Iranian sociologist trained in France, and other Iranian intellectuals who provided new, revolutionary interpretations of familiar texts. It was as though these leaders blew the dust off a thousand years of Islamic teaching, and people were able to see and interpret its fundamental power.

After returning to Iran, Shariati taught in schools and mosques, explaining the problems of Muslim societies in the light of Islamic principles. Shariati also translated Franz Fanon's *Wretched of the Earth.* But the most important works were those of banned Iranian intellectuals, many of whom were executed by the SAVAK. It is impossible to overemphasize Shariati's value to the resistance. He excited people by his wide vision and analysis that their own culture and religion could be the source of fresh and vital ideas. (Shariati moved to England and died there in 1977 under mysterious circumstances.)

Around 1977, about eighty thousand clergy at various levels of authority became leaders in the resistance, adding their considerable nationwide structure and bureaucracy. From exile, Khomeini sent to Iran tapes of instruction; these were copied, distributed, and played in mosques around the country. Khomeini provided explicit instructions, calling for strikes, boycotts, and noncooperation. He stated that members of the armed forces should be viewed as brothers.

By this time, numerous groups in Iran were ready to commit themselves to revolution: students, the small armed underground movement, clergy, and the new rootless urban poor thrown off the land. In addition, the bazaar merchant community, itself a significant middle-class group, followed the clergy's lead. When demonstrators were killed, the bazaar offered financial support to their families. The bazaar also supported striking workers.

In June 1977, three leaders sent the shah an open letter, pleading for individual freedom, freedom of the press and association, and the establishment of a freely elected government. The shah ignored the letter, but ten thousand copies were circulated widely. In October, Khomeini's son, Mostafa, was killed in Iraq under mysterious circumstances. A month later, a dinner party was held by one of the signers of the letter. The party was disrupted by members of SAVAK and the army, and three hundred people were injured. This event drew many urban middle-class people into the revolution. On New Year's Eve, President and Mrs. Carter were in Tehran, toasting the shah's health. A week later, a national newspaper accused Khomeini of being "connected with a foreign power."

On January 8, 1978, people in Qom demonstrated to protest this attack against Khomeini. People were injured and killed as the police and army responded brutally. This is the event that dates open resistance and revolution. The Islamic tradition of public mourning forty days after a death meant that from this date the momentum of popular resistance steadily built. If people were killed in a demonstration, others knew there would be another demonstration forty days later. As resistance grew and deaths occurred more frequently, these forty-day periods overlapped, and the pace of the resistance accelerated. Over the following months, demonstrations occurred in Tabriz, Tehran, Qom, Kazerun, Mashad, and Isfahan. By late July, thirteen cities saw people injured and killed in demonstrations.

People carried huge posters with photographs of leaders such as Khomeini and Shariati and of people killed in earlier demonstrations. After so many Iranians had been killed, Khomeini sent back this message: "The blood of martyrs will become fields of tulips [signifying hope as well as martyrdom] that will cover the countryside." Little wonder that the first coin struck by the new regime had tulips on one side. For women, black *chadors* (women's traditional cloth worn over other clothing, covering the head and the rest of the body) became the symbol of resistance and solidarity.

Two events in 1978, the Abadan fire and "Black Friday," proved to be major turning points. On August 20, 1978, at the Cinema Rex theater in Abadan, eight hundred people were locked inside and the theater was set on fire. Four hundred and ten people died. In spite of numerous government explanations, the belief spread that the fire was set by government officials.

In early September, marches were held in Tehran and in other cities to mourn the dead in Abadan and elsewhere. On Friday, September 7, martial law was declared and a curfew was imposed. But many people did not learn of the curfew. So when about fifty thousand people gathered at Jaleh Square in Tehran, they did so without encouragement from religious leaders. However, at 8:30 A.M., Ayatollah Nouri asked people to sit down at the square, and they did. When the army launched tear gas, people rose and moved toward the army. At the sound of machine gun fire, people panicked, regrouped, and again moved toward the soldiers. Soldiers opened fire, some shooting into the air, some aiming at people; many people were injured, and some were killed. In one instance, when a soldier was ordered to fire into the crowd, he refused, killed his commanding officer, and turned the gun on himself. All over Tehran, little knots of demonstrators and soldiers, grieving, angry, and frightened, spontaneously battled each other. By the end of the day, three thousand people had been killed. These events catalyzed the revolution. By early October, Behesht Zahara Cemetery outside Tehran became off limits to soldiers; the people's spirit of resistance was so high that soldiers dared not enter. Workers in state-run hospitals in Tehran struck for "higher pay," joining other striking public employees. Two days later, two major newspapers ceased publication to protest the imposed censorship. A general strike was called in Mashad. On October 31, oil workers struck. Within a week, this strike cost the government $60 million a day. On November 5, Prime Minister Jafan Sharif-Emami resigned, and martial law was imposed nationwide.

On November 14, demonstrators clashed with soldiers and the bazaar was closed down for a week. A week later, two hundred workers at the Shahryar power station in Tehran staged a walkout. The shah's representative would regularly give propaganda radio speeches each night. And each night, technical workers would cause a "power failure" at 8:30 when the program was scheduled. When the speech was over at 9:00, power would be restored.

In early December, people marched in Tehran despite the curfew and despite troops firing on the marchers. On December 14, there were demonstrations in fifteen cities. Khomeini called for a day of mourning and a general strike to support the striking oil workers. Two weeks later, the oil workers shut down the oil industry completely. The next day, December 29, the central bank and the oil refineries were shut down.

On January 16, 1979, the shah left the country. On February 1, Imam Khomeini returned to Iran, and a few days later he appointed a prime minister of the new government.

Lynne Shivers

References

Albert, David, ed. *Tell the American People: Perspectives on the Iranian Revolution.* Rev. ed. Philadelphia: New Society, 1980.

Graham, Robert. Iran: *The Illusion of Power.*
New York: St. Martin's, 1979.

Halliday, Fred. Iran: *Dictatorship and Development.* New York: Penguin, 1979.

Islam and Revolution: Writings and Declarations of Imam Khomeini. Translated by Hamid Algar. Berkeley, Calif.: Mizan, 1981.

Jansen, G.H. *Militant Islam.* New York: Harper Colophon, 1979.

Nobari, Ali-Reza, ed. *Iran Erupts.* Stanford, Calif.: Iran-America Documentation Group, 1978.

Shariati, Ali. *Marxism and Other Western Fallacies: An Islamic Critique.* Translated by R. Campbell. Berkeley, Calif.: Mizan, 1980.

———. *On the Sociology of Islam.* Translated by Hamid Algar. Berkeley, Calif.: Mizan, 1979.

See also JIHAD; REVOLUTION

Iraq Uprising, 1948

Predominantly nonviolent resistance to British and Iraqi government attempts to persuade the population to accept a reformulated treaty that protected British interests in Iraq. Demonstrations and strikes led to the resignation of Prime Minister Salih Jabr and the repudiation of the treaty.

In 1947, British officials revised the Anglo-Iraqi Treaty of 1930, allowing for the continuation of British influence and military presence in Iraq. Prime Minister Salih Jabr and the Iraqi delegation signed the new treaty in Portsmouth, England on January 15, 1948.

The 1948 treaty was only one of several issues in contention for Iraqis. A serious food shortage, economic inequalities, a corrupt administration, and an unpopular prime minister fueled the popular unrest. When word of the treaty signing reached Baghdad, the capital of Iraq, high school and university students staged demonstrations and a three-day student strike. Soon workers were striking as well. Iraqis were protesting food shortages as well as demanding Jabr's resignation. Daily demonstrations were staged on Rashid Street, the main thoroughfare of Baghdad. Some violent attacks were made on British businesses, such as the newspaper *Iraq Times.*

Prime Minister Jabr returned from England, but was forced to land at the British air force base in Habbania and to travel in disguise to Baghdad. On January 26, 1948, Jabr ordered police to use machine guns to disperse protest demonstrations. In response to this threat, thousands of Iraqis poured into the streets in protests, and police fired on crowds throughout the day. Over a hundred protesters were killed and several hundred wounded, but the demonstrations continued. Students who were killed by police were given public funerals attended by thousands. One of the most inspirational aspects of the resistance was the political poetry of two famous Iraqi poets, al-Jawahiri and Bahr al-Ulum. They recited poems during demonstrations and incited the resistance movement.

Although much of the protest activity was nonviolent, several violent actions occurred, including the killing of one policeman and the burning of the American Information Center. The street clashes reached a climax on January 27 with many deaths and injuries and a large crowd demanding Jabr's resignation. Finally, soldiers refused to fire on the civilians and, at eight o'clock, the resignation of the Jabr regime was announced over the radio. Jabr fled for his life to Jordan and later to England. People celebrated throughout Baghdad.

Strikes and demonstrations continued for ten days after Jabr's resignation to maintain pressure against the treaty. Business in Baghdad was completely disrupted. Finally, the entire Iraqi government repudiated the treaty. It announced that the British Military Mission would withdraw in May. The gains won during the January 1948 uprising did not last long, however. The pro-treaty leaders reestablished a military dictatorship later that year, reforms were overturned, and left-wing activists were persecuted. But the 1948 Anglo-Iraqi treaty was never enacted, and Britian was forced to form a collective agreement with a coalition of Arab countries. The predominantly nonviolent uprising also led to the resignation of an unpopular regime.

Brad Bennett

References

Bennett, Brad. "Arab-Muslim Cases of Nonviolent Struggle." In *Arab Nonviolent Political Struggle in the Middle East,* edited by Ralph E. Crow, Philip Grant, and Saad E. Ibrahim. Boulder, Colo.: Lynne Rienner, 1990.

Longrigg, Stephen Hemsley. *Iraq, 1900 to 1950: A Political, Social, and Economic*

History. London: Oxford University Press, 1953.

Italy, Social Movements and the Evolution of Strategy

Social movements emerging in Italy in the 1960s on such issues as educational reform, women's rights, nuclear energy, marginalized youth, and armaments, pursued strategies in which violent action was dominant for almost two decades but eventually became subordinated to nonviolent forms of struggle. If in several characteristics these movements were very similar to those that developed, on the very same issues, in other Western democracies, they also reflected some peculiarities of the contemporary Italian political system. In particular, institutional politics was highly polarized between one of Western Europe's strongest Communist parties, which was perpetually excluded from national power, and the uninterrupted rule of Christian Democracy, despite frequent cabinet failures. This ideological divide between the Old Left and institutionalized conservatism strongly influenced the political alliances and repertoires of action undertaken by the movement leaders of the New Left that emerged in the 1960s.

In the history of social movements during the Italian Republic, nonviolence was, for a long time, confined to tiny and largely marginal groups. From the 1960s through the 1970s, the political alliance of the New Left with the labor-based movement of the Old Left, the ideological commitment of the Old Left to confrontation including the acceptance of violence, and the harsh repression of social challengers by state agents and actors, led to a dominance of violent action in the strategies of the new social movements. Only after the shock of terrorism in the 1970s did nonviolent forms of protest come to dominate the repertoire of collective action in the 1980s. Even during the most radical confrontations, however, criticisms of violent repertoires as well as nonviolent forms of action were present in the Italian left-libertarian movements. Thus, the contemporary history of Italian social movements provides a view of the role existing political structures play in the evolution of strategies and actions by social movements.

Old Allies and New Movements: Students, Labor, and Women in the 1960s

A wave of strikes in the country's large factories at the beginning of the 1960s was a prelude to the widespread mobilization later in the decade. In the mid-1960s, the student movement set off what Sidney Tarrow has described as part of a "cycle of protest," as collective action expanded to different sectors of the society. The students' protest against a government proposal to reorganize the university system soon expanded to include aims other than the reform of the academic structures.

At the beginning of their protest, the students used forms of action that combined traditional means of exerting pressure within the institution and innovations such as sit-ins and "go-ins" (occupations of buildings), some of which were adapted from the U.S. civil rights movement and student movement. Their repertoire of action and the ideology of their protest gradually changed as the movement faced the reactions it sparked—both the hostility of "normal citizens" and the support of the organizers active in factories and labor struggles. Violence appeared with attacks by neo-fascists and in some instances brutal assaults by the police. Consequently, the "need for self-defense" became a relevant issue, although also a contested one. For, if the "necessity of a revolution" in the future was a common belief among activists, opinions on how to face repression in the present diverged widely. Thus, although the student movement's repertoires of action followed the principle of a "limited violation of the rules," a subculture began to justify violence as a "necessity" for facing state repression and the violence of social adversaries.

Those groups that consistently refused to adopt violent methods during this time were mainly active on the issue of nuclear armament. Among them were such Christian groups as the Movimento Italiano di Riconciliazione—the Italian branch of the International Fellowship of Reconciliation—and Pax Christi. Moreover, there were the nonviolent organizations, such as the Community of the Arca (founded after World War II by Lanza del Vasto), the Nonviolent Movement (founded by Aldo Capitini in 1961 and affiliated with War Resisters International), and the Lega per i diritti dei popoli (League for People's Rights), a member of the Bertrand Russell Foundation. These groups understood and practiced nonviolence as a way of life, a "total revolution," which, in the words of Aldo Capitini, had to be "open," "alive," and "creative." They aimed at converting individuals by way of personal examples, and at creating the "new" human being through a permanent process of education about nonviolence.

By the end of the 1960s, the main organizations of the so-called New Left emerged in the coordination of protest activities in the various universities and, later on, in the expansion of protest outside the university. Building an alliance with the Old Left, the student movement also radicalized its initial demands for reform. The expansion of protest to the most diverse social groups heightened political tensions and favored the dominance of the ideological view of the New Left activists on the emerging social movements. These activists—particularly in the student movement, which had expanded to include high school students—couched their hopes for radical social change in a traditional discourse of class conflict. Like most European student movements and the American New Left, the Italian students aimed at linking their anti-authoritarian sentiments with working-class revolution, and therefore looked for allies in the large factories. But in Italy, unlike the experience elsewhere in Western Europe and North America, the ties between students and workers became close and numerous. However unrealistic the hope of a stable alliance between students and workers was, the prevailing outlook among the student activists as the events of 1969 unfolded was a great enthusiasm for the "United Front of Workers and Students."

The students' encounter with the working class influenced their tactics—since, in these same years, the industrial conflicts assumed more and more radical forms. Generally, the hope for radical political change fueled cooperation between the New Left and the Old Left, as well as a fierce antagonism toward the state. If the leftist movements imported forms of protest developed by the American student movement, they also borrowed many tactics from the Old Left, such as strikes and pickets, as well as an ideological orientation.

Even the women's movement, which in its initial phase at the end of the 1960s, was composed of very small study groups and other informal associations, adopted the prevailing New Left orientation and acquired several contacts with the Old Left. And whereas the early groups, modeled on the American and European women's movements, had developed forms of civil disobedience and concentrated on problems of contraception (still illegal at the time) and women's health, the women's collectives that emerged in the early 1970s took up more strictly political issues and accepted more radical forms of action.

Political violence tended to be accepted both strategically and tactically. In the late 1960s, violence had been mainly random, unplanned (usually triggered by confrontations with neo-fascists or the police), and justified as defense against the attacks from outside. By the beginning of the 1970s, however, the concept of "defensive violence" was losing its appeal. Small group forms of violence increased and in fact predominated at the end of the decade. There was however an increasing strategic differentiation between movement organizations. Some portions of the movements criticized the use of violence, even for "defensive aims," because it increased the risk of social and political isolation. Other factions thought that "the best defense was attack" and shifted to a model of organized violence. According to this latter model, specialized groups were to use violent repertoires in order to "win" the battles that would be part of a strategy of continuous confrontation. At the margin of the student movement, the emergence in 1970 of the first underground group, the Red Brigades (Brigate Rosse), expressed this strategy in its most extreme form—terror attacks, kidnaping, and murder. In this radicalized climate, the groups advocating nonviolent action, with their refusal to justify the means through the aims, remained marginal.

Ironically, however, these were not only the years of the radicalization of social conflicts, but also the years of some political reforms. It was, in fact, in 1972 that the nonviolent movement won its first victory when the Italian Parliament passed a law introducing the *servizio civile*. Under the new law, those who refused to serve as draftees in the armed forces on a moral basis could—if their motivations were accepted by a special committee—substitute an "alternative" service in the civil sector. In 1973, nonviolent activists founded the League of the Conscientious Objectors (Lega degli Obiettori di Coscienza) to help those who refused to serve in the army.

The 1970s: Mobilization Decline and Rising Terrorism

Between 1974 and 1976, the left-libertarian movements underwent partial institutionalization and experienced a *riflusso* (low ebb). At the same time, there was an increase in some radical forms of protest. Particularly in the factories, the international economic crisis of the early 1970s pressured activists to concentrate on defending gains won in previous years. In schools and universities, the turbulent situation normalized, although it never returned to the calm of the 1950s and early 1960s. Triggered by the church-sponsored campaign for the repeal of the law governing divorce in 1973–1974, mass mobilization in support of legal abortion lasted until 1976. Because of the presence of a strong Left, both old and new, analyses of the role of women in society continued to borrow some traditional categories of class conflict: "exploitation" of women as sex objects and housewives, "imperialism" via macho values, and the "structural nature" of the "contradiction" between the sexes. The women's issues, however, also created strains within the organizations of the New Left, which had serious problems in coping with the decline of mobilization. Some organizations gradually disappeared; others contested local and national elections.

As mobilization declined, especially in the factories, relations between the New Left organizers and the trade unionists of the Old Left deteriorated. Some organizations responded to continuing harsh repression by the state with a radically confrontational posture; others began to take advantage of the new channels for political participation. Various organizations within the diverse social movements split over the question of "which level of violence" was appropriate to the "historical phase." Small groupings of the New Left radicalized their ideology and strategy. In daily confrontations with radical conservative groups and in violent fights with the police, the factions specializing in the use of violence gained greater influence within their organizations. The quasi-military structure of these groups had a particular appeal for the younger militants, socialized into the polarized politics of the early 1970s.

Afraid of the negative consequences of the violent escalation, other groups of the New Left began a long process of "self-criticism," and became more integrated in the political institutions. On the Left, in general, the moderate turn of the Italian Communist Party after the 1968 Soviet-led invasion of Czechoslovakia to crush liberalizing reforms paved the way for a repudiation of the idea of a final revolution and of the need for violent forms of collective action. The Radical Party—the main organizer of the campaigns on divorce and abortion, and represented in Parliament—emerged as one of the main voices of the nonviolent movement, promoting the ideas of Gandhi.

From 1977 to 1980, the mass movements generally were dormant. The women's movement, for one, reached a turning point in 1976–1977. During the parliamentary debate on the abortion law in 1976, the movement largely abandoned active political engagement. Although a few of its constituent groups took advantage of the new institutional opportunities and began to act as interest groups, the majority of the participants in the movement succumbed to a pessimism generated by both the economic crisis and the loss of mobilization capacity. The women's movement split into a number of small, informal collectives—including several consciousness-raising groups—that turned inward (concentrating on, for example, "search for the self"), and showed no interest in advertising their existence or recruiting new members.

The movement organizations that retained a more political orientation had to operate within a hyper-radicalized atmosphere. Still influenced by the New Left organizations, many small groups, especially those devoted to youth issues, radicalized their tactics and adopted the "autonomist" ideology (precariously combining old Leninist frames with pessimistic images of a totalitarian society), which encouraged loosely organized acts of extreme violence. For these groups, the working class became less and less important as a point of reference, and even the Old Left came to be seen as an enemy. But the autonomous groups that tried to promote youth protest failed to articulate political campaigns. Their daily fights with neo-fascists, drug dealers, and police led to rapid radicalization manifested in dramatic forms of violence. The youth groups provided new recruits first for the various tiny underground groups and, eventually, for the larger terrorist organizations. Protest activities collapsed, in particular, after the Red Brigades kidnaped and killed the president of the Christian Democratic Party, Aldo Moro, in 1978. In response, the so-called government of national unity (the Christian Democratic–led national government elected in 1978 with the external support of the Communist Party) issued an antiterrorist emergency policy. Until 1980, the only organizations that seemed to be on the rise were terrorist groups.

The Revival of Nonviolent Action in the 1980s

In this very difficult period of the late 1970s, nonviolent strategies started to appeal to a large segment of the left-libertarian movements. The importance of nonviolent repertoires of action increased, in particular, when a wave of protests followed approval of the National Plan for Energy, which provided for the construction of twenty nuclear power plants, the first of which was to be built in Montalto di Castro. Under the auspices of the Radical Party, individuals concerned about animal rights and environmental protection mobilized small groups of intellectuals and scientists. In these political groups the debate on nonviolence became a central one. A main cleavage in the movements divided those who promoted nonviolence as a "strategy"—or, better, as the very essence of the movement—and those who accepted it as only a "tactic"—as they put it in those years. The first group included the traditional nonviolent organizations as well as the League for Unilateral Disarmament, founded in 1979; the second group was represented mainly by the surviving New Left.

The situation began to change between 1981 and 1983 as the protest campaign against NATO's plan to deploy cruise missiles in several European countries gained strength. Half a million people participated in two protest marches in Rome in 1981 and 1983. Several hundred thousand took part in the march from Milan, in northern Italy, to Comiso, Sicily, the designated Italian base for the missiles. With nearly six hundred peace committees and a few coordinating meetings, the peace movement was able to (re)mobilize in a single political campaign the collective actors who had been vital participants of social movements in previous years—student activists, feminist groups, some surviving youth centers, and the environmental groups. The peace issue was framed in a variety of ways so as to appeal to a variety of groups: "peace and economic welfare" for the Communist Party and trade unions; "peace and aid for the Third World" for the Radical Party; "peace and individual consciousness" for the religious groups; "peace and motherhood" for the women's groups; "peace and critique of the adult world" for the student groups; "peace and natural equilibrium" for the ecologists; and "peace and anti-imperialism" for the radical fringe groups.

The peace movement marked the first time after the radicalization of the political conflicts in the 1970s that the Old Left, the New Left, and the more general new social movements cooperated in a political campaign. Unlike the mobilizations of the previous decade, this campaign relied on conventional forms of pressure (petitions, parliamentary initiatives), public education and awareness-building (conferences, courses, hunger strikes), civil disobedience (tax boycotts), and nonviolent direct actions (such as the international March Catania-Comiso, organized in January 1983 by the International Camp for Peace, that culminated in a blockade of the military base at Magliocco). Traditional nonviolent groups (such as the Fondazione Capitini and the Nonviolent Movement) contributed to the new political repertoires with, in particular, the organization of the Marches for Peace from Perugia to Assisi, joined by religious groups and trade unions, as well as by the government of the Region Umbria.

Although the number of violent attacks against people remained high during this period, the terrorist organizations resented the changed atmosphere. Most of them disappeared, and even the two major groups—the Red Brigades and Front Line—experienced serious setbacks when a few of their members began to collaborate with the police.

The decade following 1984 was characterized by a profound change in the left-libertarian movements. The protest that spread in the 1980s, after the lull in the late 1970s, assumed very different characteristics. The impact of socialist ideology waned with the decline of New Left groups. The most important event in this phase was the rise of the ecological movement with its pragmatic political orientation. Although the movement sometimes reached a very high capacity for mass mobilization—for instance when it attracted 150,000 people for a march in Rome after the Chernobyl disaster in 1986—it did not seem to be very interested in organizing national campaigns. It usually limited the scope of its actions, focusing on a neighborhood or other small area, although some attempts were made to coordinate campaigns at the city level. The campaigns were often defensive (protesting laws that would endanger the natural and artistic heritage), but they occasionally took an offensive tack as well (as in the campaigns to establish and expand pedestrian areas in city centers).

The environmental activists used mostly conventional forms (petitions and debates) but also took quite innovative symbolic actions. These included "constructive" exemplary actions (such as working as volunteers to manage a park, or organizing "work camps" in impoverished areas) as well as nonviolent direct action (such as "harassing" hunters by making noise to alarm the birds). Other movements—especially the student movement and the women's movement—joined forces with environmentalists in several campaigns, among them, the anti-Mafia campaign of the late 1980s. In these campaigns, the forms of protest often were highly symbolic—such as hanging white sheets in home windows to testify a refusal of the Mafia, or planting a tree in front of the home of a judge killed by the Mafia—and there was no violence. In addition, traditional nonviolent groups continued to organize protest related to peace issues—in particular, a campaign for the "tax objection" against military spending, protests of military expositions in Genoa, and actions against the arms trade.

In conclusion, nonviolent forms of action eventually came to dominate the political repertoire of Italian social movements. The disastrous consequences of terrorism had triggered both a revulsion and a learning process. In the 1990s, with very few exceptions, social movements in Italy strongly oppose the use of violence.

Donatella della Porta

References

Capitini, Aldo. *Il potere di tutti*. Firenze: La Nuova Italia, 1967.

Della Porta, Donatella. *Il terrorismo di sinistra*. Bologna: Il Mulino, 1990.

Della Porta, Donatella, and Sidney Tarrow. "Unwanted Children: Political Violence and the Cycle of Protest in Italy, 1966–1973." *European Journal of Political Research* 14 (1987): 607–632.

Diani, Mario. *Isole nell'arcipelago: Il movimento ecologista in Italia*. Bologna: Il Mulino, 1988.

Ergas, Yasmine. *Nelle maglie della politica: Femminismo, istituzioni e politiche sociali nell'Italia degli anni '70*. Milano: Angeli, 1986.

Fraser, Ronald, ed. *1968: A Student Generation in Revolt*. New York: Pantheon, 1988.

Lodi, Giovanni. *Uniti e diversi: Le mobilitazioni per la pace nell'Italia degli anni '80*. Milano: Unicopli, 1984.

Melucci, Alberto. *Altri codici: Aree di movimento nella metropoli*. Bologna: Il Mulino, 1984.

Tarrow, Sidney. *Democracy and Disorder: Protest and Politics in Italy, 1965–1975*. Oxford: Clarendon, 1989.

See also FRANCE, POLITICS AND PROTEST; SOCIAL MOVEMENTS

I

J

Jagerstatter, Franz (1907–1943)

Celebrated Austrian conscientious objector executed in 1943 for refusing to serve in Hitler's armed forces. Franz Jagerstatter, a simple peasant born in 1907, lived most of his life in the tiny Upper Austrian village of St. Radegund. Married to a woman from a neighboring village, he fathered three daughters (in addition to an illegitimate daughter from an earlier union). A devout Catholic and daily communicant, he served as sexton to the village church. Long before Hitler's forces invaded Austria, he had recognized the evil of National Socialism and, when the time came, his was the only "no" vote cast in the village for the *Anschluss* plebiscite that made Austria part of the Greater Third Reich. His vote, needless to say, went uncounted. Twice he served briefly in the armed forces, both times being released to return to his essential farm work. Returning from his second stint he told friends and family he would never go again, that merely putting on the Nazi uniform "made him feel dirty." Ordered back to duty in March 1943, he reported only to announce that he could not serve in an unjust war being waged by an immoral regime. After his arrest and several months in the military prison at Linz, he was transferred to Berlin for trial and sentencing before the Supreme Military Tribunal. On August 9, 1943, he was beheaded.

Jagerstatter was a conscientious objector, not a pacifist. He would have taken up arms eagerly to defend his beloved Austria against the Nazi invaders had resistance been attempted. There is nothing to indicate that he had ever heard about the theory or principles of classic nonviolence (though a reference in his final statement from prison suggests that months of meditation in solitary confinement had led him, as a Christian, to reject violence). The link we seek lies in the power of total personal commitment, the power upon which effective and successful nonviolent action ultimately must depend. It was, moreover, his religious judgment that prevailed. The priests he consulted, even his bishop in a private audience, told him he had no right as an ordinary citizen to make such a decision and to place himself and his family at risk by defying the power of "legitimate authority." If today this has changed and the Austrian Church is promoting his cause for canonization as a martyr and saint, it only serves to enhance his stature as witness to the absolute primacy of the individual conscience and commitment to what one recognizes as the truth.

Gordon C. Zahn

References

Zahn, Gordon. *In Solitary Witness: The Life and Death of Franz Jagerstatter.* Collegeville, Minn.: Liturgical Press, 1981.

See also CONSCIENTIOUS OBJECTION; NAZISM, CIVILIAN RESISTANCE, 1939–1945

Japan, Security Treaty Protests, 1959–1960

Movement to prevent the revision and ratification of the Japan–U.S. Security Treaty of 1960 that evolved into widespread antigovernment agitation provoking a crisis in Japanese political leadership. Led by a leftist coalition, the antitreaty movement employed strikes, political boycotts, and a variety of demonstrations. Despite the fact that the treaty was eventually signed and ratified, the protest campaign did push Prime Minister Kishi Nobusuke to resign.

The initial postwar security treaty between Japan and the United States in September 1951, among other things, granted the United States the right to maintain military bases and troops in Japan without a commitment to defend the country. In the late 1950s, pressure for the revision of the treaty began to rise out of a resurgence of Japanese nationalism and a growing dissatisfaction with the presence of the U.S. military bases in Japan. Activists launched "base struggles," in which squads of people were sent to villages surrounding U.S. military bases to educate and organize local citizens against the continuing presence of the bases. These efforts proved to be ineffective in that the base struggles never became a national movement.

In 1957, Kishi Nobusuke became prime minister and expressed a desire to revise the treaty. This stirred considerable debate throughout Japan, and an antirevision movement emerged in the late 1950s out of a coalition of socialists, Communists, *Sohyo* (the General Council of Japanese Trade Unions), and *Zengakuren* (the All-Japan Federation of Student Self-Government Associations). The coalition, called the People's Council for Preventing Revision of the Security Treaty, was created in March 1959.

In the early days of the antitreaty movement, the People's Council organized ten "United Action" days in 1959. These days consisted of strikes and "workshop rallies" by Sohyo unionists, demonstrations, automobile parades, public rallies, petition campaigns, and sit-down protests. Most of the activity was concentrated in Tokyo, but protests occurred in other major cities and some towns as well. During 1959, the propaganda war that would last into the next year began in earnest, as thousands of pamphlets, handbills, essays, articles, and booklets were published and distributed by the antitreaty movement and the Japanese government.

The United Action campaign peaked on November 27, 1959, when thousands demonstrated at the Japanese Diet to protest the Diet's consideration of the proposed revised treaty. Their initial intention was to present mass petitions to their representatives, but part of the crowd, led primarily by students, broke through police lines and stormed into the Diet compound. They stayed all day, singing, shouting, and dancing. This tactical shift provoked considerable debate in the People's Council over

whether to escalate the force and violence of their direct action. Another major militant Zengakuren demonstration occurred on January 15, 1960, when thousands of students occupied part of the Haneda airport in an unsuccessful attempt to prevent Kishi's departure for the United States.

The treaty was signed on January 19, and from that time until mid-May, anti–Security Treaty agitation gradually increased. On May 19, the socialist Diet members staged a sit-in to physically block the speaker of the Diet from entering the room to initiate a vote to extend the session and approve the treaty. Police were called in to carry off the blockaders, and the majority Liberal Democratic Party called a "snap vote" that approved the treaty. This action proved to be the catalyst for the transformation of the antitreaty movement into a more general opposition to the Kishi government.

Demonstrations became even larger and more forceful. Socialist members boycotted the Diet from May 20 to July 18, threatening to resign en masse. Sohyo organized three massive general strikes on June 4, June 15, and June 22 with accompanying demonstrations. During the largest clash between demonstrating students and police, on June 15, a female student from Tokyo University was killed. This incident seemed to awaken widespread outrage throughout the general population. As a result of this protest, President Eisenhower's visit to Japan was cancelled, and, although the treaty was ratified on June 23, Kishi resigned that same day.

One of the consequences of more than two hundred demonstrations from April 1959 to July 1960 and countless tactical discussions was the genesis of a series of new direct-action struggle methods. The People's Council employed a variety of types of demonstrations, for instance. One demonstration favored by Zengakuren activists was the "snake-dance," in which long columns of students would swerve around, bumping into obstacles and police. Other demonstrations included auto caravans and nighttime lantern parades. For many protests, portable religious shrines were brought to the streets to provide guidance for the demonstrators. The demonstrators also utilized "sit-ins" and "break-ins," in which they would break through police lines to occupy cordoned-off areas.

The demonstrations subsided after ratification. Although Kishi was driven from office by the protest movement, he retained much of his political power within the Liberal Democratic Party. However, the anti–Security Treaty protest created a crisis in Japanese politics that led to the resignation of the prime minister. The protest also left a legacy of massive protest and served to boost membership of leftist groups tremendously. Antitreaty protest surfaced again in June 1970, although it was not nearly as widespread or powerful as its predecessor.

Brad Bennett

References

Krauss, Ellis S. *Japanese Radicals Revisited: Student Protest in Postwar Japan.* Berkeley: University of California Press, 1974.

Packard, George R., III. *Protest in Tokyo: The Security Treaty Crisis of 1960.* Princeton: Princeton University Press, 1966.

Jefferson, Thomas (1743–1826)

Third president of the United States, author of the Declaration of Independence, and human rights and peaceable coercion activist. He was born on April 13, 1743, in Shadwell, Virginia, and died on July 4, 1826—on the fiftieth anniversary of the Declaration of Independence.

Thomas Jefferson's parents, Colonel Peter Jefferson and Jane Randolph, gave their son great educational opportunities, from his early private education to his attendance at the College of William and Mary, where he studied the classics. After college, Jefferson studied law for five years under one of the most noted law teachers in Virginia, George Wythe. Jefferson was admitted to the bar at the age of twenty-four.

Like his father, Jefferson was a major Virginia landowner. With ten thousand acres of land, Jefferson was also a planter and was expected, therefore, to play an active role in local government. When he was twenty-five he was elected to the Virginia House of Burgesses and served there until the Revolution.

In May 1774, Jefferson and several of the other young members of the Virginia House of Burgesses met to consider how Virginia could take a bold stand in solidarity with Massachusetts, where the British government was about to close the port of Boston in retaliation for the Boston Tea Party. Jefferson wrote of the meeting: "We were under conviction of the necessity of arousing our people from the lethargy into which they had fallen as to passing events; and thought that the appointment of a day of general fasting and prayer would be most likely to call up and alarm their attention." On May 24, 1774, the House declared June 1, 1774, a day of "Fasting, Humiliation, and Prayer." The governor of Virginia responded to this "hostile" action by dissolving the House two days later. When June 1 finally came, its effect, Jefferson wrote, "was like a shock of electricity, arousing every man and placing him erect and solidly on his centre."

Jefferson's mission was to protect the liberties of his countrymen. To Jefferson, the American Revolution was not only a struggle for independence from Britain, but also a fight for the rights of individuals. As a policymaker, he worked toward a government free of aristocracy and based instead on talent and virtue. One of Jefferson's priorities in his pursuit of freedom was his Bill for Establishing Religious Freedom, which was passed in 1786. This legislation called for the separation of church and state and the freedom for every person to think independently without being chastised.

Jefferson was elected president in 1800. During his two terms as president, Jefferson's political philosophy was twofold. He was dedicated to the democratic principle, which allowed for majority rule and guaranteed basic freedoms such as independent worship and thought.

Jefferson also founded his politics on "conquering without war." He was determined that the United States be a powerful empire of liberty without being a wager of war. When Britain and France in October 1807 assumed the right to seize neutral merchant ships, Jefferson attempted an "experiment in peaceable coercion." He imposed an embargo on all American vessels, which prevented the selling of U.S. products to Britain and its colonies in the West Indies. Since Jefferson saw the British king as the primary offender, the embargo was aimed more at Britain. This was Jefferson's attempt to avoid war while still retaliating. Jefferson used this form of nonviolent direct action to try to regain respect for neutral rights and halt the intrusion on U.S. commerce. Eventually, opposition of U.S. shippers steadily increased, and after two years the embargo was repealed with little coercive effect.

Kimberley A. Pyles

References

Burstein, M.L. *Understanding Thomas Jefferson: Studies in Economics, Law and Philosophy.* New York: St. Martin's, 1993.

Peterson, Merrill D., ed. *Thomas Jefferson: A Reference Biography.* New York: Scribner, 1986.

Sharp, Gene. *The Politics of Nonviolent Action.* Boston, Mass.: Porter Sargent, 1973.

Tucker, Robert W., and Davis C. Hendrickson. *Empire of Liberty: The Statecraft of Thomas Jefferson.* New York: Oxford University Press, 1990.

See also UNITED STATES, INDEPENDENCE MOVEMENT, 1765–1775

Jewish Resistance to the Holocaust

Actions taken by Jews that stood in contradiction to Nazi policy, orders, or perceived intentions. Jewish resistance, both armed and unarmed, was fairly widespread.

Individual resistance included actions such as trying to hide, which in Eastern Europe typically took the form of building underground hiding places in the Jewish ghettos. Very few of these hideouts went undetected, and only a handful of people survived until liberation. Those who survived were hiding in the ghettoes that were the last to be annihilated (Vilno, Kovno, and a number of small places in western Belarus of today). Others hid as Jews among non-Jews, on the "Aryan side" (in Eastern Europe). This depended on continuous support from non-Jewish individuals, and the number of these who were willing to give such support was small in Eastern Europe. Probably about twenty to thirty thousand Jews survived by hiding in Poland, which is less than 1 percent of all Polish Jews who were under Nazi rule before or by 1941. In the West, by contrast, the numbers of Jews rescued were large, in some cases very large. Over two-thirds of the Jews in France survived, largely by hiding. In Belgium, over one-half survived in this way. In the Netherlands, probably over 11 percent of the Jews survived in hiding, in Italy 83 percent. All of these figures also include those who survived by hiding their Jewish identity, which was a common phenomenon especially in the East. Organized efforts to hide Jews in non-Jewish surroundings were limited; an organization

(Zegota) was set up by the Polish underground in Warsaw and elsewhere, whose secretary and many of whose activists were Jews.

The most common Jewish reaction that can be defined as resistance in accordance with the definition offered above was that of organized efforts to maintain a modicum of economic, political, cultural, and religious life in Eastern European ghettos—in Poland (prewar borders), Lithuania, and Latvia—where about 3.3 million Jews were incarcerated, some from 1939 on, others from June of 1941 (the German invasion of the USSR). There were ghettos where smuggling food to supplement the starvation rations supplied by the Germans took an organized form. In others, food smuggling was an individual expression of a determination not to submit to what was perceived as a Nazi desire to starve the Jews to death. The organization of hospitals, of health services generally, of care for orphans, of soup kitchens for the vast numbers of starving people—all these were efforts that stood in contradiction to what were perceived to be Nazi policies. At the hospital in Vilno (Vilnius), for example, the fact that the hospital was treating cases of typhoid was hidden from the Germans by camouflaging a wing of the hospital so that the enemy did not realize it existed. Had the fact of a typhoid epidemic been known, the likelihood was that the whole ghetto would have been destroyed. In Shavli *(Siauliai),* pregnant women were hidden or operated on to cause abortions because pregnancies were forbidden and pregnant women faced death sentences.

In many ghettos schooling was forbidden, though not everywhere and not always. In Warsaw and Vilno, for instance, many small groups of children were taught by professional teachers who were paid pieces of bread for their work. In Warsaw, there was an underground high school that prepared its students for twelfth-grade final examinations. Cultural work was understood to resist a perceived Nazi desire to destroy the morale of the Jews. Over one thousand house committees in Warsaw organized not only social aid and care for preschool children by older youngsters, usually from the Zionist and Bundist youth movements, but also concerts, lectures, and the like. In Vilno, there was a theater, a library, and evenings of singing and musical presentations. Political parties and youth movements organized themselves in underground groups, and in many places they published papers and booklets, as in Warsaw, in Cracow, and in Lithuanian ghettos.

In Poland, the local branch of the U.S-based Jewish philanthropic agency, the Joint Distribution Committee (JDC), was very active in trying to alleviate suffering and organize unarmed resistance to perceived Nazi policies. In Warsaw, it organized house committees, provided an umbrella organization for the underground political parties, financed soup kitchens, and offered social aid. It raised its funds by promising wealthy members of the community that they would receive dollars for their contributions in Polish currency if they survived the war. One of the JDC directors was the famous historian Emmanuel Ringelblum, who was in charge of house committees and political parties and who also organized an underground archive called *Oneg Shabbat* (Delight of Shabbat, the traditional Jewish Friday-evening festivity). There he collected thousands of pages of testimonies from all over Poland of the Jewish fate under the Nazis. Economists, journalists, rabbis, and others were asked to write treatises on specific issues and events. Two-thirds of the archive, which was buried in the ghetto area of Warsaw, were found after the war. This effort to preserve evidence of what the Nazis were doing to the Jews was a major manifestation of unarmed resistance.

In Western Europe, social aid programs emerged, sometimes organized by the Jewish councils under German control. Most activities, however, were organized by underground groups: the JDC, the children's aid organization *Oeuvre secours aux enfants* (OSE) in France, the underground Belgian Jewish-Gentile organization *Comite de Defense des Juifs* (CDJ), and the Italian-Jewish organization *Delegazione Assistenza Emigranti e Profughi Ebrei* (Delasem). Other groups, such as the Jewish Scouts *(Eclaireurs Juifs)* and the *Mouvement de Jeunesse Sioniste* (MJS) in France were engaged in a massive program of hiding Jews, especially Jewish children. In Western Europe, where the general atmosphere was much more friendly than in Eastern Europe, Jewish initiative for rescue, aid, and hiding led in some cases, as in France and Belgium, to armed resistance.

Armed resistance was much more widespread than is usually known, though the effect of Jewish armed resistance on the Germans was almost nil. It was more a way of protest, a desire to be remembered, and a way to take a very small revenge for the horrors committed by the Nazi regime and its supporters. Jews had no arms and no access to arms, because they had no standing in the national resistance movements where these existed. In Poland, the official underground *(Armia Krajowa,* controlled by the London government-in-exile) refused to arm Jews or to help them, with the exception of some token demonstrations during the Warsaw ghetto rebellion. Jews had no government-in-exile, no arms were dropped to them, and no financial help was extended to them by the Allies. The hostility or indifference toward them in the East made armed resistance all but impossible. Yet, once they realized that their fate was to be annihilated, rebellions broke out, and large numbers tried to escape into the forests in order to fight. There were armed groups in seventeen ghettos in central Poland and Lithuania, and there were rebellions in three death camps: Sobibor, Treblinka, and Auschwitz. There were sixty-three ghettos in Belarus with armed groups, most of which tried to escape into the forests. Some seven thousand Jews managed to escape from the ghetto of Minsk into the forests, with the help of the Minsk *Judenrat* (Jewish Council). Up to thirty thousand Jews fought the Germans in East European forests, but most of them perished.

Yehuda Bauer

References

Krakowski, Shmuel. *The War of the Doomed.* New York: Holmes and Meier, 1984.
Trunk, Isaiah. *Judenrat.* New York: Macmillan, 1972.

See also DENMARK, EVACUATION OF DANISH JEWS, 1943; LE CHAMBON SUR LIGNON, FRANCE; NAZISM, CIVILIAN RESISTANCE, 1939–1945; ROSENSTRAßE PROTEST, 1943

Jihad

Key concept in Islamic teaching, related to the obligation of the faithful to spread the faith—the *da'wa,* or "call to Islam," that the Prophet Mohammad required of all followers. It is clear that the catchword of *jihad,* however popular in the Western news media, does not necessarily mean holy war, or violence. The Koranic word for war is *qital,* not *jihad. Jihad* can be interpreted, as it is by leading contemporary Muslim scholars, as a peaceful effort in the pursuit of human needs. Islamic fundamentalists, on the other hand, who subscribe to violence for toppling their governments and silencing their rivals, interpret *jihad* to mean the use of force that serves to legitimate violence for achieving political goals.

The relationship of Islam to nonviolence and nonviolent action is not obvious. In part because the Koran is not explicit on these matters there exist divergent trends. There is also a lack of an accepted authoritative interpretation that links scripture to both its historical context and to the contemporary role of Islam in the world. This is due to the fact that Islamic revelation is believed to be above history. However, as with any scripture, Islamic scripture can be interpreted as open text that permits extremely divergent interpretations. The glorification of violence by some contemporary fundamentalists, however, who selectively reinterpret scripture, without attention to the historical nature of the text as a guide to its meaning, is based on an arbitrary interpretation.

The Koran does not include any consistent or unequivocal general concept for determining violence and nonviolence, for each Koranic verse is related to very specific historical events. Thus, there are Koranic verses that call for nonviolence while others call for war. Historically speaking, this is not a contradiction but a reflection of the specific historical situation in which the respective Koranic verses were revealed in the years between A.D. 610 and 632 in Arabia. In early Meccan Islam, prior to the establishment of the first Islamic polity in Medina, one fails to find Koranic precepts related to violence or nonviolence. Most Meccan verses focus on spiritual issues.

Following the *hijra* (exodus) of the Islamic Prophet and his supporters in 622, he established in Medina the first Islamic political *umma* (community). The relations between this new polity and the surrounding tribes, as a hostile environment, had to be defined in terms of violence and nonviolence. All Koranic verses revealed between 622 and 632 (the Medina years until the death of the Prophet) were the expression of the unfolding process of establishing the polity of Medina as the center of Islam in the violent struggle against the surrounding enemies. Thus there are important differences in teachings on violence and nonviolence between the Meccan and Medinese parts of the Koran.

Furthermore, as noted above, the Koran distinguishes between fighting *(qital)* and *jihad*.

But it is not entirely consistent about whether Muslims should, or must, use violence and force in their obligation to spread the faith. On the one hand, the Koran prescribes fighting for the spread of Islam: "Fighting is obligatory for you, much as you dislike it" (al-Baqara 2:216). On the other hand, while *jihad* encompasses a resort to violence, it is not restricted to violent action. Literally *jihad* means to exert oneself while making an effort to reach a goal. Therefore it is utterly wrong to single out the military meaning of the term and to translate *jihad* exclusively as holy war. *Qital* (fighting) is the proper Koranic term for identifying war against the enemies of Islam. In other words, it is justifiable to interpret *jihad* as an Islamic concept of nonviolence, as do the modern Islamic scholars of al-Azhar.

Textual support for this perspective on nonviolence in Islam can be found in various places. For example, "Do not yield to the unbelievers and use the Koran for your *jihad* (effort) to carry through against them" (al-Furqan 25:52). This Koranic verse clearly shows that *jihad* is not used in the meaning of war. That was, however, in Mecca, where the greatest force that the Koran asked believers to use was the power of argument. In Medina the Koran moved gradually—rooted in its historical context—to provide precepts to *jihad* in the more narrow meaning of *qital* as military fighting.

Violence and Nonviolence in Modern Islam

The duality of violence and nonviolence in Islam takes shape in modern Islam. The nineteenth-century Muslim scholar Ibn Khalid al-Nasiri argued that Islam is simultaneously a "*shari'a* of war" and a "*shari'a* of peace." His preference for the Koranic verse "if they incline to peace then make peace with them" is based on his understanding of the notion of "Islamic interest" *(al-maslaha)*. In his view, Muslims—under the then prevailing conditions of political and social weakness—must come to the conclusion that it is their *maslaha* (interest) not to wage war against unbelievers. This conformism leads to setting nonviolence as the highest priority of Islam.

In the twentieth century, the Sunni Islamic establishment as represented by al-Azhar continues the earlier tradition of Islamic conformism. This tradition includes an interpretation of *jihad* to preclude violence and any use of force. Contrary to this peaceful interpretation of Islamic ethics, Islamic fundamentalists revive the ethics of war in Islam as well as the classic dichotomization of the world. Writing in 1984, for example, Nabil 'Abdulfattah argues that *jihad* is, for Islamic fundamentalists, a call to violence equally against present rulers and the West. In their rebellion against political rulers, fundamentalists introduce a new legitimacy for resisting political authority in Islam.

The Fundamentalist Interpretation of *Jihad*
Unlike the al-Azhar tradition, which seeks to read the scripture in the light of the present, Islamic fundamentalists are inclined to restore the literal authority of the text as *sola scriptura*. For them, a true Muslim has to view reality in the light of the text. Islamic fundamentalists ought not to be equated with Islam as a whole as is usually done by the news media in the West—Islam is a thirteen-centuries-old civilization, whereas fundamentalism is a recent trend within Islam. In terms of mass movements, Islamic fundamentalism dates only to the 1970s, though its roots can be traced back to the late 1920s, when the Muslim Brotherhood (al-Ikhwan-al-Muslimun) was founded in Egypt by Hasan al-Banna. Al-Banna, along with Sayyid Qutb, the movement's major ideologue, remain the leading authorities in the formulation of the political thought of Islamic fundamentalism.

Among the treatises of Hasan al-Banna is his *risalat al-jihad* (treatise on *jihad*), republished in 1990, in which he makes literal use of the Koran and the *hadith* to support conclusions radically different from those of the al-Azhar tradition. This treatise begins with the assertion that the *jihad* is a "*farida* (obligation) for every Muslim." As shown earlier, *jihad* and *qital* are used in the Koran with different meanings and nuances. However, al-Banna uses *jihad* and *qital* interchangeably and as equivalent to the use of force, whether in pursuit of resistance against existing regimes or of war against "unbelievers." Al-Banna begins his treatise in quoting the al-Baqara verse "Fighting is obligatory for you, much as you dislike it" (2:216) and continues with another verse: "If you should die or be slain in the cause for Allah, his mercy will surely be better than all the riches they amass" ('Imran 3:158).

These quotes and others provide the basis for the glorification of fighting and death for the "cause of Allah" as understood by al-Banna, who assures his followers of the Koranic promise in al-Nisa': "We shall richly reward them," regardless of "whether they die or conquer" (4:74). Instead of referring to the tolerant Koranic verses from al-Kafirun, "You have your religion and I have mine," al-Banna extends his notion of the obligation of the *qital* even against the *ahl al-kitab* (people of the book—that is, Christians and Jews) as he introduces the following Koranic verse: "Fight against those who neither believe in Allah nor in the Last Day . . . until they pay tribute out of hand and are utterly subdued" (al-Tauba 9:29).

In a subsequent section with the heading "Why do Muslims Fight?" he again emphasizes the equation of *jihad* and *qital* and adds: "Allah has obliged Muslims to fight . . . to secure the pursuit of *al-da'wa* and thus of peace, while disseminating the great mission which God entrusted to them." It becomes clear that al-Banna views peace in an inclusivist manner—nonviolence is possible only under the banner of Islam, and non-Muslims can live only "utterly subdued" as *dhimmi* (protected minorities) under global Islamic rule. In all other cases, the use of force is an unavoidable religious duty. Al-Banna also distinguishes between *al-jihad al-asghar* ("low" *jihad*) and *al-jihad al-akbar* ("high" *jihad)*. He ridicules those Muslims who consider *qital* to be low *jihad* in comparison to "*jihad al-nafs,*" meaning to exert oneself. We are now familiar with the fact that the latter term (exertion) is the original meaning of *jihad* in the Koran. In al-Banna's view, those who downgrade *qital* as fighting "make an effort to distract the people from the importance of *qital* as the intention of the *jihad*. . . . The great reward for the Muslims who fight is to kill or to be killed for the sake of Allah."

Al-Banna concludes his treatise with the rhetoric of the glorification of violence. The major fundamentalist groups currently active in the world, whether in Algeria or Egypt, not only commit themselves ethically to an interpretation of *jihad* as violent but also practice this view in killing their Muslim adversaries. They renounce the al-Azhar interpretation of *jihad* as a legitimation of the existing political regimes that these fundamentalists seek to overthrow.

The al-Azhar Interpretation of *Jihad*
The more traditional Islamic interpretation of *jihad* is found in the texts of one of the former Azhar sheikhs, Mahmud Shaltut, published in 1980. Here we find the assertion that Islam is a religion intended to be embraced by all humanity, but combined with an acknowledgment of Islam's openness to pluralism. Supporting

pluralism, Shaltut quotes the Koran: "We have created you as peoples and tribes to make you know one another" (al-Hujrat 49:13). He also rejects the notion that Islam needs to resort to violence for the spread of its beliefs, again quoting the Koran: "Had Allah wanted, all people of the earth would have believed in him, would you dare then force faith upon them?" (Jonah 10:99). From this interpretation it follows that violence is an improper instrument for pursuing the *da'wa*. Shaltut presents the authoritative view that Muslims must live with non-Muslims in peace, since "war is the immoral situation." Shaltut thus established nonviolence as the authentic Islamic view of morality.

The most recent authoritative two-volume textbook edited by the former sheikh of al-Azhar, the late Jadul-haq Ali Jadulhaq, continues the effort to establish an understanding of the ethics of nonviolence in Islam that takes precedence over any use of force. In the chapter on *jihad* in the first volume, the textbook asserts that *jihad* in itself does not mean war. If we want to talk about war, the Azhar textbook argues, then we have to add: *"al-jihad al-musallah* (armed *jihad)"* in contrast to the everyday *"jihad* against ignorance, *jihad* against poverty, *jihad* against disease. . . . The search for knowledge is the highest level of *jihad."*

Having interpreted *jihad* in this manner as nonviolence, the authoritative textbook downgrades the meaning of "armed *jihad*" since the *da'wa* for Islam can be pursued without fighting. The Azhar textbook states in this regard: "In earlier ages the sword was necessary for securing the path of the *da'wa*. In our age, however, the sword has lost its importance, albeit the resort to it is still important for the cause of defense against those who wish to do evil to Islam and its people. However, for the dissemination of the *da'wa* there are now a variety of ways. . . . Those who focus on arms in our times are preoccupied with weak instruments. . . ."

This textbook also does not present the *da'wa* as requiring the violent imposition of Islam on others: "The *da'wa* is an offer to join in, not an imposition. . . . Belief is not for imposition with force." Earlier Meccan verses (such as "You have your religion, I have mine," or "There is no compulsion in religion") are quoted repeatedly in an effort to separate the *da'wa* from any notion of *qital* or *jihad musallah*. Despite this substantial reinterpretation, the textbook of al-Azhar nevertheless continues to maintain that Islam is a mission for all

of humanity in quoting the Koran: "We have sent you forth as a blessing to mankind" (al-Anbiya' 21:107).

Conclusion

In sum, while the Koran does not prescribe an explicit ethic of nonviolence, neither does it give higher value to actions of violence. An interpretation following from current teaching of the scholars of al-Ahzar nevertheless shows that both in its historical roots and in its teaching for the contemporary world, Islam tends to give moral precedence to nonviolence. One can conclude that the pursuit of even religiously oriented or informed struggle in the modern world by the methods of nonviolent action is fully consistent with both scripture and this teaching. And the politically narrow interpretation of *jihad* by contemporary fundamentalists should not be misconstrued as providing the guidance for the behavior of Muslims as Islamic civilization adapts to contemporary circumstances.

The necessary cultural accommodation by Muslims to a changed international environment, in which an Islamic commitment to an ethic of nonviolence is urgently needed, is one of the great challenges facing Islamic civilization at the end of the twentieth century. International relations scholars who study the culturally divergent attitudes toward war and peace fear the separation of the international system into parts committed to nonviolence and others that glorify violence. Enlightened Muslims are challenged to reverse this trend and to reestablish the Islamic commitment to nonviolence.

Bassam Tibi

References

'Abdulfattah, Nabil. *Al-mashaf wa al saif.* Cairo: Madbuli, 1984.

Al-Banna, Hasan. *Five Tracts of Hasan al-Banna (1906–1949): A Selection from the Majmu'at Rasa'il al-Imam al-Shahid Hasan al-Banna.* Translated by Charles Wendell. Berkeley: University of California Press, 1978.

———. *Majmu'at Rasa'il al-Imam al-Shahid Hasan al-Banna.* Cairo: Dar al-Da'wa, New Legal Edition, 1990.

Bell, Richard, and William Montgomery Watt, eds. *Introduction to the Qur'an.* Edinburgh: University Press, 1970.

Husni, 'Abdullatif. *Al-Islam wa al-'alaqat al-duwaliyya. Namudhaj Ahmed ben Khalid al-Nasiri.* Casablanca:

Afriqya al-Sharq, 1991.

Jadulhaq, Jadul-haq 'Ali. *Bayan ila al-nas.* 2 vols. Cairo: Al-Azhar, 1984, 1988.

Khadduri, Majid. *War and Peace in the Law of Islam.* Baltimore: Johns Hopkins University Press, 1955.

The Koran (Arabic). Tunis: Mu'assasat 'Abdulkarim ben 'Abdullah. n.d.

The Koran. English translation by N.J. Dawood. 4th rev. ed. New York: Penguin Book Classics, 1974.

Lewis, Bernard. "Politics and War." In *The Legacy of Islam,* edited by Joseph Schacht and C.E. Bosworth. 2nd ed. Oxford: Clarendon, 1974.

Shadid, Muhammed. *Al-jihad fi al-Islam.* 7th ed. Cairo: Al-Risalah, 1985.

Shaltut, Mahmud. *Al-Islam aqidah wa shari'a.* 10th ed. Cairo: Dar al-Shuruq, 1980.

Tibi, Bassam. *Conflict and War in the Middle East.* New York: St. Martin's, 1993.

———. *The Crisis of Modern Islam: A Preindustrial Culture in the Scientific-Technological Age.* Salt Lake City: University of Utah Press, 1988.

———. *Islam and the Cultural Accommodation of Social Change.* Boulder, Colo.: Westview, 1990.

———: "The World View of Sunni Arab Fundamentalists." In *Fundamentalisms and Society,* edited by Martin Marty and Scott Appleby. Chicago: University of Chicago Press, 1993.

Watt, William Montgomery. *Islamic Fundamentalism and Modernity.* London: Routledge, 1988.

See also RELIGION AND NONVIOLENT ACTION

Jones, "Mother" Mary Harris (1830–1930)

Labor organizer, born in Cork, Ireland, on May 1, 1830, and died in Silver Spring, Maryland, on November 30, 1930.

Mary Harris emigrated from Ireland to North America with her father, a railroad construction worker, and spent her youth in Toronto, Canada. After leaving home she lived in Michigan, where she worked as a teacher, and then in Chicago, where she opened a dressmaking business. She became a teacher again in Tennessee, where she married George Jones, an active member of the Iron Molders' Union, in 1861.

The next decade was marked by tragedy. In 1867, her husband and four children died in a yellow fever epidemic in Memphis. After helping other victims of the epidemic, she moved to Chicago and worked as a dressmaker, but she lost everything in the Great Fire of 1871. While sheltered with others made homeless by the fire, Mary Jones began to attend lectures by members of the Knights of Labor. From that time on, she devoted her life to the cause of workers' rights.

In 1877 she worked in support of the striking railroad employees in Pittsburgh, but, from 1880 on, she was an itinerant labor organizer, moving from one place to another to help the workers. She became most closely aligned with coal miners. On many occasions, she mobilized an "army of women"—strikers' wives who brought their babies, brooms, and mops to the picket lines to improve the morale of the miners and to attract public attention to their cause. Jones told the women: "Whatever the fight, don't be ladylike!" In 1895, she helped start a socialist labor paper, *Appeal to Reason,* which she used for many years as an organizing tool.

At the turn of the century, she carried the *Appeal* to labor struggles in West Virginia, Nebraska, Kansas, and Tennessee. About this time, she came to be known as "Mother Jones." In the first two decades of the twentieth century, Jones supported or helped organize various struggles by miners in the Pennsylvania and Colorado coalfields, workers in the copper mines of Idaho and Arizona, and garment workers and streetcar workers in New York City. Jones had no permanent address. She said, "I abide wherever there is a fight against wrong."

In the spring of 1903, Mother Jones worked toward the abolition of child labor and organized the March of the Mill Children, accompanying young workers from the textile mills of Kensington, Pennsylvania, to the home of Theodore Roosevelt on Long Island in an unsuccessful attempt to confront the president. As with other actions, Jones succeeded in stirring news media attention and inspired a lively debate about child labor in the United States.

Well into her nineties, Jones continued to travel the country delivering fiery speeches. In 1921, Jones was hailed a heroine at the Pan-American Federation of Labor congress in Mexico City. Her motto was "Pray for the dead and fight like hell for the living." She died seven months after a celebration of her one hundredth birthday, muttering "what the hell, what the hell," and was buried in the Miners' Cemetery in Mt. Olive, Illinois.

Pam McAllister

References

Jones, Mary Harris. *The Autobiography of Mother Jones*. Chicago: Charles H. Kerr, 1925/1980.

Long, Priscilla. *Mother Jones, Woman Organizer: And Her Relations with Miners' Wives, Working Women, and the Suffrage Movement*. Boston: South End, 1976.

K

Kapp Putsch (Germany), 1920

Mass nonviolent noncooperation by citizens of the Weimar Republic to defend against a putsch (coup d'état) led by Wolfgang Kapp and top military officers. Encouraged by a government-in-exile, the popular resistance was widespread and included a mass general strike and other forms of noncooperation. Refusal to consent to an illegitimate authority led to the defeat of Kapp and his supporters.

Following the signing of the Peace Treaty of Versailles in June 1919, resentment began to build in certain rightist political parties and military circles. Military officers and troops were especially opposed to troop reduction deadlines imposed by the Allies on March 10 and April 10, 1920. In early March 1920, representatives from the opposition parties demanded the resignation of President Friedrich Ebert, the dissolution of the National Assembly, and the organization of new elections. Ebert's cabinet threatened to call a general strike if the rightists used military force to attempt to overthrow the republic, but they refused to call for military steps to prevent such a coup.

After Ebert rejected rightist demands on March 9 and unsuccessfully attempted to arrest suspected coup leaders, civil servant Wolfgang Kapp and several army officers led by General Baron Walter von Luttwitz set out for Berlin on March 12 with a contingent of recently dismissed soldiers. The Ebert government fled to Dresden, while insurgent troops occupied government buildings without resistance on March 13. Kapp then declared a new government of "order, freedom and action."

The government-in-exile immediately proclaimed that the German people would refuse to cooperate with the Kapp regime and would heed only the legal government and called for a general strike. This proclamation precipitated a general strike throughout Berlin, which virtually paralyzed economic life and significantly hampered the new regime's ability to control the population. Not even "essential services" were exempt from this general strike. Berlin printers, for example, went on strike after paramilitary units occupied two newspapers. Strikes spread to several other German cities, despite shootings of workers by the coup forces. By the afternoon of March 14, participation in the general strike was almost total. Kapp attempted to break the strike and outlaw picketing but without success.

Popular resistance to the Kappists took several forms. Many bureaucrats and political experts refused to collaborate with Kapp. New government posts were left unfilled as people rejected appointments. The national bank refused Kapp's request for money to pay his soldiers. Military loyalty seemed split between Ebert and Kapp. Some troops and staff officers refused orders from the new regime. During the general strike, workers fraternized with Kappist troops in an effort to persuade them to join the resistance. The Berlin Security Police demanded Kapp's resignation.

On March 15, President Ebert rejected Kapp's proposals for compromise. Leaflets calling for mass resistance to Kapp's regime were dropped over Berlin by airplane. Realizing the futility of governing without the participation of civil servants and the consent of the German people, Kapp and Luttwitz resigned on March 17 and fled Berlin. The next day, occupying troops left Berlin at the behest of the Ebert government. On their way out, troops shot at civilians, killing and wounding some.

Ebert and his government reassumed ruling powers on March 20, soon after the successful four-day campaign of nonviolent noncooperation. On March 23, the strike ended in spite of conflict between trade unions and the Ebert regime over reforms. The noncooperation campaign represents a significant example of the successful use of nonviolent civilian defense to prevent coup leaders from gaining political power and control.

Brad Bennett

References

Eyck, Erich. *A History of the Weimar Republic.* Translated by Harlan P. Hanson and Robert G.L. Waite. Cambridge: Harvard University Press, 1962.

Goodspeed, D.J. *The Conspirators: A Study of the Coup D'état.* New York: Viking, 1961.

Halperin, S. William. *Germany Tried Democracy: A Political History of the Reich from 1918 to 1933.* Hamden, Conn.: Archon, 1946.

See also CIVILIAN-BASED DEFENSE

Khan Abdul Ghaffar Khan (1890–1988)

Pathan leader and Muslim follower of Mahatma Gandhi, founded the Khudai Khidmatgars, "Servants of God," the world's first nonviolent "army." Abdul Ghaffar Khan, later known as Badshah Khan and the "Frontier Gandhi," was born in the village of Utmanzai near Peshawar in the North-West Frontier Province of British India, a rugged area around the Khyber Pass kept under heavy military governance because of its strategic importance as the "gateway to India." The son of a pious mother and a respected village headman, Ghaffar Khan early on showed a passionate desire to help his proud but impoverished people, who were divided by a violent code of vendetta binding from generation to generation. In 1910, he opened a school in his village and began experiments in rural development including education, public health, and the emancipation of women—all activities regarded by the British as seditious on the rebellious North-West Frontier Province.

Like Martin Luther King, Jr., Abdul Ghaffar Khan had an important religious experience before committing his life to nonviolence, which came when he was observing a *chilla,* a period of intense prayer and fasting, in 1914. British authorities had just closed his schools,

and it was evident that the social and political development and elevation of his people required freedom from foreign rule. Mahatma Gandhi was organizing India to seek independence through satyagraha, completely nonviolent civil resistance, and Ghaffar Khan was deeply drawn to his ideas. Again like King, he said later that he came to understand the nonviolent teaching of his own religion through Gandhi: "[Nonviolence] was followed fourteen hundred years ago by the Prophet [Mohammed] all the time he was in Mecca. . . . But we had so far forgotten it that when Gandhi placed it before us, we thought he was sponsoring a novel creed." To the astonishment of British and Indians alike, large numbers of the fierce Pathans responded to Gandhi's call to national nonviolence in 1919 under the leadership of Ghaffar Khan. Such activities were dealt with harshly in the Frontier, and Ghaffar Khan spent much of the 1920s in prison.

By 1929, the whole of India was ready for revolution. Gandhi secured a commitment to complete nonviolence. Ghaffar Khan finally met Gandhi toward the end of the year, but apparently did not confide in him that he had already embarked on one of the most astonishing experiments in history: five hundred of his countrymen had laid down their guns and become nonviolent soldiers in an "army" dedicated to village service. Uniformed, disciplined, but unarmed, they swore to uphold nonviolent principles. Their pledge read, in part: "I am a Khudai Khidmatgar [servant of God], and as God needs no service . . . I promise to serve humanity in the name of God. I promise to refrain from violence and from taking revenge. I promise to forgive those who oppress me or treat me with cruelty. I promise to devote at least two hours a day to social work."

The Khudai Khidmatgars had been organized for public service; they organized village work projects and opened schools. But within months they were called on for much more heroic action. On December 31, 1929, the Indian National Congress declared independence from Great Britain. Gandhi launched nationwide civil disobedience—the epic "salt satyagraha"—and millions were arrested in nonviolent resistance. The volatile Frontier was immediately sealed off, but when reliable reports began to come in, Indians were astonished to learn that despite mass firings on unarmed crowds, torture, and the systematic destruction and pillaging of whole villages by British troops, the Khudai Khidmatgars had kept the pledge of nonviolence and faced their oppressors without retaliation but without retreat. Such was the Pathan spirit that as repression mounted, so did enrollment in the Khudai Khidmatgars: at the height of the movement, more than eighty thousand Pathans had joined, including many women and children. Even Gandhi was amazed. "That such men," he wrote, "who would have killed a human being with no more thought than they would have for killing a sheep or a hen, should at the bidding of one man have laid down their arms and accepted nonviolence as the superior weapon sounds almost like a fairy tale."

In January 1931, the British viceroy, Lord Irwin, released Gandhi and negotiated a remarkable truce, the so-called Gandhi–Irwin Pact. Resistance was called off and political prisoners were released. Abdul Ghaffar Khan was released from prison and returned to the Frontier to resume his life's work of village uplift and development. To the Pathans he was now Badshah Khan, their "king"; to the rest of India he was the "Frontier Gandhi," the embodiment of what Gandhi himself called "the nonviolence of the brave."

By December 1931, the truce had broken down under a new viceroy and India entered a fresh round of repression—in the North-West Frontier, the worst in the history of the Raj. Badshah Khan was again imprisoned and British troops began a brutal, systematic attempt to destroy the Khudai Khidmatgars and provoke the Pathans to violence. Gandhi finally suspended satyagraha again in 1934, and Abdul Ghaffar Khan was released but banned from the Frontier. Ironically, the ban allowed him and his brother, Dr. Khan Saheb, a deeply fruitful stay at Mahatma Gandhi's ashram in Sevagram.

In 1935, the long years of satyagraha bore first fruit in the Government of India Act, which conceded elections for provincial parliaments throughout India. Badshah Khan had been imprisoned again to keep him from public speaking, but the Muslim Frontier voted overwhelmingly in support of the Indian National Congress over the Muslim League. For the first time since foreign domination, the Pathans had their own government, with Dr. Khan Saheb as chief minister. Badshah Khan was released and resumed his rural reforms. In 1938, Gandhi visited the province twice and, typically, exhorted the Pathans to even greater effort in demonstrating to the world the "nonviolence of the brave." By this time, with Jawaharlal Nehru and a few others, Badshah Khan was part of Gandhi's most intimate circle of advisers and Congress party leaders.

World War II divided Indian loyalties sharply. Gandhi's "Quit India" movement in 1942 was immediately joined by Badshah Khan, and both were again imprisoned; but when the war was over, all political prisoners were released and the new Labour government in London began preparations for Indian independence. The transition was marked by fearful riots over Muslim League demands for a separate Muslim state. Badshah Khan, like Gandhi, pleaded for unity. The Frontier, though overwhelmingly Muslim, had never aligned itself with the Muslim League; but Indian leaders, under intense pressure, gave in to a referendum that the Khudai Khidmatgars boycotted, and in the fever of the times the rest of the Frontier elected to become part of Pakistan.

Badshah Khan's struggles continued to the end of his life. The new Pakistani government immediately disbanded the elected ministry of the Frontier and silenced Badshah Khan's journal. Within a year he was in prison again—this time in his own country—for seeking democratic rights for his people, including a province of their own as was enjoyed by the other ethnic populations of Pakistan. In the next three decades, he spent fifteen years in prison and seven in exile, while Pakistan suffered through periods of military dictatorship and martial law. Whenever he was freed, he resumed working for the rights and welfare of his people. In 1956, between periods of imprisonment, he joined other leaders to found Pakistan's first social democratic party. In 1962, Amnesty International declared him Prisoner of the Year. He visited India in 1969 as a guest of the government for the Gandhi birth centenary, and again in 1987 to receive India's highest civilian honor, the Jewel of India award, from Prime Minister Rajiv Gandhi. He was nominated for the Nobel Prize for Peace in 1983 and 1984. The "Frontier Gandhi" died in Peshawar on January 20, 1988, after almost eighty years of public service, more than thirty of which were spent in jail.

Besides the significance of the Khudai Khidmatgars for the growing movement toward nonviolent peace brigades, Badshah Khan's life refutes three common myths: that nonviolence is a weapon of the weak, that it works only against "civilized" adversaries, and—of particular interest today—that it is not part of Islam.

Eknath Easwaran

References

Desai, Mahadev. *Two Servants of God*. Delhi: Hindustan Times, 1935.

Easwaran, Eknath. *A Man to Match His Mountains: Badshah Khan, Nonviolent Soldier of Islam*. Petaluma, Calif.: Nilgiri, 1984.

Khan, Abdul Ghaffar. *My Life and Struggle*. Delhi: Hind, 1969.

Tendulkar, D.G. *Abdul Ghaffar Khan: Faith Is a Battle*. Bombay: Gandhi Peace Foundation (Popular Prakashan), 1967.

Yunus, Mohammed. *Frontier Speaks*. Hind Kitabs, 1947.

Zutshi, G.L. *Frontier Gandhi: The Fighter, the Politician, the Saint*. Delhi: National Publishing House, 1970.

See also GANDHI, MOHANDAS KARAMCHAND; INDIAN NATIONAL CONGRESS; INDIAN NATIONAL MOVEMENT; JIHAD; PATHAN DEFIANCE, 1929–1938

Coretta Scott King. Photo © Coretta Scott King Collection.

King, Coretta Scott (b. 1929)

Wife of Martin Luther King, Jr., civil rights activist, and the founding president and chief executive officer of the Martin Luther King, Jr., Center for Nonviolent Social Change. She was born on April 27, 1929, in Marion, Alabama, the town in which she was also raised.

Although Coretta Scott's parents were not well educated, they dedicated themselves to the education of their three children. Coretta Scott graduated from Lincoln High School as valedictorian in 1945. She continued her education at Antioch College in Ohio, where she received a partial scholarship and was treated relatively equally to white students.

Coretta Scott had long been interested in music, and in college that interest developed into a passion. When she decided to become a music teacher, Antioch offered her a student teacher position at an all-black, Antioch-affiliated demonstration elementary school. She, however, wanted to teach at a white public school, but the college rejected the idea. Coretta Scott vehemently protested this. She encouraged her classmates to join the protest, but they would not for fear of expulsion. Coretta Scott sought help from several Antioch officials including the president, but she received no encouragement. She eventually gave in and took the teaching position at the all-black school.

In 1951, while studying on a fellowship at the New England Conservatory of Music in Boston to become a concert singer, Coretta Scott met Martin Luther King, Jr., who was then a doctoral student in theology at Boston University. After a sixteen-month courtship, they were married on June 18, 1953, in Alabama. The following year, Coretta received a Bachelor of Music degree. She and Dr. King then settled in Montgomery, Alabama, where Martin was pastor of the Dexter Avenue Baptist Church.

As Dr. King became a prominent leader in the civil rights movement, Coretta often substituted for her husband as a speaker and as a leader of marches. She also frequently addressed groups independent of Dr. King's work and often performed Freedom Concerts, which consisted of poetry and prose that described the civil rights movement. In 1958, when Dr. King was stabbed in New York City while autographing books, Coretta Scott King immediately traveled to the hospital and stayed with him while he recovered. When she was not at her husband's bedside, she was working in the office that was set up in the hospital for her to conduct civil rights business.

In 1968, when Martin was assassinated, although she was devastated, Coretta Scott

King remained strong. Through her strength and composure, she helped the country to mourn the loss of a great leader. She maintained her courage in the face of her husband's death and dedicated herself to keeping his spirit and work alive through her continued efforts for civil rights. Coretta Scott King has carried on the message of Dr. King in many ways, but one of the most tangible is through the Martin Luther King, Jr., Center for Nonviolent Social Change in Atlanta, Georgia, which she established in 1969. The center serves not only as a memorial to the fallen leader but also as a place for teaching generations about the life and work of Dr. King and his commitment to nonviolent action.

Coretta Scott King has traveled throughout the world on several peace missions both with her husband and independently. She has led goodwill missions in Latin America and Africa and has addressed two of the world's largest peace rallies in Germany and New York. In addition, she worked for broader peace issues, such as when she served as a delegate for a Women's Strike for Peace to the seventeen-nation Disarmament Conference in Switzerland in 1962.

Kimberley A. Pyles

References

Garrow, David J. *Bearing the Cross: Martin Luther King, Jr. and the Southern Christian Leadership Conference*. New York: Vintage, 1988.

Vivian, Octavia. *Coretta*. Philadelphia: Fortress, 1970.

See also KING, MARTIN LUTHER, JR.

King, Martin Luther, Jr. (1929–1968)

African-American civil rights and religious leader, proponent of Gandhian concepts of nonviolent political activism, and recipient of the 1964 Nobel Prize for Peace.

Martin Luther King, Jr., was a product of and a major contributor to the African-American tradition of social gospel Christianity. From the time of his birth on January 15, 1929, in the Atlanta home his parents shared with his grandparents, he was immersed in the tradition of politically engaged religion. His grandfather, the Reverend A.D. Williams, had been a founder of Atlanta's chapter of the National Association for the Advancement of Colored People (NAACP)

Martin Luther King, Jr. Photo © The Martin Luther King, Jr., Estate.

and often used his pastorate at Ebenezer Baptist Church as a base for political activism. After Williams's death in 1931, Martin Luther King, Sr., succeeded him as Ebenezer's pastor and also became an NAACP leader, organizing voting rights marches during the mid-1930s and later guiding efforts to bring the salaries of African-American teachers to the level of those of white teachers.

Youthful religious skepticism initially caused the younger King to reject his inherited calling, but his growing concern about social justice issues was evident in high school orations and undergraduate writings at Atlanta's Morehouse College (1944–1948). The summer after his sophomore year in college, he responded to a wave of postwar antiblack violence by proclaiming in a letter published in the *Atlanta Constitution* that African Americans were "entitled to the basic rights and opportunities of American citizens." During his senior year, King joined the Intercollegiate Council, an interracial student discussion group that met monthly at Atlanta's Emory University. He also responded readily to the weekly talks of Morehouse President Benjamin E. Mays, who urged students to pursue lives of service and undoubtedly informed them about his travels in India and his interest in

Gandhian protest methods. Religion professor George Kelsey exposed King to biblical criticism, strengthening his rebellion against religious fundamentalism while also encouraging him to believe "that behind the legends and myths of the Book were many profound truths which one could not escape." King later remarked that he saw Mays and Kelsey as deeply religious yet also learned men—"the ideal of what I wanted a minister to be." By the beginning of his senior year, King later recounted, such academic role models and the "noble example" of his father led him to overcome earlier doubts and respond to an "inner urge" calling him to "serve humanity" by becoming an ordained minister.

After enrolling at Pennsylvania's Crozer Theological Seminary (1948–1951), King refined his eclectic social gospel perspective. Marxist readings reinforced his "anti-capitalist feelings," but King rejected Marx's materialism and ethical relativism in favor of a synthesis of liberal and orthodox Christian perspectives. As he later explained in his first book, *Stride toward Freedom* (1958), his determined search for religious cogency led him to the theology of personalism as a "grounding for the idea of a personal God" and as a "metaphysical basis for the dignity and worth of all human personality." Despite King's continuing identification with social gospel Christianity, he nevertheless recalled that at Crozer he "despaired of the power of love in solving social problems." Listening to A.J. Muste argue for pacifism, he remained unpersuaded, believing that war "might be preferable to surrender to a totalitarian system—Nazi, Fascist, or Communist." King later claimed that a 1949 sermon on Gandhi by Howard University President Mordecai Johnson had a more positive impact, and family friend J. Pius Barbour recalled that King often argued for Gandhian methods during his Crozer years. These recollections suggest that, even if King's understanding of Gandhian principles remained cursory during his college years, he was familiar with the well-established African-American Gandhian tradition, as exemplified in Mays, William Stuart Nelson, and Howard Thurman.

He did not join any pacifist group while a seminary student or as a graduate student at Boston University (1951–1955), where he studied systematic theology. Indeed, as a student, King was less involved in pacifist politics than was his future wife, Coretta Scott (married in 1953), who had associated with pacifist groups during her undergraduate years at Antioch and

had attended the 1948 Progressive Party convention as a student delegate. In contrast, King remembered struggling during the early 1950s with Reinhold Niebuhr's argument that pacifism was based on a naive sectarian perfectionism that does not fully account for the "reality of sin on every level of man's existence." In response to Niebuhr's critique, King recalled that he sought "a realistic pacifism" that would be cognizant of "the complexity of man's social involvement and the glaring reality of collective evil."

After accepting the pastorate of Dexter Avenue Baptist Church in Montgomery, Alabama, King unexpectedly became the principal spokesman for the bus boycott movement that began in December 1955 when Rosa Parks refused to give up her seat on a segregated bus. As president of the Montgomery Improvement Association (MIA), King strengthened his commitment to and comprehension of Gandhian ideas, consistently basing his advocacy of nonviolence on Christian beliefs. As he explained in his first address to an MIA mass meeting, "We believe in the teachings of Jesus. The only weapon that we have in our hands this evening is the weapon of protest." After white racists bombed his home in late January 1956, he restrained angry black residents by citing Christian admonitions against retaliatory violence: "He who lives by the sword will perish by the sword. Remember that is what God said. We are not advocating violence. We want to love our enemies." As King later commented in *Stride toward Freedom,* Gandhian ideas were not mentioned in his initial MIA speeches: "It was the Sermon on the Mount, rather than a doctrine of passive resistance, that initially inspired the Negroes of Montgomery to dignified social action."

After the bombing, however, King gradually moved toward an explicit advocacy of Gandhian precepts. This movement was encouraged by the arrival in Montgomery of two veteran pacifists: Bayard Rustin, executive secretary of the War Resisters League, and Glenn E. Smiley, field secretary of the Fellowship of Reconciliation. Rustin and Smiley were at first disturbed that King saw no inconsistency between promoting nonviolence and arranging for an armed bodyguard but also found him receptive to their advice. As Smiley wrote in late February to an associate: "At first King was asked to merely be the spokesman of the movement, but as sometimes happens, he has really become the real leader and symbol of growing magnitude. If he can really be won to a faith in nonviolence there is no end to what he can do." By the spring of 1956, King was in contact not only with Rustin and Smiley but also with other knowledgeable Gandhians, including Richard Gregg, Harris Wofford, and William Stuart Nelson. King's first article on the boycott, written with Rustin's help and published in the pacifist journal *Liberation* (April 1956), described the boycott as a "movement of passive resistance" utilizing "the instrument of love." Increasingly, King cited Gandhi's example to demonstrate the potential effectiveness of nonviolent methods. "A little brown man in India tried it," he commented in May. "He decides to confront physical force with soul force." Even as King became more familiar with Gandhian methods, however, his guiding ideas remained a distinctive blend of Gandhian precepts, Christian teachings, and tactical exigencies. During this period, King explained that "the spirit of passive resistance came to me from the Bible, from the teachings of Jesus. The techniques came from Gandhi."

As Montgomery black residents sustained their boycott movement, King expanded his influence as a successful practitioner of Gandhian protest techniques. A November 1956 memorandum written by King indicates that by this time he had formulated the nonviolent strategy that he would follow for the remainder of his life. His listing of five basic principles of nonviolence codified ideas that would be restated in later speeches and writings. This formulation derived from Gandhi's teachings as interpreted by American proponents who had been in contact with King. First, King noted a distinction between nonresistance to evil and militant nonviolent opposition to evil: "This is not a method of cowardice or stagnant passivity; it does resist." Second, King insisted that the goal of nonviolent action was not "to defeat or humiliate the opponent" but to "win his friendship and understanding." Third, he distinguished between seeking to defeat the "forces of evil" and "persons caught in the force." Fourth, King asserted that nonviolence "not only avoids external physical violence, but also internal violence of spirit." Later, in *Stride toward Freedom,* he would expand upon this point, merging Christian and Gandhian principles in the concept of *agape*—that is, "an overflowing love which seeks nothing in return." Fifth, King expressed his conviction that

nonviolent methods would ultimately triumph because "the universe is on the side of justice," an assertion that in *Stride toward Freedom* he would transform into a religious affirmation that "God is on the side of truth and justice."

King's basic commitment to Gandhian nonviolence remained steadfast after the successful conclusion of the Montgomery boycott movement. As the president of the Southern Christian Leadership Conference (SCLC, founded in 1957), King often sought to guide local protest movements that utilized nonviolent tactics yet resisted outside control. The expanding southern civil rights movement produced tactical and strategic competition. During the early 1960s, student activists in the Student Nonviolent Coordinating Committee (SNCC) challenged King's charismatic leadership style by insisting that the guiding ideas of the southern civil rights struggle should come from the grassroots level rather than be imposed by national leaders such as King. SNCC activists also pushed King toward more aggressive use of direct action tactics, especially sit-ins and other forms of civil disobedience. James Lawson, a Gandhian proponent who exerted considerable influence in the Nashville student movement and was one of SNCC's founders, initially exerted greater influence than King over SNCC, although, as the southern desegregation campaign expanded during the early 1960s, many student activists came to accept nonviolence on tactical rather than philosophical grounds.

Recognizing that he had only limited ability to guide the wave of southern protests culminating in the 1963 Birmingham campaign, King became only one of the black struggle's many ideological leaders. In addition to challenges from within the civil rights movement, King was aware that black nationalist leaders such as Malcolm X were attracting growing support from frustrated African Americans. In his famous "Letter from Birmingham City Jail," written in the spring of 1963, he described himself as standing between the opposing forces of "complacency" on the one hand, and "bitterness and hatred" on the other. Arguing against the admonitions of whites who called for patience and restraint, he insisted that nonviolent protests provided a vital outlet for the resentments of black Americans: "If this philosophy had not emerged, I am convinced that by now many streets of the South would be flowing with floods of blood."

K

On many occasions he warned that non-violent proponents would have to demonstrate the effectiveness of their methods in order to retain mass black support. In September 1963, shortly after four black children died in a Birmingham church bombing, King told President John F. Kennedy, "If something isn't done to give the Negro a new sense of hope and a sense of protection, there is a danger we will face the worst race riot we have ever seen in this country." King's sense of despair about the political effectiveness of nonviolence continued to grow as the result of the shift in the focus of the black struggle from desegregation to political and economic issues. Explaining in 1964 that "nonviolence thrives best in a climate of justice," King derided the slow pace of civil rights reform: "The longer our people see no progress, or halting progress, the easier it will be for them to yield to the counsels of hatred and demagoguery."

Such warnings were indicative of King's growing willingness to undertake mass marches and civil disobedience despite federal restraining orders and despite the risk that such protest might lead to violence. Responding to violent racial rebellions in urban centers, to the "white backlash" he had witnessed during SCLC's Chicago campaign of 1966, and to the rise of "Black Power" militancy, King felt an increasing urgency to mobilize nonviolent campaigns that would offer an alternative to riot and revolution. In 1967, King insisted that "even very violent temperaments can be channeled through nonviolent discipline, if the movement is moving, if they can act constructively and express through an effective channel their very legitimate anger." Given the reluctance of government leaders to confront the underlying economic causes of racial violence, he contended that a nonviolent protest campaign could be effective only when "it has achieved the massive dimensions, the disciplined planning, and the intense commitment of a sustained, direct-action movement of civil disobedience on the national scale." By the end of 1967, King was prepared to launch a Poor Peoples' Campaign that would force national leaders to respond to the plight of the poor. "We will prod and sensitize the legislators, the administrators, and all the wielders of power until they have faced this utterly imperative need."

King and his advisers did not expect the Johnson administration and its liberal supporters to respond as readily to antipoverty protests as they had to civil rights activism. King's estrangement from Johnson became more evident after King's April 1967 address at New York's Riverside Church attacked the nation's involvement in the Vietnam War. King did not base his antiwar stand entirely on generalized opposition to war, although by this time he rejected killing in principle. Instead, King defended his position by pointing to the hypocrisy of a nation more willing to pay for warfare than for antipoverty programs. He also noted the difficulty of advocating nonviolence to "a society gone mad on war." He recounted the questions of young black men who saw the Vietnam War as a demonstration of the nation's dominant values. King remarked, "I knew that I could never again raise my voice against the violence of the oppressed in the ghettoes without having first spoken clearly to the greatest purveyor of violence in the world today—my own government."

Caught between escalating racial violence in urban centers and an unresponsive federal government, King's final years were marked by his increasingly fervent advocacy of militant nonviolence as the only workable alternative to destructive violence. In his last book, *Where Do We Go from Here: Chaos or Community?* (1967), King affirmed that his belief in nonviolence remained strong despite suggestions that he was losing touch with urban blacks. He described "a genuine leader" as "not a searcher for consensus but a molder of consensus." He sometimes noted that his status as a Nobel laureate compelled him to speak out regarding controversial issues such as the Vietnam War that were not directly related to civil rights. Rather than losing faith in nonviolent solutions, he contended that violence was an aspect of "modern civilization" that had to be supplanted by better methods. "Humanity is waiting for something other than blind imitation of the past," he wrote. "If we want truly to advance a step further, if we want to turn over a new leaf and really set a new man afoot, we must begin to turn mankind away from the long and desolate night of violence."

By the time of his assassination on April 4, 1968, King had become an internationally recognized advocate of nonviolence. Although during his last years he came under severe attack from both militant black activists and cautious white liberals, King continued to argue for ever wider application of nonviolent tactics not only in the United States but also throughout the world. In *The Trumpet of Conscience* (1967),

King noted that African Americans had "experimented with the meaning of nonviolence," but added that "the time has come for man to experiment with nonviolence in all areas of human conflict and that means nonviolence on an international scale." His universal perspective derived from his ecumenical Christian beliefs. "Now the judgment of God is upon us, and we must either learn to live together as brothers or we are all going to perish together as fools."

King's contribution to the tradition of nonviolent civil disobedience was more as a popularizer of Gandhian ideas than as a tactical or philosophical innovator. Indeed, his most developed statements of the ideas underlying his nonviolent strategy consisted not of philosophical treatises but of homilies, such as those contained in *Strength to Love* (1963). For example, in the sermon "Loving Your Enemies," King provided a pithy statement of his position on the redemptive quality of unmerited suffering: "We shall match your capacity to inflict suffering by our capacity to endure suffering. . . . One day we shall win freedom, but not only for ourselves. We shall so appeal to your heart and conscience that we shall win you in the process, and our victory will be a double victory."

King's appeals for nonviolence and his confidence in its potency ultimately derived from his Christian faith. Critics of King's arguments for nonviolence have pointed to his tendency to oversimplify vexing theological issues, such as the nature of *agape* as a social force and the notion of original sin. King also rarely acknowledged the coercive effects of nonviolent protest or the difficulty of convincing powerful groups to act according to conscience rather than self-interest. King was an adept synthesizer whose statements on nonviolence were typically discursive rather than systematic, persuasive not because of their logical consistency but because they blended Christian and democratic principles in ways that broadened the appeal of nonviolence. More concerned with promoting Gandhian and social gospel ideas than with reformulating them, King symbolized an African-American civil rights movement that represented a massive, sustained, and somewhat successful application of nonviolent methods.

After King's death, his associates in the SCLC had only modest success in continuing his work. His successor as SCLC president, Ralph David Abernathy, concluded the Poor Peoples' Campaign without achieving its goals, and

SCLC's national influence continued to decline after 1968. In 1969, Coretta Scott King founded the Atlanta-based Martin Luther King, Jr., Center for Nonviolent Social Change, Inc., and spearheaded a successful effort for a national holiday in King's honor. King's intellectual legacy remains a lasting influence on nonviolent, mass movements in many nations. Indeed, King's influence has been more evident outside African-American politics than within, where mass protest activities declined in frequency during the 1980s and 1990s and discontented youth were attracted to the rhetorical militancy of Malcolm X and other black nationalists.

Clayborne Carson

References

Carson, Clayborne, Ralph E. Luker, and Penny A. Russell, eds. *The Papers of Martin Luther King, Jr.* Volume 1, *Called to Serve, January 1929–June 1951.* Berkeley: University of California Press, 1992.

Carson, Clayborne, Ralph E. Luker, and Penny A. Russell, and Peter Holloran, eds. *The Papers of Martin Luther King, Jr.* Volume II, *Rediscovering Precious Values, July 1951–November 1955.* Berkeley: University of California Press, 1994.

King, Martin Luther, Jr. *Strength to Love.* New York: Harper and Row, 1963.

———. *Stride toward Freedom: The Montgomery Story.* New York: Harper and Row, 1964.

———. *The Trumpet of Conscience.* New York: Harper and Row, 1968.

———. *Where Do We Go from Here: Chaos or Community?* New York: Harper and Row, 1967.

———. *Why We Can't Wait.* New York: Harper and Row, 1964.

Washington, James M., ed. *The Essential Writings and Speeches of Martin Luther King, Jr.* San Francisco: Harper San Francisco, 1986.

See also ALBANY, GEORGIA, 1961–1962; BIRMINGHAM, ALABAMA, 1963; CIVIL RIGHTS MOVEMENT; FREEDOM RIDES, 1961; KING, CORETTA SCOTT; MARCH ON WASHINGTON, 1963; MONTGOMERY BUS BOYCOTT, 1955–1956; NOBEL PEACE PRIZE; SELMA-TO-MONTGOMERY MARCH, 1965; SOUTHERN CHRISTIAN LEADERSHIP CONFERENCE

King-Hall, Baron Stephen (1893–1966)
British naval commander, writer, and broadcast journalist, born January 21, 1893, and died June 2, 1966. His 1958 book, *Defence in the Nuclear Age,* may be the first systematic attempt to propound a policy of national defense by means of "non-violent resistance" (later called "civilian-based defense"). The central argument of *Defence in the Nuclear Age* was first presented as a lecture in the spring of 1957 at the Royal United Services Institute. This version was later reprinted in both the *King-Hall News-Letter* and *Peace News,* where Gene Sharp, another early proponent of civilian defense, was then an editor. The initial lecture and its subsequent development into a book excited a great deal of public comment, perhaps fueled by an April 1957 defense ministry white paper that admitted candidly that Britain lacked any adequate means of protecting its citizens from the effects of a nuclear weapons exchange.

King-Hall's thesis was that nuclear weapons had so changed the nature of warfare that a totally new conception of international conflict was needed. The new construct would need to include nonsuicidal means of confronting international communism and demonstrating to its adherents the advantages of a free and democratic "way of life," gradually eroding the competing system. He envisioned that psychological warfare techniques might be used in an offensive mode, and methods of passive resistance (in the parlance of the time) could be used for defense if this policy provoked a military attack.

He argued that all previous experience with nonviolent resistance had been gained in response to a crisis, and had not resulted from carefully prepared policies enjoying the combined support of both a government and an entire people. Nor had cases up until this time involved a systematic effort to arouse and exploit third-party support or to foment rebellion on the opponents' own home front. Nonviolent resistance movements in the past had simply not been able to generate sufficiently high costs for their opponents so as to prevent or counter military aggression.

King-Hall therefore argued for the creation of a royal commission of inquiry to investigate civilian resistance as a possible basis for Britain's defense policy, claiming that there was sufficient evidence in favor of this approach, especially from the resistance experiences of the Second World War years, to warrant its further investigation. Such a commission was never established, but the proposal was vigorously debated. Discussions stimulated by *Defence in the Nuclear Age* helped many new commentators to distinguish between the policy potential of nonviolent action and the claims of normative pacifism.

Christopher Kruegler

References
King-Hall, Stephen. *Defence in the Nuclear Age.* London: Victor Gollancz, 1958.
———. *Power Politics in the Nuclear Age.* London: Victor Gollancz, 1962.

See also CIVILIAN-BASED DEFENSE; CLAUSEWITZ, CARL VON; LIDDELL HART, CAPTAIN SIR BASIL HENRY; STRATEGY

Korea, Democratic Struggle in the South
Movement to establish democratic rights, driven largely by church and university activists, the new middle class, and an emerging young intelligentsia, beginning with the 1960 student-led revolution and culminating in the June 1987 mass demonstrations that gave birth to the first popular democratic elections for the presidency since independence. Although a certain amount of violent protest erupted during the early 1980s, the success of democratic transition, or the failure of the authoritarian regime to contain the tide of popular democratic demands, was due in large part to the nonviolent organizational activity over the previous two decades. This nonviolent protest movement was rooted in, and sustained by, church-based activists, even as it attracted nationwide support at its peak. Thus the transition to democracy in 1987 reflected a subtle interplay of nonviolent and violent protest tactics.

The Origins of the Nonviolent Movement in South Korea
To a significant extent, the nonviolent protest movement in South Korea received its inspiration from Martin Luther King, Jr.'s philosophy and strategy of nonviolent direct action in the United States. Many ecumenical church activists in South Korea—a majority of leaders of the National Council of Churches of Korea (KNCC) and others who led the democratic human rights movement in the 1970s and 1980s—were schooled and influenced by the civil rights movement in the United States in the

1960s. Although their political influences on the protest movement were sometimes indirect and intermittent (as was the case in the 1980s), leading church activists who advocated nonviolent direct action were well known among the dissident circles as well as the domestic security agencies of the Park Chung Hee and Chun Doo Hwan governments. Their considerable influence extended the antimilitary protest movement beyond the confines of the church community, with which a quarter of South Korea's population identified in the 1970s. During the repressive Yushin period (1972–1979) of President Park, they emerged as a powerful parallel group, along with campus activists, to resist the increasingly ruthless regime. The Christian activists were joined by some Buddhist leaders who, although coming from different theological and educational backgrounds, found much in common with the former, especially in terms of their belief in and advocacy of nonviolent tactics and strategies against the violent military-controlled dictatorship in Korea.

The two top leaders of South Korea's nonviolent protest movement in the 1970s and 1980s were Dr. Kim Chae-jun, founder and longtime president of Hanguk Theological College, and the Reverend Ham Sokhun, an internationally known Quaker leader and the head of the pacifist movement in Korea. Other prominent pro-democracy church leaders in South Korea during the same period were, among others, the Reverend Park Hyong-Kyu of Seoul First (Presbyterian) Church and chairman for many years of KNCC's Human Rights Committee; the Reverend Kim Kwansok, a longtime general secretary of KNCC; the Reverend Moon Ik-Hwan, an aggressive advocate of North–South unification; the Reverend Dr. Kim Chankook, former dean of the theology school and vice president of Yonsei University; and Dr. Kim Donggil, former vice president of Yonsei and member of the National Assembly from 1992 to 1996. Other influential leaders of the ecumenical pro-democracy movement in South Korea included Professors An Pyong-Mu (Hanguk Theological College), Han Wan-Sang (Seoul National University), Hyung Yong-Hak (Ewha Women's University), Yi Mun-yong (Korea University) and Chang Ul-byong (Sungkyunkwan University). Also, Dr. Yi T'ae-yŏng, a human rights lawyer, and Kang Munkyu, longtime secretary general of the Korean YMCA, were deeply—although not overtly—involved in the pro-democracy movement.

These leaders were subjected to sometimes physically violent repression at the hands of the Park and Chun governments. Most of them were imprisoned, some of them repeatedly, for their determined involvement in the pro-democracy movement, which was carried out in the name of the Christian human rights movement (inkwon undong).

A Chronology of Protest

During the 1960s—a tumultuous decade that was opened with the April 1960 student revolution and the subsequent May 1961 military revolution or "counterrevolution"—Korean church leaders were deeply involved in the theological debate over the relationship between the text and context of the Gospel. The so-called Mission Dei (Mission of God), which emerged out of this theological debate and became the mainstream position of the KNCC by the late 1960s, called for the activist involvement of the Church to humanize the inhumanity of the modernization process under military-controlled authoritarianism. The Christian human rights movement of the time was also based on the political theology of ecumenical activists who, for instance, defended on theological grounds their 1969 struggle against the constitutional revision for President Park's third term in office. In the July 1967 issue of *Sasangge,* an influential intellectual journal, Dr. Kim Chae-jun wrote: "We do not tolerate the silence against injustice, regardless of which side and who is responsible for it. It is the essence of our faith to establish justice in this land." In 1968, the KNCC commentator justified the political involvement of Korean Christians on the grounds that "it is the expression of the theological awareness of Korean Christians, in the traditions of Bonhoeffer's theology of action against the theology of secularization and of the African-American human rights struggle and the anti–Vietnam War movement in the United States."

The pivotal role of the Korean ecumenical church in the defense of human rights and democratic reform in the 1970s can be attested to by the fact that during the initial protest period following the introduction of the repressive Yushin Constitution by President Park in 1972, church activists accounted for the largest of the different occupational groups among the political prisoners incarcerated in Korean prisons.

On March 1, 1976 (the fifty-seventh anniversary of the March 1, 1919, nonviolent uprising against Japanese colonial rule), twelve prominent dissidents led by Cardinal Kim Su Hwan of the Seoul Diocese and the Rev. Kim Kwansok, general secretary of the KNCC, issued the "Declaration for Democracy and National Salvation" at Seoul's Myŏngdong Catholic Cathedral. This open challenge to the infamous Presidential Emergency Decree No. 9 of May 1975 barring any discussion on the constitutionality of the Yushin system called for popular nonviolent resistance against "a one-man dictatorship [by President Park] that tramples on human rights." The signers of the declaration demanded an immediate repeal of the repressive 1975 decree and the freedom of political prisoners who were unjustly incarcerated for opposing the Yushin dictatorship.

The rise of the new military dictatorship (Shin kunbu) led by General Chun Doo Hwan after President Park Chung Hee's assassination by his intelligence chief in 1979 and the subsequent bloody massacre in Kwangju in May 1980 for all practical purposes shifted the leadership of the protest movement to the university activists. The period of intermittent violent confrontation and radical ideological struggle between the Chun regime and the increasingly well organized university activists began in early 1984. Nonviolent actions took a back seat in the Korean protest movement during much of the period of gradually intensifying popular protest from 1984 through 1987. But the occasional protest suicide and the increasingly challenging student demonstrations—characterized by volleys of molotov cocktails, stones, and tear gas—erupted into nationwide demonstrations in the spring of 1987. Hence, the popular impression that the onset of democratic transition in the late 1980s was essentially the result of a violent mass movement. The unfolding drama in the Philippines during 1985 and 1986 of a nonviolent challenge to a U.S.-backed authoritarian regime, however, did not go unnoticed by democratic activists in Korea.

The success of the celebrated "Democratic Revolution (Minju Hyokmyong)" of 1987 was made possible by the selective and goal-directed use of violent tactics by the radical front of the mainstream university activists, on the one hand, and a persistent and extensive utilization of sophisticated, nonviolent tactics (as functional alternatives to violence) that a large university population and a majority of their adult supporters resorted to, on the other.

Among the more effective tactics adopted in the 1987 mass protests was the evocation of national symbols portraying the U.S.-backed military regime as anti-Korean. In particular, a massive protest funeral procession was held for a student victim of police torture, winding its way for more than a hundred miles to the student's home town near Kwangju. Protesters also occupied the grounds of the Myŏngdong Cathedral, strategically located in the center of Seoul. This site served to focus mass protest in May and June and clearly reflected the Philippine "experience" of nonviolent occupation. Finally, on June 29, in a stunning nationwide broadcast that riveted the nation, General Roh Tae Woo, the presidential candidate of the ruling Democratic Justice Party, announced a direct presidential election, reversing the earlier decision of President Chun Doo Hwan. A certain, violent confrontation waiting to happen was narrowly averted with this announcement, and the nation proceeded on its road to democratization.

Wonmo Dong

References

Dong, Wonmo. *Korean-American Relations at the Crossroads.* Princeton, N.J.: Association of Korean Christian Scholars in North America, 1982.

See also INDEPENDENCE CLUB MOVEMENT, 1896–1898; KWANGJU UPRISING, 1980; MARCH FIRST INDEPENDENCE MOVEMENT, 1919

Kosova, Albanian National Movement

Nonviolent political movement organized by ethnic Albanians in Kosova (Kosovo) and advocating independence from Serbia. The movement, led by prominent literary critic Ibrahim Rugova, emerged in 1990 in response to Serbia's rollback of self-government in Kosova. It rejects the legitimacy of Serbia's rule over the 2 million ethnic Albanians and relies on nonviolent methods to resist what it terms Serbian colonial rule and Serbian attempts to change the ethnic structure of the region's population. The movement has established a shadow government and parallel institutions aimed at meeting the population's most basic needs.

Kosova has long been a bone of contention between Serbs and Albanians, both of whom claim the region on historical and ethnic grounds. In medieval times, Kosova was part of the Serbian state. The Albanian national movement in the 1870s had its origins in Kosova, and it was there that the Albanians waged the major struggle that led to the proclamation of Albania's independence from Turkey in 1912. Relations between Albanians and Serbs have fluctuated from periods of uneasy coexistence to outright hostility. Throughout the 1960s and the 1970s, the situation continued at a low level of conflict, as Kosova, formally an autonomous province within the Republic of Serbia, gained increasingly wide powers of self-rule. The 1974 Yugoslav Constitution recognized Kosova as a constituent federal unit, but stopped short of granting the region an equal status with the country's six federal republics. While ethnic Albanians pushed for greater autonomy, demanding Kosova be recognized as a separate republic within the federation, local Serbs complained of discrimination by the Albanians. Violence erupted in spring 1981 when the federal government used the army to crush ethnic Albanian demonstrations. Serbia responded by taking measures to circumscribe Kosova's autonomy. In 1989, in contravention of Yugoslavia's constitution, Serbia suspended Kosova's autonomy and declared martial law in the province. In July 1990, Albanian members of the provincial parliament declared Kosova an independent unit within the Yugoslav federation. In response, Serbian strongman Slobodan Milosevic suspended the local parliament and government, fully integrating Kosova into the republic of Serbia. Serbian authorities also shut down the Albanian-language TV and radio stations and the daily newspaper *Rilindja* and launched a policy of political, economic, and cultural marginalization of ethnic Albanians, who make up more than 90 percent of the region's population. In a widespread "bureaucratic" ethnic cleansing, Albanians in leading government and administrative positions were replaced by Serbs. More than 120,000 Albanian workers were fired; many were also evicted from their apartments. The police force was cleansed of all Albanians. And when Albanians refused to accept Serbian programs, the Albanian-language university and all other educational institutions, including elementary schools, were closed down.

In the wake of the abolishment of Kosova's autonomy and the disintegration of the local League of Communists, new political parties emerged. In December 1989, a group of intellectuals led by Rugova who had publicly opposed Serbia's abolishment of Kosova's autonomy, created the Democratic League of Kosova, the first non-Communist party to be formed in Kosova

since the Second World War. Under Rugova's leadership, the Democratic League rapidly expanded its membership, becoming the dominant political force in the region. Initially, the party, which resembled more a mass movement than a modern political party, called for the restoration of Kosova's autonomous status. In the face of increased Serbian repression, the party called for Kosova's separation from Serbia, but stopped short of calling for immediate union with Albania. Ethnic Albanians refused to accept the legitimacy of what they termed Serbia's colonial rule. In a clandestine meeting in September 1990, Albanian deputies approved a constitution for the Kosova republic. In a referendum a year later, ethnic Albanians voted overwhelmingly for independence. A government was set up in exile, with Bujar Bukoshi, a prominent activist, serving as prime minister. In the most serious challenge to Serbia's rule to date, in May 1992, ethnic Albanians organized multiparty elections and Rugova was elected president. Serbia termed the elections illegal and thwarted Rugova's plans to convene the parliament and set up a government in Prishtina, the capital of Kosova. Bukoshi continued to serve as prime minister in exile.

Ethnic Albanians, nevertheless, proceeded to establish parallel institutions, creating a state within a state. Although the Serbs continued to maintain a heavy army presence in the region, the only authority the Albanians recognized was that of Rugova. The Albanians' closely knit family structure and national solidarity made it possible for them to stave off Serbia's economic pressures. A private educational system was set up. Instruction in the Albanian language was carried out in private homes, mosques, churches, restaurants, garages, barns, and other temporary locations. A Solidarity Fund, financed by the diaspora in Western Europe and the United States, provided assistance to the most needy and the families of Albanians imprisoned on political charges. Teachers and doctors working at private clinics received token financial assistance from the Solidarity Fund. Successful Albanian entrepreneurs at home and abroad adopted needy families, providing them with year-round material assistance. Rugova, the architect of the nonviolent resistance against Serbia, sees Kosova's independence from Serbia as a long-term process and not an objective that can be achieved overnight. He has stressed the importance of Albanian national institutions and self-confidence.

Rugova's demands have evolved. Before Yugoslavia's disintegration, he insisted that

K

Kosova become a republic within the federation, deferring indefinitely unification with Albania. After the secession of Slovenia and Croatia, Rugova called for the establishment of an independent Kosova state that would remain neutral and have close ties with both Serbia and Albania. But by late 1994, Rugova seemed to be moving away from the notion of an independent Kosova state to advocate for confederation with Albania. If Serbs from Bosnia and Croatia join a confederation with Serbia, maintained Rugova, then ethnic Albanians of Kosova should have the right to enter into a similar relationship with Albania.

Rugova's nonviolent resistance has come under increasing attack. Critics say that the situation of the ethnic Albanians has become much worse than it was in 1990 when Serbia suspended Kosova's autonomy. Some have advocated violent resistance, arguing that continued Serbian repression is likely to lead to a situation in which the Albanians will be unable to mount any resistance. Rugova, however, has insisted on the use of nonviolent methods and has urged his followers to desist from actions that could cause Kosova to descend into the violence that has consumed Bosnia.

Elez Biberaj

References

Biberaj, Elez. "Kosova: The Balkan Powder Keg." *Conflict Studies* 258 (1993): 26.

Dragnich, Alex, and Slavko Todorovich. *The Saga of Kosovo: Focus on Serbian-Albanian Relations.* Boulder, Colo.: East European Monographs; New York: Columbia University Press, 1984.

Pipa, Arshi, and Sami Repsiht, eds. *Studies on Kosova.* Boulder, Colo.: East European Monographs; New York: Columbia University Press, 1984.

See also BOSNIA-HERZEGOVINA, RESISTANCE TO CIVIL WAR, 1991–1992; SERBIA, ANTIWAR ACTIVITY, 1991–1994

Kwangju Uprising (Korea), 1980

One of the most significant events in modern Korean history. The proximate cause of the uprising was the imposition by General Chun Doo Hwan of martial law across South Korea on May 17, 1980, to silence his critics. One of those arrested was opposition leader Kim Dae-jung, a native of the Honam region of southwestern Korea, in which the most important city is Kwangju. In response to repression and violence by the Chun government, hundreds of thousands of Kwangju citizens filled the streets and, for a short time, seized control of the city. Although they were unsuccessful in protecting democracy at the time, in retrospect it is clear that the Kwangju incident produced a seachange in Korean attitudes toward the military and government, as well as the United States. The events of May 1980, while not entirely nonviolent, became a touchstone for the prodemocracy movement and the student demonstrations that reemerged in 1987 and ultimately led to the restoration of democratic civilian rule by the early 1990s.

Honam historically has been a region whose citizens feel neglected by the central government and discriminated against by Koreans from other parts of the country. In the 1970s, Kim Dae-jung's status as a regional hero grew out of his near-success in the presidential election of 1971, when he won 45 percent of the popular vote against the incumbent president (and former general) Park Chung Hee. After the election and throughout the 1970s, Park punished Kim by treating him like a security risk. When the president began ruling by decree in 1972, he used South Korea's extensive secret police apparatus, the Korean Central Intelligence Agency (KCIA), against Kim, continually harassing him. In 1973, for example, during one of Kim's speaking trips abroad, KCIA agents kidnaped him from a Tokyo hotel and spirited him across the Sea of Japan to Korea, at one point threatening to throw him overboard. On March 1, 1976, Kim was arrested along with other dissidents in Seoul's Myŏngdong Catholic Cathedral after reading a declaration demanding democracy in Korea. For this "anti-state activity," defined as a crime under Park's decrees, Kim went to prison. Indeed, Kim spent most of the 1970s in one form of detention or another. Nevertheless many Koreans, especially in Honam, believed that Kim would be president if Korea were a true democracy. In and out of prison, he served as the rallying point for the opposition.

President Park Chung Hee's assassination in October 1979 was followed by a brief period of liberalization in South Korea. Nearly two decades after the coup d'état that brought Park's junta to power, the Korean people seemed determined never to permit a return to military rule. During the winter and "Seoul

Spring" of 1980, Park's most draconian decrees were lifted. People blacklisted by his regime resumed their jobs and the fear that had circumscribed most political activity faded quickly. Democracy seemed to be on track again.

However, beneath the surface a new army faction, led by Major General Chun Doo Hwan, had begun marching to power. In December 1979, General Chun and his circle of Korean Military Academy classmates took control of the ROK military. This "coup-like incident," as it came to be called, was a frightening sign of Chun's determination to control events far beyond the investigation.

Chun went further in April 1980 when he assumed the directorship of the KCIA, breaking the law against military control of the agency. Fearing that Chun was taking Korea back to military rule, demonstrators took to the streets demanding immediate reform and democratic elections. In May 1980, after weeks of public unrest, Chun decided to crush his critics. On May 17 he reimposed martial law and ordered the arrest of people who had spoken out against his rise to power—journalists, intellectuals, student leaders, and opposition leaders including Kim Young Sam (later elected president in 1993) and Kim Dae-jung.

With the news of Kim Dae-jung's arrest a furor erupted in Honam. To meet surging crowds of demonstrators in the streets of Kwangju on May 18, General Chun ordered paratroopers from the ROK Army's Special Warfare Command (SWC) to the city. The SWC "Black Berets," specially trained to wreak deadly havoc on infiltrating North Korean agents, were told that the uprising in Kwangju was Communist-inspired, and with fixed bayonets they proceeded to attack the city's citizens in what amounted to a military operation. Their initial attack cost the lives of dozens of Kwangju citizens. According to hospital eyewitnesses, some of those who died were obviously bystanders, including children.

The Black Berets' actions brought more than 200,000 Kwangju citizens from all walks of life into the streets on May 20 and 21. The army's response was to send helicopter gunships circling the city and firing down into the crowds, causing a renewed wave of casualties. However, by storming the police armory and seizing weapons, and by commandeering vehicles and otherwise marauding against the police and Black Berets, the Kwangju rebels managed to drive the troops from the city by May 22. Kwangju then remained in their hands—outside central government control—for five days until May 27.

In Seoul, the central government, driven by General Chun and his cohorts, briefly considered negotiation with the rebels—a course favored by the United States, whose primary interest in the situation was maintaining stability on the peninsula and deterring any move by North Korea to take advantage of the civil unrest in the South. When the Korean government decided to forgo negotiation and crush the Kwangju uprising with regular troops, it removed the ROK Army's 20th Division, a force trained in riot control, from joint Korean-American Combined Forces Command. Because this was a use for "domestic duty," the Americans could not object on technical grounds. However, their failure to use their considerable moral and political influence over the Korean government and army to prevent the bloody crushing of the Kwangju rebellion left bitter sentiments.

The assault of the ROK 20th Division against Kwangju on May 27 was not as violent as many had feared; but it did cost a number of lives, including those of thirty holdouts barricaded in the provincial office building downtown. After the fighting, the Korean people were given only part of the story, being told that the incident had been caused by Communists and North Korean sympathizers and that the loss of life had been light. In fact, the precise death toll has never been established. The government, in a series of investigations over the years, has maintained that there were fewer than two hundred lives lost. Independent Korean and foreign sources claim more, perhaps as many as two thousand.

General Chun maneuvered himself into the presidency in August 1980, then rewrote the South Korean constitution and had himself elected to a full presidential term beginning in 1981. His term coincided with the Reagan administration in the United States, which praised him as an ally in the worldwide confrontation with communism. Ronald Reagan's televised embrace of Chun on the steps of the White House in 1981 suggested that the Americans were indifferent to the way Chun had seized power. In the years that followed, American officials in Seoul refused to discuss the question of American involvement in the Kwangju affair, calling it an "internal matter." It was not until 1989 that the State Department gave a detailed accounting of its role and accused Chun of having lied about the U.S. role and the Carter administration's repeated attempts to restrain the ROK military.

Anti-authoritarian protest erupted again in 1987, led largely by students. This renewed pro-democracy movement succeeded in forcing a change on the Korean government in a way that the events of 1980 had not. General Chun was succeeded as president in 1988 by General Roh Tae woo, who won the presidency honestly in a three-way race with opposition leaders Kim Young Sam and Kim Dae-jung. Roh's term, from 1987 to 1993, saw major strides toward democracy. However, because he was part of the Chun apparatus—and commanded key units in support of General Chun during the "coup-like incident" of December 12, 1979—

he never shook off the stigma of association with Chun and was obliged to govern in the shadow of public mistrust and anger over Chun's bloody rise to power. Elections in 1993, which were contested by the two former opposition leaders and no candidate of the military, brought Kim Young Sam to the presidency.

Donald N. Clark

References

Clark, Donald N., ed. *The Kwangju Uprising: Shadows over the Regime in South Korea.* Boulder, Colo.: Westview, 1988.

See also KOREA, DEMOCRATIC STRUGGLE IN THE SOUTH; MARCH FIRST INDEPENDENCE MOVEMENT, 1919

L

La Boétie, Etienne de (1530–1563)

Sixteenth-century French lawyer and author of the essay *Discours de la servitude volontaire* (Discourse on Voluntary Servitude). La Boétie was born in Sarlat in the Dordogne into a family of lawyers and royal officials. Having studied at the Orléans law school, he served in the Bordeaux Parliament. La Boétie probably composed the *Discours* while still a student. It circulated as a manuscript, but was not published by La Boétie himself. Although his political views seemed to have changed later in life, this essay contained the seeds of a radical theory of power that remained influential well into the twentieth century.

Paul A. Chilton

References

La Boétie, Etienne de. *The Politics of Obedience: The Discourse of Voluntary Servitude (De la servitude volontaire)*. Introduction by Murray M. Rothbard; translated by Harry Kurz. Montreal: Black Rose Books, 1975.

See also SOCIAL POWER; VOLUNTARY SERVITUDE, DISCOURSE ON

Land Seizure

Nonviolent expropriation of land legally belonging to someone else, and the utilization of that land, with the intent to create a public de facto change of ownership. Often, these seizures are conducted by peasants against large landowners. Land seizures are also sometimes carried out against the government. The land in dispute may have been owned by an unpopular government or may have been confiscated by the government as punishment for previous antigovernment actions. In any of these instances, the seizure may be accompanied by nonviolent invasion (deliberate nonviolent ingress to a forbidden area), nonviolent occupation (refusing to leave a particular place), or "squatting" (illegal habitation). By seizing the land, the nonviolent actionists intend to change their situation by manipulating physical resources and coercing the opponent into transferring ownership. Sometimes predominantly nonviolent land seizures may be accompanied by violence against landowners or their agents.

Many instances of land seizure have taken place in Latin America. In 1933, Colombian peasants capitalized on a law that required landowners to compensate tenants for any improvements they made on the land. These peasants planted coffee trees on the land, preventing repossession by the landlord without payment to the tenants. In one area, these land seizures proved successful, and the peasants kept the land. Also in Colombia, around 1961, over five hundred peasant families seized large abandoned *haciendas* (large plantations) in Cunday. The governmental Land Reform Institute divided these haciendas among the families. In Bolivia, major land seizures were endorsed by revolutionary nationalist governments in 1945 and 1952 as the beginning step in campaigns to expropriate *latifundios* (large estates). More recently, in the 1970s and 1980s, landless peasants in Honduras conducted successful "recuperaciones" (recoveries) of idle land when the government failed to enact promised agrarian reform.

References

Schlabach, Gerald. "The Nonviolence of Desperation: Peasant Land Action in Honduras." In *Relentless Persistence: Non-violent Action in Latin America,* edited by Philip McManus and Gerald Schlabach. Philadelphia: New Society, 1991.

Sharp, Gene. *The Politics of Nonviolent Action.* Boston: Porter Sargent, 1973.

Lanza del Vasto, Joseph Jean (1901–1981)

French-speaking Italian writer and pioneer of nonviolence in Europe. He was born in San Vito dei Normanni on September 29, 1901, and died in Murcie, Spain, on January 5, 1981.

Joseph Jean Lanza del Vasto studied philosophy at the universities of Florence and Pisa and wrote a dissertation on the question of the Trinity. After reading Saint Thomas Aquinas's *De Trinitate* in *Summa Theologica,* he experienced what he described as his "conversion" to Catholicism.

Prompted by a spiritual quest and a rejection of the industrial world, he traveled to Asia in 1936. Meeting Mohandas Gandhi in India in 1937 was the turning point of his life. Gandhi introduced him to nonviolence and convinced him that it was the primary truth of Christianity. Gandhi gave him the name *Shantidas* (Servant of Peace).

Lanza del Vasto returned to Europe with the dream of founding a community after the example of the Gandhian ashrams. Rather than considering nonviolence only as a technique of action, he saw it as a personal rule for reaching inner self-unity, which required a communal way of life to be achieved.

In 1948, Lanza del Vasto founded the first "Community of the Ark." This original community continues to operate at La Borie Noble, Hérault, in southern France. Striving to achieve self-sufficiency, the Ark community was created "as a patriarchal, nonviolent, hard-working, and ecumenical order." Like Gandhi, Lanza del Vasto rejected the industrial world and the division of labor, believing that people should produce what they want to consume, which Lanza del Vasto thought possible only in a small, rural community. Other Ark communities were established in Spain, Italy, Belgium, Quebec, and Argentina.

Neither Lanza del Vasto nor the other members of the Ark community intended to retire from the world. They organized several nonviolent direct actions, such as a fast protest-

Lanza del Vasto. Photo by Jim Forest.

ing the use of torture by French military officers in Algeria in 1957, the occupation in 1958 of the nuclear facility in Marcoule, which produced plutonium for the French atomic weapons program, and protests against the prison camps for Algerian suspects in France in 1961. In 1972, Lanza del Vasto was instrumental in inducing the peasants of Larzac, France, to employ nonviolent methods of resistance against expansion of the local military camp.

Lanza del Vasto wrote in many literary genres, including poetry, travel literature, drama, textual analysis and exegesis, and essays on nonviolent action and spiritual issues. He published his autobiography, *Enfance d'une Pensée,* in 1970.

Jacques Semelin

References

Lanza del Vasto, Joseph Jean. *Gandhi to Vinoba, the New Pilgrimage.* Translated by Philip Leon. London: Rider, 1956; New York: Schocken, 1974.

———. *Make Straight the Way of the Lord.* Translated by Jean Sidgwick. New York: A.A. Knopf, 1974.

———. *Principles and Precepts of the Return to the Obvious.* New York: Schocken, 1974.

———. *Return to the Source.* New York: Schocken, 1972.

———. *Warriors of Peace.* Edited by Michel Random. Translated by Jean Sidgwick. New York: A.A. Knopf, 1974.

See also LARZAC, 1971–1981

Larzac (France), 1971–1981

Nonviolent resistance by peasant farmers in southern France against government plans to expand a military base by expropriating their land. Inspired by a Gandhian advocate of nonviolent action, the Italian Lanza del Vasto, the farmers and their supporters used a wide variety of methods of nonviolent action. The protest is considered the first large, sustained, intentional campaign of nonviolent struggle in France, in which Larzac farmers linked their campaign to issues of antimilitarism, labor, and the Third World. The movement eventually achieved complete success in 1981, when the government abandoned its plans to expand the military base.

In October 1970, the secretary of state for defense revealed the army's decision to enlarge the military camp in Larzac, an expansion that would require many farmers to surrender their property. Farmers organized their first demonstration to protest the government's plan in September 1971, when they dumped manure in front of the house of a local mayor who was pro-extension. Solidarity "Larzac Committees" began to spring up around the country in 1971 and 1972. In March 1972, Lanza del Vasto gave a talk on "active nonviolence" and conducted a two-week fast with local farmers. This proved to be a major catalyst in the farmers' decision to choose nonviolent resistance over constitutional or violent means. On March 28, Larzac farmers created the "Manifesto of the 103," in which they resolved not to sell their land to the army.

From 1972 until 1981, "the 103" organized many expressions of protest and countermeasures to government enforcement actions. The demonstration was one of the most important methods in terms of garnering public support. On October 25, 1972, Larzac farmers took sixty sheep with "Save the Larzac" written into their fleece to Paris to graze under the Eiffel Tower. In August 1974, 100,000 people came to Larzac for a long rally that included the harvesting of wheat for starving people in Upper Volta, Africa. Solidarity demonstrations occurred throughout France and even in other European cities during the late 1970s. Often the demonstrations were accompanied by some form of nonviolent obstruction. For example, in October 1972, two thousand sheep were used to block access to a government-sponsored inquiry at La Cavalerie town hall. In January 1975, farmers engaged in a sit-in, blocking traffic on the major road through the Larzac. Blockades were used throughout the 1970s.

During the mid-1970s, farmers, conscientious objectors, and others began to occupy farms that had been bought by the army but were unused. Afraid of fueling positive publicity for the Larzac cause, French authorities rarely attempted to evict these squatters. On October 4, 1975, several people occupied a farm and set up a research center, called "Le Cun," to study nonviolent action. Other forms of intervention occurred during the 1970s. In February 1975, a group of women farmers entered government inquiry offices and destroyed files. In March 1975, farmers nonviolently invaded the town hall of Maillau and led the inquiry commissioner out of the building. In June 1976, another group entered La Cavalerie military camp and occupied the land purchaser's office and destroyed files. Larzac supporters also tried to interfere with army maneuvers by conducting sit-ins, erecting barricades, deflating tires, and painting graffiti on army vehicles.

The farmers and their supporters engaged in many forms of nonviolent noncooperation. In 1973, sixty farmers who were in the military reserve returned their military papers, inspiring many other supporters around the country to do likewise. Some supporters of the Larzac farmers led a Tax-Refusal-Redistribution Movement, whereby French citizens withheld 3 percent of their taxes and gave the money to peacemaking projects. Often, Larzac farm owners and town mayors boycotted meetings with government representatives. After expropriation was officially sanctioned in spring 1979, Judge Grenet attempted to view the land and speak with farm owners to determine compensation, but he was met with boycotts, sit-ins, demonstrations, and widespread noncooperation everyplace he visited.

The farmers also engaged in "reverse strikes" and similar constructive projects, whereby they erected buildings and cultivated the land illegally. Formed in 1973, the Development of Agriculture on the Larzac built over fourteen farm buildings without permits and financed illegal maintenance on roads. In August 1974, farmers spontaneously and illegally plowed a field belonging to the army. Squatters and Larzac farmers continued to use this method throughout the 1970s. In January 1975, farmers finished connecting a water-supply pipe that the government was delaying. The farmers worked on the project despite police attempts to physically pull them away from the work.

After ten years of widespread and varied resistance, the Save the Larzac movement won total victory in June 1981, when the Council of Ministers, on advice from newly elected President Francois Mitterand, annulled the military expansion project and the army soon evacuated. Participants in the Larzac campaign continued their research into nonviolent struggle, however. In August 1981, they hosted an International Meeting for Peace. Three thousand people attended, including Japanese peasants struggling nonviolently against the development of the Narita airport. Meeting participants made an international call for the formation of a coalition of grassroots movements against nuclear weapons.

Some of the important aspects of the Larzac campaign include the use of a wide variety of nonviolent methods of protest, noncooperation, and intervention, the steadfast unity of the farmers throughout the campaign, and the important network of Larzac Committees across France. The Larzac campaign remains one of the most successful sustained, nonviolent struggles in world history.

Brad Bennett

References

Mellon, Christian. "Peace Organisations in France Today." In *Defence and Dissent in Contemporary France*, edited by Jolyon Howorth and Patricia Chilton. London and Sydney: Croom Helm, 1984.

Rawlinson, Roger. *Larzac—A Victory for Nonviolence*. London: Quaker Peace and Service, 1983.

See also LAND SEIZURE; LANZA DEL VASTO, JOSEPH JEAN

Le Chambon Sur Lignon, France

A village in the south of France not far from Lyon, it became a place of refuge for five thousand Jews, many of them children escaping the Holocaust. Most of the people in Le Chambon were Huguenots, French Protestants, whose ancestors had been persecuted in France following their emergence as dissenters from Roman Catholicism in the seventeenth century. As a group, they remained conscious of their position as outsiders in French society. From the fall of France in 1940 until 1942, when Germany took over the entire country, the Lyon region was part of the unoccupied zone of France ruled by the puppet French government located in Vichy. The Protestant pastor of Le Chambon, André Trocmé, was instrumental in building a network of people in Le Chambon and its neighboring villages who sheltered Jews in their homes and farmhouses. Local Roman Catholic convents and monasteries also participated in the rescue effort.

The leaders were known as *responsables*—those who are accountable. They were motivated by their religious beliefs as well as humanitarian feelings. Trocmé preached the ethics of the Good Samaritan: "You shall love the Lord your God with all your heart, with all your strength, with all your mind; and your neighbor as yourself."

Resistance in Le Chambon began with a few small steps. At first, Trocmé urged village students to refuse to salute the flag of Vichy France. He refused to sign an oath of unconditional loyalty to Pétain, the head of the Vichy government. Church bells were silenced. Trocmé's example inspired the young. When French police deported stateless Jews from Paris, the students of Le Chambon delivered a protest letter to a visiting minister of state: "If our comrades, whose only fault is to be born in another religion, received the order to let themselves be deported, or even examined, they would disobey the orders received, and we would try to hide them as best we could." The transformation of Le Chambon into a place of refuge began with a simple act. Magda Trocmé, the pastor's wife, recalled how it happened: "A German woman knocked at my door. It was in the evening, and she said she was a German Jew, coming from northern France, that she was in danger, and that she had heard that in Le Chambon somebody could help her. Could she come into my house? I said, 'Naturally, come in, come in.' Lots of snow. She had a little pair of shoes, nothing . . ."

Throughout Le Chambon, welcome was natural. Solidarity with the refugee was seen as routine, nothing more than the correct and expected mode of behavior. Years later, when Philip Hallie interviewed the citizens of Le Chambon, they shrugged aside praise for what they had done. He paraphrased their response: "How can you call us 'good?' We were doing what had to be done. Who else could help them? And what has all this to do with goodness? Things had to be done, that's all, and we happened to be there to do them. You must understand that it was the most natural thing in the world to help these people."

Michael Berenbaum

References

Hallie, Philip P. *Lest Innocent Blood Be Shed: The Story of the Village of Le Chambon.* New York: Harper and Row, 1979.

Rittner, Carol, and Sondra Myers, eds. *The Courage to Care: Rescuers of Jews during the Holocaust.* New York: New York University Press, 1986.

See also NAZISM, CIVILIAN RESISTANCE, 1939–1945

Leadership

Process of performing multiple roles and functions for the purpose of achieving some set of goals reflecting the needs, concerns, or desires of a group, including a social movement. Leadership has long been studied by philosophers, social scientists, business leaders, and other scholars of collective action. Their concerns generally revolve around a series of key questions, including: What is the role of individual human agency in social change and historical causation? Is a leader born or made? Does leadership depend more upon the possession of unique individual skill or personality traits, or upon the social contexts and organizational relationships in which individuals are embedded? Efforts to address these questions have produced three major perspectives on leadership, all of which can be applied, with some utility, to social movements engaged in nonviolent struggle.

A group or movement pursuing its goals by the methods of nonviolent action, however, appears to challenge the ability of any of the major perspectives on leadership to explain either the empirical phenomenon or offer prescriptive advice. Nonviolent social movements have had a variety of leadership structures. For example, Martin Luther King, Jr., and many of the Southern Baptist ministers who made up the leadership cadre in the U.S. civil rights movement, were accustomed to a highly centralized, hierarchical leadership structure. However, many younger civil rights, student, and women's movement leaders advocated and experimented with "new" forms of decentralized, nonhierarchical leadership structures popularly termed "participatory democracy" and "collectivism." While there is a rich historical and sociological literature on leadership, contemporary social movement scholarship has not made leadership a central focus of its theoretical analysis. In particular, the gender, race, and class biases inherent in traditional conceptualizations of leadership remain poorly explored.

The three major contemporary social movement theories—classical collective behavior, resource mobilization, and political process—either exclude leadership as an important factor in the emergence of collective action or view leadership as merely one of several "resources" provided and determined by movement organizations. In general, there is little consensus about the definition, identification, or measurement of leadership. Early literature, especially in European scholarship, understood leadership as a property of individuals who were limited in number and "gifted" with extraordinary attributes. Until the 1930s, American scholars followed this individualistic orientation and conceptualized leadership in terms of individual personality traits. During the 1940s, however, research began to focus on leadership behavior within the context of social circumstances and developed the notion of leadership as a combination of situational circumstances. The 1950s and 1960s ushered in major conflicts over the definition of leadership, conceived of as group process, personality, compliance inducement, influence, persuasion, power relationship, goal achievement, interaction, differentiated roles, and initiation of structure. Such definitions suggest that leadership may be active or latent, may change or remain stable over time, and may be exercised in small groups or in institutional settings. Over time, heroic, charismatic, and symbolic approaches to leadership developed.

Heroic Leadership

The heroic or "great man" theory of leadership, most forcefully advocated by Thomas Carlyle, assumes that individual leaders are the movers and shapers of history and that large-scale social changes are caused by the purposes, actions, decisions, and innate skills of "heroic" and "great" men. Individual traits, such as intelligence, initiative, integrity, physique, and motivations (whether for greed, ambition, power, or public service) are crucial for many theorists, including Nicoló Machiavelli, Friedrich Wilhelm Nietzsche, John Stuart Mill, and John Kenneth Galbraith. For Galbraith and Carlyle, leaders possess intuitive insight; they are followed, admired, and obeyed to the point of worship; they are the most important factor in collective action. Similarly, Machiavelli viewed leadership as a combination of cunning, manipulation, and brute force of a "prince," who is both "lion" and "fox." For Nietzsche, leadership is the achievement of self-actualization by an extraordinary "superman." Such elitist, patricentric views of leadership, however, obscure to the point of invisibility the significant leadership roles that women and members of the poor and working class performed in many social movements, such as the civil rights movement in the United States.

Charismatic Leadership

Similarly rooted in the European, romantic tradition of Carlyle and holding a central place in modern studies of leadership in collective action, Max Weber's theory of charisma is based on a view of leadership as legitimate authority. According to Weber, leadership is manifested in three types: (1) legal-rational leadership, which is vested in a particular office or position; (2) traditional leadership, which is based on customs; and (3) charismatic leadership, which is generated by extraordinary personal qualities and skills bestowed by the divine. For Weber, charismatic leadership is "a certain quality of an individual personality by virtue of which he is set apart from ordinary men and treated as endowed with supernatural" traits or gifts of grace. Charismatic qualities, however, may be present in the routine functioning of society as well as in individuals and may work to maintain order as well as to disrupt it. For instance, in the U.S. civil rights movement, Martin Luther King, Jr., was not unlike most of the African-American civil rights leaders who were ministers, student activists, and heads of organizations, all educated and experienced in public speaking and articulating the needs and concerns of African Americans, in formulating tactics and strategies, and in mobilizing resources (especially money, publicity, and information channels). Like the focus on heroic qualities, however, the emphasis on charismatic ministers as leaders in the civil rights movement has resulted in the failure of the public and scholars to consider as significant the organizing and leadership roles of African-American women, among others, in the movement.

Symbolic Leadership

Representing both an antiheroic and anticharismatic view, Emile Durkheim's theory of symbolic leadership assumes that leaders are created by their society—they are "totems" representing the collective psyche and primordial needs of the larger group, community, or society. Depending upon the collective needs of society, an ordinary ("profane") thing or individual can be transformed into a totem ("sacred") thing or human. Durkheim wrote that if society "happens to fall in love with a man, and if it thinks it has found in him the principal aspirations that move it, as well as the means of satisfying them, this man will be raised above the others and, as it were, deified." For Durkheim and other writers, such as Orrin Klapp, Sydney Hook, Ralph Waldo Emerson, and Arthur Schlesinger, the leader is not a conscious innovator but a symbol used to convey the thoughts and ideas of the collective, whose values and social needs determine the goals and strategies of collective actions.

We search after great leaders, according to Emerson, because they show us "new possibilities" for resolving conflict. Being like ourselves, symbolic leaders actively pull out whatever virtue is in individuals and make them think of themselves in new ways. Such leaders call individuals to new purposes, create new consciousness, and give the society universal ideals.

The heroic, charismatic, and symbolic perspectives are limited in that they neglect or minimize the structural factors that provide the opportunities for and the constraints on the actions of individual leaders, particularly those holding subordinate status characteristics. While symbolic theories are correct in recognizing that great leaders are not always those individuals who possess the extraordinary skills and charismatic qualities of the Weberian hero, their primary focus on the cultural and psychological complex of the society in which leaders emerge obfuscates the significance of the structural contexts within which movement leaders operate.

In social movements, leadership operates within a complex web of changing sociostructural contexts. What constitutes leadership and its basis varies with different historical periods, sociostructural contexts, cultures, and circumstances that require, impose, constrain, or facilitate the performance of a range of leadership roles. These roles can be performed by a variety of individual actors and within a variety of structural contexts; however, the race, gender, and class biases inherent in traditional notions of leadership limited the opportunities for women and non-elites to perform leadership roles in modern social movements, such as the civil rights movement, and limited the recognition of those roles when they were in fact performed by women, particularly African-American women, and non-elites, such as poor and working-class women.

Bernice McNair Barnett

References

Barnett, Bernice McNair. "Black Women's Collectivist Movement Organizations: Their Struggles during the Doldrums." In *Feminist Organizations: Harvest of the New Women's Movements,* edited by Myra Marx Ferree and Patricia Yancey Martin. Philadelphia: Temple University, 1994.

———. "Invisible Southern Black Women Leaders in the Civil Rights Movement: The Triple Constraints of Gender, Race, and Class." *Gender and Society* 7, no. 2 (1993): 162–182.

Burns, James MacGregor. *Leadership.* New York: Harper and Row, 1978.

Carlyle, Thomas. *Heroes, Hero-Worship and the Heroic in History.* Lincoln: University of Nebraska, 1966.

Durkheim, Emile. *The Elementary Forms of Religious Life* [1915]. New York: Free Press, 1965.

Hull, Gloria T., Patricia Bell Scott, and Barbara Smith, eds. *All of the Women Are White, All of the Blacks Are Men—But Some of Us Are Brave.* Old Westbury, N.Y.: Feminist Press, 1982.

Klapp, Orrin E. *Symbolic Leaders: Public Dramas and Public Man.* Chicago: Aldine, 1964.

McAdam, Doug. *Political Process and the Development of Black Insurgency, 1930–1970.* Chicago: University of Chicago, 1982.

Morris, Aldon. *The Origins of the Civil Rights Movement.* New York: Free Press, 1984.

Stodgill, R.M. *Handbook of Leadership: A Survey of Theory and Research.* New York: Free Press, 1974.

Weber, Max. *Theory of Social and Economic Organization.* Translated by A.M. Henderson and Talcott Parsons. New York: Free Press, 1947.

See also CIVIL RIGHTS MOVEMENT; KING, MARTIN LUTHER, JR.; ORGANIZATION IN SOCIAL MOVEMENTS; SOCIAL MOVEMENTS; SOLIDARITY

L

Liddell Hart, Captain Sir Basil Henry (1895–1970)

British military historian, journalist, and pundit whose strategic thought and observations on civilian resistance had a formative influence on the strategic approach to nonviolent action. Liddell Hart was born in Paris on October 31, 1895. As a young officer in 1916, he survived Britain's disastrous first offensive on the Somme and derived from that experience and his subsequent studies of the First World War a lifelong hatred for senseless carnage in warfare. In more than thirty books, a huge body of journalism, and voluminous correspondence, he developed over the course of his career a dual approach to the problem of war. On the one hand, he reasoned, all efforts should be made to prevent its occurrence. On the other hand, one should be prepared to wage war as decisively and humanely as possible, in the event that preventative measures fail.

Liddell Hart's earliest and best-known efforts were concentrated on the second half of this dual approach. He was an ardent crusader for military reform in the interwar period. He was also a leading advocate of tank development, hoping that mechanization would restore mobility and decisiveness to the modern battlefield. His most famous work, *Strategy: The Indirect Approach,* argued that a single underlying lesson could be derived from all of military history. It was that one should never engage an opponent in a well-entrenched position, and that if one fought in a way, time, or place that was calculated to unbalance the opponent psychologically, a decision might be produced without undue violence or human cost.

Even while developing such methods and doctrines for their efficient use, Liddell Hart was a consistent and articulate critic of the system of "total war" as it was emerging in the mid-twentieth century. He felt that strategic bombing, mass conscription, economic blockade (when it had the effect of starving innocents), and unconditional surrender as an objective in war were both brutalizing and counterproductive, and could not be justified by any political goal. This critique only became sharper and more focused as the nuclear era dawned. Thus, he was open throughout his career to discussions of alternative sanctions that might replace aspects of the war system. He was also a pioneer among advocates of qualitative disarmament, an early forerunner of today's defensive or nonprovocative defense, which envisioned nations limiting themselves by agreement to weapons systems with little or no inherent offensive capability. That this approach was in apparent tension with the indirect approach to strategy and the mechanization of warfare was an irony lost on neither Liddell Hart nor his critics.

It was precisely Liddell Hart's struggle with the dual necessities of preventing war and being ready to wage it decisively that led to his involvement with the topic of nonviolent action and to discussions with some of its leading proponents. Notable pacifists of the interwar period, including Richard Gregg, Aldous Huxley, Bertrand Russell, and Kingsley Martin corresponded with Liddell Hart about the possible use of nonviolent action as an alternative to war, or as a means to mitigate its destructiveness. His contributions to these discussions were repetitive and not especially profound. His misgivings about the ultimate value of nonviolent action in extreme conflicts were two: that (in his view) it could only be practiced by people with the courage and self-restraint of saints, and that it was dependent for success on the opponents' having comparatively high moral standards. But these exchanges did make Liddell Hart alert to manifestations of nonviolent struggle during the coming war years, in which there were abundant examples of ordinary people using such methods effectively against ruthless opponents.

After the Second World War, having observed and commented on civilian resistance campaigns in places like Norway, Denmark, and the Netherlands, Liddell Hart was ready to reopen the question of defense by nonviolent means. He was ahead of his time in noticing that the advent of nuclear weapons made both guerrilla warfare and civilian struggle more, rather than less, likely and relevant. As a journalist, he interviewed more than one hundred German generals imprisoned in England after the war. He reported that they often professed to have been bewildered by the appearance of nonviolent action, and to have found violent partisan resistance easier both to counter and to punish. These insights led him to write a supportive review of Sir Stephen King-Hall's *Defence in the Nuclear Age,* which presented one of the first thorough arguments for a full-fledged national defense based on nonviolent resistance, and to encourage a younger generation of scholars working on civilian-based defense, including Gene Sharp and Adam Roberts.

In 1964, at the Civilian Defence Study Conference at Oxford University, of which Sharp and Roberts were among the principal organizers, Liddell Hart presented a paper entitled "Lessons from Resistance Movements— Guerrilla and Nonviolent." The paper reviewed some familiar territory, but it offered one new argument that has had enduring importance for the subject. He observed that many conflicts, de facto, will involve both violent and nonviolent means of resistance. Since these have the capacity to undermine each other's effectiveness, his minimal prescription was for the achievement of tactical separation in time and space of the two sets of methods. Thus, invading soldiers would not be attacked by snipers in civilian resistance areas, nor would civilian actions be planned for areas wherein, say, one's own bridges or military installations were being preemptively blown up as a means of denying their use to opponents.

Liddell Hart never made his own systematic study of the nature and requirements of nonviolent action. But his occasional insights about it, which were widely published and quoted, and the influence of his general strategic thought on some of the key authors in this field, earn him a place in the history of its emergence. Some have suggested that strategies based on nonviolent action may be the ultimate fulfillment of Liddell Hart's conception of the indirect approach.

Christopher Kruegler

References

Bond, Brian. *Liddell Hart: A Study of His Military Thought.* New Brunswick: Rutgers University Press, 1977.

Liddell Hart, Captain Sir Basil Henry. *Deterrent or Defence.* London: Stevens and Sons, 1960.

———. "Lessons from Resistance Movements—Guerrilla and Nonviolent." In *The Strategy of Civilian Defence,* edited by Adam Roberts. London: Faber and Faber, 1967.

———. *Strategy: The Indirect Approach.* 3rd ed. London: Faber and Faber, 1954. First published as *The Decisive Wars of History.* G. Bell and Sons, 1929.

Mearsheimer, John J. *Liddell Hart and the Weight of History.* Ithaca, N.Y.: Cornell University Press, 1988.

See also CIVILIAN-BASED DEFENSE; CLAUSEWITZ, CARL VON; KING-HALL, BARON STEPHEN; STRATEGY

Lightning Strike

A spontaneous strike staged to "let off steam" or a short strike intended as a protest over a minor issue. Also known as "quickie walkouts," they commonly last several hours and involve a small group of workers. They often occur in contexts where major strikes are banned. Thus, "wildcat strikes" (not union authorized) sometimes take the form of lightning strikes. While most labor strikes act to manipulate resources and coerce management into giving in to their demands, the lightning strike acts more as an appeal to management or the general public in that it does not affect the opponent's resources to the extent that a longer traditional strike does.

Lightning strikes were common in the United States during World War II because major strikes were banned under certain emergency conditions. In 1963, Paris Metro transportation workers conducted a lightning strike that provoked the government to propose legislation requiring five days' strike notice.

References
Sharp, Gene. *The Politics of Nonviolent Action.* Boston: Porter Sargent, 1973.

See also STRIKES

Lutuli, Albert John (1898–1967)

Born in 1898, the son of a black missionary in Rhodesia, Lutuli was a teacher, Zulu tribal chief, leader of the antiapartheid movement, and recipient of the 1960 Nobel Prize for peace. Albert John Lutuli descended from a line of Zulu leaders. His grandfather and his uncle both had been tribal chiefs in Natal, a province of the Republic of South Africa. For a time, however, he followed neither this heritage, nor the ministry of his father, who died when he was eight. After graduating with training as a teacher from Adams College in Natal in 1927, Lutuli taught Zulu history and literature at the College for fifteen years. In 1936, at the request of elders of his tribe, he became the chief. The tribal chief was an elective position subject to approval by the South African government, which paid the salary. This new position brought him into the politics of the tribe and, increasingly, into conflict with the white minority regime that ruled South Africa.

Escalating restrictions on Africans brought Lutuli into active opposition. In 1944 he joined the African National Congress (ANC) and in 1951 was elected president of the Natal branch. In this position he helped organize nonviolent measures of resistance, such as boycotts, strikes, and noncompliance with discriminatory policies. When the South African government demanded that he withdraw from either the ANC or from his office as tribal chief, Lutuli refused to do either, and in 1952 the government deposed him. A month later he was elected to the presidency of the ANC and became the national leader of the struggle for racial equality. In 1960, the police opened fire at Sharpeville on a mass demonstration against the Pass Laws, which limited where nonwhites could live and work—69 were killed and 180 were wounded. Lutuli publicly burned his pass in solidarity with the victims, for which he was given a jail sentence that was suspended because of his health. His award of the Nobel Prize came while he was living under restrictions in Groutville, near Durban. He accepted the award on behalf of the people of South Africa and called for a new Africa "enriched by the diversity of cultures she enjoys . . . building a non-racial democracy that shall be a monumental brotherhood."

Irwin Abrams

References
Lutuli, Albert John. *Let My People Go.* New York: McGraw-Hill, 1962.

See also AFRICAN NATIONAL CONGRESS OF SOUTH AFRICA; NOBEL PEACE PRIZE; SOUTH AFRICA, OPPOSITION TO RACIAL OPPRESSION

M

Madres de Plaza de Mayo

An Argentinean human rights group, organized in 1977, a year after the Argentine armed forces took power and imposed a brutal and repressive dictatorship. It was composed of women, most of them mothers of children who had been kidnaped by paramilitary or military personnel and had seemingly vanished, or "disappeared." All fifteen mothers who began the group had failed to find out what had happened to their children, and their initial purpose was to force the authorities to answer a simple question: "Where are our children?"

They took their name from Plaza de Mayo, a central square in Buenos Aires in front of the Presidential Palace, isolated by barriers and heavily guarded, where any kind of public demonstration was strictly forbidden. Yet it was precisely in the plaza that the women first met and, defying military orders, began to walk silently for half an hour, every Thursday afternoon, around the small column that celebrates the independence of Argentina. Repeatedly ejected by force from the plaza, ignored by the general public, ridiculed, dismissed as "madwomen" by the government, imprisoned and

Mothers of the Plaza de Mayo march in front of the Government House in Buenos Aires, Argentina, December 12, 1985. AP/Wide World Photos.

even "disappeared"—such was the fate of Azucena Villaflor de Vicenti in December 1977—they continued to walk, a white kerchief on their heads, holding signs with the names and photographs of their children and the date of their disappearance.

Their persistent actions, always nonviolent but increasingly militant, gained them the support of international human rights and peace organizations. They succeeded in publicizing human rights abuses in international arenas and forced the military junta to address their questions about the "disappeared." After the Argentine armed forces embarked on a disastrous war with England over the Malvinas/Falkland Islands in 1982, the Madres spearheaded the massive mobilizations that accelerated the end of the military dictatorship. They went on to use their Thursday marches to demand justice and led the movement that brought to trial the members of the three military juntas.

The return to democracy in Argentina in 1983 created divisions among the Madres. Once the military were defeated, personality differences, partisan politics, and disagreements over the role of their organization in "normal politics" surfaced. One faction favored an independent stance, while another preferred a close alliance with left-wing political parties.

Presently two organizations call themselves Madres de Plaza de Mayo, and there is also a separate group formed by grandmothers, Abuelas de Plaza de Mayo. They were mothers of disappeared women who were kidnaped with their children or gave birth after their disappearance. Having given up hope of finding their children, they are still searching for their grandchildren.

Marysa Navarro

References

Navarro, Marysa. "The Personal Is Political: Las Madres de Plaza de Mayo." In *Power and Popular Protest: Latin American Social Movements,* edited by Susan Eckstein. Berkeley: University of California Press, 1989.

See also DESAPARECIDOS MOVEMENT IN LATIN AMERICA; HUMAN RIGHTS

Mandela, Nelson Rolihlahia (b. 1918)

Leader of the African National Congress (ANC) and the antiapartheid movement in South Africa, beginning in the 1950s. After almost twenty-eight years in prison for his political activities, in 1994 he was elected president of the Republic of South Africa in the country's first all-race election. Mandela shared the 1993 Nobel Prize for Peace with F.W. de Klerk (the last white president of South Africa, who moved the political system away from apartheid).

Nelson Mandela was born on July 18, 1918, at Qunu, near Umtata in the Transkei, into a leading family in the Temba tribe of the Xhosa people. In his early twenties, he rebelled against the tribe's traditions and moved to Johannesburg, where he obtained a law degree from the University of Witwatersrand in 1944. It was also in 1944 that Mandela joined the ANC. With Walter Sisulu and Oliver Tambo, he organized the Youth League to promote more militant policies against racial discrimination. Mandela rose through the ANC to become deputy to ANC President Albert Lutuli, where he was key to creating the nonviolent antiapartheid campaigns involving civil disobedience, protests, and strikes in the 1950s.

Following the Sharpeville massacre in 1960, however, Mandela turned toward armed insurrection to oppose apartheid. By the end of 1961, he was the commander-in-chief of the ANC guerrilla army, Umkhonto we Sizwe (Spear of the Nation). Mandela traveled abroad for two years, seeking military and economic assistance for the armed struggle and training recruits for the new army. When he returned to South Africa in 1963, he was arrested, tried, and convicted for acts of sabotage, charges he did not deny. During his trial he articulated his creed: "I have fought against white domination and I have fought against black domination. I have cherished the ideal of a democratic and free society in which all persons live together in harmony and with equal opportunities. It is an ideal which I hope to live for and to achieve. But if need be, it is an ideal for which I am prepared to die."

Sentenced to prison for life, Mandela grew to embody the national and international struggle to end apartheid, becoming a substantial embarrassment for the various white South African administrations. From prison Mandela opened negotiations with the government, which offered him freedom if he would renounce violence. Mandela refused to disavow the armed struggle. Finally, in February 1990, President F.W. de Klerk freed Mandela unconditionally, in the most significant step of the process of creating a democratic South Africa. After almost twenty-eight years of confinement, Mandela left prison without any show of bitterness, and, statesmanlike, prepared to work together with de Klerk and to oppose the violent methods advocated by more militant factions. Together they organized and then competed in the country's first all-race elections in 1994, and de Klerk became one of the country's two vice presidents under President Mandela. With his election, Mandela attained the new responsibilities of overcoming the social and economic devastation created by decades of apartheid, while reconciling the interests of all of the republic's citizens.

Irwin Abrams

References

Abrams, Irwin. "The Nobel Prize in Peace." In *The Nobel Prize Annual for 1993,* edited by International Merchandising Group. New York: IMG, 1994.

Mandela, Nelson. *Long Walk to Freedom: The Autobiography of Nelson Mandela.* London: Little, Brown, 1994.

———. *The Struggle Is My Life.* 3rd ed. London: IDAF, 1990.

See also AFRICAN NATIONAL CONGRESS OF SOUTH AFRICA; LUTULI, ALBERT JOHN; NOBEL PEACE PRIZE; SOUTH AFRICA, ANTIAPARTHEID SANCTIONS; SOUTH AFRICA, OPPOSITION TO RACIAL OPPRESSION

Maori Movement, 1870–1900

Resistance movement of native Maori tribes in New Zealand against colonization by European settlers. Upset by expropriation of land, resources, and sovereignty by *pakeha* (whites), tribal chief Te Whiti O Rongomai and his followers pursued a policy of obstruction to prevent New Zealand government-sponsored development and settlement projects from being completed. From 1872 through 1883, Te Whiti's nonviolent movement maintained a highly effective resistance to colonization.

Although the first Europeans visited the Maori-inhabited islands in 1642, attempts to colonize and exploit the resources of New Zealand did not begin in earnest until the New Zealand Company settlers and British military arrived in the nineteenth century. Clashes with the Maori natives erupted into the Land Wars of 1860–1872, which provoked several Maori leaders to stop fighting because they could not win. During the postwar years, several movements emerged, including the King and Kota-

hitanga movements, to promote tribal unification and to petition the government for more than token Maori representation.

One charismatic Maori leader, Te Whiti, began to preach "passive resistance" and separation of the races. Like other leaders, he had arrived at his pacifist views after experiencing the futility of fighting the European military might. Claiming land previously seized by the government in 1865, he and his followers built a model village called *Parihaka* in Taranaki Province and urged Maoris not to allow Europeans to buy, seize, or build on Maori land. Employing obstructionist tactics, they hampered road and lighthouse construction and telegraph line installation. In 1879, Te Whiti's followers plowed up land claimed by *pakeha* farmers to demonstrate Maori opposition to government confiscation of their land. In 1880, Maoris built fences across roads being constructed through their territory. The primary governmental response to these actions was to jail the nonviolent actionists—hundreds of Maoris were arrested.

The confrontation came to a head in November 1881, when fifteen hundred armed constables met twenty-two hundred unarmed Maoris who were sitting en masse in front of their meeting house. Te Whiti and other leaders were arrested, demonstrators were dispersed, and Parihaka was destroyed over the next two weeks. When Te Whiti was arrested, soldiers were confronted at the gates of Parihaka by a group of singing children. Te Whiti was detained without trial for two years and the movement lost momentum.

Maoris won nominal compensation for their land claims in 1926, but European settlers had already secured a majority of the land in New Zealand. Followers of Te Whiti have commemorated his legacy by assembling at a rebuilt Parihaka and holding ritual feasts. Te Whiti became a symbol of Maori nonviolent resistance to *paheka* colonialism.

Brad Bennett

References

Mamek, Alexander, and Ahmed Ali. *Race, Class and Rebellion in the South Pacific.* Sydney: George Allen and Unwin, 1979.

Walker, Ranginui. *Ka Whawhai Tonu Motou: Struggle without End.* Auckland: Penguin, 1990.

See also LAND SEIZURE

March First Independence Movement (Korea), 1919

Spontaneous uprising that occurred on March 1, 1919, first in Seoul and then across the country, as crowds of unarmed Koreans confronted the Japanese colonial police and gendarmerie in demonstrations for independence. The best-known manifestation of Korean nationalism during the thirty-five years of Japanese rule, the March First Independence Movement, though it did not actually achieve independence, is nonetheless recognized as the central event of the resistance.

Between the fall of the Korean monarchy in 1910 and the Allied victory over Japan in 1945, Korea was a Japanese colony. Korean nationalism developed rapidly during the period in a movement that divided into left and right and ultimately led to the establishment of rival regimes and North and South Korea.

The occasion for the March First Movement was a gathering of mourners from across Korea in Seoul to attend the funeral of Kojong, former emperor of Korea (who reigned from 1864 to 1907). Other influences contributing to the outbreak were the Bolshevik Revolution in Russia (stressed in the North Korean version of Korean history), Wilsonian idealism at Versailles (stressed by the South), and a proclamation of resistance earlier in the year by Korean students in Japan where, ironically, they were free to express their political opinions. The public reading of a declaration on March First was planned largely by leaders of the Korean Ch'ŏndogyo religion, who gathered support from leading Christians and Buddhists as signers of the document. These ingredients made the March First Movement a truly national expression; thus historians, especially in South Korea, generally point to it as the genesis of modern Korean politics.

The movement began when a group of religious leaders drafted and proclaimed a declaration of independence before a crowd in downtown Seoul on March 1, 1919. A few copies of the declaration had already been circulated in secret to other cities, such as P'yŏnyang, and in the days following, more copies appeared in other locations, where attempts to read them turned into confrontations with the colonial police and gendarmerie.

The demonstrators, who were unarmed, displayed uncommon courage, for the first decade of Japanese rule had been one of ruthless repression, and all Japanese officials—bureaucrats and even teachers, in addition to the police and military—wore swords to intimidate the Koreans. The Japanese were shaken by the fervor and apparent unanimity of the demonstrators, and, fearing that they were facing a highly organized movement rather then a loosely coordinated series of spontaneous protests, they responded to the rallies with all the force at their disposal, going so far as to employ firemen's pikes to scatter the demonstrators.

The March First Movement is known as a nonviolent uprising. However, as the confrontation unfolded, many Koreans fought back with whatever weapons they could find and some of the encounters became pitched battles, joined by frightened Japanese civilians as well as officials. Japanese reprisals continued throughout Korea and even in southeastern Manchuria, where Korean émigré settlements were used to harbor fugitives. When the movement ended in 1920, the Japanese regime estimated that over a million Koreans had participated (Koreans say 2 million) in 848 outbreaks during the first two months. Korean sources put the death toll between March 1919 and March 1920 at 7,645, with 45,562 wounded. Japanese sources note many fewer Korean casualties, and show nine Japanese killed and 1,409 injured during the first two months of the uprising.

The results of the March First Movement were disappointing to the Koreans, since independence was not achieved. Historians differ on many points. In South Korea, the movement is thought to have been the reason for the reforms that lightened the burden of Japanese rule in the 1920s, including permission to gather more freely, open schools, and publish Korean newspapers. In North Korea, the Korean left wing points to the bourgeois leadership of the movement and its paltry results, accusing the Korean right wing of collaboration and arguing that nothing less than armed resistance by peasants and workers could have rid Korea of Japanese oppression. These differing interpretations of the March First Movement reflect the conflicting ideologies that divide Koreans and are part of the bitter estrangement between left and right that was exacerbated by the Allied partitioning of Korea in 1945 and the subsequent Korean War. They are a reminder that reunification of Korea in the future will have to involve negotiations between North and South Korea not only about the terms of reunification, but also about the facts and interpretations of the shared Korean past.

Donald N. Clark

The March on Washington as seen from the Lincoln Memorial, August 28, 1963. AP/Wide World Photos.

References
Lee, Chong-Sik. *The Politics of Korean Nationalism.* Berkeley: University of California Press, 1963.

March on Washington, 1963

Significant demonstration of the African-American civil rights movement held on August 28, 1963, during which Martin Luther King, Jr., gave his now famous "I Have a Dream" speech. In early July, labor leader A. Philip Randolph and five other civil rights leaders called for a march and rally in Washington, D.C., for jobs and freedom. After a march from the Washington Monument, approximately 250,000 people assembled in front of the Lincoln Memorial to listen to civil rights leaders, entertainers, and politicians. At the time, it was the largest political demonstration in U.S. history, and some historians claim that it represents the peak of the civil rights movement. The event was unmarred by violence, partially due to the presence of over one thousand trained "peace marshals." The March received unprecedented press coverage, exceeding any prior Washington event. The March on Washington is also generally credited as being the major catalyst behind the passage of the 1964 Civil Rights Act by Congress.

Brad Bennett

References
Gentile, Thomas. *March on Washington: August 28, 1963.* Washington, D.C.: New Day, 1983.
Yette, Frederick Walton, and Samuel F. Yette. *Washington and Two Marches 1963 and 1983: The Third American Revolution.* Silver Spring, Md.: Cottage Books, 1984.

See also CIVIL RIGHTS MOVEMENT; KING, MARTIN LUTHER, JR.

Mau Noncooperation (Western Samoa), 1924–1936

Nationalist noncooperation campaign of native Samoans against the colonial New Zealand government. Characterized by almost complete adherence to pacifist principles, the *Mau* ("opposition movement") resisted authoritarian government and police repression with demonstrations, boycotts, tax withholding, noncooperation, and the creation of alternative political institutions. Despite their best efforts, New Zealand administrators could not force the Samoans to submit to their will.

Western Samoa was annexed by Germany in 1900 and, when Germany surrendered to end World War I, New Zealand was given a mandate by the League of Nations to administer the territory. This mandate, which ignored native Samoan aspirations for self-government, combined with a huge influenza epidemic in 1918 brought to the islands from abroad, provoked widespread criticism of New Zealand. In 1924, Tupua Tamasese Lealofi III, one of the highest ranking tribal chiefs, was involved in a conflict with a London Missionary Society pastor. As a result, Native Affairs Secretary Harry Griffin banished Tamasese to a village north of his home of Apia. Tamasese's refusal to comply with the banishment order, his subsequent arrest, and the removal of his title by the New Zealand administrator, General George Spafford Richardson, became the initial catalyst that inspired twelve years of resistance. Samoans began to protest authoritarian district councils appointed by the government and a legal double standard based on racism.

Coinciding with a March 27, 1927, ordinance suppressing free speech, Samoans founded the "Samoan League," dedicated to pacifist principles and democratic change. This opposition movement came to be known by its Samoan name of *Mau* and continued to grow during 1927. *Mau* supporters began to camp in and around the capital of Apia and started organizing their resistance. They staged demonstrations, and when told by police to disperse, they refused and their leaders were banished from Apia. They wore uniforms consisting of white shirts, purple turbans, and white and purple skirts. The *Mau* continuously petitioned Administrator Richardson for representation. They refused to pay poll and medical taxes and refused to cooperate with government inspectors and district commissioners. Tax resistance was so widespread that virtually no tax was paid by Samoans to the New Zealand administration during 1927. Some parents kept their children from attending government schools.

Noncooperation continued during 1928. In January, the *Mau* movement imposed a *sa* (boycott) on all white-owned stores in Apia. This boycott turned out to be economically ineffective but politically effective, because it provoked Richardson to take action. He stepped up repression, called for military aid, and two battleships arrived in February. On February 24, naval personnel arrested four hundred people gathering on the Apia beach. Cognizant of the limited size of Samoan jails, many more *Mau* activists asked to be arrested so as to overload the jails. Because of the strain on the system and the continued noncooperation of the activists while in jail, the prisoners' six-month sentences were remitted and they were released on March 7. Tamasese came to leadership while in prison during this period, and the *Mau* movement crystalized around the ultimate goals of New Zealand withdrawal and Samoan self-government.

Noncooperation continued into 1929, and police gradually started to use more violent repression. This rising tension culminated in what Samoans call "Black Saturday" on December 28, 1929. During peaceful gatherings to welcome important people arriving by ship, police opened fire on Samoans who they thought were attacking them. Tamasese was fatally shot trying to stop the onslaught by calling for peace. Thousands attended his funeral and, because Samoans operated with a largely collective leadership style, the *Mau* movement continued with new leaders.

In 1930, the new administrator, Colonel Stephen Shepard Allen, initiated what Samoans called a "campaign of terror," in which troops ransacked houses and raided the countryside in search of *Mau* supporters. During this period, *Mau* men hid in bush camps and continued their strategy of nonviolent noncooperation by evading search parties and avoiding violence. The "Women's *Mau*," led by Ala Tamasese, the widow of the slain *Mau* leader, organized the open political activity during this period while the men remained underground. This activity continued during the next several years. New Zealand began to ease restrictions on civil liberties as the administration realized that noncooperation was widespread and resolute. In 1936, the order declaring the *Mau* movement seditious was revoked.

While not all Samoans opposed the mandate, most Samoans at least wanted greater political representation. There were some violent acts in the midst of the nationalist campaign, but the *Mau* movement was predominantly nonviolent. Western Samoa did not gain independence until 1962, but resistance had hampered authoritarian measures through an effective campaign of nonviolent noncooperation.

Brad Bennett

References

Davidson, J.W. *Samoa Mo Samoa: The Emergence of the Independent State of Western Samoa.* Melbourne: Oxford University Press, 1967.

Field, Michael J. *Mau: Samoa's Struggle for Freedom.* Auckland: Polynesian Press, 1984; revised and reprinted, 1991.

May Fourth Movement (China), 1919

Movement for cultural and political modernization, involving student-led demonstrations and strikes, that emerged rapidly in Beijing and Shanghai on May 4, 1919. It was the first time in modern China that nonviolent direct action was used on a large scale.

The immediate motivations for the student-led demonstrations were the combination of Japanese demands made upon a compliant Chinese government, Asian aspects of the negotiations at the Paris Peace Conference, and general political anarchy in the country. Patriotic sentiments were the principal factors mobilizing students and other sectors of Chinese society, but students and intellectuals also called for broad social reforms, such as the adoption of Western approaches to science and the use of the vernacular language in literature. The movement succeeded in inducing the government to reject the peace treaty with Germany that was drafted in Paris. However, the movement did not achieve its broader social change goals.

Despite a largely liberal and nationalist revolution in 1911, China was in political turmoil and was relatively weak economically. Yuan Shikai, one of several competing warlords who gained power during this period, seized the position of president of the new republic from Sun Yatsen. Yuan's ambitions had little to do with maintenance of the republic, and he collaborated with Japanese imperialists, seeking political and economic support. The Japanese government used the circumstances of World War I to increase its influence in China at the expense of German claims. In 1915, Japan imposed a series of secret demands on Yuan, which became known as the "Twenty-one Demands." The principal elements of the demands were the replacement of German economic rule by the Japanese in Shandong province, a region that almost cut China in two, and direct participation of Japanese nationals in many aspects of economic and political life, including police functions.

The practical effect of the demands was to reduce China to virtual colonial status. After numerous threats of war, Yuan agreed at last to the demands. Popular opposition to the treaty, however, led to the collapse of Yuan's government. Its successor, however, was not notably stronger or more assertive.

At the Paris Peace Conference following World War I, the Chinese delegation asked to take back all the privileges that Germany had enjoyed in Shandong, and to abolish all the privileges enjoyed by other foreign powers in China. Western diplomats, however, favored the Japanese, and so the peace treaty was drafted to satisfy Japanese rather than Chinese interests. The events of May 4 were prompted by the news of the Chinese government's plans to accept these terms.

After receiving the news from Paris, students at Beijing University convened a conference of representatives of all the schools in Beijing on May 4. The conference was held in the morning, and the students decided to demonstrate that afternoon. At two o'clock in the afternoon, more than three thousand students gathered before the Tiananmen Gate (the "Gate of Heavenly Peace"). Their slogans reflected their patriotic feelings: "Eliminate the traitors and fight against imperialists!" and "Take back Qingdao!" (a famous city of Shandong province). The parade marched toward the neighborhood of the embassies. When their way was blocked by soldiers and police, they went to the residence of Cao Rulin, deputy minister of foreign affairs and the Chinese government's negotiator with the Japanese. The students considered him a traitor. Some of the students stormed into the house, damaged property, and beat one of the inhabitants. Thirty-two students were arrested and one died of injuries inflicted by the police.

After the demonstration, the government prepared to close Beijing University and forbade students to intervene in government politics. Meanwhile, people from all ranks of society asked the government to release the arrested students. More than thirty colleges and universities in Shanghai protested the government's actions and asked that the students be released. Chinese students in France, Japan, and Southeast Asia also protested. Several Chinese students in Japan were imprisoned.

On May 19, students in Beijing declared a strike. On May 26, students in Shanghai went on strike as well. Eight students were beaten to

M

death in Wuhan (a large city in Hubei province). On June 2 and 3, students in Beijing, Shanghai, Tianjin, and other cities went on strike under the direction of the National Student Association, established in Shanghai on June 1. More than one thousand students were arrested in Beijing, and one hundred in Shanghai. Then the whole nation became indignant. Students, workers, and merchants all went on strike. The government retreated before such immense pressure, released the arrested students, dismissed the three officials who were responsible for negotiating the treaty with Japan, and refused to sign the Peace Treaty of Paris. On these specific issues, the movement won a complete victory.

The influence of the May Fourth Movement was substantial. It animated the patriotism of the Chinese people, who would continue to struggle against imperial and military threats. The movement also opened a new era of nonviolent action in China. The May Fourth Movement became an inspiring symbol of student activism, and new student mobilizations often occur on its anniversary. Finally, the call for broad social reforms, in science and literature, as well as in politics, pushed China forward toward modernization. In very concrete terms, the influence of the West was seen in the formation of the Chinese Communist Party in 1921 and the Party of the Youth of China in 1923, as well as in the creation of a more coherent nationalist movement.

Li Fang

References

Chow Tse-Tsung. *The May 4th Movement: Intellectual Revolution in Modern China.* Cambridge: Harvard University Press, 1960.

Hu Sheng. *From the Opium War to the May Fourth Movement.* Beijing: Foreign Languages Press, 1991.

See also CHINA; DEMOCRACY WALL MOVEMENT; MARCH FIRST INDEPENDENCE MOVEMENT, 1919; TIANANMEN SQUARE, DEMOCRACY MOVEMENT, BEIJING, 1989

Mechanisms of Direct Action

The underlying processes by which particular methods of direct action operate to effect change in a conflict situation or in the behavior of another party. These mechanisms illuminate how various methods "work" to effect or resist change and reveal the distinctive nature of nonviolent direct action. Generally, methods of direct action engage one or more mechanisms of action, which may also vary from place to place, and from time to time. One critical divide, however, separates the mechanisms based on methods of violence from those rooted in nonviolent action. Specifically, the bases of social power that drive nonviolent action are clearly distinct from the physical power of violence.

Specifying the mechanisms of direct action in a particular method facilitates the assessment of both the potential and limits of the method under different conditions. The (negative) threat of a strike may be effective, for example, when the labor to be withheld is critical to the protagonist's interests. An appeal based upon positive interests, however, may be more effective when mutual interests are at stake.

Thus the action mechanisms collectively provide a framework with which to assess the processes through which direct actions operate. The assessment of the roles of these mechanisms in direct action yields an analytical profile of how the action appears to be "working." The assessment, however, is not focused on outcomes (for example, whether the process of coercion is effective). Rather, it is focused on the process itself (that is, whether direct action requires coercion to operate).

We can identify four mechanisms of direct action: demonstrative appeals, public coercion, discrete manipulation, and physical force.

A demonstrative appeal involves the invocation of positive, common/mutual/unified interests in support of the advancement of a position, plea, or objective. Some appeals may be characterized as intellectual persuasion in that they invoke a purportedly common set of assumptions, rules, logic, or evidence. Other appeals may be characterized as authoritative in that they invoke a purportedly mutual authority from which some legitimacy is drawn. Finally, certain appeals may be characterized as altruistic in that they invoke a purportedly unified identity such that the other party can identify with, and be influenced by, the actionist's self-imposed risk or sacrifice. Whatever the basis of purported commonality, however, all demonstrative appeals operate through the invocation of positive interests.

In contrast to the positive interests invoked in appeals, public coercion involves the threatened imposition/infliction of negative interests (for example, social, political, or economic costs; psychological harm; physical injury; or death). The notion of public as opposed to explicit threats is used in recognition that many threats are veiled or otherwise less than explicitly communicated, even as they remain potent. Note also that the threat may be directed at any party, including the actionist (as in a threatened hunger strike).

Discrete manipulation differs from both appeals and coercion in that it is directed at the physical environment, the conflict situation, or opportunities available to another party rather than at the opponent's will. To simply threaten, "your money or your life," is to coerce, but to hold a loaded gun to another's head with the same threat adds a credibility lent by the manipulation of the situation. Needless to say, virtually all threats entail some manipulation to bolster their credibility. On the other hand, an act of discrete manipulation can stand alone, without any public threat, either implicit or explicit. A protest occupation of an office, for example, operates to manipulate the physical environment by making it difficult if not impossible to conduct normal office activities. No threat is needed for the action to operate in this manner.

Because discrete manipulation targets things—the physical environment, the situation, or opportunities—rather than people, it is always a unilateral act, though more often than not, it operates in conjunction with another mechanism of action. The coercion mechanism, as noted above, often relies on manipulation, but so do many appeals: for example, while appealing to the positive interests of another (with a fast), an actionist may simultaneously seek to manipulate the conflict situation such that the other's choices are more constrained—by conducting the fast in the limelight of the international press, for example.

The last mechanism of direct action that is assessed here, physical force, also operates much if not all of the time in conjunction with discrete manipulation: an actionist can physically (re)move or injure, or even kill another. The target of the use of force is always another party's (including any third party's) body, as opposed to mind. The use of physical force differs from the other mechanisms in that the party doing the direct action rather than the party against whom the action is directed must conduct or carry out the desired change. Force

often is used preemptively to prevent the target from acting. In any case, the isolated use of physical force is rarely encountered; the coercive use of physical force is much more common. Direct actionists wield physical force coercively when they inflict injury upon another's body (the target's or a third party's) as a means of imposing a negative interest in combination with a threat of continuance or worse. As with all coercion, the target then is confronted with two or more negative interests.

A useful distinction between methods of nonviolent and violent direct action can be made by examining the operative mechanisms of action. Methods relying on physical force wield physical rather than social powers. Violent methods act against people's bodies, ignoring both their human interests and will. It is important to note, however, that methods of nonviolent direct action can provoke and even bring about great harm, even death. Witness the painful and indiscriminate consequences of economic sanctions against a country.

In contrast, by working through the will of others, social powers affect the interests of those other parties. These interests may be symbolic or material; they may be social, political, or economic; and as noted above, they may be affected by the wielding of social or physical power. Both positive or negative sanctions affect these interests. Direct action employs sanctions to affect interests in ways that involve costs, threats, or risks for one or more parties. Except for the isolated use of physical force, all of the mechanisms of direct action work through the will of others, even as their immediate target may be the environment (manipulation). Also, the coercive use of physical force is important as a mechanism in that it targets bodies in an effort to affect the interests and ultimately break the will of another.

These costs, threats, or risks constitute sanctions. While the specific methods of direct action are context bound and vary greatly from setting to setting, the processes or mechanisms of action through which they operate are comparable. The analytical framework of mechanisms of direct action facilitates contextualized comparative assessments of the interminable number of different forms of direct action across the world. A careful assessment of the ways a method operates can facilitate precise targeting and leveraged application of the social power wielded by a nonviolent actionist. In other words, one can begin to optimize the strategic performance of nonviolent action by drawing upon these analytical insights.

Doug Bond

References

Wehr, Paul, Heidi Burgess, and Guy Burgess, eds. *Justice without Violence*. Boulder, Colo.: Lynne Reinner, 1994.

See also METHODS OF NONVIOLENT ACTION; SOCIAL POWER

Menchú Tum, Rigoberta (b. 1959)

Born in Guatemala on January 9, 1959, to a poor Indian peasant family and raised in the Quiché branch of the Mayan culture, Rigoberta Menchú became involved in the social reform activities of the Catholic Church and was prominent in the women's rights movement when still only a teenager. She was awarded the 1992 Nobel Prize for Peace for her work on behalf of human rights for native peoples.

Following her father, in 1979 Rigoberta joined the Committee of the Peasant Union (CUC). Her family's activities for social reform brought increasing repression from the government and the military forces. That year her brother was arrested, tortured, and killed by the army. The following year her father was killed when security forces in the capital stormed the Spanish Embassy, where he and some other peasants were staying. Shortly afterwards, her mother also died after having been arrested, tortured, and raped. Rigoberta became increasingly active in the CUC, and taught herself Spanish as well as several Mayan languages other than her native Quiché. In the early 1980s, she participated in demonstrations in the capital, Guatemala City, and joined the radical group 31st of January Popular Front, for which she educated Indian peoples in resistance to the military oppression.

In 1981, Rigoberta Menchú went into hiding in Guatemala and then fled to Mexico, where she organized opposition to the Guatemala government and support for Indians' rights throughout the region. Her award of the Nobel Peace Prize recognized her work on behalf of oppressed peoples in the face of brutalizing violence. The Nobel committee drew some criticism on the award because of Menchú's associations with radical groups. Menchú made the case herself, however, when

she said succinctly, "If I had chosen the armed struggle, I would be in the mountains now."

Irwin Abrams

References

Menchú, Rigoberta. *I, Rigoberta Menchú: An Indian Woman in Guatemala*. Edited and introduced by Elisabeth Burgos-Debray. Translated by Ann Wright. London: Verso, 1984.

See also HUMAN RIGHTS; NOBEL PEACE PRIZE

Merton, Thomas (1915–1968)

Catholic priest and Trappist monk from the abbey of Gethsemani in Kentucky. The most popular Catholic author of his era, Merton wrote on peace, nonviolence, and the spiritual life, exerting a tremendous influence on Catholics around the world and on Christians in the United States.

Although sequestered on the margins of society in a monastery, Merton wrote copiously, encouraging and cajoling Christians to combine prayer with action in response to war and racial and economic injustices. Claiming that the duty of the Christian is to work for the abolition of war, he saw experiments in nonviolence as a central aspect of that duty.

Merton advocated a spirituality of protest and nonviolent resistance to the nuclear arms race that stood in stark contrast to the accommodationist elements prominent in much of Christendom. When his religious superiors briefly refused Merton permission to write on peace-related themes in 1962, his writings circulated underground in mimeograph form throughout the religious peace movement.

A trenchant critic of the U.S. war in Vietnam, Merton provided the burgeoning nonviolent movement in the United States in 1965 with an edited collection of topically arranged quotations from Gandhi on various aspects of nonviolence. His 1966 essay for *Fellowship* magazine, "Blessed Are the Meek: The Christian Roots of Nonviolence," was widely distributed in pamphlet form by the Catholic Peace Fellowship in its organizing efforts on behalf of conscientious objectors to the Vietnam War.

The starting point of Merton's nonviolence, following Gandhi, was self-knowledge. He taught that nonviolence ultimately has to do with an inner search to root out the violence in one's own heart. Consequently, he urged that nonviolent actions include a deep respect for the adversary. No stranger to the power inherent in ritual and symbol, Merton nevertheless insisted that nonviolent direct actions be conceived and conducted in such a way that communication with the adversary be maintained and enhanced. For Merton, the test of sincerity in nonviolence is whether one is "willing to learn something from the adversary. If a new truth is made known to us by or through the adversary, will we accept it?"

A proponent of interfaith dialogue, Merton was keenly interested in Buddhism and other Eastern religions. He died tragically in Bangkok, Thailand, in 1968 by accidental electrocution.

Patrick G. Coy

References

Coy, Patrick G. "The Personalist Nonviolence of Thomas Merton." In *The Universe Bends toward Justice: A Reader in Christian Nonviolence,* edited by Angie O'Gorman. Philadelphia: New Society, 1989.

Merton, Thomas. *The Nonviolent Alternative.* Edited by Gordon Zahn. New York: Farrar, Straus, Giroux, 1980 (revised edition of *Thomas Merton on Peace,* 1971).

Mott, Michael. *The Seven Mountains of Thomas Merton.* Boston: Houghton Mifflin, 1984.

See also NONVIOLENCE, PRINCIPLED; PACIFISM; RELIGION AND NONVIOLENT ACTION

Methods of Nonviolent Action

Discrete individual patterns of direct action intended to challenge an opponent without threatening or inflicting physical injury. Methods of nonviolent action are used for purposes of making a symbolic protest or persuading others, pressuring an adversary, and directly sanctioning persons or groups. Familiar examples of methods of nonviolent action are demonstrations and protest marches, labor strikes and lockouts, consumer boycotts, hunger strikes, human cordons surrounding a building or public space, and civil disobedience.

The idea of methods is basic for research into the nature, dynamics, and effects of nonviolent struggle. Nonviolent action as used in actual disputes consists largely of the employment of methods in more or less conscious and explicit, and more or less strategically informed, ways. Because of this, the concept of methods has important research utility as an indicator that nonviolent action is being used and as a means for determining and understanding the course of strategic interaction in cases. Some researchers argue that methods that damage or destroy the property of others, with no violence to persons, should be included among the methods of nonviolent action. An example is low-level sabotage. This essay does not include these methods in the concept of nonviolent action, but assumes that they are a distinct approach to action in conflict—neither violent nor nonviolent action.

The history of nonviolent action as such is quite lengthy, but the history of systematic thought about the subject is much shorter. Thinking about nonviolent action began with the recognition that means of political action exist that can directly place constraints upon others without violence. In the 1760s and 1770s, for example, political activists in North America recognized that acts of protest and noncooperation had some distinctive features that distinguished them from both violence and political acquiescence. This idea was explored further by nonresistance thinkers in the nineteenth century, for whom nonviolent action was viewed primarily as a means of moral or spiritual persuasion. The British Chartists explored similar ideas in their quest for a means of expressing their dissent.

The twentieth-century concept that nonviolent means of action are not simply persuasive but can also impose sanctions upon another party or limit others' freedom of action can be traced partly to Henry David Thoreau (1817–1862). Thoreau proposed in the essay "Resistance to Civil Government" (1848–1849) that even a minority may create "friction" or "counterpressure" against the policies of a majority invested with governing power. Thoreau is often recognized for his ideas about the duty to resist oppressive government, but he was also addressing the problem of effective action in conflicts. His idea of friction is a way of stating the view—perhaps even hypothesis—that nonviolent resistance could have an effect by interfering with the smooth conduct of the majority's policies. Once such general concepts about the distinctiveness of nonviolent means were established, thinkers could also begin to see the diversity of distinctive methods within it.

This idea of multiple and differing forms of nonviolent action that can be used in conflict is found in the writings of Mohandas K. Gandhi, Clarence Marsh Case, and others before World War II. Krishnalal Shridharani, in a study of Gandhi's technique of satyagraha, identified a small number of methods, as did Anthony de Crespigny in a 1964 study of "nonviolent coercion."

Case's comments are particularly salient from the standpoint of research. He used the idea of nonviolent constraint or coercion as a kind of test to determine if active protest and resistance was actually happening in a given situation, no matter what an activist might have said. (He used this test to argue that some "nonresistance" thinkers did not advocate any sort of resistance at all.) These and other studies raised two significant issues taken up by Gene Sharp in *The Politics of Nonviolent Action* (1973). These issues were, first, the relationship of the methods to a general definition of nonviolent action and, second, the extent of the methods themselves.

Definition and Classification

Case wrote, in *Non-Violent Coercion* (1923), that the best approach to understanding efforts to compel an adversary through nonviolent means is to look at "methods of social pressure" used in the "exercise of social constraint by nonviolent means." Likewise, Sharp argues in *The Politics of Nonviolent Action* that the "methods" of social, political, and economic constraint (that he identifies) "collectively constitute the technique of nonviolent action." Both scholars argue that there is an identity between the phenomenon of nonviolent action as a whole and its typical components. The significance, therefore, of the concept of methods of nonviolent action is twofold: (1) it provides a working definition of the concept of nonviolent action based upon observable phenomena that is independent of views of nonviolence that vary according to time and locality, and (2) it provides a marker or indicator for the occurrence of nonviolent action in conflicts, thus allowing verifiable and replicable research findings to be made. In short, the methods taken together constitute the operational definition of nonviolent action as a technique.

Consequently, the task of identifying the range and breadth of the methods, developing a scheme of classification, and estimating their number is a pressing one. The definition of method is best approached by analyzing its components. First, a method of nonviolent action is a contentious action used within a conflict, generally between groups. More or less explicitly, it is used to influence the course and outcome of conflict. Second, a method does not consist of the use of reason, discussion, or persuasion exclusive of direct contentious action. Third, it is not conducted through the use or credible threat of violence to persons or the destruction of others' property as a sanction. Methods are nonviolent in a behavioral sense; they do not engage in direct physical bodily injury to human beings, but certainly may be disorderly and disruptive or entail economic or emotional costs to persons or groups. The methods' principle of action is rather based upon the effects of symbolic protest and communication, withdrawal of expected compliance or cooperation, or direct interference with normal operation of a system. Fourth, the influence and outcome of a method is not comprehensively provided for either in the law or in institutionalized political procedures.

Because nonviolent action may be used as an instrument of political power and the control of power, states and legal systems attempt to manage and limit the ways in which methods are used. In regulating strikes and demonstrations, for example, a government may be preserving public order or protecting a privileged constituency against their effects. But the state does not determine the procedures used in the method. It does not determine whether demonstrations are persuasive or strikes effective in the way that, for example, it legitimately certifies the outcome of an election. Nor does government enforce the outcome of an action as it enforces a legal finding, although when these outcomes are expressed in law it certainly may enforce that law.

In summary, methods of nonviolent action are individual or collective, active efforts to influence and pressure others conducted by nonviolent means as part of an effort to affect the course and results of a conflict.

The Classes of Methods

A classification scheme that makes the concept of methods usable in research includes the full range of actions that fit the characteristics that have been discussed, excludes whatever does not fit, and makes adequate distinctions among what it includes. These distinctions must also not be so overly detailed as to multiply the number unnecessarily.

In trying to achieve these goals, Sharp proposes a classification scheme based on two organizing principles. First, methods of nonviolent action may be divided into three classes according to whether they are primarily symbolic expression with communicative content (methods of nonviolent protest and persuasion), active withdrawal of customary or expected participation in a setting or relationship or conjoint activity (methods of noncooperation), or an interposition (methods of nonviolent intervention). Second, methods of nonviolent action may be subclassified by their similarities, such as whether they are individual or group undertakings or whether they appear in the social, political, or economic arena.

Methods of Protest and Persuasion. These methods are not simply verbal, but involve symbolic expression in individual, group, or impersonal and even disembodied form. This class includes protest delegations and speeches, letter-writing campaigns, poetry, and music. Methods of protest and persuasion that have been used prominently in recent conflicts include protest songs, mock elections, and protest funerals. Protest songs were very important in the South African freedom movement, along with processions, marches, and the expressive, defiant dances called *toyi-toyi*. The civil rights movement in the United States used mock elections on several occasions, notably during the voting rights campaign in the state of Mississippi in 1963–1964. So many African Americans voted in these mock elections that a new political alignment, the Mississippi Freedom Party, grew out of the protests. Protest funerals and mourning for political martyrs have occurred regularly in recent decades. In China, for example, dissidents used the recognized period of national mourning for Zhou Enlai in 1975 and Hu Yaobang in 1989 to condemn the policies of the government. Clearly, such methods are not limited to rational or orderly persuasion, but may be tumultuous and disorderly and involve many thousands of people engaging in an intense criticism and condemnation of an existing order.

Methods of Noncooperation. Sharp suggests dividing the methods of noncooperation into social, economic, and political forms. All involve a cessation, usually temporary and reversible, of the willingness to continue some activity that others have come to expect. Socially, this may mean refusal to participate in relationships and institutions. During the international ban on South African participation in international sports, for example, many countries prohibited their teams from playing rugby, cricket, or soccer matches against South African teams. In New Zealand, activists tried to prevent tours by South African teams, which expanded into several highly contentious public campaigns when some local teams would not join the boycott. Perhaps the most extreme version of social noncooperation—certainly with a political tinge—involves a population simply getting up and leaving a country. Such mass emigration, as happened in the former German Democratic Republic in 1989, can place enormous pressures on a regime.

Methods of economic noncooperation are numerous and are pursued not only for economic reasons, but also to utilize economic relationships between parties as a context for making political or social demands. In addition, relations of power and the capacity to inflict countersanctions have shaped the emergence of methods of economic noncooperation. Illustrations of each of these can be found in studies of boycotts and labor strikes. Boycotts within a country are sometimes used to support strikes and labor organizing. Boycotts may expand the constituency using a method beyond those most directly affected by a campaign, which happened in the United States in the late 1960s when consumers boycotted table grapes in support of California migrant farm workers. In similar campaigns, activist groups worldwide have called boycotts of companies' products with the goal of pressuring them to change how they sold products that were potentially dangerous to people or to the natural environment.

Economic boycotts are among the methods of nonviolent action used in the international sphere and in intergovernmental relations. The boycott by the Arab League states against Israel, for example, pursued the general hostilities against Israel that had broken out into warfare at the time of that country's independence. This boycott not only involved a primary embargo on trade with Israel, but also a secondary boycott that tried to stop dealings with firms that traded with Israel, and to an extent a tertiary boycott against businesses that dealt with the boycotted firms. In addition to this example, governments regularly use various economic sanctions against other states. Sanctions have become a regular tool of foreign policy not only to press demands aimed at economic relations as such, but also to express concern about human rights abuses and similar issues.

Strikes, which are the refusal to continue to supply labor to another party, illustrate the extent to which factors of power and sanctions may determine the form methods take. The most direct form of strike, which is putting down tools and walking off the worksite, is common enough, but it is also open to various countersanctions by the employer, the courts, or the state. Consequently, several forms of limited strike involve temporary work stoppage, or perhaps working inefficiently or doing less than expected rather than actually leaving the workplace. Public employees' unions in the United States have sometimes chosen to limit strike action this way. Teachers have refused to do more than the contract requires (work-to-rule) or declined to participate in normal extra work, such as writing college recommendations or supervising after-school activities. Forbidden to strike, police officers have sometimes held collective sickouts, "blue flu," for much the same purpose.

The opposite approach to these limited strikes is to maximize the number and breadth of workers, occupations, and industries engaged in strike action—in short, general strikes. These strikes in particular are apt to involve political demands, or politically tinged economic ones. Further, general strikes may reduce the risk of reprisals by spreading the dangers among greater numbers of people. A prominent example in North American history is the Winnipeg, Canada, general strike of 1919. Although largely based on economic concerns, the Winnipeg strike was also motivated by workers' interest in organizing "one big union," a single industrial union representing all workers. During the general strike, strikers largely controlled the remaining economic life of the city for several days until defeated by an aroused professional class in league with the Royal Canadian Mounted Police. More recent history also offers examples of politically oriented general strikes, as in Nigeria, which has seen several. Nigeria's 1994 general strike protested the arrest of Moshood Abiola, whom many considered the properly elected president, by the government of coup-maker General Sani Abacha. This general strike was brief, but there was also a lengthier strike that crippled the oil industry (although neither action removed the military government).

The last subcategory of these methods is political noncooperation. To Americans, nearly all political noncooperation is "civil disobedience," but there are in fact many other ways of refusing to comply with political institutions or procedures whose legitimacy is questioned. Reaching back into U.S. history, we find that white citizens of northern states refused to obey the laws demanding that fugitives from slavery must be returned to their masters. In Boston in the 1840s, abolitionists went further, putting up posters identifying Southerners who came to search for escapees, so that people could avoid even inadvertent cooperation in the hunt for people fleeing slavery. Political noncooperation may be practiced by individuals, formal groups, loosely associated groups, institutions, or even by governments themselves. An example of governmental noncooperation is refusal to recognize another state diplomatically or admit it to an organization, as a sanction against its actions or policies, even though it may otherwise be eligible.

As with economic noncooperation, there are also methods of partial and indirect political noncooperation. "Schweikism," which means playing dumb while limiting cooperation as much as possible, is such a method. Political noncooperation thus does not imply simply opposition, but can also be used for the defense and extension of rights. In the Anglo-American legal tradition, for example, the principle that a jury cannot be punished for its decisions was confirmed as a result of the trials of Quaker William Penn in the seventeenth century. When Penn's jury found him not guilty despite the prosecutor's expectations, the jurors were placed under house arrest to compel them to recant. They nevertheless refused to retract the verdict and were finally released, after which authorities accepted as a general rule that juries could not be punished for lawfully determined verdicts.

Methods of Nonviolent Intervention. The boundaries of this category are not completely clear in Sharp's work. In part, his explanation of these methods in *The Politics of Nonviolent Action* relies upon an implied assessment of their effects. Sharp states that these methods either "disrupt . . . established behavior patterns" or "establish new behavior patterns."

Perhaps it would be preferable to approach the definition in ways more similar to ones in which protest and persuasion and noncooperation are defined. This would mean asking what participants concretely do that adds a perceptible "intervention" to the qualities of protest and noncooperation found in their actions. In short, these methods try to step more directly between the adversary and the achievement of its purpose than the other methods (leaving aside the question of whether they achieve either disruption or the creation of new institutions).

Psychological and physical intervention share this quality. The best-known of these methods is the hunger strike or coercive fast, which tries to compel a response from others largely by making them responsible for the lives of the fasters. As is known from British Prime Minister Margaret Thatcher's reaction to the 1980–1981 prison hunger strikes in Northern Ireland, the target may well refuse to accept this responsibility or may contend that higher responsibilities take priority over acquiescing to fasters' demands. Despite this, the aspect of intervention—creating a changed situation the other side cannot ignore—is present. Physical intervention also has been prominent on both sides of the conflict in the United States over abortion. Activists opposing abortion often obstruct normal access to places where abortions are performed, while those on the other side have made human blockades to keep out abortion opponents trying to force their way in. The struggles of the 1980s in Eastern Europe also offer many examples of physical nonviolent intervention, beginning with occupation strikes conducted by Solidarity in the shipyards of Gdansk and continuing through the human cordons that defended houses of legislature from Lithuania to Moscow.

Many methods of social, economic, and political nonviolent intervention share the features of a blockade, occupation (such as sit-down strikes), or obstruction. Sharp quite rightly points out, however, that many of the actions he considers nonviolent intervention create new political and social patterns and behaviors. Such "alternative" institutions include establishing underground economies and markets. At the extreme end of the scale of intervention, the actions termed "dual sovereignty and parallel government" offer direct competition to established government for the allegiance of a people. Among the more successful examples of this is the provincial government created in Massachusetts when it was a British colony. Established in the autumn of 1774, it brought together a new lower house of the legislature, chosen by resistance committees, and the legitimate upper house, which had been done away with by Britain. Its successes included a resolution to withhold taxes from the legal government that achieved broad compliance and actually led to financial problems for the colony's treasury.

Methods and Research

The relationship between the idea of methods and attention to research problems on the dynamics and effects of nonviolent action as a means of contention in acute conflicts can be explored first by clarifying the place of the idea of methods in the concept of nonviolent action. To do this, there should first be a brief discussion of objections that have been raised to the ideas presented earlier. Some argue, for example, that the list of methods identifies something important about nonviolent action, but not something useful for defining and identifying it. From this point of view, approaching the study of nonviolent action purely as a behavioral phenomenon is reductionist, because nonviolent action must embody a quality of nonviolence in itself that is not captured in the ideas of methods or technique. Compared to understanding the individual's commitment to refraining from harming people while combating injustice, the problem of identifying differing actions and their dynamics is an important, but a secondary point. Viewed empirically, however, the great majority of examples of nonviolent action have been done by people and groups not motivated by commitment to an ethic of nonviolence. From the standpoint of research, diverse motivations for engaging in nonviolent action therefore need to be taken into account. This encourages researchers to use an approach that sees the employment of methods as a central identifying feature of nonviolent action, which minimizes the number of assumptions they need to accept and opens up for examination questions like the centrality of ethical nonviolence to nonviolent actions.

Other objections are that some individual methods, and the categories themselves, are not mutually exclusive or exhaustive. Sharp distinguishes among kinds of economic boycotts, for example, by whether they are performed by consumers, labor, producers, handlers, or merchants. He takes it that the location of the parties within an economic structure (or in other cases, a political or social structure) differentiates among methods. It might be that this qualification is not necessary, because the refusal to purchase, supply, handle, or trade something in itself constitutes an economic boycott. If so, the distinctions among types of boycotts might be overlapping.

In a sense, the list also is incomplete. Sharp does not mention, for example, a method used in Russia, China, and other places, in which protest speeches, or the texts of wall posters and statements, are recorded on audiocassette and distributed to other activists. Of course, one reason for the absence of this method is that it is a very recent invention. Indeed, any list of methods is incomplete because more methods are being developed or discovered all the time. What is important is the logic of discovery and classification, not the completeness of the roster.

Another conceptual problem with the cassette method (*magnitizidat* in Russian), is that it appears to mix protest and noncooperation (the protest message versus illegal distribution). Indeed, Sharp admits that methods may appear to "merge" categories because a legal action can be made illegal. These problems might raise doubts about the logical status of the distinctions among methods and the categories. However, the concept of methods of nonviolent action performs in a different way from a logically comprehensive, deductive set of propositions. It serves as an orienting device so that nonviolent action can be recognized and studied empirically to understand its nature, dynamics, and effects. For this reason, the concept rather than the classification is central because it enables researchers to identify nonviolent action when it occurs, even in circumstances where the methods in use have not been observed before (innovations) or where they occur in modified or combined form. What is stressed is their conceptual distinctiveness from each other and from the surrounding universe of forms of direct action.

Generating Research Questions. The intellectual role of the idea of methods as an indicator is to orient the researcher toward the domain of nonviolent action as a research problem. Its contribution toward building a community of researchers in the field is that it permits them to develop research protocols that include mutually agreed upon standards for defining and identifying nonviolent action, for formulating significant research questions, and for developing methods that pick up the course and conduct of nonviolent action comparatively. Although these may seem rather basic requirements of doing good research, in fact this kind of intersubjective validation largely is lacking in the history of research on nonviolent action. The idea of methods of nonviolent action can help to generate research questions in three areas, including the history and modification of the methods themselves, establishing the external conditions under which nonviolent action takes place, and research on strategies, dynamics, and outcomes.

Looking first at the history, innovation, and communication of methods we find, for example, that several researchers have looked at this question from the point of view of tactical innovation in U.S. civil rights campaigns. They suggest that innovation was slow and uncertain originally, as the sit-ins, bus boycotts, and early freedom rides of the World War II era were not readily emulated. McAdam has found that rates of favored "tactics" (bus boycotts, public facilities sit-ins, freedom rides, mass protests) rose and fell sharply and successively during the 1950s and 1960s. His explanation of this variation is that methods were adopted as "negative inducements," or sanctions, that served to "disrupt [the] opponent's realization of interests." The opponent, in turn, had an incentive to discover ways to adapt to, evade, or effectively respond to each new method. Thus, each action was innovated, communicated to a broader activist population, answered by the adversary, and modified over time.

The factors that encourage innovation are not completely clear, but this research shows that the capacity of the other side to neutralize a method's effects, or punish the activists, is part of the answer. What other factors explain trends in the innovation and use of methods, and what kinds of historical research could clarify this problem? How do strategic and tactical objectives drive the search for new methods? How do technological changes afford opportunities for innovative action? Do certain cultural assumptions underlie certain methods, or can they be universalized? As suggested earlier, the history of the ways in which methods have been created and used is complex, lengthy, and of world scope. Research to track this history and to relate it to social and economic conditions, to the capacities of activists and adversaries, and to cultural factors, would be a central contribution to understanding nonviolent action.

Beyond this, the concept of methods has significance for understanding the wider domain of nonviolent action and its nature, dynamics, and effects. The methods in use are the manifest features of nonviolent action. They are what researchers actually perceive when studying conflicts, particularly if these cases are not already in the literature of nonviolent action. An example of this is the research done by Conser and his colleagues on the early period of the American independence movement. They were alerted to this case by the many examples of methods from this era in Sharp's work.

Therefore, a research strategy of identifying nonviolent action operationally as the use of methods during contentious action is a way of generating a variety of basic research questions. Considering that the primary variables are actions and their effects, not movements as such, the focus on methods pushes research questions toward considering the dynamics of struggle rather than the traditional social movements questions of mobilization patterns, collective behavior, structural opportunities, and the like.

One set of research questions goes to the incidence, prevalence, distribution, and scope of nonviolent action. Where and when does nonviolent action appear? Is it rare or common, and in what contexts both historically and sociopolitically? Is it found primarily in certain cultures, societies, or economic settings? Eastern or Western? Core states or periphery? In democracies, dictatorships, colonial polities, or other political systems? Is it found to be a means used primarily in conflicts concerning issues that are not in some sense "fundamental" to the parties, or is it found equally often among the central conflicts that characterize a social or political system? What explains the emergence and change of nonviolent action in the long view, as well as the short?

Nonviolent action can be taken as a dependent variable or as an independent variable, depending on whether the question relates to its causes or purposes. In addressing causal questions, researchers ask what typical intrasocietal, economic, or political relationships shape the resort to nonviolent struggle (as distinct from, perhaps, acquiescence, violence, or normal political forms of assertion). Questions where nonviolent action is the independent variable are more concerned with agency and choice. What

objectives are facilitated by the choice of certain methods? Under what conditions? Are methods chosen by a conflict group on the basis of their sense that there exists a wider setting of nonviolent action? Are they selected piecemeal? How do political commitments shape and structure choices of actions?

Factors describing the course of interaction during conflicts can be derived in part from observing patterns of change in the use of methods. What is the rate of change in innovation? What factors explain this? What outcomes appear to be associated with what choices of methods, given the broader context of strategic thinking employed by the protagonists?

Conclusion

To summarize, the concept of methods was implied in much thought about nonviolent action long before it was developed explicitly in this century. Once being clearly stated, in the work of Sharp and others, it has played a central role in the development of a research field focusing on nonviolent action as a technique of struggle. This is because it functions in research as a readily observable indication that nonviolent struggle is taking place. Provided with such an indicator, researchers can develop operational definitions, form research questions central to understanding the dynamics and outcomes of nonviolent struggle, and gather data in ways that promise to reveal much about the significance of nonviolent action as one of the basic ways in which human beings pursue and settle their conflicts.

Ronald M. McCarthy

References

Case, Clarence Marsh. *Non-Violent Coercion: A Study of Methods of Social Pressure.* Chicago: Century, 1923; New York: Garland, 1972.

Conser, Walter H., Ronald M. McCarthy, David J. Toscano, and Gene Sharp, eds. *Resistance, Politics, and the American Struggle for Independence, 1765–1775.* Boulder, Colo.: Lynne Rienner, 1986.

McAdam, Doug. *Political Process and the Development of Black Insurgency.* Chicago: University of Chicago Press, 1982.

McCarthy, Ronald M., and Gene Sharp. *Nonviolent Action: A Research Guide.* New York: Garland, 1996.

Sharp, Gene. *The Politics of Nonviolent Ac-*

tion. Boston: Porter Sargent, 1973.

Smuts, Dene, and Shauna Westcott. *The Purple Shall Govern: A South African A to Z of Nonviolent Action*. Cape Town, South Africa: Oxford University Press, 1991.

198 Methods of Nonviolent Action

The Methods of Nonviolent Protest and Persuasion

Formal Statements
1. Public speeches
2. Letters of opposition or support
3. Declarations by organizations and institutions
4. Signed public statements
5. Declarations of indictment and intention
6. Group or mass petitions

Communications with a Wider Audience
7. Slogans, caricatures, and symbols
8. Banners, posters, and displayed communications
9. Leaflets, pamphlets, and books
10. Newspapers and journals
11. Records, radio, and television
12. Skywriting and earthwriting

Group Representations
13. Deputations
14. Mock awards
15. Group lobbying
16. Picketing
17. Mock elections

Symbolic Public Acts
18. Displays of flags and symbolic colors
19. Wearing of symbols
20. Prayer and worship
21. Delivering symbolic objects
22. Protest disrobings
23. Destruction of own property
24. Symbolic lights
25. Displays of portraits
26. Paint as protest
27. New signs and names
28. Symbolic sounds
29. Symbolic reclamations
30. Rude gestures

Pressures on Individuals
31. "Haunting" officials
32. Taunting officials
33. Fraternization
34. Vigils

Drama and Music
35. Humorous skits and pranks
36. Performances of plays and music
37. Singing

Processions
38. Marches
39. Parades
40. Religious processions
41. Pilgrimages
42. Motorcades

Honoring the Dead
43. Political mourning
44. Mock funerals
45. Demonstrative funerals
46. Homage at burial places

Public Assemblies
47. Assemblies of protest or support
48. Protest meetings
49. Camouflaged meetings of protest
50. Teach-ins

Withdrawal and Renunciation
51. Walk-outs
52. Silence
53. Renouncing honors
54. Turning one's back

The Methods of Social Noncooperation

Ostracism of Persons
55. Social boycott
56. Selective social boycott
57. Lysistratic nonaction
58. Excommunication
59. Interdict

Noncooperation with Social Events, Customs, and Institutions
60. Suspension of social and sports activities
61. Boycott of social affairs
62. Student strike
63. Social disobedience
64. Withdrawal from social institutions

Withdrawal from the Social System
65. Stay-at-home
66. Total personal noncooperation
67. "Flight" of workers
68. Sanctuary
69. Collective disappearance
70. Protest emigration *(hijrat)*

The Methods of Economic Noncooperation:
    Economic Boycotts

Actions by Consumers
71. Consumers' boycott
72. Nonconsumption of boycotted goods
73. Policy of austerity
74. Rent withholding
75. Refusal to rent
76. National consumers' boycott
77. International consumers' boycott

Action by Workers and Producers
78. Workmen's boycott
79. Producers' boycott

Action by Middlemen
80. Suppliers' and handlers' boycott

Action by Owners and Management
81. Traders' boycott
82. Refusal to let or sell property
83. Lockout
84. Refusal of industrial assistance
85. Merchants' "general strike"

Action by Holders of Financial Resources
86. Withdrawal of bank deposits
87. Refusal to pay fees, dues, and assessments
88. Refusal to pay debts or interest
89. Severance of funds and credit
90. Revenue refusal
91. Refusal of a government's money

Action by Governments
92. Domestic embargo
93. Blacklisting of traders
94. International sellers' embargo
95. International buyers' embargo
96. International trade embargo

The Methods of Economic Noncooperation:
    The Strike

Symbolic Strikes
97. Protest strike
98. Quickie walkout (lightning strike)

Agricultural Strikes
99. Peasant strike
100. Farm workers' strike

Strikes by Special Groups
101. Refusal of impressed labor
102. Prisoners' strike
103. Craft strike

104. Professional strike

Ordinary Industrial Strikes
105. Establishment strike
106. Industry strike
107. Sympathetic strike

Restricted Strikes
108. Detailed strike
109. Bumper strike
110. Slowdown strike
111. Working-to-rule strike
112. Reporting "sick" (sick-in)
113. Strike by resignation
114. Limited strike
115. Selective strike

Multi-Industry Strikes
116. Generalized strike
117. General strike

Combination of Strikes and Economic Closures
118. Hartal
119. Economic shutdown

The Methods of Political Noncooperation
Rejection of Authority
120. Withholding or withdrawal of allegiance
121. Refusal of public support
122. Literature and speeches advocating resistance

Citizens' Noncooperation with Government
123. Boycott of legislative bodies
124. Boycott of elections
125. Boycott of government employment and
     positions
126. Boycott of government departments, agencies,
     and other bodies
127. Withdrawal from government educational
     institutions
128. Boycott of government-supported organiza-
     tions
129. Refusal of assistance to enforcement agents
130. Removal of own signs and placemarks
131. Refusal to accept appointed officials
132. Refusal to dissolve existing institutions

Citizens' Alternatives to Obedience
133. Reluctant and slow compliance
134. Nonobedience in absence of direct supervision
135. Popular nonobedience
136. Disguised disobedience
137. Refusal of an assemblage or meeting to
     disperse

M

138. Sit-down
139. Noncooperation with conscription and deportation
140. Hiding, escape, and false identities
141. Civil disobedience of "illegitimate" laws

Action by Government Personnel
142. Selective refusal of assistance by government aides
143. Blocking of lines of command and information
144. Stalling and obstruction
145. General administrative noncooperation
146. Judicial noncooperation
147. Deliberate inefficiency and selective noncooperation by enforcement agents
148. Mutiny

Domestic Governmental Action
149. Quasi-legal evasions and delays
150. Noncooperation by constituent governmental units

International Governmental Action
151. Changes in diplomatic and other representations
152. Delay and cancellation of diplomatic events
153. Withholding of diplomatic recognition
154. Severance of diplomatic relations
155. Withdrawal from international organizations
156. Refusal of membership in international bodies
157. Expulsion from international organizations

The Methods of Nonviolent Intervention
Psychological Intervention
158. Self-exposure to the elements
159. The fast
    a. Fast of moral pressure
    b. Hunger strike
    c. Satyagrahic fast
160. Reverse trial
161. Nonviolent harassment

Physical Intervention
162. Sit-in
163. Stand-in
164. Ride-in
165. Wade-in
166. Mill-in
167. Pray-in
168. Nonviolent raids
169. Nonviolent air raids
170. Nonviolent invasion
171. Nonviolent interjection
172. Nonviolent obstruction

173. Nonviolent occupation

Social Intervention
174. Establishing new social patterns
175. Overloading of facilities
176. Stall-in
177. Speak-in
178. Guerrilla theater
179. Alternative social institutions
180. Alternative communication system

Economic Intervention
181. Reverse strike
182. Stay-in strike
183. Nonviolent land seizure
184. Defiance of blockades
185. Politically motivated counterfeiting
186. Preclusive purchasing
187. Seizure of assets
188. Dumping
189. Selective patronage
190. Alternative markets
191. Alternative transportation systems
192. Alternative economic institutions

Political Intervention
193. Overloading of administrative systems
194. Disclosing identities of secret agents
195. Seeking imprisonment
196. Civil disobedience of "neutral" laws
197. Work-on without collaboration
198. Dual sovereignty and parallel government

Source: Gene Sharp, *The Politics of Nonviolent Action* (3 vols.). Boston: Porter Sargent, 1973.

Mexico, Nonviolent Action and Political Processes

Interaction between nonviolent struggle and reform of the political process, which has increasingly influenced political change in Mexico since the 1988 presidential election. Both the major center-right opposition party, the Partido Acción Nacional (PAN), and the principal center-left opposition party, the Partido de la Revolución Democrática (PRD), employed nonviolent techniques, sometimes jointly, during federal elections in 1988 and 1991 and in state elections between 1990 and 1993 to protest the ruling party's use of electoral fraud. Mexico represents a special case for scholars of nonviolence, since both sides of the conflict employ nonviolent techniques. The ruling party, the Partido Revolucionario Institucional (PRI), utilizes the extraconstitutional technique of electoral fraud to maintain its domination over Mexican society, while the main opposition parties mostly have used nonviolent techniques of protest and persuasion, sometimes in conjunction with those of nonviolent intervention, to challenge the PRI's authoritarian regime.

Nonviolent opposition to Mexico's lack of effective suffrage peaked in the six-month postelectoral period following the 1988 presidential election. At that time both the PAN and the Frente Democrático Nacional (FDN), the loosely formed precursor to the PRD consisting of a coalition of center-left opposition parties under the leadership of Cuauhtémoc Cárdenas Solórzano, strongly challenged Mexico's political status quo with massive nonviolent demonstrations of protest.

During the summer and autumn of 1988 hundreds of thousands of organized citizens throughout Mexico participated in marches, parades, sit-ins, roadblocks, protest meetings, and other methods of nonviolent protest to demand that the federal government respect their constitutional right to elect their leaders democratically. Suspicion of considerable electoral fraud grew during the presidential election of July 6, 1988, when government electoral officials blamed the continuously extended delay in reporting the official vote tally on the supposed collapse of the main computer system, located at the Federal Electoral Commission, just hours after the closing of voting stations. For the first time in over sixty-five years, Mexico's ruling party came very close to losing its authoritarian control of the political system.

A nonviolent movement developed semi-spontaneously. Leaders of the FDN—a coalition of four registered opposition parties (Partido Auténtico de la Revolución Mexicana, Partido Popular Socialista, Partido Mexicano Socialista, and Partido Frente Cardenista de Reconstrucción Nacional) had barely prepared their supporters to defend their right to free elections with proconstitutional means during Cuauhtémoc Cárdenas's final campaign speech. Other than Cárdenas's initial plea to fight electoral fraud within Mexico's legal framework, the FDN had but a very sketchy and loosely organized nonviolent strategy. The FDN had not anticipated receiving the tremendous support evidenced by the massive public demonstrations organized within hours of the electoral delays. Nevertheless, the coalition organized at least 105 discrete nonviolent actions: 88 nonviolent actions of protest and persuasion, 6 actions of political noncooperation, and 11 actions of nonviolent intervention.

Despite officially losing the 1988 presidential election, the FDN's nonviolent actions guaranteed some of its electoral victories in the federal Chamber of Senators and Chamber of Deputies by pressuring the PRI-controlled government into acknowledging the FDN's overwhelming electoral support in many urban centers where most of the large demonstrations occurred. The FDN thus acquired the legislative authority to challenge the PRI-controlled government. Moreover, the FDN's electoral success in the Chamber of Senators represented the first time in Mexico's postrevolutionary history that an opposition party had secured seats in the senate. By augmenting social pressure for effective suffrage at the national level, the FDN made tremendous progress in transforming Mexico's authoritarian regime into an authentic democracy.

Given the nature of Mexico's regime, the opposition movement faced certain risks, including the potential injury or death of activists, from the sophisticated and extreme electoral manipulation by the PRI-controlled government in this and future municipal, state, and federal elections. Additionally, in 1988 the FDN was alienated from foreign governments which, although fully aware of the electoral abuses conducted by Mexico's ruling party, officially recognized the fraudulently imposed PRI president-elect. Despite the risks and lack of international support, the nonviolent actions of the FDN demonstrated the courage, determination, and creativity of its supporters. In particular, two powerful methods of nonviolent action conveyed the FDN's bold resourcefulness in confronting the PRI's power: "muralism" (the display of important themes in large public murals) and the creation of a new political party.

On July 17, 1988, muralists took to the streets of Mexico City in support of democracy and against electoral fraud. Thirty plastic artists created a forty-meter-long project at the Centro Escolar Revolución, pictorially denouncing the electoral fraud of the ruling party. Muralism represents one of Mexico's unique artistic contributions with deep roots in the country's revolutionary tradition. Orozco, Rivera, Siqueiros, and Tamayo are Mexico's best-known muralists and are artists of interna-

M

tional renown. The use of this tradition as a form of nonviolent protest achieved a powerful degree of visually vivid persuasion.

In October 1988, the leaders of the FDN created a new political party called the Partido de la Revolución Democrática (PRD). This represented the most important nonviolent tactic undertaken by the FDN to continue its political battle for democracy in Mexico. Some of the main leaders and founders of the FDN, such as Cuauhtémoc Cárdenas Solórzano and Porfirio Muñoz Ledo, had served as high-ranking PRI members before leaving the ruling party to establish the FDN. Cárdenas had completed terms as a federal senator and as governor for the state of Michoacán. Muñoz Ledo had served as Mexico's ambassador to the United Nations and as president of the PRI. Only these former PRI enthusiasts, with their inside knowledge of the PRI's character, methods, and ideals, could have designed a viable nonviolent national campaign against the official party's despotic rule.

The FDN's knowledge of the social, cultural, and artistic traditions of its supporters was key to its nonviolent strategy. For example, the FDN realized that muralism could function as a nonviolent method, and that given the presence of main squares in almost every Mexican town or city there existed a logistical propensity and idiosyncratic preference for protest meetings to become the principal vehicle for demonstrating dissatisfaction with the PRI-controlled government. The FDN also endorsed the evolution of the peaceful occupations of municipal buildings into festive affairs with singing and dancing. These joyous attributes formed intrinsically appealing elements of the action and helped persuade more citizens to join the demonstration. Uncommitted third parties realized they could participate in the FDN's demonstrations against the PRI's violation of their constitutional right to effective suffrage without alienating themselves from their colloquial culture or involving themselves in violence.

The FDN demonstrated that by choosing the correct methods a national nonviolent campaign could prosper in Mexico. By adhering to its nonviolent stance the FDN succeeded in focusing on and exposing the PRI's blatant disrespect for the electorate's right to elect the nation's leaders freely. The FDN's leaders also understood their limits in terms of nonviolent strategy. They adopted mostly the less coercive nonviolent methods of protest and persuasion, so as not to violate self-imposed constitutional and legal constraints and to maintain the image of the PRI as the transgressor of the nation's constitution. If the FDN and its supporters had adopted more forceful and illegal nonviolent methods they would have secured fewer electoral victories than they officially won.

The FDN's use of nonviolent sanctions after the 1988 elections was not an isolated application of these techniques in contemporary Mexico. Other examples reveal that different groups of Mexicans, who have strongly disagreed with the PRI's authoritarian rule of government, have opted for nonviolence as a technique for articulating their dissatisfaction. In the 1920s and early 1930s, the "Cristero" movement in the state of Jalisco mounted resistance to the state's persecution of the Catholic Church. On October 2, 1968, approximately ten thousand people gathered on the square of Tlatelolco, in Mexico City, to listen to unarmed student leaders protest against one-party rule, the detention of hundreds of political prisoners, and police repression. Five thousand police and soldiers surrounded the crowd. The police opened fire, killing approximately 325 people.

Another development of popular participation, which grew in the aftermath of the devastating earthquake that destroyed parts of Mexico City on September 19, 1985, evolved through forms of nonviolent protest. Seamstresses, whose workshop had collapsed as a result of inadequate maintenance, formed a union, the 19th of September Garment Workers Union, to fight for better working conditions. Urban grassroots organizations also emerged to challenge city officials about the corrupt maneuvers that allowed for the continued suffering of earthquake victims for months after the disaster. For a few key days after the earthquake, the population of Mexico City spontaneously organized massive rescue and relief efforts while the government virtually went into hiding. City inhabitants formed citizen groups that, unusual for Mexico, remained unaffiliated with and independent of the PRI-controlled government. Many of these groups actively rallied in support of the FDN both before and after the 1988 presidential election.

A conservative opposition party, the Partido de Acción Nacional (PAN), conducted nonviolent protest activities in the state of Chihuahua in 1986 to express dissatisfaction with the gubernatorial and mayoral elections held that year. Three prominent Chihuahuan citizens, one of whom at the time served as mayor of the state capital, fasted in the most publicized protest. Other nonviolent actions included closing the international bridges to the United States with sit-ins, and holding silent vigils in front of the homes of individuals who had taken part in the electoral fraud. According to Inda, this movement aroused the latent desires of many Mexicans for authentic political participation and led the way for the subsequent expression of popular grievances with the Mexican political regime, such as the demands articulated within the PRI by Cuauhtémoc Cárdenas and Porfirio Muñoz Ledo through their Corriente Democrática.

The 1988 nonviolent civil movement to defend the vote transformed Mexico's political setting. Elections ceased to represent a period of negotiation between one strong party and a number of smaller minority parties, becoming instead a struggle for political power between more or less equivalent social forces. By 1993 the PRD had become the most powerful political challenge the PRI ever faced. For example, after the fraudulently conducted gubernatorial race of 1992 in the state of Michoacán, the PRD sustained a relentless campaign of sit-ins and protest meetings making it impossible for the PRI governor-elect to assume office. Similar episodes occurred in the states of Hidalgo, Guanajuato, Guerrero, Puebla, Quintana Roo, San Luis Potosí, Sinaloa, and Tamaulipas.

The FDN's use of protest and persuasion as its principal nonviolent technique represents a typical response of nonviolent movements operating under authoritarian regimes that discourage genuine opposition. The movement primarily organized public assemblies and protest meetings.

Thomas D. Rojas

References

Inda, Caridad. "Between Apathy and Revolution: Nonviolent Action in Contemporary Mexico." Paper presented at the Meeting of the American Political Science Association, September 1989.

Monsiváis, Carlos. *Entrada Libre: Crónicas de la Sociedad que se Organiza*. Mexico, DF: Ediciones Era, 1989.

Poniatowska, Elena. *Massacre in Mexico*. New York: Viking, 1975.

Rojas, Thomas D. "The Use of Nonviolent Sanctions by the Frente Democrático Nacional (FDN) to Protest the Alleged Fraud during the Mexican Presidential Election of 1988." Ph.D. Dissertation, Fletcher School of Law and Diplomacy, Tufts University, 1992.

Monkeywrenching

Sabotage and disruption designed to protect natural wilderness areas and biodiversity, predominantly used by North American radical environmentalists since the early 1980s against the timber industry and other development projects. These activists were inspired by Edward Abbey's *The Monkey Wrench Gang,* a novel about monkeywrenching. Although the method is largely associated with one environmentalist organization, Earth First! it is usually an act that is individually initiated and conducted.

Monkeywrenching (also called ecotage) consists of a whole series of tactics, all of which are intended to destroy or interfere with machinery, so as to increase operating costs to the point where they cut into profits and eventually stop production or development. The average monkeywrenching incident costs the opponent $60,000, according to one estimate. The major targets are the U.S. Forest Service, private logging companies, energy development companies, and off-road vehicles.

The most common of the tactics is tree spiking, in which ecoteurs hammer nails or other objects into trees so as to break saws and make logging prohibitively expensive. The second most common tactic employed is road spiking, placing sharp objects in dirt road wheel ruts to puncture the tires of heavy machinery or off-road vehicles. Monkeywrenching also includes pulling up survey stakes, sabotaging power lines, flattening tires, removing snowmobilers' signs, and blockading roads with boulders and trees. Sometimes ecoteurs disable or destroy vehicles. In 1985, a $250,000 wood chipper was firebombed in Hawaii to prevent it from destroying rainforest to produce wood fuel, and the company who owned it went bankrupt.

Monkeywrenching is a controversial tactic within the environmental movement. Proponents of the tactic consider it nonviolent because it is directed only at machines and tools and not humans or other forms of life. Care is taken to minimize the risk to people, both opponents and monkeywrenchers. However, critics charge that the most common form, tree spiking, is violent because not only can it break a chainsaw, but in so doing it can also injure or kill the unsuspecting chainsaw operator. Because monkeywrenching is illegal, strategy, timing, and security are crucial. Few ecoteurs have been prosecuted, in spite of increased efforts to catch them. Monkeywrenching has been successful on an individual basis in disrupting various business endeavors in the wilderness.

Brad Bennett

References

Davis, John, ed. *The Earth First! Reader: Ten Years of Radical Environmentalism*. Salt Lake City: Peregrine Smith, 1991.

Foreman, Dave, and Bill Haywood, eds. *Ecodefense: A Field Guide to Monkeywrenching*. 2nd ed. Tucson, Ariz.: Ned Ludd, 1987.

See also ENVIRONMENTAL MOVEMENTS; GREENPEACE

Montgomery Bus Boycott, 1955–1956

Year-long boycott of public buses by blacks in Montgomery, Alabama, in an attempt to modify the state law that required segregated seating on buses and to protest the mistreatment of black patrons. The protest resulted in a U.S. Supreme Court decision striking down the Alabama bus segregation law and calling for an integrated bus system.

The boycott was prompted by the refusal of Rosa Parks, a Montgomery seamstress, to give up her bus seat for a white passenger. Police arrested her, and she was later released on bail posted by E.D. Nixon, a friend and former state chairman of the National Association for the Advancement of Colored People.

After Mrs. Parks's release, leaders in the black community proposed a boycott of city buses, beginning December 5, to protest the ongoing mistreatment of black patrons. Black leaders formed the Montgomery Improvement Association (MIA) to organize a movement that gave solidarity to the fifty thousand blacks participating in the boycott. Martin Luther King, Jr., was chosen as president. Other leaders included Nixon, Ralph Abernathy, and Robert Graetz, a white pastor.

The goals of the boycott were simple: (1) blacks must be treated with courtesy, (2) passengers would be seated on a first-come, first-served basis with blacks filling seats from the back forward and whites taking the seats from the front back, and (3) there would be black drivers for the mostly black routes. Such goals were modest—they were intended to achieve merely a more flexible color line, not necessarily complete integration.

The MIA coordinated alternative means of transportation for protesters. Those who could walk to their destinations would do so, but for many boycotters, the distance was too great. The black churches, therefore, bought cars and donated them to function as taxis for protesters.

The economic impact of the boycott was substantial, since blacks made up almost three-quarters of all bus patrons. The bus company's revenues declined dramatically, which forced increased fares and curtailed schedules. In addition, downtown stores lost business since fewer blacks were traveling to shop.

Some white extremists retaliated violently to the boycott, which resulted in the bombing of the homes of King, Nixon, and Graetz. In the face of the outright cruelty by whites, King encouraged blacks not to retaliate with violence, but to "love our white brothers no matter what they do to us." The bombings and King's response brought immediate sympathy for Montgomery blacks from all over the world. This, in turn, prompted thousands of dollars in contributions to the Montgomery Improvement Association, which helped replace the nearly $31,000 that was spent providing alternative means of transportation for boycotters.

After a year of conflict, the U.S. Supreme Court on November 13, 1956, upheld a lower federal court ruling that the Montgomery bus segregation law was unconstitutional. Almost simultaneously, a state court injunction on the church-sponsored carpools took effect. For the next month, as the city made its final petition to the Supreme Court for reconsideration, the boycott continued with a hastily arranged ride sharing system. On December 20, the desegregation order was served to the city officials and the next morning a completely desegregated bus service began.

Kimberley A. Pyles

References

Branch, Taylor. *Parting the Waters: America in the King Years, 1954–63*. New York: Simon and Schuster, 1988.

Cooney, Robert, and Helen Michalowski, eds. *The Power of the People: Active Nonviolence in the United States*. From an original text by Marty Jezer. Culver

City, Calif: Peace Press, 1977; 2nd ed, Philadelphia: New Society, 1987.

Garrow, David J. *Bearing the Cross: Martin Luther King, Jr. and the Southern Christian Leadership Conference.* New York: William Morrow, 1986.

Gibson Robinson, Jo Ann. *The Montgomery Bus Boycott and the Women Who Started It.* Edited by David J. Garrow. Knoxville: University of Tennessee Press, 1987.

See also BOYCOTTS; CIVIL RIGHTS MOVEMENT; KING, MARTIN LUTHER, JR.; NIXON, E.D.; PARKS, ROSA

Mott, Lucretia Coffin (1793–1880)

Social reformer, abolitionist, women's rights activist, pacifist, born on January 3, 1793, in Nantucket, Massachusetts, and died on November 11, 1880, at Roadside, her home outside of Philadelphia.

Lucretia Coffin, whose father was a sea captain and whose mother was a shopkeeper, was educated in a Quaker boarding school near Poughkeepsie, New York. She worked as a teacher until 1811, when she married James Mott in Philadelphia and began to raise a family, eventually giving birth to six children. Her grief at the death of her first son, Thomas, in 1817, inspired Mott to speak at a Quaker Meeting. Her eloquence was appreciated by the congregation, which encouraged her to preach, and in 1821 Mott was recognized as a minister. Later, in the 1830s, Mott, a Hicksite, began to travel to address tensions that had arisen from the Hicksite–Orthodox schism in the Society of Friends, though she was sometimes persecuted and ostracized for her efforts.

Increasingly aware of slavery and of the work of the abolitionists, Lucretia and her husband, after personally boycotting products of the slave trade, helped form the Philadelphia Free Produce Society in 1826 to encourage patronage of stores that did not sell goods produced by slave labor—cotton, sugar, molasses. She attended the founding convention of the American Anti-Slavery Society in 1833 and, within days, organized the Philadelphia Female Anti-Slavery Society. Her passion for the anti-slavery cause antagonized many Quakers, who attempted to strip her of her ministry and membership, but Mott persisted. In 1837, she helped organize the first Anti-Slavery Convention of

Lucretia Coffin Mott (Photo by Isaac G. Tyson). Friends Historical Library/Swarthmore College.

American Women held in New York City and was instrumental in calming racial tensions and mob violence that surrounded the convention in subsequent years.

In 1840, Lucretia and James attended the World Anti-Slavery Convention in London, but encountered strong opposition to women's rights. Female delegates, excluded from the proceedings, were forced to sit at the back of the meeting hall, and it was here that Mott met Elizabeth Cady Stanton. Eight years later, in 1848, Mott and Stanton convened the Seneca Falls Woman's Rights Convention, which passed a "Declaration of Sentiments" calling for an end to the oppression of women. In 1849, Mott wrote "Discourse on Woman" in defense of women's rights, education, and suffrage, later published as a pamphlet. Widely regarded as the mother of the women's rights movement, Mott organized, wrote, spoke, and traveled promoting feminism. In 1852, while presiding over a women's rights convention in Syracuse, New York, she met Susan B. Anthony, who became a lifelong friend.

Mott believed firmly that "there is no true Peace that is not founded on justice and right," and so was active in challenging many forms of oppression. She collected clothing and raised money for ex-slaves during the Civil War; helped organize a Women's Association for the Aid of the Freedmen; objected to capital punishment; preached eloquently against war; served as president of the American Equal Rights Association; was instrumental in 1867 in founding the Free Religious Association, a radical group of Jews and Christians dedicated to religious reform; and met with President Ulysses S. Grant in 1873 to urge him to pardon six Native Americans who had been condemned to death for resisting resettlement in California. In 1876, to protest the exclusion of women from the official Centennial Celebration of the Declaration of Independence, Mott presided over a women's counter-celebration.

When she died, several thousand people gathered at her graveside and stood in silence.

Pam McAllister

References

Bacon, Margaret Hope. *Mothers of Feminism: The Story of Quaker Women in America.* San Francisco: Harper and Row, 1986.

———. *Valiant Friend: The Life of Lucretia Mott.* New York: Walker, 1980.

See also ABOLITIONIST MOVEMENT; ANTHONY, SUSAN BROWNELL; STANTON, ELIZABETH CADY; WOMEN'S SUFFRAGE

Movement for a New Society

A loose community of activists founded in West Philadelphia in 1971. It spread to at least eight cities in the United States and established worldwide connections for nonviolence training and action.

By living as groups, buying food through a cooperative, and sharing child care, big appliances, and a few cars, they were freed from the pressure to make more money just to survive. Many had part-time jobs, which allowed them time to write manuals, act as trainers, and participate in social and political actions. Moreover, a certain sense of joie de vivre pervaded their lives through dancing and group singing.

While it was a predominantly secular organization, certain prominent Quaker activists (including Ross Flanagan, George Lakey, Berit Lakey, Gail Pressberg, Richard Taylor, and George Willoughby) provided a spiritual base to MNS.

The philosophy of "living simply that others may simply live" undergirded all MNS ac-

tions. Those against nuclear power (such as demonstrations at the Seabrook, New Hampshire, plant) are only one example. This philosophy of living is particularly relevant in our era of ecological deterioration, as most Westerners continue to expect a constantly expanding gross national product—while the gross earth product continues to decline.

Nonviolent training and action focused predominantly on social and political problems. Gandhian, Quaker, and ad hoc methods were practiced—a fusion emerging from group consensus within MNS. The aim was to systematize what had been learned in the past through single-issue campaigns. Nonviolent training and action were the visible part, but community was the internal holistic vision; it enabled MNS members to continually interact and learn to live together on an ongoing basis.

It was a time when leaderlessness and consensus decision making were in vogue in progressive social movements. MNS used these principles in discussions of divisive issues such as classism, ethnocentrism, racism, and sexism. But these discussions often highlighted the prejudices of many members, thus undermining the organization's coherence and contributing to MNS's eventual demise. George Lakey, for example, cites MNS's inability to fully use its developed leadership, an inability influenced by the antileader currents of the period, as the most important factor in its decline.

Perhaps the most dramatic and well-organized nonviolent MNS action was the 1971 blockade of U.S. arms exports to West Pakistan. Richard Taylor's *Blockade* describes the campaign in full during the civil war with East Pakistan (now Bangladesh). More than two hundred people took part in the campaign, which ran up and down the East Coast of the United States. Actions included marches, picketing, paddling canoes in front of Pakistani freighters, and all-night vigils at the White House. The campaign succeeded in blockading Philadelphia's port, preventing the shipment of such material until the war ended in 1972.

Crucial to the victory was support from the head of the International Longshoreman's local union, an African American sympathetic to the victims of West Pakistani genocide, who cooperated in getting longshoremen to refuse to load Pakistani ships. The most important achievement, says Taylor, was helping to educate the public, whose outrage eventually led to a cutoff of U.S. government aid to Pakistan.

MNS was "laid down" in 1988, but a number of members continued to participate in nonviolent training and action all over the world. Some worked on an individual basis as consultants; others joined groups such as Witness for Peace, which struggled for peace in Nicaragua. New Society Publishers continues to flourish in West Philadelphia.

Marjorie Hope
James Herbert Young

References
Taylor, Richard. *Blockade.* New York: Orbis, 1977.

See also BLOCKADES

Muste, Abraham John (1885–1967)

Clergyman, labor organizer, civil liberties advocate, champion of racial justice, and leader of antiwar movements. Born in the Netherlands on January 8, 1885, raised in Michigan, educated at Hope College and New Brunswick Theological Seminary, Muste became minister of a Dutch Reform Church in New York City in 1909. He married Anna Huizenga that year. They had three children, Anne Dorothy Muste Baker, Constance Muste Hamilton, and John Muste. Muste soon departed from his conservative upbringing for a life of activism that he compared to the journey of the biblical Abraham, who "went out looking for a city which existed—and yet had to be brought into existence."

In 1914, Muste assumed a Congregational pastorate in Newtonville, Massachusetts, which he lost four years later when his opposition to World War I clashed with the views of his parishioners. He found employment, and the religious tradition that would remain his "spiritual home" for the rest of his life, by becoming a Quaker minister in Providence, Rhode Island. In 1919, Muste led a successful workers' strike in the textile mills of Lawrence, Massachusetts, and began fifteen years of leadership in the labor movement, as dean of Brookwood Labor College in Katonah, New York (1923–1933) and head of the Conference for Progressive Labor Action. In 1935–1936, Muste was executive secretary of the Trotskyist American Workers Party. In 1936, a mystical experience returned him to Christian pacifism.

As industrial secretary of the Fellowship of Reconciliation (FOR) 1936–1937 and then di-

Abraham John Muste. Fellowship of Reconciliation Archives.

rector of the Presbyterian Labor Temple in New York City until 1940, Muste called on workers to forgo violence. In World War II, he was executive secretary of the FOR, supporting draft resistance and conscientious objection, while pleading for U.S. assistance to the victims of persecution in Europe. In the 1950s, his leadership extended to the War Resisters League and the Committee for Nonviolent Action, where he advocated unilateral disarmament, refused to pay income taxes, defied civil defense laws, and practiced other civil disobedience against atomic testing and construction of nuclear weapons.

Muste helped to organize the Society for Social Responsibility in Science, the Council for Correspondence, and the Church Peace Mission. He worked in Asia and Africa as co-chair of the World Peace Brigade and played a significant role in three major transnational walks for peace—San Francisco to Moscow (1960–1961); Quebec to Guantanamo (1961); and New Delhi to Peking (1963–1964).

Muste advised the founders of the Congress of Racial Equality and was esteemed by Martin Luther King, Jr., as a critical link between the civil rights struggle and nonviolence.

In his final years, he helped to create the strongest antiwar coalition in U.S. history, the mobilization against the war in Vietnam. Muste died on February 11, 1967.

Jo Ann Ooiman Robinson

References

Hentoff, Nat. *Peace Agitator: The Story of A.J. Muste.* New York: Macmillan, 1963.

Muste, A.J. *The Essays of A.J. Muste.* New York: Bobbs-Merrill, 1967.

Robinson, Jo Ann Ooiman. *Abraham Went Out: A Biography of A.J. Muste.* Philadelphia: Temple University Press, 1981.

———. "A.J. Muste, Prophet in the Wilderness of the Modern World." In *Peace Heroes in Twentieth Century America,* edited by Charles DeBenedetti. Bloomington: Indiana University Press, 1986.

See also Brookwood Labor College; Congress of Racial Equality; Fellowship of Reconciliation; Pacifism; Vietnam War Opposition; War Resisters' International

Mutiny

Collective military insubordination. Traditionally, the main motivation for mutiny has concerned issues of living and working conditions, such as food, pay, and discipline. More recently, however, troops have been prone to mutiny for ethical, political, or moral reasons.

The word *mutiny* frequently connotes violence, and some mutinies have indeed produced their share of bloodshed. Yet most mutinies involve little loss of life or even physical injury. In fact, the industrial wildcat strike is the most reasonable civilian analogy to military mutiny.

The typical mutiny tends to be short, measured in hours, or occasionally days. Mutiny has self-limiting characteristics: soldiers and sailors exist in an environment in which all their physical and many of their emotional needs are provided for. Therefore, after an initial period of blowing off steam, there is usually a desire to bring the outbreak to some resolution, if only to provide the customary food and quarters.

Leadership in mutinies, like leadership in other social situations, gives rise to the chicken-or-egg conundrum of whether the leader makes the mutiny or the mutiny makes the leader.

There is no clear answer. Leaders themselves typically assert that they assumed the leadership role through happenstance. The authorities, however, usually favor the conspiracy theory, tending to overemphasize the importance of the leaders and contending that the mass of the troops were led astray by a few ringleaders. The mass of troops themselves tend to run the gamut from true believers to opportunists to swimmers-with-the-tide; some are simply intimidated.

The most immediate response to an outbreak comes from the officers of the units involved. Although there are instances of particularly stalwart officers facing down the mutineers, the evidence suggests that the larger the mutiny, the less likely are the officers to take any action that can possibly be avoided. Indeed, when the numbers are large, there is little that can be done other than to attempt to assert some moral authority. This rarely has much, if any, effect, and it is left to the threat, or more rarely, the application of force to resolve the issue. Troops are understandably reluctant to use arms against their own comrades and when force has become necessary, it has usually been exercised by elite units or other formations least likely to show sympathy for the mutineers.

Classically, mutiny was the most serious crime a soldier or sailor could commit, punishable, in the military code of most countries, by death. In earlier times this was no doubt the case. But in the twentieth century there has been a trend toward greater leniency in military punishment. Execution was used through World War I, but since that time the death penalty has been rarely employed and prison terms have been progressively shorter, a phenomenon that reflects the shift in social norms to recognize the rights of soldiers as citizens. The inhibition to the use of the word *mutiny* increasingly restricted the ability of the military to inflict the legally appropriate penalties. Then too, in mutiny, as in other areas of life, there is safety in numbers. One simply cannot shoot a whole regiment or hang a whole fleet. The ancient expedient of executing every tenth man—hence the term *decimation*—would hardly be countenanced in today's world.

Mutiny—any mutiny—is so profound a trauma to the military psyche that the high command cannot help but respond. Internal investigations conducted by boards of inquiry almost invariably follow mutinies, and the sources of discontent are usually addressed. Thus, in recent years, mutiny can be said to have been an effective means by which troops could seek redress of their grievances.

Elihu Rose

References

Guttridge, Leonard F. *Mutiny: A History of Naval Insurrection.* Annapolis, Md.: Naval Institute Press, 1992.

James, Lawrence. *Mutiny in the British and Commonwealth Forces, 1797–1956.* London: Buchan and Enright, 1987.

Rose, Elihu. "The Anatomy of Mutiny." *Armed Forces and Society* 8 (Summer 1982): 561–574.

See also METHODS OF NONVIOLENT ACTION; RUSSIAN REVOLUTION OF 1905

M

N

Namibia, Campaign for Freedom

Internal and international nonviolent organizing in support of the liberation struggle of the Namibian people from the 1960s until independence was achieved in 1992.

Namibia (formerly South-West Africa), the last colony in Africa and the last League of Nations–mandated territory, became a focus of international concern uniting anti-apartheid movements, environmentalists, and antinuclear activists against the occupying army and administration of South Africa. While the South-West African People's Organization (SWAPO) led an armed resistance against the South African Defence Force from bases in Angola, a national campaign of nonviolent resistance was mobilized internally by SWAPO and the labor and religious sectors of the population.

The modern struggle against South African occupation began in the late 1940s when Namibians who had managed to escape or smuggle messages out of the territory appealed to the United Nations, asking the UN to directly administer the League of Nations mandate for the territory, which had been left under South African supervision. When South Africa refused to acknowledge the UN as the legitimate successor to the League of Nations, the UN established a Council for Namibia as the internationally recognized governing authority for the territory. The council issued a decree in 1974 outlawing all treaties and contracts with South Africa concerning Namibian natural resources. This decree became the basis for protests and legal challenges against companies and governments exploiting Namibian products and raw materials.

In 1959, South African police cracked down brutally on a boycott and peaceful demonstration organized by women protesting their forced removal from Windhoek to "bantustan" reservations, killing eleven. This police violence led to the formation of liberation organizations within Namibia and a gradually stronger and more unified labor movement. In 1971–1972, fifteen thousand Namibian workers struck for two months against the contract labor system that controlled the movement and employment of Namibians. The strikers won modest concessions, but the apartheid-based occupation system remained. Repeatedly, throughout the 1970s and 1980s, the Namibian people organized effective boycotts of South African–run elections aimed at perpetuating South African control. Eventually, by the mid-1980s, the growing unity and activism among the religious denominations and the political, labor, and student forces culminated in massive nonviolent demonstrations against the South African presence in several cities, despite widespread use of intimidation, torture, and assassination as well as military actions against civilian populations by the South African government.

Throughout this period, growing international awareness of the Namibian occupation and the special circumstances of the imposition of apartheid in a territory ostensibly under international supervision for the good of the indigenous population led to international activist efforts in support of Namibian independence.

In 1974, the War Resisters' International conference in Holland endorsed Operation Namibia, an effort to challenge and publicize South African control of Namibia by delivering books—many of them banned by South Africa—to political groups within Namibia. This effort gained support from anti-apartheid activists worldwide and received endorsements and contributions of books from individuals, social and charitable organizations, and several West African governments. The crew sailing to deliver the books carried UN visas granted by the Council for Namibia. Eventually, the books were delivered through United Nations auspices to Namibian refugee camps in Angola.

Labor groups in Australia, Belgium, Britain, Canada, France, Japan, and West Germany exposed their own government and multinational corporate involvement in the importation of Namibian raw materials, especially uranium, and demanded that the traffic stop. These groups researched and documented the routes and carriers of Namibian uranium ore, and attempted to intercept these cargoes and bring suit in the International Court for violation of UN Decree No. 1 for the Protection of the Natural Resources of Namibia.

Foreign multinational corporations importing products as varied as karakul furs and pilchard sardines were confronted with demonstrations and stockholder resolutions protesting their involvement. Anti-apartheid groups labeled food products on grocery shelves with "Stolen from Namibia" stickers and presented customer petitions asking that the products be withdrawn.

Publicity generated by the Soviet government and anti-apartheid activists prevented the South African government from testing a nuclear device in Namibia's Kalahari Desert in 1977, and the anti-apartheid movement led the effort to draw attention to the explosion of a nuclear device in the South Atlantic Ocean in 1979 and to the ongoing nuclear collaboration among South Africa, the United States, France, Great Britain, and Israel.

Student and community activists throughout the United States pushed resolutions through academic, labor, and social organizations and through municipal and state legislatures, preventing these organizations and institutions from investing monies in their trust in corporations doing business in South Africa and Namibia. These and other elements of the anti-apartheid movement drew public attention to the efforts of the U.S. government to relieve pressure on South Africa through a policy of "constructive engagement" with the apartheid state.

These efforts, combined with the failure of South African military adventures in Angola, increased the cost and diminished the economic value of South African occupation. Faced with economic and military loss, the South African government finally allowed the protracted negotiations with the United Nations to reach an agreement on a UN-monitored election for an independent Namibia in 1992, a conclusion that presaged and in some ways modeled the ending of minority rule in South Africa itself.

Ken Martin

References

American Friends Service Committee. *Namibia*. Philadelphia: AFSC, 1987.

Katjevivi, Peter. *A History of Resistance in Namibia*. Paris: UNESCO, 1988.

Moleah, Alfred. *Namibia: The Struggle for Liberation*. Wilmington, Del.: Disa, 1983.

South West African People's Organization. *To Be Born a Nation: The Liberation Struggle for Namibia*. London: Zed, 1981.

———. *Trade Union Action on Namibian Uranium: Report of a Seminar for West European Trade Unions Organized by SWAPO of Namibia in Co-operation with the Namibia Support Committee*. London: Namibia Support Committee, 1982.

United Nations Commissioner for Namibia. *Efforts to Implement Decree No. 1 for the Protection of the Natural Resources of Namibia*. New York: United Nations, 1985.

See also SOUTH AFRICA, ANTIAPARTHEID SANCTIONS; SOUTH AFRICA, OPPOSITION TO RACIAL OPPRESSION

National Woman Suffrage Association

Organization primarily devoted to procuring voting rights for women through passage of a federal amendment to the U.S. Constitution. Led by Elizabeth Cady Stanton and Susan B. Anthony, the group engaged in national lobbying and demonstrating, and encouraged women to vote despite the fact that women were not allowed to vote at the time. Members promoted nonviolent direct action by voting and running for office illegally. The organization also promoted women's rights in other arenas, including marriage, social life, and the work place.

Elizabeth Cady Stanton and Susan B. Anthony were among several members of the American Equal Rights Association who believed that women as well as blacks deserved the

Members of the National Woman Suffrage Association march up Pennsylvania Avenue in Washington, D.C., March 3, 1913. The Schlesinger Library/Radcliffe College.

right to vote. When their colleagues did not put woman's suffrage on the agenda, the two formed the National Woman Suffrage Association (NWSA) in 1869. In a speech at the first national woman's suffrage convention in Washington, D.C., Stanton called for "impolite" tactics against male speakers who refused to listen to women.

Soon after NWSA was formed, the American Woman Suffrage Association (AWSA) was founded by Lucy Stone and Henry Blackwell. The AWSA adopted a more conservative strategy, focused solely on woman's suffrage, and believed that this goal was best achieved at the state level. The NWSA, however, engaged in more radical tactics, including direct action, efforts to pass a federal amendment to the U.S. Constitution, and advocacy for women's rights in other venues as well.

Before the NWSA was formed, Stanton had run for a seat in the U.S. House of Representatives in 1866. She claimed that, although she was disenfranchised, she could still run for public office. She received only twenty-four votes out of over twenty thousand cast. At a January 1872 NWSA convocation, Stanton announced a change of tactics from their traditional focus on annual lobbying conferences in Washington, D.C. She claimed that women were already enfranchised under the Fourteenth and Fifteenth amendments. Therefore, Stanton

encouraged women to vote "illegally." In 1872, the NWSA supported the presidential campaign of Victoria Woodhull and her Cosmo Political Party. Woodhull agreed with Stanton that women could vote and run for office. Although she did not campaign much and received little support outside her circle of delegates, Woodhull's effort constituted the first time a woman had run for president of the United States. NWSA members tried to vote in several communities around the country but were denied. They then cast ballots in separate special boxes in protest. Sixteen women, including Anthony, voted in this manner in Rochester, New York. Charges were brought against Anthony, and she was subsequently fined one hundred dollars plus court costs. Refusing to pay, Stanton castigated the authorities for their behavior, and they did not enforce the fine.

The NWSA also encouraged tax refusal and organized public demonstrations. In 1876, members interrupted the national Centennial celebration in order to present a Declaration of Women's Rights. The organization also published a woman's suffrage newsletter called *Revolution,* which addressed women's issues in politics, social life, religion, finances, and labor.

The NWSA merged organizations and strategies with the AWSA in 1890 to become the National American Woman Suffrage Association (NAWSA). Anthony remained the leader, but the association's strategy gradually moved away from focusing on a federal amendment and the use of direct action. In 1920, the Nineteenth Amendment was enacted granting suffrage for women. At that time, the NAWSA changed its name to the League of Women Voters.

Brad Bennett

References

Evans, Sara M. *Born for Liberty: A History of Women in America*. New York: Free Press, 1989.
Kugler, Israel. *From Ladies to Women: The Organized Struggle for Woman's Rights in the Reconstruction Era*. New York: Greenwood, 1987.

See also ANTHONY, SUSAN BROWNELL; STANTON, ELIZABETH CADY; WOMEN'S SUFFRAGE

Native American Treaty Rights Movements, 1950s–1990s

Protest actions by Native American nations in the United States and Canada to prevent land exploitation and to procure treaty rights. Employing a variety of nonviolent and violent tactics, including occupations (nonviolent and armed), sit-ins, "fish-ins," and blockades, the protests of various Native American nations have met with mixed success.

During the 1800s, many Native American tribes were relegated to small reservations controlled by bureaucratic branches of the federal government. This was accompanied by the signing of treaties that granted the Native American nations certain land and self-governance rights. When the federal government and private businesses began making claims on these lands in the late 1950s, Native American resistance emerged. On April 16, 1958, New York State troopers and police invaded the Haudenosaunee Iroquois lands to force the Iroquois to succumb to plans to flood the Tuscarora River for the New York Power Authority. The Iroquois responded with a nonviolent blockade of the major road leading into the area. Authorities arrested leader Mad Bear and two others. But the bad publicity that was generated forced the Power Authority to scrap its plan to flood the river. In March 1959, one thousand Haudenosaunee occupied the council house of the Six Nations reservation near

Brantford, Ontario, to protest the council's complicity with the Canadian government. They ousted the tribal council and Canadian Mounted Police and declared sovereignty. After six days, Mounties used force to regain the council house.

During the 1960s, several Pacific Northwest tribes staged a series of fish-ins to protest increasingly narrow legal interpretations of off-reservation fishing rights granted in treaties. Nisqually, Puyallup, and Muckleshoot tribe members deliberately fished in areas banned to them. The fish-ins happened primarily between 1964 and 1970, and were accompanied by demonstrations, marches, international support, and some celebrity involvement (by actor Marlon Brando and comedian Dick Gregory). During one encounter in the spring of 1966, Yakima Indians made a citizen's arrest of a Washington State police officer, claiming he was trespassing. Most of these conflicts were decided in court, with mixed results. While Native Americans secured some protection of fishing rights in Oregon, arrests of fish-in participants continued in Washington.

One of the primary organizers of Native American agitation in the United States was the American Indian Movement (AIM), founded in 1968 in Minneapolis, Minnesota. Perhaps their most important and effective tactic was occupation. AIM organized and supported numerous occupations during the early 1970s. Most were nonviolent occupations, though several were armed. The first large AIM occupation was the seizure of an abandoned federal prison on Alcatraz Island in San Francisco Bay in November 1969. They held the area for nineteen months "in the name of all Indian people." In August 1971, the Milwaukee AIM chapter occupied an abandoned Coast Guard station and proceeded to organize a detox center and community school.

During the fall of 1972, members of many Native American nations traveled to Washington, D.C., in "Trail of Broken Treaties" caravans. When their demands were ignored by the Bureau of Indian Affairs (BIA), four hundred Indians occupied BIA offices, barricaded entrances, destroyed offices, and painted slogans on walls. After four days, they left as part of a negotiated agreement, but they took a truckload of BIA files with them.

On February 27, 1973, AIM responded to a plea by traditional elders of the Oglala Sioux tribe of the Pine Ridge reservation in South Dakota to seize the town of Wounded Knee to protest land and treaty violations. The armed occupation lasted seventy-one days, and the Oglala were under siege by a combination of federal marshals, FBI men, BIA police, and local vigilantes. This confrontation received huge publicity, despite a governmental order to ban television coverage. In March, the community declared itself the sovereign Independent Oglala Nation and assigned a delegation to the United Nations. They also set up committees to run housing, medical care, and other community services. The occupation ended on May 7, and over five hundred people were arrested on charges related to the occupation. During the early 1970s, the U.S. government directed a campaign to distrupt and discredit AIM, and many leaders were arrested, shot, or forced underground.

Despite the loss of many of the founders, AIM grew in popularity partly because of publicity from the Wounded Knee confrontation. Key nonviolent occupations were organized on the U.S.-Canadian border in the spring of 1974 by Mohawks; at the Alexian Brothers Novitiate, an abandoned monastery in Gresham, Wisconsin, in January 1975, by Menominees; and at the Fairchild Camera and Instrument Company Plant in Shiprock, Arizona, in the spring of 1975 in support of Navajo and Hopi grievances. All three were successful in winning some of their demands. On April 4, 1981, Native Americans initiated an occupation called Yellow Thunder Camp in the Black Hills of South Dakota. Although the U.S. Forest Service gained an injunction against the camp that declared it illegal, they did not attempt to forcibly remove the occupants.

In Canada, also, there were a series of resistance actions starting with a Mohawk action in the summer of 1990, barricading land near Montreal to prevent the expansion of a golf course. A bungled police raid led to a seventy-eight-day armed standoff, which was settled through negotiations. Other tribes organized nonviolent sympathy demonstrations and blockades during that time.

Occupations, demonstrations, and blockades by Native American tribes over the last thirty years have garnered many small successes, including compensation, land, and protection of treaty rights. The issue of sovereignty of Native American nations in the United States and Canada remains an area of controversy, however.

Brad Bennett

References

American Friends Service Committee. *Uncommon Controversy: Fishing Rights of the Muckleshoot, Puyallup, and Nisqually Indians.* Seattle: University of Washington Press, 1970.

Weyler, Rex. *Blood of the Land: The Government and Corporate War against First Nations.* Philadelphia: New Society, 1992.

See also BLOCKADES; LAND SEIZURE

Nazism, Civilian Resistance, 1939–1945

Spontaneous process of struggle by the civil society through unarmed means, through the mobilization either of its main institutions, or of its populations, or even through the action of both simultaneously. One of the fundamental characteristics of the resistance to Nazism is the strong overlapping between means of armed struggle and means of unarmed struggle. Unarmed resistance was in most cases adopted because of the lack of other means, such as lack of weapons. Nevertheless, it is possible to identify more or less autonomous acts of civilian resistance—those that aimed at mainly civilian goals, such as maintaining the independence of given institutions outside the control of the occupying power, or of protecting persons persecuted by the occupiers or their collaborators. Throughout the war civilian resistance occurred in all countries dominated by the Nazi regime, although predominantly in the countries of Western Europe and Scandinavia, and most frequently in the years up to 1943, when Germany was at its peak of power. Resistance took various forms, including clandestine education, public protests such as strikes, smuggling and protecting Jews, and overt social noncooperation. In the end, civilian resistance provided a crucial element of a strategy of survival, rather than liberation, from Nazism.

The Forms of Civilian Resistance

Civilian resistance was fundamental in the concept of resistance generally; it often appeared first, given the fact that those who started to resist had no weapons. It also played an important role in structuring resistance processes, through political, economic, or cultural actions. In particular, civilian resistance had an essential ideological aspect through the development of underground newspapers, which played a major role in challenging the legitimacy of the occupier and the power of collaborating governments. In this regard, the French resister Claude Bourdet drew a distinction between movement and network: The first objective of the "movement . . . is . . . to sensitize and organize the population on the broadest level possible," while the network "is an organization created with the aim of specific military work . . . by definition . . . in close contact with an organ of the leadership of the forces for which it works."

Civilian resistance sometimes appeared in anonymous and underground ways—working slowly, industrial sabotage, diverting orders, civil disobedience movements against compulsory labor service, and enrollment of civil servants in resistance movements. It also took public forms, mostly strikes, demonstrations, church or court protests, as well as various kinds of opposition carried out by educational, medical, cultural, and religious organizations. These also included, of course, the most significant acts of aid to and rescue of Jews, the most famous example of which was the saving of the Danish Jewish community in October 1943.

Cases of civilian resistance occurred predominantly in France, Belgium, Luxembourg, the Netherlands, Denmark, and Norway, but they also appeared in Germany, Poland, Czechoslovakia, and Bulgaria. These examples included public protests. Some occurred in the heart of Germany, such as when German bishop Clement-August Von Galen openly denounced the "assassination" of the mentally ill in August 1941, and German spouses married to Jewish men demonstrated in February 1943 in front of the jail where their husbands were held.

Factors in Development

Several social and political factors facilitated the development and expansion of civilian resistance: the structure of the occupied society, the logistics of action, and the conduct of the resistance action itself. Civilian resistance developed more fully in democratic societies (Western Europe and Scandinavia), in areas of urban and industrial concentration, as well as within groups with a strong preexisting social cohesion (such as miners), or within bodies with a certain ethic or professional practice (such as doctors and teachers). Civilian resistance benefited from a common language in its development. The role of symbols was most important in this respect. Shared symbolism was a means of recognition between members of the resistance movement, such as the "V" for victory campaign

launched by the BBC in 1941, or the Norwegian practice of wearing a paper clip on one's jacket.

Clandestine organization and a clandestine system of communication facilitated the ability of resisters to face repression. In order to last, resistance movements needed human, financial, and material resources (especially food and money) as well as international support to avoid being isolated. A legitimate authority was an important factor. It stimulated action, but did not totally create, out of the blue, a resistance movement. The resistance created its own legitimacy, which it derived from the situation of the occupation itself. Thus General De Gaulle progressively acquired legitimacy, as did the French domestic resistance. Each one needed the other.

The Problem of Repression

Resistance eventually led to confronting repression. There was no resistance without repression. However, under the German occupation, various factors determined the intensity of repression. It is important to understand the differences, other than racial considerations, in Germany's occupation politics toward Western and Eastern Europe. Overall, the societies of Western Europe were wealthier and more advanced technologically than those in the East, and thus were highly desirable to Germany as supplementary resources for winning the war. The many specialized workers and technicians provided a labor source for the Reich that could not be obtained elsewhere, at least not to the same degree. The objective of economic exploitation, and therefore the requirement to obtain at least tacit cooperation, was a general factor that moderated repression in the West.

The high levels of economic development in the West also required very complex social systems. The efficiency of state services, from government ministries to local communities, rested on the cooperation of competent agents, a cooperation that was not directly available to the occupying power. Since the main German concern was that society continue to "function," the occupiers had to avoid going too far with their repressive policies. That was why the method of encouraging state collaboration fit so well with German objectives for Western Europe, even though Berlin had not thought the policy out ahead of time. State collaboration ensured minimal compliance in the occupied countries, without which exploiting their economic wealth and human resources would have been far less effective.

The German attitude toward the societies of Eastern Europe was completely different. There, Hitler saw only a *Lebensraum* for his people, and the Slavic populations presented an obstacle to his project's achievement. No moral restraints mitigated the politics of repression in Poland or the Soviet Union. On the contrary, the rule was to eliminate the *Untermenschen* or, at least, to enslave them. Furthermore, the Reich wanted to create space for the arrival of the German colonists. Accordingly, the collaboration formula held little interest for the occupying power that thought it more advantageous to administer these new "colonial territories" directly. Thus, the general level of repression was higher in the East than in the West.

Many acts of civilian resistance faced repression, especially the spontaneous strikes. However, acts of civilian resistance appear to have been repressed less severely than armed opposition, such as sabotage or guerrilla warfare. One possible explanation for this difference is that the civilian resistance actions, such as a symbolic demonstration, did not directly threaten the occupiers' principal concerns, whereas an armed attack against its own troops certainly did. The first sort of resistance could be tolerated, if necessary, but not a repetition of the second; in the latter case, repression could not fail to be ferocious.

If civilian resistance provoked less repression, it may also be because of the indirect nature of these particular means of action. The English military historian Basil Liddell Hart's opinion on this subject is particularly illuminating. When he had the opportunity to interrogate German generals during their captivity in Great Britain after the war, he asked their opinions on the different forms of resistance that they had encountered: "Their evidence also showed the effectiveness of nonviolent resistance. . . . Even clearer, was their inability to cope with it. They were experts in violence, and had been trained to deal with opponents who used that method. But other forms of resistance baffle them—and all the more as the methods were subtle and concealed. It was a relief to them when nonviolent forms were mixed with guerrilla action, thus making it easier to combine drastic and suppressive action against both at the same time."

Resisting to Survive

Most civilian resistance movements took place before 1943, at a time when Nazi Germany was still triumphant. Civilian resistance, therefore, could not, and did not, strive for liberation as such. If it nevertheless developed mass characteristics, it was because it had another objective—survival, or saving what could be saved. The most obvious case is naturally the protection and saving of Jews, but there are others. In the great strikes of May and June 1941, the miners in northern France struggled to survive in a region that was poorly supplied. In 1940, Polish resistance began a great movement of underground education. By this means they attempted to save their culture and their intellectuals, which the Nazis were striving to destroy. In France, symbolic demonstrations were held as early as July 14 and November 11, 1942, aimed at preserving national identity. Thus, the ultimate goal of civilian resistance was to preserve the political, social, and cultural integrity of the societies experiencing aggression, to preserve the legitimacy of their institutions, and to sustain the values on which they were built. In this respect, the fight of the Norwegian teachers in 1942 against the Quisling collaborationist government was one of the most significant examples of anti-Nazi civilian resistance.

Under a regime of occupation, two societies are formed. One is the official, legal, formal, society of the occupying power, and the other is the legitimate, hidden, autonomous society. Daily life is composed of the coexistence of both societies, between which there are separations but also bridges. For the period of Europe's occupation, common behaviors existed with increasing degrees of risk—listening to the BBC, followed by reading the clandestine press, working slowly, refusing to obey received orders, protecting persons being hunted down, refusing to submit to the labor service, and occasional or permanent participation in resistance movements. Resistance was made up of the whole fabric of society, in which the life of civil society absorbed the official society. The aspects of mass civilian resistance—strikes, church protests, courts of justice, and so on—were key moments through which the independent society expressed itself publicly.

Facing Genocide

What can be said about civilian resistance when faced with the extermination of six million Jews? First, of course, the roots of genocide preceded the war. Germany was not the only country in which anti-Semitism was common, but the war acted as a springboard for extreme anti-Semitic policies. As Raoul Hilberg demonstrated in *The*

Destruction of European Jews, there can be no genocide without a latent collective assent. The whole process developed in an atmosphere of such general indifference that when the war began the genocide intensified. But by this time, prevention was impossible—the process was like a train going at full speed that can no longer be stopped. At the same time, Allied governments did nothing to stop the genocide, not even bombing the known railroads leading to concentration camps. The only thing possible, then, was to limit the destruction. It was at this stage that civilian resistance played a part.

There was a logic of war and a logic of civilian resistance that were not necessarily parallel. Churchill, Roosevelt, and Stalin appeared to remain passive in the face of the "Final Solution." Their problem was to win the war by all means, and all their efforts were concentrated toward that goal. For these leaders Auschwitz did not represent a strategic goal. But while waiting for liberation, the survival of Jews depended first of all on civilian resistance that could protect them in an immediate way, rather than on an uncertain military victory.

A Strategy of Liberation

Could civilian resistance have been anything other than a resistance for survival? Could it have been an actual strategy for liberation? Liberation required a coherence of collective action not unlike that required for victory by a sports team. To win, the team must be united, coordinated, should assess the strength of the opponents and profit from their weaknesses, and so on. Victory, or liberation, requires both coherence and strategic direction. A survival strategy, by contrast, permitted more autonomous action and did not demand the same consistent choices on the part of individuals and groups.

Thus, in the occupied societies of Europe, some people chose noncooperation while others played the game of collaboration, and still others awaited the outcome of the struggle, presumably to then join the victor. The major weakness of occupied societies consisted in this dislocation of the institutions' and people's roles in the struggle. Coordination of effort and a united commitment to resistance rather than collaboration or individual survival did not occur. In fact, civilian resistance had not been thought about, and thus had not been prepared for, prior to the need to employ its techniques. Before the war, European leaders refused to recognize the Nazi threat; they naively thought that their actions of appeasement would prevent another major war and they did not consider the possibility that their countries could be occupied. Thus civilian resistance could only be improvised.

The whole framework of civilian resistance rests on the assumption that, in case of a crisis, mass mobilization of the attacked or threatened society is possible. The period of the German occupation in Europe from 1939 to 1945 shows how difficult it was to enforce this process of collective mobilization, as well as how hazardous that action can be.

Jacques Semelin

References

Haestrup, Jorgen. *European Resistance Movements (1939–1945): A Complete History.* Westport, Conn.: Meckler, 1981.

Hart, Basil Liddell. "Lessons from Resistance Movements." In *Strategy of Civilian Defense,* edited by Adam Roberts. London: Faber and Faber, 1968.

Hilberg, Raul. *The Destruction of the European Jews.* New York: Holmes and Meier, 1985.

Semelin, Jacques. *Unarmed against Hitler. Civilian Resistance in Europe (1939–1945).* Westport, Conn.: Praeger, 1993.

Skovdin, Magne, "Norwegian Non-Violent Resistance during the German Occupation." In *Strategy of Civilian Defense,* edited by Adam Roberts. London: Faber and Faber, 1968.

See also DENMARK, RESISTANCE TO NAZI OCCUPATION; LE CHAMBON SUR LIGNON, FRANCE; NORWAY, RESISTANCE TO GERMAN OCCUPATION, 1940–1945; ROSENSTRAßE PROTEST, 1943; WHITE ROSE

Nehru, Jawaharlal (1889–1964)

Lawyer, politician, and prominent leader of the Indian nationalist movement against British colonialism from 1919 to 1947. Nehru was born on November 14, 1889, in Allahabad, in the Uttar Pradesh state, India, and died on May 27, 1964. He was president of the Indian National Congress several times and was Mohandas K. Gandhi's disciple and later designated political heir. Nehru was a key negotiator in Indian independence and partition talks and became India's first prime minister in 1947.

Nehru first met Gandhi at an Indian National Congress meeting in 1916. He became an

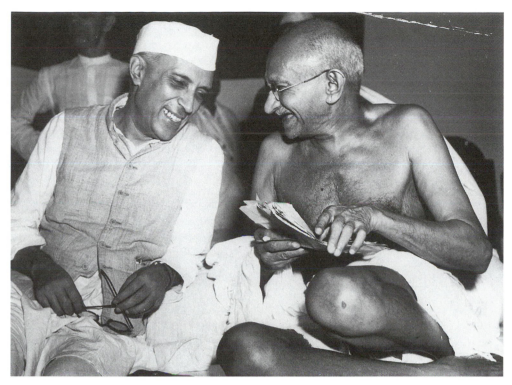

Jawaharlal Nehru with Mohandas K. Gandhi. AP/Wide World Photos.

active disciple of Gandhi's in early 1919 when he set up the local Allahabad chapter of the national Satyagraha Society. In response to the Amritsar massacre of April 11, 1919, in which hundreds of unarmed people were gunned to death by forces led by General Reginald E.H. Dyer, Nehru solidified his total opposition to British rule. From 1919 to 1947, when India gained independence, Nehru was one of the major political leaders of the nationalist movement. He pushed the Indian National Congress to adopt a goal of complete independence in 1929. He was president of the Congress several times in the 1930s and 1940s. He organized and led numerous civil disobedience campaigns, and as a result spent years in jail. In November 1928, Nehru was beaten by troops carrying *lathis* (sticks) during a civil disobedience campaign.

Although he was at first Gandhi's disciple and later his chosen political heir, Nehru disagreed with Gandhi on several key positions. First, unlike Gandhi, Nehru was not an absolute pacifist. He commended the ethical and spiritual basis of satyagraha (Gandhi's doctrine of nonviolent resistance) and believed in it as the most appropriate practical strategy for the Indian nationalist movement. Nehru was a non-

violent revolutionary, but he did not rule out the possibility of armed resistance if it was the only alternative to submission. Second, Nehru was a democratic socialist, and put much more emphasis on peasant and labor issues and on building a socialist economic state than did Gandhi. Third, Nehru criticized some of Gandhi's strategic choices, namely his autocratic suspension of both the noncooperation movement of 1922 and the civil disobedience campaign of 1934 and his signing of a truce with Viceroy Irwin in 1931.

After being imprisoned almost continuously from October 1940 to June 1945, Nehru emerged to help negotiate India's independence and partition. He served as vice president of the interim government and then as the first prime minister of independent India from 1947 until his death in 1964. His daughter, Indira Gandhi, served as prime minister from 1966 to 1977 and 1980 to 1984. Nehru wrote *An Autobiography,* published in 1962, which chronicled his life as well as the nationalist struggle for freedom. Nehru remains one of the most prominent proponents of nonviolent action and political leaders of the twentieth century.

Brad Bennett

References

Copland, Ian. *Jawaharlal Nehru of India, 1889–1964*. Queensland: University of Queensland Press, 1980.

Gupta, R.C. *Indian Freedom Movement and Thought: Nehru and the Politics of "Right" Versus "Left" (1930–1947)*. New Delhi: Sterling, 1983.

Patil, V.T. *Nehru and the Freedom Movement*. New Delhi: Sterling, 1977.

See also GANDHI, MOHANDAS KARAMCHAND; INDIAN NATIONAL CONGRESS; INDIAN NATIONAL MOVEMENT; SATYAGRAHA

Nepal, Movement for Restoration of Democracy, 1990

Nonviolent prodemocracy movement that began on February 18, 1990, in response to deteriorating economic conditions within Nepal and the long-term repressive political regime of the country. Ruled by an autocratic king, Nepal suffered from feudal economic relations, a thirty-year-old ban on political parties, authoritarian legislation, and a corrupt political structure of patronage and elite control known as the *Panchayat* system. The movement demanded the dismantling of the *Panchayat* system, the restoration of parliamentary democracy, and the reduction of the king's powers to those of a constitutional monarch. On April 8, 1990, after several weeks of strikes, demonstrations, and blockades, King Birendra lifted a ban on political parties. Multiparty elections followed a year later.

The movement was led by a coalition of the major banned political parties: the Nepali Congress and the United Left Front (a coalition of seven Communist parties). The movement also included the active participation of trade unions, professional organizations (such as doctors, lawyers, journalists, and artists), and student organizations. These set up action committees that worked in liaison with the political parties. Although the movement was widespread throughout Nepal, the principal sites of struggle were located within the Kathmandu Valley, particularly in the capital of Kathmandu and the surrounding towns of Patan, Kirtipur, and Bhaktapur. This was due to the concentration of population, as well as transportation and communication facilities, in the cities, and the fact that Kathmandu represented the political heart of the country.

Historically, the political parties involved in the MRD had engaged in armed struggle against the autocratic *Panchayat* regime of Nepal. Two strategic considerations account for the movement's shift in 1990 to nonviolent struggle—the desire to enhance the credibility of the movement internationally, and the goal of de-legitimizing the state's use of violence against the movement. The movement adopted a variety of nonviolent methods, ranging from protest and persuasion to nonviolent intervention and noncooperation. In the use of many of these methods, the movement articulated specific cultural expressions of resistance. Several countrywide strikes *(Bandhs)* were called that mobilized employees in both private and state sectors. During the strikes, participants engaged in sit-ins and demonstrations. These strikes were notable because of the participation of a wide cross-section of Nepali society, including doctors, lawyers, teachers, bank employees, government employees, trade unions, peasants, and students.

In addition, mass demonstrations were held frequently in the major urban areas, and many spontaneous "corner demonstrations" were held throughout Kathmandu. Small groups of students would assemble at a strategic location within the city, shout antigovernment slogans, and distribute movement literature. If the police arrived, they would disappear and reassemble at another location. Often many of these corner demonstrations occurred simultaneously at various locations so as to stretch police capabilities of dispersal. Various diversionary tactics also were employed by activists (such as running through the streets with *mashals* [burning torches]) to draw police attention away from movement meeting sites.

The most dramatic (and influential) expression of nonviolent resistance occurred when the town of Patan, located two kilometers from Kathmandu, was defended against incursion by government forces for a period of one week during the democratic revolution. Patan, a Communist stronghold, served as the base for the movement's underground leadership for the duration of the MRD. The seven approach roads to the town were barricaded, and trenches were also dug to prevent the entry of government vehicles and personnel. These barricades were staffed around the clock. Within Patan, the inhabitants *gheraoed* (surrounded) and captured the main police station, holding over 120 policemen in "custody" for the duration of Patan's "liberation."

Women's blockade in the town of Patan during the prodemocracy movement in Nepal, 1990. Photo by Paul Routledge.

The movement consciously used the urban topography of Patan to accommodate the exigencies of underground activism. The narrow streets of the town prevented any mass deployment of government force, while the interconnected network of backstreets that traversed the town enabled activists to move unhindered from one end of Patan to the other, and from Patan to Kathmandu without detection. The numerous open squares *(chowks)* within the web of streets acted as excellent meeting places out of the purview of the government.

Another potent expression of nonviolent resistance was the use of citywide blackouts during the evening curfews that were imposed by the government. Although the blackouts were called by the movement leadership, the communication of the action was conducted by city residents from rooftop to rooftop across Kathmandu and the other towns in the valley. The blackouts were important for several reasons. They symbolically communicated popular resistance to the government, especially since in Nepal black represents the color of revolt and disagreement. The blackouts also enabled city residents to grasp the extent of popular support for the MRD. Finally, they enabled increasing

numbers of people to challenge the curfew and join demonstrations under cover of darkness without fear of being arrested. It was also during the blackouts that the barricading of Patan took place.

The movement made use of a well-developed underground press to disseminate information concerning movement activities and the government's human rights abuses. The movement also used traditional folk songs *(Jhyaura)* to communicate political propaganda, altering the words to articulate the causes and demands of the resistance. "Voice dramas," which were recorded onto cassettes in activists' homes and then distributed throughout the urban centers of Nepal, became vehicles of political satire.

The government's response to the movement ranged from arrest and detention to torture and police shootings of activists. Police and security forces were deployed massively in Kathmandu and curfews were imposed. On April 6, 1990, during a Nepal *bandh* called by the movement, 200,000 people demonstrated against the king outside the Royal Palace in Kathmandu. During the demonstration, security forces opened fire, killing at least 50 people and injuring hundreds of others in what became known as the "Massacre of Kathmandu." On April 8, 1990, the king lifted the ban on political parties, and the next day the movement celebrated a new "Democracy Day."

Paul Routledge

Nhat Hanh, Thich (b. 1926)

Vietnamese Buddhist monk, Zen master, and poet, born October 11, 1926. An exponent of engaged Buddhism, he came to great international attention during the 1960s as a spokesperson for the Unified Buddhist Church and its opposition to the war in Vietnam. Through his poetry, his numerous books, and speaking tours, Thich Nhat Hanh articulated the suffering of the Vietnamese people and called for an end to the war. Opposed by the governments of both South and North Vietnam, he has been forced to live in France in exile up to the present time.

Thich Nhat Hanh. Photo by Jim Forest.

In 1963, after the fall of President Ngo Dinh Diem, Nhat Hanh returned to Vietnam from Columbia University to address the social and economic needs of his people and to work to end the war. He helped found Van Hanh University, created the School of Youth for Social Service, wrote peace poetry, and engaged in various publishing ventures. He worked with other monks and with Catholic priests to mobilize religious opposition to the war.

In *Love in Action* Nhat Hanh described the many forms of nonviolent action in Vietnam. These included fasts, carrying family altars into the streets to oppose tanks, shaving one's head as a sign of protest, noncooperation, use of folk poetry and satirical songs, and self-immolation. These actions were combined with constructive work—relief, reconstruction, and self-help efforts to build a cooperative social order.

In 1966, Nhat Hanh began traveling throughout the United States, Europe, Australia, New Zealand, and Asia under the auspices of the International Committee of Conscience on Vietnam, created by the Fellowship of Reconciliation to mobilize world opinion against the war. Nhat Hanh's book *Vietnam: Lotus in a Sea of Fire,* printed in eight languages and nine countries, became a best-seller. One hundred thousand legally printed copies were sold in South Vietnam. He also wrote *The Cry of Vietnam, The Path of Return Continues the Journey, Zen Keys,* and, with Daniel Berrigan, *The Raft Is Not the Shore.*

Nhat Hanh advocated the Buddhist "third solution" that opposed the war. This third way of the Unified Buddhist Church called for compassion, and offering food, shelter, and medical aid to all in need. It was a nonpartisan policy of reconciliation, a position that was vilified by both sides in the conflict, even by many in the antiwar movement.

In 1969, the Unified Buddhist Church sent a peace delegation to Paris to influence the peace talks informally. Nhat Hanh, exiled from South Vietnam, headed the peace delegation during the war years and also became a vice chairperson of the Fellowship of Reconciliation.

Prohibited from returning to Vietnam at the end of the war, Thich Nhat Hanh has lived in southern France in Plum Village, a community of persons committed to practicing mindfulness and service. He and his co-worker, Cao Ngoc Phuong (now called Chân Không), are in great demand as retreat leaders in the United States and in other countries. Author of sixty-six books, his recent writings include *Miracle of Mindfulness, A Guide to Walking Meditation,* and *Being Peace.* He was nominated for the Nobel Peace Prize by Martin Luther King, Jr.

Richard L. Deats

References

Nhat Hanh, Thich. *Cry of Vietnam: Poetry.* Santa Barbara, Calif.: Unicorn, 1968.
———. *Love in Action: Writings on Nonviolent Social Change.* Berkeley, Calif.: Parallax, 1993.
———. *Vietnam: Lotus in a Sea of Fire.* New York: Hill and Wang, 1967.

See also VIETNAM WAR OPPOSITION

Nicaragua, Civic Strike, 1944

Part of an unsuccessful movement to unseat dictator Anastasio Somoza García between June 27 and July 7, 1944. The strike consisted of a partial shutdown of the offices of physicians, dentists, and lawyers in Managua (the capital) and León on July 5, followed by the suspension of one newspaper and walkouts by commercial employees, hospital interns, and some secondary and normal school students the following day. Shops remained open, though unstaffed.

Somoza's opponents mobilized in response to a pending constitutional amendment that would have permitted him to seek another term as president. They found inspiration in the successful nonviolent insurrection in El Salvador (May 1944). University students led several hundred people in the first demonstration on June 27. The opposition "Conservative" party organized two larger demonstrations the next day.

The government squelched the attempted insurrection by arresting demonstrators and other known dissidents en masse, closing the university, and warning business proprietors in Managua that they would lose their property and licenses if they closed in response to the call for a strike that circulated on July 3. The support of Nicaragua's infant labor movement, which Somoza had courted, also helped the president prevail. The strike had no working-class participation. Somoza also placated some opponents with a statement on July 5 that he would veto the disputed constitutional amendment and restore civil liberties—promises that in the long run proved to be empty.

Patricia Parkman

References

Parkman, Patricia. *Insurrectionary Civic Strikes in Latin America, 1931–1961.* Cambridge, Mass.: Albert Einstein Institution, 1990.

See also CIVIC STRIKE

Nicaragua, Nonviolence and Revolution

Actions employed by Nicaraguans during both the Sandinista revolution of 1979 and the "contra" war in the decade that followed. In addition, international efforts to support Nicaragua and limit the civil war used a variety of innovative and effective nonviolent tactics.

A wide cross-section of the Nicaraguan people had been involved in the 1979 overthrow of the Somoza regime, which had a notorious record of corruption and human rights violations. Leading the revolution and heading the new government after the triumph was the Sandinista National Liberation Front (FSLN). Many of the revolutionary leaders and participants were inspired by liberation theology, which combines Catholic faith and teachings with a Marxist analysis. The Sandinista efforts to rebuild Nicaraguan society and politics were opposed by a group of counterrevolutionaries (contras), composed mostly of former Somoza National Guard members who received substantial monetary support from the U.S. government. This led to a decade of postrevolutionary civil war that was compounded by a U.S.-led international embargo against Nicaragua. The strategy was to wreak havoc on the civilian population to create discontent with the FSLN government while simultaneously weakening the country's economy.

Nonviolent Action during the Sandinista Revolution

Despite brutal repression, thousands of Nicaraguans participated in the insurrection to oust the regime of Anastasio Somoza-Debayle without taking up arms. They organized and carried out work stoppages, general strikes, international protests, and marches. During the final months of the revolution, general strikes within urban areas were estimated to be 80 to 90 percent effective, essentially paralyzing Somoza's control. Many participated in rearguard activities such as constructing street barricades from paving stones to protect civilians and guerrillas from the National Guard. These actions, however, were virtually indistinguishable from the armed struggle and some argue it is dubious whether such activities qualify as nonviolent. Many Nicaraguans maintain that these unarmed actions were the only means available to the majority since no individual or group was able to organize a nonviolent campaign of resistance during this period.

The climate after the revolution, however, was oriented to curtailing the cycle of violence and creating the conditions for reconciliation. After obtaining power, the Sandinistas proclaimed a "generosity in victory" and sought to break the pattern of oppressed peoples retaliating with vengeance against their former oppressors. One of their first legislative acts was to abolish the death penalty and prohibit torture. The spirit of forgiveness was also exemplified in the story of Comandante Tomás Borge, the only surviving member of the FSLN's founders who was appointed as minister of the interior in the new government. Shortly after the revolution, Borge was overseeing the treatment of captured members of Somoza's national guard. He recognized one of the imprisoned officers, who had been responsible for the torture, rape, and murder of his wife. Borge himself had been subjected to torture during his incarceration in the mid-1970s. When Borge summoned the man to him, the officer probably anticipated severe punishment or even execution. According to the account, Borge told him, "My revenge will be to pardon you." The story reflects the type of revolution many Nicaraguans hoped to engender.

Nonviolent Action during the Contra War
Upon his inauguration in 1981, President Ronald Reagan placed Nicaragua at the top of U.S. foreign policy concerns. He secured substantial U.S. funding for the contras and the civil war in Nicaragua escalated rapidly. At the same time, Nicaragua's new foreign minister, Father Miguel D'Escoto, was leading a newly emergent nonviolent movement for peace. A disciple of Gandhi and Martin Luther King, Jr., D'Escoto attempted to find effective and pragmatic responses to the contra war. He used both international diplomatic efforts as well as grassroots approaches. Internationally, D'Escoto charged the United States with violations of international laws for its aggression against Nicaragua, bringing the case to the International Court of Justice in 1984. By June 1986, the world court ruled that the U.S. war against Nicaragua, which included such acts as mining harbors, was illegal and violated international law. The United States government, however, had declared that it was not bound by the court's ruling in this case, and the judgment had no practical effect on U.S. policy.

At the local level, D'Escoto initiated the "Evangelical Insurrection" in 1985. This event offered many Christian base communities a chance to repond to the contra war and defend their nation's sovereignty. D'Escoto began this nonviolent campaign with a month-long fast, which was followed with the *Via Crucis* (Way of the Cross), a two-hundred-mile religious pilgrimage for peace. Along the way, the marchers visited war-torn villages and invited those who had joined the contras to accept the government's amnesty to return and live safely in their communities. D'Escoto also prayed publicly for the contras.

While D'Escoto, a Maryknoll priest, led many of the Catholic Christian base communities, Protestants also joined in nonviolent action aimed at ending contra aggression. In mid-1986, the Nicaraguan Protestant church council began a Campaign of Fasting and Prayer for Peace and Justice in Nicaragua. The campaign lasted several months and brought together Protestants of very different traditions, including conservative evangelicals and Pentecostals. The action culminated in an all-night vigil in the capital where more than ten thousand prayed for peace.

Dialogue also took place between the warring factions at both the official and grassroots levels. In March 1988, the Sandinista government entered negotiations with contra leaders. While these talks eventually broke down, the dialogue continued in communities throughout the country. Local reconciliation commissions had begun after the Esquipulas Peace Accord of 1987 and these groups continued their efforts through face-to-face dialogue between opposing military factions. These groups worked in the spirit of participatory democracy during ceasefires, not relying upon or waiting for the government to negotiate a peace.

Nonviolent Efforts in the International Community
While the Reagan administration's position toward the Sandinistas grew increasingly bellicose, there were also many U.S. citizens who were inspired by changes the revolution had initiated and who supported Nicaragua's right to sovereignty. A movement emerged in North America that aimed to stand in solidarity with the people of Nicaragua and to oppose the hostile foreign policy of the U.S. government, which fueled the civil war.

One of the most notable organizations in this campaign of nonviolent solidarity and intervention was Witness for Peace (WFP). Formed in 1983 in response to a peace vigil held on the Nicaraguan-Honduran border, a permanent nonviolent presence in the war zones began when WFP vigilers noticed that fighting decreased when North Americans were present. Contras, who were heavily financed by the U.S. Congress, did not want to jeopardize their monetary backing by killing U.S. citizens.

Witness for Peace volunteers also took on other tasks. One of the most devastating effects of the war had been the loss of the coffee crop, Nicaragua's central export. Since the largest coffee regions were along the northern border, where contra attacks were most frequent, harvesting was a matter of risking one's life. WFP volunteers worked the coffee harvest to add security to local farmers and to help the economy. In other instances, volunteers aided in negotiations for the release of citizens who had been kidnaped by contras. Witness for Peace also attempted to serve as an unarmed peace monitoring force in a demilitarized zone in southern Nicaragua.

Witness for Peace volunteers furthermore helped nurture the movement within the United States in two ways. First, long-term volunteers began documenting contra attacks. They investigated and recorded the contra atrocities by interviewing survivors and collecting photographic evidence. This information was sent back to the United States to challenge the misinformation propagated about Nicaragua. In addition, these reports let the Reagan administration know that, as Griffin-Nolan observed, "The use and abuse of American military power will be under continuing scrutiny by non-combatant pacifist American observers." Secondly, Witness for Peace sponsored short-term delegations of North Americans who would work and worship with Nicaraguans as well as learn about the sociopolitical context. Thousands traveled to Nicaragua and then returned to the States, motivated by their firsthand experience to change U.S. foreign policy.

Alongside of the direct action of WFP, legal battles were being fought against Reagan's policies. A civil suit was brought against officials of the U.S. government for the harm and suffering caused by the U.S.-sponsored contra forces. The plaintiffs were a group calling themselves the Committee of U.S. Citizens living in Nicaragua, and they were asking for the United States to be held legally responsible for the repercussions and human costs of its foreign policy goals. While the plaintiffs did not win their case, they represented a challenge and force of resistance through the legal system that strengthened and complemented the direct action.

As the contra war escalated in the early 1980s, representatives of the Christian peace movement in the United States met to develop a contingency plan entitled "A Pledge of Resistance." This plan, announced in 1984, stated that in hopes of preventing or ending an invasion of Nicaragua, a coordinated plan of massive public resistance had been organized that would undertake nonviolent direct action against Congress on the largest scale possible. Over forty thousand activists signed this pledge and an "urgent action" network was put in place to relay information to every congressional district within the United States whenever the country acted aggressively toward Nicaragua. Local Pledge of Resistance affinity groups undertook sit-ins, protests, vigils, blockades of trains carrying munitions to Central America, and acts of civil disobedience. The result was a cadre of thousands who were rapidly mobilized and who effectively stood in resistance to Reagan's hostile policies.

Despite the nonviolent efforts of Nicaraguans and North Americans, the contra war and the economic embargo devastated Nicaragua. Approximately forty thousand died during the civil war and over five thousand were disabled from mines and bombings. In February 1990, elections were held in compliance with the Esquipulas Peace Accord and the FSLN lost. A diverse coalition of fourteen groups, that together composed the UNO Party, won—resulting in an end to both the war and the embargo.

Sharon Erickson Nepstad

References

Chomsky, Noam. *Turning the Tide: U.S. Intervention in Central America and the Struggle for Peace.* Boston: South End, 1985.

Griffin-Nolan, Edward. *Witness for Peace.* Louisville, Ky.: Westminster/John Knox, 1991.

McManus, Philip, and Gerald Schlabach. *Relentless Persistence: Nonviolent Action in Latin America.* Philadelphia: New Society, 1991.

Wehr, Paul, and Sharon Erickson Nepstad. "Violence, Nonviolence, and Justice in Sandinista Nicaragua." In *Justice without Violence,* edited by Heidi Burgess, Guy Burgess, and Paul Wehr. Boulder, Colo.: Lynne Reinner, 1994.

See also WITNESS FOR PEACE

Nixon, E.D. (1899–1987)

Human rights activist before and during the U.S. civil rights movement. Born Edgar Daniel in Montgomery, Alabama, on July 12, 1899, Nixon was a central figure in that city's civil rights struggles in the 1950s when he served as treasurer of the Montgomery Improvement Association (MIA) and a major leader in the 1955–1956 bus boycott. He also was president of the Progressive Democratic Association, a leader in the Brotherhood of Sleeping Car Porters, and a former president of the state and local branches of the National Association for the Advancement of Colored People. Nixon died February 25, 1987, in Montgomery, Alabama.

E.D. Nixon was highly respected by both blacks and whites in Alabama and well known for standing up to the judicial system on behalf of people whose rights he felt had been violated. In 1944, as president of the Voters' League of Montgomery, Nixon organized a protest of the discriminatory restrictions that denied blacks their electoral rights. In 1954, he ran for a seat on the executive committee of Montgomery County, losing only narrowly. Nixon often bailed out of jail black townspeople who he believed had been discriminated against due to their skin color. In fact, Nixon was the man who bailed Rosa Parks out of jail when she was arrested for refusing to give her bus seat to a white passenger. Although blacks had been mistreated on the Montgomery bus system for a long time, this was the incident that finally convinced black leaders to launch a bus boycott.

After Mrs. Parks was released from jail, Nixon contacted Ralph Abernathy, pastor of the First Baptist Church of Montgomery, and suggested a one-day boycott of city buses to protest the mistreatment of Mrs. Parks and other blacks. About forty local black leaders immediately met to plan the boycott. They informed black residents and urged full participation. They also arranged for taxis to provide alternative transportation for the same cost as the bus.

After the great success of the one-day protest, black leaders created the Montgomery Improvement Association, of which Dr. Martin Luther King, Jr., was elected president, and Nixon was elected treasurer. Many people wanted Nixon to be president because he was such a dynamic, strong leader. His job as a railroad porter, however, demanded frequent out-of-town travel, which made the prospect impossible.

The MIA decided to continue the boycott because it had a highly visible impact on the city, as 75 percent of bus patrons were black. During the boycott, which continued for a year, Nixon maintained his passionate pursuit of equality for blacks. He was hailed when he made the point that "Negroes stopped riding the bus because they were arrested, and now they are being arrested for not riding them."

Kimberley A. Pyles

References

Cooney, Robert, and Helen Michalowski, eds. *The Power of the People: Active Nonviolence in the United States.* From an original text by Marty Jezer. Culver City, Calif.: Peace Press, 1977; 2nd ed. Philadelphia: New Society, 1987.
Robinson, Jo Ann Gibson. *The Montgomery Bus Boycott and the Women Who Started It: The Memoir of Jo Ann Gibson Robinson.* Knoxville: University of Tennessee Press, 1987.

See also MONTGOMERY BUS BOYCOTT, 1955–1956; PARKS, ROSA

Nobel Peace Prize

Specified in the will of Alfred Nobel as one of the five fields of human progress in which prizes were to be given to those "who shall have conferred the greatest benefit on mankind." The peace prize was to be awarded to "the person who shall have done the most or the best work for fraternity between nations, for the abolition or reduction of standing armies and for the holding and promotion of peace congresses." The last two clauses referred to the activities of the peace activists, who were organizing internationally when Nobel wrote his will in 1895. It was the clause "fraternity between nations" that enabled the Norwegian Nobel Committees to expand their mandate and to make the prize they administer the most prestigious in the world for service to humanity. Many of the early prizes were given to leaders of the organized peace movement, but humanitarians and statesmen were also early winners. In recent times champions of human rights have been recognized, with the acknowledgment that they pursue their objectives by nonviolent means.

Notably missing from the Nobel rolls are the century's major advocates of nonviolence, Leo Tolstoy (1828–1910) and Mohandas K. Gandhi (1869–1948). Tolstoy was on the committee's short list twice in the first decade of the prize. In 1909 he was nominated by five members of the Norwegian parliament and received a very favorable report from the committee's adviser, who predicted that Tolstoy's exaggerations would be forgotten, but that what would be remembered was that he had placed humanity face-to-face with its own conscience. The committee was not persuaded, however; nor did Tolstoy receive the literature award, for which his candidacy did not receive a fair hearing. Gandhi was not named by the committee because of unfortunate timing. He was a strong candidate in 1947, the year India was liberated by nonviolent methods, but the confusion over his position in the subsequent conflict between India and Pakistan apparently led the committee to postpone the decision, and the next year Gandhi was assassinated.

Nevertheless, several activists for peace and social change did receive the peace prize in the first half of the twentieth century. Jane Addams shared the prize in 1931, after having been nominated repeatedly since her efforts for peace during the First World War. While the committee spokesman in his presentation speech spoke favorably of her opposition to the entry of the United States into that war, it was that very action, deemed "unpatriotic" during the war fervor, that cost Addams her popularity and may well have delayed the decision to grant her the prize.

This was not the case with Emily Greene Balch, the colleague of Addams and her successor as leader of the Women's International League for Peace and Freedom, who received the divided prize of 1946. Balch also opposed U.S. intervention in the First World War, declaring that "the way of war is not the way of Christianity." This cost her her professorship at Wellesley College. During World War II, however, with some anguish she decided that the evil of Hitlerism had to be vanquished. "I am not an absolute pacifist," she declared. This was duly noted by committee chairman Gunnar Jahn in his presentation speech.

In 1947, however, the committee gave the prize to the U.S. and British Quaker organizations for their relief work during and after the war, emphasizing the spirit in which it had been carried out. Jahn, in his speech, referred to the Quaker antiwar declaration of 1660 and lauded the Quakers for having shown "the strength to be derived from faith in the victory of spirit over force." Both Quaker representatives in their Nobel lectures emphasized the religious basis of Quaker work, and Henry J. Cadbury, the representative of the American Friends Service Committee, gave the clearest explanation of absolute religious pacifism that has ever been heard from a Nobel peace laureate.

In 1952 the committee honored Albert Schweitzer, who as a medical missionary in Africa was living out his commitment to nonviolent "reverence for life." In his Nobel lecture Schweitzer declared that we must reject war for the ethical reason that it "makes us guilty of the crime of inhumanity." Not institutions, he said, but only the spirit can bring true peace.

The year 1961 marked a shift in perspective as the committee made its first award to a leader in the struggle for human rights by nonviolent means. Albert Lutuli, Zulu chief and president of the African National Congress, received the postponed 1960 prize. Lutuli declared in his Nobel lecture that he could not just look on while every attempt was being made "to debase the God-factor in man or to set a limit beyond which the human being in his black form might not strive to serve his Creator to the best of his ability." In working against apartheid and for freedom and equal rights, Lutuli preached the brotherhood of man and never felt hatred. As Chairman Jahn declared, "Never has he succumbed to the temptation to use violent means in the struggle for his people." In the next human rights award, in 1964, to Martin Luther King, Jr., the theme of nonviolence was even more explicit. Chairman Jahn explained that the prize was not for leading a racial minority in their struggle for equality, but in the way he waged that struggle: "He is the first person in the Western world to have shown us that a struggle can be waged without violence. He is the first to make the message of brotherly love a reality in the course of his struggle, and he has brought this message to all men, to all nations and races." King himself was just as clear about the meaning of his prize, accepting it on behalf of the civil rights movement as "a profound recognition that nonviolence is the answer to the crucial political and racial questions of our time—the need for man to overcome oppression without resorting to violence and oppression." In his Nobel lecture King explained that nonviolence seeks "to secure moral ends through moral means." It was a "weapon unique in history, which cuts without wounding and ennobles the man who wields it."

In some subsequent human rights awards, such as the prize given to Lech Walesa (1983) for his struggle for workers' rights in Poland against a repressive government, the Nobel Committee recognized that the recipients were not seeking their aims by violent methods. In the speech Walesa sent to Oslo, he declared that "we can effectively oppose violence only if we ourselves do not resort to it." This is very different from King's emphasis upon the moral value of nonviolence as a path to peace in itself. The committee recognized the significance of nonviolence in the prize for Adolfo Pérez Esquivel (1980), Argentine leader of the Latin American nonviolent organization *Servicio Paz y Justicia* (Service for Peace and Justice). Committee chairman John Sanness declared that Pérez Esquivel worked for far-reaching social and political reforms and that, as with Gandhi, nonviolence "involves much more than a mere passive acceptance of the world as it is. It is a strategy in a struggle to change the world, using means that will not stifle the good intentions and the results one aims to achieve." Pérez Esquivel, a deeply committed Roman Catholic who had denounced the violence of both governmental and antigovernmental forces, explained that his organization acts "by means of evangelical nonviolence, which we see as a force for liberation."

In the struggle against apartheid, Archbishop Desmond Mpilo Tutu (1984) did not take Lutuli's absolutist position against violence, but prescribed peaceful means to achieve racial equality in South Africa. Nelson Mandela was repeatedly nominated when he was in prison and his candidacy enjoyed much support. The committee may have delayed naming him because he refused to deny that violence could be used to combat the violence of government repression. When he left prison unembittered, a moral giant, and worked peacefully with President F.W. de Klerk to end apartheid in South Africa and establish democracy and equal rights, there could be no question but that he was destined for the prize. The committee granted it jointly to Mandela and De Klerk in 1993.

In naming Rigoberta Menchú Tum, a Mayan Indian, in 1992, the committee had to consider the charge by conservative critics that she had supported the armed struggle of the Guatemalan guerrillas. She certainly had every provocation to do so, both parents and her brother having been brutally murdered by the government forces. Two of her sisters had indeed joined the guerrillas. Menchú, however,

had taken up political and social work for her people. "If I had chosen the armed struggle," she said, "I would be in the mountains now."

Committee chairman Francis Sejerstad emphasized the significance of this choice. "Whoever commits an act of violence," he said, "will lose his humanity. Thus violence breeds violence and hate breeds hate." The only way out of this vicious circle is when people like Menchú "manage to preserve their humanity in brutal and violent surroundings." Betty Williams and Mairead Corrigan (now Maguire), who received the postponed 1976 prize in 1977, performed a similar service, but in different circumstances. They led a revulsion against violence in Northern Ireland after the tragic accidental death of three little children. The spokesman of the Nobel Committee praised them for acting "in the name of humanity and love of their neighbor; someone had to start forgiving." It was especially important to demonstrate the spirit of human brotherhood at a time and place when "hatred and revenge threaten to dominate." In the Nobel lecture, which Williams presented, nonviolence took a prominent place. "We are deeply, passionately dedicated to the cause of nonviolence," she declared, "to the force of truth and love, to soulforce. To those who say we are naive, utopian idealists, we say that we are the only realists, and that those who continue to support militarism in our time are supporting the progress toward total self-destruction of the human race."

Finally, there are the two Buddhist laureates, the Fourteenth Dalai Lama of Tibet (1989) and Aung San Suu Kyi of Burma (1991), the latter of whom was under house arrest for more than five years for daring to lead a political movement against the repressive military government. Aung San Suu Kyi was granted the prize "for her nonviolent struggle for democracy and human rights." Both this goal and the nonviolent means to attain it, she says, are closely related to Buddhist tenets. The Dalai Lama, whose religious convictions even prevent him from swatting a fly, explained in his Nobel lecture that "love and compassion are the foundation of human existence," and "altruism and forgiveness are the basis for bringing humanity together."

Such a philosophy of life has no place for violence. In one of the most perceptive Nobel lectures, Alva Myrdal (1982), the Swedish proponent of disarmament, pointed out how the increase of violence throughout the world has made our age "one of barbarism and brutalization." She showed how the accepted legitimacy of war resulted in a proliferation of arms and militarization which, along with the violence in the mass media, had brought an increase in "everyday violence, violence in the streets and in the home."

While in their awards the Nobel committees have recognized many paths to peace, the political, the humanitarian, the scientific, the economic, and the religious, and they have rightly acknowledged that peace must be based upon justice and human rights, up until World War II they largely overlooked advocates of nonviolence and practitioners of nonviolent struggle. In the subsequent forty years, this omission has been corrected.

Irwin Abrams

References

Abrams, Irwin, ed. *The Nobel Peace Prize and the Laureates: An Illustrated Biographical History, 1901–1987.* Boston: G.K. Hall, 1988.

———, ed. *Words of Peace: Selections from the Speeches of the Winners of the Nobel Peace Prize.* New York: Newmarket, 1990.

Haberman, Frederick, ed. *Nobel Lectures. Peace: 1901–1970.* 3 vols. Amsterdam: Elsevier, 1972. Vols. 4–5, edited by Irwin Abrams, are to be published by World Scientific Publishing Co., Singapore.

See also ADDAMS, JANE; AMERICAN FRIENDS SERVICE COMMITTEE; AUNG SAN SUU KYI; BSTAN-DZIN-RGYA-MTSHO, DALAI LAMA XIV; CORRIGAN, MAIREAD, AND BETTY WILLIAMS; KING, MARTIN LUTHER, JR.; LUTULI, ALBERT JOHN; MANDELA, NELSON ROLIHLAHIA; MENCHÚ TUM, RIGOBERTA; PÉREZ ESQUIVEL, ADOLFO; TUTU, ARCHBISHOP DESMOND MPILO; WALESA, LECH

Nonviolence, Principled

A form of nonviolence in which practitioners (a) explicitly state their intention to conduct and resolve conflict without violence, (b) adopt many precautions to demonstrate and carry out that intention, and (c) are prepared to suffer, even sacrifice their lives, if need be, rather than inflict suffering on others while holding fast to the truths they believe. As such it characteristically develops out of religious or ethical rather than political or practical considerations and is expressed in witness for ideals.

Principled advocates of nonviolence are not first concerned about the likely success of their witness but rather wish to express moral rejection of a governmental or societal practice. In challenging such institutions as slavery, gender discrimination, war, and racial discrimination their witness has initiated many social change movements. They differ from practitioners of tactical nonviolence in that the latter may abandon either nonviolence or their objective in the face of an inadequate response or violent repression. Principled activists also differ from advocates of violence who seek to make others change their objectives through inflicting suffering and the loss of life. Advocates of principled nonviolence distinguish between the person and the evil they may do, seeking to draw out the moral capacity of each person.

To the extent that they participate in efforts to achieve social change, principled advocates face profound political, moral, and tactical issues. Perhaps all would agree that Mohandas K. Gandhi and Martin Luther King, Jr., successfully extended principled nonviolence into societal conflict, achieving fundamental change without violence, but there is far less agreement about answers to questions such as these:

1. Is the principle "thou shalt not kill" applicable to all situations and found in all religions and secular systems of ethics? How should those who accept this principle resolve conflict with those who threaten their lives, property, country, or other values with violence? Can both pacifist and just war principles undergird principled nonviolence? Are there other principles as well?

2. Is principled nonviolence a contribution to anarchistic, revolutionary, or democratic political ideologies? Is it a distinct ideology of its own?

3. Once affirmed, what is the range of problems and situations to which it is applicable? What are the circumstances and situations that try advocates of principled nonviolence?

4. Is there a distinctive strategy for conducting conflict without violence embodied in the principle itself or is there a wide range of not-violent tactics that qualify as principled nonviolence?

5. Who in the twentieth century has led principled, nonviolent movements and

how have they developed the tactics and strategies of nonviolent action?

6. Is nonviolence successful only within democratic societies or can it, in certain conditions, successfully change dictatorships?

7. Can nonviolence concepts of conflict resolution be extended into world politics, demonstrating how a world without war is possible?

Principles

The core value or principle underlying nonviolence is "thou shalt not kill," which is found in every religion, in secular humanism, and in philosophically based systems of ethics—for example, that of Socrates. The "golden rule"— do unto others as you would have them do unto you—precludes killing for most people in most circumstances.

In the Christian tradition, according to Geoffrey Nuttall's *Christian Pacifism in History,* five principles lead to the rejection of violence: (a) fear of idolatry—the refusal to worship a head of state, obey a military commander, or other leader; (b) the law of Christ, especially as stated in the "Sermon on the Mount"; (c) the ministry of suffering—Christianity entails the belief that people may suffer for their faith; (d) the dignity of man—participation in war requires subordination to authority and the demonization of the enemy; and (e) the redemptive power of love. Leyton Richards's *Christian Alternative to War* weaves together these principles in a set of contrasts: "War seeks to overcome evil by the infliction of injury on the evildoer or his agents, Jesus on the Cross by the endurance of the utmost injury that the evildoer cares to inflict; war treats men as things, Jesus always treated them as living souls capable of responding to the love of God; war operates by killing the enemy, Jesus sought to kill the enmity; war crushes men to achieve victory, Jesus lost the battle to win men." But others have said that this underestimates the role of power between political communities, the ability of modern ideologies to blind their believers to the evil deeds they do, and those states that adopt this device will be defenseless against aggressors who would impose their creeds. Those advocating principled nonviolence have responded that the alternative of civilian-based defense is available, that whatever else the state can do, it cannot force one to kill, and they would rather deal with persecution than wage even a defensive war.

An alternative interpretation of Scriptures is the Catholic just war tradition that permits violence in self- or national defense if certain conditions are satisfied and thus provides a set of standards designed to limit the use of violence. The just war tradition, according to George Weigel's *Tranquilatas Ordinis,* provides a principled basis from which nonviolence ought to be pursued because one of the just war standards is that all nonmilitary options must be exhausted before violence can possibly be justified. Thus, as the peace research and nonviolent action communities develop additional options, like civilian-based defense, there is moral space in which nonviolence can operate while the option of violence and war is made harder to justify, although not abandoned altogether.

In the Protestant tradition, the Brethren, Mennonite, and Quaker faiths have rejected violence as incompatible with their understanding of the divine. The Islamic, Jewish, Hindu, and Buddhist traditions, at least, have their pacifist as well as just war traditions. In the contemporary world, the collapse of movements that accepted mass killing (such as Nazism and communism) could open a time of experimentation with principled nonviolence in resolving the many ethnic, nationalistic, class, religious, and other conflicts for which violence remains an all too available means.

Anarchy, Revolution, and Democracy?

The application of principled nonviolence to social change questions is varied and difficult. Does, for example, nonviolent action further anarchist, revolutionary, or democratic agendas? For some advocates, the principle guarantor of evil practices is the state, and their witness shades over into and is associated with anarchist thought understood in the maxim that that government is best which governs least. Others find themselves in apparent agreement with revolutionary goals, whether justified in the Puritan, Jeffersonian, or Marxist/Leninist traditions and seek to "humanize" the revolution, making the inevitable revolution as nonviolent as is possible. Still others believe democracy is the political system that best embodies the principled nonviolent value of conducting and resolving conflict without violence. These advocates seek in their witness to engage in "civil disobedience" that expresses a commitment to the community. Out of the latter group has come an attempt to extend principled nonviolence into conflict between states.

Advocates of principled nonviolence who share anarchist, revolutionary, or democratic goals disagree about the source of evil (in the state, in capitalism, or in human nature) but share a concern that the individual not get lost in the larger categories of historical conflict. They share a personal rejection of violence and a desire that the social change movements in which they are engaged remain nonviolent. They risk compromising their witness, however, when those movements become coalitions with others committed to violence in some circumstances. Each of these forms of principled nonviolence claims Mohandas K. Gandhi's development of a distinctive strategy for conducting conflict, satyagraha, as a precursor of their own. Following Gandhi's example, each has sought to extend principled nonviolence beyond witness to provide an effective alternative to violence as a means of removing tyrannical governments, achieving significant social change, extending democracy, or resolving conflict in world politics. Each attempt to extend principled nonviolence beyond witness raises questions about whether its core values and central dynamics are retained.

When Is Principled Nonviolence in Question?

The question of whether nonviolence should be the norm in all situations arises only after it is acknowledged that nonviolence is the norm in most situations. Nonviolence is the principle on which we judge whether parent–child, spouse, small group, and domestic conflict is appropriately conducted. Conflict between business and labor, among ethnic groups, races, classes, and genders is expected to be processed and change achieved through democratic institutions and social practices. In these cases the principle of nonviolence was stated long ago and is now embodied in custom, administrative practices, and laws. The question of principled nonviolence is faced in these areas only in gaining recognition of the law's applicability, or challenging administrative practices that deny the law, or in punishing violators of societal norms.

At the root of the various principles rejecting or restricting the use of violence is the question of whether love can be extended from family, friends, and community to one's enemies. Is it possible to act in such a way as to express love toward those full of hatred and prepared to use violence against us? Since the outcome depends upon the response of others, it is inherently uncertain. Is it better to risk your own life and that of your followers than to inflict suffering on your enemies? Advocates of principled nonviolence have said yes, while seeking to address and change the adversary's will to use violence.

Among the circumstances most likely to try an advocate of principled nonviolence are self-defense against a violent attack, risking killing someone who is in the act of killing others, challenging unjust social or political practices almost certain to be defended by violence (humanitarian intervention, for example, against genocide, mass starvation, widespread murder, or other human rights violations), and in conflicts between states for which violence remains the norm.

In response to the first two troubling situations above, advocates of principled nonviolence will disagree. The absolutist will say that in all cases violence is to be rejected, while others maintain that there is a sharp distinction between what an individual does when attacked or what one may do to prevent an individual from killing others and what one does on social issues when groups of people are involved. More selective advocates would conclude that self-defense or disarming a lethal adversary may well save lives and, in some circumstances, risk taking the adversary's life.

In social settings, civil disobedience to laws considered unjust is a strategy that principled advocates of nonviolence often adopt. Individuals and groups can acknowledge that democratic institutions have established laws that they consider unjust. After exhausting legal means to change the laws, and when obedience to the law impinges on conscience, principled advocates of nonviolence justify civil disobedience. In committing civil disobedience they do so in ways that respect the institutions that make laws but reject a specific law and refuse to obey it whatever the consequences. Thus, they seek to act in ways that affirm the need for law, knowing that the fabric of society can unravel once disrespect for law becomes widespread. For disobedience to laws to be civil it must be open, its practitioners must accept the penalty of the law, and it must be done in a manner that accepts the legitimacy of government. Henry David Thoreau's essay *On Civil Disobedience* is an eloquent defense of the legitimacy of civil disobedience, although he grounds his case on the anarchist principle that he "doesn't belong to any organization I didn't join" and therefore lacks an obligation to obey laws. Bayard Rustin, a precursor and colleague

N

of Martin Luther King, Jr., developed the concept of civil disobedience and applied it in the civil rights movement, which challenged laws and built a consensus that they should be changed.

Induction notices to the army and taxes that support war, abortions, or other activities that impinge on fundamental beliefs also may raise the question of principled nonviolence. Induction notices, for example, used to include the question: "Are you a conscientious objector to war?" Some advocates of principled nonviolence thought through their response, making the case that their commitment to nonviolence precluded their participation in an army, but their commitment to the society enabled them to accept alternative service. Others, such as Jehovah's Witnesses, objected to all service on principled grounds.

Practitioners

Mohandas Gandhi and Martin Luther King, Jr., are the twentieth century's most prominent and successful advocates of principled nonviolence. In American social change movements, Jane Addams, Kirby Page, Alfred Hassler, A.J. Muste, Bayard Rustin, A. Philip Randolph, Joan Baez, Robert Pickus, Jim Forest, and Cesar Chavez are among those who initiated or led significant nonviolent movements for social change. In other countries, Danilo Dolci (Sicily), Albert Camus (Algeria), Lanzo Del Vasto (France), Thich Nhat Hanh (Vietnam), Dom Helder Camara (Brazil), Kenneth Kaunda (Zambia), Lech Walesa (Poland), and Václav Havel (Czechoslovakia) have led significant nonviolent movements for social change, each in a significant way acting out of principled commitment.

Two figures in American academic life have contributed to the understanding and practice of nonviolent action. Joan Bondurant, in *Conquest of Violence: The Gandhian Philosophy of Conflict,* carefully distinguishes principled nonviolence from coercive nonviolent strategies of change. Gene Sharp has extended the concept of nonviolence and with insight advanced the discussion of nonviolence as a means of national defense. They work in opposite directions. Bondurant, by clarifying Gandhi's concept of satyagraha as a strategy that Gandhi described as "intended to replace methods of violence" with a movement "based entirely upon truth," makes Gandhi the standard against which all others are measured. Sharp extends and catalogues as nonviolent al-

most two hundred forms of social change, protest, or witness activities. While Bondurant sharply contrasts Gandhi's form of nonviolence as a method designed to transform an adversary with other forms of nonviolence that are coercive in seeking to limit the power, authority, or presence of an adversary, Sharp sees great benefit in including all nonviolent tactics as part of the nonviolent tradition. Bondurant maintains that Gandhi knew nonviolence was coercive and that the practitioner needed to state clearly what needed to change to enable the coercion to be removed. In addition, Gandhi, in his pursuit of truth, believed practitioners needed to admit the possibility that they might be wrong and also need to change.

Sharp, on the other hand, seeks an exhaustive list of situations and problems to which nonviolence might be applicable, making the concept, strategy, and tactics accessible to everyone. The principle involved is very much like the just war concept—the means, nonviolence, is an attempt to explore and implement all the alternatives to violence before violence can possibly be justified. Combined, both scholars have built a rich legacy of theory and interpretation of practice for new practitioners to draw upon.

The attempt to apply nonviolence to conflict between states has been explored by Robert Pickus. The extension of principled nonviolence from its origins in domestic conflict to world politics poses significant challenges. Traditional peace movement politics have rejected intervention in contests for power whether the adversary was Nazi Germany or a North Vietnam led by Ho Chi Minh. While that stance avoids participation in the horrors of conflicts like World War II and Vietnam, it leaves unaddressed the Holocaust and the tyranny imposed by Ho Chi Minh, from which more than 500,000 Vietnamese lost their lives in flight over the South China seas or in reeducation camps. Pickus argued that a nonviolent strategy could have been applied to the Vietnam conflict and more broadly to the cold war.

The Basic Concepts of Principled Nonviolence: Within Political Communities

M.K. Gandhi and Martin Luther King, Jr., developed nonviolence into a coherent strategy of change within their political communities. They offered theoretical arguments for principled nonviolence and demonstrated in specific campaigns how it might work. Both Gandhi and King brought into the political arena profound religious commitments. They argued that, despite the enormous coercive power of the state, governments cannot compel individuals to act. Whatever the state may do to you, you choose to obey its dictates. Individuals, when they withhold their consent to unjust laws, release a powerful dynamic into politics. If properly managed, this dynamic can be a powerful tool for achieving change without violence; if improperly managed, it can destroy a political community inviting rule by the most violent.

Gandhi's approach to conflict can be inferred from his *Autobiography* and from his newspaper articles. In *Conquest of Violence,* Joan Bondurant identifies "truth, nonviolence and self-suffering" as the key values in Gandhi's concept of satyagraha, which she defines as holding fast to truth. These values are applied in Gandhi's nonviolent campaigns in ways that ensure the campaigns will remain nonviolent and that open the possibility of success. These values are:

1. Dialogue: Gandhi opened dialogues with persons or representatives of institutions that he wanted to change. He entered into a dialogue with a willingness to reformulate his own position should the person persuade him that he was, in part, mistaken.
2. Nonviolent tactics: A wide variety of nonviolent measures could be adopted to open communication. These included fasting, personal witness, vigils, pickets, marches, even civil disobedience.
3. Courage: A commitment by both leaders and followers to refrain from violence, not out of fear, but out of a conviction that accepting suffering, even death if need be, is preferred to either acquiescing to the injustice or inflicting suffering on those whom you would change.
4. Love: A rejection of rhetorical or other forms of symbolic violence while expressing love and support for the adversary but rejecting the evil they may be doing.
5. Persistence: A commitment to pursue an objective for the long run in the face of obstacles while exploring a mutually acceptable solution.

The idea of accepting rather than inflicting suffering is clear in this set of principles, but the value of truth may be less obvious. Without attempting to state, much less unravel, the un- derlying epistemological assumptions, it is clear that the crucial element is the belief that you might be wrong. Making your own statement of objectives clear and getting from an adversary their statement is one element in this approach to realizing a higher truth than either of you enter into the conflict holding. Truth can be approached only when all the voices in the discussion are taken into account. Thus, Gandhi could engage in civil disobedience and encourage others to do so to open dialogues with adversaries; in doing so, a discussion of each party's partial truths would ensue with an agreement achieved, it is hoped, representing a higher truth. Violence does not advance truth; it ends the possibility of approximating it. Only through nonviolence and the discipline it imposes on yourself and the pressures it brings to bear on an adversary can the dialogue take place that can result in a higher truth's being achieved. These practices Gandhi referred to as his "experiments with truth."

In the early days of the civil rights movement, between 1948 and 1963, Bayard Rustin, Martin Luther King, Jr., and others sought to apply similar ideas to achieving needed change in race relations in the United States. Gandhi's picture adorned the King family home. Gandhi's influence as well as King's understanding of Christianity can be seen in the following rules excerpted from a "commitment card" signed by every volunteer in the King-led Southern Christian Leadership Conference campaign in Birmingham, Alabama:

I hereby pledge myself—my person and body—to the nonviolent movement. Therefore, I will keep the following ten commandments:

1. Meditate daily on the teachings and life of Jesus.
2. Remember always that the nonviolent movement in Birmingham seeks justice and reconciliation not victory.
3. Walk and talk in the manner of love, for God is love.
4. Pray daily to be used by God in order that all men might be free.
5. Sacrifice personal wishes in order that all men might be free.
6. Observe with both friend and foe the ordinary rules of courtesy.
7. Seek to perform regular service for others and for the world.

8. Refrain from the violence of fist, tongue, or heart.

9. Strive to be in good spiritual and bodily health.

10. Follow the directions of the movement and of the captain on a demonstration.

The explicit statement of principle, signed by every volunteer in the campaign, was communicated to friend and foe alike. The central dynamics of accepting, rather than inflicting suffering, of reconciliation, of dialogue, are all affirmed. In a specific demonstration, practitioners of principled nonviolence adopt precautions like the following:

1. Asking permission to hold a demonstration, indicating that it will be nonviolent and seeking the cooperation of the police.

2. Announcing in the call to the demonstration that nonviolence will be strictly adhered to—those who cannot commit to such a discipline are asked not to come; those who do come and find they cannot hold their commitment, to leave.

3. Planning in advance specific precautions against the demonstrators becoming violent, even in response to violence:

   a. appointing monitors with arm bands to be responsible for a portion of the line of march.

   b. sitting down if provoked by outsiders.

   c. going limp but not resisting arrest in other ways.

   d. checking rumors and planning how best to call off the demonstration if discipline breaks down.

   e. expressing a willingness to end the demonstration should negotiations open a more fruitful method of pursuing your objectives.

These values and procedures help ensure that principled nonviolence can be a powerful and successful instrument of social change within a political community. Can they be transposed to conflicts between political communities?

Principled Nonviolence: Between Political Communities

The prevailing voices in the discussion of nonviolence have recommended the withdrawal of one side in contests for power between political communities. They and others skeptical about the applicability of principled nonviolence to international conflict point out that one obtains power in national politics only if one persuades the public that one can provide security and advance the national interest against adversary states, and that now means through the threat or use of violence. Compromise between states appears more difficult given that land, status, and economic benefits are less divisible in conflict between political communities than within them. But given the high stakes involved in waging war in the nuclear era and with conventional weapons of mass destruction, if there is a way to apply principled nonviolence to world politics it should be tried. A few thoughtful scholars, such as Charles Osgood, Amatai Etzioni, and Robert Pickus, have explored such a route. In discussion with peace movements as well as governmental leaders that application of principled nonviolence has been called a peace initiatives strategy.

In outline form, a peace initiatives strategy initiates a cease-fire in a conflict and combines that with a systematic and detailed attempt to bring pressure to bear on an adversary to reciprocate that cease-fire. In addition, a peace initiatives strategy seeks to open other, nonmilitary arenas in which the dialogue over what is at issue in the war can be carried on. Robert Pickus, for example, advocated such a strategy for world politics during the cold war. Such a strategy enunciates a commitment to and opens for discussion a commitment to the goals essential to a world without war: reforming and transforming international organizations into instruments of world governance; strengthening a sense of world community to sustain those instruments; progress toward general and complete disarmament down to police levels; a world economic development effort capable of enabling the majority who are destitute to achieve self-sustained economic growth within broadening political freedoms sustained by democratic governments; developing nonviolent ways to force needed change; reaffirming basic shared political and religious values; and leadership by one country toward each of these goals. That leadership should be expressed in a series of interrelated initiative acts designed to induce reciprocation from whomever dialogue and negotiations do not bring into agreement.

Initiatives initiate (hence the name) progress toward each of the goals above by behavioral acts. These acts demonstrate a willingness to take risks, suffer, or bear costs for peace but invite reciprocation from others. As the first initiatives are reciprocated, additional initiatives are taken, building momentum toward the overall goals. Progress can be halted, reversed, or accelerated depending upon reciprocation. Initiatives may be partial measures, for example a commitment to 10 percent of a total goal in disarmament or development objectives, with an additional 10 percent offered to help induce reciprocation. Initiatives may be taken for a specified period of time and then rescinded if not reciprocated. Finally, initiatives may be mutually rewarding or positive, they may be neutral, or, in cases where the alternative appears to be war, coercive. Coercive initiatives include the use of many kinds of sanctions.

The vision of such a peace initiatives strategy—composed of a commitment to achieve the conditions essential to a world without war, of calibrated steps toward those goals designed to induce reciprocation, and of combining steps into an overall strategy—is a significant contribution to the discussion of how principled nonviolence can be applied in world politics. Critics point out, however, that such a strategy is principled in setting goals and in taking nonviolent steps toward them, but when it requires reciprocation for continued progress toward the goals, it becomes a form of tactical nonviolence. Advocates respond that they could become witnesses at that point, realizing that the conflict could not be resolved at that time by a nonviolent strategy, and yet would have demonstrated how such might be achieved. An initiative strategy would at least clarify who was responsible for the violence, and how, when they were willing, they could cooperate in resolving the conflict. In addition, many nonviolent measures could be developed and implemented that might help them become willing participants. Exploring those possibilities, not lamenting the response of the adversary or withdrawing, is what the advocates of principled nonviolence recommend.

Developing and Implementing a Nonviolent Strategy

If there are concepts and disciplines to prepare for a principled nonviolent strategy of change, how does one decide to develop and implement such a strategy? The first question is, is this a setting in which an adversary is likely to be changed by such a strategy? Nonviolent strategies were successful in overthrowing Communist regimes in 1989. In Czechoslovakia the commitment to nonviolence was explicit and principled. But such a strategy worked only after the Communist Party elite lost faith in its own invincibility. Earlier efforts to reform communism from within were unsuccessful, and some of them, violently repressed. A nonviolent challenge to Nazism as well as communism, might well have exposed many followers to death. Whether a discipline could have held a nonviolent movement together and succeeded with fewer deaths than occurred in World War II is unknown but unlikely.

Principled nonviolence between political communities can be enhanced by the emergence of regional and global international organizations, such as the European Union and the United Nations. The UN has as one of its purposes "eliminating the scourge of war" from humanity's affairs. Such international organizations, especially as they are increasingly influenced by democratic ideas, can serve as mediators or peacekeeping agencies. The UN has provided lightly armed peacekeeping forces to patrol borders and keep belligerents apart. Forces trained in nonviolent techniques might do more than this, but the world community has yet to agree to and apply the moral considerations that would make such a force and such institutions the instruments of principled nonviolence. Exploring in each religious tradition and ideology the basis of nonviolence may establish the needed consensus. More likely, the demonstration of successful, principled nonviolence on specific issues or conflicts will provide the impetus to reexamine and extend principled nonviolence into world politics.

Principled nonviolence is not universally applicable at this time. Few individuals or groups, much less entire political communities, are capable of the discipline. It has, however, proved remarkably successful within the democratic tradition. Skillful practitioners such as Gandhi, King, and Havel have demonstrated how change can be achieved in ways that express love for an enemy and build community among antagonists. The attempt to apply principled nonviolence to conflicts between states has been conceptually mapped out and isolated applications have been attempted. While the key concepts are clear in principled nonviolence, its applications to conflict between states is in the early stages of development. Much remains to be accomplished.

Robert Woito

References

Bondurant, Joan V. *Conquest of Violence: The Gandhian Philosophy of Conflict*. Princeton: Princeton University Press, 1958 (rev. ed. 1988).

Gandhi, Mohandas K. *All Men Are Brothers: Autobiographical Reflections*. Completed by Krishna Kripalani. New York: Continuum, 1980.

Havel, Václav, William M. Brinton, and Alan Ringler, eds. *Without Force or Lies: Voices from the Revolution of Central Europe in 1989–90*. San Francisco: Mercury House, 1990.

King, Martin Luther, Jr. *Why We Can't Wait*. New York: Harper and Row, 1964.

Nuttall, Geoffrey Fillingsham. *Christian Pacifism in History*. Oxford: Blackwell, 1958.

Pickus, Robert, and Robert Woito. *To End War: An Introduction*. Rev. ed. New York: Harper and Row, 1970.

Richards, Leyton. *The Christian's Alternative to War: An Examination of Christian Pacifism*. New York: Macmillan, 1929.

Rustin, Bayard. *Down the Line: The Collected Writings of Bayard Rustin*. Chicago: Quadrangle, 1971.

Sharp, Gene. *The Politics of Nonviolent Action*. Boston: Porter Sargent, 1973.

Weigel, George. *Tranquilas Ordinis: The Present Failure and the Future Promise of American Catholic Thought*. New York: Oxford University Press, 1987.

See also CIVIL DISOBEDIENCE; GANDHI, MOHANDAS KARAMCHAND; KING, MARTIN LUTHER, JR.; METHODS OF NONVIOLENT ACTION; PACIFISM; RELIGION AND NONVIOLENT ACTION

Nonviolent Alternatives

International network that operated from 1977 until about 1982. It was established to improve communications between individuals and groups promoting nonviolent action for peace and justice.

NVA originated in a request by Dom Helder Camara, archbishop of Recife, Brazil, that people committed to nonviolence should concentrate their forces and work together. Pax Christi International responded to this by organizing an international conference in Driebergen, Netherlands, in 1972. It was entitled "The Power of Peace Forces." This was followed, in 1977, by an international consultation in Derry, Northern Ireland, that focused on three main issues: how to bridge the gap between peace activists and peace researchers; how to improve communications between nonviolent peace activists themselves; and how to make nonviolence a more realistic option in the public mind.

As a result of this consultation, the Nonviolent Alternatives network was established with an office in Antwerp, Belgium. The executive secretary was Mr. Coen de Vocht and the follow-up committee included Elias Chacour (priest and Palestinian Arab), Jim Forest (secretary of the International Fellowship of Reconciliation), Ciaran McKeown (Peace People, Northern Ireland), Devi Prasad (War Resisters' International), Adolfo Perez Esquivel (Servicio Paz y Justicia, Argentina), Liljana Markovic-Vlasnic (journalist, Yugoslavia), Thomas Gumbleton (American bishop), and Etienne de Jonghe (secretary of Pax Christi International).

Nonviolent Alternatives started to collect information about nonviolent activities by means of a worldwide enquiry, "Mapping Peace Forces." This enabled NVA to produce a series of directories on various subjects, and to create a documentation center of journals and other resources. Apart from exchange between activists and researchers, NVA was concerned about public education and communication with and through the mass media. A quarterly bulletin, *Peace Action News,* was published, supplemented by occasional pamphlets. Titles included *Nonviolence—Theory and Practice* by Gerard A. Vanderhaar, and *Nonviolence—Gandhi and the Minority Struggles* by Devi Prasad.

One of the goals of NVA was to hold further international meetings. In 1979, there was a regional consultation that brought together Jews, Muslims, and Christians in Ibillin, Israel. Another major conference took place in Nassogne, Belgium, in 1981 on the theme "Moral Pressure for Liberation." NVA provided a personal as well as an institutional network, encouraging and even helping to fund some isolated individuals working in their local communities.

Funding problems were, however, one of the reasons why NVA came to an end. The prolonged absence of the executive secretary after a road accident also made survival more difficult. But many aspects of NVA's work were by

1982 being covered by other organizations and new initiatives. The documentation center, for example, had been taken over by IPIS, the International Peace Information Service, created in 1981 and also based in Antwerp. Eventually, *Peace Action News* subscribers were invited to transfer to journals such as *Disarmament Campaigns* (started by NVA in 1980), and NVA itself was allowed to fade away while its work was carried on through other channels.

Valerie Flessati

See also Camara, Dom Helder; Pax Christi International

Nonviolent Struggle: The Contemporary Practice of Nonviolent Action

Surveying global news media shows both the persistence and universality of nonviolent forms of struggle in conflicts, but also reveals important variations among countries, regions, and types of political systems. By analyzing reports of nonviolent direct action in news stories for the years between 1984 and 1995, we can provide tentative answers to several important questions: Just how common is nonviolent struggle in the world today? What differences are there among countries and regions? Under what kinds of political conditions and for what different purposes has nonviolent action been used? Has nonviolent struggle become more or less common in recent years?

First and foremost, nonviolent action appears in nearly every country in the world, regardless of culture, type of political system, or level of economic development. Nevertheless, nonviolent action is not equally common in all countries. Finally, the "surprising outbreak" of nonviolent struggle in 1989 does not appear to be an indicator of a rising trend toward greater use of nonviolent action over all. Rather, 1989 represented a momentary surge of activity in a number of closely related states.

Where and Why Is Nonviolent Action Used?

Nonviolent direct action is one means by which people and groups engage each other in conflict. Like violence, nonviolent action operates outside of the established parameters of institutionalized political interaction. "Direct action," both violent and nonviolent, has certain characteristics that set it apart from what might be called "routine," "institutional," or "normal" politics.

The key feature of direct action is the indeterminacy of its outcome, owing to the fact that no rules, norms, or procedures prescribe the outcome. For example, a fair election has an unknown outcome in the sense that the winner cannot be predicted in advance. However, the election process has known and predictable rules that will determine the outcome—the person receiving more than half the votes cast will win, for example. In contrast, direct actions have no procedural rules governing the results. When workers engage in a labor strike, a very common form of nonviolent direct action, or terrorists begin bombing public buildings, a form of violent direct action, there is no established procedure or norm that says, "You will win if you stay on strike for x number of days (or if you blow up x number of buildings)." The outcomes depend on factors related to the strategic and bargaining interaction between the parties to the conflict.

The degree to which conflicts are being waged in the streets rather than through existing political institutions and procedures provides an indicator of the capacity of those institutions to resolve conflicts effectively—higher levels of direct action indicate both intensified social conflict and the breakdown of established institutions. Similarly, the relative portions of nonviolent and violent direct action will indicate very generally the strategies and tactics people use to wage their conflicts.

News stories regularly report political behavior and conflict engagements, and implicitly distinguish between direct and routine action. Thus, it is possible to construct a global survey that focuses, on the one hand, on the relative amounts of direct action taking place around the world, and on the other hand on the uses of nonviolent struggle in these conflicts. News stories, of course, offer only a limited and selected reflection of reality. We know, for example, that the level of news media attention varies significantly among countries and that much more of any kind of behavior occurs than is reported. Nevertheless, news stories provide a source of data from which broad comparisons can be drawn.

Between 1984 and 1995 the Reuters world press news service reported direct action (either violent or nonviolent) in almost a third of its stories (approximately 30 percent). Nonviolent direct action accounted for somewhat less than one half of the stories concerning direct action (approximately 45 percent), or roughly 14 percent of all news stories.

Nonviolent action appears in virtually every country in the world, lending support for a very basic proposition—the use of nonviolent action is a ubiquitous phenomenon in social conflicts, cutting across cultures and histories. However, the distribution of reported nonviolent direct action is hardly uniform across the globe. One explanation is simply that the volume of new stories is much greater in some countries than in others, making the relative portions of the types of events reported somewhat skewed. Among countries that receive a high level of news attention, where the overall level of reported social conflict is low (as indicated by the portion of all direct action reports), nonviolent action tends to be the predominant means of expression. Notably, this group includes countries that are very different—such as the United States and the Soviet Union. In countries like the United States, where political processes are open and broadly accepted, violent direct action is delegitimized in favor of nonviolence when a conflict moves into the streets. In very repressive countries like the former USSR, social conflict in general, and violent opposition in particular, is strongly repressed. These important differences in the manifestations of conflict within different social and political systems are explored below.

Issues

As with the overall distribution of nonviolent direct action, the distribution of issues over which people struggle using nonviolent action varies rather dramatically. For the decade, the least frequently reported issues involved moral issues, such as abortion or obscenity, and explicitly communal or ethnic conflicts. The most frequently reported issues under contention involved human rights, economic disparities and poverty, peace or terrorism, and military and weapons concerns.

Just as the incidence of nonviolent action varied among countries and regions, the issues on which nonviolent action was used varied geographically. For example, in the Middle East and Central America, by far the most common issues involved peace, violence, and terrorism. In the former region, however, the next most prominent concerns were either military issues or self-determination, whereas in Central America the next level of concerns involved political legitimacy. This pattern makes sense in light of the regions' conflicts—each had ongoing armed conflicts over the decade; in the Middle East the struggle for Palestinian independence focused events; in

Central America guerrilla insurgencies challenged the military-backed regimes then in power. In South America, the issues of poverty and crime dominated the news. Across the North Atlantic community of states (including Western Europe and North America) military issues predominated, reflecting the public concerns with nuclear weapons deployments during the 1980s. Finally, whereas issues of communal and ethnic strife ranked low in the global pattern of conflict issues, in southern Europe, which includes the Mediterranean countries and the Balkans, matters of self-determination, communal conflict, and human rights were as common as reports about violence and terrorism.

Political Systems

As noted above, the reported incidence of nonviolent direct action tends to vary with two factors—the overall level of conflict reported and the nature of the country's political system. Countries in which conflicts take up an increasing portion of the total news are experiencing greater stress and challenge than those with a lower portion of reports. The rising frequency of demonstrations, marches, strikes, and other forms of protest and noncooperation, as well as bombings, assassinations, and armed clashes, suggest that the institutional channels for resolving conflicts are not working effectively.

Part of the variation in both conflict levels and the ways conflict is prosecuted can be attributed to their varying political conditions. Insofar as countries affording greater freedoms to their peoples generally have more efficient and effective institutional processes for resolving disputes and making decisions, we would expect to find less recourse to "protest politics" (both violent and nonviolent) and greater reliance on established procedures. Countries with few freedoms, on the other hand, provide people with fewer institutional opportunities, and, perhaps, greater grievances. However, while the incentives for opposition may be higher in countries lacking freedoms, repression by the government also raises the cost of opposition, especially of violent opposition. This does not mean that opposition does not emerge under repressive regimes—both violent and nonviolent expressions of opposition can sometimes be quite powerful, as in Eastern Europe or China in 1989. However, overall, the tendency for opposition actions, as reflected in news reports, will be diminished.

Between the extremes of the most and least free countries are those countries with some degree of civil and political freedoms, but far from open and accessible institutions or substantial personal liberties. These countries may have some combination of moderately competitive political systems, partially free media institutions, or relative protections of human rights. Some of these countries may be undergoing transitions from less to more free political and social systems. In these partially free countries, the tendency for conflict to spill over into the streets is great because the institutional arrangements provide inadequate avenues for resolution, and yet the repressive response of the government is not likely to be as powerful as in very repressive regimes.

We can group the countries of the world into three clusters corresponding to the relative levels of freedom suggested above. In the most free group we find countries like the United States, Canada, Japan, Western European states, and Czechoslovakia after 1989. In the partially free cluster we find countries such as Bangladesh, Chile before 1987, Egypt, Sri Lanka, and Taiwan. The least free grouping includes Cambodia, China, Iraq, Syria, Poland before 1989, and the Soviet Union (before its dissolution in late 1991). Because the level of freedom in some countries changes, sometimes dramatically, a grouping may have different members at different times. Therefore the discussion below characterizes the reporting of conflicts according to general types of political systems, rather than any one country.

Over the decade as a whole, conflict is least frequently reported in the most free countries, and most frequently reported in the partially free group. The expression of conflict through nonviolent methods is most common in the most free countries and least common in those that are partially free.

On an annual basis, a slightly different pattern emerges. While the portion of news stories reporting conflict in the most free group remained almost unchanged from year to year, those in the other two shifted. Beginning in 1989, the portion of stories reporting direct action in the least free countries increased slightly, indicating rising challenges to the world's most autocratic regimes. For example, the portions of news stories reporting conflict in Poland, East Germany, and Czechoslovakia all increased dramatically in 1989. And, despite the well-known tendency of the news media to be attracted to and emphasize violence, the degree to which that conflict was expressed by nonviolent methods also increased.

After 1990, however, in countries in the least free group the level of reported nonviolent direct action declined, even as reports of conflicts continued to increase, suggesting either that new challenges were being expressed in more violent terms or that repression by governments increased in response to opposition. For example, both conflict and violence increased in Angola, Iran, and Pakistan.

Generally, the most turbulence was experienced in those countries in the partially free group. The level of conflict reported, always higher than either other group, varied over the decade within a range of about 5 percentage points up and down. Significantly, however, the reported level of nonviolent struggle declined after 1989. For example, beginning in 1990 Algeria began to experience a rising intensity of conflict and a decrease in the degree to which methods of nonviolent action were used. In 1992, it shifted from the partially free to least free grouping as the conflict continued. Similarly, news reporting in Egypt showed a rising level of conflict and a diminishing resort to nonviolent struggle beginning about the same time, although the political system did not become increasingly repressive, as it did in Algeria. Finally, in South Africa, the reported level of conflict remained high throughout the decade; and even as the country moved away from apartheid and toward nonracial elections in 1994, there was a decrease in the use of nonviolent direct action.

Trends and Conclusions

The patterns and descriptive data discussed above lead to the conclusion that although nonviolent direct action has been a prominent and important element in social conflicts throughout the world in recent years, the "surprising" events of 1989 did not presage a trend of rising use of nonviolent action. Over the past decade the general portion of direct action reported in Reuters news stories remained relatively constant at about 30 percent; the degree at which direct action was expressed nonviolently was about 45 percent. Significant variation in these portions existed among regions, countries, and political regimes.

The events of 1989 were a pivotal transitional moment in world politics, dramatically helping to restructure the global political order.

N

The results of the revolutions in Europe in 1989 and 1990 encouraged people suffering under the remaining tyrannical regimes to mount new challenges, both nonviolent and otherwise.

William B. Vogele
Doug Bond

References

Program on Nonviolent Sanctions and Cultural Survival. *Transforming Struggle: Strategy and the Global Experience of Nonviolent Direct Action.* Cambridge, Mass.: Program on Nonviolent Sanctions and Cultural Survival at Harvard University, 1992.

See also CONFLICT RESOLUTION; CONFLICT THEORIES; ETHNIC CONFLICT; MECHANISMS OF DIRECT ACTION; METHODS OF NONVIOLENT ACTION; REVOLUTIONS OF 1989

Northern Ireland Civil Rights Association

Founded on January 29, 1967, by a diverse group of political activists, for five years the Northern Ireland Civil Rights Association (NICRA) engaged in political lobbying, electoral participation, and nonviolent direct action in pursuit of legal equality for Catholics and Protestants in the six counties of Northern Ireland (also known as Ulster). Its members included both Protestants and Catholics from a wide variety of backgrounds. Many activists were drawn from existing lobbying and legal reform organizations. Other participants came from liberal political parties, like the British Labour Party, as well as from Catholic nationalist groups. This political diversity was both a strength and a weakness of the association. For a time, NICRA, with its strategy of applying pressure through nonviolent action as well as political lobbying, defined both the republican movement (those seeking political unity with the Republic of Ireland in the south) and the reform movement. By the early 1970s, however, factional divisions between moderates and radicals within NICRA, combined with violence by the country's military police, undermined and finally ended the association.

Although NICRA failed to secure a lasting resolution to the conflict, it was successful in securing significant, if limited, concessions from the Northern Irish government, including reforms of the electoral system and the allocation of public housing, which improved the social and political environment for the Catholic minority. The civil rights campaign also succeeded in mobilizing not only the vast majority of the nationalist Catholic minority, but also segments of the Protestant unionist community in support of a more democratic and just system of government. However, the final stage of the civil rights movement (between 1970 and 1972) was characterized by an escalation in the intensity of conflict on the part of all parties to the conflict as political action and appeals were increasingly replaced by reliance on public coercion and physical and coercive force.

Heavily influenced by the civil rights movement in the United States, the uprisings in Paris and Prague, and the anticolonial movements in Vietnam and Algeria, NICRA employed a campaign of civil disobedience and nonviolent direct action that was designed to force the state to implement major social, economic, and political reforms. They wished to create a new situation in which the Catholic and Protestant working class could transform sectarian differences into class unity in a new democratic state. The basic demands of NICRA were: (a) one person–one vote in local elections; (b) the removal of gerrymandered electoral boundaries; (c) enactment of new laws prohibiting discrimination by local government, and the provision of machinery to deal with complaints; (d) allocation of public housing on a points system; (e) repeal of the Special Powers Act; and (f) the disbandment of the "B-Specials" (the entirely Protestant paramilitary reserve security force).

In the first stage of the civil rights movement, between 1964 and 1968, NICRA relied exclusively on political and nonviolent direct action. The moderates within NICRA attempted to secure reforms by using publicity campaigns and by lobbying supportive organizations such as the National Council for Civil Liberties in Britain and the Irish Congress of Trade Unions. This faction, led by John Hume, also encouraged the Catholic minority to make use of its limited access to political power by electing nationalist MPs to both the British parliament and the Ulster legislature at Stormont. Nationalist MPs joined in the civil rights marches to emphasize that the movement was seeking only the same rights and protections enjoyed by other residents of the United Kingdom. By working through existing institutional channels, these moderates sought to reassure Stormont that NICRA was seeking merely to reform the system.

The more radical activists, who doubted the willingness of the state to implement even modest reforms without some external pressure, employed a wide range of nonviolent direct actions, including boycotts, house squats, sit-down protests, pickets, and marches. Like their American counterparts, NICRA activists, by explicitly avowing a commitment to nonviolent struggle, sought to reach across the sectarian divide to appeal to working-class and liberal Protestants to join the movement.

Twenty-five thousand people participated in NICRA's first civil rights march in Northern Ireland on August 24, 1968, from the nationalist town of Coalisland to Dungannon. The demonstration proceeded peacefully, despite the heavy presence of the Royal Ulster Constabulatory (RUC), and members of the Ulster Protestant Volunteers, a militant Protestant sectarian organization led by the Reverend Ian Paisley. The RUC nevertheless prevented marchers from entering Dungannon.

Inspired by the success of their initial marches, NICRA, on September 8, 1968, notified the RUC of its intention to stage a march in Derry on October 5. Two days prior to the march and rally, the Northern Ireland home affairs minister, William Craig, issued a ban prohibiting the march and any other protest that was being planned. The ban prompted the first real signs of splits between the moderates and radicals in NICRA. The more cautious members on the NICRA executive became worried that events were moving too fast. After the announcement of the ban, this group wanted to call off the march. Local activists, however, were determined to go ahead, arguing that the ban was precisely the type of sectarian action that demanded protest. When it became clear that the march would go ahead without them, NICRA's more moderate leaders agreed to support the event.

Despite the official ban on the march, two thousand civil rights advocates assembled on the afternoon of October 5, 1968. The plan was to march from the Protestant Waterside district of Derry across the main Craigavon Bridge to the city center. As the marchers approached the bridge they confronted a cordon of RUC men. The marchers halted briefly while NICRA leaders consulted with the RUC. NICRA spokespersons urged the demonstrators to disband, maintaining that they had made their point, and many demonstrators did begin to leave. As they departed, however, they encountered another cordon of police who had sealed off the street at the other end. The marchers were trapped between two groups of police, who proceeded to charge the demonstrators. During the charge nationalist Westminster M.P. Gerry Fitt's head was badly gashed by a baton. Interviewed by reporters on the scene, the image of Fitt, a member of the British parliament, wounded during an unprovoked police charge as he attempted to march in support of one person–one vote, shocked the world and mobilized the nationalist community onto the streets.

Both moderates and radicals within NICRA were shocked by the brutality of the attack by the state security forces on the civil rights demonstrators, as they had assumed the presence of three Westminster MPs would ensure respect for democratic prerogatives. However, the assault on the marchers demonstrated the effectiveness of nonviolent protest as a strategy by which to mobilize all shades of nationalist opinion in the North of Ireland. So successful was NICRA's strategy, that the Irish Republican Army (IRA) remained largely on the sidelines and allowed NICRA to speak for the Catholic minority.

On November 22, Stormont Prime Minister Captain O'Neill, under pressure from British Prime Minister Harold Wilson, whose government had been stung by the international publicity given to the bloodied Gerry Fitt and to the bruised and drenched civil rights protesters, announced a five-point reform program meeting NICRA demands. These reforms were sufficient to appease Hume and the moderate faction of NICRA.

The reform package further divided the various factions within NICRA and exacerbated growing tensions within the republican movement. The Hume faction within NICRA argued that since the organization had achieved its goals further protests would serve only to heighten divisions between the Catholic and Protestant communities. The more radical faction, led by the student-organized People's Democracy and northern republican activists, however, regarded the implementation of reforms as the beginning, not the end of the civil rights struggle. This group argued that there was no guarantee those limited reforms would be enforced, much less extended to encompass the whole range of demands they were intent on raising. Therefore, when People's Democracy decided to sponsor a march across the breadth of Northern Ireland, from Belfast to Derry on New Year's Day 1969, Hume called for the march to be abandoned, and the Dublin-based IRA leadership ordered republicans not to take part.

The seventy-five-mile march was modeled on the 1965 civil rights procession that Martin Luther King, Jr., led from Selma to Montgomery, Alabama. Indeed, the demands of both sets of marchers were remarkably similar: each was calling for an end to discrimination against a long-oppressed minority, and each urged unity among working people, regardless of their color or creed.

On January 4, the demonstrators came to Burntollet Bridge, approximately eight miles from Derry. There, they were attacked by about 350 Protestant loyalists as the RUC, which had been monitoring the march, looked on. Unarmed marchers were punched, kicked, beaten, and driven into the freezing river as they attempted to escape the attack. Those who could still walk continued on to Derry, where they received a heroes' welcome from the nationalist community.

Following Burntollet, the Dublin-based IRA leadership rescinded its prohibition on IRA members participating in future civil rights protests, noting that the struggle for civil rights was developing into a struggle for national rights.

Given the differences regarding both goals and strategies it appears likely that NICRA, were it not for the unifying effect of the violent attack against members of the nationalist community, would have disintegrated. As it was, however, the attacks on the movement fostered continued cooperation between the various factions of the opposition movement.

Between August 12 and 14, 1969, Catholic–Protestant violence erupted in Derry, in what became known to Catholics as the "Battle of the Bogside." Precipitating events included vandalism of Catholic homes by Protestant paramilitary groups and a Protestant loyalist march around the wall of the old Derry, even while Catholic marches remained banned. RUC units intervened but were met with blockades and showers of bricks, bottles, and firebombs. The inability of the RUC to restore order in Derry and the rapid spread of protests to other cities in the North led the British Government, on August 14, to order regular British troops, absent from the counties since the 1920s, once again into the streets of Northern Ireland. Nevertheless, in the aftermath of the Catholic "victory," RUC and Protestant paramilitary groups launched revenge attacks on other Catholic neighborhoods,

in all destroying over two hundred homes and killing ten people.

August 1969 would mark the first major turning point in the civil rights campaign and the beginning of the second phase of the struggle, which was characterized by a marked shift both in the goals and strategy of the movement. Although NICRA had begun by demanding modest social-democratic reforms from the Stormont government, after August, few Catholics believed that even those demands could or would be granted by a Stormont administration. Thus, despite the massive mobilization of the Catholic minority in response to the attacks in Derry, Burntollet, and Belfast, the division between the moderate and radical factions of NICRA prevented the organization from devising a strategy capable of maintaining the high level of mobilization.

By the end of 1969, the failure of the British forces to protect nationalist areas had convinced many within the nationalist community that they had little choice but to defend themselves against state violence with violence. Thus it was that the inadequacy of the state's response to violent attacks on the Catholic minority initiated the shift in the nationalist community's political strategy from one of strict nonviolence to one in which the use of physical and coercive force would also play a significant role and midwife the rebirth of the IRA.

Perhaps the strongest evidence in support of the transformational nature of the nonviolent struggle of the civil rights movement is revealed in the attitudes of republican activists who participated in NICRA and were active twenty-five years later in Sinn Fein, the political party that represents the interests of the IRA.

Leading figures within Sinn Fein, such as Gerry Adams, have publicly acknowledged that participation by republicans in the broad-based nonviolent civil rights campaigns and the hunger strike campaigns in the 1980s broke down the traditional republican anathema to any form of protest except physical force and their fear of betrayal by those unwilling to support the armed struggle of the IRA. Thus, as a consequence of the participation by members and supporters of the IRA in these campaigns, the republican movement came to endorse a wide range of tactics that made it possible for increasing numbers of people to actively contribute to and participate in the nationalist movement. Throughout the 1980s, the increasing recognition, by supporters of the armed struggle of the

IRA, of the capacity of both political and nonviolent struggle to empower the nationalist community, as evidenced in the civil rights movement, the hunger strike campaigns of 1980–1981, and the electoral campaigns of Sinn Fein in 1985 and 1989, enabled those within the republican movement who recognized the limited potential of the armed struggle to effect a transformation of power relations within Northern Ireland to assume leadership of the republican movement. It is this leadership, cognizant of the power of nonviolent transforming struggle, which, as of midnight on August 31, 1994, secured the first ceasefire of the IRA since 1975 and has succeeded in securing an equal role for the nationalist community in negotiations with the British and Irish government regarding the resolution of the conflict.

Cynthia L. Irvin

References

Adams, Gerry. *The Politics of Irish Freedom.* Dingle, Ireland: Brandon, 1986.

Bew, Paul, and Henry Patterson. *The British State and the Ulster Crisis.* London: Verso, 1985.

Farrell, Michael. *Northern Ireland: The Orange State.* 2nd ed. London: Pluto, 1980.

O'Malley, Padraig. *The Uncivil Wars.* Belfast: Blackstaff, 1983.

See also CORRIGAN, MAIREAD, AND BETTY WILLIAMS; IRA HUNGER STRIKES, 1980–1981; PEACE PEOPLE, COMMUNITY OF THE;

Norway, Resistance to German Occupation, 1940–1945

Resistance against the Nazi occupation of Norway during World War II, predominantly waged by nonviolent means. After Norway was invaded by German forces on April 9, 1940, the armed resistance was defeated within two months and the king and the government eventually fled to the United Kingdom. Until the end of the war the German physical military occupation was seen by most Norwegians as something that could not be eliminated without external military assistance. Thus, although there was armed resistance, it came to play a marginal role until the end of the war was approaching. Instead, a variety of nonviolent resistance activities were employed, both spontaneously by individuals and in larger, planned campaigns. The objective of these resistance activities was to counter and resist the attempts of "Nazification" of society. Such activities were described by the term *holdningskamp* (attitude struggle), used to denote the nationalist, noncooperative, and adversarial attitude toward the occupying power as well as the various symbolical manifestations and acts of noncooperation. Such acts and manifestations were often employed regardless of military considerations and were considered as ends in themselves.

On the day of the German invasion, the leader of the national socialist party *Nasjonal Samling* (NS), Vidkun Quisling, proclaimed himself prime minister of Norway. NS had received only marginal support before the war, and it soon became clear that its government was subordinate to the German occupation authorities. Still, there was a widespread fear that power would be transferred to the Quisling government, which could then come to sign a peace agreement with Germany. In such a situation Norwegian citizens might be drafted and mobilized to fight against the countries they saw as Norway's allies. Therefore, Norwegians felt it was necessary to show that they would not let themselves be organized by the NS and to make impossible the implementation of Quisling's ambitious plans to organize Norway as a corporative state along the lines of Mussolini's Italy.

The resistance took place in a context of censorship and insecurity. All the means of communication were in the hands of the Nazi authorities, and all opposition information had to be transmitted through personal channels or by secretive means. Although repression in "Germanic" Norway was less severe than in many other occupied areas, arbitrary terror was still widely used to spread fear throughout the population. The risk involved in a minor manifestation of resistance or protest could be anything from a small fine to death. The police and *hirden,* the paramilitary section of the NS, were widely used to attack open opposition. Collective punishment and random executions were common. Goebbels, the German minister of propaganda, is quoted as having said, "If the Norwegians cannot come to love us, they will at least learn to fear us."

On an individual level different symbols were used to express opposition to the occupants and loyalty to the king. Some were obvious, like displaying small Norwegian flags, whereas others were subtle and indirect like paper clips worn on jackets (meaning "we stick together"), a comb in the front pocket (a pun on the double meaning of the Norwegian verb *greie,* meaning "to comb and to manage"), and the use of a traditional Norwegian winter headgear, the red woolen cap *topplue.* The use of this was later outlawed. Other individual acts of resistance included pretending not to speak German and refusing to sit alongside Germans on public transport. Such practices were seen as contributing to the creation of an "ice-front."

After control of the political institutions had been seized by the Nazis toward the end of 1940, the government employed new measures to erode all possible basis for social opposition. All voluntary organizations were to be placed under NS administration, and their former leadership was replaced with people loyal to the NS. These attempts at Nazification were met by massive withdrawals of membership.

One of the first cases was the sports strike beginning in 1940, when the leadership of the National Sports Federation resigned in protest against the attempts of converting it into a new organization subordinated to the Nazi ministry of sports and labor service. The strike was highly successful, and no major sports event was held until the end of the war. People refused to attend official sports events and, instead, organized alternative, clandestine competitions. This pattern of withdrawing from membership continued in other fields, often followed by letters of protest. The process culminated in the joint protest letter of forty-three organizations (representing approximately 750,000 members) in May 1941. The Nazi authorities responded first with massive arrests and finally with a declaration of martial law. All opposition was declared illegal, and the civilian resistance was forced to go underground. Increased repression was employed, but far from quelling the resistance, these measures actually seemed to strengthen it. Successful acts of collective resistance greatly strengthened the sense of community in the population.

In 1942 a new law, making membership in one's corresponding labor or civic organization compulsory, was met with renewed threats of withdrawal. In ten days, between 100,000 and 150,000 members left the Federation of Labour. Finally, Quisling was told by the Germans to drop the attempts at establishing a corporative state. The Germans feared that economic chaos would result.

The church was another center of resistance. Norway is very homogenous in terms of religious affiliation; at that time 96 percent of the population belonged to the Lutheran state church. On January 15, 1941, a letter of protest from the Lutheran bishops condemned abuses committed by *hirden* as well as the government's attempts to violate religious principles (such as the confidentiality of information confided to clergy in the performance of their pastoral duties). When the Ministry of Education failed to respond in a way the bishops thought appropriate, the bishops published the correspondence in a pastoral letter, distributed all over the country and read aloud in the churches. In February 1942, when the authorities wanted to hold a Mass in the Nidaros Cathedral to commemorate the formation of Quisling's "national government," the local bishop, Arne Fjellbu, announced that he would perform his regular service later the same day. While only a few NS members attended the official mass, thousands came to the regular service until the police ordered the doors to be shut. Several thousands braved the biting cold weather and remained outside the cathedral singing psalms, refusing to follow the police's order to disperse. Fjellbu was dismissed, and all the bishops and later the entire clergy resigned their official posts. While they refused to fulfill their state duties, they continued to perform their spiritual duties privately and did not cease to criticize the Nazi regime in public. The hymn "A Mighty Fortress Is Our God" became widely used in demonstrations and protests to overwhelm the orders of the police.

The best-known single incident in the resistance movement involved the schools and the national teachers' resistance. In 1941 the government planned to require a declaration of loyalty to the NS from all teachers. The demand, however, was preempted by a counter-declaration from the teachers stating that each one would first of all "remain faithful to one's vocation as a teacher and to one's conscience." In February 1942 two laws established a mandatory youth service in the NS for all children and compulsory membership in *Norges lærersamband* (the Nazi-controlled teachers federation), which also was given the power to fire teachers. Between eight thousand and ten thousand of the twelve thousand teachers in Norway refused to join the new organization. After repeated threats most teachers still refused, and about eleven hundred teachers were arrested and sent to a labor camp in northern Norway. Despite the appalling conditions, hardship, and even torture, nearly all the teachers remained firm. The Quisling regime then issued a declaration that was seen as nearly a complete defeat, saying that all teachers would be considered members of the *lærersamband* whether they had signed or not. When the teachers resumed work, however, they read aloud in class a declaration stating that membership in the *lærersamband* and teaching were incompatible. "Our task," the statement read, "is to give each one of you the necessary knowledge and training to attain fulfillment as a human being. . . . Teachers must teach their pupils to believe in and uphold truth and justice. Therefore, teachers cannot, without betraying their calling, teach anything that violates their consciences." In a speech at Stabæk high school, Quisling later declared: "You teachers have destroyed everything for me!"

During the occupation former political cleavages largely lost their importance, and great unity and support were achieved in the resistance—with the partial exception of the Communists. Opposition became a mark of honor, and individuals and groups all wanted to contribute. The civilian resistance was to some extent organized through different coordinating groups known as *siv.org,* but their role was advisory rather than actually commanding. Communication and cooperation went through various relationships. One of the reasons for the strength of the resistance was its success in mobilizing politically along a wide variety of different networks. Formerly apolitical groups, like the sports federation, had large memberships with networks stretching all over the country, and through the conflict with the authorities they became nuclei for resistance groups in many places. Clandestine papers and information from allied broadcasts were circulated, and funds were raised to support those who lost their employment due to their opposition. The authorities were unable to recruit replacements for the teachers and clergy who refused to collaborate.

Although the resistance was largely nonviolent, it was not motivated by pacifist beliefs. Acts of sabotage and armed resistance were explicitly discouraged by leading figures in the resistance, so as to avoid actions that could bring collective punishment. Similarly, many teachers insisted that their campaign should not assume the character of a general strike, but remain limited to refusing membership in *lærersambandet.* Still, Norwegians as a whole expressed no moral inhibitions against the use of violence. They wanted the Allies to win the war, and most were willing to employ armed struggle at a later stage in the liberation. In contemporary Norway, the military sides to the resistance are usually emphasized, together with the slogan of "Never again April 9," implying that the country must never again commit the mistake of making itself vulnerable to invasion and must rely on a strong conventional defense to deter aggressors.

Nonviolent action in Norway did not defeat the occupying power; the occupation was brought to an end through military defeat by the Allied powers. But the civilian resistance was highly successful in fighting Nazi rule. By the end of 1942, *holdningskampen* had largely defeated the plans for a corporative state, at precisely the time when Germany seemed to be winning the war. Still, there remains the critical question of how vital these attempts of Nazification were to the Germans. In sharp contrast to the negative and often hateful resistance to individual German occupiers, economic relations were largely characterized by collaboration in order to "keep the wheels running." The way this potential economic leverage was left unused illustrates how the resistance to some extent directed its struggle against the person rather than the issue. Morale-building and symbolic manifestations, however powerful and successful, may have come at the expense of applying more effective sanctions.

Kristian Skrede Gleditsch

References
The literature on the German occupation and the resistance is vast and continues to grow. Most of the relevant research literature is naturally in Norwegian. The following five items are particularly useful:

Grimnes, Ole Kristian. "Komplementerende forsvarsformer: Erfaringer fra den norske motstandskampen under den annen verdenskrig [Supplementary Forms of Defense: Lessons from the Norwegian Resistance during World War II]." In *Komplementerende forsvarsformer.* Proceedings from a Seminar on Supplementary Forms of Defense. Oslo: Den norske atlanterhavskomite, 1989.

Hackman, Gene. "Lehren des norwegischen Widerstandes [Lessons of the Norwegian Resistance]." In *Civilian Defence: Gewaltloser Widerstand als form der*

Verteidigungspolitik [Civilian Defense: A Non-violent Form of Security Policy]. Proceedings from a Workshop organized by the Association of German Scientists. Bielefeld: Bertelsmann Universitatsverlag, 1967.

Nokkelby, Berit. *Holdningskamp* [Attitude Struggle]. Vol. 4 of the series *Norge i krig: Fremmedak og frihetskamp, 1940–1945 [Norway in War: Foreign Domination and Liberation Struggle, 1940–1945]*. Edited by Magne Skodvin. Oslo: Aschehough, 1986.

Sharp, Gene. *Tyranny Could Not Quell Them*. London: Peace News, 1958.

Skodvin, Magne. "Norwegian Non-violent Resistance during the German Occupation." In *The Strategy of Civilian Defence: Non-violent Resistance to Aggression,* edited by Adam Roberts. London: Faber and Faber, 1967.

See also DENMARK, EVACUATION OF DANISH JEWS, 1943; DENMARK, RESISTANCE TO NAZI OCCUPATION; JEWISH RESISTANCE TO THE HOLOCAUST; NAZISM, CIVILIAN RESISTANCE, 1939–1945

Nuclear Energy Opposition

Social movement that emerged in the 1970s in opposition to the construction, licensing, and operation of nuclear power plants used to generate electricity. It propagated and practiced nonviolent direct action explicitly and rigorously. But, instead of touching the deep structure of America's social fabric, this movement, born out of ennui rather than suffering, remained a phenomenon specific to its generation and time.

The antinuclear movement is a true child of the 1970s, when the energy crisis and the discovery of ecology put an end to the postwar liberal–conservative consensus that more and bigger is better. Risky and complex large-scale technologies such as nuclear energy came to be seen as evidence that modern capitalism and technological development were out of control. The 1970s were also what writer Tom Wolfe had labeled the "me-decade," in which young and affluent college students became preoccupied with questions of lifestyle and ecological correctness. The new awareness of ecological limits and lifestyle concerns fused into a politics that sought to protect the most immediate—the integrity of the local community—from the most distant—the threat-ening anonymity of market and state. Nuclear energy served as a projection of such time- and generation-specific fears and desires. Therefore, a closer look at the antinuclear movement also allows us to encapsulate an era.

In the political culture of America, which is deeply distrustful of state power and does not tolerate European-style *arcana imperii,* nuclear energy was bound to become a target of opposition, even without the counterculture. This is a technology whose risky and complex nature makes centralized control and a certain amount of secrecy imperative. Qualities so clearly uncongenial to American political norms were tolerated only so long as they were justifiable by "national security" concerns, such as the need to build a nuclear bomb to defeat Nazi Germany. Once it went civilian, and thus became devoid of its exceptionalism, nuclear power had to fall prey to the usually competitive and centrifugal bent of the American political process. The campaign against civilian nuclear energy that followed is somewhat ironic, because the Atoms for Peace program was designed by a guilt-plagued scientific and political elite as compensation for the horrible destruction that the atomic bomb had unleashed. Early opposition to nuclear energy was invited by the openness of the regulatory process itself, which was designed to allow the "full, free, and frank discussion" of all things nuclear. Out of this institutionally supported, legal opposition to the local "backyard" plant, a public interest movement of dissident scientists and concerned local citizens emerged in the late 1960s that proved extraordinarily effective in thwarting the initially expansive fantasies of the nuclear lobby.

One of the great ironies of the nuclear energy debate in the United States is that the spectacle of nonviolent direct action in the late 1970s appeared just when, in economic terms, nuclear power entered its slump, from which it has yet to recover. The counterculture that entered the nuclear controversy saw it differently: all legal avenues of stopping nuclear power had failed, so direct action was justified as the "last resort" of desperate citizens. This view obscures the dramatic event in West Germany that was responsible for radically transforming the meaning of the nuclear debate. In 1975, an unlikely coalition of peasants, vintners, and students in the southwestern German village of Wyhl had occupied the construction site of a nuclear power plant and wrung a set of unprecedented concessions from the state government.

Suddenly the nuclear debate, previously arcane, expert-driven, and legalistic, was a highly tangible struggle between the people and the state. The post-student movement New Left, which then was everywhere without a cause and a proletariat, found both in the popular opposition to nuclear energy. In response to the globally televised images of the rebellious peasants in distant Wyhl, direct action alliances sprang up around contested plants all across the United States, such as the Clamshell Alliance around the Seabrook nuclear plant then under construction in New Hampshire and the Abalone Alliance around the Diablo Canyon nuclear project in central California. But whereas the entry of the New Left into the nuclear controversy would lead to violent confrontations between the antinuclear movement and the state in Germany, France, and Japan, strict nonviolent discipline was maintained for the most part in the United States. Why?

First, American political culture is rich in consensus symbols that were eagerly embraced and exploited by the direct action movement. It is no accident that the so-called new social movements of the 1970s and 1980s turned violent in those societies that had succumbed to fascist or authoritarian regimes before or during World War II, such as Germany, Italy, Japan, or Vichy France. This experience destroyed the consensual bases of political culture in these societies, and the young protesters often saw themselves as delivering the belated acts of "antifascist" resistance that their parents' generation had failed to deliver. In the United States, which has been democratic from the start and has been spared such breaks in historical continuity, the consensual founding symbols provided a common platform for even the bitterest political opponents. In the nuclear controversy, Sam Lovejoy chose Washington's Birthday for his spectacular toppling of a 550-foot utility weather tower at a proposed nuclear plant site; the Clamshell's Declaration of Nuclear Resistance opened with the all-American "We the People"; and an Abalone activist admitted that the U.S. Constitution "looks like a pretty good piece of paper" if only its ideals were turned into reality. Compare this astonishing affirmation of basic American political principles with a German left-wing terrorist's characterization of her political opponents: "This is the generation of Auschwitz. You can't argue with them."

Second, the commitment to nonviolence was reinforced by learning processes within the movement. The Clamshell Alliance was actually destroyed over the initial question of whether nonviolence was a firm moral principle or merely a tactic. A radical minority in Clamshell became dissatisfied with what they characterized as the "complacency and passivity" demanded by nonviolence and decided to "shut down nuclear power" by means of physical obstruction. Other direct action alliances, such as California's Abalone, learned from this failed experiment, and committed themselves to a "philosophical" understanding of nonviolence. In addition, the violent dead end of the "Weatherman" Underground, into which the late student and antiwar movement had locked itself, was a widely shared negative reference point for left-wing activism in the late 1970s. Finally, the direct action movement could build on a strong activist subculture that had emerged with the civil rights struggles and that espoused nonviolent civil disobedience. By the same token, if the Martin Luther King legacy of civic inclusion, rather than the Malcolm X gospel of separatist black power, inspired the antinuclear movement, this revealed its innermost, while nervously denied, substance: white, middle class, and American to the bone.

Third, and perhaps most important, nonviolence resonated with the project of community building that remains the direct action movement's most enduring legacy. In contrast to the legal opposition to nuclear energy, the direct action movement was oriented much more to process than results, pursuing a politics of exemplary action and communal empowerment. More than stopping the neighborhood plant, or redirecting national energy policy, the movement sought to build a perfect community. The transparent and egalitarian "small is beautiful" society of the future was to be visible in the movement that propagated it. The antinuclear movement became a laboratory of participatory democracy and community building like no other social movement in recent American history. No decision, however trivial, was to be reached unless every movement member consented to it—an obviously unwieldy and time-consuming process that often prevented the antinuclear movement from responding effectively to the exigency of the moment. In addition to a commitment to decision making by consensus, the movement divided its membership into small "affinity groups" that were required to undergo rigorous nonviolence training and functioned as support groups during major protest actions. The American Friends

Service Committee, a long-established pacifist Quaker organization, was instrumental in building this communal infrastructure, and thus in committing the antinuclear movement to strict nonviolence.

Regarding the enduring community-building objectives, Mary Douglas and Aaron Wildavsky have argued that the direct action movement followed the logic of religious sects: an external threat is invoked and hypostatized in order to stabilize the small egalitarian group and demarcate it from the "polluted" outside world. Thus, the community of nuclear resisters could flourish only in the shadow of the nuclear threat—that is, in an environment where imminent disaster commanded the firm solidarity of the group. The movement literature is full with descriptions that celebrate the collective jail experience after aborted blockade attempts or protest marches. To be carried away by state troopers from nuclear construction sites, and to be collectively imprisoned, underlined the strict dichotomy between the group and the outside world, and sanctified and strengthened the bonds within the exemplary community of resisters.

Yet this culture of direct action possessed an elitism and closure that contradicted the broader egalitarian philosophy of the movement: "community building" necessarily was limited to small circles of committed activists. Contrary to its intention, the culture of direct action erected a sharp boundary between a dedicated elite of (white, middle class) activists and those who should have been its natural allies: minorities, low-income groups, and labor. Rather than wooing the latter to a generalized opposition against the "system" that nuclear power epitomized, the rituals of direct action further alienated the movement from other social groups.

An observer of an Abalone Alliance protest action lucidly described the self-referential closure of direct action: "It was painfully obvious that the blockade had attracted very few 'people of color' or working-class, suburban types. The projected style of the 'visible' antinuke movement tends to isolate it from millions of people who hold antinuclear views but just don't recognize themselves in the cultural norms of the movement. . . . One blockade custom that seemed a bit strange was the habit of hugging anyone who happened to come within a ten-yard radius. Some would argue that this 'builds community.' . . . I wound up feeling emotionally homogenized."

A habit of social movement researchers is to measure and evaluate the "impacts" of movements on their targets of mobilization. In the case of the antinuclear direct action movement, the question of success or failure is only vaguely related to the stopping of a nuclear power plant. Because the medium was the message, even an aborted plant blockade was successful if it helped to "build community." In characteristic fashion, an Abalone activist summed up the successes of direct action: "We achieved all our goals but one, and that was stopping Diablo. We definitely empowered people, we maintained a commitment to nonviolence, we built community groups. My closest friends are people I have met through the movement, and they are still my closest friends today."

In retrospect, the images of tie-dye shirted, long-haired antinuke activists marching hand-in-hand against the nuclear menace, armed only with guitar, Pete Seeger songbook, and sleeping bag, may extort at best a pitiful smile from the cynical contemporary of rap, crack, and urban violence. And one would probably find these once outraged flower children to be the mild-mannered social workers, college teachers, and marriage counselors of today. Even within the nuclear energy opposition movement, direct action was merely an episode that vanished as quickly as it had appeared after Wyhl. Ironically, the influx of a mass membership in the wake of the nuclear accident at Three Mile Island in 1979—with Jane Fonda, Jerry Brown, and the "No Nukes" concert in Madison Square Garden—helped destroy a movement that needed to be "small" to be alive and "beautiful."

In addition, the end of geopolitical détente in the early Reagan years channeled the antinuclear energies of most activists into the revitalized peace movement, which operated independently and at a deliberate distance from the nuclear energy opposition. In San Francisco, for example, the liberation and refugee movements of Central America became a new focus of attention, thus foreshadowing the ethnic "minority rights" movements of the 1990s. In the end, it was clear that America's decentralized, pluralistic polity offered manifold, and highly effective, points of entry, which often made "acts of resistance" unnecessary, even for many of those citizens mobilized by social concerns. Thus, in the 1990s it is state governors and attorneys general who support local citizens' groups and the proverbial "little old ladies in tennis shoes" in their opposition to an unwanted radioactive waste dump or an unsafe nuclear power plant.

Christian Joppke

References

Douglas, Mary, and Aaron Wildavsky. *Risk and Culture.* Berkeley: University of California Press, 1982.

Gyorgy, Anna. *No Nukes: Everyone's Guide to Nuclear Power.* Boston: South End, 1979.

Jasper, James. *Nuclear Politics: Energy and the State in the United States, Sweden and France.* Princeton: Princeton University Press, 1990.

Joppke, Christian. *Mobilizing against Nuclear Energy: A Comparison of Germany and the United States.* Berkeley: University of California Press, 1993.

See also CLAMSHELL ALLIANCE

Nuclear Weapons Opposition

Consistent protests against the nuclear arms race by small groups of activists around the world, using both conventional political means and nonviolent direct action, that have occasionally generated substantial public support and reached mainstream political institutions. The high points in the cycles of mass antinuclear protest have occurred when there is a broad public perception both that issues of nuclear weaponry are particularly significant and that there is the possibility that grassroots activism might actually affect the arms race. Periods of mass protest have occurred at roughly the same time in the United States and Western Europe at times of perceived crises in the arms race, although the claims and tactics of movements have varied in accord with national issues and opportunities.

At times of intense peace activism, a broad range of actors engage in unconventional action in pursuit of a wide range of goals, and at the same time, large numbers of institutionally oriented political figures engage in more conventional activity, generally in pursuit of arms control. The political context shapes the decisions of activists, both inside and outside government, about the urgency and opportunity of particular issues. External political circumstances also shape the decisions of elite actors about whether to sponsor, tolerate, or repress protest activity, and whether to pursue their own goals through institutional or extra-institutional activity.

Protest against nuclear weapons has been generally confined to states in which the issue seemed particularly urgent and opportunities for significant protest appeared available. In less industrialized nations more distant from the nuclear arms race, protest about foreign policy and national security concerns generally has focused on issues other than nuclear weapons. In the former Soviet Union and Eastern Europe, nascent movements against nuclear weapons were either repressed or coopted by state-sponsored "Peace Committees." Such groups criticized only Western capitalist nuclear weapons and became organs for state policy. Independent activists in the former Communist bloc thus addressed themselves more directly to human rights. Independent protest against nuclear weapons, then, has generally taken place within the United States and its advanced industrialized allies in Western Europe and the Pacific, including Japan, New Zealand, and Australia.

Protest movements employ diverse means, potentially including institutional political action, extra-institutional protest, political violence, public education efforts, and cultural activities. These take place in very visible venues, such as the floor of the United States House of Representatives or outside the Greenham Common missile base in Great Britain, and far less visible ones, including local governments and activist living rooms. Despite this, there is a broad consensus among both scholars and activists about the peaks and troughs of mobilization against nuclear weapons. Two broad-based international mass movements against the arms race developed, one running from 1955 to 1963, focusing primarily on nuclear testing, the next emerging in 1981 and declining in the middle 1980s. There were also two smaller challenges. One ran from 1945 to 1947, in response to the immediate shock of the Hiroshima bomb, the other from 1968 to 1972, during the debate on antiballistic missile deployment. These were confined largely to the United States and composed of elite-based campaigns with less extensive mass support and political visibility. Each campaign left behind organizations and political networks that would support its successors.

Nuclear weapons opponents march down 42nd Street in New York City, June 12, 1982. Photo © Ellen Shub 1995.

Scientists Campaign for International Control of Nuclear Arms

The introduction of nuclear weapons into the calculus of United States foreign and military policy and world politics mandated a radical departure from previous policies. Even before 1945, among those few people actually aware of work to develop the bomb, there was no consensus about either the use of atomic weapons or their eventual role in foreign policy. In 1944, Danish physicist Neils Bohr and a number of other scientists asked U.S. leaders to share information about the development of nuclear weapons with their allies in order to begin building an international atomic weapons control regime to commence after the war. American officials were suspicious and dismissed the ideas, placing Bohr under surveillance. Similarly, early in 1945 the Franck report, calling for a demonstration of the bomb rather than its use against Japan, was dismissed without much thought. The war's end, marked by the use of nuclear weapons at Hiroshima and Nagasaki, allowed debates that had been kept within a small circle of experts to reach the mass media and the general public.

Mass media attention to the devastating new weapon was understandably overwhelming. The horrific destruction at Hiroshima seemed to usher in an era of new possibility and urgency. Almost immediately after the news became public, newspapers, magazines, and movies grappled with the bomb. Norman Cousins's influential essay "Modern Man is Obsolete," published in the *Saturday Review* just a week after the Nagasaki bomb, was in many ways a characteristic response. The bomb raised existential questions. Cousins wrote, "Is war in the nature of man?" For Cousins, nuclear weapons represented a new problem for which there was only one solution: "In the absence of world control as part of world government, [the atomic bomb] will create universal fear and suspicion." Cousins, along with numerous other writers, called for moral consideration and unspecified political action.

Atomic weapons came to the head of the agenda in both academia and mass culture. Magazines and academic journals published special issues, academic and cultural organizations sponsored symposia, and politicians inside and outside of government called for mass education on nuclear weapons. There were two essential components to the American response to atomic weapons—fear, and what Boyer describes as an "unfocused conviction that an urgent and decisive response was essential," although there was no clarity on what this response might be. The most frequently articulated alternative policies were those Cousins proposed, namely international control of nuclear weapons and world government. Several local groups of scientists formed by the end of 1945, all concerned with public education on nuclear weapons, most notably through the new *Bulletin of the Atomic Scientists,* and supportive of international control. Nonscientists—including future president Ronald Reagan—joined the United World Federalists, also formed shortly after the war, pressing for international cooperation and political action. Importantly, none of these groups provided blueprints for government policy or citizen action.

Within government, the debate about policy was more focused and more heated. Secretary of State James A. Byrnes formed a high-profile commission under the direction of Dean Acheson and David Lilienthal to consider the new issues of the nuclear age. The Acheson–Lilienthal "Report on International Control of Atomic Energy" called for the United Nations to establish an international atomic control regime. The administration was divided on the issue, however, and President Harry Truman's appointment of Bernard Baruch as special ambassador on international atomic weapons control doomed the plan to failure. Negotiations with the Soviet Union in the UN stalled over Baruch's insistence on a system that would effectively nullify the Soviets' UN veto. By early 1948, the UN proposal was dead, and division within the administration prevented bilateral agreements with the Soviet Union.

The debate about new policies, however, never reached the general public. For most people, the war's end meant demilitarization and remobilization of the American economy. Domestic affairs dominated government and public attention in the United States, and nuclear weapons seemed horrifying yet distant to activists elsewhere. Activist leaders demanded public attention and action, but failed to provide attractive or even potentially efficacious strategies for action. The most visible proposal for responding to the new nuclear threat was an ill-defined plan for the international control of nuclear weapons, sometimes expressed as a demand for world government. The Truman administration, particularly Byrnes and Truman, was skeptical of these plans, but it ostensibly pursued them in the UN. Disarmament advocates were coopted or preempted by the "Baruch plan," and the general public was never engaged. The administration, and indeed most of the public and many peace activists, blamed the failure of international control on Soviet intransigence. Truman responded by developing a strong and permanent national security establishment, operating both abroad and in the United States, and securing a network of alliances to contain Soviet expansionism.

In response to developing Soviet policies—and the harsher and more critical domestic political environment—most activists perceived little alternative but to support U.S. policies. The road to disarmament and international cooperation led through the Soviet Union, a path foreclosed in foreign policy by Soviet action, and in the West by a new obsession with internal security. Internationalism gave way to unilateralism. Cord Meyer, Jr., first head of the World Federalists, joined the CIA to pursue a new internationalist vision. Many supporters of international control also supported the Korean War, imagining a new era of international cooperation springing from the multilateral military effort. Fear of nuclear weapons was outstripped by fear of the Soviet Union and ameliorated with optimism about the promise of atomic energy. Antinuclear activism disappeared from public debate as a new cold-war order emerged. Nonetheless, even as protest faded, activists left behind organizations, such as the Federation of Atomic Scientists, outlets such as its *Bulletin,* and networks that would prove critical to subsequent antinuclear activists.

The Test Ban

The test ban campaign was the result of a coincidence of a new provocation, demonstrable evidence of the dangers of atmospheric testing, and enhanced political opportunity. The end of the Korean War and the censure of Senator Joseph McCarthy opened space for political debate inside and outside government in the United States. Lessened fear of repression allowed dissidents to question government policy openly and to propose new alternatives. Stalin's death in 1953 seemed to promise a new openness in the Soviet Union as well, and thus broader possibilities. In March 1954, the BRAVO tests in the Bikini Islands catapulted nuclear weapons and the arms race to mass public attention. Radioactive fallout from one test covered *The Lucky Dragon,* a Japanese tuna trawler, contaminating its crew and catch, and drawing international attention to the hazards of atomic testing. Almost immediately, Pope Pius XII, Jawaharlal Nehru, the British Labour Party, and the Japanese Diet all appealed to the United States to stop testing and negotiate a test ban. Activists in Japan and Great Britain marched in opposition to nuclear testing specifically, and the arms race more generally. International efforts were echoed and amplified in the United States; hundreds of letters arrived daily at the White House supporting a test ban, and doctors and scientists debated the dangers of radioactive fallout in both specialized journals and mass market magazines.

The Eisenhower administration was divided on test ban proposals, and even on whether or not to release complete information on radioactive fallout from the recent tests. In February 1955, physicist Ralph Lapp published detailed information on the BRAVO fallout in the *Bulletin of the Atomic Scientists,* nearly a week before the Atomic Energy Commission released its own report, helping to undermine public confidence in the Eisenhower administration. Shortly afterward, a group of international scientists issued the "Einstein-Russell Manifesto," calling for an end to both testing and the arms race. Public debates among scientists and military experts raged about the necessity of continued testing, the dangers of fallout, and the reliability of nonintrusive means to detect testing.

More than in earlier years, these debates found a broad and interested audience. Public recognition of the dangers of nuclear fallout provided an opening for peace activists to lodge claims against the nuclear arms race and the United States' role in it. Fear of fallout, coupled with increased anxiety about U.S. preparations for war with the Soviet Union, especially a large domestic civil defense campaign, provided a fertile base of support upon which activists could draw. The federal government's neglect of growing public concern opened political space for dissent, space first claimed by pacifist activists. On June 15, 1955, when New York City conducted its first annual air raid drill, several members of the Catholic Worker, led by Dorothy Day, refused to take cover in a shelter. Instead they sat on park benches and waved placards emphasizing the futility of fallout shelters and the dangers of nuclear war. Twenty-nine protesters were arrested and the trial judge set bail at $1,500, denouncing them as "murderers."

Responding to public pressure for a test ban, Eisenhower appointed Harold Stassen as a special adviser on disarmament. In 1956, as the Senate held hearings on testing, activists pressed Democratic presidential candidate Adlai Stevenson to support a test ban. Against the advice of his campaign staff, Stevenson made the issue a central point in his campaign. Eisenhower, personally ambivalent about a test ban, refused to discuss it, arguing against politicizing matters of national security. Shortly after winning reelection, however, he instructed his staff to explore more vigorously the possibilities for negotiated limits on testing.

Stevenson's defeat spurred further anti-testing activism, as it dashed hopes that meaningful reform could be achieved through the electoral process. Test ban advocates sought other routes for influence, as two broad wings of a movement emerged. One called for international agreements coupled with unilateral restraint, and pressed its claims through public education efforts. Its adherents issued appeals, staged international conferences, including the first Pugwash meeting, organized rallies, and ran newspaper and television advertisements. SANE, the National Committee for a Sane Nuclear Policy, founded in 1957, typified this liberal internationalist approach. Concurrently, several groups drawing from smaller left-wing and pacifist bases of support, including religiously motivated pacifist groups like the American Friends Services Committee, the Fellowship of Reconciliation, and the secular Women's International League for Peace and Freedom, launched a campaign of civil disobedience and direct action aimed at raising the political costs of continued testing. Activists again disrupted civil defense exercises in New York City by sitting on benches outside City Hall with signs such as "End War—the only defense against Atomic Weapons." Similar protests against civil defense spread to other cities over the next five years. Pacifist leader A.J. Muste organized a series of trespass campaigns at the Nevada test site.

Muste also helped raise money for a more dramatic trespass effort, pacifist Albert Bigelow's attempt to sail the *Golden Rule* into the Pacific atomic test site in 1958. Repeatedly arrested during his voyage, Bigelow and his crew did not get close to the test site. But his example inspired anthropologist Earle Reynolds to try a similar effort with his boat, the *Phoenix.* Dramatically trying to demonstrate the jeopardy they saw facing the world, these efforts won extensive coverage in the U.S. press. The effect, however, was to encourage a more politically moderate public education campaign, not further protest. SANE, for example, conducted educational exhibits about nuclear weapons in New York, and held large mass meetings. Dramatic nonviolent direct action efforts expanded the boundaries of legitimate public discourse. Subsequently, pacifist activists organized peace walks, sit-in demonstrations, and other acts of civil disobedience. Activists believed that two wings of the movement working in concert would heighten the visibility and effectiveness of both. Thus, for example, some of SANE's founders also simultaneously organized the Committee for Nonviolent Action to coordinate more radical pacifist efforts.

By the middle of 1957, officials in the United States and Great Britain were open to negotiating a test ban, largely because of domestic political fallout in the West, and what Secretary of State John Foster Dulles described as the "propaganda drubbings" the United States was taking on the issue. Eisenhower and Khrushchev presided over a testing moratorium from 1958 to 1960. In the 1960 presidential campaign both candidates promised to secure an arms control agreement on testing. Formal negotiations stalled, however, and Eisenhower emphatically advised incoming President Kennedy to resume testing. At roughly the same time, British activists formed the Campaign for Nuclear Disarmament (CND) to coordinate their efforts for nuclear disarmament.

A period of increased testing on both sides early in Kennedy's term spurred protest and activism, including trespass at military sites and more conventional political activity such as rallies and demonstrations. Nobel prize–winning scientist Linus Pauling was a visible antinuclear activist, pressing his claims both at a White House dinner in 1962 and outside the White House in protest the following evening. Inspired by *Lysistrata,* women in New York organized the Women's Strike for Peace, which led protests and sent delegations abroad to press for disarmament.

The Cuban missile crisis underscored the urgency of managing the nuclear rivalry with the Soviet Union and accentuated the administration's drive to establish an arms control regime. Kennedy used antinuclear activist Norman Cousins to open a back channel for negotiations with Khrushchev, securing an agreement to ban atmospheric testing. The agreement stopped the immediate dangers of atmospheric testing, but it also effectively ended the antinuclear movement.

The limited test ban addressed the symptoms of the arms race, but not its essential conduct. By moving nuclear tests underground, it allowed all of the parties actually to increase the number of tests they conducted absent nuclear fallout—and public scrutiny. Nonetheless, the institutional wing of the peace movement, led by SANE, actively lobbied the Senate to secure ratification, a ratification President Kennedy bought with a commitment to an accelerated underground testing program. The end of superpower atmospheric testing and the establishment of an ongoing arms control process also restored a new elite consensus, institutionalizing both arms control and an arms race. It effectively protected the arms race from strong criticism both within and outside the nuclear powers.

The Antiballistic Missile Debate

Soviet deployment of a primitive antiballistic missile (ABM) system outside Moscow in 1966 provoked a policy debate within the Johnson administration about deploying an American system. Secretary of Defense Robert McNamara proposed a "light" system, ostensibly to guard against China and other small nuclear forces. McNamara's decision, clearly devised more as a political than a strategic move, made powerful political capital for ABM supporters, who charged the Johnson administration with leaving America undefended. At the same time scientific opponents of the ABM actively publicized their differences with the administration through articles in scientific journals and testimony before Congress. They also pressed peace activists to address the issue. Early in 1968, David Inglis, then senior physicist at Argonne National Laboratories, urged SANE to oppose the ABM. Unable to achieve their goals through conventional politics, institutionally oriented scientists turned, often reluctantly, to mass politics.

Upon his election, President Nixon proposed accelerated ABM development to defend both U.S. weapons and major metropolitan areas. This engendered a wave of activism among both atomic scientists, who doubted the wisdom and feasibility of such systems, and local residents who opposed deployment of nuclear weapons near their homes. Activists sponsored teach-ins and rallies in cities where ABMs were to be deployed, including Chicago, Seattle, and Boston. Coordinated by groups like the new Union of Concern Scientists, formed to organize scientific opposition to the war in Vietnam, ABM opponents testified before Congress, giving cover to Congressional opponents, and conducted public education campaigns to buttress opposition at the grass roots.

Nixon's staff was surprised that the strongest opposition came from cities due to be "protected" by ABMs—they had expected protests from the cities left "undefended." In response, Nixon redefined the ABM's mission to defend weapons rather than cities, relocating potential sites from metropolitan areas to remote missile fields in less politically risky locales like Grand Forks, North Dakota. He also began negotiations to limit ABM systems as a precursor to the 1972 SALT Treaty. Nuclear weapons issues moved to the back burner of most activist agendas around the world.

Disarmament Campaigns of the 1980s

The arms race continued unabated throughout the 1970s, even as the United States and the Soviet Union negotiated a series of arms control agreements. Western leaders could claim they were doing everything possible to limit nuclear armaments and the possibility of nuclear war, as both superpower tension and military spending declined from the Vietnam-era peak of 1968. In the United States, activists were able to mount several campaigns against particular weapons, most notably the B-1 bomber and the MX missile. The AFSC and FOR, both key groups in the test ban campaign, successfully linked nuclear weapons to nuclear power in their civil disobedience campaign to shut down the Rocky Flats nuclear power plant. Under the slogan, "Rocky Flats: Local Hazard, Global Menace," demonstrators attempted to emphasize the connections between environmental problems nearby and the dangers of nuclear war. They staged repeated attempts to occupy the site.

In the South Pacific, peace activists worked to disengage New Zealand and Australia from the nuclear elements of the Western alliance. In Western Europe, activists often turned to environmental issues, organizing visible and effective campaigns against nuclear power. In Eastern Europe, activists used detente to lodge claims about human rights, often in the context of the Helsinki Accords of 1976.

By the end of his term, Carter visibly retreated from his announced inaugural goal of eliminating nuclear weapons altogether and initiated a military buildup. He endorsed several controversial nuclear weapons systems and announced NATO's "dual track" decision to deploy intermediate range nuclear missiles in Europe. Carter was responding, in part, to increased domestic political pressure, particularly the successfully organized campaigns of opponents to detente and SALT. Activists who brought a "nuclear freeze" proposal to the Democratic national convention in New York City were rebuffed by both candidates.

The new Reagan administration repeatedly and forcefully demonstrated its commitment to policies peace activists saw as bellicose. Administration officials were also candid in their assessments of the prospects of limited nuclear wars, the necessity of strategic superiority, and the futility of arms control; their rhetoric was untempered by qualifiers or guarded language about "options." Reagan appointees spoke cavalierly about fighting and winning nuclear wars, and worked to provide the weapons to do so.

At the same time, the administration purged from the State and Defense departments moderate scientists and strategists unconvinced of the possibility or desirability of a war-winning strategic posture or interested in arms control at all. Many experts, who lost access to the administration, sought a broader public audience. Mass media followed this elite criticism of the Reagan program, subjecting the president's policies and advisers to an unusual degree of scrutiny.

Activists in the United States and Western Europe also challenged the Reagan program. Antinuclear movements in Western Europe emerged strongly in 1981, focusing specifically on stopping the NATO plan to deploy intermediate-range nuclear missiles in five European countries. Demonstrations in Amsterdam, Brussels, Paris, London, Rome, and Bonn each attracted hundreds of thousands of activists. European activists, most notably historian E.P. Thompson, appealed explicitly to their counterparts in the United States for help. Pacifists began direct action campaigns at military contractors, submarine bases, missile sites, and even the Pentagon.

Among the more dramatic efforts: Daniel and Philip Berrigan, in conjunction with a group of Catholic activists, broke into a General Electric plant in Pennsylvania, smashed computer keyboards and missile nosecones with hammers, then waited for arrest. This was the first of more than two dozen similar "Plowshares" actions, directed at bearing witness against the arms race. The Women's Pentagon Action, consciously modeled after Women's Strike for Peace, but informed with a more explicitly feminist sensibility, staged annual attempts to shut down the Pentagon. Hundreds of women demonstrated outside the building, chanting, screaming, weeping, and culminating their efforts by trying to "weave a web of life" around the building, blocking the entrances until removed by arrest. At weapons laboratories in Berkeley and Cambridge, activists staged both regular vigils and site invasions, sometimes garnering mass arrests and successfully employing "competing harms" defenses, which weighed the dangers of nuclear war against the dangers of trespass, in their trials. Outside Seattle, nonviolent activists attempted to block the delivery of nuclear warheads to Trident missile submarines by sitting on railroad tracks when a specially marked "White Train" was scheduled to pass. Successful in garnering attention, and sometimes delaying the train, the effort spurred similar ones all along the route of the White Train from Amarillo, Texas, across the United States.

The weapons themselves served as targets for antinuclear protest all around the world. In Great Britain, women formed a "peace camp" at Greenham Common, where NATO cruise missiles were scheduled to be based. Other peace camps sprang up at missile bases throughout the United Kingdom, some women-only, others devoted to families, and others mixed. This strategy spread across the continent. In New Zealand, activists sought to declare their home a nuclear free zone, and for years met every U.S. naval ship visit with a "peace squadron," composed of yachts, small boats, kayaks, and surfboards—all directed at blocking entry to New Zealand ports. The movement succeeded in winning the endorsement of three of four major parties in the 1984 election, and the victorious Labour Party actually followed through on its campaign commitment to ban ships that might carry nuclear weapons from New Zealand's shores.

At the same time arms control advocates held educational events, sponsored symposia and teach-ins, pressed local governments to adopt resolutions opposing the Reagan program, and organized referenda campaigns. Although activists espoused a broad variety of ultimate goals and means, mass media grouped virtually all opponents of the Reagan administration's security policies under the banner of the "nuclear freeze." As articulated by Randall Forsberg, a freeze proposal was the first step in a complicated and comprehensive program to remake world politics. The broad movement coalition made this struggle particularly important, and activist efforts to control it especially difficult. As the movement grew, staging a June 1982 rally in New York City attended by some one million people, activists were increasingly divided on the meaning of the proposal so many had supported.

As the movement made inroads in institutional politics, the freeze coalition began to fray. Institutionally oriented arms control groups

cultivated their Washington connections and tried to influence Congress on a variety of budget issues, urging Congress to push the President on arms control. This approach seemed a more direct route to political influence than public education or mass demonstrations. At the same time, many pacifist and left-liberal groups continued their activities, but shifted to more salient issues, such as supporting economic sanctions against South Africa or preventing U.S. military intervention in Nicaragua. When NATO began to deploy intermediate-range missiles in the fall of 1983, many peace groups were dealt a devastating blow. Nonetheless, campaigns continued, including "peace camps" in the United States and Western Europe, that coordinated ongoing opposition to the nuclear arms race. Finally, a number of peace groups were fully engaged in electoral efforts, albeit without much visible success, as conservative governments won elections almost everywhere in Western Europe. These governments, however, expressed considerably more moderate profiles in response to their political challenges.

In the United States, for example, the Reagan administration worked to ensure the election was not a referendum on either the freeze or its own national security policies. In January of 1984, Reagan announced his new commitment to arms control negotiations, and to restoring summit meetings with the Soviet Union, offering conciliatory rhetoric to both freeze supporters and the Soviets. At the same time, a somewhat strengthened congressional opposition prevented the most aggressive aspects of the Reagan buildup, limiting growth of the budget, and effectively mandating arms control. European allies, while endorsing the deployment of the intermediate range missiles, made it clear that they would not tolerate a subsequent round of nuclear modernization.

This most recent wave of antinuclear activism did not end the arms race, as activists intended. Nonetheless, it effectively rescued the previous bipartisan policy consensus, restricting the Reagan administration's initiatives. It returned legitimacy and institutional access to advocates of arms control and nuclear restraint. On one level, a return to an arms control regime and a technological arms race seems a meager achievement. Reagan's arms control proposals, however, offered more for domestic political reasons than for an international response, had extensive unexpected effects. The new posture offered incoming Soviet General Secretary

Gorbachev a lever with which to reopen detente. When Gorbachev accepted the disproportionate cuts in nuclear forces Reagan had proposed, the administration was cornered. It couldn't reject its own proposals. This forced flexibility on arms control proved to be critical in ending the cold war. The movements won far less than they hoped, yet turned out to be far more significant than anyone involved would have guessed, playing a critical role in precipitating and shaping the events that marked the end of the cold war.

Protest cycles are related to the broader political context and the policy-making process. The cases suggest that policy shifts can provide political space for protest movements, and that governments may alter their policies in order to reclaim that political space. Elite actors, particularly scientists and strategic experts, mediate between the state and protest movements, identifying which aspects of policy are most vulnerable to assault, legitimating and sometimes aiding insurgent movements, and framing solutions to the political problems movements cause. Peace movements emerge when institutionally oriented actors lose faith in the efficacy of institutional politics. At such times, they may forge alliances with activists making broader claims and engaging in extra-institutional action. The resultant movements lodge broad claims against the state, but generally disperse after an administration re-integrates dissident elite into institutional politics, often by restoring previous policies. The cyclic nature of movement challenges reflects the shifting attention of elite actors from institutional venues to extra-institutional ones. Movements may then have the odd effect of preserving policies they find abhorrent. Whether peace activists can mobilize challenges after the cold war, during a period of military demobilization when all policy positions are subject to debate and intense scrutiny, is a critically important, and open, question.

David S. Meyer

References

Boyer, Paul. *By the Bomb's Early Light: American Thought and Culture at the Dawn of the Nuclear Age.* New York: Pantheon, 1986.

Clements, Kevin P. *Back from the Brink: The Creation of a Nuclear-Free New Zealand.* Winchester, Mass.: Allen and Unwin, 1988.

Divine, Robert A. *Blowing on the Wind: The Nuclear Test Ban Debate, 1954–1960.* New York: Oxford University Press, 1978.

Forsberg, Randall. "The Freeze and Beyond: Confining the Military to Defense As a Route to Disarmament." *World Policy Journal* 1 (1984): 287–318.

Meyer, David S., *A Winter of Discontent: The Nuclear Freeze and American Politics.* New York: Praeger, 1990.

———. "Peace Protest and Policy: Explaining the Rise and Decline of Antinuclear Movements in Postwar America." *Policy Studies Journal* 21 (1993): 1–21.

Meyer, David S., and Sam Marullo. "Grassroots Mobilization and International Politics: Peace Protest and the End of the Cold War." *Research in Social Movements, Conflicts, and Change* 14 (1992): 99–140.

Rochon, Thomas R. *Mobilizing for Peace: The Antinuclear Movements in Western Europe.* Princeton: Princeton University Press, 1988.

Smith, Alice Kimball. *A Peril and a Hope: The Scientists' Movement in America, 1945–1947.* Chicago: University of Chicago Press, 1965.

Swerdlow, Amy. *Women Strike for Peace: Traditional Motherhood and the Radical Politics of the 1960s.* Chicago: University of Chicago Press, 1993.

Thompson, E.P., and Dan Smith, eds. *Protest and Survive.* New York and London: Monthly Review, 1981.

Wittner, Lawrence. *Rebels against War: The American Peace Movement, 1933–1983.* Philadelphia: Temple University Press, 1984.

———. *The Struggle against the Bomb.* Vol. 1. *One World or None.* Stanford, Calif.: Stanford University Press, 1993.

See also CAMPAIGN FOR NUCLEAR DISARMAMENT; CATHOLIC WORKER MOVEMENT; CIVIL DISOBEDIENCE; FELLOWSHIP OF RECONCILIATION, INTERNATIONAL; PLOWSHARES MOVEMENT; VOYAGES, PROTEST; WOMEN STRIKE FOR PEACE

Nullification and Interposition

Acts of noncompliance by subnational governments against acts, policies, or court decisions by agents of the federal government. Nullification is the declaration by a state or local government that a federal act is unconstitutional and invalid, and, hence, nullified. This action is primarily an expression of protest and noncooperation. Interposition is the operationalization of nullification, in which the subnational actor asserts its authority and articulates how it will withhold cooperation with federal authorities. There are two types of interposition: the noncompliance of subnational officials by refusing to enforce a federal act or court decision, and the intervention of state or local officials to prevent federal agents from enforcing an act or court decision. The ultimate extension of interposition is secession from the larger union or federation.

Primarily an American phenomenon, these nonviolent methods were used by Southern states in the Union vs. Confederacy struggles in the early 1800s and again by those same states to oppose racial integration beginning in the 1950s. Politician John C. Calhoun of South Carolina was the chief exponent of nullification and interposition in support of free trade in the first half of the nineteenth century. In opposition to the Tariff Acts of 1828 and 1832, Calhoun authored the South Carolina Exposition and Protest of 1828 and the South Carolina Ordinance of Nullification of 1832. The first resolution articulated nullification and the second called for interposi-

tion, which lasted four months until a compromise was attained. South Carolina even threatened secession at that time.

The methods were revived by southern states in the 1950s in response to the 1954 Supreme Court decision *Brown* v. *Topeka Board of Education*. States opposed federally sanctioned and enforced integration by resorting to nullification and interposition. Perhaps the most famous incidents include the interposition by Governor Ross Barnett to deny African American James Meredith admission to the University of Mississippi and the physical blockade of the entrance to the University of Alabama by Governor George Wallace.

Brad Bennett

References

Peterson, Merrill D. *Olive Branch and Sword—The Compromise of 1833*. Baton Rouge: Louisiana State University Press, 1982.

Tipton, Diane. *Nullification and Interposition in American Thought*. Albuquerque: University of New Mexico, Division of Government Research, Institute for Social Research and Development, 1969.

See also CIVIL RIGHTS MOVEMENT

Organization in Social Movements

The more or less formally structured collectivities of people who seek change of the social order. Social movement organizations vary in terms of their form (firms, bureaus, or associations), their organizational features (centralization, hierarchy, formalization of rules and procedures), the strategies and tactics they employ to pursue change, their beliefs and frames of reference regarding the alternative social order they seek, and their life cycle (growth, development, and decline). Countermovements also develop organizations to resist social change and maintain the status quo. Examples of social movement organizations seeking peace or justice include the United Farm Workers Union, the National Organization for Women, Peace Action (formerly SANE/Freeze), the Women's International League for Peace and Freedom, the African National Congress, Solidarity, the Palestine Liberation Organization, and Servicio Paz y Justicia en America Latina. Countermovement organizations seeking to retain the status quo or restore the old social order include the Moral Majority, the Ku Klux Klan, Accuracy in Academia, English Only, and the Eagle Forum.

Movement organizations are often described as the carriers of social movements because they provide the infrastructure for a movement to undertake its activities in the pursuit of change more effectively, whether it be lobbying, demonstrating, organizing a boycott, educating the public, or any other action. However, social movement organizations are distinct from social movements. The organizations constitute a part of a movement, but they are not identical; all individuals who are part of a movement do not belong to movement organizations. Conversely, movement organizations may continue to exist long after the movement's pressures for change have subsided. For example, many socialist and Communist labor party organizations continue to exist in the United States today, even though the socialist movement peaked in the 1930s. Movement organizations are often criticized as having a stultifying effect on a social movement's energies or as a diversion of resources toward internal organizing concerns and away from challenging the system. However, Gamson's study of social protest movements shows that those organizations that stayed in the battle for the long haul were more likely to attain some of their goals.

The forms that social movement organizations may take vary widely, depending on factors such as movement goals and strategies, the political and cultural context, and the already existing organizational environment. Analysts of movement organizations generally use three broad classifications to capture some of their key differences: firms, bureaus, and associations. Firms operate to generate revenues (either as profits or as nonprofit-making institutions) through the sale of products or services in order to support the movement members who lead them. Publishers such as South End Press and merchandisers such as Donnelly/Colt (a major producer of many movements' bumper stickers and buttons) and COOP America (direct mail seller of products and services produced by organizations that meet social responsibility criteria) are examples of social movement firms.

Bureaus are formally organized components of larger institutions that have full-time paid staff members who undertake movement activities as part or all of their job responsibilities. One type of movement success leads to the establishment of government-supported bureaus to carry on the mission of the movement with the expenses being paid by taxpayers. The Environmental Protection Agency and the U.S. Institute of Peace are examples of the environmental and peace movements' longstanding efforts, respectively, to force the U.S. government to implement their objectives of preventing further environmental degradation and developing methods for nonviolent conflict resolution. Religious and educational institutions may also devote portions of their resources to pursuing social movement goals. For example, the Roman Catholic Church's Campaign for Human Development has been a major supporter of poor peoples' community organizations, and the Religious Society of Friends has supported civil rights, peace, and women's groups through its affiliated American Friends Service Committee offices. Educational institutions provide support for faculty who teach courses that promote movement goals (such as peace studies or women's studies courses) and direct some students' resources toward movement objectives through educational programs such as community service activities and law schools' legal clinics. Another type of bureau has been labeled a "halfway house" or "movement mentoring organization." These include organizations such as the Highlander Folk School, the labor colleges, and the Midwest Academy, which train activists on effective organizing techniques and promote connections among social justice causes.

Most movement organizations, however, take on the form of voluntary associations in which most or all of the participants engage in movement activities as volunteers. These associations may have varying degrees of paid, professional staff member involvement who assume some responsibilities for undertaking the work of the organization. At one extreme, the organization might be made up only of volunteers; this has been the case for the large majority of grassroots civil rights, students', women's, peace, and environmental groups. At the other extreme, the work of the organization may be almost entirely carried out by a professional staff whose salaries are paid by members' voluntary contributions. Many of the Washington, D.C., lobbying offices of the grassroots groups named above are staffed by full-time professionals and rely relatively little on the efforts of volunteers. Over time, there has been an increasing trend toward professionalization of social movement organizations, but this varies greatly depending on the

movement's goals and resources and the affluence of the society in general.

Social movement organizations vary in terms of their features. Some organizations rely very heavily on a small core of leaders or a single leader to make decisions and undertake activities, whereas others are more decentralized and rely more on members' involvement. During the height of the U.S. civil rights movement in the 1960s, the Southern Christian Leadership Conference, headed by Martin Luther King, Jr., was highly centralized, whereas the Student Nonviolent Coordinating Committee was much more decentralized, enabling more student input in decision making. The second characteristic is the degree of hierarchy; some organizations have many layers of personnel who possess different amounts of responsibility and authority within the organizations, whereas others have only one or two levels. In general, social movement organizations tend to have relatively few layers of hierarchy, in part because of members' beliefs in participatory decision making and in part because of their more general distrust of authority. The third characteristic, formalization, refers to the degree to which written rules and procedures are adopted and implemented. Highly formal organizations are incorporated, have written by-laws and job descriptions, and rely on formal decision-making procedures (whether it be majority voting or consensus rules). Professionalized, large, national scope social movement organizations tend to be more formal, whereas small, grassroots groups may be less formal. However, as social movement organization analysts have found, the mere fact of incorporating for tax status purposes and applying for nonprofit bulk mail privileges in itself has the effect of defusing dissent. As groups apply for and receive such official recognition by the state, they become more cautious in terms of the types of activities they undertake for fear of losing these benefits.

In their pursuit of social change, movements pursue a wide range of strategies and tactics. Strategies vary at the nonviolent level from education to persuasion to coercion, and at the violent level from coercive threats to outright use of force. Gene Sharp documented 198 nonviolent methods of social change, ranging from making formal statements to direct intervention in the economic, social, and political system. Various organizations within a movement tend to espouse or specialize in a particular strategy. This specialization helps explain why there are often so many organizations within a movement—movement members possess different beliefs as to how to make change occur and subsequently join or create organizations that operate in accord with those beliefs. The flourishing of organizations within a movement, ostensibly pursuing the same goal, leads to competition for resources among the groups as they each try to recruit members, raise funds, and gain recognition. The activities the organizations undertake can be directed toward the authorities, at bystander publics, potential funders, other movement organizations, countermovements, or the news media. Within their strategic frameworks, organizations generally try to achieve multiple objectives with their actions and appeal to several audiences at once.

Although there has been much speculation regarding the relationship between movement organizational forms and the actions they undertake, research on the U.S. peace movement shows only modest correlations between structure and action. Thus, while it is true that direct actions such as civil disobedience are often taken by small affinity groups, which tend to be more egalitarian, loosely structured, and to operate under informal consensual norms, it is also the case that large, centralized, professional, and bureaucratic organizations engage in civil disobedience. And while it is true that some types of actions may require more resources than others in order to be effective—for example, a boycott is more likely to succeed when it is organized by a larger group—it is nevertheless true that even small groups engage in boycotts. The organizational characteristic most likely to distinguish between groups that engage in nonviolent direct action and those that do not is whether they articulate a social change model that is grassroots-based rather than one based on pluralist or elitist perspectives.

Social movements embrace a vision of an alternative society that they believe is better than the one that now exists. This of course varies across movements, but generally movements are guided by social justice values; concern for democracy, freedom, and human rights; and egalitarian principles. Movement organizations often try to embody these values within the organizational structure and operations, as well as appeal to them in the recruitment process. This leads to the development of some prefigurative organizations that attempt to live by the values they espouse, resulting in communal arrangements, affinity groups, or base communities. These are often characterized by consensus decision making, egalitarian gender roles, and little specialized division of labor. They represent a counterculture to the mainstream society, enabling members to "live in truth," in Václav Havel's phrase, as if state oppression did not exist.

It is useful to think of social movement organizations as having life histories as long as the analogy is not pushed too far. Organizations are born as a result of the conjoining of a collective grievance and the mobilization of resources (people, time, money, interests), they grow as further resources are brought in to nourish them, and they decline or die as interest fades—which could be the result of winning the movement's objective, being crushed, or growing lack of interest. However, we must be careful to recognize that not all groups proceed through all of the stages, and that there is not necessarily a linear or cyclical progression through them. The emergence of a social movement requires not only a grievance—for these are always and everywhere present—but also a catalyzing idea or agent that organizes people and resources around the belief that the situation can be made better.

The forms organizations can take depend in part on the political opportunity structure and the already existing organizational sector. Organizations with the right ideas, abilities to mobilize resources, and strategies for change might grow and compete with other such organizations. They are also likely to muster opposition on the part of the authorities or countermovements by those who fear they have something to lose if the proposed change is implemented. The organization must mobilize resources that can be used to effect change in the larger system as well as recruit and retain resources to sustain itself.

Research on the U.S. peace movement shows that larger, more formalized groups with professional staff are better able to survive the decline of the movement than are small, informal, and fully volunteer organizations. If an organization is unable to successfully meet the dual challenges of mobilizing resources for its own maintenance as well as the pursuit of its goals, it will fade and disappear.

Ironically, even if the movement has some success, many organizations disappear because members no longer feel the need to stay involved. The submergence of the U.S. anti–nuclear weapons movement in the mid-1960s occurred as a result of the partial success of the ban-the-bomb movement—once atmospheric nuclear testing was halted through the partial test ban treaty, many movement organizations ceased operations. Contrary to the movement's larger aims, however, the nuclear arms race escalated in the late 1960s as nuclear weapons development continued through underground testing. Later, the movement reemerged in the 1980s as the nuclear freeze campaign. However, since the political opportunity structure was different, and because there was an already well-established peace and arms control movement, the issue was framed differently, yielding newly created organizations that operated differently and that took on different forms. This also had the effect of altering the peace movement as a whole, as numerous longstanding organizations altered their goals, strategies, and activities as well.

Sam Marullo

References

Edwards, Bob, and Sam Marullo. "Organizational Mortality in a Declining Movement: The Demise of Peace Movement Organizations in the End of the Cold War Era." *American Sociological Review* 60 (December 1995): 908–927.

Gamson, William. *The Strategy of Social Protest.* Homewood, Ill.: Dorsey, 1975; 2nd ed. Belmont, Calif.: Wadsworth, 1990.

Havel, Václav. "The Power of the Powerless." In *The Power of the Powerless,* edited by Václav Havel. Armonk, N.Y.: M.E. Sharpe, 1985.

Lofland, John. *Protest: Studies of Collective Behavior and Social Movements.* New Brunswick, N.J.: Transaction, 1985.

McAdam, Doug, John D. McCarthy, and Mayer N. Zald. "Social Movements." In *Handbook of Sociology,* edited by Neil Smelser. Newbury Park, Calif.: Sage, 1988.

Sharp, Gene. *The Politics of Nonviolent Action.* Part Two: *The Methods of Nonviolent Action.* Boston: Porter Sargent, 1973.

Tilly, Charles. *From Mobilization to Revolution.* Reading, Mass.: Addison-Wesley, 1978.

See also LEADERSHIP; SOLIDARITY

Outing

Politically motivated disclosure of a person's homosexual orientation against his or her will. Outing is usually done to public figures like celebrities or politicians. Some "outers" are antigay and intend to damage the career of the "outee." Others are journalists from the mainstream press who claim to be reporting news they have uncovered. The outer can also be a gay and lesbian rights activist or journalist. In this context, the outee is believed to be gay and homophobic. By outing this public figure, the activist hopes to expose hypocrisy and stop homophobic behavior. The outer also intends to show to both the gay and lesbian community and the larger straight population that many highly respected, powerful people are gay and lesbian. Sometimes the activist tries to coerce the outee into coming out by threatening to out him or her publicly.

There have been isolated historical incidents of outing, but the tactic gained major prominence within the gay and lesbian rights movement since 1989. Members of two gay rights organizations, ACT-UP (AIDS Coalition to Unleash Power) and Queer Nation, have used this tactic to publicize the issues of homophobia and lack of official response to the AIDS epidemic. Sometimes, outing occurs after someone's death, as in the outing of New York journalist and multimillionaire Malcolm Forbes in 1990. The tactic of outing is controversial in both the general public and the gay and lesbian community, as it touches issues of privacy, coercion, slander, and libel.

Brad Bennett

References

Gross, Larry. *Contested Closets: The Politics and Ethics of Outing.* Minneapolis: University of Minnesota Press, 1993.

Johansson, Warren, and William A. Percy. *Outing: Shattering the Conspiracy of Silence.* New York: Haworth, 1994.

See also ACT-UP; GAY RIGHTS MOVEMENT; QUEER NATION

P

Pacifism

A personal and social philosophy that seeks to replace diverse forms of violence, especially war, with a state of social justice and reconciliation. Pacifism utilizes persuasive and coercive nonviolent methods of conflict management and conflict resolution. Pacifism is neither a state of passivity (as in nonaction or "passivism"), nor a state of militarism (as in the threatened or actual shedding of blood).

Historical Context

Although the concept of pacifism is ancient, the word "pacifism" is of twentieth-century origin (F. *pacifisme*). Hence, especially since World War I, pacifism has been popularly interpreted to connote individual resistance to war through conscientious objection to military service. In fact, however, pacifism enjoys a much older history and includes several varieties that address a wide spectrum of personal and social issues.

The Latin root of pacifism is *pacificio (pax and facio),* which means "to make peace." Pacifism has existed, in various forms, in many ancient cultures and civilizations and is found in aboriginal and preliterate societies. Forms of pacifism exist even in some societies that are warlike in nature. As in contemporary nation-states, some preliterate societies require pacific practices in internal matters, while glorifying militaristic practices in external relations.

Pacifism as "peacemaking" has roots in ancient Hinduism, which—despite its acceptance of violence—required a vow of ahimsa (noninjury) of those who would undertake yogic practices. Buddhism and Jainism (sixth century B.C.E.) more explicitly rejected killing in their requirement that ahimsa be rooted in monastic and daily life and in their teaching of compassion for all living things. The Chinese were receptive to Buddhism in part because the Taoist concept of *wu-wei* connotes the absence of aggression and the ideal of peaceful living.

In the West, pacifism has foundations in the universalist thought of the Stoics and the mystery cults of Hellenistic and Roman times, which looked to a "Golden Age" of ubiquitous peace. The Greek concept of *eirene* connoted a sense of harmony or order in society. The Romans sought through the *Pax Romana* to establish peace through war and conquest. This led to the narrow concept that peace was a "pact" or agreement not to fight or to wage war, or that peace was the result primarily of military conquest.

The Hebrew concept of *shalom* referred to a state of physical and spiritual wholeness. Central to the achievement of peace in Hebrew thought was the presence of justice both in an individual and social context (the Arabic, *salaam,* has a similar meaning). While justifiable war was certainly a feature of Hebrew thought, the prophetic literature (Isaiah, Micah, Jeremiah) clearly looked to a time when there will be no more war among nations (Isaiah 4:2–4). Later rabbinic thought recoiled from the glorification of war. Central to the desired relations between people and nations was a peace based on respect and dignity.

Based on the teaching of Jesus of Nazareth, the early Christian communities associated peacemaking with resistance to violence and the reconciliation of enemies. In the Sermon on the Mount (Matthew 5; Luke 6), Jesus commanded his followers to overcome evil through love of their enemies. Since this love precluded bloodshed (the "an eye for an eye" ethic), love must manifest itself through the performance of good works: "Love your enemies, do good to those who hate you. . . ." (Luke 6:27). Hence, Jesus urged his followers not to resist evil in the manner of the Zealots, who were a violent political movement in his time. Jesus' counsels to "turn the other cheek," to "give your cloak as well," and to "go also the second mile" however, are counsels of nonviolent resistance to various oppressors of his time, including the Roman occupation forces. Hence, both good works and resistance to enemies are the hallmarks of the Christian peacemaker. Or, stated another way, for the Christian, active nonviolent resistance to injustice is itself a "good work" toward one's enemy.

The Acts of the Apostles relates that the early Christians held "all things in common" and that they "would sell their goods and possessions and distribute them among all according as anyone had need" (Acts 2:44–45 and 4:32–35). Later forms of monastic pacifism and, in modern times, Christian socialism have linked the "love your enemies" command with the concept that goods should be held "in common" to fashion a pacifism that not only opposes war and injustice, but also promotes social justice in the economic and political structures of society. Indeed, in the early church, Greek and Latin Fathers fiercely opposed the injustice of the rich, and some proscribed Christian participation in war and gladiatorial contests.

Pacifism as a mainstream Christian posture ended with the promulgation of Christianity as the religion of Rome in 380 and with the concomitant teaching of Ambrose of Milan and Augustine of Hippo that Christians could participate in "just" wars to defend both the empire and the faith. Christian pacifism continued in the clerical and monastic life, however, since priests and monks were forbidden to shed blood. Gradually, Christians became warriors and war fought by knights was common among Christian princes in the Holy Roman Empire. In the medieval period, the *Peace of God* and the *Truce of God* were introduced to restrict who could be killed in battle, and to limit the periods of fighting effectively to the summer months. In 1095, Pope Urban II launched the Crusades to conquer the Holy Land from the followers of Islam, and even priests and monks participated in battle. A Crusade was preached in Europe itself against the Cathari, a pacifist sect in southern France.

In the thirteenth century, a pacifist movement for both monks and laypeople was begun by Francis of Assisi. Francis linked reverence for life with nature, and his thought is a source of "environmental" pacifism in the late twentieth century. The Reformation in the sixteenth century led to the founding of the historic peace churches: Brethren, Mennonites, and Friends (Quakers). During the Renaissance, the humanist Desiderius Erasmus held that war was opposed to every purpose for which humanity was created and his thought is foundational for many humanist pacifists. In seventeenth-century Russia, the Great Schism in the Orthodox Church resulted in the creation of the pacifist sects the Doukhobors and the Molokans, who used nonviolent methods to oppose participation in war.

In the nineteenth century, pacifists played a leading role in the suffrage and antislavery movements and organized societies that pressed for international arbitration as an instrument to abolish war. At the turn of the century, some pacifists proposed socialism, and some socialists adopted pacifism, as an alternative to capitalist greed, which, they believed, sought to profit from war itself. This was especially evident in the Social Gospel and Progressive movements prior to World War I.

In the twentieth century, World War I convinced many pacifists that war could be abolished only with the creation of international juridical institutions along with socially democratic economic systems. The Gandhian experiments with nonviolence in South Africa and India persuaded many that nonviolence was an active personal and political force that could also be used effectively by nonpacifists. Pacifist organizations like the Fellowship of Reconciliation (1915), the American Friends Service Committee (1917), the American Civil Liberties Bureau (1917), the Women's International League for Peace and Freedom (1919), the War Resisters League (1921), and the Catholic Worker (1933) have inspired, and collaborated with, many other nonpacifist movements and organizations to promote international peace and social justice. Movements for racial justice, labor unions, and women's rights have all been aligned with pacifist causes. In the United States, the successes of Martin Luther King, Jr.'s nonviolent campaigns for civil rights demonstrated the power of a strategy that, while coercive, can also result in reconciliation. Indeed, as the twentieth century ends, with its numerous successful nonviolent struggles, both the aims and the means of pacifism have broadened considerably since the beginning of the century.

Varieties of Pacifism

Throughout history, three types of pacifism have developed: anarchist, utilitarian, and transformational. Anarchist or communitarian pacifists believe that people should live in small, self-reliant communities as free from the interference of the state as possible. Some anarchists have been active in politics and have advocated the abolition or severe restriction of governmental powers, especially the power to draft people into military service. Some religious anarchists hold that the divide between the virtuous "City of God" and the decadent "City of Man" is so severe that it is useless to try to reform the social order. The ancient practices of Buddhist and Christian monks, the rejection of the state found in some Mennonite communities, and the more recent teachings of Leo Tolstoy, Emma Goldman, and Peter Maurin of the Catholic Worker are examples of anarchist pacifism.

Utilitarian or reform pacifists believe that the use of nonviolent methods is tactically superior and more efficient than the use of violence. Utilitarian pacifists believe that war and systems of oppression have outlived their usefulness and can, consequently, be abolished through the wide variety of nonviolent methods now available for popular use. Generally, there is no "grand design" in the utilitarian's thought. Hence, nonviolence may result in some degree of social change but is designed primarily to solve a particular problem in a specific situation. Strategists of "civilian-based defense," many of whom disavow the label of pacifism for themselves or their ideas, advocate the use of nonviolent methods by nonpacifist citizens to provide for national security. In the nuclear age, some people referred to themselves as "nuclear pacifists," since they held that nuclear war must not be waged under any circumstances. The philosophers Immanuel Kant and Jeremy Bentham and the National Committee for a Sane Nuclear Policy (USA, 1957) are examples of utilitarian pacifist individuals and organizations.

Transformational or reconstructionist pacifists believe that there must be a radical shift in consciousness that looks to intellectual, psychological, and spiritual means of dispute settlement. Transformational pacifists stress the spiritual unity of all people, both with each other and with the cosmos. They seek not only the abolition of war, but also the creation of an international juridical, political, and economic order that will promote the rights of all species. Consequently, transformational pacifists have historically been critical of sovereign empires and nation states and of economic systems that place profit over person. Both "humanistic" and "religious" pacifists envision socially just societies in a world of harmony and tolerance. Siddartha Buddha, Jesus, Mohandas K. Gandhi, and Muriel Lester and such organizations as the International Fellowship of Reconciliation, the War Resisters League, and the Buddhist Peace Fellowship, are examples of transformational pacifist individuals and organizations.

Joseph J. Fahey

References

Ackerman, Peter, and Christopher Kruegler. *Strategic Nonviolent Conflict: The Dynamics of People Power in the Twentieth Century.* Westport, Conn.: Praeger, 1994.

Bainton, Roland H. *Christian Attitudes toward War and Peace.* New York: Abingdon, 1960.

Chatfield, Charles, and Ruzanna Ilukhina. *Peace/Mir: An Anthology of Historic Alternatives to War.* Syracuse, N.Y.: Syracuse University Press, 1994.

Ferguson, John. *War and Peace in the World's Religions.* New York: Oxford, 1977.

Josephson, Harold, Sandi E. Cooper, Solomon Wank, and Lawrence Wittner, eds. *Biographical Dictionary of Modern Peace Leaders.* Westport, Conn.: Greenwood, 1985.

Mayer, Peter, ed. *The Pacifist Conscience.* Chicago: Regnery, 1967.

Montagu, Ashley. *Man and Aggression.* 2nd ed. New York: Oxford, 1973.

Musto, Ronald G. *The Peace Tradition in the Catholic Church: An Annotated Bibliography.* New York: Garland, 1987.

Sharp, Gene. *Making Europe Unconquerable: The Potential of Civilian-Based Deterrence and Defence.* Cambridge, Mass.: Ballinger, 1985.

Sibley, Mulford Q., ed. *The Quiet Battle: Writings on the Theory and Practice of Non-violent Resistance.* New York: Doubleday, 1963.

Wink, Walter. *Engaging the Powers: Discernment and Resistance in a World of Domination.* Minneapolis, Minn.: Fortress, 1992.

See also ALLEN, DEVERE; AMERICAN FRIENDS SERVICE COMMITTEE; BALLOU, ADIN; BURRITT, ELIHU; CATHOLIC WORKER MOVEMENT; DAY, DOROTHY; FELLOWSHIP OF RECONCILIATION, INTERNATIONAL; GANDHI, MOHANDAS KARAMCHAND; KING, MARTIN LUTHER, JR.; MUSTE, ABRAHAM JOHN; NONVIOLENCE, PRINCIPLED; PEACE PLEDGE UNION; QUAKERS; RELIGION AND NONVIOLENT ACTION; SANE; SAYRE, JOHN NEVIN; TOLSTOY, LEO; WAR RESISTERS' INTERNATIONAL; WOMEN'S INTERNATIONAL LEAGUE FOR PEACE AND FREEDOM, U.S. SECTION

Palestine, Arab Revolt, 1936–1939

Longest sustained grassroots protest by Arabs against Jewish nationalist aspirations in Palestine prior to Israel's establishment as a state. Great Britain's pro-Zionist policy, symbolized by the Balfour Declaration of 1917, calling for the establishment of a Jewish homeland in Palestine, threatened Arab political prospects, as did the rapid influx of Jews into Palestine in response to widespread persecution in central Europe. The initial goal of the revolt was to force Britain, which had gained mandatory control of Palestine at the end of World War I with the collapse of the Ottoman Empire, to halt Jewish immigration, prohibit the transfer of Arab lands to Jews, and establish an independent, representative national government in Palestine. In its first stage, which lasted six months, the rebellion had both violent and nonviolent elements, including acts of sabotage, riots, a general strike, nonpayment of taxes, an economic boycott against Jewish merchants, and other forms of civil disobedience. After a lull of nearly a year, the revolt heated up again in September 1937; Britain finally crushed the uprising in the spring of 1939.

The Arab Revolt began with a series of physical attacks and counterattacks by Palestinians and Jews, triggered by the murder of two Jews by Palestinians on April 15, 1936. Riots and instability in Jerusalem, Jaffa, and other urban areas followed. The newly formed Arab Higher Committee for Palestine (AHC), an uneasy alliance of six family-based Palestinian political parties headed by Amin Husseini, quickly moved to take control of the situation and, working in cooperation with local committees, attempted to channel Palestinian anger into nonviolent activities such as strikes in the commercial and transportation sectors.

By May, the uprising had moved into the villages and encompassed virtually all of Palestine. To restore their position of control, the British sent in thousands of troops. The British soldiers demolished homes of suspected activists and those who provided them a hiding place, seized property for nonpayment of taxes, instituted emergency regulations that granted the mandatory government extraordinary powers, and imposed collective fines, curfews, and other punitive measures against villages that joined the revolt. Rather than discourage support for the uprising, however, these actions increased cohesion between the activists and the general population and spurred the growth of a Palestinian national consciousness.

Under pressure from the leaders of several Arab states, Palestinians suspended the revolt pending the outcome of deliberations by the Palestine Royal Commission (the Peel Commission) set up by Britain to investigate the situation in Palestine. This allowed the Palestinians a face-saving retreat in the face of a British cabinet decision on September 2, 1936, to send additional troops to Palestine and increase repression, including the imposition of martial law, to suppress the revolt. When the AHC called off the strike on October 11, it had lasted 175 days and had put tremendous economic pressure on the Palestinian population.

Tensions eased somewhat with the end of the strike, although debate continued within the AHC and among activists over whether force or diplomacy and nonviolent action was the most effective method to achieve Palestinian goals. The announcement in July 1937 of the Peel Commission's proposal to divide Palestine into separate Arab and Jewish states sparked a renewal of the revolt, with the additional goal of preventing partition. Rebels directed their opposition not only against British and Zionist forces but also against Arabs who supported the partition plan. Hostility to the Peel Commission report was particularly intense in the Galilee region, because the partition proposal called for the Arab population living there to be forcibly removed to make way for the Jewish state. On September 26, Palestinians murdered L.A. Andrews, acting district commissioner for Galilee, and a new period of violence erupted. In response, Britain dissolved the AHC and arrested or expelled virtually all the significant Palestinian leaders.

The revolt subsided briefly, then strengthened again. Unlike the first stage of the revolt, during which urban nationalists such as members of the AHC exercised significant political control, in 1937 and 1938 small bands of fighters operating in the rural areas held most of the power. By the summer of 1938, the region was in complete turmoil, with Zionist, British, and Palestinian forces fighting for control. In large portions of Palestine, the British civil authorities lost all ability to manage the day-to-day affairs of the population as the Palestinians established many elements of an autonomous government, including a separate court system.

Britain further intensified pressure against the revolt, sending in additional troops and virtually occupying the country. Zionist forces also began to take a more active role in repressing the uprising. Eventually, support for the rebels among the demoralized Palestinian population declined and the revolt ended. According to estimates by Khalidi, at least 3,073 (and probably closer to 15,000) Palestinians died during the revolt, along with 463 Jews, and 101 British soldiers.

Deborah J. Gerner

References

Hurewitz, J.C. *The Struggle for Palestine.* New York: Norton, 1950; New York: Schocken, 1976.

Khalidi, Walid, ed. *From Haven to Conquest: Readings in Zionism and the Palestine Problem until 1948.* Beirut: Institute for Palestine Studies, 1971; Washington, D.C.: Institute for Palestine Studies, 1987.

Porath, Yeshoshua. *The Palestinian Arab National Movement: From Riots to Rebellion.* London: Frank Cass, 1977.

Sacher, Howard M., ed. *The Rise of Israel: A Documentary Record from the Nineteenth Century to 1948.* Vols. 20–27. New York: Garland, 1987.

See also INTIFADA, 1987–1990; PALESTINE, ILLEGAL JEWISH IMMIGRATION, 1939–1948

Palestine, Illegal Jewish Immigration, 1939–1948

Organized Jewish immigration to Palestine in defiance of restrictive policies imposed by British authorities governing the territory. While individual acts of illegal entry occurred in the twenty years prior to 1939, organized illegal immigration grew during World War II and reached its peak between 1945 and 1948. Some immigrants traveled to Palestine by land, but most traveled by sea. This widespread defiance of British policies was a significant factor in the United Nations vote to partition Palestine to create a Jewish state in November 1947, and the subsequent British decision to terminate its mandate over Palestine in May 1948.

The organized Jewish immigration to Palestine from 1939 to 1948 was not considered illegal by Zionists working toward the creation of a Jewish state. The organizers of the movement, termed *aliyah beth* (illegal and clandestine immigration in Hebrew), were motivated by a desire to help fellow Jews escape the Holocaust during the war and to provide a homeland for homeless Jewish refugees after the war. From 1939 to 1945, over 16,000 illegal immigrants reached Palestine.

From 1945 to 1948, over 70,000 illegal immigrants attempted the journey to Palestine. During this period, Britain enforced a policy outlined in a 1939 White Paper that put a ceiling on the total number of legal immigrants permitted and tied immigration quotas to consent by Arabs living in Palestine. Jews attempting *aliyah beth* from 1946 were confronted by a major British prevention campaign, which included diplomatic pressure on other countries to stop ships from sailing, a blockade of Palestinian ports from 1946 to 1948 using almost forty Royal Navy ships, and deportation of Jews to detainment camps on Cyprus.

While there were many individuals and groups who engaged in *aliyah beth* activities, most of the larger efforts were organized by the Mossad Le' Aliyah Bet, an underground group established by the Zionist Jewish leadership of Palestine to facilitate "alternative" immigration. They formed operations in over twenty countries on four continents, and used emissaries to contact, assist, and organize immigrant Jews for secret voyages on ships that were bought and outfitted for the specific purpose of transporting illegal immigrants to Palestine. One of the main activities of the organized *aliyah beth* campaign was the forging of visas from various countries, and the forging of entry certificates to Palestine on genuine passports. Mossad recruits underwent training in ship operations and in assisting immigrants to land on the Palestine coast. Immigrants underwent training in defense against British tactics and created their own committees to organize discipline and cultural activities.

P

During the war, most of the illegal immigrants sailed in small vessels. After the war, the Mossad stepped up its efforts, and larger groups on larger vessels attempted the trip. Some of the largest and better-known efforts included the *Fede* and *Fenice*, sailing from Italy in 1946, the *Exodus* sailing from France in 1947, and the *Pan Crescent* and *Pan York* sailing from Romania in 1947.

In the spring of 1946, Mossad organizers had outfitted the *Fede* (renamed *Elahu Golomb*) and the *Fenice* (renamed *Dov Hos*) in the Italian port of La Spezia. The police caught wind of and stopped a secret convoy transporting immigrants to the ship in May. Allowed to board the ship but not set sail, refugees began a several day hunger strike on board. Fifteen Jewish leaders in Palestine conducted their own sympathetic hunger strike. After an agreement was reached, the hunger strike was concluded, and many of the passengers were allowed to sail for Haifa.

The incident of *aliyah beth* that garnered the most international attention was the voyage of the *Exodus* in 1947. Defying French naval authorities, the ship and its forty-five hundred immigrants sailed illegally from France in July. On the seventh day, the ship reached the Palestinian coast, and a British flotilla of destroyers attacked the *Exodus,* rammings its sides and firing on the passengers. A three-hour battle ended in a cease-fire and surrender with four dead and over two hundred wounded. The British told the refugees they were going to detention camps in Cyprus, but instead they transported all of them back to France. In the ensuing months, France refused to assist the British in deporting the refugees, the refugees refused to leave the British ships and demanded their return to Palestine, and Great Britain received much negative publicity. The British finally unloaded the refugees in Hamburg, Germany, amid international condemnation.

Given the large number of surviving Jews in Romania, one of the Mossad's biggest operations was spearheaded there. The British attempted to persuade Romanian authorities not to allow two large ships carrying over fifteen thousand hopeful Jewish immigrants, the *Pan Crescent* and *Pan York,* to sail for Palestine. The British attempt failed and the ships finally left port in December 1947, but were diverted to Cyprus by a British flotilla.

The defiance of British immigration policies was widespread and well organized. While over 100,000 eventually made it to the new Jewish state of Israel (most after months of detainment on Cyprus), over two thousand died in the attempt, either by drowning or at the hands of the British Navy. Illegal immigrants constituted one-sixth of the Jewish inhabitants in pre-Israel Palestine. From the birth of Israel in May 1948, immigration was no longer illegal; Israel welcomed refugees and encouraged immigration.

Brad Bennett

References

Hadari, Ze'ev Venia. *Second Exodus: The Full Story of Jewish Illegal Immigration to Palestine, 1945–1948*. London: Valentine Mitchell, 1991.

Ofer, Dalia. *Escaping the Holocaust: Illegal Immigration to the Land of Israel, 1939–1944*. Oxford: Oxford University Press, 1990.

See also JEWISH RESISTANCE TO THE HOLOCAUST

Panama, Civic Crusade, 1987–1989

Effort by the Panamanian population to dislodge the military dictatorship of Manuel Noriega through the creation of political organizations and the mobilization of numerous demonstrations. A period of intense protest brought some concessions in the form of a transition election, which failed to change the regime. Noriega was removed from power by a United States military invasion on December 20, 1989.

Panama's military dictatorship began in 1968. Ten years later, General Omar Torrijos decided to return the military to an indirect political role and place responsibility for economic management in civilian hands. Torrijos's plan entailed a series of steps: municipal elections in 1980, enactment of a new electoral code, and finally, in 1984, presidential and legislative elections. However, Torrijos died in 1981. Thereafter, General Manuel A. Noriega and his allies used civilian political figures and institutions, not for democratization, but to assert their own control.

During the 1984 election, Noriega and key officers, principally Col. Roberto Diaz Herrera, suspended the vote count and then took ten days to announce a narrow electoral margin for their candidate, Nicolas A. Barletta. The military regime was determined to use any means to protect its interests. In retrospect, the volume of votes for the opposition and the alleged electoral fraud of 1984 were the first concrete signs that the popular base claimed by the military was a sham. However, neither the organized opposition nor the populace was able or willing to struggle to defend its electoral victory. The time was not yet ripe for nonviolent struggle.

With their victory stolen by Noriega's party in the 1984 elections, civilian opponents concluded that normal political means would not suffice to return the Panama Defense Forces (PDF) to the barracks. However, despite opportunities that arose during 1985, full-time opposition remained largely confined to a few traditional political parties until mid-1987.

During 1985, the most significant opportunity resulted from a bitter antagonism between Gen. Noriega and a revolutionary activist, Hugo Spadafora. Unlike others who criticized the military privately, Spadafora made public accusations about Noriega's involvement in drug trafficking and political scandals. Spadafora was brutally tortured and allegedly murdered by PDF officers in September. The manner of his death breached the bounds of Panamanian normalcy. His assassination, the family's demands for an accounting, and public commemorations of his murder turned Hugo Spadafora into a heroic figure and rallying symbol for many grievances against the regime.

Public nonviolent opposition began in September 1985 when the Spadafora family led protests, symbolic actions, and religious observances to demand justice for Hugo. Although Hugo's father had considerable political party experience, the Spadafora family took pains to make their protests nonpartisan. This, plus the fact that party leaders did not direct but only supported the movement, made it easier for nonpartisan leaders and followers to join in commemorative and protest activities. In sum, the Spadafora crisis exposed the brutality and venality of the regime, created an opposition hero and family support group, constituted an "investigation" of regime crimes, and initiated a nonviolent protest movement. Nevertheless, after about six months, protests diminished, public attention faded, and the military appeared to have weathered the political storm.

In June 1987, the PDF experienced its worst crisis yet. Col. Diaz Herrera accused Noriega and the PDF of electoral fraud, Spadafora's murder, drug trafficking, the sale of visas to Cuban refu-

gees and high technology goods to Cuba, and other crimes. Diaz Herrera's defection constituted a serious blow to the PDF: he was Omar Torrijos's cousin, the highest-ranking officer behind Noriega, and he violated the institutional norm of "quietly accepting the inevitable" when the PDF power center (Noriega) turned against him.

Much more significant, however, was the popular reaction to Diaz Herrera's confessions, which were aired on radio and television and printed in La Prensa on June 7, 1987. The metaphor most commonly used to characterize the popular response to Diaz Herrera's "spark" is "detonation." Although widespread opposition had been steadily building since 1985, it had found no outlet. On June 8, a movement radiated in waves, first to leaders, immediately to the news media covering activists in the streets, and then throughout the capital.

On June 7, Diaz Herrera had telephoned widely known opposition party leaders and clergy, inviting them to join him at his house. Incredibly, they came. Even Hugo Spadafora's brother Winston responded, and took a public stand with Diaz Herrera. Soon the house was filled with party leaders, clergy, activists, and journalists. This created a bizarre scene: the man responsible for much of the dictatorship's repression was being championed by the very figures he kept out of power in 1984. Diaz Herrera was transformed from an oppressor into an opposition cult figure.

Radio journalists broadcast opposition announcements, urging people to take to the streets to demand justice and defend freedom of expression. Concurrently, a second "explosion" occurred: thousands of people flooded the streets, venting pent up grievances and demanding justice. At the end of three days, Panama's capital had been seized by the people: the movement created a popular insurrection.

Diaz Herrera's defection and its effects posed a severe crisis for the regime. Not only did it pit Torrijistas against Noriega's loyalists, it also posed the first instance in which the PDF had to consider repressing one of its own. It took a month for Noriega to decide that he had no choice but to attack Diaz Herrera's fortified home and arrest him and his followers. By that time, however, a new opposition organization, the Civic Crusade, was established and a vigorous movement was well under way.

Superficially, Panamanian politics appeared to be experiencing a spontaneous movement.

P

Certainly this was the moment when conflict between civilians and the military became actively acute and a nonviolent struggle commenced. Nonetheless, the organization and movement born on June 8–9, 1987, were the products of several legacies. Panama has a tradition of nonviolent protest, as evidenced in the teachers' movement of 1979, sovereignty demonstrations in 1959, and various women's political actions. The business and medical communities also have a tradition of initiating movements to support civic and moral values. More immediately, the Spadafora crisis set important precedents in terms of symbolic actions and the use of nonviolent protest.

Coincidentally, the leaders who spearheaded the Civic Crusade had just planned to create an umbrella organization for election monitoring, based on the NAMFREL model used successfully in the Philippines. These were Aurelio Barria, president of the Chamber of Commerce, and Fr. Fernando Guardia, who served as a point of coordination with the Catholic Church. After visiting the Philippines in early May 1987, they planned to replicate the NAMFREL experience in Panama by creating a similar organization called MODELO.

Before Diaz Herrera made his accusations, Barria had called a meeting of representatives from professional groups, labor organizations, civic associations and churches to launch MODELO on June 8, 1987. On June 7, when the confessions appeared in print, Barria and his colleagues decided to use their meeting to make even more dramatic plans. They seized the moment, realizing that the two-year plan they had envisioned (focused on the May 1989 presidential election) would have to be considerably compacted. The founders appeared to be riding, rather than guiding, a wave of popular protest.

The Nonviolent Organization: The National Civic Crusade

The Cruzada Civilista Nacional (CCN) was established on June 9, 1987. Three objectives were announced: (a) that all those accused by Diaz Herrera, civilian and military, be separated from their positions pending an investigation; (b) that an independent commission be formed to conduct the investigation; and (c) that reconstruction begin of institutions that would guarantee justice and a truly democratic system. Later, CCN objectives evolved into demands for deeper changes; initially, however, the leaders hoped to remove Noriega in order to resume the stalled transition, not to overthrow the military regime.

As an umbrella organization, the CCN comprised numerous organizations whose representatives sat as a general assembly; a smaller number sat as an executive committee. During the first three months, the executive committee deliberated almost constantly, with members consistently contributing fifteen-to-sixteen-hour days. Initially, every organization that joined the CCN automatically gained a seat on the executive committee; later, as membership exceeded one hundred and then two hundred, this procedure was untenable, so the executive committee was capped while the assembly functioned as a broader representative body.

The CCN experienced several shifts at the leadership level. The first group, under Barria's tenure, functioned vigorously during the first few months and then, as the regime threatened them with arrest, they went into exile. Several relocated to Washington, D.C., acting as lobbyists to influence U.S. policy. Meanwhile, six new leaders (executive committee members) were selected. Thereafter, persons in these positions were changed every six months; during particularly difficult times, leaders were rotated every thirty days.

Initially, the CCN was headquartered in the Chamber of Commerce. After that building was closed by the PDF, CCN leaders met at other locations, such as the Dentists' Association Building, with members, some in disguise, arriving at staggered intervals. One participant characterized the clandestine stage as "long meetings without conclusion" that sometimes took up to eight hours to make a decision.

The Opposition Movement

Between June 1987 and December 1989, various groups and numerous individuals participated in opposition activities called by the CCN, political parties, other groups, and independent activists. Many of these non-CCN actors also pursued their own opposition tactics and strategies. The parallel performance, and often disconnected nature of these groups and individuals, gave the opposition a fragmented character that accurately reflected the political situation. These other groups and individuals were also much more representative of Panamanian society than were the CCN executive committee and assembly; their participation gave the movement a much broader base than the CCN per se could claim.

Numerous groups opposed the military regime during this period, many of which joined the CCN. University and secondary school student organizations and national federations from public and private institutions intensively participated during the early stage of the struggle. Some labor unions (excluding many public sector employees but not those in IRHE, the state power and light company), particularly the CTRP (the Confederation of Workers, Republic of Panama) used strikes and other forms of noncooperation. During several political crises, some IRHE activists cut power supplies in Panama City. When U.S. economic sanctions caused a cash shortage, CTRP employees negotiated partial payment plans with employers.

Some professors, both through their associations and as individuals, were active. During the cash shortage, faculty at the Catholic University of Santa Maria Antigua accepted greatly reduced salaries in order to keep the university open in defiance of regime pressures. Associations of nonuniversity teachers, which had the most established record of opposition protest besides political parties, joined the CCN and were particularly active in "appeals" initiatives.

Women's associations, such as the Cuidadanias de Panama (similar to the League of Women Voters) and the Mujeres Civilistas of San Miguelito (Civic Women of San Miguelito), were particularly active. Medical personnel and dentists associations, which had, like teachers associations, opposed certain policies of the Torrijos regime, took a leadership role in the CCN as well as continuing their own protest activities. Dr. Mauro Zuniga and Dr. Marisin Villalaz de Arias are the best-known activists from this sector.

Finally, individual activists without organizational bases also continued their protests during the crisis years. The best-known were radio journalist and legislator Mayin Correa, law professor and radio commentator Miguel Antonio Bernal, opinion columnist Guillermo Sanchez-Borbon, philosophy professor Roberto Arosemena Jaen, and lawyer Winston Spadafora, brother of the assassinated activist Hugo.

Stages of the Struggle

Roberto Brenes, an initial CCN leader, identified four stages in the civilista opposition: (1) nonviolent direct action between June and August 1987; (2) neighborhood work from January 1988 through early 1989; (3) the electoral effort from March to May 1989; and (4) the postelectoral period, in which "everyone stood with the winners." Together, Brenes considers the first three as a grand strategy designed to challenge the military regime, build an opposition network at the neighborhood level, and then translate that network into an electoral victory.

Many participants and observers characterized Brenes's first stage as the apex of the civilista movement. Hopes were high as people expected a decisive end to an intensive but short struggle. Several business-led strikes were held. Protests occurred daily along major avenues in the commercial district. Thousands of people, many of whom worked in and around the financial district, joined in during their lunch hour or before going home. This tactic, however, had distinct limitations, confining the breadth of the civilista movement and providing predictable targets for the PDF to attack. On "Black Friday," July 10, 1987, heavily armed riot squads attacked the protesters, marking both a climax in civilista activity and a turning point in the movement. The last large demonstration was scheduled in October 1987.

During Brenes's second stage, the regime mounted an effective response which, though mild by regional standards, was the worst repression Panamanians had ever experienced. The opposition press was severely curtailed, political freedoms were denied during a "State of Urgency," and protesters faced consistently severe sanctions. Brenes explained the objective of neighborhood organizing during this period: "If successful, then we could have called on people any day, any hour." What the CCN hoped to achieve was an ability to deploy protests at various unexpected locations. Brenes believed that such protests would have been much more effective because "the hunting pack" feels safer away from home (such as in the financial district). He felt that targeting certain highways could have "driven the Dobermen crazy." Several training seminars were devoted to grassroots organization building. Part of the neighborhood strategy also involved using teachers, recruited through their professional associations (which had joined the CCN) to talk to PDF living in their neighborhoods. The idea was to appeal to personal acquaintances to stop the repression and reform the institution.

During the electoral stage, in 1989, the CCN formally joined the Democratic Opposition Alliance (ADO), which was then called ADO-Civilista (or ADO-C). The CCN organization had no candidate on the slate (one president, two vice presidents), but its symbols, resources, and legitimacy were devoted to the campaign. After ADO-Civilista gained a three-to-one margin on election day, Noriega halted the vote count and then annulled the election. By controlling the rules of normal politics, Noriega successfully blocked the opposition's electoral victory; the cost, however, was very high. After installing a provisional president on September 1, 1989, the PDF had no remaining claim to legitimacy.

During the final postelectoral stage, public protest almost ceased, although negotiations between regime and opposition leaders continued. Brenes characterizes this fourth period as "everyone stood with the winners." The opposition did, indeed, appear to be standing still, its tactics and resources exhausted but not entirely eliminated.

External Support

Beginning in late 1987, the United States provided various types and degrees of support for the civilian opposition. The National Endowment for Democracy funded CCN applications for support ($30,000 for organizational support and civic education; $60,000 to support the electoral strategy). The Department of State gave frequent verbal support, but also actively undercut the CCN and opposition party leaders by negotiating directly with Noriega. Military assistance was canceled; official U.S. military contacts were downgraded to the lowest level possible. At the Department of Defense's Southern Command headquarters in Panama, the progress of the civilista movement and other regime opponents was closely monitored as an indicator of changes in Noriega's domestic power base. Covert U.S. operations were also used to encourage and finance military coups by PDF officers in and outside of Panama; none succeeded.

Finally, on December 20, 1989, a U.S. invasion brought an abrupt end to stage four. The ADO-Civilista slate took office as Panama's new government. Some CCN leaders assert that with more time, their strategy (along with all of the other concurrent pressures on the regime) could have succeeded. Whether nonviolent action could have toppled Noriega will never be known.

Margaret E. Scranton

References

Scranton, Margaret E. "Panama's Democratic Transition." *Midsouth Journal of Political Science* 13 (Spring 1992): 107–128.

See also CIVIC STRIKE

Parks, Rosa (b. 1913)

American civil rights activist. When Rosa Parks was arrested for refusing to move from her seat on a city bus in deference to a white passenger, her action contributed to the initiation of the Montgomery Bus Boycott of 1955–1956.

However, Rosa Parks was not the first African American arrested for refusing to "move to the back of the bus," as Alabama state law required prior to the civil rights movement. Soon after a 1954 Supreme Court ruling *(Brown v. Board of Education)* gave impetus to desegregation in the South, two other women had been arrested in Parks's hometown of Montgomery, Alabama. For various reasons, however, the National Association for the Advancement of Colored People (NAACP) and other local organizations active on behalf of desegregation chose not to take their case to court. With Rosa Parks, the NAACP decided that the time had come; pleasant and unassuming, she was "humble enough to be claimed by the common folk," as Taylor Branch wrote, "yet dignified enough in manner, speech, and dress to command the respect of the leading classes."

The citywide bus boycott precipitated by Parks's arrest on December 1, 1955, led, in turn, to local clergy's forming the Montgomery Improvement Association and electing as its chair a twenty-six-year-old minister, the Reverend Dr. Martin Luther King, Jr. The boycott lasted from December 1955 to December 1956, when the Supreme Court declared the state law unconstitutional.

Born February 4, 1913, in Tuskegee, Alabama, Rosa Louise McCauley moved two years later with her family to her grandparents' farm in the same state. She recalls "going to sleep as a girl hearing the Klan ride at night and hearing a lynching and being afraid the house would burn down." At eleven, she enrolled in an industrial school for girls, founded by white women from the North. In 1932, she married Raymond Parks, who was already working for civil rights for African Americans. Later she attended what is now Alabama State University and worked with the Montgomery Voters

League. In 1943, she was elected secretary of the local NAACP, the same year that a bus driver tried to make her step off the bus, after paying her fare at the front, and enter again by the back door. He confronted her once again on that historic day in 1955.

Threatened personally and eventually fired from her job in Montgomery after her arrest, Rosa Parks and her husband moved to Detroit in 1957. They endured several years of ill health and low-paying jobs, until Congressman John Conyers, Jr., hired her to work in his office in 1965. In 1987, she initiated the Rosa and Raymond Parks Institute for Self Development, which fosters young people's awareness of and involvement in issues associated with African-American history. Its annual Reverse Freedom Tour retraces the Underground Railroad that slaves took to Canada in the nineteenth century and the Freedom Rides of the 1960s, including the spot where Parks "would not be moved."

The story of Rosa Parks is powerful not only because of her courage in risking arrest, but also because of her preparations for that moment: her day-to-day organizing as secretary of the local NAACP; earlier study with Myles Horton and Septima P. Clark at the Highlander Folk School, a Tennessee training institute for organizers; and even, as she said, her choice of a husband, who had defended the Scottsboro Boys, nine African Americans falsely charged with rape in Alabama in the early 1930s.

Michael True

References

Branch, Taylor. *Parting the Waters: America in the King Years, 1954–63.* New York: Simon and Schuster, 1988.

Parks, Rosa. *Rosa Parks: Mother to a Movement.* New York: Dial, 1992.

See also CIVIL RIGHTS MOVEMENT; MONTGOMERY BUS BOYCOTT, 1955–1956; NIXON, E.D.

Pathan Defiance, 1929–1938

Satyagraha campaign by Pathan tribespeople against British rule in the Peshawar Valley of the North-West Frontier in India (now part of Pakistan). Led by Abdul Ghaffar Khan, known as the "Frontier Gandhi," Pathan leaders organized the *Khudai Khidmatgar* ("Servants of God"), a nonviolent army devoted to freedom and service to the people.

The Muslim Pathan tribe living in the Peshawar Valley had never been fully subjugated by the British, and sporadic fighting occurred between the British and the Pathans in the late nineteenth and early twentieth centuries. Because the Pathans lived under *badal,* a code of honor demanding revenge for transgressions, the British were caught off guard by the campaign of nonviolent action in the 1930s. Formed in 1929, the Servants of God were composed of men and women who pledged to refrain from violence and to devote two hours a day to social service. They patterned themselves after the military. They were trained, disciplined, and uniformed, and if any volunteer broke the rule against using violence, he or she was instantly dismissed from the organization. The Servants of God picketed liquor stores and legal courts and organized processions, *hartal,* and general nonviolent resistance to British decrees. Women volunteers often conducted sit-ins in front of police lines. The Servants of God also engaged in a variety of constructive projects and local peacekeeping.

On April 1930, in a town called Naki, Khan called for total nonviolent civil resistance to British rule and he was arrested. In reaction, the Servants of God led thousands of Pathans in demonstrations throughout the province. A spontaneous general strike erupted in the city of Peshawar. The British responded to these protests quickly and forcefully. Almost three hundred people were killed and many more were wounded at the Kissa Khani Bazaar in Peshawar when British troops opened fire on an unarmed crowd. During the following weeks, martial law was declared in the province and the Servants of God were banned. Volunteers were subjected to beatings and arrests, and their headquarters were burned and looted. In spite of this severe repression, the Servants of God remained almost completely nonviolent.

This discipline seemed to unnerve the British, as they failed in their attempt to provoke the Pathans to further violence. Before Khan's arrest, the Servants of God numbered only one thousand recruits. In defiance of British repression, by the summer of 1930 the number of Servants of God volunteers had swelled to eighty thousand. Khan was released in 1931, arrested again, released in 1934, and banned from the North-West Frontier. Although the British declared the North-West Frontier a full-fledged Indian province in 1933 with parity with other provinces, they continued to repress the Servants of God and other independence activity. In 1938, the number of Servants of God had risen to over 100,000. Khan continued to promote satyagraha throughout India during the next three decades, spending a total of fifteen years in jail. The Servants of God historically represent one of the largest and most effective nonviolent armies designed to effect social transformation.

Brad Bennett

References

Bennett, Brad. "Arab-Muslim Cases of Nonviolent Struggle." In *Arab Nonviolent Political Struggle in the Middle East,* edited by Ralph E. Crow, Philip Grant, and Saad E. Ibrahim. Boulder, Colo.: Lynne Rienner, 1990.

Bondurant, Joan V. *Conquest of Violence: The Gandhian Philosophy of Conflict.* Princeton: Princeton University Press, 1958, 1988.

Easwaran, Eknath. *A Man to Match His Mountains: Badshah Khan, Nonviolent Soldier of Islam.* Petaluma, Calif.: Nilgiri, 1984.

See also Khan Abdul Ghaffar Khan

Alice Paul. Friends Historical Library/Swarthmore College.

Paul, Alice (1885–1977)

Women's rights activist and social reformer, born in Moorestown, New Jersey, on January 11, 1885, and died in Moorestown on July 9, 1977.

Paul was raised in the Quaker faith. After attending private schools, Paul graduated from Swarthmore College in 1905. She did graduate work at the New York School of Social Work and, in 1906, went to Europe for three years to work with Quakers in the settlement movement and to study the working conditions of women. There she became involved in Britain's militant women's suffrage campaign and was jailed several times for her activities. Continuing her studies, she received both an M.A. degree and her Ph.D. from the University of Pennsylvania.

After working for a year with the National American Woman Suffrage Association (NAWSA), Paul was critical of policies she considered too timid, especially since women's suffrage had not been debated in Congress since 1887. It was time for women to stop begging for the vote, Paul insisted. In 1913, she helped found the Congressional Union for Woman Suffrage, which merged in 1917 with the Woman's Party to form the National Woman's Party (NWP). Under Paul's leadership, the NWP grew to a membership of fifty thousand with headquarters in Washington, D.C. From 1913 to the passage of the Nineteenth Amendment in 1920, Paul headed an intensive women's suffrage campaign in the United States.

Under her leadership, the NWP employed dramatic nonviolent tactics—picketing the White House, processing with banners, organizing a cross-country automobile cavalcade, lobbying, disrupting congressional events, publicly burning copies of presidential speeches, and engaging in hunger strikes. Though they did not throw rocks or break windows as did the suffragists in England, women suffrage activists in the United States were imprisoned and endured brutal treatment. On three occasions, Paul was sent to prison for her suffrage activism. In 1917, during one of her hunger strikes, Paul was detained in a psychopathic ward and denied legal counsel. This tactic was, Paul believed, an attempt by U.S. government forces to discredit her as the leader of the women's suffrage movement, but it was subsequently used by suffrage activists to promote outrage and gain sympathy for their cause.

After the passage of the Nineteenth Amendment granting women the right to vote, Paul studied law, receiving her degree in 1922 from the Washington College of Law. She subsequently earned further law degrees at American University. In 1923, in an attempt to amend the U.S. Constitution, she drafted and introduced into Congress the first Equal Rights Amendment (ERA) on behalf of women.

In the 1920s and 1930s, Paul devoted her efforts to gaining global support of women's rights and founded the World Party for Equal Rights for Women with headquarters in Geneva. Paul continued her involvement in the National Woman's Party and worked tirelessly for the ERA. In 1970, this amendment passed Congress and went to the states for ratification where it again failed passage. Paul was successful, however, in introducing a statement affirming the equal rights of women and men into the preamble to the charter of the United Nations.

Pam McAllister

References

Bacon, Margaret Hope. *Mothers of Feminism: The Story of Quaker Women in America.* San Francisco: Harper and Row, 1986.
Irwin, Inez Hayes. *The Story of Alice Paul and the National Woman's Party.* Fairfax, Va.: Denlinger's, 1964, 1977.

See also NATIONAL WOMAN SUFFRAGE ASSOCIATION; WOMEN'S SUFFRAGE

Pax Christi International

Catholic peace movement with national sections in eighteen countries. Pax Christi (Latin for "the peace of Christ") informs Roman Catholics about their church's teachings on peace and encourages them to work for disarmament, human rights, a just world order, and nonviolent alternatives to war.

Pax Christi was founded in France by Maria-Marthe Dortel-Claudot toward the end of the Second World War. The first president, Bishop Pierre-Marie Théas, later bishop of Lourdes, had already experienced the need for reconciliation between enemies when he was imprisoned for denouncing the deportation of Jews from France in 1942. After the war, Pax Christi organized pilgrimages and acts of atonement between France and Germany. Activities for young people became popular traditions: annual *routes* (hiking trips with a discussion theme), pen-pal schemes, hostels, and centers fostering international exchanges. The movement spread to other European countries, and in 1952 Pope Pius XII gave it his approval as the international Catholic peace movement.

Pax Christi contributed in particular to new thinking on conscientious objection and the morality of weapons of mass destruction. The Second Vatican Council (1962–1965) and the encyclicals of Pope John XXIII and Pope Paul VI endorsed this. They deepened Catholic understanding of peacemaking by linking it to economic and social development, human rights, and support for the United Nations. Pax Christi brought these insights to Catholics at the local level. Unlike the national Justice and Peace Commissions appointed by the hierarchy, Pax Christi is an independent membership organization open to all laypeople and priests. Priority is given to peace education in parishes and schools and to developing the theology and spirituality of peace.

At the request of Archbishop Helder Camara of Brazil, Pax Christi arranged consultations at Driebergen, Netherlands (1972), and Derry, Northern Ireland (1977), on the theme "In Search of Nonviolent Alternatives." From these evolved a network called Nonviolent Alternatives (NVA). Nonviolence has been a recurring theme of Pax Christi seminars and publications, and several sections have provided training for specific nonviolent actions. In 1985, Pax Christi U.S.A. initiated a "Vow of Nonviolence" that many Christians have adopted.

Since 1972, when sections formed in Australia and the United States, Pax Christi has expanded and is represented on four continents. National sections are autonomous in the organization of their activities. The international movement is headed by a bishop or cardinal, an international secretary, and an executive committee, with headquarters currently in Belgium. Delegates meet every two years in an international council.

International commissions work on the priorities of the movement. There is one, for example, on security, demilitarization and the arms trade, and another on human rights and development. During the cold war years the Commission for East European Contacts established dialogue with Christians in Eastern Europe and the Soviet Union. From 1972 onwards a unique series of meetings took place between Pax Christi International and the Russian Orthodox Church. Since the dissolution of the Soviet bloc, previous contacts have generated new Pax Christi groups in Poland, Hungary, Slovakia, and the Czech Republic.

Pax Christi has consultative status at the United Nations, UNESCO, and the Council of Europe. In 1983, it received the UNESCO Peace Education Prize and in 1987, it received the UN Peace Messenger Award.

Valerie Flessati

References

de Jonghe, Etienne. "Pax Christi International: The Role and Perspectives of an International Catholic Peace Movement." *Cross Currents* 33, no. 3 (1983): 323–329.

Lalande, Bernard, and Carel ter Maat. *Reflections by Two Pioneers*. Brussels: Pax Christi International, 1992.

See also CAMARA, DOM HELDER; NONVIOLENT ALTERNATIVES; RELIGION AND NONVIOLENT ACTION

Peace Brigades International

Human rights and peacekeeping organization founded in 1981 by Gandhians and Quakers long active in international peace efforts. Significant deployments of Peace Brigades International (PBI) teams have occurred in Guatemala (1983–present), El Salvador (1986–1992), and Sri Lanka (1989–present). Operating where political space is contested and democratic freedoms are compromised, PBI attempts to secure political space within which human rights and nonviolent struggle may be more safely exercised by local activists. Relying on foreign nationals who volunteer their services for at least six months, the organization has pioneered a model of nonviolent protective accompaniment in national conflicts.

The protective accompaniment technique rests on the idea that the presence of unarmed international escorts alongside local activists is a deterrent since violence or freedom restrictions directed toward foreign nationals often result in higher political costs than the same actions directed at local citizens. Moreover, PBI's escorts function as international observers. Trained in nonviolence, armed with cameras and notebooks, their presence often reduces the level of violence and allows PBI to publicize eyewitness accounts of events.

The organization also maintains an Emergency Response Network (ERN) that consists of hundreds of people across the globe who are signed on to computer networks and phone trees to receive fast-breaking PBI information calling for immediate action. That action takes the form of letters, telexes, faxes, and phone calls calling for the correction of the perceived injustice.

Peace Brigades International teams usually enter a region upon invitation of an organization engaged in nonviolent struggle. An international nongovernmental organization with associative status at the United Nations, PBI adopts a stance of nonpartisanship in its work. Typical PBI clients include journalists, trade unionists, human rights workers, indigenous peoples, health workers, refugee communities, religious figures, opposition politicians, and various local civil associations and nongovernmental organizations under threat as a result of their activities.

Nonviolent protective accompaniment by PBI takes many forms, depending on the social and political dynamics of the conflict and on PBI's resources in the field. PBI's international escorts may provide constant, twenty-four-hour accompaniment. They may be present only when a client engages in public activities or demonstrations and feels under increased threat. Or PBI personnel may simply visit the offices of an organization or the home of an activist every week in a public fashion. Such periodic visits are designed to heighten the international visibility of the client, and thereby to provide safer political space within which they can operate.

PBI's Guatemala team provided especially significant levels of accompaniment over many years to *Grupo de Apoyo Mutuo* (GAM) (Mutual Support Group for Families of the Disappeared and Detained), and to *Consejo de Comunidades Etnicas "Runujel Junam"* (CERJ) (Council of Ethnic Communities "Everyone Equal"), an organization of Mayan farmers who resist forced service in the military's civil patrols. Whenever Rigoberta Menchu, the 1993 Nobel Peace Prize winner and an exiled leader of Guatemala's indigenous peoples, returned to Guatemala in the 1980s, she asked for and received PBI accompaniment. PBI itself has been the target of intimidating violence on a few occasions. The team house and office in Guatemala City was bombed in 1989, three PBI team members were attacked and stabbed in 1988 outside the house, and death threats were phoned in to PBI in January 1993, following PBI's accompaniment of the first mass return of Guatemalan refugees.

PBI's organizational structure is broadly decentralized. All decisions are made by consensus, including on the teams in the field. The teams usually consist of four to twelve members, and are seen as an experiment in international community living and working. There are independent PBI chapters in fourteen countries, with an international office in London that serves as a clearinghouse. Decisions regarding operations of the various projects are taken by international project committees consisting of returned team members, regional experts, and PBI staff and volunteers. The general assembly, with representation from country groups and the projects, meets every three years for policy and mandate issues, while an international council makes decisions in the interim. Finally, the organization publishes a monthly newsletter, *Project Bulletin,* as a vehicle to inform its members and the attentive public. The *Bulletin* contains news of the field projects and provides political analysis of various human rights situations.

Patrick G. Coy

References

Clark, Daniel N. "Transnational Action for Peace: The Peace Brigades International." *Transnational Perspectives* 9, no. 4 (1983): 7–11.

Coy, Patrick G. "Protective Accompaniment: How Peace Brigades International Secures Political Space and Human Rights Nonviolently." In *Nonviolence: Social and Psychological Issues,* edited by V.K. Kool. Lanham, Md.: University Press of America, 1994.

Dijkstra, Piet. "Peace Brigades International." *Gandhi Marg* 7 (October 1986): 391–406.

Siedle-Khan, Robert. "Peace Brigades International, 1981–1992: A Significant Presence." Paper presented at the Sri Lanka Seminar of the Swedish Foreign Office and the European Human Rights Foundation, Lund, Sweden, April 22, 1992.

Wiseberg, Laurie. "Protecting Human Rights Activists and NGOs: What More Can Be Done?" *Human Rights Quarterly* 13 (November 1991): 525–544.

See also HUMAN RIGHTS; WITNESS FOR PEACE

Peace People, Community of the (Northern Ireland)

The most internationally renowned of Northern Ireland's grassroots organizations advocating peace and nonviolent action in pursuit of justice. Two of its founders, Mairead Corrigan and Betty Williams, received the 1976 Nobel Peace Prize (awarded to them in 1977). The Peace People's aim is to create a "nonviolent movement towards a just and peaceful society" in Northern Ireland. They have waged their nonviolent struggle for justice in the midst of a violent, protracted civil conflict that has now lasted over a quarter-century.

Northern Ireland is locked in a sovereignty dispute in which a primarily Protestant majority of the population supports continued union with Great Britain and a primarily Catholic minority of the population desires incorporation with the Republic of Ireland. The more than three thousand who have died in this conflict have been victims of violence committed by majority and minority paramilitary groups as well as security forces. The spark for founding the Peace People was the August 1976 deaths of three children and the serious injury of their mother, Ann Maguire, all struck accidentally by the getaway car of a dying Provisional Irish Republican Army (PIRA) volunteer. It was founded by Mairead Corrigan (Ann Maguire's sister), Betty Williams, a bystander to the tragedy, and Ciaran McKeown, a journalist.

The early days of the Peace People were remarkable both in their community and cross-community contexts. The Maguires were Catholics living in the Andersonstown area of Belfast, an area historically supportive of the PIRA (a nationalist group engaged in armed struggle as a means to incorporate Northern Ireland with the Republic of Ireland). However, the day following the tragedy more than one thousand women of Andersonstown gathered at the site to demonstrate for a halt to violence, from whatever source. Despite PIRA hostility, rallies for peace in Northern Ireland throughout the summer and autumn attracted upwards of twenty-five thousand Protestant and Catholic supporters. Peace People activities attracted attention in Europe and the United States. The Peace People's financial requirements were initially met by award of the Norwegian People's Peace Prize, a populist alternative to the Nobel Peace Prize.

The Peace People's transition from mobilizing support for peace and nonviolence to institutionalizing nonviolence programs and projects for attaining social justice was marked by local political leaders' criticisms. The Peace People's grassroots, cross-sectarian orientation led its leadership to conclude that the political system in Northern Ireland, having crystallized into separate Protestant and Catholic political parties with only one biconfessional party regularly contesting elections, was itself part of the problem. Peace People ambivalence toward political solutions that maintained the party system status quo alienated some of its "peace at any price" supporters. Dilemmas posed by pressing nonviolently for social justice in a society embroiled in violent conflict created organizational tensions that were subsumed throughout 1977 by international tours and news media attention, community outreach programs to teach nonviolence, creation of a loan program to provide funding for community-initiated programs, launch of the journal *Peace by Peace,* and preparations for the first annual peace assembly. One of the most innovative of the Peace People's efforts to promote nonviolent alternatives was their paramilitary "escape route" project. They provided shelter and the means to leave Northern Ireland to paramilitary members not wanted for specific offenses who wished to abandon violence. Mairead Corrigan and Betty Williams subsequently received the 1976 Nobel Peace Prize, but public opinion critical of their decision to keep the cash prize led to decreased local popular support. Also, controversial British security and imprisonment practices in Northern Ireland once again pitted justice against peace in popular debate over the relationship between peace and justice. These controversies, along with disagreements over financial management of community projects brought matters to a head in 1980. Betty Williams and the organization's chairperson resigned, and a few months later Ciaran McKeown resumed outside employment. Of the three founders, only Mairead Corrigan remained involved with the Peace People.

Today the Peace People, with a much smaller membership, continue their direct involvement in promoting nonviolence. They advance their peace education mission by operating cross-community youth education programs and by campaigning for nonviolent alternatives in the community. They also continue their community and justice work. For example, they operate a ride service to prisons for family members of imprisoned paramilitary members to lessen their dependence on, and thus support

for, these organizations. They continue their justice mission by working for repeal of the Emergency Powers Act (which suspends in Northern Ireland several of the civil liberties and rights in place in Britain) and educating people about their rights and responsibilities under the act.

Nathalie J. Frensley

References

Bell, J. Bowyer. *The Irish Troubles: A Generation of Violence, 1967–1992.* New York: St. Martin's, 1993.
Deutsch, Richard. *Mairead Corrigan, Betty Williams.* Woodbury, N.J.: Barron's, 1977.
McKeown, Ciaran. *The Passion of Peace.* Belfast: Blackstaff, 1984.

See also CORRIGAN, MAIREAD, AND BETTY WILLIAMS; IRA HUNGER STRIKES, 1980–1981; NORTHERN IRELAND CIVIL RIGHTS ASSOCIATION

Peace Pledge Union (Great Britain)

Pacifist organization composed of individuals willing to sign a formal pledge of renunciation of all wars. Influenced at various stages by the theories of Richard Gregg, Barthélemy de Ligt, and Mohandas Gandhi, members of the Peace Pledge Union attempted to apply the principles and strategy of pacifist nonviolent action to the British context. Membership reached a high point in 1940, but the successes of Hitler prompted many to give up their pacifist beliefs and withdraw their union membership.

The Sheppard Peace Movement was founded in July 1935 by Dick Sheppard, as a pacifist response to emerging European military crises. That group became the Peace Pledge Union (PPU) in May of 1936. The PPU was founded as a pacifist society composed of persons willing to sign a pledge renouncing all wars. Initially, members embraced the strategy of "nonviolent coercion" found in Richard Gregg's *Power of Nonviolence* (published in Britain in 1935) and attempted to apply this strategy to the European context. They believed in the efficacy of training highly disciplined pacifists willing to engage in individual nonviolent direct action that would eventually lead to the end of war. Sheppard also founded the *Peace News,* a pacifist newspaper that served as the official publication of the organization until 1961.

By April 1937, dissent had risen regarding "Greggism," and PPU members became engaged in a struggle about the nature of pacifism that would last for decades. By the end of 1937, PPU shifted its focus in favor of creating a mass movement to prevent war. In February 1937, the pacifist socialist organization No More War Movement merged with the PPU, and, in a March 1938 policy manifesto, the PPU outlined a more militant strategy, promoting, among other actions, demonstrations, "seditious acts," and tax resistance. That spring, for example, they advocated noncooperation with air raid precaution procedures. During the Munich crisis in the summer of 1938, PPU offered to dispatch five hundred trained pacifists to the Sudetenland region of Czechoslovakia to intervene for peaceful resolution. The offer was rebuffed.

In the late 1930s, the PPU shifted away from pacifist practice to a more religiously based and apolitical pacifism. Many members formed a stance of "pacifist appeasement" to avoid war with Germany and were criticized as pro-Nazi. A 1939 "Stop the War" campaign and their support of conscientious objectors incurred the wrath of many. Nonetheless, PPU's membership peaked at 136,000 in 1940, and it was considered the largest pacifist organization ever at that time. However, in the light of Hitler's military and political expansion and the difficulties PPU encountered in applying pacifist theories to combating fascism, membership began to decline. The PPU was reluctant to oppose the war effort, and devoted much of their energy to relief work.

Although the union lost members and influence during World War II, the group continued to advocate for pacifist causes. During the decades after the war, they often focused on preventing the production of atomic and hydrogen bombs. At a PPU conference in London in November 1949, one of the study groups established was a Non-violence Commission devoted to the philosophical study and practical application of Gandhian principles of nonviolence in Britain. This commission launched "Operation Gandhi" in January 1952 and organized antimilitarism and antinuclear civil disobedience actions in Britain. It was this group that later formed the nucleus for the foundation of the Direct Action Committee in 1957.

Although the PPU is still active in Great Britain, its influence has never been as great at it was prior to World War II. From 1936 to the late 1950s, the PPU was the dominant organization in Great Britain applying theories of nonviolent resistance to a pacifist agenda.

Brad Bennett

References

Ceadel, Martin. *Pacifism in Britain, 1914–1945: The Defining of a Faith*. Oxford: Clarendon, 1980.

Taylor, Richard. *Against the Bomb: The British Peace Movement, 1958–1965*. Oxford: Clarendon, 1988.

See also DIRECT ACTION COMMITTEE AGAINST NUCLEAR WAR; GREGG, RICHARD

Peace Studies

A field of study focused on war prevention, social and economic justice, and environmental health, and requiring the integration of interpersonal and systems-oriented approaches through the contribution of a variety of disciplines. In the United States the discipline emerged in the aftermath of World War I, a war that shocked many intellectuals' sensibilities, as it was the first European world conflict in nearly a century. Long in infancy, the field blossomed in the aftermath of the Vietnam War, a war many considered especially notable for its brutality and meaninglessness. By the mid-1980s, peace studies could be said to have come of age, with approximately three hundred programs in colleges and universities across the nation.

As defined by Dan Thomas in the *Guide to Careers and Graduate Education in Peace Studies,* peace studies "analyzes the causes of war, violence, and systemic oppression, and explores processes by which conflict and change can be managed so as to maximize justice while minimizing violence." It encompasses "the study of economic, political and social systems at the local, national and global levels, and of ideology, culture, and technology as they relate to conflict and change." These many dimensions of human life are investigated from a wide range of ideological and philosophical perspectives. As a field of inquiry, peace studies draws its methods and scholars primarily from the traditional disciplines in the social and behavioral sciences—anthropology, economics, history, psychology, political science, and sociology. However, the humanities and natural sciences both make significant contributions.

A few fundamental assumptions underlie this broadly defined new field: an orientation to nonviolent social change; a belief in interdisciplinary study; a concern for policy formulation; and a willingness to be value-explicit. The last item signifies a commitment to making explicit the values and the assumptions of the researcher. Central among such widely shared values is a commitment to peace as a value in itself. As John Hurst writes in the *World Encyclopedia of Peace,* peace studies have as their ultimate purpose making a contribution to a "just and peaceful world that will sustain human life in full dignity into the indefinite future."

Beyond these core assumptions are some sharp differences among those engaged in peace studies. Members of the field have widely divergent views on the meaning of peace itself. They worry much about such issues as an "implicit ideological bias" and the "activist orientation" of peace studies curricula. A central question has been whether or not peace can be defined simply as the absence of war ("negative peace") or whether the concept encompasses not only the absence of war but the presence of social justice ("positive peace"). Those wanting peace to be narrowly defined hold that broadening the concept reduces its clarity. The peace researchers most often held emblematic of the two poles of this debate are Johan Galtung, who coined the phrase "positive peace," and Kenneth Boulding, who argued for the more narrow definition of peace.

A field so broadly defined in both its negative and positive meanings mandates for its practitioners something beyond the traditions of established academic fields of study. Faculty in peace studies generally hold to nontraditional pedagogical beliefs: its professors dare to think aloud with students; both the facilitator and the class unabashedly struggle to find coherence, answers, and meanings in the complex processes of social change; both accept that there are no simple unified answers. Such an approach demands much of faculty and students. It calls for liberal sprinklings of rationalism, idealism, optimism, and spirituality, as well as healthy doses of empiricism, pluralism, skepticism, and materialism. It demands recognition of the role personal values play in all analyses of economic, political, and social issues, as well as an ability to grasp the fundamental economic, political, and social structures that give shape to issues.

This pedagogy favors a Socratic approach to learning, a consciousness of worldviews, a high tolerance for the perplexities of the human condition, a sensitivity to issues of gender, race, and class, and a global vision. It requires some humility, a recognition that none of us can think about the process of peace in its entirety and that being a jack of all trades is to be master of none. Peace studies courses and programs often have titles that suggest their particular definitional positions within the field. These include peace and security studies (or global or world security studies); peace and justice studies; women, war, and peace; peace and world order studies; peace and global studies; peace and conflict studies; peacemaking and conflict resolution studies. Underlying each of these approaches are discourses on the interrelationship of peace (in both its negative and positive connotations) research, education, and action.

The field has been moving steadily toward the "positive peace" approach as articulated by Galtung, with its broad understanding that global security encompasses many more threats to human survival than war. In fact, Third World poverty, environmental degradation, inequities based on gender, class, and race, violence against women, political oppression, and human rights violations are now woven into most peace studies programs. At this particular moment of post–cold war history, however, the direction of evolution is less clear. Conflict resolution, with particular emphasis on the use of third parties and mediation, is becoming a focus of many programs. Thus, many approaches encompass training in settings that range from neighborhood centers to divorce mediation facilities to institutions dealing with mediation in public budgetary and environmental disputes to the building of university-level training and research programs related to national and international relations.

Particularly problematic for the field, however, is the absence of consensus on just where and how peace studies intersects with nonviolent action theory and practice. George Lopez poses three central questions for post–cold war peace studies curriculum development. First, in what ways are people actually dying from political and social violence in this post–cold war world? Second, what forces and factors bring forth this violence? And, third, what role can nonviolent approaches to conflict have in such a world? Despite an impressive list of successful or partially successful nonviolent struggles in the international arena (the Philippines in 1986, the Eastern European revolutions in 1989, the defeat of apartheid and the election of Nelson Mandela in South Africa in 1993, to mention a few), Carolyn Stephenson argues that neither the peace studies community nor the general public has a real appreciation of nonviolent action. What notice is taken is mere "lip service," without any clear appreciation of how successful the strategy of "large numbers of people withdrawing support from a repressive government or an invading state" can be. While the hope for some is that strategic planning for nonviolent action will become as effective as it is for "military action or more conventional political action," Stephenson nevertheless concludes: "We are left with tremendous inconsistencies in our thinking. We alternately advocate and hesitate over humanitarian intervention but seem unable to imagine more powerful methods—perhaps equally costly but less violent."

The future success of peace studies requires that the field respond to a complex mélange of global economic, social, religious, gender, and environmental conflicts. This circumstance precludes any simple explanation or moralistic naiveté. As many peace studies scholars have pointed out, one should not pretend that models for a peaceful world order are readily available, and it would be equally disingenuous to suppose that ideas of peace and community have much of a chance unless peace studies can wholly and vigorously embrace nonviolence in theory and practice.

Linda Rennie Forcey

References

Alger, Chad. "Peace Studies at the Crossroads: Where Else?" *Peace Studies: Past and Future* 504 (July 1989): 117–127.

Forcey, Linda Rennie, ed. *Peace: Meanings, Politics, Strategies.* New York: Praeger, 1989.

Hurst, John. *World Encyclopedia of Peace.* New York: Pergamon, 1986.

Lopez, George A. "Challenges to Curriculum Development in the Post–Cold War Era." In *Peace and World Security Studies: A Curriculum Guide,* edited by Michael T. Klare. Boulder, Colo.: Lynne Rienner, 1994.

Stephenson, Carolyn M. "New Approaches to International Peacemaking in the Post–Cold War World." In *Peace and World Security Studies: A Curriculum Guide,* edited by Michael T. Klare. Boulder, Colo.: Lynne Rienner, 1994.

Thomas, Daniel C., ed. *Guide to Careers and Graduate Education in Peace Studies.* Amherst, Mass.: Five College Program in Peace and World Security Studies, 1987.

See also FEMINISM; PACIFISM

Peck, James (1914–1993)

United States labor organizer, conscientious objector, war resister, and civil rights activist. He helped organize and participated in numerous nonviolent direct action campaigns for over forty years.

In the early 1930s, Peck left Harvard University after one year, rejected his affluent background, and found work as a seaman. He helped organize the National Maritime Union, and was beaten by New York police during a 1936 seaman's strike. Thereafter, he continued to support union activities in a new capacity as a reporter for the Federated Press.

On the first day of registration for the draft in 1940, Peck declared himself a conscientious objector. He spoke out against war, worked actively with the War Resisters League, and wrote a labor column for *The Conscientious Objector.* During the war, Peck was jailed for over two years for his antiwar activities. While at the federal prison in Danbury, Connecticut, he helped organize a successful inmate's strike against racial segregation in the mess hall. He was among a group who burned their draft cards at the White House in February 1947.

After World War II, Peck began to participate in direct action campaigns against racial segregation. An active member of the Congress of Racial Equality (CORE) from 1946, he edited the *CORElator* for seventeen years and organized many civil rights protests. Peck was part of the 1947 Journey of Reconciliation, cosponsored by CORE and the Fellowship of Reconciliation, in which an interracial group rode buses through the upper South to test the 1946 Supreme Court decision outlawing segregation on interstate travel. He also participated in the 1961 Freedom Ride, during which he received a severe beating by a mob of people in Birmingham, Alabama. Peck used the beating to his advantage to publicize the civil rights cause. He published *Freedom Ride* in 1962, a partially autobiographical chronicle of direct action campaigns for civil rights during the late 1950s and early 1960s.

Peck also continued to engage in nonviolent struggle against war as a long-time member of the War Resisters League. He organized demonstrations against nuclear tests and civil defense drills and in support of prisoner amnesty and conscientious objectors. During the Vietnam War, Peck helped organize protest demonstrations and counseled young men to resist the draft. He was arrested several times for antiwar civil disobedience in Washington, D.C., including the May Day demonstration in 1971.

James Peck was an important leader in progressive causes for over forty years. A proponent of "revolutionary nonviolence," he consistently advocated for and organized nonviolent direct action for labor, antiwar, civil rights, and other movements throughout his lifetime. Peck died in Minneapolis, Minnesota, on July 12, 1993.

Brad Bennett

References

Cooney, Robert, and Helen Michalowski, eds. *The Power of the People: Active Nonviolence in the United States.* From an original text by Marty Jezer. Culver City, Calif.: Peace Press, 1977; 2nd ed. Philadelphia: New Society, 1987.

Peck, James. *Freedom Ride.* New York: Simon and Schuster, 1962.

See also CIVIL RIGHTS MOVEMENT; CONGRESS OF RACIAL EQUALITY; FREEDOM RIDES, 1961; VIETNAM WAR OPPOSITION

Pérez Esquivel, Adolfo (b. 1931)

Secretary-general and founder of Servicio, Paz y Justicia (Service for Peace and Justice), the Latin American human rights organization, and recipient of the 1980 Nobel Prize for Peace. Pérez Esquivel was born in Buenos Aires, Argentina, in 1931. After training as an architect and sculptor he was appointed professor of architecture in 1956. In 1974, he relinquished his teaching post in order to devote all his time and energy to the work of coordinating the activities of various nonviolent human rights organizations in Latin America.

Pérez Esquivel, a devout Catholic, was inspired by the writings of Thomas Merton and the example of Charles de Foucauld, founder of the Little Brothers of Jesus. Through his professional training and experience he became involved in pre-Colombian art and culture, and

Adolfo Pérez Esquivel. Photo by Jim Forest.

he became aware of the perilous conditions of poverty and oppression of many native peoples of Latin America. In the late 1960s, Pérez Esquivel became associated with a Gandhian religious communitarian group.

The escalating violence in Argentina in the late 1960s and early 1970s had a deep effect upon him. Pérez Esquivel met with other human rights activists at several conferences of church, labor, student, and communitarian groups. At one of these, in Costa Rica in 1971, *Servicio de Paz y Justicia en Latina America* was founded. In 1972, he took part in a public fast to protest the violence on the part of both leftist and rightist guerrilla groups, and the next year he started the periodical *Paz y Justicia* (Peace and Justice). In 1974, Pérez Esquivel became the secretary-general of *Servicio,* and the group adopted his periodical as its official organ.

Civil strife in Argentina intensified after 1976 when the leaders of a military junta took power and began a vicious campaign of repression against alleged left-wing elements. Thousands were jailed, tortured, and "disappeared" by the police, the armed forces, and death squads in the following years of the "dirty war." Pérez Esquivel denounced these crimes and helped organize weekly demonstrations by mothers of the many children and husbands who had disappeared. In April 1977, he was detained and imprisoned for fourteen months.

Pérez Esquivel accepted the Nobel Prize "in the name of the people of Latin America . . .

in the name of my indigenous brothers and sisters, the peasants, workers, and young people—in the name of the thousands of members of religious orders and of men and women of goodwill who relinquish their privileges to share their life and path of the poor, and who struggle to build a new society." Describing his work he said: "We have denounced the killing of generals, colonels, and innocent relatives of military officials. We have no connections with political parties of any sort, much less armed groups. We act by means of evangelical nonviolence, which we see as a force for liberation."

Irwin Abrams

References

Pérez Esquivel, Adolfo. *Christ in a Poncho.* Edited by Charles Antoine. Translated by Robert R. Barr. Maryknoll, N.Y.: Orbis, 1983.

See also HUMAN RIGHTS; MADRES DE PLAZA DE MAYO; MERTON, THOMAS; NOBEL PEACE PRIZE

Persia, Reform Movement, 1880–1909

Reformist movement that evolved into a constitutionalist revolution in Persia. Led by merchants and *ulama* (Shi'ite theologians), the consititutionalists primarily employed two major methods of nonviolent direct action to pressure the shah for reforms: merchants' general strikes and taking *bast* (seeking sanctuary in protest). The movement was eventually successful when the shah was deposed in July 1909 and a new constitution endorsed.

In late-nineteenth-century Persia, the ultimate law according to which the shah ruled was the divine law of Shi'ite Islam. The *ulama* were the interpreters of that law. Reformers began to advocate the establishment of a parliament alongside the religious law. This was the largest issue of contention from 1880 to 1909. In addition, Persia was beginning to move from isolation to international cooperation, which some orthodox religious figures resisted. In the 1880s, the shah had begun to sell trade concessions to foreign figures, provoking the wrath of Persians who didn't like this foreign presence.

In 1890, the shah sold the right to monopoly over tobacco collection, manufacture, and export to a British businessman, triggering widespread discontent. A chief religious figure issued a decree prohibiting the smoking of to-bacco until the concessions were abolished. In February, merchants presented petitions to the shah. The government eventually capitulated to the pressure by religious leaders and merchants, withdrew from the contract, and paid compensation to the British company.

During the 1890s, the economy took a turn for the worse. In 1895, riots arose in Tabriz over grain-hoarding. The *ulama* led opposition to proposed foreign loans in October 1897, primarily by putting up posters accusing the prime minister, Amin al-Dawla, of being a traitor. In March, 1898, *ulama* led crowds in Shushtar in a clash with troops that led to the resignation of the governor. In May unpaid troops posted placards of complaint near their barracks. The shah dismissed Amin al-Dawla in June 1898. Agitation increased, fueled by economic unrest, opposition to the growth of foreign influence, and dissatisfaction with the shah.

By September 1900, the Persian administration had raised customs tariffs, provoking opposition from merchants and riots in early 1901 in three major cities. In August 1902, religious leaders in Tehran threatened to withdraw their allegiance to the shah if the current prime minister, Amin al-Sultan, remained in office. Amin al-Sultan resigned due to this and other pressure, but opposition continued toward the new prime minister, 'Ain al-Daula. New customs regulations permitting the employment of foreigners as customs officials in March 1903 fomented even more resistance. Protests occurred in major cities in 1904.

By 1905, opposition to specific policies had evolved into a widespread constitutionalist revolution movement. In April, leading merchants in Tehran closed their shops and took *bast* in a shrine to protest the customs administration. Taking *bast* is a traditional Persian practice of seeking sanctuary in mosques or shrines in order to gain religious protection from arbitrary justice and to draw attention to a certain issue. Governmental attempts to limit this custom had led some *bastis* to begin seeking sanctuary in foreign embassies as well. On January 12, 1906, two thousand people took *bast,* demanding the establishment of a state house of justice. By the middle of June, opposition to the government was widespread, led by religious leaders preaching to large congregations.

On July 11, 1906, Prime Minister 'Ain al-Daula ordered the arrest of a leading constitutionalist in Tehran, a group of students attempted to rescue him, and guards shot one of the students. Shops closed in protest and several huge processions were staged. On July 19, fifty merchants and students took *bast* in the British embassy. By August 2, the *bastis* grew to fourteen thousand, and included many guild workers. During negotiations of July and August, the protesters demanded the removal of 'Ain al-Daula and the establishment of a National Consultative Assembly and a constitution. The shah agreed to the demands, the *bast* ended on August 10, and shops opened the next day. Elections occurred in September and the Assembly opened in October.

Fundamentalist opposition to the Assembly began to grow, however, as militancy increased and secret societies proliferated. From June to September 1907, five hundred anticonstitutionalists took *bast* in a shrine in Tehran. The new shah (the last had died in early 1907) also opposed the constitution and Assembly. Violent clashes occurred and former Prime Minister Amin al-Sultan was shot. In December 1907, the Assembly building was attacked, but the Assembly deputies and their supporters successfully defended themselves. In June 1908, the Assembly deputies were successful in preventing a coup by the shah's soldiers.

Following this overthrow, constitutionalism reemerged. Demonstrations were staged and petitions were made to the shah. Another constitutionalist *bast* occurred in the Ottoman embassy in December 1908 accompanied by shop closings. Finally, on May 5, 1909, the shah restored the constitutional government, and in July, an Extraordinary General Council deposed the shah and opposition to the constitution was suppressed. The new Assembly was opened by the new shah in November 1909. Thus, the constitutionalist movement was eventually successful in applying pressure for reform primarily by employing *basts* and merchants' general strikes.

Brad Bennett

References

Bakhash, Shaul. "The Failure of Reform: The Prime Ministership of Amin al-Dawla 1897–8." In *Qajar Iran: Political, Social and Cultural Change, 1800–1925*, edited by Edmund Bosworth and Carole Hillenbrand. Edinburgh: Edinburgh University Press, 1983.

Browne, Edward G. *The Persian Revolution of 1905–1909*. London: Frank Cass, 1966.

Martin, Vanessa. *Islam and Modernism: The Iranian Revolution of 1906*. London: I.B. Tauris, 1989.

See also IRANIAN REVOLUTION, 1963–1979; SANCTUARY MOVEMENT

Philippines People Power Revolution, 1986

Popular uprising transpiring over several days in February 1986 at military camps Crame and Aguinaldo located on Epifanio de los Santos Avenue in Quezon City, the nation's capital. At its peak it was a stand-off between troops loyal to President Ferdinand Marcos and a small faction of the armed forces led by Defense Minister Juan Ponce Enrile and General Fidel Ramos, in which the latter were surrounded and protected by thousands of unarmed civilians.

Although it appeared to the outsider to be a sudden event, it was the climax of a long struggle to unseat Marcos. After enduring thirteen years of martial law, the assassination of Benigno Aquino—Marcos's chief political rival—and another corrupt and violent national election in early February 1986, the Filipinos' otherwise remarkable tolerance of abusive power at last had reached its limit. Aware of the opposition but still confident that the vast majority would support him, Marcos announced a snap presidential election for February 7. Corazon Aquino, wife of the late Benigno Aquino, ran against Marcos under the banner of LABAN, an acronym for *Lakas ng Bayan* ("Power of the People").

The uprising began when, during the counting of votes, thirty of the government's tabulators walked out in protest against the election fraud. Whereupon, the Catholic Bishops Conference of the Philippines issued a document that was read from pulpits throughout the nation, condemning the election as fraudulent and declaring it the people's duty to resist, nonviolently, a regime that had lost its credibility and therefore its authority to govern. A few days later, Minister Enrile and General Ramos, protected by two battalions of soldiers led by well-trained officers associated with the Reform the Armed Forces Movement (RAM), suddenly mutinied, declaring Mrs. Aquino the true winner of the election. The discontent in the military, which had given rise to the Reform Movement, resulted from endemic poor pay and the general lack of professionalism. The average soldier's pay was less than that of a garbage collector in Manila, and promotions were based on personal connections with the commander in chief rather than on the performance of duty.

As events transpired, the armed forces faction led by Enrile and Ramos seized control of the two major Philippine military camps—first Camp Aguinaldo and later Camp Crame. This became possible because soon after Enrile and Ramos took their stand and announced to the mass media that they could no longer in good conscience remain loyal to a corrupt regime, hundreds and later hundreds of thousands of civilian sympathizers assembled along the wide avenue separating the two camps, creating a human barricade. Deciding it would be easier to defend themselves from Camp Crame, and encouraged by the overwhelming support of the masses, Ramos and Enrile moved across the avenue to take their stand at Crame.

Marcos's response was swift, as expected. By this time, the whole nation was emotionally involved because all the major TV networks and radio stations were covering the events. In fact, the news media played a major role in mobilizing the people. Suddenly word came that two Marine battalions were approaching the camp in armored tanks and taking their positions on the avenue in front of the camp, to await the order to fire. Marcos was heard to say, "We'll wipe them out." A radio commentator said, "A shooting war between the forces unleashed by Malacanang [the presidential palace] and two battalions of soldiers loyal to Enrile and Ramos appears to be inevitable."

In addition to the tank invasion, there were threats of artillery fire and bombing overhead. But the rebels held their ground because the civilians, instead of retreating, pushed forward as the tanks rolled in to take their offensive positions. Some kneeled in prayer before the oncoming tanks while others waved familiar religious symbols. Moved by the earnest faces of their fellow countrymen and the customary religious symbols, the tank commanders were compelled to retreat in puzzlement, to the accompaniment of loud cheers from the huge crowd. "We're sitting ducks," one of Marcos's officers complained. "They're psyching our troops, and we're all falling down without a shot being fired."

Meanwhile, there was a continuing defection of officers and soldiers to the rebel cause. Commanders from seven regions of the country had defected by the afternoon of the second day. There was a minimum of peripheral shooting as TV and radio stations were taken over by the rebel soldiers, resulting in only a few reported casualties. It was all over in seventy-seven hours. One day Mr. Marcos's authority looked as impregnable as ever, sheltered by loyal generals in all branches of the military. The next day part of his command structure had split away to support the nucleus of a new government. Suddenly there were two governments of the Philippines. Then Marcos lost the major news media networks, his proclamation of a state of emergency was ignored, and by the evening of the fourth day he was gone!

What Marcos did not reckon with was the mysterious power of people when united for a common cause and determined to reach their collective goal. Beginning with the evidence of election fraud, the Filipino people began to sense their own power—the power of noncooperation—to oust the dictator and set up a democratic government. This is what gave them the courage to risk their lives.

Representing all political groupings and social classes, the demonstrators eventually encircled the camp. As the armored tanks rolled in, they greeted the soldiers with hugs, sharing their food and cigarettes. Some tied yellow ribbons on the guns and inserted flowers in the gun barrels. At this display of goodwill shown toward "enemy soldiers," the latter were literally disarmed. It was the presence of their fellow countrymen, in such huge numbers and accompanied by familiar religious symbols, that caused the soldiers to retreat. Thus the "inevitable" did not occur.

While it was a face-off between two armed forces, the actual contest turned out to be one between the Marcos forces and the unarmed civilians who rallied to the support of Enrile and Ramos. What actually transpired bore no resemblance to any of the possible scenarios expected. Probably for the first time in modern history unarmed civilians were able to prevent a clash between opposing armed forces, thus forestalling a massive bloodbath. It is a striking example of how the sheer presence of living human beings linked arm in arm—though unarmed—and pursuing the same end with determination, faith, and courage, can be more powerful than the military machinery protecting a long-entrenched dictator. A desperate mutiny by a handful of officers and men, outnumbered ten to one, had mushroomed into a full-scale rebellion.

Although it was a civilian-backed military revolt during those four days of February, in a larger perspective it was a military-backed civil-

P

ian revolt. Enrile sensed this when he responded to a visiting politician who was proposing a new government by military junta. "The power is not with us," he said. "It is with the people out there." It was, in fact, the triumph of the people over the forces of repression.

How does one account for such a phenomenon? For one thing, as Gandhi taught, governments are fragile in themselves because they depend on the people for reinforcement. If people suddenly withdraw their cooperation in every detail, the government will come to a standstill. The truth is that all human power depends ultimately on the consent and cooperation of those over whom the power is wielded. This is precisely what happened to the Marcos regime. Once enough people had withdrawn their support and consistently demonstrated their protest, his government collapsed, particularly when military officers and their soldiers ignored their orders and joined the protest. The chief lesson to be learned is that consent and cooperation are not inevitable, as often supposed, not even when absolute power is wielded absolutely. Obedience to authority remains essentially voluntary, and thus it can be voluntarily withdrawn.

What transpired in that four-day scenario in February won for Filipinos high respect around the world. It was not a revolution in any total sense, as we know from hindsight, but it did begin to restore the democratic process. Under pressure from the Filipino people and given declining support from the Reagan administration, Marcos fled the country on February 25, 1986, and Corazon Aquino took her place as the Philippines' legally elected president.

Douglas J. Elwood

References

Elwood, Douglas J. *Philippine Revolution 1986: Model of Nonviolent Change.* Quezon City, Philippines: New Day, 1986.

Mamot, Patricio R. *People Power: A Profile of Filipino Heroism.* Quezon City, Philippines: New Day, 1986.

See also AQUINO, CORAZON

Picketing

Method of protest or persuasion during which one maintains a physical presence at a site that is significant to an issue being contested. Picketing consists of standing, sitting, or walking in front of a place, using the mechanism of appeal to call attention to or effect change regarding a specific concern. Placards, signs, and banners may be a part of the picketing. Sometimes, the pickets may attempt to communicate with management, employees, politicians, or bystanders to promote their position, either verbally or with leaflets. Often, the pickets walk in a circle holding signs and chanting. Picketing may or may not be illegal.

Picketing has been most often associated with labor strikes. Striking workers picket a factory in an effort to deter strikebreakers from accepting work and to deter fellow strikers from returning to work before a settlement. In this case, picketing acts as a means of informing third parties of the existence of the strike and the issues in contention, as a means of protesting management's position, and as a means of building solidarity among strikers.

Pickets are often used as a protest accompanying other political and economic noncooperation. During the Indian nationalist campaign in the 1930s, pickets were conducted at law courts to urge litigants to use the village tribunals endorsed by the Indian National Congress, at opium and liquor shops to urge people not to buy those items, and at shops selling boycotted goods to urge people not to patronize them.

References

Sharp, Gene. *The Politics of Nonviolent Action.* Boston: Porter Sargent, 1973.

See also INDIAN NATIONAL CONGRESS; METHODS OF NONVIOLENT ACTION; STRIKES

Plowshares Movement

A campaign of civil disobedience emerging in the 1980s and 1990s in the United States and Europe, in which groups of activists protested nuclear weapons and the military system by symbolic and actual property destruction. Taking its name from the biblical prophesies of Isaiah and Micah to "beat swords into plowshares," the movement began following the actions of eight men and women, including Daniel and Philip Berrigan, at the General Electric plant in King of Prussia, Pennsylvania, where nose cones for the Mark 12A nuclear warhead were manufactured and tested. Over the following decade and a half, approximately forty "plowshares actions" took place in the United States, Great Britain, Australia, Sweden, and the Netherlands.

In the 1980 protest at the GE plant, the demonstrators ripped apart blueprints marked "Top Secret," poured vials of their own blood over the nose cones and prints, and then joined together in prayer, waiting to be arrested. The group told arresting officers and, later, trial judge Samuel Salus III, that they had not come to the GE plant to break the law, but to fulfill the prophecies of Isaiah and Micah. They also intended their action to "expose the criminality of nuclear weaponry and corporate piracy.... We committed civil disobedience at General Electric because this genocidal entity is the fifth leading producer of weaponry in the U.S.... Through the Mark 12A, the threat of first-strike nuclear war grows more imminent...."

The King of Prussia action began a new and dramatic campaign of resistance to the testing, manufacturing, and deployment of nuclear weapons. The movement itself had its origins in opposition to the Vietnam War. At that time, convinced the United States was committing genocide in Vietnam and discouraged by the intransigence of government officials, the Berrigans and others decided to take direct nonviolent action by invading Selective Service offices in Baltimore, Maryland, in October 1967, and again in Catonsville, Maryland, in May 1968. Over the next few years antiwar activists held similar protests at selective service offices in Milwaukee, Wisconsin; Camden, New Jersey; and elsewhere around the country. In these events, protesters removed file drawers filled with the names of draft-eligible men, poured vials of blood over the records, and burned them with a "homemade napalm" of soap chips and gasoline, mixed from a formula from a Green Beret handbook. As the files burned, the demonstrators waited quietly for FBI agents to arrive, knowing the consequences for their actions might well be prison.

This willingness to damage or destroy government property symbolically, by the pouring of blood over planes, submarines, and missile sites, and literally, by pounding on control panels and other parts of planes and ships with hammers, bewildered some who might otherwise have supported the Berrigans and friends' opposition to nuclear weapons and militarism. Indeed, the plowshares activists use of hammers to damage planes and ships frequently angered federal judges presiding at their trials. The ac-

tivists contended that as there is no "proper" use for atomic weapons, these objects could not be considered "property." Moreover, they argued, atomic weapons are tantamount to flying concentration camps and hence are a form of potentially indiscriminate mass murder. Thus, their acts of symbolic and physical destruction may break the laws of the state, but are in obedience to a higher law.

Plowshares activists also argued in court that certain international agreements, for example the Nuremberg principles, both prohibit governments from preparing for wars of mass extermination, and oblige citizens to protest any such plans by their governments. International treaties signed by the United States and other governments offer a legitimate framework for popular resistance to crimes by the state, and provide a legal basis for defense against imprisonment or fines because, as written, they supersede national laws.

Plowshares activists' efforts to use the so-called necessity defense in their trials commonly failed. They challenged the court to acknowledge that if a house is burning, it is necessary and right, and can not be considered a crime, to break down the door and rescue people inside. By the same reasoning, they sought to convince judges and juries that nuclear weapons threaten to set the world on fire and, therefore, it is just, and necessary, for people to take immediate, direct, action to prevent this imminent danger. Federal judges, however, generally disallowed this defense and cast the protesters' actions in more narrow legal terms, such as the question of trespass.

Those who were engaged in plowshares actions were more profoundly influenced and mobilized by the convictions of their religious faith than members of more politically oriented peace and social justice groups. Before taking part in an action, plowshares activists spent long periods together studying and interpreting books of the Bible, praying, and carefully articulating the need to enact their commitment to peace in real terms and in real places. Similarly, they often tried to live their whole lives in accordance with their convictions; thus, working in soup kitchens, providing hospitality (food, shelter, clothing, moral support for the poor and homeless), and damaging submarines, planes, and missile sites, were all expressions of the same motivation.

While many plowshares activists were devout Catholics, not all were practicing Christians. Still, the plowshares movement itself was firmly grounded in the teachings of the Bible, and in the tradition of Christian pacifism as practiced by the late Dorothy Day and the Catholic Worker movement. Another important influence on the plowshares movement is the witness of priests, nuns, and Catholic laypeople in Central and South America, many of whom have given their lives in the struggles against oligarchy and dictatorship, and whose belief in "liberation theology," putting biblical teachings into everyday practice, has inspired peace and social activists throughout the world.

In many ways, referring to the acts of protest and "witness" of the Berrigans and others as a "movement" is a misnomer. Plowshares activists had no board of directors, no dues-paying members, no central office out of which business was done, and no hierarchy of leaders and followers. Most plowshares activists lived in voluntary poverty, refusing to pay taxes, and declining to own private property. They often lived together in small communities, some in Catholic Worker houses located in tough urban neighborhoods, others in more rural settings, sharing what they had with one another and with those less fortunate. Community is a very important part of the plowshares movement. By living together as a community, rather than in more traditional units, plowshares activists are more able to share housework, child care, and living expenses. When someone goes to prison for beating swords into plowshares, other members work to maintain a loving, supportive environment for the jailed activist's family. It was the common bonds of commitments and values that created a network for similar actions.

Plowshares activists had no illusions about disarming either their own nations, or a world that continued to bristle with conventional and nuclear weapons even after the cold war ended. Their numbers were small, but the impact they made on jurors, judges, their fellow peace activists, and many others was substantial.

For example, the jury foreman of the Griffiss Plowshares trial stated that, while she still believed the defendants committed a crime when they damaged B-52 bombers, their moving testimony and their witness for peace changed her views on the arms race, forcing her to rethink what it meant to be a practicing Christian in a world bristling with nuclear weapons. Thomas Gumbleton, auxiliary bishop of Detroit, said that Philip and Daniel Berrigan profoundly influenced his own thinking about

militarism, and that the Berrigans inspired the Catholic Church to reexamine, and even to alter, its views on war and peace. During the years she was confined at Alderson federal penitentiary for women, Plowshares activist Jean Gump received hundreds of letters from around the world, thanking her for resisting militarism and stating that the writers had been profoundly moved by Gump's acts of resistance.

Through their witness they transformed some of their critics, and even those who found them guilty were inclined to express admiration for their courage and dedication to nonviolence. The activists' philosophy was: "We're in it for the long haul." Working for peace and social justice was a lifetime commitment and the consequences—prison, poverty, being misunderstood and ostracized, even by some fellow activists—were simply part of the price for remaining true to the call to beat swords into plowshares.

The cold war may be over, but nations have not beat their nuclear weapons into plowshares, preferring to maintain "strength through power," or, as the Berrigans and friends would argue, strength through nuclear terror. Until the world's governments stop starving their people in order to prepare for war, say the Berrigans and others, plowshares actions will continue, both in the United States and in other parts of the world.

Fred A. Wilcox

References
Laffin, Arthur J., and Anne Montgomery, eds. *Swords into Plowshares: Nonviolent Direct Action for Disarmament*. San Francisco: Harper and Row, 1987.
Wilcox, Fred A. *Uncommon Martyrs: The Berrigans, the Catholic Left, and the Plowshares Movement*. Reading, Mass.: Addison-Wesley, 1991.

See also BERRIGAN, DANIEL; BERRIGAN, PHILIP; CATHOLIC WORKER MOVEMENT; CATONSVILLE NINE; DAY, DOROTHY; NONVIOLENCE, PRINCIPLED; NUCLEAR WEAPONS OPPOSITION; PACIFISM; VIETNAM WAR OPPOSITION

Poor People's Campaign, 1968
A campaign that began April 22, 1968, in which thousands of indigent people camped out in shanties in Washington, D.C., in what was

referred to as Resurrection City. The goal was to live in the camp until Congress felt compelled to enact a program that would alleviate widespread poverty in the United States. The campaign ended after six weeks without any tangible, positive results.

The Poor People's Campaign was initiated by Martin Luther King, Jr., and was taken over by Ralph Abernathy, president of the Southern Christian Leadership Conference, after King's assassination on April 4, 1968. The high point of the campaign was Solidarity Day, which took place on June 19. Modeled after the 1963 March on Washington, fifty thousand people marched on the mall to demand that Congress take action to help eliminate poverty. Despite the vast numbers of poor blacks, Chicanos, American Indians, and whites who camped out for six weeks on fifteen acres of park land next to the Lincoln Memorial, the campaign was a disaster.

Torrential rainfalls during twenty-eight of the forty-two nights they spent at the campsite produced ankle-deep mud and waist-deep puddles throughout the entire site. The wood shanties began to fall apart; trash could not be picked up, and sewer, water, and electrical lines could not be put in place. Resurrection City soon became completely unlivable. Between the rainy, muddy conditions, and violence against fellow campaigners by some young people who had been chosen as leaders, the campsite population went from twenty-six hundred to five hundred within ten days. The few who remained by June 24 were arrested and forcibly evicted.

Kimberley A. Pyles

References
Carson, Clayborn, David J. Garrow, Gerald Gill, Vincent Harding, and Darlene Clark Hine, eds. *The Eyes on the Prize Civil Rights Reader.* New York: Penguin, 1991.
Gilbert, Ben W. *Ten Blocks from the White House: Anatomy of the Washington Riots of 1968.* New York: Praeger, 1968.
Viorst, Milton. *Fire in the Streets: America in the 1960s.* New York: Simon and Schuster, 1979.

See also CIVIL RIGHTS MOVEMENT; KING, MARTIN LUTHER, JR.

Property, Destruction of One's Own
Method of protest in which one's own property is voluntarily and publicly destroyed in order to demonstrate opposition to an opponent's actions or policy. Usually, care is taken so as not to harm other people or their property. In some cases, the property destroyed has been issued by a government or some other political organization and people are required to carry it on their person at all times. It is thus technically owned by the government or organization, but in a practical sense, these items become the "property" of the individuals who carry them.

During Colonial resistance to England, merchants and colonists publicly burned tea in support of an antitaxation boycott movement. One radical section of the Canadian Doukhobor religious sect burned their own homes in the first half of the twentieth century to protest government intervention and repression of dissent. Examples of property technically owned by the government but carried by individuals are passes, identity cards, registration cards, and classification cards. In 1960, the African National Congress called for the burning of "reference books," which were required for all black South Africans by the white South African government. During the American anti–Vietnam War movement in the 1960s, some young men burned draft cards to protest the war and conscription. Destroying identity cards also has been a tactic of the Palestinian intifada.

Reference
Sharp, Gene. *The Politics of Nonviolent Action.* Boston: Porter Sargent, 1973.

See also DOUKHOBORS; UNITED STATES, INDEPENDENCE MOVEMENT, 1765–1775

Publishing, Underground
Publication and dissemination of pamphlets, journals, newspapers, or books that are either illegal or that express strong political views or advance certain causes that may threaten the government or other societal institution. Literature that builds a case in opposition to, or in support of, particular or general government policies under conditions of repression or acute conflict is considered a method of nonviolent protest and persuasion. Literature that calls for widespread resistance and direct action against a government is classified more appropriately as political noncooperation. If the publication of such material is illegal under a particular regime, then the underground publishing constitutes a kind of civil disobedience. The nature of the con-

text determines whether underground publishing constitutes protest or noncooperation.

The underground movements against Nazi occupation in Poland, Norway, Denmark, and the Netherlands circulated illegal newspapers, pamphlets, and protest letters. During the 1980s, works by dissident authors in the Soviet Union were published elsewhere and then smuggled into the Soviet Union. These dissident publications were called *samizdat,* and the volume of such underground works became quite large. An "underground press" flourished in the United States between 1967 and 1973. While not illegal and therefore not strictly "underground," these newspapers espoused political and social beliefs that were countercultural.

References
Buhle, Mary Jo, Paul Buhle, and Dan Georgakas, eds. *Encyclopedia of the American Left.* New York and London: Garland, 1990.
Sharp, Gene. *The Politics of Nonviolent Action.* Boston: Porter Sargent, 1973.

See also UNITED STATES, INDEPENDENCE MOVEMENT, 1765–1775; VIETNAM WAR OPPOSITION

Q

Quakers (Religious Society of Friends)

A Christian sect that has practiced nonviolence in working for religious, political, and social change since its origin in the 1650s. The Quakers' practice of nonviolence predates their official commitment to Christian pacifism. During the first year of the Quaker movement in England, nonviolence was part of a strategy used to combat evil. Friends believed that religious truth was inward and that any form of outward coercion would compromise that reality. They used many strategies to educate outsiders to experience the Inward Christ. In addition to preaching, debating, and issuing tracts against adherents of the established Church, Friends engaged in symbolic actions (refusing to doff hats or use titles, going naked), refused to pay fines, accepted imprisonment, and even courted martyrdom (as in New England) to show their commitment to religious truth. Although George Fox and other leaders often denounced the actions of political authorities and demanded basic reforms in society, they supported the English Commonwealth against monarchists and never advocated military rebellion. Before and after 1660, the Quakers obeyed what they saw as God's law and ignored any human law that contravened it.

During the English Commonwealth, a few Friends served in Cromwell's army and others advocated using military force against foreign governments. In 1660, in disavowing any connection with a revolutionary plot against King Charles II, Friends proclaimed that they were not rebels and had nothing to do with either establishing or pulling down government or with worldly wars. God, not Friends, created and destroyed monarchs, although Quakers often reminded Charles II that his actions might cause God to act. The English government unleashed persecution against all dissenters, using fines, imprisonment, and exile. Friends, because they refused to meet in secret or to curtail their proselytizing, bore the brunt of the oppression. Through use of the English legal system, intercession by prominent supporters with the king, publication of their sufferings, and defense of toleration, Quakers attempted to alleviate persecution for religion. The worst of the persecution ended with the ascension of James II, and after the Glorious Revolution, the 1689 Toleration Act. For Friends living in eighteenth-century England, the peace testimony and nonviolent activity remained of little importance, because they did not actively contest being barred from political office and the government did not want them in the army or navy.

The situation was very different in the English colonies in North America, particularly in Pennsylvania, where Friends had control of the Assembly. Here the peace testimony became wedded to nonviolent activities because Quakers in the Assembly refused to authorize a militia from 1682 until 1755. William Penn designed his colony to provide religious freedom; so there was no established church, no tithe, and no coercion in religious matters. So long as morality was preserved, religious differences would have no effect on the government. In order to forestall hostility by the Lenni Lenape (Delaware) Indians, Penn attempted to buy the lands used for settlement, to guarantee justice in all business transactions, to respect Native American customs, and—above all—not to threaten the Indians by military force. During the early years of settlement, Penn's plans were successful and there was no armed conflict with

Quakers vigil at the White House as a witness against the Vietnam War, May 4, 1969. Theodore B. Hetzel Photograph Collection/Swarthmore College Peace Collection.

the Indians. Eventually, Penn's nonviolent approach to the Lenni Lenape came to symbolize the Quaker attitude to politics.

Beginning in 1691, the English government fought a series of wars with France with only brief intervals of peace. The Crown expected colonies, including Pennsylvania, to contribute men and money to the war effort. The colonial governors attempted to persuade the Quaker-dominated Assembly to meet the royal requisitions. With great reluctance, the Assembly voted money in 1696, 1711, and 1740, but always with some restrictions involved so that the funds were not directly used for war matériel. The Assembly's policy was criticized by non-Quakers as leaving the colony open to attack. On those rare occasions when they openly discussed their lack of war policy, the Assembly stressed pragmatic reasons and religious liberty rather than pacifism. Outside of Pennsylvania, the Quakers prominent in government, as in Rhode Island, made no attempt to implement a pacifist policy.

After William Penn's death, the Indians in Pennsylvania were pushed back in the west and north and exploited by fur traders, new settlers, and the proprietary government. In

1755, a force of French and Indians defeated General Edward Braddock's attempt to seize Fort Duquesne. The Native Americans now began attacks upon frontier settlements. The Quaker-dominated Assembly initiated a war tax and a militia. Philadelphia Yearly Meeting, the highest administrative level comprising Friends' meetings from Pennsylvania, New Jersey, and Delaware, upset at the betrayal of pacifism, brought pressure on Quaker assemblymen to resign. Additional pressure came from England, where propaganda from non-Quakers in Pennsylvania convinced the government that Friends had neglected the defenses of the colony and would not vigorously prosecute the war. An arrangement was worked out in 1756 with enough Quakers resigning or not seeking reelection to guarantee a non-Quaker majority in the Assembly during wartime.

Friends who believed that God's bestowing peace and prosperity on Pennsylvania stemmed from their control of government sought to understand why the war occurred. They blamed the Indian attacks upon the proprietors' unjust dealing over land (particularly the 1737 Walking Purchase fraud) and formed an association to deal justly with Indians. Friends also began a policy of sending observers to conferences with the Native Americans to make sure there was no deception by the Colonial governments. A second cause of the war, according to Friends, was Quaker complicity in the slavery of Africans. In 1755, Philadelphia Yearly Meeting condemned slavery as evil and formed a committee to visit Quaker slave holders to convince them to manumit the blacks. Before the American Revolution, Friends sought to persuade members to free slaves; then, beginning with New England Yearly Meeting's decision in 1770, all American yearly meetings, including those in Maryland and North Carolina, decided that all Quakers must free their slaves or be disowned.

After 1765, Friends throughout the colonies disapproved of the new British taxes. Pennsylvania Friends, through the Assembly and through contacts with English Friends, sought to persuade Parliament to repeal the Stamp, then the Townshend, and finally the Tea Tax. Quakers began to draw back from the antitax agitation when they concluded that war rather than compromise might be the outcome. By 1775, virtually all Quakers in the Middle Colonies had withdrawn from government positions and the yearly meetings had announced opposition to war and independence. After July 1776, Friends declared that they were neutral, playing no role in either the pulling down or establishing of governments. Members who deviated from the policy of impartiality by taking a loyalty oath or joining either army would be disowned. Ultimately, nearly one-third of the eligible Quaker males in Pennsylvania would be declared nonmembers. Friends insisted that religious liberty meant that pacifists should not serve in the military nor pay for a substitute. Refusing either to sell any goods to both armies or to seek compensation for goods seized, Friends claimed that suffering a loss of property was a witness to the purity of their faith. When Quakers refused to pay taxes to a government of uncertain legitimacy, American rebels seized Quaker property. Quakers saw themselves as neutral, but the rebels thought they were really Tories, who supported the British crown.

During the war, Friends from England sent relief to America; Philadelphia Quakers did the same for New England. Quakers nursed the wounded of both sides after the battles of the Brandywine and Guilford Courthouse. Even as they freed their own slaves, Friends began agitating against the slave trade and the practice of slavery. Repudiating any political role and demanding religious liberty for their distinctive beliefs and practices, Friends during and immediately after the Revolution redefined their position in American society as agitators for good and reformers of institutions.

During the early nineteenth century, Friends made few efforts to proselytize for pacifism. Indian rights and abolition were the causes that Friends officially endorsed. A few Quakers lived among the Seneca Indians in an effort to teach them "civilized" ways of agriculture and to promote schooling. Friends constituted the overwhelming majority of members of the manumission societies. Having used peaceful persuasion to free their own slaves, Friends sought to use similar tactics in the South. English Friends began cooperating with evangelicals such as William Wilberforce and Thomas Clarkson to petition Parliament to abolish the slave trade and then to end slavery. A few American Quakers worked through abolition societies or courts to protect the rights of freed blacks, and others helped escaping slaves on the Underground Railroad.

In the nineteenth century, in England and America the general pattern was for individual Friends to work to change institutions without the official involvement of the yearly meetings. Quakers helped create penitentiaries to reform criminals, asylums for the insane, and public schools for the poor. They supported temperance and ending lotteries. Lucretia Mott symbolized those Quaker women active in Garrisonian antislavery, women's rights, and nonresistance and peace societies.

Beginning in 1827, American Quakers experienced a whole series of schisms that destroyed the unity of Friends and weakened their influence in American society. The different meetings of Friends became so hostile to each other that they could not present an effective peace witness to outsiders. Fear of secular contamination and additional schisms turned Friends inward. Opposing slavery and yet fearing war, Friends played little role in the crises that led to the Civil War. Friends showed ambivalence during the war, with the meeting officially supporting pacifism but showing sympathy for and reluctance to disown soldiers. Indiana Yearly Meeting essentially stopped enforcing the peace testimony because, of 4,500 men of military age, 1,198 served in Union ranks. Eastern Friends either paid a fee for a substitute, joined the army, or remained steadfast. The Union officials showed sympathy for the Friends' dilemma; but not so in the South, where Friends were less well known. North Carolina Quakers who refused to serve endured persecution from the Confederacy. Civilian Quakers sought to provide for the freedman. A few Quaker women began working as nurses for the soldiers and then transferred their energies to providing relief and teaching school for free blacks. Throughout the period of Reconstruction, yearly meetings sent supplies and funds to the South, with the major emphasis upon education.

In 1869, President Grant, seeking to find honest Indian agents, asked Friends to administer federal Indian agencies in Kansas and Nebraska. The government had forced the Native Americans onto reservations and now wanted Quakers to stop raids and to persuade the Indians to adopt white culture. Caught between avaricious whites and unhappy Indians and backed up with the force of the U.S. Army, the Quaker experiment in Indian relations was not a success and was ended in 1879. Eastern and midwestern Friends continued lobbying the government on behalf of severalty legislation, which they assumed was in the Native Americans' best interest.

During the nineteenth century, English Friends provided relief to civilians during the Irish potato famine and the Crimean, Franco-Prussian, Balkan, and Boer wars. These early Quaker relief efforts were small-scale, individually initiated affairs in which workers with limited resources faced enormous need. English Friends argued that with rational, good, and Christian men in charge of governments and with economic bonds created by free trade, war was becoming obsolete. Joseph Sturge and John Bright organized opposition to the Crimean War. During the Boer War, English Friends rediscovered how unpopular pacifist witness was in wartime. Late-nineteenth-century English and American Friends joined peace societies, supported arbitration and the Hague conferences, and remained optimistic that a new era was dawning.

During World War I, English Quakers drew upon their tradition of relief efforts in creating the Friends Ambulance Unit and the Friends War Victims Relief Committee (FWVRC). They sought to protect German war refugees in England and to provide food for the Belgians. In 1917, American Friends adopted the relief techniques pioneered in France in 1914 by the FWVRC, as conscientious objectors from both nations worked together. Most American and British Quaker men eligible for conscription served, but yearly meetings reaffirmed the peace testimony, worked for alternative service for those unwilling to fight, and supported the absolutists who went to jail.

In 1920, Friends from all over the world met in London to rethink the implications of the peace testimony. They concluded that it was inadequate to focus upon individual evil as the cause for war. Imperialism, racism, poverty, oppression, and nationalism had to be confronted. The primary institutional methods for reconciling peoples and working for justice would be the American Friends Service Committee and Friends Service Council in Britain, and these national organizations would be aided by local and yearly meetings' peace committees.

The peace testimony became in the twentieth century a crucial element in distinguishing Friends from other churches, even though a majority of eligible Quakers joined the military during World War II. Because of their peace testimony, Friends forged ties with other peace churches—the Brethren, Mennonites, and Amish—and with secular organizations working for arms control and disarmament. Modern Quakers have learned techniques from labor unions and civil rights workers and theory from Gandhi, A.J. Muste, Dorothy Day, and Martin Luther King, Jr. They have expanded the peace testimony to deal with issues of violence within the family and sought to foster peaceful child-rearing techniques. In the United States, the Friends Committee on National Legislation, founded in 1942, seeks to lobby Congress on a wide variety of foreign and domestic issues. Continuing theological divisions among American Friends hamper the peace witness. Fundamentalist and evangelical Friends stress Christian missionary activities. Liberal Friends in England and America support peace and social justice work. Also, the general numerical decline of American Friends both absolutely and as a percentage of the population has weakened their political clout. Friends in their 350 years have produced few distinguished theologians; their primary creativity has come in rethinking the meaning and implications of being peacemakers.

J. William Frost

References

Barbour, Hugh, and J. William Frost. *The Quakers*. Westport, Conn.: Greenwood, 1988.

Brock, Peter. *The Quaker Peace Testimony: 1660 to 1914*. York, England: Sessions Book Trust, 1990.

Greenwood, John Ormerod. *Quaker Encounters: Friends and Relief,* vol. 1. York, England: Sessions Book Trust, 1975.

Orr, E.W. *The Quakers in Peace and War, 1920–1967*. Sussex, England: W.J. Offord, 1974.

Yarrow, C.H. *Quaker Experiences in International Conciliation*. New Haven: Yale University Press, 1979.

See also AMERICAN FRIENDS SERVICE COMMITTEE; NOBEL PEACE PRIZE; NONVIOLENCE, PRINCIPLED; PACIFISM; RELIGION AND NONVIOLENT ACTION

Queer Nation

Radical social movement organized in New York City in April 1990 by Alan Klein, Tom Blewitt, Karl Soehnlein, and, most significantly, Michelangelo Signorile. Signorile was a journalist, author, former editor of *Outweek* magazine, and creator of the practice of "outing" (the practice of exposing the "homosexual identities" of famous or powerful people who are not generally known to be gay or lesbian). Queer Nation (QN) was originally founded in response to the disenchantment many gays and lesbians felt for the organization AIDS Coalition to Unleash Power (ACT-UP), because of the latter group's narrow focus on issues surrounding the AIDS epidemic. Part of the "second wave" of gay activism, the most militant surge of lesbian/gay activism since the 1970s, Queer Nation employs direct confrontation and guerrilla theater tactics to increase awareness and visibility of gay and lesbian people and to combat the homophobia they face. Although it reached its peak in 1990–1991, many QN chapters around the country are still active today. Queer Nation is most notable for its use of modern technology and its innovative appropriation of public space to further its political agenda.

QN chapters spread quickly from the gay meccas of New York and San Francisco to many cities and towns across the United States. Frustrated by the slow pace of gay rights legislation and what many QN activists (sometimes called Queer Nationalists) perceived as government indifference to discrimination and violence directed at gays and lesbians, Queer Nationalists originated the slogan "We're Here, We're Queer, Get Used to It" to symbolize the merger of their personal identities with the political struggle for social justice and legal equality. A highly decentralized organization, QN's strategies and priorities vary from chapter to chapter. Strategies include using updated civil rights era techniques such as sit-ins, boycotts, and picket lines. The new spin that Queer Nation gives to these conventional tactics is that often QN activists engage in these activities dressed and cross dressed as "go-go boys," "motorcycle dykes," and "drag queens," forcing heterosexuals to confront openly their stereotypes of who and what gays and lesbians are. Queer Nationalists have gone further, engaging in the more confrontational tactics of disrupting public ceremonies and taunting closeted public figures with calls to "come out."

Queer Nation was also the first gay/lesbian organization to employ modern technology to share information and organize demonstrations and protests. An Internet computer network called Queernet allows QN chapters to pass information between local chapters and to other interested individuals in all parts of the United States and around the world with great speed. QN uses this technology to inundate a targeted company, government agency, or elected official with phone calls and faxes. Called "phone-zaps," or "fax zaps," these creative uses of modern technology can register instantaneously the nationwide disapproval of gays and lesbians to a homophobic policy or discriminatory practice. Some QN chapters also have used "fax-zaps" to "out" closeted celebrities and government officials, circulating their names to local news media outlets. The best-known occasion of this was the 1991 outing of Pete Williams, a top-ranking Defense Department official.

Although the goals of Queer Nation and other gay/lesbian political organizations are the same—to increase social and cultural acceptance of gays and lesbians—they differ widely on how best to accomplish these goals. For example, QN activists are critical of what they call the assimilationist attitudes of mainstream gay and lesbian organizations that prefer to work within the political system. Consequently, QN's radical tactics such as outing have alienated many within the gay and lesbian community who would ordinarily be supportive of attempts to create social change.

By 1993, many QN chapters had suffered serious splintering around charges of racism and sexism. Many discontented members claimed that the gay white men who dominated Queer Nation's leadership tended to neglect the concerns of women and minorities. Differences over QN's agenda further divided the organization. For example, many wanted Queer Nation to take a pro-choice stand on abortion. QN/San Francisco, once one of the most active, first split into two competing chapters, then disbanded altogether. The future of other chapters is unclear, but QN's attempt to "queer" the mainstream has succeeded in its effort to change the way gays and straights alike see and talk about gays and lesbians.

Gary L. Lehring

References

Lehring, Gary. "Difference and Identity, Difference As Identity: Theoretical Strategies in American Politics and Policy." Ph.D. dissertation, University of Massachusetts, Amherst, 1993.

Signorile, Michelangelo. *Queer in America: Sex, The Media, and the Closets of Power.* New York: Random House, 1993.

See also ACT-UP; GAY RIGHTS MOVEMENT; OUTING

R

Rainbow Warrior

Ship used by the group Greenpeace for protest voyages and nonviolent blockades in various environmentalist campaigns. The *Rainbow Warrior* was used for numerous maritime protest blockades from 1979 until it was sunk by two bombs in Auckland, New Zealand, in July 1985. Crewman Fernando Pereira was killed in the explosion. A large New Zealand police investigation of the bombing resulted in the conviction of two French agents of the General Directorate for External Security (DGSE), the firing of the chief of the DGSE, and the resignation of French Defense Minister Charles Hernu. The *Rainbow Warrior* was in the middle of a "Pacific Peace Tour" and had stopped in Auckland to support Prime Minister David Lange's "nuclear free" policy and to coordinate a flotilla of vessels to sail to the French nuclear testing site at Moruroa Atoll. They had intended to monitor and interfere with the testing of a neutron bomb. Greenpeace received much publicity and many financial donations as a result of this famous incident of state-sanctioned sabotage against an organization devoted to nonviolent direct action. In 1989, a new *Rainbow Warrior* was launched to continue the work of the original as a vital tool in Greenpeace campaigns.

Brad Bennett

References

Gidley, Isobell, and Richard Shears. *The Rainbow Warrior Affair.* Sydney: Counterpoint, 1985.

King, Michael. *Death of the Rainbow Warrior.* Auckland: Penguin, 1986.

The Greenpeace ship Rainbow Warrior *was used for protest voyages and nonviolent blockades in various environmentalist campaigns from 1979 until it was sunk by two bombs in Auckland, New Zealand, in July 1985. Photo © 1985 Greenpeace/Pereira.*

See also BLOCKADES; ENVIRONMENTAL MOVEMENTS; GREENPEACE; NUCLEAR WEAPONS OPPOSITION; VOYAGES, PROTEST

Religion and Nonviolent Action

People who connect religion with nonviolent action can be classified into three types: pacifists motivated solely by religious conviction, pacifists motivated by both religious and pragmatic considerations, and a large number of nonpacifists who support nonviolent action in certain situations because of nonviolent motifs within their religious traditions and for pragmatic reasons.

Many religious pacifists engage in nonviolent actions because of faithfulness to a religious belief or value system without intending to achieve a political effect. Some examples of such pacifists include most Christians during the first three centuries of the Church, Franciscans and Waldensians during the medieval period, the historic peace churches (Friends, Mennonites, Church of the Brethren), the Doukhobors, Molikans, Schwenkfelders, Jehovah's Witnesses, Tolstoy, and many Buddhist monks. Though a political goal may not be intended by these pacifists, actions of conscience do have indirect political consequences that may significantly change a society. Buddhist monks transform societies through their role in education. The Anabaptist and free church movement undermined a monolithic Christian society (symbolized by infant baptism) by establishing the principle of voluntarism and freedom of religious belief. In the twentieth century, as a result of numerous acts of conscientious objection to war and the willingness of persons of conscience to suffer the consequences for these convictions, conscientious objection has been recognized in the laws of many countries as a fundamental human right.

Important especially for the inspiration of nonviolent movements is the leadership provided by pacifists who also seek to achieve political results. Some examples are John Woolman and William Penn within the Quaker tradition, Mahatma Gandhi and his Muslim counterpart, Ghaffar Khan, A.J. Muste, who influenced the early labor movement, Martin Luther King, Jr., and other African-American Christians in the civil rights movement, and Thich Nhat Hanh in the Buddhist tradition.

Religion nurtures, supports, and contributes to nonviolent action in four fundamental ways. First, religion can legitimate strategies of peacemaking and nonviolent action (and delegitimate violence) through its symbols, myths, belief systems, and ethical norms. Second, religious institutions (the small cell, congregation, ashram, base community, interfaith organization, mosque) can give leadership or provide "space" in a society for the development and practice of nonviolence. Third, religion can foster a spirituality of truthfulness, hope, courage, patience, and

willingness to suffer to sustain a nonviolent movement struggling for change under difficult conditions. And finally, religion contributes to the repertoire of methods of nonviolent action (prayer, fasts, vigils).

One of the major ways religion supports nonviolent action is to legitimate nonviolence and delegitimate violence. However, it must be acknowledged that the legitimation of violence is deep and pervasive in all the major world religions. The ancient mythologies of Babylonia and Greece honored tribal war gods. Both the Hebrew Bible and the Qur'an have holy war traditions. After Constantine, the Christian Church aligned itself with the secular powers of empires and kings and supported the Crusades, inquisitions, and religious persecution. The virtues of the warrior are glorified in the Zen Buddhist traditions of Japan and the *Bhagavad Gita* of India. The dominating paradigm of most religious traditions is the "myth of redemptive violence"—that peace and justice are best won or maintained through the use of violent means. Religious traditions also have a strong interest in legitimating the prevailing political authority. This happens in the Christian tradition in the interpretation of texts such as Romans 13:1–7 (submit to the authorities) or in the concept of the divine right of kings. In Hinduism the *Laws of Manu* legitimate the existing caste system.

The religions also contain stories and teachings that support peacemaking and nonviolent action and challenge the myth of necessary violence to preserve the existing order. In the last several decades, especially, there has been a conflict within many religious traditions over interpretation, whether individuals and groups can claim religious traditions for support of nonviolent struggles for justice. Since the myths, symbols, and belief systems of religions are ways of interpreting the world, nonviolent struggles are often "battles" with opposing views to define the world in ways that are consonant with peacemaking and justice.

Religions can legitimate nonviolent action in several important ways. Religious belief systems provide a transcendent frame of reference that empowers people to challenge accepted conventions, particularly the view that violence is necessary or inevitable either in maintaining or transforming the existing social order. They also provide alternative visions of a peaceful order, an alternative dream or vision of how the world can be constructed. Religions develop universal conceptions of the human race that undermine conventional divisions between insider and outsider, friend and foe. And they enliven the human imagination and open the human spirit to consider ways to engage in conflict by nonviolent means to achieve justice and reconciliation.

The Eastern religious traditions tend to search for an alternative to violence through a personal inward quest. Gandhi reinterpreted violent warfare in the *Bhagavad Gita* symbolically as an inward spiritual struggle of the soul between light and darkness. The contemporary Vietnamese monk Thich Nhat Hanh drew from the resources of the Buddhist tradition of right mindfulness and meditation to resist the Vietnam War with the spirit and practice of nonviolence. Buddha's teachings reflected in the *Dhammapada* are profoundly nonviolent. The Buddha views the root of violence as ego-centeredness. Through the detachment from self-centeredness by means of the eightfold path, human beings can achieve "right mindfulness," a state of calm that brings humans into peaceful relations not only with human beings but with the whole universe. The *Tao te Ching*, a classic Chinese text, became popular during the 1960s in the youth counterculture of the West because it turns a central value of Western culture on its head by advocating peace through humility and unassertiveness rather than through striving and the quest for power.

The monotheistic traditions search for the answer to violence by seeking a right relationship with God. Though the Hebrew Bible seems to legitimate violence by God's chosen people against God's enemies, it also contains stories of "outsiders" like Hagar and Ishmael who are objects of God's compassion and who also receive God's promises. Many interpretations, especially theologies of liberation, claim that the Hebrew Bible primarily takes the side of the poor and oppressed. Such a view can undermine existing unjust social systems, though liberation theologians differ as to whether violence or nonviolence is the appropriate means to use to pursue justice. The Hebrew prophets challenged traditional nationalism and war as well as the power of elites who did not act justly. The universalism of the Hebrew Bible is reflected in the prophet Jeremiah, who calls on Jews carried into exile in Babylon to seek the *shalom* (well-being) of their enemy, Babylon. Jewish rabbis of the diaspora interpreted faithfulness to the Torah to be the practice of deeds of loving-kindness. This view became the fundamental foundation for Jewish ethics as the Jewish community lived for centuries as a nonviolent minority in the context of repression and persecution.

Christians have reexamined the early Church before Constantine and the life and teachings of Jesus as a model of peacemaking and nonviolence. The view that Jesus advocated nonresistance or passivity before enemies in the face of injustice has been challenged by scholars like Wink, who see in Jesus' Sermon on the Mount a model of nonviolent confrontation, a third way between violent revolution and passivity.

After St. Augustine, the just war theory served to legitimate the use of violent force to preserve some semblance of order and justice in a world of sin. This view seems to be in tension with the example and teaching of Jesus, though not all scholars agree that Jesus taught and practiced absolute nonviolence. The horrors of modern warfare and the skepticism about the efficacy of revolutionary violence have caused many in the twentieth century to reassess the "just war" tradition. This tradition has become more a moral framework to foster just peacemaking and practical nonviolence, and ever less an instrument for the justification of war. This peacemaking theme is central in Pope John XXIII's encyclical *Pacem in Terris* and in the 1983 pastoral letter of the U.S. Catholic bishops, *The Challenge of Peace*. Within the World Council of Churches the reassessment of nonviolence is reflected in the 1973 study document *Violence, Nonviolence and the Struggle for Social Justice*.

A new challenge to the legitimation of violence has been advanced by many feminist theologians who believe that violence is rooted in patriarchy and the mythology of a patriarchal God. They reinterpret Christianity and other religious traditions by the development of alternative symbols and stories that emphasize equality and mutuality rather than dominance and submission. A practical example is Rigoberta Menchú's nonviolence, which is nurtured both by her own indigenous culture of Guatemala as well as by stories from the Bible.

The common perception, especially in the West, is that Islam is a religion of violence. But this interpretation has been challenged by many Muslims. Muslims can cite the example of the prophet Muhammad during the Meccan period, before his flight (Hegira) from Mecca to Medina, when he struggled nonviolently against those who wanted to suppress the faith. The Sufis and contemporary peace-minded Muslims have also emphasized that in the Qur'an the greater *jihad* (holy war) is the inner struggle of a person to be in submission to God, much more central than the lesser *jihad* of external war. The Indian Muslim Ghaffar Khan, a contemporary of Gandhi, developed a principled nonviolence.

Though religious symbols, myths, and belief systems play a critical role in shaping human behavior, these ideas are often powerless if they are not institutionalized. The ashram was central to the success of Gandhi's nonviolent struggle in India. Bishop Desmond Tutu and the South African Council of Churches have been at the forefront in advocating nonviolence in the struggle in South Africa. Religious institutions, the leaders of religious organizations, and ordinary people who practice religion daily play a very important role in nurturing and sustaining nonviolent action. As movements come and go, and the popularity of a cause begins to wane, religious organizations and leaders often provide key support and staying power. Religious institutions also represent a "space," even in the most repressive societies, that is not easily controlled by the dominating political system. They can thus become centers for teaching and organizing. Religious institutions can also model alternative ways of living that counter so-called inevitable hatreds by bringing together persons of diverse religious, national, racial, ethnic, ideological, and economic backgrounds. Out of intense loyalty grounded in the authority of religious tradition, ordinary people act and shape social reality regardless of whether they are always conscious of how they impact the world.

In the Philippine struggle against Marcos and the numerous nonviolent struggles in Latin America, archbishops, bishops, priests, nuns, and Christian base communities have played key roles. In the Philippines, for example, Sister Milar Rocco was teaching her students about active nonviolence when she learned that Defense Minister Enrile and General Ramos had defected and were expecting to be bombed. Together with her students they encountered the soldiers still loyal to Marcos by offering them food and talking to them. Fifty of the soldiers said they wanted to surrender, so the nuns formed a chain around them to "protect" them and led them to join Enrile and Ramos. In the Philippines the International Fellowship of Reconciliation provided leadership and training in nonviolent action.

In Vietnam, Thailand, and Burma, Buddhist monks have given leadership in protests against human rights violations and in movements for nonviolent social change. Aung San Suu Kyi, daughter of Burma's national hero, winner of the Nobel Peace Prize, and advocate of nonviolence and democracy, connects her struggle explicitly to the teachings and institutions of Buddhism. The Tibetan nonviolent struggle for human rights is inspired by the exiled Dalai Lama.

The revival of Islam nurtured in the mosques throughout Iran was critical in the overthrow of the shah in 1978–1979. Islamic women played a vital role in the mass protests. In the Palestinian Intifada, mosques became organizing and teaching centers. Frequently marches and demonstrations began at mosques or were linked to key religious rituals.

The civil rights struggle in the United States in the 1950s and 1960s was centrally linked to the African-American church and the African-American preacher who was the most important leader in the community. Rosa Parks and other African-American Christians did not just learn nonviolence in 1954. They had been nurtured in nonviolence through the singing of spirituals and through biblical preaching.

In 1981, a youth pastor and some young people started weekly Monday prayer services for peace at the St. Nicholai Church in Leipzig, East Germany, one of the small seeds planted early that contributed to the crumbling of the Berlin Wall. In 1988, these prayer services became the locus of increasingly larger groups of East German citizens who gathered to discuss social issues. By October 1989, 300,000 persons gathered in Leipzig to demonstrate despite police harassment and arrests.

Religion also nurtures a spirituality that is essential to nonviolence. Critical to nonviolent action is the willingness of persons to cross the barrier of fear, to be able to say "no" to illegitimate authority without fear of sanctions or death. Václav Havel's courageous action in communist Czechoslovakia is a profound demonstration of what it means "to live within the truth" rather than "living a lie."

The motto of Quaker nonviolent action is "speak truth to power." Religion nurtures virtues that are central to nonviolent movements such as courage and the willingness to suffer, overcoming hatred of the enemy, the ability to endure abuse without retaliation, hope and patience during a long period of struggle, trust in the possibility of miracle or transformation when the evidence for change appears bleak, joy even in the midst of suffering and pain, realism that guards people from disillusionment by making them aware of the depth of human evil and the persistence of systems of domination and injustice, and humility about their own lack of knowledge and need for wisdom.

Gandhi's nonviolence was integrally tied to his awareness that each position he took was an "experiment with truth." He prepared himself for action by fasting, meditation, and prayer. Dorothy Day was able to practice "the harsh and dreadful love" (one of the mottos of the Catholic Worker Movement) of Father Zosima in Dostoevsky's *Brothers Karamazov* by drawing sustenance from daily participation in the mass. The icon of the Russian Orthodox Church kept alive the spirituality of the Russian people during the dark days of communism. Thich Nhat Hanh practices disciplines of meditation and breathing exercises in order to maintain internal control and calm in the midst of hatred.

Numerous nonviolent movements draw inspiration and courage from the examples of martyrs who have died for the cause. The music of the black spiritual was central to both the joy and endurance of people in the civil rights struggle. One could name a host of religious thinkers, saints, and also artists and creators and makers of music, who have nurtured the spirituality of nonviolent movements, such as Martin Buber, Abraham Heschel, Simone Weil, Julian of Norwich, St. Francis, Thomas Merton, the art of Käthe Kollwitz, hymn writers from many traditions, and many others.

Religion also provides nonviolent movements with a repertoire of actions. Simple deeds of kindness and charity in the context of hatred and violence can disarm an opponent or undermine his morale. A symbol (a cross, salt, the spinning wheel) can become a powerful unifying force in a movement. Nonviolent movements frequently use the power of prayer, fasting, meditation, silence, religious processions, key festivals or religious rituals, remembrance of martyrs or saints, funerals, sanctuary, songs and chants, gatherings at churches, mosques, temples, or other sacred sites. Any genuine religious act is potentially an act of nonviolent protest because it brings people into relationship with a transcendent reality and power that challenges systems of injustice and violence.

One of the challenges for the world's religions is to overcome their violence toward each other. The "commitment to a culture of nonviolence," signed by some 150 religious leaders at the 1993 Parliament of the World's Religions in Chicago, may signal an era of more peaceful relationships among religious traditions.

Duane K. Friesen

References

Bondurant, Joan V. *Conquest of Violence: The Gandhian Philosophy of Conflict.* Princeton: Princeton University Press, 1958, 1988.

Brock, Peter. *Pacifism in the United States from the Colonial Era to the First World War.* Princeton: Princeton University Press, 1968.

Fellowship Magazine. Fellowship of Reconciliation. Nyack, N.Y.

Ferguson, John. *War and Peace in the World's Religions.* New York: Oxford University Press, 1978.

"Islam and Peacemaking." *Reconciliation International* (February, 1988). Magazine of the International Fellowship of Reconciliation, London.

Kraft, Kenneth, ed. *Inner Peace, World Peace: Essays on Buddhism and Nonviolence.* Albany, N.Y.: SUNY Press, 1992.

McFague, Sallie. *Models of God: Theology for an Ecological, Nuclear Age.* Philadelphia: Fortress, 1987.

Nhat Hanh, Thich. *The Miracle of Mindfulness: A Manual of Meditation.* Boston: Beacon, 1976.

Solomonow, Allan, ed. *Roots of Jewish Nonviolence.* Nyack, N.Y.: Jewish Peace Fellowship, 1981.

Washington, James M., ed. *A Testament of Hope: The Essential Writings and Speeches of Martin Luther King, Jr.* San Francisco: HarperCollins, 1991.

Wink, Walter. *Engaging the Powers: Discernment and Resistance in a World of Domination.* Minneapolis, Minn.: Fortress, 1992.

Yoder, John H. *Nevertheless: The Varieties and Shortcomings of Religious Pacifism.* Scottdale, Pa.: Herald, 1992.

See also AUNG SAN SUU KYI; BSTAN-DZIN-RGYA-MTSHO, DALAI LAMA XIV; CIVIL RIGHTS MOVEMENT; DAY, DOROTHY; DOUKHOBORS; GANDHI, MOHANDAS KARAMCHAND; INTIFADA, 1987–1990; IRANIAN REVOLUTION, 1963–1979; JIHAD; KHAN

Abdul Ghaffar Khan; King, Martin Luther, Jr.; Menchú Tum, Rigoberta; Nhat Hanh, Thich; Nonviolence, Principled; Pacifism; Philippines People Power Revolution, 1986; Quakers; Tolstoy, Leo; Tutu, Archbishop Desmond Mpilo

Reverse Strike

Deliberate action in which people voluntarily work harder or longer than usual in order to call attention to a particular concern or demand. The impact is largely psychological, in that while the reverse strike manipulates the physical resources available, it is often undertaken to appeal to third parties for support and to pressure the opponent to change a particular policy or behavior. The constructive act is intended to make it difficult for the opponent to deny the strikers' requests. The reverse strike is a relatively new method of nonviolent action.

The earliest known use of the reverse strike occurred when Italian agricultural workers circa 1950 worked harder and longer than required to support their demand for a pay raise. In 1956, nonviolent action advocate Danilo Dolci led unemployed civilians in a campaign to voluntarily repair a public road in order to publicize the area's severe unemployment problem and governmental negligence. More recently, the Congress of Racial Equality (CORE) organized unemployed black youths in Chicago to clean up a slum and left a bill with City Hall for the costs of the effort.

References

Sharp, Gene. *The Politics of Nonviolent Action.* Boston: Porter Sargent, 1973.

See also Congress of Racial Equality; Dolci, Danilo; Methods of Nonviolent Action

Reverse Trial

Method of psychological intervention in which the defendants in a trial reverse roles with the prosecution, attempting to put the prosecutor on trial. The original defendants use this reverse trial to publicize their cause and to criticize and indict the prosecution. The prosecution in these cases is usually the government or some other major societal institution. The perpetrators of the reverse trial manipulate the situation to their advantage.

Reversal of roles occurred during the trials of demonstrators in Russia in 1877, in which the accused aroused public sympathy with their courtroom demeanor and tactics. Mohandas K. Gandhi asked a judge to resign his post during a trial for sedition in 1922. Germans who were prosecuted during the Ruhrkampf spoke out during trials about the injustice of the occupation of the Ruhr by France and Belgium. Activists in the Plowshares Movement have attempted to turn the tables by putting the military-industrial complex on the defensive during their trials.

References

Sharp, Gene. *The Politics of Nonviolent Action.* Boston: Porter Sargent, 1973.

See also Plowshares Movement; Methods of Nonviolent Action; Ruhrkampf, 1923

Revolution

Term applied to a wide variety of social phenomena, often involving overthrow of a government, mass upheaval, violence, and rapid and far-reaching change in a social system; yet frequently used for events and processes lacking one or more of these five characteristics. Scholars disagree greatly on what is properly called a "revolution." Rather than having a standard "anatomy," revolution now appears to be a historically evolving and diversifying phenomenon, in which such features as the role of violence, and the tempo and extent of change, all vary. Not only do successive revolutions influence theories of revolution (as they should), but the theories and ideas people are acquainted with, whether they are sound or not, shape their assumptions and goals as proponents or opponents of revolution, and thus themselves shape future revolutions. Tracing the co-evolution of revolutionary experience and theorizing makes possible better understanding of past revolutions and prospects for future ones. The history of revolution, particularly when considered in the light of the twentieth-century development of nonviolent struggle, offers hope that future revolutions might bring greater benefits at less cost than in the past.

"Revolution" originated as an astronomical term referring to cyclical motion. When "revolution" came into political use in 1660, it meant (as Hannah Arendt has put it) "a movement of revolving back to some pre-established point," reflecting a view that society cycled inevitably through a few known forms of government; hence it was applied not to what is now called the "English Revolution" of the 1640s (then called the "Great Rebellion"), but to the restoration of the monarchy that ended the revolutionary period. England's "Glorious Revolution" of 1688 was likewise what would today be called a "restoration." The modern association of revolution with novelty, so different from its original political meaning, came about because, in order to achieve their objectives (restoring what they believed to be traditional conditions undercut and violated by recent policies), both the American colonists and the French found themselves going beyond the past, creating something unprecedented.

The French Revolution has had an influence difficult to exaggerate on subsequent images and conceptions of revolution. The crowd storming the Bastille prison on July 14, 1789; the unexpected collapse of an ancient monarchy in a powerful country, and the monarch's beheading; the proclaiming of human rights, the triumph of "reason," and the values of "Liberty, Equality, Fraternity"; the Jacobins, political club members become rulers, with their "reign of terror" against counterrevolutionaries and former allies alike; rapid movement through a succession of leaders and forms of rule; idealistic language and deadly power struggles; the 1799 coup d'état by military commander (later Emperor) Napoleon Bonaparte; the pressure of neighboring regimes' hostility adding to domestic tension, and subsequent military advances and retreats—all these were spellbinding for Europeans.

But the revolution was more than turmoil and drama. Under Napoleon numerous feudal rights and local administrative structures were swept aside and individuals were subjected to the state's direct, centralized authority; thereby a national citizen army, larger than the era's conventional professional armies, became available, aiding Napoleon's conquests and impelling neighboring states to "modernize" for their own defense. New legal codes were imposed on the countries French armies overran, with lasting effects.

A subtler influence of the French Revolution, almost equally lasting, has been suggested by Arendt in On Revolution. As event followed event in a headlong, often bloody, rush, participants felt a loss of control and began using the imagery of an overpowering "torrent." The exhilaration of the effort to deliberately, rationally remake the social order gave way to feelings of necessity and inexorability. The connotation of "revolution" as remote from human control revived. "The revolution, like Saturn, devours its children," remarked a participant, and the invoking of myth is revealing.

Such sentiments became incorporated into Hegel's philosophy of history. Looking back as a nonparticipant at the French Revolution, he formulated a problematic philosophy of historical progress toward freedom propelled (and permeated) by necessity. The "Young Hegelian" Karl Marx redefined history's goal of freedom in material terms, with change to be made by human action, but in his most famous book, Capital, retained the indefensible notion that "the natural laws of capitalist production [work] with iron necessity towards inevitable results," a conception at odds with human freedom to make our own history.

Given a complex reality—that humans do make choices, but under constraints—Marx's mixed message could both breed optimistic passivity and encourage vigorous activism, each based on confidence that one knew which way history was heading. Marx himself was uncertain about how socialist goals were most likely to be achieved, leaving ambiguities regarding strategy to be bitterly debated by later Marxists.

The Marxists Lenin and Trotsky were far from Russia when the czar's rule collapsed in February 1917. The February Revolution was "made" by hardship and war-weariness, by demonstrators and troops unwilling to fire on them, much more than by leftist strategy. Amid continuing crisis, endorsing popular sentiments for "peace, bread, and land," the Bolshevik (later "Communist") Party managed to seize control of the state in a virtually bloodless coup in the famous "October Revolution."

The coming to power in Europe's most populous country of a small, illegal party led by cosmopolitan intellectuals seemed to validate their claim to possess a scientific theory of politics, and it won the party immense prestige and authority among many people with leftist sympathies worldwide. But difficulties—internal conflicts and invasion by foreign opponents—were immediate. Regarding the large peasant majority as property-hungry and thus inherently hostile to socialist state ownership and

R

collectivism, and fearing that any organized opposition group (whether conservative, liberal, or leftist) would inevitably become a vehicle for counterrevolution, the Bolsheviks sought to suppress all opposition outside their party, and soon (by similar logic) all factions within it. By 1929 Joseph Stalin had concentrated all power in his hands, and proceeded, in one of history's worst bloodbaths, to carry out a "revolution from above" that collectivized agriculture at the cost of millions of lives, while simultaneously seeking to "purge" the party and society of all rivals and potential opponents. The Russian Revolution, wrote Arendt, "had the same profound meaningfulness of first crystallizing the best of men's hopes and then realizing the full measure of their despair that the French Revolution had for its contemporaries."

The French and Russian revolutions can be contrasted with the American. In Arendt's view all revolutions have two tasks: liberation from tyranny or oppression, and the creating of a new form of government—"the constitution of freedom." The French and Russians signally failed to constitute freedom, and consequently soon failed at the former task as well. In contrast, the American Revolution proved (for those enfranchised) a dramatic success, culminating in a deliberately devised and durable (written) "constitution" enshrining rights and permitting gradual progress. The American Founding Fathers made history on the basis of their own experience (crucially, as delegates from smaller democratic societies) and their own ideas (informed, but not dictated, by history). Their example, all flaws notwithstanding, remains in this respect relevant to those who want to work without illusion to improve the human condition, rather than serve as puppet-agents of a supposed historical necessity.

If the Russian Revolution made no fundamental advance toward freedom, it did create the model (and myth) of the "vanguard party," a tool for agitation and combat that could be used to seize power and, putatively, to remake society for the better. Of the many self-described "revolutions" of the twentieth century, some little more than military coups, Gérard Chaliand, a sympathetic, firsthand observer of several, writes: "Most of the time . . . these revolutionary explosions [in Asia, Latin America, and Africa], often restricted to 'the top,' have resulted only in nationalist regimes with statist tendencies, not in thoroughgoing revolutions affecting the social structure."

Among the most interesting (and most neglected) revolutions are ones that contradict common assumptions. In Spain (1936–1939) anarchist workers and peasants established stateless, cooperative social forms, showing revolutions do not always strengthen the state. Hungary's short-lived workers' councils in 1956 displayed an alternative to both communism and capitalism. Eritrea's liberation movement (1970–1993), originally largely Leninist, survived Soviet opposition, evolved self-reliantly in a democratic direction, and, waging war "against all odds" (as Dan Connell recounts), finally won its independence; it showed movement evolution in wartime is not inevitably authoritarian.

Although many distinctions within the phenomenon of revolution can be made, perhaps the simplest and most useful contrasts are among: (a) coups d'état, which do little more than change the personnel occupying top positions, and arguably do not merit the label "revolution"; (b) political revolutions, which change the form of a regime; and (c) social revolutions, which significantly change a society's structure, and are therefore deemed the most profound.

Many revolutions, especially social ones, remain controversial. Appraising even a single revolution requires a comprehensive review of facts that can often be ascertained only with difficulty, given frequent bias in sources; and a comparison of what actually happened with historically realistic alternatives, about which agreement may be even harder to attain. The labor, complexity, and uncertainty entailed help explain why the merits of revolutions remain so hotly disputed.

Theories of Revolution

Different elements in the definition that begins this article are considered essential by different writers. Is violent change of government crucial? Or fundamental change of the social system? Either can occur without the other. If broadly defined, revolutions become "highly varied phenomena," as Jack Goldstone and his colleagues acknowledge, which reduces chances of finding universally applicable generalizations and explanations. Narrower definitions select only a subset of these phenomena. From a 1993 book on revolutions Charles Tilly excludes "top-down social transformations"; yet Ellen Kay Trimberger devotes a whole volume to "revolution from above"—the top-down transformations that made Japan a world power and crucially influenced Turkey, Egypt, and Peru. In fact, writes Trimberger, "It now [1978] seems that mass revolutions from below are the truly exceptional . . . historical phenomena."

In addition, revolutions do not occur unhindered. Some groups seek to prevent or defeat them. Consequently, a revolution for which preconditions are developing in a typical (and thus recognizable) way might never occur for precisely that reason. John Dunn suggests, for example, "If it had been clear that Cuba [was prone to revolution] . . . it is not improbable that the Cuban revolution would not have been permitted to occur at all." Revolutions do not just vary, in this view; they vary out of necessity.

Thus, paradoxically, "unlikely" revolutions may be more "likely" to occur—consider the unanticipated overthrow in 1979 of Iran's heavily armed shah by Islamic fundamentalists. A later social revolution in the Philippines may have been successfully prevented by the multiple U.S. interventions of 1985–1986, made in explicit recognition of Iran-like potential.

The most influential book on revolution in recent decades has been Theda Skocpol's *States and Social Revolutions,* a "structural" comparative analysis of France (1787–1800), Russia (1917–1921), and China (1911–1949). Skocpol downplays ideologies, intentions, and mass emotions, and makes state breakdown and reconstruction central. She argues that states may break down under the combined fiscal strain of spending to compete militarily with other states, the inefficiency of an unmodernized economic order, and conflicting demands from domestic social classes. Squeezing the latter to increase revenues can generate opposition and erode support, leading to an inability to maintain state authority. Open struggle for control of the state may follow. A revolution has occurred if and when a new group has reconsolidated state control over society.

A contrasting, "political" theory of revolution, most identified with Charles Tilly, emphasizes the continuity of revolutionary actions with conventional politics, and the manner in which groups organize to mobilize their resources for struggle, choosing methods from their "repertoires of contention" (ways of fighting known to them). When who will get control of the state is genuinely uncertain, a condition of "multiple sovereignty" exists that defines a "revolutionary situation." When the winner of the power struggle reconstructs the state's au-

thority, this ends the revolutionary situation, in Tilly's sense. If the winner is a contender formerly outside the state elite, a revolutionary outcome has occurred.

Here the structural view, strongest in analyzing state breakdown, becomes weakest, because it downplays choice. Skocpol views a new regime's policies as largely structurally determined, but (as Rod Aya points out) "never distinguishes the structural changes made by vigilante action [such as seizures of property] *during* the revolutionary situation from those made by official fiat *after* a new government is in power." The latter actions are often more far-reaching (as Napoleon and Stalin illustrate), and are certainly often matters of choice, not inevitability.

The relations among the varied processes that make up revolutions are not simple, regular, or automatic. In contrast to Skocpol and others whose definitions assume a close linkage of state collapse, struggle, and eventual outcomes, Aya writes:

> Revolutionary situations often do not owe to revolutionary intentions, or lead to revolutionary outcomes. Those who do much to bring such situations and outcomes about often do not mean to. And those who do most to transform society often do so only after the revolutionary situation in which they take power is past. . . . [T]he outbreak of a revolutionary situation, the victory of parties with revolutionary intentions, and the "structural" transformation of state and society have different causes, which you must determine by inquiry, not dictate by definition.

Nonviolent Revolutions

Many writers have made violence part of the definition of revolution—indeed, several writers call revolution "the politics of violence"—and for them the idea of a nonviolent revolution seems obviously a contradiction in terms. Yet a surprising number of scholars who lack any evident "pro-nonviolence" sympathies have excluded violence from their definition of revolution on the grounds that it is not inherent in the concept, and therefore to include it would obstruct useful inquiry into whether revolutionary changes can occur through nonviolent struggle.

Before continuing, an ambiguity should be addressed: some use "nonviolent" to mean anything "not violent," including procedures such as elections that are often institutionalized and routine. For example, Karl Marx speculated that workers might "attain their goal by peaceful means" in countries with democratic elections—in contrast to "most countries [where] it is force to which we must someday appeal" to establish socialism. Such institutionalized procedures, while rightly contrasted with violent conflict, are excluded from the conception of nonviolent struggle on which the present volume is based. Here nonviolent struggle means an array of methods of protest, noncooperation, and intervention whose effects range from mild to so forceful (such as mass strikes, marches, and disobedience) that they have been likened to war and found to wield coercive power. Further, "nonviolent revolution" as used herein does not mean that violence from any quarter is absent (for the challenge posed by nonviolent struggle is frequently countered with violence), but rather that the means used by the would-be revolutionaries are exclusively or predominantly nonviolent. Whether or not Marx had in mind violence when saying "force," or some broader conception of popular action, nonviolent struggle is at least arguably more akin to "force" than to "peaceful means," with the latter's tranquil and orderly connotations. Nonviolent struggle is best viewed as a third alternative to electoral politics and political violence.

Mohandas Gandhi's campaigns revealed possibilities for mass action without the extensive violence of the best-known past revolutions. Even some early observers (such as Clarence Marsh Case in *Non-violent Coercion*) recognized that Gandhi's political technique, through the power of noncooperation and various constructive and assertive methods, could coerce opponents by mobilizing what Dave Dellinger would later call "force without violence." It thus appeared in principle to be capable of carrying out revolution as defined in the *Shorter Oxford English Dictionary:* "forcible substitution by subjects of new ruler or polity for the old."

But can it happen in practice? Two episodes of nonviolent struggle that fit one of the simplest definitions of revolution, the overthrow of a ruler, can be found in Central America in 1944. In both El Salvador and Guatemala dictators were forced out by widespread protests, strikes, commercial shutdowns, and finally pressure from elite elements: doctors, diplomats, and even the Salvadoran dictator's cabinet. These clearly qualify as "political" revolutions.

But what about nonviolent social revolution? Gandhi, who seems to have coined the phrase "nonviolent revolution" (but used it infrequently), has been aptly called a social revolutionary, given the efforts regarding poverty, women's status, and caste that accompanied his anti-imperial work. But Gandhi left no clear strategy for effecting the changes he desired, leaving room for the conflicting viewpoints that split the Gandhian movement after his death.

From the 1940s onward a handful of writers explored "nonviolent revolution" or "revolutionary nonviolence," among them A.J. Muste, Barbara Deming, and Dave Dellinger. In 1972 the War Resisters' International issued a "Manifesto for Nonviolent Revolution" whose author, George Lakey (a U.S. civil rights and antiwar activist), elaborated his views in *Strategy for a Living Revolution,* presenting a model of five (roughly chronological but overlapping) "stages in the development [toward possible social revolution] of a mass movement from the point of view of an activist." Although Lakey concentrated mainly on the United States, he argued for principles he deemed applicable at least in part to any society. The first two stages, "cultural preparation" and "building organizational strength," were to be accompanied by a third stage of thoughtfully planned nonviolent campaigns and demonstrations designed to dramatize the movement's goals while appealing to widely shared values and making repression by opponents difficult.

The fourth stage, mass political and economic noncooperation ("tax-refusal, rent-refusal, strikes, boycotts, civil disobedience, and so on") would occur if and when a sizable public perceived both a need and a way to act on its grievances. If sufficiently widespread, such noncooperation could create the opportunity for the political opposition to compete seriously for popular allegiance with its society's state or private power structure. In Lakey's fifth stage of "intervention and parallel institutions," the kind of movement he favors aims not to seize state power for itself, but by coordinated efforts "on *many* levels by *many* groups" to shift power from the elite-dominated state to new popular organizations operating all society's institutions and "gain[ing] their legitimacy from mass acceptance and participation. . . . [They will have no] violent means of coercing the people; they can only win the people through service."

Near this point in his book Lakey paused to ask, "Is this only fantasy?" and recounted examples to show that "*fragments* of this picture ha[d] occurred in history," even though his strategy as a whole was a projection beyond any past events. In the twenty-plus years that followed, events worldwide illustrated the possibility of nonviolent revolution.

In Iran in 1978–1979 people numbering as many as 2 million defied heavily armed forces of the shah's army by marching at (traditional) forty-day intervals through Tehran to mourn and protest government killings, which increased with each march. The degree of nonviolent discipline and fortitude shown in marching repeatedly in the face of certain violent reprisal would have been dismissed as unrealistic before these actions occurred.

By February 1979 Ayatollah Khomeini and his aides had returned from exile to compete directly with the old regime for popular allegiance, in a classic "parallel institution" and "multiple sovereignty" revolutionary situation. The Iranian opposition emphasized "nonviolence" (in the sense of a deliberate rejection of violence despite the regime's provocations). In John Foran's estimation, "The revolution witnessed the largest demonstrations against a government in human history and a sustained political general strike that may be considered the most successful in working class history"— resulting in a "triumph through the disciplined use of primarily nonviolent tactics." There was no deep ethic of nonviolence, then or in the years afterward. On February 8 huge crowds chanted "Give us arms!" and armed attacks on military bases occurred during the final weekend of the power shift. But warfare did not decide the outcome—it was nonviolent mobilization that finally impelled even the shah's top generals to declare they would not oppose the people's will. Thus Iran showed that there could be a major social revolution brought about through predominantly nonviolent struggle.

Another example of revolutionary nonviolent struggle, although offering a different lesson, comes from Poland. In 1975 Charles Tilly wrote, "If violence and revolution go together to some extent, it is not because violence is the essence of revolution, but because men turn to unlimited means of coercion in the fluidity of a revolutionary situation." The most important challenge of Poland's Solidarity movement (born in 1980, suppressed in 1981, victorious in 1990) to traditional revolutionary theory and practice was its concept of "self-limiting revolution."

Timothy Garton Ash, assessing what even in 1983 he was calling "the Polish revolution," noted with wonder that "in sixteen months, this revolution killed nobody." This remarkable self-limitation with respect to means was matched in the realm of objectives. "Solidarity *never attempted* to take over the state . . . which makes Solidarity impossible to classify without redefining [terms like] 'revolution.'"

For Garton Ash, Solidarity posed this question: "Can a self-organized society transform the political system of a state within the Soviet empire, by pressure from below, without violence?" He had the wisdom in 1983, while Solidarity was underground during martial law and written off by many "tough-minded" observers, to say it was too soon to answer "no." By 1990 the world knew that the movement had succeeded, not only in transforming Poland, but also in helping catalyze the overthrow of communism through "people power" in most of Eastern Europe (in events several journalists termed "nonviolent revolutions").

Some hesitated to call Solidarity's rise to control of the government a "revolution"—understandably, if one associates revolution with rapid change, violence, and mass upheaval. The struggle spanned a decade, and the crucial milestones in 1989 and 1990—the government's invitation to Solidarity to join roundtable discussions, the movement's relegalization, and its electoral successes—lacked the drama of the 1980 Lenin Shipyard negotiations. Yet it would be perverse if Solidarity, often called "revolutionary" when it challenged Communist policies in 1980 and 1981, were to be denied that adjective after persisting through martial law to finally succeed in ending Communist rule. If one favors a conception of revolution as major change accomplished through struggle in which mass involvement is crucial to the challengers' power, then Solidarity's achievement plainly qualifies.

The Future of Revolution

Scientists seek recurrent patterns and accurate explanations, validated by successful prediction. But most people (since we must live with the history we make) want freedom from determination by past patterns and trends, and we thereby make the social scientist's job much harder. John Dunn, arguing that powerful efforts to prevent predictable revolutions worked against their predictability, states: "What we may be *certain* lies ahead for us in future decades of revolutionary experience is surprises."

With hindsight Theda Skocpol might well agree. In the very year that she published the confident assertion that it was "quite correct" to say "Revolutions are not made; they come"—came the Iranian revolution, concerning which she soon had to acknowledge, "Their revolution did not just come; it was deliberately and coherently made."

Objective and structural factors such as earthquakes, bad harvests, geography, role in the world economy, and demographic trends are undeniably important; but ideologies (and ideas) condition what people consider legitimate and what intolerable. Because these subjective, interpretive factors decisively influence matters like participation in war and feasible rates of taxation, and thus the objective determinants of state viability and fiscal crisis, any purely structural approach (like Skocpol's original position) is misleading and wrong.

After more than two centuries, the image of necessity, inevitable stages, and lack of control bequeathed by the riveting spectacle of the French revolution—an image "of enormous practical importance in subsequent historical action"—has been challenged by both scholarly findings and historical experiences. Finally, in Dunn's words, "these hypnotic effects have begun to wear off." That does not mean there is no danger in overemphasizing subjective and voluntarist factors. Factors minimally subject to deliberate change will remain important, and people who ignore them may act unrealistically and fail.

Yet, Dunn suggests, "it may simply be the case that revolutionary process has been becoming . . . more voluntarist." It may be that "the concerted actions of revolutionaries . . . can now play a causal role in *creating* objective revolutionary situations." Rational beliefs about the potential for peace, justice, and abundance, influencing popular convictions about what is right, fair, and legitimate, might serve, in combination with skillful nonviolent campaigns that dramatize those potentials, to generate change of revolutionary depth.

The apparently growing trend to choose nonviolent struggle, instead of violence or submission, supports hope for these possibilities for the future. Stephen Zunes, in a survey of twenty-one "unarmed insurrections" in the Third World between 1978 and 1993, notes that even movements that regard violence as legitimate sometimes rely on nonviolent tactics, which have the advantage of engaging far more of the population than does armed insurrection. This shift in choices among the "repertoire of contention" may reflect a human capacity to learn. New choices also seem possible regarding the timing and goals of struggle for revolutionary change.

In the final pages of *States and Social Revolutions,* Skocpol speculated, "If a social revolution were to transform an advanced industrial nation, it would . . . probably have to flow gradually, not cataclysmically, out of a long series of [in André Gorz's phrase] 'non-reformist reforms.'" Lakey had earlier likewise argued for the importance of "limited goals" for a revolutionary movement.

Some analysts, indeed, contend that self-limiting social movements such as those associated with Gandhi, King, and Solidarity have been the most valuable innovations of twentieth-century politics. Whether future advances are called "reform," "revolution in stages," "evolutionary revolution," or "a new kind of revolution" matters less than what they accomplish for humanity's betterment.

It is possible to err by believing too little is possible, just as by believing too much. If there are revolutionaries in the twenty-first century who make unlikely breakthroughs toward human liberation, it is probable they will be acting in the spirit of Gandhi's reported reply to the objection that a planned nonviolent campaign had no precedent: "Because something has not taken place in the past, that does not mean it cannot take place in the future."

Robert A. Irwin

References

Arendt, Hannah. *On Revolution.* New York: Viking, 1963, 1965.

Aya, Rod. *Rethinking Revolutions and Collective Violence: Studies on Concept, Theory, and Method.* Amsterdam: Het Spinhuis, 1990.

Chaliand, Gérard. *Revolution in the Third World.* Paris: Editions du Seuil, 1976; New York: Penguin, 1978; expanded New York: Viking, 1989.

Connell, Dan. *Against All Odds: A Chronicle of the Eritrean Revolution.* Trenton,

N.J.: Red Sea, 1993.

Dellinger, Dave. *Revolutionary Nonviolence.* Indianapolis and New York: Bobbs-Merrill, 1970.

Dolgoff, Sam, ed. *The Anarchist Collectives: Workers' Self-Management in the Spanish Revolution, 1936–1939.* New York: Free Life, 1974; Montreal: Black Rose, 1990.

Dunn, John. "The Success and Failure of Modern Revolutions." In *Political Obligation in Its Historical Context.* Cambridge: Cambridge University Press, 1980.

———. "Understanding Revolutions." In *Rethinking Modern Political Theory: Essays 1979–1983.* Cambridge: Cambridge University Press, 1985.

Foran, John. *Fragile Resistance: Social Transformation in Iran from 1500 to the Revolution.* Boulder, Colo.: Westview, 1993.

Garton Ash, Timothy. *The Polish Revolution: Solidarity;* rev. and updated ed. New York: Viking Penguin, 1991.

Goldstone, Jack A., Ted Robert Gurr, and Farrokh Moshiri, eds. *Revolutions of the Late Twentieth Century.* Boulder, Colo.: Westview, 1991.

Keddie, Nikki R., ed. *Debating Revolutions.* New York: New York University Press, 1995.

Kimmel, Michael S. *Revolution: A Sociological Interpretation.* Philadelphia: Temple University Press, 1990.

Lakey, George. *Strategy for a Living Revolution.* New York: Grossman, 1973.

Ostergaard, Geoffrey. *Nonviolent Revolution in India.* New Delhi: Gandhi Peace Foundation, 1985.

Randle, Michael. *People Power: The Building of a New European Home.* Stroud, UK: Hawthorn, 1991.

Skocpol, Theda. *Social Revolutions in the Modern World.* Cambridge: Cambridge University Press, 1994.

———. *States and Social Revolutions.* New York: Cambridge University Press, 1979.

Tilly, Charles. *European Revolutions, 1492–1992.* Cambridge, Mass.: Blackwell, 1993.

———. "Revolutions and Collective Violence." In *Handbook of Political Science,* vol. 3, *Macropolitical Theory,* edited by Fred I. Greenstein and Nelson W. Polsby.

Reading, Mass.: Addison-Wesley, 1975.

Trimberger, Ellen Kay. *Revolution from Above: Military Bureaucrats and Development in Japan, Turkey, Egypt and Peru.* New Brunswick, N.J.: Transaction, 1978.

Zunes, Stephen. "Unarmed Insurrections against Authoritarian Governments in the Third World: A New Kind of Revolution." *Third World Quarterly* 15 (1994): 403–426.

See also INDIAN NATIONAL MOVEMENT; IRANIAN REVOLUTION, 1963–1979; PHILIPPINES PEOPLE POWER REVOLUTION, 1986; REVOLUTIONS OF 1989; SOLIDARITY (POLAND); UNITED STATES, INDEPENDENCE MOVEMENT, 1765–1775

Revolutions of 1989

Series of political upheavals in which "people power" in various forms, generally nonviolent in character, was one part of a larger overall process that undermined one-party Communist systems in the six Eastern European countries that were allied with the Soviet Union through membership in the Warsaw Treaty Organization: Poland, Hungary, East Germany, Bulgaria, Czechoslovakia, and Romania. (Some of these countries can legitimately be viewed as part of "Central Europe," but for convenience the term "Eastern Europe" is used in this survey.)

There were similarities among the events in these different countries: in all cases there was popular pressure, including demonstrations in the streets; factions favoring reform existed within the ruling Communist parties; nervous Communist regimes showed themselves incapable of rallying serious public support; the Soviet Union proved unwilling to come to the aid of the Communist establishment; attempts to create transitional regimes failed to satisfy the public's demand for change; there was either an open transfer of power, or at least a public admission that there had to be an abandonment of the existing one-party system; constitutional guarantees of the primacy of ruling Communist parties were abolished; and, by 1990 at the latest, free multiparty elections were held.

The events in the six countries were revolutions of an unusual kind. In most cases the old order was in some measure ready to yield to a new one. The revolution sought was one involving an abandonment of revolutionary ideas, a reassertion of multiparty democracy, and a preoccupation with the past. Some observers coined the term "refolution" to encompass the element of reform, as much as revolution, which was at the heart of the 1989 events.

The similarities between events in the six countries, and the fact that they all led to the end of the one-party state as it had been known, suggest a degree of inevitability and uniformity that is misleading. Events in each country had their own character and causes, and left very different legacies for the hazardous process of trying to construct a post-Communist democratic order.

In 1990–1991 comparable processes were to take place in the former Soviet Union. Also, from January 1990 onward, cautious moves toward multiparty systems began in the two Eastern European Communist-ruled countries, Albania and Yugoslavia, which had not undergone revolutions in 1989. In these countries, which were not members of the Warsaw Pact, Moscow had less influence on events; and in Yugoslavia the collapse of the federal system led to the outbreak of a series of wars of succession beginning in May 1991.

Impact of the Changes in the Soviet Union upon Eastern Europe

The changes in the Soviet Union following Mikhail Gorbachev's accession to the leadership of the Communist Party of the Soviet Union (CPSU) in 1985 provided the essential precondition for the subsequent upheaval in Eastern Europe. These changes led both to a questioning of numerous aspects of Communist rule and to a growing sense that the Soviet Union might not intervene to defend unpopular socialist regimes by force of arms.

By the summer of 1989 Gorbachev appeared to have retreated significantly from the long-standing Soviet interventionist doctrine, commonly and pejoratively known as the "Brezhnev doctrine," which had sought to justify Soviet military intervention in a socialist country when the leading role of the Communist Party was felt to be threatened there. In his book *Perestroika,* first published in 1987, Gorbachev wrote: "The time is ripe for abandoning views on foreign policy which are influenced by an imperial standpoint. Neither the Soviet Union nor the United States is able to force its will on others. It is possible to suppress, compel, bribe, break or

blast, but only for a certain period." In a number of speeches, Gorbachev intimated that the Soviet Union would not try to inhibit gradual changes in Eastern Europe. Similar indications were given by Soviet Foreign Minister Eduard Shevardnadze. The effect of such statements was to encourage those Eastern Europeans who were pressing for changes to move ahead even of the pace of the Soviet restructuring.

However, the process of abandoning of the Brezhnev doctrine was not sudden, was to some extent forced upon Gorbachev by the pace of events in Eastern Europe, and was in several respects uncertain and incomplete. The long-standing ambiguity in Soviet policy between subscription to the principle of noninterference on the one hand, and maintenance of an imposed order in Eastern Europe on the other, continued right up to 1989. There was still room for doubt as to whether in an actual crisis the Soviet Union would act in accordance with its recent words or its past practice, and whether policy would be made by Gorbachev or by others. As one leading member of Solidarity in Poland, Dr. Janusz Onyszkiewicz, was later to put it, by autumn 1989 the Brezhnev doctrine might have been buried by Shevardnadze and others, but it was not yet proved to be dead.

In addition to public statements suggesting that military intervention to prevent change in Eastern Europe was unlikely, Gerhard Wettig reports evidence of a decision by the CPSU Politburo in August 1989 that Soviet troops in East Germany, Czechoslovakia, and Poland were to stay in their barracks if conflict broke out in these countries—a decision not known about there at the time.

It was only when the Eastern European revolutions were already well under way that the Brezhnev doctrine seemed to be conclusively renounced. In an interview with U.S. television on October 25, Mr. Gennady Gerasimov, the Soviet Foreign Ministry spokesman, said: "We now have the Frank Sinatra doctrine. . . . So every country decides on its own which road to take." This statement, which referred to Frank Sinatra's line "I did it my way," attracted widespread attention and was taken as a sign that the Soviet Union would not intervene by force to prevent the changes then going on in Eastern Europe. On October 26–27, a meeting of Warsaw Treaty foreign ministers in Warsaw recognized the absolute right of each state to determine its own sociopolitical development.

It was not just through the erosion of the Brezhnev doctrine that the Soviet Union assisted the process of change in Eastern Europe. The whole process of questioning so many aspects of socialism, and of Stalin's and Brezhnev's legacies, was bound to have a strong secondary effect in those countries on which the Soviet Union had imposed socialist-type systems. This was especially so in countries whose regimes had been loudest in proclaiming their absolute loyalty to the Soviet Union: East Germany, Czechoslovakia, and Bulgaria.

Some have seen the changes in the USSR, and Gorbachev's policies, as having themselves created the changes in Eastern Europe. Soviet foreign minister Eduard Shevardnadze said at the CPSU Congress in July 1990 in perhaps something of an exaggeration: "Did we, the diplomats, the ministers and the top political leadership, know what was going to happen in eastern Europe? I have never answered this question, but now I shall answer it. Yes, we foresaw everything, we felt everything. We felt that unless serious changes were made, tragic events would follow."

Suggestions that the changes were a part of policy, that they reflected a conscious decision, or that the time scale was foreseen, need to be examined critically. In the confused conditions of the Soviet Union in 1989, Gorbachev was riding an avalanche and trying all the time to look as if he was in control. It is doubtful whether he, or his senior colleagues, can really claim so much direct responsibility for a series of events that had many causes. Inasmuch as the Soviet regime did make plans for change in Eastern Europe in 1989, evidence suggests that they were plans for controlled change to Communist reformers such as Petar Mladenov in Bulgaria, rather than fundamental change to multiparty systems.

Whatever the intentions of the Soviet leaders toward Eastern Europe may in fact have been, to outsiders it was far from clear in the summer of 1989 that the Soviet Union was ready to see Communist control disappear. Some in the West, and perhaps in the East too, were still influenced by arguments that Communist totalitarian systems were unchangeable, or at least not likely to change. Even those who correctly perceived that the changes in Moscow were very profound still had grounds for doubt about how exactly they would affect Eastern Europe. It is notorious that periods of reforming change in Moscow can presage tragedy in

Eastern Europe—as had been demonstrated dramatically in 1953 in East Germany and 1956 in Hungary. Moreover, despite all the political reforms he had introduced, Gorbachev apparently remained an advocate of one-party rule. As late as November 26, 1989, he published an article in *Pravda* defending the retention of single-party rule in the USSR.

Cautious views about prospects for change were informed by an abiding sense that the Soviet Union remained attached to a security system in Eastern Europe that had been created out of the catastrophe of the Second World War, and that had seemingly provided a greater degree of stability for the USSR than previous systems had done. In 1987, Gorbachev had been general secretary of the Communist Party of the Soviet Union for only a few years and was far from certain to stay in power; whereas the leaders of the six Eastern European member states of the Warsaw Pact had, by 1987, held power for an impressive average of over twenty years.

Many observers put more emphasis on reformist prospects in Poland and Hungary than on the possibility of mass resistance in the more orthodox countries of Eastern Europe. This was not altogether wrong: events in Eastern Europe in 1989 did begin with reform in Poland and Hungary, even though they were to continue with more active popular participation in civil resistance in East Germany and Czechoslovakia.

Poland

Poland was the first Eastern European Communist country to move decisively toward non-Communist government. On January 17–18, a meeting of the Central Committee of the Polish United Workers' Party (the ruling Communist party, PUWP) accepted proposals for political pluralism. These proposals had been articulated by Solidarity, an independent movement, founded in 1980. On June 4, 1989, in elections for the *Sejm* (parliament), candidates for Solidarity decisively beat Communist candidates. On August 24, the National Assembly elected as prime minister Tadeusz Mazowiecki of Solidarity, and on September 12 it endorsed his proposals for a new coalition council of ministers dominated by Solidarity.

This change in Poland was in part the result of pressure from below in the form of popular resistance. Over a period of more than twenty years, the civil resistance of Poles, and

R

especially of Polish workers, had contributed significantly to an evolution in the thinking of the party leadership. In this process, the strike weapon had been paramount. The strikes in the Baltic ports in the winter of 1970–1971 had shown the capacity of such action even in the face of brutal repression, and many subsequent strikes and demonstrations in the next two decades, especially in summer 1980, had added to the party's malaise, while also providing the pretext for the desperate move in December 1981 to impose martial law and outlaw Solidarity.

In Poland after 1980, civil resistance had to be used with considerable care. Solidarity showed its power as much by its ability to restrain its followers as by its ability to unleash them. In December 1988, at a time of crucial deliberations on the future of Poland, one senior party figure, Mieczyslaw Rakowski, said publicly that Solidarity leader Lech Walesa was "a different man from 1981" (the period of Solidarity's confrontation with the authorities leading to the imposition of martial law). Walesa was now said to favor gradual change and compromise with the PUWP.

The change in Poland was also the result of evolutionary changes within party and government organs. It occurred as the government slowly came to recognize that the Communist system was morally and politically bankrupt. The proposals for political pluralism, originally articulated by Solidarity, were adopted by the Central Committee of the PUWP on January 17–18, 1989, after a tense debate. The senior Politburo member and principal party ideologist, Mr. Marian Orzechowski, produced an initiative on political and trade union pluralism. After a tense and difficult debate (in which the leaders threatened to resign), this was accepted, providing the necessary basis for the elections in June and the formation of a mainly non-Communist government in August–September 1989.

Internal factors, however important, were not the only ones contributing to the Polish outcome of a non-Communist government. The changes in the Soviet Union played a crucial part, not least in increasing the willingness of the PUWP regime to search for compromise solutions with its Solidarity adversaries. The U.S.-led policy of limited sanctions, introduced by President Ronald Reagan after the 1981 imposition of martial law, may also have had some effect. These had limited objectives: the ending of emergency laws, the freeing of political prisoners, and the resumption of government dialogue with Solidarity. As these objectives were achieved, the sanctions were progressively lifted. Finally, there were reports in 1992, which aroused much controversy, that during the 1980s Solidarity had received substantial financial support from the West, including from the Vatican bank and the U.S. Central Intelligence Agency (CIA).

Hungary

Hungary too had a pioneering role in creating preconditions for change in other countries in Eastern Europe. It did so partly by pointing the way toward a pluralistic economic and political system within Hungary itself, and partly by influencing events in East Germany decisively by permitting the passage of emigrants from East Germany to Austria. The changes in Hungary were characterized, even more than in Poland, by an early and gradual evolution of ideas, including within the ruling party, the Hungarian Socialist Workers' Party (HSWP). This evolution was powerfully influenced by memories of the Hungarian Revolution of 1956 and by a strong awareness of the need to reform the economic system if the country was to be competitive internationally. Although there were many important strikes and demonstrations, there was no dramatic confrontation or sudden transfer of power of the kind that happened in other countries in 1989.

By 1988, the evolution in Hungary had reached a point where genuine political and economic pluralism was increasingly identified as the goal. In July 1988, Prime Minister Károly Grósz, during a visit to the United States, said that he could "envisage any sort of a system" in Hungary, including a multiparty system. On November 13, a coalition of opposition groups issued a call for democratic elections.

In 1989, the moves toward pluralism gathered pace. On January 11, the Hungarian parliament passed a law enabling citizens to establish independent associations. In June, various new political parties were set up. On June 21, Imre Pozsgay, the reformist leader of the HSWP, said that the party accepted the principle of a democratic electoral political system based on free elections and contested by rival political parties. In July, János Kádár, who had dominated Hungarian political life since 1956, died, freeing the way for further reforms. On September 18, a complex series of talks between the party and opposition organizations resulted, after a marathon total of 238 sessions, in a compromise agreement that provided for new presidential elections, a new constitution, and new electoral laws. Pozsgay's role in all this is a notable example of how important a part in the process of change in Eastern Europe was played by influential individuals within ruling Communist parties. On October 7, the HSWP disbanded, re-forming itself as a socialist party purportedly comparable to those in the West. On October 23, 1989, the acting head of state, Mátyás Szürös, formally proclaimed the new Hungarian Republic (no longer the "Hungarian People's Republic") and a new constitution.

Disciplined but strong popular pressure within Hungary contributed greatly to the changes by forcing the pace and making Communist reformists go beyond reform. It was manifested in many ways, including in demonstrations in June 1988 (violently dispersed by the police), and in June 1989 (assisted by the authorities), to commemorate the death of Imre Nagy in the wake of the 1956 Hungarian Revolution. At the demonstration on June 16, 1989, in front of a crowd of 200,000 and shown live on national television, Viktor Orbán of the Young Democrats said prophetically: "If we can trust our souls and strength, we can put an end to the Communist dictatorship; if we are determined enough we can force the Party to submit itself to free elections; and if we do not lose sight of the ideals of 1956, then we will be able to elect a government that will start immediate negotiations for the swift withdrawal of Russian troops."

The Hungarian changes in 1989 included the opening up of Hungary's border with Austria—a process that had started in May 1989 when the dismantling of border fences began. This had huge ramifications, both because it enabled East German refugees to escape from their country to the West via Hungary, and also because it raised hopes that the "iron curtain" could disappear along its entire length. On March 17, 1989, Hungary had become the first Eastern European state formally to accede to the terms of the 1951 UN Convention on Refugees and the follow-up Protocol of 1967—an event prompted by the influx of some thirteen thousand ethnic Hungarian refugees from Romania. This agreement was to provide a useful buttress to Hungary in autumn 1989 in reinforcing its resolve to permit East German refugees to transit Hungarian territory and go to

Austria. It provided Hungary with a good legal ground for repudiating on September 10 a secret bilateral agreement with East Germany, that had been concluded in June 1969, barring nationals of the other state from unauthorized travel to third states. After a decent interval following the September 10 decision, Hungary also received generous state-guaranteed credits from West Germany: an illustration of the significance of the foreign policies of Western states in assisting the process of change in Eastern Europe.

East Germany

In East Germany, unlike in Poland and Hungary, the Communist regime in 1989 was not of a mind to make major concessions to its reformist critics. Numerous manifestations of peaceful opposition, including election monitoring in May, mass emigration, and demonstrations of various kinds, had been increasing throughout the summer of 1989. From May onward, a flood of refugees to the West via Hungary had forced many close to the regime to radically rethink the utility of the Berlin Wall and many other key policies as well. In September, New Forum came into existence: a body without office, staff, or funds. Its members were not antisocialist, and largely limited themselves to a straightforward call for democratic reform. In October and early November, huge demonstrations in East Berlin, Leipzig, and other cities provided further proof that the regime had lost control of its own population, and also indicated a public mood that was more pro-Western than New Forum's leaders. The whole process was indeed a great triumph of nonviolent pressure from below.

On October 8, a march of thirty thousand in Dresden (where the moderate Hans Modrow was party leader) dispersed after the authorities agreed to meet a delegation for discussions. On October 9, at least fifty thousand people demonstrated in Leipzig, following the regular Monday "prayers for peace" in the Church of St. Nicholas—an event that has been called a "turning point" in the East German revolution. Violence by the authorities was widely feared, and as subsequently revealed, orders to use force against demonstrators were in fact issued by Erich Honecker, the head of state and of the ruling Socialist Unity Party (SED). The protesters undertook to remain peaceful, and there was a last-minute appeal, issued by well-known individuals, for nonviolence. On this basis the

R

local commanders argued in a dispatch to East Berlin that the use of force was not necessary, and the order was revoked.

On October 11, the SED Politburo accepted the need for dialogue with the population, and on October 18, Erich Honecker resigned as head of state and head of party after eighteen years in power, being succeeded by Egon Krenz, who was not known to be a reformer. This did nothing to stop the demonstrators, who under the leadership of New Forum wanted more fundamental change. On October 30, over 300,000 demonstrated in Leipzig, and on November 4, perhaps half a million demonstrated in East Berlin. The refugee wave continued. On November 8, the new SED leadership indicated that it would accept the idea of free elections. On November 9, travel restrictions were lifted, which meant opening up the Berlin Wall. From then on, free elections were inevitable, leading to the meeting of East Germany's first freely elected parliament on April 5, 1990, and to the unification of Germany, which came into effect on October 3, 1990.

Special circumstances made peaceful opposition possible, and effective. The popular pressure was undoubtedly assisted by pressure from outside. The East German regime, having for decades proclaimed eternal loyalty to the Soviet Union, was peculiarly vulnerable to change in Moscow. The visit by Gorbachev to celebrate the fortieth anniversary of the German Democratic Republic on October 7 was a key catalyst. In a speech in East Berlin on October 6, Gorbachev stressed that "matters affecting the GDR are decided not in Moscow but in Berlin." Some of the demonstrators later that month shouted "Gorby, Gorby." Although Soviet policy toward East Germany was opaque at times, and some influential Soviet figures favored military support for a beleaguered socialist regime, the Soviet leadership appears to have opposed all use of force against the demonstrations.

In addition, the existence of a prosperous, free, and defended country near at hand, namely West Germany, provided not just an example for East Germans to aspire toward, but also a haven to which they could flee—as some 180,000 did, by one means or another, between January 1 and November 9, 1989.

The discipline of the East German demonstrators was also a significant factor. Honecker and his colleagues tended to favor the use of force. They had congratulated the Chinese on the Tiananmen Square massacre only a few months before. They came close to repeating it at Leipzig on October 9. That they did not do so is probably due not only to some resistance from within the regime, and from Gorbachev, but also to the fact that the protests, mostly church-led, were restrained, and demonstrators gave no pretext for violent repression.

Bulgaria

The changes in Bulgaria in 1989 had more the character of a "palace coup." On November 10, the seventy-eight-year-old Todor Zhivkov, who had been first secretary of the Bulgarian Communist Party (BCP) since 1954, was ousted. His successor, and the principal engineer of his removal, was Petar Mladenov, the foreign minister. Mladenov had reportedly been outraged by the renewal in May 1989 of the repression of Bulgaria's Turkish minority. In late October, he had allegedly stopped off in Moscow while en route to China and secured backing from the Soviet leadership for a challenge to Zhivkov. On November 3, about four thousand people had taken part in a brief prodemocracy demonstration outside the National Assembly building. Overall, popular participation was much less than in the other countries of Eastern Europe. The coup's timing and direction were decisively influenced by the domino effect of events elsewhere and by the strong sense in Bulgaria that it is a country whose fate is inextricably linked with that of the Soviet Union.

The change from Communist rule in Bulgaria continued in 1990 and 1991. In June 1990, the Socialist Party (a reincarnation of the BCP) became the first such Eastern European party to win free elections. However, the new government was neither effective nor popular, and in November, a general strike, and daily demonstrations in Sofia, led to the resignation of the socialist prime minister, Andrei Lukanov, thus effectively ending Communist Party rule. In elections in October 1991, the anti-Communist Union of Democratic Forces (UDF) came out ahead of the Socialist Party.

Czechoslovakia

The "velvet revolution" in Czechoslovakia in November–December 1989 began one week after the Berlin Wall was opened. On November 17, the anniversary of a Nazi assault on Czech students, Czech police attacked demonstrators in Prague, and for a time it was believed that one student had been killed. On November 19, Civic Forum was formed, linking together various

Czech opposition groups. Mass demonstrations and strikes followed, leading to a two-hour general strike on November 27. On December 3, President Gustav Husák swore in a new federal government, and on December 9 he announced his resignation. On December 29, Václav Havel was elected president by unanimous vote of the Federal Assembly, becoming the first non-Communist head of state since 1948.

The ground for the "velvet revolution" had been prepared for many years. Its roots can be traced back to the Soviet-led invasion of Czechoslovakia in 1968. At that time there had never been any question of armed resistance. An initially strong movement of demonstrations and noncooperation in the immediate aftermath of the invasion quickly gave way to a greater degree of acquiescence. Even exiles from Czechoslovakia—who in past occupations of their country had often taken up arms—did not do so in this case.

Within the country, a small movement of peaceful and legal opposition had emerged in the late 1970s, stressing the importance of national and international legal standards. In addition, the concluding document of the Vienna meeting of the Conference on Security and Cooperation in Europe, issued on January 17, 1989, also had an influence. Statements by participants at the Vienna meeting, including U.S. Secretary of State George Shultz, appear to have inhibited the Czech riot police from continuing to attack demonstrators in Prague who were commemorating the twentieth anniversary of the death of Jan Palach, a student who had committed suicide in early 1969 in protest against the Soviet-led invasion. On January 18, some five thousand people demonstrated without interference—a serious sign that the regime was losing control.

In 1989, and especially after events in the neighboring countries of Poland, East Germany, and Hungary, people began to sense that it was safe to openly oppose the decaying system of rule of the Communist Party of Czechoslovakia (CPCz). Without the mass demonstrations, the strikes, and the evidence of growing defections from the ranks of the regime's usual supporters, it is scarcely imaginable that the CPCz leaders accustomed to a monopoly of power would have abdicated; and without the impressive nonviolent discipline of the demonstrations, it is probable that the party leadership would have found a pretext for violent repression.

What happened in Prague on the night of November 17, 1989, was more complex than appeared at the time. In May 1990, a parliamentary committee investigating the events of November 17 released its report suggesting close involvement by the Soviet Committee for State Security (KGB). The general picture that emerged was of a staged police "outrage" on November 17, in which the police used brutal violence and spread rumors of the death of a demonstrator—all with the aim of creating conditions in which the existing leadership of the CPCz would be forced to make way for a more durable replacement. There have also been various suggestions as to the identity of the Soviet Union's favored candidate for the leadership of party and country, including the name of Zdeněk Mlynář, a former Politburo colleague of Alexander Dubček (and fellow student with Gorbachev) who had been living in the West. Whatever the truth of such reports, the leadership of Civic Forum, and the mass demonstrations throughout the country, ensured that what may have been planned as a palace coup from above ended as a genuine revolution from below.

Romania

The revolution, if such it was, in Romania in December 1989 presents the most tangled picture of all. Its character was shaped above all by the fact that President Nicolae Ceauşescu, who had led the Romanian Communist Party (RCP) since 1965, had built up a nationalist-cum-Communist regime of an essentially Stalinist character.

The changes in Romania were apparently triggered by events in the town of Timişoara, beginning on December 15. When the government made efforts to exile a popular and effective ethnic Hungarian Protestant pastor, Mr. László Tökés, demonstrations began that became openly hostile to the Ceauşescu regime. On December 17, the protesters were brutally assaulted in a slaughter that was believed at the time to number in the thousands. Many observers thought this slaughter would stop the protests. Yet it did not do so.

In Bucharest two days later, in a situation that plainly could have become a bloodbath, crowds shouting "Down with Ceauşescu!" caused the Romanian dictator to panic visibly, in sight of the television cameras. The crowd then openly challenged army tanks sent in to restore order. The next day, December 22, was the decisive day of the revolution. Ceauşescu made a final disastrous effort to speak to the angry

R

crowds, then ordered the use of force. It became apparent that the army was changing sides. The crowd was, understandably, delighted to have the army as an ally, and the shout went up "The army is with us!" Ceauşescu fled from Bucharest, and a former party official, Ion Iliescu, hastily announced the formation of a body called the National Salvation Council.

A murky and violent period ensued. It appeared that the National Salvation Council's efforts to establish a new government were opposed by individuals, reportedly from Ceauşescu's hated *Securitate* forces, who showed their opposition by engaging in sniper activity. The people who had been demonstrating peacefully were pleased to have the army with them when it came to dealing with this threat. On December 25, Nicolae Ceauşescu and his powerful wife, Elena, having been captured after their attempt to escape, were summarily tried by a military tribunal and executed. This was the only Eastern European revolution of 1989 that involved an element of civil war and the only one in which former leaders were killed.

The open use of violence by both sides in December 1989 and January 1990, and various conspiracy theories regarding these events, contributed to a mood of bitterness that would continue to haunt Romanian politics. The transfer away from Communist power was, at least at first, much less complete than in other Eastern European countries: the transition did not initially get beyond that stage of controlled liberalization of a kind that might have been planned with Moscow's consent.

A major controversy about the authenticity of the Romanian revolution broke out in 1990 focusing on an interview with the former Communist dissident Silviu Brucan and the former defense minister Nicolae Militaru, published in *Adevarul* (Truth), the main official newspaper in Bucharest, on August 23, 1990. Both of them had been prominent in the National Salvation Front when it seized power in December 1989 but were later sidelined by President Iliescu, who they said had shown no interest in actually changing the Communist political system. They said they had participated in a coup plot, prepared long in advance, that sealed Ceauşescu's fate. It involved army units, many generals, and a section of Ceauşescu's *Securitate* secret police. They said it was untrue that the army, as popularly believed, had suddenly taken the side of the people in a revolu-

tion. This version of events challenged that which had been put out by the National Salvation Front, which claimed to have led a popular revolution that had started in Timişoara. It was also alleged that the threat from snipers had been greatly exaggerated by the self-appointed National Salvation Council in order to secure public support for its actions. Further, in the years after 1990, evidence emerged of some degree of Soviet involvement (including that of the KGB) in plots against Ceauşescu.

Whatever the truth of the various claims and counterclaims, it seems clear from the record that President Ceauşescu fatally lost his nerve when confronted on December 21 and 22 by an unarmed but rebellious crowd. Some of the violence of the events in Romania in subsequent days can be attributed to the fact that the Ceauşescu regime, being more nationalistic and independent of the Soviet Union than most others in Eastern Europe at the time, had built up its own domestic bases of support, which continued to fight for it even after it had effectively ceased to exist. The Ceauşescu regime could not be restrained from using extreme violence by Moscow to anything like the same degree as the more dependent regimes in East Germany and Czechoslovakia.

General Issues and Conclusions
The part played by civil resistance in the events of 1989 suggests several conclusions.

1. Civil resistance was only one aspect of a large range of factors leading to the revolutions in Eastern Europe. It did, nevertheless, shape the character, course, and outcome of these revolutions.

2. There are several explanations for why, in a particularly highly armed region of the most highly armed continent, resistance assumed a nonviolent form. These include national traditions of resistance going back decades and even centuries; the influence of churches; ethical rejection of political violence; memories of wars and civil wars, leading to a desire not to repeat their miseries; an inhibition against the use of arms where these are known to be numerous and destructive; and an awareness of the vulnerability of the system being opposed. In many cases, civil resistance was a reaction to the fact of the monopoly of power's being in the

hands of the state, and to the experience of overwhelming force. The lesson of such force, as used for example in Hungary in 1956 and Czechoslovakia in 1968, coupled with the memory of Western passivity, compelled opponents of Communist systems to resort to means other than violence to achieve their ends.

3. When a system has lost its inner belief and its dynamism, as Soviet-style socialism had done by the late 1980s (due partly to earlier episodes of civil resistance), it makes a relatively easy target. Further, an awareness that the Communist regimes were reluctant to use force, and would be restrained by the much more powerful Soviet leadership if they did so, assisted the growth and ultimate success of civil resistance.

4. The demonstrators, thanks to their restraint, discipline, and emphasis on legality, could not easily be viewed as a security threat and gave no real justification for the use of counterforce. In at least two instances in East Germany and Romania, orders from the head of state to use force against demonstrators were not implemented by senior officials.

5. The presence of free and defended countries in the West was crucial to much of the change. This was not only because these were unusual cases of revolutions in favor of actually existing types of political system (that is, as found in the West), but also because the firmness of Western countries in resisting Eastern pressure over decades contributed to the loss of dynamism of Communist systems and encouraged opposition movements.

What do the events of 1989 imply for the role of civil resistance in defense? The conclusions are not simple. If civil resistance is a form of defense, it is sometimes a very slow acting one, necessitating sometimes a long wait for the right moment to act. Societies that have just been freed from long years of externally induced repression generally want to be defended, not liberated, in future. The countries that emerged from the former Soviet empire all left the Warsaw Pact (which was formally dissolved on April 1, 1991), but they have sought an association with the North Atlantic Treaty Organization and have not put all reliance on civil resistance as a means of defense against present and possible future threats. Civil resistance was highly effective in 1989, but was implicitly understood to be a special option for special circumstances.

Adam Roberts

References

Brinton, William M., and Alan Rinzler, eds. *Without Force or Lies: Voices from the Revolution of Central Europe in 1989–90.* San Francisco: Mercury House, 1990.

Dawisha, Karen. *Eastern Europe, Gorbachev, and Reform: The Great Challenge.* 2nd ed. Cambridge: Cambridge University Press, 1990.

Garton Ash, Timothy. *In Europe's Name: Germany and the Divided Continent.* London: Jonathan Cape, 1993.

____ *We the People: The Revolution of '89 Witnessed in Warsaw, Budapest, Berlin and Prague.* Harmondsworth: Penguin, 1990.

Gati, Charles. *The Bloc that Failed: Soviet–East European Relations in Transition.* London: Tauris, 1990.

Gorbachev, Mikhail. *Perestroika: New Thinking for Our Country and the World.* Rev. ed. London: Fontana/ Collins, 1988.

Havel, Václav, et al. *The Power of the Powerless: Citizens against the State in Central-Eastern Europe.* London: Hutchinson, 1985.

Oberdorfer, Don. *The Turn: How the Cold War Came to an End: The United States and the Soviet Union, 1983–1990.* London: Cape, 1992.

Pravda, Alex, ed. *The End of the Outer Empire: Soviet–East European Relations in Transition, 1985–90.* London: Sage, 1992.

Roberts, Adam. "Civil Resistance in the East European and Soviet Revolutions of 1989–91." In *The Soviet Union in Eastern Europe, 1945–89,* edited by Odd Arne Westad, Sven Holtsmark, and Iver B. Neumann. New York: St. Martin's, 1994. (An earlier version was published as *Civil Resistance in the East European and Soviet Revolutions.* Cambridge, Mass.: Albert Einstein Institution, 1991.)

Simpson, John. *The Darkness Crumbles: Despatches from the Barricades Revised and Updated.* London: Hutchinson, 1992.

R

Wettig, Gerhard. "The Kremlin's Impact on the Peaceful Revolution in East Germany (August 1989–March 1990)." In *The Soviet Union in Eastern Europe, 1945–89*, edited by Odd Arne Westad, Sven Holtsmark, and Iver B. Neumann. New York: St. Martin's, 1994.

See also BALTIC INDEPENDENCE MOVEMENTS, 1987–1991; BERLIN WALL DESTRUCTION, 1989–1990; CHARTER 77; CHINA; CZECHOSLOVAKIA, 1968 RESISTANCE MOVEMENT; DEMOCRATIZATION; HAVEL, VÁCLAV; SOLIDARITY (POLAND); SOVIET UNION, COUP ATTEMPT, 1991; TIANANMEN SQUARE, DEMOCRACY MOVEMENT, BEIJING, 1989

Rosenstraße Protest (Germany), 1943

The only incidence of mass German opposition to the Nazi effort to exterminate the Jews. In the heart of Berlin, in early 1943, German non-Jews gathered openly to protest the arrest and imminent deportation of their Jewish family members. The vast majority of these protesters were women married to Jewish men, who met day and night on the square during the course of a week. As many as six hundred or more gathered at once, and as many as six thousand had joined in by the protest's end. London Radio characterized the scene as an ongoing demonstration procession, with women continuously arriving to join the protest, or leaving to take care of other family or work matters. Despite repeated actions of the Gestapo to scatter the women by threats to shoot them down in the street, they continued their protest. Finally, Joseph Goebbels, Nazi Party authority for Greater Berlin, ordered the release of seventeen hundred to two thousand imprisoned Jews in intermarried families.

An examination of the Nazi theory of power, incidents of Catholic resistance, and the historical circumstances surrounding the Rosenstraße protest help to clarify the Nazi dictatorship's response to the protest. Popular protest offered a possibility for resistance in part because the regime presupposed that its power derived from the Aryan people. Seldom if ever did National Socialists challenge the idea that all power derives from the conscious consent of the Aryan people. This theory encouraged Nazi use of propaganda and established limits to the use of force against its own population. The Rosenstraße protest convinced the Nazi leader-

ship that forcible deportation of the arrested Jews risked social unrest and discussion and disclosure of the Final Solution, which could endanger that entire effort.

Goebbels's deputy Leopold Gutterer said in an interview in 1986 that Goebbels had feared that the protesters might be seen as an example by other Germans. He said further that Goebbels had released the Jews because he knew that this would dissolve the protest immediately. In his diary, Goebbels rationalized that he would deport the intermarried Berlin Jews after a couple of weeks. Yet these Jews, officially released and registered, survived the war, while receiving government food rations and working in government-assigned jobs.

The Rosenstraße protest followed a decision by Reich leaders to finish the deportation of German Jews and the devastating German defeat at Stalingrad. Stalingrad was a terrible blow to the German morale as well as to the military, and Goebbels strove to improve the public mood just as the Nazi leadership decided it would have to mobilize more of the German public to compensate for war losses. Total war, declared in response to Stalingrad during the week just prior to the Rosenstraße protest, increased the dictatorship's dependency on the people in direct proportion to its summons for additional popular mobilization. A parallel development was the increasing need for secrecy around the Final Solution, the revelation of which would have damaged the public morale that the regime strove to nurture, especially during war.

Protest was very rare in Nazi Germany, but some Catholics also successfully resisted specific Nazi initiatives. In 1936 and 1941, Catholics in several villages used protests, boycotts, and civil disobedience to force the regime to rescind decrees removing crucifixes from schools. Also responding to the force of popular opinion led by Catholic Bishop Clemens August Graf von Galen, Hitler ordered a stop to the so-called euthanasia killing of the insane in August 1941. The few successful protests in Nazi Germany took place under a variety of political circumstances. Key to their impact was their solidarity. At their strongest, protesters appeared to represent not just themselves, but were an integral part of society. Second, these actions were also nonviolent. Nonviolent actions avoided the appearance of treason and did not legitimate and unleash the crushing violence of the Nazi regime. Third, opposition that succeeded in reversing Nazi policies or initiatives was overt.

Publicly expressed opposition not only drew attention to secret programs and demonstrated dissent, but also potentially transmitted knowledge about a politically powerful means of dissent.

But it is important to remember that none of these protests challenged the regime itself, only specific policies. Yet even under the extreme and closed conditions of the Nazi dictatorship, civilians did take actions that challenged the fundamental Nazi principles, and saved thousands of lives. The successes of Catholics and intermarried Germans suggest that German civilians might have extracted concessions from National Socialism of lar-ger magnitude, preventing Nazism from ruling in totality and achieving even less of the "racial purification" definitive of National Socialism.

Nathan Stoltzfus

References

Stoltzfus, Nathan. *Resistance of the Heart: Intermarriage and the Rosenstrasse Protest in Nazi Germany*. New York: W.W. Norton, 1996.

See also DENMARK, RESISTANCE TO NAZI OCCUPATION; JEWISH RESISTANCE TO THE HOLOCAUST; NAZISM, CIVILIAN RESISTANCE, 1939–1945; NORWAY, RESISTANCE TO GERMAN OCCUPATION, 1940–1945

Rowlatt Bills, Opposition (India), 1919

First nationwide satyagraha campaign in India led by Mohandas K. Gandhi against the Rowlatt bills of 1918 and 1919. Lasting for seven weeks, the campaign started nonviolently but soon became violent. Opposition to the Rowlatt bills was marked by enormous widespread participation, a turn to violence, and Gandhi's subsequent conclusion that the masses had not been adequately prepared for the discipline of satyagraha.

The Sedition Committee of 1918, headed by Sir Sidney Rowlatt, proposed two bills strengthening the power of the British authorities to control what it considered seditious and anarchic offenses. The first was passed in 1919 as the Rowlatt Act, and the second was nearing introduction to the legislature. Indians claimed that both bills were unjust and violated civil rights. The campaign launched by Gandhi intended to invoke the withdrawal of the enacted bill and the prevention of the passing of the second.

In March 1919, the campaign began in earnest with participants pledging their support and purifying themselves with a one-day fast. After appeals to the viceroy, Gandhi called for mass direct action. Over 1 million Indians throughout the country participated in civil disobedience to selected laws, demonstrations, and a nationwide *hartal* (general strike) on April 6. In reponse to growing police repression, protesters began to react violently, rioting in some areas. Martial law was declared in three states and violent clashes were widespread. Distraught with the violence, Gandhi suspended the movement and went on a three-day penitential fast to urge Indians to stop their fighting.

While the law was never rescinded, the Rowlatt Act also was never invoked by the government, and the second bill was never introduced. Despite this limited success, Gandhi considered this first experiment with mass satyagraha a failure because of the outbreak of violence, and he vowed that future campaigns would consist of well-trained cadres of volunteers.

Brad Bennett

References

Bondurant, Joan V. *Conquest of Violence: The Gandhian Philosophy of Conflict*. Princeton: Princeton University Press, 1958, 1988.

See also GANDHI, MOHANDAS KARAMCHAND; INDIAN NATIONAL MOVEMENT; SATYAGRAHA

Ruhrkampf (Germany), 1923

Resistance by the German population of the Ruhr River region to the French and Belgian military occupation between January and September 1923. The aims of German resistance were twofold: to frustrate the French objective of extracting coal in lieu of unpaid reparations obligations imposed on Germany at the peace settlements of 1919, and to end the occupation and restore Berlin's authority over the region. Noncooperation tactics prevented the removal of coal for over three months and greatly increased the cost of the occupation. Nevertheless, the German government could not bear the economic burden of the resistance campaign and noncooperation ended in September. Occupation continued for another year and a half, during which France offset its occupation costs through the removal of coal. However, the entire episode encouraged an international revision of Germany's reparations obligations through the Dawes Plan of September 1924, substantially reducing the money Germany was required to pay the victors of World War I.

The French government and public felt more aggrieved by German aggression in the war than did their allies. After the war France saw itself as a country that had paid dearly in blood and treasure, to which not even Germany could compare. They were, therefore, more demanding of reparations. French Prime Minister Raymond Poincaré's government debated policies toward the Ruhr and the Rhineland through November 1922. The Ruhr region, as the center of heavy industry, had contributed significantly to Germany's economic recovery following the First World War. For example, German coke production in the Ruhr in 1922 was virtually the same as that of the Ruhr and Rhineland combined in 1913. Similar recovery had occurred in the production of steel and in the mining of coal and related minerals. The material wealth of the region, combined with its contiguity to the French-occupied Rhineland and to France itself, made it an attractive target when Germany defaulted on its reparations payments.

The military invasion of the Ruhr between January 11 and January 16, 1923, was virtually effortless. General Jean-Marie Degoutte used three divisions (two infantry and one cavalry) to control an area of 3,300 square kilometers, containing 3.5 million people. Occupation of the major cities, such as Essen and Dortmund, took a day or less.

Although not prepared in advance, a German strategy of noncooperation rapidly emerged in response to the occupation. Owners of the large coal and chemical syndicates removed documents and other crucial materials from the Ruhr valley. Coal miners continued to work the mines, but they refused to obey the orders of the French military regime. Rail workers refused to transport coal from the mine heads. French military and political planners were unprepared for this blanket denial of cooperation. As a result, they faced a situation described by the official French military historian of the period, François-André Paoli, in the phrase "All the Ruhr is at work, but not to our benefit."

Three factors contributed to the success of the resistance during its initial six months— existing organizations, cross-class solidarity, and the willingness of the government in Berlin to subsidize the resistance economically. The population of the Ruhr was well organized by virtue of the concentrated economic activity of the region. Labor was organized along industrial lines by unions of the Left. In addition, industrial activity was organized into syndicates according to product. The most important was the Coal Syndicate, located in Essen. Others included the Syndicate of Distilled products, located in Bochum, and the Steel Syndicate in Dusseldorf. These were the peak organizations of the region's economic activity. After the war, German metallurgical industry had rapidly concentrated, both horizontally and vertically. Inflation favored the consolidation of smaller firms into very large firms. Wartime production and the need for postwar adjustment also favored the rationalization and modernization of production. From this process emerged the industrial giants that would play decisive roles in the next decades of German history, such as Thyssen and Krupp. The leaders of these firms, Auguste Thyssen, Hugo Stinnes, and others, formed a distinctive class of industrialists.

At the beginning of resistance, the unions, the syndicates, and the industrialists drew together and cooperated. The Coal Syndicate, for example, immediately removed its records from Essen as the invasion approached. Workers continued to operate the mines and factories, unless the French soldiers attempted to control them directly. Industrialists continued to pay their workers (with funds reimbursed by Berlin) and abided by German policies not to trade or cooperate with the occupation authorities. Several industrialists, including Stinnes, were jailed. Administrative personnel and railway workers, the two other crucial sectors of economic activity, also obeyed Berlin's policy of noncooperation with the occupation. The result of this cross-class and cross-sectoral solidarity was the complete frustration of French policy to control the Ruhr region in order to obtain the coal reparations France was due.

However, the resistance eventually failed. It was not able to achieve either of its principal objectives—ending the occupation or preventing the extraction of goods as reparations. Three factors contributed to this failure—the political fragility of the German government, the effectiveness of French occupation policies, and the wholesale collapse of the German currency. Politically, the Franco-Belgian invasion prompted a surge of support for the government of Wilhelm Cuno in Berlin. Although solidarity was widespread, it was not uniform across the political spectrum and Germany was far from unified. Parties of the Right tended to take a stronger anti-French and German-nationalist position; parties of the Left were more inclined to view the French as a kind of protection against the nationalist Right.

By the design at Versailles, Germany did not have a strong central government and the Center-Right government of Cuno in Berlin was attacked increasingly from the federal states. Conservative and National Socialist parties took power in Bavaria. During the Ruhr struggle these parties denounced Cuno for his alleged failure to take strong action (especially military) and condemned him as a Communist or collaborationist. In Prussia, a "great coalition" of the Left and Center (including Communists) came to power. They attacked the "passive resistance" policy for the Ruhr as not flexible enough. By August the industrialists began to pursue their own economic interests. Several negotiated independently with France. And, as the economic situation worsened, workers at individual mines chose to return to work in accordance with French directives, although others stayed out.

French policies effectively exploited weaknesses in both the German political and economic situation. Significantly, this was accomplished with very little use of direct military force or physical coercion. Military forces were used directly for coercion mostly in response to episodes of sabotage or violent attacks on French and Belgian personnel. Arguably, the principal means of control was almost purely economic, implemented by the creation of MICUM (*Mission Interalliée de Contrôle des Usines et des Mines,* the Allied Mission for the Control of Factories and Mines). Although MICUM was an instrument directly under the administrative control of General Degoutte, military power was much less important than social and economic control.

Economic pressures were applied effectively to isolate the Ruhr population from the economic life of Germany. In various ways the French replaced the administrative and communication infrastructure and reorganized economic activity so that it could not benefit unoccupied Germany. For example, the French created the *Régie,* staffed by French personnel, to provide rail transportation when German railway workers refused to operate the railroads. Similarly, German bureaucrats who refused to cooperate with occupation authorities were expelled from the region (perhaps as many as 46,000 workers and their families, totaling 147,000 people) and replaced by French workers. Customs barriers established between the Ruhr and unoccupied Germany generated income and increased the costs of intra-German trade, while keeping trade between the region and France unencumbered. At the same time, until June no restrictions at all were placed on food imports to the region. This policy reflected the goals of Degoutte to avoid fomenting a complete rebellion by workers, to avoid bringing international opprobrium upon France for starving the German population, and to split the working classes from their temporary industrialist allies.

Some forms of German resistance also provided some benefits to the occupiers. For example, railway workers refused to operate the transportation system and move coal from the Ruhr to France or Belgium. But, because they were still paid, miners continued to work the pits. The result was a stockpile of coal at the pitheads that was easily removed to France once the *Régie* was organized. Similarly, because solidarity depended on financial support from Berlin, France's ability to encumber trade between the Ruhr and unoccupied Germany placed escalating burdens on German finance. Finally, while few of the other victors of the war approved of the occupation, none was ready to act against France, and in no country was a pro-German coalition nearly strong enough to influence policy.

Resistance was made possible by the German government's willingness to compensate for the financial losses noncooperation entailed—cash from Berlin replaced wages lost by workers on strike (or replaced wages paid by industry to its workers), which in turn enabled workers to purchase food and other necessities. But Berlin could supply this "strike pay" only at the cost of aggravating a latent inflation problem. By July 1923 the government was spending 60 million marks per month supporting the resistance. Then the mark collapsed completely. In July, one American dollar could be exchanged for 100,000 marks; four weeks later that dollar bought 6 million marks—the mark had retained less than 2 percent of its previous value. The policy of financing the resistance with printed money was no longer economically supportable.

The Ruhr population remained united and supportive of the government's official policy of passive resistance through midsummer, so long as the financial support from Berlin was forthcoming. The increasingly effective French restrictions, however, and the erosion of the mark's purchasing power, split the region's political solidarity and divided it from Berlin. In August, industrialists in the Ruhr began to explore a solution to the occupation independent of Berlin; some of them sought to negotiate directly with the occupying forces on an ad hoc or firm-specific basis. The economic and political crisis also produced the collapse of the Cuno government. The new government, of Gustav Stresemann, moved rapidly to bring an end to passive resistance and to work out new arrangements with Poincaré and the occupation forces.

In the end, French strategy succeeded. The French "victory" was not without cost, however. Within France, criticism mounted against Poincaré to resolve the situation he had created by the occupation. The political Right demanded more decisive action, including forcing the greater weakening of the German republic and the more direct exploitation of the region's riches. The parties of the political Left saw the occupation as adventurism and a drain on French resources.

Indeed, the occupation may have been a net economic loss for France through 1923, or at best showed a very meager net gain. Liberman shows that France netted only 120 million gold marks during 1923, and this figure should be further reduced by the costs of normal upkeep of the troops in the Ruhr and Rhineland (between 44 and 188 million gold marks). France did not realize substantial net economic gains until after the end of "passive resistance" in September and the MICUM agreements in November.

William B. Vogele

References
Ackerman, Peter, and Christopher Kruegler. *Strategic Nonviolent Conflict.* Westport, Conn.: Praeger, 1994.
Liberman, Peter. *Does Conquest Pay?* Princeton: Princeton University Press, 1995.
Paoli, François-André. *L'armée Française de 1919 a 1939: La phase fermeté.* Paris: Ministère des Armées, Service Historique, 1969–1972.
Sternstein, Wolfgang. "The *Ruhrkampf* of 1923: Economic Problems of Civilian Defense." In *The Strategy of Civilian Defense,* edited by Adam Roberts. London: Faber and Faber, 1967.
Trachtenberg, Marc. *Reparation in World Politics.* Princeton: Princeton University Press, 1982.

Russian Revolution of 1905

Dramatic shift in governing authority from the czar to something closer to a constitutional monarchy, the result of a two-year-long process of popular upheaval involving labor and general strikes, demonstrations, and the creation of alternative political institutions. The revolution in 1905 did not remove the czar—that would wait until 1917—but it marked the end of monarchical absolutism in Russia.

The underlying causes of the revolution were the social, economic, and political problems that had been festering in Russia for a generation and more. The state had long been struggling under the strains of rapid industrial growth, an anachronistic and depressed agricultural system, and the government's need to integrate or control the diverse peoples of the Russian Empire. Labor responded to its dire conditions at the turn of the century with an increasing resort to strikes. Between 1895 and 1904, for example, 1,765 separate strikes are reported to have taken place. Similarly, Russian peasants, constituting five-sixths of the empire's total population, suffered increasingly under conditions of land scarcity, an inefficient system of communal farming, and crippling taxes that ultimately financed the burgeoning industrial infrastructure. Outbursts of peasant violence usually were directed against the landed nobility, from whom most of their lands were leased or to whom they owed "redemption dues" for the land they worked.

Opposition organizations and movements had begun to form in response to the state's failure to adjust to the new realities of industrialization. Labor sought the creation of unions (although most of these organizations remained illegal). Revolutionary and liberal political organizations emerged—such as the radical populist Social Revolutionaries, the Bolsheviks led by V.I. Lenin, and liberal reformers sympathetic with the ideas of Social Democracy from Western Europe.

January 1904 was a critical month for the Russian autocracy. The First Congress of the Union of Liberation met to elect a council that immediately began to plan an action program designed to bring liberal opposition out of the shadows of Russian life. The union was a body of liberal professionals and intellectuals with political roots in the *zemstvos,* the organizations of provincial and county self-government created in the reforms of Czar Alexander II. They proposed to hold a series of public banquets that would be used as pseudo-political forums. It was planned that petitions would emerge from them, addressed to various branches of the government, embodying the liberal agenda of four-tailed suffrage (universal, secret, direct, and equal), a constituent assembly, and basic civil rights.

The banquets originally were planned to be held on or around February 19, the anniversary of the emancipation of the Russian serfs in 1861, but with the outbreak of the Russo-Japanese War on January 27, the events were postponed until November. At the end of the year, thirty-eight such banquets were held between November 5, 1904, and January 8, 1905—the eve of Bloody Sunday.

Simultaneous with the liberal banquets were other events that increased tensions. On December 5 and 6 student demonstrations in Moscow were attacked by Cossacks and brutally dispersed. On the twentieth Port Arthur was surrendered to the Japanese after a costly struggle, in what could be construed as a cowardly act by the Russian high command. It was in this highly charged and expectant atmosphere that the drama of Bloody Sunday was about to take place. In addition, on January 2, 1905, a strike broke out at the Putilov shipbuilding and arms enterprise in St. Petersburg. Other enterprises came out in support of the Putilov workers and additional demands were advanced.

As the strike spread, one of the leaders, Father Georgii Gapon, decided it was time to unveil his idea of a petition to the czar. The procession began as planned, with an estimated 150,000 participants leaving from each of the assembly branches, intending to converge on the Winter Palace square by different routes at two in the afternoon. The crowds were weaponless and reverential, as instructed. They carried icons, portraits of Nicholas and his ancestors, and sang hymns. The various branches were all stopped by military contingents along the way and told to disperse. When the crowds pressed on, they were in several cases broken up by cavalry charges, using whips, clubs, and the flats of swords. Some gave up, frustrated, while others proceeded by smaller groups and circuitous routes to eventually reach the square itself.

The shooting began against branches of the march that were stopped fairly close to the center of St. Petersburg, including the branch led by Gapon himself. Disbelief turned to horror and rage as workers, with wives and children among them, found themselves under armed attack by the czar's own elite guard units. Those who made it to the Winter Palace were attacked and driven out of the square in the late afternoon. In the end, perhaps as many as two hundred marchers were killed, and another eight hundred wounded.

The decline of the emperor's prestige that followed Bloody Sunday continued throughout the spring and summer of 1905, as new opposition organizations emerged and more and more of society aligned itself against the government. The Union of Liberation held its second congress in March, and the Second Zemstvo Congress convened in April.

By May there were enough unions or proto-unions to form a national Union of Unions, made up primarily of professional and white-collar organizations. The central bureau of the Union of Unions, directed by Pavel Milyukov of the Union of Liberation, would presumably be capable of coordinating strike activity in the pursuance of broad political objectives. In late May it announced its support for "any and all means of struggle."

Also in May the first citywide workers' council, or soviet, was formed in Ivanovo-Voznesensk, a short way from St. Petersburg. A unique feature of the soviets, as they developed here and elsewhere, was that as the new repositories of authority for the working class, they began to usurp and exercise some of the normal prerogatives of the government. By arrogating authority and exercising power, they began to provide a kind of parallel government during the latter stages of the conflict, fulfilling vital functions and setting policies for the areas under their control. At their inception, the soviets had no exclusive ideological commitments, and were genuinely democratic vehicles of worker self-organization.

The last great strike wave of 1905 began on September 19, when printers at the Sypin press struck for an increase in wages and were supported by the newly formed Moscow Printers Union, which called out the rest of the city's printers on the following day. Harcave writes that "within ten days they were joined by the city's bakers, wood workers, machine tool workers, textile workers, tobacco workers, and workers from the railroad shops." On October 2, the Moscow Soviet, comprising representatives of five trades, was formed. Its task would be to direct the strike, which by that time seemed to be losing energy in Moscow.

The impulse to strike had spread to St. Petersburg, however. Printers there struck in sympathy with the Moscow printers, and a few large factories joined them. The momentum proved sufficient to keep the strike movement going. On October 4, the Central Bureau of the Union of Railroad Workers in Moscow called for a work stoppage. This proved to be the crucial step in extending the strike throughout the empire. Moscow was the hub of the entire Russian railway system. Its shutdown sent an irresistible message far and wide. By October 8, the strike had spread to Nizhny-Novgorod, Riazansk, Yaroslavl, Kursk, and the Urals railway system, eventually including 26,000 miles of railway line and 750,000 workers. Telegraph and telephone services shut down along with the trains, and by October 10, when a general strike was declared in Moscow and the major cities of the Baltic region joined in the movement, all normal communication in the empire had ceased.

The Great October Strike was the first of its kind and scale in history. Yet it lacked the benefit of any prior planning. Many authors have used the words "contagion" and "infection" to describe what happened, but the biological analogy is faulty in at least one respect. While germs travel from one individual to another, strikes spread by occupational groups. It is hard to imagine October 1905 without the preceding months of organization building and unionization. The St. Petersburg Soviet, convened on October 13 , was but a continuation of this trend. Everywhere members of society were exercising power collectively. Even the corps de ballet in the capital went on strike. Finally, the government realized it was faced with a serious challenge to its existence.

Czar Nicholas II consulted his chief ministers on October 14 and 15. One by one, they acknowledged that the situation was beyond their control. General Trepov opined that the armed force at his command would be sufficient to put down an armed uprising in the capital, but not enough to restore railroad traffic or to quell the widespread strike. Sergei Witte, the czar's minister of finance, could see only two alternatives. Either the czar could appoint a military dictator with unlimited power who would not hesitate to crush every sign of opposition, or he could announce the first really meaningful political reforms. Witte favored the latter, which could only amount, at this stage, to the summoning of a true constituent assembly.

Their collective admission that repression would produce "rivers of blood" and might lead only to a repetition of the cycle of the previous year shows that Nicholas, in the face of widely dispersed resistance, finally accepted that there were limits to his repressive power. It was this realization that led him to order Witte to draft the imperial manifesto of October 17. Taken at face value, the manifesto looked like a complete capitulation to the extreme liberal agenda. Its provisions were as follows:

(1) to grant the people the unshakable foundations of civic freedom on the basis of genuine personal inviolability, freedom of conscience, speech, assembly, and association; (2) to admit immediately to participation in the State Duma, without suspending the scheduled elections and in so far as it is feasible in the brief period remaining before the convening of the Duma, those classes of the population that are now completely deprived of electoral rights, leaving the further development of the principle of universal suffrage to the new legislative order; and (3) to establish as an inviolable rule that no law may go into force without the consent of the State Duma and that the representatives of the people must be guaranteed the opportunity of effective participation in the supervision of the legality of the actions performed by Our appointed officials.

The October strike was losing steam, however, at the time the manifesto was issued. A unified, confident movement might have recognized an opportunity at this critical moment and declared itself victorious. After all, the manifesto represented significant change, and it had been coerced out of the government by widespread popular noncooperation. If the czar was going to play himself false, why not let him do it after the movement had time to recoup its resources, and could thus repeat the October strike performance at full strength the moment the terms of the manifesto were threatened? But the movement was not united and there is no evidence that anyone was reasoning along these lines.

At this juncture, the leading opposition organ contending for power and legitimacy was the St. Petersburg Soviet. Having managed to perpetuate itself beyond the end of the strike, it took several initiatives in the final weeks of 1905 that forced the government's hand and impelled the crisis toward its conclusion. Shortly after the manifesto the soviet declared an end to censorship. This was not an idle boast. Printers, responsive to the call, simply refused to print anything that had gone through the censors' hands. Less successful was the attempt to initiate the eight-hour day in the same manner. Workers who walked off the job after completing eight hours were subjected to lock-outs and soon gave up the tactic. The defeat left the soviet needing to prove its strength again.

The St. Petersburg Soviet issued its response to these measures on December 2. Its "Financial Manifesto" amounted to a declaration of economic warfare against the government, so long as it remained "in open war against the whole nation." The manifesto called for mass refusal to pay taxes or government debts, insistence on gold as the medium for all major transactions, and the withdrawal (in gold) of all deposits in government banks. The government recognized this as the soviets' most serious threat since mid-October and acted accordingly. The papers that had published the "Financial Manifesto" were forcibly closed and their editors arrested. The next day the soviet's meeting place was surrounded by a massive armed force, and 250 arrests were made. These included all elected deputies to the soviet and most of its executive committee.

Members of the committee who remained free called for a new empirewide general strike to begin on December 8. The Moscow Soviet followed suit with a call to strike on the seventh, and accepted a Menshevik proposal that the strike would ultimately become an armed uprising. (The Bolsheviks had wanted to begin both simultaneously.) The strike took hold in all of the major cities of the empire within a week. It was less comprehensive than the first general strike, but much more bitter and militant.

The violent uprising turned out to be quixotic in the extreme. It began when small groups of armed workers, incensed by attempts to arrest the Moscow Soviet on December 8, erected barricades on the main streets of Moscow and began exchanging fire with the police. The violent uprising was consistent with Bolshevik theories of how change would come, but it never had popular support, and did not spread to other cities. Although two thirds of the troops garrisoned in Moscow were deemed unreliable, those remaining, with some reinforcement, were sufficient to defeat the two thousand or so rebels in just over a week. With a thousand civilians dead and their stronghold in the Presnya district shelled nearly out of existence, the Moscow Soviet halted violent resistance and called off the strike on the nineteenth.

By the spring and summer of 1906, the most important reforms gained in the czar's October Manifesto largely evaporated. Unions were legalized, improvements were made in the legal status of certain minorities, and significant improvements were made in the system of land tenure. But the elections provided only limited expansion of suffrage and the Duma remained highly circumscribed by the czar's retention of powers to veto its decisions, dissolve the body, and declare martial law. As a result, the social tensions that had generated the previous two years of popular mobilization were left unresolved and the potential for moderate reform diminished.

Peter Ackerman
Christopher Kruegler

References

Ackerman, Peter, and Christopher Kruegler. *Strategic Nonviolent Conflict: The Dynamics of People Power in the Twentieth Century.* Westport, Conn.: Praeger, 1994.

Bonnell, Victoria E. *Roots of Rebellion: Workers, Politics and Organization in St. Petersburg and Moscow, 1900–1914.* Berkeley: University of California Press, 1983.

Harcave, Sidney. *First Blood: The Russian Revolution of 1905.* New York: Macmillan, 1964.

Sablinsky, Walter. *The Road to Bloody Sunday: Father Gapon and the St. Petersburg Massacre of 1905.* Princeton: Princeton University Press, 1976.

Ulam, Adam. *Russia's Failed Revolutions.* New York: Basic, 1981.

R

S

Salt March (India), 1930

Dramatic walk led by Mohandas K. Gandhi to publicize an oppressive salt tax and promote the necessity for a civil disobedience campaign for independence from British rule. The "Salt March" served as a prelude to a nationwide satyagraha campaign organized by the Indian National Congress and helped galvanize Indian support for the cause of independence.

Gandhi chose the British monopoly on the manufacture of salt and its accompanying oppressive salt tax as the target of his nonviolent resistance campaign. Gandhi, accompanied by seventy-eight trained satyagrahis, started the twenty-five day, 240-mile march from his ashram in Ahmedabad on March 12, 1930. The purposes of the walk included promoting the Congress's appeal for national civil disobedience, educating villagers about independence, and encouraging village officials to renounce their posts as an act of noncooperation with a corrupt state. Gandhi gave speeches in many villages along the way that were attended by thousands.

The marchers arrived at Dandi, on the Gujarat coast, on April 5. The next morning, Gandhi picked up a clump of salt on the beach, thereby symbolically breaking the law. This act inaugurated a two-month-long nationwide satyagraha, during which thousands of Indians manufactured, transported, and sold salt illegally. British authorities attempted to prevent these efforts and punished the transgressors, sometimes brutally. The use of *lathis* (sticks) by troops to beat back satyagrahis raiding the salt works at Dharsana injured hundreds and brought negative publicity to the British.

Viceroy Lord Irwin did not authorize the arrest of Gandhi immediately but waited until May 5, a delay that weakened the viceroy's credibility. Gandhi was finally released on January 25, 1931, and after negotiations, a Gandhi–Irwin Pact was signed in April. While it did not revoke the salt tax, it did modify regulations and allow Congress to participate in roundtable talks concerning constitutional reform. The Salt March and subsequent salt satyagraha was an integral part of the nationwide mass movement of civil disobedience for independence in 1930–1931.

Brad Bennett

References

Bakshi, S.R. *Gandhi and Salt Satyagraha.* Kerala: Vishwavidya, 1981.

Bondurant, Joan V. *Conquest of Violence: The Gandhian Philosophy of Conflict.* Princeton: Princeton University Press, 1958, 1988.

Brown, Judith M. *Gandhi and Civil Disobedience: The Mahatma in Indian Politics 1928–34.* Cambridge: Cambridge University Press, 1977.

See also DHARASANA SALT WORKS RAID, 1930; GANDHI, MOHANDAS KARAMCHAND; SATYAGRAHA

San Francisco General Strike, 1934

Four-day general strike in San Francisco, Oakland, and surrounding communities, in July 1934, in sympathy with striking Pacific Coast longshoremen. On May 9, 1934, longshoremen up and down the coast went on strike for union control of hiring and other issues. In San Francisco, other maritime workers joined the strike and teamsters refused to handle cargo from "scabs" (strikebreakers). On July 3, ship-owners, supported by police, National Guard, and vigilantes, began a campaign to open the port by force. These forces fought with strikers, and on July 5, two strikers were killed. A massive silent funeral procession on July 9 was the catalyst for the general strike. On July 16, workers throughout the area struck in sympathy for longshoremen's demands and to protest the violence by employers, vigilantes, and government forces. The strike effectively crippled San Francisco, as over 100,000 workers from many unions and sectors of the work force walked out. The general strike ended after four days, primarily because conservative labor leaders adopted propaganda tactics and made decisions against the will of the rank-and-file workers.

The eighty-three-day coastal maritime strike and the four-day San Francisco general strike triggered an era of labor insurgency. Over a million workers across the country went on a strike in the summer of 1934 alone. The general strike also highlighted various issues, including conflicts between conservative union leadership and militant rank-and-file workers, Communist-baiting, and the potential of discipline and solidarity exemplified by such a mass action.

Brad Bennett

References

Brecher, Jeremy. *Strike!* Boston: South End, 1972.

Nelson, Bruce. *Workers on the Waterfront: Seamen, Longshoremen, and Unionism in the 1930s.* Urbana and Chicago: University of Illinois Press, 1988.

See also SEATTLE GENERAL STRIKE, 1919; STRIKES

Sanctions

Coercive actions taken by one party in a conflict to influence the behavior of another party in the conflict. Sanctions may be positive or negative, though the term is most often used in its negative sense. Positive sanctions are rewards (sometimes called "carrots") offered to an opponent in exchange for a change in behavior. Negative sanctions are penalties (sometimes called "sticks") imposed on an opponent to exact a change in behavior. To use a carrot and stick approach against an opponent, then, is to use a combination of rewards and punishments, or positive and negative sanctions, to influence the opponent's behavior.

Sanctions may be violent or nonviolent. Violent sanctions include military attacks against a country, corporal punishment, and the beating of an individual for collaborating with the enemy. Nonviolent sanctions include strikes by laborers to pressure management, boycotts by consumers to influence corporate policies, and civil disobedience by citizens to change unjust laws. The term *nonviolent sanctions* is generally used synonymously with the phrase *methods of nonviolent action*.

Sanctions may be wielded by individuals, groups, or governments. Parents who tell their children that they won't get dessert if they don't finish their vegetables are resorting to the threat of a sanction (no dessert) to influence their children's eating habits. Similarly, a union on strike may ostracize those members who continue to work in an effort to get them to join the strike. And governments use the threat of such sanctions as fines and imprisonment to encourage their citizens to comply with their laws.

While sanctions may be defined broadly, the term is most commonly used in a more narrow sense to describe coercive actions between governments. International sanctions describe a government's purposeful interruption of "normal" economic or diplomatic relations with another government in order to pressure the target government to alter a certain policy or course of action. In this negative sense, they include such actions as withholding economic aid, prohibiting imports, halting exports, closing embassies, and withdrawing diplomatic personnel. International sanctions may also be positive, though this usage of the term is less common, and may include such actions as increasing economic aid, transferring technology, lowering trade barriers, and offering educational and cultural exchanges.

Roger S. Powers

See also DIPLOMATIC SANCTIONS; INTERNATIONAL ECONOMIC SANCTIONS; METHODS OF NONVIOLENT ACTION; SOUTH AFRICA, ANTI-APARTHEID SANCTIONS

Sanctuary Movement

Movement in North America to provide refuge and asylum for people fleeing the violence of civil wars and military dictatorships in El Salvador and Guatemala. Drawing on the Judeo-Christian tradition of providing a safe haven for refugees, U.S. churches and synagogues initially organized to provide bond and offer legal assistance to the refugees. Their work shifted toward smuggling Salvadorans and Guatemalans into the country and harboring them when they realized that the legal channels of asylum application were virtually impossible to use successfully. In March 1982, a Presbyterian church in Tucson, Arizona, proclaimed itself the first official sanctuary for these Central American refugees. Over the course of several years, the sanctuary movement grew into a network of several hundred churches, synagogues, and communities with the support of tens of thousands of individuals.

The concept of sanctuary as a protective place of refuge is rooted in biblical history. The Old Testament frequently addresses the needs of refugees and aliens. Of central importance is the exodus in which God liberated the Hebrews from their enslavement to the pharaoh of Egypt. God appointed Moses to lead them out, and they wandered as sojourners for forty years. This story depicts the Judeo-Christian God as a God of action, deliverance, and liberation from oppression. Upon reaching the promised land, Moses was commanded by God to set aside cities as places of refuge (*arey miklat* in Hebrew) where individuals could find asylum from those seeking to take their lives in revenge.

In addition to harboring those who were in danger, the Israelites were to take up their cause and defend them. Sanctuary, therefore, is considered not only a protective community but also a prophetic platform from which to speak out. The New Testament broadens the concept of sanctuary to include hospitality. The stranger is to be taken in and cared for, since the Israelites were also once strangers in the land of Egypt. Thus, the sanctuary movement drew upon these ancient laws by invoking the name of God and declaring their communities holy, thereby not allowing trespass by violent powers that would profane them.

The Political Context

Civil strife, violence, and governmental repression escalated in El Salvador and Guatemala in the late 1970s. Both countries had experienced decades of political dominance by military governments as well as economic dominance by a very small wealthy elite. Challenges to this economic and political structure in either country were severely repressed by the governments. Throughout this period, the regimes in El Sal-

vador and Guatemala operated with the political and material support of the U.S. government, which viewed Central America as a cold war battleground. In Guatemala, for example, the U.S. Central Intelligence Agency engineered the overthrow of the democratically elected president, Jacobo Arbenz, in 1954, leading to more than four decades of military rule. The political context became even more polarized following the successful socialist revolution in Nicaragua in 1979 and the presidential victory of Ronald Reagan in the United States in 1980.

The number of refugees fleeing El Salvador and Guatemala began to increase dramatically in 1980. Guatemalans flooded into Mexico at the rate of between two thousand and thirty-five hundred per week. El Salvador's violence grabbed world headlines when Archbishop Oscar Romero, an outspoken opponent of the military and champion of the poor, was assassinated while saying mass in San Salvador. The plight of Salvadorans gained further publicity in the United States that year when a professional smuggler collected his payments and abandoned twenty-six Salvadorans in the Arizona desert. By the time they were found, half had died of thirst and heat exposure; the others were arrested by the Immigration and Naturalization Service (INS) and were to be deported back to El Salvador. Two local churches in the Tucson area posted bond for the refugees while decisions were pending on their asylum applications.

As awareness grew about the conditions in Central America, peace and justice organizations in the United States responded. The Tucson Ecumenical Council organized weekly prayer vigils outside the INS office, established community-based legal services to advise refugees of their rights, and began raising money for bonds and legal expenses. Other communities of faith throughout the country worked together on initiatives including legislative and judicial projects and educational programs. Shareholder resolutions successfully forced all U.S. airlines to refuse to carry any Salvadoran refugees back to their country, where many would face death.

The work of these groups shifted when they realized that virtually all applications for political asylum were being rejected. In the first half of the 1980s, only 2.5 percent of Salvadorans and fewer than 1 percent of Guatemalans who applied were granted asylum. In addition, the INS continued deportations and increased bond amounts. The official reason given by the U.S. government for the rejection of the majority of applicants was that these people sought economic prosperity, not safety from political persecution. The sanctuary movement, however, argued that the Reagan administration refused to acknowledge that it was supporting oppressive regimes both financially and militarily and that asylum decisions reflected a political bias that conferred political asylum on refugees only from Communist countries and other "adversaries" of the United States. In contrast to the statistics for Central American refugees, for example, over 60 percent of Iranians, 38 percent of Afghans, and 34 percent of Poles fleeing their countries were given political refugee status during the 1980s.

The Refugee Act of 1980 was supposed to eliminate this element of political discrimination in granting asylum. The act incorporated the United Nations' definition of refugee as anyone who has a "well-founded fear of persecution for reasons of race, religion, nationality, membership in a particular social group or political opinion." Nevertheless, the act still allowed for the admission of refugees of particular humanitarian concern to the United States, enabling the government to give preference to specific refugee groups.

Prompted by the futility of efforts to gain political asylum through the established legal channels, a group of churches decided they needed to change their actions to aid those who they felt fit the description of a refugee according to the UN, the U.S. Refugee Act, and the Geneva and Helsinki Accords on human rights. Activists decided to smuggle Salvadoran and Guatemalan refugees into the country, transport them to places of safety, and harbor them in order to prevent arrests and deportations. The first church to declare itself a safe sanctuary for Central American refugees was Southside Presbyterian Church in Tucson in March 1982. Numerous other churches, communities, and synagogues followed suit, eventually expanding to a network of hundreds from Arizona to Washington state, Chicago, and Boston. The INS was keenly aware of the public disdain for making arrests within religious places and thus largely respected the sanctuaries. By the mid-1980s, the sanctuary movement became the largest grassroots civil disobedience action in the United States since the 1960s. It was also an expression of moral protest against the Reagan administration's bellicose policies in Central America, which included funding covert military action against Nicaragua.

The INS eventually did act to suppress the sanctuary movement by pressing charges against some of its participants. INS investigators infiltrated Bible studies and meetings of sanctuary groups to compile evidence against them. Several sanctuary workers were arrested when their automobiles were intercepted while carrying refugees. Others were indicted on felony charges of conspiracy, concealing illegal aliens, encouraging the entry of illegal aliens, and unlawful entry. Nonetheless the sanctuary movement continued until the flow of refugees subsided in the late 1980s when severe repression in both El Salvador and Guatemala diminished somewhat and some groups of refugees began to return home.

The sanctuary movement was both a humanitarian effort to assist victims of war and an act of political protest against the Reagan administration's policy toward Central America. It expanded the idea of sanctuary to be a holy and protective community for people whose basic human rights were being violated by government officials and military regimes. Many refugees were transported successfully to Canada while others were kept safe within the United States. Above all, the movement drew national attention to the U.S. role in Central America and the injustice of its actions toward those fleeing the violence and persecution in Guatemala and El Salvador.

Sharon Erickson Nepstad

References

Crittenden, Ann. *Sanctuary: A Story of American Conscience and the Law in Collision.* New York: Weidenfeld and Nicholson, 1988.

Golden, Renny, and Michael McConnell. *Sanctuary: The New Underground Railroad.* Maryknoll, N.Y.: Orbis, 1986.

MacEoin, Gary, ed. *Sanctuary: A Resource Guide for Understanding and Participating in the Central American Refugees' Struggle.* San Francisco: Harper and Row, 1985.

SANE (National Committee for a Sane Nuclear Policy)

Citizens' group opposed to U.S. nuclear weapons policies, 1957–1990. In June 1957, twenty-seven prominent citizens concerned with the health hazards of nuclear fallout met at the Overseas Press Club in New York City and formed the

"Provisional Committee to Stop Nuclear Tests." In the fall, the group adopted the name National Committee for a Sane Nuclear Policy, commonly known as SANE. At that time, it placed a full-page advertisement in the *New York Times* that read "We Are Facing a Danger Unlike Any Danger that Has Ever Existed," and quickly became the largest and most influential nuclear disarmament organization in the United States. The name of the organization had been suggested by distinguished psychologist and author Erich Fromm when he advocated that the role of informed citizens was "to try to bring the voice of sanity to the people."

For over three decades, men and women prominently associated with SANE included Norman Cousins, Clarence Pickett, Homer Jack, Lenore Marshall, Norman Thomas, Steve Allen, Dr. Benjamin Spock, H. Stuart Hughes, Sanford Gottlieb, and the Reverend William Sloane Coffin, Jr. They published full-page advertisements, wrote letters, signed petitions, staged impressive rallies, and took to the streets to pressure U.S. leaders to reduce the risk of nuclear war and move toward peace with justice. From the first large American antibomb rallies of the late 1950s and early 1960s, through organizing the largest anti–Vietnam War demonstration yet held in November 1965, to helping bring about the massive June 1982 disarmament march and rally in New York City, SANE was at the forefront of the liberal nuclear disarmament movement in the United States.

Intended by its founders to serve a temporary educational purpose, SANE was not designed to become a permanent membership organization, but the first newspaper advertisement "started a movement." The copy described in graphic detail the devastating effects of nuclear fallout and ended with a call for an immediate suspension of nuclear testing. The response was overwhelming. By the summer of 1958, SANE had about 130 chapters representing approximately twenty-five thousand Americans. Powerfully, SANE swept into a vacuum in the American peace movement, energizing people to politically relevant action on specific issues of the arms race.

The nuclear testing issue soon gave way to an emphasis upon the dangers of nuclear weapons themselves. This step was predictable, for the weapons themselves always represented the greatest concern of SANE disarmament advocates. In June 1958, pondering what would happen if the United States were to ban nuclear weapons tests, founding co-chair Norman Cousins maintained that such an action would "not represent the be-all and end-all of world peace and nuclear sanity. A truly sane nuclear policy will not be achieved until nuclear weapons are brought completely under control." Consequently, when both the Soviet Union and the United States voluntarily suspended nuclear weapons tests in 1958, SANE turned its attention to intercontinental ballistic missiles and the threat of nuclear annihilation. At a fall 1958 national conference, the organization resolved to broaden its goal from a nuclear test ban to general disarmament. These nuclear pacifists believed that the development of nuclear weapons and their sophisticated delivery systems had made the use of war as an instrument of national policy totally self-defeating, impractical, and immoral. The best hope for a world without self-destroying war, SANE argued, was in the achievement of universal, total disarmament with adequate inspection and control, reducing weapons to levels required for maintenance of internal order.

The organization conceived and implemented a strategy balanced between advocacy and acceptability and chose specific goals, at least partially, because they were "moral, realistic, politically possible, and pragmatically feasible next steps." The nuclear pacifists gathered around SANE legitimized the protest, gave it political scope and meaning, and thereby enlarged the area of accepted political action. Within American politics, SANE offered a retreat bunker for liberals who couldn't find a place to take a stand in the structure of political parties. Within the peace movement, it filled a gap that had opened among nuclear pacifists following the decline of the world government cause in the early 1950s and the shift among internationalists to the support of America's interventionist policies. SANE brought together a coalition following the McCarthy days to work for such achievements as the establishment of the Arms Control and Disarmament Agency in 1961 and the Limited Test Ban Treaty in 1963, which halted atmospheric nuclear testing. In 1965, SANE was among the leaders in opposition to President Johnson's escalation of American military involvement in Vietnam. Less than two years later, it helped form the "Dump Johnson" coalition and spearheaded the Eugene McCarthy antiwar presidential campaign in 1968.

In the 1970s and 1980s, SANE fought the proposed Anti-Ballistic Missile (ABM) system. It played a key role in the passage of the Strategic Arms Limitation (SALT) Agreement of 1972, helped bring down the costly B-1 bomber in 1977, and led the successful fight against the basing of the MX missile on a mobile platform. SANE activists also played a leadership role in the Nuclear Weapons Freeze Campaign. In 1987, these groups, the two largest peace groups in the country, merged into SANE/FREEZE: Campaign for Global Security, an organization of over 240 local groups, 24 state organizations, and 170,000 national members. The goals of the organization remained a comprehensive ban on nuclear testing as the first step toward complete disarmament and a redirection of military spending to social programs. Long-time peace activist Rev. William Sloane Coffin, Jr., served as president until the end of the cold war and the organization's demise in 1990.

Milton S. Katz

References

Boyer, Paul. *By the Bomb's Early Light: American Thought and Culture at the Dawn of the Atomic Age.* New York: Random House, 1985.

DeBenedetti, Charles. *An American Ordeal: The Antiwar Movement of the Vietnam Era.* Syracuse, N.Y.: Syracuse University Press, 1990.

Divine, Robert. *Bowing on the Wind: The Nuclear Test Ban Debate, 1954–1960.* New York: Oxford University Press, 1978.

Katz, Milton S. *Ban the Bomb: A History of SANE, the Committee for a Sane Nuclear Policy, 1957–1985.* Westport, Conn.: Greenwood, 1986.

McCrea, Francis B., and Gerald E. Markle. *Minutes to Midnight: Nuclear Weapons Protest in America.* Newbury Park, Calif.: Sage, 1989.

Wittner, Lawrence. *Rebels against War: The American Peace Movement, 1933–1983.* Philadelphia: Temple University Press, 1984.

See also NUCLEAR WEAPONS OPPOSITION

Satyagraha

A word coined by Mohandas K. Gandhi to describe his broad conception of nonviolent action.

It is a combination of two words common in both Hindi and Gujarati—*satya,* meaning "truth," and *agraha,* meaning (in this context) "the pursuit of something." As a term, *agraha* is flexible enough to be translated to mean "force," "determination," or "power," which is what most people believe Gandhi had in mind when he coined the word. However, since he also believed that no one could really know "truth" in the absolute sense, and that truth cannot be possessed but pursued, it is appropriate to conclude that what Gandhi meant by satyagraha was "the determined pursuit of truth." The principles on which satyagraha is based are *ahimsa* (nonviolence), *satya* (truth), *astheya* (determination), *brahmacharya* (abstinence), *asangraha* (nonpossessiveness), and *sarva dharma samanatva* (equality and unity of all religions).

For Gandhi, satyagraha expressed both a moral and political philosophy and a practical means of action. The latter aspect was necessarily rooted in the former, and therefore action had to reflect and be consistent with the broad philosophical meaning. This conviction was not always shared by Gandhi's contemporaries in the Indian National Congress, who often saw satyagraha in more instrumental and political terms. Nevertheless, the idea carried both moral and practical meaning, which can be seen by examining its philosophical basis as well as its applications by Gandhi in South Africa and India.

Gandhi's philosophy of nonviolence emerged through his moral reflection and his experiences with civil disobedience and passive resistance. He believed nonviolent action did not necessarily have to be protest-oriented or negative action, which was how he saw both civil disobedience and passive resistance as they were commonly used. Satyagraha, as he conceived of it, had to be dynamic, continuous, and positive.

The term *satyagraha,* therefore, meant a lifelong pursuit of truth both for the individual and for society. The human search for salvation involved an eternal process, since Gandhi believed "Truth is God" and the pursuit of "eternal truth" was the purpose of life. Service to the downtrodden and destitute, Gandhi said, was the best way to seek salvation. In this sense, satyagraha transcends the narrow connotation of nonviolent action. Gandhi saw satyagraha as a way of life, and sought to make this the way of life for all *satyagrahis,* those who engaged in satyagraha.

This concept of satyagraha was also closely linked to the Hindu concept of *swaraj,* which is again a combination of two Indian words—*swa,* meaning "self," and *raj,* meaning "to rule." Swaraj was commonly interpreted to mean self-rule or self-government only in the narrow political sense. Thus, when India became free from British imperialism, it was assumed that India had gained swaraj. This, however, was not true in the Gandhian sense, for swaraj is attained by individuals only when they are liberated from fear and the materialistic compulsions that rule their lives.

True self-rule, for Gandhi, meant overcoming many forms of injustice and violence. Injustice is not confined to politics but is manifest in economic, social, cultural, religious, and other aspects of human existence. It is greed for power, money, and status that drives some to dominate others.

Gaining only political freedom or political justice, while people continue to suffer all other forms of injustice was, in Gandhi's view, an incomplete struggle. What satyagraha sought was a change in the attitudes of people—both the dominant and the servile. Gandhi believed satyagraha helped awaken the consciousness of all people and through this awakening he sought justice and freedom for all, of all, and from all.

Gandhi described satyagraha as the trunk of a tree with many branches and leaves that represent the different forms of nonviolent action. This metaphor conveyed his sense of the intrinsic and reciprocal importance of the individual for the community, just as the health of each leaf and branch depend on the health of a tree's trunk, roots, and soil. Satyagraha becomes strong and healthy as it takes root in the hearts of individuals. And by extension, the many forms of injustice and violence can be overcome only by social transformation that grows from the ground up.

In Gandhi's life and philosophy, satyagraha assumed many forms from the very general to the very particular. For example, he believed that injustices around the world were compounded by the "imperialistic ambitions" and by greed of some nations over others. In *Nonviolence in Peace and War,* he proposed that if the people of the great powers had the will to give up their imperial ambitions and their exploitation of other so-called uncivilized and semicivilized nations—to become true satyagrahis—there would be a complete and global revolution. Similarly, individuals and groups should see themselves as "trustees" of their environment and of each other in order to manage more justly the resources available to all. He implemented many, very local, concrete forms of satyagraha as a "constructive program" for independence, including projects promoting rural self-sufficiency and intergroup harmony.

Gandhi evaluated and appreciated the strengths and weaknesses of each satyagrahi and assigned tasks to them that they could comfortably manage. For instance, Tara Mashruwala volunteered to participate in the political aspect of the "Quit India" movement in 1942, but it was soon realized that her health could not stand the rigors of prison life. She was asked to go to a remote village and start programs for women and children. She was given no funds and was permitted to take only one change of clothes. To work among the poor, you must live like the poor, Gandhi advised. Using her ingenuity and hard work Tara began classes for women and children in a dilapidated barn in 1943. Today it is a full-fledged school, kindergarten through twelfth grade, for nearly eight hundred students, a training center for one hundred women social workers, a ten-bed hospital with forty medical centers in remote villages, and economic programs for the poor. Gandhi gave basic training to hundreds of satyagrahis like Tara and sent them out into remote corners of India to work among the poor and deprived. The satyagrahis were required to evaluate the needs and find the means to provide them to the people. Gandhi considered this work as important as fighting injustice and trying to change the government.

Whatever one chose to do Gandhi insisted that a satyagrahi set attainable goals and take the next step only after the first is properly consolidated. When we aspire to achieve too much, we quickly become disheartened and give up. A satyagrahi must, therefore, learn to operate within the resources available in the area of operation.

On the political field too he considered it essential to set attainable goals and seek mass participation. For several years before the Salt Satyagraha in 1930, Gandhi led Indians through several small, sometimes regional campaigns so that satyagrahis knew what to do and how to handle themselves and felt encouraged with the success on a small scale. It was only after he was convinced the people were prepared that he launched the national campaign called the Salt March and then the "Quit India" movement in 1942. One has to build the momentum of a struggle gradually.

Gandhi also emphasized the need for individual satyagraha. He believed that people faced with injustice should not tolerate it just because they are alone. It is incumbent upon all of us not to submit to injustice of any sort, and nonviolence offers one the possibility of acting without the support of others. It also provided a link between campaigns. When there is need to regroup and plan a new campaign, individuals could continue offering satyagraha to maintain the tempo and continuity. The other side of the coin is the misunderstanding "individual" satyagraha leads to. It does not mean that one person offers satyagraha all the time, but that one person offers satyagraha at a time, every hour or every day, as prescribed by the needs of the campaign.

Arun Gandhi

References

Bondurant, Joan V. *Conquest of Violence: The Gandhian Philosophy of Conflict.* Princeton: Princeton University Press, 1958, 1988.

Gandhi, Mohandas K. *Non-violent Resistance (Satyagraha).* New York: Schocken, 1961.

Mathews, James K. *The Matchless Weapon: Satyagraha.* Bombay: Bharatiya Vidya Bhavan, 1989.

Shridharani, Krishnalal. *War without Violence: A Study of Gandhi's Method and Its Accomplishments.* New York: Harcourt, Brace, 1939.

See also AHIMSA; AHMEDABAD LABOR SATYAGRAHA, 1918; BARDOLI CAMPAIGN, 1928; BHAVE, VINOBA; GANDHI, MOHANDAS KARAMCHAND; INDIAN NATIONAL CONGRESS; INDIAN NATIONAL MOVEMENT; KHAN ABDUL GHAFFAR KHAN; NEHRU, JAWAHARLAL; NONVIOLENCE, PRINCIPLED; ROWLATT BILLS OPPOSITION, 1919; SALT MARCH, 1930; SHRIDHARANI, KRISHNAL; VYKOM CAMPAIGN, 1924–1925

Sayre, John Nevin (1884–1977)

Episcopal priest and leading figure in the religious pacifist organization Fellowship of Reconciliation (FOR). Born on February 4, 1884, in Bethlehem, Pennsylvania, John Nevin Sayre devoted almost his entire adult life to the FOR.

He served as editor of *The World Tomorrow* (1922–1924) and *Fellowship* (1940–1945). He was also secretary, co-secretary, and chairman of the American branch of the Fellowship of Reconciliation and head of the International Fellowship of Reconciliation (1946–1955). He died on September 13, 1977, in Nyack, New York, where the FOR is headquartered.

Sayre graduated from Princeton University in 1907. From 1910 to 1911, he studied at the Episcopal Theological School in Cambridge, Massachusetts. After his ordination he served as an instructor of New Testament theology at Boone University, Wuchung, China. In 1913, he studied at the University of Marburg, Germany. In 1914–1915, he returned to Princeton as an instructor in theology. Between 1916 and 1919, he was rector of Christ Church in Suffern, New York. It was during this latter period that his Christian pacifism took shape. When the United States entered World War I in 1917, Sayre joined the Fellowship.

Sayre's brother and closest friend, Francis, married President Woodrow Wilson's daughter. This family connection enabled Sayre to call upon President Wilson to order his secretary of war, Newton Baker, to issue a directive calling upon the military to desist from unfair and harsh treatment of all conscientious objectors incarcerated in federal prisons.

Between the world wars Sayre worked for the abolition of military training in colleges and schools throughout the United States. In numerous articles, campus speeches, and radio broadcasts, he argued that democracy and militarism were incompatible. In June 1926, he testified before the House Committee on Military Affairs in opposition to the National Defense Act of 1920 creating a Reserve Officers Training Corps (ROTC).

In late 1927 and early 1928, Sayre undertook a dangerous journey to Nicaragua in an effort to mediate a peace agreement between the rebel forces of Augusto Sandino and U.S. Marines stationed in the troubled nation. Accompanying Sayre were two members of the American Friends Service Committee and another member of the Fellowship of Reconciliation. Both peace groups sponsored the mission. With the cooperation of Sandino's half-brother and his father, as well as the Nicaraguan Federation of Labor, Sayre journeyed on horseback over rough mountain terrain to meet with Sandino's wife. They handed her a letter asking for an interview with the rebel leader in hiding. But before Sayre could

Robert Jones and John Nevin Sayre in Nicaragua, where they attempted to mediate a peace agreement between the rebel forces of Augusto Sandino and the U.S. Marines in 1927. Fellowship of Reconciliation Archives.

meet with Sandino a clash occurred between advancing Marines and Sandino's forces, resulting in casualties on both sides. The meeting with Sandino never took place. Sayre returned to the United States to meet with Senator William E. Borah, head of the Senate Foreign Relations Committee, and various State Department officials, asking them to call off the military's hunt for Sandino. Sayre also lectured on his mission of peace and goodwill throughout the United States. His efforts encouraged President Herbert Hoover's administration to reexamine U.S. policy in Central America.

Sayre is also known for his efforts to promote fellowship among conscientious objectors from different parts of the world. His support and aid for French conscientious objectors following World War I demonstrated how far he would go on behalf of peace and international brotherhood. Despite a formal pardon by the French government in the late 1920s, a number of conscientious objectors remained in exile in the penal colony of French Guiana, too poor to return home to their native France. Their living conditions were brutal. From 1929 to 1935, Sayre generated publicity concerning their plight and raised enough money to return all of the conscientious objectors to France.

Sayre's leadership of the International Fellowship of Reconciliation also took him to South Africa. In 1951–1952, despite South African restrictions on his speaking engagements, Sayre expressed pleasure at the peaceful actions that Africans and East Indians were taking to protest the policy of apartheid. While in South Africa he began a lasting friendship with the Reverend Arthur Blaxall, secretary of the Christian Council of South Africa. In subsequent years Sayre conferred with Blaxall about nonviolent tactics to combat apartheid.

Sayre believed that peace was something more than the absence of violence or change. Peace demanded sacrifice and communication. His nonviolent methods were developed from the Quaker emphasis on persuasion and understanding. Led by Sayre, the Fellowship of Reconciliation sought to bring Christian bodies to social action and to infuse reform groups with the ethic of pacifism. His stress on persuasion, liberalism, and individual commitment guided the Fellowship in its struggle for peace and justice, and its efforts to make power accountable and redirect it to bring about societal improvement and elevate human values. His nonviolent mission was one of global reformation through Christian pacifism.

Charles F. Howlett

References

Brittain, Vera. *The Rebel Passion: A History of Some Pioneer Peacemakers.* Nyack, N.Y.: Fellowship Publications, 1964.

Chatfield, Charles. *For Peace and Justice: Pacifism in America, 1914–1941.* Knoxville: University of Tennessee Press, 1971.

DeBenedetti, Charles. *Origins of the Modern American Peace Movement, 1915–1929.* Millwood, N.Y.: KTO, 1978.

Doenecke, Justus. "John Nevin Sayre." In *Biographical Dictionary of Modern Peace Leaders,* edited by Harold Josephson. Westport, Conn.: Greenwood, 1985.

Howlett, Charles F. "John Nevin Sayre and the American Fellowship of Reconciliation." *Pennsylvania Magazine of History and Biography* 114 (1990): 399–422.

———. "John Nevin Sayre and the International Fellowship of Reconciliation." *Peace and Change* 15 (1990): 123–149.

Swomley, John M. "John Nevin Sayre: Peacemaker." *Fellowship* 43 (1977): 9–11.

See also BROOKWOOD LABOR COLLEGE; FELLOWSHIP OF RECONCILIATION; MUSTE, ABRAHAM JOHN; PACIFISM; STRIKES

Seattle General Strike, 1919

Five-day general strike in support of shipyard workers. Frustrated by wartime inflation and inspired by the empowerment of workers in the Russian Revolution, the rank-and-file workers struck in the face of employer, government, and international union opposition. The American labor movement learned lessons regarding the strategy and logistics of a general strike.

On January 21, 1919, thirty-five thousand shipyard workers struck for higher wages. Because the federal government supported the yard owners, the workers appealed to the Seattle Central Labor Council for support for a general strike. On February 6, the General Strike Committee launched a citywide sympathy strike. The committee created a parallel government for the duration of the strike, and workers, businessmen, employers, and city officials came before the committee to ask for strike exemptions and approval for other activities. Workers organized large-scale alternative services designed to feed the strikers and the community. They also formed a "Labor War Veteran's Guard" to keep peace using "persuasion only" during the strike. Under pressure from the Seattle mayor, backed by federal troops, powerful employers, and international union leadership, the committee ended the general strike on February 11. The shipyard workers did not receive any concessions, but workers, employers, and government officials alike were surprised at the potential power of this general strike.

Brad Bennett

References

Brecher, Jeremy. *Strike!* Boston: South End, 1972.

See also SAN FRANCISCO GENERAL STRIKE, 1934; STRIKES

Selma-to-Montgomery March, 1965

Civil rights march to gain voting rights for African Americans in the South. The fifty-four-mile march from Selma, Alabama, to the state capitol in Montgomery is widely credited with facilitating passage of the Voting Rights Act of 1965.

Martin Luther King, Jr., announced plans for the march on March 5, 1965, to enliven a flagging voter registration drive that the Southern Christian Leadership Conference (SCLC) had launched two months before. After weeks of demonstrations and more than three thousand arrests, few African Americans had been registered to vote. More militant demonstrations were called for.

The march was attempted three times before it was completed. The first attempt was led by Hosea Williams on Sunday, March 7. More than five hundred marchers made their way from Brown's Chapel African Methodist Episcopal Church to the outskirts of Selma, where they were halted on the Edmund Pettus Bridge by about five hundred state troopers wearing steel helmets and gas masks and a few dozen sheriff's possemen. The troopers and possemen charged the protesters, forcing them to retreat. They were chased back to Brown's Chapel, trampled by horses, tear gassed, and beaten with nightsticks and bullwhips as they ran. Some one hundred protesters were injured and sixteen were hospitalized. The day became known as "Bloody Sunday."

On March 9, Martin Luther King, Jr., led 1,500 people, including more than 450 religious leaders from across the country, in the second attempt of the march. However, faced with a court injunction against the march, King struck a compromise between defying the court injunction entirely and calling off the march. He led the marchers across the Edmund Pettus Bridge to the other side, where state troopers and possemen were again waiting. But instead of pressing on to Montgomery and risking another bloody attack, he and the marchers stopped, knelt in prayer, and then turned back. That night a group of white thugs attacked three white ministers, killing the Reverend James Reeb from Boston. Reeb's death attracted national attention and put more pressure on Washington to enact voting rights legislation.

Civil rights activists, meanwhile, continued to seek permission and federal protection from the courts for the Selma-to-Montgomery march. On March 17, a U.S. district court judge upheld their right to undertake the march in a peaceful manner. President Lyndon Johnson federalized the Alabama National Guard to provide protection for the marchers. The successful march left Selma on March 21 with three thousandparticipants and ended without incident on March 25 with a rally of twenty-five thousand marchers and supporters in front of the state capitol building. Just hours after the march, however, a white thirty-nine-year-old activist from Detroit was shot dead by Klansmen as she drove from Selma to Montgomery to pick up some marchers. This brought national outrage, and ultimately, more congressional support for voting rights. Four months later, on August 6, the Voting Rights Act of 1965 was signed into law.

Kimberley A. Pyles

References

Colaiaco, James A. *Martin Luther King, Jr.: Apostle of Militant Nonviolence.* New York: St. Martin's, 1988.

Cooney, Robert, and Helen Michalowski, eds. *The Power of the People: Active Nonviolence in the United States.* From an original text by Marty Jezer. Culver City, Calif.: Peace Press, 1977; Philadelphia: New Society, 1987.

Fager, Charles E. Selma, 1965: *The March that Changed the South.* Boston: Beacon, 1985.

See also CIVIL RIGHTS MOVEMENT; KING, MARTIN LUTHER, JR.; SOUTHERN CHRISTIAN LEADERSHIP CONFERENCE

Serbia, Antiwar Activity, 1991–1994

Nonviolent peace action in Serbia that brought together women opposing the wars in Croatia and Bosnia-Herzegovina, student protest, an underground antiwar youth culture, and young men avoiding conscription. As a coordinator in this process of war resistance, the Center for Antiwar Action (CAWA) became the nerve center of nonviolent organizations and activity, providing political infrastructure and establishing international contacts. This nonviolent antiwar action did not succeed in bringing peace. However, these efforts articulated a broader quest for political freedom and more active participation in the political process, providing a foundation for a more diverse civil society when peace returns.

Peace activity in Serbia grew out of dissatisfaction with Serbian President Slobodan Milosevic's policies that contributed to setting off the war and the Yugoslav/Serbian government's support for war in Croatia and in Bosnia-Herzegovina. It was fueled by the pain of economic sanctions imposed by the international community and fear that the ongoing wars of secession could spread to Serbia itself. The parallel development of nonviolent war resistance and opposition parties, such as the Serbian Renewal Movement (SPO) and the Democratic Party, merged issues of peace, human rights, and challenges to Milosevic's ruling Socialist Party of Serbia (SPS). Therefore, Serbian antiwar activism both benefited from and provided a base for broader political opposition.

Nonviolent peace action in Serbia between 1990 and 1994 was a movement from below. During this period, three groups were major antiwar players: the Center for Antiwar Action (CAWA), women, and draft-age war resisters along with the broader underground youth culture. While their shared goal of establishing a permanent peace on the territory of the former Yugoslavia was similar, their activities and roles in the antiwar movement were somewhat different. CAWA had a political infrastructure and better organization than the other two groups. It coordinated domestic events and international cooperation. It was the icebreaker in the Serbian political arena that led to the Civic Alliance of Serbia. This party's openly antiwar character differed from other opposition parties in its emphasis on nonviolent peace struggle, human rights, and assistance to refugees, which broadened the Serbian political spectrum.

The Center for Antiwar Action was founded because of felt citizen need to resist war and its escalation. The antiwar organization grew out of a people's movement. Mothers demanded that their sons stay home; young men hid to avoid the draft. There were mass antiregime demonstrations and clashes with police. In this context, organizations such as the European Movement for Yugoslavia, the Helsinki Citizen's Assembly, and the Belgrade Women's Lobby came together to support the establishment of the center.

The CAWA stressed negotiations instead of war. It worked to develop civil society in Serbia, to create respect for individual and minority rights, and to provide education in nonviolent conflict resolution. More broadly the goals were security, peace, pluralism, and the creation of democratic institutions in the Balkans. Initially, the center offered legal help to draft resisters and held antiwar information meetings. As the civil war in Croatia intensified, however, CAWA took a more active role in mobilizing and organizing domestic nonviolent action. It coordinated the best-known Serbian antiwar events: the September 28, 1991, Peace Caravan that gathered representatives of European countries and peace movements into a peace convoy that traveled throughout Yugoslavia, local concerts for peace, and protest meetings by groups such as Citizens of Belgrade for Dubrovnik, Black Veil, and Don't count on us.

In addition to its role as a domestic antiwar organizer, CAWA networked with organizations internationally; it established contacts with human rights groups such as Helsinki Rights Watch, the UN Center for Human Rights, and the Lawyers Committee for Human Rights.

The founder of CAWA, Vesna Pesic, has gone beyond the usual activity of a nongovernmental antiwar organization into a more political arena. CAWA became the political base for her leadership of the Civic Alliance of Serbia, the only party in Serbia that has become an important political vehicle for the antiwar movement at the governmental level. In 1993, the party's legitimacy and reputation increased when Mrs. Pesic received the National Endowment for Democracy Award in Washington for her contribution to the causes of democracy and peace.

CAWA's long-term agenda includes (a) education for peace and nonviolent conflict resolution via studies on the negative impact of nationalism, war, and ethnocentrism; (b) public education on human rights and their protection; (c) an SOS telephone line for the victims of discrimination; (d) monitoring hate speech in the Yugoslav media; (e) integration of refugees, especially children traumatized by the war, into Serbian society.

It is important to recognize that CAWA's political nature and activities would be impossible without the close cooperation of women in providing active support for refugees and war resisters. Indeed, women played a leading role in Yugoslav antiwar activity, they founded almost all of the peace movement organizations in Serbia, including such groups as "Mothers for Peace," "Women in Black," "Belgrade Women's Lobby," and "Women's Parliament," which actively opposed the war from its beginning by mobilizing nonviolent opposition to the militaristic regime, compulsory mobilization, and war-mongering.

These women's organizations were especially active in the November 1991–March 1992 marathon antiwar demonstrations, weekly protests in front of the Federal Parliament that are still going on, and open support to draft resisters. In January 1992, they took part in organizing a widespread signature campaign calling for a referendum against the war.

Serbian women sought to create solidarity with women from the other republics of the former Yugoslavia, inviting them to participate in the meetings of "Network of Women and Solidarity against War." The guests included women from eighteen countries, giving these meetings a broad international character. In addition, they published antiwar works in several languages including *The Women for Peace Anthology, The Women's Peace Calendar 1994,* and a *Women's Quarterly Women against the War.* Regarding the issue of refugees, women's organizations launched a comprehensive program, "Let's Be Creative Together," with the goal of offering emotional, moral, and material help to these war victims.

War resisters, especially youth, were the third major group of nonviolent antiwar protesters on the Serbian political stage. Their strongest peace activity was in avoiding the military draft and in joining mass protests for peace that were at the same time anti-Milosevic political demonstrations. Draft resisters were most active during the period from October 18, 1991, to May 22, 1992, while Yugoslavia still existed and the Yugoslav armed forces and federal government were fighting a civil war in Croatia. An estimated 200,000 young men avoided conscription. Between fifteen and twenty thousand Serbian war resisters have been subjected to criminal proceedings because of their refusal to fight.

Mass protests that started with the March 9, 1991, demonstrations (almost three months before the civil war broke out in Croatia) and have continued throughout the war reinforced young people's antiwar orientation. This underground youth culture was based on alienation against the war, against the prowar government, and against the war propaganda that swept Serbia daily. Youth radio stations such as B92 and Radio Yugoslavia as well as the Independent TV program Studio B often were closed due to their antigovernment, antiwar programs. In addition, peace rock concerts and euphoria over contemporary Croatian rock music manifested youth antiwar sentiments.

High points of the broad antiwar and opposition activity include protesters holding a mile-long mourning streamer stretching along a main downtown street, Marsala Tita (subsequently renamed street of Serbian Rulers), as a symbol of Yugoslav tragedy, the June 1992 student blockade of Belgrade's university during the final examination period, followed in July by a 200,000-strong demonstration organized by opposition parties.

In Serbia in 1995, nonviolent antiwar protesters are criticized because they have not accomplished their goal of stopping the Yugoslav wars of secession. Several explanations are offered such as fragmentation of these organizations due to focusing on too many political issues at once, apathy created by Milosevic's status quo regime, hyperinflation, and UN economic sanctions. There is some truth to such criticism; however, according to Vesna Pesic, one can only imagine how much worse the already tremendous bloodshedding and ethnic hatred would be if there were no nonviolent peaceful organizations struggling to stop it.

Dragan Matic

References

Bjoren, Johanna. "NGO and Media Directory." *Balkan War Report: Bulletin of the Institute for War and Peace Reporting* 22 (October/November 1993).

Cohen, Leonard. *Broken Bonds: The Disintegration of Yugoslavia.* Boulder, Colo.: Westview, 1993.

Galtung, Johan. "Ex-Yugoslavia." In *Europe and the Disintegration of Yugoslavia,* edited by Radmila Nakarada. Begrade: Institute for European Studies, 1994.

Simic, Predrag, ed. *Crisis and Reform: State and Civil Society in Transition.* Zug-Belgrade: Peace and Crisis Management Foundation, 1994.

See also BOSNIA-HERZEGOVINA, RESISTANCE TO CIVIL WAR, 1991–1992; KOSOVA, ALBANIAN NATIONAL MOVEMENT

Sharp, Gene (b. 1928)

Researcher, writer, and lecturer on nonviolent direct action and civilian-based defense, born January 21, 1928, in North Baltimore, Ohio. Gene Sharp, who has been called "the Clausewitz of nonviolent warfare," emphasized the "technique approach" to nonviolent action. He argued that nonviolent action is a means of wielding power in a conflict and is more often used for pragmatic reasons than for religious or ethical ones.

Sharp is best known for his three-volume work *The Politics of Nonviolent Action* (1973), which was immediately hailed as a landmark study of nonviolent struggle. In the first volume, he resurrected and elaborated upon the premise of sixteenth-century writer Etienne de la Boétie that a government's power depends on the consent and cooperation of the governed and that to the extent that consent and cooperation are withdrawn the government's power is correspondingly undermined. Surveying historical examples of nonviolent struggle, Sharp identified 198 methods of nonviolent action, which he compiled in the second volume. In the third and final volume, he examined the dynamics of nonviolent action when used against a violent, repressive opponent.

Gene Sharp began studying issues of war, peace, and nonviolence as a student at Ohio State University, where he received a B.A. in social sciences (1949) and an M.A. in sociology (1951). His senior honors thesis was on war

Gene Sharp. Photo by Joe Wrinn.

and his master's thesis was on nonviolence. Following graduation, he moved to New York City, where he supported himself doing a variety of part-time jobs while studying the thought and political struggles of Mohandas K. Gandhi. By 1953, he had written his first book, *Gandhi Wields the Weapon of Moral Power*, which was eventually published in India in 1960 with a foreword by Albert Einstein.

It was also in 1953, during the Korean War, that Sharp was imprisoned for his stand as a conscientious objector. He served nine months and ten days of a two-year sentence. In 1954, while on parole, he served briefly as personal secretary to the American pacifist A.J. Muste. Following parole, in 1955, he moved to London.

He spent the next ten years in England and Norway studying and writing about nonviolent action. He served first as assistant editor of *Peace News* in London, and later studied at the Institute of Philosophy and the History of Ideas, University of Oslo; the Institute for Social Re-

search at Oslo; and St. Catherine's College, University of Oxford. In 1964, while a doctoral student at Oxford, Sharp helped to organize an international Civilian Defence Study Conference, which brought together military strategists, historians, and others to consider the problems and prospects of applying nonviolent resistance to the problem of national defense. This conference ultimately resulted in the publication of *The Strategy of Civilian Defence* (1967), edited by Adam Roberts.

In 1965, Sharp returned to the United States to be a research fellow at Harvard University's Center for International Affairs. There he completed his doctoral thesis for Oxford University, receiving his D.Phil. in political theory in 1968. He was a member of the faculty at the University of Massachusetts at Boston and taught courses at Boston University and Brandeis University, before accepting an appointment in 1970 at Southeastern Massachusetts University.

In 1983, Sharp founded two organizations to promote research, policy studies, and education concerning the strategic use of nonviolent action in acute conflicts: the Program on Nonviolent Sanctions at Harvard University's Center for International Affairs and the Albert Einstein Institution. That same year, Manhattan College awarded him an honorary doctorate.

Through the 1980s and 1990s, Sharp continued his research and writing and began consulting with leaders of nonviolent "people power" movements and with governments interested in civilian-based defense. For example, in Burma, he consulted with prodemocracy leaders interested in undermining the SLORC dictatorship through nonviolent "political defiance." In Thailand, he consulted with government officials interested in nonviolent means of preventing coups d'état. And in the Baltic states of Lithuania, Latvia, and Estonia, he consulted with defense ministers about the relevance of civilian-based defense for their countries.

Sharp is the author of several books on nonviolent struggle, power, political problems, and defense policy. An international lecturer, his writings have appeared in more than twenty languages.

Roger S. Powers

References

Sharp, Gene. *Civilian-Based Defense: A Post-Military Weapons System*. Princeton: Princeton University Press, 1990.

———. *Gandhi as a Political Strategist.* Boston: Porter Sargent, 1979.

———. *Making Europe Unconquerable: The Potential of Civilian-Based Deterrence and Defense.* New York: Ballinger, 1985.

———. *Social Power and Political Freedom.* Boston: Porter Sargent, 1980.

———. *The Politics of Nonviolent Action.* Boston: Porter Sargent, 1973.

Shridharani, Krishnalal (1911–1960)

Veteran of the 1930 Salt March campaign, journalist, and author of *War without Violence,* an analysis of the technique of satyagraha. Published just before World War II, the book advocated Gandhian satyagraha as a pragmatic technique of concerted social action against totalitarianism and as an equivalent to war. Shridharani was born in Bhavnagar, India, on September 16, 1911, and died on July 23, 1960.

In Part I of *War without Violence,* Shridharani explains the general processes of satyagraha. He diagrams the stages of a successful campaign, defining and describing various methods of nonviolent action (including demonstrations, strikes, sit-ins, boycotts, noncooperation, civil disobedience, and parallel government). In Part II, he illustrates real applications of the technique. Part III offers a theory of satyagraha and contrasts it with pacifism, internationalism, and war as strategies for social change.

Shridharani's technique approach to nonviolent action represents an important pioneering contribution to the field of pragmatic nonviolent struggle.

References

Sharp, Gene. *Gandhi As a Political Strategist.* Boston: Porter Sargent, 1979.

Shridharani, Krishnalal. *War without Violence: A Study of Gandhi's Method and Its Accomplishments.* New York: Harcourt, Brace, 1939.

See also GANDHI, MOHANDAS KARAMCHAND; SATYAGRAHA

Sit-ins, Sit-downs, and Building Occupations

Physical occupation of a facility with the intent of disrupting its normal operation or of presenting a visible presence to other occupants. Sit-ins generally imply occupying a place literally by sitting, either on chairs or stools, steps, or on the floor. Sit-downs often refer to labor actions in which strikers take lasting possession of a factory or other facility, with the purpose either of preventing its normal use or, rarely, of taking over production themselves. Building occupations are similar, involving an effort to mount a physical presence either in an entire building or only certain offices or spaces, often to physically exclude others from entry.

Because people enter the designated space and refuse to leave, they are using their bodies to intervene nonviolently and to make an appeal to their opponents to examine and change their behavior or policies. The method may be applied as one single event, or as part of a series of actions. It may be conducted temporarily or indefinitely. The sit-in is used to protest a specific pattern of economic or political interaction or is intended to begin to establish a new pattern of social activities.

Sit-down strikes were held in the factories of several U.S. auto manufacturers in the labor movement in the 1930s. In 1936, for example, auto workers occupied General Motors plants for four months, followed in the next year by sit-downs at Ford Motor Company's River Rouge and Flint, Michigan, facilities. For union organizers, the concept of the sit-down strike included both its capacity to exclude replacement workers from taking over the positions of strikers and a measure of protection from anti-striker violence by company agents or police. British and European sit-downs in the 1970s and 1980s were more concerned with protesting or preventing shops from being closed or subjected to reductions in the labor force as a response to economic change. An example of this kind of sit-down is the Lip Factory occupation of 1973, in which skilled workers facing layoffs actually tried to operate the plant themselves and produce goods against the wishes of the owners.

Sit-ins were widely used during the civil rights movement in the United States in the 1940s, 1950s, and especially the 1960s to open previously forbidden facilities like lunch counters and restaurants. The actionists entered facilities, occupied seats, and refused to leave until all African-American members of the group were served, the facility was closed by the owners, or the actionists were arrested. The Southern Regional Council reported that, during a seven-month period in the early 1960s, over seventy thousand people had participated in sit-ins, and over thirty-six hundred had been arrested. In 1961, a U.S. Supreme Court decision outlawed the use of disorderly conduct statutes as grounds for arresting actionists who sat in.

Sit-ins have also been used in other campaigns in the United States. Abolitionists proposed sit-ins as part of their campaign to eradicate slavery. In 1938, members of the Chippewa tribe conducted a sit-in at the Bureau of Indian Affairs headquarters to protest the commissioner's decision to move the office off the reservation to Duluth. The Chippewa argued that this decision constituted a violation of the U.S. government's policy of Indian self-government. United States Secretary of the Interior Harold L. Ickes eventually stepped in to order a binding tribal referendum on the issue. Sit-ins were also used in the "Free Speech Movement" in the 1960s. Over eight hundred people were arrested in Berkeley, California, in December 1964 following a sit-in called to demand freedom of speech. Also in 1964, at the Democratic National Convention, the predominantly African-American Freedom Democratic Party of Mississippi sat in the seats designated for the originally elected Democratic Party delegates, refusing to leave. They claimed that they were more supportive of the Democratic Party's national platform than the white Mississippi delegation. More recently, in the 1980s, sit-ins were conducted in government offices across the United States to protest federal policies regarding intervention in Central American politics.

Lofland and Fink coin the term "symbolic sit-ins" to refer to occupations conducted with a lower level of intensity than some of those mentioned in other examples. Studying several efforts to establish a personal or group presence in California's state capitol building, Lofland and Fink classify these deescalated sit-ins as pack-ins, lone-ins, one-night stands, spirited sieges, and long-term vigils. Unlike the examples given earlier, the intention of the actors was to establish a presence and show their determination rather than to exclude users of the building or disrupt the workings of government.

There are several other methods of physical intervention that are so similar to the sit-in as to merit descriptions here. These methods are attempts to adapt the objectives and logistics of a sit-in to unique situations. For example, a "stand-in" is conducted like a sit-in, the only difference being that the actionists remain standing as they enter a place and refuse to leave. A stand-in was used to help end discrimination at a swimming pool in New Jersey in 1947 as African Americans peacefully lined up in front of the ticket booth upon being refused admission. The "ride-in" is a sit-in adapted to transportation vehicles (such as trains and buses). Also known as "Freedom Rides" during the 1960s, they became a large part of the civil rights campaign to integrate buses. The "wade-in" occurs when people use a body of water and its abutting beach despite restrictions or prohibitions against them from using the area. Sometimes a "mill-in" is used instead of a sit-in. Actionists remain in a designated space for some time, but they remain mobile, constantly moving around within a place, sometimes interchanging individuals. The mill-in may achieve the goal of impeding the normal activities of the people who work in that place without engaging in direct confrontation. "Pray-ins" are specifically designed to protest religious restrictions—people enter a church or other religious institution from which they have been banned in order to worship and pray there. This method was used during the abolition movement in parts of New England.

References

Fine, Sidney. *Sit-down: The General Motors Strike of 1936–1937*. Ann Arbor: University of Michigan Press, 1969.

Greenwood, John. *Worker Sit-ins and Job Protection: Case Studies of Union Intervention*. Farnborough, UK: Gower, 1977.

Kraus, Henry. *The Many and the Few: A Chronicle of the Dynamic Auto Workers*. Los Angeles: Plantin, 1947.

Levinson, Edward. *Labor on the March* [1938]. New York: University Books, 1956.

Lofland, John, and Michael Fink. *Symbolic Sit-Ins: Protest Occupations at the California Capitol*. Washington, D.C.: University Press of America, 1982.

Nash, Diane. "Inside the Sit-ins and Freedom Rides: Testimony of a Southern Student." In *The New Negro*, edited by Mathew H. Ahmann. Notre Dame, Ind.: Fides, 1961.

Oppenheimer, Martin. *The Sit-in Movement of 1960*. Edited by David J. Garrow. Brooklyn, N.Y.: Carlson, 1989.

Proudfoot, Merrill. *Diary of a Sit-in*. Chapel

Hill: University of North Carolina Press, 1962.

Reuther, Victor. The *Brothers Reuther and the Story of the UAW*. Boston: Houghton Mifflin, 1976.

Sharp, Gene. *The Politics of Nonviolent Action*. Boston: Porter Sargent, 1973.

See also ABOLITIONIST MOVEMENT; CIVIL RIGHTS MOVEMENT; FREEDOM RIDES, 1961

Sivaraksa, Sulak (b. 1933)

Prominent and outspoken Thai social critic, Buddhist scholar, human rights campaigner, and democracy advocate, born March 27, 1933. Sulak Sivaraksa has written over one hundred books and monographs, founded an important Thai intellectual magazine, established a publishing house, and worked for indigenous, sustainable economic development in Thailand. He is a proponent of nonviolence as a Buddhist ethical precept, and promotes nonviolent action in agitating for social transformation.

On August 5, 1984, Sivaraksa was arrested on charges of *lèse-majesté* (criticizing the king). After an outpouring of international protest, however, the government dropped charges. Prior to the May 1992 pro-democracy movement in Thailand, Sivaraksa gave a speech on August 22, 1991, criticizing the coup leaders of the National Peace Keeping Council (NPKC). He was again charged in September with *lèse-majesté* and for defaming coup leaders. He avoided arrest by going into self-imposed exile until December 14, 1992. He returned to fight the charges in court and was acquitted on April 26, 1995.

During his three decades of social activism and scholarship, Sivaraksa has become one of the leading human rights and democracy campaigners in Asia. He was nominated by Irish Peace People activist and Nobel Peace Prize winner Mairead Maguire for the 1994 Peace Prize.

Brad Bennett

References

Sivaraksa, Sulak. *Seeds of Peace: A Buddhist Vision for Renewing Society*. Edited by Tom Ginsburg. Berkeley, Calif.: Parallax, 1992.

———. *When Loyalty Demands Dissent: Sulak Sivaraksa and the Charge of Lèse Majesté in Siam, 1991–1993*. Bangkok: Santi Pracha Dhamma Institute, 1993.

See also THAILAND, DEMOCRACY MOVEMENT, 1992

Skywriting and Earthwriting

Method of protest and persuasion in which words or symbols are communicated to people by "writing" them in the sky or on the earth so that they can be seen from afar. Airplanes may create messages in the sky by leaving smoke trails in the shape of words or symbols. Creating messages on the earth may be accomplished by plowing the soil, or by using plants or rearranging the landscape (moving rocks or other materials into desired shapes). This method uses the mechanism of appealing to the target audience to persuade them to change their policy or behavior.

Anti–Vietnam War activists used skywriting to create a huge nuclear disarmament symbol over a rally in Boston, Massachusetts, in 1969. A California rancher, Edwin Frazer, plowed the word "quiet" into his field to protest the sonic booms from planes flying in and out of nearby Miramar Naval Air Station. In 1987, participants in a national nonviolence conference near Rapid City, South Dakota, formed peace and ecology symbols out of painted rocks so that Air Force pilots would see them when they landed.

References

Sharp, Gene. *The Politics of Nonviolent Action*. Boston: Porter Sargent, 1973.

See also GRAFFITI

Social Boycott

Method of noncooperation characterized by a refusal to continue normal or customary social relations with a person or group. This is the most common type of social noncooperation and is also known as "ostracism." Proponents do not speak or interact with the designated targets in any way or may subject them to a more limited refusal of recognition. This method has often been associated with religious or ethnic conflict, in which one sect or ethnic group ostracizes another. The effects of this method depend on how valued or vital the relations being tested are to the person(s) being ostracized. The social boycott is designed to pressure the target into a desired behavioral change by using the mechanism of coercion. Social boycotts are usually used within an acute political struggle and hence are used temporarily. In certain societies, however, a specific group is subjected to a continuous and long-lasting social boycott (such as the "untouchables" in India).

Social boycotts have often been used to achieve three major goals within resistance movements. First, they are used to induce reluctant people within one's own cohort group to join the resistance campaign. In a Cape Cod, (Massachusetts) community, for example, churchgoers refused to follow the deacon in prayer as a sanction against his support of the British Colonial government in 1774. American colonists struggling against British rule, Finns resisting Czar Nicholas's 1901 abolition of the Finnish constitution, and Indian nationalists resisting British rule all used the social boycott to pressure those who had not joined their movements to do so. Second, these boycotts are used to induce specific people to stop collaborating with the opponent. For example, unionists in the United States in the early part of the twentieth century often tried to ostracize strikebreakers by avoiding any contact with them. Third, social boycotts are used to apply pressure on the opponent's representatives or agents (such as police or troops). During the 1923 occupation of the Ruhr, Germans boycotted French and Belgian troops. For instance, when soldiers entered a tavern, German guests would leave. Danish citizens also routinely ignored Nazi soldiers during the four years of occupation. Some close-knit religious societies use social boycotts as a way of punishing members who deviate theologically or who break social norms. In certain U.S. sects of German origin, the practice of *Meiden,* or shunning, may even require a spouse to decline to speak to the object of the sanction.

Other related methods of nonviolent social noncooperation include the selective social boycott and "Lysistratic nonaction." The social boycott may be applied selectively by restricting the refusal to interact to a specific aspect or aspects of the relationship. For example, venders may be willing to speak to occupation troops but not to sell to them. The emphasis here is on the refusal to sell to a specific person, not the refusal to sell a specific item, thus classifying this act as a selective social boycott rather than an economic boycott. Refusing to shake hands with somebody at a political rally may constitute a selective social boycott of a specific interaction. Lysistratic nonaction, as prescribed in Aristophanes' play *Lysistrata,* is a unique form of selective social boycott in which women refuse sexual relations with their male partners to protest political violence or war. In North America during the early 1600s, women of the Iroquois Nation boycotted sexual relations until the men conceded to them the tribal power to decide on issues of war and peace.

References
Sharp, Gene. *The Politics of Nonviolent Action.* Boston: Porter Sargents, 1973.

See also DENMARK, RESISTANCE TO NAZI OCCUPATION; RUHRKAMPF; UNITED STATES, INDEPENDENCE MOVEMENT, 1765–1775

Social Movements
Ongoing collective efforts aimed at bringing about consequential change in a social order. Countermovement, on the other hand, are collective efforts aimed at resisting or reversing major change in a social order. Significant factors in determining the boundaries of movements and countermovements include (1) self-identification by individuals and groups with the movement; (2) treatment of the collective effort as a movement by outsiders, especially elites, countermovements, and the state; and (3) the sharing among movement elements of common social change goals.

National European labor movements served as the original social movement prototype. The U.S. civil rights movement is an important prototype for much of the recent scholarship on social movements. The U.S. and Canadian pro-life and pro-choice movements are social movements, as are the German antinuclear and the Basque separatist movements, the Salvadoran revolutionary movement, the British women's movement, the Indian nationalist movement, the Kenyan "Greenbelt" movement, and the anti-apartheid movement in South Africa.

Relatively unplanned outbursts, such as urban commodity riots, soccer riots, or rural grain riots, are not social movements. Nor are fads that sweep through populations, nor are broad cultural tendencies such as romanticism or McCarthyism. Neither established interest groups with broad, if informal, access to national decision-making structures nor corporatist groups with formal representation in governmental structures are social movements, although each may have been movements before they achieved such access. Social movements are the seedbed of the more stable, institutionalized structures of civil society.

A social movement is composed of a set of constituent elements. These include activists, who devote extensive effort to the ongoing movement struggle; constituents, who provide labor and material resources to support these collective endeavors by joining groups and taking part in movement activities; and adherents, or those individuals and groups who support the goals of the movement yet may never or only now and then actively work to bring them about. Movement activists work to transform adherents into constituents. It must be strongly emphasized, however, that only a tiny proportion of the adherents who form the sentiment pool of any movement are ever mobilized as constituents.

Movements also include social movement organizations (SMOs), the more or less formal organizations dedicated primarily to the pursuit of movement goals. These mobilizing structures—the carriers of movements—take a variety of forms ranging from small, local networks of activists to highly bureaucratized national structures that coordinate and direct hundreds of dispersed local chapters. The structures also vary in their permanence, including many variations on temporary issue campaign structures, illustrated, for instance, by the several European national anti–cruise missile campaigns of the 1980s and the U.S. nuclear test ban campaign of the early 1960s. SMOs, like all organizations, are quite likely to ossify as they mature. In wealthy, industrialized nations, movement structures are increasingly professionalized, especially in their reliance upon paid professional staff. Movements may be characterized by their demographic and ecological features since they vary dramatically from one another in the scope and diversity of their respective mobilizing structures. For instance, some movements, such as the antitoxic movement for environmental justice that emerged in communities across the United States in recent years, are mostly based in small local grassroots groups. Others are dominated by more highly centralized national level professional structures, illustrated by the central role of groups associated with Ralph Nader in the U.S. consumer movement.

Movements also contain a variety of action elements. These include, but are not limited to, the mobilization of support and resources, mass demonstrations, door-to-door canvassing, lobbying authorities, nonviolent civil disobedience, organizing local groups, silent vigils, and terrorist campaigns. Social movements typically have been cast as users of unconventional or unruly tactics. And, while movements are likely to employ unruly tactics since their adherents and constituents are liable to be denied access to formal decision-making processes, movements characteristically rely upon an evolving mix of tactical elements that include more or less of the unconventional ones, depending both upon circumstances and movement dynamics. Most tactical elements, even unconventional ones, are simply not violent, rather than being rooted in principled nonviolence. Characteristic repertoires of collective action that include widely known and relatively standardized mixes of action elements emerge and come to dominate particular movements as well as national and historical eras.

Social movements vary in the amount of effort and resources they devote to effecting structural social change directly (that is, changing regimes, laws, or reward distributions, and so forth). Movements normally develop a characteristic mix of approaches that also includes extensive public education aimed at creating wider support for change goals and efforts, thereby indirectly affecting the potential for direct change. As well, such mixes include organized attempts to provide direct assistance to suffering movement constituents—the "mutual aid" strategy—while awaiting longer-term success in goal achievement. A division of labor usually develops in large diverse movements where constituent SMOs emphasize one or another of the approaches. The relative emphasis of a movement, as well as its constituent SMOs, on these three strategic approaches usually varies over its life as a result of many factors, including, for instance, changing political alliances, changes in rules of access, and levels of repression.

Social movements are sometimes characterized by the nature of their goals. Reform versus revolutionary movements and single-issue versus multiple-issue movements, for instance, are widely used classification schemes. Large, diverse movements, however, are usually composed of a wide range of SMOs such that movements dominated by reform groups can also include revolutionary groups, and movements dominated by single-issue groups usually include groups working to broaden the goals of the movement. As with strategic emphases, a division of labor develops in more established, older movements whereby constituent SMOs develop specialized goal emphases.

The appropriateness of one or another goal can be a source of extensive conflict between movement subconstituencies. The importance of a "radical flank," usually denoted by its use of unruly tactics or the pursuit of revolutionary goals, has been widely recognized as helpful to the more conventional reform wing of many movements. The reformers come to be perceived as more moderate—and therefore more appealing as negotiating partners—by opponents and authorities in contrast to the radicals. The Southern Christian Leadership Conference and the Congress on Racial Equality, central movement organizations to the U.S. civil rights movement, are widely viewed as having benefited from a comparison with groups using and counseling violent tactics.

Social movements may form around chronic social cleavages such as social class, religion, region, language, and ethnicity—cleavages that are important in defining the boundaries of social and geographical collectivities and their attendant intragroup grievances. They also form increasingly around emergent socially constructed categories of shared identity (such as countercultural values, commitments to participatory democracy, or pacifism) or grievances as associational structures replace more traditional communal structures as the locus of personal identity. As a result, movements are now more apt to include conscience constituents—those active supporters who gain only indirectly if the goals of the movement are achieved—since adherence becomes more a matter of individual choice than the automatic result of ascribed group status. Many modern movements do not have any beneficiary constituents—those who stand to gain directly from goal achievement by the movement, such as black South African constituents of the antiapartheid movement—among their adherents or constituents. Examples would include the many animal rights movements.

The dynamics of movement emergence have been given scholarly attention. It is widely recognized, however, that individual movements and clusters of related movements, once formed, typically move through cycles of growth, stability, decline, and, often, resurgence. The recent study of these patterns among movements of many kinds has disconfirmed the widely embraced beliefs in the existence of a typical "natural history" of emergence, growth, and decline of movements, as well as any inevitable trend toward institutionalization and conservatism.

Social movement dynamics are best understood as more or less strategic interactions between the elements of movements and the other institutions, organizations, groups, and individuals of the societies they seek to change. Analysts of movements try to explain the dynamic qualities of social movements (that is, their changing structures, strategies, tactics, and social locations as well as their temporal trajectories) with reference to several features: the broader social structures from which they emerge and that they aim to change; the role of human agency; the centrality of political processes; and the importance of cultural framing.

Existing Social Structures

Social movements are most likely to develop out of networks of adherents who had been in ongoing contact with one another before their movement activism. Movements are less likely to develop and are more difficult to maintain if they are based upon adherents who are not embedded in such preexisting social networks. Networks based upon the most common forms of everyday activity such as work, religious practice, education, associational life, and neighborliness are the typical social sites of movement activity. These networks must be cooptable to the purposes of the movement, however, since they are originally created in the pursuit of other shared social purposes. Religious structures are particularly cooptable since their congregants are likely to share high levels of consensus on many social issues. Mobilizing adherents is more efficient when it can utilize dense preexisting networks than when it must depend upon finding and communicating with isolated adherents. As well, the groups and organizations that embody them typically control other important resources that can help facilitate movement activity. Mass movements are always developed to a great extent out of such social building blocks. The central role of African-American Protestant churches in the U.S. southern civil rights movement and that of villages and ashrams in the Indian nationalist movement illustrates this process. Movements that bank, instead, upon enlisting isolated constituents in order to expand typically remain small and socially marginal.

Broad historical shifts in social structure, therefore, can help to account for the changing fortunes as well as social locus of emergent and expanding social movements. The increasing labor force participation of women, for instance, has been seen as important to the dynamics of many national feminist and lesbian rights movements. Similarly, the widening availability of higher education, the expansion of professional employment, and the emergence of gay neighborhoods have been thought to provide the social infrastructural underpinnings for the expanding mobilization of student movements, "new" social movements, and gay rights movements, respectively.

Agency

Explanations of the variable features of social movements are incomplete without an appreciation of the central role of human agency. Social movements cannot emerge and develop without the ongoing efforts of cadres of activists—those organizers, leaders, and SMO officers who take on large personal costs and sometimes risks in order to devote time and resources to the many mundane tasks of movement life. Wide variation exists across movements in important aspects of these activist cohorts that can affect the level of movement effort as well as its effectiveness. A strong cadre structure is important for internal control of movements, and this is especially the case for movements committed to the use of principled nonviolence coupled with negotiated compromise.

Cohorts vary importantly, for instance, in their previous activist experience, the extent to which their personal lives facilitate or discourage activism, the relative proportion of activists who are paid for their movement labor, the typical costs and rewards they confront as a result of their activism, and their access and receptiveness to new ideas about how to pursue social change. Careers of full-time paid activism are becoming increasingly common in affluent, democratic societies with high levels of movement activity. Once engaged, activists read their own social, cultural, and political environment more or less productively in order to develop strategic plans for bringing about change. Activists' perceptions of shifting environmental

opportunities can sometimes be translated by their effort and enthusiasm into surges of movement vitality. And, activists are often the source of innovation in standard repertoires of contention, especially in their role of adaptor/inventor of new SMO forms.

Political Processes

The emergence, shape, and trajectory of social movements must be understood with reference to the political processes of the nation-states within which they exist. Influencing state action is an aim of most movements, and in turn their broad goals, tactics, and even their organizational forms are shaped to some extent by the stable institutionalized rules of politics under which they pursue change. Cross-national differences in, for instance, legitimate forms of association, rules of group access, and systems of party representation, have been shown to be tied to comparative differences between corresponding national movements as well as the shape of national movement sectors.

As well, the actions of state functionaries, changes in the institutional structure, and in the informal power relations of a national political system can affect movement prosperity. Changes in access rules can spur movements as can important regime changes. High levels of state repression directed toward movements can lead to demobilization, and can affect choices of movement tactics, for instance, undermining a movement's ability to remain nonviolent. These factors operate in affecting movements both by encouraging or discouraging social movement actors in their social change efforts and by advantaging or disadvantaging them in their ability to successfully produce the changes they seek.

Cultural Framing

Movements depend upon the development of a mobilizing frame that defines a problem collectively rather than individually, identifies an antagonist, and defines a line of action that, if pursued, will bring about a social change that is seen as a solution to its problems. Framing consists of conscious attempts to create shared meanings that will legitimate and motivate collective action. A sense of injustice and optimism about the potential of collective action are widely construed as central features of a successful mobilizing frame. Mobilizing frames are best fashioned out of existing cultural materials, and are more likely to resonate widely the more such content they include. Frames successful in mass mobilization include goals that are well aligned with broadly accepted social values, and means that are consistent with common, legitimate, goal-seeking practices in a social milieu. The more idiosyncratic the movement's goals and means are, from the perspective of the broader culture, the more limited will be their appeal.

Media of mass communication are increasingly pivotal, in nations where newspaper reading and television viewing are common features of daily life, for the communication of cultural frames, including movement mobilization frames. The high cost of developing private communication links with large pools of adherents, along with the near indispensability of mass media for communicating with large bystander publics—those neutral groups not aligned with the goals of either the movement or countermovement—has made movements increasingly reliant on national mass media. Consequently, movement activists can find their efforts at influencing the framing of public discourse subject to both the whims of news media institutions, motivated primarily by profit or social control ends, and the counterframing efforts of opponents, hostile elites, and government functionaries. Activists are disadvantaged compared to established elites in contests aimed at legitimizing new social goals or collective action means.

Until recently, in spite of the best hopes of many of the founders of the archetypal European labor movements, social movements have been primarily national in focus. Increasingly, however, movements have begun to coalesce across national boundaries as international political institutions have become more important and influential actors in global politics. As a consequence, it can be expected that nation-states' influence on social movement dynamics will be increasingly mitigated by international political opportunity structures that define global political processes involving both state and nonstate actors. Trends in the globalization of mass media institutions, corporations, voluntary associations, and religious organizations suggest, as well, a more general upward shift in the locus of institutional power. There seems no reason to doubt that the conceptual apparatus developed to explain national social movements should be adequate to the task of making sense of newly emergent international social movements and their carrier organizations.

John D. McCarthy

References

Freeman, Jo. *The Politics of Women's Liberation*. New York: McKay, 1975.

Gamson, William A. *The Strategy of Social Protest*. 2nd ed. Belmont, Calif.: Wadsworth, 1990.

Lofland, John. *Protest: Studies of Collective Behavior and Social Movements*. New Brunswick, N.J.: Transaction, 1985.

McAdam, Doug. *Political Process and the Development of Black Insurgency, 1930–1970*. Chicago: University of Chicago Press, 1982.

McAdam, Doug, Mayer N. Zald, and John D. McCarthy. "Social Movements." In *Handbook of Modern Sociology*, edited by Niel Smelser. Beverley Hills, Calif.: Sage, 1989.

Oberschall, Anthony. *Social Conflict and Social Movements*. Englewood Cliffs, N.J.: Prentice-Hall, 1973.

Olzak, Susan. "Contemporary Ethnic Mobilization." *Annual Review of Sociology* 9 (1983): 355–374.

Snow, David A., B. Rochford, Jr., S.K. Worder, and R.D. Benford. "Frame Alignment Processes, Micromobilization and Movement Participation." *American Sociological Review* 51 (August 1986): 464–481.

Tarrow, Sidney. *Struggle, Politics and Reform: Collective Actions, Social Movements and Cycles of Protest*. Western Societies Program Series, No. 21 (2nd ed.). Cornell University, Ithaca, N.Y., 1991.

Tilly, Charles. *From Mobilization to Revolution*. Reading, Mass.: Addison-Wesley, 1978.

Turner, Ralph H., and Lewis M. Killian. *Collective Behavior*. 3rd. ed. Englewood Cliffs, N.J.: Prentice-Hall, 1987.

Zald, Mayer N., and John D. McCarthy. *Social Movements in an Organizational Society*. New Brunswick, N.J.: Transaction, 1988.

See also CIVIL RIGHTS MOVEMENT; LEADERSHIP; ORGANIZATION IN SOCIAL MOVEMENTS

Social Power

Social power is both multifaceted and pervasive in society. It is most commonly understood in one of its facets, namely as manifest in the resources held by particular actors in society. Individuals and groups are powerful to the extent that they are able to shape the preferences of other parties in society by making alternative courses of action either more or less attractive. In other words, social power works by affecting others' interests, and is commonly wielded through physical, economic, social, and political influences.

Understanding the location and basis of different types of social power is critical to understanding the existing structural relations of a society as well as the potential for political action. Both existing power relations and challenges to the status quo are functions of the structured and implicit facets of social power.

Additionally, and more critical to the potential for activism and nonviolent direct action, social power is imbedded within the particular set of institutions and values that define each society and that serve to legitimate its existence internally. In this respect, power permeates the structures and relations defining society. This relational nature of social power means that there are always at least two parties to social discourse. We return to these omnipresent relationships among social actors below.

We can identify three basic ways in which power in society is understood. These explanations of social power are associated with the pluralist, elitist, and relational schools of thought. Both individually and collectively, these three views of power contribute to our understanding of power in society.

According to the pluralist school, which evolved with the desire to make democratic states secure against totalitarian incursions, the fundamental resources necessary to exert power in democratic societies were to be found in collective action. Writing chiefly about the United States, the pluralists, including Robert Dahl and David Truman, held that shares of political power are held by different and competing groups rather than being concentrated in the hands of any particular segment of society. The absence of concentrated power, combined with an explicit understanding that the state serves as an unbiased arbiter in the conflicts of societal actors, ensures that the system remains both open to challengers, and responsive to their demands, while inhibiting the violent repression of opponents. In other words, it is by identifying and acting collectively that individual interests are combined into groups that are the fundamental building blocks of power in society,

both through institutional and noninstitutional forms of political participation. In the pluralist model, group interests overlap and follow no rigid class pattern, and organizations tend to dissipate once the issues that brought them together are resolved.

One response to pluralism was an explicit shift in focus toward the study of elite actors and their decision-making processes. An implicit premise of this realist criticism is that pluralism understates the power held by elite groups in society.

A second criticism of pluralism held that vast inequalities in property ownership and income in turn raise profound barriers to political mobilization. This criticism formed the basis of subsequent relational theories of power. Social critics like C. Wright Mills and Charles Lindbloom argued that principal aspects of the political power of the elite include the set of strong social networks among elite groups, and their ties to local decision-making centers. Students of democracy writing since the mid-1960s have focused attention on this fundamental power disequilibrium that characterizes pluralist societies.

There remained a fundamental tension between the pluralist and elitist views of the nexus of power in society. The disproportionate power held by political elites in any given society and the close ties between groups of elite actors suggest that contemporary industrial democracies are better understood as elitist rather than pluralist states. Commenting on this tension, Doug McAdam commented: "There may exist a political arena in America but it is not the teeming convention hall depicted by the pluralists, but rather a restricted club reserved for the wealthy and powerful. Only those with sufficient political capital need apply."

Working from another perspective, Marxist analysts also identify large power disparities between elite and excluded groups in capitalist societies. Rather than believe that this state of affairs is inevitable, Marxists assert that the dominance of the elites over the masses cannot last. Instead, the rise of the masses is inevitable, once these (individually weak) challengers are galvanized through collective identification into a force for political change. Thus Marxist analysts often argue that power relations permeate and sustain the existing structure of society.

A productive dialogue can be identified between these two positions. On the one hand, pluralists assume that, by virtue of multiple loyalties, power in society is diffused among multiple groups with (often) overlapping memberships and (often) competing interests; the freedom to compete is the leveling force that diffuses power, and its requisite resources, throughout society. Elite theorists, on the other hand, focus on the inevitably greater share of resources held by elites, and their consequently enhanced capacity to exert influence—powerful members of society control more resources and therefore have the competitive advantage. In contrast, Marxist analysts offer the potential for social mobilization, despite power disequilibrium, through the collective identification and action of the masses.

The third principal reading of social power is careful to identify the relational nature of social control mechanisms in any given society. According to Michael Schwartz, structural power is recognizable in two ways. First, power must be wielded. Second, power must be accepted. Schwartz tells us that social structures "could not function without the consistent and routinized exercise of power." In other words, social structures can be undermined when their legitimacy is challenged. When their vulnerability becomes apparent, Schwartz suggests, "any threat to structural power becomes a threat to [the entire social] system itself." By extension, then, "any system contains within itself the possibility of a power strong enough to alter it."

It is this relational aspect of social power that provides the opening needed for challengers to mount political challenges against the dominant political order. When a system ceases to be responsive to the interests of all constituents, nonviolent direct action—a unilaterally initiated engagement of social power—may offer the only viable approach to gaining representation. Philip Green suggests that participation through such "democratic direct action" is not simply a right, but an "essential element in the search for the conditions of self-determination that democracy is all about."

This relational view of social power was developed by Etienne de la Boétie in "Discourse on Voluntary Servitude" in the sixteenth century. In this seminal essay, Boétie sought to understand why so many people "suffer under a single tyrant who has no other power than that which they give him." This deceptively simple premise of the relational view of power found a voice in Gene Sharp who argued some four hundred years later, "By its very nature, political power must come from outside the persons of the rulers. . . . If rulers are to wield political power, they must be recognized as possessing authority."

Clearly the relationships between rulers and the ruled shift over time, creating many differently shaped social relations as well as openings for political challenge. But these openings are not constant. Particularly in sociology, there has been a concerted effort to identify and systematize the aspects of political context that advantage particular types of challengers while disadvantaging others across time and across sociopolitical contexts. Students speak of a set of "political opportunity structures" that affect a people's desire both to undertake collective action and their expectations for success. Paraphrasing Sidney Tarrow, the defining features of political opportunity structures include shifts in ruling alignments, the availability of influential allies, and cleavages within and among elite groups. Shifts in political opportunity structures affect both the likelihood that protest will develop and its likelihood of success. Changes in opportunity structures can affect a political system's degree of openness to participation by challengers.

In 1973 Eisinger employed the concept of opportunity structures to explain why protest is most likely to occur under regimes that are moderately accessible to citizen claims and participation. A complete lack of tolerance for dissent deterred protest while extremely open and accessible governments preempted it. According to the political opportunity literature, challengers rely on both internal resources, such as money, power, and organization, as well as on the external resources made available by the shifts in national and international political opportunity they confront.

The political opportunity approach places activists in their social and political context and, in this sense, it recognizes the relational nature of social power. This way of explaining social power has overshadowed for the most part the pluralist and elitist views. The numerous revolutions against long-entrenched totalitarian states since 1989, many of which were largely nonviolent, could not be anticipated with either of the former views. Thus, we had a major global phenomenon, people power, being characterized as a surprising outbreak or as an anomaly.

When protesters adopt nonviolent tactics, they challenge the rules and conventions of political engagement, and in so doing, are positioned to gain political advantage. The strategic use of nonviolent direct action affords seemingly powerless challengers a way of leveraging their numbers into a counterhegemonic social force.

By stepping beyond the standard repertoire of accepted actions, challengers redefine the rules of engagement. In defining new terms of engagement, and maneuvering on them, challengers are capable of throwing powerful adversaries off balance. This process has been characterized by Gene Sharp as political jiu-jitsu. Transcending prescribed cultural and political constraints leaves nonviolent strategists without a clear sense of the responses their action will generate. In consequence, engaging in extra-institutional contention involves high levels of risk. Activists may capture the public imagination, gain elite support and achieve desired concessions. They also risk marginalization and persecution.

In other words, those who would wield social power through direct action, both violent and nonviolent, challenge system norms. The threat of nonviolent struggle or people power to the status quo, however, is qualitatively different than the threat of violence. Violent direct action works through threatened and applied coercive physical power. The resource being controlled here is the capacity to inflict physical harm; those who resist can be killed. Nonviolent direct action, by contrast, allows for a much broader repertoire of influences employing both positive and negative interests, and drawing upon diverse sources of power, including altruistic, authoritative, and intellectual appeals, as well as the threatened and actual imposition of nonviolent (social, economic, and political) sanctions.

Sharp argued in 1973 that nonviolent direct action can serve as a functional substitute for violent conflict. Nonviolent action may also serve to dampen levels of violence by forging communities of active and politically savvy participants. In this respect, socialization may operate differently between violent and nonviolent struggles. The social power wielded in nonviolent direct action represents a democratic practice capable both of dampening divisive conflict and nurturing inclusive political communities.

This relational perspective on power is premised upon an explicit recognition of the diverse sources of power in society. Social power is located throughout society. The diversity of social powers can affect another's interests by imposing or threatening to impose negative sanctions. Social power can also operate with positive appeals. In any case, social power encompasses the totality of all influences and pressures, including physical, economic, social, and political, that may be brought to bear upon anothers interests.

Doug Imig
Doug Bond

References

Eisinger, Peter K. "The Conditions of Protest Behavior in American Cities." *American Political Science Review* 67 (March 1973): 11–28.

Green, Philip, ed. *Democracy.* Atlantic Highlands, N.J.: Humanities, 1993.

Gregg, Richard. *The Power of Nonviolence.* New York: Schocken, 1934.

La Boétie, Etienne de. *The Politics of Obedience: The Discourse of Voluntary Servitude (De la servitude volontaire).* Introduction by Murray M. Rothbard. Translated by Harry Kurz. Montreal: Black Rose, 1975.

Lakey, George. *Strategy for a Living Revolution.* San Francisco: Freeman, 1973.

McAdam, Doug. *Political Process and the Development of Black Insurgency.* Chicago: University of Chicago Press, 1982.

Nye, Joseph S. *Bound to Lead: The Changing Nature of American Power.* New York: Basic, 1990.

Rummel, R.J. *Understanding Conflict and War: The Conflict Helix.* New York: John Wiley and Sons, 1976.

Schwartz, Michael. *Radical Protest and Social Structure: The Southern Farmers Alliance and Cotton Tenancy, 1880–1890.* Chicago: University of Chicago Press, 1976.

Sharp, Gene. *The Politics of Nonviolent Action.* Boston: Porter Sargent, 1973.

Tarrow, Sidney. *Power in Movement: Social Movements, Collective Action and Politics.* New York: Cambridge University Press, 1994.

Wrong, Dennis H. *Power: Its Forms, Bases, and Uses.* Chicago: University of Chicago Press, 1988.

See also MECHANISMS OF DIRECT ACTION; METHODS OF NONVIOLENT ACTION

Solidarity

Collective commitment to the goals of a social movement and the willingness to sacrifice time, effort, and self-interest in pursuit of group goals. Solidarity entails a sense of shared fate, of collective identity, of concern for the welfare of fellow movement activists. In a nonviolent movement, solidarity implies a group commitment to nonviolent means of achieving collective goals and protecting one's fellow activists.

Movement groups are usually not-for-profit entities that do not have the material resources to hire large numbers of employees. Instead they must depend on volunteer recruits who believe in the urgency of the movement cause and are willing to sacrifice their personal welfare for that cause. They must persuade people to give up their daily round of activities for a time in order to devote themselves to movement activities. This often means sacrificing time at work, at play, or in one's family for the cause. Unless the movement activists convince potential recruits of the urgency of the cause, the movement will not grow.

Caring about the cause is not enough. People care about a lot of issues; they usually act to try to solve problems only when they believe such actions will work. This gives nonviolent movements several additional tasks. They must convince potential participants that the normal operation of social institutions will not solve the problem they are concerned about. This task may require that the movement first attempt to deal with the issue through normal institutional processes. If this fails, the movement must then convince recruits that nonviolent tactics such as sit-ins, boycotts, marches, and forms of civil disobedience will advance the movement toward the realization of its goals.

Participants express solidarity with a nonviolent movement when they believe in the urgency of the cause and in the effectiveness of nonviolent means of promoting that cause. Movement leaders use a variety of methods of promoting this kind of solidarity; because of the precariousness of the mobilization of any movement, they must do this throughout the entire process of movement development. There are at least three key factors in the promotion of solidarity in a nonviolent movement: (1) the creation of a small core group of activists in a haven, a social setting isolated from the elite target; (2) educational efforts designed to convince potential movement recruits of the urgency of the cause; and (3) the willingness of leaders and participants to suffer repressive acts by the targets of protest.

Movements often have their origins among small groups of like-minded people. Commitment to a particular issue or set of issues often emerges among such groups in social settings isolated from decision-making elites. These havens or free social spaces are pockets of critical thinking where people question rationalizing ideologies. They are meeting places where people can talk about their common problems without having to defer to the ideological pronouncements of those in power. Already-existing political groups may not be the best settings for such critical thinking because such groups often must accept the legitimacy of the system in order to gain advantages within it. Such critical thinking is more likely in nonbureaucratic informal group settings. All societies, no matter how totalitarian, have potential sites of such critical thinking and planning. Examples include block clubs and tenant associations in the community, bars and saloons in the labor movement, student lounges and hangouts, and women's consciousness-raising groups.

Havens such as southern black churches and colleges were crucial to the mobilization of the U.S. civil rights movement. A great sense of solidarity and empowerment came out of these black institutions and grew under the impact of black urbanization in the post–World War II period. The church provided protected meeting places where tactics and strategy could be planned in a setting isolated from the repressive actions of white elites. Black ministers preached a gospel of black liberation from the yoke of segregation and provided much of the leadership of the movement. Whites could not fire the insurgent leaders of black-owned and controlled institutions. Members of black congregations were the crucial source for recruitment into the movement rank and file.

Southern black colleges were also havens for the development of a critical consciousness regarding segregation. Students were also free of pressure from white employers and generally did not have families dependent on them. Campuses were closely knit socially with excellent opportunities for communication; consciousness of racism and how to fight it spread quickly throughout the network of black colleges. Black college students ultimately had an extraordinarily high level of participation in the sit-ins, freedom rides, marches, and other activities of the southern civil rights movement.

Generating solidarity in a small isolated group is no prescription for political success. In order to be effective, such groups must communicate their perspective, their analysis of injustice, to a larger circle of potential supporters. People are not likely to become active in a movement unless they understand in some depth the issues of concern to that movement. Movement activists often design educational events in order to get potential activists to understand the injustices being addressed by the movement.

A good example is the teach-ins that were so important to the beginnings of the anti–Vietnam War movement. The idea was to generate intensive discussion of the escalating U.S. war in Southeast Asia. Forty-nine faculty members at the University of Michigan organized the first teach-in on March 24, 1965. Three thousand attended the event, which focused student attention on the issue and convinced many of them of the urgency of the Vietnam War issue. Columbia University, the University of Chicago, the University of California at Berkeley, the University of Pennsylvania, New York University, the University of Wisconsin, and Harvard subsequently held teach-ins. They were designed as educational events, and not as straightforward attempts to recruit into the antiwar movement; however, many of those who attended the teach-ins probably joined the struggle against the war. Some of the most active campuses in the antiwar movement were those where teach-ins had been held. College campuses are not the only sites of such educational events; community activists often sponsor candidates' forums where housing or poverty issues are discussed; women's groups hold discussions on rape and battered women; environmental groups educate about threats to the ecological balance.

One of the ways in which movement leaders persuade others to sacrifice for the cause is to do so themselves. The example of self-sacrifice convinces others that the cause must be urgent and important. It makes formerly uninvolved bystanders pay attention to the issue; they believe that people would not sacrifice their own welfare or even their lives unless the cause they were fighting for was an important one. Promoting solidarity is not simply a matter of arguing a position; it's a matter of putting oneself on the line, of demonstrating to people that the issue is an urgent, crucial one that is deserving of their time, energy, and sacrifice. Participation in risky protest indicates that there is a group of people who are so concerned about an issue that they are willing to risk their own welfare—through arrest, physical injury, or even death—for their cause. Repression of a nonviolent movement often draws attention to the injustices the movement is fighting against and persuades bystanders to choose sides. The growing circle of solidarity becomes the key to movement success. Nonviolent movements strive to make this circle include even the targets of their protest, to achieve the beloved community.

A good example is the 1980s anti-apartheid movement at Columbia University. The movement, led by the Coalition for a Free South Africa (CFSA), called for divestment by Columbia University of all stocks in companies doing business in South Africa. In 1982 and 1983 the CFSA held workshops, sponsored forums with speakers from the African National Congress, organized antiapartheid rallies, started a petition drive, and testified at university senate hearings on divestment. When the university's trustees rejected a unanimous vote for divestment by the university senate, the CFSA organized a nonviolent protest. The students chained shut the doors of the major Columbia College classroom and administration building, Hamilton Hall (later renamed Mandela Hall), and blocked the entrance with their bodies. Hundreds of students soon joined this blockade because they saw it as a powerful way to show their outrage, to get the trustees and others to pay more attention to the apartheid issue.

Most of those on the blockade believed they would be arrested immediately on the first day of the protest. However, they were not arrested and the costs of participation in the blockade soon began to rise. The severe sacrifices involved included facing cold, rain, and lack of sleep, getting sick and losing study time. The most important threat was to the protesters' academic careers; the administration threatened to suspend or expel them from Columbia. But rather than ending the protest, the threat of disciplinary action increased its strength. The common threat forced the blockaders to draw together for protection; it gave them a powerful sense of common fate.

As the threats raised the stakes, those uncertain about the divestment issue and the blockade tactic felt compelled to make a decision and to choose to defend the blockaders or to support the administration's position. More and more people on and off campus focused their attention and activity on the issues of apartheid and divestment. This resulted in further opportunities for the generation of solidarity. The students distributed more fliers, sponsored more speeches by civil rights activists, and participated in more campus discussions on South Africa.

Hundreds of individuals and organizations sent statements of support to the protesters including representatives from Harlem community groups and churches, faculty members, Bishop Desmond Tutu, the African National Congress and the United Nations, Jesse Jackson, several labor unions, civil rights leaders, and elected officials from New York City. Students on other campuses–including Berkeley, Rutgers, Cornell, Wisconsin, the State University of New York, and the City University of New York—began to engage in similar actions. This support legitimized the protest and encouraged the blockaders to continue it to keep the growing struggle alive. The growing circle of solidarity with the divestment movement led to its success; the Columbia trustees divested in September of 1985.

Eric L. Hirsch

References

Hirsch, Eric L. "Sacrifice for the Cause: Group Processes, Recruitment, and Commitment in a Student Social Movement." *American Sociological Review* 55 (April 1990): 243–254.
Morris, Aldon. *The Origins of the Civil Rights Movement.* New York: Free Press, 1984.
Zaroulis, Nancy, and Gerald Sullivan. *Who Spoke Up? American Protest against the War in Vietnam 1963–1975.* New York: Holt, Rinehart, Winston, 1984.

See also CIVIL RIGHTS MOVEMENT; LEADERSHIP; ORGANIZATION IN SOCIAL MOVEMENTS; SOUTH AFRICA, OPPOSITION TO RACIAL OPPRESSION; TEACH-IN; VIETNAM WAR OPPOSITION

Solidarity (Poland)

A Polish federation of trade unions that arose out of the industrial strikes that swept Poland in August 1980. Although strikes occurred in several regions, notably Lublin, Szczecin, Jastrzębie, and Wrocław, the workers of the city of Gdansk on the Baltic coast opened the way to free trade unions for the rest of Poland. There on the morning of August 14, 1980, activists of the Free Trade Unions of the Baltic sparked a strike among the fifteen thousand workers of the Lenin Shipyard. The strike rapidly spread to other workplaces and turned into a general strike of the region under the leadership of the Interfactory Strike Committee based in the shipyard. The central strike tactic called for the work teams to remain in the workplace until their demands were settled—a stay-in, or sit-down, strike. The strike committee formulated a program in the form of twenty-one demands and negotiated with government teams sent from Warsaw. These unexpected events in a Leninist party dictatorship that permitted no spontaneous social organization of any significance commanded the attention of the world. Many expected these strikes would end in a bloody suppression of the workers by state security forces.

Instead, the negotiations culminated on August 31, 1980, in the signing of the Gdansk Accords, which most significantly recognized the right of workers to organize themselves in trade unions independent of the state. Almost as important, in that it provided a means to protect this primary achievement, was the second of the workers' demands—the right to strike.

Because the Polish party-state was essentially the only employer in the country and had a monopoly of association and control, this settlement carried enormous political implications if the nascent movement should sustain itself and grow beyond Gdansk.

Solidarity now burned like a firestorm across Poland. The party's attempts to halt the blaze through such devices as reforming old unions, creating new, supposedly independent, unions, imposing a news blackout, or simply using intimidation not only failed but, in fact, provoked more strikes and more union organizing by Polish citizens in all walks of life.

Within two weeks of the Gdansk settlement, representatives of thirty-five regions and factories gathered in Gdansk and voted to create a nationwide federation to be called NSZZ *Solidarność.* The NSZZ stood for Independent Self-Governing Trade Unions *(Niezalezny Samorządny Związki Zawodowe).* The title *Solidarność* (Solidarity) had been the name of the Gdansk strike bulletin in August. *Solidarność* became even more popular because of the evocative graphic design created by an unemployed artist, Jerzy Janiszewski, who joined that strike.

This federation had three levels of organization, the workplace, the regional committee, and finally, the national coordinating commission (KKP), made up of representatives of the

Solidarity supporters march in Warsaw, June 30, 1989. AP/Wide World Photos.

thirty-eight or so regions. By statutes, extensive powers were removed to the workplace and regions and the role of the national coordinating commission was in theory quite limited. In practice, the struggle against the centralized party-state forced power of decision upwards to the commission and its chairman Lech Walesa and his advisors.

By late fall, a majority of Poland's active working population had joined the popular movement, some 9.5 million people in a total population of 35 million. Scores, then hundreds and later thousands of forums of free expression surfaced throughout Poland, including hundreds of newspapers. Other new self-organized social formations such as Rural Solidarity for farmers and peasants and associations for students, pensioners, and small business persons arose, all affiliated with the workers movement.

The overall effect was huge—Solidarity turned existing organizations upside down. The Communist party's mass membership was gravely weakened as roughly half of its 3 mil-

lion rank and file joined the union and disobeyed party orders not to strike. Moreover, elite organizations previously under tight party control, such as the Union of Journalists, the Artists' Union, the Writers and Actors Associations, all held Solidarity congresses in the autumn of 1980 that swept out the old leaders and set about to implement far-reaching reforms. Although the commanding heights of state power—the central party committee, the army, and the security police—remained intact, Solidarity had captured virtually all of the rest of Polish society. It was clear in the fall of 1980 that Solidarity was not solely a union movement in the sense of an economic association, but rather a national coalition striving for fundamental labor, civil, and national rights. In short, the movement shook the foundations of Communist power in Poland and all its Communist neighbors.

By the end of 1980, Soviet and Polish state resistance stiffened. While Solidarity had created a vast zone of civil freedom, its only weapon other than symbolic and moral pressure was the threat of a general strike. As all knew, this was a most dangerous option, for its implicit power to drive the entire economy to a halt raised the stakes to an almost apocalyptic level. If employed, the general strike offered the very real prospect of ending in civil war and Soviet-led invasion.

Solidarity's weaknesses were cruelly exposed in the Bydgoscz crisis in March 1984, when Solidarity, in order to defend activists brutally and illegally beaten by security police, took the country to the brink of a general strike. Both the state and Solidarity drew back at the last moment and a fragile and ambiguous settlement was patched together. After the euphoria of the original surge, Solidarity realized there were very real limits to the amount of significant change it could achieve, given party monopoly of effective power. Even more ominously, the new social movement could not defend its members. Increasingly, party leaders called on the only argument they had to justify the continuation of their own rule: "If not us, then Soviet tanks." This hardline advocacy was somewhat balanced by another influence, a growing movement for reform of the party through the efforts of the party's own rank and file. This tendency within the party acquired an increasing measure of organization and soon, a name: the Horizontal Movement.

In the summer of 1981, the party's traditional leadership, encouraged by threatening letters from the Soviet party leadership, engineered a special party congress in which the party's own reform movement was summarily terminated.

Soon thereafter, in September–October 1981, Solidarity held its first national congress at which nearly one thousand delegates, elected by 9.5 million members, debated the state of Poland for two weeks. These were the first free elections and free assemblies in Eastern Europe since the beginning of the cold war. Though a signal achievement in itself, the other major achievement was considerably more programmatic: the union adopted a program for a new Poland, deemed the "Self-Governing Republic," which took the country to the limits of geopolitical realities. It called for democratic associations at all levels of society and made specific demands for free local and regional elections and the formation of a second house of Parliament. The program preserved the leading role of the party in the state, but in a symbolic Queen Elizabeth–like role—to reign but not to rule.

In one extraordinary burst of international revolutionary agitation comparable to Lenin's Decrees at the Bolshevik seizure of power in 1917, the congress sent a "Letter to the Workers of the East," in which the union proclaimed its solidarity with and support for the peoples of the entire Soviet bloc and exhorted the formation of free trade unions in Leninist states. Democracy in only one former Leninist dictatorship did not seem viable. International isolation would lead to domestic defeat.

The success of the Solidarity congress could not conceal the fact that the movement itself did not possess the means to compel the Polish state to effect fundamental political change. On the other hand, at that time in the fall of 1981, the union's leadership believed that suppression of Solidarity could not be carried out by the party because such an action would provoke a mass strike that would also bring an end to the government. Solidarity leaders erroneously believed the Polish armed forces could not be used against what had clearly become the sole authentic representative of the Polish people.

On the night of Saturday/Sunday, December 12–13, 1981, the Polish state struck what it hoped would be the final blow against Solidarity. At midnight, Polish security troops and armed forces began to arrest union leaders across the country. By six o'clock that morning, about five thousand local, regional, and national representatives of Solidarity, including Lech Walesa, were in prisons or concentration camps. Early that Sunday morning, Poles awakened to find that Poland was now under the rule of an extraordinary body, the "Military Council of National Salvation," headed by General Wojciech Jaruzelski.

A so-called state of war was proclaimed. All places of work were militarized and placed under the command of a commissar. Failure to obey their orders entailed severe consequences, including summary military justice. Cities were patrolled by mixed units of police and military. All newspapers and radio stations were closed. Indeed, all forms of mass media were put directly under military control and most were suspended. Travel was prohibited, except by permission of workplace commissars. Telephone conversations began with this recording: "your conversation is controlled." At the same time, troops of the Soviet Union, Czechoslovakia, and East Germany mobilized on the Polish borders to help the Polish martial law forces, if needed.

These developments did not proceed without resistance. In the first week of martial law, Polish security and military troops faced and defeated a nationwide strike. The news blackout was so effective that the extent of the protest, and its suppression, became evident only months later. Work crews who had barricaded themselves behind factory gates surrendered only when confronted by security troops armed with automatic weapons, helicopters, and tanks. All factories were isolated and, one by one, coerced into surrender. There were relatively few casualties, though nineteen miners died in one bloody incident at the Wujek Mine in Silesia.

As the strikes faded out at the end of 1981, the Polish party exulted in the restoration of the established order and with fewer casualties than might have been expected. Many Solidarity members despaired and wondered if they had been permanently defeated.

Rebirth

At the end of January 1982, street protests erupted against the "state of war" in major Polish cities. It soon became apparent that— under difficult clandestine conditions—a new underground Solidarity was forming. The catalyst was loyalty to the imprisoned five thousand leaders and to the union's leader, Lech Walesa, who had been isolated from everyone but police and party personnel in a remote cabin near the Soviet border.

Solidarity's rebirth as an underground organization progressed through most of 1982. It occurred from below as members and sympathizers labored to re-create union structures in workplaces, cities, and regions. It also occurred from above as those national leaders who had escaped arrest tried to contact their followers. On April 22, 1982, four of these nationally recognized spokesmen announced the formation of an Interim National Commission *(Tymczasowa Krajowa Komisija),* whose publicly proclaimed purpose was to restore the union and work toward a self-governing republic. Widespread street demonstrations occurred on May 1 and 3 and, finally, August 31, the occasion of the anniversary of the Gdansk Accords. These demonstrations suggested Solidarity's growing strength, and conceivably, its renewed capacity to force a showdown.

Underground Solidarity created a rich repertoire of nonviolent action. Much of it was symbolic. In some factories workers marched to their shifts like automatons out of nightmare science fiction movies. Sympathizers wore electronic resistors in place of the banned Solidarity badges. Solidarity masses were held in churches. At the hour when official government news was aired on television, one town, Swidnik, which was built around a helicopter factory, organized citywide promenades as a public demonstration of the population's nonresponse to party propaganda. When forced to stay at home by the imposition of the earliest curfew in Poland, they faced their television sets out their apartment windows to blare to the empty (save for police cars) winter night.

Polish society undertook to enforce its own social norms. In a manner reminiscent of resistance efforts under World War II German occupation, professional and trade groups established and enforced codes of ethics under the "state of war." These set out acceptable conduct and published blacklists of offenders. Such moral pressure was formidable. A prominent children's author who supported martial law found himself unable to emerge from his apartment because his lifetime readers dumped his books in front of his door. Polish actors boycotted any work on state television, turning television, the visible mouthpiece of the regime, into an embarrassing sign of government impotence. The longest-running and best-loved Polish serial, *The Family Matusiak,* slowly disintegrated week by week as reruns could no longer be shown and one boycotting actor after another had to be written out of the script. The explanations concocted by desperate script writers, "gone to study" or "died," became instruments of self-ridicule. The deceptions were laughable—and all Poland laughed. Eventually the Actors' Union was dissolved.

In such an environment, underground publishing became one of the grand successes of banned Solidarity. The first work published by the underground presses after the declaration of martial law was a translation of *The Problem of Evil* by Karl Jaspers. Several dozen independent publishing firms concentrated their energies on the blank spots in Polish history, politics, and culture. By their continued presence, these efforts effectively undermined the official media. The viability of clandestine organizations essentially turned on the ability of their participants to communicate among themselves. The numbers fluctuated over the long years of illegality, but the institutions they created numbered in the high hundreds—from bulletins and newsletters to thick learned journals. The titles of some of these publications give a glimpse into the ethos of the movement: *Where To?; Phoenix; Voice of Extremists; Unity; We Are; Next Time Around; Mini-Independence; The New Republic; Stand Up Poland and Smash Your Chains; Free Culture; Free Thought from the Underground; We Will Triumph; Without Violence; The Independent Group for Non-Violence-Wrocław; Voice of the Free Cab Drivers; Ten Million; The Dawn; Protest; Against; The Truth of Free Poles; The Whisper; In the Trenches; Freedom; In Spite of Everything; The Free Word; The Shout; Solidarity in Combat; Artists in Wartime; Word and Action; Barricade;* and *We Were, We Are, We Will Be.* One of the most important journals was the weekly *Tygodnik Mazowsze,* which was printed continuously from 1982 to 1989, when it was legalized and turned into the leading national newspaper, *Gazeta Wyborcza.*

Another area of activity was the payment and collection of funds for persecuted and imprisoned activists. Clandestine membership reached the low millions in 1983, but declined precipitously thereafter as mass organization could not be sustained. But that which could not be expressed positively could often be asserted passively. In due course, social resistance coalesced around popular refusal to participate in state-sponsored activities.

In the early days of martial law, the state hoped it could persuade some of Solidarity's leaders, including Walesa, to abandon the movement, given the hopelessness of their cause. Over the years of resistance, repression, and imprisonment, the government's lack of success in this endeavor was remarkable. In order to establish some sort of contact with and control over Polish society, the regime acted on three fronts. It tried to rebuild the mass party. It attempted to create a new mass organization for participation in public life—the Patriotic Movement for the Salvation of the Country, or PRON. Finally, it strove to create a new national trade union organization, the OPZZ, that would act in concert with the party and be loyal to it. Each of these initiatives floundered in the face of a popular boycott. In relative numbers the new government trade union made the best showing because it could dispense vital benefits, housing, vacation facilities, even consumer goods, which it used to persuade people to join.

The Strategic Dilemma

The December night in 1981 when the regime had struck had been an unmitigated disaster for the Solidarity movement. In the immediate aftermath of martial law it was by no means self-evident what the now-illegal movement should do.

The conundrum that plagued Solidarity in its original legal phase of 1980 was taken up anew through a widely discussed debate between Jacek Kuron, the most eminent political oppositionist in Poland, writing through smuggled notes out of his prison cell, and Wladysław Kulerski and Zbigniew Bujak, two leaders of the underground. Kuron argued that Poland had entered a revolutionary situation and that those who had Solidarity's legitimacy behind them should begin creating an underground state in preparation for overthrowing the occupation regime by concerted collective action. In reply, Kulerski recommended that underground Solidarity continue on the nonviolent human rights road (which Kuron himself had played such an important role in formulating); Solidarity and the Poles should renounce conspiracy and violence, and organize instead an underground society. In contrast to Kuron's proposal for a centralized underground institution, Kulerski thought that Poles should create a loosely structured, decentralized movement composed of mutually independent groups and associations that would be largely autonomous and self-directed.

In the months that followed, Kuron's program was widely discussed but never accepted. Although some small groups, such as Solidarity in Combat *(Solidarność Walcząca),* took it up in theory, most Poles continued their nonviolent resistance or turned toward what was called "internal migration"—a calculated disassociation from all officially sponsored activities.

The second option (an underground society), although explicitly rejecting violence, turned out to have two weaknesses that were not evident to most in the year of martial law in 1982. While rejecting political aims and violence, the Solidarity underground worked toward a general strike designed to force the release of the Solidarity hostages and eventually the reestablishment of their union. Yet Poles sympathetic to the underground turned out to be unwilling to follow them in what probably would have had the same result as predicted by Kuron—a violent confrontation between the society and the state. The underground's calls for a general strike on November 10, 1983, ended in a defeat that left the regime confident once again that it had the upper hand. In a demonstration of its strength, the party soon after released Lech Walesa from confinement and proceeded in the ensuing months to free the rest of the Solidarity prisoners. By July 1983, the regime felt it could afford to officially bring the "state of war" to an end.

A second weakness in the dominant strategy of the opposition lay in its concept of an underground society. Simply put, it was impossible to involve the active population of an entire country in a clandestine organization. In terms of what actually happened in the years of martial law, Solidarity looked remarkably like Kulerski's description—"mutually independent groups and committees largely autonomous and self-directed." At a national level, this association of committees and groups was headed up by the clandestine Interim National Commission (TKK), chaired by Walesa after his release. It had a public rostrum in the form of the Interim Social Council (TRS), which acted above ground as an open critic of the regime and an advocate of Solidarity's relegalization. But inevitably, under the siegelike conditions that prevailed, these groups proved unable to sustain their mass character. Resistance seemed to become the activity of an alienated elite engaged in cultural opposition.

In such mundane, if grudging ways, Poland seemed set on a course of surly stability. In 1984, the regime succeeded in holding nationwide local elections, followed by national elections to the Parliament. Although Solidarity was able to carry out various protests, there was no denying the fact that elections constituted a victory of sorts for the regime. Polls seemed to show a drop in Solidarity's prestige. In fact, the regime was illegitimate and Solidarity embodied a second sovereignty. It was a revolutionary situation lacking only a perceived split within ruling elites in Warsaw and Moscow that would allow the challenge to rise.

At the end of 1984, a nationally known priest, Jerzy Popieluszko, who held widely attended masses for Solidarity in his parish in the center of Warsaw, was abducted and murdered by a secret police death squad. In the wave of moral revulsion that followed, the regime permitted a trial and even conviction for the four police perpetrators, although it excluded punishment of their superiors who had given the orders. For the Polish regime, this murder and trial closed off the option of death squad terror, torture, and murder by the dictatorship against its challengers from the society.

By 1985, the environment surrounding Solidarity had slowly begun to change. Just as Walesa and those around him increasingly began to look like generals without an army, the party found itself once again in uncontested command of an economy that did not work. The structural crisis in the Polish economy, slowly deepening since the mid-1960s, remained unaddressed throughout the mid-1980s. By 1987, the economy was again in precipitous decline. The state confronted a fiscal crisis that could not be resolved without some popular legitimacy and societal cooperation. Subsidized basic goods may have been so irrationally priced as to be a major disincentive to production, but the regime lacked credibility to change the situation.

Forced to adopt austerity measures, on February 1, 1988, the regime raised food prices by 40 percent, placing insupportable pressure on family budgets. In April, major factories, including the gigantic steel combine at Nowa Huta, went out on strike. Finally and dramatically, the Gdansk Lenin Shipyard went on a sit-down strike that lasted nine days. The Solidarity leadership had nothing to do with these strikes, which took them by surprise. As Lech Walesa joined the Lenin Shipyard strike, he said: "I am your general. Tell me where to and I will lead you."

The regime was now faced with waves of industrial strikes, which its opponent Solidarity did not instigate or fully control. The Communists discovered they could not effectively rule; they could neither stop the strikes nor persuade Poles to work. Nor could they reimpose martial law, as the police and security troops might well divide and crumble if that task were given to them again.

In a very real sense, the Polish party was immobilized. There was, however, a potentially transformative new ingredient present in the mid-1980s that had been at work when the party had been similarly immobilized in the late 1970s. In the Brezhnev years, the Soviet party had pushed a hard line that precluded any kind of cooperative accommodation with the nonparty majority sector of society. But in the mid-1980s, a very different signal from Moscow began to be heard in Warsaw party circles: the Gorbachev doctrine to the effect that Com-

S

munist parties everywhere should seek functioning partnership with society. The effect of this stance, for Poland, was to remove coercion as a workable option of party policy.

Meanwhile, in August, a second wave of wildcat strikes materialized. The Polish government now decided, haltingly, to try to solve this grave crisis politically. In exchange for Solidarity's aid in quelling industrial unrest, they offered to discuss legalizing the union. This offer came on August 31, 1988, the eighth anniversary of the original Gdansk Accords.

Many of Solidarity's leaders feared the union would destroy its credibility by ending strikes for the government when they received no real concession in return. But Walesa thought the opportunity to enter negotiations with the government should be seized. He accepted a challenge to a national debate with Alfred Miodowicz, the head of the official trade union, OPZZ. The latter, badly in need of restoring credibility with workers and hoping his "militance" in opposing Walesa would serve such an end, played a predictable demagogic role. For his part, Walesa came armed with statistics and arguments crammed into his head by erudite experts and academicians, which he immediately forsook in favor of an utterly disarming question: "Why in the West do they ride in Mercedes and we Poles push bicycles?" In short, the Leninist corpse on the throne of power could never deliver to the people the material blessings of modern science and technology.

Like Gorbachev and the Soviet Communists and Marcos in the Philippines in 1986, the Polish regime hoped that it could manage an electoral mandate for its rule. Such rulers were so alienated from their subjects that they had no feel for public opinion. They now proposed not only to legalize Solidarity but to draw it into the system of power through the electoral process, making it co-responsible for the state's decisions—including such ringing failures as those symbolized by food price increases.

In a series of negotiations known as the Round Table, which lasted from February 6 to April 6, 1989, the Polish party, several nominally independent parties, the Church, the PRON, and Solidarity hammered out an agreement in which the union was formally legalized. Freedom of the press and association were liberalized, but also—and it turned out most significantly—major changes were made in the structure of government in preparation for the new elections. Poland's legislature was to consist of two houses—the Senate and the Sejm. The upper house, the Senate, with less power, was to be freely elected. In the Sejm, elections were to be contested in 35 percent of the seats. The remaining 65 percent were reserved for the Communists and their parties: 38 percent for the Communists and 27 percent for the satellite Democratic and United Peasant parties. Both houses together would elect a president who would have strong executive powers. These elections were to be held within thirty days.

The regime seems to have hoped that Solidarity would trade its status of illegal moral opposition for that of a legal opposition boxed into a perennially outvoted position. But the regime underestimated how utterly discredited it was before the Polish population (their opinion polls failed to uncover the depth of this sentiment), and it underestimated Solidarity's capacity to organize for the elections within a short thirty-day period, during which time the party would retain control over massive media, organizational, and financial resources. The Solidarity leaders, on the other hand, modestly hoped that they could turn in a credible performance in 1989 and be ready to contest power in 1993. It seems clear that the Round Table agreement was only possible because each side did not appreciate its own real strength or weakness or those of its adversary.

In the bare four weeks before the first round of elections, the union assembled national lists of Solidarity candidates. The election technique was simple: the candidate was photographed with Walesa! Solidarity excelled in self-representation. The outstanding election poster of the 1989 campaign showed Gary Cooper as sheriff on his way to the showdown at high noon, but instead of a tin star, he wore a Solidarity badge, and instead of a gun in his hand, he had a ballot.

The first and second rounds of voting results astounded everyone. In the upper house, the Senate, Solidarity won 99 of 100 seats. In the lower house, the Sejm, Solidarity won all 161 seats that it was allowed to contest, but these, as agreed, came to only 35 percent of all the seats.

The real sensation was that thirty-three of the thirty-five leading Polish Communists—who were the sole candidates for seats reserved for them—lost. The electors had crossed out their names or invalidated their ballots, so they failed to win 50 percent of all votes cast. The defeated included such notorious Polish Communists as the premier of Poland, Mieczysław Rakowski, the minister of the interior, Czesław Kiszczak, and the head of the government unions, Alfred Miodowicz.

Now the rejected Communists were forced to try to bring Solidarity into a coalition government that the Communists would head. As agreed, Jaruzelski was elected president but found that the Communists could not form a viable government. Their own ranks were in disorder and their satellite parties, the Democratic and United Peasant parties, began to break ranks.

Meanwhile, as the economy and political system continued to flounder, new industrial strikes broke out, increasing the pressure on the Communists. Walesa proposed a resolution: Solidarity would form a coalition government with the Democratic and Peasant parties. These parties had been little more than fig leaves on Communist rule for forty-five years. Now they abandoned their masters and joined the Solidarity coalition government formed by Premier Tadeusz Mazowiecki on August 24, 1989. Key posts, such as interior, defense, and foreign affairs were given to the Communists. This was Solidarity in a last guise as electoral machine and leader of a ruling coalition.

Within one year political quarrels led first to the resignation of Mazowiecki's Solidarity-led government, and then to a campaign for president in which Mazowiecki, Walesa's loyal adviser, ran against Walesa. Solidarity had been a national coalition of the whole society against the Communists for nine years. With democratic victory Poland was fated to enter the mundane world of ordinary politics. In 1991, in the Parliamentary elections, seven major parties, all more or less legitimate descendants of Solidarity, contested for seats. A trade union, Solidarność, continued as a successor union, but now in opposition to Walesa and to most of the Solidarity parties.

This constituted the end of Solidarity as a social movement. In nine years, it had carried out the most sustained and most sophisticated opposition to Communist rule generated in any nation since the Bolsheviks first seized power in 1917. Solidarity's capacity for resistance was a key element in discrediting and weakening Soviet power. The character of this resistance—the nonviolent endurance of millions of people carried on for many years—makes Solidarity a remarkable achievement in modern history that is remembered with awe and longing by all who had the chance to be in contact with it. A Spanish proverb says: Humanity is as God made it and worse than that much of the time *(El hombre es como Dios le hizo y aún peor muchas veces)*. Solidarity was a rare moment when many people acted above their human possibilities.

Religion and Solidarity

The religious factor in Solidarity is most easily treated as two components: (1) the influence of the Polish Catholic Church in the nation's politics and social life, and (2) the underlying religious dynamism that functioned within Solidarity itself.

The first element needs to be approached historically. After World War II, Communists quickly subjugated all independent civic associations but were unable to destroy the independence of the Catholic Church. Led by an exceptional leader, Jan Cardinal Wyszynski, the Polish Episcopate adroitly worked out a modus vivendi with the regime that succeeded in preserving the relative independence of the Church as a nonparty institution. After 1956, the Church went on the offensive in organizational and ideological terms. At times of crisis—1956, 1970, 1976, and 1980 until 1989—the government would call on the primate for support. Each time the political influence of the Church grew. This role was in fact codified within Polish political tradition; when there was no legitimate ruler, the primate became the interrex, the regent. From 1970, responding to the Baltic seacoast strikes, the Polish Church became even more active in defense of Polish society's basic human rights. This development was part of a dramatic worldwide engagement of the Catholic Church for human rights. In Poland, a special factor was the influence of a current within Catholicism, Emmanuel Mounier's personalism, that held that it was the responsibility of a Christian to be engaged in the civic and political realms.

In 1975, the bishop-cardinal of Krakow, Karol Woytyla, a distinguished representative of these currents, became Pope John Paul II. As Anna Walentynowicz, the crane operator in the Gdansk Lenin Shipyard whose firing was the catalyst for the 1980 strike, once put it, "The election of John Paul shows us that we Poles can be more than layabouts and drunkards." Soon after his election, the pope returned to Poland and presided at gigantic meetings that gave many a feeling of Polish society's inherent power and moral purpose. The decade also saw the rapid extension of Church-sponsored seminars and associations, particularly effective among youth and student groups. As an ideology and worldview, Marxism was wiped off the Polish map in that decade. It is therefore possible to speak of a moral and religious revival, a development that underlay Solidarity.

In 1980, the year of Solidarity, John Paul II published one of his most important encyclicals, *Laborens Exercens,* on the dignity and meaning of labor. Subsequently, during the creation and later repression of Solidarity, the Church was extremely important for the union movement. In many dioceses, individual bishops or priests facilitated Solidarity activity. The pact of John Paul II and President Reagan to assist underground Solidarity was a helpful, although not determining, factor in Solidarity's survival under martial law. The Church's major role was as mediator between the state and Polish society as organized in Solidarity.

Nonetheless, the Church and Solidarity remained organizationally distinct. Solidarity insisted on remaining a secular union, and a resolution that it declare itself a Catholic trade union lost overwhelmingly at the 1981 Solidarity congress. Solidarity also was not a clerical movement. Clergy appeared as chaplains, advisors, indeed martyrs, but they were not its leaders. When Primate Wyszynski, probably panicked by government stories of imminent national catastrophe (invasion by the Warsaw Pact), gave a nationwide speech against the August strikes, workers ignored it; they either condemned him or claimed his words had been twisted by the government news media.

Was Solidarity a religious movement or, less extremely, were there religious elements in Solidarity? There were fundamental features of the movement that it is difficult to analyze in terms of secular political analysis. For example, the description of Solidarity as trade union, civil rights, and national liberation movement, or as a national coalition or front, leaves out the way the decision to strike and join Solidarity in 1980 was for most a moral rebirth—a choice of a radically new way of life. In this sense, the strikes were rituals of purification and separation opening new authentic individual and social identities for those who chose them. They experienced themselves as discarding the two-faced life of bowing before power and hating or excusing one's complicity. At one of the first strikes in the Gdansk region, the factory del-

egate to the recent party congress confessed how he had lied there, and now joining his mates he kissed the cross swearing to be true. Ordinary political science is unable to account for the extraordinary avalanche quality of Solidarity's rise, as millions of people rejected the way they had lived up until then and did so at considerable risk to themselves. Indeed, two characteristics, the speed of Solidarity's membership growth and the majority proportion of people who joined the movement, may well be unprecedented in the history of collective behavior. From nothing, on August 14, 1980, Solidarity became a majority of the population of Poland within three months. Solidarity's other remarkable feature was its rejection of violence, which was adhered to by the movement—by millions of people—over nine years.

Solidarity seems to fall within the general category of what Emile Durkheim, in his work *The Elementary Forms of the Religious Life,* called "collective effervescence." This religious element in Solidarity links it to other revitalization and messianic movements.

Origins

Solidarity was part of the worldwide turn away from political ideologies toward human rights as the only ideology (as it seems). This tendency became quite evident in the 1970s and it was given a strong impulse in Poland and the rest of Eastern Europe by the rise of detente and the Helsinki process.

The turn to human rights emphasized the individual's innate moral dignity. It prescribed engagement of the individual in civic association for the defense of basic rights through legal and nonviolent means. Particularly eloquent descriptions of this stance were given by Václav Havel in *The Power of the Powerless* and Leszek Kolakowski in his essay "Hope and Hopelessness."

As the crucible of the most extreme forms of fascism and communism in the twentieth century, Eastern Europe early on exhausted the myths of revolution and purification by violence. Early tries at a violent expulsion of the Communists as in the Hungarian Revolution had failed and seemed suicidal, given the power of the Soviet Union. By 1968, hopes that the political system could be adjusted or reformed died with the crushing of the Prague Spring. But in the 1970s, changes that had occurred in Communist power in Poland, particularly the regime's weakness and desire to look civilized, created an opening for a nonviolent strategy. In earlier times that strategy would have brought on merciless and swift punishment. Indeed, in the same decade, those attempting it in the USSR or China or Romania ended up dead, or in prisons, or in psychiatric hospitals.

The Polish turn to human rights as the true basis of politics was unique because it was originated and led by industrial workers. In Poland, a political opening came in December 1970, when the Polish state signed a peace treaty with West Germany that guaranteed the western borders. Only ten days later, workers in the great shipyards of Gdansk, Gdynia, and Szczecin started protests against sudden food price rises. These developed very rapidly from protest marches and burnings of party and police buildings to citywide general strikes. The Polish Armed Forces, commanded by General Wojciech Jaruzelski, mobilized and crushed the strikes. Nonetheless, a second wave of strikes followed in January. Apparently suppressed, the seacoast strikes marked a critical moment for Polish workers as they developed new forms of resistance against the state. These were at the same time organizational, strategic, and programmatic.

Prophetically, the program of the strikers in Szczecin was written down in the form of twenty-one demands. The key programmatic point that emerged in Gdansk and Gdynia and Szczecin was the prescription to organize trade unions independent of the state, party, and workplace management. This was to be the first and really the essential point of the twenty-one demands of August 1980.

The organizational and strategic prescription to accomplish this was twofold: to organize sit-down strikes and to unite in territorial associations of workplaces against the state. These were to be known as the interfactory strike committees. In 1980, these programmatic and strategic prescriptions were successfully passed on by the Interfactory Committees of the Baltic coast to the rest of Poland.

Other sectors of Polish society entered the fray in 1975–1976. A maladroit attempt by the Polish state to amend the constitution galvanized Church and intellectual circles. In 1976, Polish intellectuals formed the Committee for the Defense of Workers (KOR) to bring material and legal aid to workers repressed for industrial protests. The committee was strongly supported by the Catholic Church and cemented the alliance of former Communists, social

democrats, and Catholic activists that was so characteristic of Solidarity. After one year of activity, KOR changed its name to the Committee for the Self Defense of Society, hence the acronym KSS-KOR. KOR became the most active group within a broad front of social activity that developed in Poland before Solidarity. KOR organized an intervention bureau to monitor civil and legal rights. It founded a clandestine book publishing firm and published several bulletins and journals, including the newspaper *Robotnik* for industrial workers. It was the patron of an incipient peasant union and the Trade Unions of the Baltic, with its three members in Gdansk. It was at the center of a broad front of intellectuals' resistance that developed in Poland after 1976—which included such groups as Young Poland, the Students Solidarity Committees, and the Association for Scientific Courses, better known as the Flying University. KOR and the opposition played a major role in preparing the Polish technical and cultural intelligentsia for the coalition with Polish workers that developed in 1980.

Roman Laba

References

Garton Ash, Timothy. *The Polish Revolution Solidarity*. New York: Vintage, 1985.
Goodwyn, Lawrence. *Breaking the Barrier: The Rise of Solidarity in Poland*. New York: Oxford University Press, 1991.
Laba, Roman. *The Roots of Solidarity*. Princeton: Princeton University Press, 1991.

See also REVOLUTIONS OF 1989; WALESA, LECH

South Africa, Antiapartheid Sanctions

A thirty-two-year international sanctions campaign to replace white minority rule with democracy in South Africa. Measured against the three bedrock propositions of sanctions effectiveness—coherence, universal application, and economic impact—the imposition of sanctions against South Africa would have to be judged a failure. The only problem is, most observers, from former National Party leaders to antisanctions stalwarts such as Helen Suzman to antiapartheid campaigners, now agree that sanctions were an important factor in building pressure for change. "I was skeptical about sanctions," admitted *Washington Post* correspondent William Claiborne in a 1990 mea culpa op-ed piece that said candidly and publicly what many officials in Pretoria were saying. "I was wrong. . . . [President De Klerk's] reforms and promises to negotiate a new and democratic constitution are driven in large measure by the effects of the squeeze put on the country's economy since 1986." The important lesson from this sanctions exercise is understanding how these tools operate politically in different domestic circumstances. In South Africa, sanctions had effect because they targeted and pressured the attitudes of white elites.

Though the National Party came to power in 1948 pledging to institutionalize racial segregation, the international community broached the topic of sanctions in connection with apartheid only in 1960. Following a South African police massacre of sixty-four blacks demonstrating peacefully in Sharpeville, the United Nations General Assembly debated whether to impose economic and diplomatic penalties. The first of many UN sanction resolutions passed in 1962, to be repealed only in 1994, when the country's first democratic election was completed and Nelson Mandela, leader of the formerly illegal African National Congress, assumed the presidency.

To evaluate the impact of sanctions on South Africa, it is useful to measure them against conventional sanctions theory. First, a long-held assumption posits that sanctions have a greater chance of success if the sender states adopt common objectives, tactics, messages, and timetables in facing a target. The target should have a clear understanding of the focus of international attention, the minimum change required, and the conditions that would have to be met for sanctions to be lifted.

In the case of South Africa, however, the senders proved a hopelessly incoherent and disorganized lot. Over more than three decades the UN approved a variety of penalties. The European Community, for its part, imposed different sanctions, with each member state free to add punishments and monitor them as they wished. The Commonwealth states engaged in public internecine combat over the issue at each summit, with nearly all members except for Britain backing tough sanctions. The Organization of African Unity lobbied for sanctions, but many member governments approved ill-concealed trade with Pretoria.

The United States, by the end, applied not only a federal sanctions package—itself a tor-

turous legislative compromise opposed and undermined by the Reagan and Bush administrations—but also no fewer than 179 state, county, city, and local sanctions on South Africa. Each contained different policies, different objectives, and different sunset provisions. It took President Bush little more than the stroke of a pen to eliminate most federal sanctions when the administration judged the time right. It would take more than a year for all the subordinate jurisdictions to get rid of them.

In sum, sanctions against South Africa flunked the first test of effectiveness: coherence. They evolved piecemeal, in the absence of domestic or international consensus, and without being anchored to an overall policy approach to apartheid. It was surely no surprise that confusion abroad produced a measure of bewilderment, bitterness, cynicism, and defiance in South Africa's white community. The inconsistencies enabled Pretoria to characterize these policies as merely the actions of foreign politicians pandering to local constituencies with no understanding of South Africa. The National Party government and businessmen complained of shifting goal posts. Others said that the outside world carried a stick but no carrots, and that no changes would satisfy "the sanctioneers."

A second proposition holds that to be effective sanctions should be evenly applied, with the fewest possible loopholes. Even one key spoiler, such as South Africa for much of the period when the world isolated Rhodesia, or the Soviet Union for Cuba, can neutralize a sanction campaign. While Pretoria could not count on a single reliable spoiler, the sanction campaign against South Africa was rife with loopholes. Corporations from most of the developed nations found numerous ways to circumvent sanctions, taking advantage of the fact that their governments only rarely took action to police the sanctions or punish transgressors. At the same time, Pretoria encouraged its own exporters to re-label goods as manufactured in Swaziland and cooperated with countries and companies to skirt the boycotts. As a result consumers could purchase in South Africa most goods available elsewhere, if at somewhat higher prices reflecting a "sanctions premium"—the extra charges involved in busting the boycott.

A third proposition asserts that sanctions, in order to achieve the desired outcome, must impose economic costs on the target that outweigh the benefits it derives from maintaining the offending policies in place. It was over this question—the measurement of the economic consequences of sanctions and whether they were potent enough to overturn apartheid—that debate revolved in the West. Experts jousted over the numbers to project whether sanctions were a worthwhile tactic. Indeed, some made the case that sophisticated new tools of economic analysis, such as the Social Accounting Matrix, could at long last "settle the disputes about effectiveness" of sanctions. In general, those who predicted minimal financial consequences concluded that sanctions would be ineffective. Those who believed that the economic impact would be greater generally supported the use of sanctions. However, there were chronic inconsistencies in some arguments. For example, opponents would contend that sanctions would have little economic impact, but that at the same time they would cause massive black unemployment and force whites "into the laager" (to adopt a siege mentality). Supporters often complained about how weak and loopholed sanctions were, but when apartheid fell they took a measure of credit for the outcome.

The most thoroughgoing study of the impact of sanctions concluded that South Africa's economy in 1990 was 20 to 35 percent smaller that it would have been without restrictions on the flow of capital and without the expensive import substitution strategies Pretoria had adopted since 1967 to reduce its dependence on the outside world and evade the threat of sanctions. The bottom line was that sanctions cost the country between 15 and 27 billion dollars, which economists Charles M. Becker and Patricia S. Pollard described as a disruptive and high, but not crippling, impact on South Africa. Not surprisingly, this estimate of the economic loss imposed by sanctions has settled nothing. Proponents and opponents continue to dispute whether the economic loss contributed to, retarded, or had no influence on political change.

What led analysts on both sides astray may have been a fixation on the economic, rather than political, measurements of sanctions. The objective of sanctions on Pretoria was not to cause economic harm. That might have been a characteristic of the sanctions campaign, but it was a means, not an end. This is a critical distinction. The objective in this case was political change—persuading the white minority government to yield power. But this central and perhaps obvious assumption was often lost, so that debates on the effectiveness of sanctions became battles over financial statistics that were beside the point. It was as if one were to try to determine the success of a military mission by counting the number of missiles fired instead of checking if the target was hit. The number of missiles is not irrelevant, just as the economic consequences of sanctions are not, but the conclusions can be imprecise and misleading. In short, many of the diagnostic tools used by protagonists in the debate were inappropriate for assessing whether sanctions worked.

To illustrate the point, it is worth recalling instances in which sanctions caused massive economic damage but failed to achieve their political ends. The U.S. effort to oust Panama's Manuel Noriega through an economic embargo is a case in point. Conversely, one can cite cases where the economic harm was slight, but political objectives were met. Washington's successful drive to stop Taiwan from pursuing a nuclear weapons program in 1976–1977 is one example.

To see if sanctions worked in South Africa, then, one needs to go back to basics and ask the right question. The professed underlying objective of international sanctions was to help pressure Pretoria to abandon white rule. Therefore, the question to ask is not, How much economic damage did sanctions cause? but, Did sanctions contribute to producing the desired political results, regardless of the precise economic impact they might have had? Before attempting an answer, however, one needs to identify the characteristics of the white polity that was the true target of sanctions.

The reason for this brief exercise is simple. The effects of pressure on a dictatorship can be expected to differ from those aimed at a democracy where public opinion matters. Similarly, embargoes will have different effects depending on how politically, economically, and culturally tied the target state is to the outside world. Sanctions against an isolated country will produce different results than those directed against a state with global linkages. Indeed, relatively cost-free measures such as a sports boycott or cultural boycott can have large psychological effects in a population that considers itself part of a world community.

South Africa's apartheid government was a strange creature. For blacks, the country was for all intents and purposes an authoritarian state. But for whites, there was a strong measure of democracy. White public opinion mattered. Moreover, many, though not all, of South

Africa's whites felt closely affiliated with the West in cultural and political terms. The nation's white business community was entwined in the global economy. And the country featured a sophisticated news media establishment through which whites received communication, filtered though it was, from the outside world.

To measure the political effectiveness of sanctions, the diagnostic tools need to fit these circumstances. Specifically, they need to assess the extent to which white public opinion and behavior, influenced by sanctions, persuaded the National Party government to begin the transition to democratic rule.

For this task a reckoning of economic consequences is only indirectly relevant. Instead, it would be critical to gather data reflecting political behavior. How did whites react to external pressure: by "retreating to the laager," as sanctions opponents had predicted, or by conceding the need for radical change, as sanctions supporters hoped?

Many studies of public opinion in South Africa tried to determine something else: whether whites and blacks supported or opposed sanctions. But the more important issue was how whites reacted to sanctions, regardless of whether or not they supported the pressures. The lone exception was the 1989 project undertaken by the Washington, D.C.–based Investor Responsibility Research Center entitled *The Impact of Sanctions on South Africa: Whites' Political Attitudes*.

The study pioneered the use of focus groups, a technique used extensively in political and marketing opinion research, but never as a test of sanctions' effectiveness. IRRC 's South African partners recruited six groups of whites, most of them Afrikaners, and trained local facilitators to run them. Insights gained in the sessions then helped frame a more conventional public opinion survey of the white community.

In retrospect, the results proved an accurate gauge of how whites were responding to pressure. The report showed that whites feeling the effects of sanctions most intensely were more rather than less likely to support political concessions to the black majority. Some 75 percent expected sanctions either to be maintained or toughened, despite the apparent disunity then prevailing in the West about adding new economic pressures. Some 66 percent perceived that the long-term effect of sanctions would be

"very harmful" to the country, regardless of the public bravado their leaders were showing. And many betrayed a keen psychological vulnerability to noneconomic sanctions such as the sports boycott, or Australia's decision to grant white South Africans visas only through embassies in neighboring black-ruled states. One year before President F.W. De Klerk announced that Nelson Mandela would be released, many whites were clearly prepared to accept change. Forty-eight percent agreed that "it is sensible to seek compromise with the advocates of sanctions," while another 41 percent said that changes should be made for South Africa's own sake. Only 9 percent said that there should be no compromise at all.

Analysts might have been able to expand on the IRRC study to develop a set of measurements providing, on a regular basis, data on the political temperature of the target population. A fuller index of white behavior could have included, for instance, emigration figures, draft evasion numbers, and suicide rates. It would surely have been difficult at the outset to judge whether trends in white morale were the result of external sanctions rather than of other internal factors such as strikes, protests, and insurgency. It might have been possible nonetheless to refine these types of diagnostic tools to focus more on that linkage. At the very least, such studies might have helped reveal whether whites were moving in the right direction as the sanctions treatment took effect. But before anyone could assemble such a project, time ran out on apartheid.

With the limited evidence that we do have, however, we can return to the three pillars of sanctions theory and try to understand how the lessons of South Africa should be applied.

Application of sanctions by the West was incoherent, uncoordinated, and inconsistent in crafting a message to Pretoria that included sanctions. But South African whites, at least in 1990, perceived the sanctions threat as more potent and real than this conclusion might suggest. There was indeed a cacophony of noises in the outside world about which sanctions to adopt, when, and for what purposes. There was, too, a press and news media in South Africa that further distorted these issues. But the overall impact was powerful for three reasons. First, South Africa featured a sophisticated communications infrastructure and a relatively free press, so that news of world opinion on apartheid got channeled directly to the white public. Second, whites considered themselves very much a part of the world community. And third, international attitudes toward South Africa, though often muddled, nonetheless left whites with the sense of being isolated. The IRRC study showed a strong yearning among them to be admitted back to the club.

Sanctions clearly were not universal. Indeed, South Africa could sustain trade despite sanctions with the help of neighboring states, companies willing to undertake the minimal risk of being caught, and countries prepared to collaborate in exchange for other advantages (such as Iraq's oil for arms barter deals). Pretoria also protected itself by developing import substitution alternatives such as Sasol, the oil from coal complex. But these arrangements took a toll. South Africans knew they had to pay a premium for products and services because of sanctions. They had also to pay higher taxes to fund high-price projects that made little economic sense in the absence of embargoes. And even if the machinations businessmen had to contend with made them cynical about sanctions, they also reinforced the sense of being labeled one of the "pole cats" of the world.

Finally, studies say that sanctions had a significant but not crippling effect on South Africa's economy. This was an impact that, on its face, appeared too weak to meet the theoretical threshold of pain sufficient to persuade whites to collaborate in the ultimate political act of helping overturn their own government system. Yet in the 1990 to 1994 period the National Party government, backed by a majority of whites, did exactly that. Of course, a range of internal pressures mounted by democratic movements such as the African National Congress played a key role. But the anomaly may also be explained by the fact that the intensity of pain that sanctions caused could not be captured in the economic statistics alone.

Overall, external pressure was effective in South Africa because conditions were right. Whites could hear the outside world, wanted to be a part of it, and had enough democracy in place so that when they wished to respond by supporting policy reversals, they could do so and change would occur. With these conditions, the West's relative discord was still understood by whites as condemnation; the porousness of sanctions only marginally undermined whites' sense of isolation; and the moderate economic effects caused far deeper unease with apartheid.

The case of anti-apartheid sanctions suggests that sanctions theory needs to be updated to incorporate new understandings of the effect of international communications, better appreciation for the perceptions and psychology of the target population, and more analysis of how to shape sanctions tactics to the political, cultural, and economic characteristics of the target state. It also spotlights the need for new tools with which to monitor the effect of sanctions as they are being applied. Conventional approaches, such as checking for leaks in an embargo, should be supplemented by sophisticated public opinion measurements in target countries where public opinion matters. Once these lessons are applied, policy-makers will have a more refined paradigm for sanctions that could make them more effective the next time they are used as a tool of foreign policy.

Stephen M. Davis

References

Becker, Charles, et al. *The Impact of Sanctions on South Africa: The Economy.* Washington, D.C.: Investor Responsibility Research Center, 1990.

Davis, Stephen M. *Apartheid's Rebels: Inside South Africa's Hidden War.* New Haven: Yale University Press, 1987.

Davis, Stephen M., Jan Hofmeyr, and Merle Lipton. *The Impact of Sanctions on South Africa: Whites' Political Attitudes.* Washington, D.C.: Investor Responsibility Research Center, 1990.

Day, Erin. *Economic Sanctions Imposed by the United States against Specific Countries: 1979 through 1992.* Washington, D.C.: Congressional Research Service, 1992.

Doxey, Margaret. *International Sanctions in Contemporary Perspective.* New York: St. Martin's, 1987.

Edgar, Robert E., ed. *Sanctioning Apartheid.* Trenton, N.J.: Africa World, 1990.

Hufbauer, Gary Clyde, and Jeffrey J. Schott. *Economic Sanctions in Support of Foreign Policy Goals.* Washington, D.C.: Institute for International Economics, 1983.

Hufbauer, Gary Clyde, Jeffrey J. Schott, and Kimberly Ann Eliott. *Economic Sanctions Reconsidered.* Washington, D.C.: Institute for International Economics, 1990.

———. *Economic Sanctions Reconsidered:*

S

Supplemental Case Histories. Washington, D.C.: Institute for International Economics, 1990.

Minter, William. "South Africa: Straight Talk on Sanctions." *Foreign Policy* 65 (Winter 1986/1987): 43–63.

Miyagawa, Makio. *Do Economic Sanctions Work?* New York: St. Martin's, 1992.

Shepherd, George W., Jr., ed. *Effective Sanctions on South Africa: The Cutting Edge of Economic Intervention.* New York: Praeger, 1991.

Zartman, I. William. "Negotiations on South Africa." *Washington Quarterly* (Autumn 1988).

See also AFRICAN NATIONAL CONGRESS OF SOUTH AFRICA; INTERNATIONAL ECONOMIC SANCTIONS; MANDELA, NELSON, ROLIHLAHIA; SANCTIONS; SOUTH AFRICA, OPPOSITION TO RACIAL OPPRESSION; SOWETO UPRISING, 1976

South Africa, Opposition to Racial Oppression

Long-term struggle over most of the twentieth century by members of the nonwhite majority to overcome institutionalized racial segregation and discrimination by white minority rule. Nonviolent action was one of the important forces contributing to the end of the apartheid regime in 1994. Nonviolent militant opposition to South African racial oppression took three principal forms: civil disobedience, electoral and other kinds of boycotts, and demonstrative labor strikes.

Civil Disobedience

Before 1960, the main civil disobedience campaigns were mounted by organizations representing Indian and Chinese minorities in Transvaal and Natal between 1906 and 1914, by African women in the Orange Free State in 1913, by African organizations on the Witwatersrand just after the First World War, by the Communist Party in 1930, by Indian organizations again, between 1946 and 1948, by the African National Congress (ANC) and its allies during the "Defiance Campaign" of 1952–1953, between 1956 and 1958 by women's organizations, and in 1960 by the Pan-Africanist Congress. After 1960, civil disobedience only reappeared in the repertoire of anti-apartheid resistance in 1984 with the beginning of communal rent strikes in black "townships" that are just ending today.

More activist forms of politically motivated lawbreaking peaked in 1989 after the launch of a second Defiance Campaign by the Mass Democratic Movement. This last major instance of South African civil disobedience was followed by the opening of negotiations between the government and the African National Congress. By April 1994, when elections under universal suffrage ended minority rule, the main racist legislation had been repealed.

Before the 1980s, civil disobedience only occasionally assumed mass dimensions. The first protests were led by Mohandas Gandhi, a British-trained lawyer from India, a founder of the Natal Indian Congress (NIC) in 1894 and of the Transvaal British Indian Organization in 1903. Both these organizations represented a narrow social elite of merchants. Gandhi originally traveled to South Africa to conduct a commercial legal case against a Transvaal trader. His entry into politics was prompted by efforts in the Natal legislature to curtail Indian franchise and trading rights.

The fifteen thousand Indians in the Transvaal Republic of the 1890s were excluded from citizenship and ownership of fixed property. After the Anglo-Boer War the new British colonial administration tightened restrictions on Indian trading, residence, and entry into the province. Transvaal Indians were mainly a commercial community, whereas the majority of the 100,000 Indians in Natal were former indentured laborers or their descendants. From 1891, the Natal authorities ceased its former practice of making land grants to Indians on the expiry of their contracts and subjected them to an annual tax of three pounds sterling. Immigration legislation proposed in 1906 and enacted in 1907 was directed specifically at Transvaal Indians and required a registration process that involved both a fee and fingerprinting, in India a practice imposed only upon criminals.

In the years between the NIC's foundation and the Transvaal Immigration Restriction Act, the preferred tactics of petitions and delegations had demonstrably failed to discourage official discrimination against Indians. Between 1903 and 1906, Gandhi, inspired by the swadeshi movement in Bengal, began to develop his strategy of passive resistance. In its fullest form, satyagraha ("truthfirmness") aimed to achieve the moral conversion of the opponent through the willing acceptance of punishment for nonthreatening forms of illegal protest. Gandhi believed that ends were contained within means; that violent action could not achieve social harmony.

Resistance to the new law began with a formal written petition (signed by 45 percent of the ten thousand adult Asian men in the Transvaal) and oath taking at a mass meeting held in Johannesburg in September 1906. Subsequently, a delegation visited London. Civil disobedience began in July 1907 and initially took the form of traders inviting arrest by selling outside the designated Indian bazaars without licenses. Upon conviction, resisters refused the option of a fine and went to prison—200 of them by January 1908. Organization of the volunteers and fund-raising for the support of prisoners' families was undertaken mainly by the British Indian Association, though the Transvaal Chinese Association also played a role. Much of the funding came from India.

The campaign was interrupted for six months by negotiations between Gandhi and Prime Minister Jan Smuts. When these talks broke down organized resistance resumed, now mainly in the form of public bonfires of registration certificates as well as illegal crossing of provincial boundaries. This latter offense was punished by deporting the offenders, not just to Natal but sometimes to India, where the campaign succeeded in arousing considerable public support as well as pressure on the British government from the Indian colonial authorities. Gandhi's weekly newspaper, *Indian Opinion,* also helped to publicize the campaign.

The resistance paused for a second time in 1911 when Smuts promised a revised immigration law that would provide Indians with legal treatment equal to that of other incoming groups. The government's failure to honor this and other promises, including repeal of the tax on indentured laborers, prompted Gandhi in September 1913 to repeat the call for resistance. This time it embraced Indian colliery workers and municipal laborers in the Natal towns of Newcastle and Dundee. Their strike spread spontaneously to forty thousand workers on the Natal sugar estates. By the end of the campaign, three thousand volunteers had served prison sentences, mainly in the Transvaal.

In 1914, the government repealed the indentured labor tax and revised some of the regulations restricting Indian entry into the Transvaal. Polygamous Indian marriages were given official recognition, which allowed a significant number of dependents to join their husbands or fathers in South Africa. However, the Indian Relief Act of 1914 did not alter the restrictions governing Indian trading in the Transvaal. The act did contain sufficient concessions to Gandhi's insistence that Indians should be afforded notional legal equality for his disciples to claim a substantial victory at the start of the Mahatma's Indian political career. In the wake of his departure from South Africa, the militant organization he had helped to build withered.

Though Indian leaders in this first phase of passive resistance had been careful to enlist white sympathizers, they made no efforts to canvass African support. Nevertheless, their efforts may have helped to inspire African women in Bloemfontein, who in May 1913 launched a vigorous protest against a municipal pass system.

Orange Free State towns, confronted with labor shortages as a consequence of industrialization in the nearby Witwatersrand, had from the 1890s forced black women as well as men to carry passes, documents that recorded their owner's employment history and tax receipts and that were used to govern their residence in municipal African "locations." Black men carried these documents in most parts of "white" South Africa, but outside the Free State women were at that stage exempt from pass legislation. In Bloemfontein, increasingly onerous regulations and controls in the aftermath of the Anglo-Boer War provoked an angry meeting on May 28, 1913, at which women resolved they would refuse to carry passes.

After a delegation was told by the mayor that he could not alter the laws, women began tearing up their passes in front of the police station. Eighty were arrested, but they were released the following morning after six hundred ululating women led by a Mrs. Molisapoli, wrapped in a Union Jack, converged on the magistrate's office. Two weeks later, the attempted arrest of a woman without a pass was followed by a riot in which thirty-four women were apprehended for stoning or biting the police. In court, they refused the option of fines and served two months in prison. Several of the women were the wives of local notables; their actions were to attract considerable sympathy and support from the leadership of the African National Congress, whose founding conference, held in Bloemfontein the year before, had probably contributed to the original resolve of the protesters. For a while even local white public

S

opinion seemed to side with the women, and this helped to restrain the police in their action against subsequent protests.

In the next few months the resistance spread to smaller towns. Participants began wearing ribbon rosettes in imitation of British suffragettes, whom the newspapers had informed them they resembled. The protests continued intermittently until the outbreak of the First World War, in August 1914, when, following the ANC's lead, the women agreed to end their protests. In June, draft legislation was tabled in parliament authorizing a change in the women's pass laws in response to a petition with five thousand signatures, but this was shelved when war was declared. Instead, the women had to content themselves with the directives from the Department of Native Affairs to the Free State authorities to relax the application of pass regulations. It is likely, though, that the forcefulness and duration of the protests helped to persuade South African governments until the 1950s of the wisdom of leaving most black South African women outside the scope of the pass laws.

After the war, African men followed the example of their Free State sisters in Johannesburg in March 1919 when the African National Congress organized demonstrations against passes. Outside the pass office men shouted "Down with the passes," and "no violence." To the accompaniment of communal singing of "Rule Britannia," several hundred men surrendered their passes to the organizers, who subsequently dispatched "pickets" to collect a couple of thousand more from workers in outlying districts. In the next month, the police made seven hundred arrests. The protest was accompanied by strikes and rioting after a mounted police charge on a demonstrating crowd. On April 25, resisters attacked police escorting prisoners to jail. The pass laws remained in force, but simultaneous civil disobedience in Pretoria won for Africans the right to walk on the city's pavements.

The next attempt to challenge the pass laws was led by the Communist Party in December 1930, responding to economic recession and a harshly segregationist Afrikaner Nationalist administration. The party, whose leadership was newly Africanized as a consequence of Comintern prompting, called for pass burnings on December 16, Dingaan's Day, under the slogan "Freedom or Death." Fewer than one thousand passes altogether were incinerated in Transvaal towns, but a large crowd in Durban

(in Natal) watched three thousand passes burn before police marched in and stabbed to death local party leader Johannes Nkosi and three of his comrades. Efforts to prolong the campaign in the wake of this butchery led to fierce political suppression in which two hundred Communists were banished from Durban. Genteel African National Congress leaders, their postwar Jacobinism now a distant memory, condemned the protests. Africans could only hope to gain white respect if they acted in a moderate way, President-General Pixley Seme told his alarmed audience.

Indians threatened to resume civil disobedience in 1939 with the passage of new legislation aimed at limiting Indian landholding. They were dissuaded from doing so by Gandhi, who had been encouraged in his correspondence with Smuts to believe that there were good prospects for an "honourable settlement." Yusuf Dadoo, a young Communist doctor from Krugersdorp and leader of the "nationalist bloc" in the Transvaal Indian Congress, was at that time sufficiently impressed by Gandhi's teachings to accept his logic. "As you rightly say," he wrote, "our duty is to win our opponents with love and understanding."

During the war, the government suspended its efforts to curtail Indian property rights, and Indian radicals concentrated on building a strong labor movement in Durban factories and the Natal sugar estates. In 1946, the Asiatic Land tenure and Indian Representation Bill prohibited any land sales in Natal and Transvaal between Asians and non-Asians. The Natal and Transvaal Indian congresses began preparing for civil disobedience by training volunteer bands, publishing a newspaper, Passive Resister, setting up local action committees, and organizing well-attended fund-raising meetings.

Resistance began in June. Groups of fifty volunteers would periodically set up tents on a plot of vacant municipal land in Durban and await arrest for breach of the tenure provisions of the new law. In two years, two thousand resisters participated. Of these, nearly half were factory workers, evidence of the trade union linkages that Indian political activists had fostered during the war. A small number of African, colored, and white sympathizers joined the protest. At the beginning of 1948, resistance was extended to illegal crossings of the Transvaal-Natal border. However, activity had become very sporadic and the campaign was "indefinitely suspended" after the electoral victory of the savagely anti-Indian Afrikaner National Party.

As in the earlier Indian campaign, the organizers directed considerable effort at orchestrating external pressure on the South African government. Dadoo and Monty Naicker, president of the Natal Indian Congress, visited Gandhi in India and succeeded in persuading the Indian government to take up their cause at the United Nations. India also began a trade boycott of South Africa that caused an immediate shortage of hessian sacking. In retaliation, white Transvaal grain farmers, unable to bag their crops, began a boycott of Indian trading stores. Despite dissension within Smuts's cabinet, the legislation remained in force until it was replaced in 1950 by the more severe Group Areas Act. Dadoo and Naicker had few illusions about the possibility of victory and, indeed, by 1946 Indian political leadership included very few satyagrahis. Their purpose in mounting passive resistance was primarily mobilizational. In this they were successful. NIC membership climbed to thirty-five thousand, and in 1947 the Indian Congress leaders joined A.B. Xuma of the ANC in signing the "Doctor's Pact" committing their organizations to future collaboration.

The increasing empathy between Indian and African political notables was not reflected by much solidarity on the ground between the two communities. In 1949, racial tensions in Durban between Africans and Indians broke out in riots that caused 142 deaths. Indian participation in the 1952 Defiance Campaign of the ANC was almost entirely at the leadership level. Although three Indians joined four ANC officials in a Joint Planning Council, fewer than one hundred Indians served as volunteers. Ostensibly, the campaign sought the abolition of "five unjust laws" that represented the first phase of the National Party government's apartheid program. These laws elaborated urban segregation, imposed passes on African women, banned the Communist Party, removed mixed-race coloreds from the common voter roll, and gave to rural chiefs new authoritarian powers to implement highly unpopular land conservation measures.

The Joint Planning Council appointed a "volunteer-in-chief," Nelson Mandela, and an Indian deputy, Ismael Cachalia, to lead three stages of civil disobedience—beginning in June with small bands of resisters in the main towns, broadening the movement to embrace smaller centers and larger groups, and then extending the movement to the countryside. In the second and third phases the intention was to support passive resistance with general strikes. Action began in June 1952 with Mandela leading a group of senior ANC and Indian Congress members in a violation of Johannesburg curfew regulations. Subsequent civil disobedience mainly targeted "petty apartheid" regulations in railway stations and post offices as well as the rules governing entry into African locations.

Over eight thousand people were arrested in the defiance campaign; nearly six thousand of them in the Eastern Cape, where ANC organization had historically been facilitated by relatively liberal local government, a concentration of educational institutions, and the development of an especially strong trade union movement. In Port Elizabeth, a one-day strike in November to protest curfews and a ban on meetings closed the docks and brought armored cars onto the streets. Thousands lost their jobs afterward. But protest was not just confined to workers. In the Eastern Cape nearly half the volunteers were women. In parts of the Ciskei reserve the campaign attracted peasant support.

Reaching a peak in August, the movement lost impetus after violent riots in its two main centers, East London and Port Elizabeth. In December, just before the campaign's end, a particularly well-publicized act of defiance took place in Germiston when forty volunteers entered the African township without the required permits. The group included seven whites and was led by Gandhi's son, Manilal, and Patrick Duncan, the son of a wartime governor-general. The seven served prison sentences, the first white South Africans to be convicted for civil disobedience. Despite some expressions of sympathy for African grievances in English-language newspapers (most of the defiance was reported very dismissively), within the white community the campaign elicited either hostility or indifference. In early 1953, the Criminal Law Amendment Act was passed. The new law prescribed a maximum prison term of three years with fines and whipping for "offenses committed by way of protest." Young volunteers had already been subjected to lashings in several towns. Most activists were unprepared for such severe punishment. For ANC politicians, their following now swollen to 120,000, civil disobedience no longer seemed a practical option.

African women thought differently, however. Beginning in 1955, a series of protests

S

against the extension of passes to women were organized by the Federation of South African Women, an umbrella body to which the ANC's Women's League, various trade unions, and the left-wing white and colored organizations were affiliated. Demonstrations began in October 1955 outside the Union Buildings in Pretoria, and a series of local protests in many smaller centers followed the traveling "mobile units" that issued the new passes. In Winburg, in the Free State, in March 1956, women recalled a local historical tradition and burned the passes that had just been distributed. The federation collected money for their defense but it counseled against outright law-breaking. Refusing to accept the passes was not illegal (they were not made compulsory for women until 1963), but burning them was. A second massive demonstration in Pretoria took place in August, at which time twenty thousand women assembled outside the Union Buildings to triumphantly sing their anthem: "Strijdom you have tampered with the women, you have struck a rock." Unfortunately, Prime Minister J.G. Stijdom was absent from his office that day.

The movement spread from the cities to the towns. In Johannesburg township branches of the Women's League persuaded large numbers of women to deliberately court arrest by taking part in meetings and marches in the city center, which were then prohibited. Twelve hundred women were charged under the Criminal Law Amendment Act before an alarmed ANC leadership overruled the federation and directed that the women should not break the law. In return, the ANC undertook to organize a national campaign against passes in general. Despite the ANC's strictures, women's protest spread outside the boundaries of organized politics. In mid-1959 anger about the passes and soil conservation regulations helped to generate a series of revolts led by women in the Natal countryside. Mostly, participants concentrated on destroying cattle dipping tanks, but they also set fire to sugar cane fields and marched on police stations and magistrate's court. About twenty thousand women were involved in these events and nearly one thousand were arrested before the demoralizing effects of heavy fines and long prison sentences took their toll.

The ANC's plans to mount a nationwide offensive against the pass laws were preempted by the decision of a militant rival organization, the Pan-Africanist Congress (PAC), which urged its supporters in early 1960 to surrender themselves without passes outside police stations. Their intention was to trigger a series of insurgent protests that would culminate in an insurrectionary uprising and "independence in 1963." Believing that rhetorical emphasis on African race pride was by itself sufficient to evoke a large following, the PAC did little systematic preparation. Its branches were concentrated around the steel-making center of Vereeniging and in the African communities of Cape Town. In Sharpeville, outside Vereeniging, high rents, unemployment among school dropouts, and authoritarian administration generated angry discontent, particularly among young people. The ANC was weak in Sharpeville, and PAC activists constructed a strong network. In Cape Town, the PAC built its base among squatters and migrant laborers, the principal targets of fiercely applied "influx control" intended to reduce to a minimum the African presence in the Western Cape.

On Monday, March 21, 1960, five thousand Sharpeville residents gathered outside the police station, their leaders demanding arrest. An increasingly nervous police detachment confronted the crowd for six hours before firing into it, killing 69 and wounding 186.

After the massacre a volatile mood prevailed. Responding to a strike call by the ANC, on March 28 teenagers invaded the streets of Soweto, burning public buildings, stoning commuters, and destroying the public radio system. The greatest drama occurred in Cape Town, where the PAC succeeded in mounting a "stay-at-home" begun on March 21. A series of demonstrations climaxed on March 30 in a procession of thirty thousand people intent on assembling outside parliament. Police authorities persuaded the young Pan-Africanist, Philip Kgosana, to divert the marchers toward police headquarters. Subsequently promised an interview with the minister of justice, Kgosana led his supporters home. Later, Kgosana was arrested and soldiers and police occupied the townships. On April 8, the government banned the PAC and the ANC.

For many, these events confirmed the vulnerability of minority rule. On March 25, the government temporarily suspended the pass laws (they were back in force within a month). A cabinet minister was moved to announce that "the old book of South African history was closed." In eighteen months, there was a net capital outflow of 248 million rands and foreign exchange reserves were halved. On April 1, the

United Nations Security Council passed its first condemnation of South Africa. A turning point had been reached, as Nelson Mandela observed, for the suppression of African political organizations convinced their leaders that "it would be unrealistic . . . to continue to preach peace and nonviolence." By the end of 1961, both the ANC and the PAC were both committed to "armed struggle" against apartheid.

For the next two decades, anti-apartheid politicians made no efforts to organize civil disobedience. Its revival in the mid-1980s was partly attributable to the relaxation of political controls that accompanied government constitutional reforms. In an effort to broaden the legitimacy of officially sanctioned politics, the government enacted separate parliamentary representation for the Indian and colored minorities and additional powers for elected African local authorities. Earlier reforms had conceded legal recognition to a strengthening black trade union movement in 1979 and an expansion of African secondary education as well as the abolition of mandatory teaching in Afrikaans, the issue that had provoked a school student rebellion across the country in 1976.

In August 1983, a United Democratic Front (UDF) was formed. The UDF's leadership included many veteran ANC activists and increasingly it took on the authority of an internal surrogate for the exiled ANC. Federal in structure, its hierarchy of committees linked a nationwide network of six hundred or so organizations. These included local "civic" associations (which had recently mushroomed in townships in a series of struggles to win improvements in services), youth and school children's movements, trade unions, and, in Natal and the Transvaal, resurrections of the Indian Congresses (which had never been formally banned). The UDF's proclaimed purpose was to challenge the constitutional and local government reforms. Within a year of its foundation many of its affiliates were swept up in a tide of often violent insurrectionary opposition to the extremely corrupt local governments in African townships, sparked by heavy rent increases for public housing.

The rebellion began with rent strikes in the townships around Vereeniging. A march on municipal offices swiftly degenerated into rioting and the killing of the local mayor. Army occupation restored order, but the rebellion spread to other cities and with it the rent boycott. It became increasingly militarized in char-acter as ANC guerrilla units established themselves in its more important centers. The rent strike remained one of the UDF's more effective weapons, enduring through a state of emergency, which between 1986 and 1988 succeeded in halting most forms of militant political opposition. In 1986, despite mass evictions, fifty-four communities were affected by the boycott, a total of more than half a million households.

By the end of 1988, the government's "securocrats" seemed to have succeeded in driving UDF activists off the streets. Popular resistance was expressed mainly through guerrilla warfare, the continuation of the rent boycott, and almost universal disinclination to vote in local elections. In 1989, organized mass politics reasserted itself. A hunger strike of political detainees succeeded in persuading the minister of law and order to release nine hundred prisoners, including most of the high-level UDF leaders. These leaders joined forces with trade unionists in a "Mass Democratic Movement" (MDM). Their objective was to instigate a second "Defiance Campaign" and to challenge racial segregation in government-controlled facilities.

On August 4, processions of black defiers, ostensibly seeking treatment, arrived at the doors of eight government "whites only" hospitals in the Transvaal and Natal. Warned in advance, doctors and nurses, with the tacit consent of the authorities, admitted them. The campaign was promoted through large meetings and huge marches, which despite their illegality were only occasionally suppressed by the authorities. Police did shoot into a crowd in Cape Town in September, killing twelve. In retaliation, the MDM called for a national strike that was supported by three million workers, and on September 15, thirty-five thousand protesters took to the streets in Cape Town. The behavior of the police in Cape Town was exceptional; on the whole, government response was unprecedentedly gentle. The MDM was challenging the authorities over an issue on which the government was already willing to concede. In any case, economic degeneration, military setbacks in Angola in 1987–1988, and a fiscal crisis had succeeded in convincing key National Party leaders that the costs of white racial supremacy were unacceptable.

Boycotts

Boycotts became an important political tactic in black South African resistance only during the

1950s, though they were not new. For example, in 1922 women's *manyanos* (self-help organizations developed around church congregations) organized a remarkably cohesive boycott of rural trading stores in the Herschel district of the Eastern Cape in protest against high commodity prices. In 1944, in Brakpan on the East Rand, parents withdrew nine hundred children from a mission school in protest against the Department of Native Affairs, which had ordered the dismissal of a popular teacher who belonged to the Communist Party. Proposals for electoral boycotts began in 1936 with the introduction of a separate voting roll and indirect parliamentary representation for Africans. Despite their earlier objections to these electoral arrangements, the leaders of a specially formed All African Convention stood for election in the new advisory Native Representative Council and endorsed white "native" parliamentary representatives.

During the 1950s, black political organizations were divided over the merits of electoral boycotts. The ANC was committed to them by its 1949 Program of Action, but in fact, through the decade ANC candidates contested township "Advisory Board" elections while its white allies in the Communist Party and the Congress of Democrats attempted to mobilize colored common-roll voters and African native representative voters to secure seats in parliament. In the Western Cape the Non-European Unity Movement enjoyed a strong following among colored teachers for its advocacy of electoral boycott but made little impact upon a mainly working-class colored electorate, which regularly returned conservative white politicians to parliament.

In a rare instance of political accord, the Trotskyite Unity Movement collaborated with the Communist Party in mounting a train boycott to protest the introduction of railway apartheid in Cape Town in 1948. Three hundred volunteers sat themselves in white compartments on the first day of the new regulations, but shortly afterwards, the Train Apartheid Resistance Committee broke apart amid accusations and counteraccusations of cowardice and adventurism. The Communist Party abandoned nonviolent direct action and successfully opposed the regulations in court, compelling the government to pass new laws in 1950.

The ANC was involved in two kinds of anti-apartheid boycott in the 1950s. In 1955, it tried to counter the introduction of a demeaning syllabus of "Bantu Education" in primary schools by mounting a class boycott. The organization's initial resolve, however, was eroded by the reluctance of many Congress leaders to withdraw their own children from school. In the end, the boycott was launched and sustained in the two areas in which ANC organization was strongest and most proletarian in social ethos, Port Elizabeth and the East Rand. In these places, 12,500 children stayed out of school for up to six months, attending instead special schools run by the Congress's African Education Movement. Eventually, the children returned to official classes, but in the context of the times, this was an impressive effort.

Consumer boycotts, which had hitherto been directed at particular enterprises to bring down prices or support industrial actions, began in 1959 to assume a more politicized dimension with an ANC campaign to "Boycott Nationalist Products." The boycott achieved some improvements in the treatment of workers in vineyards and potato farms, and it also helped to inspire the opening of an international campaign of economic sanctions initiated in London the same year by Christian Action and the Africa Bureau. Adding impetus to the economic boycott movement was a series of bus boycotts; twenty-three of these boycotts were reported in the press between 1948 and 1961. Most of these boycotts were provoked by fare increases, but they often became invested with broader political concerns as ANC activists moved into their leadership committees.

In the 1950s, however, boycotts of any type by Africans could make only a limited impact, except in those services or enterprises in which Africans dominated consumption. Early apartheid governments, for example, generally were indifferent as to whether Africans chose to vote in elections, and in 1959 even the indirect 1936 franchise arrangements were abolished. As far as education was concerned, most parents tended to take the view that even "Bantu" education was better for their children than no education at all, and from 1956 the ANC concentrated its energies in this sphere on trying to win control of the newly elected school boards, which originally it had intended to embargo.

In the 1970s, the stakes were of a different order. While the quality of state education had deteriorated its provision had massively expanded to embrace the majority of urban children. After 1970, rising unemployment meant that a secondary school matriculation certificate no longer supplied a guarantee of genteel employment. If education had lost some of its status for Africans by the 1980s, black votes were to become much more important for the government with the institution of its constitutional and local government reforms. African consumption power, of limited significance in the 1950s, also had become a crucial element in the South African economy. In short, from the mid-1970s on, Africans predominated as consumers and workers, and they had a new power of veto in a policy in which the authorities were attempting to move to less repressive forms of government.

These changes were first signaled in the schoolchildren's protests that flared up in June 1976 in reaction to a recently enforced requirement that certain school subjects be taught in Afrikaans. First in Soweto and then later countrywide, the children backed up their opposition to the Afrikaans rule with a class boycott that lasted six months, cost nearly two thousand lives, and transfigured South African politics. Rescinding the Afrikaans rule nevertheless failed to end conflict in black schools—class boycotts brought out 100,000 children for eight months in 1980 and closed down two-thirds of township schools between July and December 1985 in protest against the declaration of a state of emergency. Through the 1980s, schoolchildren supplied an army of street activists to anti-apartheid resistance organizations, which themselves were often led by the graduates of the 1976 classroom rebellion.

Politicized teenagers were conspicuous in the organization and (the often coercive) enforcement of an extraordinary series of consumer boycotts that began in 1985 in small towns in the Eastern Cape. Here African residents' associations (known as "civics") announced boycotts of shops in city centers with the intention of putting pressure on businessmen to negotiate the removal of police and soldiers from townships, secure the release of detainees, and raise funds for social facilities. Threatened with bankruptcy, chambers of commerce and municipal councils, in the fifteen towns initially affected, opened negotiations with the civics and in many cases succeeded in persuading the authorities to concede to local demands.

Industrial Strikes and Demonstrations

In apartheid's final decade, black power was most dramatically manifest in industry. In brief, efforts to build African industrial organization date from the years immediately following the First World War, but the first stable organizations developed only in the late 1930s after the entry of sizable numbers of Africans into manufacturing industry. Wartime economic growth and policy reforms encouraged the growth of African trade unions, many of them under Communist Party leadership. Much of this organization declined in the postwar recession, but enough survived into the 1950s for the ANC to develop a trade union wing, the South African Congress of Trade Unions (SACTU), which then was effectively destroyed by the imprisonment or banishment of most of its officials in the early 1960s. A new generation of trade unions developed out of a second era of manufacturing growth in the 1960s. By 1976 African trade union membership had climbed to seventy-five thousand. Fifteen years later, 1.5 million African workers belonged to trade unions, many of them united in a federation allied with the ANC.

Most trade union struggles were directed against employers and ostensibly concerned workplace issues rather than political considerations. However, in the case of African labor the employer, particularly in the early history of industrial struggle, was often the government. African strikes were in any case usually illegal, and so workers found themselves in conflict with the state as much as with factory managers. Inevitably, political organizations also were drawn into industrial struggles, most dramatically in two African strikes in the gold mines in 1920 and 1946. Both the ANC and the Communist Party tried to sponsor a mine workers' trade union during the 1940s. Similarly, workers and trade unions lent support to political causes with demonstrative "stay-at-home" general strikes.

South Africa's racial urban geography facilitated the organization of these protests, as most Africans lived in densely built townships, enclosed and isolated from other suburban communities, with relatively few points of outside communication. With quite small groups of picketers outside railway and bus stations, a determined organization could quite easily control access to and departure from a township. Between 1950 and 1961, the ANC, the Communist Party, and the PAC between them summoned seven stay-at-home demonstrations, four of them on a national scale and three of them for several days. They were unevenly successful. Most workers were disinclined to spend more than a day away from work, and the strikes tended to enjoy the most backing in those cities where trade unions were especially strong, in Port Elizabeth and Durban. The tactic was revived during the 1976 schoolchildren's uprising: on three separate occasions the Soweto Students' Representative Council managed to persuade most African workers to withdraw their labor from Johannesburg factories and shops. From 1984 the UDF's revolt against the constitution was frequently punctuated by stay-away strikes, several every year, each observed by hundreds of thousands of workers. Meanwhile, conventional industrial strikes reached record levels in 1987, a year in which half a million workers were involved in 1,148 factory stoppages representing a total of nearly 6 million lost man-days.

Conclusions

How decisive was the contribution made by nonviolent "mass action" to South Africa's transition to nonracial democracy? Before the Soweto uprising the victories that could be claimed by the leaders of antiracist movements were quite modest. Mohandas Gandhi secured some fairly theoretical legal concessions from General Smuts. And African women's resistance in 1913, and later in the 1950s, helped to delay the full implementation of pass laws. Until the modern era, though, it was exceptional for Africans or blacks more generally to muster the kind of strength in their protests to convince the authorities that national interests would be served by concessions or reform.

Only very occasionally did black resistance engage the sympathies of white society. It was more successful in attracting the attention of the outside world, but with the exception of the Indian minority, external support for the political emancipation of black South Africans began to be a significant factor in their struggle only with the inception of the United Nations arms embargo in 1963. Only from 1976 did the moral stature of the anti-apartheid movement begin to be matched by the power and the resources at its disposal. And even then, the forces arrayed against minority rule by civil disobedience movements and trade union organizations in the 1980s need to be balanced against the weight of other factors that helped to predispose President de Klerk's government toward negotiations at

the end of the decade. These would have included the pressures generated by external economic sanctions, the cost of containing guerrilla insurgency, the demoralization of white South African society arising from political violence (which claimed seven thousand lives between 1980 and 1990), the effects on government perceptions of economic recession and demographic increase, and finally, sociological and cultural changes within the white population. It is true, though, that none of these factors can be explained or evaluated in isolation; they were mutually reinforcing. Certainly the progress of negotiated democratic transition was considerably accelerated and facilitated by the existence of the vigorous civil society, which was itself a by-product of assertive popular political movements. And, to the extent to which these movements drew on traditions nearly a century old, all the history recounted in this entry helps to understand South Africa's relatively peaceful passage to democracy in 1994.

Tom Lodge

References

Bagwandeen, Dowlat. *A People on Trial: The Struggle for Land and Housing of the Indian People of Natal, 1940–1946.* Durban: Madiba, 1991.

Beinart, William, and Colin Bundy. *Hidden Struggles in Rural South Africa.* Johannesburg: Ravan, 1987.

Bozzoli, Belinda, ed. *Class, Community and Conflict: South African Perspectives.* Johannesburg: Ravan, 1987.

Carter, David. *Organized Non-violent Rejection of the Law for Political Purposes: The Experience of Blacks in South Africa.* Ph.D. dissertation, University of Durham, South Africa, 1978.

Dadoo, Yusuf Mahomed. *South Africa's Freedom Struggle.* New Delhi: Sterling, 1990.

Driver, C.J. *Patrick Duncan: South African and Pan-African.* London: Heineman, 1980.

Kuper, Leo. *Passive Resistance in South Africa.* London: Jonathan Cape, 1956.

Lewis, Gavin. *Between the Wire and the Wall.* New York: St. Martin's, 1987.

Lodge, Tom. *Black Politics in South Africa since 1945.* London: Longman, 1983.

Lodge, Tom, and Bill Nasson. *All, Here, and Now: Black Politics in South Africa in the 1980s.* New York: Ford Foundation, 1991.

Marx, Anthony. *Lessons of Struggle: South African Internal Opposition*. Cape Town: Oxford University Press, 1960–1990.

Mufson, Steven. *Fighting Years*. Boston: Beacon, 1990.

Orkin, Mark, ed. *Sanctions against Apartheid*. Cape Town: David Phillip, 1989.

Roux, Edward. *Time Longer than Rope*. 2nd ed. Madison: University of Wisconsin, 1964.

Simons, H.J., and R.E. Simons. *Class and Colour in South Africa, 1850–1950*. Harmondsburg: Penguin, 1969.

Swan, Maureen. *Gandhi: The South African Experience*. Johannesburg: Ravan, 1985.

Wells, Julia. *We Have Done with Pleading: The Women's 1913 Anti-pass Campaign*. Johannesburg: Ravan, 1991.

See also AFRICAN NATIONAL CONGRESS OF SOUTH AFRICA; GANDHI, MOHANDAS KARAMCHAND; LUTULI, ALBERT JOHN; MANDELA, NELSON ROLIHLAHIA; SOUTH AFRICA, ANTIAPARTHEID SANCTIONS; SOWETO UPRISING, 1976; TUTU, ARCHBISHOP DESMOND MPILO

Southern Christian Leadership Conference

A pivotal organization of the American civil rights movement, formed in 1957 by African-American ministers in the South and led by Martin Luther King, Jr. The Southern Christian Leadership Conference (SCLC) was crucial to the development and major victories of the American civil rights movement. The SCLC led the protest campaigns directly associated with achieving the 1964 Civil Rights Act and the 1965 Voting Rights Act. It was the organizational vehicle of Martin Luther King, Jr., who became the major charismatic leader of the civil rights movement. It was also the vehicle through which many civil rights leaders worked, including Ella Baker, Wyatt Tee Walker, James Bevel, Andrew Young, Hosea Williams, Ralph Abernathy, Fred Shuttlesworth, Jesse Jackson, and many others. A key element of its success was its mass base rooted in the black church.

By the mid-1950s, the American South had been legally segregated by race for over a half-century. By law, African Americans were required to use separate public facilities such as schools, hotels, churches, playgrounds, and water fountains. When they rode public transportation they had to sit in the rear section of the buses. Additionally, blacks were excluded from the political process, especially given that they were disenfranchised. Finally, the black masses had few economic resources, for they were concentrated at the bottom of the economic order and exploited on a routine basis. Southern blacks were an oppressed people who experienced humiliation daily. Conventional avenues of social change were ineffective for this group although slow progress was being made on the legal front by the National Association for the Advancement of Colored People (NAACP). Nevertheless, it would take some extraordinary measures by southern blacks to change the system of racial oppression.

The origins of the SCLC are to be found in the Montgomery bus boycott of 1955–1956, which set the stage for the emergence of a mass movement among southern blacks. On December 1, 1995, Rosa Parks of Montgomery refused to relinquish her bus seat to a white man. Parks was arrested because her refusal to give the white man her seat violated local segregation ordinances. Mrs. Parks was a member of the local NAACP, and she was active in a black women's group known as the Women's Political Council. Upon learning of Parks's arrest, these two organizations called for a one-day boycott of local buses. The organizers of the boycott were surprised at the degree of cooperation they received from the black community. The vast majority of black Montgomerians refused to ride the buses. As a result, plans were made to extend the boycott indefinitely until the bus company agreed to meet their demands.

The organizers of the boycott understood that a mass movement was needed to accomplish this goal. The black churches, which had mass bases, were recruited through their ministers to support the boycott. The Montgomery Improvement Association (MIA), an umbrella organization composed of other local black organizations, was formed to guide and coordinate the boycott. Martin Luther King, Jr., who at the time was pastor of a local black church, was elected MIA president.

Nonviolent direct action was chosen as the method of the movement. While King was familiar with Gandhi's nonviolent movement in India, the masses of black people were not. At this time, King was not committed to nonviolence as a way of life. But there were activists associated with organizations such as the Fellowship of Reconciliation (FOR) and the Congress of Racial Equality (CORE) who were steeped in knowledge of nonviolent resistance. Glenn Smiley and Bayard Rustin were two such individuals who came to Montgomery and conducted nonviolent workshops for the black masses and for the leadership of the movement. The philosophy of nonviolence was consistent with key tenets of the black religious tradition. This consistency made it less difficult to disseminate the philosophy and method of nonviolence to the black masses.

The Montgomery bus boycott endured over a year. During this period, King proved to be an extraordinary, charismatic leader similar to Gandhi. King's influence stemmed from his connection to the black masses through the churches, his powerful personality, and his organizational position as president of the MIA. The MIA itself effectively combined charisma, organization structure, and a mass following. The movement was victorious because of the effectiveness of its year-long boycott and a Supreme Court ruling that declared segregation on buses to be unconstitutional.

The Montgomery campaign became a model for other southern black communities wishing to overthrow racial segregation. Even before the boycott achieved its goal, it inspired nonviolent movements in other cities such as Tallahassee, Florida, and Birmingham, Alabama. King and other southern leaders realized that these movements needed to be coordinated and new movements needed to be developed to overthrow the regime of racial oppression. Several northern activists including Bayard Rustin, Ella Baker, and Stanley Levison shared the beliefs of the southern leaders. The conclusion reached by the two groups was that a regional organization modeled after the Montgomery Improvement Association was needed to generate and coordinate mass nonviolent movements to overthrow racial segregation.

The Southern Christian Leadership Conference (SCLC) was formed by southern ministers in January 1957, with King as its president. Its goal was to produce mass nonviolent resistance on such a grand scale that it would topple racial segregation and usher in an era of racial integration. Charisma and nonviolent direct action by disciplined masses, combined with organizational structure, were to be the hallmark of the SCLC. Local SCLC affiliates composed of community organizations emerged in numerous southern communities, usually guided by church-based leadership.

Throughout the late 1950s the SCLC worked in local communities, preparing them to engage in nonviolent action to achieve racial desegregation and the franchise. In 1960, it helped the student lunch-counter sit-ins to become a major movement. These sit-ins generated numerous desegregation victories and led to the establishment of the Student Nonviolent Coordinating Committee (SNCC), which SCLC helped to create. The SCLC also assisted the 1961 Freedom Rides begun by the Congress of Racial Equality (CORE), which played a key role in the desegregation of interstate travel.

By the early 1960s, the SCLC decided that major community-wide protest movements were needed to defeat southern white segregationists. These segregationists used heavy repression against the movement. They controlled local governments and the means of violence and were supported by white supremacist organizations such as the Ku Klux Klan and White Citizen Councils. To overcome such powerful repressive forces, the SCLC began planning massive nonviolent protest campaigns that would disrupt local communities and force the federal government to pass national legislation outlawing racial segregation.

In 1963, the SCLC organized such a campaign in Birmingham, Alabama. During that campaign, the SCLC utilized multiple nonviolent tactics including an economic boycott, sit-ins, mass marches, picketing, mass arrests to fill the local jails, defiance of a court injunction prohibiting demonstrations, and news media coverage to generate favorable public opinion. King and the SCLC were able to create total disruption in Birmingham within a month. Thousands of people filled the jails. The economic boycott paralyzed the economic community, and daily mass marches disrupted traffic and dramatized to the nation and to the world the great injustices imposed on African Americans. Birmingham's white power structure responded by unleashing vicious violence on the demonstrators, including many children.

However, the movement had become too large and powerful to be defeated, and local economic elites yielded to the movement's demands. Within a short time additional communities throughout the nation developed Birmingham-style movements to oppose racial segregation, leading, in 1964, to the federal Civil Rights Act. The SCLC and the civil rights movement had achieved a major victory because this act removed the legal foundation of the entire regime of racial segregation. In light of this victory and the famous 1963 March on Washington, King received the Nobel Peace Prize in 1964.

Following the Birmingham campaign, SCLC turned its attention to achieving the franchise for southern blacks. In the spring of 1965, SNCC had organized a major campaign in Selma, Alabama, aimed at gaining the vote for blacks. King and SCLC were called in to assist this campaign. SCLC decided to use this campaign to achieve the national legislation that would give blacks the right to vote. The SCLC and SNCC organized major demonstrations in Selma around the right to vote. They mounted huge public marches and other nonviolent tactics in Selma and surrounding towns. As in Birmingham, Selma's white power structure responded with violence against demonstrators, causing the death of a black protester. To counter the repression, movement leaders decided to organize a mass march from Selma to Montgomery, Alabama, to dramatize the need for the vote.

Thousands of black and white demonstrators came to Selma to participate in the march. By the time the march ended, two white demonstrators from the North had been killed by white segregationists. Nevertheless, the demonstrations had been so large and dramatic and characterized by white violence that they moved the federal government to act. In August 1965, President Johnson signed into law the Voting Rights Act, which finally guaranteed the franchise to southern blacks. SCLC and the movement had achieved another major victory leading to the defeat of the regime of racial segregation.

By the late 1960s, King and other civil rights leaders had begun to realize that economic inequality between the races was a major barrier to black equality. Large numbers of blacks, especially in northern cities, began to question the efficacy of nonviolence and racial integration. They began calling for Black Power and black self-determination. They also questioned the viability of a nonviolent strategy that did not allow for black self-defense against white violence. These trends were reinforced by the urban rebellions of the late 1960s. King and the SCLC were being severely tested by these new developments. Indeed, it was not clear whether SCLC could devise an effective national strategy to solve racial oppression, especially given the defeat King and the SCLC suffered when they attempted to build a victorious movement in Chicago in 1966. Moreover, by the late 1960s, SNCC and CORE had yielded to the developing trends by embracing the goal of Black Power and approving of the right of African Americans to engage in self-defense.

Amid these changes, King and the SCLC remained firmly committed to nonviolence and the goal of racial integration. However, King and the SCLC radicalized their approach. The organization concluded that capitalism itself was largely responsible for racism and poverty more generally. The SCLC, therefore, called for the utilization of mass nonviolent resistance to achieve a redistribution of income and wealth in America. In short, the SCLC had begun to organize an interracial movement to implement a form of socialism in the United States. To this end the SCLC was to lead a Poor People's March on Washington in the fall of 1968 to eradicate wide-scale poverty and achieve social justice. All of this was to be accomplished nonviolently.

By 1968, it was not clear whether King and the SCLC could prevent violence from occurring during its demonstrations. In the spring of 1968, King and the SCLC were summoned to Memphis, Tennessee, to help lead a movement by black sanitation workers. One march King led erupted in violence that led his critics to maintain that King should not be allowed to lead protests in the nation's capital because they too would generate violence. King responded with plans to lead a peaceful march in Memphis to demonstrate that nonviolent resistance was still viable. He never had the chance. King was assassinated in Memphis on April 4, 1968.

King's death was a major loss to the SCLC, for it removed the charismatic center of the organization. But even if King had lived, there is great uncertainty as to whether the SCLC could have eradicated poverty and racial inequality in the United States through the use of nonviolent protest. SCLC under the leadership of Ralph Abernathy conducted the Poor People's Campaign in Washington, D.C., in 1968. The protests were disorganized, and SCLC experienced internecine conflict during the campaign. These protests did not achieve their goal.

SCLC remains active and is likely to be so well into the twenty-first century. However, it is not clear whether the organization will be able to utilize nonviolent direct action in a creative fashion to challenge poverty and racism, which remain deeply entrenched in American society. What is clear is that the SCLC was a major player in the dismantling of legally sanctioned racial segregation in America during the twentieth century. Bayard Rustin was right when he concluded, "Thus when judging the SCLC, one must place above all else its most magnificent accomplishment: the creation of a disciplined mass movement of Southern blacks. . . . There has been nothing in the annals of American social struggle to equal this phenomenon, and there probably never will be again."

Aldon D. Morris

References

Fairclough, Adam. *To Redeem the Soul of America: The Southern Christian Leadership Conference and Martin Luther King, Jr.* Athens: University of Georgia Press, 1987.

Garrow, David J. *Bearing the Cross: Martin Luther King, Jr., and the Southern Christian Leadership Conference.* New York: William Morrow, 1986.

Morris, Aldon D. *The Origins of the Civil Rights Movement: Black Communities Organizing for Change.* New York: Free Press, 1984.

Rustin, Bayard. *Strategies for Freedom.* New York: Columbia University Press, 1976.

See also ALBANY, GEORGIA, 1961–1962; BIRMINGHAM, ALABAMA, 1963; CIVIL RIGHTS MOVEMENT; CONGRESS OF RACIAL EQUALITY; FREEDOM RIDES, 1961; GANDHI, MOHANDAS KARAMCHAND; KING, MARTIN LUTHER, JR.; MARCH ON WASHINGTON, 1963; MONTGOMERY BUS BOYCOTT, 1955–1956; PARKS, ROSA; POOR PEOPLE'S CAMPAIGN, 1968; SELMA-TO-MONTGOMERY MARCH, 1965; STUDENT NONVIOLENT COORDINATING COMMITTEE

Soviet Union, Coup Attempt, 1991

August 1991 coup attempt by Communist hardliners, which failed after three days as a result of nonviolent resistance by Soviet citizens, noncooperation by significant elements of the military, and the ineptitude of the coup leaders themselves. The coup leaders sought to preserve the old order of a strong central government ruled by the Communist Party. But instead, the bungled coup accelerated the country's move toward democracy and decentralization, precipitating the demise of the Communist Party and the breakup of the Soviet Union.

The leaders of the coup, all members of Soviet President Mikhail Gorbachev's cabinet, called themselves the State Committee for the State of Emergency. There were eight of them: Oleg Baklanov, first deputy chairman of the Soviet Defense Council; Vladimir Kryuchkov, head of the KGB; Valentin Pavlov, Soviet prime minister; Boris Pugo, Soviet interior minister; Vasily Starodubtsev, chairman of the Soviet Farmers' Union; Alexander Tizyakov, president of the Association of State Enterprises and Industrial, Construction, Transport, and Communication Facilities of the USSR; Gennady Yanayev, Soviet vice president; and Dmitry Yazov, Soviet minister of defense.

The coup was timed to prevent the August 20 signing of the Treaty on the Union of Sovereign States, which would have weakened the Soviet central government and given the fifteen Soviet republics more power. The coup began on Sunday afternoon, August 18, when Gorbachev, vacationing in the Crimea, was taken captive in his dacha by KGB troops loyal to the conspiracy. The next morning, the Soviet news agency, TASS, reported that Gorbachev was ill and unable to perform his duties and that Soviet Vice President Gennady Yanayev had assumed the role of acting president. The State Committee for the State of Emergency, ensconced within the Kremlin, declared a six-month state of emergency, banned demonstrations, suspended political parties (except for the Communist Party), shut down independent newspapers, and took control of Soviet radio and television. The Emergency Committee sent Soviet troops into the capitals of the three Baltic republics to seize key government buildings and communication centers. Troops and armored vehicles took up positions around the Kremlin to defend the coup leaders. Tanks and armored personnel carriers rolled through the streets of Moscow.

Inexplicably, the coup leaders did not arrest Russian President Boris Yeltsin or other potential enemies of the coup to prevent them from organizing resistance. Nor did they shut down television, telephone, and other communication links with the outside world. CNN and other foreign correspondents continued to report throughout the coup. Telephone lines remained open.

When Yeltsin heard the news, he rushed from his home to the Russian parliament building, known as the "White House," which quickly became the center of resistance to the coup. Early Monday afternoon, Yeltsin climbed on top of a tank outside the White House and appealed to the Russian people to resist the coup. He declared the coup illegal and unconstitutional and called for a general strike. Coal miners in several regions of the Soviet Union responded by walking off the job, but most other industries remained in operation. In some parts of Moscow, people filled the streets in protest, surrounding tanks and other military vehicles, and even climbing on top of them to confront troops. Thousands of Muscovites built makeshift tank barricades around the Russian parliament building and kept vigil through the night. Just before midnight, a battalion of ten tanks that had been sent into Moscow to support the coup defected to Yeltsin's side and took up defensive positions around the White House.

News of the coup and the growing resistance to it spread in a variety of ways. Yeltsin was able to transmit messages via ham radio that were picked up by the BBC, Voice of America, and Radio Liberty and then rebroadcast into the Soviet Union. An independent radio station, Moscow Echo, also continued to broadcast intermittently during the coup. Journalists whose independent newspapers had been shut down used cellular phones, photocopiers, and fax machines to get the news out. Anticoup leaflets went up in Moscow subway stations and were distributed at protest rallies. At *Izvestia,* one of the newspapers left free to publish, printers refused to put out the paper unless Yeltsin's appeal to resist the coup was included. The paper came out nearly a day late with the Emergency Committee's declarations on page one and Yeltsin's call to resistance on page two. Similarly, at TASS, pronouncements of the Emergency Committee were eventually interspersed with reports of the emerging resistance. For example, TASS let the Soviet people know that Aleksei II, patriarch of the Russian Orthodox Church, had come out against the coup.

Western nations reacted to the coup cautiously at first, but eventually came around to the same position. The United States condemned the coup, halted U.S. aid, and demanded that Gorbachev be restored to power. Similarly, the European Community cut off more than $1 billion in aid and also demanded that Gorbachev be returned to office.

Midday on Tuesday, Yeltsin and other speakers addressed an anticoup rally of fifty thousand Muscovites in front of the White House. Fearful that Soviet troops would eventually storm the White House and crush the resistance, further preparations were made for the building's defense. Tens of thousands of people built barricades and formed human chains thirty deep around the White House. Roads leading to the White House were blocked, some with trolley buses as tank barriers. Barges were used to blockade the Moscow River, which runs past the White House. And volunteers from two industrial security firms helped to secure the building. Inside the White House, hundreds of armed volunteers kept watch, ready to defend the building by force if necessary.

Elsewhere in the Soviet Union, the coup also met with resistance. In Leningrad, the city council condemned the coup and Mayor Anatoly Sobchak called for widespread resistance. Workers in some twenty factories went on strike and 200,000 demonstrated against the coup in front of the Winter Palace. Mayor Sobchak also negotiated an agreement with the commander of the Leningrad military district, Col. Gen. Viktor Samsonov, not to bring tanks into the city even if ordered to by the Emergency Committee in Moscow. In Kishinev, capital of the Moldavian republic, 400,000 demonstrated, blocking entrances to the city and surrounding key government and news media centers to stave off military incursion. Leaders of both the Ukraine and Kazakhstan declared their support for Yeltsin and their opposition to the coup. In the Baltic republics, where Soviet troops blockaded harbors and highways, seized government buildings, and took control of broadcast stations and telephone exchanges, people formed human chains and erected makeshift barricades to block streets and hinder Soviet troop movements. In Lithuania, President Vytautis Landsbergis called for nonviolent resistance. And both Estonia and Latvia declared their full independence from the Soviet Union.

By Tuesday evening, the crowd surrounding the White House had swelled to 150,000. Women blocking one of the main roads to the White House held a banner saying: "Don't shoot us. We are your mothers and sisters." The Emergency Committee had announced an 11 P.M. curfew, but Muscovites defied the curfew and troops refused to enforce it. At midnight, three civilians were killed near the Russian parliament building when a crowd clashed with armored vehicles at a barricade on the Moscow ring road. Angry protesters threw Molotov cocktails and rocks at the military vehicles, setting one ablaze. That night, three battalions of KGB troops were to have attacked the White House, but the attack never came.

Internal divisions and indecision within the military and KGB were a major factor in the failure of the coup. Military officers refused to order an attack on the White House or on civilians. Troops in Moscow assured civilians they would not obey orders to shoot. Of the three military divisions sent into Moscow on Monday by the coup leaders, two of them defected to Yeltsin's side. With troops defecting, the coup leaders decided to send an elite KGB division into Moscow, but they never entered the city. Mutinies against the Defense Ministry were reported at the Leningrad Naval Base, at a paratrooper training academy in Ryazan, and in units on the Kamchatka Peninsula and Sakhalin Island. Without the full cooperation of the military and KGB, the Emergency Committee was unable to impose its will by force. To have tried with the security forces divided would have invited civil war.

By Wednesday morning, the Emergency Committee was ready to give up. The Defense Ministry ordered troops to withdraw from Moscow and the Baltic capitals. That afternoon, a three-mile column of tanks and military vehicles could be seen leaving Moscow. At the same time, four of the coup leaders, Baklanov, Kryuchkov, Tizyakov, and Yazov, left Moscow on a plane bound for the Crimea in an attempt to meet with Gorbachev. A second plane with Yeltsin's emissaries on board left Moscow in pursuit. When the Emergency Committee members arrived at Gorbachev's dacha, they were arrested. The Soviet parliament nullified the coup decrees and demanded that Gorbachev be returned to power. On Wednesday evening, Gorbachev announced to the nation that he was back in control. He and his family returned to Moscow after midnight. As for the coup leaders, seven were arrested, and one, Pugo, committed suicide.

The failed coup sounded the death knell for both the Communist Party and the Soviet Union. Yeltsin ordered the party shut down across Russia. The party headquarters in Moscow was sealed off to preserve coup evidence. On Saturday, Gorbachev resigned as general secretary of the Communist Party, ordered all party property to be turned over to the people, and urged that the party be dissolved. The same day, the Ukraine, the second-largest Soviet republic with 52 million people, dealt a crushing blow to the USSR. It declared its independence, the sixth Soviet republic to do so. In the weeks that followed, one by one, the remaining Soviet republics declared independence as well. On December 21, eleven of the former Soviet republics (Georgia and the Baltics did not participate) formed the Commonwealth of Independent States. Gorbachev resigned as president of the USSR on December 25, bringing the country's seventy-four-year history to a close.

Roger S. Powers

References

Billington, James H. *Russia Transformed—Breakthrough to Hope: August 1991.* New York: Free Press, 1992.

Bonnell, Victoria E., Ann Cooper, and Gregory Freidin, eds. *Russia at the Barricades: Eyewitness Accounts of the August 1991 Coup.* Armonk, N.Y.: M.E. Sharpe, 1994.

Gorbachev, Mikhail. *The August Coup: The Truth and the Lessons.* New York: HarperCollins, 1991.

Gwertzman, Bernard, and Michael T. Kaufman, eds. *The Decline and Fall of the Soviet Empire.* New York: Times Books, 1992.

Loory, Stuart H., and Ann Imse. *Seven Days that Shook the World: The Collapse of Soviet Communism.* Atlanta, Ga.: Turner, 1991.

Pozner, Vladimir. *Eyewitness: A Personal Account of the Unraveling of the Soviet Union.* New York: Random House, 1992.

Putsch—The Diary: Three Days that Collapsed the Empire. Oakville, Ontario: Mosaic, 1992.

Remnick, David. *Lenin's Tomb: The Last Days of the Soviet Empire.* New York: Random House, 1993.

See also CIVILIAN-BASED DEFENSE; COUPS D'ÉTAT; MUTINY

Soweto Uprising (South Africa), 1976

Mobilization of students and workers in a black township near Johannesburg against apartheid. The resistance movement began with a student boycott and demonstration, and was followed by more demonstrations, marches, general strikes, and violent direct action. The Soweto uprising became a symbol of anti-apartheid resistance and marked the beginning of a new stage of struggle by black South Africans.

On June 16, 1976, over ten thousand students gathered in Soweto for a march and rally called by the Soweto Students Representative Council to protest a recent decision by education authorities to teach part of the high school curriculum in Afrikaans (the language of the dominant white minority). Police opened fire on the marching children, killing several and wounding many. This incited three days of rioting throughout Soweto, in which rioters burned down administration buildings and liquor stores and clashed with South African police. Mass funeral processions became powerful political demonstrations, and although in early July the government retracted the order to use Afrikaans, the resistance to the educational system, and apartheid in general, intensified.

On August 4, students initiated and tried to enforce a three-day "stay-away" (general strike), but few workers participated. That same day a march by twenty thousand students and workers was effectively aborted by police action. Another three-day strike occurred August 23–25 and was more widely observed. On the first day, approximately 80 percent of Soweto workers (mostly factory employees and servants) stayed home. Another effective three-day strike was held September 13–15.

The resistance in Soweto continued in late 1976, spearheaded mainly by the students and supported by the Black Parents Association. Fifteen hundred children demonstrated in the center of white Johannesburg on September 23, and police attacked with dogs and batons and arrested 880. By mid-October, hundreds of school teachers had resigned in protest of the violent repression. Students tried to organize another strike in early November, but it never materialized. They did, however, help to launch an anti-alcohol campaign and a boycott of Christmas shopping, both of which led to economic losses among white businesses.

Although the student movement was effectively squelched by police repression by late 1977, over a quarter of a million students had participated in class boycotts, and many protests had been staged throughout South Africa. The Soweto uprising inspired a new commitment on the part of blacks throughout South Africa to fight racial oppression.

Brad Bennett

References

Gorodnov, Valentin. *Soweto: Life and Struggles of a South African Township.* Moscow: Progress, 1988.

Marx, Anthony W. *Lessons of Struggle: South African Internal Opposition, 1960–1990.* New York: Oxford University Press, 1992.

See also AFRICAN NATIONAL CONGRESS; SOUTH AFRICA, OPPOSITION TO RACIAL OPPRESSION

Sports Boycott

Method of noncooperation in which athletes, organizations, or states refuse to participate in specific sports events as a political protest. As the institution of sports has gained popularity in the twentieth century, so has the politicization of sports. The sports boycott has increasingly been utilized as a type of international political sanction. While boycotts of sports events have occurred on all organizational levels, the peak of the international sports boycott phenomenon occurred during the early 1980s, when Western nations led by the United States boycotted the 1980 Moscow Summer Olympics and Eastern Bloc nations led by the Soviet Union boycotted the 1984 Los Angeles Summer Olympics.

Unlike most other types of boycotts, sports boycotts are rarely initiated by the participants themselves. More often than not, a national government will refuse to allow its own athletes to compete in an international sports event in the target country. Sometimes these boycotts have indirect targets, as in a boycott of an event to protest the presence of another participant who is colluding with a government not represented. Often a sports boycott has a larger publicity potential than other sanctions because of the huge popularity of sports. The most internationally publicized sports boycotts have been boycotts of the Olympic Games.

There have been numerous examples of sports boycotts in the twentieth century. Between the first and second World Wars, for instance, the USSR boycotted all "bourgeois" olympics, choosing instead to compete in alternative Workers' Olympiads sponsored by the Socialist Workers' Sports International. The Irish Gaelic Athletic Association has led a boycott of Anglophile sports throughout much of this century. And Norwegian athletes and fans boycotted sports activities organized by the Nazi occupation forces from 1940 to 1945.

S

Holland, Spain, and Switzerland boycotted the 1956 Melbourne Olympics to protest the Soviet invasion of Hungary. A call for a boycott of the 1978 World Cup Football (Soccer) championships in Argentina to protest human rights violations went largely unheeded.

One of the largest international sports boycott movements was directed against South Africa, because of its apartheid policy. In 1966, the Supreme Council of African Sport (SCAS) called for a boycott of the 1968 Mexico Olympics because of the International Olympic Committee (IOC) refusal to expel South Africa from the olympic movement. Over thirty member states joined this threat, and South Africa was forced to withdraw from the 1968 Games. Primarily due to this international pressure, they were expelled from the olympic movement in 1970. Two years later, the IOC expelled Rhodesia, the other minority, white-ruled state in Africa, as a result of a threatened African boycott. This time, the Rhodesian athletes were already residing in the Olympic Village.

The international boycott of South African sports teams and events applied to other sports as well. The New Zealand rugby team's tour of South Africa during the repression of the Soweto riots by black Africans in June 1976 provoked many African nations to boycott the 1976 Summer Olympics in Montreal to protest New Zealand's participation. In 1981, the United States Special Committee against Apartheid published the *Register of Sports Contacts with South Africa,* which functioned as a blacklist of athletes who had played in that country. South African cricket and soccer organizers countered the boycott movement in the 1980s by attempting to organize "rebel" tours by players from other countries who were offered lucrative contracts to entice them into breaking the international boycott. One "rebel" soccer tour in 1982 was unsuccessful because of a boycott of the matches by black African spectators. The sanctions against South African sports teams and events continued into the 1990s and the movement created an almost total isolation of South African sports.

There are three large-scale Olympic boycotts of note. The first, organized primarily by the South African Non-Racial Olympic Committee (SANROC), was the boycott of the 1976 Summer Olympics in Montreal by many black African nations discussed above. The second was the 1980 boycott led by President Jimmy Carter of the United States, in which several nations refused to participate in the Olympics in Moscow. The major reasons given for the U.S. boycott were the trying and exiling of famous Soviet dissidents in the late 1970s and the Soviet invasion of Afghanistan in December 1979. Some other nations (like Britain) allowed individual athletes to compete on their own even though the British National Olympic Committee was boycotting. Although the United States initiated several nonviolent sanctions, the boycott was the most publicized and most powerful; the reduced news media coverage was a loss for the USSR.

On May 8, 1984, the USSR announced its withdrawal from the 1984 Summer Olympics in Los Angeles. The reasons given were the presence of an American group, "Ban the Soviets Coalition," and the "politicization" of the Olympic Movement by the United States. Fourteen nations boycotted the event, mostly Eastern Bloc nations. The 1980 and 1984 boycotts were equally effective in gaining international news media attention.

Because of the growth in popularity of sports (billions watch major international sports events on television), the institution has grown in political salience. Sports have become an important arena for interstate political struggle.

Brad Bennett

References

Allison, Lincoln, ed. *The Politics of Sport.* Manchester, UK: Manchester University Press, 1986.

Hoberman, John. *The Olympic Crisis: Sports, Politics and the Moral Order.* New Rochelle, N.Y.: Aristide D. Caratzas, 1986.

Vinokur, Martin Barry. *More than a Game: Sports and Politics.* New York: Greenwood, 1988.

See also BOYCOTTS; SANCTIONS; SOUTH AFRICA, ANTIAPARTHEID SANCTIONS

Stanton, Elizabeth Cady (1815–1902)

Feminist philosopher, social reformer, and leader of the U.S. women's rights movement, born in Johnstown, New York, on November 12, 1815, and died in New York City on October 26, 1902.

After studying at home, Elizabeth Cady attended the Johnstown Academy and then entered Emma Willard's Troy Female Seminary. She was a keen observer of her father's law practice, where she learned how women were deprived of their rights to property, child custody, and access to professions.

Defying her father, she married the prominent abolitionist Henry Stanton in May 1840, insisting that the word *obey* be dropped from the wedding ceremony. Twelve days later, the Stantons set sail for the World's Anti-Slavery Convention in London. Women were excluded from the proceedings and relegated to the back of the hall, where Stanton met feminist activist Lucretia Mott. It was a propitious meeting and a turning point in Stanton's life. Eight years later, after successfully lobbying for the New York Married Women's Property Act, Stanton joined Mott in convening the Woman's Rights Convention in Seneca Falls, New York. There, Stanton presented the "Declaration of Sentiments" modeled on the Declaration of Independence. It boldly asserted: "The history of mankind is a history of repeated injuries and usurpations on the part of man toward woman, having in direct object the establishment of an absolute tyranny over her." Her leadership at the convention placed Stanton in the vanguard of the women's rights movement.

In March 1851 she met Susan B. Anthony, who was visiting in Seneca Falls. The fifty-year friendship that resulted from that street-corner encounter is legendary in feminist history. As Stanton later said of her working relationship with Anthony: "I forged the thunderbolts, she fired them." Stanton, frequently housebound with pregnancies, housekeeping, and the care of seven children, provided the inspiration and philosophy for Anthony, who became the tactician and organizer. Stanton refused to be limited to the question of suffrage, but addressed a range of issues including divorce, prostitution, economic independence, and dress reform. She denounced church and state, claiming that both sanctioned the absolute authority of husbands over wives.

In 1861 Stanton joined Lucretia Mott, Frederick Douglass, and other abolitionists on an antislavery tour. During the Civil War, Stanton and Anthony organized the Women's Loyal National League, collecting more than 300,000 signatures on petitions demanding immediate emancipation of the slaves.

After the war, two amendments to the Constitution were proposed in Congress. Designed to ensure the new freedmen the vote, the Fourteenth Amendment would confer citizenship on males born or naturalized in the United States and the Fifteenth Amendment would give black men the right to vote, but not women of any race. The debate on these amendments split the reform community. Some activists, including Stanton, Anthony, and Sojourner Truth, urged disenfranchised men and women, regardless of race, to stand united in advocating universal suffrage. Stanton observed: "Put the word male in the constitution and it will take fifty years to get it out." Other reformers supported passage of these amendments and claimed it was the "Negro's hour," to which Stanton asked: "Do you believe the African race is composed entirely of males?" Her arguments eventually degenerated into racist slurs.

In 1866, Stanton ran for Congress, campaigning on a platform of free speech, free press, free men, free trade, and universal suffrage; she received twenty-four votes. The following year, Stanton and Anthony traveled to Kansas to promote women's suffrage. On the trip, they met a man who offered to fund a newspaper devoted to women's rights. For the next several years, Stanton wrote for *Revolution,* which had as its motto: "Men, their rights and nothing more; women, their rights and nothing less."

In 1869, Stanton helped found the National Woman Suffrage Association (NWSA) and served as its president for twenty-one years. When it merged with another organization to become the National American Woman Suffrage Association in 1890, she served as president for two years. Stanton frequently toured the country promoting women's rights. In 1880, with Anthony, she attempted to vote in Tenafly, New Jersey, arguing that, not only could she read and write, but she was three times the legal voting age.

With Matilda Joslyn Gage and Susan Anthony, Stanton coauthored several works including the "Woman's Declaration of Rights" presented at the 1876 Centennial Exposition in Philadelphia and the multivolume *History of Woman Suffrage.* In 1892 she wrote an essay, "The Solitude of Self," that is widely considered her masterpiece. She also wrote *The Woman's Bible,* which challenged religious teachings about women's inferiority, and an autobiography, *Eighty Years and More,* published in 1898.

Pam McAllister

References
DuBois, Ellen Carol, ed. *Elizabeth Cady Stanton/Susan B. Anthony: Correspon-*

dence, Writings, Speeches. Foreword by Gerda Lerner. New York: Schocken, 1981.

Griffith, Elisabeth. *In Her Own Right: The Life of Elizabeth Cady Stanton.* New York: Oxford University Press, 1984.

Nies, Judith. *Seven Women: Portraits from the American Radical Tradition.* New York: Viking, 1977.

Stanton, Elizabeth Cady. *Eighty Years and More: Reminiscences 1815–1897* [1898]. Introduction by Gail Parker. New York: Schocken, 1971.

See also ABOLITIONIST MOVEMENT; AN-THONY, SUSAN BROWNELL; DOUGLASS, FREDERICK; MOTT, LUCRETIA COFFIN; NA-TIONAL WOMAN SUFFRAGE ASSOCIATION; TRUTH, SOJOURNER; WOMEN AND NONVIO-LENT ACTION IN THE UNITED STATES SINCE 1950; WOMEN'S SUFFRAGE

Strategy

The activity, process, or plan by which parties to a conflict deploy their available resources and actions in order to obtain their objectives as efficiently as possible and at the expense of opponents who are engaged in a similar process. The logic of strategy informs the use of all types of direct action, and it is fundamentally the same for violent, nonviolent, and mixed conflicts.

As a level of analysis or activity, strategy is subordinate to policy, which refers, in this context, to the broadest decisions taken about how to conduct a given struggle: whether to fight, what to fight for, what costs one is willing to endure and to inflict, and what would constitute an acceptable settlement. Ideally, strategy is disciplined by such decisions, and goes on to maximize a group's performance in attaining its goals through an exchange of sanctions with opponents within the parameters defined by policy. Strategy, in its turn, supersedes tactics. Whereas strategy governs choices across the entire arena of conflict (regardless of whether that is a battlefield or a society), tactics refers to those decisions and actions that serve to optimize limited and particular encounters with opponents. Thus, it may be a strategic choice to use mass demonstrations and strikes to force a violent regime to recognize minimum human rights standards, but it is a tactical choice to conduct certain demonstrations in a silent and

dignified manner, as opposed to a boisterous or provocative one.

In this hierarchy of concepts, strategy does not appear as an alternative to political ethics. Rather, any given strategy will necessarily be informed if not controlled by the politics, ethics, and culture of the group waging it. Furthermore, the conduct of strategy is shaped and constrained by the social, political, and economic context in which it appears. While the successful conduct of strategy may in turn affect the context itself and create important new opportunities for the protagonists, it must begin within a set of assumptions about what is possible and likely, and it must ask questions such as the following: Are the objectives we are considering fighting for compelling to a wide public, such that social power can be amassed in support of them? Are they well defined and winnable by some reasonable criteria? Have we enough material resources and organizational strength to persist in a long and costly struggle? Whom can we motivate to come to our aid? Do we have sufficient knowledge of different nonviolent methods such that we can vary the way we deliver sanctions to the opponents in the context of a campaign?

Based on the answers to such questions, nonviolent strategists must then design nonviolent actions that can plausibly undermine the opponents' control of the situation, progressively deny them the support they need to pursue their own objectives, and ultimately cause them to relinquish those objectives and accede to the nonviolent challenge. This all supposes sufficient knowledge and a correct assessment of the opposing forces, their goals and methods, and their relative commitment to prevail in the conflict. Nonviolent strategists should be prepared to maintain the coherence, unity, and discipline of their nonviolent forces. They should continually be asking whether their efforts are appropriately offensive, defensive, or both; whether their goals are nearer or farther away as a result of particular lines of action; and whether their choices are helping them to stay in the fight and eventually win it, or imperiling those prospects.

The history of nonviolent action is characterized by a high degree of improvisation. Leading practitioners of nonviolent struggle have often not been aware of the relevant history to which their struggles might usefully be compared. Many have operated according to the notion that it was their group's rectitude or courage that would ultimately be decisive, as against the quality of their strategic choices, and so have not exhaustively asked the kinds of questions posed above. While there have certainly been many "un-strategic" violent conflicts, it is fair to say, on balance, that in nonviolent conflict strategy has tended to be less explicit, systematic, and comprehensive than in comparable violent struggles. Whereas the strategic use of violent action (such as war) is potentially informed by centuries of comparative military studies and many theoretical models, such a body of thought on nonviolent conflict is only now beginning to emerge.

Strategy is nonetheless present in nonviolent conflicts. When groups employ the methods of nonviolent action, their objectives are often implied if not expressed. They may have ideas about how acting in a certain way will bring about change in their opponents' behavior. At times they may act in more or less deliberate imitation of protagonists in other conflicts in which nonviolent actions have seemed to serve a useful purpose. Or they may adopt nonviolent action as a "last resort," or in the apparent absence of any viable military alternative. In such cases the actors often have quite clear ideas about how their choice to avoid provocative violent acts will protect their interests in the long run. But the burden on strategists does not end there. Whenever strategy is less than fully realized it does not assess, continuously and comprehensively as suggested above, all the factors that are likely to bear on the outcome of a conflict, and adjust the group's behavior to them in real time to achieve the best effect. To the extent that strategic assessment is present at all, so long as it remains unarticulated and inchoate it is unlikely to produce good guidance and optimal decisions.

In the past few decades attempts have been made to render the conduct of nonviolent struggle more strategic. Sometimes unfairly criticized as too utilitarian, these efforts have typically acknowledged the political and moral dimensions of conflict, while seeking to demonstrate that the strategic dimension is one on which the performance, and therefore the policy relevance, of nonviolent action might be dramatically improved. Such efforts have looked to contemporary or past cases of nonviolent struggle to identify "lessons" or "principles" of this technique of conflict, and many have appropriated terms and concepts from military

strategic discourse as a means of problematizing the issues and tasks facing nonviolent strategists. It is argued that since conflict is an adversarial process with an indeterminate outcome, it is therefore one in which the adversaries' skills and performance can have a positive or negative effect on the status of their goals. Strategic analysis is therefore a useful mode in which to consider nonviolent action.

An early effort in this vein was Sir Stephen King-Hall's *Defence in the Nuclear Age,* which argued that nonviolent resistance experiences of the 1940s should be built upon for future national defense purposes. He reasoned that if nonviolent action were to enjoy the forethought, strategic direction, and legitimacy that the state could provide, its net effectiveness would surely increase. *The Strategy of Civilian Defence,* edited by Adam Roberts and published in 1967, brought together much of the best thinking to date on the subject, including essays by the British military historian Sir Basil Liddell Hart and American strategist Thomas Schelling. Gene Sharp's work has been pivotal in establishing a conceptual schema with which to identify and understand the myriad factors that may affect the conduct of strategy. Building on Sharp, Ackerman and Kruegler have used a series of case studies to induce a set of principles for strategic nonviolent conflict. Boserup and Mack's *War without Weapons* made an important contribution by showing how classical military ideas like "offense," "defense," and "the objective," derived from the great theorists of war such as Carl Von Clausewitz, could be applied to nonviolent struggle.

A fruitful argument persists regarding the degree to which the outcome of predominantly nonviolent struggles is likely to be determined by superior strategy as distinct from the conditions in and around which the fight is waged. Surely a violent protagonist who enjoys massively superior resources, many allies, a favorable geopolitical situation, and reliable military forces, can prevail at will regardless of the strategic acumen of a nonviolent challenger. On the other hand, we can see many cases in which nonviolent protagonists start from an objectively inferior position and yet make choices that enhance their position and ultimately lead them to victory.

Although with hindsight it now makes a great deal of sense, no one in the late 1970s would have expected that a trade union movement called Solidarity would form itself in Poland, win official legitimacy in the summer of 1980, contend with the Polish government over a variety of issues using nonviolent action, be forced underground for a time, and then rehabilitate itself and accede to governmental responsibility within a decade. No doubt that set of events was shaped by the conditions surrounding it, not least of which was the gradual decline of communism throughout east-central Europe. But specific strategic choices made by Polish opposition leaders undeniably played their part too. The choice to struggle for autonomous unions rather than outright capitulation by the Polish Communist Party enabled Solidarity to function and to win its initial series of victories, which in turn enabled further building of the movement. The choice to escalate conflict with new demands in the autumn of 1981 contributed, if not to the government's decision to invoke martial law in December of that year, at least to the rationalization and effectiveness of that repressive campaign, from which it took Solidarity some years to recover.

To the extent, then, that the quality of strategic choices matters in relation to the outcomes of conflicts in which nonviolent methods are used, both practitioners and scholars of these methods can concern themselves productively with the logic of strategic assessment and particular strategies as they have unfolded in the cases that are now available for such scrutiny.

Christopher Kruegler

References

Ackerman, Peter, and Christopher Kruegler. *Strategic Nonviolent Conflict: The Dynamics of People Power in the Twentieth Century.* Westport, Conn.: Praeger, 1994.

Boserup, Anders, and Andrew Mack. *War without Weapons.* London: Frances Pinter, 1974.

King-Hall, Sir Stephen. *Defence in the Nuclear Age.* London: Victor Gollancz, 1958.

Roberts, Adam, ed. *The Strategy of Civilian Defence.* London: Faber and Faber, 1967; reprinted as *Civilian Resistance as a National Defence.* New York: Penguin, 1969.

Sharp, Gene. *The Politics of Nonviolent Action.* Boston: Porter Sargent, 1973.

See also CIVILIAN-BASED DEFENSE; KING-HALL, BARON STEPHEN; LIDDELL HART, CAPTAIN SIR BASIL HENRY; MECHANISMS OF DIRECT ACTION; METHODS OF NONVIOLENT ACTION; SHARP, GENE; SOLIDARITY (POLAND)

Strikes

Work stoppages expressing the economic or social grievances of laborers. Considered "spontaneous" until the rise of recognized labor organizations in modern times, strikes usually reflect an informal coordination of workplace cultures. Avoiding violence in favor of passive resistance and economic sabotage in the vast majority of cases, they may be considered the most common nonviolent social protest across the ages.

Strikes can be traced to antiquity and to the appearance of active discontent among captive populations of laborers (such as slaves) or handicraftsmen. Labor brotherhoods, often secret and based upon religious, ethnic, or fraternal ties, flourished as early as the Roman Empire and resisted the deterioration of working conditions by suspending members' participation at work sites. During the economic revival of the Middle Ages, organized handicraftsmen often successfully negotiated rules of trade and behavior, enforced by informal sanctions, by the withdrawal of services, and under extreme conditions, economic sabotage. Unskilled laborers had little organization and yet struck repeatedly, despite laws passed against such behavior. Severe deterioration in working conditions, reductions in wages, and increases in working hours turned master craftsmen against the emerging economic system and prompted them to seize entire workshops and towns, with the resulting violence committed mostly at the behest of wealthy merchants determined to recapture control.

With the rise of modern industrialism, secret labor organizations or "combinations" sought to guide or coordinate job-related actions. By the 1830s, the first citywide walkouts (or city "general strikes") had been organized in Philadelphia and elsewhere, and proposals for a national general strike, or "Grand National Holiday," could be heard in England and on the European continent. In 1868, the International Workingmen's Association (later known as the "First International") endorsed the concept of a general strike against any proposed declaration of war. Anarchists rather than their rivals, the Marxists, proved the most eager advocates of strikes intended to preempt military violence and to overthrow capitalism entirely. The syndicalist movement, heavily influenced by anarchists, promulgated a vision of men with folded arms initiating a new social system.

In the years just before World War I, this vision seemed within realization. Across large parts of Europe and the United States, unskilled workers, previously little represented by unions, rose up in mass strikes that generally were condemned by craft union leaders. In the United States, the Industrial Workers of the World led such strikes in Lawrence, Massachusetts, Paterson, New Jersey, and elsewhere, meanwhile articulating a philosophy of solidarity across race, ethnic, and gender lines.

This vision failed with the outbreak of war. Most European labor, socialist, and syndicalist organizations enthusiastically endorsed their own nations' participation in the First World War, as did the American Federation of Labor. Still, many strikes (especially in Czarist Russia) directed at the misery of wartime conditions blunted war efforts and foreshadowed social transformation.

The withdrawal of labor had long had a decisive impact upon the history of race relations in the United States. Using a slightly different interpretation of the concept of "strikes," W.E.B. DuBois claimed in *Black Reconstruction,* with some justice, that the slaves' flight from plantations had fatally weakened the Confederacy and changed the course of the Civil War. Unlike previous runaways, this had been wholesale, and unlike previous slave uprisings, it had been largely nonviolent. Similarly, in a multitude of subsequent cases, anticolonial forces conducted strikes that weakened or toppled repressive regimes, often with little violence except for that unleashed by authorities. The "general strike" sweeping the Caribbean during 1937–1938, moving apparently spontaneously from island to island, plantation to city district, provoked little violent rioting. It rendered colonialism unworkable first by demonstrating the intractability of the colonial labor force and second by providing a popular basis for the labor-oriented parties that later guided the island-nations toward independence. From Africa to Asia and the Indian subcontinent, phases of the anticolonial struggle took similar forms, influenced directly in some places, indirectly in others, by Gandhian nonviolent principles.

By the 1940s and 1950s, strikes against labor bureaucracies of the West and against the authoritarian states of the East pointed to new possibilities for social change. In the United States, predominantly African-American workers committed noteworthy "wildcat strikes" against automakers and the United Auto Workers. Hungary's 1956 General Strike succeeded, for a time, in establishing a shadow government of workers' councils. And Poland's Solidarity trade union led waves of strikes that ultimately brought down the Communist government and left Solidarity holding the reins of state power.

Certainly, strikes by privileged strata of workers have also been directed at excluding women, racial minorities, or categories of immigrants from the labor market. They have also been used by the U.S. Central Intelligence Agency and its labor clients to overthrow elected governments, especially in Central and South America. But strikes can best be seen as the last resort of those lacking other means of protest. By being able to limit profit-making activities in various ways, strikers enforce regulatory constraints in mining, agriculture, manufacture, and commerce around the world, posing restraints upon economic expansion at the cost of human life and the natural habitat. With the general failure of anticapitalist political protest movements, strikes will no doubt continue to perform this function.

Paul Buhle

References

Brecher, Jeremy. *STRIKE!* San Francisco: Rolling Stone, 1972.

Buhle, Mari Jo, Paul Buhle, and Dan Georgakas, eds. *Encyclopedia of the American Left.* New York: Garland, 1990.

Chaplin, Ralph. *The General Strike.* Chicago: Industrial Workers of the World, 1982.

DuBois, W.E.B. *Black Reconstruction* [1935]. Introduction by David Levering Lewis. New York: Athaneum, 1992.

See also CIVIC STRIKE; LIGHTNING STRIKE; REVERSE STRIKE; SAN FRANCISCO GENERAL STRIKE, 1934; SEATTLE GENERAL STRIKE, 1919

Student Nonviolent Coordinating Committee

African-American civil rights organization that stimulated mass protests and organizing efforts in many southern black communities during the 1960s.

After a student-led desegregation sit-in on February 1, 1960, in Greensboro, North Carolina, a wave of similar protests swept through the urban South and culminated in the formation of the Student Nonviolent Coordinating Committee (SNCC). More than 120 student protest leaders attended SNCC's founding conference, held in April 1960 at Shaw University in Raleigh, North Carolina. Initially intended as a coordinating body for largely autonomous local protest movements, SNCC gradually became a gathering point for full-time protesters and organizers who expanded the civil rights movement into areas of intense segregationist resistance, especially in Mississippi and Alabama.

The dominant influence within SNCC during its initial months came from a cadre of Nashville students who had attended workshops on Gandhian methods led by James Lawson. Expelled from Vanderbilt divinity school for his protest activities, Lawson was one of a number of African-American Gandhian proponents who had traveled to India and returned as advocates of nonviolent methods. At SNCC's founding conference in Raleigh, he secured adoption of a statement of purpose that expressed the religious underpinnings of student-led direct action protests:

> We affirm the philosophical or religious ideal of nonviolence as the foundation of our purpose, the presupposition of our faith, and the manner of our action. Nonviolence as it grows from Judaic-Christian traditions seeks a social order of justice permeated by love. Integration of human endeavor represents the crucial first step towards such a society.
>
> Through nonviolence, courage displaces fear; love transforms hate. Acceptance dissipates prejudice; hope ends despair. Peace dominates war; faith reconciles doubt. Mutual regard cancels enmity. Justice for all overthrows injustice. The redemptive community supersedes systems of gross social immorality. Love is the central motif of nonviolence. Love is the force by which God binds man to Himself and man to man. Such love goes to the extreme; it remains loving and forgiving even in the midst of hostility. It matches the capacity of evil to inflict suffering with an even more enduring capacity to absorb evil, all the while persisting in love. By appealing

to conscience and standing on the moral nature of human existence, nonviolence nurtures the atmosphere in which reconciliation and justice become actual possibilities.

By the fall of 1961, a cadre of sit-in leaders left college to become full-time SNCC field secretaries who sought not only desegregation but also voting rights and economic gains. SNCC soon became a staff-run group involved in initiating community organizing projects rather than being simply a coordinating body. Its earlier Christian–Gandhian orientation gradually gave way to a secular radicalism influenced by Marxian and anticolonial ideas. The group began to focus its energies on community organizing efforts in rural Mississippi and Alabama rather than on desegregation protests in the urbanized South. Although civil disobedience remained an important aspect of SNCC's activities, staff members were increasingly likely to accept nonviolence for tactical instead of philosophical reasons. Nevertheless, even as SNCC shifted its orientation from protest to community organizing, Gandhian and pacifist influences remained evident in SNCC workers' continuing reliance on civil disobedience, their far-reaching social change agenda, and their emphasis on democratic decision making within the civil rights struggle. Robert Moses, the director of SNCC's operations in Mississippi and a proponent of decentralized, grassroots leadership, was himself influenced by his contacts with Bayard Rustin and other pacifists and had attended summer camps in Japan and Europe sponsored by the American Friends Service Committee.

After 1965, SNCC abandoned many of the values that prevailed during its early years, becoming by the end of the decade a centralized, black nationalist organization competing for ideological influence in black communities. Nonviolent protest tactics gave way to consciousness-raising efforts symbolized by the "Black Power" slogan. Weakened by internal ideological conflicts and external repression, SNCC declined as a political force during the late 1960s and by the early 1970s had dissolved. Moreover, during its years of growth, SNCC's distinctive style of political activism exerted considerable influence over the student, antiwar, and women's liberation movements. Among the many individuals affiliated with SNCC who later played major roles in other movement organizations are Free Speech Movement leader Mario Savio, feminists Mary King and Casey Hayden, Pan-Africanist Kwame Touré, and Black Panther leader Kathleen Cleaver.

Clayborne Carson

References

Carson, Clayborne. *In Struggle: SNCC and the Black Awakening of the 1960s.* Cambridge: Harvard University Press, 1981.

See also CIVIL RIGHTS MOVEMENT; FREEDOM RIDES, 1961; FREEDOM SUMMER PROJECT, MISSISSIPPI, 1964

Sudan Rebellion, 1985

Mass demonstrations and general strike precipitating the overthrow of Sudanese President Ja'far Numieri in April 1985. Starting as a small popular protest against food price increases, the rebellion quickly grew into a broad opposition movement.

Since coming to power in a military takeover in 1969, Numieri had sanctioned the brutal repression of opposition leaders and had negated a previous commitment to unifying historically polarized North and South Sudan. Famine conditions, deep economic problems, and widespread political unrest contributed to solidifying opposition against Numieri. The Sudan People's Liberation Army (SPLA), led by John Garnag de Mabior, initiated armed struggle against the Sudanese government in 1983. In late March 1985, students demonstrated and set fire to fuel tanks in the capital of Khartoum to protest commodity price increases. Riots spread during the next week with over two thousand people arrested and eighteen dead in clashes with police.

The struggle then took a more nonviolent turn. Professional organizations initiated a general strike and civil disobedience campaign to protest police brutality and economic problems. On April 3, thousands demonstrated in downtown Khartoum and marched on the presidential palace. The judiciary declared a "civil rebellion." The Free Army Officers' Organization, composed of progressive young officers, declared its support for the popular revolt. The uprising included members of all sectors of the population, including housewives, farmers, and street children. The general strike, reportedly supported by 80 percent of the population, effectively paralyzed much of Khartoum, and many riot policemen refused to confront the protesters.

On April 6, Minister of Defense General Siwar al-Dhahab initiated a military coup, removing Numieri from power. The Sudanese population celebrated, but continued to demonstrate and strike until the new military government dissolved the national security forces and arrested Numieri supporters. Although Sudan continued to experience economic problems, political unrest, and continued armed resistance from the SPLA, an unpopular dictator was ousted in 1985, partly as a result of demonstrations and strikes.

Brad Bennett

References

Bennett, Brad. "Arab-Muslim Cases of Nonviolent Struggle." In *Arab Nonviolent Political Struggle in the Middle East,* edited by Ralph E. Crow, Philip Grant, and Saad E. Ibrahim. Boulder, Colo. and London: Lynne Rienner, 1990.

Garang, John. *John Garang Speaks.* Edited and introduced by Mansour Khalid. London: KPI, 1987.

See also STRIKES

Suicide, Protest

Killing oneself to express one's total protest of, or noncooperation with, an intolerable situation or oppressive regime. This suicide must be intentionally public and the protest message must be decidedly clear, in order for the suicide to be considered direct action. The question of whether this method can be considered nonviolent action is open to debate. While one is committing violence against oneself, no physical violence is directed at others. Rather, the person committing suicide intends to change public opinion or the "heart" of the opponent through an altruistic appeal. Often the death acts to rally a resistance movement, as people mourn and honor the person. The most famous examples of protest suicide have taken the form of "self-immolation," in which people set themselves on fire in a public place.

Self-immolation was used by anti–Vietnam War protesters in both the United States and Vietnam during the 1960s. For instance, Pham Thi Mai, a Vietnamese teacher, immolated herself in May 1967 and left letters pleading for a U.S. troop withdrawal. A Czech student, Jan

Palach, burned himself in January 1969 to protest the Soviet occupation of Czechoslovakia.

References

Sharp, Gene. *The Politics of Nonviolent Action.* Boston: Porter Sargent, 1973.

Zaroulis, Nancy, and Gerald Sullivan. *Who Spoke Up? American Protest against the War in Vietnam, 1963–1975.* New York: Holt, Rinehart and Winston, 1984.

See also CZECHOSLOVAKIA, 1968 RESISTANCE MOVEMENT; VIETNAM WAR OPPOSITION

T

Teach-in

Public meeting on a current topic at which viewpoints from speakers and audience are aired. This method is a form of nonviolent protest and is also a vehicle for education (of self and others) and intellectual stimulation. Debate and dialogue are encouraged and discussion from the floor constitutes an important aspect of this method. A method related to the teach-in is the "protest meeting." A teach-in differs from a public protest meeting in that various and sometimes opposing views are represented and speakers are often "experts" or high-level specialists that can provide information not readily available. Teach-ins may also contain many more speakers and last much longer than ordinary meetings.

Teach-ins were common in antiwar movements in the United States in the late 1960s and early 1970s. The first anti–Vietnam War teach-in occurred on March 24, 1965, at the University of Michigan and was followed by a national teach-in that was broadcast to 122 college campuses during the weekend of May 15–16.

References

Sharp, Gene. *The Politics of Nonviolent Action.* Boston: Porter Sargent, 1973.

Zaroulis, Nancy, and Gerald Sullivan. *Who Spoke Up? American Protest against the War in Vietnam, 1963–1975.* New York: Holt, Rinehart and Winston, 1984.

See also VIETNAM WAR OPPOSITION

Thailand, Democracy Movement, 1992

A largely nonviolent uprising in Bangkok consisting primarily of pro-democracy demonstrations. The uprising emerged after events following a February 1991 coup d'état by the National Peace Keeping Council (NPKC). Upset by what they perceived as false promises by the NPKC, the Thai people engaged in hunger strikes, mass demonstrations, and later riots to demand the removal of Prime Minister General Suchinda Kraprayoon and institute democratic elections. Due to both internal and external pressures, Suchinda resigned and a national election was held in September 1992. Civilian Chuan Leekpai became head of a coalition government composed of all of the parties that opposed the Suchinda government during the uprising.

The February 1991 coup was executed by a group of military officers, most of whom were graduates of the Chulchomklao Military Academy Class 5. They formed the NPKC and justified their overthrow with charges that the previous Choonhawan government was corrupt. Initially, there was little opposition to the coup, as the NPKC promised to strengthen democracy by revising the constitution and reinstating general elections. In March 1992, the Samakkhi Tham Party, the political wing of the NPKC, appointed one of the NPKC's most powerful leaders, General Suchinda Kraprayoon, as prime minister. This act was seen by many as a breach of trust and the perpetuation of NPKC's power.

The campaign for democracy began on April 7, 1992, when a politician named Chalard Vorachat staged a hunger strike. People began gathering around the place he chose to stage his protest and a general campaign emerged to demand a more democratically elected prime minister. During this phase of the movement, strategy was developed primarily by a broad-based organization of political opposition parties and academic groups called the Campaign for Democracy and the mass demonstration was the primary tactic utilized. These demonstrations took place at Sanam Luang, a large space next to Thammasat University, and often took on a festive nature. The composition of this campaign was different from that of similar 1970s campaigns, in that the professional class participated. They introduced fax machines, e-mail, and cellular phones to the campaign, helping to blend traditional symbols of Buddhist culture with modern communications technology.

On May 4, Major General Chamlong Srimuang, former military commander and Bangkok governor, announced that he would "fast unto death" or until Suchinda was removed from office. This act began a second phase of opposition, in which a strategic split emerged over moving the demonstrations to the streets, and Chamlong emerged as the most powerful opposition figure. Chamlong ended his fast to lead the demonstrations in the streets, and dispersed one crowd in return for a promise from the speaker of the house to amend the constitution to allow for an elected prime minister. Senior party members did not honor this promise, and on May 15, hundreds of thousands of Thais massed in protest. During this period, the Peace Information Center distributed postcards depicting "nonviolent practices" and ten thousand copies of a small pamphlet entitled "19 Secrets of Nonviolence." On May 18, suppression of demonstrators and the burning of government buildings marked a period of violent clashes in which fifty-two deaths were reported. Suchinda later resigned and a national election was held on September 13, 1992.

Chaiwat Satha-Anand

Henry David Thoreau (Alfred Hosmer photograph of 1861 Dunshee Ambrotype). Photograph courtesy of the Concord Museum, Concord, MA.

Thoreau, Henry David (1817–1862)

American essayist and naturalist, known for his essay "Civil Disobedience." Thoreau was born in Concord, Massachusetts, the son of John and Cynthia Dunbar Thoreau. Prepared in the public schools of Concord and Concord Academy, he graduated from Harvard University in 1837. After teaching for a few weeks in the Concord grammar school, he resigned rather than use corporal punishment on his pupils as his school committee demanded. Later, he established a highly successful private school that anticipated many of the educational methods of the twentieth century and did not use corporal punishment. He gave up that school in 1841 when his brother John, who had joined him as a teacher, was forced to retire because of ill health. Meanwhile, Henry had become acquainted with his Concord neighbor Ralph Waldo Emerson, a leader of the literary group known as the New England Transcendentalists. Emerson encouraged Thoreau to embark upon a literary career, introducing him to writers, editors, and publishers and even giving him room in his house for several years.

In 1845, deciding he needed more time for writing, Thoreau built a ten- by -fifteen-foot cabin on a piece of Emerson's land on the shore of Walden Pond in Concord. There he devoted himself to writing, as a memorial tribute to his brother John, an account of a rowboat excursion the two had taken together in 1839. By simplifying his life and earning what little money he needed through manual labor, he found he needed to work only about six weeks a year, while spending the rest of his time writing and observing nature. In a little over two years he not only completed *A Week on the Concord and Merrimack Rivers* (1849), but also wrote a large part of *Walden,* an account of his life at the pond. *Walden,* which was published in 1854, became his masterpiece.

Thoreau's family and many of his Transcendentalist friends had long been active in the antislavery movement, seeing slavery as intolerable in a democracy. When his neighbor Bronson Alcott refused to pay his poll tax in a protest against slavery and was arrested (although released almost immediately when someone paid his tax for him), Thoreau decided to follow Alcott's example. (They chose the poll tax, even though it was a state tax rather than a federal tax, because it was the only nonlocal tax that they had to pay directly.) Three years later, in the summer of 1846, the village tax-collector and jailer, Sam Staples, tried to collect it, and even then offered to pay the tax for Thoreau. When Thoreau replied that he was not paying it as a matter of principle, Staples led him off to jail. That night someone, most probably Thoreau's maiden aunt Maria Thoreau, who was embarrassed to find her nephew in jail, paid his tax for him. The next morning when Staples went to the jail to release him, he found Thoreau "mad as the devil" and refusing to leave because he, himself, had not paid the taxes. He left only when Staples threatened to throw him out bodily. (Staples's arrest of Thoreau had actually been itself illegal, for confiscation of property sufficient to pay the tax was what the law called for, not imprisonment.) When Emerson asked Thoreau why he had gone to jail, Thoreau aptly asked why Emerson, himself, had not. So many Concordians were puzzled by Thoreau's action that he finally wrote up an explanation and delivered it as a lecture before the local Concord Lyceum on January 26, 1848, under the title "The Relation of the Individual to the State." A year later Elizabeth Peabody, the Transcendentalist publisher, asked permission to print the lecture in her one-volume *Aesthetic Papers,* where it appeared under the title "Resistance to Civil Government" and was then almost completely ignored. By the time it was included in a posthumous volume of his uncollected papers, Thoreau had changed its title to "Civil Disobedience," apparently the first use of that now-famous phrase. That title contains a typically Thoreauvian pun; it can imply both disobedience of civil authority and also a civil, that is, a courteous, form of disobedience.

The central points of Thoreau's essay are these:

1. There is a "higher law" than the law of one's land, which is the law of the conscience.

2. On those rare occasions when this "higher law" and the law of the land come in conflict, it is one's duty to obey that "higher law" and deliberately violate the law of the land.

3. If one violates the law of the land, he must be willing to take the full consequences of that action, even to the point of going to jail.

4. However, going to jail is not necessarily the negative act it might seem, for it will serve to draw the attention of men of good will to the evil law and thus help to bring about its repeal. Or, if enough men go to jail, their acts will serve to clog the machinery of the state and thus make the evil law unenforceable.

The idea of civil disobedience was not original with Thoreau, though the phrase itself was. Antigone was committing an act of civil disobedience by sprinkling dust on the body of her brother Polyneices. Many centuries ago, Boethius expounded the philosophy in Western culture and Mencius in Eastern writings. Thoreau was familiar with all of them. But the important fact is that it was Thoreau's work that popularized the idea, though it was nearly half a century after the essay appeared in print before anyone paid serious attention to it.

Thoreau continued his antislavery activities for the remainder of his short life, speaking out strongly on the lecture platform against the Fugitive Slave Act and in support of John Brown's attempt at Harpers Ferry to incite a revolt among the slaves. Although some have claimed he endorsed Brown's use of violence, it was Brown's willingness to sacrifice his own life for a principle that Thoreau praised. He also took part in the Underground Railroad, aiding escaped slaves who were sheltered at his parents' house in Concord on their way to freedom in Canada.

Thoreau devoted the final years of his life chiefly to botanical studies, which were left largely incomplete upon his death from tuberculosis in 1862 at the age of forty-four. His friends and editors, however, were able to rescue from his magazine writings and his manuscripts five books, which were published posthumously. *A Yankee in Canada, with Anti-slavery and Reform Papers* (1866), which contains *Civil Dis-*

obedience, was among these. In 1906, the *Journal* that he had kept for twenty-five years was published in fourteen volumes. Thoreau's reputation grew slowly but steadily over the years, but it was not until at least the middle of the twentieth century that he attained his present position as one of America's major writers.

As to his theories of civil disobedience, it was Henry Salt, his British biographer, who near the end of the nineteenth century began to speak out about them. It was he who called them to the attention of Mahatma Gandhi, who utilized them first in South Africa to defeat laws segregating the immigrant Indians and then in his own native India to win the country's freedom from the British Empire. Another early proponent was the Russian novelist Leo Tolstoy, who urged the American people to adopt Thoreau's ideas rather than those of its generals and capitalists. During World War II, many of the anti-Nazi resisters, particularly in Denmark, adapted Thoreau's essay as a manual of arms and used it very effectively.

Thoreau's native country was slow to see its value. Emma Goldman and a few of her friends used civil disobedience against the conscription act of World War I, as did a few pacifists during World War II. But it was Martin Luther King, Jr., who gave it its greatest prominence when he began applying it against segregation laws in the South in the 1950s and was awarded the Nobel Prize for his activities. *Civil Disobedience* became a popular document among those who opposed the Vietnam War in the 1970s. Altogether it has had more impact around the world than any other American political document, with the possible exceptions of the Declaration of Independence and the Constitution. And Henry David Thoreau, who was ignored in his own lifetime, has become a world figure.

Walter Harding

References

Thoreau, Henry David. "Civil Disobedience" in *The Writings of Thoreau*, vol. 4. Boston: Houghton Mifflin, 1906.

———. *The Variorum Civil Disobedience.* Edited by Walter Harding. New York: Twayne, 1967.

Harding, Walter. *The Days of Henry Thoreau.* Princeton: Princeton University Press, 1993.

Woodson, Thomas. "The Title and Text of Thoreau's 'Civil Disobedience.'" *Bulletin of Research in the Humanities* (1977): 103–112.

See also ABOLITIONIST MOVEMENT; CIVIL DISOBEDIENCE

Tiananmen Square Democracy Movement, Beijing, 1989

Reemergence of the student movement of 1986, which advocated political reform, democracy, freedom, and human rights. The 1989 prodemocracy movement lasted seven weeks, from mid-April until the beginning of June, involved more than a million people, and captured the attention of the world. It began following the death of Hu Yaobang, climaxed with a large-scale hunger strike and occupation of Tiananmen Square, and ended in the tragic June 4 massacre.

On April 15, 1989, the deposed general secretary of the Communist Party and reformist leader Hu Yaobang died of a heart attack. The next day, crowds came to Tiananmen Square to publicly mourn his death. University students saw this time of public mourning as an opportunity to criticize the government of Deng Xiaoping and call for political and economic reform and an end to government corruption. The situation was similar to that of the April Fifth Movement of 1976 in which hundreds of thousands publicly mourned the death of Zhou Enlai and at the same time criticized Mao and the Gang of Four. The students organized a march to Tiananmen Square on April 17 in which thousands participated. It was clear that their mourning for Hu was also a condemnation of Deng. People broke many small bottles (the symbol of Deng) into pieces to express their hatred toward him. They insisted on Hu's rehabilitation.

The next day larger crowds gathered in the square. Some students drew up a list of demands, which included reevaluating Hu's achievements, ending government corruption, reducing inflation, and increasing press freedom. They marched to the Zhongnanhai (the party leadership compound), where they chanted for Premier Li Peng to receive their petition. Receiving no response, they returned the next night only to be beaten and arrested by police in the early morning hours of April 20.

The official funeral ceremony was set for April 22 in the Great Hall of the People. Concerned about further student demonstrations, the government forbade people from entering Tiananmen Square. However, the night before, thousands of students began flooding into the square, before the government had cordoned it off. They remained there through the funeral ceremony. Three representatives of the students knelt before the Great Hall of the People holding a petition over their heads, but not a single high official received them.

After the funeral of Hu Yaobang, Beijing students, including Wu'er Kaixi, Wang Dan, and Chai Ling, formed a new independent student organization, the Provisional Students' Federation of Capital Universities, and called for Li Peng to resign and for students to boycott classes.

The government, determined to suppress the students, published an editorial in the *People's Daily* on April 26, condemning the student protests and implying that there would be a military crackdown if they continued. Rather than discouraging the students, however, this provoked them, increasing their anger and determination to keep on demonstrating. The very next day, tens of thousands of students marched from their respective university campuses to converge on Tiananmen Square, breaking through several military police blockades along the way. News of this march spread across China and was broadcast around the world. Another major protest march occurred in Beijing on May 4, the anniversary of the 1919 student movement.

Over the next week, the protests subsided. The government had made no concessions, and students were turning their attention to upcoming final exams and graduation. The movement was losing momentum. Student leaders saw a new opportunity to capture international news media attention if they could only keep the movement going until the May 15 visit of Soviet President Mikhail Gorbachev. To galvanize the student movement, on May 12 the Beijing Autonomous Student Federation, led by Wu'er Kaixi, Wang Dan, and Chai Ling, declared that if the government did not enter into a serious dialogue, students would begin a hunger strike. The next day the hunger strike began, with four hundred students participating. The principal demands of the strike were political reform, freedom, democracy, and human rights. The students also demanded the rehabilitation of Hu Yaobang and a positive evaluation of the student movement itself.

Students demonstrated in other cities in support of the students in Beijing and sent delegates to the capital. Hundreds more students joined in the hunger strike, which became in effect an occupation of Tiananmen Square. People of different walks of life, including intellectuals and workers, organized independent associations and supported the students. Among other things, these groups organized several large-scale demonstrations, the largest being on May 17, when more than a million people converged on Tiananmen Square. The student hunger strikers who lay on the square under the hot sun, some of them refusing even water, quickly fell ill. By May 18, thirty-five hundred fasters had collapsed and been taken to hospitals. Many of them, after being revived, returned to the square to continue the hunger strike.

On May 18, Li Peng finally agreed to a nationally televised meeting with Wang Dan, Wu'er Kaixi, and other student leaders. They presented three simplified demands: renounce the April 26 *People's Daily* editorial, recognize the Beijing Autonomous Student Federation, and enter into negotiations with the students. The meeting ended with Wu'er openly and directly criticizing Li for the government's insincerity.

The next day, before dawn, Communist Party General Secretary Zhao Ziyang broke with party discipline and went to Tiananmen Square in a last-ditch effort to persuade the students to end their hunger strike. It was his last public appearance before being placed under house arrest. Later that day, the Beijing Autonomous Workers' Federation called for a general strike. This worried government officials, who feared that a broader movement was forming among students, intellectuals, workers, and Zhao supporters. The government announced that martial law would be imposed in Beijing on May 20. Hours before, the students had decided to end the hunger strike, but the government's announcement derailed their plans to leave the square.

That night, as trucks carrying troops of the People's Liberation Army attempted to move into Beijing, citizens erected barricades in the streets to prevent them from reaching Tiananmen Square. By dawn on May 20, up to 2 million Beijing citizens were in the streets blocking the troops' movements. They offered the soldiers food, tea, and cigarettes, appealed to them not to obey their orders, and lowered their morale.

At this point, the student leadership was divided. Wu'er Kaixi and Wang Dan felt that the students should declare victory and evacuate the square. Chai Ling, on the other hand, felt that the occupation of the square should continue at all costs. The students decided to remain in the square.

As the days wore on and the government took no action, morale among the students occupying the square plummeted and they gradually began to leave. On May 27, Chai Ling was finally persuaded that the students should leave the square and continue the movement by other means. The leadership decided to hold a final rally on May 30 and asked students from the Central Academy of Fine Arts to construct a statue in the square that would symbolize the movement. But students in the square who had come from outside of Beijing rejected the student leaders' plan to retreat, and Chai Ling was pressured to reconsider. They wanted to continue the occupation until June 20, the opening of the National People's Congress.

On May 30, arts students erected a thirty-seven-foot-high statue of the Goddess of Democracy in the square, which boosted the morale of the students and gave new life to the movement. On June 2, four prominent middle-aged intellectuals—Hou Dejian, a pop singer; Liu Xiaobo, a literary critic; Zhou Duo, an economist; and Gao Xin, a former editor—began their own fast in the square.

Finally, on the night of June 3–4, fresh troops and armored personnel carriers began to advance on Tiananmen Square from the outskirts of Beijing. As before, some 2 million Beijing residents filled the streets to block the advancing troops. But this time, the troops did not stop. Armored personnel carriers ran over people in their way and troops opened fire on the crowds. No one knows how many people were killed, but the general estimate is two thousand.

By three in the morning, the troops had reached the square and were preparing for their final assault. Only about four to five thousand students were still in the square, gathered around the Monument to the Martyrs of the People. Two of the older fasters, Hou Dejian and Zhou Duo, were able to negotiate permission from Colonel Ji Xingguo for a peaceful withdrawal of the students. Tired, frightened, and confused, the students were reluctant to leave. But finally, at 5 A.M., with tanks and armored personnel carriers moving across the square and closing in on them fast, the students beat a hasty retreat.

In the end, it was the relative strength and brutality of the government, rather than mistakes by the students, that led to the tragedy of Tiananmen Square. Still, some useful lessons can be drawn from the student movement. First, the movement was not well organized and its leadership was inexperienced. There were several parallel student organizations, and they were not well coordinated with the organizations of intellectuals, workers, and other strata of society to form a strong opposition to the government. Student slogans supposedly represented the demands of the entire nation, but they lacked concrete references to the interests of the workers and peasants, who make up the vast majority of the population. Second, the radicalization of the movement over time pushed it beyond the limits of what the government was willing to tolerate. The students' initial demands for reform (which the government could have addressed but didn't) evolved into demands for revolutionary change (which the government would never consider). Third, the students overestimated the strength of their movement by its scale and the support gained from Beijing residents, and they underestimated the cruelty of Deng. Indeed, his delay in suppressing the movement gave people the false impression that the government was timid and hesitant to use force.

The democracy movement of 1989 was the largest in the history of China. It was significant in that the Chinese people began to discard their traditional roundabout way of protest and called directly for freedom, democracy, and human rights and an end to the dictatorship of the Chinese Communist Party. And although Deng and his party were able to finally suppress the students, they did so at the cost of their own legitimacy. When the government finally did use force, it did so on international television and shocked the world with its brutality.

Li Fang

References

Han Minzhu and Hua Sheng, eds. *Cries for Democracy: Writings and Speeches from the 1989 Chinese Democracy Movement.* Princeton: Princeton University Press, 1990.

Li Lu. *Moving the Mountain.* London: Macmillan, 1990.

Oksenberg, Michel, Lawrence R. Sullivan, and Marc Lambert, eds. *Beijing Spring, 1989: Confrontation and Conflict. The*

Basic Documents. Armonk, N.Y. and London: M.E. Sharpe, 1990.

Schell, Orville. *Mandate of Heaven*. New York: Simon and Schuster, 1994.

Shen Tong. *Almost a Revolution*. Boston: Houghton Mifflin, 1990.

See also CHINA; DEMOCRACY WALL MOVEMENT

Tibetan Resistance, 1950–Present

Popular movement, mostly nonviolent, by Tibetans to Chinese occupation. In October 1950, the People's Liberation Army of China invaded Tibet and annexed the country. During the next forty-four years the Chinese government has attempted to integrate the political, economic, and cultural life of Tibet into the People's Republic of China. The consequences of this policy have been a systematic assault upon Tibetan culture, including the destruction of approximately 90 percent of the Buddhist monasteries that existed before 1950; the population transfer of 6 million Chinese into Tibet in order to make Tibetans a minority in their own country; and the death of between 150,000 and 1 million Tibetans due to disappearances, famine, executions, and detentions.

Faced with suppression of their culture and civil liberties, Tibetans have articulated myriad forms of resistance against the Chinese occupation, including an episodic, localized armed struggle between 1951 and 1959. Subsequently, resistance has taken a predominantly nonviolent character, including demonstrations, appeals for international assistance, and the submission of petitions to the Chinese Army requesting that they leave Tibet. However, in 1969 Tibetans engaged in violent attacks upon local Communist officials. This rebellion was suppressed. Nonviolent resistance also has been conducted among the Tibetan diaspora, particularly in India, where the Tibetan government-in-exile is located. Since he fled Tibet in 1959, the Dalai Lama has pursued a policy of soliciting international suport for Tibetan self-determination. In 1959, 1961, and 1965, the United Nations General Assembly passed nonbinding resolutions concerning human rights in Tibet, which the Chinese government ignored.

A wave of resistance occurred in late 1987, following the publication of the Dalai Lama's Peace Plan proposal for Tibet, which was supported by the U.S. government. Resistance was organized primarily by monks and nuns. These individuals were already organized in (religious) groups, thereby facilitating the coordination of collective action, and they had no families against whom the Chinese authorities could impose reprisals. The resistance took the form of several peaceful demonstrations in and around the Tibetan capital of Lhasa. On September 27, 1987, monks staged a peaceful demonstration at Jokhang Temple carrying forbidden Tibetan flags and demanding independence. They were arrested and charged with fomenting counterrevolution. On October 1, thousands of Tibetans demonstrated for independence in Lhasa, whereupon troops opened fire killing a seven-year-old girl and wounding over one hundred Tibetans. On October 6, the Chinese authorities arrested one hundred monks who were marching toward Lhasa in a demonstration. In response to the resistance, the Chinese authorities sealed off the country to foreign visitors. In October 1988, Tibetans staged demonstrations to protest the execution of two Tibetan nationals and the continuation of Chinese occupation. In one incident, over two thousand people stoned and set fire to a police station in Lhasa. In response to the demonstrations for independence, the Chinese authorities have ordered troops to fire bullets and tear gas into the crowds. Nevertheless, between 1987 and 1993 more than 178 peaceful independence demonstrations took place in Tibet.

Alongside these openly declared demands for independence, Tibetans have also articulated myriad cultural expressions of resistance to Chinese occupation. Wall posters demanding Tibetan independence have been pasted up under cover of darkness in Lhasa city. Scraps of paper asking for international support have been surreptitiously passed to tourists visiting Tibet. Traditional hand-carved woodblocks (traditionally used to depict Tibetan scriptures), have been produced by monks demanding independence. These woodblocks have then been used to run off leaflets, pamphlets, and manifestoes for distribution both inside and outside of Tibet. Among the lay population, Tibetans working on cover designs for Chinese publications have secretly located various symbols of Tibetan nationalism and culture (such as the sun rays of the Tibetan national flag) within the designs.

Other symbols of resistance are the black-and-white Rangzen (freedom/independence) bracelets that are worn by Tibetans as a protest against Chinese occupation. These bracelets are patterned after the slings used by Tibetan nomads to protect their herds from wolves. The slings symbolize the triumph of good over evil. The bracelets were originally made by Tibetan prisoners as a form of silent protest. They now are made by women who have recently escaped into exile. Songs and poems have also been composed articulating resistance to the Chinese. These are written by monks and nuns in prison and then sung at festivals. They have also been smuggled out of Tibet via the underground resistance movement in Lhasa and by refugees. These songs and poems speak of prison conditions and repression under the Chinese occupation, but also celebrate the Tibetan religion (the Dalai Lama) and articulate the desire for independence. Because the poems are written in the language of traditional Tibetan literature, the political messages contained within them have been able to bypass the Chinese censors, who do not understand this form of the Tibetan language.

Other forms of smuggling have served as nonviolent sanctions. For example, pregnant Tibetan women are smuggled across the border into India so their babies can be born and educated in exile. Also miniature versions of the U.N. Declaration of Human Rights, translated into Tibetan, have been smuggled into Tibet to be distributed among the Tibetan population. Tibetans also have created a number of hoax religious festivals (such as the "Tsampa" festival called to celebrate the Dalai Lama's receipt of the Nobel Peace Prize) in order to stage demonstrations. Finally, under conditions of attempted cultural ethnocide, the practices of everyday life—wearing traditional dress, using the Tibetan language, using religious artifacts such as prayer flags, and participating in religious rituals—have all become cultural expressions of resistance for Tibetans attempting to maintain their cultural identity.

Brad Bennett
Paul Routledge

References
Grunfeld, A.T. *The Making of Modern Tibet.* London: Zed, 1987.
Kelly, Petra K., Gert Bastian, and Pat Aiello, eds. *The Anguish of Tibet.* Berkeley, Calif.: Parallax, 1991.

See also BSTAN-DZIN-RGYA-MTSHO, DALAI LAMA XIV

Tolstoy, Leo Nikolaevich (1828–1910)
Russian writer and thinker and creator of the religious-ethical theory of nonresistance to evil, born August 28, 1828, and died November 7, 1910.

By birth, Tolstoy belonged to nobility. He inherited the title of count and a large ancestral estate, Yasnaya Polyana (now a state reservation-museum) located fourteen kilometers from the town of Tula. Tolstoy lived on the estate for most of his life. He was a very gifted person: his strong physical build was combined with a great memory, artistic genius, and a philosophical-analytical talent. He was well educated at home and brought up in the Russian Orthodox Church. According to his own words, however, Tolstoy came of age as a complete nihilist—a person who did not believe in anything.

Tolstoy attended Kazan University to study Oriental languages, and then transferred to law. He left the university as a second-year student. Between 1851 and 1855 he served as an officer in the Crimea and Caucasus and took part in military actions. After the war he returned to Yasnaya Polyana and opened a school for peasant children, at which he taught, and published a pedagogical journal from 1858 to 1863. For one year he worked as a *mirovoi posrednik,* or peace mediator, whose duties involved resolving arguments arising during the implementation of the 1861 peasant reforms. Twice he took long trips around Europe. As a landowner, Tolstoy also was engaged in property management issues.

However, being a writer, then the most prestigious occupation in Russia, became the essence of Tolstoy's life. His first autobiographical novel, *Childhood* (1852), and stories about the defense of Sevastopol (1855) made him famous in his own country. *War and Peace* (1863–1869) and *Anna Karenina* (1873–1877) brought him world renown. In 1862, he married Sofia Andreyevna Bers. In addition to being his lifelong mate, she was his friend, assistant, biographer, editor, and the mother of his thirteen children.

In the mid-1870s, Tolstoy experienced a deep spiritual crisis that led him to the conclusion that his previous moral principles were false. He even became suicidal. He found salvation in the doctrine of Jesus Christ, which he thought had been distorted by the church. While systematically criticizing dogmatic theology, Tolstoy came to the conclusion that Jesus Christ was not God but a great social reformer, and that the essence of his teaching was a commandment of nonresistance to evil. In 1909, Tolstoy was excommunicated from the church for these unorthodox views. Tolstoy devoted the second half of his life to the practice, substantiation, and preaching of the ethical-social theory of Jesus Christ. His later books reflected these ideas. The most important ones can be divided into four periods: a confessional period—*Confession* (1879–1881), *What I Believe* (1883); a theoretical period—*What Is Religion, and What Is the Essence of It?* (1884), *The Kingdom of God Is Within You* (1890–1893), *A Law of Violence and a Law of Love* (1908); a journalistic period—*Do Not Kill* (1900), *I Can Not Be Silent* (1908); and a literary period—*The Death of Ivan Ilyich* (1886), *The Kreutzer Sonata* (1887–1889), *Resurrection* (1889–1899), and *Father Sergius* (1898).

The very sudden turn in his life does not have a simple explanation. His spiritual searches continued for several years, the final turning point occurring in 1878, when Tolstoy turned fifty years old. His crisis was expressed in bewilderment and panic in the face of inescapable death, or, as he called it, the "stops of life." He became obsessed with questions about the meaning of life.

According to Tolstoy's point of view, the meaning of life is not about birth and death. Rather, Tolstoy considered the concepts of God, freedom, and kindness as central to the meaning of life. These notions direct finite human life toward its infinite origin. Tolstoy believed that Jesus Christ gives humanity the most precise understanding of the meaning of life as the ideal of moving toward the eternal. The whole doctrine of Jesus Christ, to Tolstoy, is metaphysics and an ethic of love. Side by side with the eternal ideal, Jesus in his direct debate with the laws of Moses, formulates five specific commandments, which are reflected in the Gospel of Matthew 5:21–48: do not get angry; do not leave your wife; do not swear; do not resist evil; do not consider people of different nations your enemies. These commandments Tolstoy considered to be guideposts along the infinite road to perfection. He considered the fourth commandment, "do not resist evil," the most important one, because it imposes an absolute ban on violence.

According to Tolstoy's understanding, violence is identical to evil and is the exact opposite of love. To love means to willingly do what another person wants. To use violence means to force someone to do something against his will. The commandment of nonresistance is a negative formulation of the law of love.

Nonresistance transfers human activity into the sphere of internal moral self-improvement. Every violent act, no matter how complicated its reasons, has a final stage: someone has to pull the trigger or push the button. The most reliable way to eradicate violence is to start with this final stage—that is, with the individual's refusal to participate in violence. If there is no executioner there will be no execution.

Tolstoy also analyzed the following arguments of ordinary people's consciousness against nonresistance: that nonresistance doctrine is wonderful in theory but it would be very hard to implement, that one person cannot oppose the whole world, that nonresistance entails great suffering. He attempted to reveal the logical contradictions in these arguments and their factual groundlessness. The doctrine of Jesus Christ is not only moral but also wise, he argued; it teaches us not to do stupid things.

Tolstoy's thought on nonresistance was influenced by the writings of American writers Henry David Thoreau, William Lloyd Garrison, and Adin Ballou. His writings, in turn, influenced others, including Mohandas K. Gandhi and Martin Luther King, Jr. "Tolstoy's *The Kingdom of God Is Within You* overwhelmed me," Gandhi wrote in his autobiography. "It left an abiding impression on me. Before the independent thinking, profound morality, and the truthfulness of this book, all the books given me by Mr. Coates [a Quaker friend] seemed to pale into insignificance."

Abdusalam Gusseinov

References

Tolstoy, Leo N. *The Complete Works*. Vols. 1–90. State Publishing House. "Khudozhestvennaia literatura," 1928–1958.

———. *Writings on Civil Disobedience and Nonviolence*. Philadelphia: New Society, 1987.

See also GANDHI, MOHANDAS KARAMCHAND; KING, MARTIN LUTHER, JR.; NONVIOLENCE, PRINCIPLED; PACIFISM

Training for Nonviolent Action

An educational process that prepares people for participation in strikes, civil disobedience, sit-ins, nonviolent occupations, and many other methods of nonviolent action. Training readies participants to employ such tactics to pursue social change goals, to provide nonviolent third-party intervention, and to engage in social defense strategies.

Training teaches people practical skills for engaging in conflict nonviolently. Nonviolent action involves not only an intellectual understanding of the subject, but also physical participation. Inevitably, each person who takes part becomes emotionally engaged as well. Therefore, training for nonviolent action usually entails methods of both cognitive learning (such as lectures, talks, and books) and experiential learning (such as role-plays, discussions, exercises, and games) and provides an opportunity to at least identify fears and other strong feelings that people may have about engaging in nonviolent action. Trainers help groups build a sense of community and mutual support. They provide opportunities for participants to express feelings and develop ways to manage them in the midst of confusion and potential violence.

A Brief History of Training for Nonviolent Action

Until this century, nonviolent action was spontaneous, at least in terms of its nonviolent aspects. Although labor strikes in the nineteenth century and other actions throughout history sometimes involved careful planning and preparation, such planning did not address the nature and dynamics of nonviolent power. Specific preparation of individuals and groups to engage in deliberate nonviolent actions began in this century. The Gandhian movement for independence in India used training sessions to prepare people to face almost certain violence from British forces. These training sessions consisted mainly of inspirational talks by the movement's leadership, including Gandhi himself.

In the United States, the civil rights movement of the 1950s and 1960s developed sophisticated training methods, including extensive use of role-plays to understand the likely actions of opponents and to develop ways to protect people as much as possible. The training movement continued and expanded during the anti-Vietnam War movement, the movements against nuclear power and nuclear weapons, and the women's movement. In recent years, training has been a regular part of the more action-oriented parts of the environmental movement and played a major role in the movements against U.S. intervention in Central America and against apartheid in South Africa.

Training for nonviolent action is an international phenomenon. Throughout the world nonviolence trainers have adapted training methods to suit their own cultural and political contexts and the powers they face. Training in a variety of modes and styles is offered in Australia, India, Thailand, Sri Lanka, Taiwan, Japan, Chile, Brazil, South Africa, Russia, Canada, the United States, and throughout most of Western Europe.

Why Training?

While history demonstrates that spontaneous mass nonviolent action can be effective, experience also shows that extended nonviolent campaigns require more sophisticated strategies and the ability to sustain activities over time in the face of highly organized and resourceful opposition. In these situations, those who engage in nonviolent action must be more intentional about preparing themselves.

Practitioners of nonviolent action must develop a nonviolent discipline and learn skills for dealing with violent situations. The effectiveness of nonviolent action can be damaged or destroyed if participants fail to maintain nonviolent discipline. Training programs provide an opportunity to communicate a nonviolent discipline and to develop methods for maintaining that discipline, even when confronted with the threat or actuality of violence. At the same time, participants need specific skills for defusing incidents of actual or potential violence and for protecting themselves and others. Workshops not only communicate the basics of a nonviolent discipline, but also provide a "laboratory" in which participants can test a range of options for their own behavior when provoked by others. Through role-playing and other exercises, people discover how certain actions and attitudes tend to escalate violence and how others tend to deescalate violence.

Training also prepares participants to face violence. Some people join a nonviolent action campaign in the mistaken belief that, because the group maintains a nonviolent discipline, no one will get hurt. Although the use of nonviolent means often reduces violence, when groups challenge power structures or threaten systems of privilege, those who stand to lose from change are likely to respond with brute force, especially if they control the means of violence, such as police forces or military units. In training sessions, participants identify how opponents are likely to respond to their nonviolent actions. They then explore how they will feel in the face of those responses: the fear, rage, and physical discomfort or pain that may occur. The training group works together to figure out how to manage such feelings and how to deal with the physical threats as well.

The Pinochet dictatorship in Chile, for example, depended on fear among the population to maintain its control. During the 1980s, a group committed to nonviolent struggle encouraged people to face their fears directly in a three-step process. People took part in small group training sessions in private homes, followed by small, hit-and-run nonviolent actions, and then thorough debriefing sessions. By teaching people to control their fear, trainers helped them to take courageous actions that contributed to the fall of the dictatorship.

Practitioners of nonviolent action must also build unity among themselves. The power of nonviolent action is proportional to the group morale of the participants. Especially when engaged in protracted struggle or when facing violent reactions, groups need a sense of community and support. Trainers design workshops to assist groups to get to know each other better, to develop stronger bonds, and to integrate all members into the group.

In 1964, the Student Nonviolent Coordinating Committee (SNCC) recruited college students from all across the United States to register voters and organize freedom schools in the "Mississippi Summer" campaign. Each student volunteer took part in a two-week-long training workshop in Ohio, each session including four to five hundred students. Community-building was a major element of the training. Midway through the second workshop, the news broke that two of the participants in the first workshop had been found murdered in Mississippi. Despite the understandable fear among the students, nearly all of them stayed with the community, completed the training, and went to Mississippi.

Practitioners of nonviolent action must understand the dynamics of nonviolent struggle and develop strategies for waging conflict. Many social movements falter because leaders and participants proceed without a clear sense of how they might achieve their goals employing nonviolent methods. They fail to develop a sophisticated analysis of the power dynamics at play in the situation—including the goals and strengths of each party involved—and how concerted nonviolent action might influence the course of events. Rather, they move from tactic to tactic without the context of a larger strategy for change. Training workshops are one setting in which participants can cultivate a deeper understanding about how nonviolent struggle works and develop broader strategies.

In 1989, the United Mine Workers of America decided to launch a nonviolent civil disobedience campaign in the course of its dispute with the Pittston Coal Company. The union organized a training workshop for fifty key "lieutenants" in the struggle. While role-playing, the staffers acted on the widely held belief that direct action is a contest with police to hold "turf," such as the road where coal trucks enter the mine. Through repeated role-plays and careful debriefing, the staff learned that nonviolent methods operate through dynamics that are more political than material, that power is complex and cannot be reduced to who physically holds what at a particular moment. The group changed their strategy and the coal miners won their campaign against heavy odds and set a new standard for labor action in the United States.

Different Levels, Formats, Time Frames, and Purposes of Training

Training for nonviolent action has been designed to work at different levels. Trainers work with individuals to help them deepen their understanding of the dynamics of nonviolent action and to confront their own fears. Training workshops help subgroups or affinity groups to prepare to give each other support during a particular action and to act in cooperation with other similar groups. Organizations engage in training to address issues of decision making, roles and responsibilities, and medium-term strategy. Trainers also work with entire movements to refine their understandings of nonviolent action and to develop more comprehensive longer-term strategies.

Training has been offered in many formats, including programs of several months' duration, intensive weekends, or a few quick hours in preparation for a specific action. It has also been provided to people who are interested in nonviolent action but have no immediate plans to use it, and to people who face imminent danger from confrontation with opponents.

Trainers have provided workshops for nonviolent action in several contexts and for different purposes: training for social change, training for nonviolent third-party intervention, and training for social defense.

Training for Social Change

Training for social change has taken several forms: training for a specific action or series of events (lasting one or two days up to a week), training to plan and strategize for a campaign (lasting several months to several years), and longer-term training to develop strategy for a movement. By far the most common training deals with a single event and the tactics to be employed in it; nonviolence trainers have a great deal of experience with this level of training. Although campaign-building workshops are less common, many trainers have extensive experience providing this kind of planning and medium-term strategizing. Training for long-term strategy is a somewhat underdeveloped mode, but is of increasing importance.

A typical training workshop for a specific nonviolent action includes a mix of some or all of the following:

- Teaching basic theory and dynamics of nonviolent action
- Gaining commitment to a group nonviolent discipline
- Organizing people for action: formation of subgroups (often called "affinity groups"), assignment of roles and responsibilities, arrangement of support systems
- Describing the scenario for the action: the methods to be used, physical layout, and so on
- Exploring potential sources of violence or disruption and formulating options for nonviolent response
- Developing communications and decision-making systems
- Providing information about logistics, potential opposition, and possible legal consequences of the action
- Building a sense of community, solidarity, and unity in the group
- Training nonviolent "peacekeepers" or marshals who handle some aspects of logistics, maintain nonviolent discipline, and intervene in tense situations during the action

In addition to some of the elements included above, a campaign-building workshop includes a combination of the following:

- Exploring the dynamics of nonviolent action in more depth

- Generating a long-term vision of the changes the campaign seeks to bring about
- Developing specific and time-bound goals for the campaign
- Performing a power analysis of all parties involved
- Analyzing resources available to the nonviolent campaign (people, money, other physical and moral "capital")
- Identifying the allies and potential allies for the campaign (various constituencies, news media, political and legal forces, and others) and designing strategies for making potential allies into actual allies and passive allies into active supporters
- Developing a campaign strategy for education, political pressure, news media exposure, recruitment of participants, and so on, including key events and nonviolent methods to be used in each
- "Testing" of the campaign strategy using strategy games and role-plays
- Creating a campaign plan, including a timeline of all actions and events, resources needed, and so on

Training for long-term strategy is similar to campaign-building, but the units of analysis are larger (social, economic, and political trends) and the time frame for action more extended. Long-term strategy may include several campaigns that build on each other toward longer term goals.

Elements of strategy workshops are the following:

- Deepening understanding of the dynamics and requirements of long-term nonviolent action
- Presenting models of broad strategies for nonviolent social change
- Analyzing social/political/economic trends affecting the social change movement in question
- Appraising the status of the movement itself (level of public awareness, percentages of population agreeing/disagreeing, degree of mobilization and organization, and so on)
- Learning the dynamics of social movements, using historical examples and case studies
- Identifying key building blocks for change (challenges to the status quo, le-

gal suits, demand for new laws, changes in public attitudes, and so on)
- Arranging building blocks into a long-term strategy for change
- Testing of the strategy through use of extended strategy exercises

Training for Nonviolent Third-Party Intervention and Social Defense

In recent decades, nonviolence trainers have worked with a variety of third-party intervenors in conflict. Some have trained police units in how to intervene in domestic disputes to defuse potential violence. Others have trained teams of volunteers who have placed themselves between military or police forces and a group protesting unjust conditions. For example, nonviolent groups placed themselves between Native Americans and local and federal authorities during the standoff at Wounded Knee in 1973. Courageous volunteers have also provided protective "accompaniment" for people under imminent threat of death in the context of civil war in Guatemala and Sri Lanka. This is clearly a growing field.

At the same time, whole communities that are under threat have looked for ways to protect their way of life. Societies have explored options for defending democratic institutions against coups d'état or other forms of oppression or repression from reactionary forces within the society.

Training for nonviolent third-party intervention and for social defense is fairly new and will certainly enjoy further development in the future. Training in these fields has included the following elements:

- Developing a thorough understanding of the theory of nonviolent action
- Presenting basic models for nonviolent third-party intervention and nonviolent social defense.
- Analyzing the social, political, and economic trends that contribute to social breakdown, crisis, alienation, and conflict
- Presenting the dynamics of third-party intervention and social defense using historical examples and case studies
- Clarifying the differences between nonviolent response to coups d'état, foreign invasion, communal violence, assassination, and so forth
- Identifying sources of support within the society in the face of crisis or social breakdown—potential allies or forces to be mobilized for nonviolent action—and developing strategies for engaging those forces
- Developing a phased plan for training and maintaining local forces for intervention, protection, or defense
- Testing of strategies through use of extended strategy exercises

New Challenges for Training

In the past, nonviolent action and training for it has been used mainly by groups in opposition to established authority—groups demanding recognition of their rights or independence from an oppressor. As national governments and international bodies recognize the effectiveness and power of nonviolent action, trainers are challenged to deal with new situations. For instance, several national governments have adopted "civilian-based defense" as an element of their national defense strategy—against external aggression or internal threats to a democratic system. In order to implement such policies on a national basis, training programs will be needed. So far, none exists at that level.

Trainers have also been challenged to assist revolutionary forces seeking to overthrow oppressive dictatorships, such as in Burma. There, rebel military leaders, having witnessed the power of spontaneous nonviolent resistance, seek to develop an effective combination of mass nonviolent campaigns by civilians coupled with continued guerrilla warfare in order to bring down the regime.

Similarly, the United Nations and other international, nongovernmental groups are beginning to realize that peacekeeping forces need other means besides military power to accomplish their goals. More sophisticated training programs for military and nonmilitary personnel in how to engage in nonviolent protection, interposition, and other relevant methods will be of vital importance in the coming years.

Peter Woodrow

References

Lakey, George. *Powerful Peacemaking: A Strategy for a Living Revolution.* Philadelphia: New Society, 1987.

See also METHODS OF NONVIOLENT ACTION; STRATEGY

Transarmament

The process of changeover from a military defense policy to a civilian-based defense policy. Transarmament always involves the replacement of one means to provide defense with another. It therefore differs from "disarmament," which is the simple reduction or abandonment of military capacity. In transarmament, military forces and weaponry are gradually replaced with psychological, social, economic, and political weapons.

As it is usually conceived, transarmament would proceed in accordance with democratically made decisions, with the government playing a major role in both the choice of civilian-based defense and its preparations. In some cases, however, especially where the government's democratic qualities are limited, the society's independent groups and institutions may proceed with preparations for civilian-based defense prior to or parallel with governmental evaluation and decision making.

The process, occasion, extent, and timing of transarmament will vary widely from one situation to another. These will depend to a significant degree on the circumstances and capacities of present policies and policy-makers. Most important, however, will be the degree of understanding of civilian-based defense and the assessment of its capacity to deter and successfully defend against potential attackers.

In most cases, given the complexity of transforming an entire country's system of defense and the relatively untested nature of a civilian-based defense policy, rapid transarmament is virtually impossible.

Transarmament is most likely to occur by a gradual, incremental approach, slowly incorporating and testing civilian-based resistance components within existing predominantly military defense policies. These limited components may be intended for use in special contingencies or to provide a complementary defense capacity for defense tasks not otherwise covered. The initial component might be aimed at a specific task, such as providing a last line of defense when military means have failed, or to defend against a coup d'état. More ambitious purposes of civilian-based defense are likely to be taken seriously only after this type of defense has gained credibility for more limited objectives.

In this incremental approach, considerable time would be required for preparations and training, and often other adjustments (including economic ones). As the civilian-based component gained merited credibility, it could then be expanded in stages. The military capacity would not be downgraded or eliminated until viable substitute civilian-based defense options were considered reliable and were in place.

The emphasis in transarmament is, therefore, primarily on the increase in effective defense capacity through the new civilian-based defense measures, rather than on the reduction of military weaponry, which would occur only in the very late stages. The new defense capacity makes it possible to reduce and eventually abandon reliance on the old weapons system.

In special situations, a very different scenario might be possible, with several neighboring countries negotiating a phased plan for mutual transarmament in their region.

The term *transarmament* seems first to have been introduced by Kenneth Boulding in a 1937 pamphlet. Although writing as a pacifist, Boulding argued that "an entirely different method of defense" was needed, which was "nonviolent resistance." This would be "more effective" than military defense, he argued:

> Hence, a non-violent defense policy must imply unilateral *transarmament*—a transformation of the present violent defense forces into trained, professional, highly skilled non-violent defense forces or "goodwill forces." The actual details of this new method when applied on a political scale will develop and improve from generation to generation, just as the details of military science have developed.

The term *transarmament* seems not to have appeared in the literature again until the early 1960s, when it was reintroduced by Theodor Ebert in English translations of his German writings. His term, *Umrustung*, was conveyed into English as "transarmament." From the time of the 1964 Civilian Defense Study Conference in Oxford, the term has become a standard part of civilian-based defense vocabulary.

Gene Sharp

References

Boulding, Kenneth. *Paths of Glory: A New Way with War.* (Pamphlet.) London: Friends Book Center, 1937.

Mahadevan, T.K., Adam Roberts, and Gene Sharp, eds. *Civilian Defense: An Introduction.* New Delhi: Gandhi Peace Foundation and Bombay: Bharatiya Vidya

Bhavan, 1967.

Roberts, Adam, ed. *Civilian Resistance As a National Defense.* Harrisburg, Pa.: Stackpole, 1967; British ed. *The Strategy of Civilian Defense.* London: Faber and Faber, 1967.

Sharp, Gene. "'The Political Equivalent of War'—Civilian-Based Defense." In *Social Power and Political Freedom.* Boston: Porter Sargent, 1980.

Sharp, Gene, with Bruce Jenkins. *Civilian-Based Defense: A Post-Military Weapons System.* Princeton: Princeton University Press, 1990.

See also CIVILIAN-BASED DEFENSE

Transformational Politics

Usually defined as work intended to bring about fundamental or radical change (in the sense of going to the root) in social and political policies, values, and institutions. Though it is revolutionary in content—in its search for a society that is egalitarian, nonviolent, ecologically sensitive, and broadly participatory in its politics—most advocates of transformational politics seek change via evolution (lawful processes), not by revolution. This change is far more basic than that sought by incremental or reformist efforts. One of the key questions about pursuing politics of transformation concerns the role of nonviolence and nonviolent action. In particular, does political transformation necessarily imply nonviolence as a goal or tactic?

There are at least two important differences between incremental and transformational approaches. First, the focus of the latter is on institutional as well as personal change; that is, transformation is sought in political, social, and economic structures of power from the community level through the state level to the international level. Second, most transformational groups or movements stress the connections between problems or goals, and while not all such groups work simultaneously on the full range of problems, they are likely to go beyond single-issue politics.

Contemporary transformational groups (such as the Greens and Green parties, the bioregional movement, and some peace groups like the American Friends Service Committee) share common values, including a commitment to social and economic justice, ecological principles, and nonviolence. In contrast, many movements of the past (such as the nineteenth-century American Populists, early conservationists, and the antiwar and civil rights movements of the 1960s), while demanding basic change in one or two issue areas, avoided a hard look at the broader, connected roots of the problems they addressed. They were thus only partially transformational.

For example, the Populists called for far-reaching economic change and demonstrated the power of collective action through formation of producer cooperatives. But they ignored the connection between the economic plight of the tenant farmer (for instance) and a political structure framed by Madisonian checks and balances and a winner-take-all electoral system. They neglected racism, sexism, and all the other "isms" in a society where most decisions were made by elites. Similarly, early conservationists neglected issues around the economy and the military; the antiwar movement, before and during the time of the Vietnam War, saw environmental concerns as irrelevant; some civil rights leaders saw the draft as a sign of society's inequities, but neglected what are now termed "environmental justice" issues. In addition, in most of these efforts, women were relegated to the secondary role that they occupied in the larger society. And very few of these movements, at least until the late 1960s, paid more than lip service to the idea of participatory democracy—that is, to building and maintaining a movement (and political institutions) from the bottom up.

Most transformationalists argue that it is impossible to solve problems of social or economic injustice without what Albert Schweitzer termed "reverence for life," a stance that includes respect for other living species with which humans are ecologically entwined. If the idea of "reverence" includes nurturing the full human potential, surely widespread empowerment—that is, the ability to participate fully in the decisions made by social, economic, and political institutions—is essential as well. (This means more to transformationalists than the act of voting; it implies deliberation and consultation from the community level on up, with representatives responsible to their constituents on a continuing basis. And it applies to voluntary associations as well as to corporations, political parties, and legislatures.) Thus a focus on broadly participatory process is usually added, by transformational activists, to the substantive transformative goals of justice, sound ecology, and nonviolence.

But what if the pursuit or preservation of one of these values seems to conflict with another? Most particularly, is nonviolence an end and an absolute? Does social transformation require that the process be pursued by nonviolent methods of struggle? Do transformational activists have the right to expect a rigid adherence to nonviolent tactics by people who call for "liberation" or "revolution" and who may insist that their goals cannot be achieved through nonviolent means?

There is disagreement on these questions among transformationalists. They fall into three categories: (1) absolute pacifists who reject even nonviolent resistance as too coercive (some members of the historic peace churches); (2) those who argue that the use of violence, even for a good cause, will subvert the goal of a nonviolent society; they also see nonviolent resistance and civil disobedience as appropriate and potentially effective tactics, and would use violence only as a "last resort" if at all (Gandhi; King; the Berrigans); (3) those who see nonviolent action as a tool that—while desirable and useful—may not be adequate in some situations, notably where whole populations face death, torture, or extreme deprivation (some liberation theologians in Central America and the United States; Malcolm X).

Those who take the second position argue that the first is irresponsible in that it amounts to turning one's back on oppression. But they see the third position, however poignant the plight of the oppressed, as self-defeating in the long run. This is because one task of transformational strategy is to model what a future transformed world can be, and that world includes a rejection of violence. Further, transformational goals dictate a politics of inclusion— including respect for oppressors as fellow humans, capable of being touched, awakened, and perhaps transformed. Nonviolent acts may reach the oppressor; violence cannot.

But what if the question is reversed: can a nonviolent world be brought into being without a broader transformation? Does a nonviolent world order depend on a basic change in existing values and institutions—that is, on the elimination of economic and social injustice, ecological abuse, hierarchical structures, and the like?

Again there are several answers. Most people who work for legal or institutional change (such as through international law, mediation, or creation of a strong federation of nations) are not directly concerned with individual empowerment or community building, ecological considerations, or substantial changes in economic behavior. Most transformationalists, however, stress the interconnected nature of their goals. They argue that, just as a sustainable economy cannot be achieved solely by shifts in the ownership of the means of production, a truly stable peace cannot be achieved without dealing with the origins of violence. A world federation supported by international law will not by itself stop sexual or racial injustice, economic exploitation of both human beings and the environment, or top-down control of (private and public) politics—all root causes of many violent outbreaks.

One of the problems caused by a lack of unity on questions about the theoretical and practical links among nonviolence, nonviolent action, and transformational politics is the difficulty in forming stable coalitions among partners with diverse tactics and priorities. Tensions have emerged among environmentalists, for example, over the distinction between nonviolent resistance (as demonstrated by opponents of nuclear power) and the "ecotage" used by the Sea Shepherds in sinking Icelandic ships, or by Earth First! in destroying bridges, roads, and equipment belonging to the U.S. Forest Service. (Both actions were efforts to protect natural resources.) Similarly, groups founded by long-time peace advocates have sometimes found it difficult to work with more militant social justice groups, in American ghettos, in planning antiwar efforts, and in opposing U.S. policy in Central America.

Nevertheless, the tactics employed by transformational activists generally include many methods of nonviolent direct action: vigils and witnesses (at defense plants, nuclear test and nuclear power sites, on the streets and in public parks and offices), boycotts, demonstrations, nonpayment of taxes, draft refusal, trespass, blocking traffic, blockading logging sites, defying segregated facilities, offering sanctuary to draft resisters and to illegal immigrants, and occasional destruction of property. But some activist groups work in more traditional ways as well, engaging in lobbying, educational outreach, litigation, and electoral work (including running for office). Thus another source of tension—within as well as among groups—concerns the relative effectiveness of different tactics. Some activists argue that resistance tactics may have a negative effect on the group's efforts at converting or influencing others through education and persuasion. More militant activists usually respond that traditional tactics seldom work—and when they do, the results are only incremental or symbolic. This argument—like those over the relationship between nonviolence and transformation—is unlikely to be resolved in the near future, given the diversity, innovative style, and inclusive nature of transformational politics as a whole.

Betty H. Zisk

References

Zisk, Betty H. *The Politics of Transformation: Local Activism in the Peace and Environmental Movements.* Westport, Conn.: Praeger, 1992.

See also AMERICAN FRIENDS SERVICE COMMITTEE; BERRIGAN, DANIEL; BERRIGAN, PHILIP; ENVIRONMENTAL MOVEMENTS; GANDHI, MOHANDAS KARAMCHAND; KING, MARTIN LUTHER, JR.; MONKEYWRENCHING; PACIFISM; VIETNAM WAR OPPOSITION

Truth, Sojourner (1797?–1883)

Abolitionist, women's rights activist, orator, thought to be born in 1797 in Hurley, New York, and died on November 26, 1883, in Battle Creek, Michigan.

Sojourner Truth was born into slavery, the ninth child of Elizabeth (Mau-Mau Bett) and James, who were enslaved by a farmer of Dutch descent. Consequently, Dutch was her first language. She was called Isabella until she changed her name at age forty-six.

Throughout her childhood, Isabella had a series of owners in the Kingston, New York, area, and, though an obedient worker, she endured severe mistreatment. In her late teens, Isabella agreed to accept an older slave, Robert, as her husband, with whom she had five children. In 1826 Isabella escaped, taking her infant daughter with her, and found shelter with a Quaker family who arranged to purchase her and grant her freedom. When she learned that her son Peter had illegally been sold out of state to a plantation owner in Alabama, Isabella filed a lawsuit and eventually won custody of her child.

In 1829, Isabella moved to New York City where she worked as a servant. There she joined the Zion African Church and became known

Sojourner Truth. Sophia Smith Collection/Smith College.

for her ability to recite Bible passages from memory. She joined a women's evangelical group, worked with homeless women, and became a follower of Elijah Pierson, an eccentric self-proclaimed minister.

In 1843, Isabella, now in her mid-forties, was inspired to become an itinerant preacher. At this point, she took the name Sojourner Truth and immediately earned a reputation as a commanding speaker. She joined the Northampton Association of Education and Industry, an experimental utopian community in Massachusetts, where she met the great abolitionists of the day including Frederick Douglass and William Lloyd Garrison, as well as the leaders of the women's rights movement. Though she was illiterate, Truth dictated her life story to Olive Gilbert, and, in 1850, *The Narrative of Sojourner Truth* was published with an introduction by Garrison. From then on, Truth supported herself by selling copies of her book at abolitionist meetings. Increasingly, Truth made connections between the causes of women's rights and the abolition of slavery in the United States. At a women's rights convention in Akron, Ohio, in 1852, Truth delivered her famous "Ain't I a Woman?" speech, which aroused national attention.

During the Civil War, Truth solicited supplies for African-American soldiers in the Union army. In 1864, she traveled to Washington, D.C., to give President Lincoln encouragement and stayed to work with the National Freedmen's Relief Association as a counselor to former slaves living in temporary refugee camps.

After the war, Truth organized a protest against the segregated seating policy of a streetcar company and, after one incident, successfully sued a conductor for assault. In 1868, Truth, then in her seventies, began a campaign to help former slaves obtain land in Western territories. Once again she traveled, urging people to sign a land-grant petition that she presented to Congress. The petition was unsuccessful. From 1875 until her death, Truth lived in Battle Creek, Michigan.

Pam McAllister

References

Krass, Peter. *Sojourner Truth: Antislavery Activist*. Introduction by Coretta Scott King. New York: Chelsea House, 1988.
Washington, Margaret, editor. *Narrative of Sojourner Truth*. New York: Vintage Books/ Random House, 1850/1993.

See also ABOLITIONIST MOVEMENT; DOUGLASS, FREDERICK; GARRISON, WILLIAM LLOYD; WOMEN'S SUFFRAGE

Tubman, Harriet (1820?–1913)

Abolitionist, conductor on the Underground Railroad, born about 1820 in Dorchester County, Maryland, and died on March 10, 1913, in Auburn, New York.

The future abolitionist was born into slavery on a plantation in Maryland, the sixth of eleven children of Ben Ross and Harriet Greene. Originally named Araminta, she eventually adopted her mother's first name. By age five, she was working long hours, cleaning houses by day and tending babies at night. In her teens, Harriet was put to work in the fields, cutting wood, plowing, planting, all the time subject to beatings and abuse. When she was about thirteen, she received a severe head trauma as she attempted to intervene between another slave and an angry overseer. For the rest of her life, Tubman suffered from periodic spells of somnolence several times a day. In 1844, she entered an unhappy marriage with John Tubman, a free man. In 1849, believing rumors that she was about to be sold, she escaped, alone, to Philadelphia, unable to convince her brothers to go with her.

"Freedom" without family or friends left Tubman lonely and restless. In 1850, she resolved to return to Maryland and escort other enslaved people to the relative freedom of the North via a network of antislavery sympathizers in the Underground Railroad. For the next ten years, Tubman guided over three hundred people out of slavery, including, in 1857, her mother and father. In nineteen trips south, she dodged slaveholders who advertised a $40,000 reward for her capture. Between trips south, she worked as a cook, maid, or laborer to raise money to finance each slave escape.

Tubman, dubbed the Moses of her people, later boasted, "I never ran my train off the track and I never lost a passenger." Her tools included a revolver or rifle, fake passes, and paregoric, a drug she used to sedate infants. Once south of the Mason-Dixon Line, she sent information throughout the slave community with secret codes in songs and prayers. Her time of departure was specific and, once set, could not be delayed. "General Tubman," as she was called, did not permit anyone to question her orders or turn back. She used the north star as a directional guide, but a cunning imagination was her salvation. Once, she put a group of fugitive slaves on a train headed south to elude their captors.

In the late 1850s, Tubman became a spokesperson at antislavery and women's rights conventions. During the Civil War, from 1862 to 1865, she served as a scout and spy for Union forces in South Carolina and a nurse in camp hospitals.

After the war, Tubman settled in Auburn, New York, where she contributed to the development of African-American schools in the South. She also opened her home to orphans and former slaves and eventually, with her military pension, established the Harriet Tubman Home for Indigent Aged Negroes.

Pam McAllister

References

Bennett, Lerone, Jr. *Pioneers in Protest*. Chicago: Johnson, 1968.
Petry, Ann. *Harriet Tubman: Conductor on the Underground Railroad*. New York: Pocket Books/ Simon and Schuster, 1955.

See also ABOLITIONIST MOVEMENT

Harriet Tubman (far left) with some of the slaves she helped to free. Sophia Smith Collection/Smith College.

Tutu, Archbishop Desmond Mpilo (b. 1931)

Anglican archbishop of Johannesburg, South Africa, leader of the anti-apartheid struggle, and recipient of the 1984 Nobel Prize for Peace. Tutu was born on October 7, 1931, in Klerksdorp, a gold-mining town in the Transvaal region of South Africa. Following his father's profession, he was trained as a teacher and joined the staff of a high school in 1954. When the white minority government restricted the education of blacks to a second-rate "bantu education," Tutu resigned in protest. At this point he decided to become an Anglican priest, although describing his motivation, he said, "I was not moved by very high ideals. It just seemed that if the church would accept me, this might be a likely means of service." As he completed his theological education, however, his spiritual life deepened.

After his ordination in 1961, Tutu studied and worked for several years in London. In 1975, he was appointed the dean of St. Mary's Cathedral in Johannesburg, the first black to be named. He next served two years as bishop of Lesotho and in 1978 was appointed general secretary of the South African Council of Churches (SACC). The SACC represented and worked with all Christian churches in South Africa, except the Dutch Reform. About 80 percent of the individual members of SACC churches are black. As SACC general secretary, Tutu led these churches in opposition to the racial segregationist government policies of apartheid, as being inconsistent with the principles of Christianity. These policies had been introduced in 1948 by the Nationalist Party with the objective of consolidating the rule of 4.5 million whites over 23 million blacks. Along with provisions for limited education, apartheid measures restricted blacks' freedom of movement and association, forced evacuation of blacks to so-called homelands, permitted detention without trial, and required all blacks to carry a pass.

Tutu refused to carry a pass and spoke out against these policies. Like Albert John Lutuli (who was awarded the Peace Prize in 1960), Tutu led his constituency in a nonviolent struggle for a "nonracial, truly democratic, and more just society." Tutu declared that the SACC deplored violence, both the structural and legalized violence of apartheid and the violence of those who would overthrow the state by armed force. His counsels of love and compassion, even for the whites who oppressed blacks, and his willingness to enter into dialogue with the government, drew attacks from radical blacks. Yet he defended the spiritual and Christian roots of his resistance and action. As he asked in his Nobel lecture: "When will we learn that human beings are of infinite value because they have been created in the image of God, and that it is blasphemy to treat them as if they were less than this and to do so ultimately recoils on those who do this?"

Irwin Abrams

References

Tutu, Desmond. *Hope and Suffering: Sermons and Speeches.* Edited by John Webster. Grand Rapids, Mich.: Eerdmands, 1984.

See also Nobel Peace Prize; South Africa, Opposition to Racial Oppression

U

United Farm Workers Organizing Committee

Association of Mexican-American farm workers led by Cesar Chavez. Chavez and other labor, church, and community leaders created and expanded this organization and a subsequent farm workers union through intensive community organizing. Primarily employing two major methods of nonviolent action, nationwide consumer boycotts and local labor strikes, the farm workers gained numerous improvements in civil rights and labor treatment in the 1960s and 1970s.

In the 1950s, California farm workers consisted of a minority of "permanent" year-round workers and a majority of "seasonal" or migrant workers, many of whom were illegal immigrants or green card holders. The national Farm Labor Union and the Agricultural Workers Organizing Committee (AWOC) had unsuccessfully attempted to organize seasonal farm workers in California during the 1950s. Both failed to mobilize a mass base of farm workers, although AWOC did organize numerous ad hoc strikes led by "flying squads" of pickets against produce growers during harvest times.

In December 1961, Cesar Chavez resigned from the Community Service Organization (a civil rights organization of urban Mexican Americans) to found the Farm Workers Association (FWA). Using a multi-issue community organizing model, he helped establish a credit union and built solidarity among California seasonal farm workers. Although initially hesitant, Chavez became increasingly involved in the farm workers' labor conflicts.

In September 1965, AWOC called a strike against grape growers in the region around Delano, California. FWA soon joined the strike

and adopted a new name, the National Farm Workers Association (NFWA). They organized mobile picket squads attempting to persuade workers to strike using bull horns and signs. Pickets were threatened and insulted, and fewer than half the workers walked out. At this point, NFWA leadership decided to defy new court injunctions against large groups picketing, and forty-four pickets were arrested on October 29. This action represented a shift from local community building to deliberate solicitation of national publicity for the NFWA cause.

The NFWA then called a nationwide consumer boycott of table grapes and products manufactured by California grape growers. This campaign included leafleting stores, obstructing store entrances, harassing store owners, and attempting to convince longshoremen and teamsters not to handle these items. In the spring of 1966, NFWA led a 300-mile religious march that ended in Sacramento on Easter. During the march, national news media displayed boycott signs nationwide, provoking some growers to negotiate. In August 1966, the NFWA became the United Farm Workers Organizing Committee (UFWOC) as part of the AFL-CIO and gradually began to win union contracts with growers. Strike and boycott activities continued, accompanied by sympathetic actions by members of other unions. Numerous "hot cargo" actions occurred, in which teamsters and others would refuse to handle grapes picked by strikebreakers. In addition, shipments were deliberately misrouted and cases of grapes were misplaced or damaged. By July 1967, a national "Great Grape Boycott" had begun, and in 1968, UFWOC shifted its strategy to rely less on strikes and more on the boycott to enlist national third party support.

In February 1968, as a result of conflict over strategy, Chavez began a twenty-five-day fast in personal penitence for dissension and talk of violent direct action. This act drew religious support and mass media coverage, furthering the cause of the farm workers. The consumer boycott gained even greater leverage as they started a secondary boycott against grocery chains carrying grapes. Activists used "shop-ins," whereby shoppers would fill grocery carts with expensive perishable items and then abandon them in aisles or initiate long vociferous protests to store managers, thereby damaging frozen foods and produce. By the end of 1968, retail grape sales had dropped 12 percent nationally, and an estimated $3 to $4 million worth of grapes were left to rot on vines.

UFWOC boycott and strike efforts continued throughout the late 1960s. During 1970, however, the organization signed a series of negotiated contracts with California grape growers to allow union organizing on their ranches. Fresh from these successes, the UFWOC turned its attention to vegetable growers as well. During the 1970s, the UFWOC and its union, the United Farm Workers of America (established in February 1972), experienced a counterattack by produce growers and the Teamsters union. Growers used the strategy of "union substitution," granting the Teamsters permission to organize farm workers into their own weaker union through "sweetheart contracts." This instigated clashes between picketing farm workers and Teamsters during the early 1970s that left several workers dead. After one death in August 1973, the UFWOC called a moratorium on pickets and strikes and turned once more to a boycott on the Safeway grocery chain. California governor Jerry Brown promoted compromise legislation, which was enacted in 1975, protecting collective bargaining by farm workers in the state. In union elections in the fall of 1975, the UFW won a majority of new union elections, but could not win over many of the sites already controlled by the Teamster union. The late 1970s were characterized by a return to local strikes and factional disputes within the UFWOC and UFW, as Chavez was criticized for autocratic behavior.

The United Farm Workers movement gained numerous policy and legislation changes through their nonviolent tactics. They achieved significant real wage increases, work rule reforms, benefit awards, and bans on dangerous pesticides. On a larger scale, the movement established institutional power for an underclass with no previous political clout.

Brad Bennett

References

Hoffman, Pat. *Ministry of the Dispossessed: Learning from the Farm Worker Movement.* Los Angeles: Wallace, 1987.

Jenkins, J. Craig. *The Politics of Insurgency: The Farm Worker Movement in the 1960s.* New York: Columbia University Press, 1985.

See also BOYCOTTS; CHAVEZ, CESAR ESTRADA

United States, Independence Movement, 1765–1775

Decade of nonviolent resistance from 1765 to 1775 that resulted in de facto political independence from the British for a majority of the American colonies. Although often overlooked by historians, the three campaigns that composed this movement operated without force of arms or violence in trying to compel the British government to change its policies. The movement was notable for its development and use of a number of nonviolent methods that challenged the existing British government's authority and ability to rule in the colonies.

Three campaigns—against the Stamp Act of 1765, the Townshend Acts of 1767, and the Coercive Acts of 1774—were the focal points of the independence movement. In each case Britain's introduction of laws affecting the taxation and governing of the North American colonies prompted a campaign of opposition. Believing that these laws threatened their liberty and prosperity, many colonists were convinced that they must resist. This resistance took many forms, including some that had nothing to do with the nonviolent resistance—for example, legal petition to Parliament through conventional constitutional channels. It also ultimately included property destruction, such as the Boston Tea Party (1773), as well as generally nonlethal violence against persons, such as tarring and feathering opponents. However, property destruction was limited and generally perceived as politically counterproductive. Furthermore, fewer than a dozen cases of tarring and feathering actually occurred between 1765 and April 1775 and usually involved customs informers and thus were seen as private matters rather than elements of the political resistance campaigns. Neither constitutional appeals nor violence, therefore, played a major role in the independence movement and its successes.

The most important types of resistance in this decade of opposition were nonviolent forms of action. Methods of protest and persuasion included demonstrations and parades in behalf of a resistance campaign, the development of political iconography supporting the campaign (such as the Liberty Tree), and the publication of broadsides naming supporters or opponents of the resistance campaign. A mock funeral in Wilmington, North Carolina, in October 1765 dramatized many of these methods. According to the contemporary newspaper account in the *North Carolina Gazette,* some five hundred Wilmingtonians (out of a total population of eight hundred) met to protest the Stamp Act. They paraded an effigy of Liberty, symbolizing the rights of the colonists that were under attack by the British Parliament. The crowd put the effigy "into a Coffin, and marched in solemn procession with it to the Church-yard, a Drum in Mourning beating before them, and the Town Bells muffled ringing a doleful Knell at the same time." Just before the crowd interred the coffin, they checked the pulse of Liberty, and were delighted to discover that Liberty was still alive. They "concluded the Evening with great Rejoicings, on finding that Liberty had still an Existence in the Colonies." Significantly, the newspaper account ended with the observation, "not the least Injury was offered to any Person." Here religious ritual, political protest, and mass action were conjoined within a nonviolent method of resistance.

Methods of noncooperation varied. Social boycotts of persons opposed to the resistance campaigns are well documented. For example, in 1768 when British troops were garrisoned in Boston, one leaflet called on the Bostonians to treat the troops, "with civility, but to provide nothing." Economic forms of noncooperation provided more powerful sanctions. Organized campaigns of nonimportation refused to import British goods—particularly finished items such as tools and clothing or other materials such as foodstuffs and liquor—for sale in the colonies. Campaigns of nonconsumption focused on the collective refusal to use certain British goods, and instead to substitute American-made goods. The use of American home-spun clothing became both an economic and symbolic statement on behalf of the resistance movement. Finally, the refusal to export American materials, particularly raw materials such as lumber and naval stores, represented an additional source of economic leverage.

Methods of political noncooperation included refusing to use existing royal political, judicial, and legislative institutions as well as refusing to dissolve colonial assemblies or intercolonial bodies such as the Continental Congress when ordered to do so. Political noncooperation also involved settling legal cases in courts or clearing the papers of incoming or outgoing ships without the required stamps as in the Stamp Act campaign. The point of these social, economic, and political methods of noncooperation, as John Dickinson wrote in 1767, was that the colonists should withhold from Great Britain "all the advantages she has been used to receiving from us."

Methods of nonviolent intervention created new colonial political institutions such as the Stamp Act Congress (1765), the Committees of Correspondence (1772–1775), and the First Continental Congress (1774–1775). These ad hoc, extralegal political bodies corresponded to extralegal judicial and legislative colonial organizations that also developed during the decade, and which, taken together, embodied the parallel government that emerged most forcefully and visibly in 1774 and 1775.

This new American government, parallel in function to the British government, provided the basis for de facto independence in the colonies. The ability of the American colonies to dispense with royal direction of their political institutions and, simultaneously, to develop replacement institutions that could fulfill the functions of government represented a major political accomplishment of the independence movement.

Five factors marked the independence movement and shaped its eventual outcome. First, the campaigns developed a shared political consciousness, which expressed the Americans' political differences with Britain. Articulation of colonial rights served at first to identify American aspirations and then later to distinguish these goals and expectations from those of the British. Although this consciousness developed slowly, and notions of independence from Britain did not emerge until late 1774 or early 1775, a shared political identity nevertheless was crucial to the success of the movement. Second, the campaigns promoted the growth of institutions and organizations that expressed colonial grievances and argued for changes in Crown policy. These organizations created space for the emergence of political leaders for the campaigns and provided structures for the organized and forceful articulation of colonial perspectives on questions of governance, taxation, and political expression. Significantly, colonial resistance remained largely improvised throughout most of the campaigns. Cities such as Boston and Philadelphia nurtured a resistance ethos and sustained informal opposition networks more than other urban or rural areas. Intercolonial organizations sporadically arose, as with the Stamp Act Congress or the merchants' boycott agreements against the Townshend Acts. Not until the First Continental Congress in 1774, however, did measures emerge that were strategically conscious, applied throughout the colonies, and equipped with political and economic sanctions for noncompliance.

Third, the campaigns encouraged open resistance to specific acts of British policy. Through various acts of confrontation with British authority, popular resistance was mobilized. These were the multitude of actions by the now nameless men and women who spun, wove, and wore home-spun clothes, who unified in the boycott of British goods, and who encouraged their neighbors to join them and stand firm. Fourth, the campaigns organized noncooperation, particularly in the economic and political spheres. Such methods as nonimportation and nonexportation or the deliberate continuation of political bodies declared illegal or dissolved by Crown officials increasingly threatened British authority. As the campaigns solidified their gains over the decade, power began to shift away from dependence upon Britain.

Fifth, the resistance campaigns developed parallel institutions, particularly the institutions of government. It was the ability of the American colonists to do without British colonial administration, largely because they replaced it with governing mechanisms of their own, that signaled the beginning of American independence. With the encouragement of the First Continental Congress, extralegal committees that effectively adopted the functions of government appeared throughout the colonies in the last months of 1774. As adopted by the Congress in October 1774, the Continental Association was a program of nonimportation, nonconsumption, and nonexportation combined with provisions for enforcement utilizing social ostracism and economic boycott. This program represented a major step toward effective resistance on the part of the colonies backed by powerful sanctions. As such it also represented a significant assertion of American political autonomy.

Each of these five factors was essential for effective opposition and each developed simultaneously throughout the decade of resistance, though to varying degrees at different times. Taking all five factors together, their sustained and organized appearance in the movement some months before the beginning of the War of Independence indicates clearly that self-government in the colonies was not gained by the war, as is often assumed. Rather, within the majority of colonies, the transfer of power from British officials to the provincial conventions and committees was clearly evident before the Battle of Lexington and Concord.

Although the Americans achieved substantial political accomplishments during their nonviolent struggle, these gains were eventually defended by military force. In 1775, in the aftermath of the Battle of Lexington and Concord, the nonviolent methods were abandoned and the colonists embarked on a military struggle that would last eight years. The reasons for this shift in strategy have gone largely unexplored and further research is needed. For when presented between 1768 and 1774 with an opportunity to vote for military measures or actually to employ them, the colonists repeatedly chose nonviolent tactics. Moreover, several incidents, might have embroiled the colonies in a military struggle much earlier than Lexington and Concord. These included a general mobilization by colonists at Cambridge, Massachusetts, on September 1, 1774, the seizure of military supplies and equipment by colonists at Portsmouth, New Hampshire, on December 14, 1774, and a confrontation between troops and colonists at Salem, Massachusetts, on February 26, 1775. These encounters, however, were contained and military exchanges avoided.

Within such a context, the adoption of military methods represents a strategic shift in tactics and not an inevitable response to changed political conditions. Such a decision on the part of the colonists might have reflected innovations within the independence movement's organization and goals. Alternatively, it might have represented a misunderstanding of the gains that the nonviolent resistance had achieved, or the judgment that nonviolent action could not succeed against the changed conditions of increased British repression.

The shift in strategy represented by the abandonment of nonviolent methods and the adoption of military ones had several repercussions. As the historian Arthur Schlesinger, Sr., noted regarding the 1774–1775 campaign of commercial pressure, after Lexington and Concord, "armed rebellion had superseded commercial coercion. . . . Thereafter the Continental Association lost its distinctive character as a method of peaceable coercion; it became subordinated to the military necessities of the times." With the shift in strategy, other dynamics changed too. For example, during the decade 1765–1775, the British mercantile community had often supported the colonial resistance campaigns. In part this was a measure of the success of the resistance campaigns, for the goal of economic noncooperation was to place pressure on the British merchants, who in turn would force the British Parliament to respond to American demands. Once military hostilities broke out, British mercantile encouragement eroded very quickly, for now support of the colonists had become tantamount to sedition. Finally, with the decision of the Second Continental Congress to form an army, political decision making shifted from the popular assemblies and broad-based committees in each colony to a command structure more able to respond to military exigencies. The shift in strategy represented an end to the use of nonviolent methods; however, the goals of the movement had in large part already been achieved.

Walter H. Conser, Jr.

References

Conser, Walter H., Ronald M. McCarthy, David J. Toscano, and Gene Sharp, eds. *Resistance, Politics, and the American Struggle for Independence, 1765–1775.* Boulder, Colo.: Lynne Rienner, 1986.

Schlesinger, Arthur M. *The Colonial Merchants and the American Revolution, 1763–1775.* New York: Atheneum, 1968.

See also METHODS OF NONVIOLENT ACTION; STRATEGY

U

V

Vietnam War Opposition

Organized opposition, including explicitly nonviolent activism, that challenged the U.S. prosecution of war in Indochina from 1965 to 1975. Grounded in established peace organizations and new constituencies, the antiwar movement (or peace movement) of the Vietnam War era built on expanding grassroots activism to significantly constrain the war policy-making of the Lyndon Johnson and Richard Nixon administrations. It was the largest opposition to an ongoing war in history, a loose, shifting coalition of disparate groups that had in common mainly the conviction that the war was morally and politically wrong and had to be stopped. The movement experimented with a wide range of nonviolent approaches, although its actions became consistent and coordinated only late in the war. Whereas dissent acquired a dominant public image as radical and confrontational by 1969, in fact it was increasingly infused into mainstream politics where it helped to mobilize popular and legislative opposition.

Organizational Basis of Opposition, 1965–1967

The core of the movement consisted of peace and pacifist groups formed well before 1965. Some of them dated from the World War I era, notably the Fellowship of Reconciliation (FOR), Women's International League for Peace and Freedom (WILPF), American Friends Service Committee (AFSC), and War Resisters League (WRL). The Friends Committee on National Legislation (FCNL) was a lobbying agency founded in 1940. Other groups were formed during the 1957–1963 challenge to the cold war and nuclear weapons testing: the Committee for a SANE Nuclear Policy (SANE), Committee for

Nonviolent Action (CNVA), Women's Strike for Peace (WSP), and Students for a Democratic Society (SDS). With the exception of SDS, these groups had considerable experience with both political activism and nonviolent action, and moreover, nonviolence had become familiar in the course of the civil rights movement.

Leaders in existing peace groups had been among the critics of Vietnam policy even before President Johnson committed U.S. forces to air and ground warfare in the spring of 1965. Military escalation led them to focus on the war and also stimulated actions such as a large SDS-sponsored demonstration in Washington, D.C., and the university teach-ins. A radical edge was given to dissent as remnants of the Old Left (Communists and members of the Socialist Workers Party, or SWP) joined New Left opponents of the war and leaders of the Student Nonviolent Coordinating Committee. On the liberal side of the movement were growing networks of dissenting religious and cultural leaders. By the fall of 1965, most elements of antiwar organization had surfaced.

By that time, too, the basic arguments against the war were in place. First, war goals were deemed unfeasible: the United States could not impose accountable, representative government upon South Vietnam, and engaging in war there would overtax U.S. resources. Second, it was held that intervention would destabilize the region: North Vietnam would become more dependent on China, which might intervene, as it had done in Korea. Third, supporting a repressive government in the South was regarded as a violation of U.S. ideals. Fourth, it seemed patently immoral for the United States to condemn Vietnam to the destructiveness of all-out war for an essentially American interest. In the

Confrontation with the Warmakers demonstration at the Pentagon, Washington, D.C., October 21, 1967.
Photo by Minoru Aoki/War Resisters League Archives.

course of the war, moral concerns became increasingly central to dissent, and an anti-imperialist argument was added by the radical Left, but a coherent position was in place at the outset.

The peace movement attracted various disaffected constituencies in 1965–1967. The SWP played an increasingly strong role on the Left, often in sharp competition with other radicals. Religious leaders organized, eventually as Clergy and Laymen Concerned about Vietnam (CALCAV), led by Richard Fernandez. Politicians and intellectuals in Americans for Democratic Action (ADA) increasingly had to choose between war and sociopolitical reform, and from their ranks emerged an antiwar core in the Democratic Party. Antiwar women created Another Mother for Peace. Antiwar cadres formed among labor leaders, social workers, scientists, writers, artists and entertainers, the Peace Corps, and even business executives. By 1967 student activists were linked through a national Student Mobilization Committee (SMC), antiwar veterans began to organize, and Martin Luther King, Jr., at least symbolically aligned the mainline civil rights movement with the antiwar movement. By then, too, elements of a youthful counterculture identified peace with assorted alternative lifestyles and associated with the cause.

All these antiwar constituencies constituted a fluid coalition of leaders and constituencies that experimented with many forms of activism. Most visible were the mass demonstrations that grew in size and number, and also draft resistance, acts of civil disobedience, confrontation with authorities, and even self-immolation. But no less important were the informational campaigns, electoral politics, and lobbying that challenged the credibility of the government, the political efficacy of the war, and its moral legitimacy.

To be sure, there was an underlying tension between liberal and radical approaches, each of which comprised an ever-changing coalition of groups. Although both wings cooperated with one another upon occasion, the tension between them was patent. In this respect, the major pacifist organizations (the FOR and AFSC) experienced special tensions because their memberships accommodated both liberal and radical pacifists.

The radical cluster generally sought immediate withdrawal from Vietnam and significant changes in U.S. political and social structures, not merely programmatic reforms. Appealing to disaffected minorities, political radicals and radical pacifists (those committed to principled nonviolent direct action) developed a multi-issue agenda, of which the war was only the most compelling part. They employed mass demonstrations, civil disobedience, draft resistance, and nonviolent direct action. The counterculture added street theater, and a small number of militants on the radical fringe felt driven to violence.

Radicals lacked cohesion. Even the most tightly organized of them, the SWP, worked through other groups because of its small membership and its preference for mass demonstrations. The SDS abandoned antiwar leadership in 1965 and became thoroughly fragmented by extremism. Indeed, many of the minorities on which radicals relied were affected by sharply conflicting priorities. Extreme advocates of black power disrupted the civil rights movement, for example; some women who experienced male chauvinism in civil rights and antiwar activism turned to women's liberation; and militant ideologues and counterculture devotees fragmented various radical groups. Leadership changed rapidly. Often it was distanced from the constituencies it professed to represent. Only the challenge of the war welded disparate radicals together, and then only occasionally and for specific purposes.

Nonetheless, the various radical elements did dramatize moral and political war issues for the American people. In doing so, they contributed the dominant mass media image of dissent, which was indiscriminately associated with the cultural iconoclasm of so-called hippies and with the confrontation, if not violence, of the 1967 action to "Confront the Warmakers" at the Pentagon, the 1968 Democratic convention in Chicago, and the 1971 May Day attempt to shut down Washington, D.C. Confrontation was largely propelled by the widespread perception that the political system was unresponsive; in turn, the image of dissenters as confrontational and subversive spurred the Johnson and (especially) Nixon administrations to paranoid, extralegal surveillance and harassment of them. In reality, political and cultural radicals were fragmented on the margin of the movement by 1970, while radical pacifists were imposing discipline on nonviolent action.

Liberals tended to concentrate on the war issue, although by 1967 they linked it to domestic social reforms on the Great Society agenda. Consistently, they attempted to mobilize the

Anti–Vietnam War march in Berkeley, California, February 23, 1966. From Critical Focus: The Black and White Photographs of Harvey Wilson Richards, *edited by Paul Richards (Oakland, CA: Estuary Press, 1987), p. 54.*

political center of the country and to channel dissent into the system. The liberal approach was important in defining the war issues in 1965–1967, and it acquired increasing force from 1968 to 1975 as radical extremism played itself out and the political system opened up, notably through Democratic Party politics.

At the beginning of the war, liberal activists were based in the existing peace groups (notably the AFSC, FOR, FCNL, SANE, WILPF, and WSP), to which CALCAV was quickly added. As public disillusionment with the war grew, cadres of liberal activists emerged among professional, civic, and political groups. Preferred tactics included programs to inform and arouse the public. Such were the 1965 teach-ins, beginning at the University of Michigan, spreading to at least 130 campuses, and replicated on national television. Recognizing that large-scale demonstrations could dramatize the war issue and legitimize dissent, liberal groups like SANE successfully sponsored their

own, as in the fall of 1965, or cooperated with radical leaders, as in the spring of 1967. Cooperation required the resolution of differences about excluding groups (like Communists) or about provocative actions that were likely to give a demonstration a negative news media image. Increasingly, demonstrations made room for various forms of protest at different venues in order to accommodate plural approaches.

Ultimately, the most important liberal strategy was political lobbying and electoral activity. In 1966, Sanford Gottlieb of SANE (with the ADA, AFSC, and FCNL) initiated a "National Voters Peace Pledge" to support peace candidates. The following summer, student volunteers canvassed local communities, informing people and raising consciousness, while SANE and ADA sponsored newspaper ads and a petition campaign, and many groups lobbied Congress. Those were small and inconclusive steps, but leaders in the ADA were building an antiwar base in the Democratic Party, from which Allard Lowenstein and others engineered a challenge to Lyndon Johnson's presidential candidacy. When Eugene McCarthy agreed to run as a peace candidate in the fall of 1967, liberals had brought the contest over the war fully into the political mainstream.

Confrontation and Mainstream Politics, 1968–1975

Confrontation was most intense from fall 1968 to spring 1971, both within the political system and outside of it. The war was challenged most visibly in the streets, where the antiwar movement acquired its dominant public image as politically and culturally radical. Probably for that reason, it was not accepted by the public, despite the fact that the American people themselves withdrew their support for the war on a massive scale.

Late in 1967 the Johnson administration, perceiving public support to be soft, launched a major campaign to reassure the people that it was winning the war. Coming on the heels of that effort, the strong Communist Tet assaults in February further undermined the president's credibility and strengthened the McCarthy campaign, which in turn persuaded Senator Robert Kennedy to announce his candidacy. Johnson withdrew from the race at the end of March, leaving a three-way competition between McCarthy, Kennedy, and Vice President Hubert Humphrey. As peace activists swarmed into the McCarthy and Kennedy campaigns, however, the country seemed to unravel. Martin Luther King, Jr., was shot in April, setting off a wave of inner-city violence, and Kennedy was assassinated in June. Against that background, the Democratic convention met in Chicago, where political activists were thwarted within the meeting hall while radical activists were caught up in street violence. The immediate result was disillusionment among both antiwar liberals and radicals, which probably contributed to Nixon's electoral victory.

The radical element was further fragmented in the months that followed. A small militant fringe spun off into the kind of violence that marked the Weathermen Underground. More important, though not covered by the news media, radical pacifists formed the National Action Group (NAG) on the initiative of the AFSC's Stewart Meacham. Determined to conduct direct action that would be carefully disciplined and coordinated with other antiwar efforts, it was a body with a great deal of experience in nonviolent theory and action, with leaders from the AFSC, FOR, WRL, CNVA, CALCAV, SANE, WILPF, the Southern Christian Leadership Conference, and the draft resistance organization RESIST. The group engaged in coordinated regional rallies on Easter weekend in 1969.

Liberal activists, meanwhile, began to assess the potential of aligning antiwar Democratic legislators against a Republican president. Nixon firmed up his direction by May: he would withdraw U.S. troops while attempting to achieve an independent South Vietnam by using a combination of South Vietnamese forces, U.S. air power, pressure from China and the USSR, and direct threat. Publicly, Nixon was not specific, but he conveyed the sense that he would withdraw U.S. troops without significantly modifying war aims.

The peace movement regrouped. Liberal activists Sam Brown, Marge Sklenkar, and David Hawk organized a nationwide moratorium for October 15. Their object was to stimulate nonconfrontational expressions of antiwar concern and discussion of war issues at local levels, expanding the program as long as the war continued. The moratorium was extraordinarily successful, and it undercut Nixon's secret demand that North Vietnam negotiate on acceptable terms or face massive violence. The president responded by appealing to the "silent majority," so that moratorium leaders cooperated in a mass rally in November. That demonstration, the Mobilization, was initially developed by a left-wing coalition, now purged of its most militant elements and influenced by the NAG group. Augmented by experienced moratorium organizers, it was the largest demonstration in U.S. history up to that time, drawing perhaps a half-million people in Washington, D.C., alone. It was disciplined and moving, and it received positive news media coverage.

Nonetheless, the movement seemed to dissipate following the Mobilization. In part this was out of exhaustion and frustration, but largely it was because many activists moved into the local campaigns of the 1970 election. A disjointed kind of militancy was rife that spring too, further reinforcing the mistaken image of all protest as confrontation. That perception fueled the tragic killings at Kent State and Jackson State universities—brutal reactions to student protest sparked by Nixon's invasion of Cambodia. The movement's immediate response was passionate and widespread; but it was political activism that was sustained. By midsummer, electoral work was coordinated by some forty groups, while congressional pressure on the administration was buttressed by antiwar lobbyists.

This context made possible a coordinated antiwar political coalition, the Campaign to Set the Date for withdrawal from Vietnam. Launched in February 1971 after months of planning, the lobbying campaign was initiated by SANE, CALCAV, and FOR, and enlisted the AFSC, ADA, and some twenty other civic and religious bodies. Antiwar veterans had become effectively organized in the Vietnam Veterans against the War (VVAW) by this time, and they opened the record of war atrocities to public view. Meanwhile, pacifists in NAG won the endorsement of CALCAV, WSP, and SANE for a People's Campaign for Peace and Justice, a public information program that contrasted the administration's negotiating terms with a peace that would reflect the mutual interests of the Vietnamese and U.S. people. Another coalition was preparing a spring demonstration to get the country "Out Now!" Finally, a remnant of the radical left, led by Rennie Davis and legitimized by radical pacifist David Dellinger, proposed to shut down Washington with May Days of mass civil disobedience. Every one of those projects and constituencies was accommodated in carefully sequenced actions from late March to early May 1971. Excepting May Days, each element was controlled and effective. The attempt at concentrated civil disobedience was disrupted, largely by security forces directed from the White House.

By 1972 opposition to the war was firmly located within the political system, notably in Democratic Party leadership, and the weight of elements within the movement had shifted to liberal antiwar organizations. They formed a pressure group that was cohesive and effective up to the end of the war in Vietnam. To the Campaign to Set the Date was added (in 1972) a Campaign to End the Air War, and (after the January 1973 peace accords) a Campaign to Stop Funding the War. In the meantime, antiwar activists worked closely with the 1972 presidential campaign of Democratic Senator George McGovern. The more they focused on political issues and worked within the system, though, the less visible they were. The radical image of protest endured, masking the extent to which the antiwar movement and active nonviolence had permeated American society.

Nonviolence in the Antiwar Protest
The U.S. war in Vietnam elicited a remarkable range of nonviolent protest from innumerable groups whose actions were coordinated far more by negotiating differences than by central planning.

The hallmark of antiwar protest was mass demonstrations that grew from about 20,000 people at the April 1965 SDS rally in Washington and 30,000 at the SANE rally in November, to perhaps 100,000 in New York in the spring of 1966, 200,000 in New York and 50,000 in San Francisco in the spring of 1967, to 500,000 each for the Washington mobilizations of 1969 and 1971.

Each demonstration was designed to dramatize broad, united opposition to the war. That cohesiveness did not really exist among antiwar organizations, so that their differences had to be negotiated or glossed over. Moreover, most citizens with strong reservations to the war were not affiliated with any national antiwar group. Indeed, every demonstration attracted people whose energy it could not really direct. Each gave the heterogeneous movement a specific focal point for public outreach.

Demonstrations were also microcosms of coalition-building. Probably the best example of this was the Fifth Avenue Peace Parade Committee, which was created in New York by individuals ranging from Old Left Communists and SWP members to radical pacifists from AFSC, CNVA, WRL, and the *Liberation* collective, and to liberals from SANE, WSP, and AFSC. Inspired by A.J. Muste, the Parade Committee focused on the war and avoided ideological polarity. Effective demonstrations required experienced, strong leaders like Muste and Norma Becker of the Parade Committee, Brad Lyttle of CNVA and WRL, Fred Halsted of SWP, and Ron Young of FOR. They had to raise funds, handle logistics, negotiate arrangements with government, and train marshals to provide self-discipline to rallies.

In order to build coalitions on a national level, demonstrations increasingly provided sequenced times and places for various forms of protest. They offered a cafeteria of nonviolent actions: legal assembly in the cause of freedom of speech, speakers and promotional literature to define the issues, mass protest to mobilize public awareness and challenge government policy, vigils as a form of moral witness, individual civil disobedience to express ethical commitment, and collective civil disobedience to express solidarity and challenge authority. Interestingly, and despite the interventions of Chicago's mayor Richard Daley in 1968, and the Nixon administration in 1971, governments and protesters on all levels learned together to manage demonstrations with the least possible threat to public order. Both sides came to conclude that chaos, violence, and provocation was not in either's best interest, with the result that nonviolent protest became further institutionalized in U.S. society.

Other means than demonstrations were used to influence public opinion. In fact, the organized antiwar movement was not alone in protesting. Challenge came independently from academic experts, leading reporters like Harrison Salisbury, legislators like Senators Wayne Morse and William Fulbright, and former members of the war-making administrations, like Ramsay Clark and Daniel Ellsberg. One function of the organized movement was, therefore, to publicize independent objections to the war and to project a body of authority alternative to that of the government. This was the role of the early teach-ins and local activism, for example, of FCNL seminars for legislators, and of the 1970–1971 VVAW hearings on war atrocities.

Besides addressing the public, antiwar organizations distributed information and ideas among their own members and contacts. Particularly striking in this regard were the antiwar papers that sprang up on military posts, on naval ships, and even in the Pentagon. An underground press evolved there and also among draft resisters, providing access to otherwise unavailable information about the war and about peace actions. Such material was weighted by the sponsoring group, of course, so that it was sometimes difficult to distinguish information from propaganda (as it was also in the news media or government "reports"). In the case of the army, literature was supplemented by coffee houses adjacent to bases.

Beyond information, the organized movement emphasized moral issues in public discourse. CALCAV effectively played that role and, indeed, much of public discourse was carried in ethical terms. Moreover, keeping the real possibility of military failure before the American people challenged the government's credibility and also the validity of military solutions for political problems. Paradoxically, antiwar protest, as it was stereotyped by the news media, served to associate the war with public dislocation and social chaos. The merit of that

association is not the point here, though probably the war did align independent stresses in the social fabric; but given its radical and confrontational popular image, organized opposition added another, threatening layer to public frustration with the war.

The classic pacifist approach of moral witness through symbolic acts was widely adopted in protesting the war. The poet Robert Lowell and others made political statements when they rejected White House invitations, while singers like Joan Baez, Judy Collins, and Phil Ochs evoked moral issues in song. In the "March against Death" at the November 1969 Mobilization, a line of forty-seven thousand stretched from Arlington National Cemetery, across the Potomac River, past the White House, to the Capitol—each person walking with a candle and a plaque bearing the name of a soldier killed or a town destroyed in Vietnam. In July 1972, two thousand women and children held hands in the rain to form a "Ring around the Congress."

In countless towns, concerned citizens fasted, held vigils, engaged in sit-ins, die-ins, public prayer and song, acted in street theater, or displayed banners and bumper stickers. Innumerable college campuses were dotted with symbolic crosses placed there by students, who also held vigils. A stream of activists journeyed to South and North Vietnam, in large measure as a witness to their solidarity with the people there. At least three Americans immolated themselves in mute testimony to the war's intolerable agony. Such acts of moral witness were responses to inner need for many people, and they also helped to legitimate protest and shape the nation's ethical agenda.

It was one thing to address public opinion, quite another to direct it to specific outcomes. Political activists engaged in lobbying and legislative work and in electoral campaigns. Overwhelmingly, political protest took place on the local level—in churches, legislative districts, city precincts, labor unions, and campuses; where people worshiped, worked, or just talked. Activism enlisted students and faculty, businessmen and labor unions, mothers and neighbors, clergy, and people in advertising and entertainment. Politics engaged people locally in the off-year elections of 1966 and 1970, and it acquired a national focus in the 1968 McCarthy and Kennedy races and the 1972 McGovern campaign. Those campaigns enlisted and trained many peace advocates who applied their organizing skills to antiwar protest, focusing ever

V

more on the Congress. Reviewing the movement's record in 1972, leading activists concluded that nonviolent direct action should have been conducted all along with a clearer, more intentional sense of its political impact. From that time on, they sought to coordinate public actions with congressional lobbying efforts—to set a specific date for withdrawal, to stop the air war, and to stop military funding for South Vietnam.

Conscientious objection to war and military service predated the Vietnam War, of course, but for the first time it was complemented by a highly organized network of young draft resisters and adult supporters. The motives of conscientious objectors (COs) ranged from personal ambition and security to principled opposition to the war or militarism itself. Whatever their motivation, a sizable number of men concluded that this war at least had no claim on them. That position (in contrast to the rejection of all warfare) was selective conscientious objection, and although it was not sanctioned under U.S. law, it gained increasing support from major religious bodies. The legal basis for objection was broadened by court decisions from religious training to religious or ethical principle.

About 170,000 persons won CO deferments and another 300,000 were denied. Perhaps 600,000 evaded the draft (some of whom had been denied as COs), of whom as many as one-sixth went underground or fled the country. The number of men claiming CO deferment increased dramatically as the war wore on, notably in the military itself, where some 17,000 applied for CO status, initially against heavy odds but after 1971 with greater facility.

Counseling services for COs expanded enormously as draft calls increased. Often sponsored by pacifist organizations such as the FOR, AFSC, and Catholic Peace Fellowship or by churches, counseling brought sympathetic lawyers, ministers, and other citizens to the movement. An extensive program was developed, for example, by WSP women who understood the advantage of associating motherly figures with conscientious objectors. On a national level, counseling was coordinated especially by the Central Committee for Conscientious Objectors and by the National Service Board for Religious Objectors. The draft was abandoned in 1971, not only for political reasons and internal mismanagement but also because of broad civilian resistance to it.

Opposition to military conscription or service moved beyond the provisions of the system to draft resistance. Not only did the draft symbolize the war, it also epitomized injustice because it was weighted disproportionately against black, poor, and less-educated men. As independent "We Won't Go" groups were organized across the country in 1966, a December conference of five hundred activists adopted draft resistance as a basic antiwar strategy. This was endorsed by the national convention of SDS two weeks later, and then by the more representative SMC.

The organization of draft resistance increased the weight of radical pacifists in the antiwar movement and added men for whom even avoiding conscription could be interpreted as antiwar activism. It also generated a constituency of supporters. Thus, when David Harris and Lennie Heller initiated a national campaign to turn in draft cards on October 16, 1964, prominent men over draft age and also women made themselves complicit with eligible draftees by signing "A Call to Resist Illegitimate Authority." People in Canada and elsewhere activated their opposition to the war by providing sanctuary to U.S. draft resisters.

A related movement was war resistance from within the military, notably after Nixon's Vietnamization policy undercut any remaining sense of mission in waging (or risking) destruction. At one extreme, soldiers resisted military authority in response to battlefield conditions by tripping on drugs, refusing orders, and even killing their own officers. Those actions accompanied a widespread collapse of morale and discipline. Entwined with them were nonviolent actions directed against the war itself or service in it—desertion, sabotage, strikes, public protest, lawsuits, and explicit support for home front protests. Military war resistance began in 1965, became highly organized in 1967, and escalated after the 1968 Tet offensive. Active-duty personnel worked with the civilian opposition, and they fed into veterans groups like the VVAW. Antiwar veterans contributed to the movement's self-discipline and public legitimacy, while the collapse of military discipline and morale served to further connect the war with social chaos.

Elements of the counterculture attached cultural nonconformity to the antiwar movement by late 1966. Characteristically associated with "hippie" appearance, drug use, sexual permissiveness, and experiments in communal living, nonconformity was interpreted as protest by its advocates. For some it was a search for an alternative, authentic lifestyle. For others it mocked the absurdity of the war with its own theater of the absurd, as when Jerry Rubin and Abbie Hoffman got news media attention by coopting the hippie image for their own Yippie style of protest. Many activists objected that provocative cultural nonconformity trivialized both the war and opposition to it, pushing the movement toward the margin of society.

Civil disobedience punishable under law was undertaken by numerous citizens for whom moral witness was not enough. There were sit-ins at the Capitol and the Pentagon, for example, troop trains were challenged bodily, induction centers were blocked, and draft cards were burned in public. Pouring blood on seized draft files, or burning them, won prison terms for Catholic priests Daniel and Philip Berrigan and for some of those who joined or emulated them, but their acts also brought the government's case into court. Protesters employing civil disobedience accepted legal judgment by way of distinguishing the authority of law itself, which they accepted, from the authority of specific laws to which they objected. Collective civil disobedience was occasionally interpreted (most articulately by David Dellinger) as a form of militant resistance to illegitimate authority, as in the 1967 march on the Pentagon or the 1971 Maydays attempt to shut down Washington. The difficulty was twofold: such actions alienated citizens who opposed the war but valued law and order, and they courted violence at the hands of prowar citizens or local police forces.

In addition to those risking violence, there were some protesters who employed it. The scale ranged from harassing presidents and government officials to burning and bombing. The use of violence occurred mostly during the Nixon administration and mainly at the fringe of the organized movement or beyond it. Although understandable as an expression of frustration in the face of intransigent authority, violence was (and was widely recognized to be) counterproductive to the central objective of mobilizing popular opposition to the war in Vietnam. In retrospect, the organized movement was much more the victim than the perpetrator of illegal harassment and violence. Most important, though not fully recognized, was the wide range of nonviolent activism employed and institutionalized in opposition to the war in Vietnam.

Charles Chatfield

References

Baskir, Lawrence M., and William A. Strauss. *Chance and Circumstance: The Draft, the War and the Vietnam Generation.* New York: Vintage, 1978.

Cortright, David. *Soldiers in Revolt: The American Military Today.* Garden City, N.Y.: Anchor Press/Doubleday, 1975.

DeBenedetti, Charles, with Charles Chatfield. *An American Ordeal: The Antiwar Movement of the Vietnam Era.* Syracuse, N.Y.: Syracuse University Press, 1990.

Hall, Mitchell K. *Because of Their Faith: CALCAV and Religious Opposition to the Vietnam War.* New York: Columbia University Press, 1990.

Lynd, Staughton, and Michael Ferber. *The Resistance.* Boston: Beacon, 1970.

Small, Melvin. *Johnson, Nixon and the Doves.* New Brunswick, N.J.: Rutgers University Press, 1988.

Small, Melvin, and William D. Hoover. *Give Peace a Chance: Exploring the Vietnam Antiwar Movement.* Syracuse, N.Y.: Syracuse University Press, 1992.

Tollefson, James W. *The Strength Not to Fight.* Boston: Little, Brown, 1993.

Wells, Tom. *The War Within: America's Battle over Vietnam.* Berkeley: University of California Press, 1994.

Zaroulis, Nancy, and Gerald Sullivan. *Who Spoke Up? American Protest against the War in Vietnam, 1963–1975.* Garden City, N.Y.: Doubleday, 1984.

See also AMERICAN FRIENDS SERVICE COMMITTEE; CATONSVILLE NINE, 1968; CIVIL DISOBEDIENCE; CIVIL RIGHTS MOVEMENT; COMMITTEE FOR NONVIOLENT ACTION; FELLOWSHIP OF RECONCILIATION, INTERNATIONAL; KING, MARTIN LUTHER, JR.; MUSTE, ABRAHAM JOHN; SANE; SUICIDE, PROTEST; TEACH-IN; WAR TAX RESISTANCE; WOMEN STRIKE FOR PEACE

Vigil

Gathering of people in a particular (usually public) place for an extended period of time to express a particular position and publicize it to a wide audience. Vigils attempt to effect change by publicizing a cause and by appealing to opponents and third parties to support that cause. The vigil is distinguished from a "picket" in that a vigil is maintained over a longer period of time and is more somber in character. Sometimes a vigil is maintained night and day, resulting in a loss of sleep among participants. This method is often undertaken by a religious group and may be accompanied by prayer.

In 1917, Dutch women maintained a vigil lasting for weeks outside the building where legislators were drafting a new constitution for the Netherlands, calling attention to their request that the constitution include suffrage for women. Women's suffrage was not included in the new constitution but was chosen as an issue that could be decided by a simple majority vote of the legislature. Another example occurred when activists protesting against germ warfare research launched a silent "Appeal and Vigil" outside the germ warfare plant at Fort Detrick in Frederick, Maryland. The vigil began on July 1, 1959, and was maintained for an entire year.

References

Sharp, Gene. *The Politics of Nonviolent Action*. Boston: Porter Sargent, 1973.

See also PICKETING

Voluntary Servitude, Discourse on (*Discours de la Servitude Volontaire*)

Written in the sixteenth century by Etienne de La Boétie, constitutes a foundational text for a historically coherent discourse of nonviolent resistance to forms of political oppression. This early text contained the seeds of a radical theory of power, the state, and nonviolent resistance, influencing insurgents, revolutionaries, and theorists into the twentieth century.

The period in which the *Discours* was written was marked by the painful formation of strong sovereign states in Europe. France, La Boétie's home, was racked by political and religious conflict. In this context, the nature of the state, of power, and of the individual subject were crucial questions. How might tyranny come about, and how should it be confronted?

The way La Boétie addressed the question was unusual, and in advance of his time, in two respects. First, he argued in universal terms about natural desires for, and rights to, freedom. Second, he discussed the nature of the power of the tyrannical state. La Boétie's radical theory was that power over subjects can be maintained through indoctrination, extended patronage, and mystification. But the foundation of power was the freely given consent and the voluntary yet unnatural obedience of the people to their rulers. It followed that tyranny could be brought down not by physical force, but by the removal of the base of the colossus. In short, by disobedience and withdrawal of consent. In this way La Boétie's *Discours* can be seen as the mirror-image of Machiavelli's *Prince*: the latter advises the prince how to induce subjection, the former offers to the subject the potential for subversion.

Whatever the motives or intentions behind it, the text has been read and applied by political resisters of various kinds over the centuries. Two years after the Saint Bartholomew massacre of 1572, part of the text was published by the Huguenots in *Le Réveil Matin des Français et de leurs voisins* (The Awakening of the French and Their Neighbors), a pamphlet attacking the monarchy and appealing directly to the people of Europe. More of it appeared in another Huguenot work in 1576 (1577, 1578), where it acquired the title *Contr'un* (Against One). During the subsequent period of absolutist rule the text became invisible, but resurfaced during the nineteenth and twentieth centuries at moments of revolution or crisis in different parts of Europe.

In 1789, at the outbreak of the French Revolution, a publication attacking the monarchy includes the *Discours* in updated French. Another similar tract appeared in 1790, *L'Ami de la Révolution* (The Friend of the Revolution), and in 1792 Marat brought out his *Chaînes de l'esclavage* (Chains of Slavery) with entire pages that look as if they are lifted from La Boétie. The *Discours* was again adopted and republished by opponents of the coup of Louis-Napoleon Bonaparte in 1852 in a collection entitled *Tyrannie, usurpation et servitude volontaire* (Tyranny, usurpation and voluntary servitude). An Italian translation *(Il Contr'Uno)* was published in 1864 during the process of the political transformation of Venice and Rome. In 1905, Tolstoy published a bitter pamphlet against the czar *(The One Thing Needful)*, which uses La Boétie extensively. In 1934, a German translation appeared one year after Hitler's seizure of power and abolition of political rights. In 1942, the English translation, *Anti-Dictator,* appeared, with headings referring to Hitler and Mussolini. It was read by the translator over shortwave broadcasts to occupied France. In 1944, the nineteenth-century Italian version reappeared, playing a part in the downfall of Mussolini. The numerous retranslations from the early 1960s to the early 1970s in English, Russian, and German suggest that the cold war stimulated interest in the *Discours.* It is also possible that the work was one of a number of sources inspiring Eastern and Central European dissidents in the final stages of the Soviet empire.

The *Discours* was thus an instrument in nonviolent resistance, serving as a vehicle for debate and as a means of rallying opponents of oppressive regimes. In addition, it fed political theorizing, since its abstract formulations could easily be extended. In particular it nourished anarchist theories of resistance to the state. For example, the German anarcho-syndicalist Gustav Landauer, a victim of the 1919 Munich uprising, expounded the *Discours* in his book *Revolution.* The text also has provided stimulus for the development of ideas on the philosophy and strategy of nonviolent resistance, whether anarchist or not. One of the most significant networks of influence to which it gave rise involved Tolstoy, Gandhi, and perhaps Thoreau. Tolstoy certainly read and reread La Boétie, and he quotes him at length in *The Law of Love and the Law of Violence,* which Gandhi knew. Thoreau's "Civil Disobedience" was known to both Tolstoy and to Gandhi, and La Boétie's work was known to Thoreau. Tolstoy's "Letter to a Hindu" (December 14, 1908) does not mention the *Discours* explicitly, but it does clearly echo its sense. These connections point to the existence of a continuous body of ideas, values, and strategies consistently developed by theorists and practitioners.

Paul A. Chilton

References

La Boétie, Etienne de. *The Politics of Obedience: The Discourse of Voluntary Servitude (De la servitude volontaire).* Introduction by Murray M. Rothbard. Translated by Harry Kurz. Montreal: Black Rose, 1975.

See also LA BOÉTIE, ETIENNE DE; SOCIAL POWER

Voyages, Protest

Naval interventions made to protest and interfere with such activities as governments' tests of nuclear weapons and environmental destruction. Beginning in the late 1950s, protest voyages have made a significant contribution to the nonviolent direct action arm of the peace and ecology movements in the United States. These voyages may be grouped into two parts: (1) protest voyages in opposition to the institution of war focusing particularly on the issue of nuclear weapons testing, beginning in 1957, and (2) protest voyages with a focus on preserving the environment and aimed at policies and practices of governments and business corporations, beginning in 1971.

The first such voyage, the *Golden Rule* project, was organized by the Committee for Nonviolent Action (CNVA), which brought together major pacifist groups including the War Resisters League, Fellowship of Reconciliation, and Quaker-related groups, such as the American Friends Service Committee. CNVA, an activist organization without formal membership, sought to undertake major nonviolent direct action campaigns with support from the pacifist and peace community. Many of the founders, including Lawrence Scott, A.J. Muste, Bayard Rustin, and Bradford Lyttle, were committed to a vision of the radical pacifist community. They were involved in various movements, such as the antidraft, ban the bomb, and civil rights movements, and actively explored nonviolent direct action as an expression of a pacifist alternative to the violence characterizing contemporary social, political, and economic institutions.

The *Golden Rule* protest voyage grew out of two small direct action projects organized by CNVA in the summer and fall of 1957. These were a weekend seminar, workshop, and civil disobedience action at Mercury Flats, Nevada, followed by a Thanksgiving Day prayer vigil in Washington, D.C. These two small events received little public attention, but generated new spirit and creative energy in the committee. The voyage of *Golden Rule* was born out of this ferment.

U.S. Peace Groups and Antinuclear Voyages

The *Golden Rule* sailed from the Los Angeles area in January 1958. When the yacht docked in Honolulu the crew was served an injunction by the federal marshal forbidding the crew to sail the ship into the bomb test area. The crew

The Golden Rule, *attempting to sail into the nuclear test zone, is intercepted by the U.S. Coast Guard a few miles outside Honolulu harbor, June 4, 1958. Honolulu Star-Bulletin.*

petitioned the U.S. District Court to lift the injunction, then appealed to the U.S. circuit court, which upheld the injunction. The crew immediately set sail for the test area. A few miles out of Honolulu harbor the U.S. Coast Guard intercepted *Golden Rule,* arrested the crew, and ordered it to turn back. The crew members were imprisoned and served out sixty-day sentences.

During the court hearings related to the injunction against *Golden Rule,* the yacht *Phoenix,* captained by Earle Reynolds and crewed by the Reynolds family and a Japanese citizen, sailed into Honolulu on the last leg of a world cruise. Its destination was Hiroshima, where Earle previously had worked for the Atomic Bomb Casualty Committee, an agency of the U.S. government. The Reynolds family, which had earlier offered to continue the protest voy-

age if the crew of *Golden Rule* was imprisoned, proceeded to sail *Phoenix* out of Honolulu. The *Phoenix* was intercepted on the high seas by a U.S. naval ship and escorted to Kwajalein. Earle Reynolds was arrested and flown back to Honolulu to be tried for violation of the regulation closing off the bomb test area to general maritime traffic.

These dramatic attempts to thwart the U.S. government program of nuclear tests succeeded in crystallizing considerable support for nuclear arms opponents in the U.S. and abroad. The drama of tiny unarmed sailboats challenging the might of the U.S. government, and the obvious courage and sincerity of their crews, touched many people. CNVA and many other peace groups such as the American Friends Service Committee and Committee for a Sane

Nuclear Policy mounted support demonstrations, resulting in considerable news coverage and public discussion.

The protest voyages of *Golden Rule* and *Phoenix* were the model for a continuing series of protest voyages against nuclear bomb tests and the institutions of war. In 1962, the *Everyman I* attempted to sail from San Francisco into the Pacific bomb test area. It was intercepted by the Coast Guard and the crew imprisoned. The voyage of *Everyman II* (1962) later that year, which sought to sail from Honolulu into the test area, was also intercepted by the Coast Guard.

The voyage of *Everyman III* (1962), which sailed from England to Leningrad harbor under command of Earle Reynolds, protested all nuclear bomb tests, including those of the USSR. The crew was met by Soviet authorities, who requested they leave. When the crew did not leave Leningrad, Soviet authorities attempted to tow the ship out to sea. The crew attempted to scuttle the ship but were stopped by the Soviets, and the ship was towed back into port where it was repaired by the Soviets. *Everyman III* then sailed back to England.

In 1969, the *Phoenix* sailed from Nagasaki, Japan, to Shanghai, China, under the command of Earle Reynolds with an American crew. It was conceived of as a voyage of friendship from the people of the United States to the people of China, but was denied entry into Shanghai by a Chinese naval patrol.

The voyage of *Mon Civitan* (1969) was commanded by Scott Herrick with a crew from the United States and was sponsored by the War Resisters League of the United States. This trip defied the U.S. economic and political sanctions against Cuba. It also was conceived of as a people-to-people goodwill trip that brought artwork from the children of the United States to the children of Cuba to initiate an exchange program. It received limited reception by Cuban authorities.

As the United States became more deeply involved in the Vietnam War in the 1960s, the pacifist wing of the peace movement, increasingly dissatisfied with the position of much of the peace movement in the United States, sought to present a nonviolent approach to peacemaking under the sponsorship of A Quaker Action Group, founded in 1966 by several Quakers, many of whom were deeply involved in the protest voyages of the Committee for Nonviolent Action in previous years. Under the command of Earle Reynolds and with an international crew, the yacht *Phoenix* undertook a voyage to North Vietnam, carrying a cargo of medical supplies as a gesture of friendship and remorse from the people of the United States. The U.S. Navy, although patrolling the seas around Vietnam, did not stop the voyage. The crew were received by North Vietnamese authorities in Hanoi. When the *Phoenix*, commanded by Robert Eaton, later attempted a similar voyage to South Vietnam, it was turned back by the Saigon government.

Greenpeace, Ecology, and Antinuclear Testing Voyages

The second series of protest voyages grew out of the Greenpeace conservation movement, which began as a small organization committed to protecting the environment and grew into an international body with groups active in many countries. Although many of Greenpeace's actions targeted nuclear weapons testing, its motivating perspective on the environmental consequences of nuclear arms distinguished the organization from earlier pacifist groups like CNVA. Greenpeace contributed a significant direct action component to the conservation movement. In September 1971, the *Phyllis Cormack* sailed from Vancouver, Canada, bound for Amchitka Island in the North Pacific to protest a U.S. nuclear test in a wildlife sanctuary. The test was completed before the ship arrived, but the public response to the protest led the United States to abandon further tests in the area.

In April 1972, the *Vega* sailed from Auckland, New Zealand, for Moruroa Atoll in the South Pacific to protest French tests in which nuclear bombs are dropped from balloons. The yacht was rammed by a French minesweeper on the high seas and had to be towed to harbor for repairs. *Vega* undertook a second voyage against French atmospheric tests, this time accompanied by the yachts *Fri* and *Spirit of Peace* and a New Zealand Navy ship, *Otago*. At the end of the bomb test series the crew of *Vega* were brutally beaten by French commandos dispatched from the French warship monitoring the scene. The ensuing world headlines and the New Zealand government's lawsuit against the French government led France to abandon atmospheric tests on the atoll and to test weapons underground instead.

As the ecology movement gained popularity through the 1970s, small groups of activists formed into a loose coalition under Greenpeace,

V

with many undertaking campaigns focusing on other conservation issues, such as the antisealing campaign on the Labrador ice pack. Greenpeace activities developed the human barrier technique in which crews in inflatable speedboats placed themselves between the whales and the harpoons of Soviet whaling fleets off the coast of California.

The purchase of *Rainbow Warrior,* a 160-foot North Sea fisheries research vessel, by Greenpeace Europe in 1977 was a major development of the direct action arm of the ecology conservation movement. *Rainbow Warrior* became the flag ship of a fleet that eventually included the trawler *Cedarlea,* a pilot boat *Sirius,* the riverboat *Belugam,* and the tug *Greenpeace.*

The epic of *Rainbow Warrior* included campaigns against whaling by Iceland, Peru, Spain, and the Soviet Union and against British dumping of radioactive wastes into the ocean. In 1985 *Rainbow Warrior* set off on a year-long voyage in the Pacific to evacuate over three hundred Marshall Islanders from Rongelap Atoll, people still suffering from fallout from U.S. nuclear tests thirty-one years earlier. In July, the *Rainbow Warrior* stopped in Auckland, New Zealand, in preparation for a voyage involving several vessels to protest (and disrupt if possible) French tests of a neutron bomb. While in the harbor, the *Rainbow Warrior* was sunk by an explosion. A crewman, Fernando Pereira, was drowned. The French government later admitted that members of its secret service had planted the bombs.

Reflecting on the thirty years of experience with protest voyages as an instrument of nonviolent direct action undertaken by both peace and conservation groups, what has been accomplished? First, the protest voyages brought into the peace and conservation movements a new sense of power and excitement and a challenge and opportunity to people to take direct action to bring about desired change. Second, the voyages often touched the hearts of people in many countries who were becoming increasingly uncomfortable with nuclear testing and the destruction of the environment. The widespread public support they sparked could not be ignored by governments. Third, CNVA and Greenpeace demonstrated their abilities to plan and carry out creditable campaigns of nonviolent action that often called for highly skilled participants and involved considerable risk to life. Fourth, CNVA and Greenpeace showed an ability to work in cooperation with other groups to achieve commonly shared goals, demonstrating the importance of direct action in supporting more conventional political action. Finally, the protest voyages increased working contacts and cooperation among peace and conservation groups around the world, thus strengthening the basis for truly international or worldwide movements for peace and conservation.

George Willoughby

References
Bigelow, Albert. *The Voyage of the Golden Rule.* New York: Doubleday, 1959.
Cooney, Robert, and Helen Michalowski, eds. *The Power of the People: Active Nonviolence in the United States.* From an original text by Marty Jezer. Culver City, Calif.: Peace Press, 1977; 2nd ed. Philadelphia: New Society, 1987.
Reynolds, Earle. *The Forbidden Voyage.* New York: McKay, 1961.
Robie, David. *Eyes of Fire: The Last Voyage of Rainbow Warrior.* Philadelphia: New Society, 1987.

See also BIGELOW, ALBERT SMITH; ENVIRONMENTAL MOVEMENTS; GREENPEACE; NUCLEAR WEAPONS OPPOSITION; *RAINBOW WARRIOR*

Vykom Campaign (India), 1924–1925

Sixteen-month-long anti-untouchability satyagraha campaign in the state of Travancore led by local members of the Indian National Congress. While the immediate objective was to open roads to the Vykom orthodox Hindu temple for use by "untouchables" (members of the lowest Hindu class), the long-range goal of the campaign was to publicize the issue and win civil rights for untouchables. Satyagrahis organized processions and vigils along a portion of a road closed to untouchables.

The Anti-Untouchability Committee of the Indian National Congress organized a satyagraha campaign that began on March 30, 1924. Despite a prohibitory order by the district magistrate, for several days volunteers attempted to walk on the road and were arrested and sentenced to prison. On April 10, police constructed a barricade and began to use violent repression against the satyagrahis. The satyagrahis then altered their strategy and maintained a vigil at the barricade, maintaining their nonviolent discipline despite violent repression by police. The satyagrahis continued to maintain the vigil during monsoon season, sometimes standing in water up to their shoulders. This stalemate lasted until the spring of 1925, when Mohandas Gandhi entered the conflict and persuaded police to remove the barricades. Although the barricades were disassembled in April 1925, the satyagrahis refused to cross the line into previously banned territory until local high-caste Brahmans had been converted to the cause of anti-untouchability. Whether they converted is debatable, but the campaign was called off in November 1925.

The success of the campaign is hard to gauge. The untouchables were granted access to three of four roads around the temple, volunteers remained totally nonviolent (as opposed to previous satyagraha campaigns), and the cause of anti-untouchability gained widespread support. But the intended conversion of Indian society, and specifically the higher Hindu classes, was not attained.

Brad Bennett

References

Bondurant, Joan V. *Conquest of Violence: The Gandhian Philosophy of Conflict.* Princeton: Princeton University Press, 1958, 1988.

Ravindran, Dr. T.K. *Vaikkam Satyagraha and Gandhi.* Trichur: Sri Narayana Institute of Social and Cultural Development, 1975.

See also GANDHI, MOHANDAS KARAMCHAND; SATYAGRAHA

W

Walesa, Lech (b. 1943)

Born on September 29, 1943, in Popowo, Po-land, Walesa became internationally known as the leader of the labor organization Solidarity through the 1980s. He was awarded the Nobel Peace Prize in 1983; he chose not to accept it in person because of his concern that the Polish government would not allow him to return, sending instead his wife and son. In 1990, Walesa became Poland's first non-Communist president since World War II.

Walesa was trained as an electrician and began working at the Lenin Shipyards in Gdansk, Poland, in 1966. Dismissed in 1976 because of his organizing activities as a shop steward during the political upheavals of the early 1970s, he continued to work at temporary jobs and remained active on labor issues.

When labor protests erupted in the summer of 1980 Walesa was thrust into the leadership of Solidarity, with his proposal that workers occupy the shipyards. He was the key negotiator in the agreement of August 31, 1980, that won labor the right to organize and strike. Following the imposition of martial law in December 1981, Walesa was arrested and detained, along with most of the Solidarity leadership.

Through the 1980s, while Solidarity was illegal and operated largely underground, Walesa remained a quiet but continuous leadership presence. When he was awarded the Nobel Prize in 1983, he had been out of jail for only a few months. He accepted the prize in the name of Solidarity, saying, in part, "When I recall my own path of life I cannot but speak of the violence, hatred and lies. A lesson drawn from such experiences, however, was that we can effectively oppose violence only if we ourselves do not resort to it."

Lech Walesa, 1983. AP/Wide World Photos.

In 1989 the union was made legal again and the government authorities entered negotiations for political reform, and ultimately elections and power sharing, with Walesa. In 1990, after a year of a Solidarity-led coalition government, Walesa was elected president.

Irwin Abrams

References

Walesa, Lech. *A Way of Life: An Autobiography*. New York: Holt, 1987.

See also NOBEL PEACE PRIZE; SOLIDARITY (POLAND)

War Resisters' International

International antiwar organization with members and affiliates in over thirty countries. Headquartered in London, War Resisters' International (WRI) copublishes the monthly *Peace News* in English and an internal bulletin, *The Broken Rifle* (in English, French, German, and Spanish).

Founded in 1921, WRI adopted the broken rifle as its symbol and a founding declaration that has remained unchanged: "War is a crime against humanity. I am therefore determined not to support any kind of war and to strive for the removal of all causes of war." Many of its founders had been involved in the resistance to the First World War: its first secretary, Herbert Runham Brown, had spent two and a half years in a British prison as a conscientious objector. Witnessing the collapse of the policy of "an international general strike against war" (adopted by the Socialist International), they decided to launch an antimilitarist international. Two years later, in 1923, John Haynes Holmes, Jessie Wallace Hughan, Tracy Mygatt, and Frances Witherspoon founded the War Resisters League in the United States.

WRI members refuse to support war or preparations for war. Their conscientious objection to war takes various forms. Some refuse to engage in military service. Others refuse to pay taxes that support the military. Still others refuse to work for military contracters. WRI has been involved in movements that have transformed these individual acts of personal witness into collective acts of noncooperation, such as draft card burnings in the United States during the Vietnam War. Each year on December 1, Prisoners for Peace Day, WRI produces an Honor Roll of those imprisoned for nonviolent action against war preparations.

If the name gives an image of a network mainly of young men resisting military service, the reality is much more varied. WRI cuts across age groups, drawing on the experience of several generations of organizers of nonviolent action and from a variety of cultures. In addition, it has organized four international women's conferences and has an active Women's Working Group.

WRI members also are fundamentally committed to promoting nonviolent action as a form of social struggle. WRI has provided training in nonviolence, held international conferences on themes such as "Nonviolent Struggle and Social Defense" and "Feminism and Nonviolence," and organized nonviolent action campaigns.

Within the WRI network, from the Dutch anarchist Bart de Ligt and the U.S. Quaker Richard Gregg onward, there have always been many people interested in nonviolent struggle as a means of social change. This, together with the organization's analysis that the injustice of colonialism was a cause of war, led to a keen interest in the Indian independence struggle and, later, close working relationships with sections of the Gandhian movement.

Peak periods of activity in WRI occurred in the 1930s, the 1960s (with the first wave of antinuclear campaigning, the U.S. civil rights movement, and the international anti–Vietnam War movement), and the 1980s. In the 1930s and 1940s, WRI helped to rescue people from persecution under Franco and under the Nazis and found them safe homes with WRI members in other countries. Under Nazi occupation, Dutch, Danish, and Norwegian members of WRI played prominent roles in organizing nonviolent resistance to frustrate the occupiers' plans and to deny them the fruits of their aggression.

During the cold war, WRI consistently sought out war resisters in the Soviet bloc: first individuals, and later groups. After the 1968 invasion of Czechoslovakia, WRI organized protest demonstrations in four Warsaw Pact capitals. In the 1980s, it adopted the idea of personal peace treaties: peace activists from the Eastern and Western blocs declared their loyalty to the values they held in common and not to the machinery of state and military that divided them; they then vowed to support each other in their struggle against the militarism of their respective blocs. Other actions were less public, such as private visits where material or information was smuggled in or out of a country.

There also have been many testing times for WRI. During the Spanish Civil War, the Second World War, the Vietnam War, and the wars in the Balkans in the 1990s, peace movements have found themselves divided. Faced by what they see as a defensive war against a brutal aggressor, many individuals have questioned their commitment not to support any kind of war.

WRI has tried to develop nonviolent strategies for effective action in such situations, trying to pose another way, an alternative between submission and taking up arms, and to find means of breaking the cycle of war and violence. In 1971, when Pakistani troops were blockading what was then East Pakistan, WRI launched Operation Omega to Bangladesh, a nonviolent direct action project to take in relief supplies. More recently, the International Deserters Network associated with WRI has offered support for people resisting the Gulf War of 1991 and, on a much larger scale, the wars in the Balkans. Currently, WRI is engaged with several other peace organizations in an experiment in international nonviolent intervention, the Balkan Peace Team, working for human rights and in support of civil society initiatives in nonviolent conflict resolution.

Howard Clark

References

Nonviolent Activist. Serial: War Resisters League, 339 Lafayette Street, New York, NY 10012, U.S.A.

Peace News. Serial: War Resisters' International, 5 Caledonian Road, London N1 9DX, England.

The Broken Rifle. Serial: War Resisters' International, 5 Caledonian Road, London N1 9DX, England.

WRI Women. Serial: War Resisters' International, 5 Caledonian Road, London N1 9DX, England.

See also CONSCIENTIOUS OBJECTION; DE LIGT, BARTHÉLEMY; GREGG, RICHARD; NONVIOLENCE, PRINCIPLED; PACIFISM; PEACE BRIGADES INTERNATIONAL; WAR TAX RESISTANCE

War Tax Resistance

Refusal to pay taxes for wars or military preparation. For many resisters, the only difference between paying for war and physically participating in it is that the former is more convenient and less threatening. Paraphrasing A.J. Muste: in order to conduct a war or build a military, the government requires two chief resources—soldiers and money. In the United States, people are drafted through the Selective Service System, and money is drafted through the Internal Revenue Service (IRS). Consequently, like draft resistance, war tax resistance is one of the strongest and most dramatic nonviolent statements an individual can make.

Individual resistance to military taxation has probably been around as long as taxes have been levied for war. There are reports of collective tax refusal as far back as the second century A.D. in Egypt. The earliest-known instance of war tax refusal in America took place in 1637 when the relatively peaceable Algonquin Indians opposed taxation by the Dutch to help improve a local Dutch fort.

There has been individual tax resistance to most wars in the history of the United States, notably the Revolutionary War (by Quakers and other peace churches). Arguably, the most famous war tax resister in American history was Henry David Thoreau, who wrote his 1848 essay "On the Duty of Civil Disobedience" after being jailed for refusing to pay a poll tax as a protest to the Mexican–American War and slavery. The modern war tax resistance movement was born at the beginning of World War II and peaked during the Vietnam War with perhaps several hundred thousand people refusing to pay the federal excise tax on telephone service and tens of thousands refusing to pay some or all of their income tax. Folk singer Joan Baez gained considerable notoriety with her refusal to pay taxes that helped finance the Vietnam War.

People become war tax resisters for a variety of reasons. Some are motivated to act because of the nuclear war threat and the immoral misuse of government spending. However, most war tax resisters also do not believe that killing or threatening to kill is an acceptable way to solve social or political problems. Veteran war tax resister Wally Nelson once explained to a visiting IRS agent: "We don't intend to cooperate with the IRS in its attempts to make us pay for killing. What would you do if I came into your office tomorrow with a cup in my hand, asking for contributions to enable me to buy guns and kill a group of people I don't like?"

Historically, war tax resisters have been moved by strong religious convictions. With the onset of the Vietnam War, however, a significant number of war tax resisters were driven by political or secular beliefs to seek ways to reduce their complicity with the war. Another motivating factor is the desire to register a protest that cannot be ignored. These resisters do not simply strive for moral purity, but seek to confront the government with their opposition. Finally, most resisters want their tax money put to constructive use. Their nonpayment and redirection of taxes is a way to correct deficiencies in government spending.

Some resisters try to prevent every possible penny from going to the government, and thus to the military. One way to guarantee no money goes to the military is to live on an income that is below the taxable level. Others feel that the number of people resisting—and especially the act of resistance itself—is far more important than the absolute amount of money denied the military. Consequently, their strategy is to encourage resistance even if the amount of money resisted is not 100 percent of the federal tax due.

In the United States, the primary source of government funding for war is the individual income tax. Though this is not a direct war tax, resisters note the unusually high percentage of the income tax, between 50 and 60 percent, that goes for past and present military spending. Consequently, the income tax is the focal point for effective resistance to paying for war. However, the government raises money for war from several other sources: excise taxes (for example, on telephone service, tobacco, and alcohol), customs duties, estate taxes, and savings bonds.

The key to resistance is having the opportunity to resist. During World War II, the IRS established the payroll tax withholding system (by which taxes are removed from paychecks before employees are paid), making it easier to raise money and more difficult to resist. To circumvent this problem, the war tax resistance movement developed three primary approaches: finding work that does not have withholding (for example, as an independent contractor), claiming sufficient "allowances" on the IRS W-4 form to reduce withholding, and forming small employment agencies that have the legal responsibility to withhold taxes, but do not.

The main dangers of tax resistance are government sanctions. Usually, the unpaid tax is augmented with penalties and interest. The IRS strategy is not to haul war tax resisters into court but to frighten them into paying (mostly by sending threatening notices). Failing that, they seek to place liens on bank accounts and to garnish paychecks. In rare instances cars or homes have been seized and auctioned. Resisters have countered these tactics by keeping bank accounts far from where they live or work, in someone else's name, or living without them altogether. Working as an independent contractor minimizes the ability of the IRS to seize money from an employer. And putting the title to property in someone else's name means it cannot be seized. Perhaps the ultimate sanction is the threat of prosecution and jail. Yet, despite the thousands of Americans who have resisted war taxes since World War II, only a couple dozen have been prosecuted or jailed for that resistance.

Though it has the potential to bring a government to its knees with even a significant minority (a few percent) of people using it, war tax resistance is seen by most resisters as only one strategy among many—albeit, one that any government would find hard to ignore. The Gandhi-led Indian independence movement used the tactic of refusing to pay the British tax on salt as a way to shake the very foundation of colonial rule in 1930. More recently, the Palestinian village of Beit Sahour voted to withhold taxes from Israel in 1989, stating: "We will not finance the bullets that kill our children." The Israeli government retaliated by cutting telephone lines, seizing property, jailing citizens, and declaring the town a "closed military zone." Furthermore, a few people doing what is perceived as an extreme tactic can be a significant motivation for many others to take more moderate actions. And finally, resisters who redirect their resisted tax money to community and other nongovernment programs guarantee an effectiveness beyond that of resistance alone.

Ed Hedemann

References

Hedemann, Ed. *War Tax Resistance*. New York: War Resisters League, 1992.

See also CIVIL DISOBEDIENCE; CONSCIENTIOUS OBJECTION; METHODS OF NONVIOLENT ACTION

White Rose (Germany)

Group of underground Munich University students who published, distributed, and posted anti-Nazi leaflets and painted anti-Hitler graffiti in Munich and other cities in Germany and Austria during World War II. The group's members were considered among the first Germans to present a clear public case against German fascism. The activities of the White Rose group support the claim that nonviolent resistance occurs even in the most repressive regimes.

Beginning in May 1942, a group of Munich University students began to write, publish, and distribute anonymous anti-Nazi leaflets. They intended to launch a moral protest to arouse the German people. The core members were Hans and Sophie Scholl (brother and sister), Christoph Probst, Alexander Schmorell, and Willi Graf. The name they chose for the leaflets and their group was *Die Weisse Rose* (The White Rose). While the exact origins of the name are unknown, it is likely that it symbolized beauty and purity in opposition to the Nazi regime. During the summer of 1942, the White

Rose distributed four leaflets, randomly stuffing mailboxes throughout Munich. In November, the group increased their activities, soliciting financial support and beginning to organize resistance groups at other German universities.

On January 13, 1943, at an assembly arranged to warn students not to resist the regime, the Nazi Party leader for the District of Munich made indecent remarks in his speech that offended the audience, primarily female students. As students disrupted the speech with shuffling and whistling, a spontaneous demonstration erupted. Students poured out onto the street, marching and chanting for freedom. Riot police eventually broke up the demonstration. News of the demonstration set off smaller student protests in Frankfurt, the Ruhr, and Vienna, Austria.

Soon after the January demonstration, the White Rose published a fifth leaflet with the help of Professor Kurt Huber. They produced ten thousand copies, and, with the help of a network of students, distributed the leaflet in seven cities, including Ulm, Stuttgart, Berlin, and Salzburg, Austria. They mailed many of the leaflets from other cities so as to conceal their Munich operations. Students at other universities supported the White Rose's distribution network or began their own resistance activities. Schmorell, Graf, and Hans Scholl painted anti-Hitler graffiti on walls and pavement in Munich. Similar anonymous graffiti showed up in Berlin. About three thousand copies of the sixth, and final, White Rose leaflet were published and distributed in early February 1943.

The German Gestapo increased their investigation of the source of these leaflets. In the view of the Nazi leadership, public support for the war effort was absolutely necessary because the German Army was experiencing major setbacks (including the loss at Stalingrad in early February). To the regime, the students' resistance threatened their own propaganda campaign for public support. The Scholls were captured on February 18, while they were distributing leaflets on campus in Munich. Along with Probst, they were charged with high treason on February 21, and executed by guillotine on February 22. The other three members of the inner circle were caught and condemned to death on April 19. Schmorell and Huber were executed on July 13; Graf was killed on October 12. Throughout 1943, the Gestapo moved quickly to arrest and sentence student resisters.

The student resistance movement was systematically and effectively repressed following the breakup of the White Rose, but their activities had both symbolic and practical importance. Symbolically, that there was such resistance to Hitler's regime was a challenge to the Nazis and to all authoritarian regimes. Practically, the effects of the group's protest were widespread and long-lasting. Copies of the leaflets were smuggled into Switzerland, Norway, Sweden, and England, and British Royal Air Force planes dropped over a million copies of the sixth leaflet over Germany. In both parts of postwar Germany, commemorative stamps were issued, schools and streets were named after the people of the White Rose, and the anniversary of the initial executions was observed for years afterward.

Brad Bennett

References

Berenbaum, Michael, ed. *The World Must Know: The History of the Holocaust As Told in the United States Holocaust Memorial Museum.* Boston: Little, Brown, 1993.

Hanser, Richard. *A Noble Treason: The Revolt of the Munich Students against Hitler.* New York: G.P. Putnam's Sons, 1979.

See also DENMARK, EVACUATION OF DANISH JEWS, 1943; DENMARK, RESISTANCE TO NAZI OCCUPATION; FREEDOM COUNCIL; JAGERSTATTER, FRANZ; JEWISH RESISTANCE TO THE HOLOCAUST; LE CHAMBON SUR LIGNON, FRANCE; NAZISM, CIVILIAN RESISTANCE, 1939–1945; NORWAY, RESISTANCE TO GERMAN OCCUPATION, 1940–1945; ROSENSTRAβE PROTEST, 1943

Williams, Betty
See CORRIGAN, MAIREAD

Withdrawal, Symbolic
Several methods in which people express political objection or disapproval by withdrawing from specific usual behavior or by renouncing a specific honor. The withdrawal is either brief or limited, hence producing a symbolic noncooperation that is more akin to forms of protest than forms of noncooperation. The mechanism of change is one of ap-

peal rather than coercion or manipulation per se. If they are extended for longer periods of time or through a larger population, they will manifest noncooperation over and above protest and persuasion.

Some of the most common forms of symbolic withdrawal include "walk-outs," "corporate silence," "renouncing honors," and "turning one's back." A walk-out occurs when an individual or group expresses objection by physically walking out of a meeting, conference, or assembly before it has ended. For example, the chief of the German High Command, Wilhelm Keitel, walked out of conferences with Hitler twice during 1940. This type of political protest is very different than a "walk-out" by workers; because they are stopping work, their action functions as a strike. "Corporate silence" is most often used to express moral condemnation. It may be used exclusively or in combination with other methods such as marches or vigils. During one incident of the free speech dispute at the University of California at Berkeley in 1964, student demonstrators responded to hecklers with silence, and the hecklers left after forty-five minutes. Another method is one of renouncing special titles, medals, honorary offices, and memberships to show disapproval for a particular government or institution. This renunciation may be intended as a self-sacrifice, an appeal for others to follow suit, or an attempt to weaken the opponent's power base. It is usually enacted by an individual or small group, but if a mass of people withdraw from an organization, then this becomes a form of social or political noncooperation. During Korean national resistance to Japanese rule in 1919–1922, some Koreans renounced their Japanese-given titles of nobility. The last method of symbolic withdrawal consists of physically turning one's back (while sitting or standing) to the opponent or agents of the opponent. One example of this occurred immediately following the East German Uprising in June 1953. East Berlin workers who had been striking returned to the factories, but they refused to work. Instead, they stayed near their machines and turned their backs on Communist Party officials to show their opposition to Soviet domination.

References

Sharp, Gene. *The Politics of Nonviolent Action*. Boston: Porter Sargent, 1973.

See also MARCH FIRST INDEPENDENCE MOVEMENT, 1919

Witness for Peace

Interfaith movement of people from the United States working nonviolently in Latin America and the Caribbean to accompany those suffering from unjust U.S. military, economic, and social policies, and at home to change those policies.

In 1983, guerrillas armed and trained by the United States attacked civilian farms, roads, and individuals in Nicaragua. Nicaraguan church leaders called on their counterparts in the United States to come there to bear witness to the violence in the war zones and go back to the United States to end government support for the "contra" guerrillas. Witness for Peace formed in response to that call and has remained in Nicaragua ever since, expanding in recent years to other countries in the region.

In October 1983, a team of volunteers trained in nonviolence were placed in the besieged town of Jalapa in the belief that the contras would not attack and risk harming citizens of the country that was their chief sponsor. Beginning in December 1983, delegations of eight to twenty volunteers came to Jalapa, and eventually dozens of threatened communities, for two-week visits.

During their stays they met with victims of the war and with civic, religious, and political leaders, both as gestures of solidarity and compassion and in order to bring their stories back to the policy debate in the United States. They shared worship, danger, and hardship and frequently helped rebuild damaged schools and clinics or plant crops in burned-out fields. They documented and brought home the stories of rape and murder by contras, stories that were, at the time, rarely told in the U.S. news media.

For the next seven years witnesses were very active in protests, lobbying, news media work, civil disobedience, and other grassroots efforts to stop a war that would eventually claim more than thirty thousand Nicaraguan lives. Witness for Peace also helped organize Pledge of Resistance. Seventy thousand people signed the pledge, which was designed to deter a U.S. invasion or further aggression in Central America with a promise of massive nonviolent resistance. Witness for Peace and other organizations in the Central America movement helped bring about an eventual end to military aid to the contras in 1988.

Witness for Peace teams and delegates frequently undertook risky nonviolent actions. In 1984, a delegation on a small shrimp boat confronted a U.S. destroyer off the coast of Corinto. A 1985 Peace Flotilla on the Nicaragua–Costa Rica border resulted in the abduction of twenty-nine witnesses by contras. Witnesses accompanied medical and pastoral workers under death threats, and regularly held marches and vigils at the site of contra massacres, vowing not to forget.

After the contra war ended, following Nicaragua's 1990 elections, Witness for Peace continued its program there and expanded to include Guatemala, southern Mexico, and eventually Haiti. In Guatemala in 1990, Witness for Peace began a nonviolent presence in Santiago Atitlan at the request of that community, which had waged a successful campaign to expel the army after a massacre in the town. Witnesses in Mexico and Guatemala continue to accompany refugees returning home after ten years in exile.

Nearly four thousand people have been part of short-term delegations in the first ten years. As it begins work in other parts of the Americas, Witness for Peace seeks to apply its three founding principles—faith-based, political independence, and nonviolence—in differing contexts.

Ed Griffin-Nolan

References

Griffin-Nolan, Ed. *Witness for Peace: A Story of Resistance.* Louisville, Ky.: Westminster/John Knox, 1991.

See also NICARAGUA, NONVIOLENCE AND REVOLUTION; SANCTUARY MOVEMENT

Women and Nonviolent Action in the United States since 1950

Process of participation and engagement by which women both struggled to define a contemporary meaning for nonviolent action and contributed substantially to various movements' successes. The changes in U.S. society following World War II, particularly the renewed "traditionalism" regarding women's roles, tended to cut women off from the long history of women's nonviolent action in the United States. As a result, over the subsequent five decades women nonviolent activists had to overcome spiritual, political, and gendered isolation inside of social change movements, as well as within the broader society. In time, the key feminist insights about hierarchy, patriarchy, and the power of nonviolent action informed the new social action movements of the 1990s.

Although many women continued to be active in nonviolent movements for social change after World War II, the dampening effects of the antifeminist backlash, concurrent with the antiradical McCarthy era of the 1950s, left most women activists relatively isolated from the majority of women and from one another. The civil disobedience, tax resistance, strikes, and other actions performed by women abolitionists, suffragists, and unionists were forgotten or minimized, often through ridicule, as women were encouraged to cede the workplace, and public life in general, to returning war veterans. Once again, a woman's place was in the home, and both government propaganda and commercial advertising proclaimed a neotraditional view of women as the guardians of the nation's morals, a task to be carried out within the confines of the home—"woman's sphere"—and the gender-identity role of woman as wife, mother, and homemaker.

Those women who continued to work in women's groups rather than in mixed-gender organizations tended to express their beliefs in terms reflecting the changed social atmosphere. Whereas suffragists had scoffed at those who recommended they "find some mild and lady-like phrases" with which to replace their blunt, political description of women's disenfranchisement, women seeking political efficacy for women's activist groups in the 1950s and 1960s chose to express their views in more moralistic, even sentimental terms. "War is not healthy for children and other living things," for example, was the slogan of the group Another Mother for Peace.

Although there were many exceptions, women using collective nonviolent action in these decades generally remained divided by class and ethnicity as well as philosophy. Middle-class white women working in women's groups opposing the arms race, nuclear weapons testing, and war combined their nonviolence with aspects of the traditional feminine role in order to claim their right as women to speak and act on policies that affected a more broadly defined "women's sphere." They often took action "as mothers," the traditional guardians of future generations. Barbara Deming described the beginnings of Women Strike for

Peace in the early 1960s: the founders, meeting together for the first time, "all knew just why they were there. To put it in the simplest terms: their children were threatened—or their friends' children, the world's children; and they were angry, and they wanted to be heard."

Other middle-class white women worked in mixed-gender groups on the same issues as the women's groups or within the framework of mainly nonwhite movements for social and economic justice such as the civil rights movement, the farm workers' unionization struggle, or the National Welfare Rights Organization. In these latter groups, they came into contact with women of color and poor white women whose philosophy of nonviolent action was expressed not in explicitly gendered terms but in the vocabularies of male-dominant social and religious traditions, specifically Christianity and the patriarchal nuclear family. The "beloved community" of the civil rights movement and other movements where religion provided the supporting structure and discourse did, however, give women a place at the table. Black women, for example, had played a major role in preserving the African-American community through slavery and its aftermath; in the civil rights movement's mass nonviolent action, they could work for political change as well as physical and cultural survival. Their example was a powerful one for white women activists, especially those from the middle class, whose gender role did not allow them to appear powerful in the presence of men except in limited and sexualized situations.

In both women's groups and mixed groups, however, the unchallenged gendering of the nonviolent philosophy kept women within bounds. The emphasis in the civil rights movement, for example, was understandably placed on empowering communities of color rather than on analyzing critically the structure of those communities. The Combahee River Collective, in a 1977 statement of how they arrived at their feminist principles, described the forces that had prevented many black women, including activists, from rebelling against male domination: "The material conditions of most Black women would hardly lead them to upset both economic and sexual arrangements that seem to represent some stability in their lives. Many Black women have a good understanding of both sexism and racism, but because of the everyday constrictions of their lives, cannot risk struggling against them both."

Although women of all ethnicities were active in mixed nonviolent movements and in fact provided the support services vital to the functioning of these movements, the incorporation of traditional sex-role stereotyping into the very structure of the movements' philosophical basis kept them from participating equally. In some cases the sex-role expectations went even further. Activist Leah Fritz (writing about the 1960s in 1975) said, "We used the roles we were assigned by the patriarchy to solicit sympathy for the movement. . . . We even went to Fort Dix, at [a male leader's] suggestion, to seduce men into opposing the army. We used our accursed femininity as a weapon in the struggle and, at the same time, we went into danger with the men on their own terms. It is a matter of history that the men responded with something less than appreciation."

Thus women activists working in all-women groups and in mixed groups experienced nonviolent action as intersecting with gender roles and expectations. In some instances the intersections supported traditional roles, while at other times they presented an implied or overt challenge to these roles. This double-natured experience parallels the "two hands" of nonviolent action. As Barbara Deming put it in her 1968 essay "On Revolution and Equilibrium," nonviolent activists "have as it were two hands upon [their adversary]—the one calming him, making him ask questions, as the other makes him move." The power of nonviolent action, she stated, arises from the fact that "we put upon [the adversary] two pressures—the pressure of our defiance of him and the pressure of our respect for his life—and it happens that in combination these two pressures are uniquely effective."

This doubleness of nonviolent action, one hand reassuring while the other hand says a firm "No," transcends the gender schism in our culture. That is an uncomfortable bridging for some men and a potentially empowering one for many women. Frequently, the power of nonviolence presented a challenge to the men, who in turn required the reassurance of their women co-workers. In order for male nonviolent activists to be "real men" (that is, in order to feel that they remained fully and exclusively within the limits of the male gender role), their female colleagues had to be "real women," willing to act out within the activist community the female gender role in relation to which the male role was defined.

This dynamic was especially public and visible in the development of the Black Power movement out of the civil rights movement. An important strategy of white racism as an institution of social control was to place black men in a feminized position, socially and politically positioned as helpless against white society. In that situation, nonviolent action made sense, whether they believed in it philosophically or not; it was the strategy that worked best while allowing for the greatest chance of survival. As the situation changed and black people had more room to maneuver vis-à-vis the white power structure, nonviolence was not their only reasonable option, and some black men opted out of what they saw as the feminizing posture of nonviolent action. There were strong women in the Black Power movement, but overall it tended toward rigid and separate sex roles, with women subordinate. A black nationalist pamphlet quoted by the Combahee River Collective, for example, asserted that "the man is the head of the house. He is the leader of the house/nation because his knowledge of the world is broader, his awareness is greater, his understanding is fuller and his application of this information is wiser. . . . After all, it is only reasonable that the man be the head of the house because he is able to defend and protect the development of his home. . . . Women cannot do the same things as men—they are made by nature to function differently." The greater success of men in using violence is equated to supposedly natural differences in male and female capacities in a wide range of areas, and nonviolence, by implication, becomes a feminine attribute. In rejecting the "feminine" attributes of nonviolence, these men were rejecting the subordinate (and therefore "feminine") position assigned to them by the institution of white racism. Inevitably, their rejection of the feminine had consequences for their female colleagues who were expected to accept a gender-role definition limiting their participation as activists.

The nonviolence practiced by committed nonviolent activists in the United States is based on belief in the intrinsic value of every person. The traditional female gender role trains women to lack self-esteem. The conflict between these two perspectives was not often openly challenged in the 1950s or early 1960s, but all women nonviolent activists experienced it nevertheless, and gradually their experience of value as activists began to overtake their experience of unworthiness as women. They began to realize that much of the strength of nonviolent action came in tactics, attitudes, and approaches that were traditionally women's: negotiation, passive resistance, reassurance simultaneous with challenge, seeking change by expressing commonalities and love, and so on. This was a source of pride but also of frustration, because these qualities had not been valued as women's qualities but only when advocated by men as part of their nonviolent activist theory. Women of all ethnicities who had gained self-respect and analytical abilities while working in mixed-gender nonviolent action groups began applying these skills to their own situations in and out of these movements. Simultaneously, some women (especially white women) realized with a shock that they had been drawn to social issues as a surrogate for working on their own situation. Women continued to be the service core of the mixed nonviolent action movements throughout the 1960s, but with increasing challenges to their subservient role and increasing anger at what they felt was the men's unwillingness to recognize the violence implicit in women's social position.

This was also a time when the new "youth culture" was challenging gender roles. For example, the well-known antiwar slogan "girls say yes to boys who say no," remembered in subsequent decades only as an expression of the rebellious "free sex" ethic of youth culture, was also a form of reassurance for men willing to renounce part of their gender role. It told men they did not have to play out the traditional masculine role in order to attract women. Women nonviolent activists within youth-oriented movements responded enthusiastically to the apparent shift in male attitudes reflected in their comrades' long hair, espousal of nonviolence, and advocacy of communal love. Like the militants in the Black Power movement, these women saw the ethic of nonviolence as having the potential to "feminize" men, an eventuality the women welcomed, hoping that eventually men would become less prone to military and interpersonal violence.

Throughout the 1960s there were arguments over the wisdom of single-issue or multi-issue campaigns, whether in relation to civil rights (as when Martin Luther King, Jr., came out against the war in Indochina) or in relation to antiwar work (a narrow "bring the boys home" approach versus a broad anti-imperialism). Women's complaints about their roles and the treatment they received within mixed non-violent activist groups were invariably denounced as divisive. Because women-only organizing was also seen as divisive, many women felt they had to distance themselves from the women-only organizations that could have served as an example and a link to earlier militant women's groups. Women's relationship to nonviolence and to their nonviolent comrades was expected to remain entirely subordinate to the "more important issues."

The feminist insight of the early 1970s that "the personal is political" drew much of its initial strength from the frustrations of women who were or had been working in mixed nonviolent action groups. They saw how their male comrades assumed a distinction between violence considered worthy of political analysis and attention, on the one hand, and, on the other hand, the violence women were experiencing in the form of gender oppression: structural and cultural violence, as well as unacknowledged physical and emotional violence. These gender-linked forms of violence most men defined as "personal" and therefore both trivial and an inappropriate focus for political analysis or action. Women began to see how "violence" had been defined to exclude certain actors from being held responsible for their violence. The injustice of this had always been obvious to people of color whose resistance to violence was considered more violent than any violence they experienced at the hands of white racists. But it took women longer to recognize the legitimacy of their anger against culturally invisible forms of violence against women.

The unleashing of this anger led some women to reject nonviolence as passivism, as particularly unsuited for women because it tended to reinforce traditional role expectations. Also, as activists in mixed groups (such as the Black Panthers, the Weathermen) rebelled against the "feminine" aspects of nonviolence, femininity was devalued along with nonviolence. Either women had to be manifestations of the traditional, supposedly passive (and therefore "nonviolent") women's role, or they had to become manlike, proving their commitment to the fight against injustice by their willingness to use violent tactics.

Some women in the mixed white antiwar movement began to see war and the arms race as specifically male problems, rooted either in the male gender role or in the essential "nature" of men. Hence the popular slogan "Take the toys away from the boys." This frustration,

combined with the other factors mentioned above, led some women antiwar activists to experimentation with other strategies and tactics, rejecting nonviolence as a symptom of traditional feminine passivity.

Women who remained nonviolent activists in the late 1960s and the 1970s struggled to persuade their male colleagues that the behavior implied by a philosophy of nonviolence should not be reserved for use only with political opponents. Nor should the ethics of nonviolence remain simply an individual spiritual discipline. The nonviolent activist approach, they insisted, must also be applied within groups of nonviolent activists. Regardless of its target, every nonviolent action must represent a challenge to institutionalized violence within the nonviolent community and beyond. Without this consistency, women activists believed, nonviolent action would lose its power, degenerating from a moral force into a sometimes pragmatically useful but hypocritical tactic incapable of sustaining a long-term social change agenda.

As feminist organizations became more abundant, some women took nonviolence theory and practice into feminist movements and began trying to weave a synthesis of the two. Others claimed their version of nonviolence as an essential expression of women's nature. This tendency, especially prevalent among middle-class white feminists, to think of women as "naturally" nonviolent, hung on for years, allowing many feminist nonviolent activists to neglect rigorous analysis of nonviolence as a theory or a set of tactics. Mab Segrest describes, for example, a campaign to disrupt the production of plutonium for nuclear weapons by blocking the entrance to the plutonium plant. The feminist all-women's contingent of the campaign wanted to use a tactic that would express female power in a more spiritual way than the traditional sequential waves of people lying down in the intersection, as planned by the mixed-gender contingent, which they referred to as "the boys." When the two groups put their tactics into operation, the police had an easy time eliminating the "mystical, feminine" presence of the women's humming spiral: "Our protest lasted from 7:00 to 7:05 A.M. The 'boys' stopped traffic for a full hour. I resolved then and there that, spirituality notwithstanding, I wanted to be more grounded in the material reality of the intersection."

There were other activists—notably, feminists and lesbians of color—whose socially marginalized lives demanded rigor in analyzing political tactics. These women, initially separate from the more mainstream elements of nonviolent action and feminism, represented a pool of sophisticated but down-to-earth clarity into which other women activists eventually dipped. This pattern repeats the earlier sequence by which the nineteenth-century women's suffrage movement was inspired and energized by association with the abolitionist struggle. The political understanding of contemporary nonviolent activist women, like that of the suffragists before them, was profoundly affected by the antiracism work of African Americans (and, in this century, by the work of Chicanas, Latinas, Native Americans, and Asian Americans). However, the pattern in both centuries has been that women's oppression was not taken seriously by the majority of antiracism (or antislavery) activists. Therefore, many activist women have chosen to work separately for a time, with the goal of eventual integration with other activists when there is a sufficient basis of unity. These separations have been most difficult for those activists whose lives cannot be removed from either camp, who are women and therefore must act against the oppression of women, but who also are of color and therefore cannot and will not attempt to put the fight against racism "on hold." During the early 1990s, white women activists increasingly came to share this perspective, realizing that the category "women" is a false and insufficient basis for political work if in fact it is used as a code for "white women only."

The effect women have had on nonviolent action in the United States can be seen most clearly in the greatly increased emphasis on group process within groups and movements committed to nonviolent action. As they resisted and rejected their traditional place on the bottom of the work and respect hierarchies, women activists began to insist on nonhierarchal methods of decision making and organization. Consensus, the rotation of roles (for example, meeting facilitator, news media spokesperson), and various means of ensuring equal participation in group discussions are now virtually standard practice in most U.S. groups practicing nonviolent action. Having outgrown their willingness to believe that raising the issue of women's oppression as a form of violence was "divisive" and damaging to work on "more important" issues, women led the way toward infusing into nonviolent ethics the injunction to interrupt any type of interpersonal violence (such as sexism, racism, and ageism) as soon as it is recognized, on the grounds that these more subtly violent forms of interaction erode one's ability to move clearly and powerfully together in nonviolent action. During the 1980s and 1990s, women carried these new emphases into a variety of burgeoning movements for social change in which women have played leading roles—for example, the environmental movement, the animal rights movement, the disability rights movement, and the psychiatric survivors' movement.

Jane Meyerding

References

Deming, Barbara. "Letter to WISP." In *We Are All Part of One Another: A Barbara Deming Reader,* edited by Jane Meyerding. Philadelphia: New Society, 1984.

———. "On Revolution and Equilibrium." In *Revolution and Equilibrium.* New York: Grossman, 1971.

Fritz, Leah. *Thinking like a Woman.* Rifton, N.Y.: WIN, 1975.

Segrest, Mab. *Memoir of a Race Traitor.* Boston: South End, 1994.

Smith, Barbara, ed. *Home Girls: A Black Feminist Anthology.* New York: Kitchen Table—Women of Color [Press], 1983.

Wagner, Sally Roesch. *A Time of Protest: Suffragists Challenge the Republic, 1870–1887.* Carmichael, Calif.: Sky Carrier, 1988.

See also ABOLITIONIST MOVEMENT; CIVIL RIGHTS MOVEMENT; DEMING, BARBARA; FEMINISM; KING, MARTIN LUTHER, JR.; VIETNAM WAR OPPOSITION; WOMEN STRIKE FOR PEACE; WOMEN'S INTERNATIONAL LEAGUE FOR PEACE AND FREEDOM, U.S. SECTION; WOMEN'S SUFFRAGE

Women Strike for Peace (United States)

Organization of American women, formed in the early 1960s to press the United States and Soviet governments to halt atmospheric nuclear testing. Over the next decade and a half, Women Strike for Peace (WSP) evolved from an active grassroots lobbying force focusing on the nuclear arms race to an activist protest organization engaged in civil disobedience, as well as political pressure, to end the Vietnam War.

On November 1, 1961, tens of thousands of mainly white, middle-class women in the United States walked out of their kitchens and off their jobs in an unprecedented nationwide strike for peace. As a radioactive cloud from a series of Soviet atomic bomb tests passed over American cities and the United States threatened to retaliate with its own cycle of nuclear explosions, the striking women, carrying placards with the slogans "Pure Milk—Not Poison" and "No Tests—East or West," marched outside the offices of their elected officials. They visited governors, mayors, congressional representatives, even school board members, to express their concern regarding the pollution of children's milk by radioactive nuclear fallout. Their mission, they declared, was to urge local politicians, Republicans and Democrats alike, to demand that President John F. Kennedy take immediate steps to "End the Arms Race—Not the Human Race." To demonstrate their impartial impatience with the leaders of both the United States and the USSR, and their belief in the civilizing influence of women, the Washington, D.C., organizers of the peace strike sent identical appeals to Jacqueline Kennedy and Nina Khrushchev urging them as mothers to press their husbands for an immediate halt to nuclear testing. One week before the strike date, Dagmar Wilson, the spokesperson for the Washington, D.C., women who organized the strike, told the *Washington Post*:

> You know how men are. They talk in abstractions and prestige and the technicalities of the bomb, almost as if this were all a game of chess. Well it isn't. There are times, it seems to me, when the only thing to do is let out a loud scream. . . . Just women raising a hue and cry against nuclear weapons for all of them to cut it out.

It is interesting to note that the letter from the women strikers to Jacqueline Kennedy produced one of her rare political statements. "I do agree that as women we should exert our great influence in the cause of world peace," Jacqueline Kennedy wrote back to Wilson. "As mothers we cannot help but be concerned about the health and welfare of our husbands and children." The extensive news media coverage of the strike and the reprinting of Mrs. Kennedy's reply to WSP in hundreds of U.S. newspapers kept the peace strike in the public eye

throughout November, and by the time the month had ended the strikers decided that they could not abandon their fight to "save the planet," which had begun so auspiciously.

In the process of transforming the strike into a viable women's peace movement with one hundred local chapters, ten regional offices, and a network of contacts in Europe, Asia, and Latin America, WSP developed an innovative and spontaneous political style. It was characterized by a nonhierarchical, loosely structured "un-organizational" format that allowed for prompt direct action on the grassroots level. Without a paid staff, professional organizers, or officially designated spokespersons, WSP created an instantly effective, but costly, telephone communications network that was paid for by the women who used it. A format for relentless political lobbying in Washington, called Lobby by Proxy, was created. Local meetings, debates, walks, marches, vigils, eloquent letters to the editor, plus a flair for public relations helped to make WSP one of the important news stories of 1961 and 1962.

Tired of the old politics of both the Right and the Left, the key women who founded and sustained WSP developed a politically sophisticated yet traditionally maternal rhetoric that attracted sympathetic attention from the press and public officials. At a time when peace dissenters were characterized by the political mainstream as either "commies" or "kooks," the image projected by WSP of respectable militant mothers, "the lady next door" type, wearing white gloves and flowered hats, picketing the White House to "save the children" helped to legitimize the movement's critique of U.S. cold war policies. By stressing the ways in which the men in power were undermining the capacity of mothers to carry out their socially assigned roles of nurturance and life preservation, WSP was able to gain support for its confrontations with such sacrosanct military institutions as the Pentagon and NATO, and to win sympathy for its defiance of the House Committee on Un-American Activities, which summoned the movement to a hearing on Communist influence in the peace movement in December 1962.

Having from its inception declared, "We are women of all races, creeds, and political persuasions," WSP had rejected political screening and the exclusion of former Communist party members from the movement as manifestations of outdated cold war thinking. It is not surpris-

Women Strike for Peace demonstration at the Nevada Test Site. From Critical Focus: The Black and White Photographs of Harvey Wilson Richards, *edited by Paul Richards (Oakland, CA: Estuary Press, 1987), p. 42.*

ing then that the women of WSP did not cower before HUAC. Instead, they boldly challenged the committee's stranglehold on Americanism, declaring: "With the fate of humanity resting on a push button, the quest for peace has become the highest form of patriotism." At the HUAC hearings WSP claimed the high ground, each witness asserting with humor and passion that mothers fighting for peace were the most loyal kind of Americans. Political theorist Jean Bethke Elshtain assesses WSP's performance at the HUAC hearings as a triumph for the deconstructive power of a politics of humor, irony, evasion, and ridicule. According to Elshtain, "The Women's Strike for Peace didn't proclaim that the Emperor had no clothes, rather they put him in a position where, to his own astonishment, he found that he had disrobed himself with his own strategy and tactics." As a result, headlines critical of HUAC appeared for the first time in newspapers from coast to coast. "Peace Gals Make Red Hunters Look Silly," "Peace Ladies Tangle with Baffled Congress," "Redhunters Decapitated," and "It's Ladies Day at the Capitol: Hoots, Howls and Charm," were typical. Eric Bentley in *Thirty Years of*

Treason, a history of the House Committee on Un-American Activities, gives WSP the credit for striking the crucial blow in "the fall of HUAC's bastille."

At its peak, in 1963, WSP estimated that it had a following of more than 150,000 women. However, the exact figure could not be verified because WSP never had an official dues-paying membership list. Any woman who took part in a WSP sponsored meeting, a rally, a letter-writing luncheon, a lobby, or a picket line was considered a WSP participant by her local group. In its campaign for a nuclear test ban treaty, and later in its opposition to the war in Vietnam, WSP tapped a reservoir of dormant female political outrage, organizational talent, political inventiveness, and a hunger for sisterly collaboration that had been repressed by the cold war consensus and the feminine mystique. Through participation in the WSP movement, thousands of women who, despite a high level of education, had identified themselves only as housewives found to their surprise and satisfaction that they could do serious research, write convincing flyers and pamphlets, speak eloquently in public, plan effective political strategies, organize successful long-range national and international campaigns, and challenge the male leaders of both the Left and the Right to whom they had previously deferred.

For WSP's most successful campaign, supporting the test ban treaty, it mobilized tens of thousands of women in every form of political pressure from lobbying in Washington and at the United Nations to leafleting at supermarkets, from petitioning at church and synagogue gates to marching in Washington, New York, and Geneva, to vigils in small towns and suburbs. Jerome Wiesner, science advisor to President John F. Kennedy, credited WSP, along with the Committee for a Sane Nuclear Policy and Nobel laureate Linus Pauling, with having more influence on the president regarding the test ban treaty than the professional arms controllers in the government.

After the test ban treaty was signed in 1963, the WSP movement turned its attention to nuclear proliferation. In May 1964, WSP organized a "NATO Women's Peace Force" demonstration at The Hague, Holland, in response to a proposed plan for a multilateral nuclear force (MLF) that would have placed the fingers of German submarine commanders on nuclear triggers. There, women from the NATO countries, including eight hundred from West Germany, met to study the MLF plan, lay out a strategy of opposition, and picket the official NATO meeting. WSP made headlines across Europe, as one of its representatives, Ava Helen Pauling, the wife of Linus Pauling, was barred from entering Holland for the NATO protest at the same time that a former Nazi general who had been involved in the bombing of Rotterdam was welcomed as a NATO official. While WSP never built a mass movement in opposition to the MLF at home or abroad, it did mobilize peace activists, artists, and opinion-makers including Otto Hahn, Max Born, Lord Boyd Orr, and Bertrand Russell in opposition to the MLF. Irish poet Sean O'Casey contributed a poem in support of the NATO Women's Peace Force: "To Hell with all arms/ Excepting those/ Grandly grafted/ To our human bodies,/ These arms are all we need/ To give glory to God/ And all honor to man." For many reasons, not the least of which was public pressure, the United States eventually abandoned the plan.

By the end of 1964, WSP was diverted from its antinuclear campaigns by the escalating war in Vietnam. For the remainder of the decade and until the United States withdrew from Vietnam in 1975, WSP took an active part in the antiwar coalition. Although WSP had been wary of civil disobedience in its early years, during the Vietnam War it found nonviolent resistance an important, and often the most appropriate, tactic with which to oppose the government's relentless escalation of what the women regarded as an illegal, immoral, and inhuman war. WSP began to stage sit-ins in congressional offices and die-ins at draft boards and at the corporate headquarters of the major arms suppliers for Vietnam.

WSP played a significant role in the antidraft movement, reaching across race and class lines to counsel more than 100,000 young men on their legal rights under the selective service system. Early in the draft counseling process, the women of WSP decided that they would counsel not only those who sought legal methods of avoiding military combat in Vietnam, but that they would also help those who were ready to resist the draft regardless of the consequences. WSP developed a statement of complicity with resisters that offered not only moral but also financial support. At a demonstration at the Selective Service Headquarters in Washington, D.C., WSP declared publicly:

> We believe that support of those who resist the war and the draft is both moral and legal. We believe that it is not we, but those who send our sons to kill and be killed, who are committing crimes. We do, however, recognize that there may be legal risks involved, but because we believe that these young men are courageous and morally justified in rejecting the war regardless of consequences, we can do no less.

WSP women were present as supporters at draft card burnings, showed up in the early hours of the morning at armed forces induction lines to distribute flyers urging men not to cross the line, and provided information and legal counseling to those draftees who had last-minute doubts. WSPers also sat in at the trials of draft resisters to show the judges that "women are watching" and visited draft resisters in jail.

Refusing to accept the government's characterization of the people of Vietnam as "the enemy," WSP members made several unauthorized trips to Hanoi and arranged three conferences with the leading women of North Vietnam and the National Liberation Front of

South Vietnam under the slogan, "Not Our Sons, Not Your Sons, Not Their Sons."

WSP built its movement on the female culture of the 1940s and 1950s. Because its key organizers were socialized in the decades after the first wave of feminism and before the second wave, the ethos of female self-sacrifice was very strong in WSP. The women felt comfortable campaigning militantly to save the children, but they had not yet learned to demand any rights or power for themselves. They had neither the consciousness, nor the language, with which to connect women's exclusion from political power with their secondary status in the family and the work force or to understand the relationship between militarism and domestic violence. What WSP did accomplish in the 1960s and early 1970s was to bring woman's voice into the arena of international affairs at a time when foreign policy dissent of any kind was muffled or ignored. WSP helped to transform the image of the concerned mother from private to public and from passive victim of war to active fighter for peace. As women in the United States have done so many times in the past, WSP built on the traditional constructions of motherhood to extend women's influence and decision-making power from the nursery and the kitchen to the body politic.

Amy Swerdlow

References

Bentley, Eric. *Thirty Years of Treason: Excerpts from the Hearings before the House Committee on Un-American Activates, 1938–1968.* New York: Viking, 1971.

Elshtain, Jean Bethke, and Sheila Tobias, eds. *Women, Militarism, and War: Essays in History, Politics, and Social Theory.* Totowa, N.J.: Rowman and Littlefield, 1990.

Hamilton, Andrew. "MIT: March 4 Revisited amid Political Turmoil." *Science* 167 (March 13, 1970): 1475–1476.

Swerdlow, Amy. *Women Strike for Peace: Traditional Motherhood and Radical Politics in the 1960s.* Chicago: University of Chicago Press, 1994.

See also FEMINISM; NUCLEAR WEAPONS OPPOSITION; VIETNAM WAR OPPOSITION; WOMEN AND NONVIOLENT ACTION IN THE UNITED STATES SINCE 1950

Women's International League for Peace and Freedom, U.S. Section

The U.S. section of an international women's peace organization that has worked for the end of war, increased international cooperation, and social justice since the World War I era. When World War I broke out in Europe in August 1914, members of the International Woman Suffrage Alliance immediately took action in efforts to achieve a mediated settlement. Two women, Rosika Schwimmer of Hungary and Emmeline Pethick-Lawrence of England, came to the United States to ask their cohorts, Jane Addams and Carrie Chapman Catt, for aid in organizing United States women to pressure President Woodrow Wilson to take on the role of mediator.

Both Jane Addams and Carrie Chapman Catt met with Wilson several times. Although unsuccessful in their primary goal, oral tradition claims that they did play a role in Wilson's creation of his famous "Fourteen Points." In addition, Addams, along with a very reluctant Catt, called a conference of women organizers. Held from January 9 to 11, 1915, in Washington, D.C., the meeting resulted in the formation of the Woman's Peace Party (WPP), which in April became the U.S. section of the International Committee of Women for Permanent Peace, founded by suffragist-pacifists meeting at The Hague. Jane Addams was elected president of both the international and national groups.

The Woman's Peace Party expressed feminist sentiments—that is, it placed women's concerns and perspectives at the center of its program. It did this in several ways. First, the organization took the stance that women, as the "mother half of humanity" had the responsibility of seeing that children were not killed or turned into governmental murderers because of war. Using traditional nineteenth-century ideas about womanhood, the WPP claimed that women had a moral revulsion to war and argued that if women had the vote and equal representation in government, war would be abolished. The organization also stressed the connection between militarism and violence against women.

The WPP did quite well in terms of membership. Within a year, the organization had grown from 85 charter members to 512, and there were thirty-three local branches by the next year, spanning the entire United States. By February 1916 membership reached a peak of 40,000, and even though numbers of women

The Women's International League for Peace and Freedom demonstrates against the Vietnam War. Swarthmore College Peace Collection.

dropped out after the United States joined the war effort on April 6, 1917, that December the organization still included two hundred local branches and affiliated groups. Once the war ended on November 11, 1918, the international group planned another meeting for Zurich, May 12–17, 1919. There they created the Women's International League for Peace and Freedom. The Woman's Peace Party became the U.S. section of WILPF.

During the interwar years, WILPF/U.S. encountered both good and bad times. The 1920s was an optimistic decade for peace activists as the United States on the whole favored many approaches for achieving world peace. WILPF/U.S. worked actively in support of all international treaties, for U.S. participation in the League of Nations and the World Court, and for international disarmament conferences. Important WILPF/U.S. leaders at the time were Jane Addams (who won the Nobel Peace Prize in 1931), Emily Greene Balch, Hannah Clothier Hull, Mildred Scott Olmsted, and Dorothy Detzer. Detzer, the organization's first paid staff member, was known as a topnotch lobbyist in Washington, D.C., and received much credit for

rallying public support (largely female) for the ratification of the Kellogg–Briand Pact in 1928 and the establishment of the Nye Commission (the Senate Special Committee Investigating the Munition Industry's Work) in 1934. The commission concluded that the munitions industry had clearly tried to influence the congressional vote for war in 1917.

The 1930s were difficult years. With the growing threats of fascism in Europe and Japanese imperialism in Asia, conflicts grew within WILPF/U.S. One of the most difficult issues to resolve was how to react to President Franklin Roosevelt's neutrality acts. At times, debate was quite intense, but in the end, the national leaders of WILPF/U.S. agreed to support neutrality in order to maintain a consensus within the organization. This decision rankled some of the local branches, especially those in the New York metropolitan area, which had recruited many Jewish, socialist, and some African-American members. To the Jewish women, neutrality was equivalent to supporting Nazism. Socialist members felt frustrated because to them supporting neutrality meant losing Spain to the fascists, and African-American members were angered because to them, it meant abandoning Ethiopia to Italy. As a result of this and World War II, WILPF/U.S. membership fell drastically, leaving only a few hundred members by the war's end.

The post–World War II McCarthy era was devastating for WILPF/U.S. Many women were afraid to join the organization for fear of being labeled Communists by the U.S. government. Worse for the organization was the internal red-baiting that took place. Although the House Committee on Un-American Activities never labeled WILPF/U.S. as subversive, the FBI did infiltrate the organization in order to discredit individual members. Tensions were particularly high in the Denver, Chicago, Detroit, and New York branches. Even though in 1946 Emily Greene Balch won the Nobel Peace Prize for her work with WILPF, the organization had difficulties reviving.

What brought it back to life was a combination of the effects of the civil rights movement, the Vietnam War, the nuclear arms race, the resurgence of feminism, and the UN Decade for Women (1975–1985).

WILPF/U.S. was a very active support group for the larger civil rights movement. Women participated in national marches and local actions. In addition, each WILPF/U.S. activity kept the issue of race on the front burner. The nuclear arms race and the Vietnam War, however, became the main thrusts of the organization's activities. Working with other groups, such as Women Strike for Peace, the War Resisters League, and the Fellowship of Reconciliation, WILPF/U.S. maintained constant pressure on Congress to end both the arms race and the war. Much of the organization's work included producing flyers and literature to educate the public. International WILPF's STAR (Stop the Arms Race) campaign raised one million dollars and one million signatures for the antinuclear campaign. U.S. women were extremely active in this effort.

The feminist movement, which really took hold in 1968, greatly affected WILPF/U.S. The organization slowly accepted the fact that women's efforts were being concentrated in feminist organizations. As a result, in 1983, the organization helped feminist peace activists purchase a farm in upstate New York, which became the Seneca Women's Peace Encampment. In 1985, International WILPF played a leading role in establishing the women's peace tent at the "World Conference to Review and Appraise the Achievements of the U.N. Decade for Women: Equality, Development, and Peace," held in Nairobi, Kenya. Many U.S. women participated in the NGO meetings at the conference.

In 1995, WILPF/U.S. celebrated its eightieth anniversary. It is the longest-lasting U.S. women's peace organization in history. Today, it continues to emphasize several issues, including an end to nuclear weapons development, an end to racial and ethnic hatred, an end to homophobia, an end to violence against women, and an end to international violence.

Harriet Hyman Alonso

References

Alonso, Harriet Hyman. *Peace As a Women's Issue: A History of the U.S. Movement for World Peace and Women's Rights.* Syracuse, N.Y.: Syracuse University Press, 1993.

Bussey, Gertrude, and Margaret Tims. *Pioneers for Peace: Women's International League for Peace and Freedom, 1915–1965.* Oxford: Alden, 1980.

Degen, Marie Louise. *The History of the Woman's Peace Party* [1939]. New York: Garland, 1972.

Foster, Carrie. *The Women and the Warriors: The U.S. Section of the WILPF, 1915–1946.* Syracuse, N.Y.: Syracuse University Press, 1995.

Foster, Catherine. *Women for All Seasons: The Story of the Women's International League for Peace and Freedom.* Athens: University of Georgia Press, 1989.

Pois, Anne Marie. "The U.S. Women's International League for Peace and Freedom and American Neutrality, 1935–1939." *Peace and Change* 14 (1989): 263–284.

Schott, Linda Kay. "The Woman's Peace Party and the Moral Basis for Women's Pacifism." *Frontiers: A Journal of Women's Studies* 8 (1985): 18–24.

Steinson, Barbara Jean. *American Women's Activism in World War I.* New York: Garland, 1982.

See also ADDAMS, JANE; FEMINISM; WOMEN AND NONVIOLENT ACTION IN THE UNITED STATES SINCE 1950; WOMEN'S SUFFRAGE

Women's Suffrage

A worldwide movement for votes for women (1848–1948) led originally by American women, many of whom used nonviolent methods in the

Suffrage parade, New York City, May 3, 1913. Sophia Smith Collection/Smith College.

struggle. Born at the time of the American Revolution and the period of Enlightment, the concept of women's suffrage was nourished in the United States by the antislavery struggle and adopted its "nonresistant" principles. Later the suffrage movement became linked with the advance of women in the professions and with the major reform movements of the day, including the burgeoning peace movement. Militant suffragists used nonviolent methods in the pursuit of votes for women in the United States and to a certain extent in England. The development of the International Woman Suffrage Alliance in 1904 led to the creation of the Women's International League for Peace and Freedom, dedicated to the worldwide pursuit of justice through nonviolent tactics.

Although a few individual voices—notably those of Abigail Adams, a Massachusetts woman of letters, Mary Wollstonecraft, an English author, and Frances Wright, a Scottish reformer—were raised for suffrage in the period from 1775 to 1825, the movement did not gain momentum until the rise of the militant antislavery movement in the United States in the 1830s. Members of the American Anti-Slavery Society (AAS), organized by William Lloyd Garrison in 1833, were committed to nonresistance and to the boycott of slave produce, both elements of nonviolence as we know it today. Originally barred from membership in the AAS and its regional constituents, because of widespread prejudice against women speaking in public, the women organized female antislavery societies that participated in the struggle. In these societies women were particularly involved in the Free Produce movement and in protecting their assemblies against hostile mobs through nonviolent actions.

Shortly after becoming organized, the female societies began to protest the ban on public speaking by women. Angelina and Sarah Grimké, two sisters from South Carolina, were the first to demand the right to speak to mixed audiences and to bring the question of the rights of women into the antislavery movement. At the World Anti-Slavery Convention, held in London in 1840, the eight women delegates from the United States were refused seats because of their gender. Elizabeth Cady Stanton, a twenty-five-year-old bride, though not herself a delegate, was very much influenced by the leader of the American women, Lucretia Mott. Mott fought these restrictions with great poise and dignity, and together with Stanton the two planned to hold a convention for the rights of women.

Eight years later, Mott and Stanton called a Woman's Rights Convention at the little town of Seneca Falls, New York. Here a Declaration of Rights was adopted, including votes for women. Thereafter, woman's rights conventions were held yearly to discuss women's educational and professional advancement, reform of the marriage laws, temperance, moral reform, and other issues including suffrage. Because the changes demanded were profound the conventions were highly unpopular, and they were sometimes disturbed or broken up by unruly mobs. Using the methods of nonresistance they had learned in the antislavery movement, the women refused police protection, which was rarely offered in any case, but defended themselves by marching fearlessly arm and arm through the crowd.

Following the Civil War, the woman's rights leaders joined with the antislavery campaigners to establish the American Equal Rights Association, committed to working for suffrage for both blacks and women. The passage of the Fourteenth and Fifteenth amendments to the United States Constitution, however, giving the vote to blacks but not women, split the group. Thus, two new organizations formed—the National Woman's Suffrage Association, dedicated solely to passage of a Sixteenth Amendment giving the franchise to women in federal elections; and an American Suffrage Association, seeking suffrage amendments state by state.

Arguing that the Fifteenth Amendment could be construed to give the vote to women, a number of suffragist women proceeded to attempt to vote anyway. In New Jersey, where women had had the vote until 1807, a group attempted to vote in 1868, then staged a protest "vote in" at the other end of the voting hall. The Grimké sisters entered a protest at their polling place in Hyde Park, New York, and Susan B. Anthony, who had joined the women's rights movement in 1851, led a delegation of sixteen women who managed to vote in Rochester, New York, in 1872. Arrested, tried, and sentenced as an example to others, Anthony was willing to accept a jail sentence rather than pay a fine for her action, but the sentence was never carried out. Four years later, at the 1876 celebration of the centennial of the founding of the United States in Philadelphia, Anthony and four other women demonstrated nonviolently, interrupting the vice president of the United States to read a Women's Declaration of Independence.

Another form of direct action employed by the women seeking suffrage was to refuse to pay taxes, arguing that it was taxation without rep-resentation. A number of women used tax refusal in this manner, and several suffered distraints (property seizures). The most notable was Abby Kelley Foster and her husband, Stephen Foster, famous for nonresistance during the antislavery crusade, who permitted their farm to be sold from under them rather than pay taxes due.

Many of the American women who worked for suffrage in the second half of the nineteenth century were also involved in other reform movements. A large number were active in the closely allied campaign for temperance, which also used nonviolent methods. The dramatic action of temperance women entering saloons, though much ridiculed, was in fact a nonviolent effort to call attention to the plight of working-class wives who saw their husbands' weekly paycheck used to buy liquor. In one particularly imaginative early protest, Amanda Way, a temperance leader in Indiana and a suffrage advocate, organized an army of fifty women that raided all the saloons in Winchester, Indiana, and invited their children, whom they had brought along, to help themselves to the free lunch. Later in the century, the Women's Christian Temperance Union (WCTU) organized a department of Peace and Arbitration that did grassroots work on pacifism.

Closely allied to the temperance movement was the Moral Purity movement, which sought to improve the conditions of prostitutes and to penalize their male customers. Many suffrage women also worked to improve conditions for women prisoners and to upgrade conditions in mental hospitals. Newly trained female doctors and college professors sought to increase educational opportunities for other young women, while they participated in several of the linked campaigns.

Following the Civil War, Lucretia Mott and other women who practiced nonresistance helped to found the Universal Peace Union along with their male colleagues. Many of the outstanding women reformers of the second half of the nineteenth century belonged to this group. In 1872, Julia Ward Howe organized a series of Woman's Peace Festivals in various cities to celebrate Mothers Peace Day. This occasion was regularly celebrated in Philadelphia by members of the Universal Peace Union and led to several nonviolent actions for peace and racial justice.

Meanwhile the struggle for suffrage proceeded slowly. In 1878, the women succeeded in having a federal amendment introduced into Congress. The "Susan B. Anthony Amendment" was reported on by House and Senate committees until 1896, but never reached debate on the floor of Congress. Thereafter it was entirely dormant until 1913. Meanwhile, a state by state campaign for suffrage was successful in the West with Wyoming, Colorado, Utah, Idaho, Washington, California, Kansas, Oregon, Arizona, and Alaska giving the franchise to women.

In 1890, the two American suffrage associations joined to form the National American Woman Suffrage Association (NAWSA), and began to work together toward a federal amendment. In the interests of political expediency, they narrowed their focus and distanced themselves from several of the more controversial reform movements, such as the antilynching campaign. Eager to cultivate votes in the South, they were no longer on the forefront of the struggle for civil rights.

Susan B. Anthony, now elderly, began to turn her principle attention to the organization and nurture of the International Woman Suffrage Alliance (IWSA), developed in Germany in 1904. On her way home from a meeting of this body she stopped in England and was interviewed by Christabel Pankhurst, daughter of Emmeline Pankhurst, who was leading a militant wing of the woman suffrage movement in Great Britain. Christabel was reportedly so influenced by Susan B. Anthony that she decided to devote more energies to suffrage.

The suffrage movement in Great Britain had, to some extent, paralleled the movement in the United States. Anne Knight, who had attended the London Antislavery Convention in 1840 and had been influenced by Mott, helped to found the Sheffield Female Political Association, which issued in 1851 the first manifesto on votes for women ever made in England. Suffrage societies were organized in Edinburgh, Bristol, Birmingham, Manchester, and London, and a national association formed. Supporters attempted to introduce woman suffrage into Parliament on several occasions, but the government consistently blocked the effort.

Like their sisters in the United States, some of the women of England argued that taxation without representation was unjust and began to refuse to pay property taxes. The tax refusers often spoke at public auctions, sometimes converting the auctioneers to their cause.

In 1903, Emmeline Pankhurst organized the Women's Social and Political Union (WSPU) in Manchester with the aid of Christabel. Within two years the new organization adopted confrontational tactics, interrupting meetings and refusing to be arrested. Later, they threw bricks and sometimes detonated bombs. They believed in destroying property, but not harming persons. Arrested, they refused to eat or to be force fed, thus creating publicity and pressure on the government. Their actions were controversial within the larger suffrage movement, where they were opposed not only by the more conservative majority but also by a smaller group dedicated wholly to nonviolent methods.

In 1914, with the advent of war, Emmeline and Christabel Pankhurst abandoned the campaign and devoted themselves to the war effort, although Sylvia, another daughter, remained a pacifist and socialist. The pacifists among England's suffragists continued to lobby, and in 1918 the government granted a limited suffrage for property-owning women over thirty, which was enlarged to universal suffrage in 1928. Suffrage was also extended to women in all the dominions and colonies except India and South Africa, although several had already obtained it independently—New Zealand in 1893, Australia in 1902, and Canada in 1918.

Participating in the Pankhurst struggle before the war was a young American woman, Alice Paul. Shortly after her return to the United States she volunteered to take part in the struggle for suffrage, now in the doldrums. Originally appointed to the Congressional Committee of the NAWSA, she planned colorful parades and marches that brought national attention to the struggle. In 1913, she organized a separate national group, the Congressional Union (CU). At first the CU functioned as an auxiliary to the NAWSA, but as the group began to introduce methods of direct action, the older organization attempted to discipline the newer branch. Friction resulted and Alice Paul and her cohorts decided to become independent and renamed their organization the National Woman's Party.

The methods of the National Woman's Party were similar to those of the British WSPU but more closely in line with nonviolence. The women picketed in front of the White House, were arrested, went to prison, and there refused to be force fed. Newspaper stories spread news of their fate across the country and resulted in many women coming to volunteer to take the places of the martyrs. By refusing to use violence, Alice Paul, a Quaker, was able to keep the sympathies of a large portion of the American public. With the entry of the United States into World War I, the leaders of the NAWSA volunteered to assist in the war effort. Alice Paul, however, was opposed to war, and she and her followers stepped up their nonviolent campaign of pressure on President Woodrow Wilson to take an active role in lobbying Congress and bringing the amendment to a vote. How much this nonviolent campaign contributed to the final outcome will be debated by historians for years to come. The amendment finally was brought to the House and Senate in 1918, with Wilson pleading for its passage. In May of 1919, it was passed by both legislative bodies. By August 26, 1920, a sufficient number of states had ratified the amendment for the constitutional change to take place.

International suffragists had continued to meet, rejoicing when women won suffrage in Finland in 1906 and in Norway in 1913. In France the struggle for women suffrage had begun with the organization of a Women's Rights Society in 1876 and its sponsorship of a tax strike in 1880. In Germany, where the suffrage movement was closely allied with socialism, the suffragists conducted marches on International Women's Day (March 8) from 1911 to 1914. Progress however was slow, and the coming of World War I seemed to doom the effort to failure. Many IWSA leaders supported the war and felt they should cancel the international meeting that had been planned for The Hague in 1915. Aletta Jacobs, president of the Dutch suffrage movement, felt differently and called an International Congress of Women in its place.

As its chair she invited Jane Addams of Hull House, organizer of the Women's Peace Party in 1915. As first vice president of the NAWSA, Jane Addams had attended the IWSA conference held in Budapest in 1913. At The Hague, the women voted to call a conference of neutral nations to offer continuous mediation to end the war. Following the end of the congress they visited the heads of state of all belligerent and neutral nations to plead for an arbitrated peace. Four years later, the women met again in Geneva, and renamed themselves the Women's International League for Peace and Freedom (WILPF), dedicated to the twin goals of working for suffrage and women's rights and working for peace through nonviolent methods.

The victories for suffragists in the United States and Great Britain following World War I reflected the broader, and continuing, international suffrage movement. Revolution, war, decolonization, the creation of new states, and dramatic social changes were part of the twentieth-century environment in which suffrage spread over the following decades. In 1917, the Russian revolution brought the vote to women in the new revolutionary state. In 1919, Germany, Austria, Poland, Czechoslovakia, and Sweden followed suit. Women in Burma, Ecuador, South Africa (white women only), Brazil, Uruguay, Thailand, Turkey, Cuba, and the Philippines gained suffrage by 1937. France, Italy, Romania, Yugoslavia, and China granted it immediately after World War II. Indian women received the vote in 1949, and Pakistani women in 1956. Not until 1973 did the women of Switzerland vote. The United Nations Commission on the Status of Women, a group for which WILPF and other organizations lobbied, now monitors those countries where women are still not empowered to vote.

As a new feminist movement evolved in the United States in the 1960s and early 1970s, young women sought out the surviving suffragists and looked for ways to incorporate nonviolence into the campaign for the Equal Rights Amendment and other aspects of the continuing struggle for full equality. A small group of women went on hunger strike or chained themselves to the White House fence in support of the ERA. In Great Britain, and elsewhere in Europe new feminists have also looked back to their foremothers. Thus the suffrage campaign has lived on as an inspiration to a younger generation.

Margaret Hope Bacon

References

Bacon, Margaret Hope. "By Moral Force Alone: The Antislavery Women and Nonresistance." In *The Abolitionist Sisterhood: Women's Political Culture in Antebellum America*, edited by Jean Fagin Yellin and John C. Van Horne. Ithaca, N.Y.: Cornell University Press, 1994.

Evans, Richard J. *Comrades and Sisters; Socialism and Pacifism in Europe 1870–1945*. New York: St. Martin's, 1987.

Flexner, Eleanor. *Century of Struggle: The Woman's Rights Movement in the United States*. Rev. ed. Cambridge: Belknap, 1975.

Fry, Amelia. "Conversations with Alice Paul: Woman Suffrage and the Equal Rights Amendment." Transcript of a tape-recorded interview. Berkeley: Regional Oral History Project of the Bancroft Library of the University of California, 1976.

Kraditor, Aileen S. *The Ideas of the Woman Suffrage Movement*. New York: W.W. Norton, 1981.

McAllister, Pam. *You Can't Kill the Spirit.* Philadelphia: New Society, 1988.

MacKensie, Midge. *Shoulder to Shoulder.* New York: Knopf, 1975.

Stanton, Elizabeth, Susan B. Anthony, and Josyln Matilda Gage. *History of Woman Suffrage.* New York: Fowler, 1881–1886.

See also ABOLITIONIST MOVEMENT; ADDAMS, JANE; ANTHONY, SUSAN BROWNELL; FEMINISM; GARRISON, WILLIAM LLOYD; GRIMKÉ, SARAH MOORE AND EMILY ANGELINA; MOTT, LUCRETIA COFFIN; NATIONAL WOMAN SUFFRAGE ASSOCIATION; PAUL, ALICE; STANTON, ELIZABETH CADY; WOMEN AND NONVIOLENT ACTION IN THE UNITED STATES SINCE 1950; WOMEN'S INTERNATIONAL LEAGUE FOR PEACE AND FREEDOM, U.S. SECTION

Z

Zambia, Anticolonial Movement, 1953–1964

Nationalist movement that used nonviolent and violent direct action to protest British-sponsored rule of Northern Rhodesia by Southern Rhodesian white settlers. Led primarily by Kenneth Kaunda, who was inspired by Kwame Nkrumah and the Tanzanian anticolonial struggle, a large portion of resistance consisted of nonviolent methods such as boycotts, strikes, and demonstrations. The movement was successful and independence was won in a relatively short time compared with other African nations.

In the late nineteenth century, Cecil Rhodes and the British South Africa Company (BSA) controlled the area of Northern Rhodesia. In 1924, the BSA turned over its administrative power to the British Colonial Office, and Northern Rhodesia became a protectorate. The British created the Central African Federation in 1953, which united Southern and Northern Rhodesia with Nyasaland and gave control to Southern Rhodesia, ruled mostly by Europeans.

In the early 1950s, prior to the establishment of the federation, the Northern Rhodesia African National Congress (ANC) led an unsuccessful antifederation struggle. The climax of the ANC's prefederation opposition campaign came in April 1953 with two days of national prayer. ANC leaders had also called for a sympathetic general strike that never materialized because they had failed to garner the support of labor. Widespread anticolonial resistance did not begin until after the federation was established.

Kenneth Kaunda became organizing secretary of the ANC in 1952. Though not an absolute pacifist, he helped instill an affirmation of "nonviolence" in the ANC constitution, and continued to call for nonviolent action throughout the anticolonial struggle. In 1953, the ANC sponsored a sit-in campaign to desegregate churches, restaurants, and other public buildings. In January 1954, ANC members began to picket and boycott butcher shops in Lusaka and other towns to end discriminatory practices. After seven weeks of continued pressure, many shops in Lusaka desegregated, but shops in other areas did not. In January 1955, the African Mineworker's Union began a two-month strike to advance the African cause and won minor pay increases. In April 1955, the ANC formed six action groups in villages in Chinsali to urge the cessation of respect for government authorities. In April 1956, Kaunda and the ANC called for a boycott of all European and Asian-owned shops. In Lusaka, the boycott virtually paralyzed one commercial district in April. Instead of pickets, women known as "watchdogs" verbally dissuaded African consumers from entering shops. These boycotts were happening simultaneously with miners' strikes in the Copperbelt. In early September 1956, the governor of the Western Provice ordered the detention of forty-five union leaders. In 1960, students in six schools organized demonstrations, strikes, and boycotts. Many Africans went to jail during these noncooperation campaigns.

Other actions sponsored by the ANC during the 1950s included petitions to the queen of England to oppose the federation, a national "Day of Mourning" when African government employees stopped work for one day, noncooperation with government-decreed forced labor and compulsory communal storage of grains, and more boycotts of shops practicing racial discrimination in 1959 and 1960.

Several nationalist groups spearheaded the resistance movements during the late 1950s and early 1960s, sometimes fighting among themselves for power. Kaunda split with the ANC over tactics and founded the Zambia African National Congress (ZANC) in October 1958. This organization was banned by the government in 1959 and was succeeded by the United National Independence Party (UNIP), which later became the ruling party of Zambia. Several other smaller splinter groups emerged in the late 1950s and early 1960s.

The anticolonial struggle included violent direct action as well as nonviolent action. Toward the end of 1955, violence in the area of the Copperbelt increased. There were clashes with security forces in 1958 over village resettlement. These attacks were followed by incidents of arson, intimidation, and malicious damage in 1958 and 1959. The Zambia African National Congress was banned four months after inception because of attacks on shops by African crowds in Lusaka, the capital. In July and August 1961, many bridges were destroyed amid widespread sabotage that was, in part, sponsored by UNIP.

Supported by Ghana Prime Minister Nkrumah, Kaunda intensified his efforts to organize mass resistance in 1959 and 1960. The government cracked down in 1959, banning ZANC and arresting and jailing Kaunda for nine months in early March 1959 after he advocated an election boycott. In the spring of 1960, UNIP was banned in the Western Province, provoking clashes with police until the ban was lifted in November. In 1961, Africans in several provinces blocked roads, burned buildings, and clashed with forces, as violent resistance increased. Also in 1961, Kaunda and UNIP called for boycotts of European beer-halls in a "keep sober" campaign. In 1962, he threat-

ened a mass mine strike and an international march by the World Peace Brigade into Northern Rhodesia if the Rhodesian government did not grant majority rule.

In response to these threats and the growing power of the violent and nonviolent anticolonial movement, the British government revised the constitution to pave the way for majority rule. The 1962 Northern Rhodesia Constitution produced an awkward coalition of UNIP- and ANC-elected leaders and the Northern Rhodesian government. In late 1963, an all-UNIP government was elected. Independence was achieved on October 24, 1964. Kenneth Kaunda was named president of Zambia, and he continued to rule until 1991. The Zambian anticolonial resistance movement was successful in gaining independence through a combination of nonviolent noncooperation and violent resistance.

Brad Bennett

References

Hope, Marjorie, and James Young. *The Struggle for Humanity: Agents of Nonviolent Change in a Violent World.* Maryknoll, N.Y.: Orbis, 1977.

Mulford, David C. *Zambia: The Politics of Independence, 1957–1964.* Oxford: Oxford University Press, 1967.

Rotberg, Robert I. *The Rise of Nationalism in Central Africa: The Making of Malawi and Zambia, 1873–1964.* Cambridge: Harvard University Press, 1965.

Tordoff, William, ed. *Politics in Zambia.* Berkeley: University of California Press, 1974.

See also GHANA ANTICOLONIAL MOVEMENT, 1947–1951; SOUTH AFRICA, OPPOSITION TO RACIAL OPPRESSION

Index

Main entries are printed in boldface type.

A

Abalone Alliance, 375, 376
Abbott, Grace, 13
'Abdulfattah, Nabil, 279
Abernathy, Ralph David, 89, 332, 354, 417, 505, 507
Abiola, Moshood, 322
Abkhazia, 170
Abolitionist Movement (United States), 3–9, 59, 156, 157, 203, 322, 333, 470, 537
Aboriginal rights, 26–28, 31
Abortion, opposition, 86
Absenteeism, 71
Abuelas de Plaza de Mayo, 310
Accra, Ghana, 214
Accuracy in Academia, 387
Acheson, Dean, 379
Action, Justice, and Peace Association, 61
ACT-UP (AIDS Coalition to Unleash Power), 9–11, 13, 209, 210, 390, 423
Adams, Abigail, 580
Adams College, 307
Adams, Gerry, 370
Adams, Massachusetts, 23
ADAPT (American Disabled for Attendant Programs Today), 11–13
Addams, Jane (1860–1935), 13–14, 355, 360, 577, 578, 583
Afghanistan, 255, 512
AFL-CIO, 541
African Mineworker's Union, 585
African National Congress (Northern Rhodesia), 585
African National Congress of South Africa, 14–16, 307, 310, 355, 387, 417, 481, 482, 492, 495, 496, 497, 498, 499, 500, 501, 502, 503, 586
African Wildlife Fund, 168
Afrikaner National Party, 499
Agape, 16, 289, 291
Agitational propaganda, 9
Agricultural Labor Relations Act, 69
Agricultural Workers Organizing Committee, 541

Ahimsa, 16–17, 196, 198, 201, 391
Ahmedabad Labor Satyagraha (India), 1918, 17
Ahmedabad, India, 16, 200, 248, 249, 250, 455
AIDS, 9, 10, 22, 208, 209, 210, 423
Air Raids, 18, 328
Alabama, 286, 518, 537
Alaska, 582
al-Azhar, 278, 279, 280
Albania, 100, 254, 255, 296, 438
al-Banna, Hasan, 279
Albany, Georgia, 1961–1962, 18, 92–93, 109, 139
Albany, New York, 23
Aldermaston, England, 63
Alexander II, 451
Algeria, 132, 153, 173, 279, 300, 360, 367, 368
Algeria, French Generals' Revolt of 1961, 19–20, 102, 132
Alianza Democrática, 71, 72
Al-Khomeini, Imam Ruhallah Al-Musavi, 264
Allen, Devere (1891–1955), 20–21
Allen, Stephen Shepard, 314
Allen, Steve, 459
Allende Gossens, Salvador, 70, 71
Allentown, Pennsylvania, 53
al-Nasiri, Ibn Khalid, 278
Alternative institutions, 258, 259
Alton, Illinois, 5
Al-Wafd al-Misri, 163
Ambedkar, B.R., 250
Amchitka, Alaska, 221
American and Foreign Anti-Slavery Society, 6
American Anti-Slavery Society, 4, 5, 23, 203, 204, 333, 580
American Civil Liberties Union, 14, 111
American Colonization Society, 3, 4
American Equal Rights Association, 23, 334, 340, 581
American Federation of Labor, 53
American Friends Service Committee, 21–23, 107, 127, 128, 355, 376, 380, 382, 388, 392, 422, 462, 518, 535, 547, 549, 550, 551, 552, 554, 557, 558
American Health Care Association, 12

American Indian Movement, 342, 343
American Legion, 53
American Peace Society, 3, 4, 5, 6, 7, 8
American Public Transit Authority, 12
American Red Cross, 21
American Relief Association, 21
American Revolution, 125, 275, 421, 432, 579
American Suffrage Association, 581
American Woman Suffrage Association, 23, 341, 513
Americans for Democratic Action, 549, 550, 552
Americans with Disabilities Act, 11, 12, 13
Amish, 125, 422
Amnesty International, 233, 285
Amritsar massacre, 249, 347
Amsterdam, 382
An Pyong-Mu, 293
Anabaptists, 125
Anglo-Irish Agreement, 261, 262
Angola, 339, 340, 367
Animal Liberation Front, 166
Animal rights movements, 165, 166–68
Anniston, Alabama, 191
Another Mother for Peace, 549
Antarctica, 221
Anthony, Susan Brownell (1820–1906), 23–24, 333, 340, 341, 342, 513, 581, 582
Antiapartheid movement, 142, 307, 321, 367, 409, 417, 495–504, 463, 472, 474, 481–82, 510–11. See also Mandela, Nelson Rolihlahia; Namibia, Campaign for Freedom; South Africa; Tutu, Archbishop Desmond Mpilo
Antigone, 85, 523
Anti-Slavery Convention of American Women, 333
Anti-Slavery Society, 233
Appeals, 527
Aquinas, Saint Thomas, 300
Aquino, Benigno, 24, 412
Aquino, Corazon (b. 1933), 24, 412
Arab, 215, 258, 266, 321, 364, 394
Arab Higher Committee for Palestine, 394, 395
Arab League, 51
Arab-Israeli conflict, 22
Arafat, Yassar, 40
Arbenz, Jacobo, 457
Arendt, Hannah, 431, 432
Argentina, 131, 149, 150, 151, 300, 309, 310, 512
Aristide, Jean-Bertrand, 227, 228, 229
Arizona, 281, 582
Armenia, 169, 170, 172
Association of Relatives of the Detained and Disappeared, 71
Atlanta, Georgia, 88, 287, 291
Atlantic Life Community, 43
Atlantis Community, 11, 12
Attlee, Clement, 251
Auberger, Mike, 11
Auburn, New York, 538
Auckland, New Zealand, 425, 559, 560

Audubon Society, 165, 166
Aung San, 24
Aung San Suu Kyi (b. 1945), 24–25, 56, 57, 58, 356, 428
Auschwitz, 277
Australia, 43, 143, 340, 350, 377, 382, 403, 415, 494, 530, 582
Australia, a History of Nonviolent Action, 25–32
Australian Freedom League, 28
Austria, 21, 236, 237, 273, 440, 441, 583
Aylwin, Patricio, 70, 73
Azerbaijan, 169, 170

B
Baez, Joan, 360, 553, 565
Baghdad, Iraq, 266
Baker, Ella, 91, 505, 506
Baker, Newton B., 126
Balaguer, Joaquín, 155, 156
Balch, Emily Greene, 355, 578, 579
Balfour Declaration, 394
Baliapal Movement (India), 1985–1992, 32–34, 213
Ballou, Adin (1803–1890), 34–35, 529
Baltic Independence Movements, 1987–1991, 35–39, 509
Baltimore, Maryland, 66
Banerjea, Surendranath, 243
Bangkok, Thailand, 319, 471, 521, 522
Bangladesh, 334, 367, 564
Banners, 9, 12, 221, 326, 553
Bardoli Campaign (India), 1928, 39–40, 200, 229
Barletta, Nicolas A., 396
Baroda, India, 164
Barria, Aurelio, 398
Baruch, Bernard, 379
Basque, 472
Baton Rouge, Louisiana, bus boycott, 89
Battek, Rudolf, 67
Battle Creek, Michigan, 537
Bearing witness, 221
Becker, Norma, 552
Beckwith, George, 7
Beijing, China, 74, 75, 76, 77, 78, 80, 140, 141, 315, 316, 525
Beijing Autonomous Student Federation, 525
Beijing University, 315
Beit Sahour (Occupied West Bank), 1988–1989, 40, 566
Belarus, 35, 37, 277
Belfast, Northern Ireland, 260, 261, 370
Belgium, 276, 277, 300, 340, 344, 364, 403, 430, 449
Belgrade Women's Lobby, 466
Belgrade, Serbia, 49
Belo, Bishop Carlos Ximenes, 162
Ben Gurion, David, 22
Bengal, 244, 246, 247, 249, 251
Bentham, Jeremy, 393
Berkeley, California, 470

Berkman, Alexander, 216
Berlin Wall Destruction 1989–1990, 40–41, 133,
231, 255, 428, 441, 442
Berlin, Germany, 18, 23, 40, 205, 218, 273, 283,
442, 446, 448, 449, 450, 567
Berrigan, Daniel (b. 1921), 41–42, 43, 65, 84, 350,
382, 414, 416, 536, 555
Berrigan, Philip (b. 1923), 42–43, 65, 66, 84, 382,
414, 416, 536, 555
Bertrand Russell Foundation, 267
Besant, Annie, 244, 248
Bethlehem, 40
Bevel, James, 505
Bhagavad Gita, 81
Bhave, Vinoba (1895–1982), 43–44
Bhoodan movement, 44
Bhoodan Yajna, 43
Bigelow, Albert Smith (1906–1993), 44, 380
Bilthoven, Holland, 178
Birmingham, Alabama, 1963, 18, **44–46**, 93–96,
289, 361, 506
Birmingham, England, 582
Bishop, Merlin D., 54
Black Panthers, 98
Black Power, 123, 124, 290, 507, 518, 571
Black, Hugo, 234
Blacklisting, 46
Blackwell, Henry, 341
Blank, Wade, 11
Blanket protests, 261, 263
Blaxall, Arthur, 463
Blewitt, Tom, 423
Blockades, 46–48, 9, 83, 228, 301, 348, 370, 385,
395, 509, 525
    antiwar, 63, 270, 334, 353, 467, 555
    antiapartheid, 481
    anticolonial, 311, 586
    and disabled activists, 11, 12
    economic, 34, 40, 186, 215, 254
    environmental movement, 81, 166, 168, 376,
    536
    as a method of nonviolent action, 254, 323,
    328
    and Native American rights, 342, 343
Bloemfontein, South Africa, 497
Bloomer, Amelia, 23
Bohlen, Jim, 221
Bohlen, Marie, 221
Bohn, Herbert G., 54
Bohr, Neils, 378
Bolivia, 82, 299
Bolshevik Revolution, 312
Bolsheviks, 35, 432
Bombay, India, 243, 244, 248, 249
Bonaparte, Napoleon, 431, 433
Bondurant, Joan, 360, 361
Bonhoeffer, Dietrich, 293
Bonn, Germany, 382
Borge, Tomás, 352
Born, Max, 576

Bose, Subhas Chandra (1897–1945), 48, 250, 251
Bosnia-Herzegovina, 170, 296, 255, 296, 465
**Bosnia-Herzegovina, Resistance to Civil War,
1991–1992, 48–51**
Boston Tea Party, 84, 542
Boston, Massachusetts, 203, 204, 205, 220, 223,
224, 257, 286, 322, 381, 458, 465, 543,
544
Bougainville, Papua New Guinea, 30
Boulding, Kenneth, 408, 534
Bourdet, Claude, 344
Boycott, Captian Charles Cunningham, 51
Boycotts, 15, 51–52, 84, 155, 204, 250, 485, 486,
525, 536
    civil rights movement, 86, 89, 90, 91, 92, 93,
    179, 289, 332, 354, 400, 505
    consumer, 18, 45, 165, 168, 456, 541, 542,
    544, 580, 585, 586
    economic, 24, 65, 75, 76, 80, 103, 214, 247,
    254, 259, 314, 323, 394, 417, 472, 502,
    506
    Indian national movement, 247, 250, 285,
    327
    as a method of nonviolent action, 319, 321,
    323, 324, 387, 389, 480
    political, 50, 163, 186, 236, 273, 339, 586
    secondary, 256
    social, 48, 215
    and South Africa, 492, 493, 494, 496, 499,
    501, 503, 510
    sports, 511–512
Boynton v. *Virginia*, 92
Brando, Marlon, 342
Brantford, Ontario, 342
Brazil, 22, 61, 62, 83, 364, 530, 583
Brenes, Roberto, 399
Brethren, 125, 126, 392, 422, 426
Brezhnev, Leonid, 438, 487
Brisbane, Australia, 30
Bristol, England, 582
British Empire, 39, 244
British Indian Association, 243
British South Africa Company, 585
Brookwood Labor College, 1921–1937, 52–55,
335
Broomfield Committee, 39
Brotherhood of Sleeping Car Porters, 88
Browder v. *Gayle*, 89
Brown v. *Board of Education*, 88, 89
Brown, Edmund G., Jr., 69, 542
Brown, Herbert Runham, 564
Brown, John, 6, 7
Brown, Sam, 551
Brussels, Belgium, 382
Bryant, Anita, 208
Bstan-dzin-rgya-mtsho, Dalai Lama XIV (b. 1935),
55–56, 356, 428, 527, 528
Buber, Martin, 429
Bucharest, Romania, 443, 444
Budapest, Hungary, 236, 583

Buddhism, 16, 25, 55, 57, 179, 220, 293, 312, 350, 356, 358, 391, 393, 426, 427, 428, 471, 522, 527. *See also* Bstan-dzin-rgya-mtsho, Dalai Lama XIV
Buddhist Peace Fellowship, 393
Buenos Aires, Argentina, 150, 309
Builders Labourers Federation, Australia, 30
Bujak, Zbigniew, 486
Bukoshi, Bujar, 295
Bulgaria, 133, 254, 344, 437, 439, 442
Bureau of Indian Affairs, 342
Burma (Myanmar), 24, 25, 356, 428, 468, 533, 583
Burma, Democracy Movement, 1988–1989, 56–58
Burnam, Burnam, 27
Burns, Sir Alan, 214, 215
Burritt, Elihu (1810–1879), 58–59
Burrowes, Robert J., 31
Bush, George, 212, 492
Butkevicius, Audrius, 37, 38, 39
Byrnes, James A., 379

C

Calcutta, India, 243, 244, 251
Caldicott, Helen, 29
Calhoun, Arthur W., 52
Calhoun, John C., 385
California, 138, 208, 257, 541, 560, 582
**Camara, Dom Helder (b. 1909), 61–62, 218, 360, 364, 403
Cambodia, 367
Cambridge, Massachusetts, 544
**Campaign for Nuclear Disarmament, 62–64, 153, 219, 381
Camus, Albert, 360
Canada, 109, 143, 154, 157, 169, 216, 221, 256, 340, 342, 343, 367, 401, 530, 554, 582
Canton. *See* Guangzhou
Cao Rulin, 315
Cap Haitien, Haiti, 228
Capitini, Aldo, 267
Cárdenas Solórzano, Cuauhtémoc, 329, 330, 331
CARE, 227
Carlyle, Thomas, 303
Carmichael, Stokely, 92, 98
Carson, Rachel, 165
Carter, Jimmy, 170, 265, 298, 382, 512
Case, Clarence Marsh (1874–1946), 64, 320, 434
Castro, Fidel, 139, 255
Catholic Peace Fellowship, 43
**Catholic Worker Movement, 64–65, 137, 380, 392, 393, 416, 429
Catonsville Nine, 1968, 42, 65–66, 84
Catonsville, Maryland, 42, 43, 65, 415
Catt, Carrie Chapman, 577
Ceausescu, Nicolae, 443, 444
Cedarville, Illinois, 13
Center for Antiwar Action, Serbia, 465, 466
Centers for Disease Control, 10
Central Committee for Conscientious Objectors, 128

Central Intelligence Agency, 263, 457
Ceresole, Pierre, 178
Chacour, Elias, 364
Chai Ling, 525, 526
Challe, Maurice, 19
Chamorro, Joaquín, 83
Champaran, Bihar, India, 200, 248
Chaney, James, 96, 192
Chang Ul-byong, 293
Chanting, 259
Chaplin, Ralph, 254
Charleston, South Carolina, 86
Charter 77 (Czechoslovakia), 66–68, 135, 230
Chatterjee, Bankim Chandra, 246
Chavez, Cesar Estrada (1927–1993), 51, 68–69, 138, 177, 360, 541, 542
Chelmsford, Lord (Frederick John Napier Thesiger), 248
Chiang Kai-shek, 74, 76, 77, 78, 170
Chicago, Illinois, 9, 10, 13, 97, 121, 122, 137, 252, 281, 290, 381, 430, 458, 549, 551, 579
Chicago Peace Society, 52
Chile, 131, 149, 150, 367, 530, 531
Chile, Civic Strike, 1931, 69–70
Chile, Transition to Democracy, 70–73
China, 21, 73–81,153, 164, 168, 170, 321, 324, 367, 433, 442, 559, 583
    Democracy Wall movement in, 140–142
    and Korea, 241
    May fourth movement in, 315–16
    and tax resistance, 173, 174, 175
    Tiananmen Square, 524–26, 366
    and Tibet, 527–28
    and Vietnam War, 547, 551
Chinese Communist Party, 74, 75, 76, 77, 78, 79, 80
Chipko Movement (India), 81–82, 165, 168, 213
Christian Citizen, 58
Christian Democrats, 70, 71, 73, 267, 269
Christianity, 16, 34, 67, 74, 157, 279, 570
    and abolitionists, 3, 34, 224
    and Australia, 25, 28, 29
    Catholicism and, 64–66, 137, 318, 403
    and civil disobedience, 84–86
    and civil rights movement, 90, 287–91
    and conscientious objection, 125, 273
    and Nicaragua, 352, 353
    and nuclear disarmament, 414–16
    and pacifism, 183–84, 358, 391–93, 426–29, 462–64
    and persecution of Jews, 145, 446
    and principled nonviolence, 361–62
    Quakers and, 335, 355, 419–22
    and sanctuary movement, 456–58
    within Solidarity (Poland), 489–90
    and South Africa, 539–40
Chun Doo Hwan, 293, 294, 296, 297
Churchill, Winston, 346
Civic Alliance of Serbia, 466

Civic Forum, 230, 231, 443
Civic Strike, 82–83, 82, 83, 106, 107, 155
Civil Disobedience, 64, 83–86, 258, 259, 368, 394,
    417
    and antiwar movements, 179, 407–10, 549,
        552, 555, 573–77
    and the civil rights movement (U.S.), 89, 289–
        91
    and gay rights, 209
    and Gandhi (Indian national movement), 151,
        197, 198, 199, 201, 249, 250, 251, 284,
        347, 460
    and homelessness, 110–12
    in Italy, 268, 270
    as a method of nonviolent action, 319, 322,
        328, 389, 434, 473
    and Nazism, 344, 446–47
    and nuclear disarmament, 63, 107–9, 153,
        267, 335, 380, 382, 557
    and opposition to nuclear power, 104–5,
        375
    as principled nonviolence, 358, 359, 360, 361
    and South Africa, 310, 496–501
    and Thoreau, Henry David, 523–24
    training for, 529–33
Civil Rights Act of 1964, 96, 97, 123, 313, 505,
    506
Civil Rights Act of 1968, 98
Civil rights movement (Northern Ireland), 368–71
Civil Rights Movement (United States), 42, 43, 52,
        86–99, 292, 472, 474
    and antiwar movement, 547, 549
    and identity, 241
    leadership in, 304, 305, 426,
    nonviolent action and, 84, 85, 114, 211, 360,
        361, 530
    religious influence on, 426, 428, 480
    women and, 549, 570, 579
    See also King, Martin Luther; March on
        Washington, 1963; Montgomery Bus
        Boycott, 1955–1956; Parks, Rosa;
        Southern Christian Leadership Confer-
        ence
Civil Society, 71, 99–101, 343
Civil war, 236, 334
Civilian-Based Defense, 101–4, 292, 306, 393,
        468, 533, 534
Clamshell Alliance, 104–5, 375
Clandestine Front, 161, 162
Clandestine papers, 373
Clark, Ramsay, 553
Clark, Septima P., 401
Clausewitz, Carl von (1780–1831), 105–6, 102,
        467, 515
Cleaver, Kathleen, 519
Clergy and Laymen Concerned About Vietnam
        (CALCAV), 42, 549, 550, 551, 552, 553
Coercive Acts, 542
Coffin, William Sloane, Jr., 459, 460
Cold war, 206, 212

Collaborate, refusal to, 283
Collins, George, 53, 54
Collins, Judy, 553
Colombia, 82, 107, 149, 173, 299
Colombia, Civic Strike, 1957, 106–7
Colorado, 281, 582
Colton, James, 216
Columbia University, 482, 483
Combahee River Collective, 570, 571
Comiso, Italy, 29, 270
Comite de Defense des Juifs, 277
Committee for National Salvation, Lithuania, 38
Committee for Nonviolent Action, 44, 107–9, 107,
        139, 335, 381, 547, 551, 552, 557, 558,
        559, 560
Committee of 100 (Great Britain) , 63, 109–10,
        153
Committee of Families of the Disappeared, 149
Committee of the Peasant Union, 318
Commonwealth of Independent States, 38
Community for Creative Non-Violence, 110–12,
        177
Community of the Ark, 267, 300
Community Service Organization, 68
Concepción, Chile, 70
Concertación de Partidos por la Democracia, 70,
        73
Concord, Massachusetts, 522, 544
Confederation of Copper Workers, Chile, 71
Conference on Security and Cooperation in Eu-
        rope, 36, 443
Conflict Resolution, 112–14, 116, 117, 120, 144,
        241, 358, 388, 391, 408, 466, 565
Conflict Theories, 115–21
Congress Alliance, South Africa, 15
Congress of Industrial Organizations, 53, 54, 231
Congress of Racial Equality, 43, 90, 91, 92, 97,
        121–24, 122, 124, 191, 192, 335, 409,
        430, 506, 507
Congress of South African Trade Unions, 16, 503
Congress Socialist Party, 245, 251
Congress Swaraj Party, 245
Congressional Union for Woman Suffrage, 402
Connecticut, 257
Connor, T. Eugene "Bull", 45, 46, 93, 95
Conscientious Objection, 21, 22, 124–28, 138,
        157, 178, 268, 273, 301, 318, 335, 360,
        391, 403, 407, 409, 422, 426, 462, 463,
        468, 554, 564, 576
Consejo de Comunidades Etnicas "Runujel
        Junam," 404
Constructive actions, 270
Constructive Program, 128–30, 199, 461
Constructive projects, 301
Continental Congress, Second, 545
Convention on International Trade in Endangered
        Species of Wild Flora and Fauna
        (CITES), 165
Convention People's Party, Ghana, 214, 215
Cook County, Illinois, 9

Copenhagen People's Strike, 148, 191
Copenhagen, Denmark, 145
Corriente Democratica, 331
Corrigan, Mairead (b. 1944), 130–31, 356, 405, 406, 567
Costa Rica, 569
Council of Europe, 232, 404
Coups d'état, 131–33, 57, 102, 228, 283, 296, 431, 432, 521, 533, 534
Court of Nations, 59
Cousins, Norman, 378, 381, 459
Crawl-in, 12
Croatia, 48, 49, 50, 236, 255, 256, 296, 465, 466, 467
Croatian Democratic Union, 49
Crusade for Citizenship, 91
Cuba, 82, 109, 137, 139, 397, 433, 492, 559, 583
Cuban missile crisis, 62
Cuidadanias de Panama, 399
Cultural Revolution, 79
Cultural Survival, 168
Cumann na nGaedheal, 223
Cumberland, Rhode Island, 34
Curzon, Lord George Nathaniel, 247
Cyprus, 395, 396
Czech Republic, 404
Czechoslovak Communist Party, 158
Czechoslovakia, 146, 158, 269, 344, 363, 407, 485, 564, 583
    and revolutions of 1989, 437, 438, 439, 442–43, 444, 445
    See also Czechoslovakia, 1968 Resistance Movement; Havel, Václav
Czechoslovakia, 1968 Resistance Movement, 102, 133–36, 367, 519–20

D

D'Escoto, Miguel, 352
Dalai Lama XIV. *See* Bstan-dzin-rgya-mtsho, Dalai Lama XIV
Daley, Richard, 97
Dancing, 220
Dandi, India, 198
Darst, David, 65
Daughters of Bilitis, 206, 207
Daughters of Temperance, 23
Davis, A.L., 90
Davis, Rennie, 552
Day, Dorothy (1897–1980), 64, 137–38, 380, 416, 422, 429
de Gaulle, Charles, 19, 132, 344
de Jonghe, Etienne, 364
de Klerk, F.W., 310, 311, 356, 492, 494
de Ligt, Barthélemy (Bart) (1883–1938), 138–39, 406, 564
De Trinitate, 300
Deak, Francis, 236
Debré, Michel, 19
DeCaux, Len, 53
Declaration of Independence, 275

Declaration of Women's Rights, 341
Defence in the Nuclear Age, 292
Defiance Campaign of 1952, South Africa, 15
Delano, California, 68, 541
Delaying payment, 24
Delegazione Assistenza Emigranti e Profughi Ebrei, 277
Delhi, India, 200, 243, 249
Dellinger, David, 552, 555
Deming, Barbara (1917–1984), 139–40, 181, 569, 570
Democracy Wall Movement (China), 79, 80, 140–42
Democratic League of Kosova, 295
Democratization, 142–45, 158, 259, 294, 314, 396
Demokratizatsiya, 36
Demonstrations, 57, 68, 71, 163, 214, 215, 236, 242, 266, 294, 295, 301, 339, 451, 521
    antiwar, 466, 467, 547, 549, 551, 552, 553
    Berlin Wall, 40–41
    civil rights movement, 45–46
    in China, 74, 75, 76, 78, 79, 80, 140, 315
    environmental movement, 166–68
    gay rights movement, 209, 423
    in Iran, 264, 265
    in Latin America, 150, 329, 396, 399
    as a method of nonviolent action, 189, 211, 213, 320, 366, 387, 536
    Native American, 342–43
    against Nazism, 343, 344, 372, 446
    against nuclear weapons, 152–53, 220, 380, 382, 459
    political, 161, 162, 185, 228, 258, 259, 273, 274, 348, 543
    religious, 157–58, 412, 428
    during the revolutions of 1989, 440, 441, 442, 443
    in South Africa, 498, 500
    in Tibet, 527, 528
    and women's suffrage, 340–42
Deng Xiaoping, 79, 80, 524, 526
Denmark, 306, 344, 418, 524
Denmark, Evacuation of Danish Jews, 1943, 145–46
Denmark, Resistance to Nazi Occupation, 146–49, 190
Denver, Colorado, 11, 579
Desaparecidos Movement in Latin America, 149–51
Desertion, 554
Detroit, Michigan, 465, 579
Detzer, Dorothy, 578
Dharasana Salt Works Raid (India), 1930, 151–52
Diaz Herrera, Roberto, 396, 397, 398
Dick Gregory, 177
Die-ins, 9, 553, 576
Ding Ling, 78
Diplomatic Sanctions, 152
Direct Action Campaign, 63
Direct Action Committee Against Nuclear War (Great Britain), 109, 152–53

Dirty protest, 261, 263
Disappearance, Collective, 153
Disarmament, 534
Discourse on Voluntary Servitude, 299, 478, 556–
57
Disrobing, Protest, 154, 158, 326
Disruption, 423
Dolci, Danilo (b. 1928), 154–55, 177, 360, 430
Dominican Republic, Civic Strike, 1961, 155–56
Dorchester County, Maryland, 538
Dortel-Claudot, Maria-Marthe, 403
Douglass, Frederick (1818?–1895), 6, 23, 156–57,
513, 537
Doukhobors (Canada), 154, 157–58, 392, 426
Dover, England, 27
Draft resistance, 84, 173, 335, 465, 467, 536, 549,
551, 554, 565
Dresden, Germany, 283
Druze, 215, 216
Duan Qirui, 76
Dubček, Alexander (1921–1992), 158–59, 133,
134, 135, 230, 443
Dube, John, 14
DuBois, W.E.B., 517
Dulles, John Foster, 381
Dunkards, 126
Dunn, Robert William, 53
Durban, South Africa, 307, 498, 499, 504
Durkheim, Emile, 304
Duvalier, François, 227
Duvalier, Jean-Claude, 227, 228
Duvalier, Michèle Bennett, 227
Dyer, Richard, 249

E

Eagle Forum, 387
Earth First!, 165, 166, 331, 536
Earthlife Africa, 222
Earthwriting, 326, 471
East India Company, 243
East Timor, Resistance to Indonesian Occupation,
161–63
Eastern Regional Coalitions of Homophile Organi-
zations, 206
Eaton, Robert, 559
Ebert, Friedrich, 283, 284
Ebert, Theodor, 534
Economic sanctions, 80
Ecuador, 149, 583
Edinburgh, Scotland, 582
Education, alternative systems, 295
Egypt, 163, 257, 279, 367, 433, 457, 565
Egyptian Demonstrations against British Rule,
1919–1922, 163
Ehrlich, Paul, 165
Einstein, Albert, 468
Eisenhower, Dwight David, 88, 205, 274, 381
El Salvador, 22, 149, 150, 151, 224, 351, 404,
434, 456, 457, 458, 472
El Salvador, Civic Strike, 1944, 163–64

Ellsberg, Daniel, 553
Embargoes, 254, 255, 256, 257, 275, 327, 493
Emergency Peace Campaign, 53
Emerson, Ralph Waldo, 304, 522, 523
Emigration, Protest (Hijrat), 153, 157, 164, 252,
321, 326, 441, 494
England, 11, 43, 59, 126, 137, 306, 310, 419, 421,
422, 431, 468, 567
English Only, 387
Enrile, Juan Ponce, 412, 413, 414, 428
Environmental Movements, 164–69, 270, 530, 557
Equal Rights Amendment, 403, 583
Eritrea, 432
Esquipulas Peace Accord, 352, 353
Estonia, 35, 36, 37, 38, 39, 102, 103, 468, 509
Ethiopia, 255, 578
Ethnic Conflict, 115, 169–73, 212, 359, 366, 471,
474
Ethnicity, 210
Etzioni, Amatai, 362
European Community, 49, 50, 184, 256
European Convention on Human Rights, 232
European Union, 172, 363
Everyday Forms of Resistance, 173–75, 528
Exodus, 396

F

Falklands Islands, 310
Fanon, Franz, 264
Farm Workers Association, 541
Farmer, James, 92, 98, 121, 122, 123
Fasting, 65, 69, 109, 111, 137, 139, 154, 177–78,
249, 250, 275, 284, 300, 323, 328, 361,
426, 429, 526, 542
Fax zaps, 423
Federal Bureau of Investigation, 10, 43, 66, 127
Federation of Atomic Scientists, 379
Federation of Relatives of the Detained-Disap-
peared (FEDEFAM), 149
Federation of South African Women, 500
Fellowship of Reconciliation, 20, 43, 52, 53, 54,
90, 107, 121, 288, 335, 350, 364, 462,
463, 506, 547, 549, 550, 551, 552, 554,
557, 579
Fellowship of Reconciliation, International, 178–
80, 217, 218, 267, 393, 428, 462
Feminism, 180–83, 475
and antiwar movements, 573–79
and conflict theory, 116, 117
and nonviolent action, 218, 225, 427, 569–73
and nuclear disarmament, 382
See also Addams, Jane; Anthony, Susan
Brownell; Corrigan, Mairead; Deming,
Barbara; Grimké, Sarah Moore and
Angelina Emily; Mott, Lucretia Coffin;
National Woman Suffrage Association;
Paul, Alice; Stanton, Elizabeth Cady;
Women's Suffrage
Feminism and Nonviolence Study Group, 181
Fennelly, Carol, 111

Fernandez, Richard, 549
Fifteenth Amendment, 513, 581
Fincke, Helen, 53
Fincke, William, 53
Finland, 35, 36, 583
First Continental Congress, 543, 544
Fisher, Bernice, 121
Fish-ins, 342
FitzGerald, Garret, 262
Flanagan, Ross, 334
Flint, Michigan, 54
Florida, 139, 208
Flynn, Elizabeth Gurley, 252, 253, 254
Fondazione Capitini, 270
Footdragging, 174
Forest, Jim, 360, 364
Forman, James, 95
Forsberg, Randall, 383
Foster, Abby Kelley, 23, 581
Foster, Stephen, 23, 34, 581
Fourteenth Amendment, 513, 581
Fox, George (1624–1691), 125, 183–84, 419
France, 74, 360, 375, 392, 396
    and conscientious objection, 126, 127, 463
    environmental movements in, 221, 559
    and Jewish resistance to the Holocaust, 276,
        277
    and Nazi Germany, 172, 344, 345, 403
    and relief organizations, 21, 22, 422
    revolution in, 143, 144, 185, 186, 189, 232,
        431, 432, 436, 556
    and Ruhr River, 430, 447–50
    and sanctions, 254, 340
    and women's suffrage, 583
    See also Algeria, French Generals' Revolt of
        1961; France, Politics and Protest;
        Larzac (France), 1971–1981; Voluntary
        Servitude, Discourse on
France, Politics and Protest, 184–90
Franklin Dam, 30, 31
Fraternization, 229, 326
Free Religious Association, 334
Freedom buses, 27
Freedom Council (Denmark), 145, 148, 190–91
Freedom Rides, 1961, 13, 18, 26, 92, 96, 122, 123,
    179, 191–92, 324, 401, 470, 480, 506
Freedom Summer Project, Mississippi, 1964, 96,
    192–94, 531
Freire, Paulo, 61
Fremantle, Australia, 30
French Guiana, 463
French Revolution, 185, 186, 232, 431, 432, 436,
    556
Frente Democratico Nacional, 329, 330, 331
Frente Patriótico Manuel Rodríguez, 73
Friends Committee on National Legislation, 422,
    547, 550, 553
Friends of the Earth, 165, 166, 168
Friends Service Council, 21, 422
Fromm, Erich, 459

Fugitive Slave Act, 6, 84, 203
Fulbright, William, 553
Fundamentalism, 279
Funerals, Demonstrative, 76, 135, 194, 294, 314,
    326, 429

G

Gage, Matilda Joslyn, 23
Galbraith, John Kenneth, 304
Galtung, Johan, 408
Gandhi, Mohandas Karamchand (1869–1948), 17,
    195–203, 561
    and ahimsa, 16–17
    as an influence, 43, 44, 61, 89, 90, 102, 121,
        139, 154, 223, 269, 284, 285, 288, 289,
        300, 318, 346, 347, 352, 406, 407, 414,
        422, 426, 468, 505, 506
    and Indian National Congress, 244, 245
    and Indian national movement, 248–251
    influences of, 84, 524, 529, 557
    methods used by, 164, 229, 320, 357, 359,
        360, 361, 363, 430, 524, 530, 536, 566,
        177
    and the Nobel Peace Prize, 354–55, 356
    opposition to, 48, 138
    and religion, 426, 427, 428, 429
    and revolution, 434, 436
    and the Rowlatt Bills, 447
    and the Salt March, 151, 455
    and satyagraha, 128–130, 460–62
    and South Africa, 496–97, 498–99, 504
    See also Ahmedabad Labor Satyagraha, 1918;
        Bardoli Campaign, 1928; Constructive
        Program; Indian National Congress;
        Nehru, Jawaharlal; Vykom Campaign,
        1924–1925
Gandhi, Rajiv, 285
García Villas, Marianella, 151
Garrison, William Lloyd (1805–1879), 4, 6, 8, 23,
    34, 156, 157, 203–4, 224, 529, 537, 580
Gaudium et Spes, 217
Gay Activists Alliance, 207
Gay Liberation Front, 207, 209
Gay Rights Movement, 140, 204–10, 475
Gaza, 22, 257, 260
Gdansk, Poland, 323, 482, 485, 487, 488, 489,
    490, 491, 563
Geisinger, Eugene, 54
General strike, 24, 56, 95, 214, 351, 447, 509, 519
    in China, 75, 77
    in Germany, 132, 283–84
    in Iran, 263, 265
    as a method of nonviolent action, 103, 322,
        327
    against Nazism, 148, 373
    in Persia, 411–12,
    in Poland (Solidarity) 484, 491
    during revolutions of 1989, 442, 443
    San Francisco, 455–56
    Seattle, 464

See also Civic Strike; *Hartal*; Lightning Strike; Reverse Strike; Strikes

Geneva, Switzerland, 403, 583

Geneva Conventions, 233

Geography and Nonviolent Action, 210–14

George, Harold Lloyd, 249

Georgia, 38

Georgia (former USSR), 170, 172

Gerasimov, Gennady, 438

Germany, 43, 50, 132, 133
  and China, 74, 75
  and democratization, 143, 144
  and economic sanctions, 254, 256
  and France, 172, 185, 186
  and gay rights, 204, 205
  and Nazism, 139, 145, 146–48, 198, 254, 302, 343–46, 371–73, 407, 446, 472, 566–67
  and opposition to nuclear energy, 374, 375, 472
  and relief organizations, 21, 22
  revolutions of 1989 and, 102, 437, 438, 439, 440, 441–42, 443
  Ruhrkampf in, 447–50
  and women's suffrage, 582, 583

Germany, East, 40, 102, 441, 442, 444, 445, 485

Germany, West, 40, 442, 491, 576

Ghana Anticolonial Movement, 1947–1951, 214–15

Glasnost, 36, 40, 133

Gligorov, Kiro, 49

Gokhale, Gopal Krishna, 247, 248

Golan Heights Druze Resistance, 1981–1982, 215–16

Gold Coast. *See* Ghana Anticolonial Movement

Golden Rule, 44, 108, 221, 380, 557, 558, 559

Goldman, Emma (1869–1940), 216, 393, 524

Gonaïves, Haiti, 227, 228

Goodman, Andrew, 96, 192

Gorbachev, Mikhail S., 36, 37, 38, 80, 133, 135, 171, 384, 438, 443, 487, 488, 508, 510, 525

Gorgey, Arthur, 236

Goss-Mayr, Hildegard (b. 1930) and Jean (1912–1991), 179, 217–18

Gottlieb, Sanford, 459, 550

Goumindang, 73, 74, 75, 76, 77–78

Government of India Act, 245

Graetz, Robert, 332

Graf, Willi, 566, 567

Graffiti, 218, 301

Gramdan, India, 44

Gramsci, Antonio, 99, 100

Grandmothers of the Plaza de Mayo, 149

Grant, Ulysses S., 334, 422

Great Britain, 35, 62, 63, 74, 75, 126, 127, 143, 185, 206, 340, 345, 368, 377, 379, 381, 383, 394, 396, 405, 415, 542, 543, 544, 582, 583

Grechko, Andrei A., 135

Greece, 131, 254

Green Ban, 30

Green, Beriah, 5

Greenham Common Peace Camp, 1981–1993, 29, 63, 110, 219–20, 377, 383

Greenpeace, 13, 47, 165, 166, 168, 220–23, 425, 559, 560

Greensboro, North Carolina, 91, 518

Gregg, Richard (1885–1974), 223, 289, 306, 406, 564

Gregory, Dick, 342

Griffith, Arthur (1871–1922), 223, 237

Grimké, Sarah Moore (1792–1873) and Angelina Emily (1805–1879), 6, 223–24, 580, 581

Grósz, Károly, 440

Grupo de Apoyo Mutuo, 404

Guangzhou, China, 76, 141

Guantanamo, Cuba, 109, 139, 335

Guatemala, 149, 150, 151, 224, 318, 404, 427, 434, 456, 457, 458, 533, 569

Guatemala, Overthrow of Jorge Ubico, 1944, 224–25

Guerrilla Theater, 27, 209, 225–26, 328, 423

Guerrilla warfare, 15

Guinn, Joe, 121

Gujarat, India, 17, 164, 195, 196, 200, 248, 249

Gulf War, 30, 260

Gumbleton, Thomas, 364

Gumede, Josiah, 14

Gump, Jean, 416

H

Ha Wan-Sang, 293

Hague, The, 576, 577, 583

Hahn, Otto, 576

Haiti, 46, 149, 254, 255, 257, 569

Haiti, Fall of Duvalier, 1985–1986, 227–29

Haitian Human Rights League, 228

Hajek, Jiri, 67

Halsted, Fred, 552

Ham Sokhun, 293

Hamas, 260

Hamilton, Alice, 13

Hanoi, Vietnam, 18, 42, 559, 576

Harassment, Nonviolent, 207, 210, 229, 271, 328, 541

Hardin, Garrett, 165

Harpers Ferry, West Virginia, 7, 204

Harriet Tubman Home for Indigent Aged Negroes, 538

Harris, David, 554

Hartal, 48, 198, 229–30, 248, 251, 401, 447

Hassler, Alfred, 360

Haunting, 229

Havel, Václav (b. 1936), 67, 135, 230–31, 360, 363, 389, 428, 443, 490

Hawaii, 331

Hawk, David, 551

Hay, Harry, 206

Hayden, Casey, 519

Hayes, Denis, 165
Haywood, William ("Big Bill"), 252, 253
Heller, Lennie, 554
Helsinki Accords of 1976, 36, 67, 135, 230, 232, 382
Helsinki Citizen's Assembly, 466
Helsinki Parliament of Citizens, 49
Hernu, Charles, 425
Heschel, Abraham, 429
Highlander Folk School, 89, 231–32, 388, 401
Hijrat, 164. *See* Emigration, Protest
Hind Swaraj, 196, 197
Hindu Mahasabha, 251
Hinduism, 16, 33, 81, 130, 177, 195, 196, 200,
    202, 244, 245, 246, 247, 250, 251, 286,
    358, 391, 426, 461, 560, 561
Hiroshima, 220, 377, 378
Hirschfeld, Magnus, 204, 205
Hitler, Adolph, 139, 170, 178, 198, 254, 345, 446,
    557
Ho Chi Minh, 360
Hodgkin, Henry, 178
Hoffman, Abbie, 555
Holmes, John Haynes, 564
Holmes, Williams, 53
Holocaust, 145, 205, 276, 302, 395
Home Rule Leagues, 244, 248
Honduras, 149, 171, 299
Honecker, Erich, 40, 442
Honolulu, Hawaii, 44, 557, 558, 559
Hook, Sydney, 304
Hopedale Community, 34
Horton, Myles, 231, 401
House Un-American Activities Committee, 46,
    206, 574, 575, 579
Houser, George, 121
Howe, Julia Ward, 581
Hu Yaobang, 80, 321, 524, 525
Hughan, Jessie Wallace, 564
Hughes, H. Stuart, 459
Hughes, William, 28
Hull House, 13
Hull, Hannah Clothier, 578
Human barricades, 24, 33
Human Rights, 161, **232–36**, 275, 408
    in Czechoslovakia, 66–68
    in Korea, 243, 292–94
    and Latin America, 71, 73, 309–10, 318, 351,
        410, 458
    and Nobel Peace Prize recipients, 354–57
    and nonviolent struggle, 359, 366, 367, 514
    and nuclear weapons opposition, 377, 382
    and peacekeeping organizations, 403, 404,
        405
    in Poland (Solidarity), 486, 489, 490, 491
    and sanctions, 255, 322, 512
    in Serbia, 465, 466
    and Tiananmen Square Democracy Move-
        ment, 524–26
Human Rights Campaign Fund, 209
Hume, A.O., 244

Hume, John, 368
Humphrey, Hubert H., 551
Hungarian National Movement, 1848–1867, 236–
    37
Hungary, 79, 102, 133, 135, 223, 236, 404, 432,
    437, 439, 440, 441, 443, 445, 490, 512,
    517, 577
Hunger strikes, 25, 48, 66, 137, 150, 154, 177,
    253, 270, 317, 319, 323, 396, 501, 521
    in China, 80, 524, 525
    IRA, 260–63, 370
    women's suffrage, 402, 582, 583
Hunter, Robert, 222
Hurley, New York, 537
Husák, Gustav, 133, 135, 158, 230, 443
Hussein, Saddam, 257
Husseini, Amin, 394
Hutterites, 126
Huxley, Aldous, 306
Hyde Park, New York, 581
Hyung Yong-Hak, 293

I

Ibáñez del Campo, Carlos, 69, 70
Idaho, 281, 582
Identity, 107, 246, 474, 480
    in conflict theory, 120
    cultural, 211–12, 213
    and ethnic conflict, 169, 171
    and feminism, 180, 183, 569
    and gay rights movement, 204, 207, 208, 209
    See also Identity Theory
Identity Theory, 239–41
Immigration and Naturalization Service, 457, 458
Independence Club Movement (Korea), 1896–
    1898, 241–43
India, 153, 164, 171, 223, 447, 530
    and democracy, 143, 144
    and evironmental movements, 168, 213
    and Khan Abdul Ghaffar Khan, 284–86,
        401–2
    and Nehru, Jawaharlal, 346–47
    Pathan defiance of, 401–2
    Salt March of, 455, 469
    and satyagraha, 460–62
    and South Africa, 496–97, 499
    and Vykom Campaign, 560–61
    and women's suffrage, 582, 583
    See also Gandhi, Mohandas K.; Indian Na-
        tional Congress; Indian National Move-
        ment
Indian Association, 243
Indian National Army, 48, 251
Indian National Congress, 48, 195, 199, 200, 201,
    202, **243–46,** 247, 248, 249, 250, 251,
    252, 284, 285, 346, 347, 414, 455, 460,
    560
Indian National Movement, 246–52, 475
Indian Round Table Conference, 250
Indonesia, 29, 161, 162

Industrial and Commercial Workers Union, South
    Africa, 14
Industrial Workers of the World, 252–54, 517
INFACT (Infant Formula Action Coalition), 52
Innis, Roy, 123
Institute for Sexual Science, 205
International Brotherhood of Teamsters, 254
International Commission of Jurists, 233
International Committee of the Red Cross, 233
International Committee of Women for Permanent
    Peace, 577
International Congress of Women, 13, 583
International Council of Women, 23
International Court of Justice, 352
International Economic Sanctions, 229, 254–57
International Ladies Garment Workers Union, 52
International League for Human Rights, 233
International Monetary Fund, 256
International Peace Convoy, 49
International Whaling Commission, 221
International Woman Suffrage Alliance, 577, 580,
    582
International Women's Suffrage Association, 583
International Workers of the World, 252, 253, 254
Interstate Commerce Commission, 18
Intervention, 81, 434, 543
Intifada (Palestinian Uprising), 1987–1990, 40,
    114, 257–60, 428
Invasion, nonviolent, 197, 299, 301
Iqbal, Mohammed, 251
IRA Hunger Strikes, 1980–1981, 260–63, 371
Iran, 263, 264, 265, 367, 428, 433, 435
Iranian Revolution, 1963–1979, 263–66, 435, 436
Iraq, 254, 255, 256, 257, 258, 263, 264, 266, 367,
    495
Iraq Uprising, 1948, 266–67
Ireland, 223, 237, 261, 262, 281, 405
Irish Congress of Trade Unions, 368
Irish Republican Army, 130, 131, 260, 261, 262,
    369, 370, 405
Iroquois, 342
Irwin, Lord (Edward F. Wood), 198, 250, 285,
    455
Isfahan, Iran, 265
Islam, 161, 162, 212, 215, 248, 260, 264, 265,
    277, 278, 279, 280, 285, 358, 392, 411,
    427, 428, 429, 433, 581
Israel, 51, 215, 216, 257, 258, 259, 321, 340, 364,
    394, 396, 566
Italian Communist Party, 269, 270
Italy, 99, 137, 154, 171, 185, 219, 254, 255, 276,
    300, 371, 375, 396, 578, 583. *See also*
    Italy, Social Movements
**Italy, Social Movements and the Evolution of Strat-
    egy,** 267–71
Izetbegovic, Alija, 48, 49, 50

J
Jack, Homer, 121, 459
Jackson State University, 551

Jackson, Jesse, 482, 505
Jackson, Mississippi, 193
Jacobs, Aletta, 583
Jagerstatter, Franz (1907–1943), 273
Jainism, 16, 196, 391
Jallianwala Bagh, 249
Janus Society, 206
Japan, 164, 367, 375
    and China, 73, 74, 75, 76, 77, 315, 316
    and democracy, 143, 144
    and desertion (peasant uprising), 164
    and Korea independence movement, 312
    and nuclear weapons opposition, 377, 378,
        379
    and sanctions, 254, 256
    See also Japan Security Treaty Protests
Japan Security Treaty Protests, 1959–1960, 273–75
Japanese Tropical Action Network (JATAN), 168
Jarpa, Sergio Onofre, 72
Jaruzelski, Wojciech, 484, 489, 491
Jefferson, Thomas (1743–1826), 275–76
Jehovah's Witness, 127, 426
Jemison, T.J., 89
Jewish Resistance to the Holocaust, 276–77
Jiang Qing, 79
Jihad, 277–81, 278, 279, 280, 428
Jim Crow laws, 86
Jinnah, Mohammed Ali, 245, 251
Johannesburg, South Africa, 195, 310, 497, 498,
    499, 500, 504, 510, 511, 539
John Paul II, 227, 489, 490
John XXIII, 403, 427
Johnson, Lyndon B., 97, 193, 290, 459, 465, 507,
    547, 549, 551
Johnson, Mark, 11
Joint Distribution Committee, 277
Jonah House, 42, 43
Jones, "Mother" Mary Harris (1830–1930), 281–
    82
Jordan, 266
Josef, Franz, 236, 237
Jouhaud, Edmond, 19
Journey of Reconciliation, 90, 92, 122, 191
Judaism, 85, 427, 518, 524
Judenrat, 277
Julian of Norwich, 429

K
K231, 230
Kádár, János, 440
KAN, 230
Kang Munkyu, 293
Kansas, 281, 582
Kant, Immanuel, 393
Kapp Putsch (Germany), 1920, 18, 132, 283–84
Kapp, Wolfgang, 283
Karadzic, Radovan, 49
Kathmandu, Nepal, 348, 349
Kaunas, Lithuania, 37
Kaunda, Kenneth, 360, 585, 586

Kazakhstan, 37, 509
Kazerun, Iran, 265
Keening, 220
Kelley, Florence, 13
Kellogg-Briand Pact, 578
Kennedy, Jacqueline, 574
Kennedy, John C., 52
Kennedy, John F., 45, 46, 92, 96, 290, 381, 574, 576
Kennedy, Robert, 92, 192, 551, 553
Kent State University, 551
Kenya, 472
Keppley, Elwood, 54
Kersner, Jacob, 216
Khaddar movement, 130
Khadi, 249, 250
Khan Abdul Ghaffar Khan (1890–1988), 284–86,
    401, 426, 428
Khartoum, Sudan, 519
Khomeini, Ayatollah Ruhollah, 264, 265, 435
Khrushchev, Nikita, 381
Khrushchev, Nina, 574
Khudai Khidmatgar, 284, 285, 401
Kim Chae-jun, 293
Kim Chankook, 293
Kim Dae-jung, 296, 297, 298
Kim Donggil, 293
Kim Il Sung, 100
Kim Kwansok, 293, 294
Kim Su Hwan, 294
Kim Young Sam, 297, 298
King and Kotahitanga Movements (New Zealand),
    311
King, A.D., 45, 46
King, Coretta Scott (b. 1929), 286–87, 288, 291
King, Martin Luther, Jr. (1929–1968), 287–91
    and antiwar protests, 549, 551, 571
    and the Congress of Racial Equality, 122, 123
    as an influence, 61, 128, 179, 352, 370, 375,
        392, 417, 422, 426, 436
    influences of, 524, 529
    methods used by, 303, 304, 357, 360, 361,
        363, 388, 536
    and the Nobel Peace Prize, 355, 356
    and the Southern Christian Leadership Con-
        ference, 505–7
    See also Civil Rights Movement; King,
        Coretta Scott
King, Martin Luther, Sr., 287
King-Hall, Baron Stephen (1893–1966), 292, 306
Klapp, Orrin, 304
Klein, Alan, 423
Kljujic, Stjepan, 49
Knight, Anne, 582
Knights of Labor, 281
KOR (Committee for the Defense of Workers), 491
Koran, (Qur'an), 278, 279, 280, 426, 428
Korea, 241, 242, 243, 312, 568
Korea, Democratic Struggle in the South, 292–94
Korea, North, 100, 297, 312
Korea, South, 296, 297

Korean Central Intelligence Agency, 296, 297
Korean Citizens Coalition for Economic Justice, 168
Korean Military Academy, 297
Korean War, 107, 127, 312, 379, 468
Kosova, Albanian Nonviolent Movement, 169,
    294–96
Kossuth, Louis, 236
Koumintang. *See* Goumindang
Kremlin, 36, 38, 39
Ku Klux Klan, 53, 387, 400, 506
Kula, Anna, 53
Kulerski, Wladyslaw, 486, 487
Kuron, Jacek, 486
Kuwait, 255, 256, 258
Kwangju Uprising (Korea), 1980, 294, 296–98
Kyrgyzstan, 39

L

La Boétie, Etienne de (1530–1563), 299, 467, 478,
    556, 557
Labor Party, Australia, 28, 29
Labour Party (UK), 62, 63
Ladder, 206
Lafontant, Roger, 228
Lahore, 249
Lake Baikal, 168
Lakey, Berit, 334
Lakey, George, 139, 334
Lambda Legal Defense Fund, 209
Land Seizure, 14, 16, 299–300, 328
Landsbergis, Vytautis, 37, 38, 509
Lange, David, 425
Lansbury, George, 178
Lanza del Vasto, Joseph Jean (1901–1981), 267,
    300–301
Larzac (France), 1971–1981, 301–2
Lathrop, Julia, 13
Latvia, 35, 36, 37, 38, 39, 102, 103, 276, 468, 509
Lawrence, Massachusetts, 53, 252, 335
Lawson, James, 91, 98, 289
Le Chambon Sur Lignon, France, 178, 302–3
Leadership, 241, 242, 273, 303–5, 329, 335, 362,
    370, 371, 372, 398, 399, 463, 518, 526
    in the civil rights movement, 86, 89, 91, 289,
        506, 507
    in the concept of civil society, 99–100
    within conflict theory, 119
    during Czechoslovakia resistance movement,
        133–136, 158
    in demonstrations, 189
    in gay rights movement, 10
    during Indian national movement, 248, 249,
        250, 251
    in mutinies, 336
    within principled nonviolence, 362
    during Solidarity (Poland), 482, 484, 487,
        563
    in South Africa, 497, 498, 499, 500, 501,
        502, 503
    in women's suffrage, 402, 513

Leafleting, 283, 326, 527, 576
League for Industrial Democracy, 20
League for Unilateral Disarmament, 270
League of Communists, Kosova, 295
League of Nations, 22, 28, 254, 314, 339, 578
League of Universal Brotherhood, 59
Lebanon, 215
Lega degli Obiettori di Coscienza, 268
Lega per i diritti dei popoli, 267
Leipzig, Germany, 428, 441, 442
Lenin, V.I., 450, 484
Leningrad, 509, 559
Lesotho, 539
"Letter From Birmingham Jail," 95
Levison, Stanley, 91, 506
Lewis, John, 97
Lewis, Thomas, 43, 65, 66
Lhasa, Tibet, 55, 527, 528
Li Peng, 524, 525
Liberation collective, 552
Liberator, 4, 6, 8, 203, 204
Liberia, 255
Libya, 255
Liddell Hart, Captain Sir Basil Henry (1895–
    1970), 102, 305–7, 345, 515
Lightning Strike, 307
Lilienthal, David, 379
Lincoln, Abraham, 59, 204
Linlithgow, Lord (John Adrian Louis Hope), 251
Lithuania, 35, 36, 37, 38, 39, 102, 103, 216, 276,
    277, 323, 468, 509
Little Rock, Arkansas, 88
Locke, John, 232
Lockout, 327
London Antislavery Convention, 582
London, England, 23, 44, 63, 152, 153, 184, 190,
    195, 196, 198, 200, 205, 250, 333, 382,
    405, 407, 446, 468, 497, 513, 582
Long March of 1934–35, 78
Mountbatten, Lord Louis Alexander, 245, 252
Lorscheider, Dom Aloisio, 218
Los Angeles, California, 9, 115, 557
Louisville, Kentucky, 86, 122
Lovejoy, Elijah, 5
Lovejoy, Sam, 375
Lowell, Robert, 553
Lucky Dragon, 379
Lunch Counter Sit-Ins, 91–92
Lusaka, Zambia, 15, 585, 586
Lutuli, Albert John (1898–1967), 307, 310, 355,
    356, 539
Luxembourg, 344
Lyons, France, 217
Lysistratic nonaction, 472
Lyttle, Bradford, 107, 108, 552, 557

M

Maathai, Wangari, 168
Machiavelli, Nicoló, 304
Madras, India, 243, 248

Madres de Plaza de Mayo, 149, 150, 151, 309–10
Mafia, 271
Maguire, Anne, 130
Malaysia, 168
Malcolm X, 98, 289, 291, 536
Malta, 163
Malthus, Thomas, 165
Malvinas, 310
Maly, Václav, 67
Managua, Nicaragua, 83, 351
Manchester, England, 582
Mandela, Nelson Rolihlahia (b. 1918), 14, 15, 16,
    310–11, 356, 409, 481, 492, 494, 499,
    501
Manila, Philippines, 24, 47
Mansell, Michael, 27
Mao Zedong, 76, 78, 79, 80, 140, 141, 142, 170,
    524
Maori Movement, 1870–1900, 311
March First Independence Movement (Korea),
    1919, 293, 312
March on Washington, 1963, 96, 313, 417, 507
Marches, 9, 185, 228, 236, 263, 265, 270, 334,
    342, 525, 541
    civil rights movement, 18, 45, 92, 93, 94, 96,
        290, 313, 506, 507
    in Latin America, 150, 225, 309–10, 329,
        351–52, 569
    as a method of nonviolent action, 321, 326,
        361, 366
    in Northern Ireland, 368, 369, 370
    nuclear disarmament, 63, 152–53, 179
    against nuclear energy, 376
    for peace, 574, 576, 579
    in South Africa, 501, 510
Marcos, Ferdinand, 24, 412, 413, 428, 488
Marcoule, France, 300
Markovic-Vlasnic, Liljana, 364
Marshall, Burke, 45
Marshall Islands, 44
Marshall, Lenore, 459
Martin Luther King, Jr. Center for Nonviolent So-
    cial Change, 286, 287, 291
Martin, Kingsley, 306
Martínez, Maximiliano Hernández, 163, 164, 224
Marx, Karl, 62, 288, 431, 434
Maryland, 257
Mashad, Iran, 265
Massachusetts, 257
Massachusetts Anti-Slavery Society, 6
Massachusetts Peace Society, 3
Massachusetts Woman Suffrage Association, 224
Mattachine Society, 206, 207, 209
Matthews, Joseph B., 54
Mau Noncooperation (Western Samoa), 1924–
    1936, 313–15
Maung Maung, 57
Maurin, Peter, 64, 137, 393
May Fourth Movement (China), 1919, 75, 76, 79,
    164, 315–16

Mazowiecki, Tadeusz, 439, 489
McAlister, Elizabeth, 43
McCarthy, Eugene, 459, 551, 553
McCarthy, Joseph, 206
McGovern, George, 552, 553
McKeown, Ciaran, 364
McManaway, Clayton E., Jr., 228
McNamara, Robert, 381
McTaggert, David, 222
Mechanisms of Direct Action, 316–318
Mehta, Pherozeshah, 247
Melbourne, Australia, 30
Melville, Marjorie, 65
Melville, Thomas, 65
Memphis, Tennessee, 98, 281, 507
Menchú Tum, Rigoberta (b. 1959), 318, 356, 404,
    427
Mendez, Chico, 168
Mennonites, 125, 126, 127, 164, 358, 392, 422, 426
Meredith, James, 97, 385
Merton, Thomas (1915–1968), 318–19, 410, 429
Mesic, Stjepan, 49
Methods of Nonviolent Action, 319–28
Mexico, 137, 149, 281, 318, 457, 512, 569. *See
    also* Mexico, Nonviolent Action and
    Political Processes
Mexico, Nonviolent Action and Political Processes,
    328–31
Meyer, Cord, Jr., 379
Michigan, 257
Milan, 270
Milford, Massachusetts, 34
Milk, Harvey, 208
Mill, John Stuart, 304
Mill-in, 470
Milosevic, Slobodan, 295, 465
Mische, George, 65
Mississippi, 92, 96, 321, 470, 518, 531
Mississippi Freedom Democratic Party, 96, 97,
    192, 193, 321, 470
Mitch Snyder, 177
Mitterand, François, 302
Mohawk, 343
Mohism, 74
Moldova, 170
Molikans, 426
Monkeywrenching, 331–32
Monteagle, Tennessee, 231
Montenegro, 255
Montgomery Bus Boycott, 1955–1956, 52, 89, 90,
    91, 92, 93, 122, 179, 231, 288, 289,
    332–33, 400, 505, 506
Montgomery Improvement Association, 89, 288,
    332, 354, 400, 505, 506
Montgomery Voters League, 401
Montgomery, Alabama, 89, 90, 92, 93, 97, 122,
    191, 286, 288, 289, 354, 370, 400, 401,
    464, 465, 506, 507
Montreal, 44
Moon Ik-Hwan, 293

Moore, Patrick, 222
Moral Majority, 387
Moral Purity movement, 581
Moratorium, 551
Moro, Aldo, 269
Morse, Wayne, 553
Moruroa Atoll, 221, 425, 559
Moscone, George, 208
Moscow, 13, 36, 37, 38, 76, 108, 134, 158, 323,
    335, 381, 439, 451, 452, 453, 487, 508,
    509, 510, 511, 512
Moses, Robert, 96, 518
Mother Earth, 216
Mott, Lucretia Coffin (1793–1880), 6, 333–34,
    421, 513, 580, 581, 582
Mouvement de Jeunesse Sioniste, 277
Movement for a New Society, 334–35
Movement of the Revolutionary Left, 72
Movimento Italiano di Riconciliazione, 267
Movimiento Democrático Popular, 72
Moylan, Mary, 65
Mujeres Civilistas of San Miguelito, 399
Mujeres Por la Vida, 71
Multilateral Force, 576
Munoz Ledo, Porfirio, 330
Murcie, Spain, 300
Muslim, 24, 48, 50, 57, 162, 177, 195, 199, 200,
    244, 245, 247–248, 249, 250, 251, 252,
    264, 277–280, 285, 364, 401, 427, 428
Muslim Brotherhood, 279
Muslim League, 245, 248, 251, 285
Mussolini, Benito, 178, 198, 255, 557
Muste, Abraham John (1885–1967), 52, 53, 107,
    108, 178, 288, 335–36, 360, 380, 422,
    426, 434, 468, 552, 557, 565
Mutiny, 19, 102, 132, 328, 336–37, 413, 510
Mutual Support Group (GAM), 149, 151
Mygatt, Tracy, 564
Myongdong Catholic Cathedral, 294, 296

N

Nader, Ralph, 473
Naess, Arne, 166
Nagasaki, 378
Nagy, Imre, 441
Nairobi, Kenya, 168, 579
NAMFREL, 398
Namibia, Campaign for Freedom, 339–40
Namphy, Henri, 227, 228
Nanjing, China, 76, 77, 78
Naoroji, Dadabhai, 246
Nash, Diane, 92
Nashville, Tennessee, 91, 289
Nasser, Gamal Adbel, 22
Natal, South Africa, 197, 307, 496, 497, 498, 499,
    500, 501
National Action Group, 551, 552
National American Conference of Homophile Or-
    ganizations, 207
National American Woman Suffrage Association,

13, 23, 341, 402, 582, 583

National Association for the Advancement of Colored People, 14, 88, 89, 90, 92, 93, 96, 287, 332, 354, 400, 401, 505

National Conference of Brazilian Bishops, 61

National Council of Churches, 193

National Council of Churches of Korea, 292, 293, 294

National Farm Workers Association, 68, 69, 541

National Freedmen's Relief Association, 538

National Gay and Lesbian Task Forces, 209

National Gay Rights Advocates, 209

National Interreligious Service Board for Conscientious Objectors, 128

National League for Democracy, 57, 58

National League for Democracy Party, Burma, 25

National Liberation Front (Algeria), 18, 19

National Organization for Women, 387

National Party of South Africa, 16, 491, 492, 539

National Security League, 53

National Service Board for Religious Objectors, 554

National Student Association, 316

National Welfare Rights Organization, 570

National Wildlife Federation, 166

National Woman Suffrage Association, 23, 340–42, 513, 581

National Woman's Party, 402, 403, 582

Nationalist Party, Australia, 28

Native American Treaty Rights Movements, 1950s–1990s, 342–43

Native Americans, 334, 419, 420, 421, 422, 533, 573

Natives' Representative Council, 14

NATO Women's Peace Force, 576

Nazism, 205, 217, 273, 276, 277, 447

Nazism, Civilian Resistance, 1939–1945, 343–46

Ne Win, 25, 56, 57, 58

Nebraska, 281

Nehru, Jawaharlal (1889–1964), 199, 245, 250, 251, 285, 346–48, 379

Nehru, Motilal, 249, 250

Nelson, William Stuart, 289

Nepal, Movement for Restoration of Democracy, 1990, 348–50

Nestlé, 51, 52

Netherlands, 43, 138, 186, 222, 276, 306, 344, 364, 403, 415, 418, 512

New Deal, 22, 88

New Delhi, India, 24

New England Anti-Slavery Society, 203

New England Non-Resistance Society, 5, 6, 34

New Forum, 40, 441, 442

New Haven, Connecticut, 216

New Jersey, 470, 581

New Left, 109, 267, 268, 269, 270

New Orleans, Louisiana, 86, 90, 191

New song movement, 71

New York, 9, 10, 34, 137, 166, 193, 216, 257, 287, 333, 342, 380, 423, 537, 552, 578, 579

New York City, 64, 137, 203, 205, 207, 216, 281, 380, 383, 423, 458, 459, 468, 482, 512

New York Peace Society, 3

New York Stock Exchange, 209

New Zealand, 36, 47, 126, 143, 166, 221, 311, 313, 314, 321, 350, 377, 382, 383, 512, 559, 560, 582

Ngo Dinh Diem, 350

Nhat Hanh, Thich (b. 1926), 350, 360, 426, 427, 429

Nicaragua, 149, 335, 351, 353, 383, 457, 458, 462, 568, 569

Nicaragua, Civic Strike, 1944, 351

Nicaragua, Nonviolence and Revolution, 351–53

Nice, France, 205

Nicholas II, 452

Niebuhr, Reinhold, 89, 288

Nietzsche, Friedrich Wilhelm, 304

Nigeria, 22, 322

Nii Kwabena Bonne III, 214

Niwano Peace Prize, 218

Nixon, E.D. (1899–1987), 89, 332, 353–54

Nixon, Richard M., 381, 547, 551, 555

Nkrumah, Kwame, 214, 215, 585, 586

Nobel Peace Prize, 24, 55, 130, 217, 285, 287, 307, 310, 318, 350, 354–57, 405, 406, 410, 471, 528, 539, 563, 578, 579

Nobusuke, Kishi, 273, 274

No-Conscription Fellowship, 126

Noel, Gérard C., 227

No-Frontier News Service, 20

Noncompliance, 307

Noncooperation, 201, 215, 216, 263, 264, 434, 543, 585, 586

Nonexportation, 544

Nonimportation, 544

Nonresistance, 25, 54, 203, 204, 528, 529

Non-Resistant, 5

Nonviolence, Principled, 357–64

Nonviolent Alternatives, 364–65, 403

Non-Violent Coercion, 64

Nonviolent Struggle: The Contemporary Practice of Nonviolent Action, 365–68

Noriega, Manuel, 396, 397, 398, 400, 493

North Atlantic Treaty Organization, 62, 206, 270, 445, 574, 576

North Star, 6, 157

Northampton Association of Education and Industry, 537

Northern Ireland, 130, 241, 262, 323, 364, 368, 403, 405, 406

Northern Ireland Civil Rights Association, 368–71

Norway, 131, 146, 221, 306, 344, 418, 468, 567, 583

Norway, Resistance to German Occupation, 1940–1945, 371–74

Nouri, Ayatollah, 265

Nuclear energy, 267, 536

Nuclear Energy Opposition, 104, 334, 374–77, 530

Nuclear weapons, 47, 62, 63, 166, 267
Nuclear Weapons Freeze Campaign, 460
Nuclear Weapons Opposition, 42, 108, 137, 152, 179, 219, 220, 302, 335, 366, 377–84, 389, 458, 530, 557, 572, 573, 574
Nullification and Interposition, 384–85

O

Occupations, 12, 26, 50, 83, 186, 294, 299, 301, 317, 323, 328, 342, 343, 529
Occupied Palestinian Territories, 257, 258, 259, 260
Ochs, Phil, 553
Oeuvre secours aux enfants, 277
Office take-overs, 9
Oglala Sioux, 342
Old Left, 267, 268, 269, 270
Olmsted, Mildred Scott, 578
One, 206
Onyszkiewicz, Janusz, 438
Operation Gandhi, 152
Opium War, 74
Oregon, 582
Organization for African Unity, 232
Organization in Social Movements, 74, 213, 258, 387–90, 574
Organization of American States, 156, 232
Orissa, India, 34
Orr, Lord Boyd, 576
Osgood, Charles, 362
Ossetia, 170
Outing, 390, 423
Overloading government agencies, 24
Oxford, England, 534

P

P'yonyang, Korea, 312
Pacem in Terris, 427
Pacifism, 13, 20, 64, 107, 137, 138, 139, 203, 373, 391–94
    and antiwar sentiments, 288, 306, 311, 406, 407, 416, 549, 553
    and civil rights movement, 90, 288
    and labor movements, 53, 54, 253
    and nuclear disarmament, 380, 459
    as principled nonviolence, 127, 358, 469, 474, 557
    and Quakers, 21, 183, 335, 355, 419–22
    and religious conviction, 416, 425–26, 462–64
    and women's suffrage, 581, 582
Padyatras, 81
Page, Kirby, 360
Pahlavi, Mohammed Reza, 171, 263, 264, 265
Pakistan, 195, 251, 252, 285, 334, 355, 367, 583
Pal, B.C., 247
Palach, Jan, 134, 194, 443, 520
Palestine, 21, 257, 260, 394, 395, 396
Palestine Liberation Organization, 40, 258, 259, 260, 387

Palestine Royal Commission, 394
Palestine, Arab Revolt, 1936–1939, 394–95
Palestine, Illegal Jewish Immigration, 1939–1948, 395–96
Pamphlets, 274, 527
Pan-Africanist Congress, 15, 496, 500
Panama, 493
Panama, Civic Crusade, 1987–1989, 396–400
Pan-American Federation of Labor, 281
Pankhurst, Christabel, 582
Pankhurst, Emmeline, 582
Parades, 84, 225, 231, 274, 315, 326, 329, 543
Paraguay, 149
Parallel institutions, 27, 40, 56, 251, 434, 435, 543, 544
Paris, 19, 301, 305, 382
Paris Peace Treaty, 75
Park Chung Hee, 293, 294, 296
Park Hyong-Kyu, 293
Parks, Rosa (b. 1913), 89, 231, 288, 332, 354, 400–401, 428, 505
Partial Test Ban Treaty, 62
Partido Accion Nacional, 328, 329, 330
Partido Autentico de la Revolucion Mexicana, 329
Partido de la Revolucion Democratica, 328, 329, 330, 331
Partido Frente Cardenista de Reconstruccion Nacional, 329
Partido Revolucionario Institucional, 329, 330, 331
Party for Democratic Action (Bosnia-Herzegovina), 48
Passaic, New Jersey, 53
Passive resistance, 236, 253, 288, 289, 292, 311, 460, 496, 497, 499
Patan, Nepal, 348
Patel, Sardar Vallabhbhai, 39
Pathan Defiance, 1929–1938, 284, 285, 401–2
Paul VI, 61, 403
Paul, Alice (1885–1977), 402–3, 582, 583
Pauling, Linus, 381, 576
Paunar, India, 43
Pax Christi International, 217, 267, 364, 403–4
Peace Action, 387
Peace and Development Foundation, Australia, 31
Peace Brigades International, 404–5
Peace Corps, 549
Peace People, Community of the (Northern Ireland), 130, 131, 364, 405–6
Peace Pledge Union (Great Britain), 406–7
Peace strike, 574
Peace Studies, 388, 407–9, 407
Peacemakers, 139
Peck, James (1914–1993), 92, 409–10
Peel Commission, 394
Penn, William, 125, 322, 419, 420, 426
Pennsylvania, 125, 164, 281
People with Immune System Disorders, 9
Pereira, Fernando, 425
Perestroika, 36, 40, 133
Perez de Quellar, Javier, 50

Pérez Esquivel, Adolfo (b. 1931), 356, 364, 410–11
Perkins, Charles, 26
Persia, Reform Movement, 1880–1909, 411–12
Persian Gulf War, 128, 206, 212
Peru, 149, 173, 433
Peshawar, India, 284, 285, 401
Pesotta, Rose, 53
Pethick-Lawrence, Emmeline, 577
Petitions, 76, 83, 85, 179, 247, 263, 270, 274,
        314, 326, 340, 411, 412, 451, 459, 481,
        496, 498, 513, 576
Phadke, Vasudeo, 246
Philadelphia Female Anti-Slavery Society, 333
Philadelphia Free Produce Society, 333
Philadelphia, Mississippi, 96, 192
Philadelphia, Pennsylvania, 10, 23, 257, 333, 420,
        538, 544, 516, 581
Philippines, 24, 57, 173, 179, 218, 294, 398, 408,
        428, 433, 488, 583
Philippines People Power Revolution, 1986, 412–14
Phillips, Wendell, 23
Phoenix, 44, 108, 221, 380, 558, 559
Phone-zaps, 423
Picketing, 53, 55, 61, 65, 69, 93, 109, 137, 209,
        252, 268, 281, 283, 326, 334, 361, 402,
        414, 423, 498, 503, 506, 556, 575, 582,
        585
Pickett, Clarence, 459
Pickus, Robert, 360, 362
Pine Ridge, South Dakota, 342
Pinochet, Augusto, 70, 71, 72, 73, 531
Pittston Coal Company, 531
Pius XII, 379, 403
Plaza de Mayo, 309
Pledge of Resistance, 353, 568
Plessy v. *Ferguson*, 86, 88
Plowshares Movement, 42, 43, 65, 66, 382, 414–
        16, 430
Poetry, 266, 528
Poincaré, Raymond, 448, 450
Poland, 21, 102, 133, 367, 404, 418, 583
        and Jewish resistance to the Holocaust, 276–
        77, 344, 345
        and Solidarity, 36, 323, 387, 435, 436, 438,
        439–40, 482–91, 515–16, 517
        See also Walesa, Lech
Political jiu-jitsu, 26
Poor People's Campaign, 1968, 98, 290, 291, 416–
        17, 507
Popieluszko, Jerzy, 487
Popular International Peace Congress, 59
Populists (U.S.), 535
Port-au-Prince, Haiti, 228
Portsmouth, New Hampshire, 544
Positive action, 214, 215
Postal campaign, 4, 203
Posters, 78, 265, 326, 527
Prague Spring, 68, 133, 134, 135, 158, 490
Prague, Czechoslovakia, 68, 134, 194, 230, 443
Prasad, Devi, 364

Prayer rally, 24
Press boycott, 24
Pressberg, Gail, 334
Pretoria, South Africa, 492, 493, 494, 495, 498,
        500
Pritchett, Laurie, 18, 93
Proano, Leonidas, 218
Probst, Christoph, 566, 567
Processions, 69, 429
Property destruction, 65, 66, 157, 542
Property, Destruction of One's Own, 326, 417
Prophet Mohammad, 277, 278, 284
Protective accompaniment, 404, 533
Providence, Rhode Island, 20, 205
Psychological warfare, 18
Publishing, Underground, 417–18, 485, 553
Punjab, 247, 249

Q

Qing Empire, 74
Qom, Iran, 264, 265
Quakers (Religious Society of Friends), 64, 221,
        419–23, 223, 224, 293, 333, 335, 355,
        402, 404, 463, 537, 565, 583
        and conscientious objection, 125, 127
        and pacifism, 358, 392, 426, 428, 559
        See also Abolitionist Movement; American
        Friends Service Committee; Fox, George
Quebec, Canada 109, 139, 300, 335
Queer Nation, 209, 210, 390, 423–24
Quisling, Vikund, 345, 371, 373
Quit India campaign, 198, 200, 201, 245, 251
Qutb, Sayyid, 279

R

Radical Party, Italy, 269, 270
Rai, Lala Lajpat, 247
Rainbow Warrior, 221, 425, 560
Rainforest Action Group, 31
Rainforest Action Network, 168
Rallies, 9, 25, 29, 68, 107, 242, 274, 459, 481,
        552, 575
Ramos, Fidel, 24, 412, 413, 428
Ranade, M.G., 243
Randolph, A. Philip, 88, 90, 91, 96, 313, 360
Rangoon, Burma, 25, 56, 57, 58, 251
Rawls, John, 85
Ray, James Earl, 98
Reading, Pennsylvania, 54
Reagan, Ronald, 110, 111, 209, 257, 297, 352,
        353, 376, 378, 382, 383, 384, 440, 457,
        458, 490, 492
Red Brigades, 268, 269, 270
Red Cross, 22
Reeb, James, 465
Regala, Williams, 227
Regional Transit District, 11
Religion, 69, 85, 125, 169, 244, 302, 474, 570
        and human rights, 234, 302
        as inspiration, 284, 287–88

and pacifism, 358, 392, 419
and principled nonviolence, 357, 358
and sanctuary movement, 456–58
and social movements, 574–75
See also Abolitionist Movement; Ahimsa;
  Bstan-dzin-rgya-mtsho, Dalai Lama XIV;
  Buddhism; Catholic Worker Movement;
  Chipko Movement; Christianity; Day,
  Dorothy; Doukhobors; Fox, George;
  Gandhi, Mohandas Karamchand; Islam;
  Jihad; King, Martin Luther, Jr.; Muslim;
  Pax Christi International; Plowshares
  Movement; Quakers; Religion and Non-
  violent Action; Satyagraha
Rent strikes, 14, 434
Resignations, 259
RESIST, 551
Reuther, Roy, 54
Reverse Strike, 154, 155, 215, 301, 328, 430
Reverse Trial, 66, 430
Revolution, 43, 96, 115, 253, 348, 430–37, 535
  American, 275, 542–45
  in China, 76, 143
  in Czechoslovakia, 133–36
  and democracy, 143, 144
  French, 143, 185, 186, 189, 232, 431, 432,
    436, 556
  Iranian, 263–66
  in Italy, 267, 268, 269
  in Nicaragua, 351–53
  in Persia, 411–12
  in Russia, 143, 450–53
  and transformational politics, 535, 536
  See also Revolutions of 1989
Revolutions of 1989, 437–46
Reynolds, Earle, 108, 380, 558, 559
Rhoads, David, 54
Rhodes, Cecil, 585
Rhodesia, 255, 307, 512, 586
Richardson, George Spafford, 314
Richmond, Virginia, 86
Ride-in, 470
Rio de Janeiro, Brazil, 61, 169
Ripon, Lord (George Frederick Samuel Robinson),
    243
Robbin Island, South Africa 15
Roberts, Adam, 306
Robinson, Jo Ann, 89
Rocco, Sister Milar, 428
Rochester, New York, 23, 216, 341, 581
Rock Hill, South Carolina, 191
Rockford Female Seminary, 13
Roh Tae Woo, 298
Rojas, Rodrigo, 72
Romania, 396, 437, 441, 443, 445
Rome, 270, 382
Romero, Archbishop Oscar, 457
Romero, Monsignor Oscar Arnulfo, 149
Roosevelt, Franklin D., 88, 178, 224, 232, 346,
    578

Roosevelt, Theodore, 281
Rosa and Raymond Parks Institute for Self Devel-
    opment, 401
Rosenstraße Protest (Germany), 1943, 446–47
Round Table Conference, 200
Rowlatt Bills, Opposition (India), 1919, 200, 229,
    248, 249, 447
Rowlatt, Sidney, **447**
Royal Ulster Constabulatory, 369, 370
Rubin, Jerry, 555
Rugova, Ibrahim, 294, 295, 296
Ruhr, Germany, 102, 472, 567
Ruhrkampf (Germany), 1923, 430, 447–50
Rumania, 583
Russell, Bertrand, 109, 110, 306, 576
Russia, 186, 433, 517
  and Baltic Independence Movements, 35, 38
  and China, 74, 75
  February Revolution 1917, 431
  and nonviolent resistance, 126, 164, 173,
    236, 324, 392, 430, 530
  October Revolution 1917, 264, 431, 432,
    464, 583
  See also Russian Revolution of 1905; Soviet
    Union
Russian Orthodox Church, 528
Russian Revolution of 1905, 450–53
Russian Socio-Ecological Union, 168
Rustin, Bayard, 90, 91, 96, 122, 128, 288, 289,
    359, 360, 361, 506, 508, 518, 557

S

Sabotage, 554
Sajudis, 37
Salan, Raoul, 19
Salem, Massachusetts, 544
Salomon, Georges, 228
Salt March (India), 1930, 250, 284, 455
Samoan League, 314
San Diego, California, 168, 253
San Francisco General Strike, 1934, 455–56
San Francisco, California, 9, 44, 108, 153, 166,
    205, 206, 208, 222, 335, 342, 376, 423,
    424, 559
San Salvador, El Salvador, 163
Sanctions, 456
  antiapartheid, 491–95, 502, 504
  and conflict theory, 116, 117
  diplomatic, 152
  international economic, 254–57, 383, 399,
    440, 465, 543
  in Latin America, 156, 330, 399
  as a method of nonviolent action, 317, 319,
    322, 324, 363, 479, 511–12, 514, 516
Sanctuary, 326, 411, 429, 536
Sanctuary Movement, 456–58
Sandinista National Liberation Front, 351
Sandino, Augusto, 462
Sands, Bobby, 260, 261, 262
SANE (National Committee for a Sane Nuclear

Policy), 107, 108, 380, 381, 387, 393,
    458–60, 547, 550, 551, 552, 559, 576
Santiago, Chile, 70, 71
Saposs, David J., 52
Sarajevo, Bosnia-Herzegovina, 49, 50
Saraswati, Dayananda, 244
Sarawak, Malaysia, 31
Sarvodaya, 81
Satyagraha, 90, 164, 177, 347, 402, 460–62, 469,
    560–61
    and Gandhi, Mohandas Karamchand, 17,
        128–30, 196–202, 284, 285, 320, 359,
        361, 447, 455, 496
    See also Indian National Congress; Indian
        National Movement
Saudi Arabia, 256
SAVAK, 263, 264
Savannah, Georgia, 86
Saw Maung, 57
Sayre, John Nevin (1884–1977), 53, 462–64
Sayyid Ahmed Khan, 244
Schlesinger, Arthur, 304
Schmorell, Alexander, 566, 567
Scholl, Hans, 566, 567
Scholl, Sophie, 566
Schwedagon pagoda, 25
Schweikism, 322
Schweitzer, Albert, 535
Schwenkfelders, 125, 426
Schwerner, Michael, 96, 192
Schwimmer, Rosika, 577
Scientific Humanitarian Committee, 204, 205
Scott, Larry, 107
Sea Shepherd Conservation Society, 166, 536
Seabrook, New Hampshire, 104, 105, 166, 334
Seattle General Strike, 1919, 464
Seattle, Washington, 222, 381, 383
Seguel, Rodolfo, 71
Sein Lwin, 57
Selective Service Act, 127
Self-immolation, 519, 549, 553
Selma, Alabama, 97, 370, 464, 465, 507
Selma-to-Montgomery March, 1965, 464–65
Semyonov, V.S., 135
Seneca Falls Woman's Rights Convention, 333
Seneca Falls, New York, 513, 580
Seneca Women's Peace Encampment, 579
Seoul, South Korea, 297, 312
Serbia, 21, 172, 255, 256, 294, 295, 296, 465, 466
Serbia, Antiwar Activity, 1991–1994, 465–67
Serbian Democratic Party, 48
Serbian Renewal Movement, 465
Servicio Paz y Justicia, 218, 356, 364, 387, 410
Shakers, 125
Shaltut, Mahmud, 279, 280
Shanghai, China, 75, 76, 78, 80, 141, 315, 316, 559
Shariati, Ali, 264, 265
Sharif-Emami, Jafan, 265
Sharp, Gene (b. 1928), 139, 177, 181, 292, 306,
    320, 321, 322, 323, 324, 325, 360, 388,

467, 467–68, 478, 479, 515
Sharpeville, South Africa, 15, 307, 310, 492, 500
Sheffield Female Political Association, 582
Sheppard, Dick, 406
Sheppard Peace Movement, 406
Shevardnadze, Eduard, 438
Shop-ins, 542
Shridharani, Krishnalal (1911–1960), 121, 320, 469
Shultz, George, 228
Shuttlesworth, Fred L., 90, 92, 93, 95, 505
Sicily, 154, 155
Siegmund-Schültze, Frederich, 178
Sierra Club, 165, 166, 221
Signorile, Michelango, 423
Silent Spring, 165
Simon Commission, 250
Sin, Jaime Cardinal, 57
Singapore, 251
Singing, 39, 220, 225, 236, 253, 274, 326, 349,
    498, 528, 538
Sinn Fein, 223, 262, 370, 371
Sisulu, Walter, 14, 310
Sit-ins, Sit-downs, and Building Occupations, 258,
    267, 301, 342, 348, 380, 469–71, 480
    and civil rights movement, 18, 45–46, 506
    by disabled activists, 12
    and environmental movements, 81, 166
    and gay rights movement, 209, 423
    in India, 33, 81,
    and labor movements, 69, 254
    in Latin America, 150, 329, 353
    as a method of nonviolent action, 324, 328
    during Solidarity (Poland), 482, 487
    against Vietnam War, 553, 555, 576
Sivaraksa, Sulak (b. 1933), 471
Sklenkar, Marge, 551
Skywriting and Earthwriting, 471
Slovakia, 404
Slovenia, 49, 50, 296
Slowdowns, 252, 254
Smiley, Glenn E., 90, 170, 288, 289, 506
Smith, Gerrit, 8
Smith, Tucker P., 52
Smuts, Jan Christian, 197, 497
Smuts, Johannes, 198
Snyder, Mitch, 110, 111
Sobibor, 277
Social Boycott, 48, 146, 148, 215, 326, 471–72,
    543
Social Democratic and Labour Party, 262
Social Movements, 94, 100, 117, 123, 211, 213,
    231, 267, 268, 270, 271, 303, 304, 305,
    325, 334, 357, 359, 375, 472–76, 532
Social Power, 115, 123, 181, 316, 317, 476–79,
    514, 535
Socialist Party (U.S.), 20, 52
Socialist Party, Chile, 71
Socialist Workers Party, 547, 549
Soehnlein, Karl, 423
Sofia Andreyevna Bers, 528

Sofia, Bulgaria, 442
Solidarity, 104, 132, 332, 466, 479–82, 532
    in Czechoslovakia, 134, 135
    and IRA (Northern Ireland), 262–63
    in labor movements, 53, 252–54, 448–49, 456
    in Latin America, 352, 568
    against Nazism, 145, 302, 446
    against occupation, 259, 448–49
    in South Africa, 307, 499
    See also Solidarity (Poland)
Solidarity (Poland), 36, 323, 387, 435, 436, 438,
    439, 440, 482–91, 515–16, 517. See also
    Walesa, Lech
Somalia, 169, 255
Somoza García, Anastasio, 351
Somoza-Debayle, Anastasio, 351
South Africa
    African National Congress of, 14–16, 417
    antiapartheid movement in, 142, 307, 321,
        367, 409, 417, 496–504, 463, 472, 474,
        481–82, 510–11
    antiapartheid sanctions and, 255, 256, 257,
        481, 491–95, 512
    environmental issues of, 169, 222
    Gandhi in, 84, 195–97, 198, 244, 248, 460,
        524
    and women's suffrage, 582, 583
    See also Mandela, Nelson Rolihlahia;
        Namibia, Campaign for Freedom; Tutu,
        Archbishop Desmond Mpilo
South Africa, Antiapartheid Sanctions, 491–95
South Africa, Opposition to Racial Oppression,
    496–504
South African Council of Churches, 428, 539
South African Native National Congress, 14
South Carolina, 580
Southern Christian Leadership Conference, 18, 44,
    45, 46, 91–98, 122, 123, 289, 290, 291,
    361, 388, 417, 464, 474, 505–8, 507,
    551
South-West African Peoples Organization
    (SWAPO), 339
Soviet Union, 108, 124, 145, 264, 345, 418, 560
    and coups d'etat, 102, 132
    and ethnic conflict, 170, 171
    and nonviolent struggle, 366, 367
    and nuclear disarmament, 377, 379, 380,
        381–82, 383, 459, 559, 574
    and Prague Spring of 1968, 133, 134, 158
    and sanctions, 255, 492, 511, 512
    and Solidarity in Poland, 483, 484, 489, 490
    See also Baltic Independence Movements;
        Revolutions of 1989; Russia; Soviet
        Union, Coup Attempt, 1991
Soviet Union, Coup Attempt, 1991, 508–10
Soweto Uprising (South Africa), 1976, 500, 503,
    504, 510–11
Spadafora, Hugo, 397
Spadafora, Winston, 399
Spain, 216, 300, 432, 512, 578

Spanish Civil War, 20, 21, 137, 139, 564
Spanish-American War, 13
Speakes, Larry, 228
Spock, Benjamin, 459
Spokane, Washington, 253
Sports Boycott, 493, 494, 511–12
Squatting, 25, 26, 299
Sri Lanka, 367, 404, 530, 533
St. Augustine, 427
St. Augustine, Florida, 96
St. Francis, 429
Stalin, Joseph, 36, 173, 346, 379, 432, 433, 439
Stamp Act, 542, 543, 544
Stanton, Elizabeth Cady (1815–1902), 23, 333,
    340, 341, 512–13, 580
Stanton, Henry, 513
Starr, Ellen Gates, 13
Starr, Mark, 52
Stassen, Harold, 380
State Law and Order Restoration Council, 24, 25,
    57, 58
Stay-at-home, 326, 500
Stay-away strikes, 504
Stay-In, 231, 482
Steele, C.K., 90
Stevenhagen, Rodolfo, 169
Stevenson, Adlai, 380
Stockholm, Sweden, 135, 168, 169
Stone, Lucy, 23, 341
Stonewall Inn, 207, 208
Stowe, Irving, 221
Strategy, 419, 496, 514–16
    of the civil rights movement, 18, 89, 90, 92–
        96, 289, 291
    and civilian-based defense, 102, 103
    "feather quilt" (France), 188
    and gay rights movement, 207
    and the Indian national movement, 247, 250
    and the IRA, 262, 369, 370
    and Italy 267–71
    and nuclear disarmament, 152–53, 383, 459
    and opposition to Nazism, 147, 343, 346
    within principled nonviolence, 357, 359, 360,
        362, 363
    training nonviolent, 529, 530, 531, 532
    and war, general theory, 105–6, 305–6, 566
    and the women's movement, 182, 571
Street theater, 553
Strikes, 336, 516–17
    antiwar, 554, 564
    in Australia, 25, 28
    in China, 74–76, 80, 315–16, 524, 525
    civic, 82–83, 155–56, 163–64, 351, 399
    within the civil rights movement, 90, 95, 98
    in Colombia, 106–7
    environmental movement, 165, 166
    general, 24, 56, 75, 77, 82, 95, 132, 186, 265,
        283–84, 322, 348, 351, 401, 411–12,
        442, 443, 447, 455–56, 464, 509, 519,
        564

in Ghana, 214–15
hunger, 177, 253, 260–63, 317, 319, 370,
    396, 402, 521, 524, 525, 583
in India, 17, 33, 229, 251, 447
labor, 53, 54, 61, 68, 71, 114, 153, 165, 228,
    231, 254, 267, 281, 339, 365, 409, 449,
    450–53, 530, 541
lightning, 307
as a method of nonviolent action, 84, 113,
    114, 117, 317, 319, 320, 322, 323, 326,
    327, 328, 365, 366, 414, 434, 435, 469,
    514, 530, 568
against Nazism, 148, 343, 344, 345, 372, 373
in Palestine, 259, 394, 396
prison, 66, 253
reverse, 155, 328, 430
sit-down, 469–70
Solidarity (Poland), 482–91, 563
in South Africa, 14, 16, 307, 310, 494, 496,
    497, 498, 499, 500, 501, 503, 504, 510,
    511
student, 75, 77, 134, 266, 268, 315–16, 326,
    524, 525
Student Mobilization Committee, 549, 554
Student Nonviolent Coordinating Committee, 18,
    91, 92, 93, 95, 96, 97, 98, 123, 128,
    191, 192, 193, 194, 289, 388, 506, 507,
    517–19, 518, 531, 547
Students for a Democratic Society, 547, 549, 552,
    554
Stuttgart, Germany, 18
Sudan, 28, 255
Sudan Rebellion, 1985, 519
Suffrage, 329, 330, 333, 341, 342, 392, 402, 451,
    452, 453, 496, 513, 556, 573
Suicide, Protest, 134, 135, 294, 443, 519–20
Sullivan, Leon, 256
Sumner, Charles, 8
Sun Ke, 77
Sun Yatsen, 77, 315
Suzman, Helen, 491
Svoboda, Ludvik, 134
Swadeshi, 130, 198, 247, 249, 496
Swaraj, 130, 202, 247, 249, 250, 461
Sweden, 11, 35, 36, 103, 145, 146, 148, 415, 567,
    583
Swim-ins, 96
Switzerland, 131, 186, 512, 567, 583
Sydney, Australia, 27, 30, 31
Symbolic protection, 81
Syria, 215, 367
Szürös, Mátyás, 441

T

Tabriz, Iran, 265
Tacoma, Washington, 222
Tadjikistan, 170
Taiwan, 367, 493, 530
Tallahassee, Florida, 90, 506
Tallinn, Estonia, 36

Tambo, Oliver, 14, 15, 310
Tanzania, 585
Taoism, 74
Tappan, Arthur, 5, 6
Tappan, Lewis, 5, 6
Tasmanian Wilderness Society, 30
Taunting, 229, 423
Tax refusal and resistance, 33, 40, 64, 84, 109,
    125, 137, 164, 174, 198, 201, 236, 250,
    258, 270, 301, 314, 335, 394, 434, 536,
    569, 581
Taylor, Richard, 334
Te Whiti O Rongomai, 311
Teach-ins, 109, 326, 481, **521,** 547, 550
Teamsters, 542
Tehran, Iran, 265, 411, 412, 435
Temperance, 203, 581
Tennessee, 281
Tent protest, 27
Terrorism, 267, 268, 271
Thailand, 25, 103, 319, 428, 468, 471, 530, 583
Thailand, Democracy Movement, 1992, 521–22
Thatcher, Margaret, 62, 261, 323
Théas, Pierre-Marie, 403
Theosophical Society, 244, 248
Thirteenth Amendment, 204
Thirty-Sixers, 230
Thomas, Norman, 53, 459
Thoreau, Henry David (1817–1862), 44, 84, 89,
    196, 319, 359, **522–24,** 529, 557, 565
Three Gorges Dam, China, 168
Three Mile Island, 376
Tiananmen Square, 47, 76, 79, 80, 315, 442
Tiananmen Square Democracy Movement, Beijing,
    1989, 524–26
Tianjin, China, 316
Tibet, 55
Tibetan Resistance, 1950–Present, 527–28
Tilak, Bal Gangadhar, 244, 246, 247, 248
Tippett, Tom, 52
Tokyo, Japan, 296
Tolstoy, Leo Nikolaevich (1828–1910), 13, 34, 196,
    354, 393, 426, 524, **528–29,** 556, 557
Tongnip Sinmun, 241, 242
Toronto, Canada, 216, 281
Torrijos, Omar, 396, 397
Touré, Kwame, 519
Townshend Acts, 194, 542, 544
Toynbee Hall, 13
Training, 254, 334, 373, 375, 403
    in civil rights movement, 90, 122, 179
    for civilian-based defense, 101–3
    conscientious objection, 128, 564
    in Palestine, 258, 395
    in peace studies, 403, 408
    in South Africa, 310, 498
    See also Training for Nonviolent Action
Training for Nonviolent Action, 529–33
Transarmament, 103, **534–35**
Transformational Politics, 535–37

Transvaal, South Africa, 197, 496, 497, 498, 499, 501
Treblinka, 277
Treepeople, 168
Tribunal, 126
Trocmé, Magda and André, 178, 302
Trujillo, Rafael, 155, 156
Truman, Harry S, 88, 379
Truth, Sojourner (1797?–1883), 6, 364, 444, 513, 537–38
Tuan Ch'i-jui. *See* Duan Qirui
Tubman, Harriet (1820?–1913), 6, 538
Tucson, Arizona, 457, 458
Tula, Russia, 528
Tupua Tamasese Lealofi III, 314
Turkey, 248, 249, 256, 264, 295, 433, 583
Tuskegee, Alabama, 400
Tutu, Archbishop Desmond Mpilo (b. 1931), 356, 428, 482, 539–40

U

Ubico, Jorge, 224, 225
Ukraine, 35, 37, 509, 510
Umkhonto we Sizwe (Spear of the Nation), 15, 310
Underground Railroad, 23, 157, 401, 421, 538
UNESCO, 404
Unified Nationalist Leadership of the Uprising, 259
Unión Cívica Nacional, Dominican Republic, 155
Unión Civilista, 70
Union of Concern Scientists, 381
Union of Democratic Forces, 442
United Auto Workers, 54, 90, 254, 517
United Democratic Front, 15, 501, 504
United Farm Workers Organizing Committee, 51, 69, 137, 165, 387, 541–42
United Gold Coast Convention, 214
United National Independence Party, Zambia, 586
United Kingdom, 368, 371, 383
United Mine Workers of America, 531
United Nations, 22, 51, 178, 221, 232, 235, 255, 256, 339, 340, 343, 363, 379, 403, 404, 467, 482, 492, 499, 504, 533, 576
United Nations Commission on Human Rights, 124
United Nations Commission on the Status of Women, 583
United Nations Conference on Environment and Development, 169
United Nations Conference on the Human Environment, 168
United Nations Convention on Refugees, 441
United Nations Decade for Women, 579
United Nations Environment Program (UNEP), 168
United Nations General Assembly, 233, 234, 256, 405, 492, 527
United Nations Human Rights Commission, 232
United Nations Secretariat, 25
United Nations Security Council, 233, 255, 256, 501
United Nations Special Session on Disarmament, 218

United Nations World Population Conference, 165
United States, 143, 234, 263, 407, 477
  and antiapartheid movement, 340, 492, 493
  and civil disobedience, 84, 85, 414
  and civil rights movement, 86–98, 122, 123, 241, 313, 332, 400–401, 464–65, 507
  and conscientious objection, 126, 127, 409, 463
  and economic sanctions, 254–57, 492, 493
  environmental movements within, 165, 220–22, 557–59
  and foreign assistance, 70, 72, 77, 78, 80, 82, 156, 224–25, 295, 297, 335, 351–53, 396, 398, 399, 527
  and homelessness, 110–12, 416–17
  and international peace movements, 178, 179, 403, 405, 563–64, 568–69, 577–79
  and Japan, security treaty protests, 273–75
  and leadership, 303, 304
  and methods of nonviolent action, 51, 177, 225, 267, 307, 321, 322, 323, 324, 331, 392, 417, 418, 433, 469–70, 472, 480, 511–12, 519, 521
  and Native American rights, 342–43, 422
  and Nobel Peace Prize, 355, 361
  and nuclear disarmament, 108, 220, 377–84, 458–60
  and nuclear energy opposition, 104, 374–77
  and racial equality, 122, 123, 172, 241, 313, 332, 400, 464–65, 507
  sanctuary movement in, 457, 458
  and the Soviet Union, 36, 216, 438, 440, 443, 509
  and strikes, 516–17
  and theories of nonviolent action, 114, 211, 212, 213, 241, 361, 366, 367
  and training in nonviolent action, 530, 531
  and Vietnam War opposition, 65–66, 109, 318, 481, 519, 521, 547–55, 559
  and women's movement, 181, 340–42, 402–3, 512–13, 579–83
  See also Abolitionist Movement; Gay Rights Movement; Industrial Workers of the World; Jefferson, Thomas; King, Martin Luther; Movement for a New Society; Organization in Social Movements; Plowshares Movement; Social Movements; United States, Independence Movement; War Tax Resistance; Women and Nonviolent Action in the United States since 1950; Women Strike for Peace
United States Civil War, 3, 8, 23, 34, 86, 125, 254, 421, 513, 517, 538, 581
United States Forest Service, 331, 343
United States, Independence Movement, 1765–1775, 542–45
United States Institute of Peace, 388
United States Supreme Court, 88, 89, 92, 96, 123, 206, 209, 332, 400, 506

United States, Independence Movement, 1765–1775, 542–45
Universal Declaration of Human Rights, 232, 233, 234, 528
Universal Peace Union, 581
University of Witwatersrand, 310
Uruguay, 83, 149, 150, 583
Utah, 168, 582
Uttar Pradesh, India, 81, 346

V

Vance, Cyrus, 50
Vancouver, Canada, 220, 221, 222, 559
Vatican Council, Second, 61, 403
Velvet Revolution, 66, 68
Venezuela, 82
Vicariate of Solidarity, 71
Vienna, Austria, 217, 236, 443, 567
Vietnam, 22, 65, 350, 368, 415, 428, 459, 519, 547, 576
Vietnam, North, 18, 22, 139, 350, 360, 547, 551, 553, 559, 576
Vietnam, South, 18, 22, 29, 350, 547, 551, 553, 559
Vietnam Veterans Against the War, 552, 553, 554
Vietnam War, 18, 42, 64, 66, 84, 97, 109, 127, 166, 179, 206, 212, 290, 318, 360, 381, 407, 410, 471, 519, 535, 559, 564, 565, 573, 575, 576, 579
Vietnam War Opposition, 65, 66, 85, 109, 125, 128, 293, 318, 415, 417, 427, 459, 481, 521, 524, 530, 547–55, 564
Vigil, 65, 152, 153, 208, 212, 326, 331, 334, 352, 353, 361, 382, 426, 457, 470, 473, 509, 536, 552, 553, 555–56, 557, 560, 568, 569, 574, 576
Villaflor de Vicenti, Azucena, 151, 310
Villalaz de Arias, Marisin, 399
Vilnius, Lithuania, 36, 104, 276
Voice of America, 36
Voluntary Servitude, Discourse on *(Discours de la Servitude Volontaire)*, 299, 478, 556–57
Von Galen, Clement-August, 344
Von Luttwitz, Walter, 283
Voting Rights Act of 1965, 97, 123, 193, 464, 465, 505, 507
Voyages, Protest, 166, 221, 557–60, 557–560
Vykom Campaign (India), 1924–1925, 560–61

W

Walesa, Lech (b. 1943), 356, 360, 440, 483, 484, 485, 486, 487, 488, 489, 563
Walker, Amasa, 8
Walker, Wyatt Tee, 93, 94, 95, 505
Walk-outs, 54, 263, 307, 326, 568
Wallace, George, 46, 385
Wang Dan, 525, 526
Wang Shi-wei, 78
War Resisters' International, 139, 267, 339, 364, 434, 563–65, 564
War Resisters League, 90, 288, 335, 392, 393, 410,

547, 551, 552, 557, 559, 564, 579
War Tax Resistance, 565–66, 565, 566
Warsaw, Poland, 276, 277, 482, 487, 490
Warsaw Treaty Organization, 158, 171, 437, 438, 445
Washington, Booker T., 86
Washington, D.C., 388, 398
    demonstrations against Vietnam War, 410, 547–549, 551
    and desegregation, 88
    and freedom rides, 122, 123, 191–92
    gay rights march on, 209
    march on (civil rights movement), 96, 313, 417, 507,
    Native American protests in, 342
    Poor People's Campaign in, 98, 416–17
    and sanctions against apartheid, 257, 494
    walk for peace, 109, 139
    and women's peace movements, 574, 577, 578
    and women's suffrage, 341, 402, 582
Washington, George, 125
Watson, A.K., 214
Watson, Paul, 166
Wavell, Lord Archibald, 251
Way, Amanda, 581
Webber, Charles C., 53
Weber, Max, 304
Weil, Simone, 429
Weimar Republic, 283
Weld, Theodore, 224
West Bank, 257, 260
West Philadelphia, 334
West Virginia, 281
Western Samoa, 313, 314
Whistle-blowing, 259
White Citizen Councils, 506
White Rose (Germany), 566–67
Whyl, Germany, 104
Wilderness Society, 166
Williams, A. D., 287
Williams, Betty (b. 1943), 130–31, 356, 405, 406
Williams, Hosea, 464, 505
Willoughby, George, 334
Wilmington, North Carolina, 543
Wilson, Dagmar, 574
Wilson, Harold, 369
Wilson, Wilson, 577, 583
Wilson, Woodrow, 127, 462, 577, 583
Winnipeg, Canada, 322
Withdrawal, Symbolic, 567–68
Witherspoon, Frances, 564
Witness for Peace, 335, 352, 353, 568–69
Wofford, Harris, 289
Wollstonecraft, Mary, 580
Woman's Declaration of Rights, 23, 513
Woman's Peace Party, 13, 577
Woman's Rights Convention, 513, 580
Woman's State Temperance Society, 23
Women and Nonviolent Action in the United States

since 1950, 569–73
Women in Black, 466
Women Strike for Peace (USA), 287, 381, 382, 547, 550, 552, 554, 570, 573–77, 579
Women's Association for the Aid of the Freedmen, 334
Women's Christian Temperance Union, 581
Women's Declaration of Independence, 581
Women's International League for Peace and Freedom, U.S. Section, 14, 355, 380, 387, 392, 547, 550, 551, 577–79, 580, 583
Women's International Terrorist Conspiracy from Hell, 207
Women's Loyal National League, 513
Women's movement, 268, 269, 271, 303, 530. *See also* Feminism
Women's Peace Party, 583
Women's Pentagon Action, 382
Women's Political Council, 505
Women's rights. *See* Feminism; Women's Suffrage
Women's Rights Society (France), 583
Women's Social and Political Union (Great Britain), 582
Women's Suffrage, 137, 177, 219, 556, 573, **579–83**. *See also* Addams, Jane; Anthony, Susan Brownell; Feminism; Garrison, William Lloyd; Grimké, Sarah Moore and Emily Angelina: Mott, Lucretia Coffin; National Woman Suffrage Association; Paul, Alice; Stanton, Elizabeth Cady
Woodhull, Victoria, 341
Woolman, John, 426
Workers' Anti-War Summer School, 53
Works Progress Adminstration, 231
World Anti-Slavery Convention, 204, 333, 580
World Bank, 256
World Conference on Human Rights, 233
World Council of Churches, 427
World Court. *See* International Court of Justice
World Federalists, 379
World Health Organization, 51
World League of Sexual Reform, 205
World Party for Equal Rights for Women, 403
World Peace Brigade, 586
World Tomorrow, 20
World War I, 28, 163, 164, 170, 199, 248, 314, 315, 336, 407, 448, 583
    conscientious objection and, 126–27
    and economic sanctions, 254, 255
    and labor movements, 253, 517
    and pacifism, 392–93, 524
    and relief organizations, 21, 422
    and South Africa, 498, 503
    and war resistance, 64, 178, 305, 335, 547, 564, 577
World War II, 14, 46, 77, 143, 212, 307, 324, 578, 583
    and civil rights movement, 88, 480
    conscientious objection and, 124, 125, 127–

28, 178, 335, 409
    and economic sanctions, 254, 255
    and gay rights movement, 205–6
    and India, 200, 245, 251, 285
    and Jewish immigration, 395–96
    and Nazi Germany, 50, 147, 355, 363, 371–73, 524
    and relief organizations, 21, 22
    and solidarity (Poland), 485, 489
    and war resistance, 43, 64, 137, 292, 355, 360, 403, 485, 564, 565–66
    See also Germany; Nazism, Civilian Resistance, 1939–1945
World Wildlife Federation, 166
World Wildlife Fund, 168
Worldover Press, 20
World's Anti-Slavery Convention, 513
Wounded Knee, South Dakota, 343, 533
Wright, Frances, 580
Wu Pei-fu, 75
Wu'er Kaixi, 525, 526
Wuhan, China,316
Wyhl, Germany, 374, 376
Wyoming, 582
Wyszynski, Jan Cardinal, 489

X
Xuma, A.B., 499

Y
Yakima Indians, 342
Yeltsin, Boris, 508, 509, 510
Yi Mun-yong, 293
Yi Tae-yong, 293
Yom Kippur War, 215
Young Democracy, 20
Young India, 40
Young, Andrew, 505
Young, Ron, 552
Yuan Shikai, 315
Yugoslavia, 170, 241, 254, 255, 256, 295, 364, 438, 465, 466, 467, 583
Yuma, Arizona, 68
YUTEL (Yugoslave Television), 49

Z
Zagreb, Croatia, 49
Zambia, 360
Zambia Anticolonial Movement, 1953–1964, 585–86
Zambian African National Congress, 586
Zeller, André, 19
Zero Population Growth, 166
Zhao Ziyang, 525
Zhou Enlai, 79, 321, 524
Zimbabwe, 173
Zinn, Howard, 42
Zuniga, Mauro, 399
Zurich, Switzerland, 578